Frommer's®

New England

13th Edition

by Paul Karr, Herbert Bailey Livesey, Marie Morris, Laura M. Reckford

Here's what the critics say about Frommer's:

"Amazingly easy to use. Very portable, very complete."

—*Booklist*

"Detailed, accurate, and easy-to-read information for all price ranges."

—*Glamour Magazine*

"Hotel information is close to encyclopedic."

—*Des Moines Sunday Register*

"Frommer's Guides have a way of giving you a real feel for a place."

—*Knight Ridder Newspapers*

Wiley Publishing, Inc.

Published by:

Wiley Publishing, Inc.

111 River St.
Hoboken, NJ 07030-5774

ISBN-13: 978-0-471-79280-2
ISBN-10: 0-471-79280-2

Editor: Margot Weiss
Production Editor: Ian Skinnari
Cartographer: Andy Dolan
Photo Editor: Richard Fox
Production by Wiley Indianapolis Composition Services

Front cover photo: Vermont, Groton State Forest: woman paddling a red canoe along Boulder Beach, autumn foliage
Back cover photo: Cape Cod: man surrounded by various lobster buoys attached to home

For information on our other products and services or to obtain technical support, please contact our Customer Care Department within the U.S. at 800/762-2974, outside the U.S. at 317/572-3993 or fax 317/572-4002.

Wiley also publishes its books in a variety of electronic formats. Some content that appears in print may not be available in electronic formats.

Manufactured in the United States of America

5 4 3 2

Contents

4 Boston & Cambridge 75

by Marie Morris

5 Side Trips from Boston: Lexington & Concord, the North Shore & Plymouth 144

by Marie Morris

6 Cape Cod 193

by Laura M. Reckford

7 Martha's Vineyard & Nantucket 263

by Laura M. Reckford

8 Central & Western Massachusetts 309

by Herbert Bailey Livesey

9 Connecticut 356

by Herbert Bailey Livesey

10 Rhode Island 414

by Herbert Bailey Livesey

11 Vermont 463

by Paul Karr

12 New Hampshire 537

by Paul Karr

13 Maine 584

by Paul Karr

Appendix: New England in Depth 665

by Paul Karr

Index 675

List of Maps

About the Authors

Paul Karr (chapters 2, 11–13 and appendix) is also the author of *Frommer's Nova Scotia, New Brunswick & Prince Edward Island; Frommer's Maine Coast; Frommer's Vermont, New Hampshire & Maine* and a contributor to *Frommer's Canada.*

Herbert Bailey Livesey (chapters 8–10) is a native New Yorker and a former NYU administrator. After leaving his career in higher education, he worked briefly as an artist before devoting himself to writing full time. He is the author of several travel guides, nine books on education and sociology, and a novel.

Marie Morris (chapters 3–5) is a native New Yorker and a graduate of Harvard, where she studied history. She has worked for the *New York Times, Boston* magazine, and the *Boston Herald,* and is also the author of *Frommer's Boston* and *Boston Day by Day.* She lives in Boston.

Laura M. Reckford (chapters 6 and 7) is a writer and editor who lives on Cape Cod. Formerly the managing editor *of Cape Cod Life Magazine,* she has also been on the editorial staffs of *Good Housekeeping* magazine and *Entertainment Weekly.*

An Invitation to the Reader

In researching this book, we discovered many wonderful places—hotels, restaurants, shops, and more. We're sure you'll find others. Please tell us about them, so we can share the information with your fellow travelers in upcoming editions. If you were disappointed with a recommendation, we'd love to know that, too. Please write to:

Frommer's New England, 13th Edition
Wiley Publishing, Inc. • 111 River St. • Hoboken, NJ 07030-5774

An Additional Note

Please be advised that travel information is subject to change at any time—and this is especially true of prices. We therefore suggest that you write or call ahead for confirmation when making your travel plans. The authors, editors, and publisher cannot be held responsible for the experiences of readers while traveling. Your safety is important to us, however, so we encourage you to stay alert and be aware of your surroundings. Keep a close eye on cameras, purses, and wallets, all favorite targets of thieves and pickpockets.

Frommer's Star Ratings, Icons & Abbreviations

Every hotel, restaurant, and attraction listing in this guide has been ranked for quality, value, service, amenities, and special features using a **star-rating system.** In country, state, and regional guides, we also rate towns and regions to help you narrow down your choices and budget your time accordingly. Hotels and restaurants are rated on a scale of zero (recommended) to three stars (exceptional). Attractions, shopping, nightlife, towns, and regions are rated according to the following scale: zero stars (recommended), one star (highly recommended), two stars (very highly recommended), and three stars (must-see).

In addition to the star-rating system, we also use **seven feature icons** that point you to the great deals, in-the-know advice, and unique experiences that separate travelers from tourists. Throughout the book, look for:

Finds	Special finds—those places only insiders know about
Fun Fact	Fun facts—details that make travelers more informed and their trips more fun
Kids	Best bets for kids and advice for the whole family
Moments	Special moments—those experiences that memories are made of
Overrated	Places or experiences not worth your time or money
Tips	Insider tips—great ways to save time and money
Value	Great values—where to get the best deals

The following **abbreviations** are used for credit cards:

AE	American Express	DISC	Discover	V	Visa
DC	Diners Club	MC	MasterCard		

Frommers.com

Now that you have the guidebook to a great trip, visit our website at **www.frommers.com** for travel information on more than 3,000 destinations. With features updated regularly, we give you instant access to the most current trip-planning information available. At Frommers.com, you'll also find the best prices on airfares, accommodations, and car rentals—and you can even book travel online through our travel booking partners. At Frommers.com, you'll also find the following:

- Online updates to our most popular guidebooks
- Vacation sweepstakes and contest giveaways
- Newsletter highlighting the hottest travel trends
- Online travel message boards with featured travel discussions

What's New in New England

BOSTON & CAMBRIDGE With each passing day, Boston loses a little more of the construction site that has dominated downtown for most of the last 2 decades. Parks, surface roads, and buildings are under construction, replacing the expressway that completely came down—finally—in 2005. The downtown area has unobstructed access to the waterfront for the first time in half a century.

The transit authority, or **MBTA** (© **800/392-6100** or 617/222-3200; www.mbta.com), has announced plans to raise fares on all of its train, bus, and ferry lines in 2007. The price hike coincides with the introduction of a new automated fare-collection system. **Silver Line** "rapid transit service" (fancy talk for electric buses) links South Station, the South Boston waterfront, and Logan Airport, with direct service to the airport terminals.

At press time, the **Westin Boston Waterfront Hotel,** 435 Summer St. (© **800/WESTIN-1** or 617/532-4600; www.westin.com), near the Boston Convention and Exhibition Center, was planning a summer 2006 opening. The **Inter-Continental Boston,** 500 Atlantic Ave. (© **800/424-6835**), on the waterfront near the Financial District, should welcome its first pampered tycoon in late 2006.

On September 17, 2006, the **Institute of Contemporary Art** (© **617/266-5152;** www.icaboston.org) was scheduled to move from the Back Bay to a brand-new 65,000-square-foot building on the South Boston waterfront. The Diller Scofidio + Renfro design is the first newly constructed art museum in Boston in almost a century.

The **Boston Tea Party Ship & Museum** (© **617/269-7150;** www.bostonteapartyship.com), which closed after a fire in 2001, plans to expand and reopen in 2007. I've written some version of that sentence at least four times, so call ahead before visiting.

Tours of **Fenway Park,** 4 Yawkey Way (© **617/226-6666;** www.redsox.com), no longer definitely include a walk on the field, but they're great fun. Since the last edition of this book, the 2004 Red Sox won the World Series, snapping an 86-year unlucky streak—and their fans *still* won't shut up about it.

Another sports venue, formerly the FleetCenter, is now **TD Banknorth Garden,** which means the Celtics and Bruins once again play at "the Garden" (or, in Bostonian, "Gah-din").

The luxury chain **Barneys New York** (© **617/385-3300;** www.barneys.com) renovated a movie theater in the upscale Copley Place mall and opened in Boston in 2006.

Boston University's new hockey rink, **Agganis Arena,** 925 Commonwealth Ave. (© **617/353-4628;** www.agganisarena.com), is turning out to be a popular concert venue with touring rock and pop artists.

SIDE TRIPS FROM BOSTON The **Liberty Ride** (© **781/862-0500,** ext. 702; www.libertyride.us), the only way to tour Lexington and Concord without driving (public transit doesn't connect the towns), has extended its season and now operates from late May through mid-October.

Rockport legalized liquor sales in July 2005, ending decades as one of the state's few remaining "dry" towns. Alcohol may only be served with a meal.

Visitors to Plymouth in 2007 can look forward to celebrations of the 50th anniversary of ***Mayflower II*** (© **508/746-1622;** www.plimoth.org), the beloved replica of the type of ship the Pilgrims sailed to the New World in 1620. Sadly, the Plymouth National Wax Museum closed in 2005.

CAPE COD Visitors driving to Cape Cod over the **Sagamore Bridge** will notice a big change. Where's the rotary? After being in the planning stage for roughly 10 years, the Sagamore Bridge "fly-over" project finally got off the ground in 2005 and is expected to be finished some time in 2006. When it's all finished, the rotary will be history and drivers may experience shorter delays when crossing onto the Cape.

The **Cape Cod Maritime Museum** has opened at 135 South St. in Hyannis. Check www.capecodmaritimemuseum.org, for more details.

The newly renovated **Provincetown Art Association & Museum** (© **508/487-1750;** 460 Commercial St., Provincetown), which has a large modern addition, is well worth a visit.

MARTHA'S VINEYARD & NANTUCKET The Vineyard's top nightclub, The Hot Tin Roof (incongruously located at the Martha's Vineyard Airport), has been sold. The new owner plans to change the name and add a restaurant, but to keep the big acts—comedy, rock, reggae, Latin music, and blues—coming. For more information, call © **508/693-1137** or check out their website, www.mvhottinroof.com.

The Vineyard's other nightclub, the Atlantic Connection, is being closed as well and turned into a games arcade. The restaurant next door, **Seasons Bar 'n' Grill** on Circuit Avenue in Oak Bluffs (© **508/693-7129**), will get a spiffy renovation.

The biggest news on the Nantucket restaurant scene is the reopening of **Chanticleer,** 9 New St., Siasconset (© **508/257-4499**). The fancy French restaurant in the rose-covered cottage had long been one of the island's most cherished fine-dining spots until it closed a couple years ago. Now it is being reinvented by Susan Handy and chef Jeff Worster, who have made the casual Black Eyed Susan's one of the island's best, and funkiest, dining choices. The style of food at the new Chanticleer is "modern bistro," and the fresh decor feels warmer and more approachable.

CENTRAL & WESTERN MASSACHUSETTS The Old Inn on the Green ★★, Route 57 (© **413/229-7924**) in bucolic New Marlborough (near Great Barrington), has sold its pre-Revolutionary tavern and the adjacent Thayer House to a gifted chef and his wife. They now operate as an entity separate from the other properties.

Great Barrington itself has become the dining locus of the southern Berkshires. New to the mix is **Aegean Breeze,** 327 Stockbridge Rd. (© **413/528-4001**), a Greek roadside taverna that exceeds expectations with admirable renditions of *mezedes, moussaka,* and *thalasina.*

In Stockbridge, the promising American Craftsman restaurant has closed.

Blantyre ★★★, Route 20 (© **413/637-3556**), long one of Lenox's most luxurious resort hotels, will now remain open year-round.

Things are stirring in Pittsfield, with an expanding social and cultural calendar and a hopeful new vitality among its citizens.

One bit of evidence is the restored **Thaddeus Clapp House,** 74 Wendell Ave. (© **413/499-6840**), a grand but friendly bed-and-breakfast run by a hearty Pittsfield booster. The sophisticated downtown wine bar and bistro **Brix** ★, 40 West St. (© **413/236-9463**), a Francophilic enterprise run with infectious enthusiasm, is further evidence of Pittsfield's revival. Barkeeps pour more than 50 wines by the glass to accompany tasty panini and small plates.

On Route 7, near the Lenox border, the folksy former Yellow Aster has been upgraded to a sleek, New York–style steakhouse, **Asters,** 1015 South St. (© **413/499-2075**). There's live jazz on the weekends.

The on-and-off resurrection of North Adams continues as well, touched off by the sprawling **Massachusetts Museum of Contemporary Art** (also known as Mass MoCA). Among the many entrepreneurs drawn here is Bill Gideon, not only chef and owner of **Gideon's** ★ at 34 Holden St. (© **413/664-9449**) but also of **Gideon's Luncheon & Nightery,** 23 Eagle St. (© **413/664-0404**), which brings a bit of after-dark pizazz to town by offering live music at week's end.

East of town, a worthwhile destination is the inn-restaurant **Jae's** ★, 1111 South State St. (Rte. 8) (© **413/664-0100**). The ebullient owner has created a menu that bounds across the borders of several Asian nations, from fresh-as-dawn sushi to Thai curries to kimchi stew. He also offers 12 rooms for rent.

CONNECTICUT Fairfield County, the "Gold Coast" in the southwestern corner of the state, has seen the closing of several once-honored restaurants, including Zanghi on Summer Street in Stamford and Amberjack's in South Norwalk. All were quickly replaced.

In Stamford, **Zinc,** 222 Summer St. (© **203/252-2352**), is a pleasurable semi-authentic replica of a Left Bank bistro complete with a zinc-topped bar and a street-side terrace for warmer days.

The Inn at National Hall, an ultra-posh hostelry in Westport, was once among the state's finest lodgings. But that image has eroded and the owner has recently sought approval to convert it into condos. In another corner of the same wealthy exurb, the **Westport Country Playhouse,** 25 Powers Ct. (© **203/227-4177**), has announced a physical expansion and a new on-premises restaurant to go with a calendar that stretches from summer into the cooler months.

South Norwalk ("SoNo") continues to be a dining destination. Of the ever-growing possibilities, check out **Matches,** 98 Washington St. (© **202/852-1088**), where the buzz has as much to do with the contemporary takes on pasta and pizza as with the bar scene. Increasingly, the neighborhood is also a postprandial choice of singles and young professionals. The **Black Bear Saloon,** 80 Washington St. (© **203/299-0711**), brings in cover bands, and the **Shacojazz Art Café,** 21 North Main St. (© **203/853-6124**), presents America's original art form in many variations, while **Relish,** 86 Washington St. © **203/854-5300**) and **SoNo Caffeine,** 133 Washington St. (© **203/857-4224**), favor folkies and singer-songwriters.

When it was serving meals, **Belgique,** 1 Bridge St. (© **860/927-3681**) in Kent, garnered giddily enthusiastic reviews. The owner pulled away from the pressures of managing a full-service restaurant, turning his attention to his earlier career as a pastry chef and chocolatier. He now sells the exquisite results in a bungalow behind the larger restaurant building.

New Haven's **Ibiza,** 39 High St. (© **203/865-1933**), began life as a casual tapas joint. The owners have upgraded to an elevated form of Nuevo Spanish cuisine, and it now draws delighted attention from critics well beyond the state borders.

Farther along the Shoreline, in Guilford, the former Esteve has morphed into **Martin's,** 25 Whitfield St. (✆ **203/458-1300**), with little change in either staff or the accomplished New American menu. One big difference: It's now open for breakfast, lunch, *and* dinner.

The tribal nations of southeastern Connecticut can't build casinos (and hotels, nightclubs, and marinas) fast enough. The cascades of money extracted from floods of eager gamblers has inspired the Mashantucket Pequots to announce yet another $700-million budget, to include a fourth hotel, a parking garage, and two golf courses.

RHODE ISLAND The state's "Renaissance City" continues to reinvent itself. The latest neighborhood to garner attention, the Downtown Arts District, is a SoHo-like area of 19th-century lofts and office buildings. Of interest to visitors is the new **Hotel Providence,** 311 Westminster St. (✆ **800/861-8990**), which combined two adjoining mid-rises into a stylish boutique hotel. The lobby and hallways are filled with artworks and antiques, and the well-regarded Italian restaurant **L'Epicureo,** 311 Westminster St. (✆ **401/521-3333**), has relocated here from a long-standing location on Federal Hill.

L'Epicureo wasn't the only popular eating place to pull up stakes and move downcity. Now at 194 Washington St., **Gracie's** (✆ **401/272-7811**) has brought along its trademark decorative stars and inventive New American cooking with barely a discernible misstep.

On the way from Providence to Newport, pull off the highway at Tiverton for lunch at the new **Boat House,** 227 Schooner Dr. (✆ **401/624-6300**). Built originally to accommodate buyers of condo units up the hill, its fresh seafood specialties and panoramic view of Sakonnet Bay brought in so many customers that the owners decided to enclose part of the terrace and extend a previously summer-only season.

In Newport, the dining room of the posh Chanler hotel has conquered some early start-up stuttering to finally match its sumptuous surroundings. **Spiced Pear,** 117 Memorial Blvd. (✆ **401/847-2244**), pursues a vision of old-world elegance with an adroit staff bringing dishes composed of such treasured ingredients as Kobe beef and Iranian caviar.

And in Westerly, at the far western tip of South County, a converted woolen mill that has operated as a restaurant under several names has opened once again as **The Up River Café,** 37 Main St. (✆ **401/348-9700**). Count this as a decided improvement on earlier occupants. While the New American menu features both seafood and meats, the river running beneath the ancient building leads to thoughts of lobster bisque and the scallops brought to dock in nearby Stonington.

VERMONT The **Vermont Raptor Center** (✆ **802/457-2779**) has reopened in Quechee, a few miles away from its former home on a Woodstock hillside.

The **American Museum of Fly Fishing** (✆ **802/362-3300**) in Manchester has also reopened in new digs, these just south of the Orvis flagship store (which stocks a wide variety of fishing equipment). It holds an impressive collection of fly-fishing memorabilia, including Ernest Hemingway's pole and tackle.

Yet another reopening: The **Vermont Ski Museum** (✆ **802/253-9911**) is now right on Main St. in downtown Stowe.

Middlebury's **Swift House Inn,** 25 Stewart Lane (✆ **802/388-9925**), has changed owners for the second time in a year, but continues to be first-rate.

NEW HAMPSHIRE On the coast in Portsmouth, **Pesce Blue,** 106 Congress St. (✆ **603/430-7766**), is a hot new Italian seafood restaurant.

Also in Portsmouth, the French bakery Café La Brioche closed down, but a great coffeehouse, **Breaking New Grounds** (✆ **603/436-9555**), has moved into its former location—and retained the outdoor tables on Market Square.

In Hanover, the big **Dartmouth Bookstore** has been acquired by the college bookstore division of Barnes & Noble, but remains mostly as it was.

The **Enfield Shaker Museum** in Enfield moved into the Great Stone Dwelling, which had formerly housed the Shaker Inn.

Bellini's in North Conway has relocated to Route 16 but still serves the same great Italian family fare.

MAINE In Ogunquit, the Shore Road restaurant known as **Five-O** has a new chef (Zachary Crosby), new ownership team, and a new twist: more French fare, as opposed to the Caribbean influences that formerly predominated. Also in Ogunquit, the legendary Perkins Cove restaurant, Hurricane, has closed (the branch in Kennebunkport's Dock Square is still going strong, however).

The **Shoreline Explorer** shuttle has started service between Amtrak's Wells Station and hotels in the Kennebunks, Wells, Ogunquit, York, and Sanford. Call ✆ **207/324-5762** to arrange a pickup.

Sadly, the early-August **Maine Festival** (previously held each year in Brunswick) has apparently ceased to exist.

The **Sea Dog Brewing Co.** brewpub has moved from its original home in Camden to a restored mill in **Topsham.**

There's a new way to view the foliage along the Maine coast during fall: by boarding the **Maine Eastern Railroad** as it runs between the coastal communities of Brunswick and Rockland. Round-trip fares run about $55 per adult, half price for children ages 5 to 12. Check the railroad's website at www.maineeasternrailroad.com for more details.

Camden lost a notable fine-dining experience when **Cork** closed. Happily, however, the new **Francine Bistro** (✆ **207/230-0083**) has moved into town at 55 Chestnut St., and is garnering rave reviews as the next great Camden dining experience.

The Kelmscott Rare Breeds Foundation just inland from Lincolnville Beach, which formerly conserved rare breeds of livestock, has transferred some of its stock to other organizations and is no longer open to the public.

The large and new **Bar Harbor Grand Hotel** (✆ **888/766-2529** or 207/288-5226) in the heart of Bar Harbor echoes the design of the town's original grand hotel—the one that helped put the town on the tourist map in the first place.

Win one, lose one: Elaine's Stardust Oasis in Bar Harbor closed, but **Eden Vegetarian Café** (✆ **207/288-4422**) has capably replaced it at 78 West St.

A number of new (and surprisingly modern) seafood and fusion restaurants have recently sprouted up in, of all places, the sparsely settled Southwest Harbor area on the western lobe of Mount Desert Island. The two best are **Red Sky** (✆ **207/244-0476**) and **Fiddlers' Green** (✆ **207/244-9416**).

1

The Best of New England

One of the greatest challenges of traveling in New England is choosing from an abundance of superb restaurants, accommodations, and attractions. Where to start? Here's an entirely biased list of our favorite destinations and experiences. Over years of traveling through the region, we've discovered that these are places worth more than just a quick stop—they're all worth a major detour.

1 The Best of Small-Town New England

- **Marblehead** (MA): The "Yachting Capital of America" has major picture-postcard potential, especially in summer, when the harbor fills with boats of all sizes. From downtown, a short distance inland, make your way toward the water down the narrow, flower-dotted streets. The first glimpse of blue sea and sky is breathtaking. See "Marblehead" in chapter 5.
- **Provincetown** (Cape Cod, MA): At the far tip of the Cape's curl, in intensely beautiful surroundings, is Provincetown. Provincetown's history goes back nearly 400 years, and in the last century, it's been a veritable headquarters of bohemia—a gathering place for famous writers and artists. It's also, of course, one of the world's top gay and lesbian resort areas. But Provincetown is a place for everyone who enjoys savory food, fun shopping, and fascinating people-watching. See "The Lower Cape" in chapter 6.
- **Nantucket** (MA): With grand 19th-century homes and cobblestone streets, it looks as though the whalers just left. Traveling to the island of Nantucket is like taking a trip to a parallel universe; you get historic charm but with 21st-century amenities. The island also has shops full of luxury goods, loads of historical sites open to the public, and miles of public beaches and bike paths. See "Nantucket" in chapter 7.
- **Oak Bluffs** (Martha's Vineyard, MA): Stroll down Circuit Avenue in Oak Bluffs with a Mad Martha's ice-cream cone and then ride the Flying Horses Carousel. This island harbor town is full of fun for kids and parents. Don't miss the colorful "gingerbread" cottages behind Circuit Avenue. Oak Bluffs also has great beaches, bike paths, and the Vineyard's best nightlife. See "Martha's Vineyard" in chapter 7.
- **Stockbridge** (MA): Norman Rockwell made a famous painting of the main street of this, his adopted hometown. Facing south, it uses the southern Berkshires as backdrop for the sprawl of the Red Lion Inn and the other late-19th-century buildings that make up the commercial district. Then as now, they service a beguiling mix of unassuming saltboxes and Gilded Age mansions that have sheltered farmers, artists, and aristocrats since the days of the French and

New England

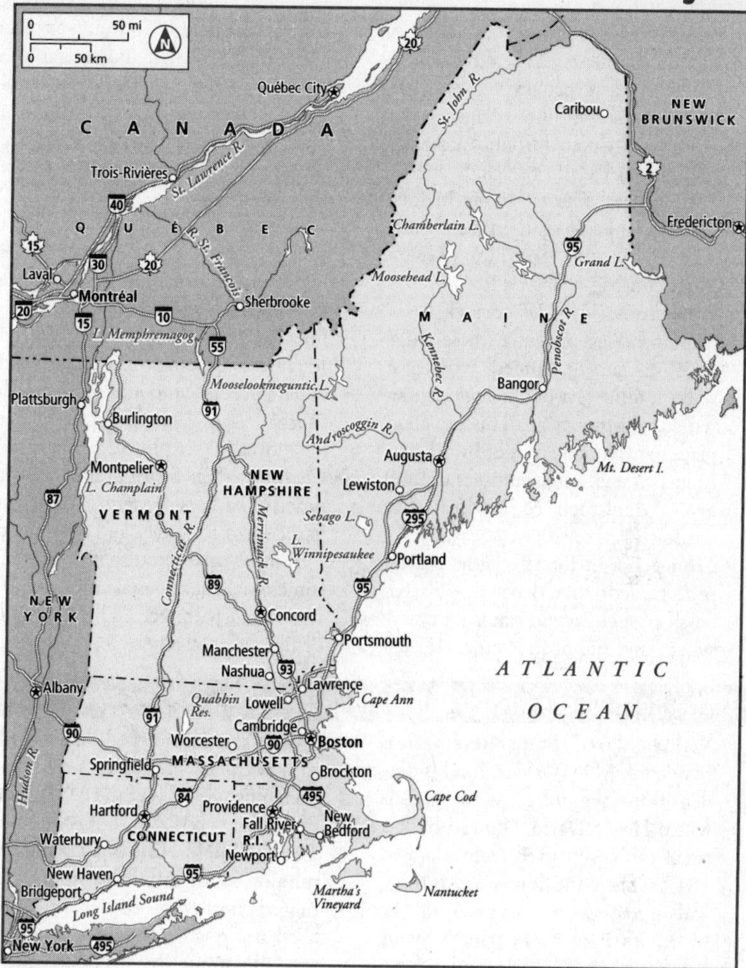

Indian Wars. See "The Berkshires" in chapter 8.

- **Washington** (CT): A classic, with a Congregational church facing a village green surrounded by clapboard Colonial houses—all of them with black shutters. See "The Litchfield Hills" in chapter 9.
- **Essex** (CT): A widely circulated survey voted Essex tops on its list of the 100 best towns in the United States. That judgment is largely statistical, but a walk past white-clapboard houses to the active waterfront on this unspoiled stretch of the Connecticut River rings all the bells. There is not an artificial note, a cookie-cutter franchise, nor a costumed docent to muddy its near-perfect image. See "The Connecticut River Valley" in chapter 9.

- **Grafton** (VT): Grafton was once a down-at-the-heels mountain town slowly being reclaimed by termites and the elements. A wealthy family took it on as a pet project, and has lovingly restored the village to its former self—even burying the electric lines to reclaim the landscape. It doesn't feel like a living-history museum; it just feels right. See "Brattleboro & the Southern Green Mountains" in chapter 11.
- **Woodstock** (VT): Woodstock has a stunning village green, a whole range of 19th-century homes, woodland walks leading just out of town, and a settled, old-money air. This is a good place to explore on foot or by bike, or to just sit and watch summer unfold. See "Woodstock & Environs" in chapter 11.
- **Montpelier** (VT): This is the way all state capitals should be: slow-paced, small enough so you can walk everywhere, and full of shops that still sell nails and strapping tape. Montpelier also shows a more sophisticated edge, with its Culinary Institute, an art-house movie theater, and several fine bookshops. But at heart it's a small town, where you just might run into the governor at the corner store. See "Exploring Montpelier & Barre" in chapter 11.
- **Hanover** (NH): It's the perfect college town: the handsome brick buildings of Dartmouth College, a tidy green, a small but select shopping district, and a scattering of good restaurants. Come in the fall and you'll be tempted to join in the touch football game on the green. See "Hanover" in chapter 12.
- **Castine** (ME): Soaring elm trees, a peaceful harborside setting, plenty of grand historic homes, and a few good inns make this a great spot to soak up some of Maine's coastal ambience off the beaten path. See "The Blue Hill Peninsula" in chapter 13.

2 The Best Places to See Fall Foliage

- **Walden Pond State Reservation** (Concord, MA): Walden Pond is hidden from the road by the woods where Henry David Thoreau built a small cabin and lived from 1845 to 1847. When the leaves are turning and the trees are reflected in the water, it's hard to imagine why he left. See p. 155.
- **Bash-Bish Falls State Park** (MA): Head from the comely village of South Egremont up into the forested hills of the southwest corner of Massachusetts. The roads, which change from macadam to gravel to dirt and back, wind between crimson clouds of sugar maples and white birches feather-stroked against banks of black evergreens. The payoff is a three-state view from a promontory above a 50-foot cascade notched into a bluff, with carpets of russet and gold stretching all the way to the Hudson River. See p. 331.
- **The Litchfield Hills** (CT): Route 7, running south to north through the rugged northwest corner of Connecticut, roughly along the course of the Housatonic River, explodes with color in the weeks before and after Columbus Day. Leaves drift down to the water and whirl down the foaming river. See "The Litchfield Hills" in chapter 9.
- **I-91** (VT): An interstate? Don't scoff (the traffic can be terrible on narrow state roads). If you like your foliage viewing wholesale, cruise I-91 from Brattleboro to Newport. You'll be overwhelmed with gorgeous terrain,

from the gentle Connecticut River Valley to the sloping hills of the Northeast Kingdom. See chapter 11.

- **Route 100** (VT): Route 100 winds the length of Vermont from Readsboro to Newport. It's the major north-south route through the center of the Green Mountains, and it's surprisingly undeveloped along most of its length. You won't have it to yourself along the southern stretches on autumn weekends, but as you head farther north, you'll leave the crowds behind. See chapter 11.
- **Crawford Notch** (NH): Route 302 passes through this scenic valley, where you can see the brilliant red maples and yellow birches high on the hillsides. In fall, Mount Washington, in the background, is likely to be dusted with an early snow. See "The White Mountains" in chapter 12.
- **Camden** (ME): The dazzling fall colors that cover the rolling hills are reflected in Penobscot Bay on the east side, and in the lakes on the west. Ascend the peaks for views out to the color-splashed islands in the bay. Autumn usually comes a week or so later on the coast, so you can stretch out your viewing pleasure. See "Penobscot Bay" in chapter 13.

3 The Best Ways to View Coastal Scenery

- **Strolling Around Rockport** (MA): The town surrounds the small harbor and spreads out along the rugged, rocky coastline of Cape Ann. From the end of Bearskin Neck, the view is spectacular—fishing and pleasure boats in one direction, roaring surf in the other. See "Cape Ann" in chapter 5.
- **Getting Back to Nature on Plum Island** (MA): The Parker River National Wildlife Refuge, in Newburyport, offers two varieties of coastal scenery: picturesque salt marshes packed with birds and other animals, and gorgeous ocean beaches where the power of the Atlantic is evident. See "Newburyport, Ipswich & Plum Island" in chapter 5.
- **Biking or Driving the Outer Cape** (MA): From Eastham through Wellfleet and Truro, all the way to Provincetown, Cape Cod's outermost towns offer dazzling ocean vistas and a number of exceptional bike paths, including the Province Lands, just outside Provincetown, that are bordered by spectacular swooping dunes. See "The Outer Cape" in chapter 6.
- **Heading "Up-Island" on Martha's Vineyard** (MA): Many visitors never venture beyond the port towns of Vineyard Haven, Oak Bluffs, and Edgartown. Though each has its charms, the scenery actually gets more spectacular "up-island," in towns like Chilmark, where you'll pass moorlike meadows and family farms surrounded by stone walls. Follow State Road and the scenic Moshup Trail to the westernmost tip of the island, where you'll experience the dazzling colored cliffs of Aquinnah and the quaint fishing port of Menemsha. See "Martha's Vineyard" in chapter 7.
- **Cruising Newport's Ocean Drive** (RI): After a tour of the fabulously overwrought "cottages" of the hyper-rich that are strung along Bellevue Avenue, emerging onto the shoreline road that dodges the spray of the boiling Atlantic is a cleansing reminder of the power of nature over fragile monuments to the conceits of men. To extend the experience, take a 3.5-mile hike along the Cliff Walk that skirts the edge of the bluff

commanded by the largest mansions. See "Newport" in chapter 10.

- **Sitting in a Rocking Chair** (ME): The views are never better than when you're caught unawares—such as suddenly looking up from an engrossing book on the front porch of an oceanside inn. Throughout the Maine chapter, look for mention of inns right on the water, such as Edwards' Harborside Inn (p. 589), Beach House Inn (p. 598), Samoset Resort (p. 632), East Wind Inn (p. 626), and the Claremont (p. 654).
- **Hiking Monhegan Island** (ME): The village of Monhegan is clustered around the harbor, but the rest of this 700-acre island is all picturesque wildlands, with miles of trails crossing open meadows and winding along rocky bluffs. See "Mid-Coast Maine" in chapter 13.
- **Driving the Park Loop Road at Acadia National Park** (ME): This is the region's premier ocean drive. You'll start high along a ridge with views of Frenchman Bay and the Porcupine Islands, then dip down along the rocky shores to watch the surf crash against the dark rocks. Plan to do this 20-mile loop at least twice to get the most out of it. See p. 641.

4 The Best Places to Rediscover America's Past

- **Paul Revere House** (Boston, MA): We often study the history of the American Revolution through stories of governments and institutions. At this little home in the North End, you'll learn about a real person. The self-guided tour is particularly thought-provoking, allowing you to linger on the artifacts that hold your interest. Revere had 16 children with two wives, supported them with his thriving silversmith's trade—and put the whole operation in jeopardy with his role in the events that led to the Revolution. See p. 121.
- **Old State House** (Boston, MA): Built in 1713, the once-towering Old State House is dwarfed by modern skyscrapers. It stands as a reminder of British rule (the exterior features a lion and a unicorn) and its overthrow—the Declaration of Independence was read from the balcony, which overlooks a traffic island where a circle of bricks represents the site of the Boston Massacre. See p. 121.
- **Faneuil Hall** (Boston, MA): Although Faneuil Hall is best known nowadays as a shopping destination, if you head upstairs, you'll be transported back in time. In the second-floor auditorium, park rangers talk about the building's role in the Revolution. Tune out the sound of sneakers squeaking across the floor, and you can almost hear Samuel Adams (his statue is out front) exhorting the Sons of Liberty. See p. 114.
- **"Old Ironsides"** (Boston, MA): Formally named USS *Constitution,* the frigate was launched in 1797 and gained fame battling Barbary pirates and seeing action in the War of 1812. Last used in battle in 1815, it was periodically threatened with destruction until a complete renovation in the late 1920s started its career as a floating monument. The staff includes sailors on active duty who wear 1812 dress uniforms. See p. 121.
- **North Bridge** (Concord, MA): British troops headed to Concord after putting down the uprising in Lexington, and the bridge (a replica) stands as a testament to the Minutemen who fought here. The Concord River and its peaceful green banks give no hint of the bloodshed that took place. On the path in from

Monument Street, placards and audio stations provide a fascinating narrative. See "Concord" in chapter 5.

- **Plymouth Rock** (Plymouth, MA): Okay, it's a fraction of its original size and looks like something you might find in your garden. Nevertheless, Plymouth Rock makes a perfect starting point for exploration. Close by is *Mayflower II,* a replica of the alarmingly small original vessel. The juxtaposition reminds you of what a dangerous undertaking the Pilgrims' voyage was. See "Plymouth" in chapter 5.
- **Sandwich** (MA): The oldest town on Cape Cod, Sandwich was founded in 1637. Glassmaking brought notoriety and prosperity to this picturesque town in the 19th century. Visit the Sandwich Glass Museum for the whole story, or tour one of the town's glassblowing studios. Don't leave without visiting the 76-acre Heritage Museums and Gardens, which has a working carousel, a sparkling antique-car collection, and a wonderful collection of Americana. See "The Upper Cape" in chapter 6.
- **Nantucket** (MA): It looks like the whalers just left, leaving behind their grand houses, cobbled streets, and a gamut of enticing shops offering luxury goods from around the world. The Nantucket Historical Association owns more than a dozen properties open for tours, and the Whaling Museum is one of the most fascinating sites in the region. Tourism may be rampant, but not its tackier side effects, thanks to stringent preservation measures. See "Nantucket" in chapter 7.
- **Deerfield** (MA): Arguably the best-preserved Colonial village in New England, Deerfield has scores of houses dating back to the 17th and 18th centuries. None of the clutter of modernity has intruded here. Fourteen houses on the main avenue can be visited through tours conducted by the organization known as Historic Deerfield. See "The Pioneer Valley" in chapter 8.
- **Newport** (RI): A key port of the clipper trade long before the British surrendered their colony, Newport retains abundant recollections of its maritime past. In addition to its great harbor, clogged with cigarette boats, tugs, ferries, and majestic sloops, the City by the Sea has kept three distinctive enclaves preserved: the waterside homes of Colonial seamen, the hillside Federal houses of port-bound merchants, and the ostentatious mansions of America's post–Civil War industrial and financial grandees. See "Newport" in chapter 10.
- **Plymouth** (VT): President Calvin Coolidge was born in this high upland valley, and the state has done a superb job preserving his hometown village. You'll get a good sense of the president's roots, but also gain a greater understanding of how a New England village works. See p. 494.
- **Shelburne Museum** (Shelburne, VT): Think of this sprawling museum as New England's attic. Located on the shores of Lake Champlain, the Shelburne features not only the usual exhibits of quilts and early glass, but also whole buildings preserved like specimens in formaldehyde. Look for the lighthouse, the railroad station, and the stagecoach inn. This is one of northern New England's "don't miss" destinations. See p. 525.
- **Portsmouth** (NH): Portsmouth is a salty coastal city that just happens to boast some of the most impressive historic homes in New England. Start at Strawbery Banke, a historic compound of 42 buildings dating from 1695 to 1820. Then visit the many

other grand homes in nearby neighborhoods, like the house John Paul Jones occupied while building his warship during the Revolution. See "Portsmouth" in chapter 12.

- **Victoria Mansion** (Portland, ME): Donald Trump had nothing on the Victorians when it came to excess. You'll see Victorian decorative arts at their zenith in this Italianate mansion built during the Civil War years by a prosperous hotelier. It's open to the public for tours in summer and also puts on outstanding Christmas-season programs in December. See p. 606.

5 The Best Activities for Families

- **Exploring the Museum of Fine Arts** (Boston, MA): Parents hear "magnificent Egyptian collections." Kids think: "Mummies!" Even the most hyper youngster manages to take it down a notch in these quiet, refined surroundings, and the collections at the MFA simultaneously tickle visitors' brains. See p. 117.
- **Experimenting in the Museum of Science** (Boston, MA): Built around demonstrations and interactive displays that never feel like homework, this museum is wildly popular with kids—and adults. Explore the exhibits, then take in a show at the planetarium or the Mugar Omni Theater. Before you know it, everyone will have learned something, painlessly. See p. 117.
- **Catching a Free Friday Flick at the Hatch Shell** (Boston, MA): Better known for the Boston Pops's Fourth of July concert, the Esplanade is also famous for family films (like *Shrek* or *Pocahontas*) shown on Friday nights in summer. The lawn in front of the Hatch Shell turns into a giant, carless drive-in as hundreds of people picnic and wait for dark. See p. 137.
- **Visiting the Heritage Museums and Gardens** (Cape Cod, MA): This site with museum buildings spread over 76 acres will delight both children and adults. Kids will especially love the gleaming antique cars, the collections of soldiers and Native American clothing, and the 1912 carousel that offers unlimited rides. Outdoor concerts free with admission take place most Sunday afternoons in season. See p. 197.
- **Whale-Watching off Provincetown** (Cape Cod, MA): Boats leave MacMillan Wharf for the 8-mile journey to Stellwagen Bank National Marine Sanctuary, a rich feeding ground for several types of whales. Nothing can prepare you for the thrill of spotting these magnificent creatures feeding, breaching, and even flipper slapping. See p. 250.
- **Deep-Sea Fishing:** Charter fishing boats these days usually have high-tech fish-finding gear—imagine how your kids will react to reeling in one big bluefish after another. The top spots to mount such an expedition are Barnstable Harbor or Rock Harbor in Orleans, on Cape Cod; Point Judith, at the southern tip of Rhode Island; and the Maine coast. See chapters 6, 10, and 13, respectively.
- **Riding the Flying Horses Carousel in Oak Bluffs** (Martha's Vineyard, MA): Some say this is the oldest carousel in the country, but your kids might not notice the genuine horsehair, sculptural details, or glass eyes. They'll be too busy trying to grab the brass ring to win a free ride. After your ride, stroll around the town of Oak Bluffs. Children will be enchanted with the "gingerbread" houses, a carryover from the 19th-century revivalist movement. See p. 275.

- **Biking Nantucket** (MA): Short, flat trails crisscross the island, and every one leads to a beach. The shortest rides lead to Children's Beach, with its own playground, and Jetties Beach, with a skate park and watersports equipment for rent; older kids will be able to make the few miles to Surfside and Madaket. See "Nantucket" in chapter 7.
- **Learning to Ski at Jiminy Peak** (MA): More than 70% of Jiminy Peak's trails are geared toward beginners and intermediates, making it one of the premier places to learn to ski in the East. The mountain is located in the heart of the Berkshires, near Mount Greylock. See p. 348.
- **Visiting Mystic Seaport and Mystic Aquarium** (CT): The double-down winner in the family-fun sweepstakes has to be this combination: performing dolphins and whales, full-rigged tall ships, penguins and sharks, and river rides on a perky little 1906 motor launch. These are the kinds of G-rated attractions that have no age barriers. See p. 402.
- **Visting the Ben & Jerry Ice Cream Factory** (Waterbury, VT): Kids and ice cream are a great combination, and the 30-minute tours that leave every 10 minutes in summer won't tax anybody's patience. Browse the small ice-cream museum, enjoy the playground and cow-viewing area, and make sure to save room for the free samples. See p. 511.
- **Exploring the Shelburne Museum** (Shelburne, VT): This museum contains one of the nation's most singular collections of American decorative, folk, and fine art. Kid favorites include the Circus Building with a 35,000 piece three-ring miniature circus; an operating vintage carousel; a collection of dolls and dollhouses; and automata, large (sometimes three feet tall), often comical wind-up toys. See p. 525.
- **Riding the Mount Washington Cog Railway** (Crawford Notch, NH): It's fun! It's terrifying! It's a great glimpse into history. Kids love this ratchety climb to the top of New England's highest peak aboard trains that were specially designed to scale the mountain in 1869. As a technological marvel, the railroad attracted tourists by the thousands a century ago. They still come to marvel at the sheer audacity of it all. See p. 577.
- **Exploring Monhegan Island** (ME): Kids from 8 to 12 especially enjoy overnight excursions to Monhegan Island. The mail boat from Port Clyde is rustic and intriguing, and the hotels are an adventure. Leave at least an afternoon to sit atop the high, rocky bluffs scouting the glimmering ocean for whales. See "Mid-Coast Maine" in chapter 13.

6 The Best Country Inns

- **Hawthorne Inn** (Concord, MA; ✆ **978/369-5610**): Everything here—the 1870 building, the garden setting a stone's throw from the historic attractions, the antiques, the eclectic decorations, the accommodating innkeepers—is top of the line. See p. 156.
- **Longfellow's Wayside Inn** (Sudbury, MA; ✆ **800/339-1776**): A gorgeous inn, an unusual setting, excellent food, the imprimatur of a distinguished New England author, nearly 300 years of history, and the schoolhouse the little lamb (supposedly) followed Mary to. What's not to like? See p. 156.
- **Captain's House Inn** (Chatham, Cape Cod, MA; ✆ **800/315-0728**): An elegant country inn dripping with

good taste, this is among the best small inns in the region. Most rooms have fireplaces, elegant paneling, and antiques; they're sumptuous yet cozy. This could be the ultimate spot to enjoy Chatham's Christmas Stroll festivities. See p. 231.

- **Charlotte Inn** (Edgartown, Martha's Vineyard, MA; ✆ **508/627-4751**): Edgartown tends to be the most formal enclave on Martha's Vineyard, and this compound of exquisite buildings is by far the fanciest address in town. The rooms are distinctively decorated: One boasts a baby grand, another its own thematic dressing room. The conservatory restaurant, **L'étoile,** is among the finest you'll find this side of France. See p. 277.
- **The Porches** (North Adams, MA; ✆ **413/664-0400**): It may be stretching the definition of the "country inn" category, but this is too much fun to ignore. It was put together with six 19th-century workmen's houses lined up opposite the Massachusetts Museum of Contemporary Art, a new veranda running across their length. The wit of the designers is evident in the use of paint-by-the-numbers pictures and sublimely kitschy accessories, but laptop rentals, DVD players, and Internet access ensure no 21st-century deprivation. See p. 354.
- **Mayflower Inn** (Washington, CT; ✆ **860/868-9466**): Not a tough call at all for this part of the region: Immaculate in taste and execution, the Mayflower is as close to perfection as any such enterprise is likely to be (points off for whiffs of excess pretension). A genuine Joshua Reynolds hangs in the hall. See p. 371.
- **Griswold Inn** (Essex, CT; ✆ **860/767-1776**): "The Griz" has been accommodating sailors and travelers as long as any inn in the country, give or take a decade. In all that time, it has been a part of life and commerce in the lower Connecticut River Valley, always ready with a mug of suds, a haunch of beef, and a roaring fire. The walls are layered with nautical paintings and memorabilia, and there's music every night in the schoolhouse-turned-tavern. See p. 394.
- **The Equinox** (Manchester Village, VT; ✆ **800/362-4747**): This is southern Vermont's grand resort, with nearly 200 rooms in a white-clapboard compound that seems to go on forever. The rooms are pleasant enough, but the real draws are the grounds and the resort's varied activities—it's set on 2,300 acres with pools, tennis courts, an 18-hole golf course, and even its own mountainside. Tried everything on vacation? How about falconry classes or backcountry driving at the Range Rover school? See p. 470.
- **Windham Hill Inn** (West Townshend, VT; ✆ **800/944-4080**): Welcome amenities such as air-conditioning in the rooms and a conference room in the barn have been added, while preserving the charm of this 1823 farmstead. It's at the end of a remote dirt road in a high upland valley, and guests are welcome to explore 160 private acres on a network of walking trails. See p. 486.
- **Jackson House Inn** (Woodstock, VT; ✆ **800/448-1890**): Constant improvements and the meticulous attention to service have made this a longtime favorite for visitors to Woodstock. The meals are stunning, the guest rooms the very picture of antique elegance. The only downside? It fronts a sometimes noisy road. See p. 488.
- **Twin Farms** (Barnard, VT; ✆ **800/894-6327**): Just north of Woodstock may be the most elegant inn in New England. Its rates are a tad

breathtaking, but guests are certainly pampered here. Novelist Sinclair Lewis once lived on this 300-acre farm, and today it's an aesthetic retreat that offers serenity and exceptional food. See p. 490.

- **The Pitcher Inn** (Warren, VT; ✆ **802/496-6350**): Even though this place was built in 1997, it's possessed of the graciousness of a longtime, well-worn inn. It combines traditional New England form and scale with modern and luxe touches, plus a good dollop of whimsy. See p. 507.
- **Basin Harbor Club** (Vergennes, VT; ✆ **800/622-4000**): Established in 1886, this lakeside resort has the sort of patina that only comes with age. It's a classic old-fashioned family resort, with golf, boating on Lake Champlain, jackets-required dining, evening lectures on the arts, and even a private airstrip. Bring books and board games, and re-learn what summer's all about. See p. 526.
- **Balsams Grand Resort Hotel** (Dixville Notch, NH; ✆ **800/255-0600**): The designation "country inn" is only half correct. You've got plenty of country—it's set on 15,000 acres in northern New Hampshire. But this resort is more castle than inn. The Balsams has been offering superb hospitality and gracious comfort since 1866. It has two golf courses, miles of hiking trails, and, in winter, its own downhill and cross-country ski areas. See p. 583.
- **White Barn Inn** (Kennebunkport, ME; ✆ **207/967-2321**): Many of the White Barn's staff hail from Europe, and guests are treated with a Continental graciousness that's hard to match. Rooms, suites, and cottages here are all a delight, and the meals (served in the barn) are among the best in Maine. See p. 600.
- **Claremont** (Southwest Harbor, ME; ✆ **800/244-5036**): The 1884 Claremont is a Maine classic. This waterside lodge has everything a Victorian resort should, including sparely decorated rooms, creaky floorboards in the halls, great views of water and mountains, and a perfect croquet pitch. See p. 654.

7 The Best Moderately Priced Accommodations

- **Newbury Guest House** (Boston, MA; ✆ **800/437-7668**) and **Harborside Inn** (Boston, MA; ✆ **888/723-7565**): These sister properties would be good deals even if they weren't ideally located—the former in the Back Bay, the latter downtown. Rates at the Guest House even include breakfast. See p. 97 and p. 91.
- **Pilgrim Sands Motel** (Plymouth, MA; ✆ **800/729-7263**): The ocean views and two pools (indoor and outdoor) make this a great deal, whether you're immersing yourself in Pilgrim lore or passing through on the way from Boston to Cape Cod. See p. 191.
- **White Horse Inn** (Provincetown, Cape Cod, MA; ✆ **508/487-1790**): The very embodiment of Provincetown funkiness, this inn has hosted such celebrities as filmmaker John Waters and poet laureate Robert Pinsky. Rooms are short on amenities but long on artiness. The apartments, cobbled together by innkeeper Frank Schaefer, are highly original and a lot of fun. See p. 255.
- **Nauset House Inn** (East Orleans, Cape Cod, MA; ✆ **800/771-5508**): This romantic 1810 farmhouse is like a sepia-toned vision of old Cape Cod. Recline in a wicker divan surrounded by fragrant flowers while the wind

whistles outside. Better yet, stroll to Nauset Beach and take a quiet walk as the sun sets. Your genial hosts also prepare one of the finest breakfasts in town. See p. 237.

- **Hopkins Inn** (New Preston, CT; ✆ **860/868-7295**): This yellow farmhouse bestows the top view of Lake Waramaug, at its best on soft summer days when robust Alpine dishes can be taken out on the terrace. The somewhat spartan rooms don't tempt winding-down guests with either phones or TVs. See p. 372.
- **Bee and Thistle Inn** (Old Lyme, CT; ✆ **800/622-4946**): Known for decades for its cuisine, this 1756 house also has a detached cottage and 11 pretty guest rooms, two of which have fireplaces. Easily one of the area's most romantic weekend getaways, it has musicians underscoring the mood in the dining rooms on weekends. See p. 393.
- **Inn at the Mad River Barn** (Waitsfield, VT; ✆ **800/631-0466**): It takes a few minutes to adapt to the spartan rooms and no-frills accommodations here. But you'll soon discover that the real action takes place in the living room and dining room, where skiers relax and chat after a day on the slopes, and share heaping helpings at mealtime. See p. 507.
- **Philbrook Farm Inn** (Shelburne, NH; ✆ **603/466-3831**): Come here if you're looking for a complete getaway. The inn has been taking in travelers since the 1850s, and the owners know how to do it right. The farmhouse sits on 1,000 acres between the Mahoosuc Mountains and the Androscoggin River, and guests can hike or relax with equal aplomb. See p. 583.
- **Franciscan Guest House** (Kennebunk, ME; ✆ **207/967-4865**): No daily maid service, cheap paneling on the walls, and industrial carpeting. What's to like? Plenty, including the location (on the lush riverside grounds of a monastery), price (doubles from $65), and a great Lithuanian-style breakfast spread in the morning. You can bike to the beach or walk to Dock Square in Kennebunkport. See p. 600.

8 The Best Restaurants

- **Legal Sea Foods** (Boston, MA, and other locations; ✆ **617/266-6800**): Newcomers ask where to go for fresh seafood, then react suspiciously when I recommend a world-famous restaurant instead of a local secret. No, it's no secret—but it's a wildly successful chain for a reason. See p. 110.
- **L'Espalier** (Boston, MA; ✆ **617/262-3023**): The city's foremost special-occasion restaurant expertly blends superb ingredients (from local produce to the finest caviar), classic preparations, a magnificent wine list, exacting service, and a gorgeous setting to create an unforgettable experience. See p. 109.
- **902 Main** (South Yarmouth, Cape Cod, MA; ✆ **508/398-9902**): With fabulous service, an elegant atmosphere, and to-die-for food, this is the place to go for fine dining in the Mid-Cape. Entrees like filet mignon with portobello mushrooms, rack of lamb with truffle mashed potatoes, and haddock with organic beets range will set you swooning. See p. 217.
- **Atria** (Edgartown, Martha's Vineyard, MA; ✆ **508/627-5840**): This fine-dining restaurant set in an 18th-century sea captain's home gets rave reviews for its gourmet cuisine and its high-quality service. This is one of those places you can just relax and

have a fantastic and memorable meal, because the staff knows exactly what they are doing. See p. 282.

- **Centre Street Bistro** (Nantucket, MA; ✆ **508/228-8470**): Two of the best chefs on the island, Ruth and Tim Pitts combine their talents at this cozy little hole-in-the-wall restaurant. The best part is that this place features wonderful, creative cuisine at fairly reasonable prices, compared to other island fine-dining restaurants. See p. 305.
- **Bistro Zinc** (Lenox, MA; ✆ **413/637-8800**): Setting the Berkshires culinary standard ever since its opening a few years back, this stylish contemporary bistro impresses on every repeat visit. It looks great, for starters, with its zinc bar, buffed woods, and flowers everywhere. Most everything that arrives on a plate is supremely satisfying, joining familiarity with the French repertoire with cunning twists in execution. There are 24 wines by the glass and an irresistible five-cheese tasting. See p. 345.
- **Union League Café** (New Haven, CT; ✆ **203/562-4299**): This august setting of arched windows and high ceilings is more than a century old and was long the sanctuary of an exclusive club. It still looks good, but the tone has been lightened into an approximation of a Lyonnaise brasserie. The menu observes the southern French tastes for curry, olive oil, pastas, lamb, and shellfish. See p. 383.
- **Scales & Shells** (Newport, RI; ✆ **401/846-3474**): Ye who turn aside all ostentation, get yourselves hence. There's nary a frill nor affectation anywhere near this place, and because the wide-open kitchen is right at the entrance, there are no secrets, either. What we have here are marine critters mere hours from the depths, prepared and presented free of any but the slightest artifice. This might well be the purest seafood joint on the southern New England coast. See p. 447.
- **Chantecleer** (Manchester Center, VT; ✆ **802/362-1616**): Swiss chef Michel Baumann has been turning out dazzling dinners here since 1981, and the kitchen hasn't gotten stale in the least. The dining room in an old barn is magical, the staff helpful and friendly. It's a great spot for those who demand top-notch Continental fare but don't like the fuss of a fancy restaurant. See p. 473.
- **T. J. Buckley's** (Brattleboro, VT; ✆ **802/257-4922**): This tiny diner on a dark side street serves up outsize tastes prepared by talented chef Michael Fuller. Forget about stewed-too-long diner fare; get in your mind big tastes blossoming from the freshest of ingredients prepared just right. See p. 483.
- **Jackson House Inn** (Woodstock, VT; ✆ **800/448-1890**): Situated in a modern addition to an upscale country inn, the Jackson House Inn serves meals that are ingeniously conceived, deftly prepared, and artfully arranged. The three-course meals cost around $55, and offer excellent value at that. See p. 491.
- **Hemingway's** (Killington, VT; ✆ **802/422-3886**): Killington seems an unlikely place for a serious culinary adventure, yet Hemingway's will meet the loftiest expectations. The menu changes frequently to ensure only the freshest of ingredients. If it's available, be sure to order the wild mushroom and truffle soup. See p. 497.
- **White Barn Inn** (Kennebunkport, ME; ✆ **207/967-2321**): The setting, in an ancient, rustic barn, is magical. The tables are set with floor-length tablecloths, and the chairs feature imported Italian upholstery. The

food? To die for. Start with lobster spring rolls, then enjoy entrees such as roasted duck with juniper sauce or Maine lobster over fettuccine with a cognac coral butter sauce. See p. 600.

- **Fore Street** (Portland, ME; ✆ **207/775-2717**): Fore Street is one of New England's most celebrated restaurants—the place was listed as one of *Gourmet* magazine's 100 best restaurants in 2001, and the chef has been getting lots of press elsewhere as well. His secret? Simplicity, and lots of it. Some of the most memorable meals are prepared over an applewood grill. See p. 609.

9 The Best Local Dining Experiences

- **Durgin-Park** (Boston, MA; ✆ **617/227-2038**): A meal at this landmark restaurant might start with a waitress dropping a handful of cutlery in front of you and saying, "Here, give these out." The surly service usually seems to be an act, but it's so much a part of the experience that some people are disappointed when the waitresses are nice (as they often are). In any case, it's worked since 1827. See p. 107.
- **Woodman's of Essex** (Essex, MA; ✆ **800/649-1773**): This busy North Shore institution is not for the faint of heart—or the hard of artery, unless you like eating corn and steamers while everyone around you is gobbling fried clams and onion rings. The food at this glorified clam shack is fresh and delicious, and a look at the organized pandemonium behind the counter is worth the (reasonable) price. See p. 170.
- **Black Eyed Susan's** (Nantucket, MA; ✆ **508/325-0308**): This is extremely exciting food in a funky bistro atmosphere. The place is small, popular with locals, and packed. Sitting at the diner counter and watching the chef in action is a show in itself. No credit cards, no reservations, and no liquor license are all an inconvenience, but if you can get past all that, you're in for a top-notch dining experience. See p. 305.
- **Louis' Lunch—The Very First (Well, Probably) Burgers** (New Haven, CT; ✆ **203/562-5507**): Not a lot of serious history has happened in New Haven, but boosters claim it was here that hamburgers were invented in 1900. This little luncheonette lives on, moved from its original site in order to save it. The patties are freshly ground daily, thrust into vertical grills, and served on white toast. Garnishes are tomato, onion, and cheese. No ketchup and no fries, so don't even ask. See p. 382.
- **Wooster Street Pizza** (New Haven, CT): New Haven's claim to America's first pizza is a whole lot shakier, but it has few equals as purveyor of the ultra-thin, charred variety of what they still call "apizza" in these parts, pronounced "ah-peetz." Old-timer **Frank Pepe's,** 157 Wooster St. (✆ **203/865-5762**), is usually ceded top rank among the local parlors, but it is joined by such contenders as **Sally's,** 237 Wooster St. (✆ **203/624-5271**) and the upstart brewpub **Brü Rm,** 254 Crown St. (✆ **203/495-1111**). See p. 382 and 384.
- **Abbott's Lobster in the Rough** (Noank, CT; ✆ **860/536-7719**): Places like this frill-free shack abound along more northerly reaches of the New England coast, but here's a little bit o' Maine a Sunday drive from Manhattan. Shore dinners rule, so roll up sleeves, tie on napkins and feedbags, dive into bowls of chowder and platters of boiled shrimp and

steamed mussels, and dunk hot lobster chunks in pots of drawn butter. See p. 405.

- **Johnnycakes and Stuffies** (RI): Sooner or later, most worthy regional food faves become known to the wider world (witness Buffalo wings). The Ocean State still clutches a couple of taste treats within its borders. "Johnnycakes" are flapjacks made with cornmeal, which come small and plump or wide and lacy, depending upon family tradition. "Stuffies" are the baby-fist-size quahog (*KWAH*-og or *KOE*-hog) clams barely known elsewhere in New England. The flesh is chopped up, combined with minced bell peppers and bread crumbs, and packed back into both halves of the shell. See chapter 10.
- **Blue Benn Diner** (Bennington, VT; ✆ **802/442-5140**): This 1945 Silk City diner has a barrel ceiling, acres of stainless steel, and a vast menu. Don't overlook specials scrawled on paper and taped all over the walls. And leave room for a slice of delicious pie, such as blackberry, pumpkin, or chocolate cream. See p. 467.
- **Al's** (South Burlington, VT; ✆ **802/862-9203**): This is where Ben and Jerry go to eat french fries—as does every other potato addict in the state. See p. 528.
- **Lou's** (Hanover, NH; ✆ **603/643-3321**): Huge crowds flock to Lou's, just down the block from the Dartmouth campus, for breakfast on weekends. Fortunately, breakfast is served all day here, and the sandwiches on fresh-baked bread are huge and delicious. See p. 555.
- **Becky's** (Portland, ME; ✆ **207/773-7070**): Five different kinds of home fries on the menu? It's breakfast nirvana at this local institution on the working waterfront. It's a favored hangout of fishermen, high-school kids, businessmen, and just about everyone else. See p. 611.
- **Silly's** (Portland, ME; ✆ **207/772-0360**): Hectic and fun, this tiny, informal, kitschy restaurant serves up delicious finger food, like pita wraps, hamburgers, and pizza. The milkshakes alone are worth the detour. See p. 612.

10 The Best of the Performing Arts

- **Symphony Hall** (Boston, MA; ✆ **617/266-1492**): Home to the Boston Symphony Orchestra, the Boston Pops, and other local and visiting groups and performers, this is a perfect (acoustically and otherwise) destination for classical music. See p. 137.
- **Hatch Shell** (Boston, MA; ✆ **617/626-1250**): This amphitheater on the Charles River Esplanade plays host to free music, dance performances, and films almost every night in summer. Around the Fourth of July, the Boston Pops provide the entertainment. Bring a blanket to sit on. See p. 137.
- **Boston's Theater District:** The area's performance spaces—which include the recently reopened Opera House—are in the midst of a nearly unprecedented boom, and this is the epicenter. Previews and touring companies of Broadway hits, local music and dance troupes, and other productions of every description make this part of town hop every night. See p. 138.
- ***The Nutcracker*** (Boston, MA; ✆ **800/447-7400** for tickets): New England's premier family-oriented holiday event is Boston Ballet's extravaganza. When the Christmas tree grows through the floor, even fidgety preadolescents forget that

they think they're too cool to be here. See p. 137.

- **The Comedy Connection at Faneuil Hall** (Boston, MA; © **617/248-9700**): Even in the Athens of America, it's not all high culture. The biggest national names and the funniest local comics take the stage at this hot spot. See p. 139.
- **The Berkshire Theatre Festival** (Stockbridge, MA; © **413/298-5576**): An 1887 "casino" and converted barn mount both new and classic plays from June to late August in one of the prettiest towns in the Berkshires. Name artists on the order of Joanne Woodward and Dianne Wiest are often listed as actors and directors in the annual playbill. See p. 336.
- **The Jacob's Pillow Dance Festival** (Becket, MA; © **413/243-0745**): Celebrated dancer/choreographer Martha Graham made this her summertime performance space for decades. Guest troupes are among the world's best, often including Dance Theatre of Harlem, the Merce Cunningham Dance Company, and the Paul Taylor Company, supplemented by repertory companies working with jazz, flamenco, or world music. See p. 338.
- **Tanglewood Music Festival** (Lenox, MA; © **617/266-1492** in Boston, 413/637-5165 in Lenox): By far the most dominating presence on New England's summer cultural front, the music festival that takes place on this magnificent Berkshires estate is itself in thrall to the Boston Symphony Orchestra (BSO). While the BSO reigns, room is made for such guest soloists as Jessye Norman and Itzhak Perlman as well as practitioners of other forms, from jazz (Dave Brubeck) to folk (James Taylor) and the Boston Pops. See p. 340.
- **Williamstown Theatre Festival** (Williamstown, MA; © **413/597-3400**): Classic, new, and avant-garde plays are all presented during the June-through-August season at this venerable festival. There are two stages, one for works by established playwrights, the smaller second venue for less mainstream or experimental plays. There is usually a Broadway headliner on hand; Frank Langella has been a frequent presence. See p. 353.
- **Norfolk Chamber Music Festival** (Norfolk, CT; © **860/542-3000**): A century-old "Music Shed" on the Ellen Battell Stoeckel Estate in this Litchfield Hills town shelters such important chamber performance groups as the Tokyo String Quartet and the Vermeer Quartet. Young professional musicians perform morning recitals. See p. 377.
- **Summer in Newport** (RI): From Memorial Day to Labor Day, only a scheduling misfortune will deny visitors the experience of an outdoor musical event. In calendar order, the highlights (well short of all-inclusive) are the July Newport Music Festival, the August Ben & Jerry's Folk Festival and JVC Jazz Festival, and the Waterfront Irish Festival in September. See p. 432.

11 The Best Destinations for Antiques Hounds

- **Charles Street** (Boston, MA): Beacon Hill is one of the city's oldest neighborhoods, and at the foot of the hill is a thoroughfare that's equally steeped in history. Hundreds of years' worth of furniture, collectibles, and accessories jam the shops along its 5 blocks. See p. 135.
- **Main Street, Essex** (MA): The treasures on display in this North Shore town run the gamut, from one step above yard sales to one step below

nationally televised auctions. Follow Route 133 west of Route 128 through downtown and north almost all the way to the Ipswich border. See "Cape Ann" in chapter 5.

- **Route 6A: The Old King's Highway** (Cape Cod, MA): Antiques buffs, as well as architecture and country-road connoisseurs, will have a field day along scenic Route 6A. Designated a Regional Historic District, this former stagecoach route winds through a half-dozen charming villages and is lined with scores of antiques shops. The largest concentration is in Brewster, but you'll find good pickings all along this meandering road, from Sandwich to Orleans. See chapter 6.
- **Brimfield Antique and Collectible Shows** (Brimfield, MA): This otherwise undistinguished town west of Sturbridge erupts with three monster shows every summer, in mid-May, mid-July, and early September. Upward of 6,000 dealers set up tented and tabletop shops in fields around town. Call ✆ **800/628-8379** for details, and book room reservations far in advance. See p. 312.
- **Sheffield** (MA): This southernmost town in the Berkshires is home to at least three dozen dealers in collectibles, Americana, military memorabilia, English furniture of the Georgian period, silverware, and weather vanes . . . even antique birdhouses. Most of them are strung along Route 7, with a worthwhile detour west along Route 23 in South Egremont. See p. 330.
- **Woodbury** (CT): More than 30 dealers along Main Street offer a diversity of precious treasures, near-antiques, and simply funky old stuff. American and European furniture and other pieces are most evident, but there are forays into crafts and assorted whimsies as well. Pick up the directory of the Woodbury Antiques Dealers Association, available in most shops. See p. 368.
- **Newfane and Townshend** (VT): A handful of delightful antiques shops are hidden in and around these picture-perfect towns. But the real draw is the Sunday flea market, held just off Route 30 north of Newfane, where you never know what might turn up. See p. 483.
- **Portsmouth** (NH): Picturesque downtown Portsmouth is home to a half-dozen or so antiques stores and some fine used-book shops. For more meaty browsing, head about 25 miles northwest on Route 4 to Northwood, where a dozen good-size shops flank the highway. See "Portsmouth" in chapter 12.
- **Route 1, Kittery to Scarborough** (ME): Antiques scavengers delight in this 37-mile stretch of less-than-scenic Route 1. Antiques minimalls and high-class junk shops alike are scattered all along the route, though there's no central antiques zone. See "The Southern Maine Coast" in chapter 13.

2

Planning Your Trip to New England

1 The Regions in Brief

BOSTON Oliver Wendell Holmes dubbed Boston the "Hub of the solar system," and the label stuck. Today, "The Hub" is the region's largest and most vibrant city. This alluring metropolis of historic and modern buildings, world-class museums, and top-notch restaurants is an important stop for travelers on any trip to New England.

CAPE COD & THE ISLANDS The ocean is writ large on Cape Cod, a low peninsula with miles of sandy beaches and grassy dunes that whisper in the wind. The carnival-like atmosphere of Provincetown is a draw, as are the genteel charms of Martha's Vineyard and Nantucket, two islands just offshore.

THE PIONEER VALLEY Extending through Massachusetts along the Connecticut River, the area takes its name from the early settlers who arrived here in the 17th century. Among the many picturesque towns is unspoiled Historic Deerfield.

THE BERKSHIRES Massachusetts's rolling hills at the state's western edge are home to historic old estates, graceful villages, and an abundance of festivals and cultural events, including the Tanglewood Music Festival and Jacob's Pillow Dance Festival.

THE LITCHFIELD HILLS The historic northwest corner of Connecticut has sleepy villages, hidden hiking trails, and a surfeit of New England charm—all just a couple of hours from New York City.

THE CONNECTICUT COAST The eastern coast is home to the historic towns of Mystic and New London, where you can get a glimpse of the shipbuilding trade at the Mystic Seaport museum and the Navy submarine base in nearby Groton.

NEWPORT, RHODE ISLAND, AREA The lifestyles of the truly rich and famous are on parade in Newport, once home to the likes of the Astors and Vanderbilts. A tour of the oceanfront mansions never fails to astonish.

GREEN MOUNTAINS Extending the length of Vermont from Massachusetts to Canada, this mostly gentle chain of forested hills and low mountains allows for great hiking, scenic back-road drives, fantastic inns, and superb bicycling.

LAKE CHAMPLAIN Pastoral and scenic, the region of Vermont that forms half the lakeshore of Lake Champlain has idyllic drives and a sense of gracious openness—along with a lot of dairy cows and great views of New York's Adirondacks.

NORTHEAST KINGDOM This is Vermont at its most remote and lost-in-time best. The state's northeastern counties are rugged and hilly, still mostly timber country, but with some wonderfully improbable grace notes, such as the St. Johnsbury Athenaeum and Bread and Puppet Museum.

COASTAL NEW HAMPSHIRE Yes, New Hampshire has a coast—18 miles of—with sand and surf, and the bonsai-perfect historic city of Portsmouth.

THE UPPER VALLEY The Connecticut River Valley between Vermont and New Hampshire is a world unto itself, full of villages, rolling hills, covered bridges, and the New England classic, Hanover (NH), home to Dartmouth College.

LAKES REGION Lake Winnipesaukee (VT) is the crown jewel of the state's Lakes Region, but other lakes and ponds that are scattered about make up in charm what they lack in size. *On Golden Pond* was filmed here, but the region's fame predates the movie.

WHITE MOUNTAINS Since the mid-1800s, New Hampshire's White Mountains have drawn travelers to their rugged, windswept peaks and forests dotted with glacial boulders and clear, rushing streams. You can find New England's best backcountry hiking and camping here.

WESTERN MAINE MOUNTAINS This oft-overlooked region—which arcs from Bethel up to Maine's highest peak at Mount Katahdin—is home to brawny hills, wide and fast rivers, and plenty of opportunity for outdoor activity.

COASTAL MAINE Maine's rocky coast is the stuff of legend, art, and poetry. The southern coast has most of the state's beaches; to the north, the Downeast region has rocky headlands and Acadia National Park.

MAINE'S NORTH WOODS With millions of acres of uninhabited terrain, the North Woods is almost entirely owned by timber companies, but there are undisturbed wildlands.

2 Visitor Information

Chamber addresses and phone numbers are provided for each region in the chapters that follow. If you're a highly organized traveler, you'll call in advance and ask for information to be mailed to you long before you depart. If you're like the rest of us, you'll swing by when you reach town and hope the office is still open.

All six New England states are pleased to send out general visitor information packets and maps to those who call or write ahead. Here's the contact information:

- **Connecticut Office of Tourism,** Department of Economic and Community Development, 505 Hudson St., Hartford, CT 06106 (© **800/282-6863** or 860/270-8080; www.ctbound.com).
- **Maine Office of Tourism,** P.O. #59 State House Station, Augusta, ME 04333 (© **888/624-6345** or 207/287-5711; www.visitmaine.com).
- **Massachusetts Office of Travel and Tourism,** 10 Park Plaza, Suite 4510, Boston, MA 02116 (© **800/227-6277** or 617/973-8500; www.massvacation.com).
- **New Hampshire Division of Travel and Tourism,** 172 Pembroke Rd. (P.O. Box 1856), Concord, NH 03302 (© **800/386-4664** or 603/271-2665; www.visitnh.gov).
- **Rhode Island Department of Economic Development,** 1 West Exchange St., Providence, RI 02903 (© **800/556-2484** or 401/277-2601; www.visitrhodeisland.com).
- **Vermont Department of Tourism,** Drawer 33, 6 Baldwin St., Montpelier, VT 05633 (© **800/837-6668** or 802/828-3237; www.travel-vermont.com).

3 Entry Requirements & Customs

ENTRY REQUIREMENTS

PASSPORTS

For information on how to get a passport, go to "Passports" in the "Fast Facts: New England" section, later in this chapter—the websites listed provide downloadable passport applications as well as the current fees for processing passport applications. For an up-to-date, country-by-country listing of passport requirements around the world, go to the "Foreign Entry Requirement" Web page of the U.S. State Department at **http://travel.state.gov**. International visitors can obtain a visa application at the same website.

VISAS

For information on how to get a Visa, go to "Visas" in the "Fast Facts: New England" section, later in this chapter.

The U.S. State Department has a **Visa Waiver Program** allowing citizens of the following countries (at press time) to enter the United States without a visa for stays of up to 90 days: Andorra, Australia, Austria, Belgium, Brunei, Denmark, Finland, France, Germany, Iceland, Ireland, Italy, Japan, Liechtenstein, Luxembourg, Monaco, the Netherlands, New Zealand, Norway, Portugal, San Marino, Singapore, Slovenia, Spain, Sweden, Switzerland, and the United Kingdom. Citizens of these nations need only a valid passport and a round-trip air or cruise ticket upon arrival. If they first enter the United States, they may also visit Mexico, Canada, Bermuda, and/or the Caribbean islands and return to the United States without a visa. Further information is available from any U.S. embassy or consulate. Canadian citizens may enter the United States without visas; they need only proof of residence.

Citizens of all other countries must have (1) a valid passport that expires at least 6 months later than the scheduled end of their visit to the United States, and (2) a tourist visa, which may be obtained without charge from any U.S. consulate.

MEDICAL REQUIREMENTS

Unless you're arriving from an area known to be suffering from an epidemic (particularly cholera or yellow fever), inoculations or vaccinations are not required for entry into the United States. If you have a medical condition that requires **syringe-administered medications**, carry a valid signed prescription from your physician—the Federal Aviation Administration (FAA) no longer allows airline passengers to pack syringes in their carry-on baggage without documented proof of medical need. If you have a disease that requires treatment with **narcotics,** you should also carry documented proof with you—smuggling narcotics aboard a plane is a serious offense that carries severe penalties in the U.S.

For **HIV-positive visitors,** requirements for entering the United States are somewhat vague and change frequently. For up-to-the-minute information, contact **AIDSinfo** (© **800/448-0440,** or 301/519-6616 outside the U.S.; www.aidsinfo.nih.gov) or the **Gay Men's Health Crisis** (© **212/367-1000;** www.gmhc.org).

CUSTOMS

WHAT YOU CAN BRING INTO NEW ENGLAND

Every visitor more than 21 years of age may bring into the United States, free of duty, the following: (1) 1 liter of wine or hard liquor; (2) 200 cigarettes, 100 cigars (but not from Cuba), or 3 pounds of smoking tobacco; and (3) $100 worth of gifts. These exemptions are offered to travelers who spend at least 72 hours in the United States and who have not claimed them within the preceding 6 months. It is altogether forbidden to bring into the country foodstuffs (particularly fruit, cooked meats, and canned goods) and plants (vegetables, seeds, tropical plants, and the like). Foreign tourists may carry in or out up to $10,000 in U.S. or foreign currency with no formalities; larger sums must be declared to U.S. Customs on entering or leaving, which includes filing form CM 4790. For details regarding U.S. Customs and Border Protection, consult your nearest U.S. embassy or consulate, or **U.S. Customs** (✆ **202/927-1770;** www.customs.ustreas.gov).

WHAT YOU CAN TAKE HOME FROM NEW ENGLAND

Canadian Citizens

For a clear summary of Canadian rules, write for the booklet *I Declare,* issued by the **Canada Border Services Agency** (✆ **800/461-9999** in Canada, or 204/983-3500; **www.cbsa-asfc.gc.ca**).

U.K. Citizens

For information, contact **HM Customs & Excise** at ✆ **0845/010-9000** (from outside the U.K., 020/8929-0152), or consult their website at **www.hmce.gov.uk**.

Australian Citizens

A helpful brochure available from Australian consulates or Customs offices is *Know Before You Go.* For more information, call the **Australian Customs Service** at ✆ **1300/363-263,** or log on to **www.customs.gov.au**.

New Zealand Citizens

Most questions are answered in a free pamphlet available at New Zealand consulates and Customs offices: *New Zealand Customs Guide for Travellers, Notice no. 4.* For more information, contact New Zealand Customs, The Custormhouse, 17–21 Whitmore St., Box 2218, Wellington (✆ 04/473-6099 or 0800/428-786; www.customs.govt.nz).

4 Money

ATMs

Nationwide, the easiest and best way to get cash away from home is from an ATM (automated teller machine), sometimes referred to as a "cash machine," or "cashpoint." The **Cirrus** (✆ **800/424-7787;** www.mastercard.com) and **PLUS** (✆ **800/843-7587;** www.visa.com) networks span the country; you can find them even in remote regions. Look at the back of your bank card to see which network you're on, then call or check online for ATM locations at your destination. Be sure you know your personal identification number (PIN) and daily withdrawal limit before you depart. ***Note:*** Remember that many banks impose a fee every time you use a card at another bank's ATM, and that fee can be higher for international transactions (up to $5 or more) than for domestic ones (where they're rarely more than $2). In addition, the bank from which you withdraw cash may charge its own fee. To compare banks' ATM fees within the U.S., use **www.bankrate.com**. For international withdrawal fees, ask your bank.

CREDIT CARDS & DEBIT CARDS

Credit cards are the most widely used form of payment in the United States: **Visa** (Barclaycard in Britain), **MasterCard** (EuroCard in Europe, Access in Britain, Chargex in Canada), **American Express, Diners Club,** and **Discover.** They also provide a convenient record of all your expenses, and they generally offer relatively good exchange rates. You can withdraw cash advances from your credit cards at banks or ATMs, provided you know your PIN.

Visitors from outside the U.S. should inquire whether their bank assesses a 1% to 3% fee on charges incurred abroad.

It's highly recommended that you travel with at least one major credit card.

Tips **Easy Money**

You'll avoid lines at airport ATMs by exchanging at least some money—just enough to cover airport incidentals and transportation to your hotel—before you leave home.

When you change money, ask for some small bills or loose change. Petty cash will come in handy for tipping and public transportation. Consider keeping the change separate from your larger bills, so that it's readily accessible and you'll be less of a target for theft.

You must have one to rent a car, and hotels and airlines usually require a credit card imprint as a deposit against expenses.

ATM cards with major credit card backing, known as **debit cards,** are now a commonly acceptable form of payment in most stores and restaurants. Debit cards draw money directly from your checking account. Some stores enable you to receive "cash back" on your debit-card purchases as well. The same is true at most U.S. post offices.

TRAVELER'S CHECKS

Traveler's checks are widely accepted in the U.S., and that includes the most heavily touristed areas of New England (Boston, Cape Cod, and so on), but foreign visitors should make sure that they're denominated in U.S. dollars; foreign-currency checks are often difficult to exchange. At smaller destinations, like backwoods camps in Maine, you might not find they are accepted—if in doubt, check in advance.

You can buy traveler's checks at most banks. Most are offered in denominations of $20, $50, $100, $500, and sometimes $1,000. Generally, you'll pay a service charge ranging from 1% to 4%.

The most popular traveler's checks are offered by **American Express** (✆ **800/807-6233** or 800/221-7282 for card holders—this number accepts collect calls, offers service in several foreign languages, and exempts Amex gold and platinum cardholders from the 1% fee); and **Visa** (✆ **800/732-1322**)—AAA members can obtain Visa checks for a $9.95 fee (for checks up to $1,500) at most AAA offices or by calling ✆ **866/339-3378;** and **MasterCard** (✆ **800/223-9920**).

If you do choose to carry traveler's checks, keep a record of their serial numbers separate from your checks in the event that they are stolen or lost. You'll get a refund faster if you know the numbers.

5 When to Go

THE SEASONS

The well-worn joke about the climate in New England is that it has just two seasons—winter and August. There's a kernel of truth in it, but it's mostly a canard to keep outsiders from moving here. In fact, the ever-shifting seasons are elements that make New England so distinctive, and with one exception, the seasons are long and well defined.

SUMMER Peak summer season runs from July 4th to Labor Day. Vast crowds surge into New England during these two holiday weekends; the level of activity remains high throughout July and August.

It should be no surprise that summers are exquisite. Forests are verdant and lush; the sky can be an almost lurid blue, the cumulus clouds painfully white. In the mountains, warm (rarely hot) days are the rule, followed by cool nights. Along the coast, ocean breezes keep temperatures down and often produce thick, soupy fogs that linger for days.

For most of the region, midsummer is the prime season. Expect to pay premium prices at hotels and restaurants. The exception is around the empty ski resorts, where you can often find bargains. Also, be aware that early summer brings out black flies and mosquitoes in great multitude in woodsy northerly areas of the region, a state of affairs that has spoiled many north-country camping trips.

AUTUMN Don't be surprised to smell the tang of fall approaching as early as mid-August, when you'll also notice a few leaves turning blaze-orange on the lush maples at the edges of wetlands. Fall comes early to New England, puts its feet up on the couch, and stays for some time. The foliage season begins in earnest in the northern part of the region by the third week in September; in the south, it reaches its peak by mid-October.

Fall in New England is one of the great natural spectacles of the United States. With its rolling hills tarted up in brilliant reds and stunning oranges, fall is garish in a way that seems determined to embarrass understated Yankees. Just keep in mind that this is another popular time of year to travel—bus tours flock like migrating geese to New England in early October. As a result, hotels are often booked solid. Reservations are essential. Don't be surprised if you're assessed a foliage surcharge of $20 or more per room at some inns.

Some states maintain recorded **foliage hot lines** to let you know when the leaves are at their peak: call **Maine** (**© 800/MAINE-45**), **New Hampshire** (**© 800/258-3608**), or **Vermont** (**© 802/828-3239**).

WINTER New England winters are like wine—some years are good, some are lousy. During a good season, mounds of light, fluffy snow blanket the deep woods and fill the ski slopes. A good New England winter offers a profound peace and tranquillity. The muffling qualities of fresh snow bring a thunderous silence to the region, and the hiss and pop of a wood fire at a country inn can sound like an overwrought symphony. During these winters, exploring the forest on snowshoes or cross-country skis is an experience bordering on magical.

During the *other* winters, the lousy ones, the weather brings a nasty mélange of rain, freezing rain, and sleet. The woods are filled with nasty, crusty snow, the cold is damp and numbing, and it's bleak, bleak, bleak.

The higher you go in the mountains, and the farther north you head, the better your odds of finding snow. Winter coastal vacations can be spectacular, but it's a high-risk venture that could yield rain rather than snow.

Naturally, ski areas are crowded during the winter months. They're especially so during school vacations, when most ski resorts take the rather mercenary tactic of jacking up rates at hotels and on the slopes.

SPRING Spring lasts only a weekend or so, often around mid-May, but sometimes as late as June. One day the ground is muddy, the trees barren, and gritty snow is still collected in shady hollows. The next day, it's in the 80s, trees are blooming, and kids are swimming in the lakes. Travelers must be very crafty and alert if they want to experience spring in New England. This is also mud season, and many innkeepers and restaurateurs close up for a few weeks for repairs or to venture someplace warm.

Burlington, VT's Average Temperatures (°F/°C)

	Jan	Feb	Mar	Apr	May	June	July	Aug	Sept	Oct	Nov	Dec
Avg. High	25/–4	27/–3	38/3	53/12	66/19	76/24	80/27	78/26	69/21	57/14	44/7	30/–1
Avg. Low	8/–13	9/–13	21/–6	33/1	44/7	54/12	59/15	57/14	49/9	39/4	30/–1	15/–9

Boston's Average Temperatures (°F/°C)

	Jan	Feb	Mar	Apr	May	June	July	Aug	Sept	Oct	Nov	Dec
Avg. High	36/2	38/3	43/6	54/12	67/19	76/24	81/27	79/26	72/22	63/17	49/9	40/4
Avg. Low	20/-7	22/–6	29/–2	38/3	49/9	58/14	63/17	63/17	56/13	47/8	36/2	25/–4

NEW ENGLAND CALENDAR OF EVENTS

January

New Year's and First Night Celebrations, regionwide. Boston, MA.; Portland, ME; Providence, RI; Hartford, CT; Portsmouth, NH; Burlington, VT; and many other cities and towns, celebrate the coming of the New Year. Check with local chambers of commerce for details. New Year's Eve.

February

U.S. National Toboggan Championships, Camden, ME. This is a raucous and lively athletic event where being overweight is actually an advantage. Held at the toboggan chute of the Camden Snow Bowl. Call © **207/236-3438.** Early February.

Dartmouth Winter Carnival, Hanover, NH. Huge, elaborate ice sculptures grace the village green during this festive celebration of winter, which includes numerous sporting events. Call © **603/646-1110.** Mid-February.

Stowe Derby, Stowe, VT. The oldest downhill/cross-country ski race in the nation pits racers who scramble from the wintry summit of Mount Mansfield into the village on the Stowe Recreation path. Call © **802/253-7704.** Late February.

March

New England Spring Flower Show, Dorchester, MA. This annual harbinger of spring presented by the Massachusetts Horticultural Society (© **617/536-9280;** www.masshort.org) draws huge crowds starved for a glimpse of green. Second or third week in March.

Maine Boatbuilders Show, Portland, ME. More than 200 exhibitors and 9,000 boat aficionados gather as winter fades to make plans for the coming summer. A great place to meet boatbuilders and get ideas for your dream craft. Call © **207/774-1067.** Mid- to late March.

April

Patriots Day, Boston area (Paul Revere House, Old North Church, Lexington Green, Concord's North Bridge), MA. The events of April 18 and 19, 1775, which signified the start of the Revolutionary War, are commemorated and reenacted. Participants dressed as Paul Revere and William Dawes ride to Lexington and Concord to warn the Minutemen. Mock battles are fought at Lexington and Concord. Call the Lexington Chamber of Commerce (© **781/862-1450;** www.lexingtonchamber.org) or the Concord Chamber of Commerce (© **978/369-3120;** www.concordmachamber.org). Third Monday in April; a state holiday in Massachusetts and Maine.

Daffodil Festival, Nantucket, MA. Spring's arrival is trumpeted with masses of yellow blooms adorning everything in sight, including a cavalcade of antique cars. Call ✆ **508/228-1700.** Late April.

May

Brimfield Antique and Collectible Show, Brimfield, MA. Up to 6,000 dealers fill several fields near this central Massachusetts town, with similar fairs in July and September. Call ✆ **800/628-8379** or 508/347-2761, or go to www.brimfieldshow.com. Mid-May, also mid-July and Sept.

Cape Maritime Week, Cape Cod, MA. A multitude of cultural organizations mount special events—such as lighthouse tours—highlighting the region's nautical history. Call ✆ **508/362-3828.** Mid-May.

Lilac Festival, Shelburne, VT. See the famed lilacs (more than 400 bushes) at the renowned Shelburne Museum when they're at their most beautiful. Call ✆ **802/985-3346.** Mid-May to late May.

Figawi Sailboat Race, Hyannis (on Cape Cod) to Nantucket, MA. The largest and wildest sailboat race on the East Coast. Intensive partying in Hyannis and on Nantucket surrounds this popular event. Call ✆ **508/362-5230.** Late May.

June

Old Port Festival, Portland, ME. A block party in the heart of Portland's historic district with live music, food vendors, and activities for kids. Call ✆ **207/772-6828.** Early June.

Yale-Harvard Regatta, on the Thames River in New London, CT. One of the oldest collegiate rivalries in the country. Call ✆ **617/495-4848.** Early June.

Taste of Hartford, Hartford, CT. One of New England's largest outdoor festivals, where many area restaurants serve up their specialties. You'll also get a "taste" of local music, dance, magic, and comedy. Call ✆ **860/728-3089.** Early June.

Market Square Weekend, Portsmouth, NH. This lively street fair attracts 300 vendors and revelers from throughout southern New Hampshire and Maine into downtown Portsmouth to dance, listen to music, sample food, and enjoy summer's arrival. Call ✆ **603/436-3988.** Early June.

Motorcycle Week, Loudon and Weirs Beach, NH. Tens of thousands of bikers descend on the Lake Winnipesaukee region early each summer to compare their machines and cruise the strip at Weirs Beach. The Gunstock Hill Climb and the Loudon Classic race are the centerpieces of the week's activities. Call ✆ **603/366-2000.** Early June.

Nantucket Film Festival, Nantucket, MA. This annual event focuses on storytelling through film and includes showings of short and feature-length films, documentaries, staged readings, panel discussions, and screenplay competitions. You may see a celebrity or two. Call ✆ **508/228-1700.** Mid-June.

Provincetown Film Festival, Provincetown, MA. Focusing on alternative film, this fete has brought out celebrities like John Waters and Lily Tomlin. Call ✆ **508/487-FILM.** Mid-June.

Boston Pride March, Back Bay to Beacon Hill, Boston, MA. (✆ **617/262-9405;** www.bostonpride.org). The largest gay pride parade in New England is the highlight of a weeklong celebration of diversity. The parade, on the second Sunday of the month, starts at Copley Square and ends on Boston Common. Early June.

Jacob's Pillow Dance Festival, Becket, MA. The oldest dance festival in America features everything from ballet to modern dance and jazz. For a season brochure, call © **413/243-0745.** Late June through August.

Williamstown Theater Festival, Williamstown, MA. This nationally distinguished festival presents everything from the classics to comedies and contemporary works. Scattered among the drama are readings and cabarets. Call © **413/597-3399.** Late June through August.

July

Tanglewood Music Festival, near Lenox, MA. The Boston Symphony Orchestra makes its summer home at this fine estate, bringing symphonies, chamber groups, and soloists to the Berkshire Hills. Call the Tanglewood Concert Line at © **413/637-1666** (July and Aug only) or Symphony Hall at © **617/266-1492;** or go to www.bso.org. July through August.

Boston Harborfest, downtown Boston (along Boston Harbor and the Harbor Islands), MA. The city puts on its Sunday best for the Fourth of July, which has become a gigantic weeklong celebration of Boston's maritime history. Events include concerts, tours, cruises, fireworks, the Boston Chowderfest, and the annual turnaround of USS *Constitution.* Contact Boston Harborfest (© **617/227-1528;** www.bostonharborfest.com). First week in July.

Boston Pops Concert and Fireworks Display, Hatch Memorial Shell on the Esplanade, Boston, MA. The big day culminates in the famous Boston Pops' Fourth of July concert. People wait from dawn 'til dark for the music to start. Visit www.july4th.org. July 4th.

Wickford Art Festival, Wickford, RI. More than 200 artists gather in this quaint village for one of the East Coast's oldest art festivals. Call © **401/294-6840,** or go to www.wickfordart.org. Weekend after July 4th.

Newport Music Festival, Newport, RI. Chamber-music concerts are held inside Newport's opulent mansions. Call © **401/846-1133.** Second and third weeks in July.

Friendship Sloop Days, Rockland, ME. This 3-day event is a series of boat races that culminates in a parade of sloops. Call © **207/596-0376.** Mid-July.

Vermont Quilt Festival, Northfield, VT. Displays are only part of the allure of New England's largest (and oldest) quilt festival. You can also attend classes and have your heirlooms appraised. See descriptions at www.vqf.org, or call © **802/485-7092** for more information. Mid-July.

Revolutionary War Days, Exeter, NH. Learn all you need to know about the War of Independence during this historic community festival, which features a Revolutionary War encampment and dozens of reenactors. Call © **603/772-2411.** Mid- July.

Barnstable County Fair, East Falmouth (on Cape Cod), MA. An old-time county fair complete with rides, food, and livestock contests. Call © **508/563-3200.** Late July.

Marlboro Music Festival, Marlboro, VT. This is a popular 6-week series of classical concerts featuring talented student musicians and seasoned artists performing in the peaceful hills outside of Brattleboro. Call © **802/254-2394** (or 215/569-4690 in winter) for information. Weekends from July to mid-August.

Maine Lobster Festival, Rockland, ME. Fill up on the local harvest and a boiled lobster or two at this event marking the importance and delectability of Maine's favorite crustacean. Call © **207/596-0376.** Late July to early August.

August

Southern Vermont Art & Craft Fair, Manchester, VT. More than 200 artisans show off their fine work at this popular festival, which also features creative food and good music. Held on the grounds of Hildene, a grand historic home. Call ✆ **802/362-2100.** Early August.

Newport Folk Festival. Newport, RI. Thousands of music lovers congregate at Fort Adams State Park for a heavy dose of performances on an August weekend. It's one of the nation's premier festivals. Call ✆ **401/847-3700,** or go to www.newportfolk.com. Early August.

Annual Star Party, St. Johnsbury, VT. The historic Fairbanks Museum and Planetarium hosts special events and shows, including night-viewing sessions during the Perseid Meteor Shower. Call ✆ **802/748-2372.** Mid-August.

Wild Blueberry Festival, Machias, ME. A festival marking the harvest of the region's wild blueberries. Call ✆ **207/794-3543** or 207/255-6665. Mid-August.

JVC Jazz Festival. Newport, RI. This 3-day jazz festival brings together some of the best in the music industry to play for a sizzling weekend at Fort Adams State Park. Call ✆ **401/847-3700.** Mid-August.

Martha's Vineyard Agricultural Fair, West Tisbury, MA. An old-fashioned country fair featuring horse pulls, livestock shows, musicians, and woodsman contests, along with plenty of carnival action. Call ✆ **508/693-4343.** Third weekend in August.

Pops Goes the Summer, Barnstable County Fairgrounds, Falmouth, MA. Cape Cod Symphony Orchestra concert followed by a huge fireworks display. Call ✆ **508/548-8500.** Late August.

September

Windjammer Weekend, Camden, ME. Come visit Maine's impressive fleet of old-time sailing ships, which host open houses throughout the weekend at this scenic harbor. Call ✆ **207/236-4404.** Labor Day weekend.

Vermont State Fair, Rutland, VT. All of Vermont seems to show up for this grand event, with a midway, live music, and plenty of agricultural exhibits. Call ✆ **802/775-5200.** Early September.

Providence Waterfront Festival, Providence, RI. Musical performances are the highlight of this weekend event, especially the jazz festival on Sunday. Call ✆ **401/621-1992.** Weekend after Labor Day.

Norwalk Oyster Festival, Norwalk, CT. This waterfront festival celebrates Long Island Sound's seafaring past. Highlights include oyster-shucking and slurping contests, harbor cruises, concerts, and fireworks. Call ✆ **203/838-9444.** Weekend after Labor Day.

Convergence International Festival of the Arts, Providence, RI. Various Providence arts organizations pull together for this weeklong citywide event, which includes sculptural installations, musical performances, and other arts events. Call ✆ **401/621-1992.** Mid-September.

Eastern States Exhibition, West Springfield, MA. "The Big E" is New England's largest agricultural fair with a midway, games, rides, rodeo and lumberjack shows, country-music stars, and lots of eats. Call ✆ **413/737-2443.** Mid- to late September.

Provincetown Arts Festival, Provincetown, MA. One of the country's oldest art colonies celebrates its past and present with local artists opening their studios. Call ✆ **508/487-3424.** Late September.

Common Ground Country Fair, Unity, ME. A sprawling, old-time state fair with a twist: The emphasis is on organic foods, recycling, crafts, and wholesome living. Call ✆ **207/568-4142.** Late September.

October

Fryeburg Fair, Fryeburg, ME. Cotton candy, tractor pulls, live music, and huge vegetables and barnyard animals at Maine's largest agricultural fair. Call ✆ **207/985-3268.** One week in early October.

Mystic Chowderfest, Mystic, CT. A festival of soup served from bubbling cauldrons set on wood fires. Call ✆ **860/572-5315.** Mid-October.

Head of the Charles Regatta, Boston and Cambridge, MA. High school, college, and post-collegiate rowing teams and individuals—some 4,000 in all—race in front of hordes of fans along the banks of the Charles River. Call ✆ **617/868-6200** or visit www.hocr.org for information. Late October.

November

Brookfield Holiday Craft Exhibition & Sale, Brookfield, CT. Thousands of unique, elegant, and artful gifts are displayed in gallery settings on three floors of a restored grist mill. Call ✆ **203/775-4526.** Mid-November through late December.

Thanksgiving Celebration, Plymouth, MA. The holiday that put Plymouth on the map is observed with a "stroll through the ages," showcasing 17th- and 19th-century Thanksgiving preparations in historic homes. Nearby Plimoth Plantation, where the colony's first years are re-created, wisely offers a Victorian Thanksgiving feast (reservations required). Call Destination Plymouth (✆ **800/872-1620;** www.visit-plymouth.com) or Plimoth Plantation (✆ **508/746-1622;** www.plimoth.org). Thanksgiving Day.

Victorian Holiday, Portland, ME. From late November until Christmas, Portland decorates its Old Port in a Victorian Christmas theme. Enjoy the window displays, take a free hayride, and listen to costumed carolers. Call ✆ **207/772-6828** or 207/780-5555. Late November to Christmas.

December

Black Nativity, Converse Hall, Tremont Temple Baptist Church, 88 Tremont St., Boston, MA. (✆ **617/723-3486;** www.blacknativity.org). Poet Langston Hughes wrote the "gospel opera," and a cast of more than 100 brings it to life. Most weekends in December.

Christmas Prelude, Kennebunkport, ME. This scenic coastal village greets Santa's arrival in a lobster boat, and marks the coming of Christmas with street shows, pancake breakfasts, and tours of the town's splendid inns. Call ✆ **207/967-0857.** Early December.

Christmas Stroll, Nantucket, MA. The island briefly stirs from its winter slumber for one last shopping/feasting spree, attended by costumed carolers and Santa in a horse-drawn carriage. The weekend event is the pinnacle of Nantucket Noel, a month of festivities starting in late November. Call ✆ **508/228-1700.** Early December.

Candlelight Stroll, Portsmouth, NH. Historic Strawbery Banke gets in a Christmas way with old-time decorations and more than 1,000 candles lighting the 10-acre grounds. Call ✆ **603/433-1100.** First two weekends in December.

Boston Tea Party Reenactment, Old South Meeting House and Congress Street Bridge, Boston, MA. Re-creates the events of December 16, 1773. Call ✆ **617/482-6439** or visit www.oldsouthmeetinghouse.org. Mid-December.

Woodstock Wassail Celebration, Woodstock, VT. Enjoy classic English grog, along with parades and dances at this annual event. Call ✆ **802/457-3555.** Mid-December.

Christmas Eve and Christmas Day, festivities throughout New England. In Newport, RI, several of the great mansions offer tours; Mystic, CT, has a program of Christmas festivities; Nantucket, MA, features carolers in Victorian garb, art exhibits, and tours of historic homes. December 24 and 25.

6 Travel Insurance

The cost of travel insurance varies widely, depending on the cost and length of your trip, your age and health, and the type of trip you're taking, but expect to pay between 5% and 8% of the vacation itself. You can get estimates from various providers through **InsureMyTrip.com**. Enter your trip cost and dates, your age, and other information, for prices from more than a dozen companies.

TRIP-CANCELLATION INSURANCE

Trip-cancellation insurance will help retrieve your money if you have to back out of a trip or depart early, or if your travel supplier goes bankrupt. Permissible reasons for trip cancellation can range from sickness to natural disasters to the State Department declaring a destination unsafe for travel.

For more information, contact one of the following recommended insurers: Access America (✆ 866/807-3982; www.accessamerica.com); Travel Guard International (✆ 800/826-4919; www.travelguard.com); Travel Insured International (✆ 800/243-3174; www.travelinsured.com); and Travelex Insurance Services (✆ 888/457-4602; www.travelex-insurance.com).

MEDICAL INSURANCE

Although it's not required of travelers, health insurance is highly recommended. Most health insurance policies cover you if you get sick away from home—but verify that you're covered before you depart, particularly if you're insured by an HMO.

International visitors should note that unlike many European countries, the United States does not usually offer free or low-cost medical care to its citizens or visitors. Doctors and hospitals are expensive, and in most cases will require advance payment or proof of coverage before they render their services. Good policies will cover the costs of an accident, repatriation, or death. Packages such as **Europ Assistance's "Worldwide**

Travel in the Age of Bankruptcy

Airlines go bankrupt, so protect yourself by **buying your tickets with a credit card.** The Fair Credit Billing Act guarantees that you can get your money back from the credit card company if a travel supplier goes under (and if you request the refund within 60 days of the bankruptcy). **Travel insurance** can also help, but make sure it covers against "carrier default" for your specific travel provider. And be aware that if a U.S. airline goes bust mid-trip, a 2001 federal law requires other carriers to take you to your destination (albeit on a space-available basis) for a fee of no more than $25, provided you rebook within 60 days of the cancellation.

Healthcare Plan" are sold by European automobile clubs and travel agencies at attractive rates. **Worldwide Assistance Services, Inc.** (© **800/777-8710;** www.worldwideassistance.com) is the agent for Europ Assistance in the United States.

Though lack of health insurance may prevent you from being admitted to a hospital in nonemergencies, don't worry about being left on a street corner to die: The American way is to fix you now and bill the living daylights out of you later.

INSURANCE FOR BRITISH TRAVELERS Most big travel agents offer their own insurance and will probably try to sell you their package when you book a holiday. Think before you sign. **Britain's Consumers' Association** recommends that you insist on seeing the policy and reading the fine print before buying travel insurance. **The Association of British Insurers** (© **020/7600-3333;** www.abi.org.uk) gives advice by phone and publishes *Holiday Insurance,* a free guide to policy provisions and prices. You might also shop around for better deals: Try **Columbus Direct** (© **0870/033-9988;** www.columbusdirect.net).

INSURANCE FOR CANADIAN TRAVELERS Canadians should check with their provincial health plan offices or call **Health Canada** (© **866/225-0709;** www.hc-sc.gc.ca) to find out the extent of their coverage and what documentation and receipts they must take home in case they are treated in the United States.

LOST-LUGGAGE INSURANCE

On flights within the U.S., checked baggage is covered up to $2,500 per ticketed passenger. On flights outside the U.S. (and on U.S. portions of international trips), baggage coverage is limited to approximately $9.07 per pound, up to approximately $635 per checked bag. If you plan to check items more valuable than what's covered by the standard liability, see if your homeowner's policy covers your valuables, get baggage insurance as part of your comprehensive travel-insurance package, or buy Travel Guard's "BagTrak" product.

If your luggage is lost, immediately file a lost-luggage claim at the airport, detailing the luggage contents. Most airlines require that you report delayed, damaged, or lost baggage within 4 hours of arrival. The airlines are required to deliver luggage, once found, directly to your house or destination free of charge.

7 Health & Safety

STAYING HEALTHY

Other than picking up a germ that may lead to a cold or flu, you shouldn't face any serious health risks when traveling in the region. Of course, you may find yourself at higher risk when exploring the outdoors, particularly in the backcountry. A few things to watch for when venturing off the beaten track:

- **Poison ivy:** The shiny, three-leafed plant is common throughout the region. If touched, you may develop a nasty, itchy rash that will seriously erode the enjoyment of your vacation. The reaction tends to be worse in some people than others. It's safest to simply avoid it. If you're unfamiliar with what poison ivy looks like, ask at a ranger station or visitor information booth for more information. Many have posters or books to help with identification.
- **Giardia:** That crystal-clear stream coursing down a backcountry peak may seem pure, but it may be contaminated with animal feces. Gross, yes, and also dangerous. Giardia cysts may be present in some streams and

rivers. When ingested by humans, the cysts can result in copious diarrhea and weight loss. Symptoms may not surface until well after you've left the backcountry and returned home. Carry your own water for day trips, or bring a small filter (available at most camping and sporting goods shops) to treat backcountry water. Failing that, at least boil water or treat it with iodine before using it for cooking, drinking, or washing. If you detect symptoms, see a doctor immediately.

- **Lyme disease:** Lyme disease has been a growing problem in New England since 1975 when the disease was identified in the town of Lyme, CT, and some 14,000 cases are reported nationwide annually. The disease is transmitted by tiny deer ticks—smaller than the more common, relatively harmless wood ticks. Look for a bull's-eye-shaped rash (3–8 in. in diameter); it may feel warm but usually doesn't itch. Symptoms include muscle and joint pain, fever, and fatigue. If left untreated, heart damage may occur. It's more easily treated in early phases than later, so seek medical attention as soon as any symptoms are noted.
- **Rabies:** The disease is spread by animal saliva and is especially prevalent in skunks, raccoons, bats, and foxes. It is always fatal if left untreated in humans. Infected animals tend to display erratic and aggressive behavior. The best advice is to keep a safe distance between yourself and any wild animal you may encounter. If bitten, wash the wound as soon as you can and immediately seek medical attention. Treatment involves a series of shots.

Those planning longer excursions into the outdoors may find a compact first-aid kit with basic salves and medicines very handy to have along.

GENERAL AVAILABILITY OF HEALTHCARE

Contact the **International Association for Medical Assistance to Travelers (IAMAT)** (© **716/754-4883** or, in Canada, 416/652-0137; **www.iamat.org**) for tips on travel and health concerns in the countries you're visiting, and for lists of local, English-speaking doctors. The United States **Centers for Disease Control and Prevention** (© **800/311-3435;** www.cdc.gov) provides up-to-date information on health hazards by region or country and offers tips on food safety. The website **www.tripprep.com**, sponsored by a consortium of travel medicine practitioners, may also offer helpful advice on traveling abroad. You can find listings of reliable clinics overseas at the **International Society of Travel Medicine** (www.istm.org).

WHAT TO DO IF YOU GET SICK AWAY FROM HOME

We list **emergency numbers** under "Fast Facts: New England," p. 59.

If you suffer from a chronic illness, consult your doctor before your departure. Pack **prescription medications** in your carry-on luggage, and carry them in their original containers, with pharmacy labels—otherwise they won't make it through airport security. Visitors from outside the U.S. should carry generic names of prescription drugs. For U.S. travelers, most reliable healthcare plans provide coverage if you get sick away from home. Foreign visitors may have to pay all medical costs upfront and be reimbursed later. See "Medical Insurance," under "Travel Insurance," above.

If you get sick, consider asking your hotel concierge to recommend a local doctor—even his or her own. You can also try the emergency room at a local hospital. Many hospitals also have walk-in clinics for emergency cases that are not life-threatening; you may not get immediate attention, but you won't pay the high price of an emergency room visit. There are large, good hospitals in all cities in this region, as well as in many small towns. Check with your hotel or the local tourism office if you're concerned about proximity to hotels.

If you suffer from a chronic illness, consult your doctor before your departure. For conditions like epilepsy, diabetes, or heart problems, wear a **MedicAlert identification tag** (© **888/633-4298;** www.medicalert.org), which will immediately alert doctors to your condition and give them access to your records through MedicAlert's 24-hour hot line.

Pack **prescription medications** in your carry-on luggage, and carry prescription medications in their original containers, with pharmacy labels—otherwise they won't make it through airport security. Also carry copies of your prescriptions in case you lose your pills or run out. Don't forget an extra pair of contact lenses or prescription glasses.

For domestic trips, most reliable healthcare plans provide coverage if you get sick away from home.

STAYING SAFE

New England—with the notable exception of parts of Boston and Hartford—boasts some of the lowest crime rates in the country. The odds of anything bad happening during your visit here are very slight. But all travelers are advised to take the usual precautions against theft, robbery, and assault.

Travelers should avoid any unnecessary public displays of wealth. Don't bring out fat wads of cash from your pocket, and save your best jewelry for private occasions. If you are approached by someone who demands money, jewelry, or anything else from you, do what most Americans do: Hand it over. Don't argue. Don't negotiate. Just comply. Afterward, immediately contact the police by dialing © **911** from almost any phone.

The crime you're statistically most likely to encounter is theft of items from your car. Don't leave anything of value in plain view and lock valuables in your trunk.

Late at night, you should look for a well-lighted area if you need gas or you need to step out of your car for any reason.

Take the usual precautions against leaving cash or valuables in your hotel room when you're not present. Many hotels have safe-deposit boxes. Smaller inns and hotels often do not, although it can't hurt to ask to leave small items in the house safe.

8 Specialized Travel Resources

TRAVELERS WITH DISABILITIES

Most disabilities shouldn't stop anyone from traveling in New England. There are more options and resources out there than ever before.

The **Golden Access Passport** gives visually impaired or permanently disabled persons (regardless of age) free lifetime entrance to all properties administered by the National Park Service, the U.S. Fish and Wildlife Service, the U.S. Forest Service, the U.S. Army Corps of Engineers, the Bureau of Land Management, and the Tennessee Valley Authority. This may include national parks, monuments, historic sites, recreation areas, and national wildlife refuges.

You may pick up a Golden Access Passport at any NPS entrance fee area by showing proof of medically determined disability and eligibility for benefits under federal law. Besides free entry, the Golden Access Passport also offers a 50% discount on federal-use fees charged for such facilities as camping, swimming, parking, boat launching, and tours. For more information, go to www.nps.gov/fees_passes.htm or call © **888/467-2757.**

Many travel agencies offer customized tours and itineraries for travelers with disabilities. Among them are **Flying Wheels Travel** (© **507/451-5005;** www.flyingwheelstravel.com); **Access-Able Travel Source** (© **303/232-2979;** www.access-able.com); and **Accessible Journeys** (© **800/846-4537** or 610/521-0339; www.disabilitytravel.com). **Avis Rent a Car** has an "Avis Access" program that offers such services as a dedicated 24-hour toll-free number (© **888/879-4273**) for customers with special travel needs; special car features such as swivel seats, spinner knobs, and hand controls; and accessible bus service.

Organizations that offer assistance to disabled travelers include **MossRehab** (www.mossresourcenet.org); the **American Foundation for the Blind (AFB)** (© **800/232-5463;** www.afb.org); and **SATH** (Society for Accessible Travel & Hospitality) (© **212/447-7284;** www.sath.org). **AirAmbulanceCard.com** is now partnered with SATH and allows you to preselect top-notch hospitals in case of an emergency.

Check out the quarterly magazine ***Emerging Horizons*** (www.emerginghorizons.com); and ***Open World*** magazine, published by SATH.

GAY & LESBIAN TRAVELERS

Parts of New England are surprisingly friendly to gay and lesbian culture, while other parts are still deeply antipathetic toward the culture. As elsewhere in the country, the larger cities tend to be more accommodating to gay travelers than smaller towns.

Provincetown, MA (at the very end of Cape Cod), is without a doubt the gay-friendliest town in New England. Rainbow flags fly proudly throughout the town, and it's safe to say this is a must-visit place for any first-time gay or lesbian traveler to the region.

Northampton, MA—home to Smith College—boasts a substantial and thriving lesbian community.

Vermont has traditionally been the most overall welcoming of the New England states; it is a specific destination for visitors who want to support the state's law acknowledging civil unions or celebrate a civil union of their own. A backlash (seen in a spate of TAKE BACK VERMONT signs) arose in response to the law, but failed to have the law repealed.

For information on Vermont civil unions, visit the state-run website www.sec.state.vt.us/otherprg/civilunions/civilunions.html.

A number of hotels and inns ranging from small B&Bs to the larger resorts welcome travelers (and their friends) who are celebrating civil unions. Check online ads and advertisements in GLBT newspapers and magazines.

Portland, ME, has a substantial gay population, attracting many refugees who have fled the crime and congestion of Boston and New York. Portland hosts a sizable Pride festival early each summer that includes a riotous parade and a dance on the city pier, among other events. In early 1998, Maine narrowly repealed a statewide gay-rights law that had been passed earlier by the state legislature. In Portland, however, the vote was nearly four to one against the repeal and in support of equal rights. Portland also has a municipal ordinance that prohibits discrimination in jobs and housing based on sexual orientation.

Ogunquit, on the southern Maine coast, is a hugely popular destination among gay travelers, and features a lively beach and bar scene in the summer. In the winter, it's still active but decidedly more mellow. A well-designed website, **www.gayogunquit.com**, is a great place to start to find information on gay-owned inns, restaurants, and nightclubs in the town.

For a more detailed directory of gay-oriented enterprises in New England, track down a copy of **The Pink Pages,** published by KP Media (66 Charles St., #283, Boston, MA 02114). Call ✆ **617/423-1515** or 800/338-6550, or visit the firm's website at **www.pinkweb.com**, which also contains much of the information in the published version.

More adventurous souls should consider linking up with the **Chiltern Mountain Club,** P.O. Box 390928, Cambridge, MA 02139 (✆ **617/869-7958;** www.chiltern.org), an outdoor-adventure club for gays and lesbians; about two-thirds of its 1,200 members are men. The club organizes trips to northern New England throughout the year.

The International Gay and Lesbian Travel Association (IGLTA) (✆ **800/448-8550** or 954/776-2626; www.iglta.org) is the trade association for the gay and lesbian travel industry, and offers an online directory of gay- and lesbian-friendly travel businesses; go to their website and click on "Members."

Many agencies offer tours and travel itineraries specifically for gay and lesbian travelers. **Now, Voyager** (✆ **800/255-6951;** www.nowvoyager.com) is a well-known San Francisco–based, gay-owned and operated travel service.

Gay.com Travel (✆ **800/929-2268** or 415/644-8044; www.gay.com/travel or www.outandabout.com), is an excellent online successor to the popular ***Out & About*** print magazine. It provides regularly updated information about gay-owned, gay-oriented, and gay-friendly lodging, dining, sightseeing, nightlife, and shopping establishments in every important destination worldwide. It also offers trip-planning information for gay and lesbian travelers for more than 50 destinations, along various themes, ranging from Sex & Travel to Vacations for Couples.

SENIOR TRAVEL

Mention the fact that you're a senior when you make your travel reservations. Although all the major U.S. airlines except America West have canceled their senior discount and coupon book programs, many hotels still offer lower rates for seniors. In most cities, people over the age of 60 qualify for reduced admission to theaters, museums, and other attractions, and discounted fares on public transportation.

New England is well suited to older travelers, with a wide array of activities for seniors and discounts commonly available. Members of **AARP** (formerly known as the American Association of Retired Persons), 601 E St. NW, Washington, DC 20049 (✆ **888/687-2277;** www.aarp.org), get discounts on hotels, airfares, and car rentals. AARP offers members a wide range of benefits, including *AARP: The Magazine* and a monthly newsletter. Anyone over 50 can join.

The **U.S. National Park Service** offers a **Golden Age Passport** that gives seniors 62 years or older lifetime entrance to all properties administered by the National Park Service—national parks, monuments, historic sites, recreation areas, and national wildlife refuges—for a one-time processing fee of $10, which must be purchased in person at any NPS facility that charges an entrance fee. Besides free entry, a Golden Age Passport also offers a 50% discount on federal-use fees charged for such facilities as camping, swimming, parking, boat launching, and tours. For more information, go to www.nps.gov/fees_passes.htm or call ✆ **888/467-2757.**

Many reliable agencies and organizations target the 50-plus market. **Elderhostel** (✆ **877/426-8056;** www.elderhostel.org) arranges study programs for those aged 55 and over. **ElderTreks** (✆ **800/741-7956;** www.eldertreks.com) offers small-group tours to off-the-beaten-path or adventure-travel locations, restricted to travelers 50 and older. **INTRAV** (✆ **800/456-8100;** www.intrav.com) is a high-end tour operator that caters to the mature, discerning traveler (not specifically seniors), with trips around the world that include guided safaris, polar expeditions, private-jet adventures, and small-boat cruises down jungle rivers.

Recommended publications offering travel resources and discounts for seniors include: the quarterly magazine ***Travel 50 & Beyond*** (www.travel50andbeyond.com); ***Travel Unlimited: Uncommon Adventures for the Mature Traveler*** (Avalon); ***101 Tips for Mature Travelers,*** available from Grand Circle Travel (✆ **800/221-2610** or 617/350-7500; www.gct.com); and ***Unbelievably Good Deals and Great Adventures That You Absolutely Can't Get Unless You're Over 50*** (McGraw-Hill), by Joann Rattner Heilman.

FAMILY TRAVEL

The family vacation is a rite of passage for many households, one that in a split second can evolve into a *National Lampoon* farce. However, it can be among the most pleasurable and rewarding times of your life.

Families will have little trouble finding fun, low-key things to do with kids in New England. The natural world seems to hold tremendous wonder for the younger set—an afternoon exploring mossy banks and rocky streambeds can be a huge adventure. Older kids may like the challenge of climbing a mountain peak or learning to paddle a canoe in a straight line, and the beach is always good for hours of afternoon diversion.

Some recommended destinations for families in New England include Weirs Beach and Hampton Beach in New Hampshire, and York Beach and Acadia National Park in Maine. North Conway, New Hampshire, also makes a good base for exploring with younger kids. The town has lots of motels with pools, and you can find nearby train rides, streams suitable for splashing around, easy hikes, and the wonderful distraction known as Story Land. And Cape Cod is filled with beaches, ice-cream stands, and the like—what it lacks in splashy amusements, it makes up for with gentler attractions.

Be sure to ask about family discounts when visiting attractions. Many places offer a flat family rate that is less than paying for each ticket individually. Some parks and beaches charge by the car rather than the head.

To locate accommodations, restaurants, and attractions that are particularly kid-friendly, refer to the "Kids" icon throughout this guide.

Familyhostel (✆ **800/733-9753;** www.learn.unh.edu/familyhostel) takes the whole family, including kids ages 8 to 15, on moderately priced U.S. and international learning vacations. Lectures, field trips, and sightseeing are guided by a team of academics.

Recommended family travel websites include **Family Travel Forum** (www.familytravelforum.com), a comprehensive site that offers customized trip planning; **Family Travel Network** (www.familytravelnetwork.com), an award-winning site that offers travel features, deals, and tips; **Traveling Internationally with Your Kids** (www.travelwithyourkids.com), a comprehensive site offering sound advice for long-distance and international travel with children; and **Family Travel Files** (www.thefamilytravelfiles.com), which offers an online magazine and a directory of off-the-beaten-path tours and tour operators for families.

Frommer's National Parks with Kids includes useful material on traveling with kids to Acadia National Park in Maine and Cape Cod National Seashore in Massachusetts.

STUDENT TRAVEL

A valid student ID will often qualify students for discounts on airfare, accommodations, entry to museums, cultural events, movies, and more. If you're planning to travel outside the U.S., you'd be wise to arm yourself with an **International Student Identity Card (ISIC),** which offers substantial savings on rail passes, plane tickets, and entrance fees. It also provides you with basic health and life insurance and a 24-hour help line. The card is available from **STA Travel** (© **800/781-4040** in North America; www.sta.com or www.statravel.com), the biggest student travel agency in the world. If you're no longer a student but are still under 26, you can get an **International Youth Travel Card (IYTC)** from the same people, which entitles you to some discounts (but not on museum admissions). **Travel CUTS** (© **800/667-2887** or 416/614-2887; www.travelcuts.com) offers similar services for both Canadians and U.S. residents. Irish students may prefer to turn to **USIT** (© **01/602-1600;** www.usitnow.ie), an Ireland-based specialist in student, youth, and independent travel.

TRAVELING WITH PETS

No surprise: Some places allow pets, some don't. We've noted inns that allow pets, but even here I don't recommend showing up with a pet in tow unless you've cleared it over the phone with the innkeeper. Note that many establishments have only one or two rooms (often a cottage or room with exterior entrance) set aside for guests traveling with pets, and they won't be happy to meet Fido if the pet rooms are already occupied. Also, it's increasingly common for a surcharge of $10 or $20 to be charged to pet owners to pay for the extra cleaning. On the positive side, all **Motel 6** hotels accept pets as a matter of policy, and so (surprisingly) do some upscale inns.

Keep in mind that dogs are prohibited on hiking trails and must be leashed at all times on federal lands administered by the National Park Service (this includes Acadia National Park in Maine). Pets are allowed to hike off-leash in the White Mountains National Forest in New Hampshire and the Green Mountain National Forest in Vermont. No pets of any sort are allowed at any time (leashed or unleashed) at Baxter State Park in Maine. Other Maine state parks do allow pets on a leash.

ECO-TOURISM

You can find eco-friendly travel tips, statistics, and touring companies and associations—listed by destination under "Travel Choice"—at the TIES website, www.ecotourism.org. **Ecotravel.com** is part online magazine and part ecodirectory that lets you search for touring companies in several categories (water-based, land-based, spiritually oriented, and so on). Also check out **Conservation International** (www.conservation.org)—which, with *National Geographic Traveler,* annually presents **World Legacy Awards** (www.wlaward.org) to those travel tour operators, businesses, organizations, and places that have made a significant contribution to sustainable tourism.

9 Planning Your Trip Online

SURFING FOR AIRFARE

The most popular online travel agencies are **Travelocity (www.travelocity.com** or www.travelocity.co.uk); **Expedia (www.expedia.com,** www.expedia.co.uk, or www.expedia.ca); and **Orbitz** (www.orbitz.com).

In addition, most airlines now offer online-only fares that even their phone agents know nothing about. This is especially true of low-fare carriers such as Southwest (with lots of flights into Manchester), JetBlue (which flies into Burlington), AirTran, and WestJet, whose fares are often misreported or simply missing from travel agency websites.

For the websites of airlines that fly to and from your destination, go to "Getting There," p. 43.

Also remember to check **airline websites,** especially those for

Other helpful websites for booking airline tickets online include:

- www.biddingfortravel.com
- www.cheapflights.com
- www.hotwire.com
- www.kayak.com
- www.lastminutetravel.com
- www.opodo.co.uk
- www.priceline.com
- www.sidestep.com
- www.site59.com
- www.smartertravel.com

SURFING FOR HOTELS

In addition to **Travelocity, Expedia, Orbitz, Priceline,** and **Hotwire** (see above), the following websites will help you with booking hotel rooms online:

- www.hotels.com
- www.quickbook.com
- www.travelaxe.net
- www.travelweb.com
- www.tripadvisor.com

It's a good idea to **get a confirmation number** and **make a printout** of any online booking transaction.

Also check on bed-and-breakfast associations in the states of New England; you can sometimes turn up gems in the rough this way.

Frommers.com: The Complete Travel Resource

For an excellent travel-planning resource, we highly recommend **Frommers.com** (www.frommers.com), voted Best Travel Site by *PC Magazine.* We're a little biased, of course, but we guarantee that you'll find the travel tips, reviews, monthly vacation giveaways, bookstore, and online-booking capabilities thoroughly indispensable. Among the special features are our popular **Destinations** section, where you'll get expert travel tips, hotel and dining recommendations, and advice on the sights to see for more than 3,500 destinations around the globe; the **Frommers.com Newsletter,** with the latest deals, travel trends, and money-saving secrets; our **Community** area featuring **Message Boards,** where Frommer's readers post queries and share advice (sometimes even our authors show up to answer questions); and our **Photo Center,** where you can post and share vacation tips. When your research is finished, the **Online Reservations System** (www.frommers.com/book_a_trip) takes you to Frommer's preferred online partners for booking your vacation at affordable prices.

SURFING FOR RENTAL CARS

For booking rental cars online, the best deals are usually found at rental-car company websites, although all the major online travel agencies also offer rental-car reservations services. Priceline and Hotwire work well for rental cars, too; the only "mystery" is which major rental company you get, and for most travelers the difference between Hertz, Avis, and Budget is negligible.

TRAVEL BLOGS AND TRAVELOGUES

To find and read a few blogs about New England, log onto:

- www.gridskipper.com
- www.salon.com/wanderlust
- www.travelblog.com
- www.travelblog.org
- www.worldhum.com
- www.writtenroad.com

10 The 21st-Century Traveler

INTERNET ACCESS AWAY FROM HOME

WITHOUT YOUR OWN COMPUTER

To find cybercafes in your destination check **www.cybercaptive.com** and **www.cybercafe.com**. Larger cities in New England, such as Boston, Hartford, Portland, and Providence always have a couple of cybercafes; in small towns, though, it's hit-or-miss (usually miss).

Aside from formal cybercafes, most **youth hostels** and **public libraries** offer Internet access. Avoid **hotel business centers** unless you're willing to pay exorbitant rates.

Most major airports now have **Internet kiosks** scattered throughout their gates. These give you basic Web access for a per-minute fee that's usually higher than cybercafe prices.

WITH YOUR OWN COMPUTER

More and more hotels, cafes, and retailers are signing on as Wi-Fi (wireless fidelity) "hotspots." Mac owners have their own networking technology, Apple AirPort. **T-Mobile Hotspot** (www.t-mobile.com/hotspot) serves up wireless connections at more than 1,000 Starbucks coffee shops nationwide. **Boingo** (www.boingo.com) and **Wayport** (www.wayport.com) have set up networks in airports and high-class hotel lobbies. IPass providers (see below) also give you access to a few hundred wireless hotel lobby setups. To locate other hotspots that provide **free wireless networks** in cities around the world, go to **www.personaltelco.net/index.cgi/WirelessCommunities**.

For dial-up access, most business-class hotels in the U.S. offer dataports for laptop modems, and a few thousand hotels in the U.S. and Europe now offer free high-speed Internet access. In addition, major Internet Service Providers (ISPs) have **local access numbers** around the world, allowing you to go online by placing a local call. The **iPass** network also has dial-up numbers around the world. You'll have to sign up with an iPass provider, who will then tell you how to set up your computer for your destination(s). For a list of iPass providers, go to www.ipass.com and click on "Individuals Buy Now." One solid provider is **i2roam** (www.i2roam.com; ✆ **866/811-6209** or 920/235-0475).

Wherever you go, bring a **connection kit** of the right power and phone adapters, a spare phone cord, and a spare Ethernet network cable—or find out whether your hotel supplies them to guests.

For information on electrical currency conversions, see "Electricity," in the "Fast Facts: New England" section at the end of this chapter.

CELLPHONE USE IN THE U.S.

Just because your cellphone works at home doesn't mean it'll work everywhere in the

Online Traveler's Toolbox

- **Airplane Food** (www.airlinemeals.net)
- **Airplane Seating** (www.seatguru.com and www.airlinequality.com)
- **Events** (www.bostonglobe.com; www.pressherald.com, www.hartford courant.com)
- **Foreign Languages for Travelers** (www.travlang.com)
- **Maps** (www.mapquest.com)
- **Subway Navigator** (www.subwaynavigator.com)
- **Time and Date** (www.timeanddate.com)
- **Travel Warnings** (http://travel.state.gov, www.fco.gov.uk/travel, www.voyage.gc.ca, www.dfat.gov.au/consular/advice)
- **Universal Currency Converter** (www.xe.com/ucc)
- **Visa ATM Locator** (www.visa.com), **MasterCard ATM Locator** (www.mastercard.com)
- **Weather** (www.intellicast.com and www.weather.com)

U.S. (thanks to our nation's fragmented cellphone system). It's a good bet that your phone will work in major cities, but take a look at your wireless company's coverage map on its website before heading out; T-Mobile, Sprint, and Nextel are particularly weak in rural areas. If you need to stay in touch at a destination where you know your phone won't work, **rent** a phone that does from **InTouch USA** (© **800/872-7626;** www.intouchglobal.com) or a rental car location, but beware that you'll pay $1 a minute or more for airtime.

If you're venturing deep into national parks, you may want to consider renting a **satellite phone ("satphones").** It's different from a cellphone in that it connects to satellites rather than ground-based towers. Unfortunately, you'll pay at least $2 per minute to use the phone, and it only works where you can see the horizon (that is, usually not indoors). In North America, you can rent Iridium satellite phones from **RoadPost** (www.roadpost.com; © **888/290-1606** or 905/272-5665). InTouch USA (see above) offers a wider range of satphones but at higher rates.

If you're not from the U.S., you'll be appalled at the poor reach of our **GSM (Global System for Mobiles) wireless network,** which is used by much of the rest of the world. Your phone will probably work in most major U.S. cities; it definitely won't work in many rural areas. (To see where GSM phones work in the U.S., check out www.t-mobile.com/coverage/national_popup.asp.) And you may or may not be able to send SMS (text messaging) home.

Your best bet for renting a phone upon arrival in New England is at Boston's Logan International Airport.

11 Getting There

BY PLANE

Airlines serving New England include **American** (© 800/433-7300; www.aa.com), **Continental** (© 800/523-3273; www.continental.com), **Delta** (© 800/221-1212; www.delta.com), **JetBlue** (© 800/538-2583; www.jetblue.com), **Northwest** (© 800/225-2525; www.nwa.com), **Southwest** (© 800/435-9792; www.southwest.com), **United**

(✆ 800/864-8331; www.united.com), and **US Airways** (✆ 800/428-4322; www.usair.com), among others. Nearly all of them serve Boston's Logan International Airport (BOS), your likely hub of arrival or connection if you're coming by air. Bradley International Airport (BDL) also does a fair bit of domestic business these days.

Commercial carriers serve smaller cities in the region, as well, such as Burlington, VT; Manchester, NH; Portland and Bangor, ME; and Providence, RI. Airlines most commonly fly to these airports from New York or Boston, although direct connections from other cities, such as Chicago, Cincinnati, and Philadelphia, are available. Many of the scheduled flights to smaller New England cities from Boston are aboard smaller prop planes; ask the airline or your travel agent if this is an issue of concern for you. Even smaller towns and cities are served by feeder airlines and charter companies, including those flying into air strips in Rutland, VT; Rockport, ME; and Trenton, ME (near Bar Harbor).

Here's a tip: If you're heading for a remote area of New England, it's often cheaper to fly into Boston's Logan Airport and then rent a car or connect by bus to your final destination. (Boston is about 2 hr. by car from Portland and Hartford each, less than 3 hr. from the White Mountains.)

Travelers should note that Boston can be very congested, and delayed flights are endemic. Following the September 11, 2001, terrorist attacks (two of the four doomed flights departed from Boston), increased security has led to periodic but massive delays during check-in and screening.

With far fewer flights, the smaller airports have not been subject to such huge disruptions, and travelers may find that the increased expense and less flexible flight times involved with using these airports are offset by the less stressful experience of checking in and boarding.

Note that discount airfares often aren't as easy to obtain to smaller airports of northern New England as to the larger cities, but notable exceptions apply. In the last few years, the airport in Manchester, NH (MHT), has grown in prominence thanks to the arrival of **Southwest Airlines,** which has brought competitive, low-cost airfares and improved service. Manchester has gone from a sleepy backwater airport to a bustling destination, recently eclipsing Portland in numbers of passengers served. Travelers looking for good deals to the region are advised to first check with Southwest (✆ **800/435-9792;** www.southwest.com) before pricing other gateways.

Upstart discounter **JetBlue** offers direct service between Burlington, Vermont, and New York City's LaGuardia Airport, with onward connections. For more information, call ✆ **800/538-2583** or check online at **www.jetblue.com**.

IMMIGRATION & CUSTOMS CLEARANCE Foreign visitors arriving by air, no matter what the port of entry, should cultivate patience and resignation before setting foot on U.S. soil. Clearing immigration control can take as long as 2 hours. This is especially true in the aftermath of the September 11, 2001, terrorist attacks, when U.S. airports considerably beefed up security clearances. People traveling by air from Canada, Bermuda, and certain Caribbean countries can sometimes clear Customs and Immigration at the point of departure, which is much faster.

FLYING FOR LESS: TIPS FOR GETTING THE BEST AIRFARE

- Passengers who can book their ticket either **long in advance or at the last minute,** or who **fly midweek** or **at less-trafficked hours** may pay a fraction of the full fare. If your schedule

Tips Prepare to Be Fingerprinted

Many international visitors traveling on visas to the United States are photographed and fingerprinted at Customs in a program created by the Department of Homeland Security called **US-VISIT.** Non-U.S. citizens arriving at airports and on cruise ships must undergo an instant background check as part of the government's efforts to deter terrorism by verifying the identity of incoming and outgoing visitors. Exempt from the extra scrutiny are visitors entering by land or those (mostly in Europe; see p. 24) that don't require a visa for short-term visits. For more information, go to the Homeland Security website at **www.dhs.gov/dhspublic**.

is flexible, say so, and ask if you can secure a cheaper fare by changing your flight plans.

- Search **the Internet** for cheap fares (see "Planning Your Trip Online," earlier in this chapter).
- Keep an eye on local newspapers for **promotional specials** or **fare wars,** when airlines lower prices on their most popular routes. You rarely see fare wars offered for peak travel times, but if you can travel in the off-months, you may snag a bargain.
- Try to book a ticket **in its country of origin.** If you're planning a one-way flight from Johannesburg to New York, a South Africa–based travel agent will probably have the lowest fares. For foreign travelers on multi-leg trips, book in the country of the first leg; for example, book New York–Chicago–Montreal–New York in the U.S.
- **Consolidators,** also known as bucket shops, are great sources for international tickets, although they usually can't beat Internet fares within North America. Start by looking in Sunday newspaper travel sections; U.S. travelers should focus on the *New York Times, Los Angeles Times,* and *Miami Herald.* U.K. travelers should search in the *Independent, The Guardian,* or *The Observer.* ***Beware:*** Bucket shop tickets are usually nonrefundable or rigged with stiff cancellation penalties, often as high as 50% to 75% of the ticket price, and some put you on charter airlines, which may leave at inconvenient times and experience delays. Several reliable consolidators are worldwide and available online. **STA Travel** has been the world's lead consolidator for students since purchasing Council Travel, but their fares are competitive for travelers of all ages. **ELTExpress (Flights.com)** (**© 800/TRAV-800;** www.eltexpress.com) has excellent fares worldwide, particularly to Europe. They also have "local" websites in 12 countries. **FlyCheap** (**© 800/FLY-CHEAP;** www.1800flycheap.com) has especially good fares to sunny destinations. **Air Tickets Direct** (**© 800/778-3447;** www.airticketsdirect.com) is based in Montreal and leverages the currently weak Canadian dollar for low fares; they also book trips to places that U.S. travel agents won't touch, such as Cuba.
- Join **frequent-flier clubs.** Frequent-flier membership doesn't cost a cent, but it does entitle you to better seats, faster response to phone inquiries, and prompter service if your luggage is stolen or your flight is canceled or delayed, or if you want to change

Tips Getting Through the Airport

- Arrive at the airport 1 hour before a domestic flight and 2 hours before an international flight; if you show up late, tell an airline employee and he or she will probably whisk you to the front of the line.
- Beat the ticket-counter lines by using airport electronic kiosks or even online check-in from your home computer, from where you can print out boarding passes in advance. Curbside check-in is also a good way to avoid lines.
- Bring a current, government-issued photo ID such as a driver's license or passport. Children under 18 do not need government-issued photo IDs for flights within the U.S., but they do for international flights to most countries.
- Speed up security by removing your jacket and shoes before you're screened. In addition, remove metal objects such as big belt buckles. If you've got metallic body parts, a note from your doctor can prevent a long chat with the security screeners.
- Use a TSA-approved lock for your checked luggage. Look for Travel Sentry certified locks at luggage or travel shops and Brookstone stores (or online at www.brookstone.com).

your seat. And you don't have to fly to earn points; **frequent-flier credit cards** can earn you thousands of miles for doing your everyday shopping. With more than 70 mileage awards programs are on the market, consumers have never had more options. Investigate the program details of your favorite airlines before you sink points into any one. Consider which airlines have hubs in the airport nearest you, and, of those carriers, which have the most advantageous alliances, given your most common routes. To play the frequent-flier game to your best advantage, consult Randy Petersen's **Inside Flyer** (www.insideflyer.com). Petersen and friends review all the programs in detail and post regular updates on changes in policies and trends.

LONG-HAUL FLIGHTS: HOW TO STAY COMFORTABLE

- Your choice of airline and airplane will definitely affect your leg room. Find more details about U.S. airlines at **www.seatguru.com**. For international airlines, the research firm Skytrax has posted a list of average seat pitches at **www.airlinequality.com**.
- Emergency exit seats and bulkhead seats typically have the most legroom. Emergency exit seats are usually left unassigned until the day of a flight (to ensure that someone able-bodied fills the seats); it's worth getting to the ticket counter early to snag one of these spots for a long flight. Many passengers find that bulkhead seating (the row facing the wall at the front of the cabin) offers more legroom, but keep in mind that bulkheads are where airlines often put baby

bassinets, so you may be sitting next to an infant.

- To have two seats for yourself in a three-seat row, try for an aisle seat in a center section toward the back of coach. If you're traveling with a companion, book an aisle and a window seat. Middle seats are usually booked last, so chances are good you'll end up with three seats to yourselves. And in the event that a third passenger is assigned the middle seat, he or she will probably be more than happy to trade for a window or an aisle.
- Ask about entertainment options. Many airlines offer seatback video systems where you get to choose your movies or play video games—but only on some of their planes. (Boeing 777s are your best bet.)
- To sleep, avoid the last row of any section or the row in front of an emergency exit, as these seats are the least likely to recline. Avoid seats near highly trafficked toilet areas. Avoid seats in the back of many jets—these can be narrower than those in the rest of coach. You also may want to reserve a window seat so you can rest your head and avoid being bumped in the aisle.
- Get up, walk around, and stretch every 60 to 90 minutes to keep your blood flowing. This helps avoid **deep vein thrombosis,** or "economy-class syndrome."
- Drink water before, during, and after your flight to combat the lack of humidity in airplane cabins. Avoid alcohol, which will dehydrate you.
- If you're flying with kids, don't forget to carry on toys, books, pacifiers, and chewing gum to help them relieve ear pressure buildup during ascent and descent.

BY CAR

Coming from the New York area (your most likely entry point, unless you're Canadian), several interstate highway corridors serve New England. **I-91** heads more or less due north from Hartford, Connecticut, through Massachusetts and along the Vermont–New Hampshire border. **I-95** parallels the Atlantic coast through Boston, after which it strikes northeast across New Hampshire and along the southern Maine coast before heading north toward the Canadian border. The Massachusetts Turnpike **(I-90)** makes a wandering east-west jaunt from Boston to the Berkshire Mountains—for a price: it's a toll road.

From Boston, you can head north on I-95 for Maine, or take **I-93** for New Hampshire and the White Mountains. In Concord, New Hampshire, **I-89** departs from I-93 northwest toward Burlington, Vermont.

If scenery is your priority, the most picturesque way to enter New England is from the west. Drive through New York's scenic Adirondack Mountains to Port Kent, New York, on Lake Champlain, then catch the car ferry across the lake to Burlington.

BY TRAIN

Getting to Boston by train is no problem, but from there train service to the rest of New England is surprisingly limited. **Amtrak's Vermonter** departs Washington, D.C., with stops in Baltimore, Philadelphia, and New York before following the Connecticut River northward. Stops in Vermont include Brattleboro, Bellows Falls, Claremont (New Hampshire), White River Junction, Randolph, Montpelier, Waterbury, Burlington/Essex Junction, and St. Albans. The Ethan Allen Express departs New York and travels northward up the Hudson River Valley

Tips High- and Low-End New York Bus Options

Many travelers find standard interstate bus service inadequate; for others, it's too swanky. Both have options on the New York–Boston route.

Business-oriented **LimoLiner** (✆ **888/546-5469**; www.limoliner.com) service connects the Back Bay Hilton, 40 Dalton St., to the Hilton New York, 1335 Ave. of the Americas (with an on-request stop in Framingham, MA). The luxury coach seats 28 and has Internet access, work tables, leather seats, and an on-board attendant. The one-way fare is $79.

At the other end of the spectrum, a number of companies run between Boston's Chinatown and New York's Chinatown. I've heard too many anecdotal accounts of poor maintenance and unsatisfactory service to give this option an unqualified recommendation, but it's madly popular with students and other bargain-hunters. The one-way fare is about $15. The largest operator is **Fung Wah** (✆ **212/925-8889**; www.fungwahbus.com), which shuttles between Boston's South Station and Canal Street in Manhattan.

and into the Adirondacks before veering over to Vermont and terminating at Rutland. Buses continue on to Killington and northward to Middlebury and Burlington.

After more than a decade of delays, Amtrak finally relaunched rail service to Maine in December 2001, restoring a line that had been discontinued in the 1960s. The **Downeaster** now operates four times daily between North Station in Boston and Portland (one-way fare: $22), with intermediate stops at Haverhill, Massachusetts; Exeter, Durham, and Dover, New Hampshire; and Wells, Saco, and Old Orchard Beach, Maine. Travel time is about 2 hours and 30 minutes between Boston and Portland, with that duration expected to decrease as track upgrades are completed. Bikes may be loaded and off-loaded at Boston, Wells, and Portland. Four trips daily are offered.

For more information on train service, contact **Amtrak** (✆ **800/872-7245**; www.amtrak.com).

There are also a number of **light rail commuter lines** radiating out from Boston, though you'll use these only rarely, if at all—the most useful ones head northeast to quiet oceanside Cape Ann.

BY BUS

Bonanza (✆ **800/556-3815** or 617/720-4110) operates largely in Connecticut. **Concord Trailways** (✆ **800/639-3317**; www.concordtrailways.com) serves New Hampshire and Maine, including some smaller towns in the Lake Winnipesaukee and White Mountains areas. **Greyhound** (✆ **800/231-2222** or 617/526-1810) is nationwide, and serves many destinations in New England. **Peter Pan** (✆ **800/343-9999** or 617/426-7838) serves western Massachusetts and Connecticut. **Plymouth & Brockton** (✆ **508/746-0378**) serves Massachusetts's south shore and onward to Cape Cod. And **Vermont Transit** (✆ **800/451-3292**; www.vermonttransit.com) is affiliated with Greyhound and serves Vermont, New Hampshire, and Maine with frequent departures from Boston. The luxury **LimoLiner** (✆ **888/546-5469**; www.limoliner.com) transports businesspeople between the Hilton hotels in Boston's Back Bay and on New York's Avenue of the Americas. No-frills **Fung Wah** (✆ **212/925-8889**; www.fungwahbus.com) connects Boston's South Station and Canal Street in Manhattan's Chinatown.

12 Packages for the Independent Traveler

Package tours are simply a way to buy the airfare, accommodations, and other elements of your trip (such as car rentals, airport transfers, and sometimes even activities) at the same time and often at discounted prices.

One good source of package deals is the airlines themselves. Most major airlines offer air/land packages, including **American Airlines Vacations** (✆ 800/321-2121; www.aavacations.com), **Delta Vacations** (✆ 800/221-6666; www.deltavacations.com), **Continental Airlines Vacations** (✆ 800/301-3800; www.covacations.com), and **United Vacations** (✆ 888/854-3899; www.unitedvacations.com). Several big **online travel agencies**—Expedia, Travelocity, Orbitz, Site59, and Lastminute.com—also do a brisk business in packages.

Travel packages are also listed in the travel section of your local Sunday newspaper. Or check ads in the national travel magazines such as *Arthur Frommer's Budget Travel Magazine, Travel + Leisure, National Geographic Traveler,* and *Condé Nast Traveler.*

13 Escorted General-Interest Tours

Escorted tours are structured group tours, with a group leader. The price usually includes everything from airfare to hotels, meals, tours, admission costs, and local transportation.

Despite the fact that escorted tours require big deposits and predetermine hotels, restaurants, and itineraries, many people derive security and peace of mind from the structure they offer. Escorted tours—whether they're navigated by bus, motorcoach, train, or boat—let travelers sit back and enjoy the trip without having to drive or worry about details. They take you to the maximum number of sights in the minimum amount of time with the least amount of hassle. They're particularly convenient for people with limited mobility and they can be a great way to make new friends.

Tips Ask Before You Go

Before you invest in a package deal or an escorted tour:

- Always ask about the **cancellation policy.** Can you get your money back? Is there a deposit required?
- Ask about the **accommodations choices and prices** for each. Then look up the hotels' reviews in a Frommer's guide and check their rates online for your specific dates of travel. Also find out what types of rooms are offered.
- Request a complete **schedule** (escorted tours only).
- Ask about the **size** and demographics of the group (escorted tours only).
- Discuss what is included in the **price** (transportation, meals, tips, airport transfers, and so on) (escorted tours only).
- Finally, look for **hidden expenses.** Ask whether airport departure fees and taxes, for example, are included in the total cost—they rarely are.

On the downside, you'll have little opportunity for serendipitous interactions with locals. The tours can be jam-packed with activities, leaving little room for individual sightseeing, whim, or adventure—plus they often focus on the heavily touristed sites, so you miss out on many a lesser-known gem.

14 Special-Interest Trips

New England is a superb destination for those who don't consider it a vacation unless they spend some time far away from their cars. Hiking, canoeing, and skiing are among the most popular outdoor activities, but you can also try rock climbing, sea kayaking, mountain biking, road biking, sailing, winter mountaineering, and snowmobiling. The best way to enjoy the outdoors is to head to public lands where the natural landscape is preserved. Wild areas in New England include the Cape Cod National Seashore, Green Mountain National Forest in Vermont, White Mountain National Forest in New Hampshire, and Baxter State Park and Acadia National Park in Maine. You can often find adventure-travel outfitters and suppliers in towns around the perimeter of these areas.

A bit of added advice: To find real adventure, plan to stay put. I advise prospective adventurers to pick just one area, then settle in for a few days or a week, spending the long summer days exploring locally by foot, canoe, or kayak. This will give you the time to enjoy an extra hour lounging at a remote backcountry lake, or to spend an extra day camped in the backcountry.

FINDING YOUR WAY

Travelers have three options: Hire a guide, sign up for a guided trip, or dig up the essential information yourself.

HIRING A GUIDE Guides of all kinds may be hired throughout the region, from grizzled fishing hands who know local rivers like their own homes to young canoe guides attracted to the field because of their interest in the environment. Alexandra and Garrett Conover of Maine's **North Woods Ways,** 2293 Elliotsville Rd., Willimantic, ME 04443 (© **207/997-3723**), are among the most experienced in the region. The couple offers canoe trips on northern Maine rivers (and as far north as Labrador), and are well versed in North Woods lore.

Maine has a centuries-old tradition of guides leading "sports" into the backwoods for hunting and fishing, although many now have branched out to include recreational canoeing and more specialized interests, such as bird-watching. Professional guides are certified by the state; you can learn more about hiring Maine guides by contacting the **Maine Professional Guides Association,** P.O. Box 336, Augusta, ME 04332. www.maineguides.org.

In Vermont, contact the **Vermont Outdoor Guide Association** (© **800/425-8747;** www.voga.org), whose members can help arrange adventure-travel tours, instruction, and lodging.

Elsewhere, contact chambers of commerce for suggestions on guides.

GUIDED TOURS Guided tours have boomed in recent years, both in number and variety. These range from 2-night guided inn-to-inn hiking trips to week-long canoe and kayak expeditions, camping each night along the way. A few reputable outfitters to start with include the following:

- **Allagash Canoe Trips,** P.O. Box 932, Greenville, ME 04441 (© **207/237-3077;** www.allagashcanoetrips.com), leads 3- to 7-day canoe trips down Maine's noted and wild Allagash River and other local rivers. You provide a sleeping bag and clothing; everything else is taken care of.

- **BattenKill Canoe Ltd.,** 6328 Historic Rte. 7A, Arlington, VT 05250 (© **800/421-5268** or 802/362-2800; www.battenkill.com), runs guided canoeing and walking excursions of between 4 and 5 nights' duration in Vermont. Nights are spent at quiet inns.
- **Bike the Whites,** P.O. Box 37, Intervale, NH 03845 (© **800/447-4345;** www.bikethewhites.com), offers self-guided biking tours between three inns in the White Mountains, with each day requiring about 20 miles of biking. Luggage is shuttled from inn to inn.
- **Country Walkers,** P.O. Box 180, Waterbury, VT 05676 (© **800/464-9255** or 802/244-1387; www.countrywalkers.com), has a glorious color catalog outlining supported walking trips around the world, including offerings in coastal Maine and north-central Vermont. Trips run 4 or 5 nights and include all meals and lodging at appealing inns.
- **Maine Island Kayak Co.,** 70 Luther St., Peaks Island, ME 04108 (© **800/796-2373** or 207/766-2373; www.sea-kayak.com), has a fleet of seaworthy kayaks for camping trips up and down the Maine coast. The firm has a number of 2- and 3-night expeditions each summer and has plenty of experience training novices.
- **New England Hiking Holidays,** P.O. Box 1648, North Conway, NH 03860 (© **800/869-0949** or 603/356-9696; www.nehikingholidays.com), has an extensive inventory of trips, including weekend trips in the White Mountains, as well as more extended excursions to the Maine coast and Vermont. Trips typically involve moderate day hiking coupled with nights at comfortable lodges.
- **Vermont Bicycle Touring,** P.O. 614 Monkton Rd., Bristol, VT 05443 (© **800/245-3868;** www.vbt.com), is one of the more established and well-organized touring operations, with an extensive bike tour schedule. VBT offers five trips in Vermont, and three in Maine.

GETTING MORE INFORMATION

Guidebooks to the region's backcountry are plentiful and diverse. L.L.Bean in Freeport, ME, and the Green Mountain Club headquarters in Waterbury, VT, have excellent selections of guidebooks for sale, as do many local bookshops throughout the region. An exhaustive collection of New England outdoor guidebooks for sale may be found on the Web at **www.mountainwanderer.com**, a company based in the White Mountains. The **Appalachian Mountain Club,** 5 Joy St., Boston, MA 02108 (© **617/523-0655;** www.outdoors.org), publishes a number of definitive guides to hiking and boating in the region.

Map Adventures, P.O. Box 15214 Portland, ME 04112 (© **207/879-4777;** www.mapadventures.com), is a small firm that publishes a growing line of recreational maps covering popular northern New England areas, including the Stowe and Mad River Valley areas and the White Mountains.

Local outdoor clubs are also a good source of information, and most offer trips to nonmembers. The largest of the bunch is the Appalachian Mountain Club (see address above), whose chapters run group trips almost every weekend throughout the region, with northern New Hampshire especially well represented. Another active group is the **Green Mountain Club,** 4711 Waterbury–Stowe Rd., Waterbury Center, VT 05677 (© **802/244-7037;** www.greenmountainclub.org).

Value For Those Who Love Historic Homes

Historic New England is a nonprofit foundation that owns and operates 35 historical properties in New England ranging from places built in the 17th century to the present, including a number of places profiled in this book. Members are eligible for free admission to all of the organization's properties and a number of other benefits, including a subscription to *Historic New England* magazine, a guide to the group's properties, and invitations to members-only events and other perks. Memberships start at $25 per year for a national membership, $35 for individuals, and $45 for a household membership. For more information on Historic New England and its properties, visit the group's website at www.historicnewengland.org, or call the organization's Boston headquarters at **✆ 617/227-3956.**

SPECIAL-INTEREST VACATIONS

A richly rewarding way to spend a vacation is to learn a new outdoor skill or add to your knowledge while on holiday. You can find plenty of options, ranging from formal weeklong classes to 1-day workshops.

- **Learn to fly-fish.** Among the region's most respected schools are those offered by **Orvis** (**✆ 888/235-9763**) in Manchester, VT, and **L.L.Bean** (**✆ 800/343-4552**) in Freeport, ME. (L.L.Bean also offers a number of shorter workshops on various outdoor skills through its **Outdoor Discovery Program;** call **✆888/552-3261.**)
- **Learn about birds and coastal ecosystems.** Budding and experienced naturalists can expand their understanding of marine wildlife while residing on 333-acre Hog Island in Maine's wild and scenic Muscongus Bay. The program has a stellar reputation. Contact the **Maine Audubon Society,** 20 Gilsland Farm Rd., Falmouth ME 04105 (**✆ 207/781-2330;** www.maineaudubon.org).
- **Sharpen your outdoor skills.** The **Appalachian Mountain Club,** 5 Joy St., Boston, MA 02108 (**✆ 617/523-0655**), has a full roster of outdoor adventure classes, many of which are taught at the club's Pinkham Notch Camp at the base of Mount Washington in the heart of the White Mountains. You can learn outdoor photography, wild mushroom identification, or backcountry orienteering for starters. In winter, ice-climbing and telemark-skiing lessons are held on the slopes of the White Mountains. Classes often include accommodations, and most are reasonably priced.

15 Getting Around New England

BY PLANE

Overseas visitors can take advantage of the APEX (Advance Purchase Excursion) reductions offered by all major U.S. and European carriers. In addition, some large airlines offer transatlantic or transpacific passengers special discount tickets under the name **Visit USA,** which allows mostly one-way travel from one U.S. destination to another at very low prices. Unavailable in the U.S., these discount tickets must be purchased abroad in conjunction with your international fare. This system is the easiest, fastest, cheapest way to see the country.

New England Driving Distances

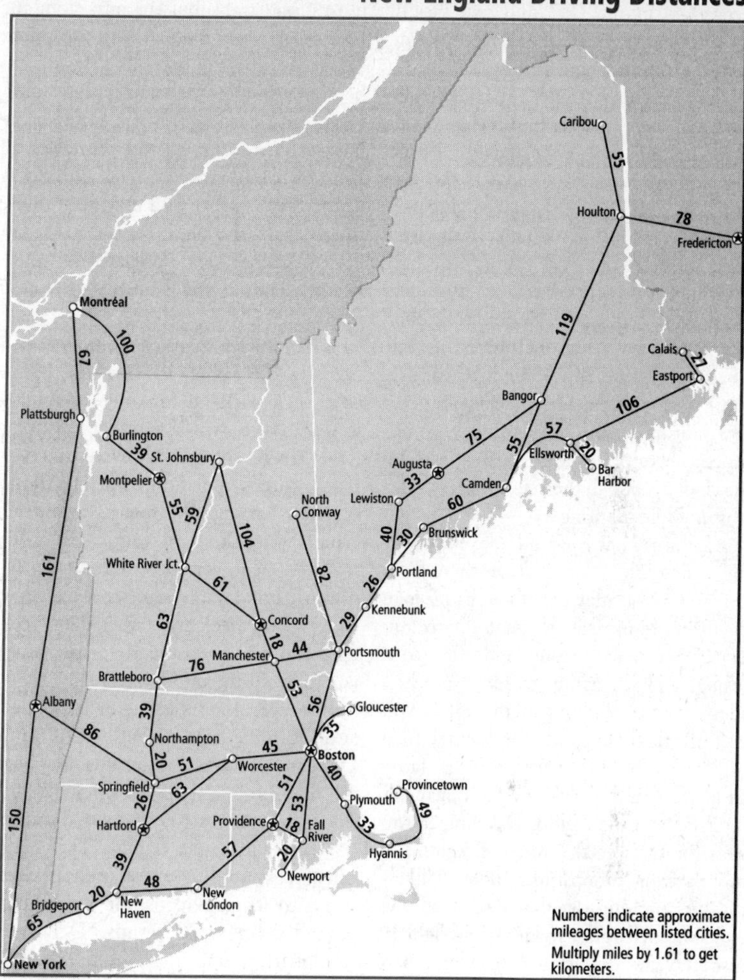

BY CAR

Unless you plan to spend the bulk of your vacation in a city where walking is the best way to get around (read: New York City or New Orleans), the most cost-effective way to travel is by car. And New England can be lovely indeed on the back roads.

If you're visiting from abroad and plan to rent a car in the United States, you probably won't need the services of an additional automobile organization. If you're planning to buy or borrow a car, automobile-association membership is recommended. **AAA, the American Automobile Association** (© **800/222-4357;** http://travel.aaa.com), is the country's largest auto club and supplies its members with maps, insurance, and, most important, emergency road service.

Note: Foreign driver's licenses are usually recognized in the U.S., but you should get an international one if your home license is not in English.

The major airports in New England (see "Getting There," earlier in this chapter) all host national car-rental chains. Some handy phone numbers and websites are **Avis** (© 800/230-4898; www.avis.com), **Budget** (© 800/527-0700; www.budget.com), **Enterprise** (© 800/736-8222; www.enterprise.com), **Hertz** (© 800/654-3131; www.hertz.com), **National** (© 800/227-7368; www.nationalcar.com), and **Thrifty** (© 800/847-4389; www.thrifty.com). You may also find independent car-rental firms in the bigger towns, sometimes at better rates than those offered by the chains. Look in the Yellow Pages under "Automobile–Renting."

A famous New England joke ends with the punch line, "You can't get there from here," but you may conclude it's no joke as you try to navigate through the region. Travel can be convoluted and often confusing, and it's handy to have someone adept at map reading in the car if you veer off the main routes for country-road exploring. North-south travel is fairly straightforward, thanks to the four major interstates in the region. Traveling east to west (or vice versa) across the region is a more vexing proposition and will likely involve stitching together a route of several state or county roads. Don't fight it; just relax and understand that this is part of the New England experience, like rain in the northwest or rattlesnakes in the southwest.

On the other hand, New England is of a size that touring by car can be done quite comfortably, at least if you're not determined to see all 6 states in a week (see chapter 3 for our suggested itineraries). Note that Maine is much larger than the other states; when making travel plans, beware of two-sided maps that alter the scale from one side to the other.

Traffic is generally light compared to most urban and suburban areas along the East Coast, but there's a big exception: Traffic anywhere in or around Boston can be sluggish anytime, and Friday afternoons and evenings in the summer are positively infuriating; the tentacles of Beantown traffic now extend all the way to the I-495, which you may need to use to get from the New York area to, say, coastal Maine. Come prepared for unexpected delays if you'll be anywhere near Boston.

A handful of other choke points, particularly on Route 1 along the Maine coast, can back up for miles as tourists jockey to cross two-lane bridges spanning tidal rivers. North Conway in New Hampshire is famed for its hellish traffic, especially during the foliage season. To avoid the worst of the tourist traffic, try to avoid being on the road during big summer holidays; if your schedule allows it, travel on weekdays rather than weekends and hit the road early or late in the day to avoid the midday crunch.

If you're a connoisseur of back roads and off-the-beaten-track exploring, **DeLorme atlases** are invaluable. These are now produced for all 50 states, but the first one was Maine, and the company's headquarters is here. The atlases offer an extraordinary level of detail, right down to logging roads and public boat launches on small ponds. DeLorme's headquarters and map store (© **800/561-5105** or 800/642-0970; www.delorme.com) are in Yarmouth, Maine, but their products are also available widely at bookstores and convenience stores throughout the region.

Travelers who are organized to a degree that sometimes alarms their family and close friends probably already know about **MapQuest** (www.mapquest.com) and **Yahoo! Maps** (maps.yahoo.com). These handy websites calculate distances and driving directions from any point in the country to any other point. Type in where you want to start and where you want to go, and the online software calculates the total distance and provides detailed driving instructions, along with maps if you want them. Before departing, you can plot your route and print out a daily driving itinerary.

BY TRAIN

International visitors can buy a USA Rail Pass, good for 15 or 30 days of unlimited travel on Amtrak (© **800/USA-RAIL;** www.amtrak.com). The pass is available through many overseas travel agents. If you're just traveling to New England, see Amtrak's website for the cost of travel within the eastern United States. With a foreign passport, you can also buy passes direct from some Amtrak locations, including New York, Boston, and most other major U.S. cities. Reservations are generally required and should be made as early as possible. Regional rail passes are also available.

BY BUS

See "Getting There" earlier in this chapter for a list of bus companies serving New England. While express bus service to major cities and tourist areas is quite good, quirky schedules and routes between regional destinations may send you miles out of the way and increase trip time significantly.

16 Tips on Accommodations

"The more we travel," said an unhappy couple next to me one morning at a New Hampshire inn, "the more we realize why we go back to our old favorites time and again." The reason for their disgruntlement? They were up and switching rooms at 2am when rain began dripping on them through the ceiling.

New England is famous for its plethora of country inns and bed-and-breakfasts (B&Bs). These offer a wonderful alternative to the cookie-cutter chain-hotel rooms that line U.S. highways coast-to-coast, but as that unhappy couple learned, there are good reasons why some people prefer cookie-cutter sameness. Predictability isn't always a bad thing. In a chain hotel, you can be reasonably certain water won't drip through your ceiling at night. Likewise, you can bet that beds will be firm, that the sink will be relatively new and lacking in interesting sepia-toned stains, and that you'll have a TV, telephone, and a lot of counter space next to the bathroom sink.

Every inn and B&B listed in this guide will yield at least a decent, and very often a high-quality, experience. Just keep in mind that every place is different, and you still need to match the personality of a place with your own personality. Some are more polished and fussier than others. Many lack the amenities to which travelers have grown accustomed in chain hotels. (In-room phones and air-conditioning lead the list.)

Note that with rare exceptions, most inns listed in this book do not allow smoking.

SAVING ON YOUR HOTEL ROOM

The **rack rate** is the maximum rate that a hotel charges for a room. Hardly anybody pays this price, however, except in high season or on holidays. To lower the cost of your room:

- **Ask about special rates or other discounts.** You may qualify for corporate, student, military, senior, frequent flier, trade union, or other discounts.
- **Dial direct.** When booking a room in a chain hotel, you'll often get a better deal by calling the individual hotel's reservation desk rather than the chain's main number.

- **Book online.** Many hotels offer Internet-only discounts, or supply rooms to Priceline, Hotwire, or Expedia at rates much lower than the ones you can get through the hotel itself.
- **Remember the law of supply and demand.** Resort hotels are most crowded and therefore most expensive on weekends, so discounts are usually available for midweek stays. Business hotels in downtown locations are busiest during the week, so you can expect big discounts over the weekend. Many hotels have high-season and low-season prices, and booking even 1 day after high season ends can mean big discounts.
- **Look into group or long-stay discounts.** If you come as part of a large group, you should be able to negotiate a bargain rate. Likewise, if you're planning a long stay (at least 5 days), you might qualify for a discount. As a general rule, expect 1 night free after a 7-night stay.
- **Avoid excess charges and hidden costs.** When you book a room, ask whether the hotel charges for parking. Use your own cellphone, pay phones, or prepaid phone cards instead of dialing direct from hotel phones, which usually have exorbitant rates. And don't be tempted by the room's minibar offerings: Most hotels charge through the nose for water, soda, and snacks. Finally, ask about local taxes and service charges, which can increase the cost of a room by 15% or more.
- **Book an efficiency.** A room with a kitchenette allows you to shop for groceries and cook your own meals. This is a big money saver, especially for families on long stays.
- **Consider enrolling in hotel "frequent-stay" programs,** which are upping the ante lately to win the loyalty of repeat customers. Frequent guests can now accumulate points or credits to earn free hotel nights, airline miles, in-room amenities, merchandise, tickets to concerts and events, discounts on sporting facilities—and even credit toward stock in the participating hotel, in the case of the Jameson Inn hotel group. Perks are awarded not only by many chain hotels and motels (Hilton HHonors, Marriott Rewards, Wyndham ByRequest, to name a few), but individual inns and B&Bs. Many chain hotels partner with other hotel chains, car-rental firms, airlines, and credit card companies to give consumers additional incentive to do repeat business.

LANDING THE BEST ROOM

Somebody has to get the best room in the house. It might as well be you. You can start by joining the hotel's frequent-guest program, which may make you eligible for upgrades. A hotel-branded credit card usually gives its owner "silver" or "gold" status in frequent-guest programs for free. Always ask about a corner room. They're often larger and quieter, with more windows and light, and they often cost the same as standard rooms. When you make your reservation, ask if the hotel is renovating; if it is, request a room away from the construction. Ask about nonsmoking rooms, rooms with views, rooms with twin, queen- or king-size beds. If you're a light sleeper, request a quiet room away from vending machines, elevators, restaurants, bars, and discos. Ask for a room that has been most recently renovated or redecorated.

If you aren't happy with your room when you arrive, ask for another one. Most lodgings will be willing to accommodate you.

17 Recommended Reading

For children, ***Make Way for Ducklings*** (Viking, 1941), by Robert McCloskey, is a classic that tells the story of Mrs. Mallard and her babies on the loose in the Back Bay and the Public Garden. Slightly older kids might know the Public Garden as the setting of part of ***The Trumpet of the Swan*** (HarperTrophy, 2000) by E. B. White. After reading it, a turn around the lagoon on a Swan Boat is mandatory. An excellent historical title is ***Johnny Tremain*** (Yearling, 1987) by Esther Forbes, a fictional boy's-eye-view account of the Revolutionary War era. The book vividly describes scenes from the American Revolution, many of which take place along the Freedom Trail.

For adults, two splendid Pulitzer Prize winners chronicle the city's history. ***Paul Revere and the World He Lived In*** (Mariner, 1999) is Esther Forbes's look at Boston before, during, and after the Revolution. ***Common Ground: A Turbulent Decade in the Lives of Three American Families*** (Vintage, 1986), by J. Anthony Lukas, is the definitive account of the busing crisis of the 1970s.

Architecture buffs will enjoy ***Cityscapes of Boston*** (Mariner, 1994) by Robert Campbell and Peter Vanderwarker; ***Lost Boston*** (Houghton Mifflin, 1999) by Jane Holtz Kay; and ***A.I.A. Guide to Boston*** (Globe Pequot, 1992) by Susan and Michael Southworth.

In the Memory House, by Howard Mansfield (Fulcrum, 1993), provides a penetrating look at New England's sometimes estranged relationship with its own past. Dona Brown, a University of Vermont professor, tells the epic tale of the rise of 19th-century tourism in New England in the uncommonly well-written study, ***Inventing New England*** (Smithsonian Books, 1997). The exhaustively researched ***Lobster Gangs of Maine*** (University Press of New England, 1988), by James M. Acheson, answers every question you'll have about lobstermen's lives. ***Northern Borders*** (Mariner, 1992), by Howard Frank Mosher, is ostensibly about a young boy living with his taciturn grandparents in northern Vermont, but the book's central character is really Vermont's Northeast Kingdom. The way to a region's character is through its stomach. John and Matt Lewis Thornes' finely crafted essays on Maine regional cooking in ***Serious Pig*** (North Point Press, 2000) are exhaustive discussions of chowder, beans, pie, and more.

FAST FACTS: New England

American Express American Express offers travel services, including check cashing and trip planning, through a number of affiliated agencies in the region. Call ✆ **800/221-7282** for the nearest location.

Area Codes Massachusetts is now divided into a number of area codes: 617 and 857 for Boston; 781 and 339 for a suburban ring surrounding Boston; 508, 978, 774, and 351 for central Massachusetts and Cape Cod; and 413 for western Massachusetts.

Connecticut uses 860 and 959 for Hartford and northern and eastern parts of the state, 203 and 475 for roughly the southwestern quarter of the state (the part closest to New York City).

Rhode Island's area code is 401. Vermont's is 802. New Hampshire's is 603. Maine's is 207.

ATM Networks See "Money," p. 25.

Automobile Organizations Auto clubs will supply maps, suggested routes, guidebooks, accident and bail-bond insurance, and emergency road service. The **American Automobile Association (AAA)** is the major auto club in the United States. If you belong to an auto club in your home country, inquire about AAA reciprocity before you leave. You may be able to join AAA even if you're not a member of a reciprocal club; to inquire, call AAA (✆ **800/222-4357**). AAA is actually an organization of regional auto clubs, so look under "AAA Automobile Club" in the White Pages of the telephone directory. AAA has a nationwide emergency road service telephone number (✆ 800/AAA-HELP).

Car Rentals See "Getting Around New England," p. 52.

Currency The most common bills are the $1 (a "buck"), $5, $10, and $20 denominations. There are also $2 bills (seldom encountered), $50 bills, and $100 bills (the last two are usually not welcome as payment for small purchases).

Coins come in seven denominations: 1¢ (1 cent, or a penny); 5¢ (5 cents, or a nickel); 10¢ (10 cents, or a dime); 25¢ (25 cents, or a quarter); 50¢ (50 cents, or a half dollar); the gold-colored Sacagawea coin, worth $1; and the rare silver dollar.

For additional information see "Money," p. 25.

Drinking Laws The legal age for purchase and consumption of alcoholic beverages is 21; proof of age is required and often requested at bars, nightclubs, and restaurants, so it's always a good idea to bring ID when you go out.

The legal age to consume alcohol is 21. In Maine, New Hampshire, and Vermont, liquor is sold at government-operated stores only; in Connecticut, Massachusetts, and Rhode Island, liquor is sold in privately owned shops. Restaurants that don't have liquor licenses sometimes allow patrons to bring in their own. Ask first.

Do not carry open containers of alcohol in your car or any public area that isn't zoned for alcohol consumption. The police can fine you on the spot. And nothing will ruin your trip faster than getting a citation for DUI ("driving under the influence"), so don't even think about driving while intoxicated.

Driving Rules See "Getting Around New England," p. 52.

Electricity Like Canada, the United States uses 110–120 volts AC (60 cycles), compared to 220–240 volts AC (50 cycles) in most of Europe, Australia, and New Zealand. Downward converters that change 220–240 volts to 110–120 volts are difficult to find in the United States, so bring one with you.

Embassies & Consulates All embassies are located in the nation's capital, Washington, D.C. Some consulates are located in major U.S. cities, and most nations have a mission to the United Nations in New York City. If your country isn't listed below, call for directory information in Washington, D.C. (✆ **202/555-1212**) or log on to **www.embassy.org/embassies**.

The embassy of **Australia** is at 1601 Massachusetts Ave. NW, Washington, DC 20036 (✆ **202/797-3000;** www.austemb.org). There are consulates in New York, Honolulu, Houston, Los Angeles, and San Francisco.

The embassy of **Canada** is at 501 Pennsylvania Ave. NW, Washington, DC 20001 (✆ **202/682-1740;** www.canadianembassy.org). Other Canadian consulates are in Buffalo (New York), Detroit, Los Angeles, New York, and Seattle.

The embassy of **Ireland** is at 2234 Massachusetts Ave. NW, Washington, DC 20008 (✆ **202/462-3939;** www.irelandemb.org). Irish consulates are in Boston, Chicago, New York, San Francisco, and other cities. See website for complete listing.

The embassy of **New Zealand** is at 37 Observatory Circle NW, Washington, DC 20008 (✆ **202/328-4800;** www.nzemb.org). New Zealand consulates are in Los Angeles, Salt Lake City, San Francisco, and Seattle.

The embassy of the **United Kingdom** is at 3100 Massachusetts Ave. NW, Washington, DC 20008 (✆ **202/588-7800;** www.britainusa.com). Other British consulates are in Atlanta, Boston, Chicago, Cleveland, Houston, Los Angeles, New York, San Francisco, and Seattle.

Emergencies In the event of an emergency, find any phone and dial ✆ **911.** You do not need a coin to make this call from a pay phone. If this fails, dial "0" (zero) and tell the operator you need to report an emergency.

Gasoline (Petrol) At press time, in the U.S., the cost of gasoline (also known as gas, but never petrol), is abnormally high but generally speaking it is probably the world's cheapest place to buy gas. In New England, expect to pay $2 to $2.50 US per gallon, more or less; taxes are already included in the printed price, though 'full-service' (pumped by an attendant) gas will cost more than self-service gas (you pump it). One U.S. gallon equals 3.8 liters or .85 imperial gallons. Fill-up locations are known as gas or service stations.

Holidays Banks, government offices, post offices, and many stores, restaurants, and museums are closed on the following legal national holidays: January 1 (New Year's Day), the third Monday in January (Martin Luther King, Jr., Day), the third Monday in February (Presidents' Day), the last Monday in May (Memorial Day), July 4 (Independence Day), the first Monday in September (Labor Day), the second Monday in October (Columbus Day), November 11 (Veterans Day/Armistice Day), the fourth Thursday in November (Thanksgiving Day), and December 25 (Christmas). The Tuesday after the first Monday in November is Election Day, a federal government holiday in presidential-election years (held every 4 years, and next in 2008).

For more information on holidays see "Calendar of Events," earlier in this chapter.

Legal Aid If you are "pulled over" for a minor infraction (such as speeding), never attempt to pay the fine directly to a police officer; this could be construed as attempted bribery, a much more serious crime. Pay fines by mail, or directly into the hands of the clerk of the court. If accused of a more serious offense, say and do nothing before consulting a lawyer. Here the burden is on the state to prove a person's guilt beyond a reasonable doubt, and everyone has the right to remain silent, whether he or she is suspected of a crime or actually arrested. Once arrested, a person can make one telephone call to a party of his or her choice. International visitors should call your embassy or consulate.

Lost & Found Be sure to tell all of your credit card companies the minute you discover your wallet has been lost or stolen and file a report at the nearest police precinct. Your credit card company or insurer may require a police report number or record of the loss. Most credit card companies have an emergency toll-free number to call if your card is lost or stolen; they may be able to wire you a cash advance immediately or deliver an emergency credit card in a day or two. Visa's U.S. emergency number is ✆ **800/847-2911** or 410/581-9994. American Express cardholders and traveler's check holders should call ✆ **800/221-7282.** MasterCard holders should call ✆ **800/307-7309** or 636/722-7111. For other credit cards, call the toll-free number directory at ✆ **800/555-1212.**

If you need emergency cash over the weekend when all banks and American Express offices are closed, you can have money wired to you via **Western Union** (✆ **800/325-6000;** www.westernunion.com).

Mail At press time, domestic postage rates were 24¢ for a postcard and 39¢ for a letter. For international mail, a first-class letter of up to 1 ounce costs 84¢ (63¢ to Canada and Mexico); a first-class postcard costs 75¢ (55¢ to Canada and Mexico); and a preprinted postal aerogramme costs 75¢. For more information go to **www.usps.com** and click on "Calculate Postage."

If you aren't sure what your address will be in the United States, mail can be sent to you, in your name, c/o General Delivery at the main post office of the city or region where you expect to be. (Call ✆ **800/275-8777** for information on the nearest post office.) The addressee must pick up mail in person and must produce proof of identity (driver's license, passport, and so forth). Most post offices will hold your mail for up to 1 month, and are open Monday to Friday from 8am to 6pm, and Saturday from 9am to 3pm.

Always include zip codes when mailing items in the U.S. If you don't know your zip code, visit www.usps.com/zip4.

Measurements See the chart on the inside front cover of this book for details on converting metric measurements to U.S. equivalents.

Newspapers & Magazines The *Boston Globe, Wall Street Journal,* and *New York Times* are distributed throughout New England, although they can sometimes be hard to find in more remote villages. Almost every small city and town has a daily or weekly newspaper covering local happenings; some of the bigger ones include the *Portland Press Herald,* the *Hartford Courant,* the *Manchester Union Leader,* and the *Burlington Free Press* (city dailies) and *Seven Days,* the *Valley Advocate,* and the *Boston Phoenix* (free weeklies). These are good sources of information for events and restaurant specials.

Passports **For Residents of Australia:** You can pick up an application from your local post office or any branch of Passports Australia, but you must schedule an interview at the passport office to present your application materials. Call the **Australian Passport Information Service** at ✆ **131-232,** or visit the government website at www.passports.gov.au.

For Residents of Canada: Passport applications are available at travel agencies throughout Canada or from the central **Passport Office,** Department of Foreign Affairs and International Trade, Ottawa, ON K1A 0G3 (✆ **800/567-6868;**

www.ppt.gc.ca). ***Note:*** Canadian children who travel must have their own passport. However, if you hold a valid Canadian passport issued before December 11, 2001, that bears the name of your child, the passport remains valid for you and your child until it expires.

For Residents of Ireland: You can apply for a 10-year passport at the **Passport Office,** Setanta Centre, Molesworth Street, Dublin 2 (✆ **01/671-1633;** www.irlgov.ie/iveagh). Those under age 18 and over 65 must apply for a €12 3-year passport. You can also apply at 1A South Mall, Cork (✆ **021/272-525**) or at most main post offices.

For Residents of New Zealand: You can pick up a passport application at any New Zealand Passports Office or download it from their website. Contact the **Passports Office** at ✆ **0800/225-050** in New Zealand or 04/474-8100, or log on to www.passports.govt.nz.

For Residents of the United Kingdom: To pick up an application for a standard 10-year passport (5-year passport for children under 16), visit your nearest passport office, major post office, or travel agency or contact the **United Kingdom Passport Service** at ✆ **0870/521-0410** or search its website at www.ukpa.gov.uk.

Safety See "Health & Safety," earlier in this chapter.

Taxes The United States has no value-added tax (VAT) or other indirect tax at the national level. However, every state, county, and city may levy its own local tax on all purchases, including hotel and restaurant checks and airline tickets. These taxes will not appear on price tags.

Current state sales taxes (as of 2006) in New England are: Connecticut, 6% (12% on lodging); Maine, 5% (7% on lodging, 10% on auto rentals); Massachusetts, 5% (local sales taxes such as Boston city or airport taxes may also apply on lodging); New Hampshire, no general sales tax but 8% tax on lodging and dining; Rhode Island, 7% (plus 5% surtax on lodging); and Vermont, 6% (9% on lodging and dining, 10% on alcohol served in restaurants).

Telephone, Telegraph, Telex & Fax Generally, hotel surcharges on long-distance and local calls are astronomical, so you're better off using your **cellphone** or a **public pay telephone.** Many convenience groceries and packaging services sell **prepaid calling cards** in denominations up to $50; for international visitors these can be the least expensive way to call home. Many public phones at airports now accept American Express, MasterCard, and Visa credit cards. **Local calls** made from public pay phones in most locales cost either 25¢ or 35¢. Pay phones do not accept pennies, and few will take anything larger than a quarter.

Most long-distance and international calls can be dialed directly from any phone. **For calls within the United States and to Canada,** dial 1 followed by the area code and the seven-digit number. **For other international calls,** dial 011 followed by the country code, city code, and the number you are calling.

Calls to area codes **800, 888, 877,** and **866** are toll-free. However, calls to area codes **700** and **900** (chat lines, bulletin boards, "dating" services, and so on) can be very expensive—usually a charge of 95¢ to $3 or more per minute, and they sometimes have minimum charges that can run as high as $15 or more.

For **reversed-charge or collect calls,** and for person-to-person calls, dial the number 0 then the area code and number; an operator will come on the line, and you should specify whether you are calling collect, person-to-person, or both. If your operator-assisted call is international, ask for the overseas operator.

For **local directory assistance** ("information"), dial ✆ **411;** for long-distance information, dial 1, then the appropriate area code and 555-1212.

Telegraph and telex services are provided primarily by Western Union. You can telegraph money, or have it telegraphed to you, very quickly over the Western Union system, but this service can cost as much as 15% to 20% of the amount sent.

Most hotels have **fax machines** available for guest use (be sure to ask about the charge to use it). Many hotel rooms are even wired for guests' fax machines. A less expensive way to send and receive faxes may be at stores such as **The UPS Store** (formerly Mail Boxes Etc.).

Time The continental United States is divided into four time zones. New England is located in **Eastern Standard Time (EST),** the same zone as New York City. There is also Central Standard Time (CST), Mountain Standard Time (MST), and Pacific Standard Time (PST). Alaska and Hawaii have their own zones. For example, when it's 9am in Los Angeles (PST), it's 7am in Honolulu (HST),10am in Denver (MST), 11am in Chicago (CST), noon in New York (EST), 5pm in London (GMT), and 2am the next day in Sydney.

Daylight saving time takes effect at 2am the first Sunday in April until 2am the last Sunday in October, except in Arizona, Hawaii, the U.S. Virgin Islands, and Puerto Rico. Daylight saving moves the clock 1 hour ahead of standard time. (A new law will extend daylight saving in 2007; clocks will change the second Sun in Mar and the first Sun in Nov.)

Tipping Tips are a very important part of certain workers' income, and gratuities are the standard way of showing appreciation for services provided. (Tipping is certainly not compulsory if the service is poor!) In hotels, tip **bellhops** at least $1 per bag ($2–$3 if you have a lot of luggage) and tip the **chamber staff** $1 to $2 per day (more if you've left a disaster area for him or her to clean up). Tip the **doorman** or **concierge** only if he or she has provided you with some specific service (for example, calling a cab for you or obtaining difficult-to-get theater tickets). Tip the **valet-parking attendant** $1 every time you get your car.

In restaurants, bars, and nightclubs, tip **service staff** 15% to 20% of the check, tip **bartenders** 10% to 15%, tip **checkroom attendants** $1 per garment, and tip **valet-parking attendants** $1 per vehicle.

As for other service personnel, tip **cabdrivers** 15% of the fare; tip **skycaps** at airports at least $1 per bag ($2–$3 if you have a lot of luggage); and tip **hairdressers** and **barbers** 15% to 20%.

Toilets You won't find public toilets or "restrooms" on the streets in most U.S. cities but they can be found in hotel lobbies, bars, restaurants, museums, department stores, railway and bus stations, and service stations. Large hotels and fast-food restaurants are often the best bet for clean facilities. If possible, avoid the toilets at parks and beaches, which tend to be dirty; some may be unsafe. Restaurants and bars in resorts or heavily visited areas may reserve their restrooms for patrons.

Visas For information about U.S. visas go to **http://travel.state.gov** and click on "Visas." Or go to one of the following websites:

Australian citizens can obtain up-to-date visa information from the **U.S. Embassy Canberra,** Moonah Place, Yarralumla, ACT 2600 (✆ **02/6214-5600**) or by checking the U.S. Diplomatic Mission's website at **http://usembassy-australia.state.gov/consular**.

British subjects can obtain up-to-date visa information by calling the **U.S. Embassy Visa Information Line** (✆ **0891/200-290**) or by visiting the "Visas to the U.S." section of the American Embassy London's website at **www.usembassy.org.uk**.

Irish citizens can obtain up-to-date visa information through the **Embassy of the USA Dublin,** 42 Elgin Rd., Dublin 4, Ireland (✆ **353/1-668-8777**; or by checking the "Consular Services" section of the website at **http://dublin.usembassy.gov**.

Citizens of **New Zealand** can obtain up-to-date visa information by contacting the **U.S. Embassy New Zealand,** 29 Fitzherbert Terrace, Thorndon, Wellington (✆ **644/472-2068**), or get the information directly from the "For New Zealanders" section of the website at **http://usembassy.org.nz**.

3

Suggested New England Itineraries

Getting to know New England requires equal amounts of patience and persistence. Your most memorable experience might come at a roadside lobster pound marked only with a scrawled paper sign, at the end of a mountainside hiking trail that overlooks a peaceful lake, or while exploring a cobblestone alley that's not on any map.

Racing around with a checklist and a beat-the-clock attitude is a recipe for disaster. The happiest visitors to New England are those who stay awhile in one spot, getting to know a manageable area through well-crafted day trips. Read on for strategies that can help you organize your time.

1 Boston & Vicinity in 1 Week

Basing yourself in Boston or Cambridge is a good way to get to know eastern Massachusetts while not limiting yourself to one destination. On this itinerary, you'll get a taste of Boston and Cambridge, then set out on day trips to the history-rich suburbs. You'll go in roughly chronological order: Start in Plymouth with the Pilgrims; move on to Lexington and Concord to learn about the rebellious colonists; and finally, visit the North Shore, which flourished after the Revolution. If you're renting a car, note that you don't need it for the full week—pick it up on (and don't start paying for it until) Day 4.

Days ❶ & ❷: Boston ★★★

Begin exploring downtown Boston by walking at least part of the 2.5-mile **Freedom Trail** (p. 118). The whole shebang can be an all-day affair, but I suggest concentrating on the first two-thirds of the trail, from **Boston Common** through **Faneuil Hall.** Break for lunch at **Faneuil Hall Marketplace** (p. 114), then head into the North End for a stroll on the main drag, **Hanover Street,** and a visit to the **Paul Revere House** (p. 121), one of my favorite Boston attractions. From there it's an easy walk to Long Wharf or Rowes Wharf, where you can take a **sightseeing cruise** (p. 124) or, if you want to save both time and money, a **ferry ride** (p. 82) to the Charlestown Navy Yard and back.

On Day 2, prearrange tickets for a **Boston Duck Tour** (p. 124), ideally one that leaves from the Prudential Center in the early afternoon. Be at the **Museum of Fine Arts** (p. 117) when it opens; consider taking a tour to give you an overview before you explore on your own. Head to the Back Bay for lunch and your Duck Tour, then make a beeline for the retail delights of **Newbury Street.** Newbury dead-ends at the **Public Garden** (p. 122), where you can unwind and perhaps go for a spin on a **Swan Boat** (p. 122).

Suggested New England Itineraries

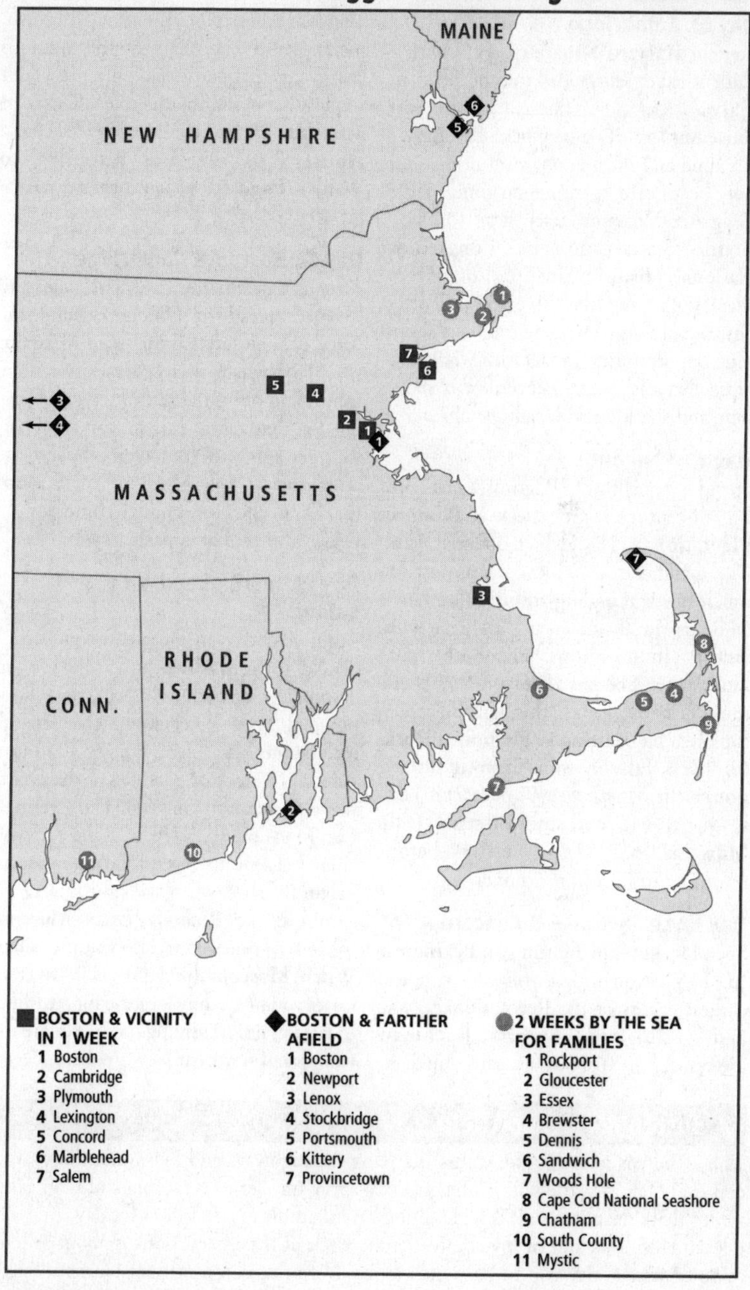
MAINE
NEW HAMPSHIRE
MASSACHUSETTS
RHODE ISLAND
CONN.
BOSTON & VICINITY IN 1 WEEK
1 Boston
2 Cambridge
3 Plymouth
4 Lexington
5 Concord
6 Marblehead
7 Salem
BOSTON & FARTHER AFIELD
1 Boston
2 Newport
3 Lenox
4 Stockbridge
5 Portsmouth
6 Kittery
7 Provincetown
2 WEEKS BY THE SEA FOR FAMILIES
1 Rockport
2 Gloucester
3 Essex
4 Brewster
5 Dennis
6 Sandwich
7 Woods Hole
8 Cape Cod National Seashore
9 Chatham
10 South County
11 Mystic

Day 3: Cambridge ★★

Start in **Harvard Square** (p. 126) with a student-led or self-guided tour of the main Harvard campus. The university **art museums** (p. 128) are up next. If you have the time and inclination, visit all three; if not, be sure to spend some time in the **Fogg Art Museum.** Then head to lovely Brattle Street and the **Longfellow National Historic Site** (p. 128). From there, walk along Mass. Ave. toward Porter Square, a route with some excellent shopping opportunities. In fact, this whole day represents a fantastic chance to mix shopping and snacking with sightseeing.

Day 4: Plymouth ★★

Spend a day with the Pilgrims. Start with a 17th-century reality check at **Plimoth Plantation** (p. 188), which opens at 9am. The hands-on activities are almost as much fun as mingling with the "settlers," who stay in character as they chat with visitors. In downtown Plymouth, have lunch at the **Lobster Hut** (p. 191), where the deck overlooks the harbor, then explore a bit, starting at **Plymouth Rock** (p. 187). Take in some historic attractions—the ***Mayflower II*** (p. 187) is next to the Rock, and the **Pilgrim Hall Museum** (p. 187) is nearby—before returning to Boston for dinner.

Day 5: Lexington ★ & Concord ★★★

Spend most of the morning in **Lexington** (p. 144), acquainting yourself with the earliest events of the Revolutionary War and visiting the historic **Buckman Tavern** (p. 148). Have an early lunch in Concord and explore the beautiful town, picking and choosing the destinations and events that particularly interest you. I suggest starting with the **Concord Museum** (p. 151), touring **Orchard House** (p. 152), and detouring to **Walden Pond** (p. 155) on the way back into town.

Day 6: Boston & Cambridge

After 2 days on the road, stick close to "home." Head to Dorchester and the **John F. Kennedy Library and Museum** (p. 116), which is accessible by public transit and offers free parking (you're paying for that rental car, so you might as well get some use out of it). Spend the afternoon at the **Museum of Science** (p. 117), allowing enough time for an IMAX film if that appeals to you.

Day 7: Marblehead ★★★ & Salem ★★

Begin your day on the picturesque streets of Old Town **Marblehead** (p. 157), a top destination for both sightseeing and shopping. If your hotel room rate doesn't include breakfast, arrive hungry and make a dent in a stack of pancakes at the **Driftwood Restaurant** (p. 161). The **Jeremiah Lee Mansion** (p. 159) is a must if you enjoy house tours. Spend the afternoon in **Salem** (p. 162), where the can't-miss destination is the **Peabody Essex Museum** (p. 164); if time allows, also visit the **Salem Witch Museum** (p. 165). This itinerary leaves you in a handy location for returning to Boston or for heading out to explore the wonders of northern New England.

2 Boston & Farther Afield

The 10-towns-in-6-days bus tours that clog the highways and byways of the Northeast every fall miss the point: The goal of a savvy traveler to New England is an experience that's deeper than it is wide. But even I'll admit to a fondness for day trips that take me just a bit out of my comfort zone. Each of these excursions is about as long as you'd want a day trip to be—and can easily work as an overnight journey. Tackle this itinerary before or after a visit to Boston and Cambridge, or as a tune-up for another of the trips in this chapter. On the first 3 days, an extra driver will come in handy; on the fourth day, there's no driving at all.

Day ❶: Newport ★★★

If you don't hit traffic, you can cover the 75 or so miles between Boston and Newport in a little over an hour. (I just happen to know.) The city's top attractions are the "cottages"—Newport-speak for "mansions"—that line Bellevue Avenue along the magnificent shore. Don't attempt to tour more than two **cottages** (p. 432) in a day, partly because they all start to run together, and partly because you'll want to leave time for exploring the picturesque downtown area. Between the glorious scenery and the serendipitous shopping, Newport is a perfect place to while away an afternoon. Linger into the evening for a drink or dinner near the water.

Day ❷: The Berkshires ★★

Try to schedule this trip to coincide with a morning rehearsal or afternoon concert by the **Boston Symphony Orchestra** at **Tanglewood** (p. 339), in Lenox. It's a long ride (at least 2 hr.) from Boston, so you'll want to get an early start, especially if you're attending a rehearsal. Spread out a blanket, picnic on the lawn, and enjoy the scene, one of the hallmarks of summer in New England. After rehearsal or before and after a concert, select one western Massachusetts town to explore, but just one—crowds and traffic dictate that you not try to get too ambitious. My choice is **Stockbridge** (p. 335), because I'm a sucker for the **Norman Rockwell Museum** (p. 336).

Day ❸: Portsmouth ★★ & Kittery ★

A little over an hour from Boston is a little gem of historic architecture, maritime sights and sounds, funky shops and cafes, and beautiful scenery. Portsmouth is worth a trip just for the **Strawbery Banke** (p. 540), where the historic buildings are the displays. Build in some time to explore the cobblestone downtown area, then cross the Piscataqua River for some serious shopping at the **Kittery** outlets and a bite to eat at **Bob's Clam Hut** (p. 590).

Day ❹: Provincetown ★★★

Ferries (conventional and high-speed) connect Boston to **Provincetown** (p. 247) every day in the summer and on weekends in the spring and fall. The trip by car is absolutely punishing, especially on a busy weekend, but an ocean voyage is always a good idea. On a day trip, you'll have time for world-class people-watching, strolling along **Commercial Street,** perusing the novelty shops and art galleries, lunching on seafood, and—if you're quick—a trip to one of the famous beaches. However, you'll have to forgo the hopping gay nightlife scene unless you've planned a longer excursion.

3 A Week by the Sea for Families

A family can easily spend a pleasant week or so exploring the beaches, boats, cobblestones, shops, museums, and attractions of coastal Maine and New Hampshire. See p. 70.

Days ❶ & ❷: Portland ★★★

Portland is a joy for families. The **Children's Museum of Maine** (p. 605) is almost exactly in the center of town, making it a good jumping-off point for a city tour. The excellent **Portland Museum of Art** (p.605), right next door, provides teens and college-age family members with something different to do.

In the historic **Old Port** (p. 604), Exchange Street is the key shopping address. Kids will enjoy the ice-cream shops, boats, and quirky gift stores. The city tourist office is on Commercial Street.

The **Maine Narrow Gauge Railroad Co. & Museum** (p. 605) combines a short train ride to the foot of the cliffs framing Portland's east end with a museum.

Another great experience is a cruise on the **Casco Bay Ferry** (p. 606) lines. You can take anything from a 20-minute run to a half-day "mail boat" cruise. Two good destinations are **Peaks Island**—a favorite among parents pushing strollers, with easy-to-cruise streets and Portland views—and **Long Island,** which has an excellent beach.

For baseball fans, an outing to Hadlock Field to watch the **Portland Sea Dogs** (p. 607) can't be beat; it's one of my favorite minor-league parks.

Finally, young and old alike enjoy the sunrises, sunsets, picnics, sailboat views, and swing sets of the park along the **Eastern Promenade** (p. 604).

Day 3: Cape Elizabeth

Plan to spend at least one afternoon hitting the string of beaches and lighthouses off Route 77 in the quiet town of **Cape Elizabeth** and surroundings, just 15 minutes from Portland.

Kids will especially enjoy the **Portland Head Light** (p. 605) and romping around in the sand and surf on **Crescent, Scarborough,** and **Willard beaches.**

Day 4: Old Orchard Beach

Drive 20 minutes south of Portland and you come to **Old Orchard Beach** (p. 613). This place may strike you as corny at first, but it rarely fails to entertain. On the pier out over the water, you can find cotton candy, french fries, and arcade games. There's also a long beach to stroll along.

Day 5: Ogunquit

About 40 minutes south of Old Orchard is **Ogunquit** (p. 591), which offers enough distractions for a few days. In addition to a main street full of shops, restaurants, and cafes, it has a main beach that's a vast stretch of powdery sand at low tide and has some of Maine's warmest ocean water (which isn't saying much!). **Perkins Cove** (p. 592) has sea views, ice-cream and candy shops, an excellent small bookstore, and lots of souvenirs for sale.

Day 6: York and Kittery

Only a 10-minute drive south, these twin towns offer a lot for families. **York** (p. 586) has a dynamite lighthouse (with homemade ice cream nearby), an amusement arcade, several excellent beaches, and the **Goldenrod** (p. 590), a candy store where kids can watch taffy being pulled. You can buy boxes to take home—half the fun is deciding which candies to buy. **Kittery** (p. 586) is more for adults, but its extensive set of outlet stores also appeals to teen shopaholics.

Day 7: Portsmouth

Portsmouth (p. 538) is a good base for exploring local parks and beaches. Be sure to visit New Castle Island for its historic streets; the outstanding collection of oceanside state parks lining Route 1A in Rye; and the **Strawbery Banke** (p. 540) by the downtown Portsmouth waterfront, with its historic buildings and restorations. Nearby is the lively **Children's Museum of Portsmouth,** with hands-on exhibits of arts and science. In town, there are plenty of shops and restaurants.

4 2 Weeks by the Sea for Families

Spend your first week in New Hampshire and Maine, as described above, then head south. The water off Massachusetts and Rhode Island is warmer than the northern New England surf (though it's all relative), but the attractions and distractions are just as enjoyable.

Days 8 & 9: Cape Ann ★★

Use your first day to explore this lovely peninsula. Visit downtown **Rockport** (p. 177) for souvenirs and fudge. Push on to **Halibut Point State Park** (p. 179), at the tip of Cape Ann, where there's plenty of room to run around and the views are spectacular. Walk the waterfront boulevard that extends north from Stage Fort Park in **Gloucester** (p. 172). Before or after blowing off some steam by running around Stage Fort Park, head west on Route 133 for fried clams at the legendary **Woodman's of Essex** (p. 170).

On Day 2, head to the beach early, before the parking lots fill. The rocky coast yields to welcoming strips of sand at several inviting spots. A good destination for families is Gloucester's **Wingaersheek Beach** (p. 170), where kids will happily while away the day. Plan on an early dinner, because you have a long drive ahead of you tomorrow.

Days 10, 11 & 12: Cape Cod ★★★

Base yourselves in **Brewster** (p. 223) or **Dennis** (p. 218); they're convenient but not in the heart of the tourist frenzy. On your first day, stick close to your home base and the child-friendly beaches that front Cape Cod Bay. On Day 4, venture to Falmouth by way of Sandwich. Be at the **Heritage Museums and Gardens** in Sandwich (p. 197) at 9am, and don't expect to get away without a carousel ride. Push on to the **Woods Hole Aquarium** (p. 202). Mix and match your routes in each direction, combining the speed and boredom of Route 6 with the pokey pace and abundant distractions of routes 6A and 28 to accommodate the level of interest in the back seat. Day 5 may just be another local beach day, but a fun option is Eastham's **Cape Cod National Seashore** (p. 259) followed by a stroll around lovely downtown **Chatham** (p. 228).

Depend on the family energy level to dictate how you fill out your days. This area abounds with options for outdoor fun; depending on your kids' ages and level of interest, you might try biking, kayaking, or fishing. Just be sure to allow for some quality beach time and that timeless Cape combo, miniature golf and soft-serve ice cream.

Days 13 & 14: South County & Mystic

Work your way west from Cape Cod along the Rhode Island coast, taking advantage of a good excuse to experience relatively undiscovered **South County** (p. 448). You'll reach Connecticut in time to explore the **Mystic Aquarium** (p. 402). That leaves a full day for a visit to **Mystic Seaport** (p. 402); fuel up first with a hearty breakfast at **Kitchen Little** (p. 406).

More Suggested New England Itineraries

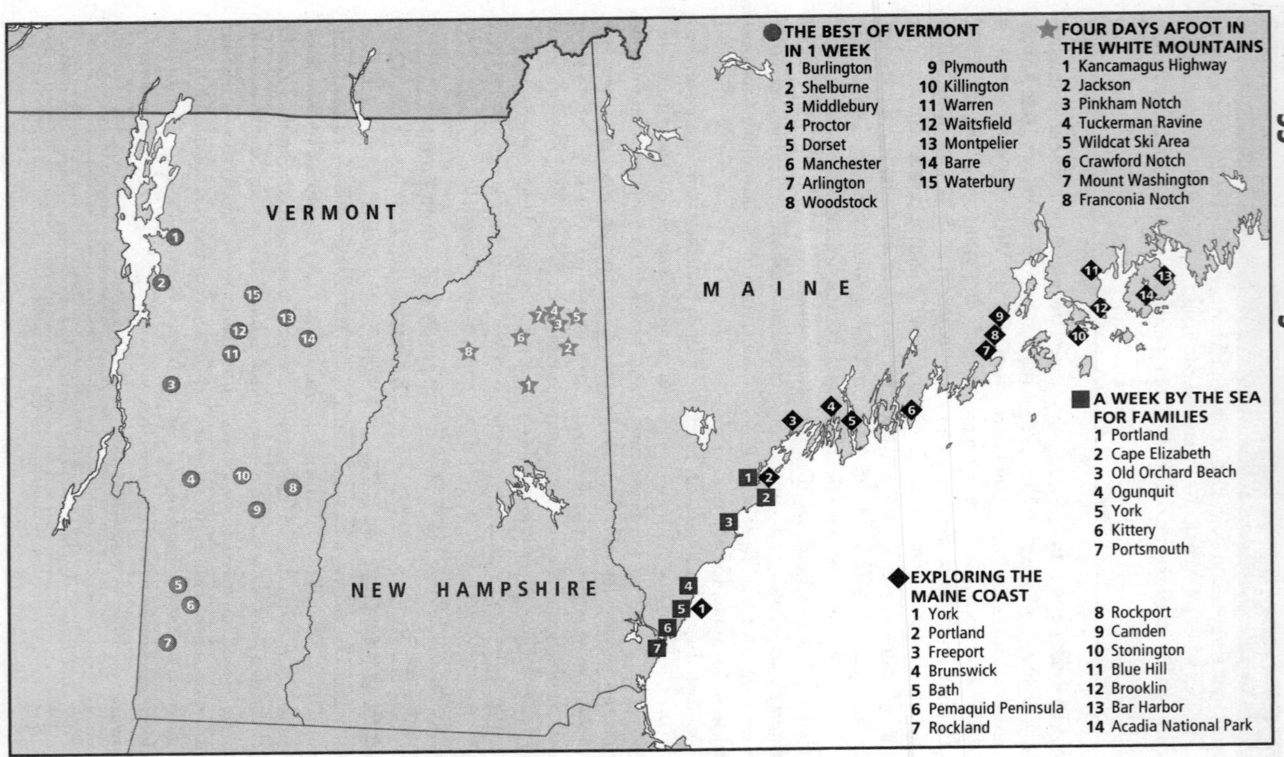

THE BEST OF VERMONT IN 1 WEEK
1 Burlington
2 Shelburne
3 Middlebury
4 Proctor
5 Dorset
6 Manchester
7 Arlington
8 Woodstock
9 Plymouth
10 Killington
11 Warren
12 Waitsfield
13 Montpelier
14 Barre
15 Waterbury
FOUR DAYS AFOOT IN THE WHITE MOUNTAINS
1 Kancamagus Highway
2 Jackson
3 Pinkham Notch
4 Tuckerman Ravine
5 Wildcat Ski Area
6 Crawford Notch
7 Mount Washington
8 Franconia Notch
A WEEK BY THE SEA FOR FAMILIES
1 Portland
2 Cape Elizabeth
3 Old Orchard Beach
4 Ogunquit
5 York
6 Kittery
7 Portsmouth
EXPLORING THE MAINE COAST
1 York
2 Portland
3 Freeport
4 Brunswick
5 Bath
6 Pemaquid Peninsula
7 Rockland
8 Rockport
9 Camden
10 Stonington
11 Blue Hill
12 Brooklin
13 Bar Harbor
14 Acadia National Park
VERMONT
MAINE
NEW HAMPSHIRE

5 The Best of Vermont in 1 Week

You can enjoy a good taste of Vermont in less than a week. This trip involves about 2 or 3 hours of driving daily, if you don't linger (though I wholeheartedly recommend it). You can also scout out places to which you'd like to return and explore in depth.

Days ❶ & ❷: Burlington ★★

Check in to the hotel and head out to explore **Burlington** (p. 522). Depending on the weather, rent bikes or in-line skates, or just put on some comfortable walking shoes—this is a great destination for pedestrians.

Budget plenty of time for exploring the pedestrian-only **Church Street Marketplace** (p. 502)—keep an eye out for the popcorn guy hawking sugared kettle corn in summer—as well as the University of Vermont campus.

Each night, have dinner at one of Burlington's many excellent mid-priced restaurants. In the evening, you can check out the **Vermont Mozart Festival** (p. 524).

Day ❸: Shelburne ★★ & Middlebury ★

Head south to **Shelburne** in the morning, and spend most of the day exploring the remarkable **Shelburne Museum** (p. 525).

Afterward, drive south to the classic town of **Middlebury** (p. 500) and spend the night at a country inn. The historic **Otter Creek** (p. 501) district, set on a steep hillside by the rocky creek, is well worth exploring and has some great crafts for sale. If you're an art lover, explore the campus and art museum of little **Middlebury College** (p. 502). For dinner, I like **American Flatbread** (p. 508), though it's open only 2 nights a week.

Day ❹: In & Around Dorset ★★ & Manchester ★★

From Middlebury, drive south on Route 7, detouring to Proctor to visit the **Vermont Marble Museum** (p. 499). You'll be amazed at the famous sculptures and edifices carved, built, enhanced, or faced with the local stone.

Later, continue west on Route 4 almost to the New York border, then go south on Highway 30 through **Dorset** and **Manchester,** both classic Vermont small towns with scenic vistas. If you're a history fan, you'll love **Hildene** (p. 468), the former estate of Robert Todd Lincoln, son of the assassinated president.

Spend the night in Manchester, Dorset, or Arlington—being sure to leave time late in the day for **outlet shopping** (p. 467) in Manchester and a stop at the flagship **Orvis** outdoors shop.

Day ❺: Woodstock ★★★

Today, head east on Highway 30 into the Green Mountains, then follow Highway 35 north to the town of **Woodstock** (p. 486). (Break out those maps if you crave back roads.)

Be sure to sit a spell on Woodstock's lovely town green, taking some photographs of the covered bridge. You can walk from the center of town to the underrated **Billings Farm and Museum** (p. 488). Drop in to a local pub or coffee shop for a pint or a cup, and try to stay overnight here or nearby.

Day ❻: The Mad River Valley

After exploring Woodstock in the morning, head west on Route 4 with a detour to **Plymouth** ★★ to visit the **President Calvin Coolidge State Historic Site** (p. 494), which is also the site of yet another **cheese factory.**

Continue through **Killington** and up scenic Route 100 to the **Mad River Valley** (p. 504). If it's winter and you're a skier, you may be in heaven; the ski hill here is Vermont's most laid-back.

Overnight in **Warren** ★★ or **Waitsfield** ★★—dropping in to the cute **Warren General Store** (p. 506) for souvenirs—and, if time permits, rent a bike or take a tour on **Icelandic ponies** (p. 506).

Day ❼: Back to Burlington ★★

Spend your final day of this tour working your way back to Burlington.

On the way, spend an hour or two in the lovely little capital city of **Montpelier** ★★. If you're interested, check out the immense working quarries in **Barre.**

You may be pressed for time, but your kids won't let you miss the **Ben & Jerry's factory tour** (p. 511) in **Waterbury** ★★. There's plenty of shopping around here, too, so give in.

End your trip with dinner in **Burlington** (p. 522) at one of the restaurants you missed on your first visit—even if it's just **Al's** (p. 528).

6 4 Days Afoot in the White Mountains

New Hampshire's White Mountains reveal extraordinary natural grandeur from the roadside, and they provide the opportunity to explore mountain crags and crystalline streams.

Day ❶: The "Kank" ★★★

Start at the town of Lincoln, at Exit 32 of I-93, and drive to North Conway via the scenic **Kancamagus Highway** (p. 560), stopping for some short hikes or a picnic. Indulge in a few shopping forays in town, and savor the views of the Mount Washington Valley. Head to the village of **Jackson** (p. 570) for the night.

Relax before dinner at **Jackson Falls**, or take a bike ride up **Carter Notch Road** or other back roads in the hills above the village.

Day ❷: Pinkham Notch ★★

Stay another night in Jackson, and spend the day exploring by foot around **Pinkham Notch** (p. 571). Stop at **Glen Ellis Falls** (p. 571) en route to the base of Mount Washington. Park at Pinkham Notch and hike to dramatic **Tuckerman Ravine** (p. 571) for a picnic lunch.

Return to your car and continue north to **Wildcat Ski Area** (p. 572). Take the chairlift to the summit for spectacular views of Mount Washington, the Presidential Range, and the Carter Range. Return to Jackson for the night.

Day ❸: Mount Washington ★★★

Retrace your path down Route 16 and back to Route 302, turn right, and drive through **Crawford Notch** (p. 575). If weather and time allow, hike to one of the scenic waterfalls.

Go to the **Mount Washington Cog Railway** (p. 577) on the far side of the Notch. Take the train ride to the summit of **Mount Washington** (dress warmly).

Day ❹: Franconia Notch ★★

Continue west on Route 302 to Route 3. Turn left (south) onto I-93, then drive through scenic **Franconia Notch** (p. 579). Visit some of the scenic attractions (such as the **Flume Gorge** [p. 579] or the **tram ride to Cannon Mountain** [p. 579]) as time permits.

7 Exploring the Maine Coast

The inlets and peninsulas of the Maine coast make it impossible to plot a straight course. This trip takes you a little more than halfway up (really across) the coast, allowing time for serendipitous detours and delays. Tack on some extra time at the end to really explore Acadia.

Day ➊: York ★★

Drive into Maine from the south on I-95, and head immediately for **York Village** (p. 586) (the first exit). Spend some time snooping around the historic homes of the **Old York Historical Society** (p. 587), and stretch your legs on a walk through town or the woods.

Drive north through **York Beach,** stock up on saltwater taffy at the **Goldenrod** (p. 590), and spend the night near the beach.

Days ➋ & ➌: Portland ★★★

Using the right route, getting to Portland can be as fun as being there. You can hit the antiques shops along parts of Route 1 as you drive north. If you're in a hurry or traveling in summer, avoid the crowds on Route 1 by taking I-95.

In **Portland** (p. 602) by afternoon, collect tourism information and devise a schedule. Plan to stay in the city or on a nearby beach, shopping for jewelry, souvenirs, or even kites; taste-testing chowder and microbrewed beer; and just soaking up the salty air and atmosphere. Don't forget a walk along the **Eastern Promenade** (p. 604) or a **day cruise** (p. 606) on a local ferry.

Day ➍: Freeport ★★★, Brunswick ★ & Bath ★★

Head north early to beat the shopping crowds at the outlet haven of Freeport. You can't leave too early for **L.L.Bean** (p. 616)—it never closes!

From Freeport, continue north to **Wiscasset** the so-called "Prettiest Village in Maine" or the **Boothbay** region (p. 618). Spend a relaxing night in a picturesque B&B.

Days ➎ & ➏: Camden ★★★ & Penobscot Bay

Heading north from the Bath-Brunswick area, detour down to **Pemaquid Point** (p. 622) for a late picnic as you watch the surf roll in. Then head back to Route 1 and set your sights on the heart of Penobscot Bay.

Rockland ★, which you'll reach first, is the workaday part of the equation. The best places here are the artsy cafes and the excellent museum and restaurants. Nearby **Rockport** ★★ is a tiny harbor town with excellent views and a small main street.

Finally, head a few miles north to wander around downtown **Camden,** poking into shops and galleries. Hike up one of the impressive hills at **Camden Hills State Park** (p. 629), hop a **ferry** to an island (North Haven and Isleboro are both great for biking), sign up for a daylong sail on a **windjammer,** or just spend a long afternoon unwinding on the deck at **The Waterfront** (p. 634). I also like getting ice cream and hot dogs down by the harbor.

Day ➐: Blue Hill ★★★ & Deer Isle

From Camden, drive up and around the head of Penobscot Bay and then down the bay's eastern shore. The roads here are great for aimless drives, but head for **Stonington** ★★, far down at the end of the peninsula.

Next, head to scenic **Blue Hill** (p. 636) for dinner and lodging. I love the views from here, and the combination of a Maine fishing town and new-blood bookshops and restaurants is quite appealing. Also take a spin around the peninsula to smaller towns such as **Blue Hill Falls** and **Brooklin,** where you'll see boatyards, old-fashioned general stores (post offices included), and ingenuity holding it all together. *This* is the real Maine.

Days ❽, ❾, ❿ & ⓫: Bar Harbor ★★ & Acadia National Park ★★★

Bar Harbor is a great base for exploring **Mount Desert Island,** which is well worth 4 (or more) days on a Maine itinerary. You may want to stay at least 2 nights in Bar Harbor, especially if you have family members along. It provides access to comforts and services such as a movie theater, souvenir shops, bike and kayak rentals, free shuttle buses all over the island, and numerous restaurants. Yes, it's a lot more developed (perhaps too much so) than the rest of the island, but think of it as a supply depot.

Hike, bike, boat, or do whatever you must to explore the island and **Acadia National Park** (p. 639), one of America's finest. What it lacks in size, it makes up for through intimate contact with nature. Explore the island at your own pace: take a beginner's **kayak trip** down the eastern shore, a **hike** out to **Bar Island,** or a **mountain bike trip** along one of the many **carriage roads** built by the Rockefeller family. Only bicycles and horses are allowed on these roads, making them a tranquil respite from the island's highways, which—almost unbelievably—do get crowded in summer.

The scenic **Park Loop Road** is a great introduction to what's in store for you later (crashing waves, big mountains, drop-dead-gorgeous views). Make sure to get a park pass that lasts more than a day.

While exploring the rest of the island, be sure to hit some of the non-park towns, too. **Northeast Harbor** ★★ and **Southwest Harbor** ★★ are fishing towns that tourism has partly transformed into tiny centers of art, music, and shopping. However, they still have tiny stores where fishermen shop for slickers and Wonder Bread.

What about those things you wanted to do but didn't have time for? Do them on your last day in Acadia. Watch a sunrise from the top of **Cadillac Mountain** (p. 643). Cap off your visit with a cold-water dip at **Sand Beach** (p. 642) and tea and popovers at **Jordan Pond House** (p. 644). Take a quick last hike up **The Bubbles** (p. 644). Or just enjoy one last lobster atop a wooden pier.

4

Boston & Cambridge

by Marie Morris

Boston embodies contrasts and contradictions—it's blue blood and blue collar, Yankee and Irish, home to budget-conscious graduate students and free-spending computer wizards. Rich in Colonial history and 21st-century technology, it's a living landmark that changes every day. The highway-construction project known as the "Big Dig" dominated downtown Boston for most of the past 2 decades. Now that it's complete, parks, open spaces, surface roads, and new buildings are springing up, mending the scar left by the demolished elevated expressway, and reuniting downtown and the North End.

Cambridge and Boston are so close that many people believe they're the same—a notion both cities' residents and politicians are happy to dispel. Cantabrigians are often considered more liberal and better educated than Bostonians, which is another idea that's sure to get you involved in a heated discussion. Harvard dominates Cambridge's history and geography, but there's more to the city than just the university.

Take a few days (or weeks) to get to know the Boston area, or use it as a gateway to the rest of New England. Here's hoping your experience is memorable and delightful.

1 Orientation

ARRIVING

BY PLANE The major domestic carriers that serve Boston's Logan International Airport are **AirTran** (✆ 800/247-8726), **American** (✆ 800/433-7300), **America West** (✆ 800/235-9292), **ATA** (✆ 800/225-2995), **Continental** (✆ 800/525-0280), **Delta** (✆ 800/221-1212), **JetBlue** (✆ 800/538-2583), **Midwest** (✆ 800/452-2022), **Northwest** (✆ 800/225-2525), **United** (✆ 800/241-6522), and **US Airways** (✆ 800/428-4322). Many major international carriers also fly into Boston.

Southwest (✆ **800/435-9792**) and several other major carriers serve New Hampshire's **Manchester International Airport** (✆ **603/624-6556;** www.flymanchester.com) and **T. F. Green Airport,** in the Providence suburb of Warwick, RI (✆ **888/268-7222;** www.pvdairport.com). Fly into Manchester if possible; **Vermont Transit** (✆ **800/552-8737;** www.vermonttransit.com) runs buses from the airport to Boston's South Station, some of which continue to Logan Airport. The fare is $18.50 one-way, $37 round-trip. Allow 60 to 90 minutes. There is no direct public transit from Boston to T. F. Green; check the website for information about getting there (Amtrak or commuter rail to Providence and local bus to Warwick).

Tips Travel Delays

Before traveling to Boston, check the latest traffic conditions, and be sure to allow plenty of time for detours and delays. A ceiling collapsed in one of the city's relatively new interstate-highway tunnels in July 2006, killing a local woman and creating unpredictable conditions that can snarl traffic downtown, at the airport, and for miles around. Ongoing repairs and inspections, which had no definite timetable at press time, have affected every mode of ground transportation. If you must drive near or around downtown Boston, don't trust online mapping sites to help you plan your route; visit the websites of the Turnpike Authority (www.masspike.com) and the Greater Boston Convention & Visitors Bureau (www.bostonusa.com) for up-to-date information on road closures and transportation options.

Logan Airport is in East Boston at the end of the Sumner, Callahan, and Ted Williams tunnels, 3 miles across the harbor from downtown. Each of the four terminals has ATMs, Internet kiosks, pay phones with dataports, fax machines, and information booths (near baggage claim). Terminals C and D have bank branches that handle currency exchange; A and C have children's play spaces.

The Massachusetts Port Authority, or **MassPort** (© **800/23-LOGAN;** www.massport.com), coordinates airport transportation. Access to the city is by bus, subway (the "T"), cab, van, and boat. The Silver Line **bus** stops at each airport terminal and runs directly to South Station, where you can connect to the Red Line subway and the commuter rail to the southern suburbs. It takes about 20 minutes, not including waiting time. The **subway** takes just 10 minutes to reach downtown, not including the shuttle-bus ride to the subway. Free **shuttle buses** run from each terminal to the Airport station on the Blue Line of the T daily from 5:30am to 1am. The Blue Line stops at State Street and Government Center, downtown points where you can exit or transfer (free) to the other lines. The fare for the bus or subway is $1.25 at press time.

A **cab** from the airport to downtown or the Back Bay costs about $22 to $30. The ride into town takes 10 to 45 minutes, depending on traffic and the time of day. If you must travel during rush hour or on Sunday afternoon, allow extra time, or plan to take the subway or water shuttle (and pack accordingly).

The Logan Airport website (www.massport.com/logan) lists numerous companies that operate **shuttle-van service** to local hotels. One-way prices start at $12 per person and are subject to fuel surcharges as gas prices fluctuate.

The trip to the downtown waterfront (near cabstands and several hotels) in a weather-protected **boat** takes 7 minutes and costs $10 one-way. The free no. 66 shuttle bus connects all terminals to the Logan ferry dock. **Harbor Express** (© **617/222-6999;** www.harborexpress.com) runs to Long Wharf, behind the Marriott Long Wharf hotel. It operates every 20 minutes on weekdays from 7am to 8pm (Fri until 11pm), and every 30 minutes from 10am to 6pm on weekends. Hours are shorter in the winter. The **City Water Taxi** (© **617/422-0392;** www.citywatertaxi.com) connects about a dozen stops on the harbor, including the airport ferry dock. The **Rowes Wharf Water Taxi** (© **617/406-8584;** www.roweswharfwatertaxi.com) serves Rowes Wharf, off Atlantic Avenue behind the Boston Harbor Hotel. Months and days of operation for water taxis are subject to change. Call ahead from the dock for water taxi pickup.

Massachusetts

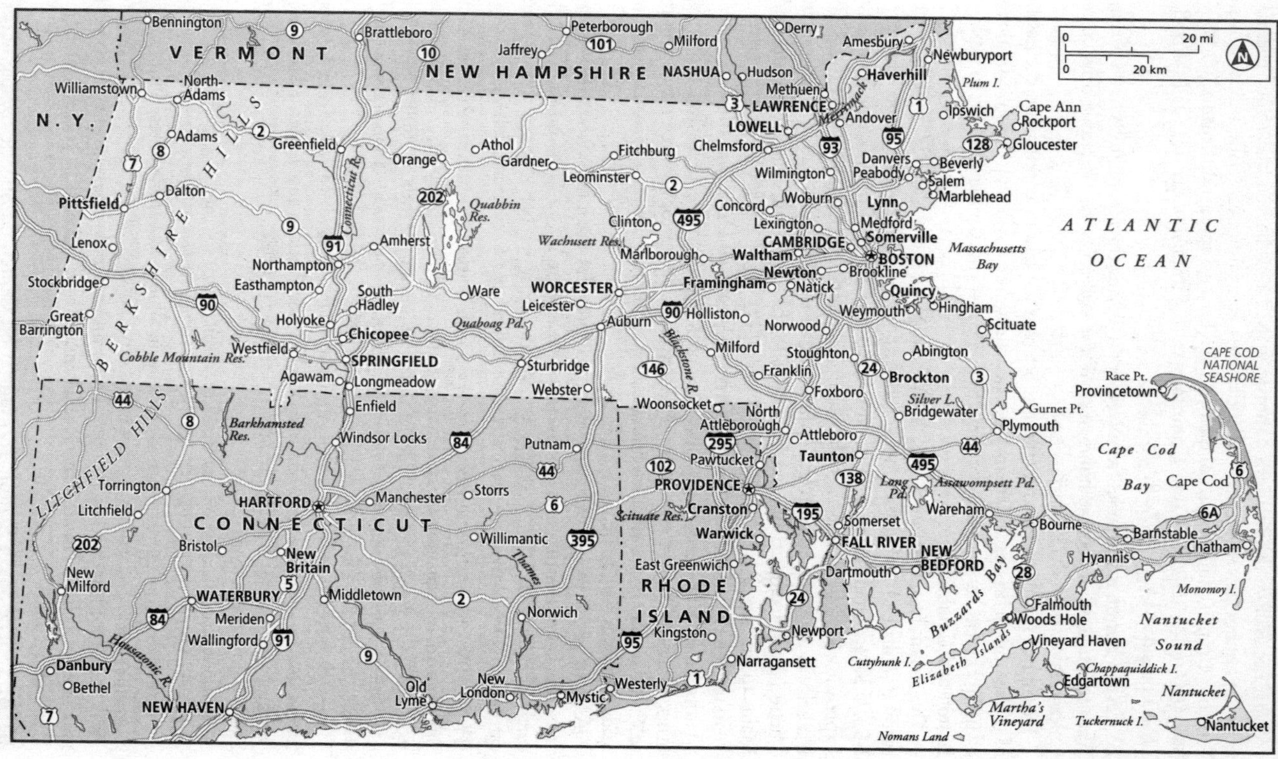

Some hotels have **limousines** or **shuttle vans;** ask when you make your reservations. To arrange private service, call ahead for a reservation, especially at busy times. Your hotel can recommend a company, or try **Carey Limousine Boston** (✆ **800/336-4646** or 617/623-8700) or **Commonwealth Limousine Service** (✆ **800/558-LIMO** outside MA, or 617/787-5575).

BY CAR Boston is 218 miles from New York; driving time is about 4½ hours. From Washington, it takes about 8 hours to cover the 468 miles; the 992-mile drive from Chicago takes around 21 hours.

Driving to Boston is not difficult, but between the cost of parking and the hassle of traffic, the savings on airfare may not be worth the aggravation. If you're thinking of using the car to get around town, think again—you won't need one to explore Boston and Cambridge.

The major highways are **I-90,** the Massachusetts Turnpike ("Mass. Pike"), an east-west toll road that runs from Logan Airport to the New York State Thruway; **I-93/U.S. 1,** which extends north to Canada; and **I-93/Route 3,** the Southeast Expressway, which connects with the south, including Cape Cod. **I-95** (MA Rte. 128) is a beltway about 11 miles from downtown that connects to I-93 and to highways in Rhode Island, Connecticut, and New York to the south and New Hampshire and Maine to the north.

To reach Cambridge, take **Storrow Drive** or **Memorial Drive** (on either side of the Charles River). The Mass. Pike's Allston/Cambridge exit connects with Storrow Drive. It has a Harvard Square exit; cross the Anderson Bridge to John F. Kennedy Street to reach the square. Memorial Drive intersects with Kennedy Street; turn away from the bridge to reach the square.

AAA (✆ **800/AAA-HELP;** www.aaa.com) provides members with maps, itineraries, and other information, and arranges free towing if you break down. The privately operated Mass. Pike arranges its own towing; if you break down, wait in your car until a patrol arrives. To reach the state police from a cellphone, call ✆ ***77.**

BY TRAIN Boston has three rail centers: **South Station,** on Atlantic Avenue; **Back Bay Station,** on Dartmouth Street across from the Copley Place mall; and **North Station,** on Causeway Street near TD Banknorth Garden. **Amtrak** (✆ **800/USA-RAIL** or 617/482-3660; www.amtrak.com) serves all three. Each train station is also a rapid-transit station. See the "Boston Transit & Parking" map on p. 83.

Amtrak serves Boston from the south and from Portland, Maine. **Acela Express** high-speed service, when it's on time, reaches New York in just under 4 hours and Washington in about 6 hours. Standard Northeast Corridor service takes 4 to 5 hours and 8 hours, respectively.

South Station is a stop on the Red Line, which runs to Cambridge by way of Park Street, the hub of the **subway** (✆ **800/392-6100** or 617/222-3200; www.mbta.com). At Park Street you can connect to the Green, Blue, and Orange lines. The Orange Line links Back Bay Station with Downtown Crossing (where there's a walkway to Park St. station) and other points. The **commuter rail** serves Ipswich, Rockport, and Fitchburg from North Station, and points south and west of Boston, including Plymouth, from South Station.

BY BUS The **South Station Transportation Center,** on Atlantic Avenue next to the train station, is the city's bus-service hub. It's served by regional and national lines, including **Greyhound** (✆ **800/231-2222** or 617/526-1801; www.greyhound.com),

Bonanza (✆ **800/556-3815** or 617/720-4110; www.bonanzabus.com), and **Peter Pan** (✆ **800/237-8747** or 800/343-9999; www.peterpanbus.com).

VISITOR INFORMATION

BEFORE YOU LEAVE HOME Contact the **Greater Boston Convention & Visitors Bureau,** 2 Copley Place, Suite 105, Boston (✆ **888/SEE-BOSTON** or 617/536-4100; 0171/431-3434 in the U.K.; www.bostonusa.com). It offers a comprehensive information kit ($10) with a planner, guidebook, map, and coupons; and a *Kids Love Boston* guide ($5). Free smaller planners for specific seasons or events are often available.

The **Cambridge Office for Tourism,** 4 Brattle St., Suite 208, Cambridge (✆ **800/862-5678** or 617/441-2884; www.cambridge-usa.org), distributes information about Cambridge.

The **Massachusetts Office of Travel and Tourism,** 10 Park Plaza, Suite 4510, Boston (✆ **800/227-6277** or 617/973-8500; www.massvacation.com), distributes the *Getaway Guide,* a free magazine with information on attractions and lodgings, a map, and a seasonal calendar.

An excellent resource for travelers with disabilities is **VSA Arts Massachusetts** (✆ **617/350-7713;** TTY 617/350-6836; www.vsamass.org). Its comprehensive website includes general access information and specifics on more than 200 arts and entertainment facilities.

IN PERSON The **Boston National Historical Park Visitor Center,** 15 State St. (✆ **617/242-5642;** www.nps.gov/bost), across the street from the Old State House and the State Street T, is a good place to start exploring. National Park Service rangers staff the center and lead free tours of the "heart" of the Freedom Trail in the spring, summer, and fall. The audiovisual show provides basic information on 16 historic sites on the trail. The center is wheelchair accessible and has restrooms; it is open daily from 9am to 5pm.

The Freedom Trail begins at the **Boston Common Information Center,** 146 Tremont St., on the Common. The center is open Monday through Saturday from 8:30am to 5pm, Sunday from 9am to 5pm. The **Prudential Information Center,** on the main level of the Prudential Center, is open Monday through Friday from 8:30am to 6pm, Saturday and Sunday from 10am to 6pm. The **Greater Boston Convention & Visitors Bureau** (✆ **888/SEE-BOSTON** or 617/536-4100) operates both centers.

There's an outdoor information booth at **Faneuil Hall Marketplace** between Quincy Market and the South Market Building. It's staffed in the spring, summer, and fall from 10am to 6pm Monday through Saturday, noon to 6pm Sunday.

In Cambridge, there's an **information kiosk** (✆ **800/862-5678** or 617/497-1630) in the heart of Harvard Square, near the T entrance at the intersection of Mass. Ave., John F. Kennedy Street, and Brattle Street. It's open Monday through Saturday from 9am to 5pm, Sunday from 1 to 5pm.

CITY LAYOUT

Parts of Boston reflect the city's original layout, a seemingly haphazard plan that can disorient even longtime residents. Old Boston abounds with alleys, dead ends, one-way streets, streets that change names, and streets named after extinct geographical features. On the plus side, every "wrong" turn **downtown,** in the **North End,** or on **Beacon Hill** is a chance to see something you might otherwise have missed.

FINDING AN ADDRESS There's no rhyme or reason to the street pattern, compass directions are virtually useless, and there aren't enough street signs. The best way to find an address is to call ahead and ask for directions, including landmarks, or leave time for wandering around. If the directions involve a T stop, be sure to ask which exit to use—most stations have more than one.

STREET MAPS Free maps of downtown Boston and the transit system are available at visitor centers around the city. *Where* and other tourism-oriented magazines, available free at most hotels, include maps of central Boston and the T. *Streetwise Boston* ($6.95) and *Artwise Boston* ($7.95) are sturdy, laminated maps available at most bookstores.

BOSTON NEIGHBORHOODS IN BRIEF

See the map on p. 88 to locate these areas. When Bostonians say **"downtown,"** they usually mean the first six neighborhoods defined here.

The Waterfront This narrow area along **Atlantic Avenue** and **Commercial Street,** once filled with wharves and warehouses, now boasts luxury condos, marinas, restaurants, offices, and hotels. Also here are the New England Aquarium and departure points for harbor cruises and whale-watches.

The North End One of the city's oldest neighborhoods has been an immigrant stronghold for much of its history. It's now less than half Italian-American, but you'll still hear Italian spoken and find many Italian restaurants, *caffès,* and shops. **Hanover Street** is the main street of the North End, which lies between Faneuil Hall Marketplace and the Waterfront. Clubs and restaurants cluster on and near **Causeway Street** in the **North Station** area (between N. Washington St. and Beacon Hill), where you shouldn't wander the side streets alone late at night.

Faneuil Hall Marketplace & Haymarket Employees aside, Boston residents tend to be scarce at Faneuil Hall Marketplace (also called Quincy Market). An irresistible draw for out-of-towners and suburbanites, the cluster of restored market buildings adjacent to the North End is the city's most popular attraction. **Haymarket,** along Blackstone Street, is home to an open-air produce market on Friday and Saturday.

Government Center Here, modern design strays into the red-brick facade of traditional Boston architecture. Across **Cambridge Street** from Beacon Hill, Government Center is home to state and federal office towers, Boston City Hall, and a central T stop.

Financial District In the city's banking, insurance, and legal center, skyscrapers surround the landmark Custom House Tower. This area is frantic during the day and practically empty at night. **State Street** separates it from Faneuil Hall Marketplace.

Downtown Crossing The Freedom Trail runs through this shopping and business district adjacent to Boston Common, which hops during the day and slows at night. The intersection that gives Downtown Crossing its name is where Winter Street becomes Summer Street at **Washington Street,** the most "main" street downtown.

Beacon Hill Narrow, tree-lined streets and architectural showpieces make up this largely residential area near the State House. **Charles Street** is the main drag of "the Hill." Two of the city's loveliest and most exclusive spots are here: Mount Vernon Street and Louisburg Square (pronounced "Lewisburg," and home to John Kerry). Massachusetts General Hospital is off

Cambridge Street. On the south side, **Beacon Street** borders Boston Common, as does **Park Street,** which is just 1 block long but looms large in the geography of the T.

Charlestown One of the oldest areas of Boston is where you'll see the Bunker Hill Monument and USS *Constitution* ("Old Ironsides"). Yuppification has brought some diversity to the mostly white residential neighborhood, but pockets remain that have earned their reputation for insularity. To get here, follow **North Washington Street** from the North End.

Seaport District (South Boston Waterfront) The city's newest neighborhood has several names; these are the most popular. Across **Fort Point Channel** from downtown, it's where you'll find the World Trade Center, Institute of Contemporary Art, Seaport Hotel, Fish Pier, federal courthouse, Museum Wharf, Boston Convention & Exhibition Center, and one end of the Ted Williams Tunnel.

Chinatown The fourth-largest Chinese community in the country abounds with Asian restaurants, groceries, and other businesses. As the "Combat Zone," or red-light district, has nearly disappeared, Chinatown has expanded to fill the area between Downtown Crossing and the Mass. Pike extension. Its main street is **Beach Street.** Also in this neighborhood, the tiny **Theater District** extends about 1½ blocks in each direction from the intersection of Tremont and Stuart streets; be careful here at night after the crowds thin out.

South End Cross **Huntington Avenue** or Stuart Street to reach this landmark district packed with Victorian row houses and little parks. Known for its ethnic, economic, and cultural diversity, as well as its galleries and boutiques, the South End has a large gay community and some of the city's best restaurants. Main thoroughfares include **Tremont** and **Washington streets,** which originate downtown, and **Columbus Avenue.** ***Note:*** Don't confuse the South End with South Boston, a residential neighborhood across I-93.

Back Bay Fashionable since its creation out of landfill in the mid–19th century, the Back Bay overflows with gorgeous architecture and chic shops. It extends from **Arlington Street,** in the plush area near the **Public Garden,** to the student-dominated sections near Massachusetts Avenue, or **Mass. Ave.** Unlike downtown, it's laid out in a grid. The main streets include the prime shopping areas of **Boylston** and **Newbury streets** and largely residential Commonwealth Avenue, or **Comm. Ave.,** and **Beacon Street.** The cross streets go in alphabetical order.

Huntington Avenue Landmarks dot the "Avenue of the Arts" (or, with a Boston accent, "Otts"). Not a formal neighborhood, Huntington Avenue is where you'll find Symphony Hall (at the corner of **Mass. Ave.**), Northeastern University, and the Museum of Fine Arts. Parts of Huntington can be a little risky; if you're leaving the museum at night, grab a cab or the Green Line, and travel in a group.

Kenmore Square The landmark white-and-red Citgo sign above the intersection of **Comm. Ave., Beacon Street,** and **Brookline Avenue** tells you you're approaching Kenmore Square. Boston University students throng its shops, bars, restaurants, and clubs. The college-town atmosphere goes out the window when the Red Sox are in town and baseball fans flock to Fenway Park, 3 blocks away.

Tips All's Fare on the T

During the lifespan of this book, the MBTA (© **800/392-6100** or 617/222-3200; www.mbta.com) plans to complete its conversion to automated fare collection and raise fares. The paper **CharlieTicket** and the plastic **CharlieCard** will replace tokens on the subway; passengers on buses and aboveground trolleys will have the option to pay cash (coins only). Elaborate instructions are posted in every T station that uses the new system. The **fare hike** is scheduled for early 2007, but details weren't set at press time. Expect to pay at least $1.50 for the subway and $1 for the bus. The new fare-collection system may include zoned fares, but that's not official, either. You can check the website or quiz the phone representatives for details before your trip.

Cambridge The backbone of Boston's neighbor across the Charles River is **Mass. Ave.,** which originates in Roxbury and extends 9 miles, into Cambridge, Arlington, and Lexington. The Red Line subway parallels Mass. Ave. in the areas you're likeliest to visit, around the following T stops: **Kendall/MIT, Central, Harvard,** and **Porter.**

2 Getting Around

It's impossible to say this often enough: When you reach your hotel, *leave your car in the garage and walk or use public transportation.* If you must drive in town, ask at the front desk for the quickest route (which may not be obvious from a map or mapping website).

BY PUBLIC TRANSPORTATION

The Massachusetts Bay Transportation Authority, or **MBTA** (© **800/392-6100** or 617/222-3200; www.mbta.com), is known as the "T," and its logo is that letter in a circle. It runs subways, trolleys, buses, and ferries in Boston and many suburbs, as well as the commuter rail. Its website includes maps, schedules, and other information.

Newer stations on the Red, Blue, and Orange lines are wheelchair accessible; the Green Line is being converted. All T buses have lifts or kneelers; call © **800/LIFT-BUS** for information. To learn more, call the **Office for Transportation Access** (© **617/222-5438** or TTY 617/222-5854).

BY SUBWAY & TROLLEY Red, Blue, and Orange line trains and Green Line trolleys make up the **subway** system, which runs partly aboveground. (The commuter rail to the suburbs is purple on system maps and is sometimes called the Purple Line; the Silver Line is a fancy name for a bus line.) The local fare at press time is $1.25—you'll need a token or, in stations that use them, a ticket (see box above, "All's Fare on the T"). Transfers are free. Route and fare information and timetables are available through the website and at centrally located stations. Service begins around 5:15am and ends around 12:30am. On New Year's Eve, closing time is 2am and service is free after 8pm. A sign on the token booth in every station gives the time of the last train in either direction.

Boston Transit & Parking

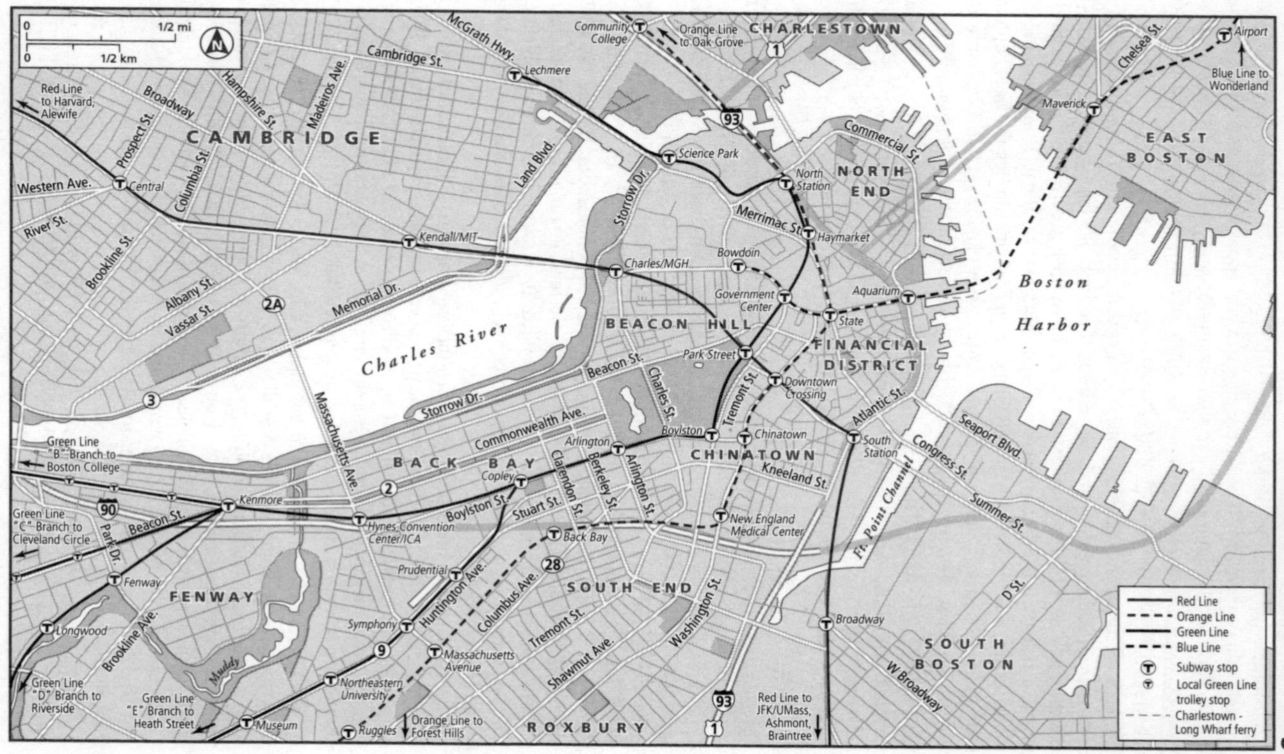

The oldest system in the country, the T dates to 1897. The Green Line is the most unpredictable—leave early if you're taking it to a vital appointment, and bring cab fare in case you have to jump off. Note that downtown stops are so close together that walking is often faster. The system is generally safe, but always watch out for pickpockets, especially during the holiday season.

BY BUS T buses and "trackless trolleys" (buses with electric antennae) provide service around town and to and around the suburbs. The local bus fare at press time is 90¢; express buses are $2.20 and up. Exact change is required; after fare collection is automated, a ticket will work, too (see box above, "All's Fare on the T"). Important local routes include **no. 1** (Mass. Ave. from Dudley Sq. in Roxbury through the Back Bay and Cambridge to Harvard Sq.); **nos. 92** and **93** (between Haymarket and Charlestown); and **no. 77** (Mass. Ave. from Harvard Sq. north to Porter Sq. and Arlington).

BY FERRY The MBTA Inner Harbor ferry connects **Long Wharf** (near the New England Aquarium) with the **Charlestown Navy Yard**—it's a good way to get back downtown from "Old Ironsides" and the Bunker Hill Monument. The fare is $1.50. Visit www.mbta.com or call ✆ **617/227-4321** for information.

BY TAXI

Taxis are expensive and not always easy to flag—find a cabstand or call a dispatcher. Stands are usually near hotels. There are also busy ones at Faneuil Hall Marketplace (on North St. and in front of 60 State St.), South Station, Back Bay Station, and on Mass. Ave. in Harvard Square near the Coop and in front of Au Bon Pain.

To call ahead, try the **Independent Taxi Operators Association** (✆ **617/426-8700**), **Boston Cab** (✆ **617/262-2227**), **Town Taxi** (✆ **617/536-5000**), or **Metro Cab** (✆ **617/242-8000**). In Cambridge, call **Ambassador Brattle** (✆ **617/492-1100**) or **Yellow Cab** (✆ **617/547-3000**). Boston Cab can dispatch a wheelchair-accessible vehicle; advance notice is recommended. If you want to report a problem or have lost something in a Boston cab, call the police department's **Hackney Hot Line** (✆ **617/536-8294**).

The fare structure: the first ¼-mile (when the flag drops), $1.75; each additional ⅛th of a mile, 30¢. Wait time is extra, and the passenger pays tolls as well as a total of $6.50 in fees on trips entering and leaving Logan. Charging a flat rate is not allowed in the city; the police department publishes a list (available at www.massport.com/logan) of distances to the suburbs that establishes the flat rate for those trips.

BY WATER TAXI From April to November, **City Water Taxi** (✆ **617/422-0392;** www.citywatertaxi.com) provides on-call service in small boats that connects a dozen stops on the Inner Harbor, including the airport. It operates daily from 7am to 7pm. One-way fares start at $10. The **Rowes Wharf Water Taxi** (✆ **617/406-8584**) connects the airport ferry dock, the federal courthouse on Fan Pier, the World Trade Center, and Rowes Wharf. It runs year-round from 7am to 7pm, daily in the summer and weekdays only from October to May. The flat fare is $10 one-way. Call ahead from the dock for pickup by either service.

Weekday-only **Seaport Express** (✆ **617/939-4802;** www.seaporttma.org) connects Central Wharf, behind the New England Aquarium, to the World Trade Center. The one-way fare is $1.50, and on-call service to other destinations around the harbor is available for $5 to $10.

BY CAR

If you plan to visit only Boston and Cambridge, you do not need a car. Construction, expensive parking, daredevil drivers, and confusing geography make Boston in particular a motorist's nightmare. If you arrive by car, park at the hotel and walk or use public transit. For day trips, you'll probably want a car.

RENTALS The major car-rental firms have offices at Logan Airport and in Boston; some have other area branches. Boston levies a $10 surcharge on car rentals that goes toward the construction of a new convention center. If you're traveling at a busy time, especially during foliage season, reserve well in advance. Most agencies offer shuttle service from the airport to their offices.

Companies with offices at the airport include **Alamo** (© 800/327-9633), **Avis** (© 800/831-2847), **Budget** (© 800/527-0700), **Dollar** (© 800/800-4000), **Hertz** (© 800/654-3131), and **National** (© 800/227-7368). **Enterprise** (© 800/325-8007) and **Thrifty** (© 800/367-2277) are nearby but not on the grounds; leave time for the shuttle ride.

PARKING It's difficult to find your way around Boston and practically impossible to park in some areas. Most spaces on the street are metered (and patrolled until 6pm on the dot Mon–Sat), have strict time limits, or both. Parking downtown usually costs $1 an hour; bring plenty of quarters. Time limits range from 15 minutes to 2 hours. The penalty is a $45 ticket, but should you blunder into a tow-away zone, retrieving the car will take at least $100 and a lot of running around. The city tow lot is at 200 Frontage Rd., South Boston (© **617/635-3900;** T: Red Line to Andrew, then grab a cab).

It's best to leave the car in a garage or lot and walk. A full day at most lots costs no more than $25, but some downtown facilities charge as much as $35. Some restaurants offer discounts at nearby garages; ask when you make reservations.

The city-run **Boston Common Garage,** off Charles Street (© **617/954-2096**), accepts vehicles under 6 feet, 3 inches tall. The **Prudential Center Garage** (© **617/267-1002**) has entrances on Boylston Street, Huntington Avenue, and Exeter Street, and at the Sheraton Boston Hotel. Parking is discounted if you buy something at the Shops at Prudential Center and have your ticket validated. The **Copley Place Garage,** off Huntington Avenue (© **617/375-4488**), offers a similar deal. Many businesses in Faneuil Hall Marketplace validate parking at the **75 State St. Garage** (© **617/742-7275**).

Good-size garages downtown are at **Government Center,** off Congress Street (© **617/227-0385**); **Sudbury Street** off Congress Street (© **617/973-6954**); the **New England Aquarium** (© **617/723-1731**); and **Zero Post Office Square,** in the Financial District (© **617/423-1430**). In the Back Bay, there's a large garage near the Hynes Convention Center on **Dalton Street** (© **617/247-8006**).

DRIVING RULES When traffic permits, you may turn right at a red light after stopping, unless a sign says otherwise. Seat belts are mandatory for adults and children, children under 12 may not ride in the front seat, and infants and children under 5 must be in car seats. Pedestrians in the crosswalk and vehicles already in a rotary (traffic circle or roundabout) have the right of way.

FAST FACTS: Boston & Cambridge

American Express The main local office is at 1 State St. (© **617/723-8400**), opposite the Old State House. Other offices are in the Financial District, 170 Federal St. (© **617/439-4400**); in the Back Bay, 432 Stuart St., around the corner from Back Bay Station (© **617/236-1331**); and in Cambridge, 39 John F. Kennedy St., Harvard Square (© **617/868-2600**).

Area Codes Eastern Massachusetts has eight area codes: Boston proper, **617** and **857;** immediate suburbs, **781** and **339;** northern and western suburbs, **978** and **351;** southern suburbs, **508** and **774.** ***Note:*** To complete a local call, you must dial all 10 digits plus a 1 at the beginning.

Car Rentals See "Getting Around," above.

Dentists Ask at your hotel's front desk or try the **Massachusetts Dental Society** (© **800/342-8747** or 508/480-9797; www.massdental.org).

Doctors Your hotel concierge should be able to help you. Hospital referral services include **Brigham and Women's** (© **800/294-9999**), **Massachusetts General** (© **800/711-4MGH**), and **Tufts–New England Medical Center** (© **617/636-9700**). An affiliate of Mass. General, **MGH Back Bay,** 388 Comm. Ave. (© **617/267-7171**), offers walk-in service and honors most insurance plans.

Drinking Laws The legal drinking age is 21. In many bars, particularly near college campuses, and at sporting events, you will probably be asked for ID.

Embassies & Consulates See "Embassies & Consulates" in chapter 2.

Emergencies Call © **911** for fire, ambulance, or police. For the state police, call © **617/523-1212** or, from a cellphone, © ***77.**

Hospitals **Massachusetts General Hospital,** 55 Fruit St. (© **617/726-2000**), and **Tufts–New England Medical Center,** 750 Washington St. (© **617/636-5000**), are closest to downtown. In Cambridge are **Mount Auburn Hospital,** 330 Mt. Auburn St. (© **617/492-3500**), and **Cambridge Hospital,** 1493 Cambridge St. (© **617/498-1000**).

Hot Lines AIDS Hotline (© **800/235-2331**); Poison Control (© **800/682-9211**); Rape Crisis (© **877/627-7700** or 617/492-7273); and Travelers Aid Family Services (© **617/542-7286**).

Information See "Visitor Information," earlier in this chapter. For directory assistance, dial © **411.**

Internet Access The ubiquitous **FedEx Kinko's** charges 10¢ to 20¢ a minute. Locations include 2 Center Plaza, Government Center (© **617/973-9000**); 187 Dartmouth St., Back Bay (© **617/262-6188**); and 1 Mifflin Place, off Mount Auburn Street near Eliot Street, Harvard Square (© **617/497-0125**). **Tech Superpowers,** 252 Newbury St., third floor (© **617/267-9716;** www.newburyopen.net), offers access by the hour ($5/hour; $3 minimum) and free wireless access at many spots near its offices.

Newspapers & Magazines The daily papers are the *Boston Globe* and *Boston Herald.* The "Sidekick" section of the daily *Globe* and the "Edge" section of the Friday *Herald* contain cultural listings. The arts-oriented *Boston Phoenix,* published on Thursday, has entertainment and restaurant listings.

Where, a free monthly magazine, contains information on shopping, nightlife, attractions, museums, and galleries. Newspaper boxes around both cities dispense the free weekly *Phoenix* and *Tab,* and the biweekly *Improper Bostonian* and *Stuff@Night. Boston* magazine is a lifestyle-oriented monthly.

Pharmacies Downtown Boston has no 24-hour pharmacy. The pharmacy at the **CVS** at 155–157 Charles St. (✆ **617/523-1028**), next to the Charles/MGH Red Line T stop, is open until midnight. The pharmacy at the **CVS** at the Porter Square Shopping Center, off Mass. Ave. in Cambridge (✆ **617/876-5519**), is open 24 hours. Some emergency rooms can fill your prescription at the hospital's pharmacy.

Police Call ✆ **911** for emergencies. For the state police, call ✆ **617/523-1212** or, from a cellphone, ✆ ***77**.

Restrooms The visitor center at 15 State St. has public restrooms, as do most tourist attractions, hotels, department stores, shopping centers, coffee bars, and public buildings. Free-standing, self-cleaning pay toilets (25¢) are scattered around downtown, but check carefully before using them; despite regular patrols, IV-drug users have been known to take advantage of the generous time limits.

Safety On the whole, Boston and Cambridge are safe cities for walking. As in any urban area, stay out of parks (including Boston Common, the Public Garden, and the Esplanade) at night unless you're in a crowd. Areas to avoid at night include Boylston Street between Tremont and Washington, and Tremont Street from Stuart to Boylston. Try not to walk alone late at night in the Theater District and around North Station. Public transportation is busy and safe, but service stops between 12:30 and 1am.

Smoking Massachusetts bans smoking in all workplaces, including clubs, bars, and restaurants. Take it outside—you'll have plenty of company.

Taxes The 5% sales tax does not apply to food, prescription drugs, newspapers, or clothing that costs less than $175; the tax on meals and takeout food is 5%. The lodging tax in Boston and Cambridge is 12.45%.

Taxis See "Getting Around," earlier in this chapter.

Transit Info Call ✆ **617/222-3200** for the T (subways, local buses, commuter rail), and ✆ **800/23-LOGAN** for MassPort (airport transportation).

3 Where to Stay

Boston's occupancy rates are nearly back to their late-1990s heights, and so—despite the addition of hundreds of rooms since then—are prices. You'll need to do some planning, especially at busy times. Rates at most downtown hotels are lower on weekends than on weeknights, when business and convention travelers fill rooms; leisure hotels offer discounts during the week. If you don't mind cold and the possibility of snow, aim for January through March, when you'll find great deals, especially on weekends.

It's always a good idea to make a reservation, especially during foliage season. The area is also busy during spring and fall conventions, July and August vacations, and college graduation season (May and early June).

Boston Accommodations

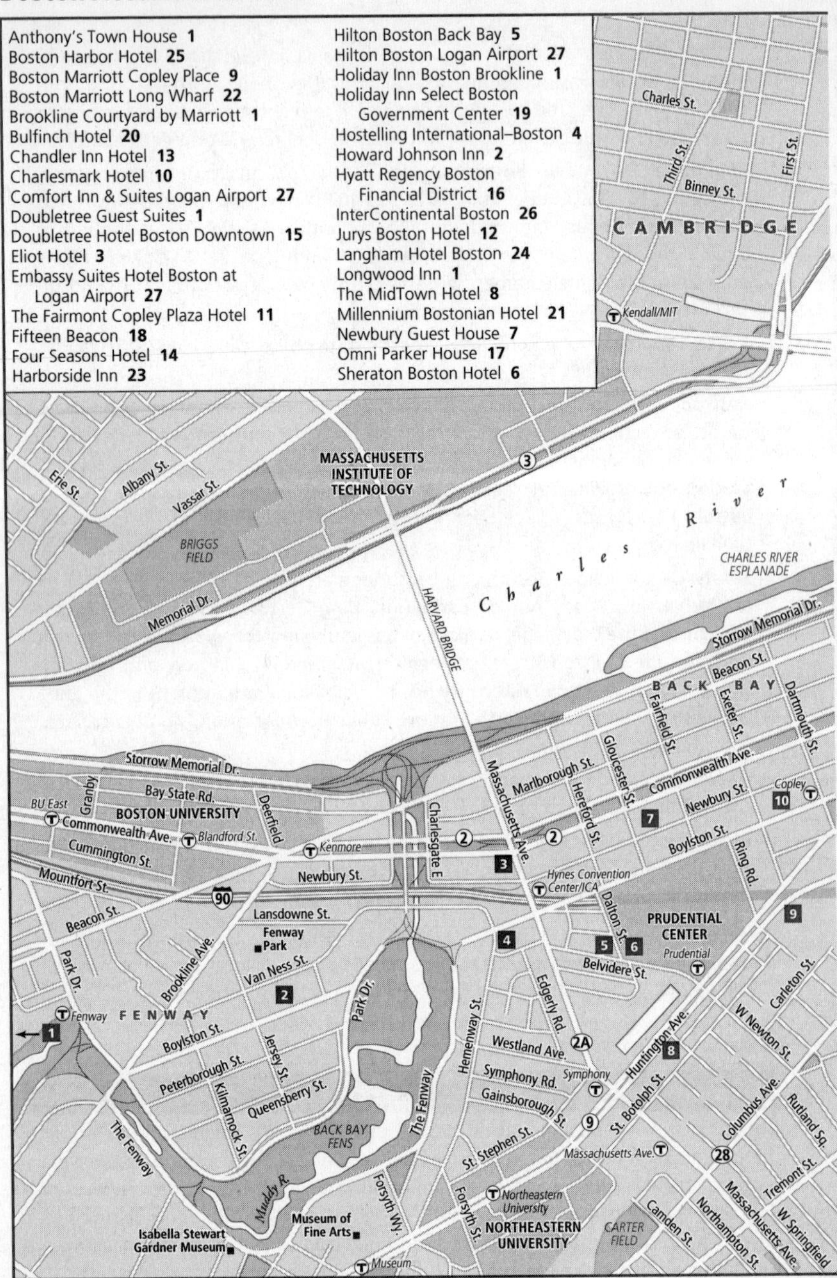

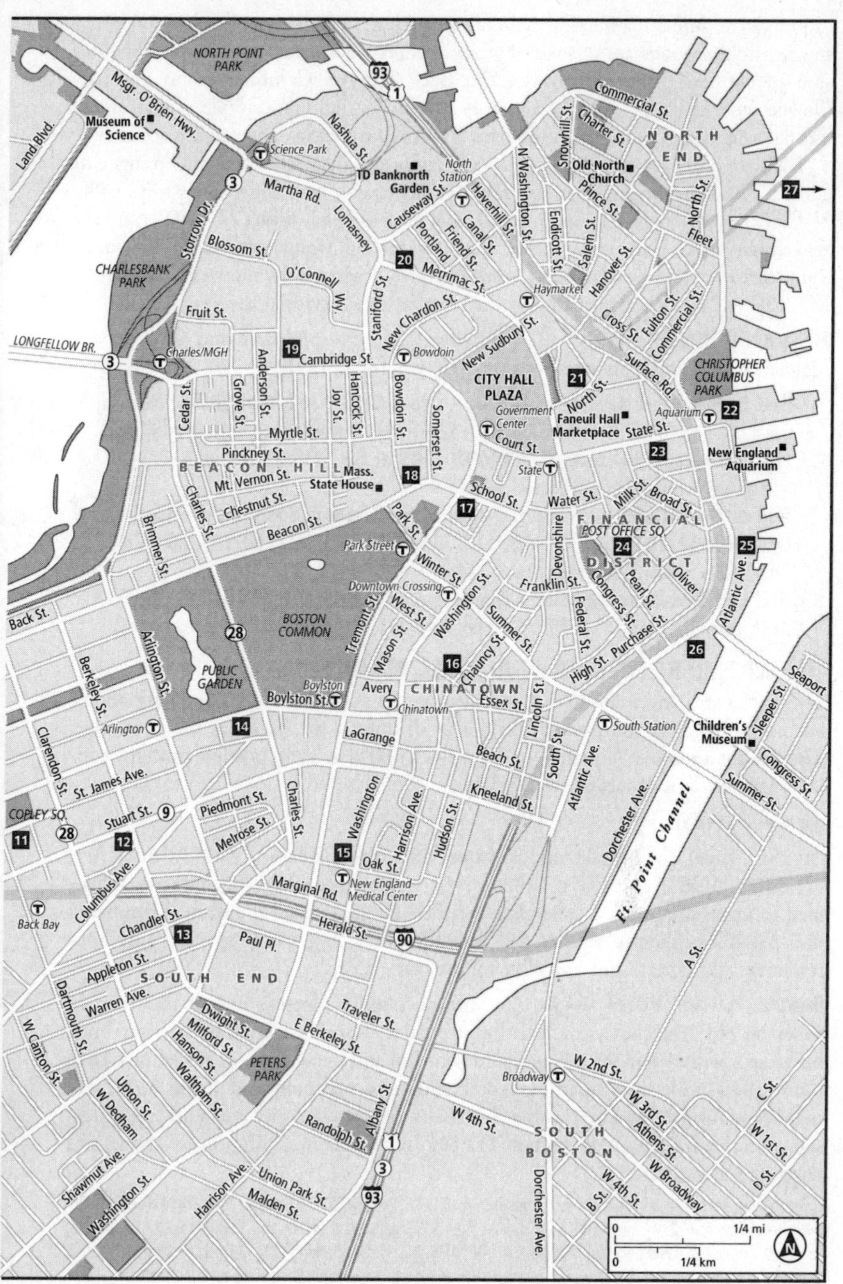

NORTH POINT PARK
Msgr. O'Brien Hwy.
Museum of Science
Land Blvd.
Science Park
Nashua St.
North Station
TD Banknorth Garden
Martha Rd.
Causeway St.
Commercial St.
Charter St.
Snowhill St.
NORTH END
Old North Church
Prince St.
N Washington St.
Haverhill St.
Canal St.
Friend St.
Portland
Lomasney
Endicott St.
Salem St.
North St.
Fleet
Storrow Dr.
Blossom St.
CHARLESBANK PARK
O'Connell Wy.
Merrimac St.
Hanover St.
Haymarket
Staniford St.
New Chardon St.
Fruit St.
Cross St.
Fulton St.
Commercial St.
LONGFELLOW BR.
Charles/MGH
Cambridge St.
Bowdoin
New Sudbury St.
Surface Rd.
CHRISTOPHER COLUMBUS PARK
CITY HALL PLAZA
North St.
Cedar St.
Grove St.
Anderson St.
Joy St.
Hancock St.
Bowdoin St.
Somerset St.
Government Center
Faneuil Hall Marketplace
State St.
Aquarium
Myrtle St.
Court St.
New England Aquarium
Pinckney St.
BEACON HILL
Mass. State House
State
Mt. Vernon St.
Charles St.
Chestnut St.
School St.
Water St.
Milk St.
Broad St.
FINANCIAL DISTRICT
POST OFFICE SQ.
Brimmer St.
Beacon St.
Park St.
Park Street
Devonshire
Winter St.
Oliver
Atlantic Ave.
Downtown Crossing
Washington St.
Franklin St.
Congress St.
Pearl St.
Back St.
BOSTON COMMON
Tremont St.
West St.
Summer St.
Federal St.
Purchase St.
Arlington St.
Berkeley St.
PUBLIC GARDEN
Mason St.
Chauncy St.
High St.
Seaport
Boylston
Boylston St.
Avery
CHINATOWN
Chinatown
Essex St.
Lincoln St.
Sleeper St.
Arlington
South Station
Children's Museum
Clarendon St.
LaGrange
South St.
Congress St.
St. James Ave.
Beach St.
Atlantic Ave.
Summer St.
Charles St.
Kneeland St.
COPLEY SQ.
Stuart St.
Piedmont St.
Melrose St.
Washington
Harrison Ave.
Hudson St.
Dorchester Ave.
Ft. Point Channel
Oak St.
Columbus Ave.
New England Medical Center
Marginal Rd.
Back Bay
Chandler St.
Herald St.
Paul Pl.
Appleton St.
SOUTH END
A St.
Warren Ave.
Dartmouth St.
Traveler St.
Dwight St.
Milford St.
E Berkeley St.
Hanson St.
W Canton St.
PETERS PARK
W 2nd St.
Waltham St.
Broadway
Upton St.
W Dedham
Albany St.
W 3rd St.
C St.
Randolph St.
W 4th St.
SOUTH BOSTON
Athens St.
W 1st St.
Shawmut Ave.
Harrison Ave.
Union Park St.
W Broadway
W 4th St.
D St.
B St.
Washington St.
Malden St.
Dorchester Ave.
0
1/4 mi
1/4 km
N

Before you rule out a hotel because of its location, consult a map. Especially downtown, neighborhoods are so small that the borders are somewhat arbitrary. The division to consider is **downtown vs. the Back Bay vs. Cambridge** and not, say, Downtown Crossing vs. the (adjacent) Financial District. For example, if your interests lie primarily in Cambridge, the Back Bay is not the most convenient place to stay.

The state **hotel tax** is 5.7%. Boston and Cambridge (like Worcester and Springfield) add a 2.75% convention-center tax to the 4% city tax, bringing the total tax to 12.45%.

The Convention & Visitors Bureau **Hotel Hot Line** (✆ **800/777-6001**) can help make reservations even at the busiest times. It's staffed Monday through Friday until 8pm, Saturday and Sunday until 4pm. If you're driving from the west, stop at the Mass. Pike's Natick rest area and try the **reservations service** at the visitor center.

BED-AND-BREAKFASTS Most lodgings require a minimum stay of at least 2 nights. The following organizations can help you find a B&B:

- **Bed & Breakfast Agency of Boston** (✆ **800/248-9262,** 0800/89-5128 from the U.K., or 617/720-3540; fax 617/523-5761; www.boston-bnbagency.com).
- **Host Homes of Boston** (✆ **800/600-1308** or 617/244-1308; fax 617/244-5156; www.hosthomesofboston.com).
- **Bed & Breakfast Reservations North Shore/Greater Boston/Cape Cod** (✆ **800/832-2632** outside MA, 617/964-1606, or 978/281-9505; fax 978/281-9426; www.bbreserve.com).
- **Bed and Breakfast Associates Bay Colony** (✆ **888/486-6018,** 08/234-7113 from the U.K., or 781/449-5302; fax 781/455-6745; www.bnbboston.com).

THE WATERFRONT & FANEUIL HALL MARKETPLACE

These areas are convenient to the Financial District and other downtown destinations, but not as handy if you plan to spend a lot of time in the Back Bay or Cambridge. ***Tip:*** Ask for a room on a high floor—you'll want to be as far as possible from the construction that has succeeded the Big Dig.

VERY EXPENSIVE

At press time, the ultraluxurious **InterContinental Boston,** 500 Atlantic Ave. (✆ **800/424-6835** or 617/747-1000; www.intercontinentalboston.com), was scheduled to open in late 2006. The glass-sheathed 424-unit hotel is already a landmark; the chain's over-the-top services and amenities, including a large spa and a 24-hour restaurant, promise to put this place on the map.

Boston Harbor Hotel ★★★ The Boston Harbor Hotel is one of the finest in town, an excellent choice for both business and leisure travelers. The 16-story brick building is within walking distance of downtown and the waterfront attractions. Each plush guest room is a luxurious combination of bedroom and living area, with mahogany furnishings and comfortable chairs. Rooms with city views are less expensive than those that face the harbor. The best units are suites with private terraces and dazzling water vistas.

Rowes Wharf (entrance on Atlantic Ave.), Boston, MA 02110. ✆ **800/752-7077** or 617/439-7000. Fax 617/330-9450. www.bhh.com. 230 units. $295–$595 double; from $455 suite. Extra person $50. Children under 18 stay free in parent's room. Weekend packages available. AE, DC, DISC, MC, V. Valet parking $25–$34; self-parking $20–$30. T: Red Line to South Station or Blue Line to Aquarium. Pets accepted. **Amenities**: Restaurant (eclectic); cafe; bar; 60-ft. indoor lap pool; well-appointed health club and spa; concierge; courtesy car; business center; 24-hr. room service; in-room massage; babysitting; laundry service; dry cleaning. *In room:* A/C, TV w/pay movies, high-speed Internet access ($10/day), minibar, hair dryer, iron, umbrella, robes.

Boston Marriott Long Wharf ★ The landmark Marriott's chief appeal is its location, a stone's throw from the New England Aquarium. It attracts business travelers with its proximity to the Financial District and woos families with its pool and easy access to downtown and waterfront attractions. Rooms are large and quite sunny (the stand-alone building has no neighbors to block the light), and units close to the harbor afford good views of the wharves and the waterfront.

296 State St. (at Atlantic Ave.), Boston, MA 02109. ✆ **800/228-9290** or 617/227-0800. Fax 617/227-2867. www.marriottlongwharf.com. 400 units. Apr–Nov $249–$450 double; Dec–Mar $159–$279 double; $450–$490 suite year-round. Packages available. AE, DC, DISC, MC, V. Parking $34. T: Blue Line to Aquarium. **Amenities:** Restaurant (seafood); cafe and lounge; bar and grill; indoor pool; exercise room; Jacuzzi; game room; concierge; tour desk; 24-hr. business center; limited room service; laundry service; same-day dry cleaning. *In room:* A/C, TV, high-speed Internet access ($10/day), coffeemaker, hair dryer, iron, safe.

EXPENSIVE

Millennium Bostonian Hotel ★★ The relatively small Bostonian offers excellent service and features that make it competitive with larger hotels. It's popular with business travelers who want a break from convention-oriented giants, and with vacationers who enjoy the boutique atmosphere and access to the adjacent spa. The traditionally appointed guest rooms contain top-of-the-line furnishings and amenities. They're soundproof, an important feature in this busy location. Half of the units have French doors that open onto small balconies; the plushest rooms are suites with working fireplaces or Jacuzzis.

At Faneuil Hall Marketplace, 26 North St., Boston, MA 02109. ✆ **800/343-0922** or 617/523-3600. Fax 617/523-2454. www.millenniumhotels.com. 201 units. $149–$299 double; $265–$450 deluxe double; $439–$775 suite. Extra person $20. Children under 18 stay free in parent's room. Packages available. AE, DC, DISC, MC, V. Valet parking $35. T: Orange Line to Haymarket, or Green or Blue Line to Government Center. **Amenities:** Restaurant (contemporary American); lounge; small fitness room; access to nearby health club ($10); in-room exercise equipment delivery on request; concierge; tour desk; car-rental desk; business center; salon; 24-hr. room service; in-room massage; babysitting; laundry service; same-day dry cleaning. *In room:* A/C, TV w/pay movies, high-speed Internet access ($10/day), minibar, hair dryer, iron, safe, umbrella, robes.

MODERATE

Harborside Inn ★★ Under the same management as the Newbury Guest House in the Back Bay, the Harborside Inn offers a similar combination of location and (for this neighborhood) value. The renovated 1858 warehouse is near Faneuil Hall Marketplace, the harbor, and the Financial District. The nicely appointed guest rooms have hardwood floors, Oriental rugs, and Victorian-style furniture. They surround a skylit atrium; city-view units are more expensive but can be noisier. Still, they're preferable to the interior rooms, whose windows open only to the atrium. Units on the top floors of the eight-story building have lower ceilings but better views.

185 State St. (between Atlantic Ave. and the Custom House Tower), Boston, MA 02109. ✆ **888/723-7565** or 617/723-7500. Fax 617/670-6015. www.harborsideinnboston.com. 54 units. $120–$210 double; $235–$310 suite. Extra person $15. Packages and long-term rates available. Rates may be higher during special events. AE, DC, DISC, MC, V. Off-site parking $20; reservation required. T: Blue Line to Aquarium or Orange Line to State. **Amenities:** Restaurant (international bistro); access to nearby health club ($15); concierge; limited room service; laundry service; dry cleaning. *In room:* A/C, TV, wireless Internet access ($10/day), hair dryer, iron.

AT THE AIRPORT

EXPENSIVE

The **Embassy Suites Hotel Boston at Logan Airport,** 207 Porter St., Boston, MA 02128 (✆ **800/EMBASSY** or 617/567-5000; www.embassysuites.com), is a 273-unit hotel with an indoor pool, exercise room, and business center. Each suite in the

10-story hotel has a living room with a pullout couch. Room rates, which start at $169, include breakfast, high-speed Internet access, and shuttle service to the airport and the Airport T stop.

Hilton Boston Logan Airport ★★ This hotel smack in the middle of the airport draws most of its guests from meetings, conventions, and canceled flights. Walkways lead directly to Terminals A (near) and E (far). The hotel is convenient for business travelers, and an excellent fallback for vacationers who don't mind a short commute to downtown. Guest rooms are large; the best units, on higher floors of the 10-story building, afford sensational views. Soundproofing throughout the hotel, which opened in 1999, is excellent.

85 Terminal Rd., Logan International Airport, Boston, MA 02128. ✆ **800/HILTONS** or 617/568-6700. Fax 617/568-6800. www.hiltonbostonloganairport.com. 599 units. $99–$399 double; from $500 suite. Children under 19 stay free in parent's room. Packages available. AE, DC, DISC, MC, V. Valet parking $26; self-parking $22. T: Blue Line to Airport, then take shuttle bus. Pets accepted; deposit required. **Amenities:** Restaurant (American); Irish pub; coffee counter; indoor lap pool; health club; 24-hr. shuttle to airport destinations (including car-rental offices and ferry dock); business center; 24-hr. room service; massage; laundry service; same-day dry cleaning. *In room:* A/C, TV w/pay movies, wireless Internet access ($10/day), minibar, coffeemaker, hair dryer, iron.

MODERATE

Comfort Inn & Suites Logan Airport Although it loses points for the misleading name—the airport is about 3½ miles south—the well-equipped Comfort Inn ranks high on service and amenities. Room rates at the eight-story hotel include high-speed Internet access, local phone calls, and continental breakfast. The somewhat inconvenient location translates to reasonable rates, and the North Shore is easily accessible if you plan to take a day trip.

85 American Legion Hwy. (Rte. 60), Revere, MA 02151. ✆ **800/228-5150,** 888/283-9300 (local toll-free), or 781/485-3600. Fax 781/485-3601. www.comfortinnboston.com. 208 units. $79–$169 double; $119–$199 suite. Rates include continental breakfast. Children stay free in parent's room. Senior and AAA discounts available. AE, DC, DISC, MC, V. Free parking. T: Blue Line to Airport; take airport shuttle bus to terminal, then hotel shuttle. Pets accepted; $20 fee. **Amenities:** Restaurant (Italian/American); lounge; indoor pool; exercise room; shuttle to subway and airport; business center; limited room service; coin-op laundry; laundry service; same-day dry cleaning. *In room:* A/C, TV w/pay movies, high-speed Internet access, coffeemaker, hair dryer, iron.

FINANCIAL DISTRICT

VERY EXPENSIVE

Langham Hotel Boston ★★ This is one of the best business hotels in the city, with a busy weekend clientele of vacationers attracted by excellent rates for luxurious accommodations and amenities, including a pool. Elegantly decorated and large enough to hold a generous work area, the well-kept guest rooms have 153 configurations, including loft suites with two bathrooms. Buildings envelop the hotel on three sides; the most desirable rooms face the lovely park in Post Office Square. Langham, a Hong Kong–based chain of luxury hotels with properties in England and the Pacific, acquired this hotel, its first North American property, in 2004.

250 Franklin St. (at Post Office Sq.), Boston, MA 02110. ✆ **800/791-7794** or 617/451-1900. Fax 617/423-2844. www.langhamhotels.com. 325 units. $225–$475 double midweek, $159–$279 double weekend; $525–$2,000 suite. Extra person $30. AE, DC, DISC, MC, V. Valet parking $25–$39; self-parking $7–$28. T: Blue or Orange Line to State, or Red Line to Downtown Crossing or South Station. Pets accepted. **Amenities:** Restaurant (French); cafe w/Sun jazz brunch and Sat "Chocolate Bar Buffet" (Sept–May); bar w/live piano most nights; 40-ft. indoor pool; well-equipped health club; Jacuzzi; sauna; concierge; business center; 24-hr. room service; in-room massage; babysitting; laundry service; same-day dry cleaning. *In room:* A/C, TV w/pay movies, high-speed Internet access ($10/day), minibar, coffeemaker, hair dryer, iron, safe, umbrella, robes.

DOWNTOWN CROSSING/BEACON HILL/NORTH STATION

The **Holiday Inn Select Boston Government Center,** 5 Blossom St., at Cambridge Street (✆ **800/HOLIDAY** or 617/742-7630), offers all the features you'd expect of the international chain, including a heated outdoor pool.

VERY EXPENSIVE

Fifteen Beacon ★★ Nonstop pampering, high-tech appointments, and outrageously luxurious rooms make this boutique hotel *the* name to drop with the expense-be-hanged set. The 10-story hotel has attracted demanding travelers, especially businesspeople, since it opened in 2000. Management bends over backward to keep them returning, with attentive service and lavish perks. The guest rooms, individually decorated in austere but plush style that's more SoHo than Beacon Hill, contain queen-size canopy beds with Frette linens, surround-sound stereo systems, gas fireplaces, and 4-inch TVs in the bathroom. "Studio" units have a sitting area.

15 Beacon St., Boston, MA 02108. ✆ **877/XV-BEACON** or 617/670-1500. Fax 617/670-2525. www.xvbeacon.com. 60 units (some with shower only). From $395 double; from $1,200 suite. AE, DISC, MC, V. Valet parking $34. T: Red or Green Line to Park St., or Blue Line to Government Center. Pets under 20 lb. accepted; refundable deposit required. **Amenities:** Restaurant (eclectic); bar; fitness room; access to nearby health club ($15); concierge; courtesy car; 24-hr. room service; in-room massage; babysitting; laundry service; same-day dry cleaning. *In room:* A/C, TV w/pay movies, fax/copier/printer, high-speed Internet access, minibar, hair dryer, iron, safe, umbrella, robes.

EXPENSIVE

Hyatt Regency Boston Financial District ★ *Value* This centrally located 22-story hotel has two lives. It's a busy convention and business destination during the week, and its excellent weekend packages make it a magnet for sightseers. Guest rooms are large enough to hold sitting areas, a desk, and a settee; they have king-size or European twin-size beds. The property is in excellent condition: Hyatt completed $10.5 million in guest-room renovations in 2005. Ask for a unit on a high floor; this neighborhood was ugly even before construction began all along nearby Washington Street.

1 Ave. de Lafayette (off Washington St.), Boston, MA 02111. ✆ **800/223-1234** or 617/912-1234. Fax 617/451-0054. www.hyattregencyboston.com. 500 units. $189–$375 double; $300–$450 suite. Extra person $25. Children under 12 stay free in parent's room. Packages available. AE, DC, DISC, MC, V. Valet parking $34; self-parking $26. T: Red Line to Downtown Crossing, or Green Line to Boylston. **Amenities:** Restaurant (American/Continental); bar; 52-ft. indoor pool; health club; sauna; concierge; tour desk; business center; 24-hr. room service; massage; babysitting; laundry service; same-day dry cleaning. *In room:* A/C, TV w/pay movies, wireless Internet access ($10/day), coffeemaker, hair dryer, iron, robes.

Omni Parker House ★ The Parker House offers a great combination of over 150 years of history (since 1855!) and extensive renovations. Wireless Internet access is available in the guest rooms and public spaces, and regular renovation (most recently, $5 million-plus in updates just in 2005 and 2006) keeps the property in excellent shape. Guest rooms, a patchwork of more than 50 configurations, aren't huge, but they are thoughtfully laid out and nicely appointed. Business travelers can book a room with an expanded work area, while sightseers can economize by requesting a smaller, less expensive unit.

60 School St., Boston, MA 02108. ✆ **800/THE-OMNI** or 617/227-8600. Fax 617/742-5729. www.omnihotels.com. 552 units (some with shower only). $189–$289 double; $249–$399 suite. Children under 18 stay free in parent's room. Packages and AARP discount available. AE, DC, DISC, MC, V. Valet parking $36. T: Green or Blue Line to Government Center, or Red Line to Park St. Pets accepted; deposit required. **Amenities:** Restaurant (New England); 2 bars; exercise room; access to nearby health club ($20); concierge; tour desk; business center; 24-hr. room service; laundry service; same-day dry cleaning. *In room:* A/C, TV w/pay movies and Nintendo, wireless Internet access, minibar, coffeemaker, hair dryer, iron, robes.

MODERATE

Bulfinch Hotel ★ One block from North Station, the Bulfinch abounds with details that enhance its "budget boutique" feel. Rooms are on the small side, but custom furnishings create the illusion of more space. Plush fabrics (including suede headboards), flatscreen TVs, and marble bathrooms set off the contemporary, uncluttered design. The hotel, which opened in 2004, offers business features such as work desks, cordless phones, and high-speed Internet access (included in the room rate). The best units are junior suites—oversize doubles—known as "nose rooms" because they're in the pointed end of the triangular building.

107 Merrimac St., Boston, MA 02114. ✆ **800/4-CHOICE** or 617/624-0202. Fax 617/624-0211. www.bulfinchhotel.com. 80 units (most with shower only). $169–$324 double; $199–$369 junior suite. Children under 18 stay free in parent's room. Packages and AAA, AARP, and military discounts available. AE, DC, DISC, MC, V. Parking $25 in nearby garage. T: Green or Orange Line to North Station. Pets under 40 lb. accepted; $50 fee. **Amenities:** Restaurant (steakhouse); exercise room; concierge; room service; same-day dry cleaning. *In room:* A/C, TV, high-speed Internet access, coffeemaker, hair dryer, iron.

CHINATOWN/THEATER DISTRICT

MODERATE

Doubletree Hotel Boston Downtown ★ *Value* Within walking distance of both downtown and the Back Bay, the Doubletree is a better deal than most competitors in either neighborhood. The six-story building is a former high school, with high ceilings and compact, well-designed rooms. Ask for a unit that faces away from busy Washington Street, and your view will be of a cityscape rather than the hospital across the street. Don't confuse this hotel with its all-suite corporate sibling near Cambridge (p. 97). This Doubletree, which opened in 2000, adjoins the Wang YMCA of Chinatown, and room rates include access to its extensive facilities.

821 Washington St., Boston, MA 02111. ✆ **800/222-TREE** or 617/956-7900. Fax 617/956-7901. www.downtownboston.doubletree.com. 267 units (some with shower only). $129–$299 double; $189–$359 suite. Extra person $10. Children under 17 stay free in parent's room. Packages and AAA, AARP, and military discounts available. AE, DC, DISC, MC, V. Valet parking $33. T: Orange Line to New England Medical Center. **Amenities:** Restaurant and lounge (American/Asian); cafe; access to adjoining YMCA w/Olympic-size pool; concierge; business center; limited room service; same-day dry cleaning; executive-level rooms. *In room:* A/C, TV w/pay movies, wireless Internet access ($10/day), minibar, coffeemaker, hair dryer, iron, safe.

BACK BAY/SOUTH END

VERY EXPENSIVE

Eliot Hotel ★★★ This exquisite hotel combines the flavor of Yankee Boston with European-style service and amenities. On tree-lined Comm. Ave., it feels more like a classy apartment building than a hotel, with a romantic atmosphere that belies the top-notch business features. Almost every unit (16 rooms are standard doubles) is a spacious suite with antique furnishings. French doors separate the living rooms and bedrooms, and bathrooms are outfitted in Italian marble. The 1925 building is near Boston University and MIT (across the river), and the location contrasts pleasantly with the bustle of Newbury Street, a block away.

370 Comm. Ave. (at Mass. Ave.), Boston, MA 02215. ✆ **800/44-ELIOT** or 617/267-1607. Fax 617/536-9114. www.eliothotel.com. 95 units (8 with shower only). $255–$315 double; $265–$435 1-bedroom suite for 2; $510–$770 2-bedroom suite. Extra person $20. Children under 18 stay free in parent's room. Packages available. AE, DC, MC, V. Valet parking $34. T: Green Line B, C, or D to Hynes/ICA. Pets accepted. **Amenities:** Restaurant (eclectic); sashimi bar; access to nearby health club; concierge; business center; 24-hr. room service; in-room massage; babysitting; laundry service; dry cleaning. *In room:* A/C, TV w/pay movies, wireless Internet access ($10/day), minibar, hair dryer, iron, umbrella, robes.

The Fairmont Copley Plaza Hotel ★★ The "grande dame of Boston" is a true grand hotel with a well-earned reputation for service. Built in 1912, the six-story Renaissance Revival building faces Copley Square. The spacious guest rooms have a residential feel, thanks largely to a $34-million overhaul completed in 2004. The custom-made traditional furnishings reflect the elegance of the opulent public spaces. Rooms that face the lovely square afford better views than those that overlook busy Dartmouth Street.

138 St. James Ave., Boston, MA 02116. ✆ **800/441-1414** or 617/267-5300. Fax 617/247-6681. www.fairmont.com/copleyplaza. 383 units. From $259 double; from $699 suite. Extra person $30. Packages available. AE, DC, MC, V. Valet parking $32. T: Green Line to Copley, or Orange Line to Back Bay. Pets accepted; $25/day. **Amenities:** Restaurant (steakhouse); lounge; exercise room; access to nearby health club ($15); concierge; tour desk; courtesy car; business center; 24-hr. room service; laundry service; same-day dry cleaning. *In room:* A/C, TV w/pay movies, high-speed Internet access ($14/day), minibar, hair dryer, iron, safe, umbrella, robes.

Four Seasons Hotel ★★★ Many hotels offer exquisite service, a beautiful location, elegant guest rooms and public areas, a terrific health club, and wonderful restaurants. But no other hotel in Boston—indeed, in New England—combines every element of a luxury hotel as seamlessly as the Four Seasons. If I were traveling with someone else's credit cards, I'd head straight here. The 16-story brick-and-glass building (the hotel occupies eight floors) blends traditional and contemporary style. The best units overlook the Public Garden; city views from the back of the hotel aren't as desirable. Children receive bedtime snacks and toys, and can ask at the concierge desk for duck food to take to the Public Garden. Small pets even enjoy a special menu and amenities.

200 Boylston St., Boston, MA 02116. ✆ **800/332-3442** or 617/338-4400. Fax 617/423-0154. www.fourseasons.com. 272 units. $425–$650 double; from $695 1-bedroom suite; from $2,200 2-bedroom suite. Packages available. AE, DC, DISC, MC, V. Valet parking $37. T: Green Line to Arlington. Pets under 15 lb. accepted. **Amenities:** Restaurant (New England), The Bristol (see "Bars & Lounges," later in this chapter); 51-ft. pool; health club and spa; concierge; tour desk; limo to downtown; business center; 24-hr. room service; in-room massage; babysitting; laundry service; same-day dry cleaning. *In room:* A/C, TV w/pay movies, high-speed Internet access ($10/day), minibar, coffeemaker, hair dryer, iron, safe, robes.

EXPENSIVE

The largest convention hotel in New England is the 1,147-unit **Boston Marriott Copley Place,** 110 Huntington Ave., Boston, MA 02116 (✆ **800/228-9290** or 617/236-5800; www.copleymarriott.com). Part of the Copley Place shopping complex, it offers complete business features and a good-size pool.

Hilton Boston Back Bay ★★ Across the street from the Prudential Center complex, the Hilton is primarily a business hotel, but families also find it comfortable. Rooms in the 26-story tower are large, soundproof, and furnished in modern style. The weekend packages, especially in winter, can be a great deal. The closest competitor is the Sheraton, across the street. It's three times the Hilton's size (which generally means less personalized service), has a better pool, and books more vacation and function business.

40 Dalton St., Boston, MA 02115. ✆ **800/874-0663,** 800/HILTONS, or 617/236-1100. Fax 617/867-6104. www.hiltonbostonbackbay.com. 385 units (66 with shower only). $149–$399 double; from $450 suite. Extra person $20; rollaway $20. Children under 18 stay free in parent's room. Packages and AAA discount available. AE, DC, DISC, MC, V. Valet parking $36; self-parking $20. T: Green Line B, C, or D to Hynes/ICA. Pets accepted. **Amenities:** Restaurant (American/Continental); bar; indoor pool; fitness center; concierge; courtesy car; 24-hr. business center; 24-hr. room service; laundry service; same-day dry cleaning. *In room:* A/C, TV w/pay movies, high-speed Internet access ($10/stay), minibar, coffeemaker, hair dryer, iron.

Jurys Boston Hotel ★★ In the former Boston Police Headquarters building, the Jurys Boston (part of the Irish chain) caters to both business and leisure travelers. The

1925 limestone-and-brick structure holds dramatic public areas and plush accommodations. The luxurious guest rooms have nice touches such as a work area with an ergonomic chair, good-size bathrooms, and windows that open but also muffle street noise. Still, light sleepers will want to face away from busy Berkeley Street. Opened in 2004, this is Jurys Doyle's first U.S. property outside Washington, D.C.

350 Stuart St. (at Berkeley St.), Boston, MA 02116. ✆ **866/JD-HOTELS** or 617/266-7200. Fax 617/266-7203. www.jurysdoyle.com. 225 units (some with shower only). $155–$435 double; $275–$575 1-bedroom suite; from $1,150 2-bedroom suite. Children under 16 stay free in parent's room. Extra person $20. Packages from $155 per night. AE, DC, DISC, MC, V. Valet parking $36. T: Orange Line to Back Bay or Green Line to Arlington or Copley. **Amenities:** Restaurant (American); Irish bar; coffee and wine bar; exercise room; business center; 24-hr. room service; laundry service; same-say dry cleaning. *In room:* A/C, TV w/pay movies, wireless Internet access, fridge, hair dryer, iron, safe, umbrella, robes.

Sheraton Boston Hotel ★ Its central location, range of accommodations, convention and function facilities, direct access to the Hynes Convention Center and the Prudential Center complex, and huge pool make this 29-story hotel one of the most popular in the city. Because it's so big, it often has rooms available when smaller properties are full. If you're on a budget, though, you may be able to get a better deal elsewhere; shop around. The fairly large guest rooms are decorated in sleek contemporary style and contain Starwood's signature pillow-top beds. Units on higher floors afford gorgeous views.

39 Dalton St., Boston, MA 02199. ✆ **800/325-3535** or 617/236-2000. Fax 617/236-1702. www.sheraton.com/boston. 1,215 units. $129–$409 double; from $309 suite. Children under 17 stay free in parent's room. Packages available. 25% discount for students, faculty, and retired persons with ID, depending on availability. AE, DC, DISC, MC, V. Valet parking $35; self-parking $33. T: Green Line E to Prudential, or B, C, or D to Hynes/ICA. Dogs under 40 lb. accepted with prior approval. **Amenities:** Restaurant (New England); lounge; heated indoor/outdoor pool; health club; Jacuzzi; sauna; concierge; airport shuttle; business center; limited room service; laundry service; same-day dry cleaning. *In room:* A/C, TV w/pay movies, high-speed Internet access ($10/day), coffeemaker, hair dryer, iron.

MODERATE

Chandler Inn Hotel ★ *Value* The comfortable, unpretentious Chandler Inn is a bargain for its location, just 2 blocks from the Back Bay. Guest rooms have individual climate control and tasteful contemporary-style furniture. Each unit holds a queen-size, double bed, or two twin beds, without enough room to squeeze in a cot. Bathrooms are tiny. This is a gay-friendly hotel—Fritz, the bar next to the lobby, is a neighborhood hangout—that books up early for foliage season and events such as the Marathon and Boston Pride March.

26 Chandler St. (at Berkeley St.), Boston, MA 02116. ✆ **800/842-3450** or 617/482-3450. Fax 617/542-3428. www.chandlerinn.com. 56 units. Apr–Dec $139–$169 double; Jan–Mar $129–$139 double. Children under 12 stay free in parent's room. AE, DC, DISC, MC, V. No parking. T: Orange Line to Back Bay. Pets under 25 lb. accepted with prior approval. **Amenities:** Lounge; access to nearby health club ($10). *In room:* A/C, TV, dataport, hair dryer.

Charlesmark Hotel ★★ *Value* In an excellent location overlooking the Boston Marathon finish line, the Charlesmark has a boutique feel and great prices. It's both luxurious and—literally, not figuratively—no frills. The contemporary design evokes a yacht, using custom furnishings to pack plenty of comfort into compact spaces. Rooms have pillow-top mattresses and enough room to hold a comfortable chair. The amenities don't challenge the perks of the large hotels in this neighborhood, but they're more than sufficient for most business or leisure travelers—rates include continental breakfast, access to a computer in the lobby, and local phone calls.

655 Boylston St. (between Dartmouth and Exeter sts.), Boston, MA 02116. ✆ **617/247-1212.** Fax 617/247-1224. www.thecharlesmark.com. 33 units (most with shower only). $99–$249 double. Rates include continental breakfast. Children under 12 stay free in parent's room. AE, DC, DISC, MC, V. Self-parking $32 in nearby garage. T: Green Line to Copley. Pets accepted with prior approval. **Amenities:** Lounge; access to nearby health club ($10); laundry service. *In room:* A/C, TV, high-speed Internet access, minifridge, hair dryer.

The MidTown Hotel ★ *Kids* *Value* Even without free parking and an outdoor pool, this centrally located two-story hotel would be a good deal for families and budget-conscious businesspeople; it also books a lot of tour groups. It's on a busy street within walking distance of Symphony Hall and the Museum of Fine Arts. The well-maintained rooms are large, bright, and attractively outfitted, although bathrooms are on the small side. Some units have connecting doors that allow families to spread out. The best rooms are on the side of the building that faces away from Huntington Avenue.

220 Huntington Ave., Boston, MA 02115. ✆ **800/343-1177** or 617/262-1000. Fax 617/262-8739. www.midtownhotel.com. 159 units. $119–$259 double; $139–$279 suite. Extra person $15. Children under 18 stay free in parent's room. Packages and AAA, AARP, and government employee discount available, subject to availability. AE, DC, DISC, MC, V. Free parking (1 car per room). T: Green Line E to Prudential, or Orange Line to Mass. Ave. **Amenities:** Restaurant (Italian); heated outdoor pool; access to nearby health club ($5–$10); concierge; airport shuttle; laundry service; same-day dry cleaning. *In room:* A/C, TV w/pay movies, wireless Internet access ($11/day), coffeemaker, hair dryer, iron.

Newbury Guest House ★★ *Value* After just a little shopping in the Back Bay, you'll appreciate what a find this cozy place is: a bargain on Newbury Street. It's a pair of brick town houses built in the 1880s and combined into a refined inn. It offers comfortable furnishings, a pleasant staff, nifty architectural details, and a buffet breakfast served in the dining room, which adjoins a brick patio. Rooms are modest in size but nicely appointed (with high-speed Internet access, included in the room rate). It operates near capacity all year, drawing business travelers during the week and sightseers on weekends. At these prices in this location, there's only one caveat: Reserve early.

261 Newbury St. (between Fairfield and Gloucester sts.), Boston, MA 02116. ✆ **800/437-7668** or 617/437-7666. Fax 617/670-6100. www.newburyguesthouse.com. 32 units (some with shower only). $140–$195 double. Winter discounts and packages available. Rates include continental breakfast. Extra person $15. Rates may be higher during special events. Minimum 2 nights on weekends. AE, DC, DISC, MC, V. Parking $15 (reservation required). T: Green Line B, C, or D to Hynes/ICA. **Amenities:** Access to nearby health club ($25). *In room:* A/C, TV, wireless Internet access, hair dryer, iron.

INEXPENSIVE

Hostelling International–Boston This hostel near the Berklee College of Music and Symphony Hall caters to students, youth groups, and other travelers in search of comfortable, no-frills lodging. Accommodations are dorm-style, with six beds per room; a couple of private units sleep one or two. The air-conditioned hostel has two kitchens, 29 bathrooms, and a large common room. It provides linens, or you can bring your own; sleeping bags are not permitted. The enthusiastic staff organizes free and inexpensive cultural, educational, and recreational programs.

12 Hemenway St., Boston, MA 02115. ✆ **800/909-4776** or 617/536-9455. Fax 617/424-6558. www.bostonhostel.org. 205 beds. Members of Hostelling International–American Youth Hostels $28–$45 per bed; nonmembers $31–$48 per bed. Members $70–$100 per private unit; nonmembers $73–$106 per private unit. Children 3–12 half price; children under 3 free. Rates include continental breakfast. MC, V. T: Green Line B, C, or D to Hynes/ICA. **Amenities:** Access to nearby health club ($6); coin laundry; Internet access (fee). *In room:* A/C, lockers, no phone.

OUTSKIRTS & BROOKLINE

Staying in this area means commuting to downtown Boston. Because of the unwieldy public transit connections, it's not a great choice if your destination is Cambridge.

EXPENSIVE

Doubletree Guest Suites ★★ *Value* This hotel is one of the best deals in town—every unit is a two-room suite. Overlooking the Charles River, the hotel is near Cambridge and the riverfront bike path, but not in a real neighborhood. Shuttle service to local destinations makes the location easier to handle. The large suites, which were renovated in 2006, surround a 15-story atrium. Most bedrooms have a king-size bed and writing desk. Each living room contains a sofa bed and dining table. The Hyatt Regency Cambridge, the hotel's nearest rival, is more convenient but generally more expensive.

400 Soldiers Field Rd., Boston, MA 02134. ✆ **800/222-TREE** or 617/783-0090. Fax 617/783-0897. www.doubletree.com. 308 units. $129–$309 double. Extra person $20. Children under 18 stay free in parent's room. Packages and AARP and AAA discounts available. AE, DC, DISC, MC, V. Valet parking $27; self-parking $20. Pets accepted with prior approval. **Amenities:** Restaurant (American); lounge; Scullers Jazz Club (see later in this chapter); indoor pool; exercise room; free access to nearby health club; Jacuzzi; sauna; concierge; shuttle service; 24-hr. business center; limited room service; coin laundry; laundry service; same-day dry cleaning. *In room:* A/C, TV w/pay movies, wireless Internet access ($10/day), fridge, coffeemaker, hair dryer, iron.

MODERATE

Options in this price range and area are chain hotels, including the **Brookline Courtyard by Marriott,** 40 Webster St., Brookline (✆ **866/296-2296,** 800/321-2211, or 617/734-1393), and the **Holiday Inn Boston Brookline,** 1200 Beacon St., Brookline (✆ **800/HOLIDAY** or 617/277-1200). The **Howard Johnson Inn,** 1271 Boylston St., Boston (✆ **800/654-2000** or 617/267-8300), is scheduled to close in late 2007.

INEXPENSIVE

Anthony's Town House The Anthony family has operated this four-story brownstone guesthouse since 1944, and a stay here feels like a visit to Grandma's. Many patrons are Europeans accustomed to accommodations with shared bathrooms, but budget-minded Americans won't be disappointed. Each floor has three high-ceilinged rooms furnished in Queen Anne or Victorian style, plus a bathroom with enclosed shower; the staff will supply a VCR, DVD player, hair dryer, or iron on request. The large front rooms have bay windows. The guesthouse is 1 mile from Kenmore Square, about 15 minutes from downtown by T, and 2 blocks from a busy commercial strip.

1085 Beacon St., Brookline, MA 02446. ✆ **617/566-3972.** Fax 617/232-1085. www.anthonystownhouse.com. 12 units, none with private bathroom. $68–$98 double. Extra person $10. Weekly rates and winter discounts available. No credit cards. Limited free parking. T: Green Line C to Hawes St. *In room:* A/C, TV, high-speed Internet access, no phone.

Longwood Inn In a residential area 3 blocks from the Boston-Brookline border, this three-story Victorian guesthouse offers comfortable accommodations at modest rates. Room rates include wireless Internet access, and guests have the use of a full kitchen, dining room, and TV lounge. There's one apartment with a private bathroom, kitchen, and balcony. Tennis courts, a running track, and a playground at the school next door are open to the public. Public transportation is within easy reach, and the Longwood Medical Area and busy Coolidge Corner neighborhood are within easy walking distance.

123 Longwood Ave., Brookline, MA 02446. ✆ **617/566-8615.** Fax 617/738-1070. www.longwood-inn.com. 22 units, 17 with private bathroom (some with shower only). Apr–Nov $109–$129 double; Dec–Mar $69–$89 double; 1-bedroom apt (sleeps 4-plus) $99–$139. Weekly rates available. AE, DISC, MC, V. Free parking. T: Green Line D to Longwood, or C to Coolidge Corner. **Amenities:** Coin laundry. *In room:* A/C, TV.

Cambridge Accommodations & Dining

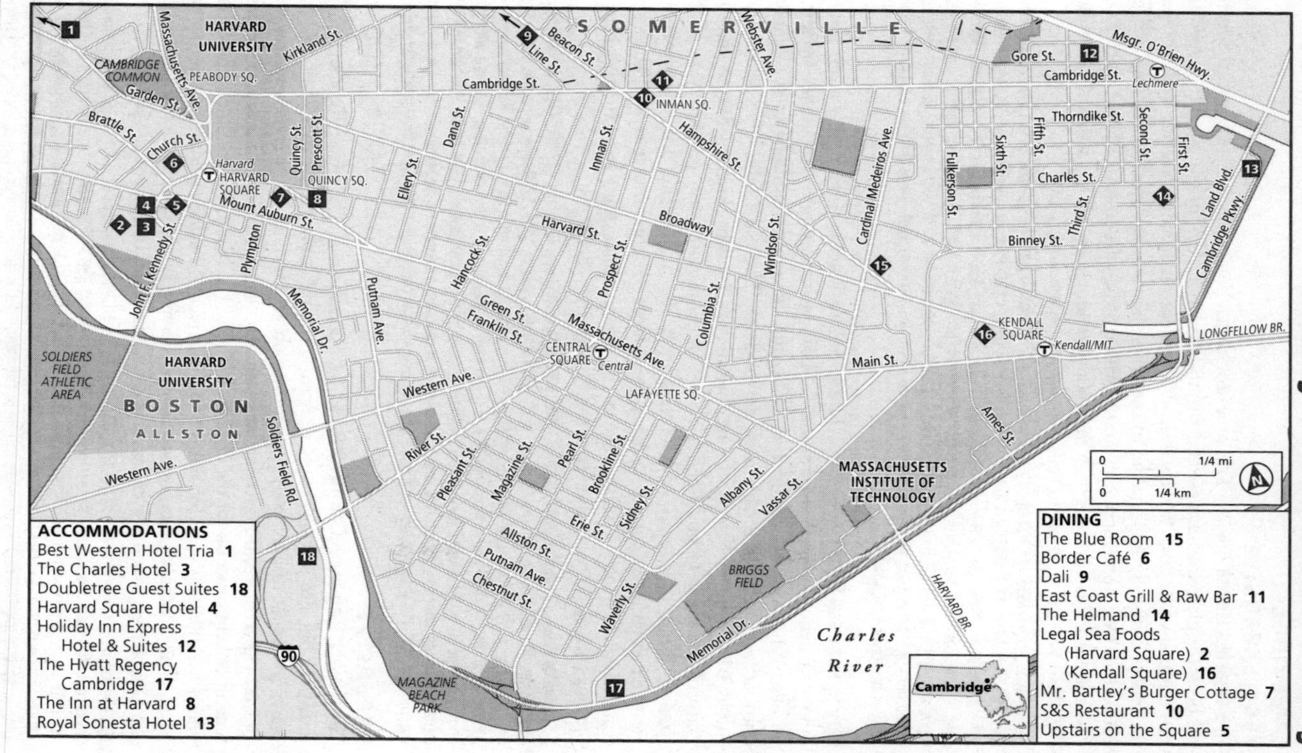

CAMBRIDGE

VERY EXPENSIVE

The Charles Hotel ★★★ This nine-story brick hotel a block from Harvard Square has been *the* place for business and leisure travelers in Cambridge since it opened in 1985. Much of its fame derives from its excellent restaurants, jazz bar, and day spa; the service is equally impeccable. In the posh guest rooms, which were renovated in 2006, the style is contemporary country, with custom adaptations of Shaker furniture. The austere design contrasts with the indulgent amenities, which include down quilts and Bose Wave radios; bathrooms contain telephones and TVs.

1 Bennett St., Cambridge, MA 02138. ✆ **800/882-1818** or 617/864-1200. Fax 617/864-5715. www.charleshotel.com. 293 units. $259–$599 double; $309–$4,000 suite. Extra person $20. Packages available. AE, DC, MC, V. Valet or self-parking $28. T: Red Line to Harvard. Pets under 25 lb. accepted; $50 fee. **Amenities:** 2 restaurants (Mediterranean, American); bar; Regattabar jazz club (p. 140); access to adjacent health club w/pool, Jacuzzi, and exercise room; adjacent spa and salon; concierge; car-rental desk; business center; 24-hr. room service; in-room massage; babysitting; laundry service; same-day dry cleaning. *In room:* A/C, TV/DVD, high-speed Internet access ($11/day), minibar, hair dryer, iron, safe.

Royal Sonesta Hotel ★★ *Kids* This luxurious hotel is close to only a few things but convenient to everything. Features for both businesspeople and families, from the business center to wireless Internet access throughout the building to the indoor/outdoor pool with retractable roof, are excellent. The CambridgeSide Galleria mall and the Museum of Science are nearby, and it's actually closer to Boston than to Harvard Square. MIT and Kendall Square are 10 minutes away on foot. Most of the spacious rooms have lovely views of the river or the city. (Higher prices are for better views.) Everything is custom designed in modern yet comfortable style. The closest competition is Hotel Marlowe, across the street, which offers less extensive fitness options (there's no pool) and fewer rooms with river views.

5 Cambridge Pkwy., Cambridge, MA 02142. ✆ **800/SONESTA** or 617/806-4200. Fax 617/806-4232. www.sonesta.com/boston. 400 units (some with shower only). $239–$279 standard double; $259–$299 superior double; $279–$319 deluxe double; $339–$1,000 suite. Extra person $25. Children under 18 stay free in parent's room. Packages available. AE, DC, DISC, MC, V. Valet and self-parking $19. T: Green Line to Lechmere; 10-min. walk. Pets accepted with prior approval. **Amenities:** Restaurant (new American/Mediterranean); cafe; indoor/outdoor pool; health club and spa; bike rental (seasonal); concierge; courtesy van; business center; limited room service; massage; laundry service; dry cleaning. *In room:* A/C, TV w/pay movies, wireless Internet access, minibar, coffeemaker, hair dryer, iron, safe, umbrella.

EXPENSIVE

The Hyatt Regency Cambridge ★ *Kids* Location is The Hyatt Regency's main drawback but also part of its appeal. Across the street from the Charles River, the dramatic pyramidal brick building is convenient to Harvard and Kendall squares and Boston University. Shuttle service, access to the bike path along the river, and plentiful amenities help make up for the distance to the T. The best of the spacious guest rooms afford breathtaking views of Boston and the river. A business destination during the week, The Hyatt Regency courts families on weekends. The closest competitor is the Doubletree, which is even less centrally located but consists of all suites.

575 Memorial Dr., Cambridge, MA 02139. ✆ **800/233-1234** or 617/462-1234. Fax 617/491-6906. www.cambridge.hyatt.com. 469 units (some with shower only). $139–$295 double; $300–$750 suite. Extra person $25. Children under 18 stay free in parent's room. Packages available. AE, DC, DISC, MC, V. Valet parking $22; self-parking $20. Pets under 25 lb. accepted; $50 fee. **Amenities:** Restaurant and lounge (eclectic); 75-ft. indoor lap pool; rooftop health club; Jacuzzi; sauna; bike rental; concierge; shuttle to Cambridge destinations; business center; limited room service; in-room massage; laundry service; same-day dry cleaning. *In room:* A/C, TV w/pay movies, fax, wireless Internet access ($10/day), coffeemaker, hair dryer, iron.

The Inn at Harvard ★★ The Inn at Harvard is adjacent to Harvard Yard, and its Georgian-style architecture would fit nicely on campus. Inside, however, there's no mistaking it for anything other than an elegant hotel, popular with business travelers and university visitors. The guest rooms were extensively renovated in 2006; they have pillow-top beds, and each has a work area with an Aeron chair. The four-story skylit atrium holds the "living room," a huge, well-appointed guest lounge that's suitable for meeting with a visitor if you don't want to conduct business in your room.

1201 Mass. Ave. (at Quincy St.), Cambridge, MA 02138. ✆ **800/458-5886** or 617/491-2222. Fax 617/520-3711. www.theinnatharvard.com. 113 units (some with shower only). $149–$359 double; $1,200 presidential suite. AAA and AARP discounts available. AE, DC, DISC, MC, V. Valet parking $30. T: Red Line to Harvard. **Amenities:** Restaurant (New England); dining privileges at the nearby Harvard Faculty Club; fitness center; room service until 10:30pm; laundry service; same-day dry cleaning. *In room:* A/C, TV, wireless Internet access ($10/day), hair dryer, iron, umbrella, robes.

MODERATE

Best Western Hotel Tria ★ This four-story establishment offers a sophisticated blend of chain-motel convenience and boutique-hotel features (such as a "soap menu"). Guest rooms are spacious, with sleek but comfy contemporary furnishings, and are at least one floor up from the busy street. Room rates include wireless Internet access and 30 minutes of local phone calls. The hotel underwent a $3-million renovation in 2003 and added an exercise room in 2005. The commercial neighborhood is unattractive but convenient: Boston is about a 15-minute drive or a 30-minute T ride away, and Lexington and Concord are less than a half-hour away by car.

220 Alewife Brook Pkwy., Cambridge, MA 02138. ✆ **866/333-8742** or 617/491-8000. Fax 617/491-4932. www.hoteltria.com. 69 units. Mid-Mar to Oct $129–$299 double; Nov to mid-Mar $109–$159 double. Extra person $10. Rates include continental breakfast. Rates may be higher during special events. Children under 17 stay free in parent's room. AE, DC, MC, V. Parking $12. T: Red Line to Alewife, 10-min. walk. Pets accepted; reservation required; $25 fee; $100 deposit. **Amenities:** Indoor pool; exercise room; Jacuzzi; tour desk; shuttle service; same-day dry cleaning. *In room:* A/C, TV, wireless Internet access, coffeemaker, hair dryer, iron, robes.

Harvard Square Hotel ★ The Harvard economics department could use this hotel to illustrate supply and demand: At busy times, including almost every night in the fall, rates seem high for such modest accommodations (supply)—but you can't beat the location (demand). Smack in the middle of Harvard Square, the six-story brick hotel is a favorite with visiting parents and budget-conscious business travelers. The unpretentious guest rooms are relatively small but comfortable; they were renovated in 2006. The front desk handles fax and copy services.

110 Mount Auburn St., Cambridge, MA 02138. ✆ **800/458-5886** or 617/864-5200. Fax 617/864-2409. www.harvardsquarehotel.com. 73 units. $99–$269 double. Extra person $10. Children under 17 stay free in parent's room. Corporate rates and AAA and AARP discounts available. AE, DC, DISC, MC, V. Parking $27. T: Red Line to Harvard. **Amenities:** Dining privileges at the Harvard Faculty Club; free access to nearby health club; car-rental desk; laundry service; dry cleaning. *In room:* A/C, TV, wireless Internet access ($10/day), fridge, coffeemaker, hair dryer, iron, umbrella.

Holiday Inn Express Hotel & Suites *Value* A limited-services lodging on a busy street, the Holiday Inn Express is comfortable and convenient—just a 5-minute walk from the Green Line—for businesspeople on tight budgets as well as vacationers. Each decent-size room has a fridge and microwave. The eight-story building sits slightly back from the street, but you'll still want to be up as high as possible to get away from traffic noise. If you're willing to do without a restaurant, business center, or exercise facility, you'll probably find that the reasonable rates, which include local phone calls and parking—a big plus in Cambridge—more than make up for the lack of extras.

250 Msgr. O'Brien Hwy., Cambridge, MA 02141. © **888/887-7690** or 617/577-7600. Fax 617/354-1313. www.hiexpress.com/boscambridgema. 112 units. From $104 double; from $125 suite. Rates include continental breakfast. Discounts for hospital patients and families available, subject to availability. AE, DC, DISC, MC, V. Free parking. T: Green Line to Lechmere. **Amenities:** Access to nearby health club ($10); laundry service; same-day dry cleaning. *In room:* A/C, TV w/pay movies, high-speed Internet access, fridge, coffeemaker, hair dryer, iron.

4 Where to Dine

Travelers from around the world relish the variety of skillfully prepared seafood available in the Boston area. Lunch is an excellent, economical way to check out a fancy restaurant without breaking the bank. At restaurants that accept reservations, it's always a good idea to make them, particularly for dinner.

WATERFRONT

EXPENSIVE

A branch of **Legal Sea Foods,** at 255 State St. (© **617/227-3115**), sits across from the New England Aquarium. See "Back Bay," later in this section.

Sel de la Terre ★★ PROVENÇAL A stone's throw from Boston Harbor, Sel de la Terre is a taste of southern France. The subtly flavorful food—scallops handled so gently that they're still sweet, juicy roasted chicken, salmon with truffled cauliflower purée—relies on fresh local ingredients. The restaurant attracts a go-go business-lunch crowd (dinner is calmer). The unusual pricing structure feels like a deal when you're tucking into a generous portion of Black Angus rib-eye, less of a bargain if you're eating pasta. Whatever you're eating, try the sublime pommes frites. There's seasonal outdoor seating, and the bakery at the entrance sells out-of-this-world breads.

255 State St. © **617/720-1300.** www.seldelaterre.com. Reservations recommended. Main courses $15 lunch, $24 dinner; sandwiches (lunch only) $8.50. Children's menu $7. AE, DC, DISC, MC, V. Mon–Fri 11:30am–2:30pm; Sat–Sun 11am–3:30pm; daily 5–10pm. Valet and validated parking available at dinner. T: Blue Line to Aquarium.

THE NORTH END

Many North End restaurants don't serve dessert, but you can satisfy your sweet tooth at a *caffè*. Favorites include **Caffè Vittoria,** 296 Hanover St. (© **617/227-7606**), and **Caffè dello Sport,** 308 Hanover St. (© **617/523-5063**). For gelato, head to **Gelateria,** 272 Hanover St. (© **617/720-4243**), which serves 50 flavors of the Italian version of ice cream.

VERY EXPENSIVE

Mamma Maria ★★★ NORTHERN ITALIAN In a town house overlooking North Square and the Paul Revere House, the best restaurant in the North End offers innovative seasonal cuisine and a level of sophistication that's unusual for this casual neighborhood. The menu changes seasonally, and portions are more than generous. Fork-tender *osso buco* is almost enough for two, but you'll want it all for yourself. You can't go wrong with main-course pastas, either, and the fresh seafood specials are uniformly marvelous. The pasta, bread, and desserts are homemade, and the shadowy, whitewashed rooms make this a popular spot for getting engaged.

3 North Sq. © **617/523-0077.** www.mammamaria.com. Reservations recommended. Main courses $24–$35; 3-course chef's menus $38 and $58. AE, DC, DISC, MC, V. Sun–Thurs 5–9:30pm; Fri–Sat 5–10:30pm. Valet parking available. T: Green or Orange Line to Haymarket.

MODERATE

Artú ITALIAN Artú is a neighborhood favorite as well as a good stop for Freedom Trail walkers. It's known for superb roasted meats and bounteous home-style pasta dishes. Roast lamb, penne alla puttanesca, and chicken stuffed with ham and cheese are all terrific. *Panini* (sandwiches) are big in size and flavor—prosciutto, mozzarella, and tomato is sublime, and chicken parmigiana is tender and filling. Artú isn't great for quiet conversation, especially during dinner in the noisy main room, but do you really want to talk with your mouth full?

6 Prince St. ✆ **617/742-4336.** www.artuboston.com. Reservations recommended at dinner. Main courses $9.50–$18; sandwiches $4.75–$7. AE, MC, V. Daily 11am–11pm. T: Green or Orange Line to Haymarket.

Daily Catch ★ SOUTHERN ITALIAN/SEAFOOD This storefront restaurant is about the size of a large kitchen (it seats just 20), but it packs a wallop—of garlic. A North End favorite for over 30 years, it has excellent food, chummy service, and very little elbow room. The surprisingly varied menu includes excellent fried calamari, fresh clams, squid-ink pasta puttanesca, and a variety of broiled, fried, and sautéed fish and shellfish. All food is prepared to order, and some dishes arrive still in the frying pan.

323 Hanover St. ✆ **617/523-8567.** Reservations not accepted. Main courses $12–$19. No credit cards. Sun–Thurs 11:30am–10pm; Fri–Sat 11:30am–11pm. T: Green or Orange Line to Haymarket.

Giacomo's Ristorante ★★ ITALIAN/SEAFOOD The line snakes out the door and down the street, especially on weekends. No reservations, cash only, a tiny dining room with an open kitchen—what's the secret? Terrific food, plenty of it, and the "we're-all-in-this-together" atmosphere. To start, try fried calamari or mozzarella with excellent marinara sauce. Take the chef's advice or put together your own main dish from the list of daily ingredients on a board on the wall. The best suggestion is salmon and sun-dried tomatoes in tomato cream sauce over fettuccine. Non-seafood offerings such as butternut squash ravioli are equally memorable. Service is friendly but incredibly swift. (Those hungry people want your seat.) After a 40-minute dinner, dessert at a *caffè* is practically a necessity.

355 Hanover St. ✆ **617/523-9026.** Reservations not accepted. Main courses $13–$18; specials market price. No credit cards. Mon–Thurs 5–10pm; Fri–Sat 5–10:30pm; Sun 4–10pm. T: Green or Orange Line to Haymarket.

La Summa ★ SOUTHERN ITALIAN Away from the restaurant rows of Hanover and Salem streets, La Summa maintains a cozy neighborhood atmosphere. It's worth seeking out for wonderful homemade pasta and desserts; more elaborate entrees are scrumptious, too. Try any seafood special, lobster ravioli, *pappardelle e melanzane* (eggplant strips tossed with ethereal fresh pasta), or the house special—veal, chicken, sausage, shrimp, artichokes, pepperoncini, olives, and mushrooms in white-wine sauce. Desserts, especially tiramisu, are terrific.

30 Fleet St. ✆ **617/523-9503.** Reservations recommended. Main courses $11–$24. AE, DC, DISC, MC, V. Sun–Fri 4:30–10:30pm; Sat 4:30–11pm. T: Green or Orange Line to Haymarket.

Piccola Venezia ITALIAN Piccola Venezia's glass front wall faces the Freedom Trail—a touristy location with a neighborhood feel. Portions are large, and the homey food tends to be heavy on red sauce. Spaghetti and meatballs, eggplant rolatini, and pasta puttanesca are always on the menu. This is a good place to try traditional Italian-American favorites such as home-style polenta, *baccala* (reconstituted salt cod), or the house specialty, tripe.

263 Hanover St. ✆ **617/523-3888.** Reservations recommended for dinner. Main courses $12–$22; lunch specialties $5–$10. AE, DISC, MC, V. Sun–Thurs 11:30am–9:30pm; Fri–Sat 11:30am–10:30pm (lunch Mon–Sat until 3pm). Validated parking available. T: Green or Orange Line to Haymarket.

Boston Dining

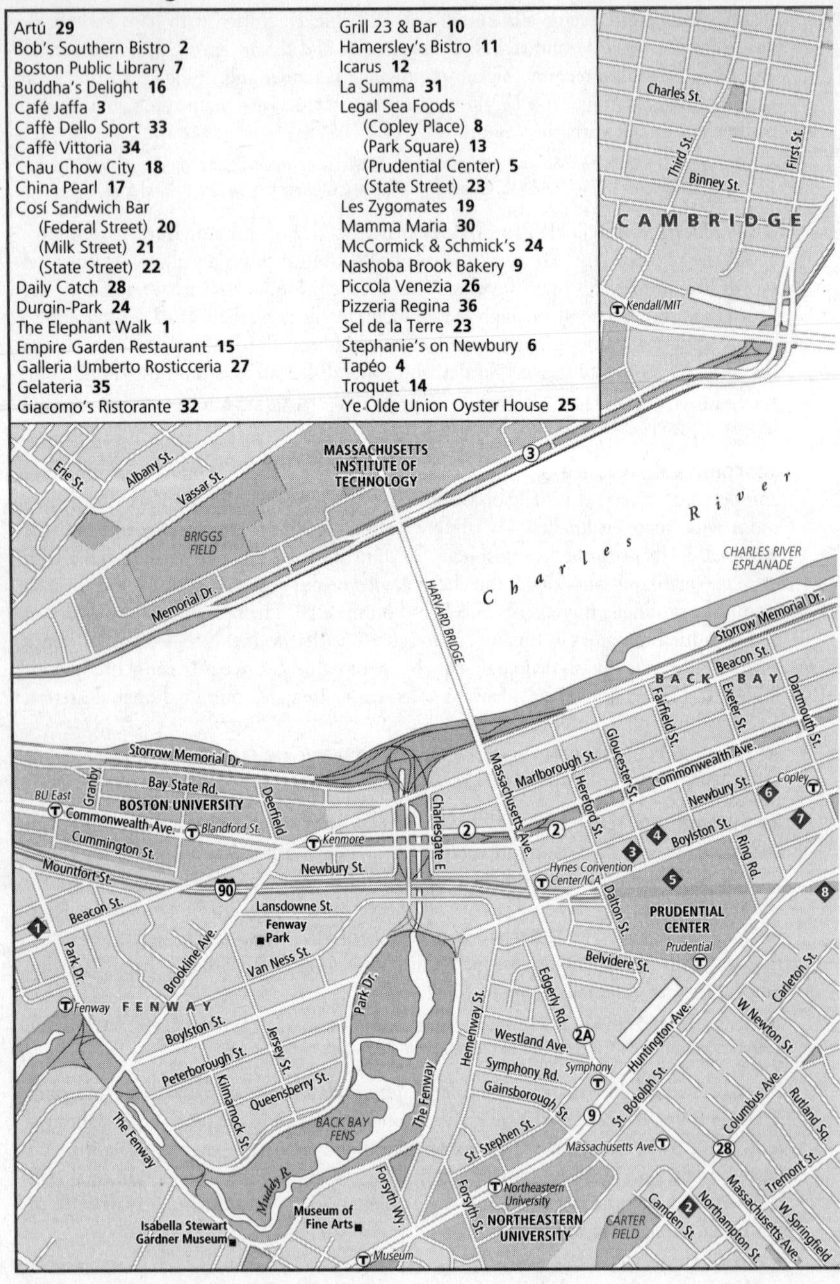

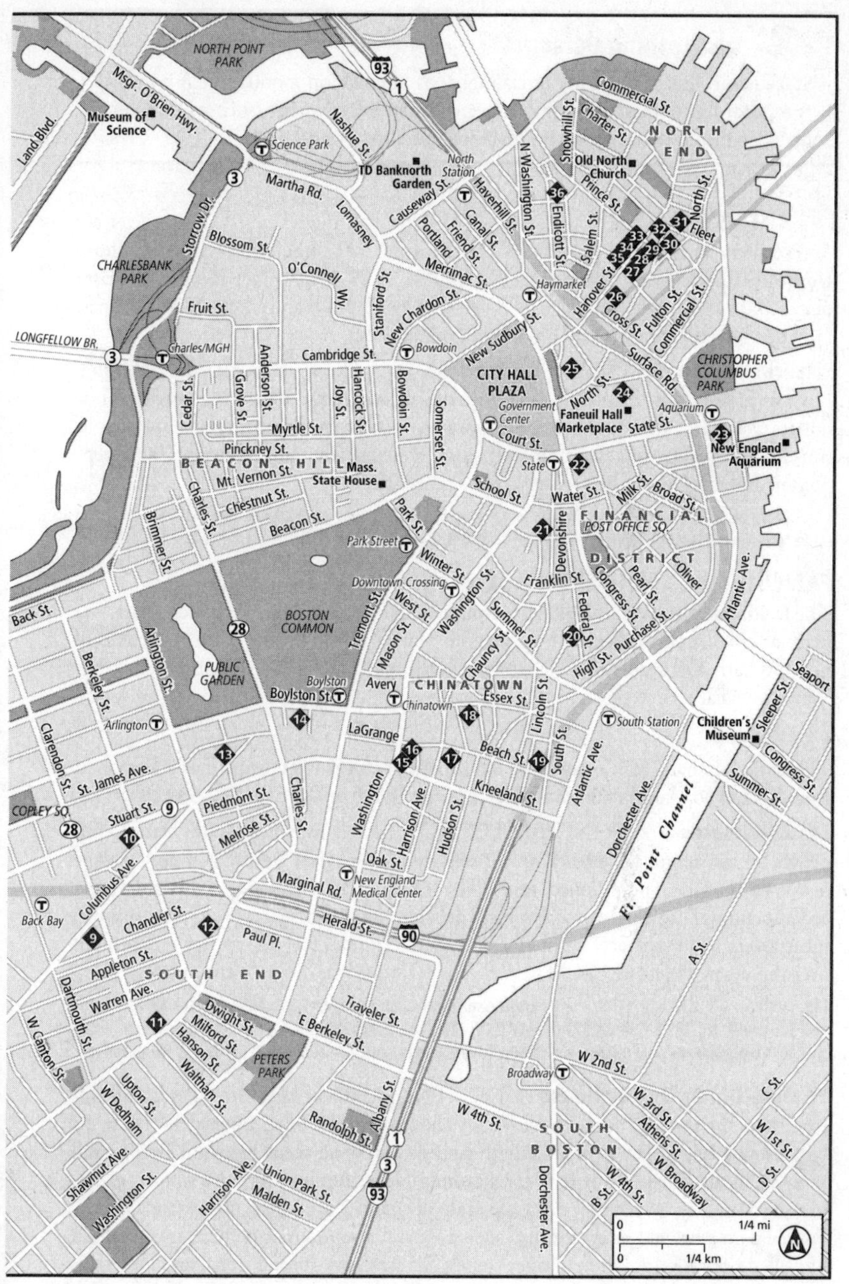

NORTH POINT PARK
Museum of Science
Science Park
TD Banknorth Garden
North Station
Old North Church
NORTH END
CHARLESBANK PARK
Haymarket
CITY HALL PLAZA
Government Center
Faneuil Hall Marketplace
Aquarium
New England Aquarium
CHRISTOPHER COLUMBUS PARK
BEACON HILL
Mass. State House
FINANCIAL DISTRICT
POST OFFICE SQ.
Park Street
Downtown Crossing
BOSTON COMMON
PUBLIC GARDEN
Boylston
CHINATOWN
Chinatown
South Station
Children's Museum
Arlington
COPLEY SQ.
New England Medical Center
Back Bay
SOUTH END
PETERS PARK
Broadway
SOUTH BOSTON
Ft. Point Channel
LONGFELLOW BR.
Charles/MGH
Bowdoin
State
0 1/4 mi
0 1/4 km

Tips It's Nothing Personal

State law requires the scary disclaimer that appears on menus to alert you to the potential danger of eating raw or undercooked meat (such as rare burgers), seafood (raw oysters, for instance), poultry, or eggs.

INEXPENSIVE

An excellent eat-and-run spot just off the Freedom Trail is the cafeteria-style **Galleria Umberto Rosticceria,** 289 Hanover St. (✆ **617/227-5709**). Join the line for tasty pizza, *arancini* (a rice ball filled with ground beef, peas, and cheese), or calzones. Lunch is served Monday through Saturday; cash only.

Pizzeria Regina ★★ PIZZA Regina's looks like a movie set, but it's the real thing. Busy waitresses weave through the boisterous dining room, delivering peerless pizza hot from the brick oven. The list of toppings includes nouveau ingredients such as sun-dried tomatoes, but that's not authentic. House-made sausage, maybe some pepperoni, and a couple of beers—now, *that's* authentic.

11½ Thacher St. ✆ **617/227-0765**. www.pizzeriaregina.com. Reservations not accepted. Pizza $10–$17. No credit cards. Mon–Thurs 11am–11:30pm; Fri–Sat 11am–midnight; Sun noon–11pm. T: Green or Orange Line to Haymarket.

FANEUIL HALL MARKETPLACE & FINANCIAL DISTRICT

The **food court** at Faneuil Hall Marketplace is a great place to pick up picnic fare. Eat here, or cross Atlantic Avenue and pass the Marriott to reach the plaza at the end of Long Wharf. Or head to the left of the hotel and dine in Christopher Columbus Waterfront Park.

EXPENSIVE

The national chain **McCormick & Schmick's Seafood Restaurant** has a branch at Faneuil Hall Marketplace in the North Market Building (✆ **617/720-5522**).

Les Zygomates ★★ FRENCH/ECLECTIC Tucked away near South Station, this delightful bistro and wine bar is worth seeking out. It offers a great selection of wine by the bottle, glass, and 2-ounce "taste." The efficient staff will guide you toward a good accompaniment for chef-owner Ian Just's delicious food. Roasted salmon is toothsome; meat-lovers will savor beef short ribs with potato purée. For dessert, try not to fight over the warm chocolate cake. There's live jazz (in its own dining room) nightly.

129 South St. ✆ **617/542-5108**. www.winebar.com. Reservations recommended. Main courses $9–$14 lunch, $18–$26 dinner; prix fixe $15 lunch, $29 dinner. AE, DC, DISC, MC, V. Mon–Fri 11:30am–1am (lunch until 2pm, dinner until 10:30pm); Sat 6pm–1am (dinner until 11:30pm). Valet parking available at dinner. T: Red Line to South Station.

Ye Olde Union Oyster House ★ NEW ENGLAND/SEAFOOD America's oldest restaurant in continuous service, the Union Oyster House opened in 1826. Its tasty New England fare is popular with tourists on the adjacent Freedom Trail as well as savvy locals. They're not here for anything fancy; the best bets are simple, classic preparations. Try oyster stew or a cold seafood sampler of oysters, clams, and shrimp. Follow with a broiled or grilled dish such as scrod or salmon, or perhaps fried seafood or grilled pork loin. A "shore dinner" (chowder, steamers, lobster, corn, and dessert) is an excellent introduction to local favorites. ***Tip:*** A plaque marks John F. Kennedy's favorite booth (no. 18), where he often read the Sunday papers.

41 Union St. (between North and Hanover sts.). ✆ **617/227-2750.** www.unionoysterhouse.com. Reservations recommended. Main courses $8–$22 lunch, $17–$29 dinner; lobster market price. Children's menu $5–$12. AE, DC, DISC, MC, V. Sun–Thurs 11am–9:30pm (lunch until 5pm); Fri–Sat 11am–10pm (lunch until 6pm). Union Bar daily 11am–midnight (lunch until 3pm, late supper until 11pm). Validated and valet parking available. T: Green or Orange Line to Haymarket.

MODERATE

Durgin-Park ★★ Kids NEW ENGLAND For huge portions of delicious food, a rowdy atmosphere where CEOs share tables with students, and famously cranky waitresses, Bostonians have flocked to Durgin-Park since 1827. Approximately 2,000 people a day join the line that stretches down a flight of stairs to the first floor of Faneuil Hall Marketplace's North Market building, and everyone's disappointed when the waitresses are nice (as they often are). They come for prime rib the size of a hubcap, piles of fried seafood, fish dinners broiled to order, and bounteous portions of roast turkey. Steaks and chops are broiled on an open fire over wood charcoal. This is the place to try Boston baked beans. For dessert, strawberry shortcake is justly celebrated.

340 Faneuil Hall Marketplace. ✆ **617/227-2038.** www.durgin-park.com. Reservations accepted for parties of 15 or more. Main courses $7–$25; specials $19–$40. Children's menu $8–$9. AE, DC, DISC, MC, V. Mon–Sat 11:30am–10pm; Sun 11:30am–9pm (lunch daily until 2:30pm). Validated parking available. T: Green or Blue Line to Government Center, or Orange Line to Haymarket.

INEXPENSIVE

Cosí Sandwich Bar ★ ITALIAN/ECLECTIC Flavorful fillings on delectable bread make Cosí a downtown lunch favorite. This location, just off the Freedom Trail, makes a delicious refueling stop. Tasty Italian flatbread is filled with your choice of meat, fish, vegetables, cheese, and spreads. The more fillings you choose, the more you pay; the total can climb, so don't go wild if you're on a budget. Other branches are at 14 Milk St., near Downtown Crossing (✆ **617/426-7565**), and 133 Federal St. (✆ **617/292-2674**), which has patio seating.

53 State St. (at Congress St.). ✆ **617/723-4447.** Sandwiches $6–$10; soups and salads $4–$7. AE, DC, MC, V. Mon–Thurs 7am–6pm; Fri 7am–5pm. T: Orange or Blue Line to State.

CHINATOWN/THEATER DISTRICT

The best way to sample Chinese food is by trying **dim sum,** the traditional midday meal featuring a variety of appetizer-style dishes. It's especially popular on weekends, when the variety of offerings is greatest. My favorite dim sum is at **Empire Garden Restaurant,** also known as Emperor's Garden, 690–698 Washington St., 2nd floor (✆ **617/482-8898**); other good destinations are **China Pearl,** 9 Tyler St., 2nd floor (✆ **617/426-4338**), and **Chau Chow City,** 83 Essex St. (✆ **617/338-8158**).

VERY EXPENSIVE

Troquet ★★ NEW AMERICAN/WINE BAR The second-floor dining room at Troquet (French slang for "small wine cafe") overlooks Boston Common, and the ground floor is a lounge that serves "creative cocktails" and small plates. Troquet offers 40-plus wines by the 2- or 4-ounce glass and hundreds more by the bottle. Because the markup is lower than usual, sampling several selections is surprisingly affordable. The menu and the helpful staff can recommend pairings; you'll want just the right thing to complement the exceptional cuisine, which emphasizes seasonal ingredients.

140 Boylston St. ✆ **617/695-9463.** Reservations recommended. Main courses $26–$38; lounge menu $9–$22. AE, DC, DISC, MC, V. Dining room Tues–Sat 5–10:30pm; lounge daily 5pm–1am (food available until midnight). T: Green Line to Boylston.

INEXPENSIVE

Buddha's Delight ★ VEGETARIAN/VIETNAMESE Fresh, healthful, cheap, and filling—what's not to like? Buddha's Delight serves "chicken," "pork," and even "lobster"—in quotes because the chefs substitute fried and barbecued tofu and gluten for meat, poultry, and fish to create more-than-reasonable facsimiles of traditional dishes. Between pondering how they do it and savoring the strong, clear flavors, you might not miss your usual protein. To start, try fried "pork" dumplings or a delectable salad. Move on to "shrimp" with rice noodles, any of the house specialties, or excellent chow fun.

3 Beach St., 2nd floor. ✆ **617/451-2395.** Main courses $6–$13; lunch specials $6.50. MC, V. Sun–Thurs 11am–9:30pm; Fri–Sat 11am–10:30pm. T: Orange Line to Chinatown.

SOUTH END

VERY EXPENSIVE

Hamersley's Bistro ★ ECLECTIC This is the place that put the South End on Boston's culinary map, a pioneering restaurant that's both classic and contemporary. It's one of the area's top special-occasion restaurants yet feels like a neighborhood hangout, mostly thanks to the huge volume of repeat business. The seasonal menu offers entrees noted for their emphasis on local ingredients and classic techniques. The signature roast chicken with garlic is a bit tame, but cassoulet with pork, duck confit, and garlic sausage is a gorgeously executed combination of flavors and textures. The kitchen also has a way with fish—perhaps mustard-crusted salmon with creamy leeks, beets, and horseradish. The wine list is excellent, and there's seasonal outdoor seating.

553 Tremont St. ✆ **617/423-2700.** www.hamersleysbistro.com. Reservations recommended. Main courses $26–$40; tasting menu varies. AE, DISC, MC, V. Mon–Fri 6–10pm; Sat 5:30–10pm; Sun 5:30–9:30pm. Closed Jan 1–10. Valet parking available. T: Orange Line to Back Bay.

Icarus ★★ AMERICAN This shamelessly romantic subterranean restaurant offers every element of a great dining experience. Chef and co-owner Christopher Douglass uses choice local ingredients to create imaginative dishes. The menu changes regularly—you might start with braised exotic mushrooms on polenta, or sublime avocado soup. Move on to seared duck breast and roasted duck leg served with wild-rice pancakes, or a scrumptious seafood special. Save room for dessert; the seasonal fruit sorbets are especially delicious. On Friday from 7 to 11pm, the bar schedules live jazz.

3 Appleton St. ✆ **617/426-1790.** www.icarusrestaurant.com. Reservations recommended. Main courses $26–$36. AE, DC, DISC, MC, V. Mon–Wed 6–9:30pm; Thurs 6–10pm; Fri 6–10:30pm; Sat 5:30–10:30pm; Sun 5:30–9:30pm. Valet parking available. T: Green Line to Arlington or Orange Line to Back Bay.

MODERATE

Bob's Southern Bistro ★ SOUTHERN/CAJUN Bob's resembles a yuppie fern bar, but it serves generous portions of delicious Southern specialties against a backdrop of jazz. The music is live Thursday through Saturday beginning at 7:30pm and at the Sunday buffet brunch. Originally Bob the Chef's, then Bob the Chef's Jazz Café, it's a perennial neighborhood favorite and well worth a trip off the beaten tourist track. The menu includes dishes such as fried chicken, served alone or with barbecued ribs; meatloaf; and "soul fish" (in cornmeal batter), as well as Creole specialties like jambalaya and shrimp étouffée. For dessert, try the amazing sweet-potato pie, which makes pumpkin pie taste like vanilla pudding.

604 Columbus Ave. ✆ **617/536-6204.** www.bobssouthernbistro.com. Reservations recommended on weekends; accepted only for parties of 4 or more. Main courses $10–$16; brunch $20 adult, $15 child. AE, DISC, MC, V.

Mon–Wed 5–10pm; Thurs–Fri 5pm–midnight; Sat 11:30am–midnight; Sun 10am–10pm (brunch until 2:30pm). T: Orange Line to Mass. Ave. or Green Line E to Symphony.

INEXPENSIVE

Nashoba Brook Bakery ★ SANDWICHES This little neighborhood cafe serves baked goods so scrumptious you'll wish the South End were your neighborhood. The soups, salads, breads, and pastries make a reverse commute every day from the original location in suburban Concord (p. 157). Everything is fresh and delicious, especially the sandwiches—like ham and cheese with the tasty addition of apple slices—on incredible artisan breads.

288 Columbus Ave. ✆ **617/236-0777.** www.slowrise.com. Most items less than $7. MC, V. Mon–Fri 6:30am–6pm; Sat–Sun 8am–5pm. T: Orange Line to Back Bay.

BACK BAY

VERY EXPENSIVE

Grill 23 & Bar ★ STEAKS/AMERICAN Wood-paneled, glass-walled Grill 23 is the best steakhouse in town. A briefcase-toting crowd fills the two levels to chow down on traditional slabs of beef and chops, traditional steakhouse side dishes, and sophisticated yet traditional desserts. The meat is of the highest quality, expertly prepared. Steak au poivre and lamb chops are perfectly grilled, crusty, juicy, and tender. Fish dishes aren't quite as memorable as the meat offerings, but hey, it's a steakhouse. The bountiful a la carte sides include creamed spinach, out-of-this-world garlic mashed potatoes, and "tater tots" drizzled with truffle oil. Desserts are toothsome but (this is *not* your father's steakhouse) don't always include cheesecake. The service is exactly right for the setting, helpful but not familiar. ***Caveats:*** The wine list is excellent but pricey, and the room can get unbelievably loud.

161 Berkeley St. ✆ **617/542-2255.** www.grill23.com. Reservations recommended. Main courses $21–$44; Kobe beef from $39. AE, DC, DISC, MC, V. Mon–Thurs 5:30–10:30pm; Fri–Sat 5:30–11pm; Sun 5:30–10pm. Valet parking available. T: Green Line to Arlington.

EXPENSIVE

The Spanish tapas restaurant **Dalí** (p. 111) has a Back Bay outpost called **Tapéo,** at 266 Newbury St. (✆ **617/267-4799**).

L'Espalier ★★★ NEW ENGLAND/FRENCH Dinner at L'Espalier is a unique experience, very much like spending the evening at the home of a dear friend who has only your pleasure in mind—and a dozen helpers in the kitchen. Chef-owner Frank McClelland presides over one of Boston's favorite special-occasion destinations, which consists of three dining rooms on the second floor of an 1886 town house. The space is formal yet inviting, the service excellent, the food magnificent. The imaginative kitchen uses classic techniques to turn the freshest and most interesting ingredients available—many from small New England purveyors of everything from seafood to game to organic produce—into unforgettable dishes. The regularly changing menu might include seared diver scallops with black truffles, red-lentil purée, and cardamom-tangerine beurre blanc; smoked chicken with roasted artichokes; or prosciutto-wrapped pheasant served with apple relish, celery-root purée, and rutabagas. The breads, sorbets, ice creams, and alarmingly good desserts (many adapted from the family's heirloom cookbooks) are made in-house. Even if you order one of the superb soufflés, ask to see the beautiful desserts. Or finish with the celebrated cheese tray, which always includes at least two local selections.

30 Gloucester St. ✆ **617/262-3023.** www.lespalier.com. Reservations recommended. *Prix fixe* (3 courses) $75; degustation menu (7 courses) $94. AE, DC, DISC, MC, V. Mon–Sat 5:30–10pm; Sat 2–3pm (tea). Valet parking available. T: Green Line B, C, or D to Hynes/ICA.

Legal Sea Foods ★★★ SEAFOOD The food at "Legal's" isn't the fanciest, cheapest, or trendiest. It's the freshest, and management's commitment to that policy has produced a thriving chain (and a private seafood-processing plant). The menu includes regular selections plus whatever looked good at the market that morning, prepared in every imaginable way. It's all splendid. The clam chowder is famous, the fish chowder lighter but equally good. Entrees run the gamut from grilled fish served plain or with Cajun spices (try the arctic char) to seafood *fra'diavolo* on fresh linguine to salmon baked in parchment with vegetables and white wine. There's even a terrific wine list.

In the Prudential Center, 800 Boylston St. ✆ **617/266-6800.** www.legalseafoods.com. Reservations recommended. Main courses $11–$19 lunch, $14–$35 dinner; lobster priced daily. AE, DC, DISC, MC, V. Mon–Thurs 11am–10pm; Fri–Sat 11am–11pm; Sun noon–10pm. T: Green Line B, C, or D to Hynes/ICA or E to Prudential. Also at 255 State St. ✆ **617/227-3115.** T: Blue Line to Aquarium. 36 Park Place (between Columbus Ave. and Stuart St.), Park Sq. ✆ **617/426-4444.** T: Green Line to Arlington. Copley Place, 2nd level. ✆ **617/266-7775.** T: Orange Line to Back Bay or Green Line to Copley. 20 University Rd., behind The Charles Hotel, Cambridge. ✆ **617/491-9400.** T: Red Line to Harvard. 5 Cambridge Center, Cambridge. ✆ **617/864-3400.** T: Red Line to Kendall/MIT.

Stephanie's on Newbury ★ AMERICAN Celebrated for "sophisticated comfort food," Stephanie's on Newbury is a neighborhood favorite. The lively bar has a clubby air, while the two-level dining room has a see-and-be-seen atmosphere. The prime people-watching spot is the outdoor patio. The extensive menu emphasizes traditional favorites like chef's salad, burgers, macaroni and cheese, chicken potpie, meatloaf (with caramelized onions), pineapple upside-down cake, and strawberry cheesecake. Prices are high, but portions are huge.

190 Newbury St. ✆ **617/236-0990.** www.stephaniesonnewbury.com. Reservations recommended. Main courses $14–$28 at lunch, $23–$35 at dinner. AE, DC, DISC, MC, V. Mon–Thurs 11am–10:30pm; Fri–Sat 11am–11:30pm; Sun noon–10pm. Valet parking available at dinner. T: Green Line to Copley or Orange Line to Back Bay.

INEXPENSIVE

The Boston Public Library, 700 Boylston St. (✆ **617/536-5400;** www.bpl.org), is home to a restaurant, **Novel,** that serves lunch and afternoon tea on weekdays only and the less expensive **Sebastian's Map Room Café,** which serves meals and snacks Monday through Saturday from 9am to 5pm.

Café Jaffa MIDDLE EASTERN A long, narrow brick room with a glass front, Café Jaffa looks more like a snazzy pizza place than the excellent Middle Eastern restaurant it is. Reasonable prices, high quality, and large portions draw crowds for traditional dishes such as falafel, baba ghanoush, and hummus, as well as burgers and steak tips. For dessert, try the baklava if it's fresh (give it a pass if not).

48 Gloucester St. ✆ **617/536-0230.** Main courses $5–$16. AE, DC, DISC, MC, V. Mon–Thurs 11am–10:30pm; Fri–Sat 11am–11pm; Sun 1–10pm. T: Green Line B, C, or D to Hynes/ICA.

KENMORE SQUARE

MODERATE

The Elephant Walk ★★ FRENCH/CAMBODIAN France meets Cambodia on the menu at this madly popular spot 4 blocks from Kenmore Square. Many Cambodian dishes have part-French names, such as *poulet dhomrei* (chicken with Asian basil, bamboo shoots, fresh pineapple, and lemon grass) and *curry de crevettes* (shrimp curry with picture-perfect vegetables). Or try *loc lac,* fork-tender beef cubes in addictively spicy sauce. On the French side, you'll find classics like filet mignon with pommes frites. The pleasant staff will help out if you need guidance.

900 Beacon St. ✆ **617/247-1500.** www.elephantwalk.com. Reservations recommended for dinner Sun–Thurs; not accepted Fri–Sat. Main courses $7–$26 lunch, $11–$27 dinner. AE, DC, DISC, MC, V. Mon–Fri 11:30am–2:30pm; Sun brunch 11am–3pm; Sun–Thurs 5–10pm; Fri–Sat 5–11pm. Valet parking available at dinner. T: Green Line C to St. Mary's St.

CAMBRIDGE

The Red Line runs from downtown Boston to Harvard Square. Many of the restaurants listed here can be reached on foot from there. To go in search of inexpensive ethnic food, head for Central and Inman squares.

Note: See the "Cambridge Accommodations & Dining" map on p. 99 for the locations of the restaurants reviewed below.

VERY EXPENSIVE

Upstairs on the Square ★★ ECLECTIC Upstairs on the Square is the reincarnation of a longtime Harvard Square favorite, Upstairs at the Pudding. It consists of two distinct spaces; I prefer the more casual one to its fancier counterpart, but both are delightful. The second-floor Monday Club Bar dining room is a relaxed yet romantic space where firelight flickers on jewel-toned walls. The food—unusual salads and sandwiches (including a daily grilled-cheese option at lunch), pizza, fried chicken, steak with baked potato and onion rings—is homey and satisfying, and the bar is a tweedy Cambridge scene. The Soiree Room, atop the four-story building, is the place for that big anniversary dinner: It's a jewel box of pinks and golds under a low, mirrored ceiling. The menu is enjoyably old-fashioned, with straightforward main courses (a slab of swordfish, luscious rib-eye steak) that contrast with bolder starters—delectable Jerusalem artichoke or watercress soup, simple but superb endive and watercress salad. In both rooms, you'll find outstanding wine selections and desserts.

91 Winthrop St. ✆ **617/864-1933.** www.upstairsonthesquare.com. Reservations recommended. Main courses $11–$26 downstairs, $24–$42 upstairs. AE, DC, DISC, MC, V. Downstairs Mon–Fri 11:30am–2:30pm; Sun brunch 11am–2pm; daily 5pm–1am. Upstairs Mon–Sat 5:30–10pm; Sun brunch 11am–2pm. Validated and valet parking available. T: Red Line to Harvard.

EXPENSIVE

Legal Sea Foods has branches in Harvard Square and in Kendall Square; see "Back Bay," above.

The Blue Room ★★★ ECLECTIC The Blue Room sits below plaza level in an office-retail complex, a slice of foodie paradise in high-tech heaven. The cuisine is a rousing combination of top-notch ingredients and aggressive flavors, the service excellent, and the crowded dining room not as noisy as it looks. Main courses tend to be grilled over a wood fire, roasted, or braised, with at least one well-conceived vegetarian choice. Roast chicken, roasted with Moroccan spices and served with garlic mashed potatoes, is world-class. Seafood is always a good choice, and grilled rib-eye is a juicy wonder. In warm weather, there's patio seating.

1 Kendall Sq. ✆ **617/494-9034.** www.theblueroom.net. Reservations recommended. Main courses $17–$26. AE, DC, DISC, MC, V. Sun–Thurs 5:30–10pm; Fri–Sat 5:30–11pm; Sun brunch 11am–2:30pm. Closed 1st week of July. Validated parking available. T: Red Line to Kendall/MIT; 10-min. walk.

Dalí ★★★ SPANISH This festive restaurant casts an irresistible spell—people wait an hour or more for a table and hardly complain. The payoff is authentic Spanish food, notably tapas. Entrees include excellent paella, but most people come in a group and explore the three dozen or more tapas offerings, all perfect for sharing. They include delectable garlic potatoes, salmon balls with not-too-salty caper sauce, pork tenderloin with blue goat cheese, and delicious sausages. The staff sometimes seems rushed but never fails to supply bread for sopping up juices and sangria for washing it all down. I like to finish with "ubiquitous flan" or *tarta de chocolates.*

The owners of Dalí also run **Tapéo,** 266 Newbury St. (✆ **617/267-4799**), between Fairfield and Dartmouth streets in Boston's Back Bay.

415 Washington St., Somerville. ✆ **617/661-3254.** www.DaliRestaurant.com. Reservations not accepted. Tapas $3–$8.50; main courses $19–$24. AE, DC, MC, V. Daily 5:30–11pm. T: Red Line to Harvard; follow Kirkland St. to intersection of Washington and Beacon sts. (20-min. walk or $5 cab ride).

East Coast Grill & Raw Bar ★★ SEAFOOD/BARBECUE Huge portions, a dizzying menu, and funky decor have made the East Coast Grill incredibly popular for over 20 years. The kitchen handles fresh seafood (an encyclopedic variety), barbecue, and grilled fish and meats with equal authority and imagination. The influence of founder Chris Schlesinger, a national expert on grilling and spicy food, is apparent in the exuberant menu descriptions ("super fresh catch o' the moment," "wings of mass destruction from hell!"). Desserts are just decent, but there's a great ice-cream store (Christina's) up the street.

1271 Cambridge St., Inman Sq. ✆ **617/491-6568.** www.eastcoastgrill.net. Reservations accepted only for parties of 5 or more, Sun–Thurs. Main courses $14–$30; sandwich plates $9–$10. AE, MC, V. Sun–Thurs 5:30–10pm; Fri–Sat 5:30–10:30pm; Sun brunch 11am–2:30pm. Validated parking available. T: Red Line to Central, 10-min. walk on Prospect St. Or Red Line to Harvard, then no. 69 (Harvard-Lechmere) bus to Inman Sq.

MODERATE

Border Cafe Kids TEX-MEX/CAJUN This unbelievably crowded restaurant has been a Harvard Square favorite for over 20 years. Patrons loiter at the bar while waiting for a table, enhancing the festival atmosphere. Portions are generous, and the beleaguered staff keeps the chips and salsa coming. Try the excellent chorizo appetizer, seafood enchiladas, or popcorn shrimp. Fajitas for one or two, sizzling noisily, are also popular. Ask to be seated downstairs if you want to be able to hear your companions. ***Tip for parents:*** This place is great for kids—even the risk-averse will devour chips—but only if you eat early. (You do that anyway, right?)

32 Church St. ✆ **617/864-6100.** Reservations not accepted. Main courses $7–$15. AE, MC, V. Daily 11am–11pm. T: Red Line to Harvard.

The Helmand ★ AFGHAN Never exactly a secret, The Helmand enjoyed a burst of publicity when Afghanistan moved into the headlines, and it's hardly had a slow night since. Unusual cuisine, an elegant setting, and reasonable prices had already made this spacious spot near the CambridgeSide Galleria mall a local favorite. Service could be more attentive, but with food this good, that's a quibble. Afghan food is vegetarian friendly, and many of the non-veggie dishes use meat as one element rather than the centerpiece. *Aushak,* pasta pockets filled with leeks or potatoes, comes topped with split-pea-and-carrot sauce or meat sauce. Other entrees include stews like *deygee kabob,* an excellent mélange of lamb, yellow split peas, onion, and red peppers. For dessert, don't miss the Afghan version of baklava.

143 First St. ✆ **617/492-4646.** Reservations recommended. Main courses $12–$20. AE, MC, V. Sun–Thurs 5–10pm; Fri–Sat 5–11pm. T: Green Line to Lechmere.

INEXPENSIVE

Mr. Bartley's Burger Cottage ★★ AMERICAN Great burgers and the best onion rings in the world make Bartley's a perennial favorite with a cross section of Cambridge. The 40-plus-year-old family business is a high-ceilinged, crowded room plastered with signs and posters. Anything you can think of to put on ground beef is available, from American cheese to grilled pineapple. Good dishes that don't involve meat include veggie burgers and creamy, garlicky hummus.

1246 Mass. Ave. ✆ **617/354-6559.** www.mrbartleys.com. Burgers $8–$13; main courses, salads, and sandwiches $5–$9. No credit cards. Mon–Sat 11am–9pm. Closed Dec 25–Jan 1. T: Red Line to Harvard.

S&S Restaurant ★★ DELI *Es* is Yiddish for "eat," and this Cambridge classic is as straightforward as its name ("eat and eat"). Founded in 1919 by the current owners' great-grandmother, the wildly popular brunch spot draws huge crowds at busy times on weekends. It looks contemporary, but the brunch offerings are traditional: fantastic omelets, pancakes, waffles, fruit salad, cinnamon rolls. You'll also find traditional deli items (corned beef, pastrami, potato pancakes, blintzes), and breakfast anytime. Arrive early for brunch, or plan to spend a chunk of your Saturday or Sunday people-watching and getting hungry. Or dine on a weekday and soak up the neighborhood atmosphere.

1334 Cambridge St., Inman Sq. ✆ **617/354-0777.** www.sandsrestaurant.com. Main courses $4–$15. AE, MC, V. Mon–Wed 7am–11pm; Thurs–Fri 7am–midnight; Sat 8am–midnight; Sun 8am–10pm (brunch Sat–Sun until 4pm). T: Red Line to Central; 10-min. walk on Prospect St. Or Red Line to Harvard, then no. 69 (Harvard–Lechmere) bus to Inman Sq.

5 Seeing the Sights in Boston

At press time, the **Institute of Contemporary Art** ★★ (✆ **617/266-5152;** www.icaboston.org) was packing up to move from the Back Bay to a brand-new museum on Seaport Boulevard at Fan Pier, on the South Boston waterfront near the federal courthouse. A $37-million project designed by the pioneering New York firm Diller Scofidio + Renfro, the 65,000-square-foot building was scheduled to open in September 2006. The ICA made its reputation—imaginative and daring yet accessible—with its rotating exhibits of 20th- and 21st-century art, including painting, sculpture, photography, and video and performance art. Offerings include films, lectures, musical performances, poetry readings, and educational programs for children and adults. In the new location, the museum will have a permanent collection for the first time. Visit the website for hours and admission fees, more details, and updates on events related to the opening.

DISCOUNT PASSES If you concentrate on the included attractions, a **CityPass** (✆ **888/330-5008;** www.citypass.com) offers great savings. It's a booklet of tickets to the Harvard Museum of Natural History, Kennedy Library, Museum of Fine Arts, Museum of Science, New England Aquarium, and Prudential Center Skywalk. The price (at press time, $39 for adults, $22 for children 3–11) represents a 50% savings for adults who visit all six attractions, and having a ticket means you can go straight to the entrance without waiting in line. The passes, good for 1 year from the date of purchase, are on sale at participating attractions, from the website, through the **Greater Boston Convention & Visitors Bureau** (✆ **800/SEE-BOSTON;** www.bostonusa.com), and from some hotel concierges and travel agents.

CityPass's main competition is the **Explorer Pass,** a spin-off of the **Go Boston Card** (✆ **800/887-9103** or 617/742-5950; www.gobostoncard.com) that covers its own list of attractions. The Explorer Pass (www.explorerpass.com) is good for 2 days and costs $45 for adults, $29 for children—a deal, but fitting in all 10 destinations to score the full savings takes serious planning. The original Go Boston card includes admission to more than 60 Boston-area and New England attractions, dining and shopping discounts, a guidebook, and a 2-day trolley pass. If you strategize wisely, it's a great value. Prices range from $49 for 1 day to $159 for 7 days, with discounts for children and winter travelers. Purchase through the website; at the office in the Ferry Terminal behind the Boston Harbor Hotel, Rowes Wharf (off Atlantic Ave.); from the Bostix booths in Faneuil Hall Marketplace (closed Mon) and Copley Square; at many concierge desks; and as part of numerous hotel packages.

THE TOP ATTRACTIONS

Faneuil Hall Marketplace ★★ Kids Since Boston's most popular attraction opened in 1976, cities all over the country have imitated the "festival market" concept. The complex of shops, food counters, restaurants, bars, and public spaces is such a magnet for tourists and suburbanites that you could be forgiven for thinking that the only Bostonians in the crowd are employees.

The five-structure complex sits on brick-and-stone plazas that teem with crowds shopping, eating, performing, watching performers, and people-watching. In warm weather, it's busy from just after dawn until well past dark. **Quincy Market** (you'll hear the whole complex called by that name) is the central Greek Revival–style building; its central corridor is an enormous food court. On either side, glass canopies cover full-service restaurants as well as pushcarts that hold everything from crafts created by New England artisans to hokey souvenirs. Here you'll also see a bar that exactly replicates the set of the TV show ***Cheers.*** In the plaza between the **South Canopy** and the South Market building is an **information kiosk,** and throughout the complex you'll find an enticing mix of chain stores and unique shops. On summer evenings, people fill the tables that spill outdoors from the restaurants and bars. One constant since the year after the original market opened (in 1826) is **Durgin-Park,** a traditional New England restaurant with traditionally crabby waitresses (p. 107). **Faneuil Hall** ★ itself—nicknamed the "Cradle of Liberty"—sometimes gets overlooked, but it's well worth a visit. National Park Service rangers give free 20-minute talks every half-hour from 9am to 5pm in the second-floor auditorium.

Between North, Congress, and State sts. and I-93. ✆ **617/523-1300.** www.faneuilhallmarketplace.com. Marketplace Mon–Sat 10am–9pm; Sun noon–6pm. Food court opens earlier; some restaurants close later. T: Green or Blue Line to Government Center, Orange Line to Haymarket, or Blue Line to Aquarium or State.

Isabella Stewart Gardner Museum ★★ Isabella Stewart Gardner (1840–1924) was an incorrigible individualist long before such behavior was acceptable for a woman in polite Boston society, and her iconoclasm paid off for art lovers. "Mrs. Jack" designed her exquisite home in the style of a 15th-century Venetian palace and filled it with European, American, and Asian painting and sculpture. You'll see works by Titian, Botticelli, Raphael, Rembrandt, Matisse, and Mrs. Gardner's friends James McNeill Whistler and John Singer Sargent. Titian's magnificent *Europa* is one of the most important Renaissance paintings in the United States.

The building holds a hodgepodge of furniture and architectural details imported from European churches and palaces. The *pièce de résistance* is the magnificent skylit

Boston Attractions

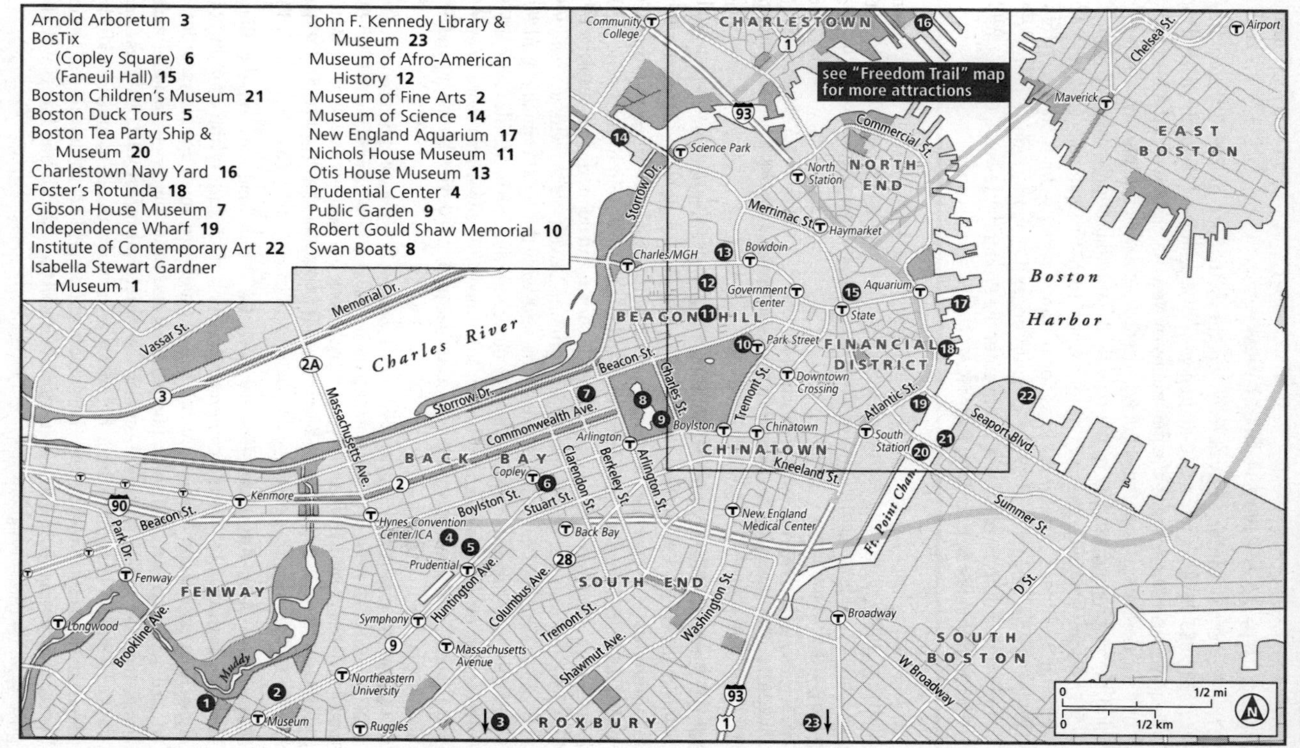

Arnold Arboretum 3
BosTix
(Copley Square) 6
(Faneuil Hall) 15
Boston Children's Museum 21
Boston Duck Tours 5
Boston Tea Party Ship & Museum 20
Charlestown Navy Yard 16
Foster's Rotunda 18
Gibson House Museum 7
Independence Wharf 19
Institute of Contemporary Art 22
Isabella Stewart Gardner Museum 1
John F. Kennedy Library & Museum 23
Museum of Afro-American History 12
Museum of Fine Arts 2
Museum of Science 14
New England Aquarium 17
Nichols House Museum 11
Otis House Museum 13
Prudential Center 4
Public Garden 9
Robert Gould Shaw Memorial 10
Swan Boats 8
see "Freedom Trail" map for more attractions
CHARLESTOWN
NORTH END
EAST BOSTON
Boston Harbor
BEACON HILL
FINANCIAL DISTRICT
CHINATOWN
BACK BAY
SOUTH END
SOUTH BOSTON
ROXBURY
FENWAY
Charles River
0 1/2 mi
0 1/2 km

Kids Up, Up & Away: A Great View

The **Prudential Center Skywalk** ★★, on the 50th floor of 800 Boylston St. (✆ **617/859-0648**), offers a 360-degree view of Boston and beyond. When it's clear, you can see as far as the mountains of New Hampshire and the beaches of Cape Cod. Away from the windows, interactive audiovisual displays—including the fascinating exhibits of the now-defunct immigration museum Dreams of Freedom—chronicle the city's history. Open 10am to 10pm daily (call before visiting; the space sometimes closes for private events). Admission is $11 for adults, $9 for seniors, and $7 for children under 12, and includes a narrated audio tour. Adults must show an ID to enter the Prudential Tower. T: Green Line E to Prudential or B, C, or D to Hynes/ICA.

courtyard, filled year-round with fresh flowers from the museum greenhouse. A special exhibition gallery features two or three changing shows a year, often by contemporary artists in residence.

280 The Fenway. ✆ **617/566-1401.** www.gardnermuseum.org. Admission $11 adults Sat–Sun, $10 adults Mon–Fri; $7 seniors; $5 college students; free for children under 18 and adults named Isabella with ID. Tues–Sun, some Mon holidays 11am–5pm. T: Green Line E to Museum.

John F. Kennedy Library and Museum ★★ Kids The Kennedy era springs to life at this dramatic library, museum, and research complex overlooking Dorchester Bay. It captures the 35th president's accomplishments in sound and video recordings as well as fascinating displays of memorabilia and photos. Far from being a static experience, it changes regularly, with temporary shows and reinterpreted displays that highlight and complement the permanent exhibits. A visit begins with a 17-minute film about Kennedy's early life. The exhibits start with the 1960 campaign and end with a tribute to Kennedy's legacy. There's a film about the Cuban Missile Crisis, along with displays on Attorney General Robert F. Kennedy, the civil-rights movement, the Peace Corps, the space program, First Lady Jacqueline Bouvier Kennedy, and the Kennedy family.

Columbia Point. ✆ **877/616-4599** or 617/929-4500. www.jfklibrary.org. Admission $10 adults; $8 seniors, college students, and youths 13–17; free for children under 13. Surcharges may apply for special exhibitions. Daily 9am–5pm (last film at 3:55pm). T: Red Line to JFK/UMass, then free no. 2 shuttle bus, which runs every 20 min. By car, take Southeast Expwy. (I-93/Rte. 3) south to Exit 15 (Morrissey Blvd./JFK Library), turn left onto Columbia Rd., and follow signs to free parking lot.

Museum of Afro-American History ★★ Kids The final stop on the **Black Heritage Trail** (p. 118) offers a comprehensive look at the history and contributions of blacks in Boston and Massachusetts. Changing and permanent exhibits incorporate art, artifacts, documents, historic photographs, and other objects—including many family heirlooms. The museum occupies the **Abiel Smith School** (1834), the first American public grammar school for African-American children, and the **African Meeting House,** 8 Smith Court. The oldest standing black church in the United States, the meetinghouse opened in 1806; bicentennial exhibits and events will take place in 2006 and throughout 2007.

46 Joy St. ✆ **617/725-0022.** www.afroammuseum.org. Free admission; donations encouraged. Mon–Sat 10am–4pm. T: Red or Green Line to Park St. or Red Line to Charles/MGH.

Museum of Fine Arts ★★★ Kids One of the world's great museums, the MFA works constantly to become even more accessible and interesting. The museum's not-so-secret weapon in its quest is a powerful one: its magnificent collections. Every installation reflects a curatorial attitude that makes even those who go in with a feeling of obligation leave with a sense of discovery and wonder. That includes children, who can launch a scavenger hunt, admire the mummies, or participate in family-friendly programs scheduled year-round.

The MFA is especially noted for its **Impressionist paintings** ★★★ (including dozens of Monets), Asian and Old Kingdom Egyptian collections, classical art, Buddhist temple, and medieval sculpture and tapestries. The American and European paintings and sculpture are a remarkable assemblage of timeless works that may seem as familiar as the face in the mirror or as unexpected as a comet. There are also magnificent holdings of prints, photography, furnishings, and decorative arts, including the finest collection of Paul Revere silver in the world. The museum has two restaurants, a cafe, and a cafeteria. Pick up a floor plan at the information desk, or take a free **guided tour** (weekdays except Mon holidays at 10:30am and 1:30pm; Wed at 6:15pm; and Sat at 10:30am and 1pm).

None of this comes cheap: The MFA's admission fees are among the highest in the country. A Boston CityPass (see the introduction to this section) is a great deal if you plan to visit enough of the other included attractions.

Tips: The Huntington Avenue entrance is usually much less busy than the West Wing lobby—though farther from the gift shop, restaurants, and garage. To use it, walk back along Huntington Avenue when you leave the T, enter from the driveway, and stop to take in the John Singer Sargent murals in the rotunda.

A $500-million expansion project began in 2005 and is expected to last 5 years. While construction proceeds, the museum is rearranging some collections and closing some exhibition spaces. Check ahead before visiting if you have your heart set on seeing a particular work of art.

465 Huntington Ave. © **617/267-9300.** www.mfa.org. Admission $15 adults, $13 seniors and students when entire museum is open ($13 and $11, respectively, when only West Wing is open); $6.50 children under 18 on school days before 3pm, otherwise free. Admission good for 2 visits within 10 days. Voluntary contribution ($15 suggested) Wed 4–9:45pm. Surcharges may apply for special exhibitions. Free admission for museum shop, library, restaurants, and auditoriums. Entire museum Sat–Tues 10am–4:45pm; Wed 10am–9:45pm; Thurs–Fri 10am–5pm. West Wing only Thurs–Fri 5–9:45pm. T: Green Line E to Museum or Orange Line to Ruggles.

Museum of Science ★★★ Kids For the ultimate pain-free educational experience, head to the Museum of Science. The demonstrations, experiments, and interactive displays introduce facts and concepts so effortlessly that everyone learns something. Take a couple of hours or a whole day to explore the permanent and temporary exhibits, most of them hands-on and all of them great fun. Among the hundreds of exhibits, you might find out how much you'd weigh on the moon, battle urban traffic (in a computer model), or climb into a space module. Activity centers focus on fields of interest—natural history (with live animals), computers, and the human body—as well as interdisciplinary approaches. **Investigate!** teaches visitors to think like scientists, analyzing questions through activities such as sifting through an archaeological dig. **Science in the Park** uses familiar tools such as playground equipment and skateboards to look at Newtonian physics.

The separate-admission theaters are worth planning for, even if you're skipping the exhibits. Buy all your tickets at once, not only because it's cheaper but also because shows sometimes sell out. Tickets are for sale in person and, subject to a service charge, over the phone and online. The **Mugar Omni Theater** ★★★, which shows IMAX movies on a five-story screen, is an intense experience. The **Charles Hayden Planetarium** ★★ takes you into space with daily star shows as well as shows on special topics that change several times a year. On weekends, rock-music laser shows take over. Science Park, off O'Brien Hwy. on bridge between Boston and Cambridge. ✆ **617/723-2500.** www.mos.org. Admission to exhibit halls $15 adults, $13 seniors, $12 children 3–11. Mugar Omni Theater, Hayden Planetarium, or laser shows $9 adults, $8 seniors, $7 children 3–11. Discounted combination tickets available. July 5 to Labor Day Sat–Thurs 9am–7pm, Fri 9am–9pm; day after Labor Day to July 4 Sat–Thurs 9am–5pm, Fri 9am–9pm. T: Green Line to Science Park.

New England Aquarium ★ Kids This entertaining complex is home to more than 15,000 fish and aquatic mammals. At busy times, it seems to contain at least that many people—try to make this your first stop of the day, especially on weekends. You'll want to spend at least half a day, and afternoon crowds can make getting around painfully slow. Also consider buying a Boston CityPass (p. 113); it allows you to skip the ticket line. The **Simons IMAX Theatre** ★★★, which has its own hours and admission fees, is worth planning ahead for, too. It shows 3-D films that concentrate on the natural world.

The focal point of the main building is the four-story, 200,000-gallon **Giant Ocean Tank.** It holds a replica of a Caribbean coral reef, a vast assortment of sea creatures, and, twice a day, scuba divers who feed the sharks. Other exhibits focus on freshwater and tropical specimens, the Aquarium Medical Center, denizens of the Amazon, a wide variety of jellyfish, and the ecology of Boston Harbor. The hands-on **Edge of the Sea** exhibit contains a tide pool with sea stars, sea urchins, and horseshoe crabs. Discounts are available when you combine a visit to the aquarium with an IMAX film or a whale-watch (see "Organized Tours," below).

Central Wharf. ✆ **617/973-5200.** www.newenglandaquarium.org. Admission $18 adults, $10 children 3–11. Free admission for outdoor exhibits, cafe, and gift shop. July to Labor Day Mon–Thurs 9am–6pm, Fri–Sun and holidays 9am–7pm; day after Labor Day to June Mon–Fri 9am–5pm, Sat–Sun and holidays 9am–6pm. Simons IMAX Theatre: ✆ **866/815-4629** or 617/973-5206. Tickets $9.50 adults, $7.50 children 3–11. Daily 10am–9pm. T: Blue Line to Aquarium.

THE FREEDOM TRAIL ★★★

A line of red paint or red brick down the center of the sidewalk, the 2½-mile Freedom Trail links 16 historic sights. Markers identify the stops, and plaques point the way from one to the next. The trail begins at **Boston Common,** where the Information Center, 146 Tremont St., distributes pamphlets that describe a self-guided tour.

The Freedom Trail Foundation (✆ **617/357-8300;** www.thefreedomtrail.org) rents hand-held digital audio players, for use with or without headphones, that allow visitors to take a narrated tour of the trail at their own pace. The 2-hour narrative includes interviews, sound effects, and music. Players rent for $15; they're available at the Boston Common Visitor Center and can be dropped off there or at several other sites.

You can also explore the **Black Heritage Trail** ★★ from here. Two-hour guided tours start at the **Robert Gould Shaw Memorial,** on Beacon Street across from the State House. They're available Monday through Saturday from Memorial Day to Labor Day and by request at other times; contact the visitor center (✆ **617/742-5415;** www.nps.gov/boaf) for starting times or to make a reservation. Or go on your own, using a brochure (available at the Museum of Afro-American History and

THE TRAVELOCITY GUARANTEE

...THAT SAYS EVERYTHING YOU BOOK WILL BE RIGHT, OR WE'LL WORK WITH OUR TRAVEL PARTNERS TO MAKE IT RIGHT, RIGHT AWAY.

To drive home the point, we're going to use the word "right" in every single sentence.

Let's get right to it. Right to the meat! Only Travelocity guarantees everything about your booking will be right, or we'll work with our travel partners to make it right, right away. Right on!

Here's a picture taken smack dab right in the middle of Antigua, where the Guarantee also covers you.

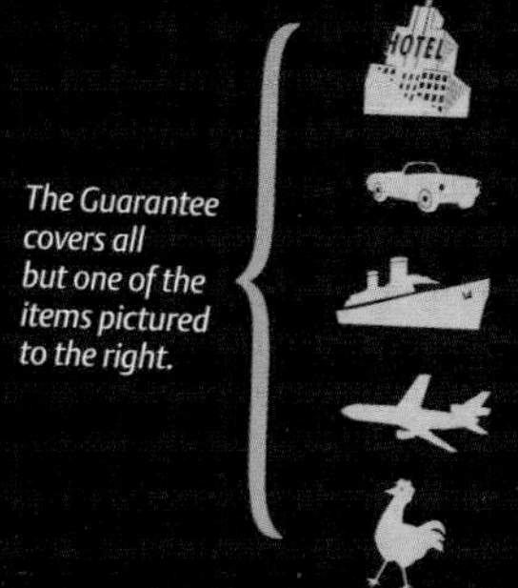

The Guarantee covers all but one of the items pictured to the right.

For example, what if the ocean view you booked actually looks out at a downright ugly parking lot? You'd be right to call – we're there for you. And no one in their right mind would be pleased to learn the rental car place has closed and left them stranded. Call Travelocity and we'll help get you back on the right track.

Now, you may be thinking, "Yeah, right, I'm so sure." That's OK; you have the right to remain skeptical. That is until we mention help is always right around the corner. Call us right off the bat, knowing our customer service reps are there for you 24/7. Righting wrongs. Left and right.

Now if you're guessing there are some things we can't control, like the weather, well you're right. But we can help you with most things – to get all the details in righting,* visit travelocity.com/guarantee.

*Sorry, spelling things right is one of the few things not covered under the Guarantee.

I'd give my right arm for a guarantee like this, although I'm glad I don't have to.

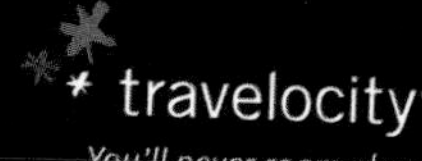

The Freedom Trail

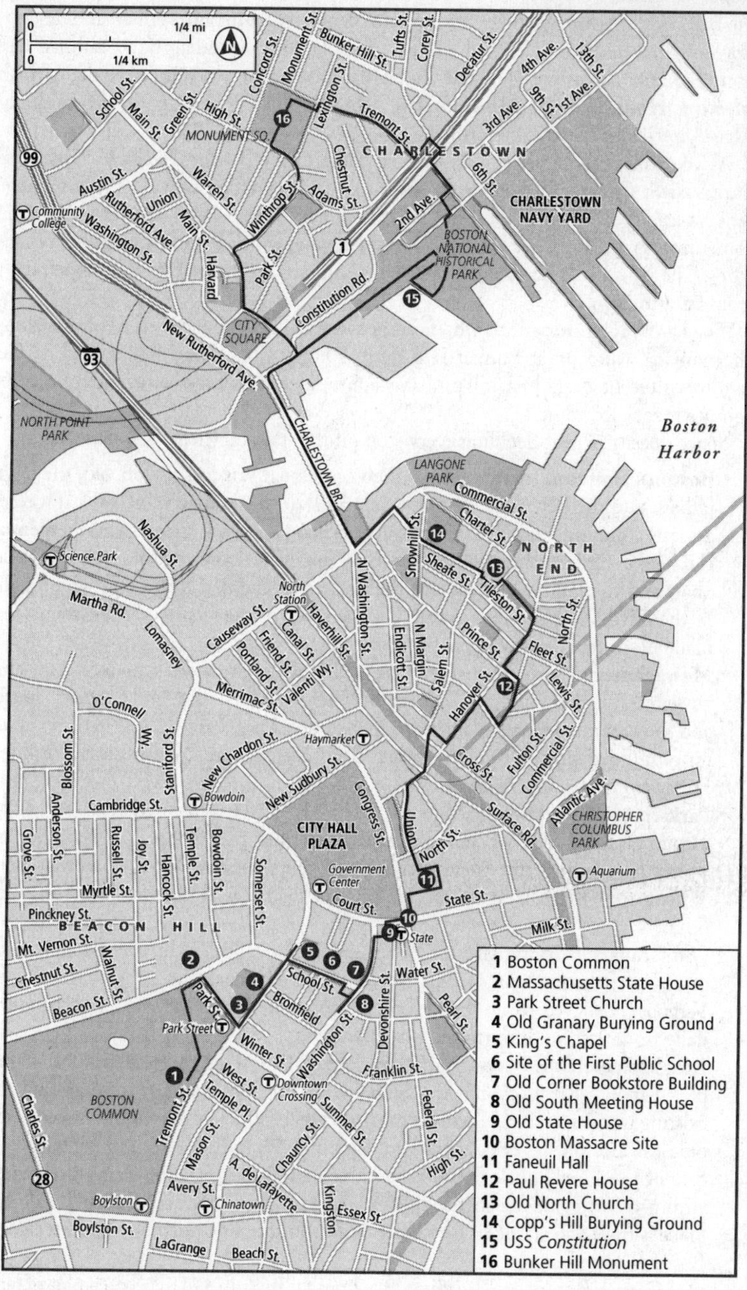

1 Boston Common
2 Massachusetts State House
3 Park Street Church
4 Old Granary Burying Ground
5 King's Chapel
6 Site of the First Public School
7 Old Corner Bookstore Building
8 Old South Meeting House
9 Old State House
10 Boston Massacre Site
11 Faneuil Hall
12 Paul Revere House
13 Old North Church
14 Copp's Hill Burying Ground
15 USS Constitution
16 Bunker Hill Monument
CHARLESTOWN
CHARLESTOWN NAVY YARD
BOSTON NATIONAL HISTORICAL PARK
MONUMENT SQ.
CITY SQUARE
NORTH POINT PARK
LANGONE PARK
NORTH END
Boston Harbor
CITY HALL PLAZA
BEACON HILL
CHRISTOPHER COLUMBUS PARK
BOSTON COMMON
CHARLESTOWN BR.

the Boston Common and State Street visitor centers) that includes a map and descriptions of the buildings. The trail includes stations on the underground railroad and homes of famous citizens. The only stops that are open to the public are the **African Meeting House** and the **Abiel Smith School,** which make up the **Museum of Afro-American History** (p. 116).

As you follow the Freedom Trail, you'll come to the **Boston National Historical Park Visitor Center,** 15 State St. (✆ **617/242-5642;** www.nps.gov/bost). From here, rangers lead free tours of the heart of the trail from mid-April to November (and sometimes in the winter). An audiovisual show provides basic information on the stops. The wheelchair-accessible center has restrooms and a bookstore. It's open daily from 9am to 5pm.

The hard-core history fiend who peers at every artifact and reads every plaque along the trail will wind up at Bunker Hill some 4 hours later, weary but rewarded. The family with restless children will probably appreciate the enforced efficiency of the 90-minute ranger-led tour.

Space doesn't permit detailing every stop on the trail, but here's a concise listing:

- **Boston Common.** In 1634, when their settlement was just 4 years old, the town fathers paid the Rev. William Blackstone £30 for this property. In 1640, it was set aside as common land. Be sure to stop at Beacon and Park streets, where a **memorial** ★★★ designed by Augustus Saint-Gaudens celebrates Col. Robert Gould Shaw and the Union Army's 54th Massachusetts Colored Regiment, who fought in the Civil War. You may remember the story of the first American army unit made up of free black soldiers from the movie *Glory.*
- **Massachusetts State House** (✆ **617/727-3676;** www.sec.state.ma.us/trs and www.mass.gov/statehouse). Charles Bulfinch designed the "new" State House, and Gov. Samuel Adams laid the cornerstone of the state capitol in 1795. Free tours (guided and self-guided) leave from the second floor Monday through Friday from 10am to 3:30pm.
- **Park Street Church,** 1 Park St. (✆ **617/523-3383;** www.parkstreet.org). The plaque at the corner of Tremont Street describes this Congregational church's storied past. In July and August, it's open for tours Tuesday through Saturday from 9:30am to 3:30pm. Year-round Sunday services are at 8:30am, 11am, 4pm, and 6pm.
- **Old Granary Burying Ground.** This cemetery, established in 1660, contains the graves of Samuel Adams, Paul Revere, John Hancock, and the wife of Isaac Vergoose, believed to be the "Mother Goose" of nursery-rhyme fame. It's open daily from 9am to 5pm (until 3pm in winter).
- **King's Chapel,** 58 Tremont St. (✆ **617/227-2155;** www.kings-chapel.org). Completed in 1754, this church was built by erecting the granite edifice around the existing wooden chapel. The **burying ground** (1630), facing Tremont Street, is the oldest in Boston. It's open daily from 8am to 5:30pm (until 3pm in winter).
- **Site of the First Public School.** Founded in 1634, the school is commemorated with a colorful mosaic in the sidewalk on (of course) School Street. Inside the fence is the 1856 statue of **Benjamin Franklin,** the first portrait statue erected in Boston.
- **Old Corner Bookstore Building,** 3 School St. Built in 1718, it's on a plot of land that was once home to the religious reformer Anne Hutchinson.

- **Old South Meeting House,** 310 Washington St. (✆ **617/482-6439;** www.oldsouthmeetinghouse.org). Originally built in 1670 and replaced by the current structure in 1729, it was the starting point of the Boston Tea Party. It's open daily, April to October from 9:30am to 5pm, November to March from 10am to 4pm. Admission is $5 for adults, $4 for seniors, and $1 for children 6 to 18.
- **Old State House** ★, 206 Washington St. (✆ **617/720-1713;** www.bostonhistory.org). Built in 1713, it served as the seat of Colonial government in Massachusetts before the Revolution, and as the state capitol until 1797. It houses the Bostonian Society's fascinating **museum** of the city's history, open daily from 9am to 5pm. Admission is $5 for adults, $4 for seniors and students, and $1 for children 6 to 18.
- **Boston Massacre Site.** On a traffic island in State Street, across from the T station under the Old State House, a ring of cobblestones marks the place where the skirmish took place on March 5, 1770.
- **Faneuil Hall** ★ (✆ **617/242-5675;** www.ns.gov/bost). Built in 1742, and enlarged using a Charles Bulfinch design in 1805, it was a gift to the city from the merchant Peter Faneuil. National Park Service rangers give free 20-minute talks every half-hour from 9am to 5pm in the second-floor auditorium.
- **Paul Revere House** ★★★, 19 North Sq. (✆ **617/523-2338;** www.paulreverehouse.org). The oldest house in downtown Boston (built around 1680) presents history on a human scale. It's open April 15 through October daily from 9:30am to 5:15pm, November through April 14 from 9:30am to 4:15pm (closed Mon Jan–Mar). Admission is $3 for adults, $2.50 for seniors and students, and $1 for children 5 to 17.
- **Old North Church** ★, 193 Salem St. (✆ **617/523-6676;** www.oldnorth.com). Paul Revere saw a signal in this church's steeple and set out on his "midnight ride." Officially named Christ Church, this is the oldest church building in Boston (1723). It's open daily from 9am to 5pm; a $3 donation is requested. Free tours of the church begin every 15 minutes. The 50-minute behind-the-scenes tour ($8 adults, $5 children under 17) includes visits to the steeple and the crypt; it's available on weekdays and on weekend afternoons from June to mid-August, and the rest of the year by appointment. Reservations are recommended. Sunday services (Episcopal) are at 9 and 11am.
- **Copp's Hill Burying Ground,** off Hull Street. The second-oldest cemetery (1659) in the city, it contains the graves of Cotton Mather and Prince Hall, who established the first black Masonic lodge. It's open daily from 9am to 5pm (until 3pm in winter).
- **USS *Constitution*** ★★, Charlestown Navy Yard (✆ **617/242-5670;** www.oldironsides.com). Active-duty sailors in 1812 dress uniforms give free tours of "Old Ironsides." They begin every half-hour between 10am and 3:30pm in summer Tuesday through Sunday, and in winter Thursday through Sunday. The **USS**

Tips **Out to Sea**

A fun way to return to downtown from Charlestown is on the **ferry** that connects the Navy Yard to Long Wharf (near the Aquarium). It costs $1.50.

Constitution **Museum** ★ (✆ **617/426-1812;** www.ussconstitutionmuseum.org) is open daily, May through October 15 from 9am to 6pm, October 16 through April from 10am to 5pm. Admission is free; donations are encouraged.

- **Bunker Hill Monument** (✆ **617/242-5641;** www.nps.gov/bost), Charlestown. The 221-foot granite obelisk honors the memory of the men who died in the Battle of Bunker Hill on June 17, 1775. A punishing flight of 294 stairs leads to the top. National Park Service rangers staff the monument, which is usually open daily from 9am to 4:30pm. Admission is free.

HOUSE MUSEUMS

The most fascinating historic home in Boston is the **Paul Revere House** (p. 121). To see three other interesting residences, you must take a guided tour. Check ahead for open days and hours.

On Beacon Hill, you'll find two houses as notable for their Charles Bulfinch architecture as for their occupants. Tours of the 1796 **Otis House Museum** ★★, 141 Cambridge St. (✆ **617/227-3956;** www.spnea.org), home of a young lawyer who was later mayor of Boston, discuss post-Revolutionary social, business, and family life. Tours cost $8. The 1804 **Nichols House Museum** ★, 55 Mount Vernon St. (✆ **617/227-6993;** www.nicholshousemuseum.org), holds beautiful antique furnishings collected by several generations of the Nichols family. Admission is $7.

Nearby, in the Back Bay, the **Gibson House Museum,** 137 Beacon St. (✆ **617/267-6338;** www.thegibsonhouse.org), is a lavishly decorated 1859 brownstone that embodies the word "Victorian." Admission is $7.

PARKS & GARDENS

The best-known park in Boston is the spectacular **Public Garden** ★★★, bordered by Arlington, Boylston, Charles, and Beacon streets. Something lovely is in bloom at the country's first botanical garden at least half of the year. For 5 months, the lagoon is home to the celebrated **Swan Boats** (✆ **617/522-1966;** www.swanboats.com). The pedal-powered vessels—the attendants pedal, not the passengers—come out of hibernation on the Saturday before Patriot's Day (the third Mon of Apr). They operate in summer daily from 10am to 5pm; in spring daily from 10am to 4pm; and from Labor Day to mid-September Monday through Friday from noon to 4pm and Saturday and Sunday from 10am to 4pm. The 15-minute ride costs $2.50 for adults, $1.50 for seniors, and $1 for children under 16.

The most spectacular garden is the **Arnold Arboretum** ★★, 125 Arborway, Jamaica Plain (✆ **617/524-1718;** www.arboretum.harvard.edu). One of the oldest

---

Finds **Eyes in the Skies**

For a smashing view of the airport, the harbor, and the South Boston waterfront, stroll along the water or Atlantic Avenue to Northern Avenue. On either side of this intersection are buildings with free observation areas. Be ready to show an ID. The first, on the 14th floor of Independence Wharf, 470 Atlantic Ave., is open daily from 11am to 5pm. Foster's Rotunda, on the ninth floor of 30 Rowes Wharf, in the Boston Harbor Hotel complex, is open Monday to Friday from 11am to 4pm.

---

parks in the United States, founded in 1872, it is open daily from sunrise to sunset. Admission is free. Its 265 acres contain more than 15,000 ornamental trees, shrubs, and vines from all over the world. Lilac Sunday, in May, is the only time picnicking is allowed. To get here, take the Orange Line to Forest Hills and follow signs to the entrance.

ORGANIZED TOURS

WALKING TOURS ★★ From May to October, the nonprofit **Boston by Foot** ★★ (✆ **617/367-2345,** or 617/367-3766 for recorded info; www.bostonbyfoot.com), conducts excellent historical and architectural tours that focus on neighborhoods or themes. The rigorously trained volunteer guides encourage questions. Buy tickets ($10 adults, $8 children 6–12; Boston Underfoot $12 per person) from the guide; reservations are not required. The 90-minute tours take place rain or shine.

The **Society for the Preservation of New England Antiquities** (✆ **617/227-3956;** www.spnea.org) offers a fascinating tour that describes life in the mansions and garrets of Beacon Hill in 1800. "Magnificent and Modest" ($12) starts at the Otis House Museum, 141 Cambridge St., at 11am on Saturdays from mid-May to October. The price includes a tour of the Otis House; reservations are recommended.

The **Boston Park Rangers** (✆ **617/635-7383;** www.ci.boston.ma.us/parks) offer free guided walking tours. The best-known focus is the **Emerald Necklace,** a loop of green spaces designed by pioneering landscape architect Frederick Law Olmsted. They include Boston Common, the Public Garden, the Commonwealth Avenue Mall, the Muddy River in the Fenway, Olmsted Park, Jamaica Pond, the Arnold Arboretum, and Franklin Park. Call for schedules.

The nonprofit **Boston History Collaborative** (✆ **617/350-0358;** www.bostonhistorycollaborative.org) coordinates several heritage trails. Presented as guided and self-guided walking tours, longer excursions by bus and boat, and information-packed websites, they focus on maritime history (www.bostonbysea.org), immigration (www.bostonfamilyhistory.net), literary history (www.Lit-Trail.org), and inventions (www.innovationodyssey.com).

TROLLEY TOURS Because Boston is so pedestrian friendly, a trolley tour isn't the best choice for the able-bodied and unencumbered making a long visit. But if you're short on time, unable to walk long distances, or traveling with children, a trolley tour can be worth the money. The narrated tour can give you an overview before you focus on specific attractions, or you can use your all-day pass to hit as many places as possible in 8 hours or so.

The various companies cover the major attractions and offer informative narratives in their 90- to 120-minute tours. Most offer free reboarding if you want to visit the sites. Tickets cost $22 to $29 for adults, $15 or less for children (subject to fuel surcharges). Boarding spots are at hotels, historic sites, and tourist information centers. Each company paints its cars a different color. They include orange-and-green **Old Town Trolley Tours** (✆ **617/269-7150;** www.trolleytours.com); **Beantown Trolleys** (✆ **800/343-1328** or 617/720-6342; www.grayline.com), which say "Gray Line" but are red; and silver **CityView Trolleys** (✆ **617/363-7899;** www.cityviewtrolleys.com). The **Discover Boston Trolley Tours** (✆ **617/742-1440;** www.discoverbostontours.com) vehicle is white; its narration is available translated into Japanese, Spanish, French, German, and Italian.

Kids Boston by Duck

The most unusual and enjoyable way to see Boston is with **Boston Duck Tours** ★★★ (✆ **800/226-7442** or 617/267-DUCK; www.bostonducktours.com). The tours, offered from April to November, are pricey but great fun. Sightseers board a "duck," a reconditioned World War II amphibious landing craft, behind the Prudential Center on Huntington Avenue or at the Museum of Science. The 80-minute narrated tour begins with a quick but comprehensive jaunt around the city. Then the duck lumbers down a ramp, splashes into the Charles River, and takes a spin around the basin. Tickets cost $26 for adults, $23 for seniors and students, $17 for children 3 to 11, and $3 for children under 3. Tours run every 30 to 60 minutes from 9am to a half-hour before sunset. You can buy tickets online or in person (at the Prudential Center, the Museum of Science, and Faneuil Hall). Try to buy same-day tickets early in the day, or ask about the limited number of tickets available 5 days in advance. Reservations are not accepted (except for groups of more than 19). No tours December through March.

SIGHTSEEING CRUISES ★★ The season runs from April to October, with spring and fall offerings often restricted to weekends. Check websites for discount coupons before you leave home. If you're prone to seasickness, check the size of the vessel (larger equals more comfortable) before buying tickets.

Boston Harbor Cruises, 1 Long Wharf (✆ **877/733-9425** or 617/227-4321; www.bostonharborcruises.com), is the largest company. Ninety-minute historic sightseeing cruises, which tour the Inner and Outer harbors, depart daily at 11am, 1pm, 3pm, and 6 or 7pm (the sunset cruise), with extra excursions at busy times. Tickets are $18 for adults, $16 for seniors, and $13 for children 4 to 12; sunset-cruise tickets are $2 more. The 45-minute USS *Constitution* cruise takes you around the Inner Harbor and docks at the Charlestown Navy Yard so you can visit Old Ironsides. Tours leave Long Wharf hourly from 10:30am to 4:30pm, and on the hour from the Navy Yard from 11am to 5pm. Tickets are $12 for adults, $11 for seniors, and $9 for children.

Massachusetts Bay Lines (✆ **617/542-8000;** www.massbaylines.com) offers 55-minute harbor tours. Cruises leave Rowes Wharf on the hour from 11am to 6pm (until 5pm after Labor Day); the price is $12 for adults, $9 for children 5 to 12 and seniors. Children under 5 are free. The 90-minute sunset cruise ($17 for adults, $13 for children and seniors) leaves at 7pm (6pm after Labor Day).

The **Charles Riverboat Company** (✆ **617/621-3001;** www.charlesriverboat.com; T: Green Line to Lechmere) offers 60-minute narrated cruises around the lower Charles River basin. Boats leave the CambridgeSide Galleria mall six times a day daily from June to August and on weekends in May and September. Sunset cruises run daily; call for times. Tickets (cash only) cost $12 for adults, $10 for seniors, and $6 for children 2 to 12.

WHALE-WATCHING ★★ For information on Cape Ann excursions, see "A Whale of an Adventure," in chapter 5.

The **New England Aquarium** (p. 118) runs whale-watching trips (✆ **617/973-5206**) daily from May to mid-October and on weekends in April and late

October. They travel several miles out to Stellwagen Bank, the feeding ground for whales as they migrate from Newfoundland to Provincetown. Allow 3½ to 5 hours. Tickets are $33 for adults; $30 for seniors, college students, and youths 12 to 18; and $26 for children 3 to 11. Children must be at least 3 years old and 30 inches tall. Reservations are strongly recommended; you can also buy tickets online.

With its onboard exhibits and vast experience, the Aquarium offers the best whale-watches in Boston. If they're booked, try **Boston Harbor Cruises** (✆ **617/227-4321;** www.bostonharborcruises.com), which has a high-speed catamaran, or **Massachusetts Bay Lines** (✆ **617/542-8000;** www.massbaylines.com).

ESPECIALLY FOR KIDS

Destinations with something for every family member include **Faneuil Hall Marketplace** (✆ **617/523-1300**) and the **Museum of Fine Arts** (✆ **617/267-9300**), which offers special weekend and after-school programs. Hands-on exhibits and large-format films are the headliners at the **New England Aquarium** (✆ **617/973-5200**) and the **Museum of Science** (✆ **617/723-2500**). A **Red Sox game** (see "Spectator Sports," later in this chapter) is another sure-fire kid pleaser.

The allure of seeing people the size of ants draws young visitors to the **Prudential Center Skywalk** (✆ **617/236-3318**). They can see actual ants—though they might prefer dinosaurs—at the Museum of Comparative Zoology, part of the **Harvard Museum of Natural History** (✆ **617/495-3045;** see "Exploring Cambridge," below).

Older children who have studied American history will enjoy a visit to the **John F. Kennedy Library and Museum** (✆ **617/929-4523**). Middle-schoolers who enjoyed Esther Forbes's *Johnny Tremain* might get a kick out of the **Paul Revere House** (✆ **617/523-2338**). Young visitors who have read Robert McCloskey's children's classic *Make Way for Ducklings* will relish a visit to the **Public Garden,** as will fans of E. B. White's *The Trumpet of the Swan,* who certainly will want to ride on the **Swan Boats.** Considerably less tame and much longer are **whale-watches** (see "Organized Tours," above, and "A Whale of an Adventure," in chapter 5); **sightseeing cruises** fall somewhere in the middle.

The **Boston Tea Party Ship & Museum** (✆ **617/338-1773;** www.bostonteapartyship.com) closed after a fire in late 2001. It's currently renovating, expanding, and planning to reopen in 2007. It makes an entertaining stop on the way to or from the Children's Museum.

The walking-tour company **Boston by Foot** ★★ (✆ **617/367-2345,** or 617/367-3766 for recorded info; www.bostonbyfoot.com) has a special program, **Boston by Little Feet,** geared to children 6 to 12. The 1-hour walk gives a child's-eye view of the architecture along the Freedom Trail and of Boston's role in the American Revolution. Children must be accompanied by an adult. Tours ($8 per person) run May through October and meet at the statue of Samuel Adams on the Congress Street side of Faneuil Hall, Saturday at 10am, Sunday at 2pm, and Monday at 10am, rain or shine.

Boston Children's Museum ★★ *Kids* A delightful destination for kids under 11, the Children's Museum is great fun for adults, too. Children can stick with the family or wander on their own. The centerpiece of the original building, a renovated warehouse, is a two-story-high maze that incorporates motor skills and problem-solving. The hands-on exhibits include, among many others, **Grandparents' Attic,** a souped-up version of dress-up; physical experiments (such as creating giant soap bubbles); and **Boats Afloat,** which has an 800-gallon play tank and a replica of the bridge of a working boat. A special room, **Playspace,** is packed with toys and activities for children under 4 and their caregivers. Check ahead for information on traveling exhibitions, participatory plays, and other special programs.

Note: The museum is scheduled to close from January through March 2007 to allow an expansion project to proceed as quickly as possible. If you plan to visit within a month or two of the closure, check ahead to make sure the museum is open and on a regular schedule.

300 Congress St. (Museum Wharf). ✆ **617/426-8855.** www.bostonkids.org. Admission $9 adults, $7 seniors and children 2–15, $2 children age 1, free for children under 1; Fri 5–9pm $1 for all. Sat–Thurs 10am–5pm; Fri 10am–9pm. T: Red Line to South Station. Walk north on Atlantic Ave. 1 block (past Federal Reserve Bank), turn right onto Congress St., walk 2 blocks (across bridge). Call for information on discounted parking.

6 Exploring Cambridge

Harvard Square ★★ is a people-watching paradise of students, instructors, commuters, shoppers, and sightseers. Restaurants and stores pack the three streets that radiate from the center of the square and the streets that intersect them. On weekend afternoons and evenings year-round, you'll hear music and see street performers. To get away from the urban bustle, stroll down to the paved paths along the Charles River.

From Boston, take the Red Line toward Alewife. In Cambridge, the subway stops at Kendall/MIT, and Central, Harvard, and Porter squares. If you're staying in or visiting the Back Bay, a longer and more colorful route is the no. 1 bus (Harvard–Dudley), which runs along Mass. Ave.

By car from Boston, follow Mass. Ave., or take Storrow Drive along the south bank of the river to the Harvard Square exit. Memorial Drive runs along the north side of the river near MIT, Central Square, and Harvard. Traffic in and around Harvard Square is almost as bad as in downtown Boston. Once you get to Cambridge, park the car and walk.

HARVARD UNIVERSITY

Harvard is the oldest college in the country, and if you suggest aloud that it's not the best, you may encounter the attitude that inspired the saying, "You can always tell a Harvard man, but you can't tell him much." The university encompasses the college and 10 graduate and professional schools in more than 400 buildings around Boston and Cambridge. Free student-led tours of the main campus leave from the **Events & Information Center,** in Holyoke Center, 1350 Mass. Ave. (✆ **617/495-1573**), during the school year twice a day weekdays and once on Saturday (except during vacations), and during the summer four times a day Monday through Saturday. Call for exact times; reservations aren't necessary. You're also free to wander on your own. The Events & Information Center has maps, illustrated booklets, and self-guided walking-tour directions. You might want to check out the university's website, www.harvard.edu.

Harvard Museum of Natural History and Peabody Museum of Archaeology & Ethnology ★ *Kids* These fascinating museums house the university's collections of items and artifacts related to the natural world. The world-famous academic resource offers interdisciplinary programs and exhibitions that tie in elements of all the associated fields. On weekends, staffed "Investigation Stations" help visitors learn through hands-on activities. You'll certainly find something interesting here, be it a

Harvard Square & Environs

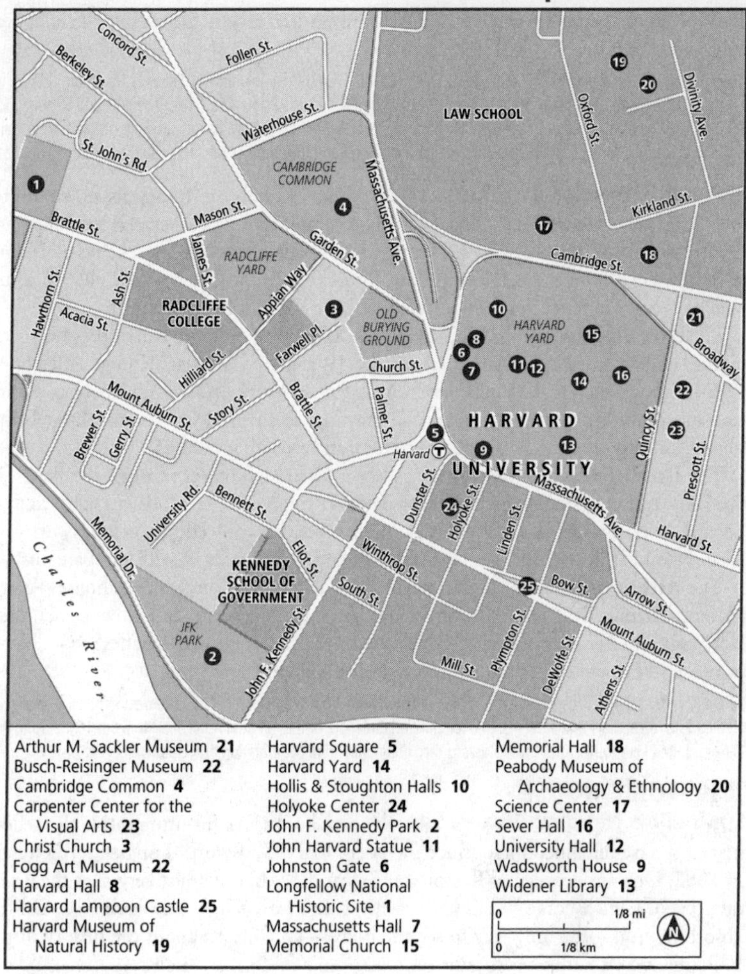

dinosaur skeleton, a hunk of meteorite, a Native American artifact, or the world-famous Glass Flowers.

The centerpiece of the **Botanical Museum,** the **Glass Flowers** ★★★ are 3,000 models of more than 840 plant species devised between 1887 and 1936 by the German father-and-son team of Leopold and Rudolph Blaschka. You may have heard about them, and you may be skeptical, but it's true: They look real. Children love the **Museum of Comparative Zoology** ★★, where dinosaurs share space with preserved and stuffed insects and animals that range in size from butterflies to giraffes. The **Peabody Museum** ★ boasts the **Hall of the North American Indian,** where artifacts representing 10 cultures are on display, and is home to the only surviving artifacts positively attributed to the Lewis and Clark expedition. The **Mineralogical Museum** is the most specialized but can be as interesting as the others, especially if gemstones hold your interest.

Museum of Natural History: 26 Oxford St. ✆ **617/495-3045.** www.hmnh.harvard.edu. Peabody Museum: 11 Divinity Ave. ✆ **617/496-1027.** www.peabody.harvard.edu. Admission to both $7.50 adults, $6.50 seniors and students, $5 children 3–18; free to all Sun until noon year-round and Wed 3–5pm Sept–May. Daily 9am–5pm. T: Red Line to Harvard. Cross Harvard Yard, keeping John Harvard statue on right, and turn right at Science Center. First left is Oxford St.

Harvard University Art Museums ★ The Harvard art museums house more than 200,000 works in three collections. The exhibit spaces also serve as teaching and research facilities. You can take a 1-hour guided tour of the Fogg weekdays at 11am, of the Busch-Reisinger weekdays at 1pm (both year-round), or of the Sackler at 2pm weekdays September through June, Wednesday only in July and August.

The **Fogg Art Museum,** 32 Quincy St., near Broadway, centers on an impressive 16th-century Italian stone courtyard. Each of the 19 galleries holds something different—17th-century Dutch and Flemish landscapes, 19th-century British and American paintings and drawings, French paintings and drawings from the 18th century through the Impressionist period, contemporary sculpture, and changing exhibits.

The **Busch-Reisinger Museum,** in Werner Otto Hall (enter through the Fogg), is the only museum in North America devoted to the art of northern and central Europe, specifically Germany. The early-20th-century collections include works by Klee, Feininger, Kandinsky, and artists and designers associated with the Bauhaus.

The **Arthur M. Sackler Museum,** 485 Broadway, at Quincy Street, houses Asian, ancient, Islamic, and Later Indian art. You'll see internationally renowned Chinese jades, superb Roman sculpture, Greek vases, Korean ceramics, Japanese woodblock prints, and Persian miniature paintings and calligraphy.

32 Quincy St. and 485 Broadway. ✆ **617/495-9400.** www.artmuseums.harvard.edu. Admission to all 3 museums $7.50 adults, $6 seniors and students, free for children under 18; free to all until noon Sat. Mon–Sat 10am–5pm; Sun 1–5pm. T: Red Line to Harvard. Cross Harvard Yard diagonally from the T station and cross Quincy St.

A HISTORIC HOUSE

Longfellow National Historic Site ★ The books and furniture inside the yellow mansion have remained intact since the poet Henry Wadsworth Longfellow died here in 1882. During the siege of Boston in 1775 and 1776, the house served as the headquarters of Gen. George Washington, with whom Longfellow was fascinated. On the absorbing tour—the only way to see the house—you'll learn about the history of the building and its famous occupants.

105 Brattle St. ✆ **617/876-4491.** www.nps.gov/long. Guided tours $3 adults, free for children under 17. Call ahead to confirm hours and tour times. Apr–May Tues–Sat 10am–4:30pm, May–Oct Wed–Sun 10am–4:30pm. Tours 10:30am, 11:30am, 1, 2, 3, and 4pm. Closed Nov–Mar. T: Red Line to Harvard, then follow Brattle St. about 7 blocks; house is on the right.

A CELEBRATED CEMETERY

Dedicated in 1831, **Mount Auburn Cemetery** ★, 580 Mt. Auburn St. (✆ **617/547-7105;** www.mountauburn.org), was the first of America's rural, or garden, cemeteries. Since the day it opened, Mount Auburn has been a popular place to retreat and reflect. The graves of Henry Wadsworth Longfellow, Oliver Wendell Holmes, Mary Baker Eddy, Winslow Homer, and many other prominent New Englanders are here. In season, you'll see gorgeous flowering trees and shrubs. The cemetery is open daily from 8am to 5pm October through April, 8am to 7pm May through September; there is no admission fee. Pets, picnicking, and jogging are not allowed. Bus route nos. 71 and

73 start at Harvard station and stop near the gates; they run frequently on weekdays, less often on weekends. From Harvard Square by car (5 min.) or on foot (30 min.), take Mount Auburn Street or Brattle Street west; just after they intersect, the gate is on the left. Stop at the office to pick up brochures and a map or to rent a tour on tape or CD ($7; a $15 deposit is required), which you can play in your car or on a portable player. The **Friends of Mount Auburn Cemetery** conducts workshops and coordinates walking tours; through June 2007, keep an eye out for events related to the cemetery's 175th anniversary. Call the main number for topics, schedules, and fees.

A STROLL AROUND CAMBRIDGE

To explore Harvard and the surrounding area, begin your walk in **Harvard Square.** Town and gown meet at this lively intersection, where you'll get a taste of the improbable mix of people drawn to the crossroads of Cambridge.

Start at the Harvard T station, with the **Harvard Coop** at your back. Walk half a block, crossing Dunster Street. To your right is **Holyoke Center,** an administration building designed by the Spanish architect Josep Luis Sert, the dean of the university's Graduate School of Design from 1953 to 1969, and a disciple of Le Corbusier.

Across the street is **Wadsworth House,** 1341 Mass. Ave., a yellow wood structure built in 1726 as a residence for Harvard's fourth president. Its claim to fame is a classic: George Washington slept here. Turn left and follow the outside of the brick wall along Mass. Ave. to another T entrance. Pass through **Johnston Gate,** which guards the oldest part of **Harvard Yard.** "The Yard" was just a patch of grass with grazing animals when Harvard College was established in 1636 to train young men for the ministry. The Continental Army, under Washington's command, spent the winter of 1775 to 1776 here.

With Johnston Gate at your back, to your right is **Massachusetts Hall** (1720), the university's oldest surviving building. It houses the president's office and rooms for first-year students. To your left is **Harvard Hall** (1765), a classroom building. The matching side-by-side buildings behind Harvard Hall are **Hollis** and **Stoughton halls.** Hollis dates to 1763 and has been home to many students who went on to great fame, among them Ralph Waldo Emerson, Henry David Thoreau, and Charles Bulfinch.

Across the Yard is **University Hall,** the college's main administration building, designed by Bulfinch and constructed in 1812 and 1813. It's the backdrop of the **John Harvard statue** ★★, one of the most photographed objects in the Boston area. Designed by Daniel Chester French in 1884, it's known as the "Statue of Three Lies" because the inscription reads "John Harvard—Founder—1638." In fact, the college was established in 1636; Harvard (one of many people involved) wasn't the founder, but donated money and his library; and this isn't John Harvard, anyway. No portraits of him survive, so the model was, according to various accounts, either his nephew or a student. Walk over to the statue and join the throng of tourists posing for pictures with the benevolent-looking gentleman.

Walk around University Hall into the adjoining quadrangle; you're leaving the "Old Yard" for the "New Yard," where commencement and other university-wide ceremonies take place. On your right is **Widener Library,** the centerpiece of the world's largest university library system. It was built in 1913 as a memorial to Harry Elkins Widener, a 1907 Harvard graduate who died when the *Titanic* sank in 1912. Legend has it that he was unable to swim 50 yards to a lifeboat, and his mother donated $2 million for the library on the condition that every undergraduate pass a 50-yard swimming test.

Facing the library is **Memorial Church,** built in 1931 and topped with a tower and weather vane 197 feet tall. You're welcome to look around this Georgian Revival–style edifice unless services are going on. The entrance is on the left. The south wall, toward the Yard, lists the names of Harvard graduates who died in World Wars I and II, Korea, and Vietnam. One is Joseph P. Kennedy, Jr., '38, the president's older brother.

Continue across the Yard onto Quincy Street. To your right is the curvilinear **Carpenter Center for the Visual Arts,** 24 Quincy St. Designed by the Swiss-French architect **Le Corbusier** and completed in 1963, it's the only Le Corbusier building in North America.

Re-enter the Yard, pass Memorial Church, and turn right. Follow the path out of the Yard to the **Science Center,** Zero Oxford St. The 10-story monolith supposedly resembles a Polaroid camera. (Edwin H. Land, founder of Cambridge-based Polaroid Corporation, was one of its main benefactors.) Sert also designed this structure, which was built from 1970 to 1972.

To your right as you face the Science Center is **Memorial Hall,** a Victorian structure built from 1870 to 1874. The hall of memorials (enter from Kirkland or Cambridge sts.) is a transept where you can read the names of the Harvard men who died fighting for the Union during the Civil War—but not those who died for the Confederacy.

With the Science Center behind you and "Mem Hall" to your left, turn right, and follow the walkway for the equivalent of a block and a half as it curves around to the right. The **Harvard Law School** campus is on your right. Carefully cross Mass. Ave. to **Cambridge Common.** Memorials and plaques dot this well-used plot of greenery and bare earth. Turn left and head back toward Harvard Square; after a block or so you'll walk near or over **horseshoes** embedded in the concrete. This is the path William Dawes, Paul Revere's fellow alarm-sounder, took from Boston to Lexington on April 18, 1775.

Turn right onto Garden Street and find **Christ Church,** Zero Garden St. The oldest church in Cambridge, it was designed by Peter Harrison of Newport, Rhode Island (also the architect of King's Chapel in Boston), and opened in 1761. Note the square wooden tower. Inside the vestibule you can still see bullet holes made by British muskets.

With the church at your back, turn right and return to Mass. Ave. Turn right again, then walk 2 blocks into the middle of the square and 1 more block on John F. Kennedy Street. Turn left onto Mount Auburn Street. Stay on the left side of the street as you cross Dunster, Holyoke, and Linden streets.

The corner of Mount Auburn and Linden streets is a good vantage point for viewing the **Harvard Lampoon Castle,** designed by Wheelwright & Haven in 1909. Listed on the National Register of Historic Places, this is the home of Harvard's undergraduate humor magazine, the *Lampoon.* The main tower looks like a face, with windows as the eyes, nose, and mouth, topped by what looks like a miner's hat.

Cross Mount Auburn Street and walk south (away from Holyoke Center) on Holyoke Street or Dunster Street to get a sense of some of the rest of the campus. Turn right on Winthrop Street or South Street, continue to John F. Kennedy Street, and turn left. Cross the street at some point, and follow it toward the Charles River, almost to Memorial Drive. On your right is **John F. Kennedy Park** and the adjacent Graduate School of Government. Walk away from the street to the fountain, engraved with excerpts from the president's speeches. This is an excellent place to take a break and plan the rest of your day.

7 Spectator Sports & Getting Outside

SPECTATOR SPORTS

Boston enjoys a well-deserved reputation as a great sports town. The New England Patriots (who play in suburban Foxboro) continued that tradition by winning the Super Bowl in 2002, 2004, and 2005, but that's not what anyone will remember about the turn of the 21st century. In 2004, the Boston Red Sox won the World Series, snapping an 86-year dry spell and making their already-rabid fan base even more obsessed.

BASEBALL In my opinion, no other experience in sports matches watching the **Red Sox** play at **Fenway Park** ★★★, which they do from April to early October, and later if they make the playoffs. The quirkiness of the oldest park in the major leagues (1912) only adds to the mystique. The team changed hands in 2002, and the new owners have invested so much in the existing structure—including building seats above the legendary left-field wall—that rumors of its impending demolition have quieted down.

The Fenway Park **ticket office** (✆ **877/REDSOX-9;** www.redsox.com) is at 4 Yawkey Way, off Brookline Avenue. Tickets go on sale in December; order early. Tickets are the most expensive in the majors—a few upper bleacher seats go for $12, but most are in the $23-to-$85 range. Forced to choose between tickets for a low-numbered grandstand section (say, 10 or below) and less expensive bleacher seats, go for the bleachers and the better view. Throughout the season, a limited number of standing-room tickets and (if you're lucky) returned tickets go on sale the day of the game. Take the Green Line B, C, or D to Kenmore or D to Fenway.

Tours (✆ **617/236-6666**) start on the hour from 9am to 4pm (or 3 hr. before game time, whichever is earlier) daily, year-round. There are no tours on holidays or before day games. The cost is $12 for adults, $11 for seniors, and $10 for children under 15.

BASKETBALL Sixteen NBA championship banners hang in TD Banknorth Garden, testimony to the history of the **Boston Celtics.** Unfortunately, the most recent is from 1986. The Celtics play from early October to April or May; when a top contender is visiting, you may have trouble getting tickets. Prices are as low as $10 for some games and top out at $150. For information, call **TD Banknorth Garden** (✆ **617/624-1000;** www.nba.com/celtics); for tickets, contact **Ticketmaster** (✆ **617/931-2000;** www.ticketmaster.com). To reach the Garden, take the Green or Orange Line to North Station. ***Note:*** Spectators may not bring any bags, including backpacks and briefcases, into the arena.

FOOTBALL The **New England Patriots** (✆ **800/543-1776;** www.patriots.com) were playing to sellout crowds even before they won the Super Bowl three times in 4 years. The Pats play from August to December or January at Gillette Stadium on Route 1 in Foxboro, about a 45-minute drive south of the city. Tickets sell out well in advance. Call or check the website for information on individual ticket sales and public-transit options.

HOCKEY The **Boston Bruins** are exciting but expensive to watch. Tickets often sell out early despite being among the priciest ($19–$155) in the league. For information, call **TD Banknorth Garden** (✆ **617/624-1000;** www.bostonbruins.com); for tickets, call **Ticketmaster** (✆ **617/931-2000;** www.ticketmaster.com). To reach the

Garden, take the Green or Orange Line to North Station. ***Note:*** Spectators may not bring any bags, including backpacks and briefcases, into the arena.

Economical fans will be pleasantly surprised by the quality of local **college hockey** ★. Even for sold-out games, standing-room tickets are usually available shortly before game time. Local teams include **Boston College,** Conte Forum, Chestnut Hill (© **617/552-3000**); **Boston University,** Agganis Arena, 928 Commonwealth Ave. (© **617/353-3838**); **Harvard University,** Bright Hockey Center, North Harvard Street, Allston (© **617/495-2211**); and **Northeastern University,** Matthews Arena, St. Botolph Street (© **617/373-4700**).

THE MARATHON Every year on Patriot's Day (the third Mon in Apr), the **Boston Marathon** ★★★ rules the roads from Hopkinton to Copley Square in Boston. An especially nice place to watch is tree-shaded Comm. Ave. between Kenmore Square and Mass. Ave., but you'll be in a crowd wherever you stand, particularly near the finish line in front of the Boston Public Library. For information about qualifying, contact the **Boston Athletic Association** (© **617/236-1652;** www.bostonmarathon.org).

ROWING In late October, the **Head of the Charles Regatta** ★ (© **617/868-6200;** www.hocr.org) attracts some 4,000 oarsmen and oarswomen. The largest crew event in the country draws hundreds of thousands of spectators who socialize and occasionally even watch the action.

GETTING OUTSIDE

The **Department of Conservation & Recreation** (www.state.ma.us/dcr) oversees activities on the state's public lands. (The DCR's Division of Urban Parks & Recreation replaced the Metropolitan District Commission, a name that survives on many signs.) The website describes properties and activities, and has a planning area to help you make the most of your time.

BEACHES The beaches in Boston proper are not worth the trouble. Boston Harbor water is not only bone-chilling, but also subject to being declared unsafe for swimming. If you want to swim, book a hotel with a pool. If you want the sand-between-your-toes experience, hit the beach on the North Shore or at Walden Pond in Concord. See chapter 5 for information on suburban beaches.

BIKING Even expert cyclists who feel comfortable with Boston's layout will be better off in Cambridge, which has bike lanes, or on the area's many bike paths. The 18-mile **Dr. Paul Dudley White Charles River Bike Path** follows the river from the Museum of Science to Watertown and back. You can enter and exit at many points along the way. Bikers share the path with lots of pedestrians, joggers, and in-line skaters. On warm-weather Sundays from 11am to 7pm, **Memorial Drive** from Central Square to west Cambridge is closed to cars.

State law requires that children under 12 wear helmets. Bicycles are forbidden on buses and the Green Line, and on other lines during rush hours.

Most rental shops charge around $5 per hour or $25 per day. They include **Back Bay Bicycles,** 366 Comm. Ave., near Mass. Ave. (© **617/247-2336;** www.backbaybicycles.com); **Boston Bicycle,** 842 Beacon St., about 3 blocks from Kenmore Square (© **617/236-0752**); and **Community Bicycle Supply,** 496 Tremont St., near East Berkeley Street (© **617/542-8623;** www.communitybicycle.com). Across the river, try **Cambridge Bicycle,** 259 Mass. Ave. (© **617/876-6555;** www.oldroads.com/cb.html),

Finds A Vacation in the Islands

Majestic ocean views, hiking trails, historic sights, rocky beaches, nature walks, campsites, and picnic areas abound in New England. The **Boston Harbor Islands** ★★ (✆ **617/223-8666;** www.bostonislands.com) have them all. Their unspoiled beauty makes a welcome break from the urban landscape, but they're not well known, even to many longtime Bostonians. Bring a sweater or jacket, and note that fresh water is available only on Georges Island. (Management strongly suggests that you bring your own.)

Thirty islands dot the Outer Harbor, and at least a half-dozen are open to the public. Ferries run to the **Georges Island,** home of Fort Warren (1834), which held Confederate prisoners during the Civil War. You can investigate on your own or take a ranger-led tour. The island has a visitor center, refreshment area, fishing pier, picnic area, and wonderful view of Boston's skyline. Allow at least half a day, longer if you plan to take the free water taxi to **Lovell, Peddocks, Bumpkin,** or **Grape Island,** all of which have picnic areas and campsites.

Harbor Express (✆ **617/222-6999;** www.harborexpress.com) serves Georges Island from Long Wharf and Fan Pier; the trip takes 45 minutes, and round-trip tickets are $10 to $12 for adults, $8 to $9 for seniors, and $7 for children 3 to 11. Cruises depart daily on the hour from 10am to 5pm in the summer, less frequently in the spring and fall. In the off season, check ahead for winter wildlife excursions (scheduled occasionally). Water taxis and admission to the islands are free.

The Boston Harbor Islands National Recreation Area (www.nps.gov/boha) is the focus of a public-private project designed to make the islands more interesting and accessible. For more information, visit the website, consult the staff at the **kiosk on Long Wharf,** or contact the **Friends of the Boston Harbor Islands** (✆ **617/740-4290;** www.fbhi.org).

near MIT. For more information, contact **MassBike** (✆ **617/542-2453;** www.massbike.org).

GOLF The **Massachusetts Golf Association** (✆ **800/356-2201** or 774/430-9100; www.mgalinks.org) represents more than 400 courses around the golf-mad state. Given a choice, play on a weekday, when you'll find lower prices and smaller crowds than on weekends.

One of the best public courses in the area, **Newton Commonwealth Golf Course,** 212 Kenrick St., Newton (✆ **617/630-1971;** www.sterlinggolf.com), is a challenging 18-hole Donald Ross design. It's 5,305 yards from the blue tees, par is 70, and greens fees are $28 weekdays, $35 weekends. Within the city limits is the legendary 6,009-yard **William J. Devine Golf Course,** in Franklin Park, Dorchester (✆ **617/265-4084**). As a Harvard student, Bobby Jones sharpened his game on the 18-hole, par-70 course. Greens fees are $26 weekdays, $34 weekends. Less challenging but with more of a neighborhood feel is 9-hole, par-35 **Fresh Pond Golf Course,** 691 Huron Ave., Cambridge (✆ **617/349-6282;** www.freshpondgolf.com). The 3,161-yard layout adjoins the Fresh Pond Reservoir (there's water on 4 holes) and charges $21, or $31 to go around twice, on weekdays; $25 and $37 on weekends.

GYMS The concierge at your hotel can recommend a health club. Hotels with good health clubs (see "Where to Stay," earlier in this chapter) include the Boston Harbor Hotel, the Four Seasons Hotel, the Hilton Boston Logan Airport, and the Royal Sonesta Hotel. The best combination of facilities and value is at the **Wang YMCA of Chinatown,** 8 Oak St. W., off Washington Street (✆ **617/426-2237**), close to downtown; or the **Central Branch YMCA,** 316 Huntington Ave. (✆ **617/536-7800**), near Symphony Hall. A day pass costs $10.

ICE-SKATING The rink at the Boston Common **Frog Pond** (✆ **617/635-2120**) is an extremely popular cold-weather destination. It's an open surface with an ice-making system and a clubhouse. Admission is $3 for adults and free for children under 14; skate rental costs $7 for adults, $5 for kids. Try to go on a weekday; huge crowds descend on weekends.

IN-LINE SKATING Unless you're confident of your ability and your knowledge of Boston traffic, stay off the streets. A favorite car-free spot is the **Esplanade,** between the Back Bay and the Charles River. It continues onto the bike path that runs to Watertown and back, but once you leave the Esplanade, the pavement in many spots is in disrepair. Your best bet is to wait for a spring, summer, or fall Sunday, when **Memorial Drive** in Cambridge closes to cars. It's a perfect surface. The **InLine Club of Boston** offers event and safety information on its website (www.sk8net.com).

Expect to pay about $15 for rentals. Try the **Beacon Hill Skate Shop,** 135 Charles St. S. (✆ **617/482-7400**), or one of the vendors who set up shop on Memorial Drive on warm-weather Sundays.

JOGGING The **Dr. Paul Dudley White Charles River Bike Path** (see "Biking," above) is the area's busiest jogging trail. It's so popular because it's car-free (except at intersections), scenic, and generally safe. The bridges along the river allow for circuits of various lengths, but be careful around abutments, where you can't see far ahead. Don't jog at night, and try not to go alone. Visit the DCR website (www.state.ma.us/dcr) to view a map that gives distances. If the river's not convenient, check with the concierge or desk staff at your hotel for a map with suggested routes.

SAILING The best deal in town is **Community Boating, Inc.,** 21 David Mugar Way, on the Esplanade (✆ **617/523-1038;** www.community-boating.org). It's open April through November, and the fleet includes 13- to 23-foot sailboats as well as windsurfers and kayaks. Visitors pay $100 for 2 days of unlimited use in the Charles River basin.

TENNIS Public courts are available throughout the city at no charge. Well-maintained courts near downtown that seldom get busy until after work are along the Southwest Corridor Park in the South End (there's a nice one near **W. Newton St.**) The courts on **Boston Common** and in **Charlesbank Park,** overlooking the river next to the bridge to the Museum of Science, are more crowded during the day.

8 Shopping

Boston-area shopping represents a tempting blend of classic and contemporary. Boston and Cambridge boast tiny boutiques and sprawling malls, esoteric bookshops and national chain stores, classy galleries and snazzy secondhand-clothing outlets.

Note: Massachusetts has no sales tax on clothing priced below $175 or on food. All other items are taxed at 5% (as are restaurant meals and takeout food). The state no longer prohibits stores from opening before noon on Sunday, but many still wait until noon or don't open at all—call ahead before setting out.

BACK BAY This is New England's premier shopping district. Dozens of upscale galleries, shops, and boutiques make **Newbury Street** ★★★ a world-famous destination. Nearby, an enclosed walkway across Huntington Avenue links **Copley Place** (✆ **617/375-4400**) and the **Shops at Prudential Center** (✆ **800/SHOP-PRU**). This is where you'll find the tony department stores **Barneys New York** (✆ **617/385-3300**), **Lord & Taylor** (✆ **617/262-6000**), **Neiman Marcus** (✆ **617/536-3660**), and **Saks Fifth Avenue** (✆ **617/262-8500**).

If you're passionate about art, set aside a couple of hours for strolling along Newbury Street. Besides being a prime location for upscale boutiques, it boasts an infinite variety of styles and media in the dozens of art galleries at street level and on the higher floors. (Remember to look up.) Most galleries are open Tuesday through Sunday from 10 or 11am to 5:30 or 6pm. For specifics, pick up a copy of the free monthly *Gallery Guide* at businesses along Newbury Street.

DOWNTOWN **Faneuil Hall Marketplace** (✆ **617/523-1300**) is the busiest attraction in Boston not only for its smorgasbord of food outlets, but also for its shops, boutiques, and pushcarts. Although it has more upscale chain outlets than only-in-Boston shops, it's a fun experience.

If the hubbub here is too much for you, stroll over to **Charles Street,** at the foot of Beacon Hill. A short but commercially dense (and picturesque) street, it's home to perhaps the best assortment of gift and antiques shops in the city. Be sure to check out the contemporary home accessories at **Koo De Kir,** 65 Chestnut St., just off Charles (✆ **617/723-8111;** www.koodekir.com); the well-edited selection at **Upstairs Downstairs Antiques,** 93 Charles St. (✆ **617/367-1950**), and the engagingly funky gifts at **Black Ink,** 101 Charles St. (✆ **617/723-3883**).

One of Boston's oldest shopping areas is **Downtown Crossing.** Now a traffic-free pedestrian mall along Washington, Winter, and Summer streets near Boston Common, it's home to **Macy's**; tons of smaller clothing, shoe, and music stores; food and merchandise pushcarts; and a branch of **Borders.** After the consolidation of the Macy's and Filene's chains and the shuttering of the Washington Street Barnes & Noble, Downtown Crossing had two big vacancies at press time. A constant since 1908 is **Filene's Basement** ★★★, 426 Washington St. (✆ **617/542-2011**). Although Macy's has replaced the original Filene's, the name survives in the Basement chain, which split off from the parent company years ago. The famed automatic markdown policy (25% off the already-discounted price after 2 weeks on the selling floor, up to 75% after 8 weeks) applies only here, at the flagship store. We happen to love this sort of thing, but you may find that battling the crowds isn't worth the payoff—the selling floors are pretty wild at busy times.

CAMBRIDGE The bookstores, boutiques, and T-shirt shops of **Harvard Square** lie about 15 minutes from downtown Boston by subway. Despite the neighborhood association's efforts, chain stores have swept across the Square. You'll find a mix of national and regional outlets, and more than a few persistent independent retailers. They include the delightful children's store **Calliope,** 33 Brattle St. (✆ **617/876-4149**); **Colonial Drug,** 49 Brattle St. (✆ **617/864-2222**), which stocks hard-to-find

Finds By the Book

Bookworms flock to Cambridge; Harvard Square in particular caters to general and specific audiences. Check out the basement of the **Harvard Book Store,** 1256 Mass. Ave. (✆ **800/542-READ** outside 617, or 617/661-1515; www.harvard.com), for great deals on remainders and used books. **Curious George Goes to WordsWorth,** 1 John F. Kennedy St. (✆ **617/498-0062;** www.curiousg.com), specializes in children's books, toys, and games. Jampacked shelves line the tiny **Grolier Poetry Book Shop,** 6 Plympton St. (✆ **617/547-4648**). Barnes & Noble runs the book operation at the **Harvard Coop,** 1400 Mass. Ave. (✆ **617/499-2000;** www.thecoop.com), which stocks textbooks, academic works, and a large general selection. One T stop away is the excellent independent shop **Porter Square Books,** in the Porter Square Shopping Center, 25 White St. (✆ **617/491-2220**).

In Boston, you'll find a huge selection of used and rare titles at the **Brattle Book Shop,** 9 West St. (✆ **800/447-9595** or 617/542-0210; www.brattlebookshop.com), near Downtown Crossing. Downtown Crossing has a **Borders,** 24 School St. (✆ **617/557-7188;** www.borders.com), and there's a **Barnes & Noble** (✆ **617/247-6959**) at the Shops at Prudential Center mall in the Back Bay. There's also a **Borders** (✆ **617/679-0887**) at the CambridgeSide Galleria mall.

perfume and other high-end cosmetics; and **Oona's,** 1210 Mass. Ave. (✆ **617/491-2654**), a trove of lovely "experienced" clothing and accessories.

For a less generic experience, walk along **Mass. Ave.** in either direction to the next T stop. The stroll takes about an hour. Heading north toward Porter Square, be sure to stop at **Joie de Vivre,** 1792 Mass. Ave. (✆ **617/864-8188**), a top-notch gift shop, and the retro home-accessories emporium **Abodeon,** 1731 Mass. Ave. (✆ **617/497-0137**). Going southeast to Central, pop into **Pearl Art & Craft Supplies,** 579 Mass. Ave. (✆ **617/547-6600**), an excellent link in the national discount chain.

And if you just can't manage without a trip to a mall, head to East Cambridge. Take the Green Line to Lechmere, or the Red Line to Kendall/MIT and the free shuttle bus to the **CambridgeSide Galleria,** 100 CambridgeSide Place (✆ **617/621-8666**).

9 Boston & Cambridge After Dark

For up-to-date entertainment listings, consult the "Sidekick" section of the daily *Boston Globe,* the "Edge" section of the Friday *Boston Herald,* or the Sunday arts sections of both papers. Three free publications, available at newspaper boxes around town, publish nightlife listings: the *Boston Phoenix,* the *Stuff@Night* (a *Phoenix* offshoot), and the *Improper Bostonian.* The *Phoenix* website (www.bostonphoenix.com) archives the paper's season preview issues; especially before a summer or fall visit, it's a worthwhile planning tool.

GETTING TICKETS Some companies and venues sell tickets over the phone or online; many will refer you to a ticket agency. The major agencies that serve Boston,

Ticketmaster (© **617/931-2000;** www.ticketmaster.com), **Next Ticketing** (© **617/423-NEXT;** www.nextticketing.com), and **Telecharge** (© **800/432-7250;** www.telecharge.com), calculate service charges per ticket, not per order. To avoid the fee—and possible losses if your plans change and you can't get your money back—visit the box office in person. If you wait until the day before or day of a performance, you'll sometimes have access to tickets that were held back and have just gone on sale.

DISCOUNT TICKETS Visit a **BosTix** (© **617/482-2849;** www.bostix.org) booth at Faneuil Hall Marketplace (on the south side of Faneuil Hall) or in Copley Square (at the corner of Boylston and Dartmouth sts.). Same-day tickets to musical and theatrical performances are half price, subject to availability. Credit cards are not accepted, and there are no refunds or exchanges. Check the board or the website for the day's offerings. The booths, which are also Ticketmaster outlets, are open Tuesday through Saturday from 10am to 6pm (half-price tickets go on sale at 11am), Sunday from 11am to 4pm. The Copley Square location is also open Monday from 10am to 6pm.

THE PERFORMING ARTS

The city's premier classical performance venue is **Symphony Hall,** 301 Mass. Ave. (© **617/266-1492;** www.bso.org), which turned 100 in 2000. It plays host to other notable groups and artists when the Boston Symphony Orchestra and the Boston Pops are away. The **Hatch Shell** on the Esplanade (© **617/626-1250;** www.mass.gov/dcr) is an amphitheater best known as the home of the Pops' Fourth of July concerts. On summer nights, free music and dance performances and films take over the stage to the delight of crowds on the lawn.

Other venues that attract big-name visitors include the **Berklee Performance Center,** 136 Mass. Ave. (© **617/747-8890;** www.berkleebpc.com); the **Boston Center for the Arts,** 539 Tremont St. (© **617/426-2787;** www.bcaonline.org); the **Cutler Majestic Theatre,** 219 Tremont St. (© **617/824-8000;** www.maj.org); New England Conservatory's **Jordan Hall,** 30 Gainsborough St. (© **617/585-1260;** www.newenglandconservatory.edu/jordanhall); and **Sanders Theatre,** 45 Quincy St., Cambridge (© **617/496-2222;** www.fas.harvard.edu/~memhall).

THE MAJOR COMPANIES

In addition to the companies listed below, the **Boston Lyric Opera** (© **617/542-6772** or 617/542-4912; www.blo.org) performs classical and contemporary works. The season runs from October to May. Performances are at the **Shubert Theatre,** 265 Tremont St., and tickets cost $34 to $166.

Boston Ballet ★★ Boston Ballet's reputation seems to jump a notch every time someone says, "So it's not just *The Nutcracker.*" The country's fourth-largest dance company performs the holiday staple from Thanksgiving to New Year's. During the rest of the season (Oct–May), it presents an eclectic mix of classic ballets and contemporary works. Because the Wang was originally a movie theater, the pitch of the seats makes the top two balconies less than ideal for ballet—paying more for a better seat is a good investment. ***Note:*** Unlike other Boston Ballet productions, *The Nutcracker* plays the **Opera House,** 539 Washington St. 19 Clarendon St. © **617/695-6955** or 800/432-7250 (Telecharge). www.bostonballet.com. Performances at the Wang Theatre, 270 Tremont St. (box office Mon–Sat 10am–6pm). Tickets $39–$98. Student rush tickets (1 hr. before curtain) $15, except for *The Nutcracker.* T: Green Line to Boylston.

Boston Pops ★★ From May to July, members of the BSO lighten up. Tables and chairs replace the floor seats at Symphony Hall, and drinks and light refreshments are served. The Pops play a range of music from light classical to show tunes to popular music, often with celebrity guest stars. Performances are Tuesday through Sunday evenings. Special holiday performances in December ($31–$107) usually sell out well in advance, but it can't hurt to check. The regular season ends with a series of free outdoor concerts at the Hatch Shell on the Esplanade along the Charles River. It includes the traditional Fourth of July concert. Symphony Hall, 301 Mass. Ave. (at Huntington Ave.). ✆ **617/266-1492** or 617/CONCERT (program information). SymphonyCharge ✆ **888/266-1200** (outside 617) or 617/266-1200. www.bso.org. Tickets $39–$74 for tables; $17–$45 for balcony seats. T: Green Line E to Symphony, or Orange Line to Mass. Ave.

Boston Symphony Orchestra ★★★ The Boston Symphony, one of the world's greatest, was founded in 1881. James Levine is the music director. You might want to schedule your trip to coincide with a particular performance, or with a visit by a celebrated guest artist or conductor. The season runs from October to April, with performances most Tuesday, Thursday, and Saturday evenings; Friday afternoons; and some Friday evenings. Explanatory talks (included in the ticket price) begin 75 minutes before the curtain. If you can't get tickets in advance, check at the box office for returns from subscribers 2 hours before showtime. A limited number of rush tickets are available on the day of the performance for Tuesday and Thursday evening and Friday afternoon programs. Some Wednesday evening and Thursday morning rehearsals are open to the public. Symphony Hall, 301 Mass. Ave. (at Huntington Ave.). ✆ **617/266-1492** or 617/CONCERT (program information). SymphonyCharge ✆ **888/266-1200** (outside 617) or 617/266-1200. www.bso.org. Tickets $28–$109. Rush tickets $8 (on sale 10am Fri, 5pm Tues and Thurs). Rehearsal tickets $16. T: Green Line E to Symphony, or Orange Line to Mass. Ave.

THEATER & PERFORMANCE ART

Boston is one of the last cities for pre-Broadway tryouts, allowing an early look at a classic (or classic flop) in the making. It's also a popular destination for touring companies of established hits. You'll find most of the shows headed to or coming from Broadway in the **Theater District,** at the **Colonial Theatre,** 106 Boylston St. (✆ **617/426-9366**); the **Opera House,** 539 Washington St. (✆ **617/880-2400**); the **Shubert Theatre,** 265 Tremont St. (✆ **617/482-9393**); the **Wang Theatre,** 270 Tremont St. (✆ **617/482-9393;** www.wangcenter.org); and the **Wilbur Theater,** 246 Tremont St. (✆ **617/423-4008**). The promoter often is **Broadway Across America** (✆ **866/523-7469;** www.broadwayacrossamerica.com).

The excellent local theater scene boasts the **Huntington Theatre Company,** which performs at the Boston University Theatre, 264 Huntington Ave. (✆ **617/266-0800;** www.huntington.org), and the **American Repertory Theatre,** which makes its home at Harvard University's Loeb Drama Center, 64 Brattle St., Cambridge (✆ **617/547-8300;** www.amrep.org).

The off-Broadway performance-art sensation **Blue Man Group** is a trio of cobalt-colored entertainers who use music, percussion, food, and audience participants—props include social commentary, Twinkies, marshmallows, breakfast cereal, toilet paper, and lots of blue paint. Older children and teenagers enjoy the mayhem as much as adults. Shows are at the **Charles Playhouse,** 74 Warrenton St. (✆ **617/426-6912;** www.blueman.com), in the Theater District. Tickets are $53 and $43 at the box office and through Ticketmaster (✆ **617/931-ARTS**).

Finds Boston Common Culture

An excellent summer diversion is a free, top-quality performance on historic Boston Common. Bring a picnic, spread out a blanket, and enjoy the sunset. The **Commonwealth Shakespeare Company** (✆ **617/532-1252**; www.commonwealthshakespeare.org) performs Tuesday through Sunday nights in July and early August. The **Boston Landmarks Orchestra** (✆ **617/520-2200**; www.landmarksorchestra.org) schedules classical concerts in parks around town, including the Common, on weekend afternoons and evenings in July and August.

THE CLUB & MUSIC SCENE

The Boston-area club scene changes constantly, and somewhere out there is a good time for everyone. Check the "Sidekick" section of the *Globe,* the *Phoenix,* the "Edge" section of the Friday *Herald, Stuff@Night,* or the *Improper Bostonian* while you're planning.

Bars close at 1am, clubs at 2am. The subway shuts down between 12:30 and 1am. The drinking age is 21; a valid driver's license or passport is required as proof of age. The law is strictly enforced, especially near college campuses (in other words, practically everywhere). Be prepared to show ID if you appear to be younger than 35 or so, and try to be patient while the amazed 30-year-old ahead of you fishes out a license.

Big-name rock and pop artists play **TD Banknorth Garden,** 100 Legends Way (Causeway St.; ✆ **617/624-1000;** www.tdbanknorthgarden.com), when it's not in use by the Bruins (hockey), the Celtics (basketball), the circus (in Oct), and touring ice shows. Concerts are in the round or on the arena stage.

COMEDY

The Comedy Connection at Faneuil Hall ★★ The oldest original comedy club in town (established in 1978) draws top-notch talent from near and far. There's one show Sunday through Thursday, two shows Friday and Saturday. The cover seldom tops $20 during the week but jumps for a big name appearing on a weekend. Quincy Market (2nd floor, off the rotunda). ✆ **617/248-9700.** www.comedyconnectionboston.com. Cover $15–$45. T: Green or Blue Line to Government Center or Orange Line to Haymarket. Validated parking available.

The Comedy Studio ★★★ *Finds* Nobody here is a sitcom star—yet. With a stellar reputation for searching out undiscovered talent, the no-frills Comedy Studio draws connoisseurs, students, and network scouts. Sketches and improv spice up the standup. Shows Tuesday through Sunday at 8pm. At the Hong Kong restaurant, 1238 Mass. Ave., Cambridge. ✆ **617/661-6507.** www.thecomedystudio.com. Cover $6–$10. T: Red Line to Harvard.

DANCE CLUBS

Avalon ★★★ A cavernous multilevel space with a spectacular light show, Avalon is either great fun or sensory overload. Friday is **"Avaland,"** with national and international names in the DJ booth and costumed house dancers on the floor. On Saturday (suburbanites' night out), expect more mainstream dance hits. Concerts (Gavin DeGraw and Belle and Sebastian have played recently) usually start in the early evening. The dress code calls for jackets and shirts with collars, and no jeans or athletic wear. Open Thursday (international night) through Sunday (gay night) from 10pm to 2am. 15 Lansdowne St. ✆ **617/262-2424** or 617/423-NEXT (for tickets). www.avalonboston.com. Cover $5–$20. T: Green Line B, C, or D to Kenmore.

Finds The Classiest Pickup Joint in Town

On the first Friday of each month, the **Museum of Fine Arts,** 465 Huntington Ave. (✆ **617/267-9300;** www.mfa.org), becomes a spirited nightlife destination. From 5:30 to 9:30pm, music, a cash bar, and a crowd of 20- and 30-somethings liven up the galleries. General admission to the museum ($13 after 5pm) includes admission to "firstfridays."

The Roxy ★★ This former hotel ballroom boasts excellent DJs and live music, a huge dance floor, a stage, and a balcony. Occasional concerts and boxing cards take good advantage of the sightlines. No jeans or athletic shoes. Open from 9pm to 2am Thursday through Saturday, plus some Wednesdays and Sundays. In the Courtyard Boston Tremont Hotel, 279 Tremont St. ✆ **617/338-7699.** www.roxyplex.com. Cover $10–$20. T: Green Line to Boylston or Orange Line to New England Medical Center.

FOLK & ECLECTIC

Club Passim ★★★ Joan Baez, Suzanne Vega, and Tom Rush all started out in this legendary basement coffeehouse. There's live music nightly, and coffee and food (but no alcohol) until 10:30pm. Open Sunday through Thursday from 11am to 11pm, Friday and Saturday until midnight. 47 Palmer St., Cambridge. ✆ **617/492-7679.** www.clubpassim.org. Cover $5–$25; most shows $15 or less. T: Red Line to Harvard.

Johnny D's Uptown Restaurant & Music Club ★★★ *Finds* This family-owned establishment draws a congenial, low-key crowd for performers on international tours as well as local acts. The music ranges from zydeco to rock, blues to ska. It's only two stops past Harvard Square on the Red Line (about a 15-min. ride at night). Open daily from 11:30am to 1am. Brunch starts at 9am on weekends; dinner runs from 4:30 to 9:30pm Tuesday through Saturday, with lighter fare until 11pm. 17 Holland St., Davis Sq., Somerville. ✆ **617/776-2004** or 617/776-9667 (concert line). www.johnnyds.com. Cover $3–$20, usually $8–$12. T: Red Line to Davis.

JAZZ & BLUES

Three restaurants that offer jazz along with excellent food are **Bob's Southern Bistro** (p. 108), **Icarus** (p. 108; Fri only), and **Les Zygomates** (p. 106). On summer Thursdays at 6pm, the **Boston Harbor Hotel** (✆ **617/439-7000**) stages performances on the "Blues Barge," which floats in the water behind the hotel.

Regattabar ★★★ The Regattabar's lineup of local and international artists is often considered the best in the area—a title that Scullers (see below) is happy to dispute. Bo Diddley, Madeleine Peyroux, and McCoy Tyner have appeared recently. The third-floor room holds about 200 and, unfortunately, can get a little noisy. Buy tickets in advance or try your luck at the door an hour before showtime. In The Charles Hotel, 1 Bennett St., Cambridge. ✆ **617/661-5000,** or 617/395-7757 for tickets. www.regattabarjazz.com. Tickets $12–$35. T: Red Line to Harvard.

Scullers Jazz Club ★★★ Overlooking the Charles River, Scullers is a lovely room that books top singers and instrumentalists—recent notables include Abbey Lincoln, Nicholas Payton, and Big Bad Voodoo Daddy. Patrons tend to be more hard-core and quieter than the crowds at the Regattabar, but it depends on who's performing. The box office is open Monday through Saturday from 11am to 6pm. Ask about dinner and overnight packages. In the Doubletree Guest Suites hotel, 400 Soldiers Field Rd. ✆ **617/562-4111.** www.scullersjazz.com. Tickets $15–$50. Validated parking available.

Wally's Cafe ★ This Boston institution, near a busy corner in the South End, opened in 1947. Its New Orleans–style all-about-the-music atmosphere draws a notably diverse crowd—black, white, straight, gay, affluent, indigent—and features nightly live music by local ensembles, students and instructors from the Berklee College of Music, and (on occasion) internationally renowned musicians. 427 Mass. Ave. ✆ **617/424-1408.** www.wallyscafe.com. 1-drink minimum. T: Orange Line to Mass. Ave.

ROCK & ALTERNATIVE

The Middle East ★★★ The best rock club in the area books an impressive variety of progressive and alternative acts in two rooms (upstairs and downstairs) every night. Showcasing top local talent as well as bands with international reputations, it's a popular hangout that gets crowded, hot, and *loud.* In the same complex are the **Corner,** a former bakery that features acoustic artists, and **ZuZu** (✆ **617/492-9181**), a Middle Eastern restaurant with its own music schedule. 472–480 Mass. Ave., Central Sq., Cambridge. ✆ **617/864-EAST,** or 617/931-2000 (Ticketmaster). www.mideastclub.com. Cover $7–$15. T: Red Line to Central.

Paradise Rock Club ★ Hard by the Boston University campus, the medium-size Paradise draws enthusiastic, student-intensive crowds for top local rock and alternative performers. You might see national names or locals who aren't ready to headline a big show. 967 Comm. Ave. ✆ **617/562-8800,** or 617/423-NEXT for tickets. www.thedise.com. T: Green Line B to Pleasant St.

Toad ★★ *Value* Essentially a bar with a stage, this narrow space attracts a savvy three-generation clientele with big local names and no cover. Toad enjoys good acoustics but not much elbow room—a plus when restless musicians wander into the crowd. 1912 Mass. Ave., Cambridge. ✆ **617/497-4950** (info line). www.toadcambridge.com. T: Red Line to Porter.

T. T. the Bear's Place ★ A mainstay of the Central Square live-music scene since it opened in 1985, "T. T.'s" has an uncanny knack for booking hot new talent. Bookings range from cutting-edge alternative rock to ska to up-and-coming pop acts. New bands predominate early in the week, with more established artists on weekends. Open until 1am Sunday to Wednesday, 2am Thursday through Saturday. 10 Brookline St., Cambridge. ✆ **617/492-0082,** or 617/492-BEAR (concert line). www.ttthebears.com. Cover $3–$15. T: Red Line to Central.

Tips Bowled Over

One of the hottest nightlife destinations in town is, of all things, a bowling alley. **Kings,** 10 Scotia St. (✆ **617/266-2695;** www.backbaykings.com), is a 25,000-square-foot complex in a former movie theater. It has 20 bowling lanes (four of them private) and an eight-table billiards room. Open until 2am daily; patrons must be 21 after 6pm. The complex includes a branch of the Cambridge restaurant **Jasper White's Summer Shack.** Scotia Street is off Dalton Street, across from the Hynes Convention Center.

BARS & LOUNGES

The Black Rose Purists might sneer at The Black Rose's touristy location, but performers don't. Sing along with the authentic entertainment at this jampacked pub and restaurant at the edge of Faneuil Hall Marketplace. 160 State St. ✆ **617/742-2286.** www.irishconnection.com. Cover $3–$5. T: Orange or Blue Line to State.

The Bristol ★★★ An elegant room with cushy seating and a fireplace, The Bristol is an oasis anytime, and it features a fabulous dessert buffet on weekend nights. There's live jazz every evening, and food until 11:30pm (12:30am Fri–Sat). In the Four Seasons Hotel, 200 Boylston St. ✆ **617/351-2037.** T: Green Line to Arlington.

Casablanca ★★ Students and professors jam this legendary Harvard Square watering hole, especially on weekends. It offers an excellent jukebox, excellent food, and excellent eavesdropping. 40 Brattle St., Cambridge. ✆ **617/876-0999.** T: Red Line to Harvard.

Cheers (Beacon Hill) Try to hide your shock when you enter "the *Cheers* bar" and it looks nothing like the bar on the TV show. (A spin-off in Faneuil Hall Marketplace fills that niche—see the next listing.) This one-time neighborhood bar is far better known as a destination for legions of out-of-towners, who find good pub grub and plenty of souvenirs. 84 Beacon St. ✆ **617/227-9605.** www.cheersboston.com. T: Green Line to Arlington.

Cheers (Faneuil Hall Marketplace) Blatantly but good-naturedly courting fans of the sitcom, this bar centers on an area that exactly replicates the set of the TV show. You know you want to. Quincy Market Building, South Canopy. ✆ **617/227-0150.** www.cheersboston.com. T: Green or Blue Line to Government Center, or Orange Line to Haymarket.

DeLux Cafe ★ Ultracool but never obnoxious about it, the DeLux is one of the classiest dives around. The funky decor (check out the Elvis shrine), selection of microbrews, and veggie-friendly ethnic menu attract a cross section of the South End, from off-duty chefs to yuppies. 100 Chandler St. ✆ **617/338-5258.** T: Orange Line to Back Bay.

Flat Top Johnny's ★★ A spacious, loud room with a bar and 12 red-topped pool tables, Flat Top Johnny's has a casual neighborhood feel despite being in a rather sterile office-retail complex. Open weekdays noon to 1am, weekends 3pm to 1am. 1 Kendall Sq., Cambridge. ✆ **617/494-9565.** www.flattopjohnnys.com. Pool $12/hour Mon–Sat, $6/hour Sun. T: Red Line to Kendall/MIT.

The Fours One of Boston's best and best-known sports bars, The Fours is about one football field away from TD Banknorth Garden. Festooned with sports memorabilia and TVs, it's a madhouse before Celtics and Bruins games—and a promising place to pick up an extra ticket. 166 Canal St. ✆ **617/720-4455.** T: Green or Orange Line to North Station.

Grendel's Den ★ A vestige of pre-franchise Harvard Square, this cozy subterranean space is *the* place to celebrate turning 21. Recent grads and grad students dominate, but Grendel's has been so popular for so long that it also gets its share of Gen Y's parents. 89 Winthrop St., Cambridge. ✆ **617/491-1050.** www.grendelsden.com. T: Red Line to Harvard.

Hard Rock Cafe Kids This link in the chain is a fun one—just ask the other tourists in line with you. The bar is shaped like a guitar, and the stained-glass windows glorify rock stars. Memorabilia of Jimi Hendrix, Elvis Presley, Madonna, local favorites Aerosmith and the Cars, and others decorates the walls. 131 Clarendon St. ✆ **617/424-ROCK.** www.hardrock.com. T: Orange Line to Back Bay or Green Line to Copley.

John Harvard's Brew House ★★ This subterranean Harvard Square hangout pumps out terrific English-style brews in a clublike setting and prides itself on its food. 33 Dunster St., Cambridge. ✆ **617/868-3585.** www.johnharvards.com. T: Red Line to Harvard.

Mr. Dooley's Boston Tavern ★★ Sometimes an expertly poured Guinness is all you need. If one of the nicest bartenders in the city pours it, so much the better. This Financial District spot offers many imported beers on tap, live music, and a menu of pub favorites. 77 Broad St. ✆ **617/338-5656.** www.somerspubs.com. Cover $3–$5 Fri–Sat. T: Orange Line to State or Blue Line to Aquarium.

The Plough & Stars ★ Although it's comically small, The Plough is a huge presence on the local pub and live-music scenes. A neighborhood hangout during the day, it's a hipster magnet at night. Saturday is bluegrass night. 912 Mass. Ave., Cambridge. ✆ **617/576-0032.** www.ploughandstars.com. T: Red Line to Central or Harvard.

Top of the Hub ★★★ The 52nd-story view of greater Boston from this appealing lounge is especially lovely at sunset. There's music and dancing nightly. Dress is casual but neat. Prudential Center, 800 Boylston St. ✆ **617/536-1775.** T: Green Line E to Prudential.

5

Side Trips from Boston: Lexington & Concord, the North Shore & Plymouth

by Marie Morris

Besides being, in the words of Oliver Wendell Holmes, "the hub of the solar system," Boston is the hub of a network of wonderful day trips and longer excursions. The destinations in this chapter are lively communities where you'll find sights and attractions of great beauty and historical significance. Exploring can take as little as half a day or as long as a week or more.

WEST OF BOSTON If time is short, combine a visit to Cambridge (see chapter 4) with a trip to Lexington and Concord for a hefty dose of American history. The route that Paul Revere took out of Boston on April 18, 1775, is tough to follow—he started by crossing the harbor in a rowboat, for one thing—but his fellow rider William Dawes cut through Harvard Square. Both proceeded to warn the colonists that British troops were on the march.

NORTH OF BOSTON Great prosperity came to eastern Massachusetts after the Revolution, as the new nation took advantage of the lifting of British trade barriers. Today, the spoils of the China trade adorn mansions and public edifices in seaside locales such as Marblehead, Salem, and Cape Ann. Fishing is still an important industry, but these days the area caters more to commuters and tourists than to those who make their living from the sea. A worthwhile detour from the north or west is Lowell, a once-decrepit mill town where tourism is now the largest industry.

SOUTH OF BOSTON The communities between Boston and Cape Cod are mostly commuter suburbs. The prime sightseeing destination is Plymouth, one of the oldest permanent European settlements in North America. It's a pleasant place where you can walk in the footsteps of the Pilgrims—and of the countless out-of-towners who flock here in summer and at Thanksgiving. Farther south, the old whaling port of New Bedford makes an interesting detour.

1 Lexington ★

9 miles NW of downtown Boston; 6 miles NW of Cambridge; 6 miles E of Concord

A country village turned prosperous suburb, Lexington takes great pride in its history. It's a pleasant town with some engaging destinations, but it lacks the atmosphere and abundant attractions of nearby Concord. Being sure to leave time for a tour of the Buckman Tavern, you can schedule as little as a couple of hours to explore downtown

Around Boston

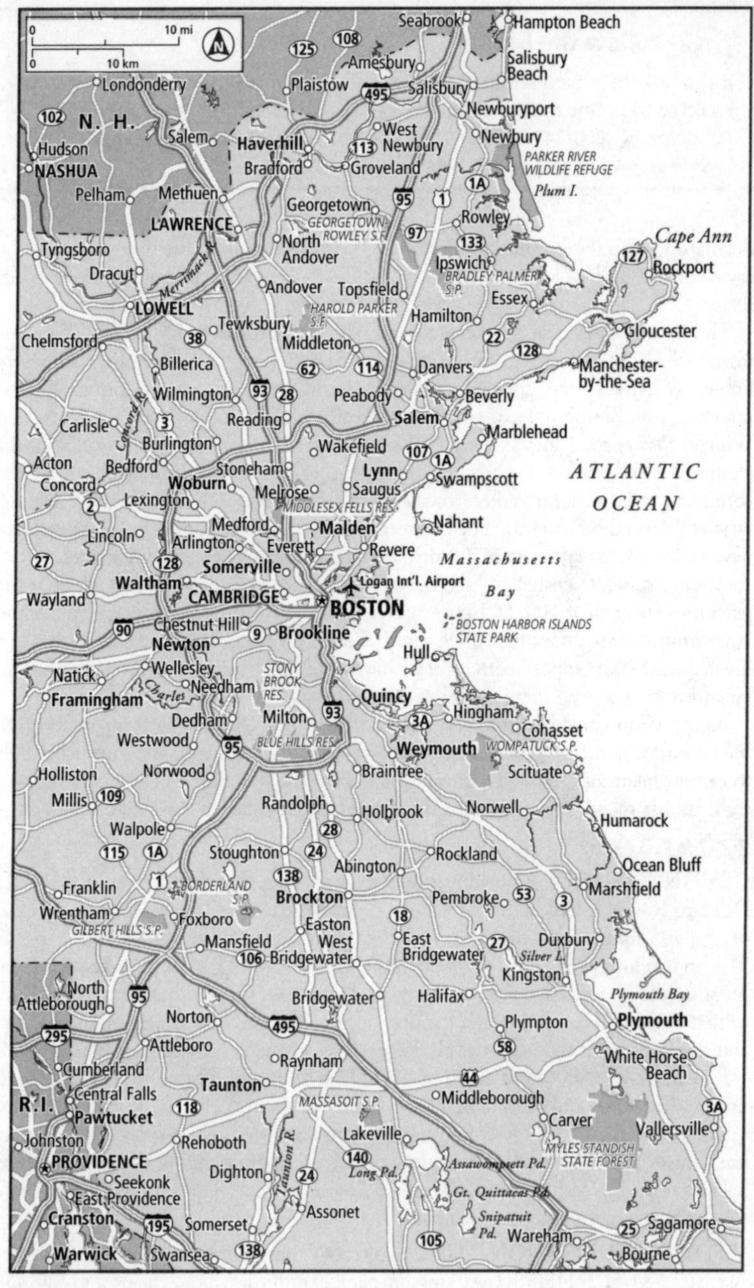

Tips Follow the Leader

If you lack the time or inclination to make your own arrangements, consider an escorted tour. One reliable company is Gray Line's **Brush Hill Tours,** 435 High St., Randolph (✆ **800/343-1328** or 781/986-6100; www.grayline.com), which offers a wide variety of half- and full-day excursions.

Lexington, possibly en route to Concord. A visit can also fill a half or full day. The town contains part of Minute Man National Historical Park, which is definitely worth a visit.

The shooting phase of the Revolutionary War started here, with a skirmish on the town green. It began when British troops clashed with local militia members, who were known as "Minutemen" for their ability to assemble on short notice. British soldiers marched from Boston to Lexington late on April 18, 1775. Tipped off, Paul Revere and William Dawes rode ahead to sound the warning. They did their job so well that the alarm came long before the advancing forces. The Lexington Minutemen, under the command of Capt. John Parker, got the word shortly after midnight, but the redcoats were still several hours away. The colonists repaired to their homes and the Buckman Tavern. Five hours later, some 700 British troops under Major Pitcairn arrived.

A tense standoff ensued. Three times Pitcairn ordered them to disperse, but the patriots—fewer than 100, and some accounts say 77—refused. Parker called: "Stand your ground. Don't fire unless fired upon, but if they mean to have a war, let it begin here!" Finally the captain, perhaps realizing as the sky grew light how badly outnumbered his men were, gave the order to fall back.

As the Minutemen began to scatter, a shot rang out. One British company charged into the fray, and the colonists attempted to regroup as Pitcairn tried unsuccessfully to call off his troops. Nobody knows who started the shooting, but when it was over, eight militia members, including a drummer boy, lay dead, and 10 were wounded.

ESSENTIALS

GETTING THERE From downtown Boston, take Storrow Drive or Memorial Drive to Route 2. Follow Route 2 from Cambridge through Belmont, exit at Route 4/225, and follow signs to downtown Lexington. Or take Route 128 (I-95) to Exit 31A and follow signs. If it's not rush hour, allow about 35 minutes. **Massachusetts Avenue** (the same "Mass. Ave." you saw in Boston and Cambridge) runs through the center of town. There's metered parking on the street and in several municipal lots, and free parking at the National Heritage Museum and the National Historical Park.

The **MBTA** (✆ **800/392-6100** or 617/222-3200; www.mbta.com) runs bus route nos. 62 (Bedford) and 76 (Hanscom) to Lexington from Alewife station, the last stop on the Red Line. The one-way fare at press time was 90¢; the trip takes about 25 minutes. Buses operate Monday through Saturday every hour during the day and every half-hour during rush periods. There's no Sunday service. The seasonal Liberty Ride tour connects Lexington and Concord.

VISITOR INFORMATION The Chamber of Commerce **visitor center,** 1875 Mass. Ave. (✆ **781/862-2480;** www.lexingtonchamber.org), distributes maps and information. The **Greater Merrimack Valley Convention & Visitors Bureau** (✆ **800/443-3332** or 978/459-6150; www.merrimackvalley.org) includes Lexington.

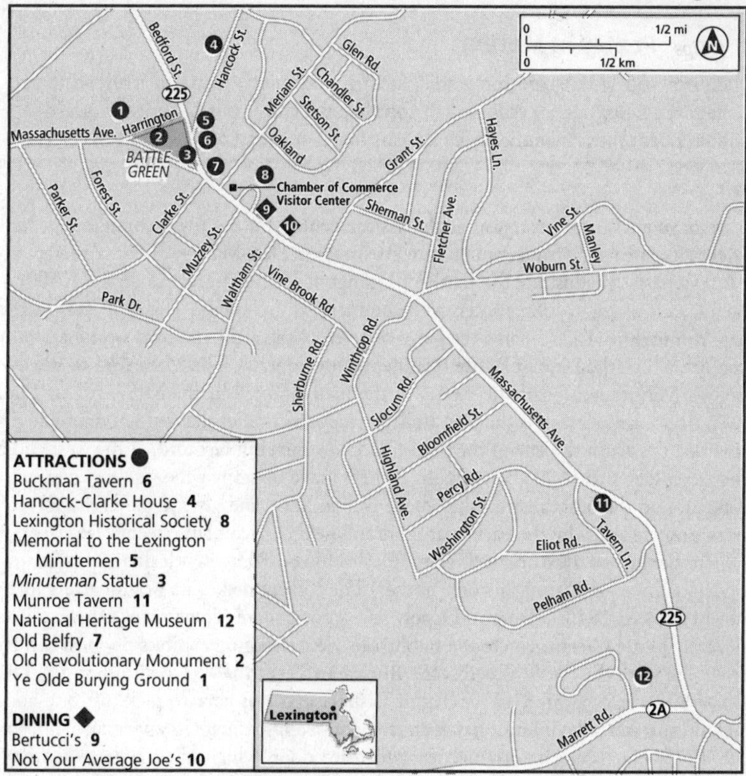

GETTING AROUND Downtown Lexington is easily negotiable on foot, and most of the attractions are within walking distance. If you prefer not to walk to the Munroe Tavern and the National Heritage Museum (see below), bus nos. 62 and 76 pass by on Mass. Ave.

The **Liberty Ride** (✆ **781/862-0500,** ext. 702; www.libertyride.us) is a narrated tour that connects the attractions in Lexington and Concord and the Concord commuter rail station. It operates from 10:30am to 3pm daily from late May through mid-October; check ahead to confirm the schedule. The fare (good for a full day) is $20 for adults, $10 for children 5 to 17, free for children under 5. There's free parking at the National Heritage Museum and the national park visitor center, and your ticket entitles you to discounts at local businesses.

SPECIAL EVENTS **Patriots Day,** a state holiday observed on the third Monday in April, commemorates the start of the Revolution. Celebrations include a reenactment of the battle and other festivities.

EXPLORING THE HISTORIC SITES

Minute Man National Historical Park is in Lexington, Concord, and Lincoln (see "Concord," below).

Tips Poetry in Motion

Before you visit Lexington and Concord, you might want to (re)read **"Paul Revere's Ride,"** Henry Wadsworth Longfellow's classic but historically questionable poem that dramatically chronicles the events of April 18 and 19, 1775.

Start your visit to Lexington at the **visitor center,** on the town common or Battle Green. It's open daily from 9am to 5pm (10am–4pm Dec–Mar). A diorama and accompanying narrative illustrate the Battle of Lexington. The **Minuteman statue** (1900) on the green is of Capt. John Parker, who commanded the militia. The **Old Revolutionary Monument** (1799) marks the grave of seven of the eight colonists who died in the conflict, which the **Line of Battle Boulder** commemorates. The **Memorial to the Lexington Minutemen** bears the names of the men who fell in the battle. Across Mass. Ave., near Clarke Street, is the **Old Belfry,** a reproduction of the free-standing bell that sounded the alarm the day of the battle. **Ye Olde Burying Ground,** at the west end of the green, dates to 1690 and contains Parker's grave. A stop at the visitor center and a walk around the monuments takes about half an hour, and gives a good sense of what went on here and why the participants are still held in such high esteem.

The **Lexington Historical Society** (**© 781/862-1703;** www.lexingtonhistory.org) operates three fascinating historic houses. The society makes its headquarters in the newly restored 1846 Lexington Depot, on Depot Square (downtown, off Mass. Ave. near the Battle Green), where the public can view changing exhibits on local history.

Across from the Battle Green is the **Buckman Tavern** ★★, 1 Bedford St. (**© 781/862-5598**), built around 1710. If time is short and you have to pick just one house to visit, this is it. The interior has been restored to approximate its appearance on April 19, 1775. You'll see the original bar and front door, which has a hole in it from a British musket ball. The Minutemen gathered here to wait for word of British troop movements and brought their wounded here after the conflict. On the excellent tour, costumed guides describe the history of the building and its inhabitants, explain the battle, and discuss Colonial life.

Within walking distance is the **Hancock-Clarke House,** 36 Hancock St. (**© 781/861-0928**). Samuel Adams and John Hancock, who had left Boston several days earlier upon learning that the British were after them, were sleeping here (or trying to) when Revere arrived. They fled to nearby Woburn. Built around 1698 by Hancock's grandfather and lavishly improved by his uncle, the house contains some original furnishings as well as artifacts of the Battle of Lexington.

The British took over the **Munroe Tavern** ★, 1332 Mass. Ave. (about 1 mile east of the green), to use as their headquarters and field hospital. The taproom ceiling still has a bullet hole made by a careless soldier. The 1690 building holds many fascinating artifacts. The furniture, carefully preserved by the Munroe family, includes the table and chair where President Washington dined in 1789. The historically accurate gardens at the rear (free admission) are beautifully planted and maintained.

All three houses are open for guided tours (the only way to see them). The Buckman Tavern is open daily from April through October; tours start every half-hour from 10am to 4pm. The Hancock-Clarke House and the Munroe Tavern are open weekends from Patriots Day weekend through June and daily from July through

October. Tours of the Hancock-Clarke House start on the half-hour from 11am to 2pm; tours of the tavern start every half-hour from 1:30 to 3pm. Admission for adults is $5 for one house, $8 for two, and $10 for all three; for children 6 to 16, $3 for one house, $5 for two, and $7 for three. Call © **781/862-5598** for information about group tours, which are offered by appointment.

National Heritage Museum ★★ Kids This fascinating museum explores history through popular culture. It makes an entertaining complement to the Colonial focus of the rest of the town. The installations in the six exhibition spaces change regularly; you can start with another dose of the Revolution, the permanent exhibit *Lexington Alarm'd.* Other topics have ranged from George Washington to mail-order catalogs to metal lunchboxes. Lectures, concerts, and family programs are also offered, and the cafe serves lunch on weekdays. The Scottish Rite of Freemasonry sponsors the museum.

33 Marrett Rd., Rte. 2A (at Mass. Ave.). © **781/861-6559** or 781/861-9638. www.nationalhaeritagemuseum.org. Free admission. Mon–Sat 10am–5pm; Sun noon–5pm. Bus: 62 or 76 from downtown Lexington to Rte. 2A.

SHOPPING

A stroll along **Mass. Ave.** near the center of town won't disappoint. Start at **The Muse's Window,** 1656 Mass. Ave. (© **781/274-6873**), an excellent crafts gallery. As you head back toward the green, check out **Waldenbooks,** 1713 Mass. Ave. (© **781/862-7870**); **Upper Story Books,** 1730 Mass. Ave. (© **781/862-0999**); and the **Crafty Yankee,** 1838 Mass. Ave. (© **800/286-3037** or 781/863-1219). One of the best-known yarn shops in eastern Massachusetts is **Wild & Woolly Studio,** 7A Meriam St., off Mass. Ave. (© **781/861-7717**).

WHERE TO STAY

Bedford is 15 minutes from downtown Lexington on Route 4/225, across I-95. The **Boston/Bedford Travelodge,** 285 Great Rd., Bedford (© **781/275-6120;** www.travelodge.com), is an affordable motel with an outdoor pool. A double room runs about $79 in high season.

Renaissance Boston Bedford Hotel ★ The sights in Lexington and Concord are convenient to this three-story, lodge-style hotel, which neatly makes the transition from a weekday business destination to a weekend family resort. There's also plenty to do without leaving the property. The well-maintained guest rooms contain oversize work desks; larger units have king-size beds. The hotel shuttle transports guests to destinations within 5 miles, including the Burlington Mall.

44 Middlesex Tpk., Bedford, MA 01730. © **800/HOTELS-1** or 781/275-5500. Fax 781/275-3042. www.marriott.com. 284 units. Sun–Thurs $129–$249 double; Fri–Sat $79–$229 double. Extra person $15. Children under 19 stay free in parent's room. Packages and senior and AAA discounts available. AE, DC, DISC, MC, V. **Amenities:** Restaurant (New England); lounge; indoor pool; indoor/outdoor tennis courts; fitness center; Jacuzzi; sauna; shuttle; concierge; business center; 24-hr. room service; laundry service; dry cleaning. *In room:* A/C, TV w/pay movies, high-speed Internet access ($10/day), minibar, coffeemaker, hair dryer, iron.

Sheraton Lexington Inn Overlooking the interstate but sheltered from the noise by a stand of trees, the two-story Sheraton is 5 minutes from downtown Lexington by car. It offers the chain's usual amenities, including pillow-top beds, but the feel is more suburban motel than downtown business behemoth—whether that's a plus or a minus is your call. Rooms are large enough to hold a wing chair or couch, and some have balconies. It's a decent choice for families, and popular with travelers who have business on the Route 128 high-tech corridor.

727 Marrett Rd. (Exit 30B off I-95), Lexington, MA 02173. ✆ **800/325-3535** or 781/862-8700. Fax 781/863-0404. www.sheraton.com. 119 units. $109–$219 double; $219–$369 suite. Extra person $10. AAA and AARP discounts available. AE, DC, DISC, MC, V. **Amenities:** Restaurant (American); lounge; exercise room; business center; limited room service. *In room:* A/C, TV, high-speed Internet access ($10/day), coffeemaker, iron.

WHERE TO DINE

If you're not continuing to Concord, which has more interesting dining options, Lexington offers some pleasant choices. The fresh soups and sandwiches at the cafe at the **National Heritage Museum** (see above) make it a popular spot for lunch on weekdays. **Bertucci's,** 1777 Mass. Ave. (✆ **781/860-9000**), is a branch of the family-friendly pizzeria chain. A branch of the reliable but somewhat generic local chain **Not Your Average Joe's,** 1727 Mass. Ave. (✆ **978/674-2828**), serves good pizza and creative American cuisine.

2 Concord

18 miles NW of Boston; 15 miles NW of Cambridge; 6 miles W of Lexington.

Concord (say "conquered") revels in its legacy as a center of groundbreaking thought and its role in the country's political and intellectual history. A visit can easily fill a day; if your interests are specialized or time is short, a half-day excursion is reasonable. For an excellent overview of town history, start your visit at the **Concord Museum.**

After just a little time in this lovely town, you may find yourself adopting the local attitude toward two of its most famous residents: Ralph Waldo Emerson, who comes across as a well-respected uncle figure, and Henry David Thoreau, everyone's favorite eccentric cousin. Long before they wandered the countryside, the first official battle of the Revolutionary War took place at the North Bridge, now part of Minute Man National Historical Park. By the middle of the 19th century, Concord was the center of the Transcendentalist movement. Homes of Emerson, Thoreau, Nathaniel Hawthorne, and Louisa May Alcott are open to visitors, as is the authors' final resting place, Sleepy Hollow Cemetery.

ESSENTIALS

GETTING THERE From Lexington (10 min. by car), take Route 2A west from Mass. Ave. (Rte. 4/225) at the National Heritage Museum; follow the BATTLE ROAD signs. From Boston and Cambridge (30–40 min.), take Route 2 into Lincoln and stay in the right lane. Where the main road makes a sharp left, go straight onto Cambridge Turnpike, and follow signs to HISTORIC CONCORD. To go directly to Walden Pond, use the left lane, take what's now Route 2/2A another mile or so, and turn left onto Route 126. There's parking throughout town and at the attractions.

The **commuter rail** (✆ **800/392-6100** or 617/222-3200; www.mbta.com) takes about 45 minutes from North Station in Boston, with a stop at Porter Square in Cambridge. The round-trip fare at press time was $10. The station is about ¾ of a mile over flat terrain from the town center. There is no bus service from Boston to Concord. For information about **Liberty Ride** tours, which cover Concord and Lexington, see "Getting Around," p. 147.

VISITOR INFORMATION The **Chamber of Commerce,** 15 Walden St., Suite 7 (✆ **978/369-3120;** www.concordmachamber.org), maintains a visitor center at 58

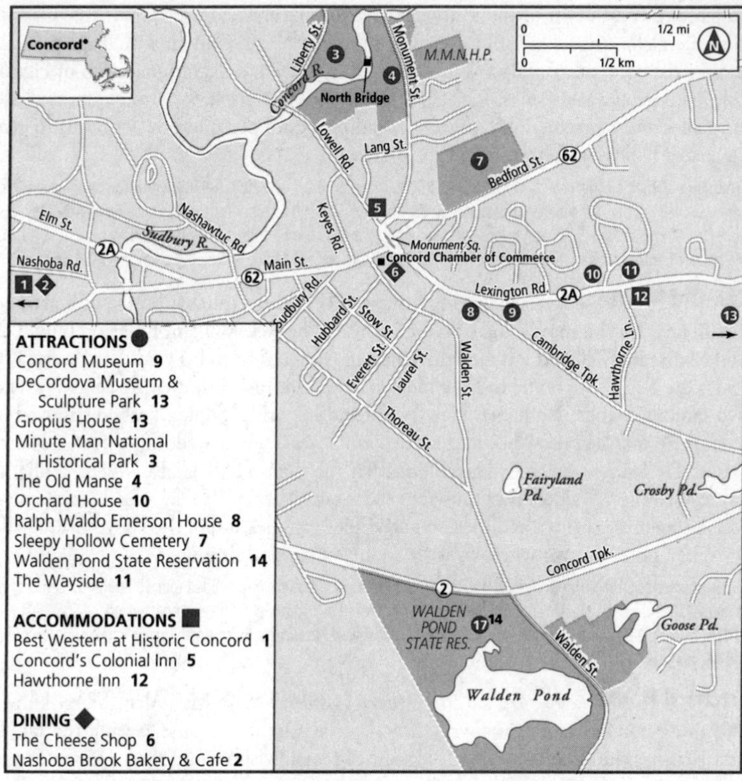

Main St., next to Middlesex Savings Bank, 1 block south of Monument Square. It's open daily 9:30am to 4:30pm from April through October; public restrooms in the same building are open year-round. Guided walking tours are available. Weekday and group tours are available by appointment. The community (**www.concordma.com**) and town (**www.concordnet.org**) websites include visitor information. You can also contact the **Greater Merrimack Valley Convention & Visitors Bureau** (© **800/443-3332** or 978/459-6150; www.merrimackvalley.org).

GETTING AROUND Major attractions are within walking distance of downtown. If you're trying to stop everywhere in a day or are visiting Walden Pond or Great Meadows, you'll need a car.

SEEING THE SIGHTS

LITERARY LANDMARKS & HISTORIC ATTRACTIONS

Concord Museum ★★ Kids Just when you're (understandably) suspecting that everything interesting in this area started on April 18, 1775, and ended the next day, this superb museum sets you straight. It's a great place to start your visit to the town. The **History Galleries** ★★ explore the question "Why Concord?" Artifacts, murals, films, maps, documents, and other presentations illustrate the town's role as a Native American settlement, Revolutionary War battleground, 19th-century intellectual center, and focal point of the 20th-century historic preservation movement. One of the lanterns that signaled Paul Revere from the Old North Church is on display. You'll also see the contents of Ralph Waldo Emerson's study and a large collection of Henry David Thoreau's belongings. Pick up a **family activity pack** ★ as you enter and use the games and reproduction artifacts (including a quill pen and powder horn) to give the kids a hands-on feel for life in the past.

Cambridge Tpk. at Lexington Rd. ✆ **978/369-9609** (recorded info) or 978/369-9763. www.concordmuseum.org. Admission $8 adults, $7 seniors and students, $5 children under 16. June–Aug daily 9am–5pm; Apr–May and Sept–Dec Mon–Sat 9am–5pm, Sun noon–5pm; Jan–Mar Mon–Sat 11am–4pm, Sun 1–4pm. Follow Lexington Rd. out of Concord Center and bear right at museum onto Cambridge Tpk.; entrance is on left. Parking allowed on road.

The Old Manse ★ The engaging history of this home touches on the military and the literary, but it's mostly the story of a family. The Rev. William Emerson built The Old Manse in 1770 and watched the Battle of Concord from his yard. For almost 170 years, the house was home to his widow, her second husband, their descendants, and two famous friends. Nathaniel Hawthorne and his bride, Sophia Peabody, moved in after their marriage in 1842 and stayed for 3 years. As a wedding present, Henry David Thoreau sowed the vegetable garden for them. This is also where William's grandson Ralph Waldo Emerson wrote the essay "Nature." Today, you'll see mementos and memorabilia of the Emerson and Ripley families and of the Hawthornes, who scratched notes on two windows with Sophia's diamond ring.

269 Monument St. (at North Bridge). ✆ **978/369-3909.** www.oldmanse.org. Guided tour $8 adults, $7 seniors and students, $5 children 6–12, $25 families. Mid-Apr to Oct Mon–Sat 10am–5pm; Sun and holidays noon–5pm (last tour at 4:30pm). Closed Nov to mid-Apr. From Concord Center, follow Monument St. to North Bridge parking lot (on right); Old Manse is on left.

Orchard House ★★★ Kids *Little Women* (1868), Louisa May Alcott's best-known and most popular work, was written and set at Orchard House. Seeing the family home brings the Alcotts to life for legions of female visitors and their pleasantly surprised male companions. Fans won't want to miss the excellent tour, copiously illustrated with heirlooms. Serious buffs can check in advance for information on special events and holiday programs, some of which require reservations.

Louisa's father, the writer and educator Amos Bronson Alcott, created Orchard House by joining and restoring two homes. The family lived here from 1858 to 1877, socializing in the same circles as Emerson, Thoreau, and Hawthorne. Other relatives served as the models for the characters in *Little Women.* Anna ("Meg"), the eldest, was an amateur actress, and May ("Amy") a talented artist. Elizabeth ("Beth"), a gifted musician, died before the family moved to this house. Their mother, the social activist Abigail May Alcott, frequently assumed the role of breadwinner—Bronson, Louisa wrote in her journal, had "no gift for money making."

Note: Call before visiting. An extensive project continuing the preservation of the house, which dates to around 1690 and has been open to the public since 1911, was underway at press time.

399 Lexington Rd. ✆ **978/369-4118.** www.louisamayalcott.org. Guided tour $8 adults, $7 seniors and students, $5 children 6–17, $20 families. Apr–Oct Mon–Sat 10am–4:30pm, Sun 1–4:30pm; Nov–Mar Mon–Fri 11am–2:45pm, Sat 10am–4:30pm, Sun 1–4:30pm. Closed Jan 1–15. Follow Lexington Rd. out of Concord Center and bear left at Concord Museum; house is on left. Overflow parking across the street.

Ralph Waldo Emerson House This house offers an instructive look at the days when a philosopher could attain the status we now associate with rock stars. Emerson, also an essayist and poet, lived here from 1835 until his death, in 1882. He moved here after marrying his second wife, Lydia Jackson, whom he called "Lydian"; she called him "Mr. Emerson," as the staff still does. The tour gives a good look at his personal side and at the fashionably ornate interior decoration of the time. You'll see original furnishings and some of Emerson's personal effects.

28 Cambridge Tpk. ✆ **978/369-2236.** Guided tours $7 adults, $5 seniors and students. Call to arrange group tours (10 people or more). Mid-Apr to Oct Thurs–Sat 10am–4:30pm; Sun 1–4:30pm. Closed Nov to mid-Apr. Follow Cambridge Tpk. out of Concord Center; just before Concord Museum, house is on right.

Sleepy Hollow Cemetery ★ Follow the signs for AUTHOR'S RIDGE and climb the hill to the graves of some of the town's literary lights, including the Alcotts, Emerson, Hawthorne, and Thoreau. Emerson's bears no religious symbols, just an uncarved quartz boulder. Thoreau is buried nearby; at his funeral, in 1862, his old friend Emerson concluded his eulogy with these words: ". . . wherever there is knowledge, wherever there is virtue, wherever there is beauty, he will find a home."

Entrance on Rte. 62 W. ✆ **978/318-3233.** www.concordnet.org. Daily 7am to dusk, weather permitting. Call ahead for wheelchair access. No buses allowed.

The Wayside ★ The Wayside was Nathaniel Hawthorne's home from 1852 until his death, in 1864. The Alcotts also lived here (the girls called it "the yellow house"), as did Harriett Lothrop, who wrote the *Five Little Peppers* books under the pen name Margaret Sidney and owned most of the current furnishings. The Wayside is part of Minute Man National Historical Park, and the fascinating 45-minute ranger-led tour illuminates the occupants' lives and the house's crazy-quilt architecture. The exhibit in the barn (free admission) consists of audio presentations and figures of the authors. Call ahead to double-check hours, which are subject to change.

455 Lexington Rd. ✆ **978/369-6975.** www.nps.gov/mima/wayside. Guided tour $4 adults, free for children under 17. May–Oct; open days and hours vary. Closed Nov–Apr. Follow Lexington Rd. out of Concord Center past Concord Museum and Orchard House. Parking across the street.

MINUTE MAN NATIONAL HISTORICAL PARK ★★

This 970-acre park preserves the scene of the first Revolutionary War battle, on April 19, 1775. After the skirmish at Lexington, the British continued to Concord in search of stockpiled arms (which the colonists had already moved). Warned of the advance, the Minutemen crossed the North Bridge, evading the "regulars" standing guard, and awaited reinforcements on a hilltop. The British searched nearby homes and burned any guns they found, and the Colonials, seeing the smoke, mistakenly thought the soldiers were burning the town. The gunfire that ensued, the opening salvo of the Revolution, is remembered as "the shot heard round the world."

The park is open daily year-round. A visit can take as little as half an hour—for a jaunt to the North Bridge (a reproduction)—or as long as half a day (or more), if you stop at both visitor centers and perhaps participate in a ranger-led program. To reach the bridge from Concord Center, follow Monument Street until you see the parking lot on the right. Walk a short distance to the bridge, stopping along the unpaved path to read and hear the narratives. On one side of the bridge is a plaque commemorating the British soldiers who died in the Revolutionary War. On the other side is Daniel Chester French's **Minute Man** statue, engraved with a stanza of the poem Emerson wrote for the dedication ceremony in 1876.

You can also start at the **North Bridge Visitor Center** ★, 174 Liberty St., off Monument Street (✆ **978/369-6993;** www.nps.gov/mima), which overlooks the Concord River and the bridge. A diorama and video illustrate the Battle of Concord; exhibits include uniforms, weapons, and tools of Colonial and British soldiers. Park rangers lead programs and answer questions. Outside, picnicking is allowed, and the scenery (especially the fall foliage) is lovely. The center is open daily from 9am to 5pm (until 4pm in winter).

At the Lexington end of the park is the **Minute Man Visitor Center** ★ (✆ **781/862-7753;** www.nps.gov/mima), off Route 2A, about ½ mile west of I-95 Exit 30B. The park includes the first 4 miles of the Battle Road, the route the defeated British troops took as they left Concord. At the visitor center, you'll see a fascinating multimedia program on the Revolution, informational displays, and a 40-foot mural illustrating the battle. Call ahead (use the phone number for the North Bridge Visitor Center, above, if there's no answer here) for open days and hours. On summer weekends, rangers lead tours of the park—call ahead for times. Pedestrians, wheelchairs, and bicycles share the **Battle Road Trail,** a 5.5-mile interpretive path. Panels and granite markers display information about the area's military, social, and natural history.

Also on the park grounds, on Old Bedford Road, is the **Hartwell Tavern.** Costumed interpreters demonstrate daily life on a farm and in a tavern in Colonial days. It's open from 9:30am to 5pm, daily June through August and weekends only in April, May, September, and October. Admission is free.

NEARBY SIGHTS

DeCordova Museum and Sculpture Park ★★ Indoors and out, this museum shows the work of American contemporary and modern artists, with an emphasis on living New England residents. The main building, on a leafy hilltop, overlooks a pond and the public sculpture park. The museum also has a roof garden and a sculpture terrace. Picnicking is allowed in the sculpture park; bring your lunch or buy it at the cafe (open Tues–Sun 11am–3pm). Free tours of the main galleries start at 1pm Thursday and 2pm Sunday year-round; sculpture-park tours run May through October on Saturday and Sunday at 1pm.

51 Sandy Pond Rd., Lincoln. ✆ **781/259-8355.** www.decordova.org. Museum: $9 adults; $6 seniors, students, and children 6–12. Tues–Sun and Mon holidays 11am–5pm. Sculpture park: Free admission when museum is closed. Daily daylight hours. From Rte. 2 east, take Rte. 126 south to Baker Bridge Rd. (1st left after Walden Pond). When it ends, go right onto Sandy Pond Rd.; museum is on left. From I-95, take Exit 28B, follow Trapelo Rd. 2½ miles to Sandy Pond Rd., then follow signs.

Gropius House ★ Architect Walter Gropius (1883–1969), founder of the Bauhaus school of design, built this home for his family in 1938. Having taken a job at the Harvard Graduate School of Design, he worked with Marcel Breuer to design the hilltop house. He used traditional materials such as clapboard, brick, and fieldstone, with components then seldom seen in domestic architecture, including glass blocks and chrome (on the banisters). Breuer designed many of the furnishings, which were made for the family at the Bauhaus. Decorated as it was in the last decade of Gropius's life, the house affords a revealing look at his life, career, and philosophy.

68 Baker Bridge Rd., Lincoln. ✆ **781/259-8098.** www.historicnewengland.org. Admission $10 adults, $9 seniors, $5 students and children. Tours on the hour June–Oct 15 Wed–Sun 11am–4pm; Oct 16–May Sat–Sun 11am–4pm. From Rte. 2 east, take Rte. 126 south to left on Baker Bridge Rd. (1st left after Walden Pond); house is on right. From I-95, take Exit 28B, follow Trapelo Rd. to Sandy Pond Rd., go left onto Baker Bridge Rd.; house is on left.

WILDERNESS RETREATS

The titles of Henry David Thoreau's first two published works can serve as starting points: *A Week on the Concord and Merrimack Rivers* (1849) and *Walden* (1854).

To see the area from water level, there's no need to take a week; 2 hours or so should suffice. Rent a **canoe** ★ at the **South Bridge Boathouse,** 496–502 Main St. (✆ **978/369-9438**), just over half a mile west of the center of town, and paddle to the North Bridge and back. Rates are about $12 per hour on weekends, less on weekdays.

At **Walden Pond State Reservation** ★★, 915 Walden St., Rte. 126 (✆ **978/369-3254;** www.mass.gov/dcr), a pile of stones marks the site of the cabin where Thoreau lived from 1845 to 1847. Today the picturesque reservation is an extremely popular destination for walking (a path circles the pond), swimming, and fishing. Although crowded, it's well preserved and insulated from development, making it less difficult than you might expect to imagine Thoreau's experience. Call for the schedule of interpretive programs. No dogs or bikes are allowed. Parking costs $5. In good weather, the lot fills early every day—call before setting out, because the rangers turn away visitors if the park has reached capacity (1,000). From Concord Center, take Walden Street (Rte. 126) south, cross Route 2, and follow signs to the parking lot.

Another Thoreau haunt, an especially popular destination for birders, is **Great Meadows National Wildlife Refuge** ★, 73 Weir Hill Rd., Sudbury (✆ **978/443-4661;** www.fws.gov/northeast/greatmeadows). The Concord portion of the 3,400-acre refuge includes 2.5 miles of walking trails around man-made ponds that attract abundant wildlife. More than 200 species of native and migratory birds have been recorded. The refuge is open daily from sunrise to sunset; admission is free. Dogs are not allowed. Follow Route 62 (Bedford St.) east out of Concord Center for 1⅓ miles, then turn left onto Monsen Road.

SHOPPING

Downtown Concord, off **Monument Square,** is a terrific shopping destination. Here you'll find the **Concord Toy Shop,** 4 Walden St. (✆ **978/369-2553**); the **Grasshopper Shop,** 36 Main St. (✆ **978/369-8295**), which carries women's clothing and accessories; jewelry and art at **Catseye,** 48 Monument Sq. (✆ **978/369-8377**); and the **Concord Bookshop,** 65 Main St. (✆ **978/371-2672**). The compact shopping district in **West Concord,** along Route 62, boasts the old-fashioned **West Concord 5 & 10,** 106 Commonwealth Ave. (✆ **978/369-9011**), which carries everything from light bulbs to lace.

WHERE TO STAY

The **Best Western at Historic Concord,** 740 Elm St. (✆ **800/780-7234** or 978/369-6100; www.bestwestern.com), is just off Route 2, about 2 miles from the center of town. The motel has a fitness room and a seasonal outdoor pool. Doubles go for $109 to $149, which includes continental breakfast.

Concord's Colonial Inn ★ The main building of the Colonial Inn has overlooked Monument Square since 1716. Like many historic inns, it's not luxurious, but it is comfortable and centrally located. Additions since it became a hotel in 1889 have left the inn large enough to offer modern conveniences (including wireless Internet access) and small enough to feel friendly. It's popular with businesspeople as well as vacationers, especially during foliage season. The 15 original guest rooms—one of which (no. 24) supposedly is haunted—are in great demand. Reserve early if you want to stay in the main inn, which is decorated in Colonial style. Rooms in the 1970 Prescott Wing have country-style decor, and four free-standing buildings hold one-, two-, and three-bedroom suites suitable for long-term stays.

Two lounges serve light meals; sit on the porch and you'll have a front-row seat for the action on Monument Square. The lovely restaurant serves salads, sandwiches, and pasta at lunch, and traditional American fare at dinner. Afternoon tea is served Friday through Sunday; reservations required (✆ **978/369-2373**).

48 Monument Sq., Concord, MA 01742. ✆ **800/370-9200** or 978/369-9200. Fax 978/371-1533. www.concordscolonialinn.com. 56 units (some with shower only). Double main inn $159–$239 May–Aug, $199–$279 Sept–Oct, $139–$199 Nov–Apr. Double Prescott Wing $139–$219 May–Aug, $179–$259 Sept–Oct, $119–$179 Nov–Apr. Suites from $245 May–Aug, from $265 Sept–Oct, from $215 Nov–Apr. Children under 13 stay free in parent's room. Discounts available for stays of 4 nights or more. Packages available. AE, DC, DISC, MC, V. **Amenities:** Restaurant (American); lounge; bar w/live jazz and blues nightly; access to nearby health club ($10); concierge; tour desk; business center; same-day dry cleaning. *In room:* A/C, TV/DVD, wireless Internet access, coffeemaker, hair dryer, iron.

Hawthorne Inn ★★ This is the quintessential country inn. Built around 1870, it sits on a tree-shaded property across the street from Nathaniel Hawthorne's home, The Wayside. Antiques and handmade quilts enhance the rooms, which aren't huge but are meticulously maintained and gorgeously decorated. My favorite is the Walden Room, which has black wallpaper, but they're all delightful. Original art is on display throughout, and there's a small pond in the peaceful garden. Personable innkeepers Gregory Burch and Marilyn Mudry, who have been in business for more than 25 years, acquaint interested guests with the philosophical, spiritual, military, and literary aspects of Concord's history.

462 Lexington Rd., Concord, MA 01742. ✆ **978/369-5610**. Fax 978/287-4949. www.concordmass.com. 7 units (some with shower only). $165–$285 double. Rates include continental breakfast. Extra person $30. Off-season discounts available. AE, DISC, MC, V. From Concord Center, take Lexington Rd. ¼ mile east; inn is on right. *In room:* A/C, wireless Internet access, hair dryer, iron, robes.

A HISTORIC INN NEARBY

Longfellow's Wayside Inn ★★ Worth a visit even if you're not spending the night, this delightful institution dates to 1716 and got its name when Henry Wadsworth Longfellow published *Tales of a Wayside Inn* in 1863. Part of a nonprofit educational and charitable trust, it claims to be the country's oldest operating inn. All 10 guest rooms are decorated in attractive, not at all fussy Colonial style and furnished with antiques, but only two (the most popular, of course) are in the original building. Reserve as early as possible.

In addition to being a popular wedding and honeymoon destination, the inn is the centerpiece of what amounts to a tiny theme park. Buildings on the 106-acre property include the Redstone School (reputedly the school in "Mary Had a Little Lamb"), a wedding chapel, and a working gristmill. The mill grinds the wheat flour and cornmeal used in the inn's baked goods. Old grindstones dot the lawn, a pleasant spot for sunbathing.

In the rambling **dining rooms** ★, costumed staff members dish up generous portions of traditional New England fare, which often incorporates produce grown at the inn. The menu changes daily; favorite choices include prime rib, lobster casserole, chicken pie, and strawberry shortcake. You'll see lots of families—this seems to be *the* place for grandparents' birthdays. Food is served Monday through Saturday from 11:30am to 2:30pm and 5 to 9pm, Sunday from noon to 7:30pm (dinner menu

Tips North of Boston: Road Rules

For convenience and flexibility, drive if you can. The trip from Boston to Cape Ann on I-93 and Route 128 takes about an hour. A more leisurely excursion on Routes 1A, 129, and 114 takes you through Marblehead to Salem. You can also follow Route 1 to I-95 and Route 128, but don't attempt it during rush hour. To take Route 1A, leave downtown through the Callahan or Ted Williams Tunnel. If you miss the entrance and wind up on I-93, follow signs to Route 1 and pick up Route 1A in Revere. The **North of Boston Convention & Visitors Bureau** (© **800/742-5306** or 978/977-7760; www.northofboston.org) publishes a visitor guide that covers many destinations in this chapter.

only). Main courses are $9 to $15 at lunch, $17 to $30 at dinner. Reservations are recommended, especially on weekends.

Wayside Inn Rd., Sudbury, MA 01776. © **800/339-1776** or 978/443-1776. Fax 978/443-8041. www.wayside.org. 10 units (some with shower only). Summer $125–$160 double. Rates include breakfast. Extra person $15. Packages and off-season discounts available. AE, DC, DISC, MC, V. Closed July 4 and Dec 25. From Main St. in Concord, follow Sudbury Rd. to Rte. 20 west; 11 miles after passing I-95, bear right onto Wayside Inn Rd.; inn is on the right. *In room:* A/C.

WHERE TO DINE

See also the **Colonial Inn** and **Longfellow's Wayside Inn,** above. For basic to lavish picnic provisions, stop in downtown Concord at the **Cheese Shop,** 25–31 Walden St. (© **978/369-5778**).

Nashoba Brook Bakery & Café ★ AMERICAN The enticing variety of artisan breads, baked goods, pastries, and from-scratch soups, salads, and sandwiches makes this airy cafe a popular destination throughout the day. The industrial-looking building off West Concord's main street backs up to little Nashoba Brook, which is visible through the glass back wall. Order and pick up at the counter, then grab a seat along the window or near the children's play area. Or order takeout—this is great picnic food.

152 Commonwealth Ave., West Concord. © **978/318-1999.** www.slowrise.com. Sandwiches $6.50; other menu items $2–$8. MC, V. Mon–Fri 7am–5:30pm; Sat 7am–5pm; Sun 8am–5pm. From Concord Center, follow Main St. (Rte. 62) west, across Rte. 2; bear right at traffic light in front of train station and go 3 blocks. For overflow parking, turn right onto Commonwealth Ave. and right onto Winthrop St.

3 Marblehead ★★★

15 miles NE of Boston; 4 miles SE of Salem

Like an attractive person with a great personality, Marblehead has it all. Scenery, history, architecture, and shopping combine to make it one of the area's most popular day trips for both locals and visitors. The narrow streets of historic "Old Town" lead down to the magnificent harbor that helps make Marblehead the self-proclaimed "Yachting Capital of America." Plaques on many homes give the dates of construction as well as the names of the builders and original occupants—a history lesson without any studying.

Many of the houses have stood since before the Revolutionary War, when Marblehead was a center of merchant shipping. Two historic homes are open for tours. Allow at least a full morning to visit Marblehead, but be flexible, because you may want to hang around.

ESSENTIALS

GETTING THERE From Boston, take Route 1A north until you see signs in Lynn for Swampscott and Marblehead. Take Lynn Shore Drive to Route 129, and follow it into Marblehead. Or take I-93 or Route 1 to Route 128, then Route 114 through Salem into Marblehead. Except at rush hour, allow 35 to 40 minutes. Parking is tough, especially in Old Town—grab the first spot you see.

MBTA (✆ **800/392-6100** or 617/222-3200; www.mbta.com) bus no. 441/442 runs from Haymarket (Orange or Green Line) in Boston to downtown Marblehead. During weekday rush periods, bus no. 448/449 connects Marblehead to Downtown Crossing. The trip takes about an hour; the one-way fare at press time was $3.45.

VISITOR INFORMATION The **Marblehead Chamber of Commerce,** 62 Pleasant St. (✆ **781/631-2868;** www.visitmarblehead.com), is open weekdays from 9am to 5pm. The **information booth** (✆ **781/639-8469**) on Pleasant Street near Spring Street is open mid-May through October, weekdays from noon to 5pm, weekends from 10am to 6pm. Before you visit, download a description of a walking tour from the chamber website.

GETTING AROUND Wear good walking shoes—the car or bus can get you to Marblehead, but it can't negotiate many of the narrow streets of Old Town. The downtown area is fairly compact and moderately hilly.

SPECIAL EVENTS Sailing regattas take place all summer. The National Offshore One Design (NOOD) Regatta, or **Race Week,** falls in mid- to late July and attracts enthusiasts from all over the country. During the **Christmas Walk,** on the first weekend in December, Santa Claus arrives by lobster boat.

EXPLORING THE TOWN

A stroll through the winding streets of **Old Town** ★★★ invariably leads to shopping, snacking, or gazing at something picturesque, be it the harbor or a beautiful home. Be sure to spend some time in **Crocker Park** ★★, on the water off Front Street. Especially in warm weather, when boats jam the harbor, the view is breathtaking. The park has benches and allows picnicking. The view from **Fort Sewall,** at the other end of Front Street, is just as mesmerizing. The ruins of the fort, built in the 17th century and rebuilt late in the 18th, are another excellent picnic spot.

Just inland, the **Lafayette House** is a private home at the corner of Hooper and Union streets. Legend has it that one corner of the first floor was chopped off in 1824 to allow Lafayette's carriage to negotiate the turn. In Market Square, on Washington Street near State Street, is the **Old Town House,** a public meeting and gathering place since 1727.

By car or bicycle, the swanky residential community of **Marblehead Neck** ★ is worth a look. Follow Ocean Avenue across the causeway. Here you can visit the **Audubon Bird Sanctuary** (✆ **800/AUDUBON** or 781/259-9500; www.massaudubon.org); look for the tiny sign at the corner of Risley Ave. Admission is free. Or continue to **Castle Rock** for another eyeful of scenery. At the end of "the Neck," at Harbor and Ocean avenues, is **Chandler Hovey Park,** which has a (closed) lighthouse and a panoramic view. Many inns and B&Bs provide bikes for guests' use; to rent, visit **Marblehead Cycle,** 25 Bessom St., 1 block off Pleasant Street (✆ **781/631-1570;** www.marbleheadcycle.com). Bikes go for $14 for a half-day, $20 for a full day.

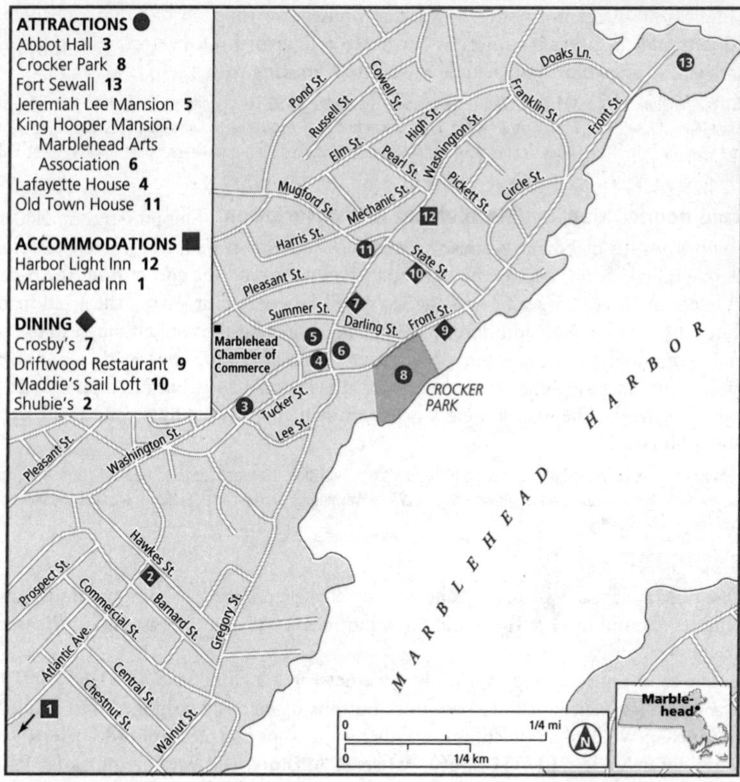

Abbot Hall A 5-minute stop here (look for the clock tower) is just the ticket if you want to be able to say you did some sightseeing. The town offices and Historical Commission share Abbot Hall with Archibald M. Willard's famous painting ***The Spirit of '76*** ★, on display in the Selectmen's Meeting Room. The thrill of recognizing the ubiquitous drummer, drummer boy, and fife player is the main reason to stop here. Cases in the halls contain artifacts from the Historical Society's collections.

Washington Sq. ✆ **781/631-0528.** www.marblehead.org. Free admission. Year-round Mon–Tues and Thurs 8am–5pm, Wed 7:30am–7:30pm, Fri 8am–1pm; May–Oct also open Fri 1–5pm, Sat 9am–6pm, Sun 11am–6pm. From the historic district, follow Washington St. up the hill.

Jeremiah Lee Mansion ★★ The prospect of seeing original hand-painted wallpaper in an 18th-century home is reason enough to visit this house, built in 1768 for a wealthy merchant and considered an extraordinary example of pre-Revolutionary Georgian architecture. Rococo woodcarving and other details complement historically accurate room arrangements, and ongoing restoration and interpretation by the Marblehead Museum & Historical Society place the 18th- and 19th-century furnishings and artifacts in context. The friendly guides welcome questions and are well versed in the history of the home. The lawn and gardens are open to the public.

Across the street is a visitor center that houses two galleries; one shows changing exhibits and the other paintings by the noted folk artist J. O. J. Frost, a Marblehead native. Call ahead for the schedule of **summer walking tours.**

161 Washington St. © **781/631-1768.** Guided tours $5 adults, $4.50 seniors and students. June–Oct Tues–Sat 10am–4pm. Closed Nov–May. Visitor center: 170 Washington St. Free admission. June–Oct Tues–Sat 10am–4pm; Nov–May Tues–Fri 10am–4pm. Follow Washington St. until it curves right and heads uphill toward Abbot Hall; mansion is on right.

King Hooper Mansion/Marblehead Arts Association Shipping tycoon Robert Hooper got his nickname because he treated his sailors so well, but it's easy to think he was called "King" because he lived like royalty. Around the corner from the home of Jeremiah Lee (whose sister was the second of Hooper's four wives), the 1728 mansion gained a Georgian addition in 1745. The period furnishings, although not original, engagingly illustrate the ubiquitous Colonial style. The Marblehead Arts Association stages exhibits, schedules special events, and runs a gift shop that sells members' work. The mansion has a lovely garden; enter through the gate at the right of the house.

8 Hooper St. © **781/631-2608.** www.marbleheadarts.org. Donation requested for tour. Tues–Sat 10am–4pm; Sun 1–5pm. Call ahead; no tours during private parties. Where Washington St. curves at the foot of hill near Lee Mansion, look for the colorful sign.

SHOPPING ★★

One of Marblehead's claims to fame is its excellent retail scene. Shops, boutiques, and galleries abound in **Old Town** and on **Atlantic Avenue** and the east end of **Pleasant Street.**

The most unusual shop in town is **Antiquewear,** 82 Front St. (© **781/639-0070**), near the town pier. It sells 19th-century buttons ingeniously fashioned into women's and men's jewelry of all descriptions. Other good stops include **Arnould Gallery,** 111 Washington St. (© **781/631-6366**); **Artists & Authors,** 108 Washington St. (© **781/639-0400;** www.artists-authors.com), which carries rare books and fine art; **Cargo Unlimited,** 82 Washington St. (© **781/631-1112;** www.cargounlimited.com), for home furnishings and accessories; **Erlich Gallery,** 96 Washington St. (© **781/631-1202**); **Lavender Home & Table,** 7 Pleasant St. (© **781/639-2238**), which specializes in French country wares; and the **Marblehead Toy Shop,** 44–48 Atlantic Ave. (© **781/631-9900**).

WHERE TO STAY

The accommodations listings of the **Chamber of Commerce** (© **781/631-2868;** www.visitmarblehead.com) include many of the town's innumerable inns and B&Bs. Contact the chamber or consult one of the agencies listed in chapter 4 under "Where to Stay."

Harbor Light Inn ★★ Two Federal-era mansions make up this gracious inn, a stone's throw from the Old Town House. From the wood floors to the 1729 beams (in a third-floor room) to the swimming pool, it's both historic and relaxing. Rooms are comfortably furnished in period style, with some lovely antiques; most have canopy or four-poster beds. Eleven have working fireplaces, and five of those have double Jacuzzis. The best rooms, on the top floor at the back of the building (away from the street), have gorgeous harbor views. If you don't book one, you can take in the scenery from the roof deck. Undeniably romantic, the inn also attracts business travelers.

58 Washington St., Marblehead, MA 01945. ✆ **781/631-2186.** Fax 781/631-2216. www.harborlightinn.com. 21 units (7 with shower only). $145–$335 double; $195–$335 suite. Rates include breakfast. Corporate rate available midweek. 2- to 3-night minimum weekends and holidays. AE, MC, V. Free parking. **Amenities:** Heated outdoor pool, access to nearby health club ($5); Jacuzzi; concierge; airport shuttle; in-room massage. *In room:* A/C, TV/VCR, wireless Internet access, hair dryer, iron, umbrella, robes.

Marblehead Inn ★ Kids This 1872 Victorian mansion just outside the historic district is an all-suite inn. Each attractive unit contains a living room, bedroom, and workstation. This is a good choice for businesspeople making an extended stay as well as families, who can make good use of the self-catering kitchenette. (Breakfast provisions are supplied.) It's not as romantic as the Harbor Light Inn, but it offers better amenities and a more family-friendly atmosphere. Most suites have Jacuzzis, and some have fireplaces and small patios.

264 Pleasant St. (Rte. 114), Marblehead, MA 01945. ✆ **800/399-5843** or 781/639-9999. Fax 781/639-9996. www.marbleheadinn.com. 10 units (2 with shower only). $109–$225 double. Rates include continental breakfast. Extra person $25. Children under 11 stay free in parent's room. Winter discounts, corporate, and long-term rates available. 2- to 3-night minimum weekends and holidays. AE, MC, V. Free parking. *In room:* A/C, TV/VCR, wireless Internet access, kitchenette, fridge, coffeemaker, hair dryer, umbrella.

A SEASIDE INN NEARBY

Diamond District Bed & Breakfast ★★ This comfortable Georgian-style mansion, built in 1911 as a private home, attracts both business and leisure travelers. The Atlantic is a block away; the 3-mile public beach (a good place to burn off the inn's generous breakfast) is popular for jogging, skating, and biking as well as swimming. It's visible from many of the good-size rooms, tastefully decorated with elaborate Victorian touches. The best are third-floor units with ocean views and Jacuzzis. Two rooms have cozy electric fireplaces. The large living room and porch overlook houses on Lynn Shore Drive and, just past them, the ocean. The whirlpool spa, on the back lawn, also has a water view.

The **1882 Stewart House,** across the street (away from the water), contains a common living room, a double room, two doubles that share a bathroom (a good choice for families), and a tiny single room.

142 Ocean St., Lynn, MA 01902. ✆ **800/666-3076** or 781/595-2200. Fax 781/599-5122. www.diamonddistrictinn.com. 15 units, 13 with private bathroom (some with shower only). $155–$285 double. Rates include breakfast. Extra person $20. Winter discounts available. 2-night minimum on busy weekends. AE, DC, DISC, MC, V. Take Rte. 1A north to signs for Swampscott/Marblehead; after rotary, take Lynn Shore Dr. north, past 2 lights and Christian Science Church. Turn left onto Wolcott Rd., then right onto Ocean St.; inn is on the right. **Amenities:** Outdoor whirlpool. *In room:* A/C, TV, dataport.

WHERE TO DINE

You can stock up for a picnic at a number of places in Old Town. **Crosby's,** 118 Washington St. (✆ **781/631-1741**), is a full-service market with a large prepared-food section. **Shubie's,** 32 Atlantic Ave. (✆ **781/631-0149**), carries a good selection of specialty foods.

Driftwood Restaurant ★ DINER/SEAFOOD At the foot of State Street next to Clark Landing (the town pier) is an honest-to-goodness local hangout. Join the crowd at a table or the counter for generous portions of breakfast (served all day) or lunch. Try pancakes or hash, chowder or a seafood "roll" (a hot-dog bun filled with, say, fried clams or lobster salad). The house specialty, served on weekends and holidays, is fried dough, a sort of New England beignet that's exactly as delicious and indigestible as it sounds.

63 Front St. ✆ **781/631-1145.** Main courses $3–$12; breakfast items under $7. No credit cards. Daily 5:30am–2pm.

Maddie's Sail Loft SEAFOOD Less than a block from the harbor, Maddie's is a friendly tavern that serves good steaks as well as excellent fresh seafood. The strong drinks are another attraction, especially during the summer boating season; this (or, alas, one of the private yacht clubs) is the place to search for that cute sailor you saw down by the water. There's live jazz on Thursday nights and a lively local scene year-round.

15 State St. © **781/631-9824.** Main courses $9–$16. No credit cards. Mon–Sat 11:45am–2pm and 5–10pm; Sun 11:45am–4pm. Bar open until 11:30pm.

4 Salem ★★

16 miles NE of Boston; 4 miles NW of Marblehead

Settled in 1626 (4 years before Boston) and later known around the world as a center of merchant shipping, Salem is internationally famous today for a 7-month episode in 1692. The witchcraft trials led to 20 deaths, centuries of notoriety, countless lessons on the evils of prejudice, and innumerable bad puns ("Stop by for a spell" is a favorite slogan). Today, the city abounds with witch-associated attractions. Most are historically accurate, but you'll also see a fair number of goofy souvenirs and opportunistic tourist traps. An excellent antidote is the **Peabody Essex Museum.** Salem is a family-friendly destination that's worth at least a half-day visit, perhaps after a stop in Marblehead; it can easily fill a day.

Visitors concentrating on wall-to-wall witches will miss another important part of the city's history. Salem's merchant vessels circled the globe in the 17th and 18th centuries, returning laden with treasures. The city peaked between the Revolutionary War and the War of 1812, with the opening of the China trade—many overseas merchants even believed that Salem was an independent country. One reminder of that era, a replica of the 1797 East Indiaman tall ship *Friendship,* is anchored near the Salem Maritime National Historic Site.

ESSENTIALS

GETTING THERE From Marblehead, take Route 114 west into downtown Salem. From Boston, take I-93 or Route 1 to Route 128, then Route 114 east. Or take Route 1A north from Boston, being careful in Lynn, where the road turns left and immediately right. There's metered street parking and a reasonably priced garage opposite the visitor center.

From Boston, the **MBTA** (© **800/392-6100** or 617/222-3200; www.mbta.com) runs commuter trains from North Station and bus no. 450 from Haymarket (Orange or Green Line). The train is more comfortable but runs less frequently. It takes 30 to 35 minutes; the round-trip fare is $7.50. The station is about 5 blocks from the downtown area. The one-way fare for the 35- to 55-minute bus trip is $3.45.

VISITOR INFORMATION A good place to start is the **National Park Service Regional Visitor Center,** 2 New Liberty St. (© **978/740-1650;** www.nps.gov/sama), open daily from 9am to 5pm. Exhibits highlight early settlement, maritime history, and the leather and textiles industries. The center distributes brochures and pamphlets, including one that describes a walking tour of the historic district, and has an auditorium where a free film on Essex County provides an overview.

The city tourism office, **Destination Salem** (© **877/SALEM-MA** or 978/744-3663; www.salem.org), produces a free visitor guide that includes a good map. The

Salem

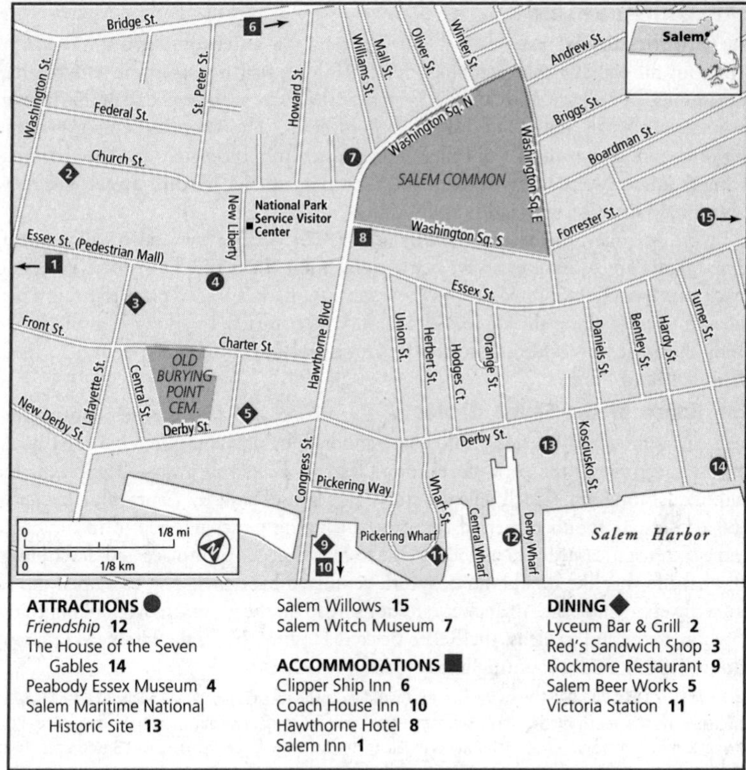

Salem Chamber of Commerce, 63A Wharf St. (✆ **978/744-0004;** www.salemchamber.org), maintains a rack of brochures and pamphlets at its office on Pickering Wharf. It's open weekdays 9am to 5pm. Salem has an excellent community website, **www.salemweb.com.**

GETTING AROUND In the congested downtown area, walking is the way to go. If it's hot or you plan lots of sightseeing, you might prefer to ride. **Salem Trolley** ★ (✆ **508/744-5469;** www.salemtrolley.com) offers a 1-hour narrated tour and unlimited reboarding at any of its 12 stops. The tour starts at the Essex Street side of the visitor center. It operates from 10am to 5pm (last tour at 4pm), daily April through October; check ahead for November hours. Tickets ($12 adults, $10 seniors, $3 children 5–14) are good all day.

SPECIAL EVENTS The city's month-long Halloween celebration, **Haunted Happenings** ★★ (www.hauntedhappenings.org), includes parades, parties, tours, and a ceremony on the big day. In July or August, the 2-day **Salem Maritime Festival** features music, food, and demonstrations of nautical crafts. During **Heritage Days,** a weeklong August event, the city celebrates its multicultural history with musical and theatrical performances, a parade, and fireworks.

EXPLORING SALEM

The **historic district** extends well inland from the waterfront; ask at the visitor center for the walking-tour pamphlet. Many 18th-century houses, some with original furnishings, still stand. Ship captains lived near the water at the east end of downtown, in relatively small houses crowded close together. The captains' employers, the shipping-company owners, built their homes away from the water (and the accompanying aromas). Many lived on the grand thoroughfare of **Chestnut Street** ★★, now a National Historic Landmark.

By car or trolley, the **Salem Willows** (✆ **978/745-0251;** www.salemwillows.com) amusements are 5 minutes away; many signs point the way. The strip of rides and snack bars has a honky-tonk air, and the waterfront park is a good place to bring a picnic and wander along the shore. Admission is free; metered parking is available. To enjoy the great view without the arcades and rides, have lunch one peninsula over at **Winter Island Park.**

The House of the Seven Gables ★ *Kids* Nathaniel Hawthorne's cousin lived here, and stories and legends of the house and its inhabitants inspired his 1851 book. If you haven't read the eerie novel, don't let that keep you away—begin with the audiovisual program, which tells the story. The house, built by Capt. John Turner in 1668, holds six rooms of period furniture, including pieces referred to in the book, and a secret staircase. Tours include a visit to Hawthorne's birthplace and descriptions of what life was like for the house's 18th-century inhabitants. The costumed guides are well versed and eager to answer questions. Also on the grounds, overlooking Salem Harbor, are period gardens, the Retire Beckett House (1655), the Hooper-Hathaway House (1682), and a counting house (1830).

54 Turner St. ✆ **978/744-0991**. www.7gables.org. Guided tour of house and grounds $12 adults, $11 seniors, $7.25 children 5–12, free for children under 5. Surcharges may apply for special exhibitions. July–Oct daily 10am–7pm; Nov–June daily 10am–5pm. Closed 1st 3 weeks of Jan. From downtown, follow Derby St. east 3 blocks past Derby Wharf.

Peabody Essex Museum ★★ *Kids* Now in its third century, the Peabody Essex has transformed itself into a national presence. All by itself, this captivating museum is reason enough to visit Salem.

Impressive collections of art from New England and around the world are the Peabody Essex's calling card, but they're just part of the story. The museum owns two dozen houses, including a well-preserved 18th-century Qing dynasty house, **Yin Yu Tang** ★, that was shipped here from China and reassembled. The only example of Chinese domestic architecture outside that country, the house captures 2 centuries of rural life. It sits outside a huge new wing designed by Moshe Safdie that allows the museum to display a significant proportion of its holdings for the first time.

Those holdings are impressive: The 1.4 million items in the permanent collections blend contemporary acquisitions with "the natural and artificial curiosities" that Salem's sea captains and merchants brought back from around the world to the Peabody Museum (1799) and local and domestic objects collected by the Essex Institute (1821), the county historical society. The displays help you understand the significance of each object, and interpretive materials (including interactive and hands-on activities) let children get involved. You might see objects related to the history of the port of Salem (including gorgeous furniture), the whaling trade, or the witchcraft trials. Other noteworthy collections include American, African, Indian,

Asian, and East Asian art and objects; photography; and the practical arts and crafts of East Asian, Pacific Island, and Native American peoples. Portraits of area residents include Charles Osgood's omnipresent rendering of Nathaniel Hawthorne.

East India Sq. © **800/745-4054** or 978/745-9500. www.pem.org. Admission $13 adults, $11 seniors, $9 students, free for children under 17. Surcharges may apply for special exhibitions. Daily 10am–5pm. Take Hawthorne Blvd. to Essex St., following signs for visitor center. Enter on Essex St. or New Liberty St.

Salem Maritime National Historic Site ★ Kids An entertaining introduction to Salem's seagoing history, this complex includes an exciting attraction: a real live ship. The ***Friendship*** ★★ is a full-size replica of a 1797 East Indiaman merchant vessel, a three-masted 171-footer that disappeared during the War of 1812. The guided ranger tour includes a tour of the ship.

Central Wharf holds a warehouse (ca. 1800) that houses the orientation center. Tours, which vary seasonally, expand on Salem's maritime history. Yours might include the Derby House (1762), a wedding gift to shipping magnate Elias Hasket Derby from his father, and the Custom House (1819). Legend (myth, really) has it that Nathaniel Hawthorne was working here when he found an embroidered scarlet "A." If you prefer to explore on your own, you can see the free film at the orientation center and wander around Derby Wharf, the West India Goods Store, the Bonded Warehouse, the Scale House, and Central Wharf.

174 Derby St. © **978/740-1660.** www.nps.gov/sama. Free admission. Guided tour $5 adults, $3 seniors and children 6–15. Daily 9am–5pm. Take Derby St. east; just past Pickering Wharf, Derby Wharf is on the right.

Salem Witch Museum ★★ Kids This is one of the most memorable attractions in eastern Massachusetts—it's both interesting and scary. The main draw of the museum (a former church) is a three-dimensional audiovisual presentation with life-size figures. The show takes place in a huge room lined with displays that are lighted in sequence. The 30-minute narration tells the tale of the witchcraft trials and the accompanying hysteria. The well-researched presentation recounts the story accurately, if somewhat overdramatically. One of the victims was crushed to death by rocks piled on a board on his chest—smaller kids may need a reminder that he's not real.

19½ Washington Sq., on Rte. 1A. © **978/744-1692.** www.salemwitchmuseum.com. Admission $7 adults, $6 seniors, $4.50 children 6–14. July–Aug daily 10am–7pm; Sept–June daily 10am–5pm; check ahead for Oct hours. Follow Hawthorne Blvd. to the northwest corner of Salem Common.

SHOPPING

Pickering Wharf, at the corner of Derby and Congress streets (© **978/740-6990;** www.pickeringwharf.com), is a waterfront complex of shops, boutiques, restaurants, and condos. It's popular for strolling, snacking, and shopping, and the central location makes it a local landmark.

Several shops specialize in witchcraft accessories. Bear in mind that Salem is home to many practicing witches who take their beliefs very seriously. The **Broom Closet,** 3–5 Central St. (© **978/741-3669**), and **Crow Haven Corner,** 125 Essex St. (© **978/745-8763;** www.crowhavencorner.net), stock everything from crystals to clothing.

Shops throughout New England sell the chocolate confections of **Harbor Sweets** ★★, Palmer Cove, 85 Leavitt St., off Lafayette Street (© **978/745-7648;** www.harborsweets.com). The retail store overlooks the floor of the factory. The deliriously good sweets are expensive, but candy bars and small assortments are available. Closed Sunday.

Trying Times: The Salem Witch Hysteria

The Salem witch trials took place in 1692, a product of old-world superstition, religious control of government, and plain old boredom.

The crisis began quietly in Salem Village (now the town of Danvers). The Rev. Samuel Parris's household included his 9-year-old daughter, Elizabeth, her cousin Abigail, and a West Indian slave named Tituba who told stories to amuse the girls during the long, harsh winter. Entertained by tales of witchcraft, sorcery, and fortunetelling, the girls and their friends began to act out the stories, claiming to be under a spell, rolling on the ground and wailing. The settlers, aware that thousands of people in Europe had been executed as witches in the previous centuries, took the behavior seriously.

At first, only Tituba and two other women were accused of casting spells. The infighting typical of the Puritan theocracy surfaced soon enough, and an accusation of witchcraft became a handy way to settle a score. Anyone "different" was a potential target, from the elderly to the deaf to the poor. A special court convened in Salem proper, and although the girls recanted, the trials began. Defendants had no counsel, and pleading not guilty or objecting to the proceedings was considered equivalent to a confession. From March 1 to September 22, of the more than 150 people who were accused, 27 were convicted.

In the end, 19 people went to the gallows, and one man who refused to plead, Giles Corey, was pressed to death by stones piled on a board on his chest. Finally, cooler heads prevailed. Leading cleric Cotton Mather and his father, Harvard president Increase Mather, led the call for tolerance. With the jails overflowing, the court called off the trials and freed the remaining prisoners, including Tituba.

The episode's lessons about open-mindedness and tolerance have echoed through the years. Salem was the backdrop for Arthur Miller's 1953 play *The Crucible.* It is both a story about the witch trials and an allegory about the McCarthy Senate hearings—another kind of witch hunt in a time when those lessons needed to be taught again.

WHERE TO STAY

The busiest and most expensive time of year is **Halloween week;** reserve well in advance if you plan to travel anytime in October.

Most major chains are represented on or near Route 1 north of I-95, within 30 minutes of downtown Salem. The **Clipper Ship Inn,** 40 Bridge St., Rte. 1A (© **978/745-8022;** www.clippershipinn.com), is a comfortable, modern motel northeast of downtown. Doubles in high season run $130 to $170.

Coach House Inn Built in 1879 for a ship's captain, this welcoming inn is 2 blocks from the harbor and 9 blocks from downtown. The three-story mansion, set back from the street by a well-kept lawn, was renovated in 2002. The good-size guest rooms are elegantly furnished in traditional style. All have high ceilings, and most have (non-working) fireplaces. Breakfast arrives at your door in a basket. The inn is 20 minutes on foot or 5 minutes by car from the center of town, up the street from Salem State College.

284 Lafayette St. (Routes 1A and 114), Salem, MA 01970. ✆ **800/688-8689** or 978/744-4092. Fax 978/745-8031. www.coachhousesalem.com. 11 units, 9 with private bathroom (2 with shower only). $115–$175 double; $170–$230 2-room suite. Rates include continental breakfast. 2- to 3-night minimum weekends and holidays. AE, DISC, MC, V. Free parking. *In room:* A/C, TV, fridge, coffeemaker.

Hawthorne Hotel ★ This historic hotel, built in 1925, is both convenient and comfortable. It attracts vacationers and business travelers, and is popular for functions. The six-story building is centrally located and well maintained, with a traditional atmosphere. The guest rooms are attractively furnished and adequate in size. The best units, on the Salem Common (north) side of the building, have better views than rooms that face the street. Ask to be as high up as possible, because the neighborhood is busy.

18 Washington Sq. W. (at Salem Common), Salem, MA 01970. ✆ **800/729-7829** or 978/744-4080. Fax 978/745-9842. www.hawthornehotel.com. 89 units (30 with shower only). $104–$209 double; $209–$309 suite. Extra person $12. Children under 16 stay free in parent's room. Packages and off-season and senior discounts available. 2-night minimum May–Oct weekends. AE, DC, DISC, MC, V. Limited self-parking. Pets accepted; $10/day; $100 deposit. **Amenities:** Restaurant (American); tavern; exercise room; access to nearby heath club; concierge; airport shuttle; business center; limited room service; laundry service; same-day dry cleaning. *In room:* A/C, TV, wireless Internet access, hair dryer, iron, umbrella.

Salem Inn ★★ The Salem Inn occupies the comfortable niche between too-big hotel and too-small B&B. Rooms in the three buildings are large and tastefully decorated; some have fireplaces, canopy beds, and whirlpool baths. The best units are the honeymoon and family suites in the 1874 Peabody House. The variety allows the innkeepers to match accommodations with guests, whether they're honeymooners, sightseers, or families. Guests of all three houses can relax in the peaceful rose garden at the rear of the main building.

7 Summer St. (Rte. 114), Salem, MA 01970. ✆ **800/446-2995** or 978/741-0680. Fax 978/744-8924. www.SalemInnMA.com. 41 units (some with shower only). Nov–Sept $119–$149 double, $169–$229 suite; Oct $180–$210 double, $220–$285 suite. Rates include continental breakfast. 2- to 3-night minimum during holidays and special events. Winter packages available. AE, DC, DISC, MC, V. Free parking. Pets accepted by prior arrangement ($15–$25/night). *In room:* A/C, TV, coffeemaker, hair dryer, iron.

WHERE TO DINE

Pickering Wharf has a food court as well as a **Victoria Station** restaurant (✆ **978/744-7644**), with a menu that features seafood and traditional American fare and a great view of the marina from the deck. The restaurant and cafe at the **Peabody Essex Museum** (p. 164) serve lunch.

Lyceum Bar & Grill ★★ CONTEMPORARY AMERICAN The elegance of the Lyceum's dining rooms matches the quality of the food, which attracts local businesspeople and out-of-towners. Grilling is a favorite cooking technique—try the signature marinated grilled portobellos. They're available as an appetizer and scattered throughout the menu—say, in delectable pasta with chicken, red peppers, and Swiss chard in wine sauce. Meat and fish dishes, such as pork tenderloin with mashed sweet potatoes or pan-seared swordfish with wild-mushroom risotto, are equally delicious. Save room for a traditional yet sophisticated dessert—the brownie sundae is out of this world.

43 Church St. (at Washington St.). ✆ **978/745-7665.** www.lyceumsalem.com. Reservations recommended. Main courses $7–$12 lunch, $18–$29 dinner. AE, DISC, MC, V. Mon–Fri 11:30am–3pm; Sun brunch 11am–3pm; daily 5:30–10pm. Validated parking available.

Red's Sandwich Shop *Value* NEW ENGLAND Locals and visitors feel equally comfortable at this diner-style no-frills hangout in an 18th-century building. Hunker down at the counter or a table and be ready for your waitress to call you "dear" as she brings you eggs and fantastic pancakes at breakfast, or soup (opt for chicken over chowder) and a burger at lunch or dinner.

15 Central St. ✆ **978/745-3527.** www.redssandwichshop.com. Most items under $7. No credit cards. Mon–Sat 5am–9pm; Sun 6am–1pm.

Rockmore Restaurant ★ SEAFOOD/AMERICAN If you're going to eat at a restaurant with a gimmick, it might as well be a good gimmick. This is: It's on a float in the middle of Salem Harbor. The Rockmore serves burgers, sandwiches, and fresh seafood in an extremely casual atmosphere, usually to local boaters. The food is fine, but nobody's here for the food. (Did I mention it's on a *float?*) If you're not traveling by boat, ferry service is available from the Congress Street Bridge, next to Pickering Wharf.

Salem Harbor. ✆ **978/740-1001.** www.rockmore.us. Main courses $8–$16. AE, DISC, MC, V. Memorial Day to Labor Day daily 11am–10pm, weather permitting.

Salem Beer Works PUB GRUB Beer is the headliner at this popular downtown restaurant (a sibling of Boston Beer Works), but the food is also worth mentioning. Piled-high burgers, salads, sandwiches, and buckets of fried delicacies such as onion rings, jalapeño poppers, and pickles complement the house-made brews.

278 Derby St. ✆ **978/745-BEER.** www.beerworks.net. Main courses $6–$17. AE, DISC, MC, V. Sun–Thurs 11:30am–midnight; Fri–Sat 11:30am–1am.

Milling Around: A Trip to Lowell

A 19th-century textile center that later fell into disrepair, Lowell is a 21st-century success story. A city built around restored mills and industrial canals will never be a glamorous vacation spot, but thousands of visitors a year find Lowell a fascinating and rewarding destination. The sights concentrate on the history of the Industrial Revolution and the textile industry. They include boardinghouses where the "mill girls" lived; the workers, some as young as 10, averaged 14-hour days weaving cloth on power looms.

Start at the **Lowell National Historical Park Visitor Center,** 246 Market St. (✆ **978/970-5000;** www.nps.gov/lowe), open daily from 9am to 5pm. Rangers lead free programs and tours, and canal cruises and free trolley tours operate in summer. Ask for a map of the area, and use it to find your way around downtown. Two interesting museums are within walking distance: the **American Textile History Museum,** 491 Dutton St. (✆ **978/441-0400;** www.athm.org), and the **New England Quilt Museum** ★, 18 Shattuck St. (✆ **978/452-4207;** www.nequiltmuseum.org). For more information, consult the **Greater Merrimack Valley Convention & Visitors Bureau,** 9 Central St., Suite 201, Lowell (✆ **800/443-3332** or 978/459-6150; www.merrimackvalley.org).

To drive to Lowell, take Route 3 or I-495 to the Lowell Connector and follow signs north to Exit 5B and the historic district. The **commuter rail** (✆ **800/392-6100** or 617/222-3200; www.mbta.com) from Boston's North Station takes about 45 minutes and cost $11 round-trip at press time.

5 Cape Ann

Gloucester, Rockport, Essex, and Manchester-by-the-Sea make up Cape Ann, a rocky peninsula so enchantingly beautiful that when you hear the slogan "Massachusetts's *Other* Cape," you may forget what the first one was. Cape Ann and Cape Cod do share some attributes—scenery, shopping, seafood, and traffic. The smaller cape's proximity to Boston and manageable scale make it a wonderful day trip and a good choice for a longer stay.

With the decline of the fishing industry that brought great prosperity to the area in the 19th century, Cape Ann has played up its long-standing reputation as a haven for artists. Along with galleries and crafts shops, you'll find historical attractions, beaches—and oh, that scenery!

Although all four towns have large year-round populations, this is hardly a four-season destination. Many establishments close in fall or early winter through April or May; some open on weekends in December.

The **Cape Ann Transportation Authority** (✆ **978/283-7916;** www.canntran.com) runs buses from town to town on Cape Ann and operates special summer routes.

The **Cape Ann Chamber of Commerce,** 33 Commercial St., Gloucester (✆ **800/321-0133** or 978/283-1601; www.capeannvacations.com), and the **North of Boston Convention & Visitors Bureau** (✆ **800/742-5306** or 978/977-7760; www.northofboston.org) provide abundant visitor information.

MANCHESTER-BY-THE-SEA

The scenic route to Gloucester from points south is Route 127, which runs through Manchester-by-the-Sea, a lovely village incorporated in 1645. Now a prosperous suburb of Boston, Manchester is probably best known for **Singing Beach** (see "Life's a Beach . . . With Very Cold Water!" below). The **commuter rail** (✆ **800/392-6100** or 617/222-3200; www.mbta.com) from Boston cost $11 round-trip at press time and stops in the center of the compact downtown area, where there are many shops and restaurants. Nearby **Masconomo Park** overlooks the harbor.

The home of the Manchester Historical Society is the **Trask House,** 10 Union St. (✆ **978/526-7230;** www.manchesterhistorical.org), a 19th-century sea captain's home. Tours show off the period furnishings, including pieces produced in Manchester, and the society's costume collections. It's specialized, but intriguing to devotees of house tours. Open Monday to Thursday from 10:30am to 1pm, and by appointment. A donation is requested.

MAGNOLIA

Pay close attention as you head north from Manchester or south from Gloucester on Route 127—Magnolia is easy to miss, but the village (technically part of Gloucester) is worth a detour. Notable for its lack of waterfront commercial property, the village center is unremarkable. The homes surrounding it, many of them former summer residences now occupied year-round, are magnificent.

Just up the coast are two noteworthy geological formations; grab your camera. **Rafe's Chasm** is a huge cleft in the shoreline rock, opposite the reef of **Norman's Woe,** which figures in Henry Wadsworth Longfellow's scary poem "The Wreck of the *Hesperus.*" About ¾ of a mile out of the center, look for a small parking area on the right. After a ¼-mile walk through the woods, you'll find a gorgeous panorama of stone and surf.

Life's a Beach . . . With Very Cold Water!

Paradoxically, Cape Ann is almost as well known for its sandy beaches as for its rocky coastline. Things to know: First, the water is *cold.* Second, parking can be scarce, especially on weekends, and pricey—as much as $22. If you can't set out before breakfast, wait until midafternoon and hope that the early birds have had enough. During the summer, lifeguards are on duty from 9am to 5pm at larger public beaches. Surfing is generally permitted outside of those hours. The beaches listed here all have bathhouses and snack bars. Swimming or not, watch out for greenhead flies in July and August. They don't sting—they take little bites of flesh. Bring or buy insect repellent.

The best-known North Shore beach is **Singing Beach** ★★, off Masconomo Street in Manchester-by-the-Sea. Because it's accessible by public transportation, it attracts the most diverse crowd—carless singles, local families, and other beach bunnies of all ages. From the train station, they walk about ½ a mile on Beach Street to find sparkling sand and lively surf. Take the commuter rail (✆ **800/392-6100** or 617/222-3200; www.mbta.com) from Boston's North Station.

Nearly as famous and popular is **Crane Beach** ★, off Argilla Road in Ipswich, part of a 1,400-acre barrier beach reservation. Fragile dunes and a white-sand beach lead down to Ipswich Bay. The surf is calmer than that at less sheltered Singing Beach, but still quite chilly. Pick up Argilla Road south of Ipswich Center near the intersection of Routes 1A and 133 or take the Ipswich Essex Explorer bus (see "Ipswich," p. 183). Also on Ipswich Bay is Gloucester's **Wingaersheek Beach** ★, on Atlantic Street off Route 133. From Exit 13 off Route 128, the beach is about 15 minutes away (mind the speed limits). Wingaersheek has beautiful white sand, a glorious view, and more dunes. Because these beaches are harder to get to, they attract more locals—but also lots of day-tripping families.

Most other good beaches in Gloucester have almost no nonresident parking. Two exceptions are **Half Moon Beach** and **Cressy's Beach,** at Stage Fort Park, off Route 127 near Route 133 and downtown. The sandy beaches and the park snack bar are popular local hangouts.

ESSEX ★

West of Gloucester (past Rte. 128) on Route 133 lies a beautiful little town known for Essex clams, salt marshes, a long tradition of shipbuilding, a plethora of antiques shops, and one celebrated restaurant.

Legend has it that **Woodman's of Essex** ★★★, 121 Main St. (✆ **800/649-1773** or 978/768-6057; www.woodmans.com), was the birthplace of the fried clam in 1916. Today the thriving family business is a great spot to join legions of locals and visitors from around the world for lobster "in the rough," chowder, steamers, corn on the cob, onion rings, and (you guessed it) superb fried clams. Expect the line to be long, even in winter, but it moves quickly and offers a view of the regimented commotion in the food-preparation area. Credit cards aren't accepted, but there's an ATM

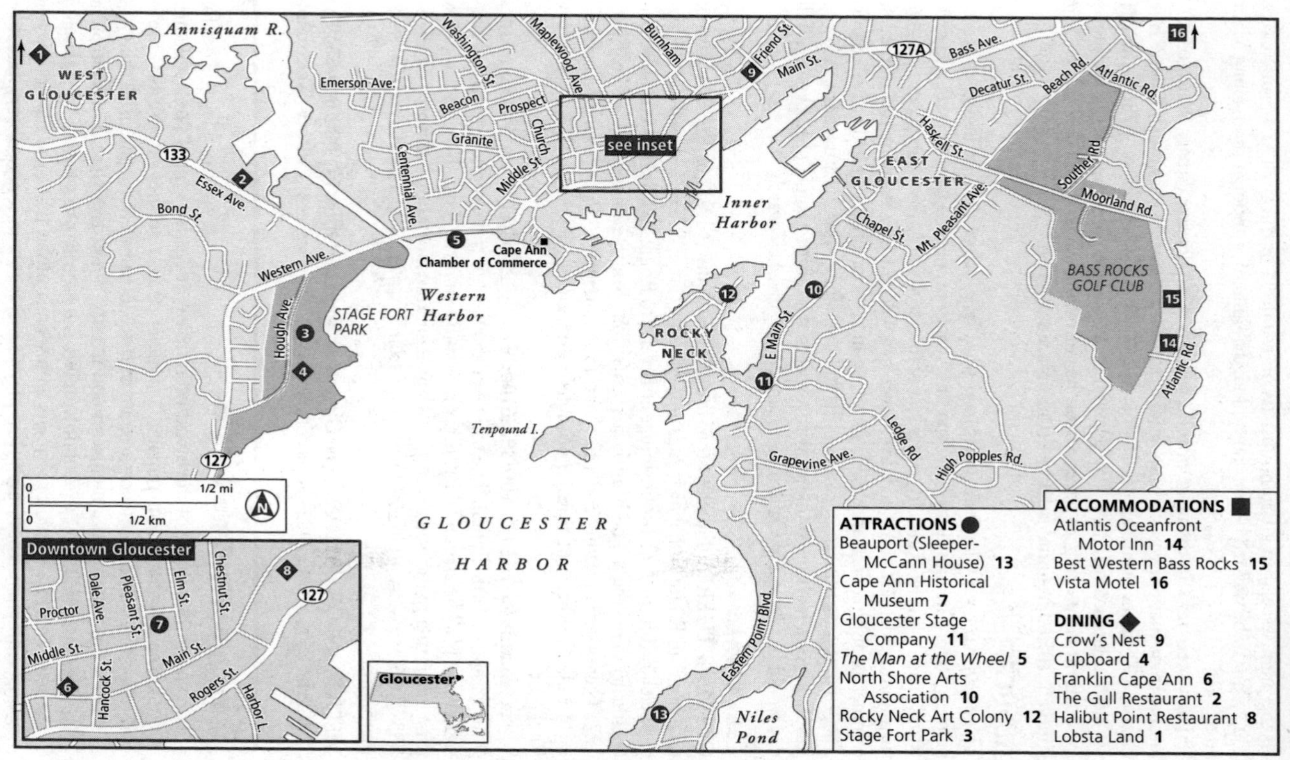
ATTRACTIONS
Beauport (Sleeper-McCann House) 13
Cape Ann Historical Museum 7
Gloucester Stage Company 11
The Man at the Wheel 5
North Shore Arts Association 10
Rocky Neck Art Colony 12
Stage Fort Park 3
ACCOMMODATIONS
Atlantis Oceanfront Motor Inn 14
Best Western Bass Rocks 15
Vista Motel 16
DINING
Crow's Nest 9
Cupboard 4
Franklin Cape Ann 6
The Gull Restaurant 2
Halibut Point Restaurant 8
Lobsta Land 1
Downtown Gloucester
Chestnut St.
Elm St.
Pleasant St.
Dale Ave.
Proctor
Middle St.
Main St.
Rogers St.
Hancock St.
Harbor L.
WEST GLOUCESTER
EAST GLOUCESTER
ROCKY NECK
Annisquam R.
Essex Ave.
Bond St.
Western Ave.
Hough Ave.
STAGE FORT PARK
Emerson Ave.
Centennial Ave.
Washington St.
Beacon
Granite
Prospect
Church
Middle St.
Maplewood Ave.
Burnham
Friend St.
Main St.
see inset
Cape Ann Chamber of Commerce
Western Harbor
Inner Harbor
Tenpound I.
GLOUCESTER HARBOR
Niles Pond
Eastern Point Blvd.
E Main St.
Grapevine Ave.
Ledge Rd
High Popples Rd.
Chapel St.
Mt. Pleasant Ave.
Haskell St.
Bass Ave.
Decatur St.
Beach Rd.
Atlantic Rd.
Souther Rd
Moorland Rd.
BASS ROCKS GOLF CLUB
Atlantic Rd.
Gloucester
1/2 mi
1/2 km
0
0

on the premises. Eat in a booth, upstairs on the deck, or out back at a picnic table. You'll want to be well fed before you explore the numerous antiques shops along Main Street.

The water views in town are of the Essex River, a saltwater estuary. Narrated 90-minute tours that put you in prime birding territory are available through **Essex River Cruises** ★, Essex Marina, 35 Dodge St. (✆ **800/748-3706** or 978/768-6981; www.essexcruises.com), daily May through October. The pontoon boat, which allows for excellent sightseeing, is screened and has restrooms. Tickets cost $22 adults, $19 seniors, $10 children under 13; reservations are suggested.

GLOUCESTER ★★

The ocean has been Gloucester's lifeblood since long before the first European settlement in 1623. The most urban of Cape Ann's communities, Gloucester (which rhymes with "roster") is a working city, not a cutesy tourist town. Miles of gorgeous coastline surround the densely populated downtown area. Gloucester is home to one of the last commercial fishing fleets in New England, an internationally celebrated artists' colony, a large Portuguese-American community, and just enough historic attractions. Allow at least half a day, perhaps combined with a visit to the tourist magnet of Rockport; a full day would be better, especially if you plan a cruise or whale-watch.

ESSENTIALS

GETTING THERE From Boston, the quickest route is I-93 (or Rte. 1, if it's not rush hour) to Route 128, which ends at Gloucester. From Salem, a slower but prettier approach is Route 1A across the bridge at Beverly to Route 127. It runs through Manchester to Gloucester. The Manchester exits from Route 128 allow access to Route 127. There's street parking and a free lot on the causeway to Rocky Neck. Gloucester is 33 miles northeast of Boston, 16 miles northeast of Salem, and 7 miles south of Rockport.

The **commuter rail** (✆ **800/392-6100** or 617/222-3200; www.mbta.com) runs from Boston's North Station. The trip takes about 1 hour; the round-trip fare at press time was $11. The station is across town from downtown, about 10 blocks, so allow time for getting to the waterfront. The **Cape Ann Transportation Authority** (✆ **978/283-7916;** www.canntran.com) runs buses from town to town as well as special summer routes.

VISITOR INFORMATION The **Gloucester Tourism Office** (✆ **800/649-6839** or 978/281-8865; www.gloucesterma.com) operates the excellent **Visitors Welcoming**

Moments ***The Perfect Storm***

Long after the release of the blockbuster movie, Sebastian Junger's best-selling book ***The Perfect Storm*** remains a popular reason to visit Gloucester. The thrilling but tragic nonfiction account of the "no-name" hurricane of 1991 centers on the ocean and a neighborhood tavern. The **Crow's Nest,** 334 Main St. (✆ **978/281-2965**), a bit east of downtown, is a no-frills place with a horseshoe-shaped bar and a crowd of regulars who seem amused that their hangout is a tourist attraction. The Crow's Nest plays a major role in Junger's story, but its ceilings aren't high enough for it to be a movie set—so the crew built an exact replica nearby.

Center at Stage Fort Park, off Route 127 at Route 133. It's open in summer daily from 9am to 5pm. The **Cape Ann Chamber of Commerce,** 33 Commercial St. (© **800/321-0133** or 978/283-1601; www.capeannvacations.com), is open year-round (summer weekdays 8am–6pm, Sat 10am–6pm, Sun 10am–4pm; winter weekdays 8am–5pm). It also operates a seasonal information booth on Rogers Street at Harbor Loop.

GETTING AROUND Downtown is fairly compact and walkable, but there's more to Gloucester than that. If you can manage it, travel by car. You'll be able to make the best use of your time, especially if you plan several stops. The **Cape Ann Transportation Authority** (see above) serves Gloucester.

SPECIAL EVENTS Gloucester holds summer festivals and street fairs that honor everything from clams to schooners. The best known is **St. Peter's Fiesta,** a colorful 4-day event at the end of June. The Italian-American fishing colony's festival has more in common with a carnival midway than a religious observation, but it's great fun. There are parades, rides, music, food, sporting events, and, on Sunday, the blessing of the fleet.

EXPLORING THE TOWN

Start at the water, as visitors have done for centuries. The French explorer Samuel de Champlain called the harbor "Le Beauport" in 1604—some 600 years after the Vikings first visited—and its configuration and proximity to good fishing gave it the reputation it enjoys to this day. Fishing is still Gloucester's leading industry (as your nose will tell you), with tourism a close second. The city is exceptionally welcoming—residents seem genuinely happy to see out-of-towners and to offer directions and insider info. The **Gloucester Maritime Trail** brochure, available at visitor centers, describes four excellent self-guided tours.

On Stacy Boulevard (west of downtown) is a reminder of the sea's danger. Leonard Craske's bronze statue of the **Gloucester Fisherman,** known as "The Man at the Wheel," bears the inscription "They That Go Down to the Sea in Ships 1623–1923." To the west is a memorial to the women and children who waited at home. As you take in the glorious view, consider this: More than 10,000 fishermen lost their lives during the city's first 300 years.

Stage Fort Park, off Route 127 near the intersection with Route 133, offers an excellent view of the harbor and has a busy seasonal snack bar, the Cupboard (© **978/281-1908**). The park is a good spot for picnicking, swimming, or playing on the cannons in the Revolutionary War fort.

To reach **East Gloucester,** follow signs as you leave downtown or go directly from Route 128, Exit 9. On East Main Street, you'll see signs for the world-famous **Rocky Neck Art Colony** ★★, the oldest continuously operating art colony in the country. Park in the lot on the tiny causeway and head west along Rocky Neck Avenue, which abounds with studios, galleries, restaurants, and people. The attraction is the presence of working artists, not just shops that happen to sell art. In summer, most galleries are open daily from 10am to 10pm. The prestigious **North Shore Arts Association,** 197 E. Main St. (© **978/283-1857;** www.northshoreartsassoc.org), founded in 1922, is open from late May to Columbus Day, Monday through Saturday from 10am to 5pm, Sunday from noon to 5pm. Admission is free.

Also in East Gloucester, the **Gloucester Stage Company** ★, 267 E. Main St. (© **978/281-4099;** www.gloucesterstage.com), is one of the best repertory troupes in New England. It schedules six plays a season (June to mid-Sept).

Beauport (Sleeper-McCann House) ★★ Historic New England, which owns and operates Beauport, describes it as a "fantasy house," and that's putting it mildly. Interior designer and antiquarian Henry Davis Sleeper accumulated vast stores of American and European decorative arts and antiques in his summer home. From 1907 to 1934, he decorated the 40 rooms, most of which are open to the public, to illustrate literary and historical themes. The entertaining tour concentrates more on the house in general than on the countless objects. You'll see architectural details from other buildings, magnificent arrangements of colored glassware, the "Red Indian Room" (with a majestic view of the harbor), and "Strawberry Hill," the master bedroom. Note that the house is closed on summer weekends.

75 Eastern Point Blvd. ✆ **978/283-0800.** www.historicnewengland.org. Guided tour $10 adults, $9 seniors, $5 students and children 6–12. Tours on the hour. June to mid-Sept Mon–Fri 10am–4pm; mid-Sept to Oct 15 daily 10am–4pm. Closed Oct 16–May and summer weekends. Take E. Main St. south to Eastern Point Blvd. (a private road), continue ½ a mile to house, park on left.

Cape Ann Historical Museum ★ This meticulously curated museum makes an excellent introduction to Cape Ann's history and artists. It devotes an entire gallery to the extraordinary work of **Fitz Hugh Lane** ★★★ (also known as Fitz Henry Lane), the Luminist painter whose light-flooded canvases show off the best of his native Gloucester. The nation's single largest collection of his paintings and drawings is here. Other galleries feature works on paper by 20th-century artists such as Maurice Prendergast and Milton Avery, work by other contemporary artists, and granite-quarrying tools and equipment. There's also an outdoor sculpture court. The maritime and fisheries galleries display entire vessels, exhibits on the fishing industry, ship models, and historic photographs and models of the Gloucester waterfront. The Capt. Elias Davis House (1804), decorated and furnished in Federal style, is part of the museum.

27 Pleasant St. ✆ **978/283-0455.** www.capeannhistoricalmuseum.org. Admission $6.50 adults, $6 seniors, $4.50 students, free for children under 6. Mar–Jan Tues–Sat 10am–5pm; Sun 1–4pm. Closed Feb. Follow Main St. west through downtown and turn right onto Pleasant St.; the museum is 1 block up on right. Metered parking on street or in lot across street.

SCHOONER CRUISES

For information on whale-watches, see "A Whale of an Adventure," above.

The schooner ***Thomas E. Lannon*** ★ (✆ **978/281-6634;** www.schooner.org) is a lovely reproduction of a Gloucester fishing vessel. The 65-foot tall ship sails from Seven Seas Wharf downtown; 2-hour excursions ($35 for adults, $30 for seniors, $25 for children under 17) leave about four times a day from mid-June to mid-September, less often on weekends from mid-May to mid-June and mid-September to mid-October. Reservations are recommended. The company offers music and dining cruises, including lobster bakes on Friday.

SHOPPING

Rocky Neck (see "Exploring the Town," above) offers great browsing. If you admired the wardrobe design in *The Perfect Storm,* check out the shirts and caps at **Cape Pond Ice,** 104 Commercial St., near the Chamber of Commerce (✆ **978/283-0174;** www.capepondice.com). Downtown, Main Street between Pleasant and Washington streets is a good destination. Agreeable stops include **Mystery Train,** 178 Main St. (✆ **978/281-8911;** www.mystrain.com), which carries used LPs, CDs, tapes, and videos; **Ménage Gallery,** 134 Main St. (✆ **978/283-6030**), which shows work by

Kids A Whale of an Adventure

The waters off the Massachusetts coast are prime **whale-watching** ★★ territory, and Gloucester is a center of cruises. Stellwagen Bank, which runs from Gloucester to Provincetown about 27 miles east of Boston, is a rich feeding ground for the magnificent mammals, which dine on sand eels and other fish that gather on the ridge. The whales often perform by jumping out of the water, and dolphins occasionally join the show. Naturalists on board narrate the trip for the companies listed here, pointing out the whales and describing birds and fish that cross your path.

Whale-watching is not particularly time- or cost-effective, especially if restless children are along, but it's so popular for a reason: The payoff is, literally and figuratively, huge. This is an experience that kids (and adults) will remember for a long time.

The season runs from April or May to October. Bundle up—it's much cooler at sea than on land—and wear a hat and rubber-soled shoes. Pack sunglasses, sunscreen, and a camera. If you're prone to motion sickness, take precautions, because you'll be at sea for 4 to 6 hours.

This is an extremely competitive business—they'd deny it, but the companies are virtually indistinguishable. Most guarantee sightings, offer morning and afternoon cruises and deep-sea fishing excursions, honor other firms' coupons, and offer Internet, AARP, and AAA discounts. Check ahead for sailing times, prices ($34–$38 for adults, less for seniors and children), and reservations, which are strongly recommended. In downtown Gloucester, **Cape Ann Whale Watch** (© **800/877-5110** or 978/283-5110; www.caww.com), is the best-known operation. Also downtown are **Capt. Bill & Sons Whale Watch** (© **800/339-4253** or 978/283-6995; www.captbillandsons.com) and **Seven Seas Whale Watch** (© **800/238-1776** or 978/283-1776; www.7seas-whalewatch.com). At the Cape Ann Marina, off Route 133, is **Yankee Whale Watch** (© **800/WHALING** or 978/283-0313; www.yankeefleet.com).

artists and artisans; and the **Dogtown Book Shop,** 2 Duncan St. (© **978/281-5599**), noted for its used and antiquarian selection.

WHERE TO STAY

The 40-unit **Vista Motel,** 22 Thatcher Rd. (Rte. 127A), Gloucester (© **866/VISTA-MA** or 978/281-3410; www.vistamotel.com), is a comfortable establishment on a hilltop near the Rockport border. Summer rates run $125 to $145 for standard rooms, $155 to $175 for efficiencies.

Atlantis Oceanfront Motor Inn This motor inn sits across the street from the water, affording stunning views from every window. The well-maintained, good-size guest rooms are decorated in comfortable, contemporary style. Every unit has a terrace or balcony. The view from second-floor accommodations is a little better. The

Atlantis doesn't have the resort feel of its pricier neighbor, the Bass Rocks Ocean Inn, but the views are the same.

125 Atlantic Rd., Gloucester, MA 01930. ✆ **800/732-6313** or 978/283-0014. Fax 978/281-8994. www.atlantismotorinn.com. 40 units (7 with shower only). Late June to Labor Day $155–$185 double; spring and fall $130–$160 double. Children under 12 stay free in parent's room. Extra person $8. Off-season midweek discounts available. Closed Nov to mid-Apr. Minimum stay may be required. AE, MC, V. Follow Rte. 128 to the end (Exit 9, East Gloucester), turn left onto Bass Ave. (Rte. 127A), and follow it ½ mile. Turn right and follow Atlantic Rd. **Amenities:** Coffee shop (breakfast only); heated outdoor pool. *In room:* A/C, TV, wireless Internet access, coffeemaker, hair dryer.

Best Western Bass Rocks Ocean Inn The Bass Rocks Ocean Inn offers gorgeous views and modern accommodations in a traditional setting. The spacious guest rooms take up a sprawling, comfortable two-story motel across the road from the rocky shore. A Colonial Revival mansion built in 1899 and known as the "wedding-cake house" holds a handful of newly renovated one-bedroom suites and the public areas, including a billiard room and library. The inn has an old-fashioned resort feel that distinguishes it from the neighboring Atlantis. Each unit has a balcony or patio; second-floor rooms have slightly better views. In the afternoon, the staff serves coffee, tea, lemonade, and cookies.

107 Atlantic Rd., Gloucester, MA 01930. ✆ **800/528-1234** or 978/283-7600. Fax 978/281-6489. www.bassrocksoceaninn.com. 48 units. $160–$350 double; $450 suite. Extra person $10; rollaway or crib $12. Children under 12 stay free in parent's room. Rates include continental breakfast. 3-night minimum summer weekends, some spring and fall weekends. Closed Nov to late Apr. AE, DC, DISC, MC, V. Follow Rte. 128 to the end (Exit 9, East Gloucester), turn left onto Bass Ave. (Rte. 127A), and follow it ½ mile; turn right and follow Atlantic Rd. **Amenities:** Heated outdoor pool; free bikes. *In room:* A/C, TV/VCR, wireless Internet access, fridge, coffeemaker, hair dryer, iron.

WHERE TO DINE

See "Essex," above, for information on the celebrated **Woodman's of Essex,** which is about 20 minutes from downtown Gloucester. The Stage Fort Park snack bar, the **Cupboard** (✆ **978/281-1908**), serves excellent fried seafood and blue-plate specials in the summer. **Lobsta Land,** 10 Causeway St., near Exit 12 off Route 128 (✆ **978/281-0415**), is a summer-only destination for familiar and unusual seafood dishes and amazing french fries.

The Franklin Cape Ann ★★ BISTRO A sophisticated offshoot of a neighborhood favorite in Boston's South End, the Franklin is a welcome addition to the fried-seafood-focused local dining scene. It does serve seafood, but in inventive preparations such as panko-crusted scallops accompanied by delectable lemon sauce, and pan-seared Atlantic cod with oyster mushrooms, scallions, and ginger. Meat dishes are equally creative. The two-story restaurant also offers fabulous martinis and live jazz at least 1 night a week, making it a popular late-evening destination.

118 Main St. ✆ **978/283-7888.** www.franklincapeann.com. Reservations recommended. Main courses $10–$17. AE, MC, V. Sun–Thurs 5–10:30pm, Fri–Sat 5pm–midnight; bar daily 4:30pm–1am.

The Gull Restaurant ★★ Kids SEAFOOD/AMERICAN Floor-to-ceiling windows show off the Annisquam River from almost every seat at The Gull. The big, welcoming restaurant is known for prime rib as well as excellent seafood. It draws locals, visitors, boaters, and families for large portions at reasonable prices, and the lounge is a local hangout. The seafood chowder is famous, appetizers tend toward bar food, and the french fries are terrific. Daily specials run from simple lobster (market price) to sophisticated fish and meat dishes. At lunch, there's an extensive sandwich menu.

75 Essex Ave. (Rte. 133), at Cape Ann Marina. ✆ **978/281-6060.** www.thegullrestaurant.com. Reservations recommended for parties of 8 or more. Main courses $7–$13 lunch, $8–$22 dinner; breakfast items $4–$9; children's menu $4–$6. DISC, MC, V. Daily May to mid-Oct 6am–10pm (lounge open until 1am). Closed mid-Oct to Apr. Take Rte. 133 west from intersection with Rte. 127, or take Rte. 133 east from Rte. 128.

Halibut Point Restaurant SEAFOOD/AMERICAN A local legend for its chowders and burgers, Halibut Point is a friendly tavern that serves generous portions of good food. The "Halibut Point Special"—a cup of chowder, a burger, and a beer—hits the high points. The clam chowder is terrific, and some people come to Gloucester just for the spicy Italian fish chowder. There's also a raw bar. Main courses are simple (mostly sandwiches) at lunch, more elaborate at dinner. Be sure to check the specials board—you didn't come all this way to a fishing port not to have fresh fish, did you?

289 Main St. ✆ **978/281-1900.** Main courses $5–$12 lunch, $9–$17 dinner. AE, DISC, MC, V. Daily 11:30am–11pm.

ROCKPORT

This lovely little town at the tip of Cape Ann was settled in 1690. Over the years it has been a fishing port, a center of granite excavation, and a thriving summer community whose specialty seems to be selling fudge and refrigerator magnets to out-of-towners. But there's more to Rockport than just gift shops. It's home to a lovely state park, and it's popular with photographers, sculptors, jewelry designers, and painters. Winslow Homer, Fitz Hugh Lane, and Childe Hassam are among the famous artists who have captured the local color. At times, especially on summer weekends, you'll be hard pressed to find much local color in this tourist-weary destination. But for every year-round resident who seems genuinely startled when people with cameras around their necks descend each June, there are dozens who are proud to show off their town.

Rockport makes an entertaining half-day trip, perhaps combined with a visit to Gloucester. Out of season, from January to mid-April, Rockport is pretty but somewhat desolate, though some businesses stay open and keep reduced hours.

ESSENTIALS

GETTING THERE Rockport is north of Gloucester along Route 127 or 127A. At the end of Route 128, turn left at the signs for Rockport to take 127, which is shorter but more commercial. To take 127A, continue on 128 to the sign for East Gloucester and turn left. Parking is next to impossible, especially on summer Saturday afternoons. Make one loop around downtown, and then head to the free parking lot on Upper Main Street (Rte. 127). The shuttle bus to downtown costs $1. Rockport is 40 miles northeast of Boston, 7 miles north of Gloucester.

The **commuter rail** (✆ **800/392-6100** or 617/222-3200; www.mbta.com) runs from Boston's North Station. The trip takes 60 to 70 minutes; the round-trip fare at press time was $12. The station is about 6 blocks from the downtown waterfront. **Cape Ann Transportation Authority** (✆ **978/283-7916;** www.canntran.com) buses serve Rockport.

VISITOR INFORMATION The **Rockport Chamber of Commerce,** 33 Whistlestop Mall (✆ **888/726-3922** or 978/546-6575; www.rockportusa.com), is open daily from 9am to 5pm. From mid-May to mid-October, it operates an information booth on Upper Main Street (Rte. 127), about a mile from the town line and a mile from downtown—look for the WELCOME TO ROCKPORT sign. The Rockport

Chamber is a division of the Cape Ann Chamber of Commerce (see "Gloucester," earlier in this chapter), which is also a good source of information.

GETTING AROUND For traffic and congestion, Boston has nothing on Rockport on a summer weekend afternoon. If you can schedule only one weekday trip, make it this one. When you arrive, park and walk, especially downtown. The Cape Ann Transportation Authority (see above) runs within the town.

SPECIAL EVENTS The **Rockport Chamber Music Festival** (✆ **978/546-7391;** www.rcmf.org) takes place in June at the Rockport Art Association, 12 Main St. Events include performances, family concerts, lectures, and discussions. The annual **Christmas pageant,** on Main Street in early December, is a kid-friendly event with carol singing and live animals.

EXPLORING THE TOWN

The most famous sight in Rockport has something of an "Emperor's New Clothes" aura—it's a wooden fish warehouse on the town wharf, or T-Wharf, in the harbor. The barn-red shack known as **Motif No. 1** is the most frequently painted and photographed object in a town filled with lovely buildings and surrounded by rocky coastline. The color certainly catches the eye in the neutrals of the surrounding seascape, but you may find yourself wondering what the big deal is. Originally constructed in 1884 and destroyed during the blizzard of 1978, Motif No. 1 was rebuilt using donations from residents and visitors. It stands again on the same pier, duplicated in every detail, reinforced to withstand storms.

Nearby is **Bearskin Neck,** named after an unfortunate ursine visitor who washed ashore in 1800. It holds perhaps the highest concentration of gift shops anywhere. The narrow peninsula has one main street (South Rd.) and several alleys crammed with galleries, snack bars, antiques shops, and ancient houses. The peninsula ends in a plaza with a magnificent water view.

Throughout town, more than two dozen **art galleries** ★ display the work of local and nationally known artists. The **Rockport Art Association,** 12 Main St. (✆ **978/546-6604;** www.rockportartassn.org), sponsors exhibitions and special shows. It's open daily in the summer, Tuesday through Sunday in the winter.

The 1922 **Paper House,** 52 Pigeon Hill St., Pigeon Cove (✆ **978/546-2629**), is an unusual experience. Everything in it (including the furniture) was built entirely out of 100,000 newspapers. Every item is made from papers of a different period. It's open April through October, daily from 10am to 5pm. Admission is $1.50 for adults, $1 for children. Follow Route 127 north from downtown about 1½ miles until you see signs at Curtis Street pointing to the left.

SHOPPING

Bearskin Neck is the obvious place to start. Dozens of little shops stock clothes, gifts, toys, jewelry, souvenirs, inexpensive novelties, and expensive handmade crafts and paintings. Another enjoyable stroll is along **Main** and **Mount Pleasant streets.** Good stops include the nonprofit **Toad Hall Bookstore,** 47 Main St. (✆ **978/546-7323**); **New England Goods,** 57 Main St. (✆ **978/546-9677**), where the stock is exclusively local; and **Willoughby's,** 20 Main St. (✆ **978/546-9820**), a women's clothing and accessories shop.

Two favorite stops are retro delights. Downtown, you can watch taffy being made at **Tuck's Candy Factory,** 7 Dock Sq. (✆ **800/569-2767** or 978/546-6352), a local

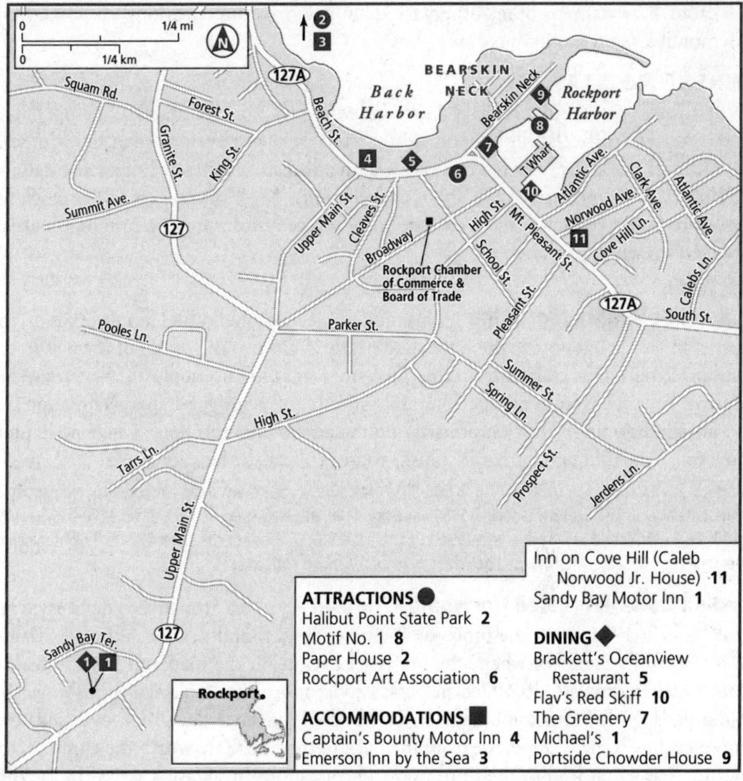

landmark since the 1920s. Near the train station, **Crackerjacks,** 27 Whistlestop Mall, off Railroad Avenue (✆ **978/546-1616**), is an old-fashioned variety store with a great crafts department.

A TRIP TO THE EDGE OF THE SEA

The very tip of Cape Ann is accessible to the public, and well worth the 2½-mile trip north on Route 127 to **Halibut Point State Park** ★★ (✆ **978/546-2997;** www.mass.gov/dcr). The surf-battered point got its name not from the fish, but because sailing ships heading for Rockport and Gloucester must "haul about" when they reach the jutting promontory. This is a great place to wander around and admire the scenery. On a clear day, you can see Maine.

About 10 minutes from the parking area, you'll come to a huge water-filled quarry next to a visitor center, where staffers dispense information, brochures, and bird lists. Swimming in the quarry is absolutely forbidden. There are walking trails, tidal pools, a World War II observation tower, and a rocky beach where you can climb around on giant boulders. To take a self-guided tour, pick up a brochure at the visitor center or the Chamber of Commerce. Call ahead for information about other special programs, scheduled from May through September. The park is open daily from Memorial Day to Labor Day 8am to 8pm, otherwise daily dawn to dusk; parking costs $2 from Memorial Day to Columbus Day.

WHERE TO STAY

When Rockport is busy, it's very busy, and when it's not, it's practically empty. The town's dozens of B&Bs fill in good weather and empty or even close in the winter. If you haven't made summer reservations well in advance, cross your fingers and call the Chamber of Commerce to ask about cancellations. Most innkeepers will arrange for guests to be picked up at the train station; if you're not driving, be sure to ask about this service when you reserve.

In Town

Captain's Bounty Motor Inn This modern, recently renovated motor inn is on the water. In fact, it's almost *in* the water, and nearly as close to the center of town as to the harbor. Each rather plain unit in the three-story building overlooks the water and has its own balcony. Rooms are spacious and soundproof, with good cross-ventilation but no air-conditioning. The best units are on the adults-only top floor. Kitchenette units are available. Although it's hardly plush, you can't beat the location.

1 Beach St., Rockport, MA 01966. ✆ **978/546-9557.** Fax 978/546-9993. www.captainsbountymotorinn.com. 24 units. Late May to late Sept $150 double, $160 efficiency, $180 efficiency suite; spring and fall $100–$120 double, $110–$125 efficiency, $125–$135 efficiency suite. Extra adult $10; $5 for each child over 5. 2- to 3-night minimum weekends and holidays. MC, V. Closed Nov–Mar. *In room:* TV, fridge, coffeemaker.

Inn on Cove Hill (Caleb Norwood Jr. House) ★ This attractive Federal-style inn was built in 1771 using the proceeds of pirates' gold found nearby. Although it's just 2 blocks from the town wharf, the inn is set back from the road and has a hideaway feel. Guest rooms are decorated in period style; most have Colonial furnishings and handmade quilts, and some have canopy beds. Innkeeper Betsy Eck overhauls one room each winter. Water views from the back of the house are worth the climb on the narrow stairs that lead to the third floor. The generous breakfast is served in the dining room or, in good weather, in the pleasant garden. A harbor-view apartment across the street is available for long-term (1 week or more) stays.

37 Mount Pleasant St., Rockport, MA 01966. ✆ **888/546-2701** or 978/546-2701. Fax 978/546-1095. www.innoncovehill.com. 7 units (some with shower only). $110–$165 double. Extra person $25. Rates include continental breakfast. 2-night minimum June–Oct weekends. Off-season discounts available. MC, V. *In room:* A/C, TV, no phone.

Sandy Bay Motor Inn ★ About ½ mile from downtown Rockport, this modern motor inn offers comfortable accommodations and a variety of recreational facilities at a good price. One of the largest lodgings in town, it's a sprawling two-story complex with attractively landscaped grounds on a hill next to Route 127, which is busy during the day but not at night. Still, units that face away from the road are preferable. Guest rooms are large and conventionally furnished—nothing fancy, but well maintained and large enough to hold a cot. The restaurant is a local hangout.

183 Main St. (Rte. 127), Rockport, MA 01966. ✆ **800/437-7155** or 978/546-7155. www.sandybaymotorinn.com. 79 units (some with shower only). Mid-June to early Sept $125–$170 double; off season $110–$155 double. Extra adult $15; extra child $4. Cot $6. Senior discount available. 2-night minimum summer weekends. AE, MC, V. Pets accepted; $10 fee. **Amenities:** Restaurant (breakfast only); heated indoor pool; putting green; 2 outdoor tennis courts; whirlpool; saunas. *In room:* A/C, TV.

On the Outskirts

Emerson Inn by the Sea ★★ Somewhere in an old guest register, you might find Ralph Waldo Emerson's name—the philosopher stayed at the original (1840) inn. He wouldn't recognize it today: The oceanfront building expanded in 1912, and innkeepers Bruce and Michele Coates have transformed it into a miniresort. Still, the inn retains a relaxing old-fashioned feel, with modern conveniences like an outdoor pool. Traditional furnishings such as four-poster beds grace the rooms, which are nicely appointed but not terribly large. If you can manage the stairs, the view from the top floor is worth the exertion. The best units have private balconies, fireplaces, or hot tubs; the regular oceanview rooms offer the same scenery. Two three-bedroom cottages nearby each rent for $1,800 to $4,500 a week. The public dining room (✆ **978/546-9500**) enjoys a good reputation for contemporary American cuisine. It serves dinner daily in the summer and on weekends in the off season; reservations are required.

1 Cathedral Ave., Rockport, MA 01966. ✆ **800/964-5550** or 978/546-6321. Fax 978/546-7043. www.emersoninnbythesea.com. 35 units (some with shower only). May–Oct $299–$379 "best" double; $229–$229 oceanview double; $159–$179 double without view. Off-season discounts available. Extra person $25; crib or cot $25. Rates include full breakfast May–Oct, continental breakfast Nov–Apr. Weekly rates available. 2- or 3-night minimum weekends May–Oct. AE, DC, DISC, MC, V. Follow Rte. 127 north from the center of town for 2 miles; turn right at sign on Phillips Ave. **Amenities:** Dining room; outdoor pool; sauna. *In room:* A/C, TV, dataport, hair dryer.

WHERE TO DINE

In 2005, Rockport lifted its ban on alcohol after years of being one of the few remaining "dry" towns in Massachusetts. A good way to experience the town is to arrive before the tourist hordes descend and enjoy a hearty breakfast. Two tasty destinations are **Flav's Red Skiff,** 15 Mount Pleasant St. (✆ **978/546-7647**), and **Michael's,** at the Sandy Bay Motor Inn, 183 Main St./Rte. 127 (✆ **978/546-9665**).

The birthplace of the fried clam, **Woodman's of Essex** (see "Essex," earlier in this chapter), is about half an hour from Rockport.

Brackett's Oceanview Restaurant *Kids* SEAFOOD/AMERICAN The dining room at Brackett's has a gorgeous view of the water. The nautical decor suits the seafood-intensive menu, which offers enough variety to make this a good choice for families—burgers are always available. The service is friendly and the fresh seafood quite good, if not particularly adventurous. Try the moist, plump codfish cakes if you're looking for a traditional New England dish, or something with Cajun spices for variety. The most exciting offerings are on the extensive dessert menu, where anything homemade is a great choice.

29 Main St. ✆ **978/546-2797.** www.bracketts.com. Reservations recommended for dinner. Main courses $7–$20 lunch, $10–$26 dinner. AE, DC, DISC, MC, V. Mid-Apr to Memorial Day Wed–Sun 11:30am–8pm; Memorial Day to Oct Sun–Fri 11:30am–8pm, Sat 11:30am–9pm. Closed Nov to mid-Apr.

The Greenery ★ SEAFOOD/AMERICAN The Greenery could get away with serving so-so food because of its great location near Bearskin Neck—but it doesn't. The cafe at the front serves light fare to stay or go; the dining rooms, at the back, boast great harbor views. The food ranges from tasty crab-salad quiche at lunch to lobster at dinner to steamers and fresh-caught fish anytime. As in any town with a fishing fleet, check out the daily specials. All baking is done in-house. When the restaurant is busy, the cheerful service tends to drag. This is a good place to launch a picnic on the beach, and an equally good spot for lingering over coffee and dessert while watching the action around the harbor.

15 Dock Sq. ✆ **978/546-9593.** www.greenery-restaurant.com. Reservations recommended for dinner. Main courses $9–$19 lunch, $10–$25 dinner; breakfast items $2–$13. AE, DC, DISC, MC, V. Spring–fall daily 8am–9:30pm; call for winter hours.

Portside Chowder House ★ CHOWDER/SEAFOOD In an unbelievably touristy location, this busy restaurant on Bearskin Neck is a favorite with locals as well as out-of-towners. The crowds are here for chowder—clam, corn, and whatever else looked good that day. Equally enjoyable are seafood platters, burgers, and lobster rolls, all served in a dining room with a great view of the harbor or (seasonally) on the deck. 7 Tuna Wharf, off Bearskin Neck. ✆ **978/546-7045.** Reservations not accepted. Most items less than $9. AE, MC, V. Late June to Labor Day daily 11am–8pm; after Labor Day to late June daily 11am–3pm. Off-season hours may vary; call ahead.

6 Newburyport, Ipswich & Plum Island

The area between Cape Ann and the New Hampshire border is magnificent, with outdoor sights and sounds that can only be described as natural wonders, and enough impressive architecture to keep any city slicker happy.

In a part of the world where the word "charming" is used almost as often as "hello," Newburyport is a singular example of a picturesque waterfront city. Downtown Newburyport is on the Merrimack River. On the town's Atlantic coast, Plum Island contains one of the country's top nature preserves. On the other side of Ipswich Bay, Ipswich is a lovely town that's home to Crane Beach, on another wildlife reservation.

NEWBURYPORT ★★

To get here directly from Boston, take I-93 (or Rte. 1 if it's not rush hour) to I-95—*not* Route 128, as for most other destinations in this chapter—and follow it to Exit 57, a solid 45-minute ride. Signs point to downtown, where you can park and explore. The **commuter rail** (✆ **800/392-6100** or 617/222-3200; www.mbta.com) from North Station takes about 75 minutes and cost $12 round-trip at press time. The no. 51 **bus** (✆ **978/469-6878;** www.mvrta.com) stops at the train station en route to and from downtown and Plum Island; the fare is $1.

Newburyport has a substantial year-round population that lends it a less touristy atmosphere than its appearance might suggest. Start your visit at the **Greater Newburyport Chamber of Commerce and Industry,** 38R Merrimac St. (✆ **978/462-6680;** www.newburyportchamber.org), in the red-brick downtown shopping district. It also runs a seasonal information booth on Merrimac Street near Green Street. Visit the website to download a map of a walking tour.

Market Square, at the foot of State Street near the waterfront, is the center of a neighborhood packed with boutiques, gift shops, plain and fancy restaurants, and antiques stores. You can also wander to the water, take a stroll on the boardwalk, and enjoy the action on the river. Architecture buffs will want to climb the hill to High Street, where the **Charles Bulfinch**–designed building (1805) that houses the Superior Court is only one of several Federal-era treasures. Ask at the Chamber of Commerce for the walking-tour map.

If you haven't gone out to sea yet, now is a good time, and here's a good place: **Newburyport Whale Watch** ★★, Hilton's Dock, 54 Merrimac St. (✆ **800/848-1111** or 978/499-0832; www.newburyportwhalewatch.com), offers 4½-hour cruises on a 100-foot boat with onboard marine biologists as guides. Tickets are $35 for adults, $30 for seniors, and $20 for children 4 to 12; reservations are suggested. (See "A Whale of an Adventure," on p. 175, for more information.)

Or head to the ocean using an inland route: From downtown, take Water Street south until it becomes Plum Island Turnpike and follow it to the Parker River National Wildlife Refuge.

PARKER RIVER NATIONAL WILDLIFE REFUGE ★★

The 4,662-acre refuge (✆ **978/465-5753;** www.fws.gov/northeast/parkerriver) on **Plum Island** is a complex of barrier beaches, dunes, and salt marshes, one of the few remaining in the Northeast. The refuge is flat-out breathtaking, whether you're exploring the marshes or the seashore. More than 800 species of plants and animals (including more than 300 bird species) visit or make their home on the narrow finger of land between Broad Sound and the Atlantic Ocean.

The refuge offers some of the best **birding** ★★★ anywhere, as well as observation of mammals and plants. Wooden boardwalks with observation towers and platforms wind through marshes and along the shore—most lack handrails, so this isn't an activity for rambunctious children. Birders come from around the world hoping to see native and migratory species such as owls, hawks, martins, geese, warblers, ducks, snowy egrets, swallows, monarch butterflies, Canada geese, foxes, beavers, and harbor seals.

The ocean beach closes April 1 to allow piping plovers, listed by the federal government as a threatened species, to nest. The areas not being used for nesting reopen July 1; the rest open in August, when the birds are through. The currents are strong and can be dangerous, and there are no lifeguards—swimming is allowed but not encouraged. Surf fishing is popular, though; striped bass and bluefish are found in the area. A permit is required for night fishing and vehicle access to the beach.

The refuge is open from dawn to dusk year-round. The daily entrance fee is $5 for motorists, $2 for bikers and pedestrians. The seven parking lots fill quickly on weekends when the weather is good, so plan to arrive early. South of lot 4 (Hellcat Swamp), the access road is flat and well maintained but not paved.

IPSWICH ★

Across Ipswich Bay from Plum Island is the town of Ipswich. It's accessible from Route 1A (which you can pick up in Newburyport or at Rte. 128 in Hamilton) and from Route 133 (which intersects with Rte. 128 in Gloucester and I-95 in Georgetown). The **MBTA** (✆ **800/392-6100** or 617/222-3200; www.mbta.com) commuter rail serves Ipswich; the round-trip fare is $11, and the trip from Boston takes about an hour. The **Cape Ann Transportation Authority** (✆ **978/283-7916;** www.ipswichessexexplorer.com) runs the summer-only Ipswich Essex Explorer bus, which connects the station to the attractions, including Crane Beach. The fare is $1; an all-day pass costs $3.

The **visitor center,** in the Hall Haskell House, 36 S. Main St., Rte. 133 (✆ **978/356-8540**), is open daily from Memorial Day weekend to Columbus Day, and weekends through early December. Information is also available from the **Ipswich Business Association** (✆ **978/356-9055;** www.ipswichma.com).

Settled in 1630, Ipswich is dotted with **17th-century houses** ★—reputedly the largest concentration in the United States. Many are private homes; ask at the visitor center for a map of a tour that passes three dozen of them. House-tour aficionados can go inside the **John Whipple House,** 1 South Village Green (✆ **978/356-2811;** www.ipswichmuseum.net). Built between 1655 and 1700, it's decorated with period furnishings. Tours ($4) are offered Wednesday through Saturday from May through October; call for schedules.

Ipswich is also known for two more contemporary structures. The **Clam Box,** 246 High St., Rte. 1A/133 (✆ **978/356-9707**), is a restaurant shaped like—what else?—a red-and-white-striped takeout clam box. It's a great place to try Ipswich clams, and not easy to sneak past if you have children in the car. Heading south from Newburyport, it's on the right. Closed December through February.

South of Ipswich Center, near the intersection of Routes 1A and 133, look carefully for the Argilla Road sign (on the east side of the street). If you're traveling west on Route 133 from Gloucester and Essex, watch for a sign on the right pointing to Northgate Road, which intersects with Argilla Road. Follow it east to the end, where you'll find the 1,400-acre Crane Estate.

The property is home to **Crane Beach** (see "Life's a Beach . . . With Very Cold Water!," on p. 170), the **Crane Wildlife Refuge** ★★, a network of hiking trails, and **Castle Hill,** 290 Argilla Rd. (✆ **978/356-4351;** www.thetrustees.org). One of the Boston area's most popular wedding locations, the exquisite Stuart-style seaside mansion known as the Great House was built by Richard Teller Crane, Jr., who made his fortune in plumbing and bathroom fixtures early in the 20th century. If you can't wangle an invitation to a wedding, tours of the house ($10 for adults, $8 for seniors and children 6–12) are given June to October on Wednesday and Thursday from 10am to 4pm and Friday 9am to noon. You can also explore the estate ($8 per car on summer weekends, otherwise $5 per car) without entering the house.

Children who can't get excited about a tour might be pacified by a stop just before Castle Hill. **Russell Orchards Store and Winery** ★, 143 Argilla Rd. (✆ **978/356-5366;** www.russellorchardsMA.com), is open daily May through November. It has a picnic area, farm animals, and an excellent country store. Depending on the season, you might go on a hayride or taste fruit wines. Be sure to try some cider and doughnuts.

7 Plymouth ★★

Everyone educated in the United States knows at least a little about Plymouth—about how the Pilgrims, fleeing religious persecution, left Europe on the *Mayflower* and landed at Plymouth Rock in 1620. Many also know that the Pilgrims endured disease and privation, and that just 51 people from the original group of 102 celebrated the first Thanksgiving in 1621 with Squanto, a Pawtuxet Indian associated with the Wampanoags, and his cohorts.

What you won't know until you visit is how small everything was. The *Mayflower* (a replica) seems perilously tiny, and when you contemplate how dangerous life was at the time, it's hard not to be impressed by the settlers' accomplishments. The *Mayflower* passengers weren't even aiming for Plymouth. They originally set out for what they called "Northern Virginia," near the mouth of the Hudson River. On November 11, 1620, rough weather and high seas forced them to make for Cape Cod Bay and anchor at Provincetown. The captain then announced that they had found a safe harbor and refused to continue to their original destination. On December 16, Provincetown having proven an unsatisfactory location, the weary travelers landed at Plymouth.

Plymouth is in many ways a model destination, where the 17th century coexists with the 21st, and most historic attractions are both educational and fun. Tourists jam the downtown area in summer, but the year-round population is so large that Plymouth feels more like the working community it is than like a warm-weather day-trip destination. It's a manageable excursion from Boston, particularly enjoyable if you're traveling with children. It also makes a good stop between Boston and Cape Cod.

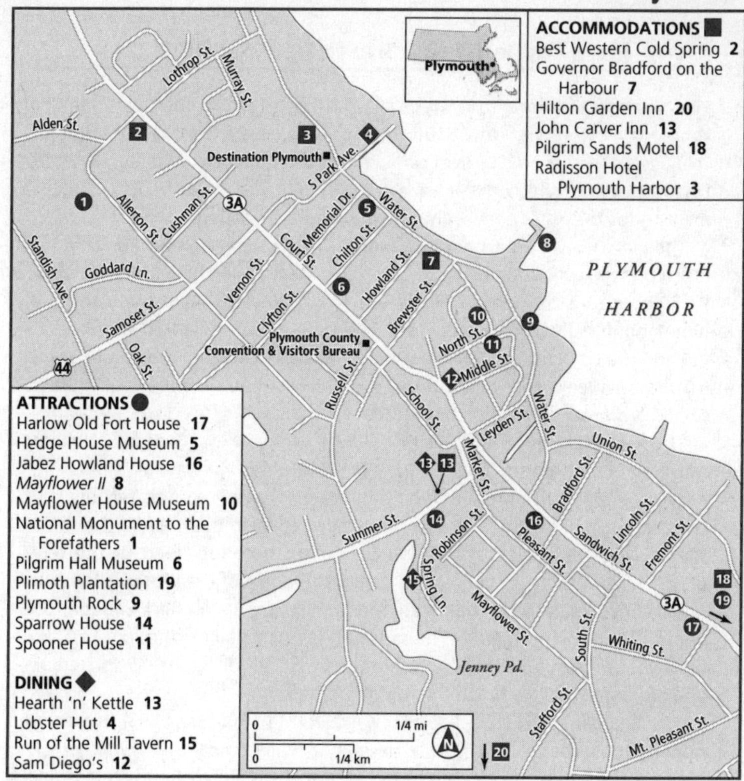

ESSENTIALS

GETTING THERE By car, follow the Southeast Expressway (I-93) from Boston to Route 3. From Cape Cod, take Route 3 north. Take Exit 6A to Route 44 east, and follow signs to the historic attractions. The 40-mile trip from Boston takes 45 to 60 minutes if it's not rush hour. Take Exit 5 to the **Regional Information Complex** for maps, brochures, and information. Take Exit 4 to go directly to **Plimoth Plantation.**

The **commuter rail** (**© 800/392-6100** or 617/222-3200; www.mbta.com) serves Cordage Park, on Route 3A north of downtown, from South Station. The round-trip fare at press time was $12. The **Plymouth Area Link bus** (**© 508/746-0378;** www.gatra.org/pal.htm) runs between the train station and downtown. The fare is $1.

Plymouth & Brockton buses (**© 617/773-9401** or 508/746-0378; www.p-b.com) run more often and cost more than the train: $12 one-way, $22 round-trip. The ride takes about an hour from South Station.

VISITOR INFORMATION If you haven't visited the Regional Information Complex (see "Getting There," above), pick up a map at the **visitor center** (**© 508/747-7525**), open seasonally at 130 Water St., across from the town pier. To plan ahead, contact Plymouth Visitor Information, known as **Destination Plymouth** (**© 800/USA-1620** or 508/747-7533; www.visit-plymouth.com). The **Plymouth County**

Finds More Whale Tales: A Trip to New Bedford

The masses that flock to eastern Massachusetts aren't yet swarming the cobblestone streets of New Bedford, which makes it a good destination for families on the verge of crowd-phobia. The **New Bedford Whaling National Historical Park,** which encompasses the downtown historic district, commemorates the city's past as the world's leading whaling port.

The downtown area near the waterfront has been restored, and the attractions are reasonably close together. Start your visit at the **National Park Service Visitor Center,** 33 William St. (© **508/996-4095;** www.nps.gov/nebe), open daily from 9am to 5pm. The exhibits include a film about whaling and the city's history. Take a guided walking tour (daily in summer, some off-season weekends) or pick up a brochure that describes self-guided excursions around the historic district.

The centerpiece of the Historical Park is the **New Bedford Whaling Museum** ★, 18 Johnny Cake Hill (© **508/997-0046;** www.whalingmuseum.org). It's the world's premier whaling museum, which sounds terribly specialized but is actually quite absorbing. On display in the lobby is the skeleton of a 65-foot juvenile blue whale, Kobo (short for "king of the blue ocean"). Admission to the lobby is free, but the rest of the museum is worth a visit. Children love the half-scale model of the whaling bark *Lagoda,* the world's largest ship model. The museum is open daily from 9am to 5pm, until 9pm on summer Thursdays. Admission is $10 for adults, $9 for seniors and students, and $6 for children 6 to 14.

The **Seamen's Bethel,** 15 Johnny Cake Hill (© **508/992-3295**), a nondenominational chapel described in Herman Melville's classic novel *Moby-Dick,* is across the street. Up the hill from the water, the **Rotch-Jones-Duff House & Garden Museum,** 396 County St. (© **508/997-1401;** www.rjdmuseum.org), is an 1834 Greek Revival mansion with magnificent formal gardens. Admission is $5 for adults, $4 for seniors and students, $2 for children under 13.

To get there, take the Southeast Expressway south to I-93 (Rte. 128), then Route 24 south. Follow signs to Route 140 south to I-195. From Plymouth, take Route 44 west to Route 24 south. **Dattco** (© **800/229-4879;** www.dattco.com) buses take 75 minutes from Boston's South Station ($20 round-trip). For more information, contact the **New Bedford Office of Tourism** (© **508/979-1745;** www.ci.new-bedford.ma.us, click "visitors") or the **Bristol County Convention & Visitors Bureau** (© **800/288-6263** or 508/997-1250; www.bristol-county.org).

Convention & Visitors Bureau (© **800/231-1620** or 508/747-0100; www.seeplymouth.com) publishes a vacation guide.

GETTING AROUND The downtown attractions are accessible on foot. A shallow hill slopes from the center of town to the waterfront. **Plymouth Rock Trolley Company** (© **508/747-4161;** www.plymouthrocktrolley.com) offers a 40-minute narrated tour and unlimited reboarding daily from Memorial Day to October and weekends until Thanksgiving. It serves marked stops downtown (every 20 min.) and Plimoth Plantation (once an hour in summer). Tickets are $15 for adults, $12 for children 3 to 12.

EXPLORING THE HISTORIC SITES

No matter how many times you suffered through elementary-school pageants wearing a big black hat and paper buckles on your shoes, you can still learn something about Plymouth and the Pilgrims. The logical place to begin (good luck talking children out of it) is where the Pilgrims first set foot—at **Plymouth Rock** ★★. The rock, accepted as the landing place of the *Mayflower* passengers, was originally 15 feet long and 3 feet wide. It was moved on the eve of the Revolution and several times thereafter. In 1867, it assumed its present position at tide level. The Colonial Dames of America commissioned the portico around the rock, designed by McKim, Mead & White and erected in 1920. The rock isn't much to look at, but the accompanying descriptions are interesting, and the atmosphere curiously inspiring.

To get away from the waterfront crowds, cross though Brewster Park (from the Rock, walk away from the *Mayflower II* and turn away from the water) and make your way to **Town Brook Park,** at Jenney Pond, across Summer Street from the John Carver Inn. It's a good place to unwind—ducks and geese live in the pond, and there's room to run around.

A short distance from the waterfront is the **National Monument to the Forefathers** (**© 508/866-2580**), a granite behemoth inscribed with the names of the *Mayflower* passengers. Heading away from the harbor on Route 44, look carefully on the right for the turn onto Allerton Street, and climb the hill. The 81-foot-high monument is elaborately decorated with figures representing moral and political virtues and scenes of Pilgrim history. The monument is incongruous in its little park in a residential neighborhood, but it's also quite impressive. The view from the hilltop is excellent.

In 2005, the beloved **Plymouth National Wax Museum** closed. Plenty of other places in town can help you get your Pilgrim fix, but it's still a great loss. Check with Destination Plymouth (above) when you arrive to see whether the engaging exhibits, which illustrate scenes from the lives of the early settlers, are on display elsewhere.

Mayflower II ★ Kids Berthed a few steps from Plymouth Rock, *Mayflower II* is a full-scale reproduction of the type of ship that brought the Pilgrims from England to America in 1620. Even at full scale, the 106½-foot vessel seems remarkably small. Constructed in England from 1955 to 1957, the ship will be the focus of 50th-anniversary events in 2007. Although little technical information about the original *Mayflower* survives, William A. Baker, designer of *Mayflower II,* incorporated the few references in Governor Bradford's account of the voyage with other research to re-create the ship as authentically as possible. Costumed guides provide interesting first-person narratives about the vessel and voyage. Displays describe and illustrate the journey and the Pilgrims' experience, including 17th-century navigation techniques.

State Pier. **© 508/746-1622.** www.plimoth.org. Admission $8 adults, $7 seniors, $6 children 6–12. Plimoth Plantation (good for 2 consecutive days) and *Mayflower II* admission $24 adults, $21 seniors and students, $14 children 6–12, $72 families. Apr–Nov daily 9am–5pm.

Pilgrim Hall Museum ★ This is a great place to get a sense of the day-to-day lives of Plymouth's first European residents. Many original possessions of the early Pilgrims

Tips A Presidential History Twofer

A worthwhile detour en route to Plymouth is the **Adams National Historical Park** in Quincy, about 10 miles south of Boston. The park preserves the birthplaces of Presidents John Adams and John Quincy Adams, the house where four generations of the family lived, and eight other buildings associated with the political dynasty. A trolley connects the buildings, which are open for guided tours daily from 9am to 5pm in season (mid-Apr to mid-Nov). Admission is $5 for adults, free for children under 16. The grounds and the visitor center, 1250 Hancock St. (© **617/770-1175**; www.nps.gov/adam), are open in the winter Tuesday through Friday 10am to 4pm. The center is across the street from the Quincy Center stop on the Red Line; call or surf ahead for driving directions.

and their descendants are on display, including Myles Standish's sword, Governor Bradford's Bible, and an uncomfortable chair (you can sit in a replica) that belonged to William Brewster. Regularly changing exhibits explore aspects of the settlers' lives, such as home construction or maritime history. Among the permanent exhibits is the skeleton of the *Sparrow-Hawk,* a ship wrecked on Cape Cod in 1626 that lay buried in the sand until 1863. (It's even smaller than the *Mayflower II.*)

75 Court St. © **508/746-1620.** www.pilgrimhall.org. Admission $6 adults, $5 seniors and AAA members, $3 children 5–17, $16 families. Feb–Dec daily 9:30am–4:30pm. Closed Jan. From Plymouth Rock, walk north on Water St. and up the hill on Chilton St.

Plimoth Plantation ★★ *Kids* Allow at least half a day to explore this re-creation of the 1627 village, which children and adults find equally interesting. Enter by the hilltop fort that protects the "villagers" and walk down the hill to the farm area, visiting homes and gardens constructed with careful attention to historical detail. The "Pilgrims" are actors who, in speech, dress, and manner, assume the personalities of members of the original community. You can watch them framing a house, splitting wood, shearing sheep, preserving foodstuffs, or cooking a pot of fish stew over an open hearth, all as it was done in the 1600s. Wear comfortable shoes—you'll be walking a lot.

The plantation is as accurate as research can make it. The planners combined accounts of the original colony with archaeological research, old records, and the history written by the Pilgrims' leader, William Bradford (who often used the spelling "Plimoth"). There are daily militia drills with matchlock muskets that are fired to demonstrate the community's defense system. In fact, little defense was needed, because the Native Americans were friendly. Local tribes included the Wampanoags, who are represented near the village at a replica of a homesite (included in plantation admission). Museum staffers show off native foodstuffs, agricultural practices, and crafts.

At the main entrance are two modern buildings that house exhibits, a gift shop, a bookstore, a cafeteria, and an auditorium that shows a film produced by the History Channel. There's also a picnic area. Call or surf ahead for information on special events, lectures, tours, workshops, theme dinners, and family programs.

137 Warren Ave. (Rte. 3). ✆ 508/746-1622. www.plimoth.org. Admission (good for 2 consecutive days) $21 adults, $18 seniors, $12 children 6–12. Plimoth Plantation and *Mayflower II* admission $24 adults, $21 seniors and students, $14 children 6–12, $72 families. Apr–Nov daily 9am–5pm. From Rte. 3, take Exit 4, Plimoth Plantation Hwy.

THE HISTORIC HOUSES

You can't stay in Plymouth's historic houses, but they're worth a visit to see the changing styles of architecture and furnishings since the 1600s. Costumed guides explain the homemaking and crafts of earlier generations. When they're not undergoing renovation, most of the houses are open Memorial Day through Columbus Day, during Thanksgiving celebrations, and around Christmas; call for schedules.

Tip: Unless you have a sky-high tolerance for house tours, pick just one or two from eras that you find particularly interesting. This advice applies especially if you're sightseeing with children.

Six homes are usually open to visitors. The 1640 **Sparrow House,** 42 Summer St. (✆ **508/747-1240;** www.sparrowhouse.com; admission $2 adults, $1 children under 13), and the 1667 **Jabez Howland House,** 33 Sandwich St. (✆ **508/746-9590;** www.pilgrimjohnhowlandsociety.org; $4 adults, $2 children), are most engaging for those curious about the original settlers. Other houses that are open to the public include the 1749 **Spooner House,** 27 North St. (✆ **508/746-0012;** $4.50 adults, $2 children), and the 1754 **Mayflower House Museum,** 4 Winslow St. (✆ **508/746-2590;** www.mayflower.org; $2.50 adults, 75¢ children). The **Harlow Old Fort House,** 119 Sandwich St., and the 1809 **Hedge House Museum,** 126 Water St., were closed for renovation at press time. Contact the **Plymouth Antiquarian Society** (✆ **508/746-0012;** www.plymouthantiquariansociety.org), which owns both buildings, for updates.

ORGANIZED TOURS & CRUISES

To walk in the Pilgrims' footsteps, take a **Colonial Lantern Tour** ★ (✆ **800/698-5636** or 508/747-4161; www.lanterntours.com). Participants carry pierced-tin lanterns on a 90-minute walking tour of the original settlement under the direction of a knowledgeable guide. It might seem a bit hokey at first, but it's fascinating. Tours run nightly April through Thanksgiving. Tickets are $15 for adults, $12 for children 5 to 12; check the meeting place when you call for reservations. The company offers special tours for Halloween and Thanksgiving.

Narrated cruises run from April or May to November. **Capt. John Boats,** 10 Town Wharf (✆ **800/242-2469** or 508/747-2400; www.captjohn.com), offers several tours. The *Pilgrim Belle* paddle-wheeler is the vessel for 75-minute narrated tours of the harbor ($12 for adults, $10 for seniors, $8 for children under 13) leave from State Pier. **Whale-watches** ($34 adults, $30 seniors, $22 children) run from April through October. Dining and entertainment cruises and ferry service to Provincetown (p. 247) are available.

A LEGENDARY ATTRACTION NEARBY

Edaville USA ★, 7 Eda Ave., South Carver (✆ **877/EDAVILLE** or 508/866-8190; www.edaville.com), is a longtime favorite with young New Englanders. The main attraction is an entertaining 45-minute train ride on a 5½-mile loop of narrow-gauge railroad tracks that takes you past cranberry bogs. Also on the premises are a carousel, kiddie rides, railroad museum, and cafe. It's a retro experience—no high-tech multimedia stuff, just good clean fun.

The railroad, which dates to 1947, reopened in 1999 after being shuttered for 7 years, and management has tinkered with the schedule ever since. Definitely call ahead to confirm hours. It's currently open weekends and holidays June through September; for the Cranberry Festival on Columbus Day weekend; and for the Holiday Festival of Lights, on weekends in November and daily in December. The railroad is extremely crowded when the weather is good; try to arrive when it opens. Admission is $16, free for children under 2. From Plymouth, follow Route 44 west to Route 58 south, continue about 3 miles to Rochester Road, and turn right.

SHOPPING

Water Street, on the harbor, boasts an inexhaustible supply of souvenir shops. A less kitschy destination, just up the hill, is Route 3A, known as Court, Main, and Warren Street as it runs through town. **Lily's Apothecary,** 6 Main St. Extension, in the old post office (© **508/747-7546;** www.lilysapothecary.com), carries a big-city-style selection of skin- and hair-care products. **Main Street Antiques,** 46 Main St. (© **508/747-8887**), is home to dozens of dealers. **Pilgrim's Progress,** 13 Court St. (© **508/746-6033**), carries women's and men's clothing. **Great Giraffe Graphic Co.,** 11 Court St. (© **508/830-1990**), is an entertaining card and gift shop.

WHERE TO STAY

Just about every establishment in town participates in a **Destination Plymouth** (© **800/USA-1620;** www.visit-plymouth.com) program that piles on the deals and discounts. Especially in the off season, this can represent great savings. On busy summer weekends, it's not unusual for every room in town to be taken; make reservations well in advance.

The 175-unit **Radisson Hotel Plymouth Harbor,** 180 Water St. (© **800/333-3333** or 508/747-4900; www.radisson.com), is the only chain hotel downtown. On a hill across the street from the waterfront, it offers the usual amenities, including a pool in the atrium lobby. Doubles in high season run $180 to $225. At press time, a **Hilton Garden Inn,** 4 Home Depot Dr. (© **877/782-9444** or 508/830-0200; www.hiltongardeninn.com), was scheduled to open in mid-2006 near Route 3 Exit 5, about 10 minutes from downtown. Check ahead for opening specials at the hotel, which has an exercise room, an indoor pool, and extensive business features, including wireless Internet access.

Best Western Cold Spring ★ Convenient to downtown and the historic sights, this fastidiously maintained motel and the adjacent cottages surround nicely landscaped lawns. Rooms are pleasantly decorated and big enough for a family to spread out; if you want some privacy, book a two-bedroom cottage. The location makes the Cold Spring a good deal: The two-story complex is 1 long block inland, set back from the street in a quiet part of town.

188 Court St. (Rte. 3A), Plymouth, MA 02360. © **800/678-8667** or 508/746-2222. Fax 508/746-2744. www.bwcoldspring.com. 58 units (10 with shower only), 2 2-bedroom cottages. $99–$159 double; $139–$199 suite; $109–$159 cottage. Extra person $10. Rollaway $10. Crib $5. Children under 12 stay free in parent's room. Rates include continental breakfast. Packages, AAA and off-season discounts available. AE, DC, DISC, MC, V. Closed Dec–Mar. Pets accepted; $10 fee. **Amenities:** Outdoor pool. *In room:* A/C, TV, wireless Internet access, coffeemaker, hair dryer, iron.

Governor Bradford on the Harbour This well-maintained motor inn occupies a great location across the street from the waterfront and only a block from Plymouth Rock and the *Mayflower II.* Each attractively decorated room contains modern furnishings. The more expensive units on the top floor offer excellent water views—if that's what you care about, they're worth the money.

98 Water St., Plymouth, MA 02360. ✆ **800/332-1620** or 508/746-6200. Fax 508/747-3032. www.governorbradford.com. 94 units (some with shower only). From $125 double. Rates include continental breakfast. Extra person $10. Children under 16 stay free in parent's room. Off-season, AAA, and AARP discounts available. 2-night minimum weekends and holidays. AE, DC, DISC, MC, V. **Amenities:** Small heated outdoor pool; coin laundry. *In room:* A/C, TV, dataport, fridge.

John Carver Inn *Kids* A three-story Colonial-style building with a landmark portico, this hotel offers comfortable, modern accommodations and plenty of amenities, including two pools. The indoor "theme pool," a big hit with families, has a large water slide and a Pilgrim ship model. Business features, including meeting space, make this the Radisson's main competition for corporate travelers. The good-size guest rooms are decorated in Colonial style. The best units are the lavish suites with private Jacuzzis; "four-poster" rooms contain king-size beds. The inn is within walking distance of the main attractions on the edge of the downtown business district.

25 Summer St., Plymouth, MA 02360. ✆ **800/274-1620** or 508/746-7100. Fax 508/746-8299. www.johncarverinn.com. 85 units. Early Apr to mid-June and mid-Oct to Nov $119–$219 double, $259–$299 suite; mid-June to mid-Oct $159–$249 double, $299–$329 suite; Dec to early Apr $99–$199 double, $239–$279 suite. Extra person $20; rollaway $20; cribs free. Children under 19 stay free in parent's room. Packages and senior and AAA discounts available. AE, DC, DISC, MC, V. **Amenities:** Restaurant (American/seafood); outdoor pool; fitness center; Jacuzzi; concierge; business center; limited room service; laundry service; dry cleaning. *In room:* A/C, TV w/pay movies, wireless Internet access, hair dryer, iron.

Pilgrim Sands Motel ★★ *Kids* This attractive, regularly updated motel sits on its own beach 3 miles south of town, within walking distance of Plimoth Plantation. If you want to avoid the bustle of downtown and still be near the water, it's an excellent choice. The good-size rooms are tastefully furnished and well maintained; all but four are nonsmoking, and most have wireless Internet access. If you can swing it, book a beachfront room—the view is worth the money, especially when the surf is rough.

150 Warren Ave. (Rte. 3A), Plymouth, MA 02360. ✆ **800/729-7263** or 508/747-0900. Fax 508/746-8066. www.pilgrimsands.com. 64 units. Summer $155–$195 double; spring and early fall $134–$169 double weekends, $114–$149 double weekdays; Apr and late fall $114–$134 double weekends, $94–$114 double weekdays; Dec–Mar $84–$99 double. Extra person $6–$8 (suite $10–$15). Up to 2 children under 7 stay free in parent's room. Rates include continental breakfast. 2-night minimum holiday weekends. Rates may be higher on holiday weekends. AE, DC, DISC, MC, V. **Amenities:** Coffee shop; indoor and outdoor pools; access to nearby health club ($10); Jacuzzi; business center; private beach. Rooms for travelers w/disabilities are available. *In room:* A/C, TV, dataport, fridge, hair dryer.

WHERE TO DINE

Plimoth Plantation (p. 188) has a cafeteria and a picnic area, and occasionally schedules theme dinners. The family-friendly **Hearth 'n' Kettle** chain has a branch at the John Carver Inn (p. 191), and there's a lively Southwestern restaurant, **Sam Diego's** (✆ **508/747-0048**), at 51 Main St.

Lobster Hut ★ SEAFOOD The Lobster Hut is a busy self-service restaurant with a great view. It's popular with both locals and sightseers. Order and pick up at the counter, then head to an indoor table or out onto the large deck that overlooks the bay. To start, try clam chowder or lobster bisque. The seafood "rolls" (hot-dog buns with your choice of filling) are excellent. The many fried seafood options include clams, scallops, shrimp, and haddock. There are also boiled and steamed items, burgers, chicken tenders—and lobster, of course. Beer and wine are served, but only with meals.

25 Town Wharf. ✆ **508/746-2270.** Reservations not accepted. Lunch specials $7–$9; main courses $6–$15; sandwiches $3–$7; clams and lobster priced daily. MC, V. Summer daily 11am–9pm; winter daily 11am–7pm. Closed Jan.

Run of the Mill Tavern ★ AMERICAN This friendly restaurant sits 3 blocks inland, across from Town Brook Park. You won't mind not having a water view—the food is tasty and reasonably priced, making the comfortable tavern a popular hangout. The unconventional clam chowder, made with red potatoes, is fantastic. Other appetizers include nachos, potato skins, and mushrooms. Entrees are well-prepared versions of familiar meat, chicken, and fish dishes, plus burgers, fresh seafood (fried, broiled, or baked), and sandwiches (at lunch).

6 Spring Lane, off Summer St. ✆ **508/830-1262.** Reservations accepted only for parties of 6 or more. Main courses $8–$19; children's menu $4–$6. AE, DC, DISC, MC, V. Sun–Thurs 11:30am–9:30pm; Fri–Sat 11:30am–10pm. Bar closes at 1am.

6

Cape Cod

by Laura M. Reckford

Only 75 miles long, Cape Cod is a curving peninsula encompassing miles of beaches, hundreds of freshwater ponds, more than a dozen richly historic New England villages, scores of classic clam shacks and ice-cream shops–and it's just about everyone's idea of the perfect summer vacation spot.

More than 13 million visitors flock to the Cape to enjoy summertime's nonstop carnival. In full swing, the Cape is, if anything, perhaps a bit too popular for some tastes. Connoisseurs are discovering the subtler appeal of the off season, when prices plummet along with the population. For some select travelers, the prospect of sunbathing en masse on sizzling sand can't hold a candle to a long, solitary stroll on a windswept beach with only the gulls as company. Come Labor Day, the crowds clear out—even the stragglers are gone by Columbus Day—and the whole place hibernates until Memorial Day weekend, the official start of "the season."

We've listed mostly summer rates for the accommodations in this chapter, because that's when the vast majority of travelers plan their trips, but if you decide to explore the Cape off season, you'll get the added benefit of lower prices everywhere you go.

The **Cape Cod Chamber of Commerce,** Routes 6 and 132, Hyannis (© **888/332-2732** or 508/862-0700; fax 508/362-2156; www.capecodchamber.org), is a clearinghouse of information. You can also stop in at the Route 25 Visitor Center (© **508/759-3814;** fax 508/759-2146), open daily year-round.

1 The Upper Cape

Because the Upper Cape towns are so close to Boston by car (just over an hour), they've become bedroom as well as summer communities. They are perhaps a bit more staid than those towns farther east, but they are also spared some of the fly-by-night qualities that come with a transient populace. Shops and restaurants tend to stay open year-round.

SANDWICH ★★

Sandwich is both the oldest town on the Cape and the most quaint. Towering oak trees, 19th-century churches, and historic houses line its winding Main Street. A 1640 gristmill still grinds corn beside bucolic Shawme Pond. Farther east, Sandy Neck, one of the Cape's most beautiful beaches, extends out into Cape Cod Bay.

Sandwich's claim to fame is its prominence as the home to the nation's first glass factories in the early to mid–19th centuries. The town still supports a number of highly skilled glassmakers.

Cape Cod

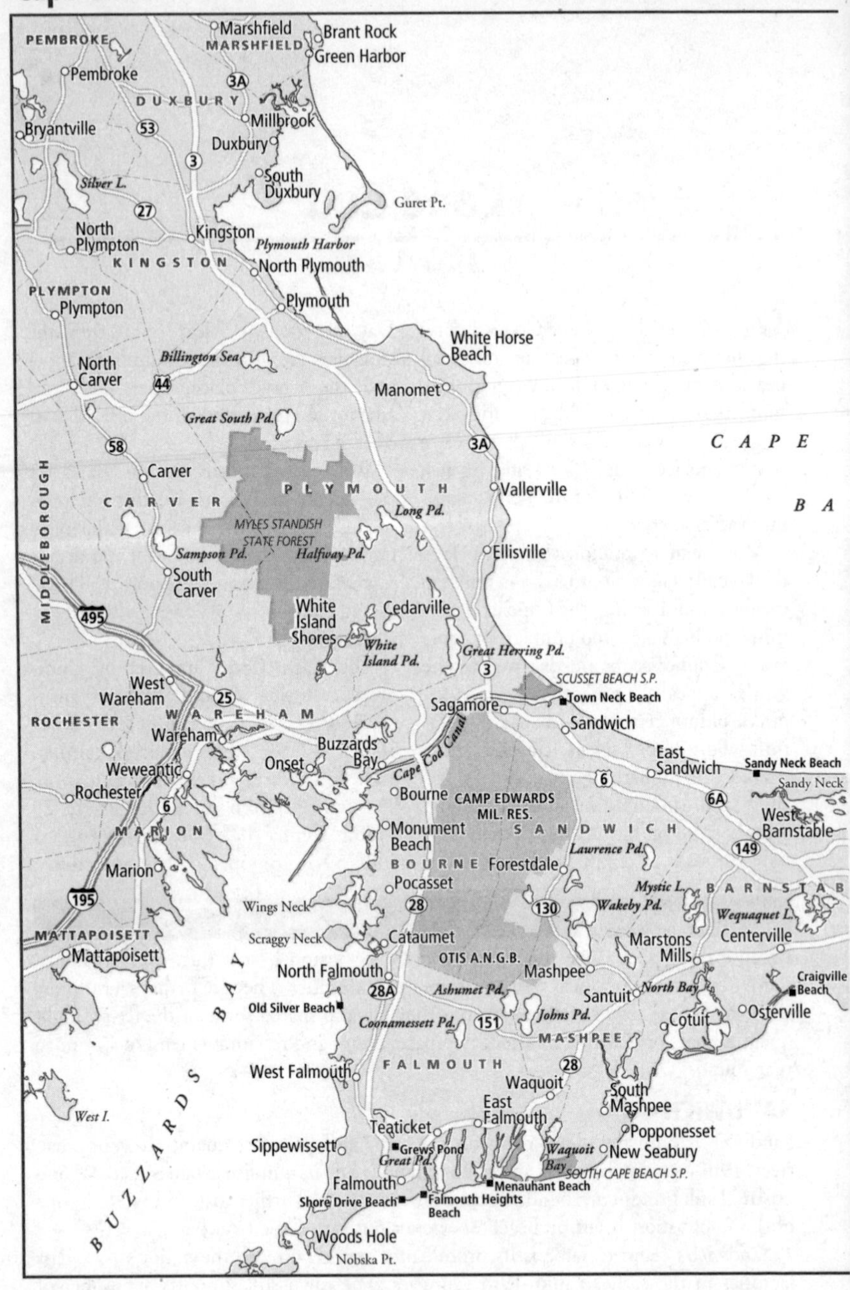
PEMBROKE
Pembroke
Marshfield
MARSHFIELD
Brant Rock
Green Harbor
DUXBURY
Millbrook
Bryantville
Duxbury
South Duxbury
Silver L.
Guret Pt.
North Plympton
Kingston
Plymouth Harbor
KINGSTON
North Plymouth
PLYMPTON
Plympton
Plymouth
White Horse Beach
Billington Sea
North Carver
Manomet
Great South Pd.
CAPE
Carver
PLYMOUTH
Vallerville
BA
CARVER
Long Pd.
MYLES STANDISH STATE FOREST
Sampson Pd.
Halfway Pd.
Ellisville
MIDDLEBOROUGH
South Carver
White Island Shores
Cedarville
White Island Pd.
Great Herring Pd.
SCUSSET BEACH S.P.
Town Neck Beach
West Wareham
WAREHAM
Sagamore
ROCHESTER
Wareham
Sandwich
Buzzards Bay
Onset
Cape Cod Canal
East Sandwich
Sandy Neck Beach
Sandy Neck
Weweantic
Bourne
CAMP EDWARDS MIL. RES.
Rochester
West Barnstable
MARION
Monument Beach
SANDWICH
Lawrence Pd.
BOURNE
Forestdale
Marion
Pocasset
Mystic L.
BARNSTAB
Wings Neck
Wakeby Pd.
Wequaquet L.
MATTAPOISETT
Scraggy Neck
Cataumet
Marstons Mills
Centerville
Mattapoisett
OTIS A.N.G.B.
North Falmouth
Mashpee
Craigville Beach
Ashumet Pd.
Santuit
North Bay
Old Silver Beach
Coonamessett Pd.
Johns Pd.
Cotuit
Osterville
MASHPEE
BUZZARDS BAY
West Falmouth
FALMOUTH
Waquoit
South Mashpee
West I.
East Falmouth
Teaticket
Popponesset
Sippewissett
Grews Pond
Great Pd.
Waquoit Bay
New Seabury
SOUTH CAPE BEACH S.P.
Falmouth
Menauhant Beach
Shore Drive Beach
Falmouth Heights Beach
Woods Hole
Nobska Pt.

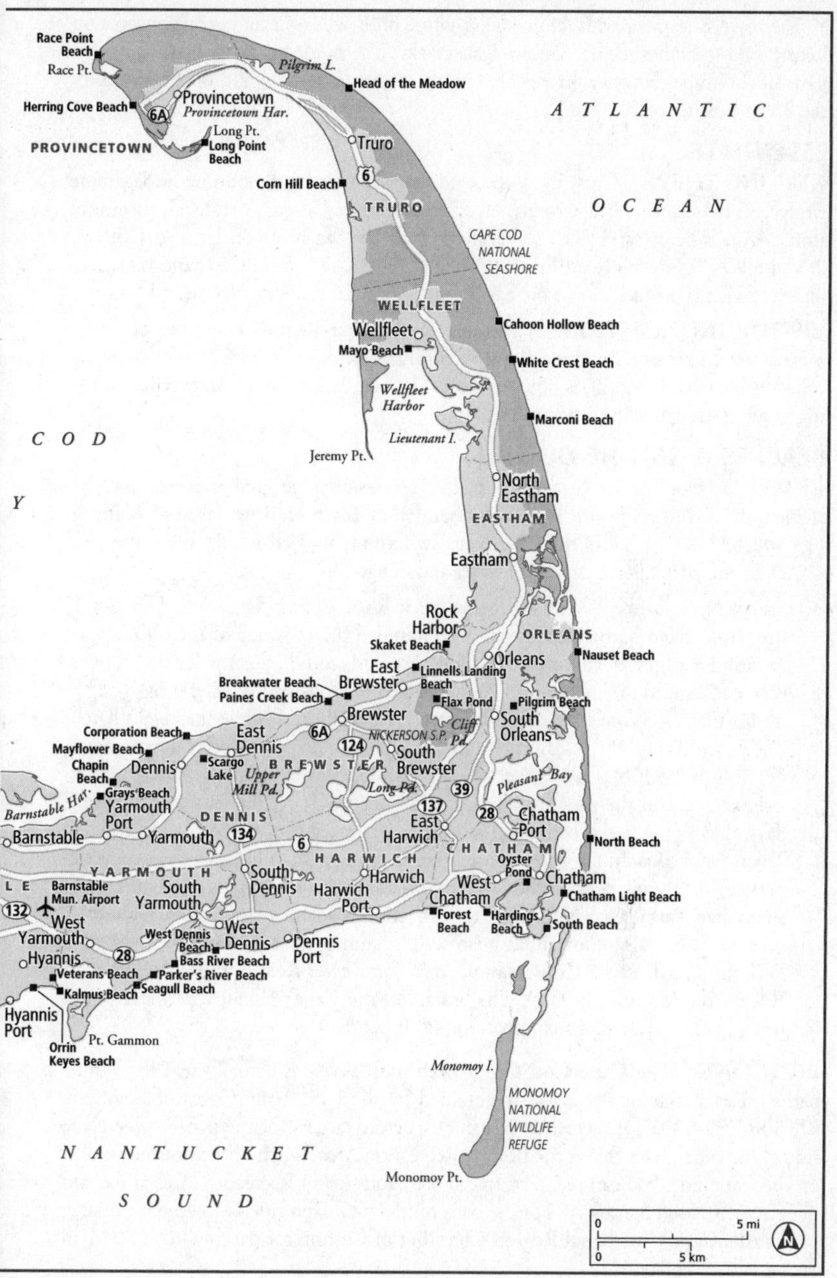

Race Point Beach
Race Pt.
Pilgrim L.
Head of the Meadow
Provincetown
Herring Cove Beach
6A
Provincetown Har.
ATLANTIC
Long Pt.
Long Point Beach
PROVINCETOWN
Truro
6
Corn Hill Beach
TRURO
OCEAN
CAPE COD NATIONAL SEASHORE
WELLFLEET
Wellfleet
Cahoon Hollow Beach
Mayo Beach
White Crest Beach
Wellfleet Harbor
Marconi Beach
COD
Lieutenant I.
Jeremy Pt.
North Eastham
Y
EASTHAM
Eastham
Rock Harbor
Skaket Beach
ORLEANS
Orleans
Nauset Beach
East Brewster
Linnells Landing Beach
Breakwater Beach
Paines Creek Beach
Flax Pond
Pilgrim Beach
Brewster
Cliff Pd.
South Orleans
Corporation Beach
East Dennis
NICKERSON S.P.
124
Mayflower Beach
South Brewster
Chapin Beach
Dennis
Scargo Lake
Upper Mill Pd.
BREWSTER
Long Pd.
39
Pleasant Bay
Grays Beach
Barnstable Har.
Yarmouth Port
DENNIS
137
28
Chatham Port
East Harwich
Barnstable
Yarmouth
134
North Beach
CHATHAM
HARWICH
Oyster Pond
YARMOUTH
South Dennis
Harwich
Chatham
LE
Barnstable Mun. Airport
South Yarmouth
West Chatham
Chatham Light Beach
132
Harwich Port
Forest Beach
Hardings Beach
South Beach
West Yarmouth
West Dennis Beach
West Dennis
Dennis Port
Hyannis
Veterans Beach
Bass River Beach
Parker's River Beach
Kalmus Beach
Seagull Beach
Hyannis Port
Pt. Gammon
Orrin Keyes Beach
Monomoy I.
MONOMOY NATIONAL WILDLIFE REFUGE
NANTUCKET
Monomoy Pt.
SOUND
0
5 mi
0
5 km
N

The town is popular with families and nature buffs who will find excellent spots for hiking, biking, and canoeing. Sandwich also makes a convenient base for exploring other parts of the Cape that may offer more lively activities, like the nightlife of Hyannis or the ocean beaches of Wellfleet.

ESSENTIALS

GETTING THERE Cross the Cape Cod Canal on either the Bourne or Sagamore Bridge. At the Bourne Bridge rotary, take Sandwich Road along the canal; it turns into Route 6A as it nears Sandwich Center. If you cross the Sagamore Bridge, take Exit 1 or 2, and follow Sandwich Road/Route 6A or Route 130, respectively, to Sandwich Center. Sandwich is 3 miles east of the Sagamore Bridge, 16 miles northwest of Hyannis.

VISITOR INFORMATION The **Cape Cod Canal Region Chamber of Commerce,** 70 Main St., Buzzards Bay (© **508/759-6000;** fax 508/759-6965; www.capecodcanalchamber.org), is open year-round, daily 9am to 5pm. An excellent walking guide is available at most inns in town.

BEACHES & GETTING OUTSIDE

BEACHES For the beaches listed below, nonresident parking stickers—$40 for the length of your stay—are available at **Sandwich Town Hall Annex,** 145 Main St. (© **508/833-8012**). Note that there's no swimming allowed within the Cape Cod Canal, as the currents are much too swift and dangerous.

- **Sandy Neck Beach** ★★★, off Sandy Neck Road in East Sandwich: This 6-mile stretch of silken barrier beach with low, rounded dunes is one of the Cape's most beautiful beaches; in summer, its parking lot tends to fill up early. It's also popular with endangered piping plovers—and their nemesis, off-road vehicles (ORVs). That means that ORV trails are closed for some of the summer while the chicks hatch. ORV permits ($100 per season for nonresidents) can be purchased at the gatehouse (© **508/362-8300**). ORV drivers must be equipped with supplies like a spare tire, jack, shovel, and tire-pressure gauge. Parking costs $10 per day in season. Up to 3 days of camping in self-contained vehicles is permitted at $10 to $12 per night.
- **Town Neck Beach,** off Town Neck Road in Sandwich: A bit rocky but ruggedly pretty, this narrow beach offers a busy view of passing ships, plus restrooms and a snack bar. Parking costs $10 per day, or you could hike from town (about 1½ miles) via the community-built boardwalk spanning the salt marsh.
- **Wakeby Pond,** Ryder Conservation Area, John Ewer Road (off South Sandwich Rd. on the Mashpee border): The beach, on the Cape's largest freshwater pond, has lifeguards, restrooms, and parking ($10 per day).

BICYCLING The **Cape Cod Canal bike path** ★★★ is actually two flat 7-mile paths on each side of the canal, maintained by the U.S. Army Corps of Engineers (© **508/759-5991** for recreation hot line). For easy access for the path on the Cape side of the canal, park free at the Bourne Recreation Area, north of the Bourne Bridge, on the Cape side. You can also park free at the Sandcatcher Recreation Area at the end of Freezer Road in Sandwich. For the path on the mainland side of the canal, you can park at the **Cape Cod Canal Region Chamber of Commerce** parking lot at 70 Main St., in Buzzards Bay.

The closest bike-rental shop is on the mainland side of the canal at **P&M Cycles** at 29 Main St. in Buzzards Bay (© **508/759-2830**), opposite the railroad station. The shop also offers free parking.

BOATING To explore by canoe, rent one in Falmouth (see below) and paddle around Old Sandwich Harbor, out to Sandy Neck, or through the salt-marsh maze of Scorton Creek, which leads out to Talbot Point.

FISHING Sandwich has eight fishable ponds; for licenses, inquire at **Town Hall** in the center of town (✆ **508/888-0340**). No permit is required to fish from the banks of the Cape Cod Canal. Call the **Army Corps of Engineers** (✆ **508/759-5991**) for canal tide and fishing information.

NATURE & WILDLIFE AREAS The **Shawme-Crowell State Forest,** off Route 130 in Sandwich (✆ **508/888-0351**), offers 298 campsites and 742 acres to roam. Entrance is free; parking costs $2. The **Sandwich Boardwalk** links the town and Town Neck Beach by way of salt marshes that attract many birds, including great blue herons.

The 57-acre **Green Briar Nature Center & Jam Kitchen** ★, 6 Discovery Hill Rd., off Rte. 6A (✆ **508/888-6870**), has a mile-long path crossing marsh and stands of white pine.

MUSEUMS

Heritage Museums and Gardens ★★★ *Finds* *Kids* This is one of those rare museums that appeals equally to adults and children. The 76 beautifully landscaped acres are crisscrossed with walking paths and riotous with color in late spring, when the museum's famous collection of towering rhododendrons are in bloom. Scattered buildings house a wide variety of collections, from Native American artifacts to Cape Cod Baseball League memorabilia. The high point for most kids will be a ride on the 1912 carousel. There's also a replica Shaker round barn packed with gleaming antique automobiles. Outdoor summer concerts are usually held Sundays around 2pm.

Grove and Pine sts. (about ½ mile southwest of the town center). ✆ **508/888-3300.** Admission $12 adults, $10 seniors, $6 children 6–16, free for 5 and under. AE, DISC, MC, V. Fri–Wed 9am–6pm; Thurs 9am–8pm.

Sandwich Glass Museum ★★ *Finds* Even if you don't consider yourself a glass fan, make an exception for this fascinating museum, which captures the history of the town above and beyond its legendary industry. A brief video introduces Deming Jarves's brilliant 19th-century endeavor to bring glassware—a hitherto rare commodity available only to the rich—within reach of the middle classes. All went well until Midwestern factories undercut Jarves by using coal to fire their furnaces. Unable to keep up with their level of mass production, Jarves switched back to handblown techniques just as his workforce was ready to revolt. An excellent little gift shop stocks Sandwich-glass replicas and original glassworks. In summer, volunteers demonstrate glassblowing techniques.

129 Main St. (in the center of town). ✆ **508/888-0251.** www.sandwichglassmuseum.org. Admission $4.50 adults, $1 children 6–14, free for children under 6. Apr–Dec daily 9:30am–5pm; Feb–Mar Wed–Sun 9:30am–4pm. Closed Jan, Thanksgiving, and Christmas.

WHERE TO STAY

Many motels line Route 6A in Sandwich, but the one with the best location is **Sandy Neck Motel** at 669 Rte. 6A, East Sandwich (✆ **800/564-3992** or 508/362-3992; www.sandyneck.com), which sits at the entrance to the road leading to Sandy Neck, the best beach in these parts. Rates are $89 to $99 double and $135 to $235 for one- and two-room efficiencies. Closed November to mid-April.

The Belfry Inne ★★ *Finds* This inn right in the center of Sandwich Village has about the most creative renovation on Cape Cod. The turreted 1879 rectory, called The Drew House, is the gaudiest "painted lady" in town. The rooms are romantic, with queen-size retrofitted antique beds, a claw-foot tub (or Jacuzzi), and a scattering of fireplaces and private balconies. Next door is the Abbey, a former church that owner Chris Wilson has converted into six unique deluxe guest rooms, and one very fine restaurant (see below). The Abbey rooms are painted vivid colors and tucked cleverly into sections of the old church. All of the Abbey rooms have Jacuzzis. Mr. Wilson also owns the Village House, next door, with eight rooms decorated in a French country style. He recently purchased and renovated a former meetinghouse nearby that used to be the home of the Doll House Museum. The three deluxe guest rooms in The Meeting House are priced at $350 per night. Children cannot be accommodated in The Meeting House.

8 Jarves St. (in the center of town), Sandwich, MA 02563. ✆ **800/844-4542** or 508/888-8550. Fax 508/888-3922. www.belfryinn.com. 22 units. Summer $139–$275 double. Rates include continental breakfast. AE, MC, V. **Amenities:** Restaurant (New American).

The Dan'l Webster Inn ★★ This large, popular inn is a dependable bet for a comfortable stay or a hearty meal. The main building sits on the site of a Colonial tavern favored by Daniel Webster, the famous orator and Boston lawyer. Guest rooms are ample and nicely furnished with reproductions. Deluxe suites, some in nearby historic houses, offer perks like balconies, gas fireplaces, oversize whirlpool tubs, and heated tile bathroom floors. The inn's common spaces are convivial, if bustling; the restaurant is a tour bus lunch spot that turns out surprisingly sophisticated fare.

149 Main St. (in the center of town), Sandwich, MA 02563. ✆ **800/444-3566** or 508/888-3622. Fax 508/888-5156. www.danlwebsterinn.com. 54 units. Summer $159–$229 double; $219–$359 suite. Off-season rates include full breakfast. AE, DC, DISC, MC, V. **Amenities:** Restaurant (New American); tavern/bar; small outdoor heated pool; access to local health club; limited room service. *In room:* A/C, TV, dataport, hair dryer, iron.

Isaiah Jones Homestead ★ *Value* Of the many B&Bs in Sandwich Center, this one is a particularly good value, though the fancier rooms tend to be more expensive (and more elegant) than those at other small B&Bs in town. Innkeepers Jan and Doug Klapper have carefully appointed this courtly 1849 Victorian with fine antiques and reproductions. Many rooms have additional romantic touches like fireplaces and whirlpool baths. Two minisuites in the Carriage House have sitting alcoves. The room named for industrial magnate Deming Jarves boasts an inviting floral-curtained half-canopy bed and an oversize whirlpool tub. The gentility that prevails at the candlelight breakfast, served with fine china and crystal, completes the picture.

165 Main St. (in the center of town), Sandwich, MA 02563. ✆ **800/526-1625** or 508/888-9115. Fax 508/888-9648. www.isaiahjones.com. 7 units. Summer $115–$175 double. Rates include full breakfast. AE, DC, DISC, MC, V. No children under 12. *In room:* A/C, hair dryer, no phone.

Spring Hill Motor Lodge ★ This motel boasts all sorts of amenities, like night-lit tennis court and a large pool. The interiors are cheerfully contemporary, the grounds beautifully landscaped. In addition to the motel rooms, there are four cottages that are light, airy, and comfortable.

351 Rte. 6A (about 2½ miles east of the town center), East Sandwich, MA 02537. ✆ **800/647-2514** or 508/888-1456. Fax 508/833-1556. www.sunsol.com/springhill. 24 units (20 tub/shower), 4 cottages (shower only). Summer $115–$165 double; $180–$275 efficiency; $185–$265 or $1,100 weekly for 1-bedroom cottage; $235–$350 or $1,400 weekly for 2-bedroom cottage. AE, DC, DISC, MC, V. **Amenities:** Heated outdoor pool; night-lit tennis court. *In room:* A/C, TV, fridge, coffeemaker.

Wingscorton Farm Inn ★★ Kids Finds This Colonial farmhouse on 7 acres will delight youngsters and animal lovers of all ages. It's been a working farm since 1758 and still houses a brood of sheep, goats, dogs, cats, chickens, a pet turkey, and a potbellied pig. The paneled guest rooms have canopy beds, working fireplaces, and braided rugs. Modernists might prefer the carriage house, with its skylight-suffused loft bedroom, kitchen (with woodstove), and private deck. A private bay beach is a short walk down a country lane.

11 Wing Blvd. (off Rte. 6A, about 5 miles east of the town center), East Sandwich, MA 02537. ✆ **508/888-0534.** Fax 508/888-0545. 3 units, carriage house, cottage. Summer $175 suite; $200 carriage house. Rates for suites and carriage house include full breakfast. AE, MC, V. Pets welcome. *In room:* A/C, TV, fridge, no phone.

WHERE TO DINE

Aquagrille ★ SEAFOOD Overlooking the town's picturesque marina and not-so-picturesque power plant, this place wants to be the premier place for fish in Sandwich. The towering lobster salad with *haricot vert,* tomato, avocado, chives, and crème fraîche is the perfect antidote to a steamy summer night. Those with larger appetites may want to try the baby-back pork spareribs with peach barbecue sauce, which comes with—what else?—potato salad and Boston baked beans. Ask for a table that doesn't face the power plant.

14 Gallo Rd. (next to Sandwich Marina). ✆ **508/888-8889.** www.aquagrille.com. Reservations recommended. Main courses $8–$20. AE, DC, MC, V. Apr–Oct Mon–Fri 11:30am–2:30pm and 5–9pm, Sat–Sun noon–9pm; call for off-season hours.

The Bee-Hive Tavern ★ INTERNATIONAL A cut above the rather characterless restaurants clustered along this stretch of road, this tavern employs atmospheric old-time touches: Green-shaded banker's lamps illuminate the dark wood booths, and vintage prints convey a clubby feel. The food is straightforward but tasty, and well priced for what it is. Steaks, chops, and fresh fish among the pricier choices, while burgers, sandwiches, and salads cater to lighter appetites (and wallets). At lunch, try the lobster roll, one of the Cape's best.

406 Rte. 6A (about ½ mile east of the town center), East Sandwich. ✆ **508/833-1184.** Main courses $7–$16. MC, V. Mon–Sat 11:30am–3pm and 5–9pm; Sun 8am–3pm and 5–9pm.

The Belfry Bistro ★★ Finds NEW AMERICAN Sandwich's most romantic dining option is in a renovated abbey, formerly a Catholic church. The Gothic space is quite spectacular, with flying buttresses supporting the ceiling's high arches. Once seated, guests can concentrate on the snowy, dense linens, intimate lighting, and pleasing menu. Portions are generous and elegantly presented. The menu changes seasonally, but among the appetizers you might find a Thai crab and baby shrimp cake or mini-barbecue pork empanadas, which are braised and wrapped in pastry. The entrees run from an unusual black grouper roasted in a banana leaf to the traditional grilled filet of beef over whipped potatoes with green beans. Because this restaurant hosts many weddings and other events, it is sometimes closed to the public, so be sure to call ahead. While The Belfry Bistro serves dinner only, the more casual **Painted Lady Café** next door serves lighter, less expensive ($8–$25) fare, like brie cheese burgers and chicken potpie, from 11:30am to 9pm.

8 Jarves St. (in the center of town). ✆ **508/888-8550.** Reservations recommended. Main courses $20–$32. AE, MC, V. Feb–Dec Tues–Sat 5–10pm; call for off-season hours. Closed Jan.

The Dan'l Webster Inn ★★ Kids AMERICAN You have a choice of four main dining rooms—from a casual, Colonial-motif tavern to a skylight-topped conservatory fronting a splendid garden. The atmospheric Tavern at the Inn, with its own pub-style menu, is the most popular. A restaurant on this scale could probably get away with ho-hum food, but the output is on a par with that of the Cape's best boutique restaurants. Try a classic dish like the *fruits de mer* in white wine.

149 Main St. (in the center of town). ✆ **508/888-3622.** Reservations recommended. Main courses $18–$29; Tavern menu $7–$14. AE, DC, DISC, MC, V. Daily 8am–9pm; call for off-season hours.

Marshland Restaurant Value DINER Locals have been digging this diner for 2 decades. This is home-cooked grub, slung fast and cheap. You'll gobble up the hearty breakfast and be back in time for dinner.

109 Rte. 6A. ✆ **508/888-9824.** Most items under $10. No credit cards. Sun–Thurs 6am–8:30pm; Fri–Sat 6am–9pm. Open year-round.

FALMOUTH & WOODS HOLE ★★★

Falmouth is a classic New England town, complete with church steeples encircling the town green and a walkable and bustling Main Street. With over 32,000 year-round residents, it's the second-largest town on the Cape, after Barnstable.

Woods Hole ★★★, one of eight villages in Falmouth, has been a world-renowned oceanic research center since 1871, when the U.S. Commission of Fish and Fisheries set up a primitive seasonal collection station. Today the various scientific institutes crowded around—the National Marine Fisheries Service, the Marine Biological Laboratory, and the Woods Hole Oceanographic Institute—employ thousands of scientists. They offer a unique opportunity to get in-depth—and often hands-on—exposure to marine biology. Woods Hole is also one of the hipper communities on the Cape, with a number of restaurants, bars, and shops making crowded Water Street (don't even think of parking here in summer) a very pleasant place to stroll.

Falmouth Heights ★★★, a cluster of shingled Victorian summer houses on a bluff east of Falmouth's harbor, is as popular as it is picturesque; its narrow ribbon of beach is a magnet for all, especially families.

ESSENTIALS

GETTING THERE After crossing the Bourne Bridge, take Route 28 south. It's 18 miles south of the Bourne Bridge, 20 miles southwest of Hyannis.

Falmouth's bus station near the center of town is serviced by **Bonanza Bus Lines** (59 Depot Ave.; ✆ **508/548-7588;** www.bonanzabus.com). There are daily buses from Boston, Logan Airport, Providence, and New York.

GETTING AROUND To get around Falmouth and Woods Hole (where parking in summer is a mathematical impossibility due to ferry traffic to Martha's Vineyard), use the **Whoosh Trolley,** which makes a circuit every 20 minutes down Falmouth's Main Street to Woods Hole. You can flag it down anywhere along the route.

The **Sea Line Shuttle** (✆ **800/352-7155**) connects Woods Hole and Falmouth, with Hyannis year-round (except holidays). The fare ranges from $1 to $3.50, depending on distance.

VISITOR INFORMATION Contact the **Falmouth Chamber of Commerce,** Academy Lane, Falmouth, MA 02541 (✆ **800/526-8532** or 508/548-8500; fax 508/548-8521; www.falmouth-capecod.com).

SPECIAL EVENTS

The **Falmouth Road Race** (www.falmouthroadrace.com), on the second Sunday in August, is a 7.3-mile run from the Captain Kidd Bar in Woods Hole to The British Beer Company in Falmouth Heights. It all started nearly 30 years ago when two buddies decided to race from one bar to the other. Now the race attracts 10,000 participants from all over the world. Those who want to run need to apply to a lottery in April.

BEACHES & GETTING OUTSIDE

BEACHES While Old Silver Beach, Surf Drive Beach, and Menauhant Beach will sell a day pass, most other Falmouth public beaches require a parking sticker. Day passes to Old Silver are $20 and passes to Surf Drive and Menauhant are $10. Renters can obtain temporary beach parking stickers for $60 per week or $90 per month at **Falmouth Town Hall,** 59 Town Hall Sq. (✆ **508/548-7611**), or at the **Surf Drive Beach Bathhouse** in season (✆ **508/548-8623**). The town beaches for which a parking fee is charged all have lifeguards, restrooms, and concession stands. Falmouth's public shores include:

- **Falmouth Heights Beach** ★★★, off Grand Avenue in Falmouth Heights: Once a rowdy spot, this is now primarily a family beach. Parking is sticker-only. This neighborhood supported the Cape's first summer colony. The grand Victorian mansions still overlook the beach.
- **Grew's Pond** ★★, in Goodwill Park off Palmer Avenue in Falmouth: This freshwater pond in a large town forest stays fairly uncrowded, even in the middle of summer. While everyone else is trying to find parking at Falmouth's popular saltwater beaches, here you can park for free and wander shady paths around the pond. There's a playground, picnic tables, barbecue grills, lifeguard, and restrooms.
- **Menauhant Beach** ★, off Central Avenue in East Falmouth: A bit off the beaten track, Menauhant is a little less mobbed than Falmouth Heights Beach and better protected from the winds. Parking costs $10.
- **Old Silver Beach** ★★★, off Route 28A in North Falmouth: Western-facing (great for sunsets) and relatively calm, this warm Buzzards Bay beach is a popular, often crowded, choice. It's the chosen spot for the college crowd. Families with young children cluster on the opposite side of the street where a shallow pool formed by a sandbar is perfect for toddlers. Parking costs $20.
- **Surf Drive Beach** ★★★, off Shore Street in Falmouth: About a half-mile from downtown, this is an easy-to-get-to choice. The tidal beach between the jetties is a shallow, calm area called "the kiddie pool." Parking is limited and costs $10.

BICYCLING The **Shining Sea Bicycle Path** ★★★ (✆ **508/548-8500**) is a 3.3-mile beauty skirting Vineyard Sound from Falmouth to Woods Hole with plenty of swimmable beach along the way. (Unfortunately, most of the beach along this stretch is rocky.) You can park at the trail head on Locust Street in Falmouth or at any spot in town (parking in Woods Hole is scarce). The closest bike shop is **Corner Cycle** at Palmer Avenue and North Main Street (✆ **508/540-4195**) near the Village Green.

BOATING **Patriot Party Boats,** 227 Clinton Ave. (at Scranton Ave. on the harbor), Falmouth (✆ **800/734-0088** or 508/548-2626; www.patriotpartyboats.com, www.TheLiberte.com), offers scenic cruises around Vineyard Sound aboard the three-masted schooner ***Liberte*** ★★. Two-hour sails cost $20 to $25 for adults and $15 to $25 for children 12 and under. Also offered in July and August are 2-hour sunset cruises on the *Patriot Too.*

Cape Cod Kayak (✆ **508/563-9377;** www.capecodkayak.com) rents kayaks and offers lessons and eco-tours. **Waquoit Kayak Company** at **Edward's Boat Yard,** 1209 E. Falmouth Hwy., East Falmouth (✆ **508/548-9722**), rents out canoes for exploring Waquoit Bay (see "Nature & Wildlife Areas," below). **Washburn Island** ★★★, a protected reserve with wooded trails and pristine beaches, is about a 1-hour paddle via canoe.

FISHING Falmouth has six fishable ponds. A free guide is available from the Falmouth Chamber of Commerce. Freshwater fishing and shellfishing licenses can be obtained at **Falmouth Town Hall,** 59 Town Hall Sq. (✆ **508/548-7611,** ext. 219). Freshwater fishing licenses can also be obtained at **Eastman's Sport & Tackle,** 150 Main St. (✆ **508/548-6900**).

Surf Drive Beach is a great spot for surf-casting, once the crowds have dispersed. Other good locations are the jetties off Nobska Point in Woods Hole and Bristol Beach on Menauhant Road in East Falmouth.

To go after bigger prey, head out with a group on one of the **Patriot Party Boats** (✆ **800/734-0088** or 508/548-2626; www.patriotpartyboats.com). Boats leave twice daily in season. The clunky *Patriot Too,* with an enclosed deck, is ideal for family-style "bottom fishing" (4-hr. sails $30 adults, $20 children under 12; equipment provided).

For sportfishing out of Falmouth Inner Harbor, call Captain Dan Junker of **Cool Running Charters** (✆ **508/457-9445**).

NATURE & WILDLIFE AREAS **Ashumet Holly and Wildlife Sanctuary** ★★, operated by the Massachusetts Audubon Society at 186 Ashumet Rd., off Route 151 (✆ **508/362-1426**), is an intriguing 49-acre collection of more than 1,000 holly trees, along with over 130 species of birds and a kettle pond that's covered with a carpet of Oriental lotus blossoms in summer. The trail fee is $3 for adults and $2 for seniors and children under 16.

Near the center of Falmouth (follow Depot Rd. to the end) is the 650-acre **Beebe Woods** ★★, a treasure for hikers and dog walkers. From here, you can wend your way to the 90-acre **Peterson Farm** ★★ (entrance off Woods Hole Rd.; take a right at the Quisset farm stand) with paths through woods and fields, as well as a flock of sheep and a llama grazing in a meadow. Bluebird boxes (special birdhouses for bluebirds) line the path on the way to a quiet pond.

The 2,250-acre **Waquoit Bay National Estuarine Research Reserve (WBNERR),** at 149 Waquoit Hwy. in East Falmouth (✆ **508/457-0495;** www.waquoitbayreserve.org), maintains a 1-mile nature trail. Also inquire about the boat ride to **Washburn Island** ★★★ on Saturdays in season by reservation. After the 20-minute boat trip to the island, naturalist-led guided walks are offered.

WATERSPORTS Falmouth is something of a sailboarding mecca, prized for its unflagging southwesterly winds. While Old Silver Beach in North Falmouth is the most popular spot for windsurfing, the sport is allowed there only prior to 9am and after 5pm. The Trunk River area on the west end of Falmouth's Surf Drive Beach and a portion of Chapoquoit Beach are the only public beaches where windsurfers are allowed during the day.

SEA SCIENCE

Woods Hole Aquarium ★ Kids A little beat-up after more than a century of service, this aquarium—the first such institution in the country—may not be state of the art, but it's a treasure nonetheless. The displays, focusing on local waters, might make you think twice before taking a dip. Children show no hesitation, though, in getting up to their elbows in the "touch tanks." A key exhibit concerns the effect of plastic trash on the marine environment. The seals who live here are fed at 11am and 4pm.

Albatross St. (off the western end of Water St.), Woods Hole. ✆ **508/495-2001.** Donations accepted. Mid-June to early Sept Tues–Sat 11am–4pm; mid-Sept to mid-June Mon–Fri 10am–4pm. You need a picture ID to enter.

Woods Hole Oceanographic Institution Exhibit Center and Gift Shop This world-class research organization—locally referred to by its acronym, WHOI (pronounced "Hooey")—is dedicated to the study of marine science. Kids might enjoy looking through microscopes at organisms or listening to sounds of marine animals on a computer. *Titanic* fans be interested in the brief video, displays, and the life-size model of the submersible that discovered the wreck. Walking tours of WHOI are offered twice a day on weekdays in July and August, reservations required; call ✆ **508/289-2252.**

15 School St. (off Water St.), Woods Hole. ✆ **508/289-2663.** $2 donation requested. Late May to early Sept Mon–Sat 10am–4:30pm, Sun noon–4:30pm; call for off-season hours. Closed Jan–Mar.

WHERE TO STAY

EXPENSIVE

Beach Breeze Inn ★ This inn has a great location, just steps from Surf Drive Beach and a short and pleasant stroll to Main Street with its many shops and restaurants. Guests here beat the summer traffic blues, because with beach and town within walking distance, you never need to use your car! Rooms are sunny and spacious with motel-style privacy; many of them have separate entrances. The inn was built in 1858, and spent many years as a run-down boardinghouse. In recent years, it has been thoroughly freshened up and is now a terrific lodging option, particularly for families.

321 Shore St. (about ¼ mile south of Main St.), Falmouth, MA 02540. ✆ **800/828-3255** or 508/548-1765. www.beachbreezeinn.com. 20 units. Summer $169–$279 double; $1,250–$1,600 weekly efficiencies. MC, V. **Amenities:** Unheated pool. *In room:* TV, fridge.

Coonamessett Inn ★★ A gracious inn built around the core of a 1796 homestead, the Coonamessett Inn is Falmouth's most traditional lodging choice. Set on 7 lush acres overlooking a pond, it has the feel of a country club. Some of the guest rooms, decorated in reproduction antiques, can be a bit somber, so try to get one with good light. (The rooms with the best light are room nos. 1 through 6 of the Village Rooms; they have large picture windows overlooking a pond). Most have a separate sitting room attached. On-site is a restaurant featuring a very comfortable tavern room as well as a more formal dining room. The extensive buffet brunch here on Sundays brings out people from all over town.

Jones Rd. and Gifford St. (about ½ mile north of Main St.), Falmouth, MA 02540. ✆ **508/548-2300.** Fax 508/540-9831. www.capecodrestaurants.org. 27 units, 1 cottage. Summer $150–$200 double; $175–$230 2-bedroom suite; $200–$260 cottage. Rates include continental breakfast. AE, MC, V. **Amenities:** 2 restaurants (1 fancy, 1 tavern w/entertainment). *In room:* A/C, TV, coffeemaker, hair dryer.

Inn at West Falmouth ★★ One of the loveliest small inns on the Cape, this shingle-style house is set high on a wooded hill with distant views to Buzzards Bay. The large living room has heaps of bestsellers begging to be borrowed, while the guest rooms are lavished with custom linens and unusual antiques. Some units have small balconies and whirlpool tubs. After a leisurely breakfast, you might carry off a tome to the small deck pool set in the deck or wander the landscaped grounds. Chapoquoit Beach is about a 10-minute walk away.

66 Frazar Rd. (off Rte. 28A), West Falmouth, MA 02574. ✆ **508/540-7696.** www.innatwestfalmouth.com. 7 units. Summer $280–$375 double. Rates include continental breakfast. AE, MC, V. **Amenities:** Small outdoor heated pool; clay tennis court; billiard room, masseuse on staff (fee). *In room:* A/C, cable TV, hair dryer, iron.

Scallop Shell Inn ★★ *Finds* This deluxe B&B just steps from Falmouth Heights Beach, is one of Falmouth's best. Guests are often found lounging on the wide front porch. Several rooms have wonderful views of Vineyard Sound and Martha's Vineyard. Some have gas fireplaces and two-person whirlpool tubs. Two units have balconies; several have private entrances. In the billiard and sitting room guests can enjoy a drink from the wet bar; they also have free rein of the guest kitchenette, stocked with beverages and homemade treats. The four-course gourmet breakfast could include an omelet with lobster, asparagus, and Gruyère.

16 Massachusetts Ave., Falmouth Heights, MA 02540. ✆ **800/249-4587** or 508/495-4900. Fax 508/495-4600. www.scallopshellinn.com. 7 units. Summer $285–$360 double. Rates include full breakfast. AE, DISC, MC, V. **Amenities:** Free laundry room. *In room:* A/C, TV/VCR, safe.

MODERATE

For a basic motel with a great location, try the **Tides Motel** (✆ **508/548-3126**) at the west end of Grand Avenue in Falmouth Heights. The 1950s-style no-frills (no air-conditioning, no phone) motel is a good value. It sits on the beach at the head of Falmouth Harbor facing Vineyard Sound. Rates in season are $140 to $150 double, $195 suite. Closed late October to mid-May.

The **Red Horse Inn** ★ (✆ **508/548-0053;** www.redhorseinn.com) is a family-friendly option just a short walk from Falmouth Harbor in Falmouth Heights. The 22 rooms are priced from $150 to $250, and kids will love the large outdoor pool.

Inn on the Sound ★★ *Finds* The ambience here is as breezy as the setting, high on a bluff beside Falmouth's premier sunning beach, with a sweeping view of Vineyard Sound from the large front deck. There's none of the usual frilly/cutesy stuff in these well-appointed guest rooms, most of which have ocean views, several with their own private decks. The focal point of the inn's living room is a handsome boulder hearth (nice for those nippy nights). Most guests enjoy having their breakfast, which features lots of home-baked goodies, on the front deck.

313 Grand Ave., Falmouth Heights, MA 02540. ✆ **800/564-9668** or 508/457-9666. Fax 508/457-9631. www.innonthesound.com. 7 units (5 tub/shower, 2 shower only). Summer $200–$295 double, $3,500 a week. Rates include continental breakfast. AE, DISC, MC, V. No children under 16. *In room:* TV, hair dryer, robes, no phone.

Sands of Time Motor Inn & Harbor House ★★ This property, across the street from the ferry terminal for Martha's Vineyard, consists of a two-story motel in front of a shingled 1879 Victorian mansion. The motel rooms feature crisp, above-average decor, plus private balconies overlooking the harbor. The rooms in the Harbor House are more lavish—some with four-poster beds and working fireplaces.

549 Woods Hole Rd., Woods Hole, MA 02543. ✆ **800/841-0114** or 508/548-6300. Fax 508/457-0160. www.sandsoftime.com. 36 units, 2 with shared bathroom. Summer $150–$200 double. Rates include continental breakfast. AE, DC, DISC, MC, V. Closed Nov–Mar. **Amenities:** Small heated pool; 2 tennis courts. *In room:* A/C, TV.

INEXPENSIVE

Inn at One Main Though built back in 1892, this shingled house with Queen Anne flourishes still has a youthful air. The bedrooms embody barefoot romance, rather than the Victorian brand. Lace, chintz, and wicker have been laid on lightly, leaving plenty of room to kick about. The Turret Room, with its big brass bed, is perhaps the most irresistible. Breakfasts feature gingerbread pancakes, orange-pecan French toast, homemade scones—it's a good thing the Shining Sea bike path is right at hand.

1 Main St. (1 block northwest of the Village Green), Falmouth, MA 02540. ✆ **888/281-6246** or 508/540-7469. Fax 603/462-5680. www.innatonemain.com. 6 units. Summer $110–$150 double. Rates include full breakfast. AE, DISC, MC, V. *In room:* A/C, hair dryer, no phone.

WHERE TO DINE

EXPENSIVE

Fishmonger's Cafe ★★ NATURAL This sunny cafe jutting out into the harbor attracts local young people, scientists, and tourists, for an array of imaginatively prepared dishes, with vegetarian choices a specialty. Lunch could be a tempeh burger or a regular beef version. The eclectic, changing dinner menu includes some Thai entrees. Regulars sit at the counter to enjoy a bowl of the fisherman's stew while newcomers usually go for the tables by the window, where you can watch boats come and go from Eel Pond.

56 Water St. (at the Eel Pond drawbridge), Woods Hole. ✆ **508/540-5376.** Main courses $15–$25. AE, MC, V. Mid-June to Oct Wed–Mon 7am–10pm; Tues noon–10pm. Call for off-season hours. Closed mid-Dec to mid-Feb.

La Cucina Sul Mare ★★ ITALIAN Locals and tourists alike line up outside this popular Main Street restaurant, craving its hearty Italian fare. The interior features cheerful murals and a tin ceiling, and large picture windows overlook Main Street. Chef/owner Mark Ciflone's signature dishes include classic Italian specialties like lasagna, braised lamb shanks, *osso buco,* lobster *fra diablo* over linguine, *zuppa de pesce,* rigatoni a la vodka, chicken Parmesan, and veal piccata, among others. The desserts here are homemade and truly delicious.

237 Main St., Falmouth. ✆ **508/548-5600.** Reservations required. Main courses $15–$25. AE, MC, V. Tues–Sun 11:30am–2pm and 5–10pm. Open year-round.

Phusion Grille ★ NEW AMERICAN/ASIAN This place is one of Falmouth's best restaurants, combining excellent food, professional service, and a terrific location on Eel Pond in Woods Hole. The interior is all blond wood and Asian screens, but nothing blocks the views of the wraparound floor-to-ceiling windows. The menu changes nightly depending on the catch of the day, but keep an eye out for the bouillabaisse and the sautéed sea scallops tossed with artichokes and a lobster sherry cream sauce. There's also a sushi bar.

71 Water St., Woods Hole. ✆ **508/457-3100.** Reservations not accepted. Main courses $21–$27. AE, MC, V. Daily 11:30am–2pm and 5–10pm. Call for off-season hours.

Roo Bar ★★ NEW AMERICAN Roo Bar is the top restaurant in town, for service, food, and atmosphere. The arty decor of this stylish bistro features handblown glass lamps over the bar and metal sconce sculptures on the walls. The food is exceptionally yummy, if pricey. Creative appetizers include Thai wontons with ginger chicken and a crispy tuna stick with a spicy dipper sauce. As a main course, try the snapper pie, which is a braised snapper in a puff pastry. Pizzas from the wood-burning oven come with unusual toppings like scallop and prosciutto. They don't take reservations, but if you call a half-hour ahead, you can put your name on the waiting list.

285 Main St. (at Cahoon Court). ✆ **508/548-8600.** Reservations not accepted. Main courses $11–$26. AE, MC, V. Daily 5–10pm; call for off-season hours.

MODERATE

Chapoquoit Grill ★★ NEW AMERICAN One of the few worthwhile dining spots in sleepy West Falmouth, this little roadside bistro has Californian aspirations: wood-grilled slabs of fish accompanied by trendy salsas, and crispy personal pizzas delivered straight from the brick oven. People drive here from miles around for the flavorful food. A no-reservations policy means long waits nightly in season and weekends year-round.

410 Rte. 28A, West Falmouth. ✆ **508/540-7794.** Reservations not accepted. Main courses $10–$18. MC, V. Daily 5–10pm.

Landfall ★★ AMERICAN A waterfront setting and good service make this Woods Hole seafood restaurant stand out. Besides the usual fish and pasta dishes, there's "light" fare like burgers and fish and chips. This is a great place to bring the kids; a children's menu comes with games and crayons. Or come for a drink at the half-dory bar to enjoy this massive wooden building constructed of salvage, both marine and terrestrial. A large bank of windows looks out onto the harbor, and the Martha's Vineyard ferry, when docking, appears to be making a beeline straight for your table.

Luscombe Ave. (½ block south of Water St.), Woods Hole. ✆ **508/548-1758.** Reservations recommended. Main courses $7–$26. AE, MC, V. Mid-May to Sept daily 11:30am–9pm; call for off-season hours. Closed late Nov to mid-Apr.

Peking Palace ★★ CHINESE/JAPANESE/THAI This popular Chinese restaurant has been given a major renovation from the ground-up with an expanded menu with Japanese and Thai food. There are also three regional Chinese cuisines (Cantonese, Mandarin, and Szechuan), as well as Polynesian. The decor is modern and sophisticated. Sip a fanciful drink to give yourself time to take in the menu, and be sure to solicit your server's opinion: That's how I encountered some heavenly spicy chilled squid.

452 Main St. (a few blocks east of the center of town), Falmouth. ✆ **508/540-8204.** Reservations for parties of six or more only. Main courses $5–$15. AE, MC, V. Daily 11:30am–midnight. Open year-round.

INEXPENSIVE

Betsy's Diner ★ *Finds* *Kids* AMERICAN This is hearty food like your mother used to make, if your mother was a variation of June Cleaver. The menu features turkey dinner, breakfast all day, and homemade pies. Some say the fried clams here are the best in town. Each red vinyl booth is equipped with its own jukebox with retro hits.

457 Main St. (in the center of town). ✆ **508/540-0060.** No reservations accepted. All items under $11. AE, MC, V. Mon–Sat 6am–9pm; Sun 6am–2pm; call for off-season hours.

The British Beer Company ★ PUB FARE/PIZZA The view is great at this faux British pub across the street from Falmouth Heights beach. Best choices are the fish and chips, burgers, and pizzas. The lobster bisque is also good and has won local awards. Of course, there is beer, 23 drafts available, like Guinness and John Courage, as well as bottled selections.

263 Grand Ave. (across from the beach), Falmouth Heights. ✆ **508/540-9600.** Reservations not accepted. All items under $15. AE, DC, DISC, MC, V. Mon–Sat 11:30am–10pm; Sun noon–10pm.

The Clam Shack ★ *Kids* SEAFOOD This classic clam shack at the head of Falmouth harbor offers steaming plates of fried seafood that you carry to a picnic table inside, outside, or up on the roof deck. It's basic fare, but the fish is fresh and you can't beat the view.

227 Clinton Ave. (off Scranton Ave., about 1 mile south of Main St.). ✆ **508/540-7758.** Reservations not accepted. Main courses $5–$15. No credit cards. Daily 11:30am–7:45pm. Closed early Sept to late May.

FALMOUTH AFTER DARK

The Boathouse (✆ **508/548-7800**) at 88 Scranton Ave. on Falmouth Inner Harbor features live bands in season, from classic rock to jazz, and dancing is popular here. God knows whom you'll meet in the rough-and-tumble old **Cap'n Kidd** ★, 77 Water St., in Woods Hole (✆ **508/548-9206**): maybe a lobsterwoman, maybe a Nobel prize winner. Good grub, too. Everyone heads to **Liam Maguire's Irish Pub** ★, on 273 Main St. in Falmouth (✆ **508/548-0285**), for a taste of the Emerald Isle. Live music on weekends year-round, often by Liam himself. **Grumpy's,** at 29 Locust St. (✆ **508/540-3930**), is a good old bar/shack with live music (rock, blues, and jazz) Thursday to Saturday nights. Cover is $2 to $10.

2 The Mid-Cape

Visitors who want to be centrally located on Cape Cod choose the Mid-Cape, which is just over an hour from Boston (without traffic), an easy (less than an hour) drive to the Outer Cape, and a 1-hour ferry ride from Nantucket. This is the Cape's most populous area and also the prime location for its cheapest motels, which line Route 28 from Hyannis to Dennis.

Hyannis is the Cape's unofficial capital. It's a sprawling concrete jungle of strip malls and chain stores where the Kennedy mystique of the 1960s had the unfortunate side effect of spurring heedless development over the ensuing decades—a period during which the Cape's year-round population doubled to more than 200,000. The summer population is about three times that, and you'd swear every single person had daily errands to run in Hyannis. And yet this overrun town still has plenty of pockets of charm, especially the waterfront area and Main Street.

The real beauty of the Mid-Cape lies in its smaller places: old-money hideaways like **Osterville** ★ to the west, and charming villages like **West Barnstable** ★★ and **Yarmouth Port** ★★, which can be found along the **Old King's Highway (Rte. 6A)** ★★★ on the northern bay side of the Cape. A drive along this winding two-lane road reveals the early architectural history of the region, from humble Colonial saltboxes to ostentatious captains' mansions. Scores of intriguing antiques shops subtly compete to draw a closer look, and each village seems a throwback to a kinder, gentler era.

HYANNIS & ENVIRONS ★

Hectic Hyannis is the commercial center and transportation hub of the Cape, with the large Cape Cod Mall and busy Barnstable Municipal Airport. It also has a diverse selection of restaurants, bars, and nightclubs. But if you were to confine your visit to this one town, you'd get a warped view of the Cape. Along Routes 132 and 28, you could be visiting Anywhere, USA: The roads are lined with the standard chain stores and mired with maddening traffic.

While Hyannis's impersonal hotels and motels have more beds at better prices than anywhere else on the Cape, there's little reason to choose them unless you happen to have missed the last ferry out to Nantucket. We recommend staying in Hyannisport or heading due north to Barnstable Village, where you'll find myriad charming B&Bs along the scenic Old King's Highway. Once you're settled, you can visit Hyannis to sample some of the Cape's best restaurants and nightlife. See "Barnstable Village & Environs," below.

ESSENTIALS

GETTING THERE After crossing the Sagamore bridge, head east on Route 6 or 6A. Route 6A passes through Barnstable Village; Route 132 (Exit 6 off Rte. 6) leads to Hyannis. You can also fly into Hyannis, and there is good bus service from Boston and New York.

VISITOR INFORMATION Contact the **Hyannis Area Chamber of Commerce,** 1481 Rte. 132, Hyannis, MA 02601 (✆ **800/449-6647,** 877/492-6647, or 508/362-5230; fax 508/362-9499; www.hyannis.com).

BEACHES & GETTING OUTSIDE

BEACHES Most of the Nantucket Sound beaches are fairly protected and offer little in the way of surf. Parking costs $12 to $15 a day, usually payable at the lot; for a weeklong parking sticker ($40), visit the Recreation Department at 141 Basset Lane, at the **Kennedy Memorial Skating Rink** (✆ **508/790-6345**).

- **Craigville Beach** ★★★, off Craigville Beach Road in Centerville: This broad expanse of sand has lifeguards and restrooms. A destination for the bronzed and buffed, it's known as "Muscle Beach." It's a short walk to Craigville Village, a former Methodist camp meeting site with Carpenter Gothic–style cottages.
- **Kalmus Beach** ★★, off Gosnold Street in Hyannisport: This 800-foot spit of sand stretching toward the mouth of the harbor makes an ideal launching site for windsurfers. The surf is tame, the slope shallow, and the conditions ideal for young kids. There are lifeguards, a snack bar, and restrooms.
- **Orrin Keyes Beach** ★★ (also known as Sea Beach), at the end of Sea Street in Hyannis: This little beach at the end of a residential road is popular with families.
- **Veterans Beach,** off Ocean Street in Hyannis: A small stretch of harborside sand adjoining the John F. Kennedy Memorial, this spot is not tops for swimming. Parking is usually easy, though, and it's walkable from town. The snack bar, restrooms, and playground will see to a family's needs.

FISHING Among the charter boats berthed in Barnstable Harbor is the 36-foot ***Drifter*** (✆ **508/398-2061**), offering half- and full-day trips. **Hy-Line Cruises** offers seasonal sonar-aided "bottom" or blues fishing on boats leaving from its Ocean Street dock in Hyannis (✆ **508/790-0696**). **Helen H Deep-Sea Fishing** at 137 Pleasant St., Hyannis (✆ **508/790-0660**), offers year-round expeditions aboard a 100-foot boat with a heated cabin and full galley.

GOLF The **Hyannis Golf Club,** Route 132 (✆ **508/362-2606**), offers a 46-station driving range, and an 18-hole championship course. Smaller but scenic is the 9-hole **Cotuit High Ground Country Club,** 31 Crockers Neck Rd., Cotuit (✆ **508/428-9863**).

WATERSPORTS **Eastern Mountain Sports,** 1513 Iyannough Rd./Rte. 132 (✆ **508/362-8690;** www.ems.com), offers rental kayaks—tents and sleeping bags, too—and sponsors free clinics and walks, like a full-moon hike. Kayaks rent for about $50 a day.

SIGHTSEEING TOURS BY STEAMER

Hy-Line Harbor Cruises For a fun and informative introduction to the harbor and its residents, take a leisurely 1- to 2-hour tour aboard one of Hy-Line's 1911 steamer replicas. The Sunday "Ice-Cream Float" includes a design-your-own Ben & Jerry's sundae, while the Thursday "Jazz Boat" features a Dixieland band.

Ocean St. Dock, Hyannis. ✆ **508/790-0696.** www.hy-linecruises.com. Tickets $12–$21 adults, $19 seniors, $15 children 12 and under. Parking is $3 per car. Late June to Sept departures daily; call for schedule. Closed Nov to mid-Apr.

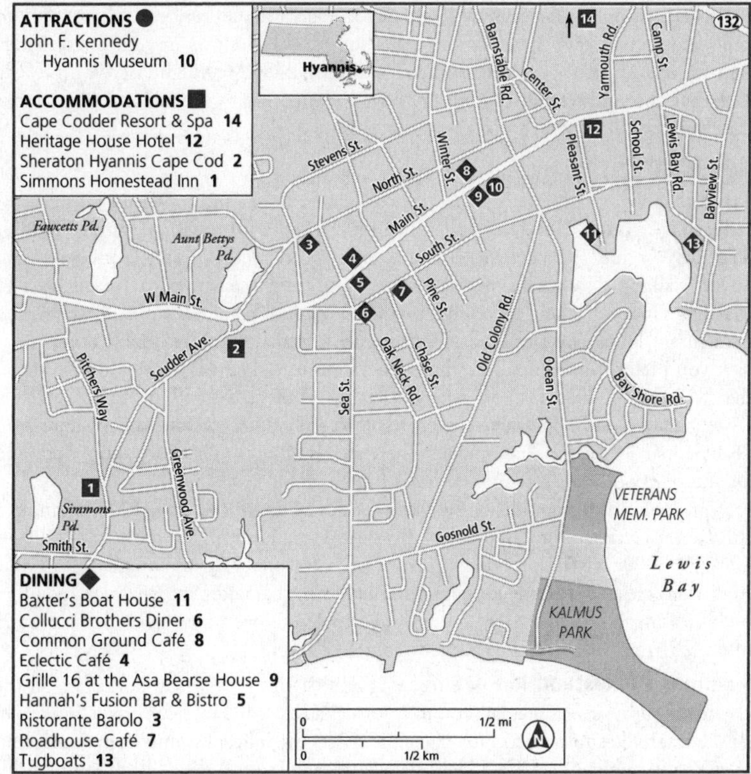

THE KENNEDY LEGACY

Don't even bother trying to track down the Kennedy Compound in Hyannisport; it's effectively screened from view. You'll see more at the following museum. Or if you absolutely must satisfy your curiosity, take a harbor cruise (see "Sightseeing Tours by Steamer," above).

John F. Kennedy Hyannis Museum *Overrated* This multimedia display captures the Kennedys during the glory days from 1934 to 1963.

397 Main St., Hyannis. © **508/790-3077.** Admission $5 adults, $2.50 for children 10–16 and seniors. Mid-Apr to Oct Mon–Sat 9am–4:30pm; Sun and holidays noon–4:30pm; last admission at 3:30pm. Call for off-season hours.

SHOPPING

Although Hyannis is undoubtedly the commercial center of the Cape, the stores here are fairly standard. Head to the wealthy enclaves west of Hyannis, such as Osterville, and along the Old King's Highway (Rte. 6A) to the north, to locate the real gems.

On Main Street in Hyannis, you'll find a world of wonderful kitchen products at **Nantucket Trading Company,** 354 Main St. (© **508/790-3933**).

Tao Water Art Gallery, 1989 Rte. 6A, West Barnstable (© **508/375-0428**), is a former garage converted into a very Zenlike space. It features paintings by Chinese artists as well as museum reproductions of Chinese antiques and jade.

Richard Kiusalas and Steven Whittlesey salvage antique lumber and turn it into cupboards, tables, and chairs, among other things; old windows are retrofitted as mirrors. Most of the stock at **West Barnstable Tables,** 2454 Meetinghouse Way (off Rte. 149 near the intersection of Rte. 6A), West Barnstable (✆ **508/362-2676**), looks freshly made, albeit with wood of unusually high quality.

WHERE TO STAY

There are a variety of large, generic but convenient hotels and motels in Hyannis.

Heritage House Hotel, 259 Main St. (in the center of town), Hyannis (✆ **800/352-7189** or 508/775-7000; www.heritagehousehotel.com) is ideally located on Main Street, walking distance from restaurants, shops, and the ferries to Nantucket and Martha's Vineyard. There are an indoor and an outdoor pool, hot tub and saunas, and a restaurant/lounge on-site. The 143 rooms are priced at $169 for double occupancy.

If you prefer more amenities, there's the **Sheraton Hyannis Cape Cod Resort** at the West End Circle just off Main Street (✆ **800/598-4559** or 508/775-7775; www.sheraton.com). Summer rates are $199 to $309 double. Out the back door is an 18-hole, par-3 executive golf course. There are also four tennis courts, an indoor and an outdoor pool, four restaurants, and a fitness center.

A great choice for families is the **Cape Codder Resort and Spa,** 1225 Iyannough Rd./Rte. 132 (at the intersection of Bearse's Way), Hyannis (✆ **888/297-2200** or 508/771-3000; www.capecodderresort.com), It features two restaurants (VJ's Grille Room and Hearth 'n Kettle for families), plus a wine bar and a spa (massage and other body treatments). Kids love the indoor wave pool with two water slides. Summer rates in the 261 rooms are $239 to $259 double, $479 suite.

Simmons Homestead Inn ★★ *Finds* The first thing passersby notice are all the classic red sports cars: 50 at last count. A former ad exec and race-car driver, innkeeper Bill Putman likes to collect. He's made his sports car collection into a small museum open to the public called Toad Hall, after *The Wind in the Willows.* Each room in this rambling 1820s house has an animal theme represented by stuffed toys, sculptures, even needlepoint and wallpaper. Guests who prefer privacy may book the spiffily updated "servants' quarters," a spacious wing with its own deck. This is the kind of place where you'll find everyone milling around the hearth sipping complimentary wine while they compare notes and nail down dinner plans. To help his guests plan their days, Putman has typed up extensive notes on day trips, bike routes, and his own quirky restaurant reviews.

288 Scudder Ave. (about ¼ mile west of the West End rotary), Hyannisport, MA 02647. ✆ **800/637-1649** or 508/778-4999. Fax 508/790-1342. www.SimmonsHomesteadInn.com. 14 units. Summer $200–$260 double; $350 2-bedroom suite. Rates include full breakfast. AE, DISC, MC, V. Dogs welcome. **Amenities:** 6-person hot tub; loaner bikes; billiards parlor. *In room:* Hair dryer, iron, no phone.

WHERE TO DINE

Very Expensive

Grille 16 at the Asa Bearse House ★ STEAKHOUSE There's a lot of buzz about Grille 16, Cape Cod's best new steakhouse. Rick Angelini, who started the successful Naked Oyster restaurant across town, has teamed up with Derek Sanderson, who wore the jersey number 16 for the Boston Bruins hockey team, for this ambitious endeavor. It used to be you had to head to the big city to get steaks like this: prime porterhouse, prime New York sirloin, and filet mignon. Besides premium steaks, you'll find local seafood like pan-roasted halibut on the menu. On clear nights, you'll want to sit on the patio in front. In the winter, the best tables are near the fireplaces.

415 Main St., Hyannis. ✆ **508/778-0006.** Reservations recommended. Main courses $19–$37. AE, DC, DISC, MC, V. Daily 11:30am–1am. Open year-round.

Expensive

Eclectic Cafe ★ *Finds* NEW AMERICAN Hidden down an alley off Hyannis's busy Main Street, this little jewel of a restaurant is a real find, like a secret cafe. Most of the seating is outside in a magical garden, lush with plants and flowers. Continuing the feeling that you've found an alternate universe, the waitstaff is exceptionally pleasant and skilled. Pastas are homemade and luscious. Dishes like bouillabaisse a la Eclectic or oven-roasted cod with artichokes will tempt you to recommend this one to all your friends. But, then again, you wouldn't want to give away the secret.

606 Main St., Hyannis (at the west end of Main St.). ✆ **508/771-7187.** Reservations highly recommended. Main courses $18–$29. AE, DC, DISC, MC, V. Apr–Oct daily 5:30–9pm; call for off-season hours. Open year-round.

Hannah's Fusion Bar and Bistro ★★ INTERNATIONAL/ASIAN After serving as chef at the RooBar and starting the restaurant Phusion, both in Falmouth, Chef Binh Phu has created a following for his innovative cuisine. Those people will likely flock to his new restaurant, Hannah, a labor of love for this Vietnamese native. Binh's genius comes from his creativity in blending ingredients. For example, main courses might include Mongolian coffee-encrusted pork tenderloin or pan-seared ginger and lemon grass marinated Atlantic salmon. There's also a special sushi menu. His all-chocolate dessert menu features delicacies like Key lime pie with a chocolate trellis. Those who catch the early-bird menu (4:30–6:30pm) get a choice of soup or appetizer, choice of main course, plus dessert for $20.

615 Main St., Hyannis (the west end of town). ✆ **508/778-5565.** Reservations recommended. Main courses $18–$30. AE, DC, DISC, MC, V. Apr–Oct daily 4:30–10pm; call for off-season hours. Open year-round.

The Regatta of Cotuit at the Crocker House ★★★ NEW AMERICAN One of the best restaurants on Cape Cod, The Regatta serves fine-dining cuisine in the Federal-era rooms of a 1790 Cape. The food and service are always top-notch. Specials might include roasted buffalo tenderloin with blackberry Madeira sauce served with braised fresh greens and a Stilton sage bread pudding. For budget-minded gourmands, the Regatta menu also includes several less expensive "bistro" items, like chicken fricassee and grilled pork loin medallions.

4631 Rte. 28 (near the intersection of Rte. 130), Cotuit. ✆ **508/428-5715.** Reservations recommended. Main courses $26–$35; bistro menu $16–$17. AE, MC, V. Apr–Dec daily 5–10pm; Jan–Mar Wed–Sun 5–10pm.

Ristorante Barolo ★★ NORTHERN ITALIAN This is the best Italian restaurant in town. Part of a smart-looking brick office complex, this place does everything right, from offering extra-virgin olive oil for dunking the crusty bread to getting those pastas perfectly al dente. Entrees include a number of tempting veal choices, as well as such favorites as *Linguine al Frutti di Mare,* with littlenecks, mussels, shrimp, and calamari. The desserts are brought in daily from Boston's famed North End.

1 Financial Place (297 North St., just off the West End rotary), Hyannis. ✆ **508/778-2878.** Reservations recommended. Main courses $10–$27. AE, DC, MC, V. June–Sept Sun–Thurs 4:30–10pm, Fri–Sat 4:30–11pm; call for off-season hours.

Roadhouse Café ★★ AMERICAN/NORTHERN ITALIAN This is neither a roadhouse nor a cafe but it is a solid entry in the Hyannis dining scene. The menu is split between American standards and real Italian cooking. Among the appetizers are beef carpaccio with fresh-shaved Parmesan, and vine-ripened tomatoes and buffalo mozzarella drizzled with balsamic vinaigrette. The vinaigrette also makes a tasty marinade for native swordfish headed for the grill. A less expensive, lighter-fare menu, including what some have called "the best burger in the world," is served in the snazzy bistro in back, which also features live jazz Monday nights (see "Hyannis & Environs After Dark," below).

488 South St. (off Main St., near the West End rotary), Hyannis. ✆ **508/775-2386.** Reservations recommended. Main courses $15–$26. AE, DC, DISC, MC, V. Daily 4pm–midnight.

Moderate

Tugboats ★ Kids AMERICAN Yet another harborside perch for munching and ogling, this one's especially appealing. Forget fancy dining and chow down on blackened-swordfish bites (topping a Caesar salad, perhaps) or lobster fritters. Among the desserts is a Key lime pie purportedly lifted straight from Papa's of Key West.

21 Arlington St. (at the Hyannis Marina, off Willow St.), Hyannis. ✆ **508/775-6433.** Reservations not accepted. Main courses $11–$18. AE, DC, DISC, MC, V. Late May to Oct daily 11:30am–10:30pm; Apr to late May Tues–Sun 11:30am–10:30pm. Closed Nov–Mar.

Inexpensive

Baxter's Boat House ★ Value Kids SEAFOOD A shingled shack on a jetty jutting out into the harbor, Baxter's caters to the boating crowd with fried clams and fish virtually any way you like it, served on paper plates at picnic tables.

177 Pleasant St. (near the Steamship Authority ferry), Hyannis. ✆ **508/775-7040.** Main courses $8–$14. AE, MC, V. Late May to early Sept Mon–Sat 11:30am–10pm, Sun 11:30am–9pm; mid-Apr to late May and mid-Sept to mid-Oct Thurs–Sun 11:30am–9pm. Closed mid-Oct to Apr.

Collucci Brothers Diner DINER In the tradition of great diners, this one has a tin ceiling, comfy booths, and a shiny counter. It also has sassy waitresses who pour really good coffee. Selections from the children's menu are under $4. Wash down a tuna melt with a root beer float or splurge on the roast turkey dinner. The diner is a block from Main Street and about a half-mile from the Hy-Line ferry terminal with boats to Nantucket.

50 Sea St. (at the corner of South St.). ✆ **508/771-6896.** Reservations not accepted. All items under $10. AE, MC, V. Late May to Sept Mon–Sat 6am–3pm; Sun 6am–2pm.

Common Ground Cafe ★ Value AMERICAN Talk about an out-of-body experience: Step off tacky Main Street Hyannis into this New Age-y sandwich shop run by a commune. The barn-board walls and wide-board floors surround alcoves with private booths containing amorphous tree-stump tables. But enough about atmosphere; this place makes the best iced tea on Cape Cod (the house blend—a mixture of mint teas and lemon). The sandwiches and salads are wholesome and delicious, and the burrito with turkey is a winner.

420 Main St., Hyannis. ✆ **508/778-8390.** Most items under $6. AE, DC, DISC, MC, V. Mon–Thurs 10am–9pm; Fri 10am–3pm.

HYANNIS & ENVIRONS AFTER DARK

From July to early September, try to catch a show at the **Cape Cod Melody Tent** ★★, West End rotary, Hyannis (✆ **508/775-9100**). Built as a summer theater in 1950, this billowy big top proved even better suited to variety shows. A nonprofit venture since 1990, the Melody Tent has hosted the major performers of the past 50 years, from jazz greats to comedians, crooners to rockers. There's children's theater Wednesday at 11am.

The congenial **Baxter's Boat House,** 177 Pleasant St. (see "Where to Dine," above), Hyannis (✆ **508/775-7040**), with low-key blues piano, draws an attractive crowd. A good place for after-dinner entertainment is **Roadhouse Café** ★, 488 South St. (see "Where to Dine," above), Hyannis (✆ **508/775-2386**), a dark-paneled bar that stocks 48 boutique beers. Insiders show up Monday nights to hear local jazz great Dave McKenna. **Roo Bar,** 586 Main St., Hyannis (✆ **508/778-6515**), feels very Manhattan, with ultra-cool servers, a long, sleek bar area, and lots of attitude. The bistro food is good, too.

The cramped dance floor makes for instant camaraderie at **Harry's** ★★, 700 Main St., Hyannis (✆ **508/778-4188**), which features live blues and rockabilly nightly in season and about 5 nights a week the rest of the year. The cover is $3 to $4 Thursday through Saturday.

BARNSTABLE VILLAGE & ENVIRONS ★★

Just a couple miles from Hyannis, the bucolic village of Barnstable houses the county courthouse and government offices for the region. In this peaceful setting are some of the most charming B&Bs around. The bay area along historic Route 6A, the Old King's Highway, unfolds in a blur of greenery and well-kept Colonial houses.

BEACHES & GETTING OUTSIDE

BEACHES Barnstable's primary bay beach is **Sandy Neck,** accessed through East Sandwich (see "The Upper Cape," earlier in this chapter).

BOATING You can rent a canoe from **Eastern Mountain Sports** (see "Watersports," under "Hyannis & Environs," earlier in this chapter) and paddle around Scorton Creek, Sandy Neck, and Barnstable Harbor.

FISHING Barnstable has 11 ponds for freshwater fishing; for permits, visit **Town Hall,** 367 Main St., Hyannis (✆ **508/790-6240**), or **Sports Port,** 149 W. Main St., Hyannis (✆ **508/775-3096**). Shellfishing permits are available from the **Department of Natural Resources,** 1189 Phinneys Lane, Centerville (✆ **508/790-6272**). Surf-casting without a license is permitted on Sandy Neck. Among the charter boats berthed in Barnstable Harbor is the ***Drifter*** (✆ **508/398-2061**), a 36-foot boat offering half- and full-day trips.

SHOPPING

Today only one weaver in the United States creates Jacquard designs by hand, and that's Bob Black, who began his trade at age 14 and refined it at the Rhode Island School of Design. He works out of **The Blacks' Handweaving Shop,** 597 Rte. 6A, about ⅔ mile west of Rte. 149, West Barnstable (✆ **508/362-3955**).

Tao Water Art Gallery, 1989 Rte. 6A, West Barnstable (✆ **508/375-0428**), is a former garage converted into a very Zenlike space. It features paintings by Chinese artists as well as museum reproductions of Chinese antiques and jade.

Richard Kiusalas and Steven Whittlesey salvage antique lumber and turn it into cupboards, tables, and chairs, among other things at **West Barnstable Tables,** 2454 Meetinghouse Way, off Route 149 near the intersection of Route 6A, West Barnstable (✆ **508/362-2676**).

WHERE TO STAY

Ashley Manor Inn ★ A lovely country inn along the Old King's Highway, this 1699 mansion still retains many of its original features, including a hearth with beehive oven and wide-board floors, many of them brightened with Nantucket-style splatter paint. The rooms, all but one with working fireplace, are spacious and inviting. A deluxe unit has a separate entrance, whirlpool bath, and canopy bed. The 2-acre property includes a Har-Tru tennis court. Breakfast on the brick patio is worth waking up for.

3660 Rte. 6A (just east of Hyannis Rd.), Barnstable, MA 02630. ✆ **888/535-2246** or 508/362-8044. Fax 508/362-9927. www.ashleymanor.net. 6 units. Summer $150–$165 double; $200–$215 suite. Rates include full breakfast. AE, DISC, MC, V. **Amenities:** Har-Tru tennis court; loaner bikes. *In room:* A/C, dataport, coffeemaker, hair dryer.

Beechwood Inn ★★ *Finds* Look for a butterscotch-colored 1853 Queen Anne Victorian all but enshrouded in weeping beech trees. Admirers of late-19th-century decor are in for a treat: The interior is dark and rich, with a red-velvet parlor and a tin-ceilinged dining room. Two of the upstairs bedrooms embody distinctive period styles from the 1860s and 1880s. Each affords a distant view of the bay. Rooms range from quite spacious (Lilac) to romantically snug (Garret).

2839 Rte. 6A (about 1½ miles east of Rte. 132), Barnstable, MA 02630. ✆ **800/609-6618** or 508/362-6618. Fax 508/362-0298. www.beechwoodinn.com. 6 units (4 tub/shower, 2 shower only). Summer $160–$180 double. Rates include full breakfast. AE, DISC, MC, V. *In room:* A/C, minifridge, hair dryer, no phone.

Lamb and Lion Inn ★ This is an unusual property: part B&B, part motel. From the roadside, it's one of those charming old Cape Cod cottages (ca. 1740) along the Old King's Highway. Inside, it's a motel-like space with units encircling a pool and hot tub. The rooms are all individually decorated, and six rooms have kitchenettes. All rooms in the main inn building are air-conditioned. The multilevel barn suite, with three loft-type bedrooms, is a funky historic space (built in 1740), filled with rustic nooks and crannies.

2504 Main St. (Rte. 6A), Barnstable, MA 02630. ✆ **800/909-6923** or 508/362-6823. Fax 508/362-0227. www.lambandlion.com. 10 units (6 tub/shower, 4 shower only). Summer $145–$250 double. Rates include continental breakfast. MC, V. Well-behaved pets allowed (40-lb. limit). **Amenities**: Pool; hot tub. *In room:* A/C, TV.

WHERE TO DINE

Dolphin Restaurant ★★ NEW AMERICAN Never mind the corny decor in what looks like just another run-of-the-mill eatery. The finesse is to be found in the menu, where amid the more typical fried fish you'll find such delicacies as Chilean sea bass with roasted corn salsa and lime vinaigrette, roast duck with mango glaze and toasted coconut.

3250 Rte. 6A (in the center of town), Barnstable. ✆ **508/362-6610.** Main courses $17–$23. AE, MC, V. May–Oct Mon–Sat 11:30am–3pm and 5–9:30pm; Sun 5–9:30pm.

Mattakeese Wharf ★ SEAFOOD This place, with great views and average food, is always packed; don't even bother on summer weekends. The outdoor seating fills up first, and no wonder, with Sandy Neck sunsets to marvel over. The bouillabaisse is always good, and you can't go wrong if you stick to the varied combinations of pasta, seafood, and sauce—from Alfredo to *fra diablo.* There's live piano music most nights in season.

271 Mill Way (about ½ mile north of Rte. 6A), Barnstable. ✆ **508/362-4511.** Reservations recommended. Main courses $14–$28. AE, DC, DISC, MC, V. June to mid-Oct daily 11:30am–10pm; call for off-season hours. Closed mid-Oct to mid-Apr.

YARMOUTH ★★

Yarmouth represents the Cape at its best—and worst. **Yarmouth Port** ★★, on Cape Cod Bay, is an enchanting village, whereas the sound-side villages of West and South Yarmouth are a lesson in unbridled development run amuck. This section of Route 28 is a nightmarish gauntlet of mostly tacky accommodations and attractions.

ESSENTIALS

GETTING THERE After crossing the Sagamore bridge, head east on Route 6 or 6A. The section of Route 6A north of Route 6's Exit 7 passes through the village of Yarmouth Port. The villages of West Yarmouth, Bass River, and South Yarmouth are located along Route 28, east of Hyannis; to reach them from Route 6, take Exit 7 (Yarmouth Rd.) or Exit 8 (Station St.) south.

VISITOR INFORMATION Contact the **Yarmouth Area Chamber of Commerce,** 657 Rte. 28, West Yarmouth, MA 02673 (✆ **800/732-1008** or 508/778-1008; fax 508/778-5114; www.yarmouthcapecod.com).

BEACHES & GETTING OUTSIDE

BEACHES Yarmouth boasts 11 saltwater and two pond beaches open to the public. The body-per-square-yard ratio can be pretty intense along the sound, but so's the social scene, and no one seems to mind. The beachside parking lots charge $12 to $15 a day and sell weeklong stickers ($45).

- **Bass River Beach** ★, off South Shore Drive in Bass River (South Yarmouth): At the mouth of the largest tidal river on the eastern seaboard, this sound beach offers restroom facilities and a snack bar, plus a wheelchair-accessible fishing pier. The beaches along the south shore (Nantucket Sound) tend to be clean and sandy with comfortable water temps, but they can also be crowded. You need a beach sticker to park here.
- **Grays Beach,** off Center Street in Yarmouth Port: This isn't much of a beach, but tame waters make this tiny spit of dark sand good for young children. It adjoins the Callery–Darling Conservation Area with a 2.5-mile trail. The Bass Hole boardwalk offers one of the most scenic walks in the Mid-Cape. Parking is free, and there's a picnic area.
- **Parker's River Beach,** off South Shore Drive in Bass River: The usual amenities are available, like restrooms and a snack bar, plus a gazebo for the sun-shy.
- **Seagull Beach** ★, off South Sea Avenue in West Yarmouth: Rolling dunes, a boardwalk, and all the necessary facilities, like restrooms and a snack bar, attract a young crowd. Bring bug spray, though: Greenhead flies get the munchies in July.

FISHING Of the five fishing ponds in the Yarmouth area, Long Pond near South Yarmouth is known for its largemouth bass and pickerel; for details and a license (shellfishing is another option), visit **Town Hall** at 1146 Rte. 28 in South Yarmouth (✆ **508/398-2231**), or **Riverview Bait and Tackle** at 1273 Rte. 28 in South Yarmouth (✆ **508/394-1036**). Full-season licenses for out-of-state residents cost $39. You can cast for striped bass and bluefish off the pier at Bass River Beach (see "Beaches," above).

NATURE & WILDLIFE AREAS For a pleasant stroll, follow the 2 miles of trails maintained by the **Historical Society of Old Yarmouth.** Park behind the post office. The in-season trail fee (50¢ adults, 25¢ children) includes a keyed trail guide. Your path will cross the 1873 Kelley Chapel, said to have been built by a Quaker grandfather to comfort his daughter after the death of her child.

MUSEUMS

The Edward Gorey House ★★ *Finds* The Cape's newest attraction is a museum devoted to the life and works of whimsically mischievous illustrator Edward Gorey, whose best known work may be the animated opening to the television series *Mystery!* on PBS. He was also the author of many illustrated books, including *The Doubtful Guest* and *The Gashlycrumb Tinies.* Gorey died in the spring of 2000 and his home on the Yarmouth Port Common off Route 6A (the Old Kings Hwy.) has been converted into an intimate museum displaying original artworks, photographs, and first editions from his career as an author, playwright, illustrator, and costume and set designer. Gorey's passion for animals is also a focus of the collection.

8 Strawberry Lane (off Rte. 6A, on the Common), Yarmouth Port. © **508/362-3909.** www.edwardgoreyhouse.com. Admission $5 adults, $3 students and seniors, $2 children 6–12, free for under 6. Mar–Jan Wed–Sat 11am–4pm; Sun noon–4pm. Closed Feb.

Winslow Crocker House ★★ The only property on the Cape currently preserved by the prestigious Society for the Preservation of New England Antiquities, this house, built around 1780, deserves every honor. Not only is it a lovely example of the shingled Georgian style, it's packed with outstanding antiques collected in the 1930s by Mary Thacher, a descendant of the town's first land grantee. Anthony Thacher and his family had a rougher crossing than most: Their ship foundered off Cape Ann in 1635, and though their four children drowned, Thacher and his wife were able to make it to shore, clinging to the family cradle. You'll come across a 1690 replica in the parlor.

250 Rte. 6A (about ½ mile east of the town center), Yarmouth Port. © **617/227-3957**, ext. 256. www.spnea.org. Admission $4 adults, $4 seniors, $2.50 children 6–12, free to Yarmouthport residents and SPNEA members. June–Oct 1st Sat each month, tours hourly 11am–5pm (last tour at 4pm). Closed Nov–May.

SHOPPING

Driving Route 6A, the Old King's Highway, in Yarmouth Port, you'll pass a number of antiques stores and shops for the home. Check out **Town Crier Antiques,** 153 Rte. 6A (in the center of town), Yarmouth Port (© **508/362-3138**), for fun stuff including well-priced quilts, glassware, and attendant paraphernalia. The most colorful bookshop on the Cape is **Parnassus Books,** 220 Rte. 6A, Yarmouth Port (© **508/362-6420**), housed in an 1858 Swedenborgian church. New stock, including the Cape-related reissues published by Parnassus Imprints, is offered alongside the older treasures. The outdoor racks, maintained on an honor system, are open 24 hours a day.

WHERE TO STAY

There are so many hotels and motels lining Route 28 and along the shore in West and South Yarmouth that it can be hard to make sense of the choices. For those staying on Route 28, the town runs frequent beach shuttles in season. Families looking for a reasonably priced beach vacation may want to consider one of the following options, all near or on the beach.

The attractive 101-unit white clapboard **Tidewater Motor Lodge,** 135 Main St. (Rte. 28), West Yarmouth (© **800/338-6322** or 508/775-6322; www.tidewaterml.com), has indoor and outdoor pools. Double rates go for $170 in summer. The 114-unit **All Seasons Motor Inn,** 1199 Main St. (Rte. 28), South Yarmouth (© **800/527-0359** or 508/394-7600; www.allseasons.com), has a game room and indoor and outdoor pools. Summer rates are $145 to $160 for a double room. The 63-unit **Ocean Mist** ★, 97 S. Shore Dr., South Yarmouth (✆ **800/248-6478** or 508/398-2633; www.capecodtravel.com/oceanmist), is right on the beach. There's also an indoor pool, in case it rains. Doubles range from $189 to $209 double, and suites are $259.

Captain Farris House ★★ Sumptuous is the only way to describe this 1845 inn, improbably set a block off bustling Route 28. Fine antiques and striking contemporary touches elevate the interiors beyond the average B&B decor. Some suites are apartment-size, with fireplaces and whirlpool tubs. Welcoming touches include chocolates, fresh flowers, and plush robes. Next door, the Elisha Jenkins House contains an additional suite with its own deck.

308 Old Main St. (just west of the Bass River Bridge), Bass River, MA 02664-4530. ✆ **800/350-9477** or 508/760-2818. Fax 508/398-1262. www.captainfarris.com. 10 units (9 tub/shower, 1 shower only). Summer $150–$190 double; $195–$275 suite. Rates include full breakfast. AE, DISC, MC, V. *In room:* A/C, TV/VCR, dataport, hair dryer, iron.

Red Jacket ★★ Kids Of the huge resort motels lining Nantucket Sound in South Yarmouth, Red Jacket has the best location. It's at the end of the road and borders Parker's River on the west, so sunsets are particularly fine. Families who want all the fixings will find them, though the atmosphere can be a bit impersonal. All rooms have a balcony or private porch.

1 S. Shore Dr. (P.O. Box 88), South Yarmouth, MA 02664. ✆ **800/672-0500** or 508/398-6941. Fax 508/398-1214. www.redjacketinns.com/redjacket. 150 units, 14 cottages. Summer $295–$395 double; $325–$550 cottages. Cottages weekly: $3,000–$5,500. MC, V. Closed Nov to mid-Apr. **Amenities:** Restaurant; bar/lounge; ice-cream shop; indoor and outdoor heated pools; putting green; tennis court; exercise room; whirlpool; sauna; full concierge service. *In room:* A/C, TV/VCR, hair dryer, fridge.

WHERE TO DINE

At **Hallett's,** 139 Rte. 6A, Yarmouth Port (✆ **508/362-3362**), an 1889 drugstore, you can get a float from the original marble soda fountain.

Expensive

902 Main ★★★ NEW AMERICAN Our vote for best new restaurant on Cape Cod. With fabulous service, an elegant atmosphere, and to-die-for food, this is the place to go for fine dining in the Mid-Cape. Entrees like filet mignon with portobello mushrooms, rack of lamb with truffle mashed potatoes, and haddock with organic beets will make you swoon.

902 Main St./Rte. 28, South Yarmouth. ✆ **508/398-9902.** Reservations required. Main courses $18–$33. AE, MC, V. Daily 5–10pm.

abbicci ★★ MEDITERRANEAN This sophisticated spot serves cuisine that's a cut above most of the New England-y fare you'll find around these parts. While the exterior is a modest 18th-century Cape, the stylish interior features mosaic floors and mural-covered walls. The menu offers seafood dishes, as well as veal, lamb, and, of course, pasta, all in a delicate Northern Italian style. A taste of the veal *nocciole* (with toasted hazelnuts and a splash of balsamic vinegar), and you'll be transported straight to Tuscany. This small restaurant can get overrun on summer weekends, so expect a wait even with a reservation.

43 Main St./Rte. 6A (near the Cummaquid border), Yarmouth Port. ✆ **508/362-3501.** Reservations recommended. Main courses $18–$28. AE, MC, V. Daily 11:30am–2:30pm and 5–10pm.

Inaho ★★ Finds JAPANESE What better application of the Cape's oceanic bounty than fresh-off-the-boat sushi? From the front, Inaho is a typical Cape Cod cottage, but park in the back so you can enter through the Japanese garden. The decor is minimalist with traditional shoji screens and crisp navy-and-white banners softened by tranquil music and service. On chilly days, opt for the tempura or a steaming bowl of shabu-shabu.

157 Main St./Rte. 6A (in the village center), Yarmouth Port. ✆ **508/362-5522.** Reservations recommended. Main courses $13–$23; sushi pieces and rolls $3–$7. MC, V. Tues–Sun 5–10pm; call for off-season hours.

Old Yarmouth Inn NEW ENGLAND If a traditional Cape Cod atmosphere is what you are looking for, you can't do much better than this old stagecoach inn serving Yankee basics like prime rib and baked scrod. The food is fresh and hearty and the preparations are tasty. People are catching on that this is good food at reasonable prices, so it can be crowded on weekends in season. There's also a lighter-fare menu. One of the most requested dishes is the deluxe lobster roll, with big chunks of fresh lobster. The Sunday brunch, a combination buffet and a la carte meal, is popular.

223 Rte. 6A (in the center of Yarmouth Port). ✆ **508/362-9962.** Reservations recommended. Main courses $14–$25. AE, DC, DISC, MC, V. June–Oct Tues–Sat 7–11am and 11:30am–2:30pm, Sun 10am–1pm, daily 4:30–9pm; call for off-season hours. Open year-round.

DENNIS ★★

In Dennis, as in Yarmouth, virtually all the good stuff—pretty drives, inviting shops, and restaurants with real personality—is in the north, along Route 6A. Route 28, on the other hand, is chockablock with generic motels and strip malls.

ESSENTIALS

GETTING THERE After crossing the Sagamore Bridge, head east on Route 6 or 6A. Route 6A passes through the villages of Dennis and East Dennis (which can also be reached via northbound Rte. 134 from Exit 9 off Rte. 6). Route 134 South leads to South Dennis; if you follow Route 134 all the way to Route 28, the village of West Dennis will be a couple of miles to your west, and Dennisport a couple of miles east. Or fly into Hyannis (see "Getting There," in chapter 2).

VISITOR INFORMATION Contact the **Dennis Chamber of Commerce,** 242 Swan River Rd., West Dennis, MA 02670 (✆ **800/243-9920** or 508/398-3568; www.dennischamber.com).

BEACHES & RECREATIONAL PURSUITS

BEACHES Dennis harbors more than a dozen saltwater and two freshwater beaches open to nonresidents. The bay beaches are charming and a big hit with families. The beaches on the Sound tend to attract wall-to-wall families, but the parking lots are usually not too crowded, because many beachgoers stay within walking distance. The lots charge $15 per day; for a 1-week permit ($50), visit **Town Hall** on Main Street in South Dennis (✆ **508/394-8300**).

- **Chapin Beach** ★★, off Route 6A in Dennis: A nice, long bay beach pocked with occasional boulders and surrounded by dunes. No lifeguard, but there are restrooms.
- **Corporation Beach** ★★, off Route 6A in Dennis: This bay beach boasts a wheelchair-accessible boardwalk, lifeguards, snack bar, restrooms, and a children's play area.
- **Mayflower Beach** ★★, off Route 6A in Dennis: This 1,200-foot bay beach has the necessary amenities, plus an accessible boardwalk. The tide pools attract lots of children.

- **Scargo Lake in Dennis:** This large kettle-hole pond (formed by a melting fragment of a glacier) has two pleasant beaches: Scargo Beach, accessible right off Route 6A; and Princess Beach, off Scargo Hill Road, where there are restrooms and a picnic area.
- **West Dennis Beach** ★★, off Route 28 in West Dennis: This long (½-mile) but narrow beach along the sound has lifeguards, a playground, a snack bar, restrooms, and a special kite-flying area. The eastern end is reserved for residents; the western end tends, in any case, to be less packed.

BICYCLING The 25-mile **Cape Cod Rail Trail** ★★★ (✆ **508/896-3491**) starts here, on Route 134, a half-mile south of Route 6, Exit 9. Once a Penn Central track, this paved bikeway extends all the way to Wellfleet (with a few on-road lapses), passing through woods, marshes, and dunes. At the trail head is **Bob's Bike Shop,** 430 Rte. 134, South Dennis (✆ **508/760-4723**), which rents bikes and in-line skates and does repairs. Rates are $10 for a couple hours and up to $22 for the full day. Another bike path runs along Old Bass Road, 3.5 miles north to Route 6A.

FISHING Fishing is allowed in Fresh Pond and Scargo Lake; for a license (shellfishing is also permitted), visit **Town Hall** on Main Street in South Dennis (✆ **508/394-8300**), or **Riverview Bait and Tackle** at 1273 Rte. 28 in South Yarmouth (✆ **508/394-1036**). Plenty of people drop a line off the Bass River Bridge along Route 28 in West Dennis. Several charter boats operate out of the Northside Marina in East Dennis's Sesuit Harbor, including the ***Albatross*** (✆ **508/385-3244**).

NATURE & WILDLIFE AREAS Behind the town hall parking lot on Main Street in South Dennis, a half-mile walk along the **Indian Lands Conservation Trail** leads to the Bass River, where blue herons and kingfishers often take shelter. Dirt roads off South Street in East Dennis, beyond the Quivet Cemetery, lead to Crow's Pasture, a patchwork of marshes and dunes bordering the bay; this circular trail is about a 2.5-mile round-trip.

WATERSPORTS On small, placid Swan River, **Cape Cod Waterways,** 16 Rte. 28, Dennisport (✆ **508/398-0080**), rents canoes, kayaks, and paddle boats for exploring 200-acre Swan Pond (less than a mile north) or Nantucket Sound (2 miles south). A full-day canoe or kayak rental costs $50.

MUSEUMS

Cape Cod Museum of Art ★★ Part of the prettily landscaped Cape Playhouse complex, this museum has done a great job of acquiring hundreds of works by representative area artists dating back to the turn of the 20th century.

60 Hope Lane (off Rte. 6A in the center of town). ✆ **508/385-4477.** www.cmfa.org. Admission $8 adults, free for children under 18, admission by donation Weds 10am–1pm and Thurs 5–8:30pm. MC, V. Mon–Sat 10am–5pm; Sun noon–5pm..

SHOPPING

Dennisport has a growing cluster of flea market-style antiques shops, but you may want to save your time and money for the better shops along Route 6A, where you'll also find fine contemporary crafts.

More than 136 dealers stock the co-op **Antiques Center of Cape Cod,** 243 Rte. 6A, about 1 mile south of Dennis Village center, Dennis (✆ **508/385-6400**); it's the largest such enterprise on the Cape.

Kids Especially for Kids

If the kids get sick of all the miscellaneous go-cart and minigolf concessions on Route 28, they can take in a show. On Friday mornings in season, at 9:30 and 11:30am, the **Cape Playhouse** ★★ (✆ **508/385-3911**), 820 Rte. 6A, Dennis, hosts visiting companies that mount theater geared toward children 4 and up. At only $7 to $8, tickets go fast.

Dennis along Route 6A has become a magnet for interesting small galleries. Among the finest is **Scargo Stoneware Pottery and Art Gallery,** 30 Dr. Lord's Rd. S. (off Rte. 6A, about 1 mile east of the town center), Dennis (✆ **508/385-3894**).

WHERE TO STAY

Corsair & Cross Rip Resort Motels ★ Kids Of the many family-oriented motels lining this part of Nantucket Sound, these two neighbors are among the nicest, with fresh contemporary decor, two beach-view pools, and their own chunk of sand. As a rainy-day backup, there's an indoor pool, a game room, and a toddler playroom equipped with toys.

41 Chase Ave. (off Depot St., 1 mile southeast of Rte. 28), Dennisport, MA 02639. ✆ **800/201-1072** or 508/398-2279. Fax 508/760-6681. www.corsaircrossrip.com. 47 units (all with tub/shower). Summer $175–$285 double; $265–$375 efficiency. Special packages and family weekly rates available. AE, MC, V. Closed mid-Oct to Apr. **Amenities:** 2 outdoor pools, indoor pool; outdoor Jacuzzi; game room; toddler playroom and kids' playground; coin-op washers and dryers. *In room:* A/C, TV w/HBO, fax, dataport, fridge, coffeemaker, hair dryer, iron.

Isaiah Hall B&B Inn ★★ This inn's location on a quiet side street in a residential neighborhood bodes well for a good night's sleep, but it's also just a short walk to restaurants, entertainment options, and Corporation Beach. Breakfasts are served at the long plank table that dominates the 1857 country kitchen. Room styles range from 1940s knotty pine to spacious and spiffy.

152 Whig St. (1 block northwest of the Cape Playhouse), Dennis, MA 02638. ✆ **800/736-0160** or 508/385-9928. Fax 508/385-5879. www.isaiahhallinn.com. 10 units (5 with tub/shower, 5 with shower only). Summer $115–$155 double; $185 suite. Rates include continental breakfast. AE, DISC, MC, V. Closed mid-Oct to late Apr. No children under age 7. *In room:* A/C, TV/VCR, dataport, hair dryer.

Lighthouse Inn ★★ Kids Set on placid West Dennis Beach on Nantucket Sound, this resort has been welcoming families for over 60 years. In 1938, Everett Stone acquired a decommissioned 1855 lighthouse and built an inn and a 9-acre cottage colony around it. With amusements such as miniature golf and shuffleboard right on the premises, as well as a heated outdoor pool and tennis courts, there's plenty to do. The rooms aren't what you'd call fancy, but some have great views. Lunch is served on the deck overlooking Nantucket Sound, a delightful setting in which to enjoy a club sandwich. The Sand Bar, a classic bar with cabaret-style entertainment, serves as onsite nightspot.

1 Lighthouse Inn Rd. (off Lower County Rd., ½ mile south of Rte. 28), West Dennis, MA 02670. ✆ **508/398-2244.** Fax 508/398-5658. www.lighthouseinn.com. 44 units, 24 cottages (all with tub/shower). Summer $244–$270 double; $447–$583 2-bedroom cottage; $480–$690 3-bedroom cottage. MC, V. Rates include full breakfast and all gratuities. Closed mid-Oct to mid-May. **Amenities:** 2 restaurants (large dining room, pool snack bar); bar w/entertainment; outdoor heated pool w/sunning deck, chairs, umbrellas, and pool house/changing rooms; outdoor tennis court; "InnKids," a free supervised play program (ages 3–11) offered July and Aug; game room; shuffleboard; volleyball; and minigolf. *In room:* A/C, TV, fridge, hair dryer, iron, safe.

WHERE TO DINE

For a time-travel treat, visit **Sundae School** ★, 381 Lower County Rd., at Sea Street, about ½ mile south of Route 28, Dennisport (✆ **508/394-9122**). The spacious barn has been retrofitted with a turn-of-the-20th-century marble soda fountain and other artifacts from the golden age of ice cream.

EXPENSIVE

Gracie's Table ★ *Finds* SPANISH TAPAS Just steps from the Cape Playhouse and Cape Cinema, Gracie's Table offers something different on Cape Cod: Spanish-style dining. Preparations by chef/owner Ann Austin are inspired by cuisine from the Basque region, as well as southwest France. While there are plenty of full meals to choose from, the specialty here is tapas, small unusual dishes. The best way to enjoy tapas is for each diner to choose several smaller dishes and share the different tastes with their dining companions. Tapas choices include hot lobster roll, sushi style; potato and chorizo tortilla; and tuna carpaccio with horseradish sorbet. The dining room is sleek and sophisticated, and is staffed by professional servers, pleased to recommend their favorite tapas.

800 Main St./Rte 6A (at Theatre Marketplace in front of the Cape Playhouse complex), Dennis Village. ✆ **508/385-5600.** Reservations recommended. Tapas $5–$15; main courses $18–$30. AE, MC, V. Daily 5–10pm; call for off-season hours. Open year-round.

The Ocean House New American Bistro and Bar ★★ *Finds* NEW AMERICAN This restaurant set on the beach overlooking Nantucket Sound has long had a stellar reputation, and now it's better than ever. There's a buzz around this creative cuisine, making this oceanfront restaurant a must-go location. One appealing thing about The Ocean House is that you can come for a multicourse fine-dining meal or just nibble on some appetizers. Favorites are the lemon-grass battered gray sole and the grilled beef tenderloin with Maytag blue cheese. With the dining room's large arches framing the beach beyond, this is a wonderful place to spend the evening.

3 Chase Ave. (at Depot St., on the beach), Dennisport. ✆ **508/394-0700.** Reservations strongly recommended. Main courses $18–$29. MC, V. June–Sept Tues–Sun 5–9:30pm; call for off-season hours. Open year-round.

The Red Pheasant Inn ★★ CONTEMPORARY AMERICAN An enduring Cape favorite since 1977, this handsome space—an 18th-century barn turned chandlery—has managed not only to keep pace with trends, but also to remain a front-runner. Popular dishes include roast rack of lamb, sole meunière, and in the fall, game specials like venison. Two massive brick fireplaces tend to be the focal point in the off season. In fine weather, you'll want to sit out in the garden room.

905 Main St. (about ½ mile east of the town center). ✆ **508/385-2133.** Reservations required. Main courses $18–$30. DISC, MC, V. Apr–Dec daily 5–10pm; Jan–Mar Wed–Sun 5–10pm.

MODERATE

Center Stage Café & Backstage Pub ★ NEW AMERICAN In the same complex as the Cape Playhouse and Cape Cinema, this place could get away with so-so food and service. Instead, the Center Stage has become a destination in itself, in addition to being *the* place to go after a show. The beauty of this place is you can get anything from a burger or sandwich to a full multicourse meal. Hours are extended for convenient bites before or after a show. From a fresh lobster roll to a barbecue chicken pizza to a Delmonico steak, it's all here. This is also a great place to grab a drink before or after a show; the bar is cozy and convivial.

36 Hope Lane (on the grounds of the Cape Playhouse). ✆ **508/385-7737.** www.centerstagedennis.com. Reservations suggested. Main courses $8–$22. AE, MC, V. June to late Aug Mon–Sat 4–11pm; Apr–May and late Aug to Nov Wed–Sun 4–11pm. Closed Dec–Mar.

Gina's by the Sea ★★ ITALIAN A landmark amid Dennis's "Little Italy" beach community since 1938, this intimate restaurant specializes in traditional Italian comfort food. Save room for Mrs. Riley's Chocolate Rum Cake, made daily by the owner's mother. This popular place fills up fast, so if you want to eat before 8:30pm, arrive before 5:30pm.

134 Taunton Ave. (about 1½ miles northwest of Rte. 6A; turn north across from the Public Market and follow the signs). ✆ **508/385-3213.** Reservations not accepted. Main courses $10–$23. AE, MC, V. June to late Aug daily 5–10pm; Apr–May and late Aug to Nov Thurs–Sun 5–10pm. Closed Dec–Mar.

Scargo Cafe ★ INTERNATIONAL Formerly a sea captain's house, this lively bistro has a menu split into "traditional" and "adventurous" categories. Traditionalists will find surf and turf, and the popular grilled lamb loins served with mint jelly (talk about traditional!); adventurous dishes include "wildcat chicken" (a sauté of sausage, mushrooms, and raisins, flambéed with apricot brandy). Serving food until 11pm makes this one of only a couple of options in the neighborhood to go after a show at the Cape Playhouse across the street.

799 Main St./Rte. 6A (opposite the Cape Playhouse). ✆ **508/385-8200.** Reservations accepted for parties of 6 or more. Main courses $14–$22. AE, DISC, MC, V. Mid-June to mid-Sept daily 11am–3pm and 4:30–11pm; mid-Sept to mid-June daily11am–10pm.

INEXPENSIVE

The Marshside ★ AMERICAN Overlooking a picturesque marsh, this is one of the Cape's best diners. There's a relaxed atmosphere here that comes from having a year-round staff that knows what it's doing (a rarity on the Cape). The food is fresh and tasty, be it a fried-fish platter, cheeseburger, or veggie melt. The homemade desserts are good, too.

28 Bridge St. (at the junction of Routes 134 and 6A), East Dennis. ✆ **508/385-4010.** Reservations not accepted. Main courses $7–$17. AE, DC, DISC, MC, V. Daily 7:30am–9pm. Open year-round.

DENNIS AFTER DARK

The oldest continuously active straw-hat theater in the country and still one of the best, the **Cape Cod Playhouse** ★★, 820 Rte. 6A (✆ **877/385-3911** or 508/385-3911; www.capeplayhouse.com), was the 1927 brainstorm of Raymond Moore, who'd spent a few summers as a playwright in Provincetown and quickly tired of the strictures of "little theater." Salvaging an 1838 meetinghouse, he plunked it amid a meadow and got his New York buddy, designer Cleon Throckmorton, to turn it into a proper theater. It was an immediate success, and a parade of stars has trod the boards in the decades since, from Humphrey Bogart to Julie Harris. Not all of today's headliners are quite as impressive, but the theater can be counted on for a varied season of polished work. Performances are staged from mid-June to early September. Tickets range from $25 to $45.

The **Cape Cinema** ★★, 36 Hope Lane, off Route 6A in the center of town (✆ **508/385-22503** or 508/385-5644; www.capecinema.com), is an Art Deco surprise, with a Prometheus-themed ceiling mural. George Mansour, curator of the Harvard Film Archive, sees to the art-house programming. The setting and seating—black leather armchairs—may spoil you forever.

3 The Lower Cape

The Lower Cape has fewer year-rounders than the Mid and Upper Cape towns, so the communities on this part of Cape Cod are more summer-oriented. There are also several upscale and expensive resorts and restaurants in this section of the Cape.

Along the easternmost portion of historic Route 6A, **Brewster** still enjoys much the same cachet that it boasted as a high roller in the maritime trade. But for the cars, it looks much as it might have in the late 19th century, with its general store still serving as a social center. Perhaps because excellence breeds competition, Brewster has spawned several fine restaurants and has become something of a magnet for gourmands.

Realtors tout **Chatham,** the Cape's most chichi town, as "the Nantucket of the Cape." Its Main Street offers appealing shops and eateries, complemented by a scenic lighthouse and plentiful beaches nearby.

As the gateway to the Outer Cape, where all roads merge, **Orleans** is a bustling town in the summer. The village of East Orleans is a destination itself, offering a couple of fun restaurants and—best of all—a goodly chunk of magnificent, unspoiled Cape Cod National Seashore.

BREWSTER ★★

With miles of placid Cape Cod Bay beaches and acres of state park, Brewster is an attractive place for families. Route 6A, the Old King's Highway, becomes Brewster's Main Street and houses a bevy of B&Bs, pricey restaurants, and the Cape's finest antiques shops. The town has managed to absorb a huge development within its borders, the 380-acre condo complex known as Ocean Edge. Brewster also welcomes the tens of thousands of campers and day-trippers headed for Nickerson State Park.

ESSENTIALS

GETTING THERE After crossing the Sagamore Bridge, head east on Route 6 or 6A. Route 6A on the north side of the Cape passes through the villages of West Brewster, Brewster, and East Brewster. You can also reach Brewster by taking Route 6 to Exit 10 north, along Route 124.

VISITOR INFORMATION Contact the **Brewster Chamber of Commerce Visitor Center** behind Brewster Town Hall, 2198 Main St./Rte. 6A, Brewster (✆ **508/896-3500;** fax 508/896-1086; www.brewstercapecod.org).

BEACHES & GETTING OUTSIDE

BEACHES Brewster's eight bay beaches have minimal facilities. When the tide is out, the beach extends as much as 2 miles, leaving behind tide pools to splash in and explore. On a clear day, you can see the whole curve of the Cape, from Sandwich to Provincetown. Purchase a beach parking sticker ($15 per day, $40 per week) at the **Visitor Center** behind Town Hall at 2198 Main St. (Rte. 6A; ✆ **508/896-4511**).

- **Breakwater Beach** ★★, off Breakwater Road, Brewster: Only a brief walk from the center of town, this calm, shallow beach (the only one with restrooms) is ideal for young children.
- **Flax Pond** ★★ in Nickerson State Park (see "Nature & Wildlife Areas," below): This freshwater pond has a bathhouse and offers watersports rentals. The park contains two more ponds with beaches—Cliff and Little Cliff. Access and parking are free.

- **Linnells Landing Beach** ★, on Linnell Road in East Brewster: This is a ½-mile, wheelchair-accessible bay beach.
- **Paines Creek Beach** ★, off Paines Creek Road, West Brewster: With 1½ miles to stretch out on, this bay beach has something to offer sun lovers and nature lovers alike. Your kids will love it if you arrive when the tide's coming in—the current will give an air mattress a nice little ride.

BICYCLING The **Cape Cod Rail Trail** ★★★ intersects with the 8-mile **Nickerson State Park** trail system at the park entrance, where there's plenty of free parking; you could follow the Rail Trail back to Dennis (about 12 miles) or onward toward Wellfleet (13 miles). In season, **Idle Times** (✆ **508/255-8281**) provides rentals within the park. Another good place to jump in is on Underpass Road about a half-mile south of Route 6A. Here you'll find **Brewster Bicycle Rental,** 442 Underpass Rd. (✆ **508/896-8149**); and **Brewster Express,** which makes sandwiches to go. Just up the hill is the well-equipped **Rail Trail Bike & Blade,** 302 Underpass Rd. (✆ **508/896-8200**). All three shops offer free parking. Bicycle rentals start at around $14 for 4 hours and go up to about $22 for 24 hours.

BOATING You can rent a canoe from **Goose Hummock** ★ in Orleans (✆ **508/255-2620**) and paddle around Paines Creek and Quivett Creek, as well as Upper and Lower Mill ponds.

Moments Biking the Cape Cod Rail Trail

The 25-mile **Cape Cod Rail Trail** ★★★ is one of New England's longest and most popular bike paths. Once a bed of the Penn Central Railroad, the trail is relatively flat and straight. On weekends in summer, you'll have to contend with dogs, in-line skaters, families, and bikers who whip by you on their way to becoming the next Lance Armstrong. Still, if you want to venture away from the coast and see some of the Cape's countryside without having to deal with motorized traffic, this is one of the best ways to do it.

The trail starts in South Wellfleet on Lecount Hollow Road or in South Dennis on Route 134, depending on which way you want to ride. Beginning in South Wellfleet, the path cruises by purple wildflowers, flowering dogwood, and small maples, where red-winged blackbirds and goldfinches nest. In Orleans, you'll have to ride on Rock Harbor and West roads until the City Council decides to complete the trail. Fortunately, the roads provide a good view of the boats lining Rock Harbor. Clearly marked signs lead back to the Rail Trail. You'll soon enter Nickerson State Park bike trails, or continue straight through Brewster to a series of swimming holes—Seymour, Long, and Hinckleys ponds. A favorite picnic spot is the Pleasant Lake General Store in Harwich. Shortly afterward, you'll cross over Route 6 on Route 124 before veering right through farmland, soon ending in South Dennis.

—by Stephen Jermanok

FISHING Brewster offers more ponds for fishing than any other town: 14 in all. Among the most popular are Cliff and Higgins ponds (within Nickerson State Park). For a license, visit the town clerk at **Town Hall** at 2198 Rte. 6A (✆ **508/896-3701**).

GOLF The 18-hole championship **Ocean Edge Golf Course** at 832 Villages Dr. (✆ **508/896-5911**) is Brewster's most challenging, followed closely by **Captain's Golf Course** at 1000 Freemans Way (✆ **508/896-5100**).

NATURE & WILDLIFE AREAS Admission is free to the two trails maintained by the Cape Cod Museum of Natural History (see below). The **South Trail,** covering a .75-mile round-trip south of Route 6A, crosses a natural cranberry bog beside Paines Creek to reach a hardwood forest of beeches and tupelos; toward the end of the loop, you'll come upon a "glacial erratic," a huge boulder dropped by a receding glacier. Before heading out on the .25-mile **North Trail,** stop in at the museum for a free guide describing the local flora. Also accessible from the museum parking lot is the **John Wing Trail,** a 1.5-mile network traversing 140 acres of preservation land, including upland, salt marsh, and beach. (***Note:*** This can be a soggy trip. Be sure to heed the posted warnings about high tides, especially in spring, or you might very well find yourself stranded.)

As it crosses Route 6A, Paines Creek Road becomes Run Hill Road. Follow it to the end to reach **Punkhorn Park Lands,** an undeveloped 800-acre tract popular with mountain bikers; it features several kettle ponds, a "quaking bog," and 45 miles of dirt paths.

The short jaunt around the **Stony Brook Grist Mill** is especially scenic. In spring, you can watch the alewives (freshwater herring) vaulting upstream to spawn, and in the summer, the millpond is surrounded and scented by honeysuckle.

The 1,955-acre **Nickerson State Park** at Route 6 and Crosby Lane (✆ **508/896-3491**) encompasses 418 campsites (reservations pour in a year in advance, but some are held open for new arrivals willing to wait a day or two), eight kettle ponds, and 8 miles of bicycle paths.

WATERSPORTS Sailboats, kayaks, canoes, and more are available seasonally at **Jack's Boat Rentals** (✆ **508/896-8556**) on Flax Pond in Nickerson State Park.

BREWSTER MUSEUMS

Cape Cod Museum of Natural History ★★★ Kids Long before "ecology" became a buzzword, noted naturalist writer John Hay helped found a museum dedicated to Cape Cod's unique landscape. The children's exhibits include a "live hive"—like an ant farm, only with busy bees and marine-room tanks. The bulk of the museum is outdoors, where 85 acres invite exploration (see "Nature & Wildlife Areas," above). There's an on-site archaeology lab on Wing Island, thought to have sheltered one of Brewster's first settlers—the Quaker John Wing, driven from Sandwich in the mid–17th century by religious persecution—and before him, native tribes dating back 10 millennia. The museum sponsors lectures, concerts, marsh cruises, bike tours, seal cruises, and "eco-treks"—including a sleepover on uninhabited Monomoy Island off Chatham.

869 Rte. 6A (about 2 miles west of the town center). ✆ **800/479-3867** (eastern MA only), or 508/896-3867. www.ccmnh.org. Admission $8 adults, $7 seniors, $3.50 children 3–12. June–Sept daily 10am–4pm; Oct–Mar Wed–Sun 11am–3pm; Apr–May Wed–Sun 10am–4pm.

SHOPPING

Brewster's stretch of Route 6A offers the best antiquing on the entire Cape. The artifacts gathered at **Kingsland Manor Antiques,** 440 Rte. 6A, about 1 mile east of the Dennis border (✆ **800/486-2305** or 508/385-9741), tend to be on the flamboyant side, which makes browsing all the more fun.

No one should miss **The Brewster Store,** 1935 Main St./Rte. 6A, in the center of town (✆ **508/896-3744**), built as a church in 1852. You'll find everything from penny candy to comics to the bestselling Brewster Store coffee. Neighbors meet on the wide front porch to catch up on village gossip.

WHERE TO STAY

Captain Freeman Inn ★★ This mint-green 1866 Victorian has a terrific location, right next to The Brewster Store and within walking distance of a pretty bay beach. The "luxury rooms" incorporate every extra you could hope to encounter: a canopied, four-poster bed; a fireplace; a TV/VCR; and a private porch with a two-person hot tub. The plainer rooms are just as pretty.

15 Breakwater Rd. (off Rte. 6A, in the town center), Brewster, MA 02631. ✆ **800/843-4664** or 508/896-7481. Fax 508/896-5618. www.captainfreemaninn.com. 12 units (all with tub/shower). Summer $165–$225 double. Rates include full breakfast and afternoon tea. MC, V. No children under 10. **Amenities:** Outdoor pool; loaner bikes. *In room:* A/C, hair dryer.

Michael's Cottages ★ *Value* These cottages on an immaculately groomed compound are small yet centrally located. Across the street is Brewster's Drummer Boy Park, which has a playground, historic windmill, and antique house. Brewster's summer band concerts are held there as well. The closest beach is Paines Creek, about 1 mile away. In July and August, rentals are available by the week only.

618 Main St./Rte. 6A, Brewster, MA 02631. ✆ **800/399-2967** or 508/896-4025. Fax 508/896-3158. www.michaelsinbrewster.com. 7 units (2 tub/shower, 5 shower only). Summer $150–$175 double. Weekly rates $775–$850 double; $1,375 2-bedroom. B&B rooms include continental breakfast. AE, DISC, MC, V. Open year-round. *In room:* A/C, TV, fridge, coffeemaker, hair dryer.

Old Sea Pines Inn ★★ *Kids* *Value* This reasonably priced, large historic inn is a great spot for families. The inn's former days as the Sea Pines School of Charm and Personality for Young Women can still be seen in the handful of rather minuscule boarding-school-scale rooms on the second floor. These bargain rooms with shared bathrooms are the only ones in the house without air-conditioning, but at $95 per night in season, who cares? The annex rooms are downright playful, with colorful accouterments, such as pink TVs. Sunday evenings from mid-June through mid-September, Old Sea Pines is the site of a dinner/theater performance by the Cape Cod Repertory Theatre.

2553 Main St. (about 1 mile east of the town center), Brewster, MA 02631. ✆ **508/896-6114.** Fax 508/632-0084. www.oldseapinesinn.com. 24 units, 5 with shared bathroom. Summer $95–$150 double; $135–$155 suite. Rates include full breakfast and afternoon tea. AE, DC, DISC, MC, V. Closed Jan–Mar. *In room:* TV, hair dryer, iron.

WHERE TO DINE

The Bramble Inn Restaurant ★★★ NEW AMERICAN Often named among the best restaurants on Cape Cod, The Bramble Inn is also one of the most expensive—but worth it for a special night out. But now the restaurant also has an a la carte bistro menu that is available Sunday to Thursday in the Hunt Room bar and in the courtyard garden. Fortunately, no matter which menu you order from, you'll be able to enjoy Ruth Manchester's extraordinary cuisine. Her assorted seafood curry (with lobster, cod, scallops, and shrimp in a light curry sauce with grilled banana, toasted almonds, coconut, and chutney) and her rack of lamb (with deep-fried beet-and-Fontina polenta, pan-seared zucchini, and mustard port cream) have been written up in the *New York Times.*

2019 Main St. (about ⅓ mile east of Rte. 124). ✆ **508/896-7644.** Reservations required for fine-dining, not for bistro. Fixed-price dinner $44–$59. AE, DISC, MC, V. June to early Sept daily 5:30–9pm; call for off-season hours. Closed Jan–Mar.

Chillingsworth ★★★ FRENCH This longtime contender for the title of fanciest restaurant on the Cape has two dining options: formal dinner with jackets recommended for men, and the more casual bistro. The dining room boasts antique appointments dating back several centuries and a six-course Francophiliac table d'hôte menu that will challenge the most shameless gourmands. Specialties include steamed lobster over spinach and fennel with sea beans and lobster-basil butter sauce. Finish with warm chocolate cake with pistachio ice cream and chocolate drizzle. Or try the moderately priced bistro, which serves Sunday brunch and lunch and dinner daily in season in the adjoining greenhouse or on the shady lawn. There are also three deluxe guest rooms on the premises.

2449 Main St. (about 1 mile east of the town center). ✆ **800/430-3640** or 508/896-3640. www.chillingsworth.com. Reservations required for fine-dining; recommended for bistro. Jacket advised for men in fine-dining section. Fixed-price meals $60–$70; bistro $17–$28. AE, DC, MC, V. Early May to mid-Oct Tues–Sun 11:30am–2:30pm and 6–9:30pm (bistro opens for dinner at 5:30pm), Mon 5:30–9:30pm (dinner in bistro only on Mon); call for off-season hours. Closed Dec–Apr.

MODERATE

The Brewster Fish House ★★ NEW AMERICAN Spare and handsome as a Shaker refectory, this small restaurant bills itself as "non-conforming" and delivers on the promise. Its approach to seafood borders on genius: Consider, for instance, squid delectably tenderized in a marinade of soy and ginger; or silky-tender, walnut-crusted ocean catfish accompanied by kale sautéed in Marsala. Beef and vegetarian options are always available as well. Better get there early (before 7pm) if you want to get in.

2208 Main St. (about ½ mile east of the town center). ✆ **508/896-7867.** Reservations not accepted. Main courses $17–$29. MC, V. May–Aug Mon–Sat 11am–3pm and 5–9:30pm, Sun noon–3pm and 5–9:30pm; call for off-season hours. Closed mid-Dec to Apr.

INEXPENSIVE

Brewster Inn & Chowder House ★ ECLECTIC To get the gist of the expression "chow down," just observe the early-evening crowd happily doing so at this century-old restaurant. The draw is hearty staples at prices geared to ordinary people rather than splurging tourists. This place also makes the best martinis in town, and there's a good old bar, **The Woodshed,** out back.

1993 Rte. 6A (in the center of town). ✆ **508/896-7771.** Main courses $12–$18. AE, DISC, MC, V. Late May to mid-Oct daily 11:30am–2:30pm, Sun–Thurs 5–9:30pm, Fri–Sat 5–10pm; call for off-season hours. Open year-round.

Cobie's ★ AMERICAN Accessible to cars whizzing along Route 6A and within collapsing distance for cyclists exploring the Rail Trail, this picture-perfect clam shack has been dishing out exemplary fried clams, lobster rolls, foot-long hot dogs, black-and-white frappés, and all the other beloved summer staples since 1948.

3260 Rte. 6A (about 2 miles east of Brewster center). ✆ **508/896-7021.** Most items under $15. No credit cards. Late May to early Sept daily 11am–9pm. Closed early Sept to late May.

CHATHAM ★★★

Chatham (say "Chatt-um") is small-town America the way Norman Rockwell imagined it. Roses climb white picket fences in front of shingled Cape cottages, all within a stone's throw of the ocean. The Cape's fanciest town is also its prettiest. As a result, inn rooms are pricier here and rentals are snapped up more quickly. But those looking for a picture-perfect New England town will love Chatham's winding Main Street, filled with pleasing shops and leading to a beautiful beach with lighthouse.

Sticking out like a sore elbow, Chatham was one of the first spots to attract early explorers. Samuel de Champlain stopped by in 1606 but got into a tussle with the prior occupants and left in a hurry. The first colonist to stick around was William Nickerson of Yarmouth, who befriended a local *sachem* (tribal leader) and built a house beside his wigwam in 1656. To this day, listings for Nickersons occupy a half page in the Cape Cod phone book.

Chatham is one of the few areas on the Cape to support a commercial fishing fleet—against increasing odds. Overfishing has resulted in closely monitored limits to give the stock time to bounce back. Boats must now go out as far as 100 miles to catch their fill. Despite the difficulties, it's a way of life few locals would willingly relinquish.

ESSENTIALS

GETTING THERE After crossing the Sagamore Bridge, head east on Route 6 and take Exit 11 south (Rte. 137) to Route 28. From this intersection, South Chatham is about a half-mile west, and West Chatham is about 1½ miles east. Chatham itself is about 2 miles farther east on Route 28. The town lies 32 miles east of Sandwich, 24 miles south of Provincetown.

VISITOR INFORMATION Visit the **Chatham Chamber of Commerce,** 533 Main St., Chatham, MA 02633 (✆ **800/715-5567** or 508/945-5199; www.chathaminfo.com); or the new **Chatham Chamber booth** at the intersection of Routes 137 and 28 (no phone).

BEACHES & GETTING OUTSIDE

BEACHES Chatham has an unusual array of beach styles, from the peaceful shores of the Nantucket Sound to the treacherous, shifting shoals along the Atlantic. For beach stickers ($15 per day, $60 per week), call the **Permit Department** on George Ryder Road in West Chatham (✆ **508/945-5180**).

- **Chatham Light Beach** ★★: Located directly below the lighthouse parking lot (where stopovers are limited to 30 min.), this narrow stretch of sand is easy to get to: Just walk down the stairs. Currents here can be tricky and swift, though, so swimming is discouraged.
- **Cockle Cove Beach, Ridgevale Beach,** and **Hardings Beach** ★★: Lined up along the sound, each at the end of its namesake road south of Route 28, these family-pleasing beaches offer gentle surf and full facilities. Ridgevale Beach also has kayak and sailboat rentals.
- **Forest Beach** ★: No longer an officially recognized town beach (there's no lifeguard), this Sound landing near the Harwich border is still popular, especially among surfboarders.
- **Oyster Pond Beach,** off Route 28: Only a block from Chatham's Main Street, this sheltered saltwater pond (with restrooms) swarms with children.

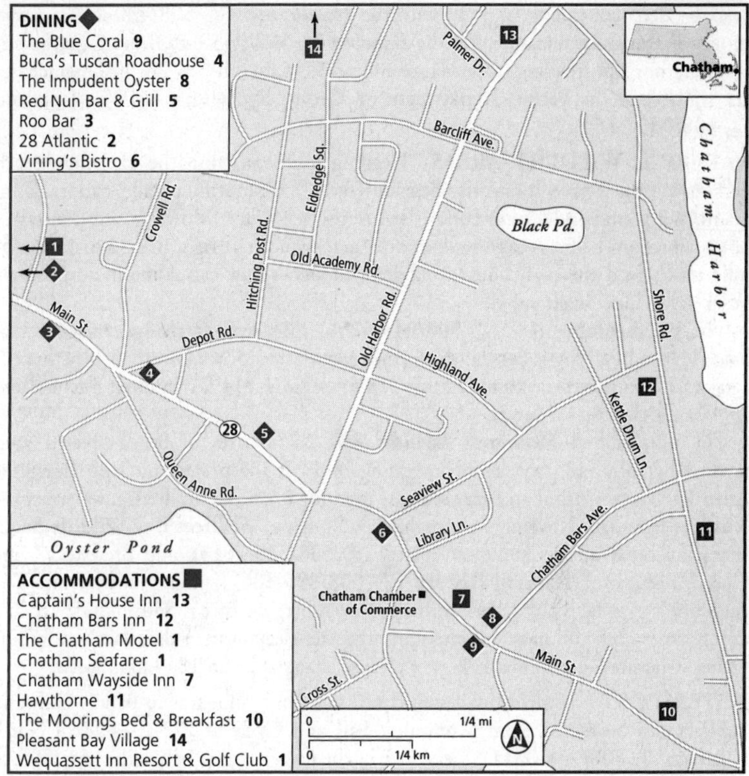

• **South Beach** ★★: A former island jutting out slightly to the south of the Chatham Light, this glorified sandbar can be dangerous, so heed posted warnings and content yourself with strolling.

• **North Beach** ★★: Extending all the way south from Orleans, this 5-mile barrier beach is accessible from Chatham only by boat; you can take the **Beachcomber** (✆ **508/945-5265**), a water taxi, which leaves from the fish pier. The round-trip costs $12 for adults, $8 for children 12 and under.

BICYCLING Though Chatham has no separate recreational paths per se, a demarcated biking/skating lane makes a scenic, 8-mile circuit of town, heading south onto "The Neck," east to the Chatham Light, up Shore Road all the way to North Chatham, and back to the center of town. A brochure prepared by the **Chatham Chamber of Commerce** (✆ **800/715-5567** or 508/945-5199) shows the route. Rentals are available at **Bikes & Blades,** 195 Crowell Rd., Chatham (✆ **508/945-7600**).

FISHING Chatham has five ponds and lakes that permit fishing; Goose Pond off Fisherman's Landing is among the top spots. For saltwater fishing without a boat, try the fishing bridge on Bridge Street at the southern end of Mill Pond. First, though, get a license at **Town Hall** at 549 Main St. in Chatham (✆ **508/945-5101**). If you hear the deep sea calling, sign on with the ***Headhunter*** (**© 508/430-2312; www.capecodfishingcharters.com**), or the ***Banshee*** (**© 508/945-0403**), both berthed in Stage Harbor. Sportfishing rates average around $725 for 8 hours. Shellfishing licenses are available at the **Permit Department** on George Ryder Road in West Chatham (**© 508/945-5180**).

NATURE & WILDLIFE AREAS Heading southeast from the Hardings Beach parking lot, the 2-mile, round-trip **Seaside Trail** offers beautiful parallel panoramas of Nantucket Sound and Oyster Pond River. Access to 40-acre Morris Island, southwest of the Chatham Light, is easy: walk or drive across and start right in on a marked .75-mile trail. Heed the high tides, as advised, though—they can come in surprisingly quickly, leaving you stranded.

The **Beachcomber** ★★ (**© 508/945-5265**) runs **seal-watching cruises** out of Stage Harbor. Parking is behind the former Main Street School on the left before the rotary. The cruises cost $20 for adults, $18 for seniors, $14 for children 3 to 15, and are free for children under 3.

The uninhabited **Monomoy Islands** ★★, 2,750 acres of brush-covered sand favored by some 285 species of migrating birds, is the perfect pit stop along the Atlantic Flyway. Harbor and gray seals are catching on, too: Hundreds now carpet the coastline from late November through May. Both the **Wellfleet Bay Wildlife Sanctuary,** operated by the Audubon Society (**© 508/349-2615**), and Brewster's **Cape Cod Museum of Natural History** (**© 508/896-3867**) offer guided trips. The Audubon's trips take place April through November; the cost is $30 to $60. About a dozen times each summer, the museum organizes sleepovers in the island's only surviving structure—a clapboard "keeper's house" flanked by an 1849 lighthouse.

WATERSPORTS Seaworthy vessels, from surf- and sailboards to paddle craft and Sunfish, can be rented from **Monomoy Sail and Cycle** at 275 Rte. 28 in North Chatham (**© 508/945-0811**). Pleasant Bay, the Cape's largest bay, is the best place to play for those with sufficient experience; if the winds don't seem to be going your way, try Forest Beach on the South Chatham shore.

SHOPPING

Chatham's tree-shaded Main Street offers a terrific opportunity to shop and stroll. Headed for such prestigious outlets as Neiman Marcus, the handblown glassworks of James Holmes originate at **Chatham Glass Company,** 758 Main St., just west of the Chatham rotary (**© 508/945-5547**), where you can literally look over their shoulders as the pieces take shape. At **Chatham Pottery,** 2058 Rte. 28, east of the intersection with Route 137 (**© 508/430-2191**), striking graphics characterize the collaborative work of Gill Wilson (potter) and Margaret Wilson-Grey (glazer).

WHERE TO STAY

Chatham's accommodations tend to be more expensive than those of neighboring towns, but you can also find several good inexpensive motel options.

Practically across the street from the Chatham Bars Inn, the very basic **Hawthorne,** 196 Shore Rd. (**© 508/945-0372;** www.thehawthorne.com), boasts one of the best locations in town: right on the water, with striking views of Chatham Harbor, Pleasant Bay, and the Atlantic Ocean. An additional perk here are the free phone calls (both local and long distance) and Internet access. Rates for the 26 rooms are $165 to $195 double.

Chatham Seafarer, 2079 Rte. 28 (about ½ mile east of Rte. 137), West Chatham (✆ **800/786-2772** or 508/432-1739; www.chathamseafarer.com), is a well-run motel on Route 28. Though it does not have a pool, it's only about a half-mile from Ridgevale Beach. Rates are $145 to $165 double.

Another inexpensive option is **The Chatham Motel,** 1487 Main St./Rte. 28, Chatham (✆ **800/770-5545** or 508/945-2630; www.chathammotel.com), 1½ miles from Hardings Beach. It has an outdoor pool, and summer rates in the 32 rooms are $145 to $185 double, $305 suites.

VERY EXPENSIVE

Chatham Bars Inn ★★ *Kids* Set majestically above the beach in Chatham with commanding views out to a barrier beach and the Atlantic Ocean beyond is the grand Chatham Bars Inn. The colonnaded 1914 brick building is surrounded by 26 shingled cottages on 20 acres. This resort also has a heated outdoor pool, tennis courts, and three restaurants. Take in the sweeping ocean views from the breezy veranda, where you can order a drink and recline in an Adirondack chair. Many guest rooms have balconies with views of the beach or the landscaped grounds. Cottage rooms are cheery with painted furniture and Waverly fabrics.

Shore Rd. (off Seaview St., about ½ mile northwest of the town center), Chatham, MA 02633. ✆ **800/527-4884** or 508/945-0096. Fax 508/945-5491. www.chathambarsinn.com. 205 units. Summer $340–$460 double; $550–$620 1-bedroom suite; $790–$1,600 2-bedroom suite. AE, DC, MC, V. **Amenities:** 3 restaurants (the formal Main Dining Room, the fireplaced Tavern, and the seasonal Beach House Grill located right on the beach); outdoor heated pool; putting green (Seaside Links, a 9-hole course open to the public, adjoins the resort; guests play for a fee, $18); 3 all-weather tennis courts ($15 an hour); boat to the outer beach for a fee; Wellness Center offering spa and massage services and fitness equipment; complimentary children's program for ages 3½ and up, available morning through night in summer; room service (7am–10pm in season, 7am–9pm off season); babysitting; concierge. *In room:* A/C, TV/VCR, dataport (free unlimited Internet access), hair dryer, iron.

Wequassett Inn Resort and Golf Club ★★★ *Kids* Fans of golf, sailing, and tennis will enjoy this 22-acre resort occupying its own little peninsula sticking out on Pleasant Bay. Adjacent is the private Cape Cod National Golf Club, where inn guests enjoy exclusive privileges. The resort's restaurant, 28 Atlantic, was recently revamped and is now one of the Cape's top dining spots (see below). Tucked amid the woods along the shore, 15 buildings, built in the 1940s, harbor roomy quarters done up in a country style. They cost a bit more than the 56 more modern "villa" rooms because of their beachfront locations. All units have either a balcony or a patio. Beachloving guests can choose the calm private bay beach just steps from the rooms or Chatham's North Beach, a 15-minute ride via the inn's Power Skiff ($12).

2173 Rte. 28 (about 5 miles northwest of Chatham center, on Pleasant Bay), Chatham, MA 02633. ✆ **800/225-7125** or 508/432-5400. Fax 508/432-5032. www.wequassett.com. 104 units. Summer $415–$775 double; $600–$1,240 suites. AE, DC, DISC, MC, V. Closed Dec–Mar. **Amenities:** 2 restaurants (28 Atlantic for fine dining and Outer Bar and Grille for casual fare, both open to the public); golf course next door ($105 a round plus $20 for a cart); pear-shaped heated outdoor pool; 4 all-weather Plexipave tennis courts ($15 an hour per person) plus a pro shop; fitness room (w/new machines and weights); rental bikes ($20–$40 per day) and watersports equipment (sailboards, Sunfish, Daysailers, and Hobie Cats) for about $40 an hour; free horseshoes, basketball, and volleyball equipment; yoga and Pilates classes for $15; Children's Fun Club, $25 for half-day, $45 for full day; concierge; room service (daily 7am–10pm); massage; secretarial and babysitting services available. *In room:* A/C, TV, minibar, coffeemaker, hair dryer, iron.

EXPENSIVE

Captain's House Inn ★★★ *Finds* This 1839 Greek Revival house—along with a cottage and a carriage house—set on 2 meticulously maintained acres is a shining example of 19th-century style. The hospitality and amenities here make this one of the top B&Bs on Cape Cod. Guest rooms are richly furnished, with atmospheric touches like canopied four-posters, beamed ceilings, and brick hearths. The inn provides a wonderful array of extras, like robes, bottled water, newspapers, early morning coffee, and room service. Many rooms have minifridges and Jacuzzis. The window-walled breakfast room is also the site of a traditional tea. Light lunches can be enjoyed poolside for an extra charge.

369–377 Old Harbor Rd. (about ½ mile north of the rotary), Chatham, MA 02633. ✆ **800/315-0728** or 508/945-0127. Fax 508/945-0866. www.captainshouseinn.com. 16 units (14 tub/shower, 2 shower only). Summer $235–$425 double. Rates include full breakfast and afternoon tea. AE, DISC, MC, V. **Amenities:** Outdoor heated pool; exercise room. *In room:* A/C, TV/VCR, dataport, coffeemaker, hair dryer, iron.

Chatham Wayside Inn ★★ Centrally located on Chatham's Main Street, this 1860 stagecoach stop, has undergone a thoroughly modern renovation. Don't expect any musty antique trappings: it's all lush carpeting, Waverly fabrics, and polished reproductions. The prize rooms boast patios or balconies overlooking the town bandstand. The restaurant serves three meals a day and is open to the public.

512 Main St. (in the center of town), Chatham, MA 02633. ✆ **800/391-5734** or 508/945-5550. Fax 508/945-3407. www.waysideinn.com. 56 units. Summer $195–$315 double, $345–$415 suite; off-season packages available. DISC, MC, V. **Amenities:** Restaurant/bar; outdoor heated pool. *In room:* A/C, TV/VCR, hair dryer, iron.

Pleasant Bay Village ★★ Across the street from Pleasant Bay, a few minutes' walk from a bay beach, this is one fancy motel. Over the past 25 years, the owner has transformed the property into a Zen paradise, where waterfalls cascade through colorful rock gardens into a stone-edged pool surrounded by whimsical Oriental gardens. Guest rooms, done up in pastels, are unusually pleasant. Many bathrooms feature marble countertops and stone floors. The suites have fully equipped kitchens, including microwave ovens, as well as two televisions, one with a VCR. In summer, the restaurant serves three meals a day. You can order lunch from the grill without having to leave your place at the heated pool.

1191 Orleans Rd./Rte. 28 (about 3 miles north of Chatham center), Chatham Port, MA 02633. ✆ **800/547-1011** or 508/945-1133. Fax 508/945-9701. www.pleasantbayvillage.com. 58 units. Summer $165–$255 double; $245–$455 1- or 2-bedroom suite (for 4 occupants). AE, MC, V. Closed Nov–Apr. **Amenities:** Restaurant (breakfast; July and Aug: lunch by the pool and dinner); heated pool and 8-person hot tub; game room (w/pinball). *In room:* A/C, TV, dataport, fridge, hair dryer, iron.

MODERATE

The Moorings Bed and Breakfast ★★ Whether you end up in the main house, a Victorian beauty, or the carriage houses out back, you'll enjoy a breakfast in the gazebo surrounded by flower gardens. Several rooms in the carriage houses are spacious, with kitchenettes and private decks or courtyards. Some units have VCRs and minifridges. All are immaculate and quaintly decorated, joined by a central courtyard. In addition, everything you need to enjoy Chatham's winding roads and beautiful beaches is provided: bikes, beach chairs, and umbrellas.

326 Main St. (at the east end of Main St.), Chatham, MA 02633. ✆ **800/320-0848** or 508/945-0848. www.mooringscapecod.com. 15 units, 1 cottage (14 tub/shower, 2 shower only). Summer $148–$215 double; $230–$235 suite; $2,200 weekly cottage. Rates include full breakfast. DISC, MC, V. **Amenities:** Loaner bikes. *In room:* A/C, TV, hair dryer.

WHERE TO DINE

VERY EXPENSIVE

28 Atlantic ★★★ NEW AMERICAN A major renovation has turned this restaurant on the grounds of the Wequasett Inn resort into one of the top places to eat on

Cape Cod. The elegant, spacious dining room overlooks Pleasant Bay through immense floor-to-ceiling glass panels. Service is professional and stylish. And the food stands out as superb, from the *amuse bouche* (a little taste teaser) offered at the start of the meal, to the exceptional desserts served at the end. Menu items use local provender as much as possible, but there are also delicacies from around the world. You might start with the Cape lobster and roasted corn bisque with sherried Devonshire cream; move on to the composed salad of mache, melon, prosciutto, grapes, goat cheese mousse, and tawny port syrup; and then get to your main course, perhaps skillet-seared local bluefish with saffron smoked mussel risotto, wilted Swiss chard, and lobster oil. You're in for a treat here; it's all exquisite.

2173 Rte. 28 (at the Wequasett Inn, about 5 miles northwest of Chatham center, on Pleasant Bay). ✆ **508/430-3000.** www.wequasett.com. Reservations recommended. Main courses $21–$44. AE, DC, DISC, MC, V. May–Nov daily 7am–10pm. Call for off-season hours. Closed Dec–Mar.

EXPENSIVE

The Blue Coral ★ NEW AMERICAN This new restaurant features "seaside cuisine" on an outdoor courtyard just off Main Street. Specialties include a three-pound lobster dinner with all the fixins, and sushi-grade blue fin tuna pan-seared with balsamic demi-glaze. One of the most popular dishes is the lobster ravioli served with a brandy cream sauce. There's live entertainment in the form of jazz and blues on Thursday through Sunday nights in season.

483 Main St., Chatham. ✆ **508/348-0485.** Reservations accepted. Main courses $18–$40. AE, DISC, MC, V. Daily 11:30am–2:30pm and 5–10pm. Closed late Sept to late June.

Roo Bar ★ NEW AMERICAN Like its sister restaurants in Hyannis and Falmouth, this new Roo Bar in Chatham has quickly become the place to see and be seen. Somehow the owners have turned a former Friendly's Restaurant into a sleek and stylish venue that features a garden patio area as well as a welcoming bar. The menu offers a wide range of options, from seafood specialties like seafood jambalaya to fine meat dishes like herb-grilled Delmonico. You may also opt for a brick-oven pizza topped with spicy prawns or barbecued chicken.

907 Main St., Chatham. ✆ **508/945-9988.** Reservations accepted. Main courses $17–$28. AE, MC, V. Daily 5–10pm. Open year-round.

MODERATE

Buca's Tuscan Roadhouse ★★ *Finds* NORTHERN ITALIAN This popular Harwich restaurant is very close to the Chatham border and well worth the drive for anyone staying in the lower Cape. It's got a great atmosphere, somehow romantic and festive at the same time; wonderful food; and superior service. The only problem is getting a reservation, even in January. But once you do, you can relax and enjoy homemade pastas, fresh-off-the-boat fish, and tender cuts of meat—it doesn't get much better than this. From basics like eggplant parmigiana to cacciucco, a mélange of seafood in a garlic-y broth, the food is delicious. Wines by the glass are also exceptional.

4 Depot Rd. (on the corner of Rte. 28, close to the Chatham border), Harwich. ✆ **508/432-6900.** Reservations recommended. Main courses $18–$25. AE, MC, V. June–Aug daily 5–10pm; call for off-season hours. Open year-round.

The Impudent Oyster ★ INTERNATIONAL All but hidden off the main drag, this perennially popular eatery cooks up fabulous fish in exotic guises, ranging from Mexican to Szechuan, but mostly Continental. The flavorful specialties of the house are the *sole picatta* (native sole with lemon, fresh herb, and caper butter sauce) the steak *au poivre,* and the *pesca fra diablo* (local littlenecks, lobster, and other seafood served in a spicy sauce over fettuccine). A tavern menu is served at the bar from 3 to 5pm with soup, salads, raw bar, chicken fingers, and burgers. This place is very busy in the summer and if you don't make a reservation, you may be out of luck.

15 Chatham Bars Ave. (off Main St., in the center of town). © **508/945-3545.** Reservations recommended. Main courses $14–$20. AE, MC, V. Mon–Thurs 11:30am–3pm and 5–9:30pm; Fri–Sat 11:30am–3pm and 5–10pm; Sun noon–3pm and 5–9:30pm.

Vining's Bistro ★★ *Finds* FUSION If you're looking for cutting-edge cuisine, venture upstairs at Chatham's minimall and into this ineffably cool cafe. The menu offers compelling juxtapositions such as the warm lobster tacos with salsa fresca and crème fraîche, or the spit-roasted chicken suffused with achiote-lime marinade and sided with a salad of oranges and jicama.

595 Main St. (in the center of town). © **508/945-5033.** Reservations not accepted. Main courses $16–$24. AE, DC, MC, V. June to mid-Oct daily 5:30–9:45pm; call for off-season hours. Closed Jan–Mar.

INEXPENSIVE

Red Nun Bar & Grill *Value* DINER There used to be lots of casual little hole-in-the-wall places like this on the Cape. Now there are precious few. With just five tables and some bar seats, this is a good place to go early, late, or off season. They serve comfort food, like Mama's meatloaf, cheeseburgers, and a fish sandwich made from this morning's catch that was probably brought in by one of the guys bellied up to the bar. There's a good selection of beers on tap, too.

746 Main St. (near Monomoy Theatre and Veterans Field). © **508/348-0469.** Under $11. No credit cards. May–Sept Mon–Thurs 4pm–1am, Fri–Sun noon–1am; call for off-season hours. Closed Jan 15–Apr 1.

CHATHAM AFTER DARK

Chatham's free **band concerts** ★★ are arguably the best on the Cape and attract crowds in the thousands. This is small-town America at its most nostalgic, as the band plays standards of yesteryear that never go out of style. Held in Kate Gould Park (off Chatham Bars Ave.) from July to early September, the concerts kick off at 8pm every Friday. Come early to claim your square of lawn, which is already checkerboarded with blankets by late afternoon. Call © **508/945-5199** for information.

A great leveler, the **Chatham Squire** ★, 487 Main St. (© **508/945-0942**), attracts CEOs, seafarers, and collegians alike. Great pub grub, too! The piano bar **Upstairs at Christian's,** 443 Main St. (© **508/945-3362**), has the air of a vintage frat house with scuffed leather couches and movie posters. Live music is offered nightly in season and weekends year-round.

ORLEANS ★★

Orleans is where the "Narrow Land" (the early Algonquin name for the Cape) starts to get very narrow indeed: From here on up—or "down," in paradoxical local parlance—the Cape is never more than a few miles wide from coast to coast. This is also where the oceanside beaches open up into a glorious expanse some 40 miles long, framed by dramatic dunes and serious surf.

The Cape's three main roads (Routes 6, 6A, and 28) converge here, too, so on summer weekends, it acts as a rather frustrating funnel. Nevertheless, Main Street boasts some appealing restaurants and shops. The village of East Orleans, near the entrance to Nauset Beach, may be the best place to base yourself. The 10-mile beach, which is the southernmost stretch of the Cape Cod National Seashore preserve, is a magnet for families and young folks.

ESSENTIALS

GETTING THERE After crossing the Sagamore Bridge, head east on Route 6 or 6A (the long but scenic route); both converge with Route 28 in Orleans. The town is 35 miles east of Sandwich, 25 miles south of Provincetown.

VISITOR INFORMATION Contact the **Orleans Chamber of Commerce,** 44 Main St. (P.O. Box 153), Orleans, MA 02653 (✆ **800/865-1386** or 508/255-1386; www.capecod-orleans.com). There's an **information booth** at the corner of Route 6A and Eldredge Parkway (✆ **508/240-2484**).

BEACHES & GETTING OUTSIDE

BEACHES From here all the way to Provincetown on the Cape's eastern side, you're dealing with the wild Atlantic Ocean. Current ocean conditions are clearly posted at the entrance to Nauset Beach. Purchase 1-week parking permits ($50 for renters) from **Town Hall** on School Road (✆ **508/240-3775**). Day passes for Nauset Beach and Skaket Beach are $15 per car. Day-trippers who arrive early enough—better make that before 10am on weekends in July and August—can pay at the gate (✆ **508/240-3780**).

- **Crystal Lake** ★, off Monument Road about ¾ mile south of Main Street: Parking—if you can find a space—is free, but there are no facilities here.
- **Nauset Beach** ★★★, in East Orleans (✆ **508/240-3780**): Stretching southward all the way past Chatham, this barrier beach, which is part of the Cape Cod National Seashore but is managed by the town, has long been one of the Cape's gonzo beach scenes—good surf, big crowds, lots of young people. Full facilities, including a terrific snack bar, can be found within the 1,000-car parking lot. The in-season parking fee is $15 per car, which is also good for same-day parking at Skaket Beach (see below). Substantial waves make for good surfing and boogie-boarding in the special section to the far left reserved for that purpose. In July and August, there are concerts from 7 to 9pm in the gazebo.
- **Pilgrim Lake** ★, off Monument Road about 1 mile south of Main Street: This small freshwater beach is covered by a lifeguard in season. You must have a beach parking sticker.
- **Skaket Beach** ★, off Skaket Beach Road to the west of town: This peaceful bay beach is a better choice for families. When the tide recedes, little kids will enjoy splashing about in the tide pools left behind. Parking costs $15, and you'd better turn up early.

BICYCLING Orleans presents the one slight gap in the 25-mile **Cape Cod Rail Trail** ★★★ (✆ **508/896-3491**): Just east of the Brewster border, the trail merges with town roads for about 1½ miles. The best way to avoid vehicular aggravation and fumes is to zigzag west to scenic Rock Harbor. Bike rentals are available at **Orleans Cycle** at 26 Main St. (✆ **508/255-9115**).

BOATING **Arey's Pond Sailing School,** off Route 28 in South Orleans (✆ **508/255-7900**), offers sailing lessons on Little Pleasant Bay. Individual lessons are $65 per hour; weekly group lessons are around $189. The **Goose Hummock Outdoor Center** at 15 Rte. 6A, south of the rotary (✆ **508/255-2620;** www.goose.com), rents out canoes, kayaks, and more, and the northern half of Pleasant Bay is the perfect place to use them.

FISHING Fishing is allowed in Baker Pond, Pilgrim Lake, and Crystal Lake. For licenses, visit **Town Hall** at Post Office Square in the center of town (✆ **508/240-3700,** ext. 305) or **Goose Hummock** (see above). Surf-casting—no license needed—is permitted on Nauset Beach South, off Beach Road. **Rock Harbor** ★★, a former packet landing on the bay (about 1¼ miles northwest of the town center), shelters New England's largest sportfishing fleet: some 18 boats at last count. One call (✆ **800/287-1771** in MA, or 508/255-9757) will get you information on them all—or go look them over in person. Rock Harbor charter prices range from $450 for 4 hours to $700 for 8 hours. Individual prices are also available ($115 per person for 4 hr.; $140 per person for 8 hr.).

> *Fun Fact* **Rock Harbor**
>
> Yes, those are trees in the middle of the harbor at Rock Harbor; and no, they are not live trees. For decades, dead trees have been erected in the harbor in order to mark the channel. At sunset, the row of narrow trees silhouetted against the horizon makes a pretty picture.

WATERSPORTS The **Pump House Surf Co.** at 9 Rte. 6A (✆ **508/240-2226**) rents and sells wet suits, body boards, and surfboards. Stop by for up-to-date reports on where to find the best waves. **Nauset Sports** at Jeremiah Square, Route 6A at the rotary (✆ **508/255-4742**), also rents surfboards, boogie boards, skim boards, kayaks, and wet suits.

SHOPPING

Though shops are somewhat scattered, Orleans is full of great finds for browsers. You'll find some 400 vintage light fixtures at **Continuum Antiques,** 7 S. Orleans Rd., Route 28, south of the junction with Route 6A (✆ **508/255-8513**). The proprietor of **Countryside Antiques,** 6 Lewis Rd., south of Main Street in the center of East Orleans (✆ **508/240-0525**), roams the world in search of stylish furnishings. Stop by **Kemp Pottery,** 9 Rte. 6A, just south of the rotary (✆ **508/255-5853**), and check out the turned and slab-built creations from soup tureens to fanciful sculptures.

WHERE TO STAY

MODERATE

A Little Inn on Pleasant Bay ★★ *Finds* Set back from a winding road that follows the coast between Orleans and Chatham, A Little Inn on Pleasant Bay sits on a hill next to a cranberry bog and overlooks the water (Pleasant Bay, naturally). The sprawling grounds are a riot of colorful flowers. The four rooms in the peaceful main house, which dates to 1798, have been completely renovated in warm tiles, light woods, and subtle colors that reflect a sort of Zen–Pottery Barn aesthetic. An adjacent building, called the "Paddock," has three additional rooms. There is also a two-bedroom suite. Breakfast (served outside, overlooking either the garden or the bay) is an extravagant affair; the spread of pastries, yogurt, muesli, cereals, fresh fruits and assorted meats and cheeses feels vaguely European. Innkeepers Bernd and Sandra are an excellent source for local restaurant recommendations. Pictures posted in the kitchen chronicle the "wildlife" spotted on the grounds—chief among them the resident Yorkie, Penny, who's a sucker for the love and attention guests routinely shower on her.

654 S. Orleans Rd., South Orleans, MA 02662. ✆ **888/332-3351** or 508/255-0780. www.alittleinnonpleasantbay.com. 9 units. $185–$275 double; $1,000 per week suite. Rates include continental breakfast and evening sherry. AE, MC, V. No children under 10 accepted. *In room:* A/C, TV (in Paddock rooms), hair dryer, no phone.

The Cove ★ This well-camouflaged motel complex on busy Route 28 also fronts placid Town Cove, where guests are offered a free minicruise in season. The interiors are adequate, if not dazzling, and a small heated pool and a restful gazebo overlook the waterfront. Some rooms have kitchenettes, and balconies with cove views.

13 S. Orleans Rd. (Rte. 28, north of Main St.), Orleans, MA 02653. ✆ **800/343-2233** or 508/255-1203. Fax 508/255-7736. www.thecoveorleans.com. 47 units. Summer $119–$189 double; $179–$209 suite or efficiency. Open year-round. AE, DC, DISC, MC, V. **Amenities:** Small heated pool. *In room:* A/C, TV/VCR, fridge, coffeemaker, hair dryer, microwave.

Nauset Knoll Motor Lodge ★★ *Value* Overlooking Nauset Beach, one of Cape Cod's most popular beaches, this nothing-fancy motel with picture windows will suit beach lovers to a T. The simple, clean rooms are well maintained, and by staying here, you'll save on daily parking charges at Nauset Beach. The whole complex is owned by Uncle Sam and is under the supervision of the National Park Service.

237 Beach Rd. (at Nauset Beach, about 2 miles east of the town center), East Orleans, MA 02643. ✆ **508/255-2364.** www.capecodtravel.com. 12 units (all with tub/shower). Summer $150 double. MC, V. Closed late Oct to early Apr. *In room:* TV, no phone.

The Orleans Inn ★ You can't miss this mansard-roofed beauty, perched right on the edge of Town Cove. Absolutely, get one of the rooms facing the water. Built in 1875, the inn has been lovingly restored and maintains its central place in the community. The simple rooms, some with twin beds or sleeper sofas, are cheerful with modern amenities and extra touches like a box of chocolates on the bureau. Downstairs is a bar and restaurant with wonderful views of the cove.

Rte. 6A (P.O. Box 188; just south of the Orleans rotary), Orleans, MA 02653. ✆ **508/255-2222.** Fax 508/255-6722. www.orleansinn.com. 11 units. Summer $175–$225 double; $250–$300 suite. Rates include continental breakfast. AE, MC, V. **Amenities:** Restaurant/bar. *In room:* TV, fridge.

INEXPENSIVE

Nauset House Inn ★★ *Value* Just a half-mile from Nauset Beach, this reasonably priced country inn is a cozy setting for those seeking a quiet retreat. Several of the rooms in greenery-draped outbuildings feature such romantic extras as a sunken bath or private deck. The most romantic hideaway here, though, is a 1907 conservatory appended to the 1810 farmhouse inn. It's the perfect place to lounge when the rain pounds down, prompting the camellias to waft their heady perfume. Breakfast would seem relatively workaday, were it not for the setting—a pared-down, rustic refectory—and innkeeper Diane Johnson's memorable muffins and pastries.

143 Beach Rd. (P.O. Box 774; about 1 mile east of the town center), East Orleans, MA 02643. ✆ **800/771-5508** or 508/255-2195. Fax 508/240-6276. www.nausethouseinn.com. 14 units, 6 with shared bathroom (4 tub/shower, 4 shower only). Summer $65 single; $75–$85 shared bathroom; $100–$170 double with private bathroom. Rates include full breakfast. DISC, MC, V. Closed Nov–Mar. No children under 12. *In room:* No phone.

WHERE TO DINE

EXPENSIVE

Abba ★★ INTERNATIONAL Abba is everyone's new favorite restaurant. It's a fresh take on fine-dining in the Lower Cape. Tables are closely packed inside, so we prefer the covered outdoor dining area behind the restaurant. Chef/co-owner Erez

Pinhas of Israel creates what can only be described as fusion cuisine, a little Middle Eastern, a little European, a little New American, plus some Thai and New England thrown in. Where else can you start with a falafel, move on to a steaming plate of shrimp pad Thai, and then end with chilled melon soup?

West Rd. and Old Colony Way (2 blocks from Main St., toward Skaket Beach). ✆ **508/255-8144.** Reservations recommended. Main courses $18–$27. AE, MC, V. June–Aug Tues–Sun 5–10pm; call for off-season hours. Open year-round.

Academy Ocean Grille NEW AMERICAN Just the basics here, fresh food prepared simply, but sometimes that's just what you want. Seafood specialties include flounder sautéed and topped with blue crab and a lemon thyme and lavender beurre blanc sauce; and local cod baked and served with a sweet beet and horseradish beurre blanc sauce. There's also veal, steak, and roast duck. On clear summer evenings, dinner is served outside on the trellised patio, which is quite lovely. The interior of the restaurant is on the bland side.

2 Academy Place (in the center of town). ✆ **508/240-1585.** Reservations recommended. Main courses $20–$30. AE, MC, V. Late June to mid-Sept daily 11:30am–2:30pm and 5:30–9:30pm; call for off-season hours. Closed Jan to mid-Apr.

MODERATE

Joe's Beach Road Bar & Grille at the Barley Neck Inn ★ NEW AMERICAN This 1857 captain's house with adjoining tavern is a favorite with locals. While the front room has a more traditional ambience, the tavern space features a huge fieldstone fireplace and World War II posters. With denim tablecloths and bandannas serving as napkins, the atmosphere is casual. The 28-foot mahogany bar is a popular meeting place. The menu varies from fancy dishes such as grilled Atlantic salmon filet with a red-pepper *coulis* and basil vinaigrette to Joe's pizza (with goat cheese, roasted peppers, and spinach) or high-falutin' fish and chips—beer-battered, with saffron aioli.

At The Barley Neck Inn, 5 Beach Rd. (about ½ mile east of the town center), East Orleans. ✆ **508/255-0212.** www.barleyneck.com. Reservations accepted. Main courses $10–$25. AE, DC, MC, V. June to early Sept daily 5–10pm; call for off-season hours. Open year-round.

The Lobster Claw Restaurant ★ *Kids* SEAFOOD This sprawling family-owned business has been serving up quality seafood for almost 30 years. Get the baked stuffed lobster with all the fixings.

Rte. 6A (just south of the rotary), Orleans. ✆ **508/255-1800.** Main courses $10–$19. AE, DC, DISC, MC, V. Daily 11:30am–9pm. Closed Nov–Mar.

Mahoney's Atlantic Bar & Grill ★ NEW AMERICAN Seafood is the specialty at this casual restaurant. Dishes like tuna sashimi, grilled sea bass, and pan-seared lobster are why you came to Cape Cod. There are also poultry, meat, pasta, and vegetarian dishes. Some nights in season, there's live jazz and blues.

28 Main St. (in the center of town). ✆ **508/255-5505.** www.mahoneysatlantic.com. Reservations recommended. Main courses $12–$21. AE, MC, V. May–Sept daily 5–10pm; Oct–Apr Tues–Sun 5–10pm.

INEXPENSIVE

Binnacle Tavern ★ *Kids* AMERICAN All sorts of strange nautical salvage adorn the barn-board walls of this popular pizzeria, where the pies—reputed to be the Cape's best—come with some very peculiar toppings (Thai pizza with chicken, ginger, cilantro, scallions, and peanut sauce, topped with mozzarella cheese!) for those so inclined. More conservative combos are available, along with traditional Italian fare. Kids love the funky atmosphere. The margaritas are marvelous, and there are homemade desserts and espresso.

20 S. Orleans Rd./Rte. 28 (north of Main St.). ✆ **508/255-7901**. Reservations not accepted. Most items under $12. AE, MC, V. Mid-May to mid-Oct daily 5–11:30pm; mid-Oct to mid-May Wed–Sun 5–11:30pm.

Cap't Cass Rock Harbor Seafood SEAFOOD Most tourists figure that a silvered shack sporting this many salvaged lobster buoys has an inside track on the freshest of seafood. The supposition makes sense, but the stuff here is about par for the area and the preparations are basic. Nevertheless, it's fun to eat in a joint left untouched for decades as time—and dining fads—marched on.

117 Rock Harbor Rd. (on the harbor, about 1½ miles northwest of the town center). No phone. Most main courses under $12. No credit cards. Late June to mid-Oct Tues–Sun 11am–2pm and 5–9pm. Closed mid-Oct to late June.

ORLEANS AFTER DARK

Joe's Beach Road Bar & Grille ★ at the Barley Neck Inn (✆ **508/255-0212;** see "Where to Dine," above) is a big old barn of a bar that might as well be town hall: It's where you'll find all the locals exchanging juicy gossip and jokes. On Sunday evenings in season, there's live "Jazz at Joe's."

There's live music Thursday through Saturday at the **Land Ho!** ★★ (✆ **508/255-5165**), the best pub in town, and on Monday and Tuesday nights as well during high season. There's usually no cover charge.

4 The Outer Cape

It's only on the Outer Cape that the landscape and even the air feel really beachy. You can smell the seashore just over the horizon—in fact, everywhere you go, because you're never more than a mile or two away from sand and surf. You won't find any high-rise hotels along the shoreline or tacky amusement arcades—just miles of pristine beaches and dune grass rippling in the wind. That's because in the early 1960s, 27,000 acres here became the federally protected Cape Cod National Seashore.

WELLFLEET ★★★

With the well-tended look of a classic New England village and surrounded by beaches, Wellfleet is the chosen destination for artists, writers, off-duty psychiatrists, and other contemplative types who hope to find more in the landscape than mere quaintness or rusticity. Distinguished literati such as Edna St. Vincent Millay and Edmund Wilson put this rural village on the map in the 1920s, in the wake of Provincetown's bohemian heyday.

To this day, Wellfleet remains remarkably unspoiled. Once you leave Route 6, commercialism is kept to a minimum, though the town boasts plenty of appealing shops, distinguished galleries, and a couple of very good New American restaurants. It's hard to imagine any other community on the Cape supporting so sophisticated an undertaking as the Wellfleet Harbor Actors' Theatre, or hosting such a wholesome event as public square dancing on the adjacent Town Pier. And where else could you find a thriving drive-in movie theater right next door to an outstanding nature preserve?

ESSENTIALS

GETTING THERE After crossing the Sagamore Bridge, head east on Route 6 to Orleans, and after the rotary, continue north on Route 6 to Wellfleet. Wellfleet is 42 miles northeast of Sandwich, 14 miles south of Provincetown.

VISITOR INFORMATION Contact the **Wellfleet Chamber of Commerce,** off Route 6, Wellfleet, MA 02663 (© **508/349-2510;** fax 508/349-3740; www.wellfleet chamber.com).

BEACHES & GETTING OUTSIDE

BEACHES Wellfleet's fabulous ocean beaches tend to sort themselves demographically: LeCount Hollow is popular with families, Newcomb Hollow with high-schoolers, White Crest with the college crowd, and Cahoon Hollow with 30-somethings. Only the latter two permit parking by nonresidents ($15 per day). To enjoy the other two, as well as Burton Baker Beach on the harbor at Indian Neck and Duck Harbor on the bay, plus three freshwater ponds, you'll have to walk or bike in, or see if you qualify for a sticker ($60 per week). Bring proof of residency to the seasonal Beach Sticker Booth on the Town Pier, or call the **Wellfleet Recreation Department** (© **508/349-9818**). Parking is free at all beaches and ponds after 4pm.

- **Marconi Beach** ★★, off Marconi Beach Road in South Wellfleet: A National Seashore property, this cliff-lined beach (with restrooms) charges an entry fee of $15 per day, or $45 for the season. ***Note:*** The bluffs are so high that the beach lies in shadow by late afternoon.
- **Mayo Beach,** Kendrick Avenue (near the Town Pier): Right by the harbor, facing south, this warm, shallow bay beach (with restrooms) is hardly secluded but will please young waders. Parking is free. You could grab a bite (and a paperback) at The Bookstore Restaurant across the street.
- **White Crest & Cahoon Hollow Beaches** ★★★, off Ocean View Drive in Wellfleet: These two town-run ocean beaches—big with surfers—are open to all. Both have snack bars and restrooms. Parking costs $15 per day, $45 for the season.

BICYCLING The end of the 25-mile **Cape Cod Rail Trail** ★★★ (© **508/896-3491**), Wellfleet is also among its more desirable destinations: A country road off the bike path leads right to LeCount Hollow Beach. At the end of the trail, the **Black Duck Sports Shop** at 1446 Rte. 6 in Wellfleet, at LeCount Hollow Road (© **508/349-9801**), stocks everything from rental bikes to boogie boards. The deli at the adjoining **South Wellfleet General Store** (© **508/349-2335**) can see to your snacking needs.

BOATING **Jack's Boat Rentals,** located on Gull Pond off Gull Pond Road, about a half-mile south of the Truro border (© **508/349-9808**), rents out canoes, kayaks, sailboards, and Sunfish, as well as sea cycles and surf bikes. Gull Pond connects to Higgins Pond by way of a placid, narrow channel lined with red maples and choked with water lilies. Needless to say, it's a great place to paddle. If you'd like a canoe for a few days, you'll need to go to the Jack's Boat Rentals location on Route 6 in Wellfleet (next to the Cumberland Farms). In addition to watercraft to go, Jack's is also the place for information about **Eric Gustavson's guided kayak tours** (© **508/349-1429**) of kettle ponds and tidal rivers from Chatham to Truro.

The Chequessett Yacht & Country Club on Chequessett Neck Road in Wellfleet (© **508/349-0198**) offers group sailing lessons. For experienced sailors, **Wellfleet Marine Corp.,** on the Town Pier (© **508/349-2233**), rents sailboats in season.

Tips Recommended Reading

In *Midnights: A Year with the Wellfleet Police,* frequent *New Yorker* contributor Alec Wilkinson chronicles his stint with the police department in this small Cape Cod town, earning the nickname "Crash." A sense of the Cape, and of New England life, is nicely captured here.

FISHING For a license to fish at Long Pond, Great Pond, or Gull Pond, visit **Town Hall** at 300 Main St. (© **508/349-0301**). Surf-casting, which doesn't require a license, is permitted at the town beaches. Shellfishing licenses—Wellfleet's oysters are world-famous—can be obtained from the **Shellfish Department** on the Town Pier off Kendrick Avenue (© **508/349-0300**).

Heading out from Wellfleet Harbor in season is the 60-foot party fishing boat ***Navigator*** (© **508/349-6003**) and three charter boats: the ***Erin-H*** (© **508/349-9663;** www.virtualcapecod.com/erinh), ***Jac's Mate*** (© **508/255-2978**), and ***Snooper*** (© **508/349-6113**).

NATURE & WILDLIFE AREAS Right in town, the short, picturesque boardwalk known as **Uncle Tim's Bridge,** off East Commercial Street, crosses Duck Creek to access a tiny island crisscrossed by paths.

The Cape Cod National Seashore maintains two spectacular self-guided trails. The 1.25-mile **Atlantic White Cedar Swamp Trail** ★★, off the parking area for the Marconi Wireless Station (see "Cape Cod National Seashore," later in this chapter) shelters a rare stand of the lightweight species prized by Native Americans as wood for canoes; the moss-choked swamp is a magical place, refreshingly cool even at the height of summer. A boardwalk will see you over the muck, but the return trip does entail a calf-testing half-mile trek through deep sand. Consider it a warm-up for magnificent **Great Island,** jutting 4 miles into the bay (off the western end of Chequessett Neck Rd.) to cup Wellfleet Harbor. Before attaching itself to the mainland in 1831, Great Island harbored a busy whaling post. Be sure to cover up, wear sturdy shoes, bring water, and venture to Jeremy Point—the very tip—only if you're sure the tide is going out.

You'll find 6 miles of very scenic trails lined with lupines and bayberries—Goose Pond, Silver Spring, and Bay View—within the **Wellfleet Bay Wildlife Sanctuary** ★★★, off Route 6 north of the Eastham border, in South Wellfleet (© **508/349-2615;** fax 508/349-2632; www.wellfleetbay.org). A spiffy, eco-friendly visitor center serves as both introduction and gateway to this 1,000-acre refuge, maintained by the Massachusetts Audubon Society. Passive solar heat and composting toilets are just a few of the waste-cutting elements incorporated into the seemingly simple building. You might see red-winged blackbirds and osprey as you follow the looping trails through pine forests, salt marsh, and moors. The sanctuary offers naturalist-guided tours and workshops for children. Inquire about canoeing, birding, and seal-watching excursions. Trail use is free for Massachusetts Audubon Society members; otherwise, the fee is $5 for adults and $3 for seniors and children 3 to 12. Trails are open July through August from 8am to 8pm, and September through June from 8am to dusk. The visitor center is open from Memorial Day to Columbus Day daily from 8:30am to 5pm; off season, it's closed Monday.

WATERSPORTS Surfing is restricted to White Crest Beach, and sailboarding to Burton Baker Beach at Indian Neck during certain tide conditions; ask for a copy of the regulations at the Beach Sticker Booth on the Town Pier.

SHOPPING

A stroll from Main Street down Bank Street and then along Commercial Street will take you past a dozen galleries worth a look. Crafts make a strong showing, too, as do contemporary women's clothing and eclectic home furnishings. But unlike Provincetown, which has something to offer virtually year-round, Wellfleet pretty much closes up come Columbus Day.

The **Cove Gallery,** 15 Commercial St., by Duck Creek (© **508/349-2530**)—with a waterside sculpture garden—carries the paintings and prints of many well-known artists, including Barry Moser and Leonard Baskin. John Grillo's work astounds every summer during his annual show in July. **Jules Besch Stationers,** 15 Bank St. (© **508/349-1231**), specializes in stationery products, including papers, gift cards, handmade journals, and unusual gift items.

WHERE TO STAY

Even'tide ★ *Kids* Set back from busy Route 6, this well-run motel is a good base for families. In case of rain, there's a 60-foot, heated indoor pool—a rarity in this part of the Cape. There are seven cottages on the property with one-, two-, and three-bedroom units. In the pines are a barbecue and picnic area. The Rail Trail goes right by, and a 1-mile footpath through the woods leads to Marconi Beach.

650 Rte. 6 (about 1 mile north of the Eastham border), South Wellfleet, MA 02663. © **800/368-0007** in MA only, or 508/349-3410. Fax 508/349-7804. www.eventidemotel.com. 40 units (39 tub/shower, 1 shower only). Summer $125–$160 double, $165–$180 efficiency; $1,100–$1,800 weekly for cottages. AE, DISC, MC, V. **Amenities:** Large heated indoor pool; playground; self-service laundromat. *In room:* A/C, TV, fridge, coffeemaker.

The Inn at Duck Creeke *Value* This historic complex is set on 5 woodsy acres overlooking a tidal creek and salt marsh. The 1880s captain's house features wide-board floors and charming but basic rooms, many with shared bathrooms; the carriage house contains a few light and airy cabin-style rooms; and the 1715 saltworks building has smaller, rooms with antique decor. In the main building, each shared bathroom adjoins two rooms, which might not suit those in search of privacy. All rooms have fans, and the third floor rooms have air-conditioning. The carriage house and saltworks building are quieter and can be downright romantic. But there's definitely a no-frills quality to this place—towels are thin, and so are walls. A big plus is that there are two good restaurants on-site: **Sweet Seasons** (see "Where to Dine," below) and the **Duck Creeke Tavern,** with live entertainment in season.

70 Main St. (P.O. Box 364), Wellfleet, MA 02667. © **508/349-9333.** Fax 508/349-0234. www.innatduckcreeke.com. 26 units (13 tub/shower, 5 shower only, 8 with shared bathroom). Summer $85–$90 double with shared bathroom; $95–$125 double with private bathroom. Rates include continental breakfast. AE, MC, V. Closed Nov–Apr. **Amenities:** 2 restaurants (seafood restaurant and tavern). *In room:* No phone.

Surfside Cottages ★★ *Kids* This is where you want to be: smack dab on a spectacular beach with 50-foot dunes, within biking distance of Wellfleet Center and a short drive from Provincetown. All of the one, two, or three bedrooms have kitchens, fireplaces, barbecues, outdoor showers, and screened porches. Some even have roof decks. From mid-May to mid-October, the cottages rent weekly. Bring your own sheets and towels; renting a set costs $10 per person.

Ocean View Dr. (at LeCount Hollow Rd.; P.O. Box 937), South Wellfleet, MA 02663. ✆/fax **508/349-3959.** www.surfsidevacation.com. 18 cottages (showers only). Summer $1,100–$1,875 weekly; off season $80–$130 per day. MC, V. Closed Nov to early Apr. Pets allowed off season. *In room:* Fridge, coffeemaker.

WHERE TO DINE

Hatch's Fish & Produce Market ★, 310 Main St., behind Town Hall (✆ **508/349-6734** for produce, 508/349-2810 for fish market), is the unofficial heart of Wellfleet. You'll find the best local bounty, from fresh-picked corn to fruit-juice Popsicles to steaming lobsters. Virtually no one passes through without picking up a little something, including the latest town gossip. It's closed from late September until May.

Mac's Seafood Market and Harbor Grill Restaurant ★ *Finds* *Kids* On the town pier, this takeout shack with picnic tables features fresh local seafood unloaded from the boats just steps away. Besides grilled fish dinners, there's homemade chowders, sushi, and a raw bar.

Wellfleet Town Pier. ✆ **508/349-9611.** Main courses $10–$20. MC, V. Daily 7:30am–10pm. Closed mid-Oct to late May.

Moby Dick's Restaurant ★ *Kids* SEAFOOD This is your typical clam shack. Order your meal at the register, sit at a picnic table, and a cheerful college student brings it to you. The fried fish, clams, scallops, and shrimp are all good; try the Moby's Seafood Special—a heaping platter of all of the above, plus coleslaw and fries. Then there's the clambake special with lobster, steamers, and corn on the cob. Bring the family and chow down.

Rte. 6, Wellfleet. ✆ **508/349-9795.** www.mobydicksrestaurant.com. Reservations not accepted. Main courses $8–$20. MC, V. Mid-June to early Sept daily 11:30am–10pm; call for off-season hours. Closed mid-Oct to Apr.

Sweet Seasons Restaurant ★ NEW AMERICAN Chef-owner Judith Pihl's Mediterranean-influenced fare is still appealing after 20-plus years, as is this dining room's peaceful pond view. Some of the dishes can be a bit heavy by contemporary standards, but there's usually a healthy alternative: Wellfleet littlenecks and mussels in a golden, aromatic tomato-and-cumin broth, for instance, as opposed to Russian oysters with smoked salmon, vodka, and sour cream. Specialties of the house include creamy sage-and-asparagus ravioli, and Seasons shrimp with feta and ouzo.

At The Inn at Duck Creeke, 70 Main St. (about ⅛ mile west of Rte. 6). ✆ **508/349-6535.** Reservations recommended. Main courses $19–$30. AE, MC, V. July–Sept Tues–Sun 5:30–10pm. Closed Oct–June.

The Wicked Oyster ★★ NEW AMERICAN This old warehouse-style building on the way to Wellfleet Center has been converted into a cool and casual year-round restaurant. Several restaurants have come and gone from this spot in recent years, but this one looks like a keeper. There are several sections: an enclosed front porch, an ample dining room, and a large bar area. With a busy to-go area for coffee and pastries, this place definitely has a bustling atmosphere. You'll see families with small children, 20-something couples, and older folks enjoying this comfortable and convenient restaurant. Breakfast is popular and features a multitude of omelets plus very strong coffee. At lunch, sandwiches and fried fish appear on the menu. Dinner choices range from burgers to more refined options, like pan-fried sole with lemon caper butter, spring risotto with mushrooms and asparagus, or, for large appetites, grilled angus tenderloin.

50 Main St. (just off Rte. 6, close to Wellfleet Center). ✆ **508/349-3455.** Reservations recommended. Main courses $6–$26. MC, V. June–Aug daily 7am–2pm and 5:30–10pm; call for off-season hours. Open year-round.

Winslow's Tavern ★★ BISTRO This new upscale bistro offers summer time treats like grilled lobster and bistro classics like steak frites in a contemporary setting. Of course they have Wellfleet oysters, the town's world famous bi-valve. But they also have wonderful salads and light meals.

316 Main St. (in the center of town). ✆ **508/349-6450.** Reservations for parties of 6 or more only. Main courses $13–$23. AE, MC, V. July–Aug daily noon–3pm and 5:30–10pm; call for off-season hours. Closed late Oct to mid-May.

WELLFLEET AFTER DARK

The Beachcomber ★, 1220 Old Cahoon Hollow Rd., off Ocean View Drive (✆ **508/349-6055;** www.beachcomber.com), arguably the best dance club on Cape Cod, is definitely the most scenic. It's right on Cahoon Hollow Beach—so close, in fact, that late beachgoers on summer weekends can count on a free concert of reggae, blues, ska, or rock. Cover varies. Closed early September to late May.

Local talent—jazz, pop, folk, and blues—accompanies the light fare at **Duck Creeke Tavern,** at The Inn at Duck Creeke, 70 Main St. (✆ **508/349-7369**). Closed mid-October to late May; no cover.

The cozy attic at the **Upstairs Bar at Aesop's Tables,** 316 Main St. (✆ **508/349-6450**), is usually inhabited by local blues and jazz performers.

The **Wellfleet Drive-In Theater,** 51 Rte. 6, just north of the Eastham border (✆ **800/696-3532** or 508/349-2520), built in 1957, is the only drive-in left on Cape Cod and one of a scant half-dozen surviving in the state. The rituals are as unbending and endearing as ever: the playtime preceding the cartoons, the countdown plugging the allures of the snack bar, and finally, two full first-run features. It's open daily from late May through mid-September; showtime is at dusk. Call for off-season hours.

The principals behind the **Wellfleet Harbor Actors' Theatre,** 1 Kendrick Ave., near the Town Pier (✆ **508/349-6835**), aim to provoke—and usually succeed, even amid this very sophisticated, seen-it-all summer colony. Performances are given from late May through October, daily at 8pm.

TRURO ★★

With only 1,600 year-round residents (fewer than it boasted in 1840, when Pamet Harbor was a whaling and shipbuilding port), Truro amounts to little more than a smattering of stores and public buildings, and lots of low-profile houses hidden away in the woods and dunes. Edward Hopper lived in contented isolation in a South Truro cottage for nearly 4 decades. If you find yourself craving cultural stimulation or other kinds of excitement, Provincetown is only a 10-minute drive away.

ESSENTIALS

GETTING THERE After crossing the Sagamore Bridge, head east on Route 6 or 6A to Orleans and north on Route 6.

VISITOR INFORMATION Contact the **Truro Chamber of Commerce,** Route 6A (at Head of the Meadow Rd.), Truro, MA 02666 (✆ **508/487-1288**). Truro is 46 miles east of Sandwich, 10 miles south of Provincetown.

BEACHES & GETTING OUTSIDE

BEACHES Parking at all of Truro's exquisite Atlantic beaches, except for one Cape Cod National Seashore access point (Corn Hill Beach), is reserved for residents and renters. To obtain a sticker ($30 for 1 week; $60 for 2 weeks), inquire at the beach-sticker office at 14 Truro Center Rd. behind the post office in Truro Center (✆ **508/487-3635**).

- **Corn Hill Beach** ★★, off Corn Hill Road: Offering restrooms, this bay beach—near the hill where the Pilgrims found the seed corn that ensured their survival—is open to nonresidents for a parking fee of $10 per day.
- **Head of the Meadow** ★★★, off Head of the Meadow Road: Among the more remote National Seashore beaches, this spot (equipped with restrooms) is known for its excellent surf. A parking lot connected by a short boardwalk to the beach makes this beach more easily accessible than other National Seashore beaches. It is also connected by a short bike path to Pilgrim Heights (see "Bicycling," below). Parking costs $15 per day, or $45 per season.

BICYCLING Although it has yet to be linked up to the Cape Cod Rail Trail, Truro does have a stunning 2-mile bike path of its own: the **Head of the Meadow Trail** ★, off the road of the same name (look for a right-hand turn about a half-mile north of where Routes 6 and 6A intersect). Part of the old 1850 road toward Provincetown, it skirts the bluffs, passing Pilgrim and ending at High Head Road.

FISHING Great Pond, Horseleech Pond, and Pilgrim Lake—flanked by parabolic dunes carved by the wind—are all fishable; for a freshwater fishing license, visit **Town Hall** on Town Hall Road (✆ **508/487-2702**). You can also call town hall for a shellfishing license. Surf-casting is permitted at Highland Light Beach, off Highland Road.

GOLF North Truro boasts the most scenic—and historic—9-hole course on the Cape. Created in 1892, the minimally groomed, Scottish-style **Highland Links** at 10 Lighthouse Rd., off South Highland Road (✆ **508/487-9201**), shares a lofty bluff with the 1853 Highland Light.

NATURE TRAILS The Cape Cod National Seashore, comprising 70% of Truro's land, offers three self-guided nature trails. The .5-mile **Pamet Trail** ★ off North Pamet Road leads you past an old cranberry-bog building and bogs that have reverted to marshland. Park in the lot to the left of the Little America youth hostel and walk back to the fire road entrance about 500 feet down North Pamet Road. The **Pilgrim Spring Trail** ★ and **Small Swamp Trail** ★ (each a .75-mile loop) head out from the National Seashore parking lot just east of Pilgrim Lake. Both paths overlook Salt Meadow, a freshwater marsh favored by hawks and osprey.

A MUSEUM & AN ARTS CENTER

Highland House Museum and Highland Lighthouse Built as a hotel in 1907, the Highland House is a perfect repository of the odds and ends collected by the Truro Historical Society: ship's models, harpoons, primitive toys, a pirate's chest, and so on. In 1996, Highland Lighthouse was moved back from its perilous perch above a rapidly eroding dune. Now the lighthouse is within 800 feet of the museum and is also operated by the Truro Historical Society. Seasonal lighthouse tours run May through October. There is a 51-inch height requirement so, unfortunately, little ones can't climb up the tower.

27 Highland Light Rd. (off S. Highland Rd., 2 miles north of the town center on Rte. 6). ✆ **508/487-1121**. www.trurohistorical.org. Admission to both museum and lighthouse $6 adults, free for children under 12. Admission to museum or lighthouse $4; free for children under 12 at museum only. Museum June–Sept Mon–Sat 10am–4:30pm; Sun 1–4:30pm. Last ticket sold at 3:30pm. Lighthouse mid-June to mid-Oct daily 10am–5:30pm. Closed mid-Oct to mid-June.

WHERE TO STAY

Days Cottages ★ *Value* Lined up along the bay beach in North Truro, these identical cottages—named after flowers—are all white clapboard with sea-foam green shutters. Although lacking frills, each has a living room, two small bedrooms, a kitchen, and a bathroom. The downside is that these accommodations are somewhat rough: The bedrooms are minuscule, and in some of the cottages, the fireplace has about 10 years' worth of graffiti written on the brick chimney. There is also the noise of passing cars on this busy stretch of road to contend with. The upside is miles of bay beach for walking and swimming with views of Provincetown's quirky skyline in the distance. In season, beginning June 1, the cottages are rented only by the week, and they usually book up far in advance.

Rte. 6A (a couple miles south of the Provincetown border), North Truro, MA 02652. ✆ **508/487-1062.** Fax 508/487-5595. www.dayscottages.com. 23 cottages (all with shower only). Summer $1,050 weekly. No credit cards. Closed mid-Oct to Apr. *In room:* Fridge.

Kalmar Village ★★ *Kids* *Value* Spiffier than many of the motels and cottages between Pilgrim Lake and Pilgrim Beach, this 1940s complex features little white cottages shuttered in black. There are picnic tables, grills, and daily maid service. Some cottages have air-conditioning. The clientele—mostly families—can splash the day away in the 60-foot freshwater pool or on the 400-foot private beach.

674 Shore Rd. (Rte. 6A, about ¼ mile south of the Provincetown border), North Truro, MA 02652. ✆ **508/487-0585.** Fax 508/487-5827. www.kalmarvillage.com. 16 units, 40 cottages. Summer $135 double, $175 2-bedroom suite; $1,295–$1,495 cottages weekly. DISC, MC, V. Closed mid-Oct to late May. **Amenities:** Outdoor pool; coin-op laundry. *In room:* TV, fridge.

WHERE TO DINE

Terra Luna ★ FUSION People come from miles around to sample the outstanding breakfasts at this modest restaurant. The muffins and scones emerge fresh from the oven, and "entrees" such as the breakfast burrito or strawberry mascarpone-cheese pancakes call for a hearty appetite. You can start in again in the evening, on well-priced Pacific Rim and/or neo-Italian fare, such as penne prosciutto sautéed with garlic, black pepper, and a splash of vodka. Main courses include local seafood and lobster dishes, like lobster risotto with asparagus and saffron. There's even a creative children's menu.

104 Shore Rd. (Rte. 6A), North Truro. ✆ **508/487-1019.** Reservations recommended. Main courses $14–$20. AE, MC, V. Late May to mid-Oct daily 8am–1pm and 5:30–10pm. Closed mid-Oct to late May.

Moments A Vineyard in the Dunes

This pastoral property just off Route 6 in Truro is one of the last working farms in the Outer Cape and the site of an honest-to-goodness vineyard. Horticulturist/innkeepers Kathy Gregrow and Judy Wimer of **Truro Vineyard of Cape Cod** (11 Shore Rd./Rte. 6A, North Truro; ✆ **508/487-6200**) uncorked their first home-grown chardonnay and Cabernet Franc in the fall of 1996, the muscadet in 1997, the merlot in 1998. Inside the main house, the living room, with its exposed beams, is decorated with interesting oenological artifacts. Late May through October, free wine tastings are held daily from noon to 5pm. Guided tours of the property take place at 1 and 3pm.

SWEETS & TAKEOUT

Jams *Finds* Seeing as this deli/bakery/grocery is basically the whole enchilada in terms of downtown Truro, and seasonal to boot, it's good that it's so delightful. It's full of tantalizing aromas: fresh, creative pizzas (from pesto to pupu); rotisseried fowl sizzling on the spit; or cookies straight from the oven. The pastry and deli selections deserve their own four-star restaurant, but are all the more savory as part of a picnic. 14 Truro Center Rd. (off Rte. 6, in the center of town). ✆ **508/349-1616.** Call for hours. Closed early Sept to late May.

PROVINCETOWN ★★★

You made it all the way to the end of the Cape, to one of the most interesting spots on the eastern seaboard. Explorer Bartholomew Gosnold must have felt much the same thrill in 1602, when he and his crew happened upon a "great stoare of codfysshes" here. The Pilgrims, of course, were overjoyed when they slogged into the harbor 18 years later. Never mind that they'd landed several hundred miles off course.

And Charles Hawthorne, the painter who "discovered" this near-derelict fishing town in the late 1890s and introduced it to the Greenwich Village intelligentsia, was besotted by this "jumble of color in the intense sunlight accentuated by the brilliant blue of the harbor."

He'd probably be aghast at the commercial circus his enthusiasm has wrought—though pleased, no doubt, to find the Provincetown Art Association & Museum, which he helped found in 1914, still going strong. The whole town, in fact, is dedicated to creative expression, both visual and verbal. The general atmosphere of open-mindedness plays a pivotal a role, allowing a very varied assortment of individuals to explore their creative urges.

That same open-mindedness may account for Provincetown's ascendancy as a gay and lesbian resort. In peak season, the streets are a celebration of the individual's freedom to be as "out" as imagination allows. But the street life also includes families, art lovers, and gourmands. In short, Provincetown has something for just about everyone.

ESSENTIALS

GETTING THERE After crossing the Sagamore Bridge, head east on Route 6 or 6A to Orleans, then continue north on Route 6 to Provincetown. Provincetown is 56 miles northeast of Sandwich, 42 miles northeast of Hyannis.

If you plan to spend your entire vacation in Provincetown, you won't need a car—everything is within walking or biking distance. And because parking is a hassle, consider leaving your car at home and taking a boat from Boston or Plymouth. You'll get to skip the horrendous Sagamore Bridge traffic jams and arrive by sea like the Pilgrims did.

Bay State Cruises (✆ **617/748-1428;** www.boston-ptown.com) makes round-trips from Boston, daily from late June through September.

The high-speed ***Provincetown Express*** boat takes 90 minutes and makes three round-trips daily from mid-May to late September. It leaves Boston's World Trade Center at 8am, 1pm, and 5:30pm. On the return trip, it leaves Provincetown at 10am, 3pm, and 7:30pm. Tickets on the high-speed boat cost $39 one-way, $60 round-trip for adults. Seniors are $33 one-way and $54 round-trip. Children 4 to 11 are $28 one-way, $49 round-trip. Reservations are recommended.

The regular 3-hour boat, called ***Provincetown II,*** leaves Boston's Commonwealth Pier on Fridays, Saturdays, and Sundays at 9:30am and arrives in Provincetown at 12:30pm. At 3:30pm, the boat leaves Provincetown, arriving in Boston at 6:30pm.

On the slow boat, round-trip fare is $30 for adults, free for children 4 to 11, and $24 for seniors.

Boston Harbor Cruises (✆ **617/227-4321;** www.bostonharborcruises.com) runs fast ferries from Long Wharf in Boston to Provincetown's Macmillan's Wharf. It's a 90-minute trip. In high season, there are three round-trips a day, leaving at 9am, 2pm, and 6:30pm from Boston and leaving from Provincetown at 11am, 4pm, and 8:30pm. In the shoulder season, beginning in late May to mid-June and from early September to mid-October, there are one or two trips a day. Ferry tickets cost $38 one-way, $59 round-trip for adults. Tickets for seniors cost $33 one-way, $54 round-trip; and tickets for children cost $28 one-way, $49 round-trip. Bikes cost $5 each way. Reservations are a must on this popular boat.

Capt. John Boats (✆ **508/747-2400;** www.provincetownferry.com) connects Plymouth and Provincetown daily mid-June through August; Tuesday, Wednesday, Saturday, and Sunday in September; and weekends only from late May to mid-June. The 90-minute boat ride leaves the state pier in Plymouth at 10am; it leaves Provincetown at 4:30pm. The adult round-trip fare is $33, seniors $28, children under 12 $23; bikes are $5 extra.

You can also fly into Provincetown. **Cape Air** (✆ **800/352-0714;** www.flycapeair.com) offers flights from Boston and from Nantucket in season. Both trips take about 25 minutes.

As far as getting around once you're settled, you can enjoy the vintage fleet of the **Mercedes Cab Company** (✆ **508/487-3333**).

GETTING AROUND

Parking is at a premium. Illegally parked cars are ticketed (even on Sun), and repeat offenders will be towed. If your inn provides parking, you may want to keep your car there and get around on foot, bicycle, or shuttle. **Provincetown's Summer Shuttle** (✆ **508/487-3424**) loops through town and to the beach daily from late June through October.

VISITOR INFORMATION Contact the **Provincetown Chamber of Commerce,** 307 Commercial St., Provincetown, MA 02657 (✆ **508/487-3424;** fax 508/487-8966; www.ptownchamber.com), or the gay-oriented **Provincetown Business Guild,** 115 Bradford St., P.O. Box 421, Provincetown, MA 02657 (✆ **800/637-8696** or 508/487-2313; fax 508/487-1252; www.ptown.org).

BEACHES & GETTING OUTSIDE

BEACHES With nine-tenths of its territory (basically, all but the downtown area) protected by the Cape Cod National Seashore, Provincetown has miles of beaches. The 3-mile bay beach that lines the harbor, though certainly swimmable, is not all that inviting compared to the magnificent ocean beaches overseen by the National Seashore. The two official access areas (see below) tend to be crowded; however, you can always find a less densely populated stretch if you're willing to hike down the beach a bit.

- **Herring Cove** ★★★: This popular west-facing National Seashore beach is known for its spectacular sunsets. The long stretches of pristine sand front a calmer beach than Race Point (see below) because Herring Cove faces Cape Cod Bay. This is a haven for same-sex couples, who tend to gather to the far left side of the beach. Parking costs $15 per day, $45 per season.

Provincetown

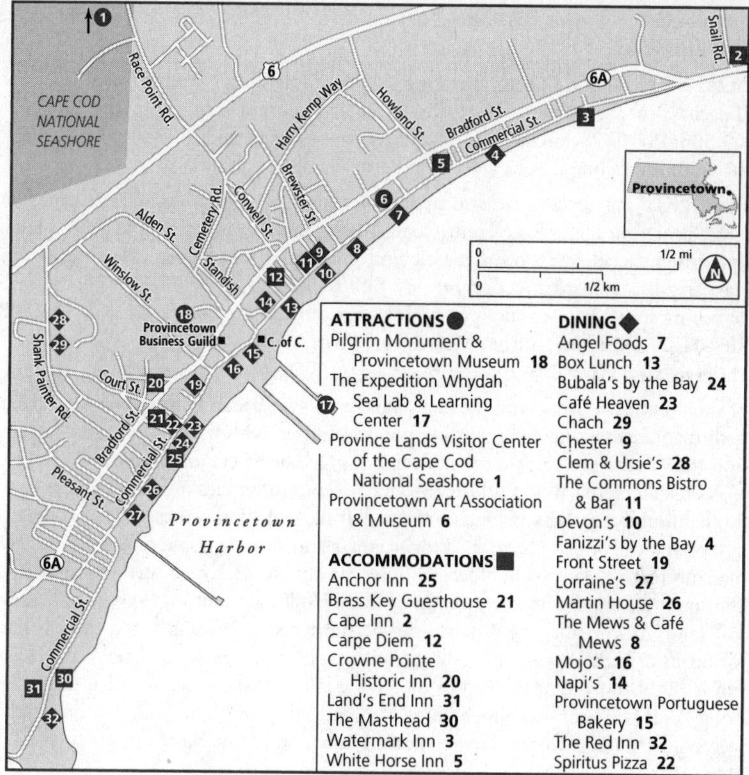

- **Long Point:** Trek out over the breakwater at the far west end of Commercial Street and walk about 1½ miles over sand—or catch a water shuttle—$8 one-way, $12 round-trip, hourly in season—from Flyer's Boat Rental (see "Boating," below) to visit this very last spit of land, capped by an 1827 lighthouse. Locals call it "the end of the earth." Shuttles run hourly in July and August.
- **Race Point** ★★★: Facing the Atlantic Ocean, Race Point offers rougher surf than Herring Cove, and you might actually spot whales en route to Stellwagen Bank. Parking costs $15 per day, $45 per season.

BICYCLING North of town, nestled amid the Cape Cod National Seashore preserve, is one of the more spectacular bike paths in New England, the 7-mile **Province Lands Trail** ★★, a heady swirl of steep dunes anchored by wind-stunted scrub pines. With its free parking, the **Province Lands Visitor Center** ★ (✆ **508/487-1256**) is a good place to start: You can survey the landscape from the observation tower to try to get your bearings before setting off amid the dizzying maze. Follow signs to follow a spur path leading to one of the beaches, Race Point or Herring Cove, lining the shore. Rentals are offered in season by **Nelson's Bike Shop** at 43 Race Point Rd. (✆ **508/487-8849**). It's also an easy jaunt from town, where you'll find plenty of good bike shops—such as **Ptown Bikes** at 42 Bradford St. (© **508/487-8735**); reserve several days in advance.

BOATING In addition to operating a Long Point shuttle from its own dock (see "Beaches," above), **Flyer's Boat Rental** at 131 Commercial St. in the West End (© **508/487-0898**) offers all sorts of craft, from kayaks and dinghies to sailboats of varying sizes; sailing lessons and fishing-gear rentals are also available.

FISHING Surf-casting is permitted at Herring Cove Beach (off Rte. 6) and Race Point Beach (near the Race Point Coast Guard Station); many people drop a handline or light tackle right off the West End breakwater. For low-cost deep-sea fishing via party boat, board the ***Cee Jay*** (© **800/675-6724** or 508/487-4330; www.ceejayfishing.com). For serious sportfishing, sign on for the ***Shady Lady II*** (© **508/487-0182**). Both depart from MacMillan Wharf.

NATURE TRAILS Within the Province Lands (off Race Point Rd., ½ mile north of Rte. 6), the National Seashore maintains the 1-mile **Beech Forest Trail** ★, a shaded path that circles a shallow freshwater pond blanketed with water lilies before heading into the woods. You can see the shifting dunes gradually encroaching on the forest.

A walk along the **West End breakwater** ★★ out to the end of **Long Point** is about 5 miles round-trip. Walking just to the end of the wide breakwater, located at the end of Commercial Street next to the Provincetown Inn, is quite popular. You'll see all ages maneuvering the layered boulders, about a 30-minute walk each way. If you want to continue to Long Point, the very tip of Cape Cod, it's about a 1½-hour walk across soft sand. At low tide, the distance can be shortened by cutting across the salt flats. **Wood End Lighthouse** is directly across the spit of sand near the breakwater. **Long Point Lighthouse** is at the end of the point. Hikers determined to reach the end of Long Point will want to bring a hat, water, and sunscreen. The inside of the arm has views of Provincetown and Provincetown Harbor and a couple of shipwrecks.

ORGANIZED TOURS & CRUISES

Art's Dune Tours ★★ is at the corner of Commercial and Standish streets (© **800/894-1951** or 508/487-1950; www.artsdunetours.com). In 1946, Art Costa started

Whale-Watching in P-town

Stellwagen Bank, 8 miles off Provincetown, is a rich feeding ground for whales. The **Dolphin Fleet** ★★★, MacMillan Wharf (© **800/826-9300** or 508/349-1900), was the first, and by all accounts still the best, outfitter running whale-watching trips to Stellwagen. Most cruises carry a naturalist to provide running commentary.

Tickets for the 3½-hour trips are $28 for adults, $26 for seniors, $22 for children 7 to 12, and free for children under 7. Call to reserve. Closed late October through March.

Tips for first-timers: Dress very warmly, in layers, and take along a waterproof windbreaker. If you're prone to seasickness, consider taking a motion-sickness pill at the start of the trip. (They are provided free as you board the vessel.)

driving sightseers out to ogle the decrepit "dune shacks" where such transient luminaries as Eugene O'Neill, Jack Kerouac, and Jackson Pollock found their respective muses. The park service wanted to raze these eyesores, but luckily saner heads prevailed: They're now National Historic Landmarks. The tours typically take about 1 to 1½ hours. Tickets are $18 to $26 for adults, $13 to $16 for children 6 to 11. Additional tours offered include a sunset clambake dune tour ($66), a barbecue tour ($56), and a Race Point Lighthouse tour ($26 adults, $16 children 6–11).

A recommended boat tour is on the ***Bay Lady II*** ★ (✆ **508/487-9308;** www.sailcapecod.com), which leaves from Macmillan Wharf. The sunset trip aboard this 73-foot reproduction gaff-rigged Grand Banks schooner is especially spectacular. Tickets cost $20 for adults, $10 to $20 for children under 12. There are four 2-hour sails daily from mid-May to mid-October.

MUSEUMS

The Expedition Whydah Sea Lab & Learning Center *Overrated* Though the subject matter is fascinating, this site is a bit of a tourist trap. Cape Cod native Barry Clifford made headlines in 1984 when he tracked down the wreck of the 17th-century pirate ship *Whydah* (pronounced *Wid*-dah, like Yankee for "widow") 1,500 feet off the coast of Wellfleet, where it had lain undisturbed since 1717. Only 10% excavated to date, it has already yielded over 100,000 artifacts. In this museum/lab, visitors can supposedly observe the reclamation work being done, though it's unusual to actually see scientists or scholars at work.

MacMillan Wharf (just past the whale-watching fleet). ✆ **508/487-8899.** www.whydah.com. Admission $8 adults, $6 children 6–12. June–Sept daily 9:30am–9pm; Oct–Dec and mid-Apr to May weekends only 10am–5pm. Closed Jan to mid-Apr.

Pilgrim Monument & Provincetown Museum ★★ Anywhere you go in town, this granite tower looms, ever ready to restore your bearings. Climb up the 60 gradual ramps interspersed with 116 steps—a surprisingly easy lope—and you'll get a gargoyle's-eye view of the spiraling coast and, in the distance, Boston against a backdrop of New Hampshire's mountains. Definitely devote some time to the curious exhibits in the museum, chronicling P-town's checkered past as both fishing port and arts nexus. Among the memorabilia, you'll find polar bears brought back from MacMillan's expeditions and early programs for the Provincetown Players.

High Pole Hill Rd. (off Winslow St., north of Bradford St.). ✆ **508/487-1310.** www.pilgrim-monument.org. Admission $7 adults, $3.50 children 4–12. July–Aug daily 9am–7pm; off season daily 9am–5pm. Last admission 45 min. before closing. Closed Dec–Mar.

Province Lands Visitor Center of the Cape Cod National Seashore ★ Though much smaller than the Salt Pond Visitor Center, this satellite does a good job of explicating this special environment, where plant life must fight a fierce battle to maintain its hold amid shifting sands buffeted by salty winds. Be sure to circle the observation deck for great views. Inquire about special events, such as guided walks, family campfires, and canoe programs (reservations required).

Race Point Rd. (about 1½ miles northwest of the town center). ✆ **508/487-1256.** Free admission. Mid-Apr to late Nov daily 9am–5pm. Closed late Nov to mid-Apr.

Provincetown Art Association & Museum ★★ *Moments* This extraordinary cache of 20th-century American art began with five paintings donated by local artists, including Charles Hawthorne, the charismatic teacher who first "discovered" this picturesque outpost. Founded in 1914, only a year after New York's revolutionary Armory Show, the museum was the site of innumerable "space wars," as classicists and modernists vied for square footage. In today's less competitive atmosphere, it's not unusual to see a tame still life next to an unrestrained abstract. The museum sponsors a full schedule of concerts, lectures, readings, and classes.

460 Commercial St. (in the East End). ✆ **508/487-1750.** www.paam.org. Admission $2 adults, free for members and children under 12. July–Aug daily noon–5pm and 8–10pm; call for off-season hours. Open year-round.

SHOPPING

ART GALLERIES Of the several dozen galleries in town, only a handful are reliably worthwhile. In season, most of the galleries and even some of the shops open around 11am, then take a siesta from around 5 to 7pm, reopening and greeting visitors up to as late as 10 or 11pm. Shows usually open on Friday evenings, prompting a "stroll" tradition spanning the many receptions.

Berta Walker is a force to be reckoned with, having nurtured many top artists through her association with the Fine Arts Work Center, before opening her own gallery in 1990, the **Berta Walker Gallery** ★, 208 Bradford St. in the East End (✆ **508/487-6411**). Closed from late October to late May.

DNA (Definitive New Art) Gallery ★, 288 Bradford St. above the Provincetown Tennis Club in the East End (✆ **508/487-7700**), has attracted such talents as photographer Joel Meyerowitz, Provincetown's favorite portraitist, known for such tomes as *Cape Light;* sculptor Conrad Malicoat, whose free-form brick chimneys and hearths can be seen around town; and local conceptualist/provocateur Jay Critchley. Readings by cutting-edge authors add to the buzz. Closed from mid-October to late May.

Julie Heller started collecting early P-town paintings as a child—and a tourist at that. She chose so incredibly well, her roster at **Julie Heller Gallery** ★, 2 Gosnold St. on the beach in the center of town (✆ **508/487-2169**), reads like a who's who of local art. Hawthorne, Avery, Hofmann, Lazzell, Hensche—all the big names from Provincetown's past are here, as well as some contemporary artists. Closed weekdays January to April.

Schoolhouse Center for Art and Design, 494 Commercial St. in the East End (✆ **508/487-4800**), is an impressive setup with two galleries, studios, arts programs, and an events series.

DISCOUNT SHOPPING

Marine Specialties, 235 Commercial St. in the center of town (✆ **508/487-1730**), is packed to the rafters with useful stuff, from discounted Doc Martens to cut-rate Swiss Army knives. Hung from the ceiling are some real antiques, including several carillons' worth of ship's bells.

FASHION

Giardelli/Antonelli Studio Showroom, 417 Commercial St. in the East End (✆ **508/487-3016**), is filled with Jerry Giardelli's unstructured clothing elements in vibrant colors and inviting textures. They demand to be mixed and matched with Diana Antonelli's statement jewelry.

Mad as a Hatter, 360 Commercial St. (✆ **508/487-4063**), has hats to suit every style and inclination. Closed January to mid-February.

Moda Fina, 349 Commercial St. (© **508/487-6632**), specializes in women's clothing and accessories, including shoes and lingerie, and unique summer dresses.

WHERE TO STAY

VERY EXPENSIVE

Anchor Inn ★★ This waterfront property centrally located on Commercial Street recently underwent a multi-million-dollar face-lift. Many rooms feature deluxe showers, whirlpool baths, and fireplaces. Sixteen guest rooms have waterfront balconies overlooking the harbor. Four have separate entrances through private porches. Some of the rooms, called "yacht cabins," are quite small, but have fabulous views. Others are large suites with king-size beds, two-person whirlpool baths, and French doors leading to a private balcony. Breakfast is an elaborate affair that could include quiche or eggs Benedict.

175 Commercial St. (in the center of town), Provincetown, MA 02657. © **800/858-2657** or 508/487-0432. Fax 508/487-6280. www.anchorinnbeachhouse.com. 23 units. Summer $255–$275 double; $375 suite. Rates include continental breakfast. AE, MC, V. Closed Jan–Mar. *In room:* A/C, TV/VCR, CD player, dataport, fridge, hair dryer.

Brass Key Guesthouse ★★★ Brass Key is the fanciest place to stay in Provincetown. With Ritz-Carlton–style amenities and service in mind, the innkeepers have created a paean to luxury. They've thought of everything: down pillows, jetted showers, and free iced tea and lemonade delivered poolside. Rooms in the 1828 Federal-style Captain's House and the Gatehouse are decorated in a playful country style, while the Victorian-era building is classically elegant, with materials like mahogany, walnut, and marble. Most deluxe guest rooms have gas fireplaces and oversize whirlpool tubs. In high season, the clientele here is primarily gay men, though all are made to feel welcome.

67 Bradford St. (in the center of town), Provincetown, MA 02657. © **800/842-9858** or 508/487-9005. Fax 508/487-9020. www.brasskey.com. 29 units, 4 cottages (9 tub/shower, 22 shower only, 2 with tub and shower). Summer $245–$445 double; $295–$445 cottage. Rates include continental breakfast and afternoon wine-and-cheese hour. AE, DISC, MC, V. Closed late Nov to early Apr. No children under 18. **Amenities:** Outdoor heated pool; 17-ft. hot tub. *In room:* A/C, TV/VCR, dataport, fridge, hair dryer, safe.

Crowne Pointe Historic Inn ★★ This newly restored property perched high on Bradford Street is exquisitely maintained with deluxe commons areas and attractive gardens. The staff is accommodating and professional. Rooms are spacious and some of the deluxe rooms and suites have fireplaces, wet bars, and whirlpool spas. Buffet breakfast is served in the large living room, which has plenty of overstuffed couches for lounging while you plan your day.

82 Bradford St. (in the center of town), Provincetown, MA 02657. © **877/CROWNE1** or 508/487-6767. Fax 508/487-5554. www.crownepointe.com. 40 units. $195–$450 double. Rates include continental breakfast, afternoon tea, and wine-and-cheese hour. AE, MC, V. **Amenities:** Heated outdoor pool; 10-person outdoor spa. *In room:* A/C, TV/VCR, dataport, hair dryer, iron.

EXPENSIVE

Land's End Inn ★★★ *Finds* Enjoying a prime perch atop Gull Hill in the far West End of Commercial Street, this whimsical 1907 bungalow is bursting with outlandish antiques. Some rooms would suit a 19th-century sheik. In other words, the place is unique in a way that will delight some guests and overwhelm others. There are three deluxe rooms that make use of the inn's soaring towers. The two-bedroom loft tower suite, entered through an armoire (very Narnia) must be one of the most unusual and spectacular lodging spaces on the Cape. From the spacious living room, climb the ironwork spiral stairway to the bedroom, where an immense stained-glass window serves as your headboard. There's also a wonderful octagonal tower room with bay-view decks on two sides. Some of the other rooms are small, but all are filled with kitschy Victorian and Deco *objets.* Though the inn is predominantly gay, cosmopolitan visitors will feel welcome. The breakfast, an elaborate continental spread, features fresh fruits and homemade baked goods.

22 Commercial St. (in the West End), Provincetown, MA 02657. © **800/276-7088** or 508/487-0706. Fax 508/487-0755. www.landsendinn.com. 16 units. Summer $165–$195 double; $295–$495 tower rooms. Rates include continental breakfast and wine-and-cheese hour. AE, MC, V. Closed Nov–Apr. *In room:* A/C, no phone.

The Masthead ★★ Kids This is one of the few places in town, other than the impersonal motels, that actively welcomes families, and the placid 450-foot private beach will delight young splashers. The cottages are fun, some with wicker furniture and antiques. In the water-view rooms perched above the surf, with their 7-foot picture windows overlooking the bay and Long Point, you may feel as though you're onboard a ship.

31–41 Commercial St. (in the West End), Provincetown, MA 02657. © **800/395-5095** or 508/487-0523. Fax 508/487-9251. www.themasthead.com. 21 units (3 tub/shower, 16 shower, 2 with shared bathroom), 4 cottages. Summer $86–$93 double with shared bathroom; $102–$249 double; $179–$235 efficiency; $265 2-bedroom apt. $1,750–$2,541 cottage weekly. AE, DC, DISC, MC, V. Open year-round. *In room:* A/C, TV, fridge, coffeemaker.

Watermark Inn ★★ Kids If you'd like to experience P-town without being stuck in the thick of it (the carnival atmosphere can get tiring at times), this contemporary inn at the peaceful edge of town is the perfect choice. This beachfront hotel contains dazzling suites; the prize ones, on the top floor, have picture windows and sweeping deck views. Handmade quilts brighten up clean, monochromatic rooms.

603 Commercial St. (in the East End), Provincetown, MA 02657. © **508/487-0165**. Fax 508/487-2383. www.watermark-inn.com. 10 units. Summer $130–$270 suite. From mid-May to mid-Sept, suites rent by the week only ($1,200–$2,440 per week). AE, MC, V. Open year-round. *In room:* TV, fridge, coffeemaker.

MODERATE

Cape Inn ★ This no-surprises motel on the waterfront at the far eastern edge of town is a good choice for first-timers not quite sure what they're getting into. Guests in waterfront rooms get a nice view of town. In season free movies are shown in the restaurant/lounge on a 100-foot screen and dinner is served in the restaurant. There's also a poolside bar and grill. Though this motel is a bit of a hike from the town's center, an in-season town shuttle will whisk you down Commercial Street or to the beaches.

698 Commercial St. (at Rte. 6A, in the East End), Provincetown, MA 02657. © **800/422-4224** or 508/487-1711. Fax 508/487-3929. www.capeinn.com. 78 units. Summer $119–$179 double. Rates include continental breakfast. AE, DC, DISC, MC, V. Closed Nov–Apr. Dogs allowed. **Amenities:** Restaurant; outdoor pool. *In room:* A/C, TV, dataport, fridge, coffeemaker, hair dryer, iron.

Carpe Diem ★★ The theme of this stylish B&B is "seize the day." The location, a quiet side street right in the center of town, will suit most P-town habitués to a "T." Guest rooms are exquisitely decorated with European antiques and brightly painted walls and wallpapers. All rooms have down comforters and pillows, as well as bathrobes, and all but one has a minifridge. There are two deluxe garden suites with private entrances, Jacuzzis, and fireplaces. The cottage has a two-person whirlpool, a fireplace, a private patio, and a wet bar. The full breakfast features homemade pastries served at the dining-room table. On clear days, sun worshippers prefer the patio where there's a six-person hot tub.

12 Johnson St. (in the center of town), Provincetown, MA 02657. ✆ **800/487-0132** or ✆/fax 508/487-4242. www.carpediemguesthouse.com. 14 units. Summer $140–$185 double; $225–$265 suites; $325 cottage. Rates include full breakfast and wine-and-cheese hour. AE, DISC, MC, V. Open year-round. **Amenities:** 8-person hot tub. *In room:* A/C, TV/VCR, dataport.

INEXPENSIVE

White Horse Inn ★★ *Value* Look for the house with the bright yellow door in the East End. The rates are terrific, especially given that this inn is the very embodiment of Provincetown's bohemian mystique. Frank Schaefer has been tinkering with this late-18th-century house since 1963. The rooms may be a bit austere, but each is enlivened by some of the 300 to 400 paintings he has collected over the decades. A number of his fellow artists helped him cobble together the studio apartments out of salvage: There's an aura of beatnik improv about them still. Guests over the years have embodied a range of low and high art: Cult filmmaker John Waters stayed here often, as did poet laureate Robert Pinsky.

500 Commercial St. (in the East End), Provincetown, MA 02657. ✆ **508/487-1790.** 24 units, 10 with shared bathroom. Summer $60 single with shared bathroom; $70–$80 double; $125–$140 efficiency. No credit cards. *In room:* No phone.

WHERE TO DINE

Spiritus Pizza, 190 Commercial St. (✆ **508/487-2808**), is an extravagant pizza parlor open until 2am. The pizza's good, as are the fruit drinks and premium ice cream. For a peaceful morning repast, check out the little garden in back.

Peruse the scrumptious meat pies and pastries at **Provincetown Portuguese Bakery,** 299 Commercial St. (✆ **508/487-1803**). Both establishments are closed November to early April.

VERY EXPENSIVE

Chester ★★★ NEW AMERICAN Step through the columned portico for a singular dining experience. Chester specializes in local seafood, meats, and vegetables prepared simply yet with a flourish. Service is exceptional; the food is beautifully presented. Starters like spinach and scallop risotto take advantage of local provender, as does the main course of Chatham cod with prosciutto and sage. The extensive wine list has won *Wine Spectator* awards. For dessert, look no further than the warm chocolate cake with homemade ice cream.

404 Commercial St. ✆ **508/487-8200.** www.chesterrestaurant.com. Reservations recommended. Main courses $19–$34. AE, MC, V. Late June to mid-Sept daily 6–10pm; mid-Apr to late May Thurs–Mon; late May to late June and mid-Sept to Oct Thurs–Tues 6–10pm. Call for off-season hours. Closed Jan to mid-Apr.

Martin House ★★★ CONTEMPORARY NEW ENGLAND/INTERNATIONAL Easily one of the most charming restaurants on the Cape, this snuggery of rustic soft-lit rooms happens to contain one of the Cape's most forward-thinking kitchens. The chef favors local delicacies, such as the littlenecks that appear in a kafir-lime–tamarind broth with Asian noodles. Main courses might include local-lobster-stuffed squash blossoms with a warm porcini-saffron vinaigrette. In season, there's seating in the rose-covered garden terrace for both dinner and, on Saturdays and Sundays, breakfast.

157 Commercial St. ✆ **508/487-1327.** www.themartinhouse.com. Reservations recommended. Main courses $16–$33. AE, DC, DISC, MC, V. May–Oct daily 6–11pm, Sat–Sun 9am–12:30pm; Feb–Apr and Nov–Dec Thurs–Sun 6–10pm. Closed Jan.

The Red Inn ★★ NEW AMERICAN New owners have turned this property at the far west end of Commercial Street into one of the toughest reservations to get in town. The dining room with its wraparound floor-to-ceiling windows has great beach views. The refined atmosphere makes this a favorite for special occasions, when your dinner might begin with a glass of champagne and end with a soufflé. This is fine dining on the calorie-rich side, with entrees like grilled thick pork chops with tomatillo salsa and pepper-crusted filet mignon with truffle mashed potatoes and Jack Daniel's sauce. There are always fresh fish and vegetarian main courses on the menu also.

15 Commercial St. ✆ **508/487-7334.** Reservations required. www.theredinn.com. Main courses $21–$38. AE, DC, DISC, MC, V. Mid-June to early Sept daily 5:30–10pm, Sat–Sun 10am–2:30pm; call for off-season hours.

EXPENSIVE

Devon's ★★ NEW AMERICAN You can tell which one is Devon. He's the one seating people, acting as line cook, busing tables, taking reservations, and chatting with customers. The force behind Devon's is a multi-talented restaurateur with a great attitude. The tiny restaurant itself, a former boat shack, has fewer than 10 tables inside, all next to the open kitchen. In good weather, the choice seats are on the patio out front. Service is professional and the food elegantly prepared and nicely presented. The menu changes often but features wonderful fish, steak, chicken, and vegetarian meals. One favorite is sole with a simple beurre blanc sauce. This is a romantic option, but you definitely need a reservation. It's also a good choice for breakfast for those staying in the far East End of town.

401½ Commercial St. (in the East End). ✆ **508/487-4773.** Reservations recommended. Main courses $18–$25. DISC, MC, V. June–Sept Thurs–Tues 8am–1pm and 6–10pm; call for off-season hours. Closed Nov–Apr.

Front Street ★★ MEDITERRANEAN FUSION/ITALIAN For years, this restaurant has delivered high-quality food and service, and locals consider it a cherished locale. Located in a belowground space on Commercial Street, this cozy restaurant feels most comfortable in the chilly days of spring and summer. Chef Donna Aliperti is constantly improving her menu, inspired by trips to Italy and southern France. The fusion menu, available in season, has creative items like soft-shell crabs with corn-studded risotto and Chinese five-spice grilled duckling. There is also a traditional Italian menu with pastas available every night.

230 Commercial St. ✆ **508/487-9715.** www.frontstreetrestaurant.com. Reservations recommended. Main courses $18–$25. DISC, MC, V. June–Sept daily 6–10pm. Call for off-season hours.

Lorraine's ★★ MEXICAN/NEW AMERICAN Long heralded by year-rounders as a spot for creative food and a festive atmosphere, Lorraine's is on the far west end of Commercial Street. Even those who shy away from Mexican restaurants should try the truly unique food here. Maryland soft-shell crabs are lightly dusted in flour with Chimayo chile powder and pan-sautéed and served with a jalapeño aioli. For a main course, consider *viere verde*—sea scallops sautéed with tomatillos, flambéed in tequila, and cloaked in a green-chile sauce. For a treat, check out the extensive tequila menu; shots are served with a wonderful tomato juice-based chaser.

133 Commercial St. (in the West End). ✆ **508/487-6074.** Reservations suggested. Main courses $17–$26. DISC, MC, V. June–Sept daily 6–10pm; call for off-season hours. Closed mid-Dec to Mar.

The Mews & Cafe Mews ★★ INTERNATIONAL/AMERICAN FUSION Bank on fine food and suave service at this beachfront restaurant, an enduring favorite since 1961. Upstairs is the cafe with its century-old mahogany bar and lighter menu. The dining room downstairs sits right on the beach. The best soup in the region is The Mews' scrumptious summertime special, chilled cucumber-miso bisque with curry shrimp timbale. Among the showier entrees is "captured scallops": prime Wellfleet specimens enclosed with a shrimp-and-crab mousse in a crisp wonton pouch and served atop a petite filet mignon with chipotle aioli. Desserts and coffees—take them upstairs in the cafe to the accompaniment of soft-jazz piano—are delectable.

429 Commercial St. ✆ **508/487-1500.** Reservations recommended. www.mews.com. Main courses $18–$29. AE, DC, DISC, MC, V. Mid-June to early Sept daily 6–10pm, Sun 11am–2:30pm; late Sept to mid-June daily 6–10pm only. Open year-round.

MODERATE

Bubala's by the Bay ★ ECLECTIC This trendy bistro promises "serious food at sensible prices." And that's what it delivers: from buttermilk waffles to creative focaccia sandwiches to fajitas, Cajun calamari, and pad Thai. This is a big operation for Provincetown, and the huge outdoor patio facing Commercial Street is particularly popular in the morning. In season, there's entertainment nightly from 10pm to 1am.

183 Commercial St. (in the West End). ✆ **508/487-0773.** Main courses $10–$21. AE, DISC, MC, V. Apr–mid-Oct daily 8am–11pm. Closed late Oct to Apr.

Café Heaven ★ AMERICAN Prized for its leisurely country breakfasts (served until midafternoon, for reluctant risers), this modern storefront—adorned with big, bold paintings by acclaimed Wellfleet artist John Grillo—also turns out substantial sandwiches, such as avocado and goat cheese on a French baguette. For dinner, Café Heaven becomes a Thai restaurant.

199 Commercial St. (in the center of town). ✆ **508/487-9639.** Reservations not accepted. Most items $11–$18. No credit cards. July–Aug daily 8am–3pm and 6:30–10pm; call for off-season hours. Closed Feb–May.

The Commons Bistro & Bar ★★ ECLECTIC/FRENCH BISTRO It's a tossup: The sidewalk cafe provides an optimal opportunity for studying P-town's inimitable street life, while the plum-colored dining room is a refuge adorned with the owners' extraordinary collection of Toulouse-Lautrec prints. Either way, you'll get to partake of tasty and creative fare. At lunch, the lobster club sandwich on country bread is unbeatable. The Commons boasts the only wood-fired oven in town to date, which comes in handy in preparing the popular gourmet pizzas with unique toppings. At dinner, try the paella with roasted chicken, chorizo, clams, mussels, and shrimp. The Commons also serves as an all-day coffee shop, with cappuccinos and baked goods.

386 Commercial St. ✆ **508/487-7800.** www.commonsghb.com. Reservations recommended. Main courses $10–$26. AE, MC, V. Mid-June to mid-Sept daily 8am–3pm and 6–10:30pm; call for off-season hours. Closed Nov–Mar.

Fanizzi's By The Sea ★ *Value* ITALIAN/SEAFOOD This waterfront restaurant in the far East End of town is the perfect place to get away from all the hustle and bustle in the town center. The beauty of this casual restaurant is that you can have a burger and fries, comfort food like Mom's meatloaf, or splurge on shrimp scampi, and it's all very reasonably priced. The view from the large wraparound plate glass windows is among the best in town. The $13 buffet brunch, served until 2pm on Sundays, is a good deal.

539 Commercial St. (in the far east end of town). ✆ **508/487-1964.** Reservations accepted. Main courses $9–$21. AE, MC, V. Mid-June to mid-Sept Mon–Sat 11:30am–10pm, Sun 10am–9pm; call for off-season hours. Open year-round.

Napi's ★★ INTERNATIONAL Restaurateur Napi Van Dereck can be credited with bringing P-town's restaurant scene up to speed—back in the early 1970s. His namesake restaurant still reflects that zeitgeist, with its rococo-hippie carpentry, select outtakes from his sideline in antiques, and some rather outstanding art. The cuisine is a lot less granola than it was, or maybe we've just caught up—hearty peasant fare never really goes out of style. And these peasants really get around, culling dumplings from China, falafel from Syria, and, from Greece, shrimp feta flambéed with ouzo and Metaxa. Unusual in Provincetown, this restaurant has its own parking lot (around back).

7 Freeman St. (at Bradford St.). ✆ **800/571-6274** or 508/487-1145. Reservations recommended. Main courses $14–$26. DISC, MC, V. May to mid-Sept daily 5–10pm; mid-Sept to Apr daily 11:30am–4pm and 5–9pm.

INEXPENSIVE

Chach ★ *Finds* DINER A diner run by a chef instead of a cook means the omelets are divine, the BLTs are heavenly, and there are all kinds of little surprises on the menu, like Mexican specials. It's a little off the beaten track, but it's worth seeking out Chach's for reasonably priced dining without the crowds you find on Commercial Street.

73 Shankpainter Rd. (off Bradford St., a few blocks south of town). ✆ **508/487-1530.** Under $10. No credit cards. May–Aug Thurs–Tues 7am–3pm; Sept–Feb and Apr 8am–2:30pm. Closed Mar.

Clem and Ursie's ★ *Kids* *Finds* SEAFOOD /BARBECUE Grab a picnic table for a big family dinner of fried seafood and barbecue ribs. More elaborate choices include bouillabaisse and Japanese udon (fish, shellfish, and vegetables in a dashi broth over noodles). The children's menu offers a choice of $5 entrees with fries, drink, dessert, and a surprise. Takeout is popular here, as is the separate ice cream section.

85 Shankpainter Rd. (off Bradford St., a few blocks south of town). ✆ **508/487-2333.** Main courses $6–$17. MC, V. Apr to mid-Oct daily 11am–10pm. Closed mid-Oct to Mar.

TAKEOUT & PICNIC FARE

Mojo's ★, 5 Ryder St. Ext. (✆ **508/487-3140**), is a seafood shack known for its lightly breaded fried fish and hand-cut fries. There are also veggie burgers, burritos, and chicken tenders. Eat at one of the six picnic tables on the patio or take it to the beach. Closed mid-Oct to early May.

The best gourmet shop is **Angel Foods,** 467 Commercial St., in the East End (✆ **508/487-6666**), which offers Italian specialties and other prepared foods.

The rollwiches—pita bread packed with a wide range of fillings—at **Box Lunch,** 353 Commercial St., in the center of town (✆ **508/487-6026**), are ideal for a strolling lunch.

CYBERCAFE

To check your e-mail, surf online, or just hang out with techies, stop by **Cyber Cove,** an Internet lounge on the second floor of Whalers' Wharf on Commercial Street (✆ **508/487-7778;** www.cybercove-ptown.com).

PROVINCETOWN AFTER DARK

To order tickets for any of the shows at Provincetown's nightclubs and cabarets, call **Ptown Tix** (✆ **508/487-9793;** ptowntix.com).

An on-again, off-again contender for hottest club in town is **Club Euro,** 258 Commercial St., 2nd floor, beside Town Hall (✆ **508/487-8800**), the current home of "Two Fags and a Drag" and the ever-popular all-star musical comedy drag revue "Big Boned Barbies," starring Kandi Kane. Closed October to May.

Perhaps the nation's premier gay bar, **The Atlantic House** ★, 6 Masonic Place, off Commercial Street (✆ **508/487-3821**), is open year-round. The "A-House" also welcomes straights, except in the leather-oriented Macho Bar upstairs. In the little bar downstairs, check out the Tennessee Williams memorabilia, including a portrait *au naturel.*

Come late afternoon, if you're wondering where all the beachgoers went, it's a safe bet that a number are attending the gay-lesbian tea dance held daily in season from 3:30 to 6:30pm on the pool deck at the **Boatslip Beach Club** ★, 161 Commercial St. (✆ **508/487-1669**). The action then shifts to the **Pied,** 193 Commercial St. (✆ **508/487-1527**; www.pied.com), for its After Tea T-Dance from 5 to 10pm, but returns to the Boatslip later in the evening for disco. Closed November through April.

Crown & Anchor ★, 247 Commercial St. (✆ **508/487-1430;** www.thecrownand anchor.net), houses a number of bars spanning leather, disco, comedy, drag shows, and cabaret. Facilities include a pool bar and game room. Closed November through April.

One of P-town's top clubs, the **Post Office Café and Cabaret,** 303 Commercial St. (✆ **508/487-3892**), despite its cramped space, can be depended on for amusing drag and comedy shows. In recent years, the B-Girlz (Hard Kora, Barbie-Q, and Belle Bottom) have been the featured act. The cover is $20. Closed November to April.

The chic women's bar, **Vixen,** at the Pilgrim House, 336 Commercial St. (✆ **508/487-6424**), features local and national jazz, blues, and comedy acts, including such favorites as Lea DeLaria and Melissa Ferrick a couple times a season. There are also pool tables. Closed November to April.

Governor Bradford, 312 Commercial St. (✆ **508/487-2781**), is a good old bar, featuring pool tables, drag karaoke (summer nights at 9:30pm), and disco.

CAPE COD NATIONAL SEASHORE ★★★

No trip to Cape Cod would be complete without a visit to the **Cape Cod National Seashore** on the Outer Cape. Take an afternoon barefoot stroll along the "The Great Beach," and see why the Cape attracts so many artists and poets. On August 7, 1961, President John F. Kennedy signed a bill designating 27,000 acres in the 40 miles from Chatham to Provincetown as the Cape Cod National Seashore. However, as early as the 1930s, the National Park Service had been interested in Cape Cod's ocean beach; back then the land would have cost taxpayers about $10 an acre! Unusual for a national park, the Seashore includes 500 private residences, the owners of which lease land from the park service. Convincing residents that a National Seashore would be a good thing for Cape Cod was an arduous task back then, and Provincetown still grapples with Seashore officials over town land issues.

ESSENTIALS

GETTING THERE Take Route 6, the Mid-Cape Highway, to Eastham; it's about 50 miles from the Sagamore Bridge.

VISITOR INFORMATION Pick up a map of the National Seashore at the **Salt Pond Visitor Center,** in Eastham (✆ **508/225-3421**). It's open daily: late May to early September from 9am to 5pm, early September to late May from 9am to 4:30pm. A $3-million rehab of the visitor center was completed recently. There is also the **Province Lands Visitor Center** (p. 249), a smaller site, in Provincetown. Both centers have ranger activities, gift shops, and restrooms. Seashore beaches are all clearly marked off Route 6. Additional beaches along this stretch are run by individual towns; you must have a sticker or pay a fee to park.

BEACHES & GETTING OUTSIDE

BEACHES The Seashore's claim to fame is its spectacular beaches—in reality, one long beach—with dunes 50 to 150 feet high. This is the Atlantic Ocean, so the surf is rough (and cold), but a number of the beaches have lifeguards. A $45 pass will get you into all of them for the season, or you can pay a daily rate of $15. Most of the Seashore beaches have large parking lots, but you'll need to arrive early (before 10am) on busy summer weekends to claim a spot. If the beach you want to go to is full, try the one next door—most of the beaches are 5 to 10 miles apart. Don't forget your beach umbrella—the sun can get intense.

- **Coast Guard Beach** ★★★ and **Nauset Light Beach** ★★★, off Ocean View Drive, Eastham: Connected to outlying parking lots by a free shuttle, these pristine beaches have lifeguards and restrooms. With the old Coast Guard building on one and the striped lighthouse on the other, these two strands are among the most scenic in the Seashore.
- **Head of the Meadow Beach** ★★, off Head of the Meadow Road, Truro: Among the more remote National Seashore beaches, this spot (with restrooms) is known for its excellent surf. Because beachgoers don't have to traverse steep dunes to get here, Head of the Meadow is easier for seniors or those with disabilities to access.
- **Marconi Beach** ★★, off Marconi Beach Road in South Wellfleet: The bluffs are so high here that the beach lies in shadows by late afternoon. Restrooms are available.
- **Race Point Beach** ★★★ and **Herring Cove Beach** ★★★, off Route 6, Provincetown: Race Point has rough surf, and you might even spot a whale on its way to Stellwagen Bank, a breeding ground. Herring Cove, with much calmer waters, is a good place to watch sunsets, and is popular with same-sex couples.

BICYCLING Some say the best bike path on Cape Cod is the **Province Lands Trail** ★★★, 5 swooping and invigorating miles at Race Point Beach. There is also a 2-mile, relatively flat path linking Head of the Meadow Beach to High Head Beach in Truro.

FISHING Surf-casting is allowed from the ocean beaches. Race Point is a popular spot.

NATURE TRAILS The Seashore has a number of walking trails—all free, all picturesque. In Eastham, **Fort Hill** ★★★, off Route 6, has one of the best scenic views on Cape Cod, as well as a popular boardwalk trail through a red maple swamp. Following the trail markers around Fort Hill, you'll pass "Indian Rock" (bearing the marks of untold generations who used it to sharpen their tools) and enjoy scenic vantage points overlooking the channel-carved marsh and out to sea. The Fort Hill Trail hooks up with the .5-mile Red Cedar Swamp Trail, offering boardwalk views of an ecology otherwise inaccessible.

The **Nauset Marsh Trail** ★ is accessed from the Salt Pond Visitor Center, on Route 6 in Eastham. **Great Island** ★★, on the bay side in Wellfleet, is one of the finest places to have a picnic; you could spend the day hiking the trails. On **Pamet Trail** ★, off North Pamet Road in Truro, hikers pass the decrepit old cranberry-bog building on the way to a trail through the dunes. Don't try the old boardwalk trail over the bogs here; it has flooded and is no longer in use. The **Atlantic White Cedar Swamp Trail** ★★ is located at the Marconi Wireless Station site (described below). **Small Swamp** ★ and **Pilgrim Spring** ★ trails are found at Pilgrim Heights Beach. **Beech Forest Trail** ★★ is located at Race Point in Provincetown.

Tips Recommended Reading

Henry David Thoreau's *Cape Cod* is an entertaining account of the author's journeys on the Cape in the late 19th century. The writer/naturalist walked along the beach from Eastham to Provincetown, and you can follow in his footsteps. Henry Beston's *The Outermost House,* originally published in 1928 (Henry Holt, 2003), describes a year of living on the beach in Eastham in a simple one-room dune shack. The shack washed out to sea about 20 years ago, but "The Great Beach" remains. Michael Cunningham's *Land's End: A Walk in Provincetown* (Crown, 2002) is a brief, engrossing meditation, travelogue, and memoir about the little town at the tip of Cape Cod.

SEASHORE SIGHTS The **Old Harbor Lifesaving Station** ★, Race Point Beach off Race Point Road, Provincetown (✆ **508/487-1256**), was one of 13 lifesaving stations mandated by Congress in the late 19th century. This shingled shelter with a lookout tower was part of a network responsible for saving some 100,000 lives. Before the U.S. Lifesaving Service was founded in 1872 (it became part of the Coast Guard in 1915), shipwreck victims lucky enough to be washed ashore were still doomed unless they could find a "charity shed"—a hut supplied with firewood—maintained by the Massachusetts Humane Society. The six valiant "Surfmen" manning each lifesaving station took a more active approach, patrolling the beach at all hours and rowing out into the surf to save all they could. Their old equipment is on view at this museum. Admission is free; there's a parking fee for Race Point Beach (see "Beaches," above). It's open daily from 3 to 5pm in July and August; call for off-season hours. Closed November through April.

The **Marconi Wireless Station,** on Marconi Park Site Road (off Rte. 6), South Wellfleet (✆ **508/349-3785**), tells the story of the first international telegraphic communication. It's from this spot that inventor Guglielmo Marconi sent the world's first wireless communiqué: "Cordial greetings from President Theadore [sic] Roosevelt to King Edward VII in Poldhu, Wales." It was also here, in 1912, that news of the *Titanic* first reached these shores. There's scarcely a trace left of this extraordinary feat of technology (the station was dismantled in 1920); still, the outdoor displays convey the leap of imagination that was required.

The **Captain Edward Penniman House** ★, at Fort Hill off Route 6 in Eastham, is a grandly ornate 1868 Second Empire mansion. It's open for tours in season, but the exterior far outshines the interior. Call the visitor center (✆ **508/255-3421**) for times. Check out the huge whale jawbone gate before crossing the street to the trails (see "Nature Trails," above).

Five lighthouses, all automated now, dot the Seashore. In 1996, both Nauset Light, in Eastham, and Highland Light, in Truro, were successfully moved from precarious positions on the edge of dunes in order to save the beloved lighthouses. **Nauset Light** ★, with its cheerful red stripe, was originally moved to Eastham from Chatham in 1923. The lighthouse flashes an alternating red and white light that can be seen for 23 miles; public tours are offered.

Highland Light ★★, also known as **Cape Cod Light,** is the site of the first light in this area, dating back to 1798. The present structure was built in 1857. Follow signs from Route 6 in North Truro to the end of Highland Road. This lighthouse, set high on a cliff, was the first light seen by ships traveling from Europe. Now that the structure has been moved back from the eroding cliff, visitors are allowed to climb the staircase to the top with a guide. ***Note:*** There's a minimum 4-foot height requirement for climbing the lighthouse. Nearby is the 1907 **Highland House** ★★, home of the collections of the Truro Historical Society. Admission to both lighthouse and museum is $5 for adults, free for children under 12. Both are open June through September, daily from 10am to 5pm.

Wood End Light, on Long Point in Provincetown, is an unusual square lighthouse built as a "twin" to Long Point Light in 1873. Hearty souls can hike first across the breakwater at the west end of Commercial Street and then about a ½ mile over soft sand to see this lighthouse.

Long Point Light, established in 1827, is isolated at the very tip of Cape Cod. It's about a 1½-hour walk from the breakwater, or a short boat ride from the center of Provincetown. Its fixed green light can be seen for 8 miles. This lighthouse was once the center of a thriving fishing community in the 1800s. Storms and erosion led the community to float their houses across the bay to Provincetown's West End, where a couple of the houses—some of the oldest in town—are still standing.

7

Martha's Vineyard & Nantucket

by Laura M. Reckford

Megastars and CEOs, vacationing families, and penniless students all seek refuge on Martha's Vineyard and Nantucket, two picturesque islands off the coast of Cape Cod. Both islands have much to offer families with children and couples seeking a romantic getaway. Their fame as summer resorts doesn't begin to take into account their rich history, diverse communities, and artistic traditions. But the popularity of these islands means that if you must go in the middle of summer, expect crowds and even—yikes!—traffic jams.

While only about 25 nautical miles apart, each island has its own distinct personality. Martha's Vineyard, large enough to support a year-round population spanning a broad socioeconomic spectrum, is not quite as rarefied as Nantucket. Vineyarders pride themselves on their liberal stances. True, a prime oceanside estate might fetch millions here, but the residents still dicker over the price of zucchini at the local farmers' market.

Nantucket, flash-frozen in the mid–19th century through zealous zoning, has long been considered a Republican haven. It's rich and traditional. Social scene aside, Nantucket has more pristine public shores than the Vineyard, as well as the best upscale shopping in the region. But there's something for everyone on both islands, and an island vacation is bound to be one that's cherished for many years.

1 Martha's Vineyard ★★★

With 100 square miles, Martha's Vineyard is New England's largest island, yet each of its six communities is blessed with endearing small-town charm. When the former First Family vacationed here, locals joked that the Clintons tested their reputed nonchalance toward famous faces. But don't visit the Vineyard for the celebrities. Instead, savor the decidedly laid-back pace of this unique place.

Most visitors don't take the time to explore the entire island, staying in the "down-island" towns of **Vineyard Haven** ★ (officially called Tisbury), **Edgartown** ★★★, and **Oak Bluffs** ★★★. The "up-island" towns—**West Tisbury** ★★, **Chilmark** ★ (including the fishing village of **Menemsha** ★★★), and **Aquinnah** ★ (formerly known as Gay Head)—tend to be less touristy.

By all means, admire the regal sea captains' homes in Edgartown. Stroll down Circuit Avenue in Oak Bluffs with a Mad Martha's ice-cream cone, then ride the Flying Horses Carousel, said to be the oldest working carousel in the nation. Check out the cheerful "gingerbread" cottages behind Circuit Avenue, where the echoes of 19th-century revival meetings still ring out from the imposing tabernacle.

But don't forget to journey "up-island" to marvel at the red-clay cliffs of Aquinnah, a national historic landmark. Or bike the country roads of West Tisbury and Chilmark. Buy a lobster roll in the fishing village of Menemsha. There's a surprising degree of diversity here, for those who take the time to discover it.

ESSENTIALS

GETTING THERE

BY FERRY Most visitors take a ferry from the mainland to the Vineyard. You'll most likely catch the ferry from the village of Woods Hole in the town of Falmouth on Cape Cod; however, boats also run from Falmouth Inner Harbor, Hyannis, New Bedford, Rhode Island, and Nantucket. It's easy to get a passenger ticket on almost any of the ferries, but space for cars is extremely limited, especially on summer weekends, when reservations must be made months in advance. Unless you absolutely must have your car with you, leave it on the mainland. Traffic and parking on the island can be brutal in summer, and it's easy to take shuttle buses (see below) from town to town or simply bike around.

From Woods Hole in Falmouth The state-run **Steamship Authority** (**© 508/477-8600** for reservations and information from Apr 4–Sept 7 daily 7am–9pm, and reduced hours the rest of the year; or 508/693-9130 daily 8am–5pm; www.steamshipauthority.com) operates daily, year-round, weather permitting. It maintains the only ferries to Martha's Vineyard that accommodate cars. These large ferries make the 45-minute trip to Vineyard Haven throughout the year; some boats go to Oak Bluffs from late May to late October (call for seasonal schedules). The cost of a round-trip car passage from mid-May to mid-October is $124 to $144; in the off season it drops to $78 to $98. The higher rates are for vehicles more than 16 feet long. Car rates do not include drivers or passengers.

Although you can buy tickets over the phone, it's much faster to purchase them online at the boat line's website **www.steamshipauthority.com**.

Many people prefer to leave their cars on the mainland, take the ferry (often with their bikes), and then travel around the island by shuttle bus or taxi, or rent a bicycle, car, or jeep on the island. You can park your car at the Woods Hole lots (always full in the summer) or at one of the many lots in Falmouth and Bourne that absorb the overflow of cars. Parking costs $10 per day. Free shuttle buses (some equipped for bikes) run regularly from the outlying lots to the Woods Hole ferry terminal. If you're leaving your car on the mainland, plan to arrive at the parking lots at least an hour before sailing time to allow for parking, taking the free shuttle bus to the ferry terminal, and buying your ferry ticket.

The cost of a round-trip passenger ticket on the ferry to Martha's Vineyard is $14 for adults and $8 for children 5 to 12. Bringing a bike costs an extra $6 round-trip. You do not need a reservation on the ferry if you're traveling without a car, and there are no reservations needed for parking.

From Falmouth Inner Harbor, you can board the ***Island Queen*** (**© 508/548-4800;** www.islandqueen.com) for a 35-minute cruise to Oak Bluffs (passengers only). The boat runs from late May to mid-October; round-trip fare is $12 for adults, $6 for children under 13, and an extra $6 for bikes. There are seven crossings a day in season (eight on Fri and Sun), and no reservations are needed. Parking runs $15 a day. Credit cards are not accepted.

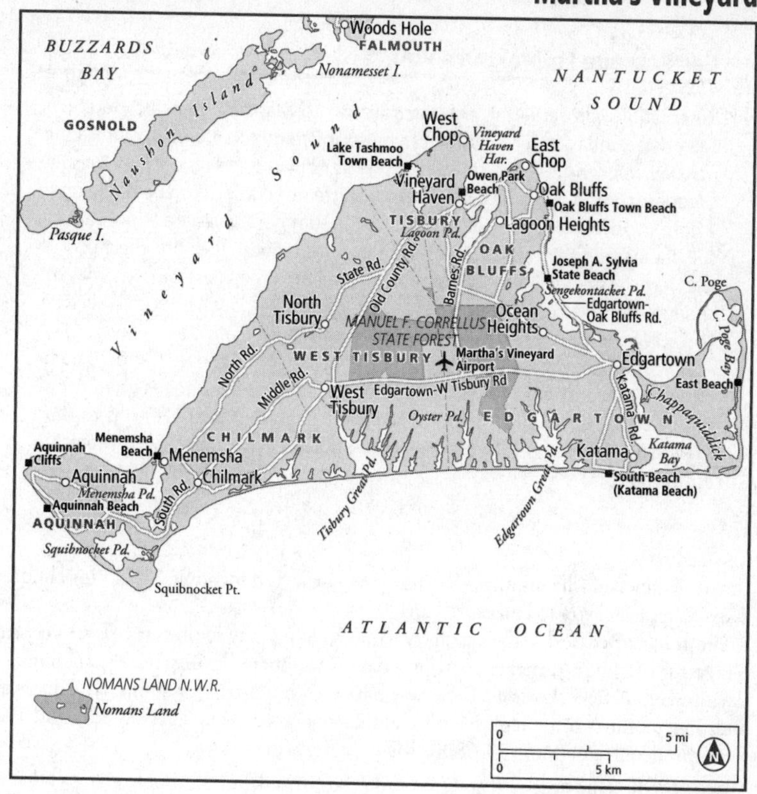

The **Falmouth–Edgartown Ferry Service,** 278 Scranton Ave. (**© 508/548-9400;** www.falmouthferry.com), operates a 1-hour passenger ferry, called the ***Pied Piper,*** from Falmouth Harbor to Edgartown. The boat runs from late May to mid-October; reservations are required. In season, there are five crossings a day (six on Fri). Round-trip fares are $30 for adults and $24 for children under 12. Bicycles are $8 round-trip. Parking is $18 per day.

From Hyannis Early June through late September, **Hy-Line,** Ocean Street Dock (**© 508/778-2600;** www.hy-linecruises.com), operates from the Ocean Street dock to Oak Bluffs on Martha's Vineyard. It runs three trips a day; travel time is about 1 hour and 45 minutes. A round-trip costs $32 for adults and $17 for children 5 to 12 ($10 extra for bikes). It's a good idea to reserve a parking spot in Hyannis; the all-day fee is $10.

Hy-Line also operates a **fast ferry** from Hyannis to Martha's Vineyard. It departs five times daily in season and takes 55 minutes. Round-trip tickets cost $53 for adults, $40 for children.

From Nantucket From early June to mid-September, **Hy-Line,** Ocean Street Dock (**© 508/778-2600;** www.hy-linecruises.com), runs three passenger ferries to Oak Bluffs on Martha's Vineyard. There is no car-ferry service between the islands. The trip

Car Passage to Martha's Vineyard

Reservations are required to bring your car to Martha's Vineyard on Friday, Saturday, Sunday, and Monday from mid-June to mid-September, plus Memorial Day weekend. During these months, standby is in effect only on Tuesday, Wednesday, and Thursday. Technically, vehicle reservations can be made up to 1 hour in advance of ferry departure, but in summer ferries are almost always full. Be aware that your space may be forfeited if you have not checked into the ferry terminal 30 minutes prior to sailing time. Reservations may be changed to another date and time with at least 24 hours' notice; otherwise, you will have to pay for an additional ticket for your vehicle.

If you arrive without a reservation on a day that allows standby, come early and be prepared to wait in line for hours. Your passage is guaranteed if you're in line by 2pm on designated standby days. For up-to-date **Steamship Authority** information, check out their website (www.steamship authority.com).

time is 2 hours and 15 minutes. The one-way fare is $16 for adults, $8.25 for children 5 to 12, and $5 extra for bikes.

From New Bedford The fast ferry M/V Whaling City Express travels to Martha's Vineyard in 1 hour. It makes six trips a day in season and is in service year-round, 7 days a week. A ticket costs $20 one-way and $40 round-trip for adults, $17 one-way and $34 round-trip for seniors and children under 12. Contact New England Fast Ferry for details (✆ **866/453-6800;** www.nefastferry.com).

From North Kingstown, Rhode Island From mid-June through October **Vineyard Fast Ferry** (✆ **401/295-4040;** www.vineyardfastferry.com) runs the high-speed catamaran, *Millennium,* to Oak Bluffs two to three round-trips daily. The trip takes 90 minutes. The ferry leaves from Quonset Point, about 10 minutes from Route I-95, 15 minutes from T.F. Green Airport in Providence, and 20 minutes from the Amtrak station in Kingston. There is dockside parking. Rates are $72 round-trip for adults; $54 round-trip for children 4 to 12; free for children under 4; and $10 round-trip for bikes. Parking next to the ferry port is $8 per day.

BY PLANE You can fly into **Martha's Vineyard Airport,** also known as Dukes County Airport (✆ **508/693-7022**), in West Tisbury, about 5 miles outside Edgartown.

Airlines serving the Vineyard include **Cape Air/Nantucket Airlines** (✆ **800/352-0714** or 508/771-6944), which connects the island year-round with Boston (trip time 34 min.; hourly shuttle service in summer costs about $240 round-trip), Hyannis (trip time 20 min., cost $80), Nantucket (15 min., $89), and New Bedford (20 min., $83); and **US Airways** (✆ **800/428-4322**), which flies from Boston for about $215 round-trip and also has seasonal weekend service from La Guardia (trip time 1 hr. 15 min.), which costs approximately $400 round-trip.

Year-round charter service is offered by **Direct Flight** (✆ **508/693-6688**). **Westchester Air** (✆ **800/759-2929**) runs some charters out of White Plains, New York.

BY BUS **Bonanza Bus Lines** (✆ **888/751-8800** or 508/548-7588; www.bonanzabus.com) connects the Woods Hole ferry port with Boston (from South Station), New York

City, and Providence, Rhode Island. The trip from South Station in Boston takes about 1 hour and 35 minutes and costs about $17 one-way, $30 round-trip; from Boston's Logan Airport, the cost is $22 one-way, $40 round-trip; from New York, the bus trip to Woods Hole takes about 6 hours and costs approximately $52 one-way or $93 round-trip.

BY LIMO **King's Coach** (© **800/235-5669** or 508/563-5669) will pick you up at Boston's Logan Airport and take you to meet your ferry in Woods Hole (or anywhere else in the Upper Cape area). The trip takes about 90 minutes depending on traffic, and costs about $125 one-way plus a gratuity for a carload or a vanload of people. You'll need to book the service a couple of days in advance. **Falmouth Taxi** (© **508/548-3100**) also runs limo service from Boston and the airport to the Woods Hole ferry terminal.

GETTING AROUND

BY BICYCLE & MOPED The best way to explore the Vineyard is on two wheels. There's a little of everything for cyclists, from paved paths to hilly country roads (see "Exploring the Vineyard on Two Wheels," later in this chapter, for details on where to ride).

Mopeds, which you need a driver's license to rent and a helmet to ride, are also a way to navigate Vineyard roads, but be aware they are considered quite dangerous on the island's busy, winding, and sandy roads—the number of accidents involving mopeds seems to rise every year. Also, islanders tend to feel quite negatively about mopeds.

Bike-rental shops are clustered in all three down-island towns. Scooter- and moped-rental shops are only in Oak Bluffs and Vineyard Haven. Bike rentals cost about $20 a day (the higher prices are for suspension mountain bikes), scooters and mopeds $46 to $85. For bike rentals in Vineyard Haven, try **Strictly Bikes,** Union Street (© **508/693-0782**); or **Martha's Bike Rentals,** Lagoon Pond Road (© **508/693-6593**). For mopeds, try **Adventure/Thrifty Rentals,** Beach Road (© **508/693-1959**). In Oak Bluffs, there's **Anderson's,** Circuit Avenue Extension (© **508/693-9346**), which rents bikes only; **DeBettencourt's Bike Shop,** 31 Circuit Ave. Extension (© **508/693-0011**), which is across from the Island Queen ferry landing; and **Sun 'n' Fun,** Lake Avenue (© **508/693-5457**). In Edgartown, you'll find bike rentals only at **R. W. Cutler Bike,** 1 Main St. (© **508/627-4052**); **Edgartown Bicycles,** 190 Upper Main St. (© **508/627-9008**); and **Wheel Happy,** 204 Upper Main St. and 8 S. Water St. (© **508/627-5928**).

BY CAR If you're here for a long visit or you want to do some exploring up-island, you may want to bring a car or rent one on the island. Keep in mind that car-rental rates can soar during peak season, and gas is also much more expensive on the island. Representatives of national car-rental chains are located at the airport and in Vineyard Haven and Oak Bluffs. Local agencies also operate out of all three port towns, and many of them rent jeeps, mopeds, and bikes in addition to cars. The national chains include **Budget** (© **800/527-0700** or 508/693-1911), **Hertz** (© **800/654-3131**), and **Thrifty** (© **800/874-4389**).

For local agencies, in Vineyard Haven, you'll find **Adventure Rentals,** Beach Road (© **508/693-1959**); and in Edgartown, **AAA Island Rentals,** 141 Main St. (© **508/627-6800**). Operating out of the airport is **All Island Rent-a-Car** (© **508/693-6868**).

BY SHUTTLE BUS In season, shuttle buses certainly run often enough to make them a practical means of getting around. They are also cheap, dependable, and easy.

The **Martha's Vineyard Regional Transit Authority** (✆ **508/693-9440;** www.vineyardtransit.com) operates shuttle buses year-round on about a dozen routes around the island. The buses, which are white with purple logos, cost about $2 to $5 depending on distance. The formula is $1 per town. For example, Vineyard Haven to Oak Bluffs is $2, but Vineyard Haven to Edgartown (passing through Oak Bluffs) is $3. A 1-day pass is $6; a 3-day pass is $15. The Edgartown Downtown Shuttle and the South Beach buses circle throughout town or out to South Beach every 20 minutes in season. They also stop at the free parking lots just north of the town center—this is a great way to avoid circling the streets in search of a vacant spot on busy weekends. The main down-island stops are Vineyard Haven (near the ferry terminal), Oak Bluffs (near the Civil War statue in Ocean Park), and Edgartown (Church St., near the Old Whaling Church). From late June to early September, they run more frequently from 6am to midnight every 15 minutes or half-hour. Hours are reduced in spring and fall. Buses also go out to Aquinnah (via the airport, West Tisbury, and Chilmark), leaving every couple of hours from down-island towns and looping about every hour through up-island towns.

For bus tours of the island, call **Island Transport** (✆ **508/693-0058**) or hop on one of the Island Transport buses that are stationed at the ferry terminals in Vineyard Haven and Oak Bluffs in the summer.

BY TAXI Upon arrival, you'll find taxis at all ferry terminals and at the airport, and there are permanent taxi stands in Oak Bluffs (at the Flying Horses Carousel) and Edgartown (next to the Town Wharf). Most taxi outfits operate cars as well as vans for larger groups and travelers with bikes. Cab companies on the island include **Adam Cab** (✆ **800/281-4462** or 508/693-3332), **Accurate Cab** (✆ **888/557-9798** or 508/627-9798; the only 24-hr. service), **All Island Taxi** (✆ **800/693-TAXI** or 508/693-2929); and **Marlene's Taxi** (✆ **508/693-0037**). Rates from town to town in summer are generally flat fees based on where you're headed and the number of passengers on board. A trip from Vineyard Haven to Edgartown would probably cost around $15 for two people. Late-night revelers should keep in mind that rates double after midnight until 7am.

THE CHAPPAQUIDDICK FERRY From June to mid-October, the **On-Time ferry** (✆ **508/627-9427**) runs the 5-minute trip from Memorial Wharf on Dock Street in Edgartown to Chappaquiddick Island. It leaves every 5 minutes from 7am to midnight. Passengers, bikes, mopeds, dogs, and cars (three at a time) are all welcome. The one-way cost is $3 per person, $10 for one car/one driver, $6 for one bike/one person, and $5 for one moped or motorcycle/one person.

VISITOR INFORMATION

Contact the **Martha's Vineyard Chamber of Commerce** at Beach Rd., Vineyard Haven (P.O. Box 1698 Vineyard Haven, MA 02568; ✆ **508/693-0085;** fax 508/693-7589) or visit their website at **www.mvy.com**. There are also information booths at the ferry terminal in Vineyard Haven, across from the Flying Horses Carousel in Oak Bluffs, and on Church Street in Edgartown. For information on current events, check the two local newspapers, the **Vineyard Gazette** (www.mvgazette.com) and the **Martha's Vineyard Times** (www.mvtimes.com), for information on current events.

In case of an **emergency,** call ✆ **911** and/or head for the **Martha's Vineyard Hospital,** Linton Lane, Oak Bluffs (✆ **508/693-0410**), which has a 24-hour emergency room.

A STROLL AROUND EDGARTOWN ★★★

A good way to acclimate yourself to the pace and flavor of the Vineyard is to walk the streets of Edgartown. This walk starts at the Dr. Daniel Fisher House and meanders along for about a mile; it takes about 2 to 3 hours.

If you're driving, park at the free lots at the edge of town (you'll see signs on the roads from Vineyard Haven and West Tisbury) and bike or take the shuttle bus (it only costs 50¢) to the Edgartown Visitor Center on Church Street.

The **Dr. Daniel Fisher House** ★, 99 Main St. (✆ **508/627-8017**), is a prime example of Edgartown's trademark Greek Revival opulence. A key player in the 19th-century whaling trade, Dr. Fisher amassed a fortune sufficient to found the Martha's Vineyard National Bank. Built in 1840, his proud mansion boasts such classical elements as colonnaded porticos and a delicate roof walk.

Note: The only way to view the interior (now headquarters for the Martha's Vineyard Preservation Trust) is with a guided **Vineyard Historic Walking Tour** (✆ **508/627-8619**). This tour, which also takes in the neighboring Old Whaling Church, originates next door at the **Vincent House Museum.** Tours are offered June through September, Monday through Saturday noon to 3pm. The cost is $7 to $10 for adults, free for children 12 and under.

The **Vineyard House Museum** ★, off Main Street between Planting Field Way and Church Street, is a transplanted 1672 full Cape and is considered the oldest surviving dwelling on the island. The **Old Whaling Church** ★★, 89 Main St., is a magnificent 1843 Greek Revival edifice designed by local architect Frederick Baylies, Jr., and was built as a whaling boat would have been, out of massive pine beams; it boasts 27-foot windows and a 92-foot tower. Maintained by the Preservation Trust and still supporting a Methodist parish, the building is now primarily used as a performance venue.

Continuing down Main Street and turning right onto School Street, you'll pass another Baylies monument, the 1839 **Baptist Church,** which, having lost its spire, was converted into a private home with a rather grand, column-fronted facade. Two blocks farther is the **Vineyard Museum** ★★, 59 School St. (✆ **508/627-4441**), a fascinating complex assembled by the Dukes County Historical Society. This cluster of buildings contains exhibits of Native American crafts; an entire 1765 house; an extraordinary array of maritime art, and the Gay Head Light Tower's decommissioned Fresnel lens.

Give yourself enough time to explore the museum's curiosities before heading south 1 block on Cooke Street. Cater-cornered across South Summer Street, you'll spot the first of Baylies's impressive endeavors, the 1828 **Federated Church.** One block left are the offices of the ***Vineyard Gazette,*** 34 S. Summer St. (✆ **508/627-4311**). Operating out of a 1760 house, this exemplary small-town newspaper has been going strong since 1846.

Walk down South Summer Street to Main Street and take a right toward the water, stopping at any inviting shops along the way. Veer left on Dock Street to reach the **Old Sculpin Gallery,** 58 Dock St. (✆ **508/627-4881**), open from late June to mid-September. The output of the Martha's Vineyard Art Association is displayed. The real draw is the stark old building itself, which started out as a granary and spent the better part of the 20th century as a boat-building shop.

Cross the street to survey the harbor from the second-floor deck at Town Wharf. You can watch the tiny On-Time ferry make its 5-minute crossing to **Chappaquiddick Island** ★★. Don't bother looking for the original **Dyke Bridge,** infamous scene of the Kennedy/Kopechne scandal; it has been dismantled and, at long last, replaced.

Stroll down North Water Street to admire the many formidable captain's homes, several of which have been converted into inns. Each has a tale to tell. The 1750 **Daggett House** (no. 59), which is now a private inn, started out as a 1660 tavern, and the original beehive oven is flanked by a "secret" passageway. Nathaniel Hawthorne holed up at the **Edgartown Inn** (no. 56) for nearly a year in 1789 while writing *Twice Told Tales*—and, it is rumored, romancing a local maiden who inspired *The Scarlet Letter.* On your way back to Main Street, you'll pass the **Gardner–Colby Gallery** (no. 27), filled with beautiful island-inspired paintings.

After all that walking, stop for a drink at **The Newes from America,** 23 Kelley St., off N. Water St. © **508/627-4397**). This Colonial basement pub serves up specialty beers and the best French onion soup on the island (see "Where to Dine," later in this chapter).

BEACHES & OUTDOOR PURSUITS

BEACHES Most down-island beaches in Vineyard Haven, Oak Bluffs, and Edgartown are open to the public and are just a walk or a short bike ride from town. In season, shuttle buses make stops at **State Beach** between Oak Buffs and Edgartown. Most of the Vineyard's magnificent up-island shoreline is privately owned or restricted to residents, and thus off-limits to visitors. Renters in up-island communities, however, can obtain a beach sticker (around $35–$50 for a season sticker) for those private beaches by applying with a lease at the relevant **town hall:** West Tisbury, © **508/696-0147;** Chilmark, © **508/645-2115** or 508/645-2100; or Aquinnah, © **508/645-2300.** Also, many up-island inns offer the perk of temporary passes to the beautiful up-island beaches. In addition to the public beaches listed below, you might also track down a few hidden coves by requesting a map of conservation properties from the **Martha's Vineyard Land Bank** (© **508/627-7141**). Below is a list of visitor-friendly beaches.

- **Aquinnah Beach** ★★★ (Moshup Beach), off Moshup Trail: Parking costs $20 a day in season at this peaceful half-mile beach just east (Atlantic side) of the colorful cliffs. Although it is against the law, nudists tend to gravitate toward this beach. Because of rapid erosion, climbing the cliffs or taking clay for a souvenir is forbidden. Restrooms are near the parking lot, which is a 10-minute walk from the beach.
- **East Beach** ★★, Wasque (pronounced *Way*-squee) Reservation, Chappaquiddick: Relatively few people bother biking or hiking (or four-wheel driving) this far, so you should be able to find all the privacy you crave. Take the On-Time Ferry to Chappaquiddick, then go straight 2½ miles, and continue straight for another ½ mile on a dirt road. Biking on Chappaquiddick is one of the great Vineyard experiences, but the roads can be quite sandy and are best suited to a mountain bike. Along the dirt road, you'll pass **Mytoi,** a 14-acre Japanese garden open to the public, which is an oasis of flora and fauna. Because of its exposure on the east shore of the island, the surf here is rough. Pack a picnic; there are no stores on Chappy.

Edgartown

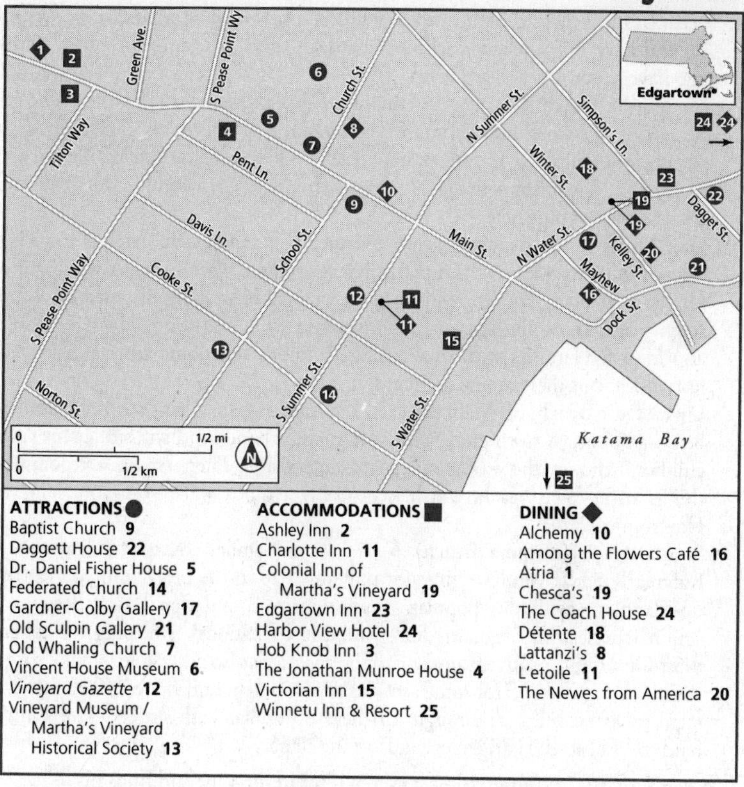

There is a portable toilet in the parking lot. Most people park their car near the Dike Bridge and walk the couple hundred yards out to the beach. Admission is $3 per person.

- **Joseph A. Sylvia State Beach** ★★★, midway between Oak Bluffs and Edgartown: Stretching a mile and flanked by a paved bike path, this placid beach has views of Cape Cod and Nantucket Sound and is prized for its gentle and (relatively) warm waves, which make it perfect for swimming. The drawbridge is a local landmark, and visitors and islanders alike have been jumping off it for years. Be aware that State Beach is one of the Vineyard's most popular; in midsummer, it's packed. The shuttle bus stops here, and roadside parking is also available—but it fills up fast, so stake your claim early. Located on the eastern shore of the island, this is a Nantucket Sound beach, so waters are shallow and rarely rough. There are no restrooms, and only the Edgartown end of the beach, known as Bend-in-the-Road Beach, has lifeguards.
- **Lake Tashmoo Town Beach** ★, off Herring Creek Road, Vineyard Haven: The only spot on the island where lake meets ocean, this tiny strip of sand is good for swimming and surf-casting but is somewhat marred by limited parking and often brackish waters. Nonetheless, this is a popular spot, as beachgoers enjoy a choice

between the Vineyard Sound beach with mild surf or the placid lake beach. Bikers will have no problem reaching this beach from Vineyard Haven; otherwise, you have to use a car to get here.

- **Menemsha Beach** ★★, next to Dutchers Dock in Menemsha Harbor: The gentle surf of this small but well-trafficked strand, with lifeguards and restrooms, is popular with families. In season, it's virtually wall-to-wall umbrellas. Nearby food vendors in Menemsha—selling everything from ice cream and hot dogs to shrimp cocktail—are a plus here.
- **Oak Bluffs Town Beach,** Seaview Avenue: This sandy strip extends from both sides of the ferry wharf, which makes it a convenient place to linger while waiting for the next boat. This is an in-town beach, within walking distance for visitors staying in Oak Bluffs. The surf is consistently calm and the sand smooth, so it's also ideal for families with small children. Public restrooms are available at the ferry dock, but there are no lifeguards.
- **Owen Park Beach,** off Main Street in Vineyard Haven: A tiny strip of harborside beach adjoining a town green with swings and a bandstand will suffice for young children, who, by the way, get lifeguard supervision. There are no restrooms, but this is an in-town beach, which is probably a quick walk from your Vineyard Haven inn.
- **South Beach (Katama Beach)** ★★★, about 4 miles south of Edgartown on Katama Road: If you have time for only one trip to the beach and you can't get up-island, go with this popular, 3-mile barrier strand that boasts heavy wave action (check with lifeguards for swimming conditions), sweeping dunes, and, most important, relatively ample parking space. It's also accessible by bike path or shuttle. Lifeguards patrol some sections of the beach, and there are sparsely scattered toilet facilities. The rough surf here is popular with surfers. ***Tip:*** Families tend to head to the left, college kids to the right.

A word about Aquinnah: Almost every visitor to the Vineyard finds his or her way to the cliffs, and with all the tour buses lined up in the huge parking lot and the rows of tacky concession stands and gift shops, this can seem like a rather outrageous tourist trap. You're right; it's not the Grand Canyon. But the observation deck, with its view of the colorful cliffs, the adorable brick lighthouse, and the Elizabeth Islands beyond, will make you glad you bothered. Instead of rushing away, stop for a cool drink and a clam roll at the snack bar with the deck overlooking the ocean.

FISHING For shellfishing, get information and a permit from the appropriate town hall (for the telephone numbers, see "Beaches," above). Popular spots for surf-casting include **Wasque Point** on Chappaquiddick, South Beach, and the jetty at Menemsha Pond.

Moments Menemsha Beach Sunset

This beach is the ideal place to watch a sunset. Get a lobster dinner to go at the famous **Home Port restaurant** right next to the beach in Menemsha (see "Where to Dine," later in this chapter), grab a blanket and a bottle of wine, and picnic here for a spectacular evening.

Exploring the Vineyard on Two Wheels

Biking on the Vineyard is a memorable experience, not only for the smooth, well-maintained paths, but also for the long stretches of virtually untrafficked up-island roads that reveal breathtaking country landscapes and sweeping ocean views.

A triangle of paved bike paths, roughly 8 miles to a side, links the down-island towns of Oak Bluffs, Edgartown, and Vineyard Haven. The Vineyard Sound portion along Beach Road, flanked by water on both sides, is especially enjoyable. From Edgartown, you can also follow the bike path to South Beach. For a more woodsy ride, there are paved paths and mountain-biking trails in the **Manuel F. Correllus State Forest (© 508/693-2540)**, a vast spread of scrub oak and pine in the middle of the island. The bike paths are accessible off Edgartown–West Tisbury Road.

The up-island roads leading to West Tisbury, Chilmark, Menemsha, and Aquinnah are a cyclist's paradise, with unspoiled pastureland, old farmhouses, and brilliant sea views reminiscent of Ireland's countryside. But keep in mind that the terrain is often hilly, and the roads are narrow and a little rough around the edges. From West Tisbury to Chilmark Center, try **South Road**—about 5 miles—which passes stone walls rolling over moors, clumps of pine and wildflowers, verdant marshes and tidal pools, and, every once in awhile, an Old Vineyard farmhouse. **Middle Road** is another lovely ride with a country feel and will also get you from West Tisbury to Chilmark. (It's usually less trafficked, too.)

Our favorite up-island route is the 6-mile stretch from Chilmark Center out to Aquinnah via **State Road** and **Moshup Trail** ★. The ocean views along this route are spectacular. Don't miss the **Quitsa Pond Lookout,** about 2 miles down State Road, which provides a panoramic vista of Nashaquitsa and Menemsha ponds, beyond which you can see Menemsha, Vineyard Sound, and the Elizabeth Islands. A bit farther, just over the Aquinnah town line, is the Aquinnah spring, a roadside iron pipe where you can refill your water bottle with the freshest and coldest water on the island. At the fork after the spring, turn left on Moshup Trail—in fact, a regular road—and follow the coast, which offers gorgeous views of the ocean and the sweeping sand dunes. You'll soon wind up in Aquinnah, where you can explore the red-clay cliffs and pristine beaches. On the return trip, you can take the handy bike ferry ($7 round-trip) from Aquinnah to Menemsha. It runs daily in summer and on weekends in May.

There are lots of bike-rental operations near the ferry landings in Vineyard Haven and Oak Bluffs, as well as a few rental shops in Edgartown. For information on rentals, see "Getting Around," earlier in this chapter.

A very good outfitter out of Boston called **Bike Riders (© 800/473-7040;** www.bikeriderstours.com) runs 6-day island-hopping tours of Martha's Vineyard and Nantucket. Stays are at various inns on the islands. It's a perfect way to experience both islands.

The party boat ***Skipper*** (✆ **508/693-1238**) offers half-day trips out of Oak Bluffs harbor in season. The cost is $35 for adults and $25 for children 12 and under. Deep-sea excursions can be arranged aboard **Big Eye Charters** (✆ **508/627-3649**) out of Edgartown, and **Summer's Lease** (✆ **508/693-2880**) out of Oak Bluffs. Up-island, there are **North Shore Charters** (✆ **508/645-2993;** www.bassnblue.com) and **Flashy Lady Fishing Charters** (✆ **508/645-2462;** www.flashyladycharters.com) out of Menemsha, locus of the island's commercial fishing fleet.

Cooper Gilkes III, proprietor of **Coop's Bait & Tackle** at 147 W. Tisbury Rd. in Edgartown (✆ **508/627-3909**), which offers rentals as well as supplies, is another acknowledged authority. He's available as an instructor or charter guide.

GOLF The 9-hole **Mink Meadows Golf Course** off Franklin Street in Vineyard Haven (✆ **508/693-0600**), is open to the general public, while the championship-level 18-hole **Farm Neck Golf Club** off Farm Neck Road in Oak Bluffs (✆ **508/693-3057**) is semi-private.

NATURE TRAILS About a fifth of the Vineyard's landmass has been set aside for conservation, and it's all accessible to bikers and hikers. The **West Chop Woods,** off Franklin Street in Vineyard Haven, comprise 85 acres with marked walking trails. Mid-way between Vineyard Haven and Edgartown, the **Felix Neck Wildlife Sanctuary** ★★ includes a 6-mile network of trails over varying terrain, from woodland to beach.

The 633-acre **Long Point Wildlife Refuge** ★★ off Waldron's Bottom Road in West Tisbury (gatehouse ✆ **508/693-7392**) offers heath and dunes, freshwater ponds, a popular family-oriented beach, and interpretive nature walks for children.

Up-island, along the sound, the **Menemsha Hills Reservation** off North Road in Chilmark (✆ **508/693-7662**) encompasses 210 acres of rocks and bluffs, with steep paths, lovely views, and even a public beach. **The Cedar Tree Neck Sanctuary,** off Indian Hill Road southwest of Vineyard Haven (✆ **508/693-5207**), offers some 300 forested acres that end in a stony beach. Swimming and sunbathing are prohibited.

Some remarkable botanical surprises can be found at the 20-acre **Polly Hill Arboretum** ★★, 809 State Rd., West Tisbury (✆ **508/693-9426**). Legendary horticulturist Polly Hill has developed this property over the past 40 years and allows the public to wander the grounds Thursday to Tuesday from 7am until 7pm. This is a magical place, particularly mid-June to July when the Dogwood Allee is in bloom. Wanderers will pass old stone walls on the way to The Tunnel of Love, an arbor of hornbeam. There are also witch hazels, camellias, magnolias, and rhododendrons. To get there from Vineyard Haven, go south on State Road, bearing left at the junction of North Road. The arboretum entrance is about a half-mile down, on the right. There is a requested donation of $5 for adults.

WATERSPORTS **Wind's Up,** 199 Beach Rd., Vineyard Haven (✆ **508/693-4252**), rents out canoes, kayaks, and various sailing craft, including windsurfers, and offers instruction on a placid pond; it also rents surfboards and boogie boards. Canoes and kayaks rent for $20 per hour.

MUSEUMS & HISTORIC LANDMARKS

Cottage Museum ★ This little museum, a cottage in the center of Oak Bluffs' famous "campground," displays 19th-century artifacts, like bulky black bathing costumes and a melodeon used for informal hymnal singalongs. The campground consists of a 34-acre circle with more than 300 multicolored, elaborately trimmed

Carpenter Gothic cottages, which look very much the way they might have more than a hundred years ago. These adorable little houses were loosely modeled on the revivalists' canvas tents that inspired them. In the 1860s, when many of the cottages were built, campers typically attended three lengthy prayer services daily. Opportunities for worship remain at the 1878 Trinity Methodist Church within the park or, just outside, on Samoset Avenue, at the non-sectarian 1870 Union Chapel, a magnificent octagonal structure with superb acoustics.

At the very center of the Camp Meeting Grounds is the striking **Trinity Park Tabernacle** ★★. Built in 1879, the open-sided chapel is the largest wrought-iron structure in the country. Thousands can be accommodated on its long wooden benches, which are usually filled to capacity for the Sunday-morning services in summer, as well as for community sings (Wed in July–Aug) and occasional concerts.

1 Trinity Park (within the Camp Meeting Grounds), Oak Bluffs. © **508/693-7784.** Admission $1.50 (donation). Mid-June to Sept Mon–Sat 10am–4pm. Closed Oct to mid-June.

Flying Horses Carousel ★★ Kids You don't have to be a kid to enjoy what is considered to be the oldest working carousel in the country. Built in 1876 at Coney Island, this National Historic Landmark predates the era of horses that "gallop." Lacking the necessary gears, these mounts merely glide smoothly in place to the joyful strains of a calliope. Take a moment to admire the intricate hand carving and real horsehair manes, and gaze into the horses' glass eyes for a surprise: tiny animal charms glinting within.

33 Circuit Ave. (at Lake Ave.), Oak Bluffs. © **508/693-9481.** Tickets $1 per ride, or $8 for 10. Late May to early Sept daily 10am–10pm; call for off-season hours. Closed mid-Oct to mid-Apr.

The Martha's Vineyard Historical Society ★ All of Martha's Vineyard's colorful history is captured here, in a compound of historic buildings. To acclimate yourself chronologically, start with the pre-Colonial artifacts—from arrowheads to colorful Gay Head clay pottery—displayed in the 1845 **Captain Francis Pease House.** The **Gale Huntington Reference Library** houses rare documentation of the island's history, from genealogical records to whaling-ship logs. Some extraordinary memorabilia, including scrimshaw and portraiture, are on view in the adjoining **Francis Foster Maritime Gallery.**

To get a sense of daily life during the era when the waters of the East Coast were the equivalent of a modern highway, visit the **Thomas Cooke House,** a shipwright-built Colonial, built in 1765, where the Customs collector lived and worked. The Fresnel lens on display outside the museum was lifted from the Gay Head Lighthouse in 1952, after nearly a century of service. Though it no longer serves to warn ships of dangerous shoals (that light is automated now), it still lights up the night every evening in summer, just for show.

59 School St. (corner of Cooke St., 2 blocks southwest of Main St.), Edgartown. © **508/627-4441.** www.marthasvineyardhistory.org. Admission in season $7 adults, $4 children 6–15. Mid-June to mid-Oct Tues–Sat 10am–5pm; mid-Oct to late Dec and mid-Mar to mid-June Wed–Fri 1–4pm, Sat 10am–4pm; early Jan to mid-Mar Wed–Fri by appointment, Sat 10am–4pm.

ORGANIZED TOURS & CRUISES

Hugh Taylor (James's brother) alternates with a couple of other captains in taking the helm of ***Arabella*** ★, docked in Menemsha Harbor at the end of North Road (© **508/645-3511**). This swift 50-foot catamaran makes daily trips to Cuttyhunk

Island, and offers sunset cruises around the Aquinnah cliffs. It's a great way to see lovely coves and vistas otherwise denied the ordinary tourist. Daily sails are $60 for adults, $30 for children under 12. From mid-June to mid-September, departures are daily at 10:30am and 6pm (or 2 hr. before sunset). Reservations required.

The Trustees of Reservations, a statewide land conservation group, offers fascinating 2½-hour **Natural History Tours** ★★★ (✆ **508/627-3599;** www.thetrustees.org) by safari vehicle or canoe around Cape Poge on Chappaquiddick Island. The canoe tour on Poucha Pond and Cape Poge Bay is designed for all levels. The cost for the safari tour is $30 for adults and $15 for children 15 and under. The cost for the canoe tour is $35 for adults and $15 for children. There's also a tour of the Cape Poge lighthouse that costs $20 for adults and $12 for children. Two-hour kayak tours around Long Point cost $35 for adults and $18 for children. Call ✆ **508/693-7392** for details on the Long Point trips.

SHOPPING ★

ANTIQUES/COLLECTIBLES For the most exquisite Asian furniture, lamps, porcelains, and jewelry, visit **All Things Oriental** at 123 Beach Rd. in Vineyard Haven (✆ **508/693-8375**). The owner handpicks the treasures in China.

ARTS & CRAFTS No visit to Edgartown would be complete without a peek at the wares of scrimshander Thomas J. DeMont, Jr., at **Edgartown Scrimshaw Gallery** at 43 Main St. (✆ **508/627-9439**). All the scrimshaw in the gallery is hand-carved using ancient mammoth ivory or antique fossil ivory.

The Field Gallery, State Road (in the center of town), West Tisbury (✆ **508/693-5595**), is where Marc Chagall meets Henry Moore and where Tom Maley's playful figures have enchanted locals and passersby for decades. You'll also find paintings by Albert Alcalay and drawings and cartoons by Jules Feiffer. The Sunday-evening openings are high points of the summer social season. Closed from mid-October to mid-May.

Don't miss the **Granary Gallery at the Red Barn,** Old County Road (off Edgartown–West Tisbury Rd., about ¼ mile north of the intersection), West Tisbury (✆ **800/472-6279** or 508/693-0455), which displays astounding prints by the late longtime summerer Alfred Eisenstaedt and dazzling color photos by local luminary Alison Shaw.

Another unique local artisans' venue is **Martha's Vineyard Glass Works,** State Road, North Tisbury (✆ **508/693-6026**). The three resident artists—Andrew Magdanz, Susan Shapiro, and Mark Weiner—have shown nationwide to considerable acclaim. Their output is decidedly avant-garde and may not suit all tastes, but it's an eye-opening array and all the more fascinating once you've witnessed a work in progress.

GIFTS/HOME DECOR **Craftworks,** 149 Circuit Ave. (✆ **508/693-7463**), is filled to the rafters with whimsical, contemporary American crafts.

Carly Simon's **Midnight Farm,** 18 Water-Cromwell Lane, Vineyard Haven (✆ **508/693-1997**), offers a world of high-end, imaginative gift items from candles to children's clothes to furniture and glassware.

WHERE TO STAY

When deciding where to stay on Martha's Vineyard, you'll need to consider the type of vacation you prefer. The down-island towns of Vineyard Haven, Oak Bluffs, and Edgartown provide shops, restaurants, beaches, and harbors within walking distance, and frequent shuttles to get you all over the island. But all three can be overly crowded on busy summer weekends. Vineyard Haven is the gateway for most of the ferry traffic; Oak Bluffs is a raucous town with most of the Vineyard's bars and nightclubs; and many visitors make a beeline to Edgartown's manicured Main Street. Up-island inns provide more peace and quiet, but you'll probably need a car to get around. Also, you may not be within walking distance of the beach.

We've provided only summer rates below, because the Vineyard is so seasonal. If you do visit in the off season, you may find substantial discounts at the establishments that remain open year-round.

EDGARTOWN

Very Expensive

Charlotte Inn ★★★ Ask anyone to recommend the best inn on the island, and this is the name you're most likely to hear. It's one of only two Relais & Châteaux properties on the Cape and islands. Linked by formal gardens, each of the 18th- and 19th-century houses has a distinctive look and feel, though the predominant mode is English country. All but one of the rooms have TVs; some have VCRs. The bathrooms are luxurious, and some are bigger than most standard hotel rooms. The restaurant on-site is **L'étoile,** the island's best fine-dining restaurant (p. 282).

27 S. Summer St. (in the center of town), Edgartown, MA 02539. ✆ **508/627-4751.** Fax 508/627-4652. 25 units (all with tub/shower). Summer $295–$695 double; $695–$895 suite. Rates include continental breakfast; full breakfast offered for extra charge ($15). AE, MC, V. Open year-round. No children under 14. **Amenities:** Fine-dining restaurant. *In room:* A/C, TV, hair dryer.

Harbor View Hotel ★★ Grander than grand on the outside but hotel-standard on the inside, this shingle-style complex started out as two Gilded Age waterfront hotels, later joined by a 300-foot veranda that overlooks Edgartown Harbor and the lighthouse. Front rooms with that pretty view cost substantially more. In back, there's a large pool surrounded by newer annexes, where some rooms and suites have kitchenettes. The hotel is just far enough from "downtown" to avoid the traffic, but close enough for a pleasant walk past regal captain's houses. **The Coach House** (p. 282) serves three meals in an elegant setting.

131 N. Water St. (about ½ mile northwest of Main St.), Edgartown, MA 02539. ✆ **800/225-6005** or 508/627-7000. Fax 508/627-8417. www.harbor-view.com. 124 units (all with tub/shower). Summer $330–$625 double; $490–$710 one-bedroom suite; $750–$875 two-bedroom suite; $950 three-bedroom suite. AE, DC, MC, V. Open year-round. **Amenities:** 2 restaurants (fine-dining; more casual bar open daily for lunch and dinner, you can ask to be served by the pool); heated outdoor pool; 2 tennis courts; concierge; room service (seasonal only: breakfast, lunch, and dinner); babysitting; same-day laundry. *In room:* A/C, TV, fridge, hair dryer, iron, safe.

Hob Knob Inn ★★ Owner Maggie White has reinvented this 19th-century Gothic Revival inn as an exquisite destination that vies for top honors as one of the Vineyard's best places to stay. Her style is peppy/preppy, with crisp floral fabrics and striped patterns creating a clean and comfortable look. The farm breakfast is a delight and is served at beautifully appointed individual tables in the sunny, brightly painted dining rooms. Bovine lovers will enjoy the agrarian theme, a decorative touch throughout the inn. The attentive staff will pack a splendid picnic basket or plan a charter fishing trip on Maggie's 27-foot Boston Whaler.

128 Main St. (on upper Main St., in the center of town), Edgartown, MA 02539. ✆ **800/696-2723** or 508/627-9510. Fax 508/627-4560. www.hobknob.com. 20 units, 4-bedroom cottage. Summer $270–$550 double. Rates include full breakfast and afternoon tea. AE, MC, V. Open year-round. **Amenities:** Exercise room; rental bikes ($20 per day); room service; massage (extra charge). *In room:* A/C, TV, hair dryer.

The Winnetu Inn & Resort ★★ This large luxury hotel sits on 11 acres overlooking South Beach in Katama. Guests can walk down a 250-yard path to get to the private beach, which is next to South Beach on the Atlantic Ocean. A 3-mile bike path links the inn to Edgartown, but the inn also runs a shuttle service that can pick up inn guests at the Edgartown ferry. Most rooms are two- and three-bedroom suites with kitchenettes, and there is one deluxe cottage with a four-person hot tub and a roof deck. Some guest rooms have ocean views and washer/dryers. Many have private decks or patios. The fine-dining restaurant, Lure, is a treat.

South Beach, Edgartown, MA 02539. ✆ **978/443-1733** (reservations line), 508/627-4747. www.winnetu.com. 48 units. Summer $320 double; $570–$1,200 suite. AE, MC, V. Closed Dec to mid-Apr. **Amenities:** Fine-dining restaurant; outdoor heated pool; putting green; tennis courts w/pro (6 Har-Tru, 4 all-weather); fitness room; children's program (late June to early Sept complimentary 9am–noon; fee in evenings for 3-year-olds through preteens); concierge; laundry facilities. *In room:* A/C, TV/VCR, fridge, coffeemaker, iron, microwave.

Expensive

Ashley Inn ★ *Value* On Upper Main Street in Edgartown, this attractive B&B is just a short walk to the many shops and restaurants on Main Street and picturesque Edgartown Harbor. Innkeepers Fred and Janet Hurley have decorated the bedrooms in the 1860 captain's house with period antiques and quilts, and some rooms have canopy or four-poster beds. Thoughtful extras at this B&B include a little box of Chilmark Chocolates left on your pillow. A carriage house offers suites with a kitchen and whirlpool bath. In the morning, breakfast is served at individual tables in the dining room.

129 Main St., Edgartown, MA 02539. ✆ **508/627-9655.** Fax 508/627-6629. www.ashleyinn.net. 10 units. Summer $195–$295 double, Rates include full breakfast. MC, V. Open year-round. *In room:* A/C, TV.

Colonial Inn of Martha's Vineyard ★★ *Kids* This 1911 inn in the center of Edgartown has been transformed into a fine modern hotel and recent extensive renovations have elevated it to what can accurately be described as "affordable luxury." Its lobby serves as a conduit to the Nevins Square shops beyond. The guest rooms are decorated in soothing, contemporary tones with pine furniture, crisp fabrics, hardwood floors, and beadboard wainscoting. Suites have VCRs (complimentary videos) and kitchenettes. Many rooms have gas fireplaces. Be sure to visit the roof deck, ideally around sunset or, if you're up for it, sunrise.

38 N. Water St., Edgartown, MA 02539. ✆ **800/627-4701** or 508/627-4711. Fax 508/627-5904. www.colonialinnmvy.com. 28 units. Summer $225–$385 double; $390–$435 suite or efficiency. Rates include continental breakfast. AE, MC, V. Closed Dec–Mar. Pets allowed in designated rooms for $30 per day. **Amenities:** 2 restaurants; fitness room and spa; shopping arcade. *In room:* A/C, TV, dataport, hair dryer, iron.

The Jonathan Munroe House ★★ *Finds* With its graceful wraparound, colonnaded front porch, The Jonathan Munroe House stands out from the other inns and captain's homes on this stretch of upper Main Street. Inside, the formal parlor has been transformed into a comfortable gathering room with European flair. Guest rooms are immaculate, antique-filled, and dotted with clever details. Many rooms have fireplaces. At breakfast, don't miss the homemade waffles and pancakes, served on the sunny porch. Request the garden cottage if you are in a honeymooning mood.

100 Main St., Edgartown, MA 02539. ✆ **877/468-6763** or ✆/fax 508/627-5536. 7 units, 1 cottage. Summer $195–$255 double; $295 cottage. Rates include full breakfast and wine-and-cheese hour. AE, MC, V. Open year-round. No children under 12. *In room:* A/C, hair dryer.

Victorian Inn ★★ Do you long to stay at a quaint, reasonably priced inn that is bigger than a B&B but smaller than a Marriott? The Victorian Inn is a freshened-up version of those old-style hotels that used to exist in every New England town. There are enough rooms here so you don't feel like you are trespassing in someone's home, yet there's a personal touch. With three floors of long, graceful corridors, the Victorian could serve as a stage set for a 1930s romance. Several rooms have canopy beds and balconies. The innkeepers are always quick to dispense helpful advice with good humor.

24 S. Water St. (in the center of town), Edgartown, MA 02539. ✆ **508/627-4784.** www.thevic.com. 14 units. Summer $185–$385 double. Rates include full breakfast and afternoon tea. MC, V. Open year-round. Dogs welcome Nov–Mar. *In room:* A/C, TV, hair dryer, no phone.

Moderate

Edgartown Inn ★ *Value* This lovely, centrally located 1798 Federal manse, a showplace even here on captain's row, offers perhaps the best value on the island. Nathaniel Hawthorne holed up here for nearly a year, and Daniel Webster also spent time here. The rooms are no-frills but pleasantly traditional; some have TVs and harbor views. Modernists may prefer the two cathedral-ceilinged quarters in the annex out back, which offer lovely light and a sense of seclusion. Service is excellent; be sure to say hello to Henry King, who has been on the staff for over 50 years.

56 N. Water St., Edgartown, MA 02539. ✆ **508/627-4794.** Fax 508/627-9420. www.edgartowninn.com. 20 units, 4 with shared bathroom. Summer $110 shared bathroom; $155–$250 double. No credit cards. Closed Nov–Mar. No children under 8. *In room:* A/C, no phone.

OAK BLUFFS

Those looking for a basic motel with a central location, can try **Surfside Motel** across from the ferry dock on Oak Bluffs Avenue in Oak Bluffs (✆ **800/537-3007** or 508/693-2500). Summer rates are $165 to $205 double; $305 for suites. Well-behaved pets are allowed.

Expensive

The Oak House ★★ *Finds* An 1872 Queen Anne bayfront beauty has preserved all the luxury and leisure of the Victorian age. Innkeeper Betsi Convery-Luce trained at Johnson & Wales; her pastries are sublime. The common rooms are furnished in an opulent Victorian mode, as are the 10 guest rooms. Those toward the back are quieter, but those in front have Nantucket Sound views. This inn is very service oriented, and requests for feather beds, down pillows, or non-allergenic pillows are accommodated. Anyone intent on decompressing is sure to benefit from this immersion into another era—the one that invented the leisure class.

75 Seaview Ave. (on the sound), Oak Bluffs, MA 02557. ✆ **800/245-5979** or 508/693-4187. Fax 508/696-7385. www.vineyardinns.com. 10 units (1 tub/shower, 9 shower only). Summer $205–$260 double; $320–$325 suite. Rates include continental breakfast and afternoon tea. AE, DISC, MC, V. Closed late Oct to early May. *In room:* A/C, TV.

Moderate

The Dockside Inn ★ *Kids* Set close to the harbor, The Dockside is perfectly located for exploring the town of Oak Bluffs and is geared toward families. The welcoming exterior, with its colonnaded porch and balconies, duplicates the inns of yesteryear. Once inside, the whimsical Victorian touches will transport you into the spirit of this rollicking town. Most of the cheerfully decorated rooms have either garden or harbor views; some have private decks. Location, charm, and flair make this a popular place, so book early.

9 Circuit Ave. Extension (Box 1206), Oak Bluffs, MA 02557. ✆ **800/245-5979** or 508/693-2966. Fax 508/696-7293. www.vineyardinns.com. 22 units. Summer $175–$220 double; $280–$370 suite. Rates include continental breakfast. AE, DISC, MC, V. Closed late Oct to early Apr. *In room:* A/C, TV, hair dryer, iron.

The Oak Bluffs Inn ★ This homey Victorian inn has a fun location at the top of Circuit Avenue, Oak Bluff's main drag. The inn stands out with its colorful Victorian paint scheme and its prominent cupola, from which guests can enjoy a 360-degree view of Oak Bluffs. It's a 2-minute stroll from the inn to all the Oak Bluffs attractions, like the gingerbread cottages, the tabernacle, the Flying Horses Carousel, the waterfront park, and the ferries. Some of the rooms are a tad on the small side, but others are spacious and even have comfortable seating areas.

64 Circuit Ave. (at the corner of Pequot Ave.), Oak Bluffs, MA 02557. ✆ **800/955-6235** or 508/693-7171. Fax 508/693-8787. www.oakbluffsinn.com. 9 units. Summer $215–$300 double. Rates include continental breakfast. AE, MC, V. Closed Nov–Apr. *In room:* A/C, hair dryer, no phone.

Wesley Hotel ★ *Value* Formerly one of the grand hotels of Martha's Vineyard, this imposing 1879 property, right on the harbor, is now a solid entry in the good-value category, especially with its low off-season rates. It occupies a terrific location in Oak Bluffs, across the street from the harbor, in the center of the action. The only drawback here can be the noise from revelers on the boats in the harbor or traffic on busy Lake Avenue. Most of the rooms are fairly compact and basic, though some are roomy with harbor views. The Wesley Arms, behind the main building, contains 33 air-conditioned rooms with private bathrooms, accessible by elevator. Eight suites and executive suites have kitchenettes. Reserve early to specify harbor views, which do not cost more than regular rooms. This is one of the few Vineyard hotels that does not require a minimum stay in season.

70 Lake Ave. (on the harbor), Oak Bluffs, MA 02557. ✆ **800/638-9027** or 508/693-6611. Fax 508/693-5389. www.wesleyhotel.com. 95 units (all with shower only). Summer $195–$235 double; $290 suite. AE, DC, MC, V. Closed late Oct to Apr. *In room:* A/C, TV, no phone.

VINEYARD HAVEN (TISBURY)

Expensive

The Mansion House Inn ★★ *Finds* After a fire burned down the 200-year-old Tisbury Inn several years ago, the owners decided to rebuild, making this one of the island's most full-service inns. The building, occupying a prominent corner location in Vineyard Haven, is a community hub, with a restaurant, health club, and shops. The three-story hotel is comfortable with generous amenities. The rooms range in size from cozy to spacious and prices vary accordingly. Many have kitchenettes, plasma-screen TVs, and extra-large bathtubs. Some have harbor views. All the rooms are equipped with high-speed Internet service. One of the most unusual features of the inn is the 75-foot mineral spring (no chlorine) swimming pool in the health club in the inn's basement. The restaurant, **Zephrus,** is open to the public for lunch and dinner, and also supplies room service for guests until late in the evening.

9 Main St., Vineyard Haven, MA 02568. ✆ **800/332-4112** or 508/693-2200. Fax 508/693-4095. www.mvmansionhouse.com. 32 units. $269–$319 double; $319–$479 suite. Rates include full buffet breakfast. AE, MC, V. Open year-round. **Amenities:** Restaurant (Zephrus, a fine-dining New American–style restaurant); health club and spa w/75-ft. pool. *In room:* A/C, TV, fridge.

CHILMARK (INCLUDING MENEMSHA), WEST TISBURY & AQUINNAH

Very Expensive

Beach Plum Inn ★★ *Finds* This family-owned country inn is set on 8 lush acres, with a lawn sloping gracefully down to Vineyard Sound. The room decor is predominantly cottage-y, though some rooms lean toward elegance. All but one room have decks or patios, some with views of Menemsha Harbor. Some units have canopied beds and are quite romantic. Linens are 275 count and above; towels are Egyptian cotton. Five of the rooms have a whirlpool bath. The inn's restaurant is one of the best fine-dining spots on the island (see "Where to Dine," below).

Beach Plum Lane (off North Rd., ½ mile northeast of the harbor), Menemsha, MA 02552. ✆ **877/645-7398** or 508/645-9454. Fax 508/645-2801. www.beachpluminn.com. 11 units. Summer $250–$400 double or cottage. Rates include full breakfast in season; continental off season. AE, DC, DISC, MC, V. Closed Jan–Apr. **Amenities:** Restaurant (fine-dining); private beach passes; tennis court; croquet court; laundry service for a charge. Babysitting and in-room massage by arrangement. *In room:* A/C, TV, dataport, fridge, hair dryer, iron.

Expensive

Lambert's Cove Country Inn ★★ Set far off the main road and surrounded by apple trees and lilacs, this secluded estate suggests an age when time was measured in generations. A dedicated horticulturist created this haven in the 1920s, expanding on a 1790 farmstead. You can see the old adzed beams in some of the upstairs bedrooms. New owners have upgraded the rooms and the decor substantially. Among the showpieces is the Greenhouse Room, a bedroom with its own conservatory. You'll find an all-weather tennis court on the grounds, and the namesake beach 1 mile away. The inn's restaurant is known for skillfully prepared New American dinners prepared by one of the island's best chefs.

Lambert's Cove Rd. (off State Rd., about 3 miles west of Vineyard Haven), West Tisbury, MA 02568. ✆ **508/693-2298.** Fax 508/693-7890. www.lambertscoveinn.com. 15 units. Summer $195–$295 double. Rates include full breakfast. AE, MC, V. Open year-round. **Amenities:** Restaurant (New American cuisine dinner only); tennis court; private beach passes. *In room:* A/C, TV/DVD, CD, dataport.

Menemsha Inn and Cottages ★★ There's an almost Quaker-like plainness to this weathered waterside compound set in the pines near Menemsha Harbor, though many of the rooms are quite inviting. Mostly it's a place to revel in the outdoors (on 11 seaside acres) without distractions. The property is about a half-mile walk through a wooded path to the beach. There's no restaurant—just a restful breakfast room. Cottages have hair dryers, TVs, VCRs, dataports, outdoor showers, barbecue grills, and kitchenettes. The most luxurious suites are located in the Carriage House, which has a spacious common room with a fieldstone fireplace. All rooms have private decks; most have water views. Guests have access to complimentary passes and shuttle bus service to the Lucy Vincent and Squibnocket private beaches.

Off North Rd. (about ½ mile northeast of the harbor), Menemsha, MA 02552. ✆ **508/645-2521.** Fax 508/645-9500. www.menemshainn.com. 15 units, 12 cottages. Summer $240–$310 double; $575 2-bedroom suite daily; $2,200–$3,100 cottages weekly. Rates include continental breakfast for rooms and suites. MC, V. Closed Dec to mid-Apr. **Amenities:** Beach passes; tennis court; fitness room (step machine, treadmill, exercise bike, and free weights). *In room:* TV.

Moderate

The Captain R. Flanders House ★ *Finds* Set amid 60 acres of rolling meadows crisscrossed by stone walls, this late-18th-century farmhouse has remained much the same for 2 centuries. The living room, with its broad-plank floors, is full of astonishing antiques. Two countrified cottages overlook the pond. The owners will provide you with a coveted pass to nearby Lucy Vincent Beach.

North Rd. (about ½ mile northeast of Menemsha), Chilmark, MA 02535. ✆ **508/645-3123.** www.captainflanders.com. 5 units, 3 with shared bathroom; 2 cottages. Summer $80 single with shared bathroom; $175 double with shared bathroom; $195 double with private bathroom; $275 cottage. Rates include continental breakfast. AE, MC, V. Closed Nov to early May. **Amenities:** Private beach and shuttle bus passes. *In room:* No phone.

WHERE TO DINE

Outside Oak Bluffs and Edgartown, all of Martha's Vineyard is "dry," including Vineyard Haven, so bring your own bottle; some restaurants charge a small corkage fee.

EDGARTOWN

Very Expensive

L'étoile ★★★ CONTEMPORARY FRENCH Every signal (starting with the price) tells you that this is going to be one very special meal. To get to the restaurant, you pass through a pair of sitting rooms before coming to a summery conservatory, sparkling with the light of antique brass sconces and fresh with the scent of potted citrus trees. Everything is just right, from the table settings (gold-rimmed Villeroy & Boch) to the nouvelle-cuisine menu. Chef Michael Brisson is determined to dazzle with an ever-evolving seven-course menu of delicacies flown in from the four corners of the earth. Sevruga usually makes an appearance—perhaps as a garnish for chilled leek soup. An étouffée of lobster with lobster, cognac, and chervil sauce might come with littlenecks, bay scallops, and roasted corn fritters.

At the Charlotte Inn, 27 S. Summer St. (off Main St.). ✆ **508/627-5187.** Reservations required. Collared shirts requested for men. Fixed-price menu $78; Chef's Tasting Menu $120. AE, MC, V. July–Aug seatings daily 6:30–9:30pm; May–June and Sept–Oct Tues–Sun 6:30–9:45pm; mid-Feb to Apr and Nov–Dec Thurs–Sat 6:30–9:45pm. Closed Jan to mid-Feb.

Expensive

Alchemy ★★ FRENCH BISTRO This spiffy restaurant is a slice of Paris on Main Street. Such esoteric choices as oyster brie soup and Burgundy Vintners salad share the bill with escargot-and-chanterelle fricassee. As befits a true bistro, there's a large selection of cocktails, liqueurs, and wines. In addition to lunch and dinner, a bar menu is served from 2:30 to 11pm. This choice isn't for everyone, but sophisticated diners will enjoy the Continental flair.

71 Main St. (in the center of town). ✆ **508/627-9999.** Reservations accepted. Main courses $22–$33. AE, MC, V. Apr–Nov daily noon–2:30pm and 5:30–10pm; call for off-season hours. Open year-round.

Atria ★★★ NEW AMERICAN This fine-dining restaurant set in an 18th-century sea captain's house gets rave reviews for its gourmet cuisine and high-caliber service. Pronounced with the emphasis on the second syllable (ah-TRE-ah), the name refers to the brightest of three stars forming the Southern Triangle constellation. You can sit in the elegant dining room, the rose-covered wraparound porch, or the brick cellar bar downstairs for more casual dining. The menu offers a variety of creative dishes with influences from around the country and around the world, with stops in the Mediterranean, Middle East, and Asia. It features organic island-grown produce, off-the-boat seafood, local shellfish, and aged prime meats. Two popular starters are the miso soup with steamed crab dumplings and the Thai lemon-grass mussels. Unusual main courses include wok-fried Martha's Vineyard lobster or cracklin' pork shank with Southern collard greens. There is live entertainment in the bar, along the lines of acoustic guitar, on weekends.

137 Main St. (a short walk from the center of town). ✆ **508/627-5850.** www.atriamv.com. Reservations recommended. Main courses $22–$33. AE, MC, V. June–Sept daily 5:30–10pm; call for off-season hours. Open year-round.

The Coach House ★★ NEW AMERICAN This is a terrific place to have a drink or to dine, with its exquisite view of Edgartown Harbor and the lighthouse. The long and elegant bar is particularly smashing. The menu is simple but stylish. To start,

Moments **The Quintessential Lobster Dinner**

When the basics—a lobster and a sunset—are what you crave, head to the **Home Port** on North Road in Menemsha (✆ **508/645-2679**), a favorite of locals and visitors alike. At first glance, prices for the lobster dinners may seem a bit high, but note that they include an appetizer of your choice (go with the stuffed quahog), salad, amazing fresh-baked breads, a nonalcoholic beverage (remember, it's BYOB in these parts), and dessert. The decor is on the simple side, but who really cares? It's the riveting harbor views that have drawn fans to this family-friendly place for over 60 years. Locals not keen on summer crowds prefer to order their lobster dinners for pickup (less than half price) at the restaurant door, then head down to Menemsha Beach for a private sunset supper. Reservations are required. Fixed-price platters range from $26 to $60. The Home Port is open mid-June to Labor Day daily at 5pm with last reservations at 9pm. Closed mid-September to mid-May. Call for off-season hours.

there's soft-shell crab with arugula and teardrop tomatoes. As a main course, try the caramelized sea scallops with a salad of Asian pear and apple. Service is excellent; these are trained waiters, not your usual college surfer dudes. At the end of your meal, you may want to sit on the rockers on the Harbor View Hotel's wraparound porch and watch the lights twinkling in the harbor.

At the Harbor View Hotel (p. 277), 131 N. Water St. ✆ **508/627-7000.** Reservations recommended. Main courses $18–$35. AE, MC, V. Mon–Sat 7–11am and noon–2pm; Sun 8am–2pm; daily 6–10pm. Call for off-season hours. Open year-round.

Detente ★★ NEW AMERICAN Taking the French word for relaxation and good relations, this new Edgartown restaurant is working to be the new hot spot on the Vineyard. Early reviews are thumbs-up, citing the sophisticated wine bar and creative fine-dining cuisine. The menu is based on seasonal specials featuring foods from local farms and markets. For starters, you can go light with a spring watercress and spiced pecan salad, or heavy, with island lobster ravioli. The main courses are similarly varied, from pesto-marinated rack of lamb to orange curry-crusted monkfish. The wine list is extensive with numerous intriguing choices available by the glass.

Off Winter St. (in Nevin Sq. behind the Colonial Inn). ✆ **508/627-8810.** Reservations recommended. Main courses $29–$35. AE, MC, V. June–Aug Mon–Sat 5:30–10pm, Sun 11am–2pm and 5:30–10pm; call for off-season hours. Closed Feb–Mar.

Lattanzi's ★★ NORTHERN ITALIAN Some say Al Lattanzi cooks the best veal chops on Martha's Vineyard. This is the ideal place to eat in the dead of winter, by the glow of the paneled living room's handsome fireplace. Service is exceptional, and the wine list has a wide range of well-priced bottles. But back to that veal chop: You have two choices, *Piccolo Fiorentina,* which is hickory-grilled veal porterhouse chop with black peppercorns and lemon, or *Lombatina di Vitello al Porcini,* which pairs the chop with porcini-mushroom cream. If it's July, get the locally caught striped bass—it's luscious.

Lattanzi also owns the very good **brick-oven pizza joint** next door (✆ **508/627-9084**).

19 Church St. (Old Post Office Sq., off Main St. in the center of town). ✆ **508/627-8854.** Reservations recommended. Main courses $22–$38. DC, DISC, MC, V. June–Sept daily 6–10pm; call for off-season hours. Open year-round.

Moderate

Among the Flowers Cafe ★★ *Value* AMERICAN Everything's fresh and appealing at this small outdoor cafe near the dock. The breakfasts are the best around, and the comfort-food dinners are among the most affordable options in this pricey town. There's almost always a wait, not just because it's so picturesque, but because the food is homey, hearty, and kind on the wallet.

Mayhew Lane. ✆ **508/627-3233.** Main courses $10–$18. AE, DC, DISC, MC, V. July–Aug daily 8am–10pm; May–June and Sept–Oct daily 8am–4pm. Closed Nov–Apr.

Chesca's ★★ *Finds* ITALIAN This modern-decor restaurant at the Colonial Inn is a solid entry, with yummy food at reasonable prices. You're sure to find favorites like paella (with roasted lobster and other choice seafood), risotto (with roasted vegetables), and ravioli (with portobello mushrooms and asparagus). Smaller appetites can fill up on homemade soup and salad.

At the Colonial Inn, 38 N. Water St. ✆ **508/627-1234.** Reservations accepted for parties with 6 or more only. Main courses $13–$32. AE, MC, V. Late June to early Sept daily 5:30–10pm; call for off-season hours. Closed Nov–Mar.

Inexpensive

The Newes from America ★★ *Finds* PUB GRUB The food is better than average at this subterranean tavern, built in 1742. Beers are a specialty here. Try a rack of five esoteric brews, or let your choice of food—from a wood-smoked oyster "Island Poor Boy" sandwich with linguica (Portuguese-style sausage) relish to an 18-ounce porterhouse steak—dictate your draft; the menu comes handily annotated with recommendations. Don't miss the seasoned fries.

At The Kelley House, 23 Kelley St. ✆ **508/627-4397.** Main courses $7–$10. AE, MC, V. Daily 11:30am–11pm. Open year-round.

OAK BLUFFS

Expensive

Park Corner Bistro ★★★ *Finds* NEW AMERICAN This superb restaurant in the center of Oak Bluffs is an intimate and cozy bistro that has a definite European aura. With just 10 tables, it's a romantic space for casual fine dining. Favorite appetizers are the beet salad and the Parmesan gnocchi, which is sautéed with chanterelle and black trumpet mushrooms. Move on to the Australian lamb loin with sweet corn flan and champagne corn emulsion. For dessert, don't miss the warm fruit cobbler with vanilla ice cream.

20H Kennebec Ave. (off Circuit Ave., across from the OB Post Office). ✆ **508/696-9922.** Reservations suggested. Main courses $25–$37. AE, MC, V. July–Aug daily 9am–3pm and 6–10pm; call for off-season hours. Open year-round.

Sweet Life Cafe ★★★ FRENCH/AMERICAN Locals are crazy about this pearl of a restaurant, set in a restored Victorian house on upper Circuit Avenue. In season, the most popular seating is outside in the gaily lit garden. Fresh island produce is featured, with seafood specials an enticing draw. If the roasted lobster with potato-Parmesan risotto, roasted yellow beets, and smoked-salmon chive fondue is offered, order it.

63 Circuit Ave. ✆ **508/696-0200.** Reservations recommended. Main courses $18–$35. AE, DISC, MC, V. Mid-May to Aug daily 5:30–10pm; Apr to mid-May and Sept–Nov Thurs–Mon 5:30–9:30pm. Closed Dec to mid-May.

Moderate

Lola's Southern Seafood ★ SOUTHERN This sultry New Orleans–style restaurant drips with atmosphere: crystal chandeliers; intricate wrought-iron, arched doorways; and starched linens in an ocher palette. Specialties include the chicken-and-seafood jambalaya, and the rib-eye steak spiced either "from heaven or hell." Meals are served family-style, with large helpings of side dishes. There's live entertainment nightly in season, while Sunday brunch also features live music. Off season, there's live music Friday and Saturday nights. A less-expensive pub menu is served in the bar.

At the Island Inn, Beach Rd. ✆ **508/693-5007.** www.lolassouthernseafood.com. Reservations accepted only for 5 or more. Main courses $20–$36. DC, MC, V. Sun 10am–2pm; daily 5–11pm. Open year-round.

Inexpensive

Coop de Ville ★ SEAFOOD Of the several open-air harborfront choices in Oak Bluffs, Coop de Ville has the best service and food. This outdoor fried-seafood shack serves up tasty beer-battered shrimp, grilled swordfish, lobster salad, and "world famous" chicken wings. It's a fun place to people-watch on sunny summer days as boaters cruise around the harbor.

Dockside Market Place, Oak Bluffs Harbor. ✆ **508/693-3420.** Most items $9–$20. MC, V. June–Aug daily 11am–10pm; call for off-season hours. Closed mid-Oct to Apr.

Slice of Life *Finds* DELI This deli at the upper end of Circuit Avenue is the place to head for gourmet sandwiches, salads, and soups. There are just a handful of tables inside and more tables out on the screened porch in front. The eclectic menu includes burgers and pizza. All of the food is very wholesome. There's also wine, beer, and specialty coffees.

50 Circuit Ave. ✆ **508/693-3838.** Reservations not accepted. Most items under $10. MC, V. June–Aug daily 8am–8pm; call for off-season hours. Open year-round.

VINEYARD HAVEN (TISBURY)

Just around the corner from the Black Dog Tavern on Water Street near the ferry terminal is the **Black Dog Bakery** (✆ **508/693-4786**). The doors open at 5am, and from midmorning on, it's elbowroom only as customers line up for freshly baked breads, muffins, and desserts that can't be beat. Don't forget some homemade doggie biscuits for your pooch.

Expensive

Black Dog Tavern ★ NEW AMERICAN How does a humble harbor shack come to be a national icon? Location helps. So do cool T-shirts. Soon after *Shenandoah* captain Robert Douglas decided, in 1971, that this hardworking port could use a good restaurant, influential vacationers, stuck waiting for the ferry, began to wander into this saltbox to tide themselves over with a bit of "blackout cake" or peanut-butter pie. The food is still home-cooking good, especially the seafood, and the blackout cake has lost none of its appeal. Though the lines grow ever longer, nothing much has changed at this beloved spot. Eggs Galveston for breakfast at the Black Dog Tavern is still one of the ultimate Vineyard experiences—go early, when it first opens, and sit on the porch, where the views are perfect.

Beach St. Extension (on the harbor), Vineyard Haven. ✆ **508/693-9223.** Reservations not accepted. Main courses $14–$27. AE, MC, V. June to early Sept daily 7–11am, noon–4pm, and 5–9pm; call for off-season hours. Open year-round.

Café Moxie ★ NEW AMERICAN A casual Vineyard-y atmosphere and top-notch food make this cafe a must-try. Starters like artichoke soup with fresh croutons and herbed potato gnocchi are deeply flavorful, as though all the ingredients were gathered from local gardens. Unusual combinations are a specialty, like the pan-seared scallops with pea risotto and warm apple-wood bacon sherry vinaigrette.

48 Main St. (in the center of town). ✆ **508/693-1484.** Reservations suggested. Main courses $22–$32. MC, V. Wed–Sat 11:30am–2:30pm; Tues–Sun 5:30–10pm. Open year-round.

Le Grenier ★★ FRENCH If Paris is the heart of France, Lyons is its belly—and that's where chef-owner Jean Dupon grew up on his *Maman*'s hearty cuisine. Dupon has the Continental moves down, as evidenced by such classics as steak au poivre, calves' brains Grenobloise with beurre noir and capers, and lobster Normande flambéed with Calvados, apples, and cream. Despite the fact that Le Grenier means (and, in fact, is housed in) an attic, the restaurant is quite romantic, especially when aglow with hurricane lamps. Remember: You must BYOB here.

96 Main St. (in the center of town). ✆ **508/693-4906.** Reservations suggested. Main courses $22–$32. AE, DC, DISC, MC, V. Daily 11am–2pm and 5:30–10pm. Open year-round.

Zephrus at the Mansion House Inn ★★ INTERNATIONAL This hip restaurant is a great place to go for casual fine dining. Seating is at the sidewalk cafe on Main Street or inside by the hearth in view of the open kitchen. Main-course winners are pan-roasted pork tenderloin served with sweet 'tater tots; and shrimp and farfalle pasta. Though the menu is in constant flux, there is always a good vegetarian choice like the delicious vegetable risotto with truffle vinaigrette. Bring your favorite wine; the corkage fee is $5 per table.

9 Main St., Vineyard Haven ✆ **508/693-3416.** www.zephrus.com. Reservations recommended. Main courses $20–$28. AE, DC, DISC, MC, V. July–Aug daily 11:30am–3pm and 5:30–9pm. Call for off-season hours. Open year-round.

INEXPENSIVE

Art Cliff Diner ★ ECLECTIC DINER Expect the best food you've ever had at a diner at this quirky establishment. It's a short walk from the center of Vineyard Haven. Be aware that the hours are a little unreliable and you should call to be sure it is open before making the trek. The food here is really scrumptious, whether you are having the just-caught fish of the day served with herbs from the chef's garden, or a simple burger, cooked just right. Desserts are homemade, of course.

39 Beach Rd. (a short walk from Main St.). ✆ **508/693-1224.** Reservations not accepted. Main courses all under $15. No credit cards. July–Aug daily 8am–8pm; call for off-season hours. Closed Nov–Apr.

CHILMARK (INCLUDING MENEMSHA) & WEST TISBURY

Very Expensive

The Beach Plum Inn Restaurant ★★★ INTERNATIONAL This jewel of a restaurant is on a bluff overlooking the fishing village of Menemsha. Extensive renovations and attention to quality have made this one of the island's top dining venues. Guests can dine inside in the spare, but elegant, dining room, or outside on the new tiled patio. Chef James McDonough's most popular dishes include hazelnut-encrusted halibut with Marsala wine beurre blanc sauce. The most winning appetizer is the elaborate blackened lobster tips, served with mango cream sauce and house-cured gravlax with homemade wild rice and corn pancakes. For dessert, you'll flip for the chocolate quadruple-layer cake made with white and dark chocolate mousse and Chambord. In the spring and fall, there is usually an ethereal soufflé on the menu, either Grand Marnier or chocolate.

At the Beach Plum Inn, 50 Beach Plum Lane (off North Road), Menemsha. ✆ **508/645-9454.** www.beachpluminn.com. Reservations required. Main courses $32–$40; 4-course fixed-price menu $68; off season only fixed-priced menu $50. AE, MC, V. Mid-June to early Sept daily seatings from 5:30–6:45pm and 8–9:30pm. Call for off-season hours. Closed Dec–Apr.

Bittersweet ★★ NEW AMERICAN It's a bit of an adventure to take the long drive down winding country roads into the heart of the Vineyard to this low-key fine-dining restaurant. This pricey but popular up-island venue is earning raves for the high quality of the food and service. From the outside, it looks like a modest roadhouse; the inside is simply decorated, with the work of island artists featured on the walls and tables. The menu changes often as the chef combines unusual ingredients with island produce, meats, and locally caught fish. The restaurant is in West Tisbury, a dry town, so you must BYOB. Also, no credit cards are accepted, so bring plenty of cash.

688 State Rd., West Tisbury. ✆ **508/696-3966.** Main courses $25–$36. No credit cards. July–Aug daily 6–10pm; call for off-season hours. Closed late Jan to Apr.

Lambert's Cove Country Inn Restaurant ★★ *Finds* NEW AMERICAN One of the Vineyard's favorite chefs, Joe Silva, runs the kitchen at this romantic country inn. If you are staying in one of the down-island towns such as Edgartown or Oak Bluffs, driving through the wooded countryside to this secluded inn feels like an expedition to an earlier time. The interior of the restaurant is set up with crisp white tablecloths and antique furniture. In good weather, you can dine alfresco on a deck surrounded by flowering trees and shrubs. The menu features fresh seafood and island produce and meats. You might start with a crab and asparagus napoleon, or a simple, but luscious, cream of mushroom soup. Special dinner entrees include grilled marinated duck breast casserole baked in a sherry lobster cream sauce. Desserts are homemade delicacies. Don't forget: the town of West Tisbury is "dry," so you must bring your own alcoholic beverages.

Lamberts Cove Rd. (off State Rd., about 3 miles west of Vineyard Haven), West Tisbury. ✆ **508/693-2298.** Reservations suggested. Main courses $24–$32. AE, MC, V July–Aug daily 6–9pm; call for off-season hours. Open year-round.

Moderate

The Bite ★★ *Finds* SEAFOOD It's usually places like The Bite that you crave when you think of New England. This is your quintessential "chowdah" and clam shack, flanked by picnic tables. The Bite makes superlative chowder, potato salad, fried fish, and so forth.

Basin Rd. (off North Rd., about ¼ mile northeast of the harbor), Menemsha. ✆ **508/645-9239.** Main courses $18–$30. No credit cards. July–Aug daily 11am–8pm; call for off-season hours. Closed late Sept to Apr.

MARTHA'S VINEYARD AFTER DARK

All towns except Oak Bluffs and Edgartown are dry, and last call at bars and clubs is at midnight. Hit Oak Bluffs for the rowdiest bar scene and best nighttime street life. In Edgartown, you may have to hop around before you find the evening's most happening spot.

The Vineyard's top nightclub, The Hot Tin Roof, has been sold. The new owner plans to change the name and add a restaurant, but also keep the big acts—comedy, rock, reggae, Latin, and blues—coming. The Hot Tin Roof is at the Martha's Vineyard

Airport. For more information, call ✆ **508/693-1137** or check out their website, www.mvhottinroof.com.

Young and loud are the buzzwords at the **Lamppost** and the **Rare Duck,** 111 Circuit Ave., Oak Bluffs (✆ **508/696-9352**), a pair of clubs in the center of town. The Lamppost features live bands and a dance floor; the Rare Duck, acoustic acts. This is where the young folk go, and the performers could be playing blues, reggae, R&B, or '80s. The cover is $1 to $5.

The Vineyard's first and only brewpub, **Offshore Ale Company,** 30 Kennebec Ave., Oak Bluffs (✆ **508/693-2626**), is an attractively rustic place, with oak booths and peanut shells strewn on the floor. Local acoustic performers entertain 6 nights a week in season. The cover is $5.

The Ritz Cafe, 1 Circuit Ave., Oak Bluffs (✆ **508/693-9851**), is a down-and-dirty hole in the wall that features live music nightly in season and on weekends year-round. The cover is $2 to $3.

PERFORMING ARTS

This magnificent 1843 **Whaling Church,** 89 Main St., Edgartown (✆ **508/627-4442**), functions primarily as a 500-seat performing-arts center offering lectures and symposia, films, plays, and concerts. Ticket prices vary; call for schedule.

The Vineyard Playhouse, 24 Church St., Vineyard Haven (✆ **508/696-6300** or 508/693-6450; www.vineyardplayhouse.org), is an intimate black-box theater, where Equity professionals put on a rich season of favorites and challenging new work, followed, on summer weekends, by musical or comedic cabaret in the gallery/lounge. Children's theater selections are performed on Saturdays at 10am. Townspeople often get involved in the outdoor Shakespeare production, a 3-week run starting in mid-July at the Tashmoo Overlook Amphitheatre about 1 mile west of town.

2 Nantucket ★★★

Once the whaling capital of the world, this tiny island, 30 miles off the coast of Cape Cod, still counts its isolation as a defining characteristic. At only 3½×14 miles in size, Nantucket is smaller and more insular than Martha's Vineyard. But charm-wise, Nantucket stands alone—21st-century amenities wrapped in an elegant 19th-century package.

Sophisticated Nantucket Town features bountiful stores, quaint inns, cobblestone streets, interesting historic sites, and pristine beaches. The rest of the island is mainly residential, but for a couple of notable villages. **Siasconset** (nicknamed 'Sconset), on the east side of the island, is a tranquil community with picturesque, rose-covered cottages and a handful of businesses, including a pricey French restaurant. Sunset aficionados head to **Madaket,** on the west coast of the island, for the evening spectacular.

The lay of the land on Nantucket is rolling moors, cranberry bogs, and miles of exquisite public beaches. The vistas are honeymoon-romantic: an operating windmill, three lighthouses, and a skyline dotted with church steeples.

ESSENTIALS

GETTING THERE

BY FERRY From Hyannis Ferry service to Hyannis is fairly hassle-free, unless you're bringing a car in summer. But first-time visitors will find a car more of a nuisance than a convenience, unless they're staying outside of Nantucket Town.

Nantucket

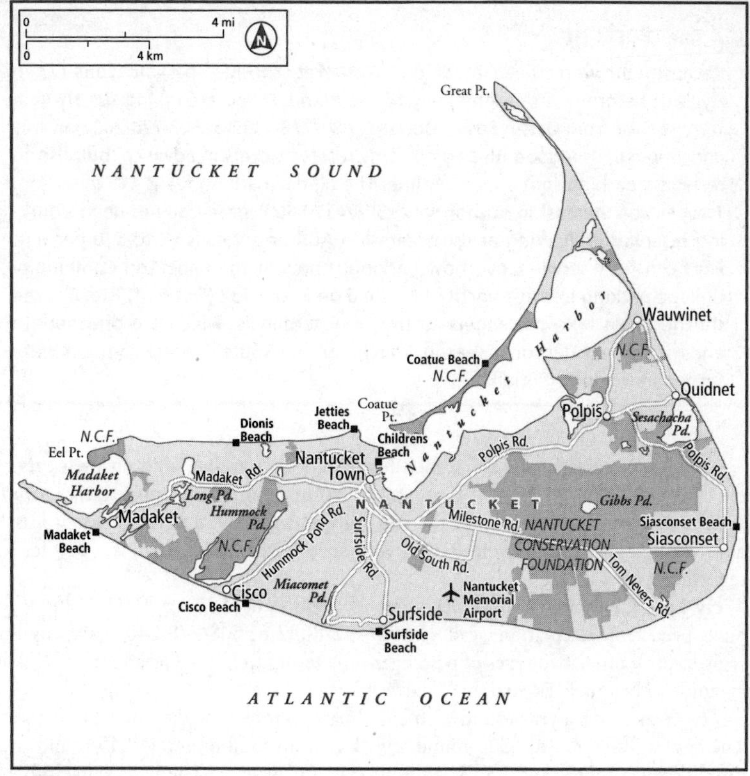

From Hyannis (South St. Dock), the **Steamship Authority** (**© 508/477-8600** in Hyannis, or 508/228-3274 in Nantucket; www.steamshipauthority.com) operates year-round ferry service for cars, passengers, and bicycles to Steamship Wharf on Nantucket using both high-speed and conventional ferries.

The Steamship Authority's high-speed ferry to Nantucket, ***The Flying Cloud*** (**© 508/495-3278**), is for passengers only. It takes 1 hour and runs five to six times a day in season. Tickets cost $30 one-way ($60 round-trip) for adults, $23 one-way ($46 round-trip) for children 5 to 12. Parking costs $8 to $10 per day. Watch for the ferry parking signs on Route 6; if lots next to the dock are full, you'll need to take Exit 6 for a satellite lot, instead of Exit 7 for the main lot. Passenger reservations are highly recommended. No pets are allowed on *The Flying Cloud.*

Total trip time on the conventional ferry that carries cars is 2 hours and 15 minutes. A round-trip fare for a car costs $350 to $400 from mid-May to mid-October; $230 to $270 the rest of the year. The higher rates are charged for vehicles more than 16 feet long. Car rates do not include drivers or passengers. Passenger tickets are $15 one-way ($29 round-trip) for adults, $7.75 one-way ($16 round-trip) for children 5 to 12; bikes cost $12 round-trip. Parking costs $8 to $10 per day; you do not need to make parking reservations.

Tips Parking

Because you won't need a car on Nantucket, consider parking your car in Hyannis before boarding the ferry to the island. If you are taking the **Hy-Line** ferry service from Ocean Street Dock (✆ **888/778-1132** or 508/778-2602) in July and August, it's a good idea to not only reserve tickets in advance, but also to reserve a parking spot ahead of time. The all-day parking fee is $15 in season. Travelers on **Steamship Authority** (✆ **508/477-8600**) vessels do not need a parking reservation. Parking at the Steamship Authority lots is $8 to $10 per day. For both ferry services, overflow parking is now at the Cape Cod Community College parking lots just north of Route 6 on Route 132 (Exit 6 off Rte. 6). Free shuttle buses take passengers to the ferry terminals, which are on opposite ends of Hyannis Harbor. In season, watch signs on Route 6 for up-to-the-minute ferry parking information.

No advance reservations are needed for passengers traveling without their cars on the conventional ferry. But if you bring your car in summer, you must reserve *months in advance*—only six boats make the trip daily and they fill up fast. Arrive at least 1 hour before departure to avoid having your space given away. There is a $10 fee for canceling a reservation.

Hy-Line Cruises, Ocean Street Dock (✆ **888/778-1132** or 508/778-2600; for high-speed ferry reservations, call ✆ **800/492-8082** or 508/778-0404; www.hy-linecruises.com), offers two types of passenger-only ferries from the Ocean Street Dock in Hyannis to Nantucket's Straight Wharf.

The Grey Lady, a year-round high-speed passenger ferry, makes the trip in 1 hour. The cost is $37 one-way ($63 round-trip) for adults, $28 one-way ($45 round-trip) for children 5 to 12, and $5 ($10 round-trip) for bicycles. The boat seats 260 and makes five to six round-trips daily in season; reserve in advance.

From early May through October, Hy-Line runs its standard 1-hour-and-50-minute ferry service. Round-trip tickets are $32 for adults, $17 for children ages 5 to 12, and $10 extra for bikes. On busy holiday weekends, the slow ferry fills up, too, so order tickets in advance; buy or pick up your tickets at least half an hour before sailing time.

The standard ferry also has a **first-class section** with a private lounge, bathrooms, a bar, and a snack bar; a continental breakfast or afternoon cheese and crackers is also served onboard. No pets are allowed in the first-class section. Tickets in the first-class section are $46 for all ages.

Hy-Line's **"Around the Sound" cruise** is a 1-day round-trip excursion from Hyannis with stops on Nantucket and Martha's Vineyard. It runs from early June to late September. The price is $45 for adults, $24 for children 5 to 12, and $15 extra for bikes.

From Martha's Vineyard From Oak Bluffs on Martha's Vineyard, Hy-Line runs three passenger-only ferries to Nantucket from early June to mid-September (there is no car-ferry service between the islands). The trip time is 2 hours and 15 minutes. The round-trip fare is $32 for adults, $6.50 for children 5 to 12, and $5 extra for bikes.

From Harwich Port You can avoid the summer crowds in Hyannis by boarding a passenger-only ferry with **Freedom Cruise Line,** 702 Rte. 28 in Harwich Port, across from Brax Landing (✆ **508/432-8999;** www.nantucketislandferry.com). From mid-May to mid-October, boats leave from Saquatucket Harbor in Harwich Port; the trip takes 1½ hours. Round-trip tickets are $51 for adults, $39 for children ages 2 to 11, $6 for children under 2, and $10 extra for bikes. Parking is free if you pick up your car the same day, but it's $12 for each night thereafter. Reservations are highly recommended.

BY PLANE You can fly into **Nantucket Memorial Airport** (✆ **508/325-5300**), which is about 3 miles south of Nantucket Road on Old South Road. The flight to Nantucket takes 30 to 40 minutes from Boston, 15 minutes from Hyannis, and a little more than an hour from New York City airports.

Airlines providing service to Nantucket include: **Business Express/Delta Connection** (✆ **800/221-1212**) year-round from Boston and seasonally from New York; **Cape Air/Nantucket Airlines** (✆ **800/352-0714**) year-round from Hyannis ($79 round-trip), Boston (about $249 round-trip), Martha's Vineyard ($76 round-trip), and New Bedford ($139 round-trip); **Continental Express** (✆ **800/525-0280**) from Newark, seasonally (about $723 round-trip); **Island Airlines** (✆ **508/228-7575**) year-round from Hyannis ($79 round-trip); and **Colgan/US Airways Express** (✆ **800/428-4322**) year-round from Boston ($316 round-trip) and New York ($535 and up round-trip).

Island Airlines and Nantucket Airlines both offer year-round charter service to the island.

GETTING AROUND

Nantucket is easily navigated on bike, moped, or foot, and also by shuttle bus or taxi. The chamber of commerce strongly suggests that visitors leave their cars behind in order to minimize congestion and environmental impact. If you're staying outside of Nantucket Town, however, or if you plan to explore the outer reaches of the island, you might want to bring your car or rent one here. Keep in mind that if you do opt to travel by car, in-town traffic can reach gridlock in the peak season, and parking can be a nightmare.

BY BICYCLE & MOPED Biking is a great way to get around Nantucket. The island is relatively flat, and paved bike paths abound—they'll get you from Nantucket Town to Siasconset, Surfside, and Madaket. There are also many unpaved back roads to explore, which make mountain bikes a wise choice. Mopeds are also available, but be aware that local rules and regulations are strictly enforced. Mopeds are not allowed on sidewalks or bike paths. You'll need a driver's license to rent a moped, and state law requires that you wear a helmet.

You can bring your own bike over on the ferries for an additional charge. Otherwise, shops that rent bikes and mopeds (all within walking distance of the ferries) include: **Cook's Cycle Shop, Inc.,** 6 S. Beach St. (✆ **508/228-0800**); **Nantucket Bike Shops,** at Steamboat Wharf and Straight Wharf (✆ **508/228-1999**); and **Young's Bicycle Shop,** at Steamboat Wharf (✆ **508/228-1151**), which also does repairs. Bike rentals average $20 to $25 for 24 hours.

BY SHUTTLE BUS From June through September, inexpensive shuttle buses, with bike racks and wheelchair lifts, make a loop through Nantucket Town and to outlying spots; for routes and stops, contact the **Nantucket Regional Transit Authority**

(© **508/228-7025;** www.nantucket.net/trans/nrta) or pick up a schedule at the visitor center on Federal Street or the chamber of commerce office on Main Street. The cost is $1 to $2, and exact change is required. A 3-day pass can be purchased at the visitor center for $10. Dogs are allowed on the bus as long as they are relatively clean and dry.

BY CAR & JEEP We recommend a car if you'll be here for more than a week or if you're staying outside Nantucket Town. Remember, though, there are no in-town parking lots; parking, although free, is limited.

Rental agencies on the island include: **Affordable Rentals of Nantucket,** 6 S. Beach Rd. (© **508/228-3501**); **Budget,** at the airport (© **800/527-0700** or 508/228-5666); **Hertz,** at the airport (© **800/654-3131** or 508/228-9421); **Nantucket Windmill Auto Rental,** at the airport (© **800/228-1227** or 508/228-1227); and **Young's 4 X 4 & Car Rental,** Steamboat Wharf (© **508/228-1151**). A standard car costs about $100 per day in season; a four-wheel-drive rental costs about $185 per day (including an Over-Sand Permit).

BY TAXI You'll find taxis (many are vans that can accommodate large groups or those traveling with bikes) waiting at the airport and at all ferry ports. During the busy summer months, we recommend reserving a taxi in advance to avoid a long wait upon arrival. Rates are flat fees, based on one person riding before 1am, with surcharges for additional passengers, bikes, and dogs. A taxi from the airport to Nantucket Town hotels will cost about $10. Reliable cab companies include **A-1 Taxi** (© **508/228-3330**), **All Point Taxi** (© **508/228-5779**), **Bev's Taxi** (© **508/228-7874**), **Lisa's Taxi** (© **508/228-2223**), and **Val's Cab Service** (© **508/228-9410**).

VISITOR INFORMATION

For information contact the **Nantucket Island Chamber of Commerce** at 48 Main St., Nantucket, MA 02554 (© **508/228-1700;** www.nantucketchamber.org). When you arrive, you should also stop by the **Nantucket Visitors Service and Information Bureau,** 25 Federal St. (© **508/228-0925**). It's open daily from June to September; and Monday to Saturday from October to May. There are also information booths at Steamboat Wharf and Straight Wharf. Always check the island's newspaper, the *Inquirer & Mirror* (known locally as "The Inky"), for information on events and activities around town.

Nantucket Accommodations, P.O. Box 217, Nantucket, MA 02554 (© **508/228-9559;** fax 508/325-7009; www.nantucketaccommodation.com), a 30-year-old private service, arranges advance reservations for inns, cottages, guesthouses, bed-and-breakfasts, and hotels; it has access to 95% of the island's lodging, in addition to houses and cottages available by the night or week (as opposed to most realtors, who will only handle rentals for 2 weeks or more). The charge for the service is $15, assessed only when a reservation is made. Last-minute travelers should keep in mind the **Nantucket Visitors Service and Information Bureau** (© **508/228-0925**), a daily referral service for available rooms. It's not a booking service, but it always has the most updated list of accommodations availability and cancellations.

ATMs can be difficult to locate on Nantucket. **Nantucket Bank** (© **508/228-0580**) has five locations: 2 Orange St., 104 Pleasant St., Amelia Street, the Hub on Main Street, and the airport lobby, all open 24 hours. **Pacific National Bank** has four locations: A&P Supermarket (next to the wharves), the Stop & Shop (open 24 hr.

seasonally), the Steamship Wharf Terminal, and Pacific National Bank lobby (open during bank hours only).

In case of a **medical emergency,** the **Nantucket Cottage Hospital,** 57 Prospect St. (**© 508/228-1200**), is open 24 hours.

BEACHES & OUTDOOR PURSUITS

BEACHES In distinct contrast to Martha's Vineyard, virtually all of Nantucket's 110-mile coastline is open to the public.

- **Children's Beach:** This small beach is a protected cove just west of busy Steamship Wharf. Appealing to families, it has a park, a playground, restrooms, lifeguards, a snack bar, and even a bandstand for free weekend concerts.
- **Cisco Beach** ★★: About 4 miles from town, in the southwestern quadrant of the island (from Main St., turn onto Milk St., which becomes Hummock Pond Rd.), Cisco enjoys vigorous waves—great for the surfers who flock here, not so great for the waterfront homeowners. Restrooms and lifeguards are available.
- **Coatue Beach** ★: This fishhook-shaped barrier beach, on the northeastern side of the island at Wauwinet, is Nantucket's outback, accessible only by four-wheel-drive vehicles, watercraft, or the very strong-legged. Swimming is strongly discouraged because of fierce tides.
- **Dionis Beach** ★★★: About 3 miles out of town (take the Madaket bike path to Eel Point Rd.) is Dionis, which enjoys the gentle Nantucket Sound surf and steep, picturesque bluffs. It's a great spot for swimming, picnicking, and shelling, and you'll find fewer children than at Jetties or Children's beaches. Stick to the established paths to prevent further erosion. Lifeguards patrol here, and restrooms are available.
- **Jetties Beach** ★★★: Located about a half-mile west of Children's Beach on North Beach Street, Jetties is about a 20-minute walk, or an even shorter bike ride, shuttle bus ride, or drive, from town (there's a large parking lot, but it fills up early on summer weekends). It's another family favorite for its mild waves, lifeguards, bathhouse, and restrooms. Facilities include the town tennis courts, volleyball nets, a skate park, and a playground; watersports equipment and chairs are also available to rent. In August, Jetties hosts an intense sand-castle competition, and the Fourth of July fireworks are held here.
- **Madaket Beach** ★★★: Accessible by Madaket Road, the 6-mile bike path that runs parallel to it, and by shuttle bus, this westerly beach is narrow and subject to pounding surf and sometimes serious crosscurrents. Unless it's a fairly tame day, you might content yourself with wading. It's the best spot on the island for admiring the sunset. Facilities include restrooms, lifeguards, and mobile food service.
- **Siasconset ('Sconset) Beach** ★★: The easterly coast of 'Sconset is as pretty as the town itself and rarely, if ever, crowded, perhaps because of the water's strong sideways tow. You can reach it by car, by shuttle bus, or via the Polpis or Milestone bike paths, about an 8-mile trip. Lifeguards are usually on duty, but the closest facilities (restrooms, grocery store, and cafe) are back in the center of the village.
- **Surfside Beach** ★★★: Three miles south of town via a popular bike/skate path, broad Surfside—equipped with lifeguards, restrooms, and a surprisingly accomplished little snack bar—is appropriately named and very popular. It draws thousands of visitors a day in high season, from college students to families, but the free-parking lot can only fit about 60 cars—you do the math, or better yet, ride your bike or take the shuttle bus.

BICYCLING ★★★ Several paved bike paths radiate out from the center of town to outlying beaches. The **bike paths** run about 6 miles west to Madaket, 3.5 miles south to Surfside, and 8 miles east to 'Sconset. To avoid backtracking from 'Sconset, continue north through the charming village, and return on the **Polpis Road bike path** ★★. Strong riders could do a whole circuit of the island in a day, but most will be content to combine a single route with a few hours at a beach.

For a free map of the island's bike paths, stop by **Young's Bicycle Shop,** at Steamboat Wharf (✆ **508/228-1151**). It's definitely the best place for bike rentals. See "Getting Around," above, for more bike-rental shops.

FISHING For shellfishing, you'll need a permit from the **harbormaster's office** at 34 Washington St. (✆ **508/228-7261**). You'll see surf-casters all over the island (no permit is required); for a guided trip, try Mike Monte of **Surf & Fly Fishing Trips** (✆ **508/228-0529**). Deep-sea charters heading out of Straight Wharf include Capt. Bob DeCosta's *The Albacore* (✆ **508/228-5074**), Capt. Josh Eldridge's *Monomoy* (✆ **508/228-6867**), and Capt. David Martin's *Absolute* (✆ **508/325-4000**).

NATURE TRAILS Through preservationist foresight, about one-third of Nantucket's shoreline is protected from development. Contact the **Nantucket Conservation Foundation** at 118 Cliff Rd. (✆ **508/228-2884**) for a map of its holdings ($4), which include the 205-acre **Windswept Cranberry Bog** (off Polpis Rd.), where bogs are interspersed amid hardwood forests; and a portion of the 1,100-acre **Coskata–Coatue Wildlife Refuge** ★★, comprising the barrier beaches beyond Wauwinet (see "Organized Tours & Cruises," below). **The Maria Mitchell Association** (see "Museums & Historic Landmarks," below) sponsors guided birding and wildflower walks in season.

WATERSPORTS **Nantucket Community Sailing** manages the concession at **Jetties Beach** (✆ **508/228-5358**), which offers lessons and rents out kayaks, sailboards, sailboats, and more. **Sea Nantucket,** on tiny Francis Street Beach off Washington Street (✆ **508/228-7499**), also rents kayaks; it's a quick sprint across the harbor to beautiful Coatue.

MUSEUMS & HISTORIC LANDMARKS

Hadwen House ★★ During Nantucket's most prosperous years, whaling merchant Joseph Starbuck built the "Three Bricks" (nos. 93, 95, and 97 Main St.) for his three sons. His daughter married successful businessman William Hadwen, owner of the candle factory that is now the Whaling Museum, and Hadwen built this grand Greek Revival home across the street from his brothers-in-law in 1845. Although locals (mostly Quakers) were scandalized by the opulence, the local outrage spurred Hadwen on, and he decided to make the home even grander than he had originally intended. It soon became a showplace for entertaining the Hadwens' many wealthy friends. The home has been furnished with period pieces, and the gardens have been maintained in period style.

96 Main St. (at Pleasant St., a few blocks southwest of the town center). ✆ **508/228-1894.** www.nha.org. Admission included in Nantucket Historical Association's History Ticket ($18 adults, $9 children under 16). AE, MC, V. June–Sept Mon–Sat 10am–5pm; Sun noon–5pm. Call for off-season hours. Closed Dec–Mar.

Jethro Coffin House ★ This 1686 saltbox is the oldest building left on the island. A National Historical Landmark, the brick design on its central chimney has earned it the nickname "The Horseshoe House." It was struck by lightning and severely

Nantucket Town

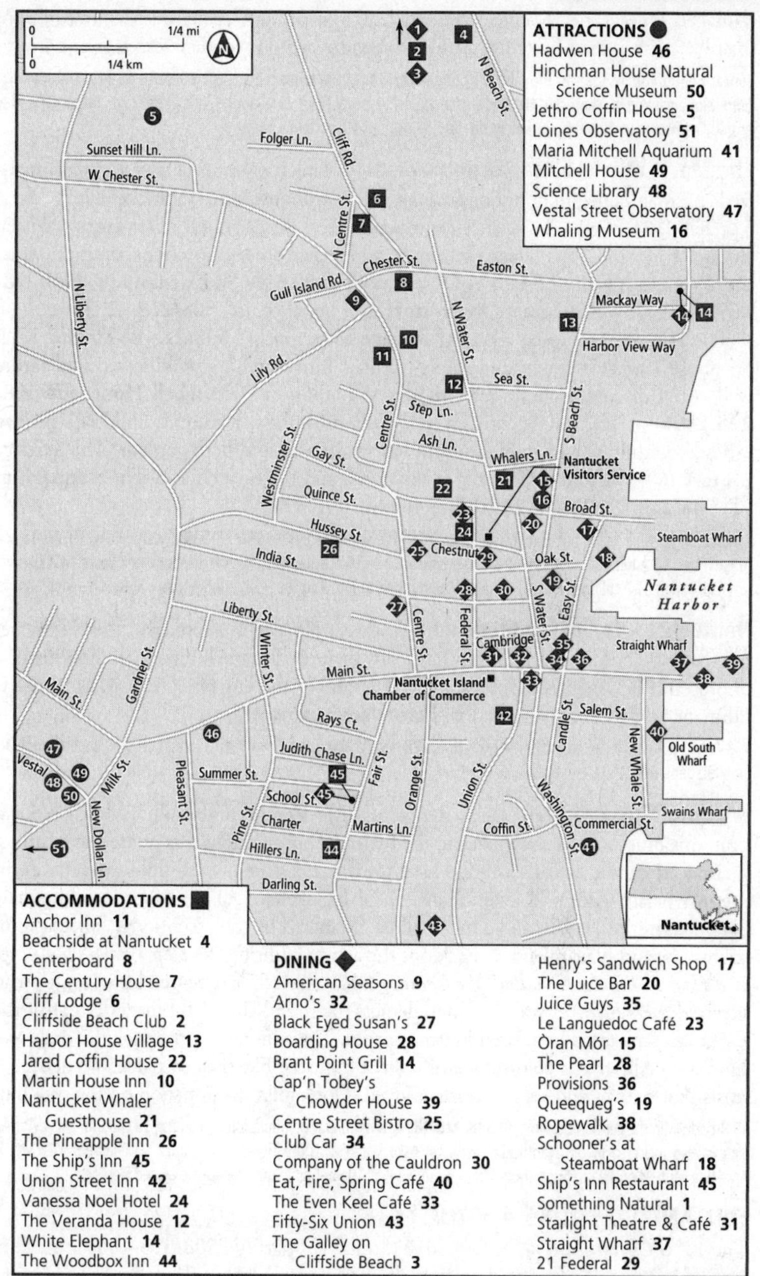

0
1/4 mi
0
1/4 km
N
ATTRACTIONS
Hadwen House 46
Hinchman House Natural Science Museum 50
Jethro Coffin House 5
Loines Observatory 51
Maria Mitchell Aquarium 41
Mitchell House 49
Science Library 48
Vestal Street Observatory 47
Whaling Museum 16
N Beach St.
Folger Ln.
Cliff Rd.
Sunset Hill Ln.
W Chester St.
N Centre St.
Chester St.
Easton St.
Gull Island Rd.
N Liberty St.
Mackay Way
Harbor View Way
Lily Rd.
N Water St.
Sea St.
S Beach St.
Step Ln.
Centre St.
Ash Ln.
Westminster St.
Gay St.
Whalers Ln.
Nantucket Visitors Service
Quince St.
Broad St.
Hussey St.
Steamboat Wharf
Chestnut
India St.
Oak St.
Nantucket Harbor
Liberty St.
Federal St.
S Water St.
Easy St.
Cambridge
Straight Wharf
Winter St.
Gardner St.
Main St.
Nantucket Island Chamber of Commerce
Rays Ct.
Salem St.
Old South Wharf
Judith Chase Ln.
Fair St.
Orange St.
Union St.
Candle St.
New Whale St.
Vestal
Milk St.
Pleasant St.
Summer St.
School St.
Washington St.
Swains Wharf
Pine St.
Charter
Martins Ln.
Coffin St.
Commercial St.
New Dollar Ln.
Hillers Ln.
Darling St.
Nantucket
ACCOMMODATIONS
Anchor Inn 11
Beachside at Nantucket 4
Centerboard 8
The Century House 7
Cliff Lodge 6
Cliffside Beach Club 2
Harbor House Village 13
Jared Coffin House 22
Martin House Inn 10
Nantucket Whaler Guesthouse 21
The Pineapple Inn 26
The Ship's Inn 45
Union Street Inn 42
Vanessa Noel Hotel 24
The Veranda House 12
White Elephant 14
The Woodbox Inn 44
DINING
American Seasons 9
Arno's 32
Black Eyed Susan's 27
Boarding House 28
Brant Point Grill 14
Cap'n Tobey's Chowder House 39
Centre Street Bistro 25
Club Car 34
Company of the Cauldron 30
Eat, Fire, Spring Café 40
The Even Keel Café 33
Fifty-Six Union 43
The Galley on Cliffside Beach 3
Henry's Sandwich Shop 17
The Juice Bar 20
Juice Guys 35
Le Languedoc Café 23
Òran Mór 15
The Pearl 28
Provisions 36
Queequeg's 19
Ropewalk 38
Schooner's at Steamboat Wharf 18
Ship's Inn Restaurant 45
Something Natural 1
Starlight Theatre & Café 31
Straight Wharf 37
21 Federal 29

damaged (in fact, nearly cut in two) in 1987, prompting a long-overdue restoration. It's filled with period furniture such as a trundle bed on wooden wheels.

Sunset Hill Rd. (off W. Chester Rd., about ½ mile northwest of the town center). © **508/228-1894.** www.nha.org. Admission included in Nantucket Historical Association's History Ticket ($18 adults, $9 children). AE, MC, V. Late May to mid-Oct Mon–Sat 10am–5pm; Sun noon–5pm. Closed mid-Oct to late May.

The Maria Mitchell Association ★★ *Kids* This is a group of six buildings organized and maintained in honor of distinguished astronomer and Nantucket native Maria Mitchell (1818–89). The science center consists of astronomical observatories, with a lecture series, children's science seminars, and stellar observation opportunities (when the sky is clear) from the **Loines Observatory** at 59 Milk St. Extension (© **508/228-8690**) and the **Vestal Street Observatory** at 3 Vestal St. (© **508/228-9273**).

The **Hinchman House Natural Science Museum** (© **508/228-0898**) at 7 Milk St. houses a visitor center and offers lectures, bird-watching, wildflower and nature walks, and discovery classes for children and adults. The **Mitchell House** (© **508/228-2896**) at 1 Vestal St., the astronomer's birthplace, features a children's history series and adult-artisan seminars, and has wildflower and herb gardens. The **Science Library** (© **508/228-9219**) is at 2 Vestal St., and the tiny, child-oriented **aquarium** (© **508/228-5387**) is at 28 Washington St.

4 Vestal St. (at Milk St., about ½ mile southwest of the town center). © **508/228-9198.** www.mmo.org. Admission to each site: $4 adults, $3 children. Museum pass (for birthplace, aquarium, science museum, and Vestal St. Observatory) $10 adults, $7 children ages 6–14. MC, V. Early June to late Aug Tues–Sat 10am–4pm; call for off-season hours.

Nantucket Life-Saving Museum ★★ *Finds* Housed in a replica of the Nantucket Life-Saving Station, the museum has loads of interesting exhibits, including historic photos and newspaper clippings, as well as one of the last remaining Massachusetts Humane Society surf boats and its horse-drawn carriage.

158 Polpis Rd. (2½ miles east of town) © **508/228-1885.** Admission $5 adults, $2 children. Mid-June to mid-Oct daily 9:30am–4pm.

Whaling Museum ★★★ *Kids* Reopened after a grand multimillion-dollar renovation, this museum is a showpiece in the region. Appropriately, it is housed in a former spermaceti-candle factory (candles used to be made from a waxy fluid extracted from sperm whales). Kids will love the awe-inspiring skeleton of a 43-foot finback whale (stranded in the 1960s), and adults will be fascinated by the exceptional collections of scrimshaw and nautical art. (Check out the action painting, *Ship Spermo of Nantucket in a Heavy Thunder-Squall on the Coast of California 1876,* executed by a captain who survived the storm.) A wall-size map depicts the round-the-world meanderings of the *Alpha,* accompanied by related journal entries. The admission price includes daily lectures on the brief and colorful history of the industry, like the beachside "whalebecue" feasts that natives and settlers once enjoyed. Don't miss the gift shop on the way out.

13 Broad St. (in the center of town). © **508/228-1894.** www.nha.org. Admission $15 adults, $8 children 5–14. Admission is also included in the Nantucket Historical Association's History Ticket ($18 adults, $9 children). AE, MC, V. Apr–Nov Mon–Wed 10am–5pm; Thurs 10am–9pm; Fri–Sat 10am–5pm; Sun noon–5pm. Closed Dec–Mar.

ORGANIZED TOURS & CRUISES

The 1926 ***Christina*** ★★, at Slip 1016, Straight Wharf (© **508/325-4000**), is a classic mahogany catboat. A sail around the harbor is probably the best entertainment bargain on Nantucket ($25 for a 1½-hr. trip). The sunset trips ($35) tend to sell out a day or two in advance. No sailings November through April.

The Trustees of the Reservations, a statewide conservation organization, runs the 3-hour **Coskata–Coatue Wildlife Refuge Natural History Tour** ★★★ (✆ **508/228-6799**). The trip via Ford Expedition takes you over sand dunes and through rare habitat out to the **Great Point Lighthouse,** a replica of the 1818 original. On the way, you might spot snowy egrets, ospreys, and terns. Tours are offered mid-May to mid-October, daily at 9:30am and 1:30pm. The cost is $40 for adults and $15 for children 15 and under; call to reserve.

***Endeavor* Sailing Excursions** ★★, at Slip 15 on Straight Wharf (✆ **508/228-5585**), offers jaunts around the harbor on the *Endeavor,* a 31-foot replica of a historic Friendship sloop. Skipper James Genthner will gladly drop you off at one the beaches for a bit of sunbathing or beachcombing. Rates are $25 to $35 for a 1½-hour sail; reservations are recommended. No sailings November through April.

SHOPPING

All of the shops listed below are right in the center of Nantucket Town.

ANTIQUES/COLLECTIBLES **Tonkin of Nantucket,** 33 Main St. (✆ **508/228-9697**), specializes in English and French antiques. Its offerings include silver, china, ship models, and majolica.

ART & CRAFTS **The Artists' Association of Nantucket** has the widest selection of work by locals, and the gallery at 19 Washington St. (✆ **508/228-0294**) is impressive. It's open April through January and by appointment only February and March.

Exquisite art glass, as well as ceramics, jewelry, and basketry, can be found at **Dane Gallery,** 28 Centre St. (✆ **508/228-7779**).

Sailor's Valentine in the Macy Warehouse on lower Main Street (✆ **508/228-2011**) houses a collection of contemporary fine art, folk art, and "outsider art." There are also new versions of the namesake craft, a boxed design of colorful shells, which 19th-century sailors used to bring back from the Caribbean for their sweethearts at home.

FASHION Martha's Vineyard may have spawned "Black Dog" fever, but this island boasts the inimitable "Nantucket reds"—cotton clothing that starts out tomato-red and washes out to salmon-pink. The fashion originated at **Murray's Toggery Shop,** 62 Main St. (✆ **800/368-2134** or 508/228-0437).

WHERE TO STAY

As with Martha's Vineyard, we've given only summer rates here, because Nantucket is so seasonal. However, if you do visit in the off season, you can find substantial discounts at any of the places that remain open. Note, though, that lodging rates on Nantucket are at high-season levels during the popular Christmas Stroll in December and Daffodil Festival in April.

VERY EXPENSIVE

Cliffside Beach Club ★★★ *Finds* Right on the beach and a 15-minute walk from town, this is the premier lodging on the island. It may not be as fancy as some, but there's a sublime beachy-ness to the whole setup, from the simply decorated rooms and the cheerful, youthful staff to the colorful umbrellas lined up on the beach. All guest rooms have such luxuries as French milled soaps, thick towels, and exceptional linens. Lucky guests on the Fourth of July get a front-row seat for the fireworks staged at Jetties Beach nearby.

46 Jefferson Ave. (about 1 mile from town center), Nantucket, MA 02554. ✆ **800/932-9645** or 508/228-0618. Fax 508/325-4735. www.cliffsidebeach.com. 25 units, 1 cottage. Summer $395–$655 double; $755–$1,535 suite; $785 apt; $955 cottage. Rates include continental breakfast. AE. Closed mid-Oct to late May. **Amenities:** Restaurant (The Galley, an elegant French bistro); exercise facility (Cybex equipment and a trainer on staff); indoor hydrotherapy spa; steam saunas; concierge; climate-controlled massage room; babysitting. *In room:* A/C, TV/VCR, fridge, coffeemaker, hair dryer.

Nantucket Whaler Guesthouse ★★ This 1850s sea captain's house is unique in that all of the rooms are suites with their own entrance and kitchen facilities. Compared to other B&Bs on the island, the Nantucket Whaler Guesthouse has a particularly private feel, almost like having your own apartment. All rooms are comfortably outfitted with cottage-y furnishings including overstuffed couches and stacks of games and books.

8 North Water St. (in the center of town), Nantucket, MA 02554. ✆ **800/462-6882** or 508/228-6597. Fax 508/228-6291. www.nantucketwhaler.com. 12 units (8 tub/shower, 4 shower only). Summer $325–$495 double; $625–$695 2-bedroom suite. AE, DC, MC, V. Closed mid-Dec to late Apr. No children under age 12. *In room:* A/C, TV/VCR, CD player, dataport, hair dryer, iron.

Vanessa Noel ★ This is Nantucket's trendiest inn. Vanessa Noel, a shoe designer whose shoe store is on the first floor, has decorated the eight rooms in this historic building with boutique hotel features like Philippe Starck fixtures, Bulgari toiletries, 15-inch flatscreen plasma televisions, and minibars stocked with the hotel's bottled water. Most of the rooms are tiny, though there are two including a fun attic space that are fairly spacious. **The Vanno Bar,** a caviar and champagne bar on the first floor, has novelties like leopard-print calfskin banquettes, two swings, and food imported from Caviarteria, the New York City caviar emporium.

5 Chestnut St. (in the center of town), Nantucket, MA 02554. ✆ **508/228-5300.** Fax 508/228-8995. www.VANNO.com. 8 units. Summer $340–$480 double. AE, DISC, MC, V. Open year-round. *In room:* A/C, TV, minibar, hair dryer.

The Wauwinet ★★ This beachfront retreat is Nantucket's only Relais & Châteaux property. The inn is next to a wildlife sanctuary and is nestled between the Atlantic Ocean and Nantucket Bay. Each lovely room is individually decorated, with pine armoires, plenty of wicker, exquisite Audubon prints, and handsome fabrics, though some are on the small side. Extras include robes, bottled water, and a personalized set of engraved note cards. The staff goes to great lengths to please, ferrying you into town, for instance, or dispatching you on a 21-foot launch across the bay to your own private strip of beach in season.

120 Wauwinet Rd. (P.O. Box 2580), about 8 miles east of Nantucket center, Nantucket, MA 02554. ✆ **800/426-8718** or 508/228-0145. Fax 508/325-0657. www.wauwinet.com. 25 units, 10 cottages (all with tub/shower). Summer $500–$1,020 double; $950–$1,200 cottage. Rates include full breakfast and afternoon wine and cheese. AE, DC, MC, V. Closed Nov to mid-May. **Amenities:** Restaurant (fine dining); 2 clay tennis courts w/pro shop and teaching pro; croquet lawn; row boats, sail boats, sea kayaks, and mountain bikes on loan; concierge; room service (8am–9pm). *In room:* A/C, TV/VCR, CD player, hair dryer, iron.

White Elephant ★★★ This luxury property, right on the harbor, is the ultimate in-town lodging. Guest rooms (distributed among one building and 12 cottages) are big and airy (the most spacious on Nantucket), with country-chic decor. About half the rooms have working fireplaces, and most have harbor views. The same company owns Breakers, a 25-room hotel next door that offers a less bustling atmosphere.

50 Easton St. (P.O. Box 1139), Nantucket, MA 02554. ✆ **800/445-6574** or 508/228-2500. Fax 508/325-1195. www.whiteelephanthotel.com. 52 units, 11 cottages (61 tub/shower, 2 shower only). Summer $525–$625 double;

$570 1-bedroom cottage; $1,450 2-bedroom cottage. Rates include full breakfast. AE, DC, DISC, MC, V. Closed Nov–Mar. **Amenities:** Restaurant (lobster and steakhouse serving lunch and dinner daily plus an afternoon raw bar); exercise room; concierge; business lounge; full room service; fee-based laundry and dry-cleaning service. *In room:* A/C, TV/VCR/DVD, dataport, fridge, hair dryer, iron, safe.

EXPENSIVE

Beachside at Nantucket ★ No ordinary motel, the Beachside has 90 guest rooms that have been lavished with Provençal prints and handsome rattan and wicker furniture; the patios and decks overlooking the central courtyard with its heated pool have been prettified with French doors and latticework.

30 N. Beach St. (about ¾ mile west of the town center), Nantucket, MA 02554. ✆ **800/322-4433** or 508/228-2241. Fax 508/228-8901. www.thebeachside.com. 90 units (all with tub/shower). Summer $280–$335 double; $650–$675 suite. Rates include continental breakfast. AE, DC, DISC, MC, V. Closed late Oct to late Apr. **Amenities:** Heated outdoor pool. *In room:* A/C, TV, fridge, hair dryer.

Harbor House Village ★★ *Kids* This property, which recently underwent a multimillion-dollar freshening-up, is now one of Nantucket's most full-service lodging options, complete with pool and two restaurants. It is just a 5-minute walk from the center of Nantucket Town. The main building, the 35-room historic Harbor House, was built 130 years ago, but few vestiges of the past remain. The rooms are decorated with pine and wicker furniture; some are quite spacious and have balconies.

South Beach St., Nantucket, MA 02554. ✆ **866/325-9300** or 508/228-1500. Fax 508/228-7639. www.harborhousevillage.com. 104 units. Summer $270–$410 double. AE, DC, DISC, MC, V. Closed early Dec to mid-Apr. **Amenities:** 2 restaurants (a seasonal Chinese restaurant and a breakfast cafe); bar/lounge (featuring Mon Night Football on the large screen TV in the fall); outdoor heated pool (in season); free children's program in summer; concierge; free shuttle from Steamship Authority ferry; babysitting; laundry service; dry cleaning. *In room:* A/C, TV, dataport, hair dryer, iron, VCR or fridge available on request.

Jared Coffin House ★★ *Kids* This grand brick manse built in 1845 is the social center of town. Accommodations range from well-priced singles to spacious doubles. The central location does have a drawback: front rooms can be quite noisy. Although the breakfast is not included in the room rate, it is known as the best in town and attracts many locals. To avoid long waits, we suggest calling ahead and putting your name on the list.

29 Broad St. (at Centre St.), Nantucket, MA 02554. ✆ **800/248-2405** or 508/228-2400. Fax 508/228-8549. www.jaredcoffinhouse.com. 60 units (52 tub/shower, 8 shower only). Summer $290–$450 double. AE, DC, DISC, MC, V. Open year-round. **Amenities:** 2 restaurants (family and tavern); concierge. *In room:* TV, dataport, fridge, coffeemaker, hair dryer, iron.

The Pineapple Inn ★★ This beautifully renovated historic inn has quickly become one of the premier places to stay on the island. The graceful Quaker entrance of the 1838 home leads to spacious guest rooms decorated with fine reproductions and antiques, Oriental rugs, marble bathrooms, and many four-poster canopy beds. Breakfast here is extra deluxe with fresh baked goods, espresso, cappuccino, and freshly squeezed orange juice.

10 Hussey St. (in the center of town), Nantucket, MA 02554. ✆ **508/228-9992**. Fax 508/325-6051. www.pineappleinn.com. 12 units (8 tub/shower, 4 shower only). Summer $165–$375 double. Rates include continental breakfast. AE, MC, V. Closed early Dec to mid-Apr. No children under age 8. *In room:* A/C, TV, dataport, hair dryer, iron.

Union Street Inn ★★ *Finds* Innkeepers Deborah and Ken Withrow have a terrific location for their 1770s property, a quiet, residential section that's just steps from Main Street. Ken's experience in big hotels shows in the full concierge service offered here. Many guest rooms have canopied or four-poster beds; half have working wood-burning fireplaces. All are outfitted with antique furniture and fixtures. Unlike many Nantucket inns that are forbidden by zoning laws to serve a full breakfast, this inn's location allows for a superb complete breakfast on the garden patio. The inn is outfitted with wireless Internet access.

7 Union St. (in the center of town), Nantucket, MA 02554. ✆ **800/225-5116** or 508/228-9222. Fax 508/325-0848. www.unioninn.com. 12 units (1 with tub/shower, 11 shower only). Summer $260–$395 double; $495 suite. Rates include full breakfast. AE, MC, V. Closed Jan–Mar. *In room:* A/C, TV, CD player, hair dryer, no phone.

The Veranda House ★★ *Finds* This newly reopened classic guesthouse, formerly known as the Overlook Hotel, has been in the same family for generations. It's in a quiet neighborhood, a short walk from the center of town. Wraparound porches surround the inn and serve as the communal area for enjoying the sunshine or meeting fellow guests. Rooms are on the small side but smartly decorated with antique photos. Beds are made with Frette linens and goosedown comforters. On the top floor are seven rooms that share bathrooms. Breakfast, which features hot delicacies like quiches and frittatas, is served on the ample front porch. The entire inn property is covered by a wireless Internet service.

Three Step Lane (a few blocks from town center), Nantucket, MA 02554. ✆ **508/228-0695.** Fax 508/374-0406. www.theverandahouse.com. 20 units, 7 with shared bathroom. Summer $229–$339 double; $339–$399 2-bedroom suite. Rates include continental breakfast. AE, MC, V. Closed mid-Oct to late May. *In room:* A/C, hair dryer.

MODERATE

Anchor Inn ★ *Value* This historic gem, an 1806 captain's home, is next to the Old North Church. Another property, 72 Centre St., is three doors down from the inn. Authentic details can be found throughout both houses, in the antique hardware and paneling, wide-board floors, and period furnishings. The five rooms in the 72 Centre St. house are a particularly good value; they are smaller and less expensive.

66 Centre St. (P.O. Box 387, in the center of town), Nantucket, MA 02554. ✆ **508/228-0072.** www.anchor-inn.net. 16 units (2 tub/shower, 9 shower only). Summer $185–$225 double. Rates include continental breakfast. AE, MC, V. Closed Jan–Feb. *In room:* A/C, TV, hair dryer.

Centerboard ★★ This updated 1886 home boasts parquet floors, Oriental rugs, lavish fabrics, plush feather mattresses, and lace-trimmed linens. Of the inn's seven bedrooms, the first-floor suite is perhaps the most romantic, with a green-marble Jacuzzi and a private living room with fireplace. Other rooms and bathrooms are small, but all have bathrobes and minifridges.

8 Chester St. (in the center of town), Nantucket, MA 02554. ✆ **508/228-9696.** Fax 508/325-4798. www.centerboardguesthouse.com 7 units. Summer $210–$295 double; $325–$425 suite. Rates include continental breakfast. AE, MC, V. Closed Nov–Apr. *In room:* A/C, TV, fridge, hair dryer.

The Century House ★ This handsome inn offers a homey atmosphere just a short walk to the center of town. One of the highlights is the immense wraparound porch, complete with rocking chairs, where you could relax away an afternoon if you like. Rooms, which are spotlessly clean, range widely in size from the garret rooms on the third floor, to more spacious expanses on the second floor. Little extras include luxury bath products and robes. The entire property is outfitted with free wireless Internet. An artist in residence program means the walls are hung with numerous interesting paintings.

10 Cliff Rd. (a few blocks from the center of town), Nantucket, MA 02554. ✆ **888/INN-0530** or 508/228-0530 (late Oct to mid-May 561/655-3127). www.centuryhouse.com. 16 units. Summer $145–$345 double; $325–$450 apt.

Rates include continental breakfast and afternoon tea. MC, V. Closed late Oct to mid-May. *In room:* A/C, TV/DVD, CD, hair dryer.

Cliff Lodge ★★ *Finds* Debby and John Bennett have freshened up this charming 1771 whaling captain's house with their own country style. The cheerful guest rooms feature colorful quilts and splatter-painted floors. Rooms range from a first-floor beauty with king-size bed, paneled walls, and fireplace to the tiny third-floor rooms tucked into the eaves. The spacious apartment in the rear of the house is a sunny delight. Climb up to the widow's walk for a bird's-eye view of the town and harbor.

9 Cliff Rd. (a few blocks from the center of town), Nantucket, MA 02554. ✆ **508/228-9480.** Fax 508/228-6308. www.nantucket.net/lodging/clifflodge. 12 units. Summer $145 single; $180–$295 double; $425 apt. Rates include continental breakfast. MC, V. Open year-round. No children under 12. *In room:* A/C, TV.

Martin House Inn ★★ *Value* This is one of the lower-priced B&Bs in town, but also one of the most stylish, with a formal parlor and a spacious side porch, complete with hammock. Some guest rooms in this historic 1803 mariner's home have four-poster beds and working fireplaces. The four garret singles with a shared bathroom are a bargain.

61 Centre St. (between Broad and Chester sts.; a couple blocks from town center), Nantucket, MA 02554. ✆ **508/228-0678.** Fax 508/325-4798. www.nantucket.net/lodging/martinn. 13 units (4 tub/shower, 5 shower only, 4 with shared bathroom). Summer $110 single; $180–$270 double; $350 suites. Rates include continental breakfast. AE, MC, V. Open year-round. *In room:* No phone.

The Ship's Inn ★ *Value* This pretty, historic inn is on a quiet side street, just slightly removed—3 blocks—from Nantucket's center. Rooms are comfortable, spacious, and charming, and offer a good variety of bed arrangements like single rooms and twin beds. The restaurant downstairs holds its own (see "Where to Dine," below).

13 Fair St. (a few blocks from town center), Nantucket, MA 02554. ✆ **888/872-4052** or 508/228-0040. Fax 508/228-6524. www.nantucket.net/lodging/shipsinn. 12 units, 2 with shared bathroom. Summer $110 single with shared bathroom; $235 double. Rates include continental breakfast. AE, DISC, MC, V. Closed late Oct to mid-May. **Amenities:** Restaurant (fine-dining) located in the basement. *In room:* A/C, TV, fridge, hair dryer, iron.

The Woodbox Inn ★ *Value* Built in 1709, this is Nantucket's oldest inn and it's an atmospheric place. In a residential section of the historic district, the inn is a short walk to Main Street. The well-known restaurant on-site serves breakfast and dinner and is famous for popovers. The rooms, decorated with both period antiques and reproductions, plus canopy beds, range from cozy to spacious. Some have refrigerators and phones. There are also one- and two-bedroom suites with working fireplaces. **The Woodbox** is a popular spot for breakfast (not included in the room rates).

29 Fair St. (a few blocks from town center) Nantucket, MA 02554. ✆ **508/228-0587.** Fax 508/228-7527. www.woodbox.com. 9 units. Summer $180–$210 double; $210 1-room suite; $310 2-room suite. (Unusual in the area, a 10% "service" fee is added to your bill here, in addition to tax.) No credit cards. Closed early Jan to late Mar. **Amenities:** Fine-dining restaurant serving breakfast and dinner. *In room:* Fridge.

WHERE TO DINE

VERY EXPENSIVE

Brant Point Grill ★★ NEW AMERICAN At this lobster, steak, and chops house, many of the signature dishes, like the cedar planked Atlantic salmon and rotisserie of prime rib, are prepared on the Fire Cone grill, a 21st-century interpretation of a Native American technique that cooks food by radiant heat and imparts it with a smoky mesquite flavor. If you can't sit on the terrace, try to snag a seat near one of the windows where you can watch the twilight fade over the harbor. Dinner at this establishment is an expensive proposition. However, the raw bar is open July through Labor Day from 4 to 7pm for light snacks.

At the White Elephant Hotel (Easton and Willard sts.). ✆ **508/325-1320.** Collared shirt and long pants requested for gentlemen. Reservations strongly recommended. Main courses $26–$39. AE, DISC, MC, V. Mid-Apr to early Dec daily noon–2:30pm and 6–10pm. Closed mid-Dec to mid-Apr.

Chanticleer Inn ★★★ MODERN BISTRO The biggest news on the Nantucket restaurant scene is the reopening of Chanticleer. The fancy French restaurant in the rose-covered cottage in 'Sconset had long been one of the island's most cherished fine-dining spots until it closed a couple years ago. Now it is being reinvented by Susan Handy and chef Jeff Worster, who have made the casual Black Eyed Susan's (see below) into one of the island's best, and funkiest, dining choices. The pair plan to freshen up the decor at Chanticleer and make the restaurant more approachable. Unlike at the old Chanticleer, jackets won't be required, but diners will likely be wearing their best casual yet elegant island attire.

9 New St., Siasconset. ✆ **508/257-4499.** Reservations recommended. Jacket preferred for men. Main courses $25–$45. AE, DC, MC, V. Mid-May to mid-Oct daily 6:30–9:30pm. Closed mid-Oct to mid-May.

Cinco Restaurant and Bar ★ INTERNATIONAL TAPAS This exquisite new restaurant is capitalizing on the new vogue for tapas, those little plates of Spanish-style food. This is not the place to come with a big appetite, but it's a great place for a light meal and to enjoy lively atmosphere. There are about two dozen choices on the menu, three or four per person would make a small meal, but you'll want to pass them around and share. The preparations and tastes are unusual and sophisticated. There are cured meats, marinated vegetables, grilled fish, and other delicacies, for example cornmeal crusted softshell crab and Nantucket fluke seviche.

5 Amelia Dr. (¼ mile from the rotary, just off South Rd.). ✆ **508/325-5151.** Reservations recommended. Tapas $11–$31. MC, V. Mid-June to Sept daily 6–10:30pm; call for off-season hours.

Club Car ★★★ CONTINENTAL For decades one of the top restaurants on Nantucket, this posh venue is popular with locals. The menu has classic French influences. Interesting offerings include a first course of Japanese octopus in the style of Bangkok and an entree of roast rack of lamb Club Car (with fresh herbs, honey-mustard glaze, and minted Madeira sauce). Some nights, seven-course tasting menus are available for $65 per person. The lounge area is within an antique car from the old Nantucket railroad.

1 Main St. ✆ **508/228-1101.** Reservations recommended. Main courses $24–$45. MC, V. July–Aug daily 11am–3pm and 6–10pm; call for off-season hours. Closed Jan–Apr.

The Galley on Cliffside Beach ★★★ NEW AMERICAN With the best setting of any restaurant on the island—on a private beach on the property of Cliffside Beach Club (see "Where to Stay," earlier in this chapter)—this restaurant offers a particularly chic yet beachy fine-dining experience. Given the setting, it's no surprise that The Galley specializes in seafood, caught locally by island fishermen. Produce comes from the restaurant's own organic garden. The menu changes often, but noteworthy menu options include the restaurant's signature New England clam chowder with smoked bacon, or the shrimp tempura served with Asian slaw. As a main course, there might be a luscious lobster risotto, native halibut with forest mushroom strudel, Black Angus filet, or simply a 2-pound lobster with all the fixings.

54 Jefferson Ave., Nantucket. ✆ **508/228-9641.** Reservations suggested. Main courses $29–$39. AE, MC, V. Daily noon–2pm and 5–10pm. Closed Oct to late May.

The Pearl ★★ NEW AMERICAN Miami Beach meets Nantucket at this swank establishment. The numerous stylish touches include appetizers and desserts served in martini glasses; a contemporary look with bluish lighting and large fish tanks; and an extensive champagne list. Skip the *grande deluxe plateau de mer;* it's not a lot of shellfish for a lot of money. Instead, go for the wild mushroom galette with white truffle cream, and for a main course, look no further than the pan-roasted striped bass with citrus tomato infusion.

12 Federal St. ✆ **508/228-9701.** Reservations recommended. Main courses $33–$45. AE, MC, V. Mid-May to mid-Oct daily 6–10pm; call for off-season hours. Closed Jan–Mar.

Straight Wharf ★★ NEW AMERICAN Straight Wharf, on the waterfront in the center of town, has long been known for its creative cuisine. Choices may include fancy appetizers like seared beef carpaccio with white truffle oil, and main courses like native lobster *a la nage,* which is prepared with a champagne sauce. Devoted regulars at Straight Wharf swear by the smoked bluefish pâté served with herb focaccia. A more affordable "summer grill" menu, served in the bar area, features simpler fare. Make your reservation for 8pm on the deck so you can watch the sun set over the harbor.

Straight Wharf. ✆ **508/228-4499.** Reservations recommended. Main courses $34–$38; summer grill menu $16–$22. AE, MC, V. July–Aug Tues–Sun 6–9:30pm; call for off-season hours. Closed late Sept to late May.

The Summer House ★★ *Finds* NEW AMERICAN The classic 'Sconset-style atmosphere distinguishes this fine-dining experience from others on the island: wicker and wrought-iron, roses and honeysuckle. A pianist plays nightly—often Gershwin standards, and the pounding Atlantic Ocean is just over the bluff. Distinctive main courses include unusual lobster cutlets with coconut-jasmine risotto timbale and mint-tomato relish. If it's blueberry season, end your meal with the blueberry pie.

17 Ocean Ave., Siasconset. ✆ **508/257-9976.** Reservations recommended. Main courses $33–$39. AE, MC, V. July–Aug daily 11:30am–3pm (weather permitting) and 6–11pm; mid-May to June and Sept to mid-Oct Wed–Sun 6–11pm. Closed mid-Oct to Apr.

Topper's at The Wauwinet ★★★ REGIONAL/NEW AMERICAN This 1850 restaurant—part of a secluded resort—is a tastefully subdued knockout, with wicker armchairs, splashes of chintz, and a two-tailed mermaid to oversee a chill-chasing fire. Try to sit at one of the cozy banquettes if you can. The menu features the finest regional cuisine: Lobster is a major event (it's often sautéed with champagne beurre blanc), and be on the lookout for specials like arctic char. Desserts, like the toasted brioche with poached pears and caramel sauce, are fanciful and fabulous. The Wauwinet runs a complimentary launch service from mid-June to mid-September to the restaurant for lunch and dinner; it leaves from Straight Wharf at 11am and 5pm, takes 1 hour, and also makes the return trip.

120 Wauwinet Rd. (off Squam Rd.), Wauwinet. ✆ **508/228-8768.** Reservations required for dinner and the launch ride over. Jacket requested for men. Main courses $34–$56. AE, DC, MC, V. May–Oct Mon–Sat noon–2pm and 6–10pm; Sun 11:30am–2pm and 6–10pm. Closed Nov–Apr.

EXPENSIVE

American Seasons ★★ REGIONAL AMERICAN This romantic little restaurant has a great theme: Choose your region (New England, Pacific Coast, Wild West, or Down South) and select creative offerings. Start, for instance, with Louisiana crayfish risotto with fire-roasted onion and fried parsnips in a sweet corn purée from Down South; then move on to the Pacific Coast's aged beef sirloin with caramelized shallot and Yukon potato hash. A lighter tapas menu is available throughout the evening.

80 Centre St. (2 blocks from the center of town). ✆ **508/228-7111.** Reservations recommended. Main courses $24–$30. AE, MC, V. late Apr–Nov daily 6–9pm. Closed early Dec to mid-Apr.

Boarding House ★★ NEW AMERICAN This centrally located fine-dining restaurant doubles as one of the most popular bars in town. You can dine in the romantic lower-level dining room or upstairs in the hopping bar area. But on clear summer nights, you'll want to get one of the tables outside on the patio. The menu has definite Asian and Mediterranean influences, but the signature dish is the classic grilled lobster tails with grilled asparagus, mashed potatoes, and champagne beurre blanc. The award-winning wine list offers a range of prices.

12 Federal St. ✆ **508/228-9622.** Reservations recommended. Main courses $26–$36. AE, MC, V. July–Aug daily 6–10pm; call for off-season hours. Open year-round.

Company of the Cauldron ★★★ CONTINENTAL Considered the most romantic restaurant on the island, this candlelit dining room features a classical harpist in season. The menu is unusual in that there is one three- to four-course fixed-price meal each night, so would-be patrons must check the menu out front or call ahead to see which night to go. Dietary preferences can be accommodated with advance notice. The main course could be seafood, a special swordfish preparation, or a meat dish, like beef Wellington.

5 India St. (between Federal and Centre sts.) ✆ **508/228-4016.** www.companyofthecauldron.com. Reservations required. Fixed-price dinner $50. MC, V. Early July to early Sept Tues–Sun, 2 seatings 6:45 and 8:45pm; call for off-season hours. Closed mid-Oct to mid-May, except Thanksgiving weekend and the first 2 weeks of Dec.

Fifty-six Union ★★ NEW AMERICAN This understated restaurant offers fine-dining without pretensions: just good service, a pleasing contemporary atmosphere, and wonderful food. Diners can sit in the bar area, which tends to be loud and lively, in the quieter Garden Room or on the outdoor patio. Intriguing appetizers include a salad with prosciutto and gilled fig, and a crabmeat spring roll with a pepper coulis. Main course choices range from Javanese fried rice to risotto with wild mushrooms to a rack of Colorado lamb.

56 Union St. (½ mile from Main St.) ✆ **508/228-6135.** www.fiftysixunion.com. Reservations suggested. Main courses $23–$32. AE, MC, V. Early July to early Sept daily 6–10pm, Sun 10am–1pm; call for off-season hours. Open year-round.

Òran Mór ★★★ *Finds* INTERNATIONAL New owners have taken over this second-floor waterfront venue that has for several years been one of the best restaurants on the island. The new chef, formerly of Topper's (see above) will likely maintain the high quality of this venue. The restaurant is known for a menu that changes often with surprising and unusual choices. Appetizer standouts in past years have been the lobster risotto and the Thai littleneck clam hot pot with *somen* (thin white Japanese noodles similar to vermicelli). Intriguing entrees include grilled buffalo tenderloin and sautéed gray sole with sauce puttanesca.

2 S. Beach St. (in the center of town). ✆ **508/228-8655.** Reservations recommended. Main courses $22–$34. AE, MC, V. July–Aug daily 6–10pm; Sept–June Thurs–Sat and Mon–Tues 6–9pm, Sun noon–9pm. Open year-round.

Ropewalk ★ SEAFOOD This open-air restaurant on the harbor is Nantucket's only outdoor raw bar, and it's where the yachting crowd hangs out after a day on the boat. While the food is a bit overpriced, the location is prime. This is a good place to enjoy a light meal or appetizers, such as fried calamari, crab cakes, or fried oysters. The dinner menu includes grilled swordfish with ratatouille and grilled breast of chicken with roasted garlic and rosemary jus.

1 Straight Wharf. ✆ **508/228-8886.** No reservations. Main courses $23–$33. MC, V. Apr to mid-Dec daily 11am–10pm. Closed mid-Oct to Apr.

Ship's Inn Restaurant ★★ NEW AMERICAN This intimate restaurant in the brick-walled basement of a 12-room inn is one of the island's most romantic dining options. The waitstaff here is professional and entertaining, a real treat. The menu features a variety of fresh fish, meat, and pasta dishes including several lighter options made without butter or cream. A flavorful starter here is the Roquefort and walnut terrine with Asian pear. As a main course, popular dishes include the pan-roasted Muscovy duck breast and the grilled yellowtail flounder. For a festive dessert, there's always the Grand Marnier soufflé.

13 Fair St. ✆ **508/228-0040.** Reservations recommended. Main courses $28–$38. AE, DISC, MC, V. July–Sept Wed–Mon 5–10pm. Call for off-season hours. Closed Nov–Apr.

21 Federal ★★ NEW AMERICAN This restaurant seems to get better every year. For melt-in-your-mouth pleasure, try the appetizer of tuna tartare with wasabi crackers and cilantro aioli. The fish entrees are the most popular here, although you might opt for the fine breast of duck accompanied by pecan wild rice and shiitake mushrooms. We love the pan-crisped salmon with champagne cabbage and beet-butter sauce, which has been a staple of the menu for years.

21 Federal St. (in the center of town). ✆ **508/228-2121.** Reservations recommended. Main courses $27–$37. AE, MC, V. Apr to mid-Dec daily 6–9:30pm. Closed mid-Dec to Mar.

MODERATE

Black Eyed Susan's ★★ *Finds* ETHNIC ECLECTIC This is supremely exciting food in a funky bistro atmosphere. Reservations are accepted for the 6pm seating only, and they go fast. Others must line up outside; the line starts forming around 5:30pm. The menu is in constant flux, as chef Jeff Worster's mood and influences change every 3 weeks. We always enjoy the spicy Thai fish cake, and the tandoori chicken with green mango chutney. There's usually a Southwestern touch like the Dos Equis beer–battered catfish quesadilla with mango slaw, hoppin' john, and jalapeño. There's no liquor license, but you can BYOB.

10 India St. (in the center of town). ✆ **508/325-0308.** Reservations accepted for 6pm seating only. Main courses $15–$25. No credit cards. Apr–Oct daily 7am–1pm, Mon–Sat 6–10pm; call for off-season hours. Closed Nov–Mar.

Centre Street Bistro ★★ NEW AMERICAN This tiny fine-dining restaurant in the center of Nantucket town is owned and operated by Ruth and Tim Pitts, who are considered top chefs on the island. This cozy place features wonderful, creative cuisine at reasonable prices, especially compared to other island fine-dining restaurants. The menu changes often, but high points in the past have included the warm goat cheese tart to start, and the Long Island duck breast with pumpkin and butternut squash risotto as a main course.

29 Centre St. ✆ **508/228-8470.** No reservations. Main courses $19–$25. No credit cards. Wed–Sun noon–2:30pm and 6–10pm. Open year-round.

Eat, Fire, Spring ★★ NEW AMERICAN This hip outdoor cafe, located past the galleries at the end of Old South Wharf, is a popular place. Unlike many of Nantucket's restaurants, this is a casual place, the perfect spot to enjoy a leisurely lunch on a sunny day, or a light dinner on a sultry night. The eclectic menu features standards like blackened tuna or steak tips, but prepared with unique sauces and sides. There's live music nightly.

12 Old South Wharf. ✆ **508/228-5756.** Reservations not accepted. Main courses $18–$25. AE, MC, V. Late June to early Sept daily noon–3pm and 6–9pm. Call for off-season hours. Closed early Sept to early June.

Le Languedoc Cafe ★★ NEW AMERICAN Nantucket's most authentic French cafe offers a cozy atmosphere and reasonable prices. An expensive dining room is upstairs, but locals prefer the casual bistro atmosphere downstairs and out on the terrace. Soups are superb, as are the Angus-steak burgers with garlic french fries. More elaborate dishes include the roasted tenderloin of pork stuffed with figs and pancetta.

24 Broad St. ✆ **508/228-2552.** www.lelanguedoc.com. Reservations not accepted for cafe; reservations recommended for dining room. Main courses $9–$19. AE, MC, V. June–Sept daily 5:30–9:30pm, Tues–Sun noon–2pm; call for off-season hours. Closed mid-Dec to Apr.

Queequeg's ★ NEW AMERICAN A cozy bistro atmosphere and good value are the hallmarks of this small restaurant, which is tucked along a side street behind the Athenaeum. Outside seating is available on the patio in good weather. As befits the Moby Dick reference in the name, the specialty here is seafood. The menu offers a range from basics to fancier fare. For example, as an appetizer, you could have the New England clam chowder or tuna tartare. The rich and flavorful pan-seared halibut with Parmesan risotto is a favorite with locals. Meat-lovers may enjoy chargrilled New Zealand lamb or New York strip sirloin. And vegetarians have options as well.

6 Oak St. ✆ **508/325-0992.** Reservations recommended. Main courses $18–$25. MC, V. June–Sept daily 5–10:30pm; call for off-season hours. Closed late Nov to late Apr.

Schooner's at Steamboat Wharf AMERICAN This casual family-friendly restaurant near the Steamship Authority dock is noteworthy for the outdoor dining on the screened-in porch. Diners who sit on the second floor have views of the harbor. Prices are reasonable and portions are generous in this casual pub. The most popular dishes are the fajitas, fried clams, fish and chips, and the lobster salad. There is a lively late-night bar scene with live acoustic music some nights in season.

31 Easy St. ✆ **508/228-5824.** Reservations accepted. Main courses $18–$24. AE, MC, V. Apr–Dec daily 11am–10pm. Closed Jan–Mar.

INEXPENSIVE

Arno's ★ Kids ECLECTIC A storefront facing the passing parade of Main Street, this institution packs surprising style between its bare-brick walls. The internationally influenced menu yields tasty, bountiful platters for breakfast, lunch, and dinner. Specialties include grilled sirloin steaks and fresh grilled fish.

41 Main St. ✆ **508/228-7001.** Reservations recommended. Main courses $15–$23. AE, DC, DISC, MC, V. Apr–Dec daily 8am–2pm and 5–9:30pm. Closed Jan–Mar.

Cap'n Tobey's Chowder House ★ SEAFOOD The specialty at this convenient eatery close to the harbor is seafood, obtained on a daily basis from local fishermen. Diners can choose between halibut, yellowfin tuna, and haddock, and have it grilled, baked, or blackened. The raw bar features oysters, littlenecks, and shrimp. Upstairs, **Off Shore at Cap'n Tobey's** has live music in season.

20 Straight Wharf. ✆ **508/228-0836.** Reservations accepted. Main courses $9–$30. AE, MC, V. Late June to Sept daily 11:30am–10pm. Call for off-season hours. Closed Jan–Apr.

The Even Keel Café ★ AMERICAN This low-key cafe in the heart of town serves breakfast, lunch, and dinner both indoors and outside on the patio in the back. Unlike much of Nantucket's dining scene, you'll find reasonable prices and non-exotic fare here, like burgers and sandwiches. There are always vegetarian choices, as well as meat and fish dishes that range from cheeseburgers to grilled salmon to veal *osso buco.* There's also a kid's menu, as well as high-speed Internet access. On Sundays, they serve a hearty brunch. Alcohol is not sold, but you can BYOB.

40 Main St. ✆ **508/228-1979.** Reservations not accepted. Main courses $10–$25. AE, MC, V. July–Aug daily 7am–10pm. Call for off-season hours. Open year-round.

TAKEOUT & PICNIC FARE

You can get fresh-picked produce right on Main Street from the traveling truck from **Bartlett's Ocean View Farm** ★, 33 Bartlett Farm Rd. (✆ **508/228-9403**), or head out to this seventh-generation farm where, in June, you get to pick your own strawberries. They also sell sandwiches, quiches, pastries, pies, and more. Closed January through March.

Henry's Sandwich Shop ★, Steamboat Wharf (✆ **508/228-0123**), which opened in 1969, is set a block away from Steamboat Wharf, where the ferries dock. They bake their own sub rolls from scratch every morning. Closed November through May.

Before you bike out of town to the beach, stop by **Provisions,** 3 Harbor Sq., Straight Wharf (✆ **508/228-3258**), a gourmet sandwich shop. Closed early November to March.

A terrific value on pricey Nantucket, **Something Natural,** 50 Cliff Rd. (✆ **508/228-0504**), turns out gigantic sandwiches, with fresh ingredients piled atop fabulous bread. Save room for their addictive chocolate-chip cookies. Closed mid-October to March.

The **Juice Bar** ★★, 12 Broad St. (✆ **508/228-5799**), is a humble hole in the wall that dishes out some of the best homemade ice cream and frozen yogurt around, complemented by superb homemade hot fudge. Closed from mid-October to mid-April.

Juice Guys, 4 Easy St. (✆ **508/228-4464**), is the spot to get your Nantucket Nectars fix. High-tech blenders mix potent combinations of fresh juice with vitamins, sorbet, yogurt, and holistic enhancers. Closed from late December to April.

NANTUCKET AFTER DARK

Acoustic performers from all over the country hold forth in the **Brotherhood of Thieves,** 23 Broad St., in the center of Nantucket Town (no phone), an atmospheric pub where you'll find live folk music just about every night in season; no cover. Closed in February. The **Chicken Box,** 12 Dave St. (✆ **508/228-9717**), is the rocking spot for the 20-something crowd. It sometimes seems like the entire population of the island is shoving their way in here. Jimmy Buffett shows up late at night about once a summer, unannounced, and jams with the band. The cover runs from $4 to $15. The **Rose and Crown,** 23 S. Water St. (✆ **508/228-2595**), draws all ages with its loud dance music. The cover for live bands on weekends is $3 to $5. Closed January through March.

The **Nantucket Arts Alliance** (✆ **800/228-8118** or 508/228-8118) operates Box Office Nantucket, offering tickets for all sorts of cultural events around town. It operates out of the Macy Warehouse on Straight Wharf, in season daily from 10am to 4pm.

Theater buffs will want to spend an evening at the **Actors' Theatre of Nantucket,** Methodist Church, 2 Centre St. (✆ **508/228-6325;** www.nantuckettheatre.com). This shoebox-size theater assays thought-provoking plays as readily as summery farces. The season runs from mid-May to mid-September. Tickets are $12 to $20. You can catch the children's productions ($12) from mid-July to mid-August.

8

Central & Western Massachusetts

by Herbert Bailey Livesey

While Boston and its maritime appendages of Cape Ann and Cape Cod face the sea and embrace it, inland Massachusetts turns in upon itself. Countless ponds and lakes shimmer in its folds and hollows, often hidden by deep forests and granite outcroppings. Farming and industry grew along the north-south valleys of the Connecticut and Housatonic rivers.

The heartland Pioneer Valley, enclosing the Connecticut River, earned its name in the early 18th century, when European trappers and farmers first began to push west from the colonies clinging to the edges of Massachusetts Bay. They were followed by ambitious capitalists who erected red-brick mills along the river for the manufacture of textiles and paper. Most of those enterprises failed or faded in the post–World War II movement to the milder climate and cheaper labor of the South, leaving a miasma of economic hardship that has yet to be completely resolved. But those industrialists also helped fund several distinguished colleges for which the valley is now known; their educated populations provide much energy and a rich cultural life.

Roughly the same pattern applied in the Berkshires, the twin ranges of rumpled hills that define the western band of the state. There is only one college of note here, however, and the development of this region in the 19th century was prompted mainly by the construction of the railroad from New York and Boston. Artistic and literary folk made a favored summer retreat of it, followed by wealthy urbanites attracted by the region's reputation for creativity and bohemianism. Many of their extravagant mansions, dubbed "Berkshire Cottages," still survive, and to this day the region attracts the town-and-country crowd, who support a vibrant summer schedule of the arts, then steal away as the crimson leaves fall and the Berkshires grow quiet beneath 6 months of snow.

1 Worcester

46 miles W of Boston; 55 miles NE of Springfield

A dispirited air clings to Massachusetts's second-largest city, especially around its often dilapidated edges. But that observation applies to many of the region's cities, most of which reached their apogees in the late 19th century, and Worcester has enough attractions to justify a stopover or an overnight on the way to or from Boston.

Its citizens support frequent bootstrapping efforts, especially downtown around the Romanesque City Hall. Over the years, local benefactors have invested in a surprising number of museums, historic buildings, and theatrical venues. One example is the costly and long-awaited renovation of the railroad station.

Worcester (pronounced *Wuss*-ter, or *Woos*-tah locally) was the site of the first National Women's Rights Convention, held here in 1850, and the city's annual music festival claims to be the oldest in the country.

ESSENTIALS

GETTING THERE Worcester is near the juncture of the east-west Massachusetts Turnpike (I-90) and I-395. **Amtrak** stops here daily each way on its route between Boston and Chicago. Call ✆ **800/USA-RAIL** (872-7245) for details on the frequently changed schedule.

VISITOR INFORMATION The **Visitor Center** is opposite the DCU Arena and Convention Center at 30 Worcester Center Blvd., Worcester, MA 1608 (✆ **508/755-7400;** www.worcester.org).

WHAT TO SEE & DO

EcoTarium *Kids* This ambitious family-oriented institution is primarily directed at children, although adults will also enjoy it. It brings together a planetarium, an observatory, an aquarium, and a zoo that includes bald eagles, polar bears, barred owls, bobcats, otters, and mountain lions. Ponds and picnic areas dot the 60 hilltop acres of woods, which are traversed by a meandering nature trail. A narrow-gauge railroad is yet another attraction. Indoors, interactive displays and computers sugarcoat messages regarding concerns about ecology and conservation.

222 Harrington Way. ✆ **508/791-9211.** www.ecotarium.org. General admission $8 adults, $6 seniors, students, and ages 3–16. Mon–Sat 10am–5pm; Sun noon–5pm. Planetarium $3.50, Explorer Express Train $2.50, Tree Canopy Walkway $7. From exit 14 of I-290, head east on Rte. 122 (Grafton St.), bearing left on Hamilton St., then left again on Harrington Way.

Higgins Armory Museum ★ The steel-and-glass structure, one of the earliest of its kind, resembles a Gothic castle shining in its coat of aluminum paint. John W. Higgins was president of a company that processed steel, no doubt accounting for his interest in medieval and Renaissance armor and heraldry. He gathered many examples over his lifetime, supplementing his collection with ancient arms, paintings, stained glass, and tapestries. The results are displayed here, in a museum that opened in 1931. Nearly 100 suits of armor, including one made for a dog, are arrayed in the Great Hall, which is fashioned after an 11th-century castle. A sound-and-light show and various demonstrations bring the age of chivalry to life, and there is a room in which visitors can try on armor and clothing of the period.

100 Barber Ave. ✆ **508/853-6015.** www.higgins.org Admission $8 adults, $7 seniors and children 6-16. Tues–Sat 10am–4pm; Sun noon–4pm. Take I-190 to Exit 1, onto MA 12 north, then turn right on Barber Ave.

Worcester Art Museum ★★ With a large modern concrete wing attached to the original building facing Salisbury Street, WAM occupies most of a large city block holding an unexpectedly large number of artworks. The diverse collections contain pieces that range from ancient Egypt to 20th-century America, for a total of over 30,000 paintings, sculptures, and related objects. Particular strengths are the American wing, housing canvases by Sargent, Whistler, Ryder, and a few memorable works by anonymous Colonial artists; the Europeans on the second floor, including Gauguin, El Greco, and Gainsborough; and the pre-Columbian artifacts are on the fourth floor, with finely wrought urns from Peru, Costa Rica, and Mexico's Monte

Alban. In the lower level of the first floor is a reconstructed 12th-century French chapter house *and* a large floor mosaic from 6th-century Antioch in what is now southeastern Turkey.

55 Salisbury St. (corner of Tuckerman St.) ✆ **508/799-4406.** www.worcesterart.org. Admission $10 adults, $8 seniors and students, free under age 17 and to all Sat 10am–noon. Wed–Fri 11am–5pm (until 8pm Thurs); Sat 10am–5pm; Sun 11am–5pm. Closed Sun July–Aug.

WHERE TO STAY

Pickings are slim, and most of what's available is chain motels. An alternative is staying in nearby Sturbridge (p. 312), which is less than 20 miles away and has a more interesting choice of accommodations.

Beechwood Hotel ★ The eye-catching feature of this relatively young red-brick building is its round core structure, which resembles a medieval keep. Public spaces and guest rooms are agreeably furnished with pieces that use wood and fabric in nearly equal proportions. Sunday through Thursday, guests are invited to a manager's reception for a free cocktail (5–7pm). A costly recent renovation added 15 executive level rooms and suites, which are accorded such extra services as continental breakfast and morning newspaper delivery. Those on the fifth floor have fireplaces and many have unstocked fridges. High-speed Internet access is available throughout, and to show they're keeping up with other technologies, guests can plug their MP3s into the clock radio.

363 Plantation St., Worcester, MA 01605. ✆ **800/344-2589** or 508/754-5789. Fax 508/752-2060. www.beechwoodhotel.com. 73 units. $149–$224 double; $194–$234 suite. Rates include breakfast. AE, DC, DISC, MC, V. **Amenities:** Restaurant (New American); bar; 24-hr. room service; modest exercise room; small business center; same-day dry cleaning/laundry service. *In room:* A/C, TV w/pay movies, dataport, coffeemaker, hair dryer, iron.

Crowne Plaza Along with its desirable location, this outlet of the well-known chain delivers on most points of expected conveniences. Fireplaces in the lobby and adjacent dining room are warming notes on a winter night, and self-parking is handy in the garage directly opposite the main entrance. Bedrooms provide more than sufficient elbow room, and contain such extras as makeup mirrors and high-speed Internet access. Complimentary newspapers are outside the door in the morning. The concierge level has a private lounge serving food and drinks morning and evening and has unstocked fridges in bedrooms. Still, the facility is overdue for a good sprucing-up.

10 Lincoln Sq. (corner of Lincoln St. and Belmont St.), Worcester, MA 01608. ✆ **800/227-7963** or 508/791-1600. Fax 508/791-1796. www.worcester-dwtn.crowneplaza.com. 243 units. $143–$169 double. AE, DC, DISC, MC, V. Valet parking $6. **Amenities:** Restaurant (Italian/Continental); bar; heated indoor/outdoor pool w/whirlpool; adequate exercise room; business center; free parking, limited room service; dry cleaning/laundry service. *In room:* A/C, TV w/pay movies, dataport, coffeemaker, hair dryer, iron.

WHERE TO DINE

Sole Proprietor ★★ SEAFOOD According to local legend, Legal Seafoods, the steamrolling seafood restaurant chain, came to Worcester to challenge Sole Proprietor, then quickly turned tail and fled, easily vanquished. The evidence of that suzerainty is clear even on a cold Tuesday night, when the large parking lot outside is like a bumper-car attraction. Part of the reason is the congenial staff, from the hostess who remains unflustered no matter how many would-be diners clog the entrance to waiters who can describe dishes in as much detail as patrons wish. But the food is key, with fish as fresh as the dawn and preparations from bare-bones simple to entrancingly complex. One side of the large rectangular bar is given over to a sushi and raw bar, while the kitchen produces such worthy inventions as tuna steak Barcelona, the fish coated with cracked peppercorns, grilled medium rare, sliced, and laid over a bed of feta cheese, sun-dried tomatoes, scallions, and basil leaves. Menus (and prices) change daily. Up to 50 wines are available by the glass.

118 Highland St. ✆ **508/798-3474.** Main courses $17–$27 (sushi $6–$12 per piece, lobster dinners $23–$59). AE, DC, MC, V. Mon–Fri 11:30am–10pm; Sat noon–11pm; Sun 4–9:30pm.

Union Station Occupying a large space at one end of the meticulously restored train station of the same name, the room has the masculine tone of an upscale steakhouse, what with the high ceilings, dark woods, maroon carpeting, velvet drapes, and dim lighting from chandeliers and guttering candles. A waitstaff dressed in black and white routinely asks if you want bread and butter—say yes, for the small loaf is fragrant with rosemary. While there are several beef dishes on the menu—which don't come in monster 2-pound sizes—there is a greater number featuring seafood or pasta. One such is the slightly misnamed lobster ravioli, in which the pasta is filled with crabmeat, but bathed in a creamy lobster sauce decorated with one-half of a small lobster tail. Starters are mostly salads, but a small grilled pizza is also offered.

In the train station, 2 Washington Sq. ✆ **508/831-7000.** AE, DC, MC, V. Tues–Thurs 5–10pm; Fri–Sat 5–11pm.

2 Sturbridge & Old Sturbridge Village

18 miles SW of Worcester; 32 miles E of Springfield

First things first: Sturbridge and Old Sturbridge Village aren't a single entity. The former is an organic community, populated by working people with real lives. But why are there so many motels and restaurants in a town of fewer than 8,000 residents? That's due to the latter, a fabricated early-19th-century village comprised of authentic buildings moved here from other locations and peopled by docents pretending to follow the pursuits of 170 years past. It is deservedly popular, one of the two most prominent tourist destinations in central Massachusetts.

ESSENTIALS

GETTING THERE Take the east-west Massachusetts Turnpike (I-90) to Exit 9, or take I-84 to Exit 3B.

VISITOR INFORMATION The **Sturbridge Area Visitors Center,** 380 Main St. (✆ **508/347-2761**), is open Monday through Friday during regular business hours.

SPECIAL EVENTS Highly popular annual occasions are the **Brimfield Antique and Collectible Shows** ★ (✆ **800/628-8379** or 508/347-2761; www.brimfieldshow.com), when over 6,000 dealers gather along a mile-long strip for up to 6 days (Tues–Sun) in mid-May, mid-July, and early September. Brimfield is an otherwise sleepy village adjoining Sturbridge on the west. Because it has few hotels, most of the dealers and seekers stay in Sturbridge, so you'll need to reserve your room at least 6 months in advance during show periods.

Thanksgiving and Christmas weeks at Old Sturbridge Village bring traditional New England dinners, concerts, and candlelit nights. Call ✆ **800/733-1830** or 508/347-3362 for details.

EXPLORING A 19TH-CENTURY VILLAGE

Sturbridge has only one sight of significance, and is otherwise a pleasantly unremarkable town. Expect crowds on holiday weekends in summer and during the October foliage season.

Old Sturbridge Village ★★★ *Kids* Only one of the more than 40 restored structures in the complex stands on its original site. The rest were transported here from as far away as Maine. All are authentic buildings, not re-creations, and they represent the living quarters and places of trade and commerce of a rural settlement of the 1830s. Among these are a Quaker meetinghouse, sawmill, bank, country store, blacksmith shop, school, cooperage, and printing office. At the edges of the village are a working farm and herb garden.

Costumed docents demonstrate hearth cooking, sheep shearing, heirloom gardening, maple sugaring, musketry, carpentry, and more. "Residents" include children who roll hoops and play games true to the period. At the children's museum, kids 3 to 7 can dress up in costumes and use their imaginations in a pretend farm kitchen and one-room school. Special events mark such dates as the Fourth of July, Thanksgiving, and the Christmas season. Weddings, militia drills, and a harvest fair are staged. The 20-minute boat ride on the adjacent Quinebaug River is popular with younger visitors.

The Village has evolved, with special seasonal events, new activities, and additional buildings. But the administration has lately had to engage in some serious belt-tightening, due to declining attendance. The Oliver Wright Tavern, opened in 2002, was a major casualty, closed in 2005.

1 Old Sturbridge Village Rd. ✆ **800/733-1830** or 508/347-3362. Fax 508/347-0375. www.osv.org. Admission (2-day pass) $20 adults, $18 seniors, $5 children 3–17. Apr–Oct daily 9:30am–5pm; Nov–Dec daily 9:30am–4pm; Jan–Mar Wed–Sun 9:30am–4pm; but there are frequent exceptions in hours and days of operation, so call ahead. Closed Dec 25. Take Exit 3B off I-84 or Exit 9 off I-90, drive west on Rte. 20, and bear right into the turnaround just before the entrance to the village.

WHERE TO STAY

If the Publick House (below) is full, try the **EconoLodge,** 682 Main St. (✆ **508/347-2324**), the **Comfort Inn & Suites,** 215 Charlton Rd. (Rte. 20) (✆ **508/347-3306**), or the **Sturbridge Coach Motor Lodge,** 408 Main St. (✆ **508/347-7327**). The first two are located near Exit 9 off I-84, the third near the entrance to Old Sturbridge Village. The **Old Sturbridge Village Motor Lodges,** part of the namesake facility described above, has around 60 rooms, but was closed indefinitely in 2006 due to money problems.

Publick House ★ This three-building complex on 60 acres is the high-profile lodging in the Sturbridge area. The main structure incorporates a tavern, heavy on the antique charm, built in 1771. Rooms there and in the adjacent **Chamberlain House** are rustic, some with canopy beds, rag rugs, and Colonial reproductions, while the contemporary **Country Motor Lodge,** a mile away, has an outdoor pool and tennis courts.

Rte. 131 (P.O. Box 187), Sturbridge, MA 01566. ✆ **800/782-5425** or 508/347-3313. Fax 508/347-5073. www.publickhouse.com. 126 units. $89–$125 double; from $125 suite. Packages available. AE, DC, DISC, MC, V. From Exit 3B off I-84, drive 1½ miles south of Rte. 20 on Rte. 131. Pets accepted in some rooms of Country Motor Lodge ($5 per night). **Amenities:** 2 restaurants (American); 2 bars; 2 heated outdoor pools; tennis courts; access to nearby health club; dry cleaning. *In room:* A/C, TV, hair dryer.

WHERE TO DINE

In addition to the establishments listed below, you might sample either of the two restaurants associated with the **Publick House** (see above).

Rom's ★ *Value* ITALIAN/AMERICAN This was once a hot dog and fried-clam roadside stand that has grown over the last half-century like a multi-generation New England farmhouse. Today, it seats 750 diners and remains a near-ideal family restaurant, with something for everyone, from homemade pastas and pizzas to full seafood dinners. The lobster roll is twice the size but about the same price as those offered on the coast. Buffets at Wednesday and Friday dinner and Sunday brunch are huge crowd pleasers and cost only $9.95 per person. On Tuesdays, a takeout window ladles "buckets of rigatoni" and passes out fish and chips and half-price pizzas.

Rte. 131, 2 miles south of Rte. 20. ✆ **800/ROM-1952** or 508/347-3349. Main courses $8.95–$17. AE, DC, DISC, MC, V. Daily 11:30am–9pm.

Rovezzi's ★ ITALIAN This new roadside trattoria is a welcome addition to the area's rather wan dining possibilities. Inside the front door is a long, brightly lit bar populated with people who know each other; the dining room, with its marble fireplace, is an attached wing in back. The two-page menu lists appetizer-size pastas and cold and hot antipasti (you might want to order something other than the two bruschettas, which are made with the same focaccia served with dinner). Pastas can be supplemented with herb-roasted chicken or with the so-called "world's best meatballs." Every night has a special soup, risotto, filet mignon, cannoli, and crème brulée. Go for the excellent crab and salmon bisque, if it's available. Of the main dish pastas, the ravioli *per lo Invierno* is a good choice, butternut squash and sweet potato envelopes with crumbled sausage and a sage cream sauce.

Rte. 20, 2 miles west of Old Sturbridge Village. ✆ **508/347-0100.** Main courses $13–$24. MC, V. Daily 5–9pm (Fri–Sat until 10pm).

3 Springfield

89 miles W of Boston; 32 miles N of Hartford

Times have been tough in this once-prosperous manufacturing city on the east bank of the Connecticut River. But its loyal citizens haven't caved under the pressures of job flight and high unemployment, and evidence of redevelopment can be seen throughout downtown, with recycled loft and factory buildings standing beside modern glass towers. Springfield remains the most important city in western Massachusetts and has enjoyed some success in attracting new enterprises. Vacationers can pass a few hours or a night here, but Springfield is primarily a stop on the way north or south.

ESSENTIALS

GETTING THERE Springfield is located near the juncture of the east-west Massachusetts Turnpike (I-90) and north-south I-91.

Bradley International (✆ **203/627-3000**), in Windsor Locks, CT, is the nearest major airport, about 20 miles to the south. Rent a car here from any of the major companies or catch a bus, cab, or limo into Springfield. Major airlines serving Bradley include **American** (✆ 800/433-7300), **Continental** (✆ 800/525-0280), **Delta** (✆ 800/221-1212), **Northwest** (✆ 800/225-2525), **United** (✆ 800/241-6522), and **US Airways** (✆ 800/247-8786).

Amtrak (✆ **800/USA-RAIL;** www.northeast.amtrak.com) trains stop daily both ways in Springfield on routes between Boston and Chicago; Boston and Washington, DC; and New York and St. Albans, VT (where there are connecting buses from Montreal), with intermediate stops in Philadelphia, New York, and Hartford, among others.

VISITOR INFORMATION The **Greater Springfield Convention and Visitors Bureau** (✆ **413/787-1548;** www.valleyvisitor.com) has two visitor information centers, at 1441 Main St., Springfield, MA 01103 (✆ **413/787-1548**) and at 1200 West

Columbus Ave., Springfield, MA 01105 (© **413/750-2980**), near the Basketball Hall of Fame.

SPECIAL EVENTS During the last 2 weeks in September the **Eastern States Exposition** (© **413/737-2443**), a huge old-fashioned agricultural fair with games, rides, a midway, and entertainment is held on a fairground on the opposite side of the Connecticut River in West Springfield. Also on the grounds is **Old Storrowtown Village,** a collection of restored Colonial buildings, accessible by guided tour Monday through Saturday from June to Labor Day, and by appointment the rest of the year. A newcomer is the **Six Flags New England** theme park.

WHAT TO SEE & DO

Naismith Memorial Basketball Hall of Fame ★★ Kids Canadian-born Dr. James Naismith invented basketball in Springfield in 1891. A feast for fans, the Basketball Hall of Fame is painless even for those who regard the game as a blur of 7-foot armpits. It has been so popular this entirely new facility was opened near the original hall in 2002. You can't miss it—there's a 136-foot spire holding a 13-foot illuminated basketball. Take one of the glass elevators to the top (third) level and work down. Up there is the Honors Ring, with biographies of the players enshrined in the Hall within the context of the times in which they lived. Displays there and on lower floors, many of them interactive, feature vast quantities of memorabilia of the sport and the history of the game—remember the Chicago Studebakers, the Indianapolis Kautskys, the Philadelphia Hebrews? On the ground floor is a large, not-quite regulation court where clinics and skill challenges are held and where anyone can pick up a ball and shoot a few. A McDonald's and a Reebok store bracket the entrance and there's a chain hotel on the other side of the parking lot.

1000 W. Columbus Ave. (at Union St.). © **413/781-6500.** Fax 413/781-1939. www.hoophall.com. Admission $17 adults, $14 seniors, $12 children 5–15. Daily 10am–5pm (until 6pm Fri).

Six Flags New England Kids A relative newcomer to the Springfield area, Six Flags New England continues to enhance its offerings since its opening. In 2006, it added two new thrill rides to the 10 roller coasters already in operation, including a soaker called "Splash Water Falls." Among the most popular are "Superman—Ride of Steel" and "Batman—The Dark Knight," which climbs to 117 feet and carries its deliriously terrified passengers over half a mile of twisting track in a little over 2 minutes. There are over 50 rides in total, varying in excitement quotient to satisfy every member of the family. There are concerts and other celebrations, often featuring Justice League superheroes and Looney Tunes characters.

1623 Main St., Agawam, MA 01114 © **413/786-9300.** General admission to the park is by size, not age: $50 "adults, $30 for heights 36"–53". Mid-June to late Aug daily 10am–10pm. Shorter hours in off season. Closed Nov to mid-Apr.

Springfield Museums at the Quadrangle ★ Kids Four museums and a library surrounding a quadrangle constitute this worthwhile resource. Enter the quadrangle from the Welcome Center (open 9am–5pm) on Edwards Street. Toward the library at the other end of the quad is the new **Dr. Seuss National Memorial Sculpture Garden,** with three groups, including the author himself (who was born in Springfield), the Cat in the Hat, and the Grinch. On the right is the first museum; the others around the quad make a counterclockwise circuit. Before setting out, note the somewhat limited hours below.

Fun Fact . . . And to Think That I Saw It on Mulberry Street

Interest in the man who called himself Dr. Seuss spiked with a Broadway show, *Seussical,* and the movies *The Cat in the Hat* and *The Grinch.* The grandparents of Theodor Seuss Geisel lived on Springfield's Mulberry Street, and in 1937, the writer and illustrator named the first of his dozens of children's books for the neighborhood. He followed up with such classics as *The Cat in the Hat* and *How the Grinch Stole Christmas.* Over 100 million copies of his books have been sold, and every title is still in print.

Geisel spent most of his adult life in California, the result of a nearly 2-decade career in documentary films, during which he won two Academy Awards. But much of his inspiration for the children's books for which he is remembered can be traced to Springfield. His drawing of Bartholomew Cubbins's castle bears a strong resemblance to the Howard Street Armory, now a community center, and certain of his landscapes look as if they were recalled from his playtimes in Forest Park, near his boyhood home at 74 Fairfield St.

Alas, Mulberry Street is no longer the august avenue it once must have been, its Victorian manses now crowded by undistinguished apartment blocks and commercial strips—and the former Central High School from which Geisel graduated is now a condominium.

First, on the right, is the **Connecticut Valley Historical Museum**, with examples of weapons made by the city's firearms manufacturers, including a blunderbuss and an unusual 1838 rifle with a revolving cartridge chamber.

Next is the **Museum of Fine Arts** ★, the most important of the lot, with 14 galleries of Colonial paintings from Gilbert Stuart and John Copley of the Revolutionary period to early-20th-century realists George Bellows and Reginald Marsh, and culminating with magic realists and abstract expressionists—Frank Stella, Helen Frankenthaler, Don Eddy, and George Sugarman. Ask if the remarkable serigraph of lower Manhattan by Richard Estes is on view at the time of your visit.

At the opposite corner, near the library, is the **George Walter Vincent Smith Art Museum**, housed in an 1896 Italian Renaissance–style mansion. Upstairs are largely sentimental pastoral scenes, with a few small landscapes by George Inness, Thomas Cole, and Albert Bierstadt. Also on display are Asian rugs, tapestries, and small jade and rose quartz figurines. On the main floor are cases of Japanese samurai weaponry surrounding a carved 1805 Shinto shrine as well as a room of full-size casts of classical Greek and Renaissance sculptures.

And last, near the Welcome Center, kids will enjoy the **Springfield Science Museum** (the sign over the door reads "Museum of Natural History"). It contains a 100-seat planetarium, dioramas of African animals, a Dinosaur Hall, and the Solutia Eco-Center. Planetarium shows Tuesday through Friday at 2pm, Saturday through Sunday at 1, 2, and 3pm.

State and Chestnut sts. ✆ **413/263-6800.** www.springfieldmuseums.org. Combined admission for all 4 museums: $10 adults, $7 seniors, $5 college students, $3 children 6–17; $3 extra each for the planetarium and dinosaur hall. Tues–Fri noon–5pm; Sat–Sun 11am–4pm.

WHERE TO STAY

Sheraton Springfield ★★ Just off the Springfield Center exit of I-91, this Sheraton can be a treat after a few nights in idiosyncratic New England B&Bs. Predictable, yes, but a hotel with conveniences like room service, two capable restaurants, and an expansive spa and fitness center can suddenly make charm seem overrated. Executive-level rooms are sometimes cheaper than standard units, so be sure to inquire. High-speed Internet access is available by request for an extra charge.

1 Monarch Place, Springfield, MA 01114. ✆ **800/426-9004** or 413/781-1010. Fax 413/747-8065. www.starwoodhotels.com/sheraton. 310 units. $159–$189 double. AE, DC, DISC, MC, V. **Amenities:** 2 restaurants (Continental/American); bar; heated indoor pool; health club; Jacuzzi; sauna; business center; shopping arcade; limited room service; same-day dry cleaning. *In room:* A/C, TV w/pay movies, dataport, coffeemaker, hair dryer, iron.

Springfield Marriott ★★ Directly across the street from the Sheraton (see above), this Marriott duplicates most of its rival's attributes. Even the room rates are essentially the same. A $3.5-million renovation has freshened guest rooms with new fabrics, carpeting, and marble bathroom floors. Among its perks are high-speed Internet access, a concierge level, and poolside food service.

1500 Main St., Springfield, MA 01105. ✆ **800/228-9290** or 413/781-7111. Fax 413/731-8932. www.marriotthotels.com. 265 units. $159–$184 double. AE, DC, DISC, MC, V. **Amenities:** 2 restaurants (Continental/American); 2 bars; heated indoor pool; health club; Jacuzzi; sauna; business center; limited room service; same-day dry cleaning. *In room:* A/C, TV w/pay movies, dataport, coffeemaker, hair dryer, iron.

WHERE TO DINE

Student Prince and the Fort ★ GERMAN/AMERICAN In 1935, German immigrants opened the Student Prince and began serving schnitzels and sauerbraten. That might not have seemed the precise historical moment to ensure the success of such an enterprise, but nevertheless, the restaurant thrived. In 1946, the Fort dining room was added next door, and in 1997 a separate deli was opened on the other side. The result is the most popular place in town. Waitresses rush about in sensible shoes, slapping plates down and tolerating no lip from playful patrons. Monster portions are the rule, with veal shanks as thick as a linebacker's forearm. Weiner schnitzel, roulade, and sauerbraten are to be expected in such a setting, but are no less tasty for that. Check out the enormous stein collection in the bar, which fills shelves all the way to the high ceiling.

8 Fort St. (west of Main St.). ✆ **413/734-7475.** Main courses $7.95–$20. AE, DC, DISC, MC, V. Mon–Sat noon–11pm; Sun noon–10pm.

SPRINGFIELD AFTER DARK

Symphony Hall, at Court Street and East Columbus Avenue (✆ **413/788-7033;** tickets@citystage.symphonyhall.com), is the venue for concerts by the Springfield Symphony Orchestra, touring performers and musicals, and productions meant for children.

A strip of ever-changing beer-and-pool joints, music bars, and hip eateries lies along downtown Worthington and Bridge streets near our two recommended hotels. Among the possibilities (with no guarantee they'll still be there when you arrive) are the **Alumni Club,** 90 Worthington (✆ **413/736-5455**), with karaoke, DJs, and pool; **Theodore's,** 201 Worthington St. (✆ **413/736-6000**), showcasing local blues bands Wednesday through Saturday; and the **Fat Cat Bar & Grill,** 232 Worthington St. (✆ **413/734-0554**), with live music and other entertainment, Wednesday through Saturday. They are only three of many.

4 The Pioneer Valley

Low hills and quilted fields channel the Connecticut River as it runs south toward Long Island Sound, forming the Pioneer Valley. The earliest European settlers came here for what proved to be uncommonly fertile soil and were followed in the 19th century by men who harnessed the power of the river and became wealthy textile and paper manufacturers.

These industrialists took the lead in funding the institutions of higher learning that are now the pride of the region. Prestigious Smith, Mount Holyoke, and Amherst are here, as are innovative Hampshire College and the sprawling main campus of the University of Massachusetts, with its 25,000 students. All five contribute mightily to the cultural life of the valley, and the towns of **Northampton, Amherst,** and **South Hadley** are invigorated by the vitality of thousands of college-age young people.

In the north, near Vermont, the living village of **Deerfield** preserves the architecture and atmosphere of Colonial New England, but without the whiff of sterility that often afflicts artificial gatherings of old buildings with costumed docents.

Interstate 91 and Route 5 both traverse the valley from south to north. The trip from edge to edge on the interstate takes less than an hour, while Route 5 tenders more of the flavor of pastoral vistas and colorful mill towns.

There are plenty of motels along the way, but if you're looking for lodgings more representative of the character of the region, contact the **Folkstone Bed & Breakfast Reservation Service** (© **800/762-2751** or 508/480-0380).

ESSENTIALS

GETTING THERE From Boston and upstate New York, take the Massachusetts Turnpike (I-90) to Springfield, then follow I-91 or Route 5 north. While there are local buses, you need a car to explore this area.

The nearest major airport is **Bradley International** (© **860/292-2000;** www.bradleyairport.com), just south of Springfield, in Windsor Locks, CT. (See "Springfield," earlier in this chapter, for a list of airlines that serve Bradley.) **Valley Transporter** (© **800/872-8752** or 413/253-1350; www.valleytransporter.com) offers van shuttles between the airport and Amherst, Northampton, Hadley, Holyoke, and Deerfield. **Peter Pan Bus Lines** (© **800/237-8747** or 413/781-2900; www.peterpanbus.com) schedules frequent connections between Springfield and the towns of the Valley.

Amtrak (© **800/USA-RAIL;** www.amtrak.com) *Vermonter* trains stop in Amherst and Northampton on the route between St. Albans, VT, and Washington, DC, with connections to New York City and Boston.

HOLYOKE

Once an important paper-manufacturing center, Holyoke (8 miles north of Springfield, 88 miles west of Boston) has suffered a long economic slide since World War II. Abandoned factories and the dissolute air of the commercial center don't bolster first impressions. Still, there are a couple of modestly worthwhile sights amid some imaginatively recycled old mills.

Canals dug during the city's mid-19th-century heyday still cut through downtown. (They were intended to allow access to the mills.) Running beside one of the canals is long and narrow **Heritage State Park** (© **413/534-1723**); the entrance is at 221 Appleton St. The interpretive center offers walking tours and exhibits, and the park

The Pioneer Valley

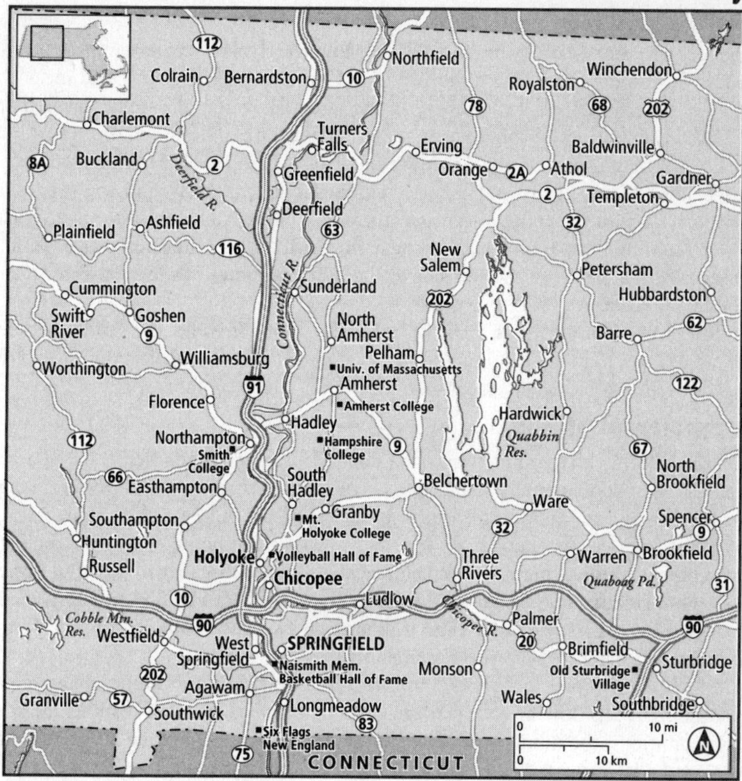

also contains a restored antique merry-go-round and the **Volleyball Hall of Fame** (✆ **413/536-0926;** www.volleyhall.org). On most Sundays from mid-June to late August, the ancient locomotive of the **Heritage Park Railroad** pulls train buffs on a 2-hour trip downriver to Holyoke Mall at Ingleside. Call Heritage State Park for more information.

The **St. Patrick's Day Parade** in Holyoke is said to be the second largest in the United States.

WHERE TO STAY & DINE

Yankee Pedlar Inn ★ If you're looking for a sedate, tranquil country inn, this isn't it. Business is thriving, and the place bustles with weddings, tour groups, and corporate get-togethers. The dining room is highly popular with locals as well as travelers. Of the five buildings in the largely Victorian complex, the 1850 House has the most modern rooms, while the Carriage House has the least expensive. Live music is presented many evenings in the Oyster Bar.

1866 Northampton St. (Rte. 5), Holyoke, MA 01040. ✆ **413/532-9494.** Fax 413/536-8877. www.yankeepedlarinn.com. 28 units. May–Oct $85–$140 double; Nov–Apr $80–$136 double. Rates include breakfast. AE, DC, DISC, MC, V. Take Exit 16 off I-91 and head east 5 blocks. **Amenities:** Restaurant (American); bar; access to nearby health club; video rentals. *In room:* TV/VCR.

SOUTH HADLEY

Pioneer educator Mary Lyon founded the Mount Holyoke Female Seminary here in 1836. Strung along the eastern side of Route 116 (College St.), the college, one of the "Seven Sisters" schools for women, is the essential reason this small town (pop. 13,600) exists. It lies 15 miles north of Springfield and 7 miles south of Amherst.

On the campus is a worthy **Art Museum** ★ (✆ **413/538-2245**), which focuses on art of the Orient, Egypt, and the Mediterranean. Recent renovation and expansion brought more of the collection into regular view. Hours are Tuesday through Friday from 11am to 5pm, Saturday and Sunday from 1 to 5pm. Admission is free. To find it, take Park Street from the east side of the Y intersection in the center of town and follow the signs.

Joseph A. Skinner State Park (✆ **413/586-0350**) straddles the border between South Hadley and Hadley. On its 390 acres are miles of trails, picnic grounds, and the historic Summit House (open Sat–Sun May–Oct), with panoramic views of the valley.

NORTHAMPTON ★★

Smith College, with its campus sprawling along Main Street slightly west of the commercial center, is Northampton's dominating physical and spiritual presence. One of the original "Seven Sisters," Smith is the largest female liberal arts college in the United States.

Northampton (also known as "NoHo") was long the home of Calvin Coolidge, who pursued his law practice here before and after his occupancy of the Oval Office. A room maintained by the **Forbes Library,** 20 West St. (✆ **413/584-6037**), contains many of his papers. Coolidge lived in houses at 21 Massasoit St. and on Hampton Terrace, but these are not open to the public.

Much else is open to visitors, however, and Northampton supplies many of the diversions of this thriving college town. Cultural events range from chamber music to art exhibitions, the number and diversity of restaurants and bars are far greater than most cities its size can flaunt, and its many stores are as kicky as any devout shopper might ask. Try to allow at least a long day and overnight in the area.

A large and growing gay and lesbian presence is apparent but not overwhelming, one manifestation being the Pride March on May 1. A well-received book by Tracy Kidder, *Home Town* (Random House; 1999), profiles Northampton and a number of its people.

WHAT TO SEE & DO

Historic Northampton Among Northampton's most popular attractions are the Museum Houses—three historic homes still standing on their original sites. They are the 1730 Parsons House, the 1796 Shepherd House, and the 1812 Isaac Damon House, which contains a furnished parlor true to 1820.

46 Bridge St. (east of the railroad bridge). ✆ **413/584-6011.** www.historic-northampton.org. Tours $3 adults, $2 seniors and students, $1 children 12 and under. Museum Tues–Fri 10am–4pm, Sat–Sun noon–4pm; house tours given Sat–Sun noon–4pm only.

Smith College ★ To a considerable extent, the campus buildings that line Elm Street are a testament to the excesses of late-19th-century architecture. Their often egregious admixtures of Gothic, Greco-Roman, Renaissance, and medieval aesthetic notions lend a Teutonic sobriety to the west end of town. On the other hand, Frederick Law Olmsted, famed for his design of New York's Central Park, laid out much of the original landscaping, and the campus contains many wooded walks and gardens.

Elm St. ✆ **413/584-2700.** www.smith.edu.

Smith College Museum of Art ★★ With the conclusion of a 3-year renovation and expansion, this facility stepped up to claim equal footing with New England's finest college art museums, including those at Williams, Harvard, and Yale. It already had an impressive permanent collection of paintings by Degas, Monet, Picasso, and Winslow Homer, among many 19th- and 20th-century Europeans and Americans. Now, there is not only more space to show them, but also ample room for an ambitious program of temporary exhibitions. The new third-floor galleries have fine views of town and campus and allow abundant light for canvases by a substantial number of French Impressionists and post-Impressionists, including Gauguin, Cézanne, Renoir, and Monet. Americans Sargent, Whistler, and Georgia O'Keeffe are also represented. On the second floor, British historical and portrait painters Benjamin West and Joshua Reynolds share space with Greek and Roman glassware, ceramics, and statuary, while the ground floor is given to traveling exhibits. There is an atrium cafe serving drinks and snacks. Parking is a challenge, but worth the effort.

Elm St. and Bedford Terrace. ✆ **413/585-2760.** www.smith.edu/artmuseum. Admission $5 adults, $4 seniors, $3 students, $2 ages 6–12. June–Aug Tues–Sun noon–4pm; Sept–May Tues–Sat 10am–4pm; Sun noon–4pm.

GETTING OUTSIDE

Three miles southwest of town on Route 10 is the **Arcadia Nature Center and Wildlife Sanctuary,** 127 Combs Rd., Easthampton (✆ **413/584-3009;** www.massaudubon.org), a 700-acre preserve operated by the Massachusetts Audubon Society. It contains marshes and woods bordering the Connecticut River, with 5 miles of trails. The sanctuary is open Tuesday through Sunday from dawn to dusk, trails from 9am to 3pm. Admission is $4 for adults, $3 for seniors and children 3 to 12.

The 8½-mile **Norwottuck Rail Trail Bike Path** follows a former railroad bed running between Northampton and Amherst. Access is via Damon Road and at Mount Farms Mall. Bicyclists, skaters, and cross-country skiers are all welcome. Bikes can be rented at **Valley Bicycles,** 319 Main St. (✆ **413/256-0880**), across the river in Amherst.

Look Memorial Park, 300 N. Main St. (✆ **413/584-5457**), is northwest of town off Route 9, with 157 acres of woods, a lake (with boats for rent), miniature golf, tennis, picnic grounds, and a small zoo. Musical and theatrical events, including puppet shows, are held in summer. Admission is $3 weekends and $2 weekdays from April to October; free from November to March.

SHOPPING

In a town with a bookstore at every other corner, **Raven Used Books,** 4 Old South St., down the hill from Main Street (✆ **413/584-9868**), stands out. Along with the usual categories, it has shelves devoted to shamanism, prophecy, and erotica.

In addition to an abundance of bookstores, Northampton enjoys the most diverse shopping in the valley. The **Antiques Center of Northampton,** 9½ Market St. (✆ **413/584-3600**), contains the stalls of more than 60 dealers; closed Wednesdays. **Ten Thousand Villages,** 82 Main St. (✆ **413/582-9338**), is part of a nonprofit Mennonite program selling handicrafts from more than 30 Third World countries.

A former department store was reconfigured into **Thorne's Marketplace,** 150 Main St. (✆ **413/584-5582**), now containing more than 30 boutiques and casual eating places. Next to the side entrance of the marketplace is **Herrell's,** 7 Old South St. (✆ **413/586-9700**), a celebrated New England super-premium ice-cream emporium, dipping scooping a huge variety of flavors, including Mudpie, Cheesecake Blueberry Swirl, and Kentucky Bourbon Vanilla; open daily.

Northampton has a reputation as a small town with an unusually vigorous arts community. Burnishing that image is the prestigious **R. Michelson Gallery,** 132 Main St. (✆ **413/586-3964**), which occupies a grand former bank.

WHERE TO STAY

Anticipate higher rates and limited vacancies during graduation and homecoming, in addition to the usual holiday weekends.

Clarion Hotel ★ This used to be called the Inn at Northampton, so there's a new sign out by the road. That makes it easier to find, because the hotel is hidden behind a gas station. Renovations have elevated it from a standard motel to something closer to a modest resort and conference center.

Rte. 5 and I-91 (just west of Exit 18), Northampton, MA 01060. ✆ **800/582-2929** or 413/586-1211. Fax 413/586-0630. www.hampshirehospitality.com. 122 units. $94–$131 double; $149 suite. Rates include continental breakfast Mon–Fri. AE, DC, DISC, MC, V. **Amenities:** Restaurant (steakhouse); bar; heated indoor pool; outdoor pool; lighted tennis court; Jacuzzi; business center; limited room service. *In room:* A/C, TV, dataport, coffeemaker, hair dryer, iron.

Hotel Northampton ★ Built in 1927, this brick building at the center of town looks older. Rooms of varying sizes contain wicker and Colonial reproductions, feather duvets, and assorted Victoriana. Many front rooms have balconies overlooking King Street, some have fridges, and a few have Jacuzzis. Downstairs, Wiggins Tavern is an atmospheric watering hole with dark beams and three stone fireplaces.

36 King St., Northampton, MA 01060. ✆ **800/547-3529** or 413/584-3100. Fax 413/584-9455. www.hotelnorthampton.com. 107 units. Apr–Nov $185–$230 double; Dec–Mar $145–$215 double. Rates include continental breakfast. AE, DC, DISC, MC, V. Free parking. **Amenities:** 2 restaurants (American); bar; exercise room; business center; limited room service; same-day dry cleaning/laundry. *In room:* A/C, TV, dataport, hair dryer, iron.

WHERE TO DINE

Eastside Grill ★★ AMERICAN Everyone agrees: this white-clapboard building with a nautical look is the best place to eat in town. For the over-40 set it's also a refuge from the prevailing collegiate tone of Northampton. The comforting menu used to feature Cajun/Creole dishes but has shifted to less regional treatments. About a third of the many entrees involve beef, such as the delicious tenderloins with Gorgonzola and fried leeks, but the seafood choices are impressive, too, especially the fried oysters with béarnaise and sesame scallops with lobster and sake.

19 Strong Ave. (1 block south of Main St.). ✆ **413/586-3347.** Reservations recommended. Main courses $14–$18. AE, DC, DISC, MC, V. Mon–Thurs 5–10pm; Fri 5–10:30pm; Sat 4–10:30pm; Sun 4–9pm.

Fitzwilly's *Value* AMERICAN Occupying an 1898 building, this ingratiating pub makes the most of its stamped-tin ceilings and ample space. Copper brewing kettles signal an intriguing selection of beers. Beyond the two bars are curtained booths where patrons dive into nachos, burgers pizzas, ribs, pastas, and such pub faves as crab cakes and fried calamari. Appetizers are half price during the 4-to-7pm happy hour, and there are blue-plate lunches for only $5.95 to $6.95. Everything is available for takeout.

23 Main St. (near Pleasant St.). ✆ **413/584-8666.** Reservations not accepted. Main courses $11–$18. AE, DC, DISC, MC, V. Daily 11:30am–1am.

Green Street Café ★ NEW AMERICAN Julia Child famously dined here, which may account for the Gallic tilt of the menu and the excellent baguettes, baked on-site.

Don't overdose on the bread, though, for there are any number of delectables emerging from the kitchen—wild caught salmon and chicken with apples and hazelnuts, for example. The restaurant grows its own vegetables in season, and the emphasis throughout the year is on fresh ingredients. Service is largely by students, and can range from sweet to snippy. While consistency can be an issue, it remains one of the town's two or three best—it's also the most expensive (compare with the prices at the Eastside Grill, above).

64 Green St. ✆ **413/586-5650.** Reservations recommended. Main courses $20–$26. MC, V. Mon–Fri noon–2pm; Sun 10am–2pm; daily 5–10pm. Follow Main St. toward the Smith campus, straight into West St., turning right on Green St.

Osaka JAPANESE There's no pretending that this new sushi and steakhouse is the equal of similar establishments in New York or Los Angeles, but it's odds-on best of breed in the Valley. Decor includes lots of blond wood, a sushi bar at the entrance and a large hibachi in back, which they'll fire up for as few as two people. The menu lists 18 special rolls, over two dozen selections of a la carte sushi and sashimi, and 13 vegetable sushi maki. Then it takes a deep breath before adding soups, chef's specials, bento boxes, teriyaki, and so on. Entrees come with uninspired miso soup and boiled rice. While it's possible to put together a conventional meal, the wiser course is to pick and choose among the many rolls and sushi options—the spicy red snapper, ebi tempura, maki, osaki, and naruto have all been good. Once you are past the taciturn male members of the staff, you will find the waitresses cheerful and accommodating.

7 Old South St. (1 block south of Main St.). ✆ **413/587-9548.** Main courses $12–$26. AE, DC, DISC, MC, V. Mon–Sat 11:30am–11pm (Fri–Sat until midnight); Sun 12:30–11pm.

Vermont Country Deli & Cafe ECLECTIC Tantalizing options often include sesame chicken, pesto tortellini, and maple-barbecued pork ribs. Nearly 20 imaginative sandwiches, including three of the strictly vegetarian persuasion, are made to order. Also on offer are plump sticky buns and sourdough baguettes.

48 Main St. (near Pleasant St.). ✆ **413/586-7114.** Main courses $5.50–$9.95. MC, V. Mon–Sat 7am–7pm; Sun 8am–6pm.

NORTHAMPTON AFTER DARK

The presence of Smith and four other area colleges only partially accounts for the large number of bars and clubs in town, making Northampton the nightlife magnet of the valley. For a rundown of what's happening, pick up a free copy of the *Valley Advocate.*

Still thriving after 100-plus years, the **Academy of Music,** 74 Main St. (✆ **413/584-8435**), shows arthouse and foreign films, and provides a venue for opera, ballet, and pop performers on tour.

Another old favorite, the **Iron Horse Music Hall,** 20 Center St. (✆ **413/586-8686**), has played host to a wide variety of artists, from Bonnie Raitt to Dave Brubeck to folkies and grunge rockers. It's open Tuesday through Sunday, when the cover for live acts is typically between $8 and $18.

Live bluegrass, jam rock, and soul-funk alternate with DJs at the **Pearl Street Nightclub,** 10 Pearl St. (✆ **413/584-7771**). There are often dance nights targeted at teenagers, as well as gay nights. Nearby is the newer **Bishop's Lounge,** 41 Strong Ave. (✆ **413/584-8513**), a sophisticated update of the funky old Bay State Hotel, with live music of scattered identity 6 nights a week. **Harry's,** 140 Pleasant St. (✆ **413/586-9155**), has music every night, mostly live, largely rock or R&B, with karaoke, open mic, and DJ interludes.

The **Calvin Theatre and Performing Arts Center,** 19 King St. (✆ **401/586-0851**), offers touring performers as diverse as the Pat Metheny Group, flamenco troupes, and children's theater. Classical and chamber music is the customary fare at Smith's **Sweeney Concert Hall,** Sage Hall (✆ **413/585-2787**).

AMHERST

Yet another Pioneer Valley town defined by its educational institutions, this one has an even larger student population than most, with distinguished Amherst College occupying much of its center, the large University of Massachusetts campus to its immediate northwest, and Hampshire College off South Pleasant Street. All three, plus Mount Holyoke and Smith College, on the other side of the Connecticut River, combine to provide a full September-to-June slate of artistic and musical events.

On the edge of the town green is a seasonal **information booth.** Its hours vary, but if it's closed, visitors can call the **Chamber of Commerce** (✆ **413/253-0700**) for information.

HISTORIC HOMES & COLLEGES

Most of the historic homes are within a few blocks of the Amity/Main/Pleasant street crossing. Amherst College lies mostly along the east side of the town green. At the northeast corner is the **Town Hall,** another fortress-like Romanesque Revival creation of Boston's H. H. Richardson.

Amherst College Named for Baron Jefferey Amherst, a British general during the last of the French and Indian Wars, the illustrious liberal-arts college was founded in 1821, with Noah Webster on its first board of trustees. Robert Frost was a member of the faculty for more than a decade.

Amherst's campus cuts through the heart of the town and contains two museums open to the public. The **Pratt Museum** ★, at the southeast corner of the main quad (✆ **413/542-2165**), contains dinosaur tracks collected from sedimentary rocks in the valley, as well as fossils and a mastodon skeleton. The **Mead Art Museum** ★, Routes 116 and 9 (✆ **413/542-2335**), displays sculptures, paintings, photographs, and antiquities. Its strengths lie in the works of 19th- and 20th-century American artists and French Impressionists. Admission to both museums is free.

S. Pleasant and College sts. ✆ **413/542-2000.** www.amherst.edu.

The Emily Dickinson Museum: The Homestead and The Evergreens ★ Designated a National Historic Monument, The Homestead is where Emily Dickinson was born in 1830 and where she lived until her family moved in 1840. (The Evergreens was the home of Emily's brother Austin and his wife.) Emily and her family returned in 1855, and the famous poet stayed here until her death 31 years later. The "Belle of Amherst" was the granddaughter and daughter of local movers and shakers, the source of her support while she produced the poetry that was increasingly celebrated even as she withdrew into near-total seclusion.

280 Main St. (2 blocks east of the Town Hall). ✆ **413/542-8161.** www.emilydickinsonmuseum.org. Admission $8 adults, $7 seniors and students, $5 for ages 6–18, free for children under 6. Guided tours only, Mar, Wed and Sat 1–4pm on the hour; Apr–May and Sept–Oct Wed–Sat 1–4pm on the hour; June–Aug Wed–Sun 1–4pm on the half-hour, Sat 10:30 and 11:30am. Reservations recommended.

University of Massachusetts Though the university was founded in 1863, this sprawling 1,200-acre campus north of the town center dates mainly from the 1960s.

Several of its buildings top out at over 20 stories. Its 25,000 students study for degrees in 90 academic fields. Six art galleries are scattered around the campus; foremost among these is the University Gallery in the **Fine Arts Center** ★, beside the pond in the quad. It focuses on 20th-century artists. The center also mounts productions in dance, music, and theater. Call the box office (✆ **413/545-2511**) for information on upcoming performances.

Rte. 116. ✆ **413/545-4237** for tour information. Campus tours available daily at 11am and 1:15pm, except Sat–Sun in June–July, Mar break, and most holidays.

GETTING OUTSIDE

An 8½-mile bicycle trail follows an old rail bed from Warren Wright Road in Belchertown, passing through Amherst, and on to Elder Island in the Connecticut River adjacent to Northampton. Bikes can be rented at **Valley Bicycles,** 319 Main St., Amherst (✆ **413/256-0880**). It operates a seasonal shop, **Valley Bicycles Trailside,** 8 Railroad St. (✆ **413/584-4466**), directly on the trail.

SHOPPING

Under new ownership, the former Atticus/Albion Bookstore has become **Amherst Books,** 8 Main St. (✆ **413/256-1547**). While it has a less rumpled aspect than it did, the operators are no less committed to books and their patrons. The nearby **Jefferey Amherst Bookshop,** 55 S. Pleasant St. (✆ **413/253-3381**), specializes in Emily Dickinson and academic texts.

WHERE TO STAY

Lord Jeffery Inn ★★ It's a running battle to keep the principal lodging in a college town from looking a little battered. At the moment, the Lord Jeff is winning, thanks to almost constant renovation and redecorating. So despite the wear and tear of more than 75 years of graduations and homecomings, the inn offers an environment that is as warm as its several fireplaces. The Sorbonne-trained chef has turned the **Windowed Hearth** into Amherst's event restaurant, open for dinner and Sunday brunch. Pub food is served in the casual **Elijah Boltwood's Tavern.**

30 Boltwood Ave. (next to the Town Hall), Amherst, MA 01002. ✆ **800/742-0358** or 413/253-2576. Fax 413/256-6152. www.lordjefferyinn. 48 units. $79–$239 double. AE, MC, V. Pets accepted ($15). **Amenities:** 2 restaurants (creative regional); bar; access to nearby health club; limited room service. *In room:* A/C, TV, dataport.

WHERE TO DINE

Additional options are the **Windowed Hearth** and **Elijah Boltwood's Tavern,** at the Lord Jeffery Inn, above.

Judie's ★★ CREATIVE AMERICAN Don't leave Amherst without eating at Judie's. The vivacious owner does her best to suit every taste. Just to keep things ticking, for example, there's a "Munchie Madness" period from 3 to 6pm, with a snacks menu of potato skins, nachos, hummus and black bean dip, and so forth. Throughout the day, folks drop by for a cup of seafood bisque and one of the trademark popovers. Typical dinner entrees are the steak, the three-mushroom risotto, and the seafood gumbo with shrimp, sausage, scallops, salmon, and lobster. This being a college town, portions run from really big to immense, the better to assuage raging young metabolisms.

51 N. Pleasant St. (north of Amity and Main sts.). ✆ **413/253-3491.** Main courses $17–$19. AE, DISC, MC, V. Sun and Tues–Thurs 11:30am–10pm; Fri–Sat 11:30am–11pm.

AMHERST AFTER DARK

Students and other young adults tend to gravitate toward the livelier music scene in Northampton, but Amherst does offer some nighttime entertainment. Close at hand is the **Black Sheep Cafe,** 79 Main St. (✆ **413/253-3442**), active with folk singers, readings, chamber music—a broad, unpredictable selection. The beer is good, the food indifferent, and the music varied at the **Amherst Brewing Company,** 24–36 N. Pleasant St. (✆ **413/253-4400**).

Amherst College's **Buckley Recital Hall** (✆ **413/542-2195**) and the **Mullins Center** (✆ **413/733-2500**) at UMass mount a variety of performances that might include, for example, the Cincinnati Symphony, Mummenschantz, or Elton John.

DEERFIELD ★★★

Meadows cleared and plowed more than 330 years ago still surround this historic town between the Connecticut and Deerfield rivers. Every morning, tobacco and dairy farmers leave houses fronting the main street to work their land nearby. Students attend the distinguished prep school, Deerfield Academy, founded in 1797. Deerfield is an invaluable fragment of American history, and it isn't one of those New England village exhibits with costumed performers who go home to their condos at night.

A town still exists here, 16 miles north of Northampton and 16 miles northwest of Amherst, because the earliest English settlers were determined to thrive despite their status as a frontier pressure point in the wars that tormented Colonial America. Massacres of Deerfield's settlers by the French and Indian enemies of the British nearly wiped out the town in 1675 and again in 1704. In the latter raid, 47 people were killed and another 112 were taken prisoner and marched to French Quebec.

The main thoroughfare, simply called **"The Street,"** is lined with more than 80 houses built in the 17th, 18th, and 19th centuries. Most are private, but 14 of them can be visited through tours conducted by Historic Deerfield, a local tourism organization (see below).

MUSEUMS & HISTORIC HOMES

The Street is a mile long, with most of the museum houses concentrated along the long block north of the central town common. There are two buildings operated by organizations other than Historic Deerfield. One is **Memorial Hall Museum,** east of the town common on Memorial Street, for which a separate admission is charged. (For the slightly higher fee of $12 adults, $5 children and students, tours of the 14 museum houses can be combined with a visit to Memorial Hall through Historic Deerfield.) The other is the **Indian House Memorial,** north of the Deerfield Inn, also maintained by a separate organization. Because it is only a 1929 reproduction of an earlier house, it is of less interest than the other structures.

Special **celebrations** in the town are held on Patriot's Day (the third Mon in Apr), Washington's Birthday, Thanksgiving, and the Christmas holidays. Call the information center in Hall Tavern (✆ **413/774-5581;** see below) for details.

Historic Deerfield ★★★ Begin with a visit to the **Hall Tavern,** opposite the post office, where tickets are sold and brochures are available. A particularly useful booklet outlines a walking tour of 88 historic locations in the village. This is also the departure point for guided tours. While there are no charges for simply strolling The Street, the only way to get inside the museum houses is on a tour.

The 14 houses on the tour were constructed between 1720 and 1850. They contain furnishings, textiles, ceramics, silver and pewter, and implements used from the early 17th century to 1900. Included are imports from China and Europe as well as items made in the Connecticut River Valley during its prominence as an industrial center.

The judicious selection at the **Museum Store,** between the post office and the Deerfield Inn (✆ **413/774-5581**), includes weather vanes, hand-dipped candles, and reproductions of light fixtures found in the village houses.

A stone building behind the Dwight House contains the **Flynt Center of Early American Life** ★, with galleries for changing exhibitions of paintings, textiles, and decorative arts relevant to the local history.

A free attraction is the **Channing Blake Meadow Walk.** Open from 8am to 6pm in good weather, the interpretive trail begins beside the Rev. John Farwell Moors House, a Historic Deerfield holding on the west side of The Street. It goes through a working farm, past the playing fields of Deerfield Academy, and through pastures beside the Deerfield River. Along the trail, sheep and cattle are seen up close; for that reason, dogs aren't allowed.

Information Center, Hall Tavern, The Street. ✆ **413/774-5581.** www.historic-deerfield.org. Admission to all museum houses (good for 2 consecutive days) $14 adults, $5 for ages 6–21. Daily 9:30am–4:30pm.

Memorial Hall Museum ★ Deerfield Academy's original 1798 building was converted into this museum of village history in 1880. A popular, if suggestively grisly exhibit is the door of a 1698 home that shows the gashes made by weapons of the French and Indian raiders in 1704. Should the point be too subtle, a hatchet is also embedded in the door. Five period rooms are also on view. Special events—plays, crafts fairs, lectures, and even ice-cream socials—are held monthly.

8 Memorial St. (between The Street and Routes 5 and 10). ✆ **413/774-3768,** or 413/774-7476 off season. www.old-deerfield.org/museum. Admission $6 adults, $3 children and students, free for children under 6. May–Oct daily 10am–4:30pm.

WHERE TO STAY & DINE

Deerfield Inn ★ Built in 1884, this inn in the middle of The Street is one of the best-known stopping places in the valley. The innkeepers have restlessly scoured the establishment, over the last few years, replacing all the bathroom fixtures, refinishing the older furniture, and installing new carpeting. Antiques and reproductions are judiciously mixed throughout. With blazes in the several fireplaces and an atmospheric tavern in which to linger, this is as pleasant a setting as can be found. That said, the food served in the dining room and in the cafeteria, truth to tell, is no better than ordinary.

81 Old Main St., Deerfield, MA 01342. ✆ **800/926-3865** or 413/774-5587. Fax 413/775-7221. www.deerfieldinn.com. 23 units. May–Oct $205–$277 double; Nov–Apr $173–$195 double. Rates include breakfast and afternoon tea. Midweek discounts available. AE, DC, MC, V. **Amenities:** Restaurant (American); cafeteria; bar. *In room:* A/C, TV, dataport, coffeemaker, hair dryer, iron.

5 The Berkshires

More than hills but less than mountains, the Taconic and Hoosac ranges that define this region at the western end of the state go by the collective name "The Berkshires." The hamlets, villages, and two small cities that have long drawn sustenance from the region's kindly Housatonic River and its tranquil tributaries are as New England as can be.

Mohawks and Mohegans lived and hunted here, and while white missionaries established settlements at Stockbridge and elsewhere in an attempt to Christianize the native tribes, the Indians eventually moved on west. Farmers, drawn to the narrow but fertile flood plains of the Housatonic, were increasingly supplanted in the 19th century by manufacturers, who erected the brick mills that drew their power from the river.

At the same time, artists and writers were attracted by the mild summers and seclusion that these hills and lakes offered. Nathaniel Hawthorne, Herman Melville, and Edith Wharton were among those who put down temporary roots. By the late 19th century and the arrival of the railroad, wealthy New Yorkers and Bostonians had discovered the region and begun to erect extravagant summer "cottages." With their support, culture and the performing arts found a hospitable reception. By the 1930s, theater, dance, and music performances had established themselves as regular summer fixtures. Tanglewood, Jacob's Pillow, and the Berkshire and Williamstown Theatre festivals draw tens of thousands of visitors every summer.

Note that many inns routinely stipulate minimum 2- or 3-night stays in summer and over holiday weekends and often require advance deposits.

ESSENTIALS

GETTING THERE The Massachusetts Turnpike (I-90) runs east-west from Boston to the Berkshires, with an exit near Lee and Stockbridge. From New York City, the scenic Taconic State Parkway connects with I-90 not far from Pittsfield., or, to reach the southern end of the county, exit before that on the Taconic at Route 20 heading toward Hillsdale, NY, and Great Barrington, MA.

Amtrak (© **800/USA-RAIL;** www.northeast.amtrak.com) operates the Lake Shore Limited daily between Boston and Chicago, stopping in Pittsfield each way.

VISITOR INFORMATION The **Berkshire Visitors Bureau,** 3 Hoosac St., Adams, MA (© **800/237-5747** or 413/443-9186), can assist with questions and lodging reservations. Local chambers of commerce and visitor centers maintain information booths at central locations in Great Barrington, Lee, Lenox, Pittsfield, Stockbridge, and Williamstown (see the sections that follow). Also check out **www.berkshires.org**.

SHEFFIELD ★

The first settlement of any size encountered when approaching from Connecticut on Route 7, Sheffield occupies a flood plain beside the Housatonic River, 11 miles south of Great Barrington, with the Berkshires rising to the west.

Agriculture has long been the principal occupation of its residents, and still is, to a degree. Everyone else sells antiques, or so it might seem driving along Route 7 (also known as Main St. or Sheffield Plain). The meticulously maintained houses cultivate an impression of prosperous tranquillity.

May through October, stop by the **Colonel Ashley House,** Cooper Hill Road, in Ashley Falls (© **413/298-3239**). Built by the colonel himself in 1735, this modified saltbox is believed to be the oldest house in Berkshire County. Ashley was a person of considerable repute in Colonial western Massachusetts, a pioneer settler, an officer during one of the French and Indian Wars, and later a lawyer and a judge. The house is open from 1 to 5pm on Saturday and Sunday, from Memorial Day to Columbus Day. Admission to the grounds is free; tours of the house are $5 for adults and $1 for children 6 to 12. To find it, drive south from Sheffield on Route 7, then veer onto Route 7A toward Ashley Falls. Bear right on Rannapo Road. At the Y intersection, turn right on Cooper Hill Road.

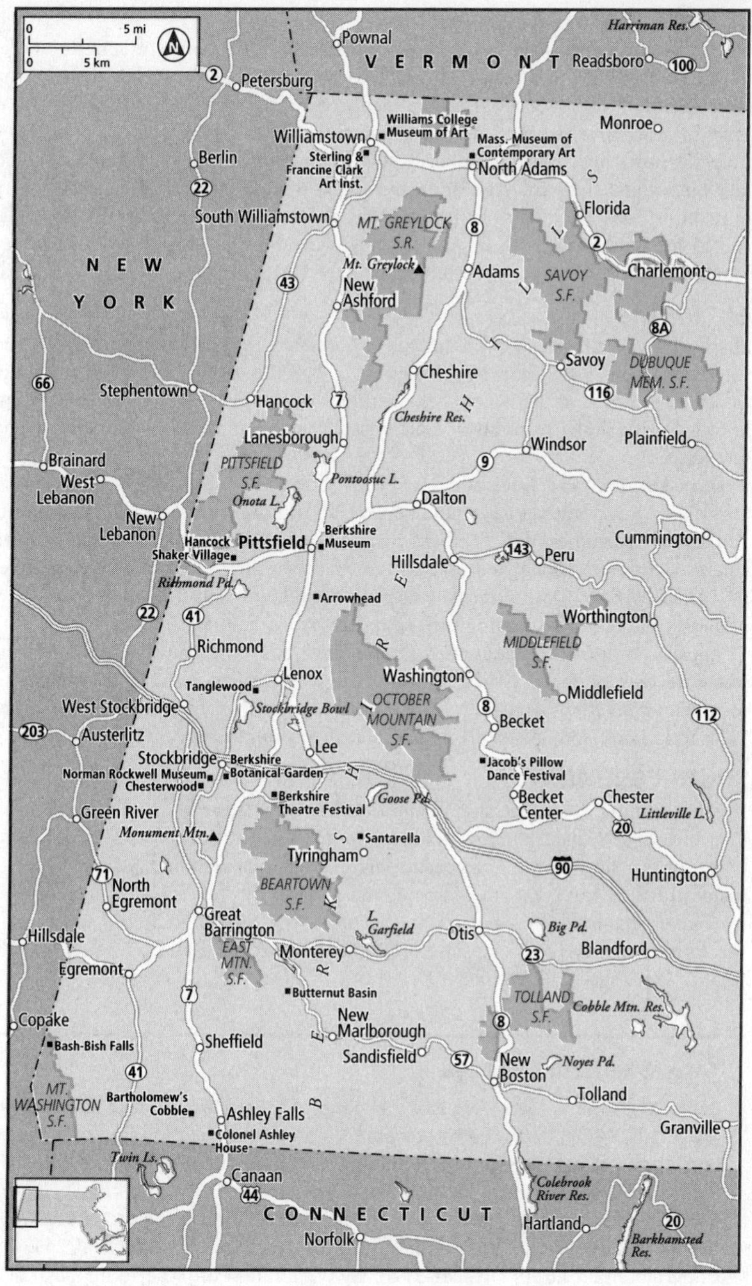
0
5 mi
0
5 km
N
VERMONT
NEW YORK
CONNECTICUT
Harriman Res.
Pownal
Readsboro
Petersburg
Monroe
Williams College Museum of Art
Williamstown
Mass. Museum of Contemporary Art
Sterling & Francine Clark Art Inst.
North Adams
Berlin
Florida
South Williamstown
MT. GREYLOCK S.R.
Mt. Greylock
Adams
SAVOY S.F.
Charlemont
New Ashford
Savoy
DUBUQUE MEM. S.F.
Cheshire
Stephentown
Hancock
Cheshire Res.
Lanesborough
Plainfield
Windsor
Brainard
PITTSFIELD S.F.
West Lebanon
Onota L.
Pontoosuc L.
Dalton
New Lebanon
Hancock Shaker Village
Pittsfield
Berkshire Museum
Cummington
Hillsdale
Peru
Richmond Pd.
Arrowhead
Worthington
Richmond
MIDDLEFIELD S.F.
Lenox
Washington
Tanglewood
West Stockbridge
Stockbridge Bowl
OCTOBER MOUNTAIN S.F.
Middlefield
Becket
Austerlitz
Lee
Stockbridge
Berkshire Botanical Garden
Norman Rockwell Museum
Chesterwood
Jacob's Pillow Dance Festival
Berkshire Theatre Festival
Goose Pd.
Becket Center
Chester
Green River
Littleville L.
Monument Mtn.
Santarella
Tyringham
Huntington
BEARTOWN S.F.
North Egremont
Great Barrington
L. Garfield
Otis
Big Pd.
Hillsdale
EAST MTN. S.F.
Monterey
Blandford
Egremont
Butternut Basin
TOLLAND S.F.
Cobble Mtn. Res.
Copake
New Marlborough
Sheffield
Bash-Bish Falls
Sandisfield
New Boston
Noyes Pd.
MT. WASHINGTON S.F.
Bartholomew's Cobble
Tolland
Ashley Falls
Colonel Ashley House
Granville
Twin Ls.
Canaan
Colebrook River Res.
Hartland
Norfolk
Barkhamsted Res.
BERKSHIRE HILLS

GETTING OUTSIDE

The 278-acre nature reservation called **Bartholomew's Cobble** ★, on Route 7A (✆ **413/229-8600**), lies beside an oxbow bend in the Housatonic. A "cobble," by local definition, is a "scenic, rocky eminence rising from the valley floor." These 6 miles of trails cross pastures, penetrate forests, and provide vistas of the river valley from the area's high point, Hurlburt's Hill. Picnicking is permitted. Birders should take binoculars. Trails are open from sunrise to sunset, and the small natural-history museum is open daily from 9am to 4:30pm. Requested donations are $5 for adults and $1 for children 6 to 12. To get here, follow the directions for the Colonel Ashley House (see above), except at the end of Rannapo Road, bear left on Weatogue Road.

ANTIQUING

Sheffield lays justifiable claim to the title of "Antiques Capital of the Berkshires"—no small feat, given what seems to be an effort by half the population of the Berkshires to sell collectibles, oddities, and true antiques to the other half. These are canny, knowledgeable dealers who know exactly what they have, so expect high quality and few bargains.

Darr Antiques and Interiors, 34 S. Main St. (✆ **413/229-7773**), specializes in 18th- and 19th-century English and American furniture. Farther north along Route 7, **Dovetail Antiques,** 440 Sheffield Plain (✆ **413/229-2628**), features American clocks. Continuing along Route 7, on the left at the edge of town, is **Susan Silver** (✆ **413/229-8169**), with meticulously restored 18th- and 19th-century English library furniture (desks, reading stands) and French accessories.

There are at least two dozen other dealers along this route. Most of them stock the **free directory** of the Berkshire County Antiques Dealers Association, which lists member dealers from Sheffield to Cheshire and across the border in Connecticut and New York. Look, too, for the pamphlet called *The Antique Hunter's Guide to Route 7.*

SOUTH EGREMONT

If you're coming to the Berkshires from the Taconic Parkway in New York, you can't help but drive through the town of Egremont. Its larger, busier half is South Egremont, once a stop on the stagecoach route between Hartford and Albany. It retains many structures from that era, including mills that utilized the stream that still rushes by. Those circumstances make it a magnet for antiques dealers and restaurateurs. In the former category, seek out **The Splendid Peasant,** on Route 23 (✆ **413/528-5755**), which specializes in folk art.

Tips Sheffield on Stage

From late June to late August, the nonprofit **Barrington Stage Company** (✆ **413/528-8888;** www.barringtonstageco.org) mounts musicals, comedies, and dramas at the **Consolati Performing Arts Center,** on Berkshire School Road and other sites. The Tony-winning *The 25th Annual Putnam County Spelling Bee* was given its premiere by the company before it moved to Broadway. On five Saturday evenings in July and August, the **Berkshire Choral Festival,** 245 N. Undermountain Rd. (✆ **413298-3926;** www.choralfest.org), performs classical works at the Berkshire School in Sheffield.

GETTING OUTSIDE

HIKING Scenic **Bash-Bish Falls State Park** ★★, on Route 23 (✆ **413/528-0330**), makes a rewarding outing for a day of hiking, birding, and fishing (no picnicking, though). To get here, drive west on Route 23 from town, turning south on Route 41, and immediately right on Mount Washington Road. Watch for signs directing the way to Mount Washington State Forest and Bash-Bish Falls. After 8 miles, a sign indicates a right turn toward the falls; look for it opposite a church with an unusual steeple. The road begins to follow the course of a mountain stream, going downhill. In about 3 miles is a large parking place next to a craggy promontory.

The sign also points off to a trail down to the falls, which should be negotiated only by reasonably fit adults. First, mount the promontory for a splendid view across the plains of the Hudson Valley to the pale-blue ridgeline of the Catskill Mountains. The falls can be heard, but not yet seen, down to the left. If this trail seems too steep, continue driving down the road to another parking area, on the left. From here, a gentler trail a little over a mile long leads to the falls. The falls themselves are quite impressive, crashing down from more than 80 feet. The park is open from dawn to dusk. It has 15 campsites.

SKIING At the western edge of the township, touching the New York border, is the **Catamount Ski Area,** on Route 23 (✆ **413/528-1262;** www.catamountski.com). Only about 2 hours from Manhattan, it is understandably popular with New Yorkers. It has 28 trails, including the daunting Catapult (the steepest run in the Berkshires) and seven chairlifts, as well as a 400-foot half-pipe for snowboarders. Night skiing and rentals are available. On weekends, full-day lift tickets cost $48 for adults, $38 for seniors and children 7 to 13, and $12 for children 6 and under.

WHERE TO STAY

Egremont Inn ★ Guests slip into this friendly former stagecoach stop as easily as into a favorite old flannel robe. The Egremont has been a tavern and inn since 1780. That longevity shows, in tilting floors and a grand brick fireplace. Rooms are simple and rustic, with iron bedsteads, rag rugs, wide-board floors, and adequate bathrooms.

Dinner is served Wednesday through Sunday year-round. A singer-guitarist performs Thursday nights, a jazz ensemble Saturday evenings. Rates are negotiable during slow periods and for long stays. Kids are welcome.

Old Sheffield Rd. (1 block off Rte. 23), South Egremont, MA 01258. ✆ **413/528-2111.** Fax 413/528-3284. www.egremontinn.com. 21 units. Weekdays $90–$160 double; weekends $115–$200 double; 2–3 nights required on peak season weekends. Rates include breakfast. Weekend packages available. AE, DISC, MC, V. **Amenities:** Restaurant (American); tavern; outdoor pool; golf course nearby; 2 tennis courts; bike rental. *In room:* A/C.

Weathervane Inn An affectionate cat welcomes new arrivals to a building that began as a 1735 farmhouse, but was renovated in Greek Revival style in 1835. Many guest rooms have four-poster beds with quilts; fireplaces have been added to two units. In summer, a 3-night stay is required on weekends. Children are welcome.

Rte. 23, South Egremont, MA 01258. ✆ **800/528-9580** or 413/528-2111. Fax 413/528-1713. www.weathervaneinn.com. 10 units. $115–$165 double; $225–$275 suite. Rates include breakfast and afternoon tea. Packages available. AE, DC, MC, V. **Amenities:** Unheated outdoor pool; public golf course next door. *In room:* A/C, dataport.

GREAT BARRINGTON

Even with a population barely over 7,500, this pleasant retail center, 7 miles south of Stockbridge, is the largest town in the southern part of the county. Rapids in the

Housatonic provided power for a number of mills in centuries past, most of which are now gone, and in 1886 this was one of the first communities in the world to have electricity on its streets and in its homes.

Great Barrington has no sights of particular significance, leaving time to browse its many antiques galleries and specialty shops. Convenient as a home base for excursions to such nearby attractions as Monument Mountain, Bash-Bish Falls, Butternut Basin, Tanglewood concerts, and the historic houses of Stockbridge, it has a number of unremarkable but entirely adequate motels north of the center along or near Route 7 that tend to fill up more slowly on weekends than the better-known inns in the area. It is something of a dining destination, too, with 55 eating places, including, at last count, *four* sushi bars!

A farmer's market is held on Saturdays from 9:00 to 1:00 in season at the train station on Castle Street.

The **Southern Berkshire Chamber of Commerce** maintains an information booth at 362 Main St. (© **413/528-1510;** www.southernberkshires.com), near the town hall. It's open Tuesday through Sunday from 10am to 5pm.

GETTING OUTSIDE

The **Egremont Country Club,** on Route 23 (© **413/528-4222;** www.egremont countryclub.com), is open to the public. Its facilities include a scenic 18-hole golf course, tennis courts, and an Olympic-size pool. Greens fees are modest; tee times required.

Butternut Basin, on Route 23, 2 miles east of town (© **413/528-2000,** or 800/438-7669 for snow conditions; www.butternutbasin.com), is known for its strong family ski programs. There's day care at $8 per hour for kids 2½ to 6 from December 23 until the end of the season, and the Mountaineer program for children 4 to 12 offers packages that include lunch, instruction, and lift tickets for $75 per day. Six double and quad chairlifts provide access to 22 trails. There are also 5 miles of cross-country trails. On weekends, full-day lift tickets cost $46 for adults, $36 for seniors and children 7 to 13, and $10 for children 6 and under. A 2-day jazz festival is presented in late August.

A little over 4 miles north of town, west of Route 7, is **Monument Mountain,** with two trails to the summit. The easier route is the Indian Monument Trail, about an hour's hike to the top; the more difficult one, the Hickey Trail, isn't much longer but takes the steep way up. The summit, called Squaw Peak, offers splendid views.

SHOPPING

Head straight for Railroad Street, the town's best shopping strip. Start on the corner with Main Street, at **T. P. Saddle Blanket & Trading Co.** (© **413/528-6500**). An unlikely emporium that looks as if it had been lifted whole from the Rockies, it's packed with boots, hats, Indian jewelry, blankets, and jars of salsa.

Mistral's, 6 Railroad St. (© **413/528-1618**), stocks Gallic tableware, linens, fancy foods, and furniture. **Church Street Trading Company,** 4 Railroad St. (© **413/528-6120**), defies easy categorization, with walking sticks, dog collars, and candles all on display. The primary wares are sturdily stylish North Country sweaters, shirts, and pants.

Recently moved from around the corner on Main St., **The Chef's Shop,** 31 Railroad St. (© **413/528-0135**), still features a bounty of gadgets and cookbooks as well as cooking classes. Across the street, **La Pace,** 313 Main St. (© **413/528-1888**), is an upmarket Bed Bath & Beyond–style store with an Italian tilt.

In the north end of town, just before Route 7 turns right across a short bridge, Route 41 goes straight, toward the village of Housatonic. In about 4 miles you'll see a shed that houses the kiln of **Great Barrington Pottery** (© **413/274-6259**). Owner Richard Bennett has been throwing pots according to ancient Japanese techniques for more than 30 years.

Stay on Route 7, going north of the center, and you'll pass a large mall with an anchoring Kmart. In that unlikely location is one of the best (and few) bookstores in the Berkshires, **The Bookloft,** Barrington Plaza (© **413/528-1521**).

WHERE TO STAY

There are several acceptable motels north of town on Route 7, the most desirable being the **Holiday Inn Express,** 415 Stockbridge Rd. (© **413/528-1810;** www.hiexgb.com), which has an indoor pool and whirlpool, and rooms with Jacuzzis and/or fireplaces; rates include breakfast. The **Chamber of Commerce** operates a lodging hot line at © **800/269-4825** or 413/528-4006.

The Old Inn on the Green ★★ This former 1760 tavern/general store and the adjacent 18th-century Thayer House are under new ownership: chef Peter Platt and his wife Meredith Kennard. The most desirable rooms are in Thayer House, some with fireplaces and all with air-conditioning, VCRs, and whirlpool tubs. Those six rooms currently have satellite TV; four more are to be added in the inn. Wireless Internet access is now available in all rooms. The five intimate dining rooms in the pre-Revolutionary tavern have fireplaces, and the only other illumination at dinner is from candles. Menus are quite sophisticated, featuring such unexpected ingredients as sea urchins, diver scallops, and squab. Reservations are strongly advised, especially on weekends. Most of the year, dinner is served Wednesday through Sunday, with Mondays added in summer. There is outdoor dining in season

Rte. 57, New Marlborough, MA 01230. © **413/229-7924.** www.oldinn.com. 11 units. $205–$365 double. Rates include breakfast. AE, MC, V. Take Rte. 23 east from Great Barrington, picking up Rte. 57 after 3½ miles. After 5¾ miles, The Old Inn is on the left. **Amenities:** Restaurant (creative American); courtyard pool at Thayer House. *In room:* A/C, hair dryer, iron.

Windflower Inn A roadside lodging built in the middle of the last century in Federal style, the Windflower commands a large plot of land opposite the Egremont Country Club, on Route 23 between Great Barrington and South Egremont. The gracious family that has owned and operated the inn through two generations makes everyone welcome. Six rooms have fireplaces; four have canopy beds. The inn is smoke-free.

684 S. Egremont Rd. (P.O. Box 25), Great Barrington, MA 01230. © **800/992-1993** or 413/528-2720. Fax 413/528-5147. www.windflowerinn.com. 13 units. $100–$225 double. Rates include full breakfast and afternoon tea. Children under 16 stay in parent's room for $25. AE. **Amenities:** Unheated outdoor pool. *In room:* A/C, TV, dataport.

WHERE TO DINE

In addition to the places listed below, you might check out the restaurant at **The Old Inn on the Green** (see above).

Aegean Breeze ★ GREEK Readers who associate Greek cuisine with roadside diners or dingy blue-and-white storefronts in strip malls will have their preconceptions swept away by this commendable taverna. Almost hidden on the heavily commercial street leading north from Great Barrington to Stockbridge, it occupies a building with an enclosed porch, an open terrace, and three dining rooms. The menu is laid out in the traditional manner, with sections for *mezedes* (appetizers), *salates,* and *thalasina* (seafood), along with pastas, poultry, and lamb. Execution is what counts here, elevating such standards as *moussaka* (potatoes, eggplant, and ground beef with béchamel) and lamb *plaki* (with mushrooms, Vidalia onions, and feta baked in a clay pot). Especially appealing are the fish and shellfish, 16 of them, utterly fresh and simply prepared. Thursday is "lobster night." *Opa!*

327 Stockbridge Rd. ✆ **413/528-4001.** Reservations advised on weekends. Main courses $14–$26. AE, MC, V. Daily 11am–10pm.

Castle Street Cafe ★★ NEW AMERICAN This storefront bistro has ruled the Great Barrington roost for some time now, and has expanded into the next building, installing what it calls a "Celestial Bar," with live jazz piano 6 nights a week in summer and on weekends the rest of the year. While a Francophilic inclination is apparent in the main room (hello, steak *au poivre*), it isn't overpowering—rack of lamb and the grilled vegetable entree are other possibilities. Have a drink at the bar in the while you're checking out the night's menu, or stay there for such casual eats as burgers, pizzas, and cheese plates. An award-winning wine list is another reason to stop in.

10 Castle St. (near the Town Hall). ✆ **413/528-5244.** Reservations advised on weekends. Main courses $20–$28. AE, DISC, MC, V. Sun–Thurs 5–9pm; Fri–Sat 5–10pm (until 10:30pm in the Celestial Bar).

Helsinki Café ECLECTIC It looks like an eastern European tearoom run by an eccentric fortuneteller, with mismatched tables and even overstuffed living room armchairs amid the assorted oddments. (In winter, try for a table near the fireplace in the back room.) There are Scandinavian items on the card to justify the name, including Finnish meatballs, "Red Square" smelts, latkes and dilled cucumber, borscht, and blini with gravlax. Refusing the straitjacket, though, the kitchen also puts together a quesadilla du jour, teriyaki ribs, and a blackened catfish po' boy with jalapeño aioli. At least they did, on last sight—expect surprises. There's full bar service.

284 Main St. (in back, down the passageway). ✆ **413/528-3394.** Reservations suggested on weekends. Main courses $15–$22. DISC, MC, V. Daily 10am–10pm.

Pearl's ★ CONTEMPORARY BISTRO A share of the credit for Great Barrington's growing rep as a gastronomic destination has to go to this self-assured enterprise. Traditionalists grumble that this follow-up to the owners' stylish Bistro Zinc in Lenox (see later in this chapter) is more Manhattan than Berkshires, and it clearly isn't country cookin'. The presence of a floor-to-ceiling painting of a bull of regal bearing and a large print of a resplendent wild turkey rightly imply that beef and game are the way to go. The New York strip, filet mignon, and 24-ounce porterhouse come with tasty sides and straightforward preparations that are hard to beat for flavor. Blackened catfish with black bean and corn salsa and tomato marmalade and triple-cut lamb chops with mint butter and white bean purée are just as satisfying. Don't resist the caramel banana strudel as a finisher. Since most of the menu items can be cooked quickly, expect to be in and out within an hour unless you purposely slow down delivery.

47 Railroad St. ✆ **413/528-7767.** Reservations suggested. Main courses $18–$27. AE, MC, V. Mon–Sat 5–10pm (until 11pm Fri–Sat); Sun 11am–3pm and 5:30–10pm.

Verdura/Dué CONTEMPORARY ITALIAN It doesn't put on airs, not with wood-only floors, tables, chairs, and ceiling beams, but this is a welcome antidote to the red-sauce-and-pizza joints that usually pass for Italian in the Berkshires. A basket of thick, chewy bread sets the tone, with a fruity olive oil for dipping, following icy, filled-to-the-brim martinis. An excellent starter is the antipasto sampler, with asparagus, marinated mushrooms, pickled beets, roasted sweet peppers with balsamic vinegar, honeyed cippolini onions, and prosciutto with fig jam. After that, a simple dish of pasta is likely to be more than enough dinner. Short, plump bucatelli tumbled with a rich veal ragout does nicely. Heartier appetites might prefer the braised lamb shank with rosemary polenta or the wood-grilled quail with sweet-potato gratin.

The dinner crowd is more often greyheaded than pierced and inked, but that ratio reverses in **Dué,** the wine bar adjoining the restaurant. The *enoteca* is for conversation with glasses of pinot grigio and tapas, pastas, or panini. Prices are gentler than next door.

44–47 Railroad St. ✆ **413/528-8969.** Reservations advised for Verdura on weekends. Main courses, Verdura $23–$42, Dué $6–$12. AE, MC, V. Verdura Thurs–Tues 5–10pm; Dué Tues–Sun 11:30am–close (summer), 5pm–close (winter).

GREAT BARRINGTON AFTER DARK

A grand old downtown cinema, the **Mahaiwe Performing Arts Center,** 14 Castle St. (✆ **413/644-9040;** www.mahaiwe.org), has been restored to some of its century-old glory, and stages a surprising variety of music, dance, and drama. The **Aston Magna Festival** features classical music performed on period instruments. Concerts are held on five Sundays in July and August at St. James Church, Main Street and Taconic Avenue (✆ **800/875-7156** or 413/528-3595; www.astonmagna.org).

Live jazz is often presented at the Castle Street Cafe, and the Union Bar & Grill brings in DJs weekends (see "Where to Dine," above). **Club Helsinki,** 284 Main St. (✆ **413/528-3394;** www.clubhelsinkiweb.com) is a more regular music venue, with as many as 6 nights a week of rock, pop, bluegrass, reggae, and other forms throughout the year. The **Triplex Cinema,** 70 Railroad St. (✆ **413/528-8886**), shows a mixed bag of independent and foreign flicks as well as major studio releases.

STOCKBRIDGE ★★

Stockbridge's ready accessibility to Boston and New York (about 2½ hr. from each and reachable by rail since the mid–19th century) transformed the original frontier settlement into a Gilded Age summer retreat for the rich. The town has long been popular with artists and writers as well. Illustrator Norman Rockwell, who lived here for 25 years, rendered the Main Street of his adopted town in a famous painting. Along and near Main Street are a number of historic homes and other attractions, enough to fill up a long weekend, even without the Tanglewood concert season in nearby Lenox. One of the Berkshires' hottest destinations, Stockbridge is inevitably jammed on warm weekends and during foliage season. A prominent event is the Christmas celebration on the first Sunday in December, when over 50 antique cars are parked along Main Street to help re-create the scene painted by Norman Rockwell decades ago.

Stockbridge lies 7 miles north of Great Barrington and 6 miles south of Lenox. The **Stockbridge Chamber of Commerce** (✆ **413/298-5200;** www.stockbridgechamber.org) maintains an information booth opposite the row of stores depicted by Rockwell. It's open May through October.

WHAT TO SEE & DO

Berkshire Botanical Garden These 15 acres of flower beds, ponds, and vegetable and herb gardens are an inviting destination for strollers and picnickers. The first weekend in October features a harvest festival.

Routes 102 and 183. ✆ **413/298-3926.** www.berkshirebotanical.org. Admission $7 adults, $5 seniors, $3 students, free for children under 12. May–Oct daily 10am–5pm. Tours offered Sat–Sun June–Aug. Drive west from downtown Stockbridge on Main St., picking up Church St. (Rte. 102) northwest for about 2 miles.

The Berkshire Theatre Festival ★★ From June to August, and occasionally at other times during the year, The Berkshire Theatre Festival holds its season of classic and new plays, often with marquee names starring or directing. Kevin Kline and Al Pacino are among the many film and theater names who have been participants. Its venue is a "casino" built in 1887 to plans by architect Stanford White. A second venue, the Unicorn Theatre, opened in 1996.

P.O. Box 797, Main St. ✆ **413/298-5576.** www.berkshiretheatre.org. Tickets: Main Stage $35–$50, Unicorn Theatre $25–$35.

Chesterwood ★ Sculptor Daniel Chester French, best known for the Lincoln Memorial in Washington, DC, used this estate as his summer home for more than 30 years. His Minute Man statue at the Old North Bridge in Concord, completed in 1875 at the age of 25, launched his highly successful career. The 122-acre grounds are used for an annual show of contemporary sculpture. Entrance to the residence and studio are by guided tour only.

4 Williamsville Rd. ✆ **413/298-3579.** www.chesterwood.org. Admission $10 adults, $9 seniors and college students, $5 children 6–18. May–Oct daily 10am–5pm. Drive west on Main St., south on Rte. 183 about 1 mile to the Chesterwood sign.

Mission House The Rev. John Sergeant had the most benevolent, if paternalistic, of intentions: He sought to build a house among the members of the Housatonic tribe, hoping to convert them to "civilized" (that is, English) ways through proximity to his godly self and his small band of settlers. The weathered Mission House, built in 1739, was the site of this Christianizing process. History buffs in particular will enjoy a visit here.

Main and Sergeant sts. (Rte. 102). ✆ **413/298-3239.** www.thetrustees.org. Admission $5 adults, $3 children 6–12. Memorial Day to Columbus Day daily 10am–5pm. Visits are by guided tour only.

Naumkeag ★ In 1886, Stanford White designed this 26-room summer house for Joseph Hodge Choate, who served as U.S. ambassador to the Court of St. James. The client dubbed it "Naumkeag," a Native American name for Salem, MA, his childhood home. His house of many gables and chimneys is largely of the New England shingle style, surrounded by impressive gardens with fabulous views to the west. Admission is by guided tour only, worth it for the glimpses of the rich interior, which features extensive use of mahogany and California redwood. One oddity is the chandelier of Murano glass in the shape of a badminton cock. Tucked away in a dark corner upstairs are several original Goya etchings.

Prospect Hill. ✆ **413/298-3239.** www.thetrustees.org. Admission $10 adults, $3 ages 6–12. Memorial Day to Columbus Day daily 10am–5pm. From the Cat & Dog Fountain in the intersection next to The Red Lion Inn, drive north on Pine St. to Prospect Hill Rd. about ½ mile.

Norman Rockwell Museum ★★ This striking building opened in 1993, at a cost of $4.4 million, to house the works of Stockbridge's favorite son. The illustrator used both his neighbors and the town where he lived to tell stories about an America now rapidly fading from memory. Most of Rockwell's paintings adorned covers of the *Saturday Evening Post:* warm and often humorous depictions of homecomings, first proms, and visits to the doctor. He addressed serious concerns, too, notably with his poignant portrait of a little African-American girl being escorted by U.S. marshals into a previously segregated school. Critics long derided his paintings as saccharine and sentimental, but today a revision of sorts has led to widespread appreciation for his deft brushwork. The lovely 36-acre grounds also contain Rockwell's last studio (closed Nov–Apr). The museum and grounds remain open year-round.

Rte. 183. ✆ **413/298-4100.** www.nrm.org. Admission $13 adults, $7 students, free for children 18 and under. May–Oct daily 10am–5pm; Nov–Apr Mon–Fri 10am–4pm, Sat–Sun 10am–5pm. Take Main St. (Rte. 102) west to the junction with Rte. 183, then turn left (south) at the traffic signal. In about ½ mile, you'll see the entrance to the museum on the left.

WHERE TO STAY & DINE

Inn at Stockbridge ★ A little over a mile north of Stockbridge center, this 1906 building with a grandly columned porch is set well back from the road on 12 acres. The innkeepers are eager to please, serving full breakfasts by candlelight and afternoon spreads of wine and cheese. Several bedrooms have fireplaces and whirlpools, and there are four suites in the newly remodeled barn. High-speed Internet access is provided.

30 East St. (Rte. 7), Stockbridge, MA 01262. ✆ **888/466-7865** or 413/298-3337. Fax 413/298-3406. www.stockbridgeinn.com. 16 units. June–Oct $180–$345 double; Nov–May $140–$260 double. Rates include full breakfast and afternoon refreshments. AE, DISC, MC, V. No children under 12. **Amenities:** Heated outdoor pool. *In room:* A/C, TV/VCR, dataport, hair dryer, iron.

The Red Lion Inn ★★ So well known that it serves as a symbol of the Berkshires, this busy inn had its origins as a stagecoach tavern in 1773. The rocking chairs on the porch are the place to while away an hour reading or people-watching. An ancient birdcage elevator carries guests up to halls and rooms filled with antiques ranging in styles of over 2 centuries. Floors creak and tilt, as might be expected, but modern comforts are provided. Six satellite buildings have gradually been added, all within 3 miles of the inn. Dining choices include the pricey traditional dining room, the casual and marvelously atmospheric **Widow Bingham Tavern,** the **Lion's Den** pub, and, in good weather, the courtyard out back. The basement Lion's Den also has nightly live entertainment, usually of the folk-rock variety. Book your room far in advance; for a quieter night, ask for an inside room.

Main St., Stockbridge, MA 01262. ✆ **413/298-5545.** Fax 413/298-5130. www.redlioninn.com. 108 units, 14 with shared bathrooms. Jan to late May $110–$205 double, $175–$395 suite; late May to late Oct $135–$220 double, $205–$430 suite; late Oct to mid-Apr $110–$195 double, $185–$395 suite. Packages available. AE, DC, DISC, MC, V. **Amenities:** 3 restaurants (eclectic/American); 2 bars; outdoor pool; golf and tennis privileges nearby; recently upgraded fitness room; limited room service; massage; babysitting; laundry; dry cleaning. *In room:* A/C, TV/VCR, dataport, unstocked fridges in suites, hair dryer.

Taggart House ★★ Ordinarily, an inn with only four guest rooms wouldn't merit space here. But what rooms! The decor of this outwardly sedate 1850 Victorian/Colonial mansion provides guests with a breathtaking immersion in the Gilded Age. Start with the theatrical main floor—the inlaid mahogany dining table was once a centerpiece in an Argentine palace. There's a paneled library, a ballroom, a harpsichord, and nine beguiling fireplaces. And upstairs, beds are decorated with fur throws, East Indian silk coverlets, and velvet canopies.

Main St. (1 block west of the Red Lion), Stockbridge, MA 01262. ✆/fax **413/298-4303.** www.taggarthouse.com. 4 units. May–Oct $250–$350 double; Nov–Apr $175–$250 double. Rates include breakfast. Packages available. 2-night minimum stay on weekends. MC, V. Young children not accepted. *In room:* A/C, dataport.

LEE

While Stockbridge and Lenox were developing into luxurious recreational centers for the upper crust of Boston and New York, Lee was a thriving paper-mill town. That meant that it was shunned by the wealthy summer people and thus remained essentially a town of workers and merchants. It has a somewhat raffish though not unappealing aspect, its center bunched with shops and offices and few of the stately homes that characterize neighboring communities.

The town's contribution to the Berkshire cultural calendar is The Jacob's Pillow Dance Festival, which first thrived as "Denishawn," a fabled alliance between founders Ruth St. Denis and Ted Shawn.

Lee is 5 miles southeast of Lenox. In summer and early fall, the **Lee Chamber of Commerce** (✆ **413/243-0852;** www.leechamber.org) operates an **information center** on the town common, Route 20 (✆ **413/243-4929**). It can help you find lodging, often in guesthouses and B&Bs—rarely as grand as those in neighboring Lenox, but nearly always cheaper. That's something to remember when every other place near Tanglewood is either booked or quoting prices of $300 a night.

WHAT TO SEE & DO

The Jacob's Pillow Dance Festival ★★★ In 1933, Ted Shawn decided to put on a show in the barn, and so was Jacob's Pillow born. After decades of advance and retreat and evolution, Jacob's Pillow is now to dance what Tanglewood is to classical music. Once a regular summer venue for Shawn and famed dancer and choreographer Martha Graham, one of his early disciples, the theater has long welcomed troupes of international reputation, including the Mark Morris Dance Group, Les Grands Ballets Canadiens, Twyla Tharp, and the Paul Taylor Dance Company. The season runs from late June to late August, and tickets go on sale April 1.

The more prominent companies are seen in the main Ted Shawn Theatre, while other troupes are assigned to the Doris Duke Studio Theatre. Admission is free to the Inside/Out, an outdoor stage. The growing campus includes a store, pub, dining room, tent restaurant, and exhibition space. Picnic lunches can be pre-ordered 24 hours in advance.

P.O. Box 287, George Carter Rd., Becket. ✆ **413/243-0745.** www.jacobspillow.org. Tickets $10–$55. From Lee, take Rte. 20 east about 9 miles, then turn north on Rte. 8 toward Becket.

Santarella ★ With no obligatory historic homes or museums to see in Lee, visitors often make the short excursion to a fairy-tale structure called Santarella, but known by most as the "Gingerbread House." Conical turrets top towers, while the shingled roof rolls like waves on the ocean. It served as a studio for sculptor Henry Hudson Kitson from 1930 to 1947, and now is used only for weddings and other special events. The garden is open to visitors.

Tyringham Rd. ✆ **413/243-3260.** Take Rte. 20 south from Lee to Rte. 102, near the no. 2 interchange of the Mass. Pike Following the signs through the complicated intersection, pick up Tyringham Rd. on the other side and drive south about 4 miles.

GETTING OUTSIDE

October Mountain State Forest (✆ **413/243-1778**) offers 50 campsites (with showers) and more than 16,000 acres for hiking, canoeing, cross-country skiing, and snowmobiling. To get here, drive northwest on Route 20 into town, turn right on Center Street, and follow the signs.

WHERE TO STAY

On the road to Lenox, the lakeside **Best Western Black Swan,** 435 Laurel St./Rte. 20 (© **800/876-7926** or 413/243-2700; www.travelweb.com), has a pool and restaurant; some of the 52 rooms have fireplaces.

Applegate ★ This B&B utilizes a gracious 1920s Georgian Colonial manse to full advantage. The nicest unit has a canopy bed, Queen Anne reproductions, sunlight filtering through gauzy curtains, a steam shower, and a fireplace (with real wood). Most rooms have phones with dataports, some have TVs, Jacuzzis, and/or gas fireplaces. Chocolates and brandy await guests at bedside. Breakfast is by candlelight, and the innkeepers set out wine and cheese in the afternoon. They are "flexible" on children.

279 W. Park St., Lee, MA 01238. © **800/691-9012** or 413/243-4451. www.applegateinn.com. 10 units plus a 2-bedroom cottage. June–Oct $150–$350 double; Nov–May $120–$260 double; carriage house rates on application. MC, V. From Stockbridge, drive north on Rte. 7 about ½ mile; take a right on Lee Rd. The inn is 2¼ miles ahead. No children under 12. **Amenities:** Heated outdoor pool; 9-hole golf course across the street; tennis court; access to nearby health club; bikes. *In room:* A/C.

Chambéry Inn ★ This was the Berkshires' first parochial school (1885), named for the French hometown of the nuns who ran it. That accounts for the extra-large bedrooms, about 500 square feet each, which were formerly classrooms. Six of them, with 13-foot ceilings and the original woodwork and blackboards, are equipped with whirlpool tubs and gas fireplaces. Some rooms have TV/VCRs, CD players, and fridges. A breakfast basket is delivered to your door each morning. No smoking.

199 Main St., Lee, MA 01238. © **413/243-2221.** Fax 413/243-0039. www.berkshireinns.com. 9 units. July–Aug and Oct $75–$119 double; $99–$239 suite. Rates include breakfast. AE, DISC, MC, V. No children under 16. **Amenities:** Limited room service from neighboring restaurant. *In room:* A/C, TV, coffeemaker, hair dryer, iron.

Devonfield From the road, there's no way to tell what this place is. The sign out front reads only "Devonfield," and the large house standing on a rise amid tall hemlocks and 29 acres could as easily be a yoga retreat or a conference center. But an inn it is, of the comfy-casual, rather than elegant, variety. When JFK and Queen Wilhemina stayed here decades ago, they were probably given the house on the other side of the pool, with its large sitting room with fireplace, kitchen, Jacuzzi, and king bedroom. Three rooms in the main house have fireplaces, too. Several common rooms invite guests inclined to cocooning. New owners have plans for upgrading the property.

85 Stockbridge Rd., Lee, MA 01238. © **800/664-0880** or 413/243-3298. Fax 413/243-1360. www.devonfield.com. 10 units. June–Oct $140–$325 double; Nov–May $95–$245 double. Rates include full breakfast. MC, V. No children under 12. **Amenities:** Heated outdoor pool. *In room:* A/C, TV, hair dryer.

LENOX ★★ & TANGLEWOOD

Stately homes and fabulous mansions mushroomed in this former agricultural settlement from the 1890s until 1913, when the 16th Amendment, authorizing income taxes, put a severe crimp in that impulse. But Lenox remains a repository of extravagant domestic architecture surpassed only in such fabled resorts of the wealthy as Newport and Palm Beach. And because many of the cottages have been converted into inns and hotels, it is possible to get inside some of these beautiful buildings, if only for a cocktail or a meal.

The reason for so many lodgings in a town with a population of barely 5,000 is Tanglewood, a nearby estate where a series of concerts by the Boston Symphony Orchestra is held every summer.

Lenox lies 7 miles south of Pittsfield. The **Lenox Chamber of Commerce** (✆ **413/637-3646;** www.lenox.org) provides visitor information and lodging referrals.

WHAT TO SEE & DO

Frelinghuysen Morris House & Studio ★ Built on 46 acres next to the Tanglewood property in the early 1940s, this Bauhaus-influenced house was the home of abstract artists Suzy Frelinghuysen and George L. K. Morris. Their chosen style was Cubism, which they pursued long after it had been abandoned by better-known practitioners. Works by some of those artists—Braque, Léger, Gris, and Picasso—can be viewed alongside the canvases of the owners. Visits are by tour only.

92 Hawthorne St. ✆ **413/637-0166.** www.frelinghuysen.org. Admission $9 adults, $3 children 5–16. June 4th to Labor Day Thurs–Sun 10am–3pm; Sept to Columbus Day Thurs–Sat call for hours. Drive south from Tanglewood on Rte. 183, turn left on Hawthorne Rd., then left again on Hawthorne St. (note 2 different streets).

The Mount, Edith Wharton Restoration ★ Wharton, who won a Pulitzer for her novel *The Age of Innocence,* was singularly equipped to write that deftly detailed examination of the upper classes of the Gilded Age and the first decades of the 20th century. She was born into that stratum of society in 1862 and traveled in the circles that made the Berkshires a regular stop on their restless movements between New York, Florida, Newport, and the Continent. Wharton had her villa built on this 130-acre lakeside property in 1902 and lived here 10 years before leaving for France, never to return. She took an active hand in the creation of The Mount, which makes the mansion a notable rarity—it's one of the few designated National Historic Landmarks designed by a woman. Wharton was, after all, the author of an upscale 1897 how-to guide called *The Decoration of Houses.* A $25-million restoration campaign continues, with work so far completed on the terrace and greenhouse and continuing on the interior and gardens.

Note: Understanding that the high admission fee helps support the ongoing restoration, it is up to the visitor to decide whether the cost is justified by what is essentially a walk through a work in progress.

2 Plunkett St. (at the intersection of Routes 7 and 7A). ✆ **413/637-1899.** www.edithwharton.org. Admission $18 adults, $9 students, free for children under 12. Late Apr to Oct 9am–5pm; guided tours given June–Oct daily 9am–5pm.

Shakespeare & Company ★★ The repertory company had long used buildings and amphitheaters on the grounds of The Mount (see above) to stage its May-to-December season of plays by the Bard, works by Chekhov and George Bernard Shaw, and efforts by new American and English playwrights. After increasingly bitter conflict with the custodians of the Wharton property, officials of the company purchased a 63-acre property on Kemble Street, closer to downtown Lenox. With construction of a new Founder's Theatre, the Spring Lawn Theatre, the tented Rose Footprint Theatre, an administration building, and planned rehabilitation of other existing buildings, the Company now enjoys its very own campus devoted to the dramatic arts. Walking trails have been developed at the north end of the grounds and a cafe in the theater lobby serves drinks and light fare. Picnickers are welcome. Free outdoor performances are staged before evening curtain times.

70 Kemble St. ✆ **413/637-3353.** www.shakespeare.org. Tickets $23–$51.

Tanglewood Music Festival ★★★ Lenox is filled with music every summer, and the undisputed headliner is the Boston Symphony Orchestra (BSO), conducted by

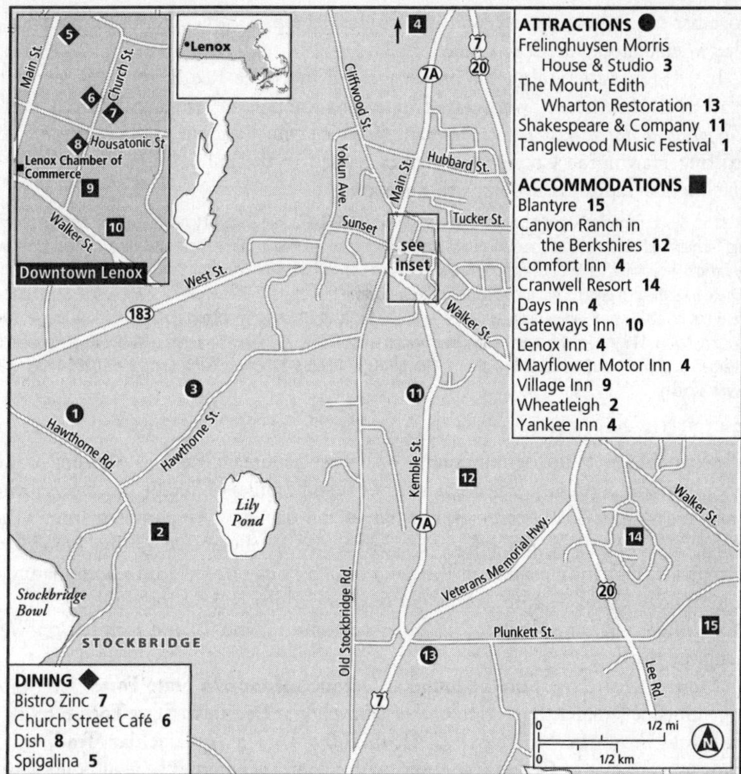

James Levine since Seiji Ozawa stepped down in 2002. Concerts are given at the famous Tanglewood estate, usually beginning in July and ending the weekend before Labor Day. The estate is on West Street (actually in Stockbridge township, although it's always associated with Lenox). From Lenox, take Route 183 1½ miles southwest of town.

While the BSO is Tanglewood's 800-pound cultural gorilla, the program features a menagerie of other performers and musical idioms. These run the gamut from popular artists (like James Taylor and Bonnie Raitt) and jazz musicians (including Dave Brubeck and Wynton Marsalis) to such guest soloists as Itzhak Perlman and Yo-Yo Ma.

The Koussevitzky Music Shed is an open auditorium that seats 5,000, surrounded by a lawn where an outdoor audience lounges on folding chairs and blankets. Chamber groups and soloists appear in the smaller Ozawa Hall. Major performances are on Friday and Saturday nights and Sunday afternoon.

Tentative programs are available after January 1; the schedule is usually locked in by March. Tickets can sell out quickly, so get yours as far in advance as possible. If you decide to go at the last minute, take a blanket or lawn chair and get tickets for lawn seating, which is almost always available. You can also attend open rehearsals during the week, as well as the rehearsal for the Sunday concert on Saturday morning.

The estate itself (✆ **413/637-5165** June–Aug), with more than 500 acres of lawns and gardens, much of it overlooking the lake called Stockbridge Bowl, was put together starting in 1849 by William Aspinwall Tappan. Admission to the grounds is free when concerts aren't scheduled.

In 1851, a structure on the property called the Little Red Shanty was rented to Nathaniel Hawthorne, who stayed here long enough to write a children's book, *Tanglewood Tales,* and meet Herman Melville, who lived in nearby Dalton. The existing Hawthorne Cottage is a replica (closed to the public). On the grounds is the original Tappan mansion, with fine views.

West St., Stockbridge. For recorded information, call ✆ **617/266-1492** Sept–June 10 (note that information on upcoming Tanglewood concerts is not available until the program is announced in Mar or Apr). www.bso.org (tentative program info available after Jan 1). Tickets $28–$96 Shed and Ozawa Hall, $16–$20 lawn. Lawn tickets for children under 12 are free; children under 5 not allowed in the Shed or Ozawa Hall. Higher prices apply for some special appearances. To order tickets by mail before June, write the Tanglewood Ticket Office at Symphony Hall, 301 Massachusetts Ave., Boston, MA 02115. After June 1, write the Tanglewood Ticket Office, 297 West St., Lenox, MA 01240. Tickets can be charged to a credit card through **Symphony Charge** (✆ **888/266-1200** outside Boston, or 617/266-1200) or at www.bso.org.

GETTING OUTSIDE

Pleasant Valley Wildlife Sanctuary, 472 West Mountain Rd. (✆ **413/637-0320;** www.massaudubon.org), has a small museum and 7 miles of hiking and snowshoeing trails crossing its 1,300 acres. Beaver lodges and dams can be glimpsed from a distance, and waterfowl and other birds are found in abundance—bring binoculars. Hours for the nature center are Tuesday through Friday from 9am to 5pm, Saturday and Sunday 10am to 4pm; admission is $3 for adults and $2 for children 3 to 15. To get here, drive north about 6½ miles on Routes 7 and 20 and turn left on West Dugway Road.

More extensive trails can be found at **October Mountain State Forest** (see "Getting Outside," under the section on Lee, above) or at **Beartown State Forest,** 69 Blue Hill Rd., in nearby Monterey (✆ **413/528-0904**). The **Appalachian Trail,** which runs from Maine to Georgia, connects with a loop trail around a small pond with a nice swimming area. To get here, take Route 7 south for 3½ miles, then turn left onto West Road. After 2½ miles, turn left at the T intersection onto Route 102 east. Turn right over the bridge onto Meadow Street, then turn right onto Pine Street and follow the signs.

SHOPPING

The Bookstore, 11 Housatonic St. (✆ **413/637-3390**), with author signings and poetry readings, helps fill a yawning gap in the Berkshires, which are curiously short on comprehensive bookstores. Those in pursuit of art and antiques, on the other hand, cannot easily exhaust the possibilities. For fashion-forward clothing for men and women, much of it Italian-made, check in at **Casablanca,** 21 Housatonic St. (✆ **413/637-2680**). L.L.Bean, it isn't. Out on Route 7, heading toward Pittsfield, serious cooks should watch for **Different Drummer's Kitchen,** 374 Pittsfield Rd. (✆ **413/637-0606**).

WHERE TO STAY

The list of lodgings below is only partial, and most can accommodate only small numbers of guests. The Tanglewood concert season is a powerful draw, so prices are highest in summer as well as during the brief foliage season in mid-October. Rates are of Byzantine complexity, set according to wildly varying combinations of seasons and days of the week as well as facilities offered. Minimum 2- or 3-night stays are usually required during the Tanglewood weeks, foliage, weekends, and holidays. ***Note:*** For visits during the Tanglewood season, reserve far in advance—February isn't too soon.

Given the substantial number of lodgings and limited space to describe them, admittedly arbitrary judgments have been made to winnow the list. Some inns, for example, are so rule-ridden and facility-free that they come off as crabby—no kids, no pets, no phones, no credit cards, no breakfast before 9am, shared bathrooms—and they cost twice as much as nearby motels that have all those conveniences. Let them seek clients elsewhere.

If all the area's inns are booked or if you want to be assured the full quota of 21st-century conveniences, Routes 7 and 20 north and south of town harbor a number of motels, including the **Mayflower Motor Inn** (✆ **413/443-4468**), the **Days Inn** (✆ **413/637-3560**), the **Lenox Motel** (✆ **413/499-0324**), and the **Comfort Inn** (✆ **413/443-4714**).

Very Expensive

Blantyre ★★★ Until recently, this sumptuous 1902 Tudor-Norman mansion was open only during the warmer months. Now it cossets its guests year-round in its undeniably luxurious public rooms, dining areas, and bedchambers. A long drive curls up through 100 acres to the main manor, where guests enter a baronial lobby packed with the sorts of imposing antique furniture, a massive fireplace, stuffed animal heads, and a carved and beamed ceiling suitable for the country home of a 19th-century blue blood. Elsewhere, decor is beholden to no uniform decorative style, the rooms by turn heavily masculine and airily feminine, but with fireplaces and chandeliers as common features. In addition to the four cottages, the main house holds eight units and the nearby carriage house 12. Dining—in several interior spaces as well as in the garden and the glassed-in wing that overlooks it—is of the highest order, as dictated by the Relais & Châteaux hotel association, of which the inn is an honored member. Coat and tie are required at dinner. If any place is worth these breathtaking tariffs, it's this one.

P.O. Box 995, Rte. 20, Lenox, MA 01240. ✆ **413/637-3556.** Fax 413/637-4282. www.blantyre.com. 25 units. $450–$550 double; $750–$1,050 suite. AE, DC, MC, V. From Exit 2 on I-90 (Mass. Pike), drive 3 miles on Rte. 20 West. **Amenities:** Restaurant (eclectic); heated outdoor pool; 4 tennis courts; golf nearby; fitness room w/sauna; spa treatments and massage available; 24-hr. room service; same-day dry cleaning. *In room:* Fireplace (some), fridge (some), balcony (some), patio or deck (some).

Canyon Ranch in the Berkshires ★★★ Resorts successfully melding turn-of-the-last-century opulence and contemporary impulses for fitness and healthy living are rare, so for those with the discretionary income or others who'd like to splurge just once, this is the place. A guard turns away the unconfirmed at the gate, so there's no popping in for a look around. The core facility is an 1897 mansion modeled after Le Petit Trianon at Versailles. A fire in 1949 left only the magnificent library untouched, but that loss has been offset by major renovations. Sweat away the pounds in the huge spa complex, with more than 50 fitness classes and related activities a day, weights, an indoor track, racquetball, squash, and all the equipment you might want. Skiing, snowshoeing, kayaking, canoeing and hiking are added possibilities. The staff includes physicians, nurses, and psychologists, as well as sports and cooking instructors and massage therapists. Guest rooms are in contemporary New England style, with every hotel convenience except tempting minibars. After you've been steamed, exhausted, pummeled, and cleansed, the next big event is mealtime: "nutritionally balanced gourmet," naturally.

P.O. Box 2170, 165 Kemble St., Lenox, MA 01240. ✆ **800/742-9000** or 413/637-4100. Fax 413/637-0057. www.canyonranch.com. 126 units. All-inclusive 3- to 7-night packages from $1,580–$5,290 double. Rates include meals and allowances for health, beauty, and fitness services. Taxes and 18% service charge extra. AE, DC, DISC, MC, V. **Amenities:** Restaurant (spa cuisine); heated indoor and outdoor pools; outdoor and indoor tennis courts; extensive health club and spa; bikes; business center; salon, limited room service; in-room massage; same-day dry cleaning/self-service laundry. *In room:* A/C, TV/VCR/DVD, dataport, hair dryer, iron, safe.

Cranwell Resort ★★★ The main building of this all-season resort looks like a castle in the Scottish Highlands, but no 17th-century laird lived this well. It stands at the center of a 380-acre property, ringed by views of the surrounding hills. That's where the most expensive rooms are; the rest are in four smaller outlying buildings. Accommodations are outfitted with less concern for adherence to a particular style than for surrounding guests in immediate comfort. In addition to the lovely grounds (which serve as cross-country ski trails in winter), there is a 60-acre golf school. Three dining rooms range from formal to pubby, and live jazz is featured Friday and Saturday nights. An enormous 35,000-square-foot spa was opened in 2002, with pool, lounges with fireplaces, and 17 spa treatment rooms. Services include facial treatments, various massage therapies, exfoliations, and healing wraps. In summer and fall, a satirical cabaret revue is added to the diversions.

55 Lee Rd. (Rte. 20), Lenox, MA 01240. ✆ **800/272-6935** or 413/637-1364. Fax 413/637-4364. www.cranwell.com. 107 units. Late May to Oct $275–$375 double, from $375 suite; Nov to mid-May $175–$275 double, from $275 suite. Golf, spa, and ski packages available. AE, DC, DISC, MC, V. From Lenox Center, go north to Rte. 20 E. The resort is on the left. **Amenities:** 4 restaurants (eclectic/grill/spa); bar; heated outdoor and indoor pools; 18-hole par-70 golf course; 4 tennis courts; extensive new health club; bike rental; salon; limited room service; in-room massage; babysitting; same-day dry cleaning. *In room:* A/C, TV/VCR, fax, dataport, fridge, coffeemaker, hair dryer, iron, safe.

Wheatleigh ★★ A fountain out front and a lobby fireplace with deeply carved garlands and cherubim set the tone. Beyond, glamorous urbanites often drape themselves in Gatsbyesque poses around the lavishly appointed great hall. Much of the time, they look elaborately bored, no easy feat in this persuasive 1893 replica of a 16th-century Tuscan palazzo, which aspires to the highest standards of the moneyed Berkshires. Happily, the interior decor is muted, not florid, utilizing neutral colors and restrained shapes. Wheatleigh has always been very expensive, even though the cheapest rooms average only 11×13 feet. But other places are catching up, and the manager is striving to give requisite value. The dining room rounds out the experience, with painstakingly conceived food presented superbly.

Hawthorne Rd., Lenox, MA 01240. ✆ **413/637-0610.** Fax 413/637-4507. www.wheatleigh.com. 19 units. $585–$1,185 double; from $1,250 suite. AE, DC, MC, V. **Amenities:** 2 restaurants (eclectic); lounge; heated outdoor pool; tennis court; exercise room; bike rental; concierge; in-room massage; babysitting; laundry service; dry cleaning. *In room:* A/C, TV/VCR, fax, hair dryer.

Moderate-Expensive

Gateways Inn ★★ Harley Procter, who hitched up with a man called Gamble and made a bundle, had this house built in 1912. Its most impressive feature is the staircase that winds down into the lobby. Designed by McKim, Mead & White, it's a stunner, just the thing for a grand entrance. Equally impressive is the suite named for conductor Arthur Fiedler, with not one but two fireplaces, a big four-poster on the sun porch, and a Jacuzzi. Eight rooms have working fireplaces. Dining here is one of Lenox's greater pleasures. The bar features 55 grappas and 130 single-malt scotches. Also, a terrace has been added for after-concert light meals and desserts. Lunch is offered on summer weekends, with light fare after dinner to midnight. This is a totally nonsmoking property.

51 Walker St., Lenox, MA 01240. ✆ **888/492-9466** or 413/637-2532. Fax 413/637-1432. www.gatewaysinn.com. 12 units. June–Oct $150–$295 double, $350–$450 suite; Nov–May $100–$190 double, $230–$350 suite. Rates include breakfast. AE, DC, DISC, MC, V. No children under 12. **Amenities:** Restaurant (eclectic); bar. *In room:* A/C, TV, dataport.

Moderate

Village Inn An inn off and on since 1775, this place hasn't a whiff of pretense. Its rooms come in considerable variety and are categorized as Deluxe, Superior, Standard, or Economy. That means four-posters in the high-end rooms, some of which have fireplaces and/or Jacuzzis, and constricted quarters with double beds at the lower prices. Claw-foot tubs are common. Ask about rooms on the renovated third floor. Afternoon tea and dinner are served in the restaurant, where prices are lower than the town average; light meals are available in the tavern. All rooms have VCRs, and there's a free video library. No smoking.

16 Church St., Lenox, MA 01240. ✆ **800/253-0917** or 413/637-0020. Fax 413/637-9756. www.villageinn-lenox.com. 32 units. Summer–fall $149–$269 double; winter–spring $109–$179 double. Discount of 30% during midweek in winter/spring. Rates include breakfast. AE, DC, DISC, MC, V. No children under 6. **Amenities:** Restaurant (American); bar. *In room:* A/C, TV/VCR.

Yankee Inn *Kids* Of the several motels strung along Route 20 east of Lenox center, this is arguably the most desirable, and a place to remember when the area's inns are filled. It is also more congenial for families; children are welcome, as they are not in most B&Bs. Housekeeping is of reasonably high standard, and furnishings, while routine in design, are as fresh-looking as might be expected in a city hotel. Some rooms have gas fireplaces and unstocked fridges. Long, empty corridors don't enhance the experience, but the indoor pool, convenient location, and moderate prices (for the Berkshires) compensate.

461 Pittsfield Rd. (Rte. 20), Lenox, MA 01240. ✆ **800/835-2364** or 413/499-3700. Fax 413/499-3634. www.berkshireinns.com. 96 units. $99–$129 double. AE, DC, DISC, MC, V. **Amenities:** Lounge; heated indoor pool w/whirlpool; modest exercise room. *In room:* A/C, TV, dataport, hair dryer, iron.

WHERE TO DINE

See also "Where to Stay," above, as many inns have dining rooms. In particular, **Blantyre** (✆ **413/637-3556**) is worth a splurge. In high season, **Spigalina,** 80 Main St. (✆ **413/637-4455**), serves imaginative Mediterranean food. Note that the restaurants recommended below serve lunch, in a region where most of the better restaurants don't open until evening.

Bistro Zinc ★★ CONTEMPORARY BISTRO Zinc leapt to the upper echelon of Berkshires dining nearly as soon as it opened. For one thing, it is the best-looking restaurant in town, with its eponymous zinc bar, faux tin ceiling, flowers, and lacquered woods, tile floor, and butcher paper over white tablecloths. Setting aside, the cuisine and wine list adhere with some rigor to the French-bistro canon. Menus have listed such appetizers as phyllo-wrapped spring rolls incorporating beefy, rare knobs of tuna, and continuing with such possibilities as sautéed halibut with saffron aioli, rack of lamb with artichokes and pistachio coulis, and honey glazed duck breast with white-bean cassoulet. A remarkable 24 wines are available by the glass, most of which go quite well with the five-cheese tasting ($15).

56 Church St. ✆ **413/637-8800.** Reservations suggested. Main courses $24–$32. AE, MC, V. Wed–Mon 11:30am–3pm and 5:30–10pm (bar until 12:30am).

Church Street Cafe ★★ ECLECTIC AMERICAN Lenox's most popular eating place delivers fanciful combinations that please the eye and pique the taste buds. Menus change with the seasons, but past options have included fried oysters with a lemony rémoulade sauce, seared duck breast chinois, and sake-soy marinated shrimp with crabmeat wontons. Lunch is a busy time here, with gumbo and black-bean quesadillas and crab-cake sandwiches among the favorites. The decor is rudimentary, the service friendly but rushed. A large deck fills up whenever the weather allows.

65 Church St. ✆ **413/637-2745.** Reservations recommended on weekends. Main courses $19–$29. MC, V. May–Oct daily 11:30am–2pm and 5:30–9pm; Nov–Feb Tues–Sat 11:30am–2pm and 5:30–8:30pm. Closed Mar–Apr.

Dish ★ NEW AMERICAN Opened in late 2003, this narrow storefront eatery was packed from the get-go. Since the decor is negligible and the accommodations cramped, the only discernible reason for its furious popularity is the food. It comes from the kitchen in stuttering intervals, the uncertainty easily compensated by the startlingly high quality of what the creative chef-owner sends forth. At dinner, the charbroiled rainbow trout and herb-roasted baby rack of lamb au jus are stars, preceded by a remarkable shrimp cake with horseradish plum tomato aioli or, perhaps, the pan-seared turkey dumplings with ginger-soy vinaigrette. Those appetizers appear as "small plates" at lunch, when all the wildly tasty sandwiches are only $7. That's another reason the locals like it—they don't need a bank loan to eat here.

37 Church St. ✆ **413/637-1800.** Reservations advised for dinner. Main courses $18–$28. MC, V. Wed–Mon 7:30am–3pm; Thurs–Sat 5:30–9pm.

PITTSFIELD

Berkshire County's largest city (pop. 44,285) gets little attention in most tourist literature, and for good reason. A commercial and industrial center, it presents little of the charm that marks such popular destinations as Stockbridge and Lenox. Still, it is a convenient base for day excursions to attractions elsewhere in the region.

A recently-discovered document banned the playing of baseball within 80 yards of the main church in 1791, giving Pittsfield claim to the invention of the game, 48 years before Cooperstown, NY. In summer, the **Berkshire Black Bears** (✆ **413/448-2255**) play minor-league baseball at Wahconah Park, a 1919 stadium with real wooden box seats.

Pittsfield lies 137 miles west of Boston, 7 miles north of Lenox. The **Berkshire Visitors Bureau** (✆ **800/237-5747** or 413/443-9186; www.berkshires.org) is in the same block of buildings as the Crowne Plaza Hotel, on Berkshire Common.

WHAT TO SEE & DO

Arrowhead Herman Melville bought this 18th-century house in 1850 and lived here until 1863. It was during this time that he wrote *Moby-Dick*. A nature trail and shop are on-site. In truth, however, the house is of limited interest to visitors other than literature students and avid readers.

780 Holmes Rd. ✆ **413/442-1793.** www.mobydick.org. Admission $8 adults, $5 students 15 and older, $3 for ages 6–14. From Fri before Memorial Day to Columbus Day daily 9:30am–5pm; rest of year by appointment only. Visits are by guided tour only, given on the hour, 10–4pm. Drive east from Park Sq. on East St., turn right on Elm St., and turn right on Holmes Rd.

Berkshire Museum ★ It began in 1903 as the "Museum of Natural History and Art," words chiseled in stone above the entrance. The holdings bounce from Babylonian cuneiform tablets to tanks of live fish to archaeological artifacts like a delicate necklace from Thebes dating to at least 1500 B.C. Included in the permanent collections are works by such 19th-century portraitists and landscapists as George Inness, Edwin Church, and Albert Bierstadt. Temporary exhibitions are frequent and professionally mounted. An auditorium seating 300 serves as the "Little Cinema," which shows art and foreign films during the warmer months.

39 South St. (Rte. 7, 1 block south of Park Sq.). ✆ **413/443-7171.** www.berkshiremuseum.org. Admission $7.50 adults, $6 seniors and college students, $4.50 ages 3–18. Mon–Sat 10am–5pm; Sun noon–5pm.

Hancock Shaker Village ★★★ The serenity of the setting, among low hills and meadows, and the carefully considered placement of the buildings and their relationships with each other are the essence of Shaker philosophy, "Order is Heaven's law." Of the 20 restored buildings that make up the village, its signature structure is easily the 1826 round stone barn. The Shaker preoccupation with functionalism joined with purity of line and respect for materials has never been clearer than it is in the design of this building—its round shape expedited the chores of feeding and milking livestock by arranging cows in a circle, and the precise joinery of the roof beams and support pillars is a joy to observe.

The second must-see is the brick dwelling that contained the communal dining room, kitchens, and sleeping quarters. Sexes were separated at meals, work, and religious services, and such features as the opposing staircases leading to male and female "retiring rooms" served equality.

Movers & Shakers in Massachusetts

Mother Ann arrived in 1774 with eight disciples just as the disgruntled American colonies were about to burst into open rebellion. The former Ann Lee, once imprisoned in England for her excess of religious zeal, had anointed herself leader of the United Society of Believers in Christ's Second Coming. The austere Protestant sect was dedicated to simplicity, equality, and celibacy. They were popularly known as "the Shakers" for their spastic movements when in the throes of religious ecstasy. By the time of her death in 1784, Mother Lee had many converts, who then fanned out across the country to form communal settlements from Maine to Indiana. One of the most important Shaker communities, **Hancock,** edged the Massachusetts–New York border, near Pittsfield.

Shaker society produced dedicated, highly disciplined farmers and craftspeople whose products were much in demand in the outside world. They sold seeds, invented early agricultural machinery and hand tools, and erected large buildings of several stories and exquisite simplicity. Their spare, clean-lined furniture and accessories anticipated the so-called Danish Modern style by a century and in recent years have drawn astonishingly high prices at auction.

All of these accomplishments required a verve owed at least in part to sublimation of sexual energy, for a fundamental Shaker tenet was total celibacy for its adherents. They kept going with converts and adoption of orphans (who were free to leave, if they wished). But by the 1970s, the inevitable result of this policy left the movement with a bare handful of believers. The string of Shaker settlements and museums that remain testify to their dictum, "Hands to work, hearts to God."

While artisans and docents demonstrate Shaker crafts and techniques, only those in the Schoolhouse and the Trustee's Office and Store dress in period clothing to portray Shaker inhabitants. All are knowledgeable about their subject, though, and dispense such nuggets as explanations of the Shaker discipline that required members to dress the right side first, to button from right to left, and to step with the right foot first.

The museum shop is excellent, and a cafe serves lunches in summer and fall, with some dishes based on Shaker recipes. On Saturday nights from July to October, the village presents tours and Shaker four-course dinners at a cost of about $40. Reservations for these are essential.

Routes 20 and 41, Pittsfield. ✆ **800/817-1137** or 413/443-0188. www.hancockshakervillage.org. Admission $15 adults, $4 children 13–17, free under 13, lower Nov–May. May–Oct daily 9:30am–5pm; rest of year daily 10am–4pm (tours on the hour). Call ahead in winter for hours and events.

GETTING OUTSIDE

Plaine's Bike, Ski, & Snowboard, 55 W. Housatonic St., at Center Street (✆ **413/499-0294;** www.plaines.com), rents bikes and carries equipment for all the sports its name suggests. It's on Route 20, west of downtown.

Pittsfield State Forest, entered on Cascade Street (✆ **413/442-8992**), is a little over 3 miles west of the center of town. Its 10,000 acres have 31 campsites, boat ramps, streams for canoeing and fishing, and trails for hiking, biking, riding, and cross-country skiing. It's open daily from 8am to 8pm. Admission is $2 per car.

BOATING **Onota Boat Livery,** 463 Pecks Rd. (✆ **413/442-1724**), rents canoes and motorboats for use on Onota Lake, conveniently located at the western edge of the city.

SKIING South of the city center, off Route 7 near the Pittsfield city limits, is the **Bousquet Ski Area,** Dan Fox Drive (✆ **413/442-8316** business office, 413/442-2436 snow phone; www.bousquets.com). Bousquet (pronounced "Bos-kay") has 21 trails, with a vertical drop of 750 feet, two double lifts, and two rope tows. Night skiing is available Monday through Saturday. Rentals and lessons are offered. Lift tickets cost $25 to $32.

Proceeding north on Route 7, watch for the turn west on Brodie Mountain Road and continue 2 miles to **Jiminy Peak** ★, Hancock (✆ **413/738-5500,** or 413/738-7325 for ski reports; www.jiminypeak.com). This expanding resort aspires to four-season activity, so skiing on 28 trails (18 open at night) with seven lifts is supplemented the rest of the year by horseback riding, trapshooting, fishing in a stocked pond, a rock-climbing wall, six tennis courts, mountain biking, pools, and golf at the nearby Waubeeka Springs course. For people staying overnight, lift tickets are included in the room rates. For day-trippers, 4-hour tickets cost adults $40 during the week, $51 on weekends; $31 and $45 for ages 7 to 19, $31 and $35 for seniors, and $17 under age 7.

The Brodie Mountain Ski Area, on Route 7 in New Ashford, was bought by Jiminy Peak in 2005, and no longer offers skiing.

WHERE TO STAY

Thaddeus Clapp House The eponymous Mr. Clapp was ahead of his time, incorporating central heating and indoor plumbing in his 1871 manse. He also rejected the excesses of High Victorian design, stripping his home to what amounted—at the time—to near-minimalism. Restoration took 18 months, and included installation of gas fireplaces and high-speed Internet access. The extra-large rooms come with CD players, robes, and fridges stocked with waters and soft drinks. The owner/manager is

Tips Pittsfield on Stage

The **Berkshire Opera Company,** 297 North St. (✆ **413/442-9955; www.berkshire opera.org**), stages its June productions at the Mahaiwe Theatre in Great Barrington, its July and August productions of both established and new operas at the Koussevitzky Arts Center of Berkshire Community College in Pittsfield. That venue is also employed by the **Albany Berkshire Ballet,** 51 North St. (✆ **413/445-5382; www.berkshireballet.org**), with up to 14 performances of two ballets from early July to mid-August.

a fervent Pittsfield booster and a font of information about the local dining and cultural scenes.

74 Wendell Ave., Pittsfield, MA 01201. ✆ **888/499-6840** or 413/499-6840. Fax 413/499-6842. www.clapphouse.com. 8 units. $125–$250 double. MC, V. *In room:* A/C, TV, coffeemaker, hair dryer, iron.

The Country Inn at Jiminy Peak *Kids* This is one of the better lodging deals in the Berkshires, if your idea of luxury is space. The units, all one- to three-bedroom suites with full kitchens and sofa beds, are perfect for families. Also great for kids are the on-site downhill skiing and abundant recreational facilities (see "Getting Outside," above). Four- and 8-hour lift tickets start any time. In summer, there's downhill mountain-bike riding for the adventurous, plus bobsled rides down the alpine slide, bungee-trampoline, a climbing wall, a giant swing, trout fishing, and minigolf. The owners recently purchased the Brodie Mountain ski area, on the other side of the hill; future plans are uncertain. A convenience store on the property has groceries, wine, beer, and a post office. No pets.

Brodie Mountain Rd. (near Rte. 43), Hancock, MA 01237. ✆ **800/882-8859** or 413/738-5500. Fax 413/738-5513. www.jiminypeak.com. 105 units. $129–$799 1–3 bedroom suite. Winter rates include lift tickets. Children under 18 stay free in parent's room. AE, DC, DISC, MC, V. **Amenities:** 2 restaurants (eclectic); 2 bars; heated outdoor and indoor pools; 6 tennis courts; exercise room; Jacuzzi; sauna; children's programs; game room; babysitting; coin-op washers and dryers. *In room:* A/C, TV/VCR, kitchenette, coffeemaker, hair dryer, iron.

Crowne Plaza *Kids* The tallest building in town at 14 stories, this former Hilton isn't hard to find, although it may take a little round-the-block maneuvering to get to the front door. It has the bells and whistles expected of upper-middle chain hotels and is more family-friendly than many smaller lodgings in the region. Kids are welcome, and readily occupied with the heated indoor pool and PlayStations in every room. With this many rooms, there's also a good chance of copping a bed on Tanglewood weekends. Free self-parking is available in the adjacent garage.

1 West St., Pittsfield, MA 01201. ✆ **877/227-6963** or 413/499-2000. Fax 413/442-0449. www.berkshirecrowne.com. 179 units. Summer $127–$242 double; off season $102–$165 double. AE, DISC, MC, V. **Amenities:** Restaurant (American); bar; heated indoor pool; fitness room w/Jacuzzi, limited room service. *In room:* A/C, TV w/pay movies, dataport, coffeemaker, hair dryer, iron.

WHERE TO DINE

Asters STEAK/SEAFOOD The former Yellow Aster has been converted to this sleek Manhattan(ish) steakhouse, complete with way too much Sinatra on the stereo. The lower floor is a raw bar, and there are several rooms upstairs, two of them with fireplaces. An outdoor firepit gathers patrons for drinks and dessert. Next to the black onyx bar is a walk-in wine cabinet, signaling the management's enthusiasm for the grape. They offer, for example, a flight of monthly featured wines—2-ounce tastings of three bottles for only $8. Wines by the glass are ample pours, too. Apart from the modest raw-bar choices, you'll find clam chowder, Caesar salad, crab cakes, and fried calamari among the expected starters, most of them competently done, a description that can be given the steaks, chops, and fish, as well. In sum, a pleasantly satisfying meal and evening can be had, accompanied by live jazz on Friday and Saturday evenings.

1015 South St. (Rte. 7) © **413/499-2075.** Main courses $11–$29. AE, MC, V. Mon–Thurs 4–9pm; Fri–Sat 4–10pm; Sun 10am–2pm and 5–9pm.

Brix Wine Bar ★ CONTEMPORARY BISTRO What a refreshing antidote to the forlorn Pittsfield dining landscape! The enthusiasm of the owners and staff for their new 34-seat enterprise is infectious, the kind that brings patrons back over and over again. Wine is a priority, obviously, and every effort is made to instruct newbies and cosset sophisticates. There are over 50 pressings available by the glass, more than you're likely to see this side of Paris. Flights of four wines cost only $10. The eats are tantalizing, and geared to the smallest or largest of appetites, running from such panini as the combination of roasted lamb, pickled red onions, and baby arugula on to plates of charcuterie, cheese, and savory tarts—simply keep ordering until sated. "Brix," by the way, is named for the inventor of a refractometer used to measure the sugar content of grapes.

40 West St. (opposite Crown Plaza Hotel). © **413/236-9463.** Most dishes under $12. AE, MC, V. Sun and Tues–Wed 5–11pm; Thurs–Sat 5pm–1am.

WILLIAMSTOWN ★★

This community and its prestigious liberal-arts college were both named for Col. Ephraim Williams, who was killed in 1755 in one of the French and Indian Wars. He bequeathed the land for creation of a school and a town. His college grew, spreading east from the central common along both sides of Main Street (Rte. 2). Over the town's long history, buildings have been erected in several styles of the times. That makes Main Street a virtual museum of institutional architecture, with representatives of the Georgian, Federal, Gothic Revival, Romanesque, and Victorian styles, as well as a few that are yet to be labeled. Inserted into this diverting display is the new **'62 Center for Theatre and Dance,** a thoroughly contemporary structure that opened in September 2005 (see below). They stand at dignified distances from one another, so what might have been a tumultuous visual hodgepodge is instead a stately lesson in historical design. The impressive Clark Art Institute is the best reason to make a special trip, perhaps in conjunction with a performance at the increasingly ambitious Williamstown Theatre Festival.

A free weekly newspaper, the *Advocate* (© **413/664-7900**), produces useful guides to both the northern and southern Berkshires. For a copy, write to the *Advocate,* 87 Marshall St., North Adams, MA 01267. An **information booth,** at North Street (Rte. 7) and Main Street (Rte. 2), has an abundance of pamphlets and brochures free for the taking.

WHAT TO SEE & DO

Sterling and Francine Clark Art Institute ★★★ Within these walls are canvases by Renoir (34 of them), Degas, Gauguin, Toulouse-Lautrec, Pissarro, and their predecessor, Corot. Look for Turner's splendid seascape, *Rockets and Blue Lights.* Also on display is the famed Degas sculpture *Little Dancer,* believed to be his only three-dimensional piece and a signature work of the Institute. In addition to these standouts, you'll find works by 15th- and 16th-century Dutch portraitists, European genre and landscape painters, and Americans Sargent and Homer, as well as fine porcelain, silver, and antiques. The Clarks were more disciplined in their acquisitions than most wealthy collectors, and their museum qualifies as one of the great cultural resources of the Berkshires and of the state.

Apart from the collection itself, the Clarks' farsighted endowment funded the modern wing added to the original neoclassical building and has covered all acquisitions, upkeep, and renovations. His stipulation that there be no admission fee was finally breached, but the charge applies only to adults, 4 months a year. A substantial bookstore in the lobby has been joined by a snack counter and an attractive cafe. An additional wing is on the drawing board.

225 South St., Williamstown. ✆ **413/458-2303.** www.clarkart.edu. Admission June–Oct $10 adults, free for students and children; free to all Tues and Nov–June. Day after Labor Day to June Tues–Sun 10am–5pm; July to Labor Day daily 10am–5pm.

Williams College Museum of Art ★ The second leg of Williamstown's two prominent art repositories exists in large part thanks to the college's collection of almost 400 paintings by the American modernists Maurice and Charles Prendergast. The museum also has works by Gris, Léger, Whistler, Picasso, Warhol, and Hopper. There are frequent special exhibitions and lecture series.

15 Lawrence Hall Dr., Williamstown. ✆ **413/597-2429.** www.williams.edu/WCMA. Free admission. Tues–Sat (and some Mon holidays) 10am–5pm; Sun 1–5pm.

GETTING OUTSIDE

Waubeeka Golf Links, 137 New Ashford Rd. (Routes 7 and 43), Williamstown (✆ **413/458-8355** for tee times, 413/458-5869 for the restaurant), is open to the public, with greens fees of $33 on weekdays, $47 weekends. Golf carts cost $15 per rider. The 18-hole course is still not widely known in the region, so last-minute tee-times are often possible.

Mount Greylock State Reservation ★ contains the highest peak (3,491 ft.) in Massachusetts as well as a section of the Appalachian Trail. A long, narrow, bumpy road allows cars almost to the summit, where the War Memorial Tower affords vistas of the Taconic and Hoosac ranges, far into Vermont and New York (parking $20). The ride down is very popular with mountain bikers. The park is open from sunrise until a half-hour after sunset, the visitor center mid-May to mid-October daily from 9am to 5pm, and mid-October to mid-May weekends and holidays from 8am to 4pm. Black bear and deer are often sighted. Trails radiate from the parking lot near **Bascom Lodge,** North Main Street off Route 7 in Lanesboro (✆ **413/743-1591** or 413/443-0011), a grandly rustic creation of the Civilian Conservation Corps in the New Deal 1930s. Simple dormitory beds ($26 per night) and four private rooms ($68–$98) accommodating at total of 32 guests are available for rent from mid-May to mid-October. Family-style dinners are available by reservation.

SHOPPING

In the small downtown shopping district, **Library Antiques,** 70 Spring St. (✆ **413/458-3436**), is filled with a wealth of English chess sets, African carvings, Peruvian alpaca sweaters, Polish stoneware, and antique American fishing lures and creels. South of the town center on Route 7, **Saddleback Antiques,** 1395 Cold Spring Rd. (✆ **413/458-5852**), features country, wicker, and Victorian furniture. Slightly south of town on Route 7, **Collectors Warehouse,** 105 North St. (✆ **413/458-9686**), has a little bit of everything—jewelry, books, dolls, furniture, and glassware.

WHERE TO STAY

This is a college town, so in addition to the usual Berkshires peak periods of July, August, and the October foliage season, accommodations fill up during graduation and on football weekends. The largest lodging in town is the 100-unit **Williams Inn,** 1090 Main St. (✆ **800/828-0133** or 413/458-9371). Despite the name, it is a standard motel, with a dining room, tavern, and indoor pool. See also the section on North Adams, below.

Field Farm Guesthouse After an extended vacation of B&B-hopping, there may come a time when one more tilted floor or wobbly Windsor chair will send even a devout inn-lover over the edge. Here's an antidote. This pristine example of postwar modern architecture rose in 1948 on a spectacular 296-acre estate with 4 miles of trails. Most guest rooms look over meadows to Mount Greylock. The living room is equipped with a telescope to view the beavers and waterfowl on the lake. The Scandinavian Modern furniture was made to order for the house, and three units have decks while two have fireplaces. Don't expect TV or phones, but there is wireless Internet access. Breakfasts are hearty meals of waffles and five-cheese omelets utilizing fruits, herbs, and vegetables grown on the property. Well-behaved children are welcome. Closed Monday through Wednesday from November to April.

554 Sloan Rd., Williamstown, MA 01267. ✆/fax **413/458-3135.** www.thetrustees.org. 5 units. $150–$200 double. Rates include breakfast. DISC, MC, V. Follow Rte. 7 to Rte. 43 and turn west, then make an immediate right on Sloan Rd. Continue 1 mile to the Field Farm entrance, on the right. **Amenities:** Heated outdoor pool; tennis court. *In room:* Hair dryer.

The Orchards ★★ A sedate choice just right for visiting Williams alumni and parents, this has an upscale country-club atmosphere, the sort of place where afternoon tea is an event. Each of its public and private rooms enjoys a mix of antique and reproduction English-style furniture. Even standard rooms are sizeable, all with separate dressing cubicles, and those with working fireplaces have chaise longues and deeply padded chairs. Some have fridges with soft drinks; safes are hidden in places we can't divulge. A 3-year renovation benefited every corner, including the exercise room, and the kitchen, too, now surpasses the merely competent operation that preceded it. There is live piano in the lounge on weekends. Providing an international touch is an internship program that brings young people from all over the world to staff the front desk and dining room.

222 Adams Rd., Williamstown, MA 01262. ✆ **800/225-1517** or 413/458-9611. Fax 413/458-9611. www.orchardshotel.com. 47 units. Mid-Nov to late May $195–$345 double; late May to mid-Nov $175–$275 double. AE, DC, DISC, MC, V. **Amenities:** Restaurant (international); bar; heated outdoor pool; exercise room w/sauna and whirlpool. *In room:* A/C, TV/VCR, coffeemaker, hair dryer, iron, safe.

WHERE TO DINE

Mezze ECLECTIC Meals here are entirely competent but less than dazzling. The enthusiasm for "small plates" is addressed in the name and on the menu, with tapas-type starters like steamed mahogany clams and plates of anchovies, prosciutto, olives, and marinated eggplant. The chef put in time at acclaimed Craft in New York, an experience reflected in such dishes as the roasted skate with sautéed arugula, gnocchi, and chanterelles and the roasted spaghetti squash with a lobster curry sauce. Less esoteric choices are beef stroganoff, hanger steak, and a serious cheeseburger. The clientele is composed primarily of professors, administrators, and students with visiting parents in tow.

16 Water St. ✆ **413/458-0123.** Main courses $13–$26. AE, DISC, MC, V. Sun–Thurs 5–9pm; Fri–Sat 5–10pm.

Spice Root *Value* INDIAN Catch an irresistible whiff of this Indian newcomer from several storefronts away and thoughts of anything but food vanish. Impecunious students like it for the bargain all-you-can-eat $6.95 lunch buffet, and while it's pretty good, choices are necessarily limited. The a la carte menu is more rewarding, with several starters, breads, curries, nine vegetarian dishes, tandoor specialties, and a half-dozen dishes from Bombay. Standouts are the curried salmon, chicken or lamb tikka masala, fiery shrimp vindaloo, and a veggie delight that involves bell peppers stuffed with mashed potatoes, paneer cheese, and spinach accompanied by yellow lentils. Of the several breads baked on-site, plain nan is certainly serviceable, but the version filled with cheese, nuts, and raisins is a particular treat.

23 Spring St. ✆ **413/458-5200.** Main courses $7–$19. AE, DISC, MC, V. Daily 11:30am–2:30pm and 5–10pm.

WILLIAMSTOWN AFTER DARK

The Williams College Department of Music sponsors diverse concerts and recitals. Call its **Concertline** (✆ **413/597-3146**) to learn of upcoming events. In addition, the Clark Art Institute (see above) hosts frequent classical-music events.

The '62 Center for Theatre and Dance ★★ Williamstown has long hosted one of The Berkshires' premier summer attractions, the **Williamstown Theatre Festival** (✆ **413/597-3400;** www.wtfestival.org), and now it has a facility that provides a proper showcase. This ambitious center opened in the fall of 2005 (the year in its name is for the class that graduated in 1962), providing three performance venues as well as studios, classrooms, and rehearsal spaces. Dramatic productions, dance, music, and related cultural events, involving students and alumni as well as professionals, can now be mounted all year. Staging classic and new plays during its season from late June to late August, the festival attracts many top actors and directors. The MainStage Theatre presents works by major playwrights, while the CenterStage often features more experimental productions. The schedule is usually announced by April. It's not too difficult to get tickets; even if a particular performance is said to be sold out, there are often cancellations in the 30 minutes before curtain. Tickets to the Festival itself range from about $20 to $55, while admission to other events are often free, and no more than $10.

1000 Main St. (P.O. Box 517). ✆ **413/597-2425** for box office. www.williams.edu/go/62center.

NORTH ADAMS

Ten years ago, it seemed impossible that this comatose mill town could recover. Its unemployment rate was the highest in the state, and over two-thirds of its storefronts were empty. A land developer once even suggested that the town be flooded to create lakefront property.

However, North Adams experienced a whiplash turnaround, and today many of those once-abandoned storefronts are taken up with restaurants, galleries, and high-tech start-ups. The unlikely reason, to almost everyone's agreement, is an art museum. An abandoned industrial complex has been converted, despite early hoots of derision, into a center for the visual and performing arts. It is called the Massachusetts Museum of Contemporary Art, and it has strikingly altered the socio-economic dynamic of North Adams.

The first Sunday of October is Fall Foliage Day, with a parade of fire engines, marching bands, and Clydesdales and balloons, hot dogs, and cotton candy on sale at sidewalk stands.

Massachusetts Museum of Contemporary Art ★★ A lot of excitement and anticipation surrounded this ambitious project, the conversion of an empty 27-building textile factory into a center for the arts. Even before its official opening, it had a nickname—MASS MoCA—and hosted performances by David Byrne, Patti Smith, and the Merce Cunningham Dance Company. Works on display are often outsized, crossing traditional aesthetic boundaries to marry elements of both performing and visual arts.

Its chief virtue—from the standpoint of those contemporary artists who choose to work on a grand scale—is the vastness of the spaces available. But additionally, the museum has hosted a variety of musical events, experimental films, even dance parties, and is attracting small tenant companies working the vineyards of technology, including software, video, and e-commerce. MASS MoCA has attracted hundreds of thousands of visitors and is certainly worth the short detour east from neighboring Williamstown.

Two restaurants operate on the sprawling museum campus: the snacky **Lickety Split** (✆ **413/663-3372**), serving coffee, ice cream, and light fare; and **Café Latino** (✆ **413/662-2004**), an airy space with terrace tables serving lunch and dinner with south-of-the-border inclinations.

87 Marshall St., North Adams. ✆ **413/662-2111.** www.massmoca.org. Admission $10 adults, $8 students, $4 children 6–16. July to early Sept daily 10am–6pm; early Sept to June Wed–Mon 11am–5pm.

WHERE TO STAY

Jae's (see below) also has accommodations.

The Porches ★★ "Retro-rural chic" might describe this row of six detached 19th-century workingmen's houses stitched together by an uninterrupted streetside veranda, the spaces in between roofed over and fitted with indoor catwalks and patios. Rooms are witty tributes to the past, with kitschy lamps and paint-by-numbers pictures on the walls, but are also equipped with DVD players and high-speed Internet access. A computer is provided for guests' use, and laptop rentals are also available. Down duvets, bathrobes, and cushy sofas make things even cozier. Ask for one of the second-floor king rooms with balcony. Coffee, croissant, and a newspaper paper in a rocking chair out on the porch on a warm autumn morning is a singular pleasure. Evening cocktails are available.

231 River St., North Adams, MA 01247. ✆ **413/664-0400.** Fax 413/664-0401. www.porches.com. 47 units. Late May to early Nov $160–$295 double, $225–$435 suite; early Nov to late May $135–$259 double, $175–$329 suite. Rates include breakfast. Packages available. AE, DC, MC, V. Find it behind the MASS MoCA complex, ½ block west of Marshall St. **Amenities:** Heated outdoor pool; fitness room, Jacuzzi; sauna; in-room massage; laundry service (Mon–Fri); free DVD library. *In room:* A/C, TV/DVD, dataport, minibar, hair dryer, iron.

WHERE TO DINE

Gideon's ★ ECLECTIC The human dynamo shaking the skillets in the open kitchen is Bill Gideon, the chef/owner. With little help and working with furious efficiency, he sends out large plates of food from an uncomplicated menu dominated by Italian pastas and meat dishes with largely Gallic origins. Tomato-and-basil angel hair, gnocchi Alfredo, and a grilled vegetable risotto are characteristic, augmented by duck confit, veal Marsala, and herbed rack of lamb. He may offer to whip up an unlisted favorite on request. Even on a Saturday night, the crowd, composed of families, friends, and couples, starts thinning out by 8:30pm. But at peak times, try for a table at the edge of the room, as the plywood floor bounces annoyingly with the foot traffic.

But Gideon's night isn't over. After the cooking is done, he walks across the parking lot to **Gideon's Luncheon & Nightery** (✆ **413/664-0404;** 23 Eagle St.) It is what it says: a lunch spot made into a club with live music Thursday through Saturday nights, usually jazz, rock, or Brazilian rhythms. Tapas and panini make up much of the light fare.

34 Holden St. ✆ **413/664-9449.** Main courses $11–$28. AE, MC, V. Tues–Sun 5–9 or 10pm.

Jae's ★ ASIAN The boundlessly cheerful Korean owner of this inn and restaurant swept from his homeland to Japan to Thailand to assemble his menu, and the result is both entertaining and delicious in almost every regard. Take the culinary journey with him, beginning with a platter of flawless maki and sushi, continue with the exceptional seafood pancake, comprised of shrimp, crabmeat, squid, and scallions, and finish with Jae's Special country curry. All fish is as fresh as the morning. Or, make a meal of appetizers, fabricated in both the kitchen and at the sushi bar. From the former, consider *mandoo* (fried meat dumplings) or *hamachi-kama* (grilled yellowtail); from the latter, *naruto* (crab stick, flying fish roe, and avocado roll), or tiger eyes (grilled squid stuffed with smoked salmon). More daring diners might try the spicy kimchi stew or the *bibim bab,* veggies and marinated chicken cooked in a hot stone pot.

There are 12 bedrooms available in the inn, all with air-conditioning, Wi-Fi, TV, and DVD players, renting for $95 to $150 per night.

1111 South State St. (Rte. 8 south). ✆ **413/664-0100.** Main courses $9–$18. AE, DC, DISC, MC, V. Sun–Thurs 11:30am–10pm; Fri–Sat 11:30am–11pm.

9

Connecticut

by Herbert Bailey Livesey

Connecticut resists generalization and confounds spinners of superlatives. It doesn't rank at the top or bottom of any important chart of virtues or liabilities, which makes it impossible to pigeonhole. The nation's third-smallest state is certainly compact—only 90 miles wide and 55 miles top to bottom—but it is still three times the size of the most diminutive of all, which happens to lie right next door. While parts of it are clogged with humanity, some corners are as empty and undeveloped as inland Maine.

By many measures, Connecticut's citizens are as wealthy as any in the country, but dozens of its towns are only shells of their prosperous 19th-century selves, beset by poverty as intractable as it gets. It can boast no dramatic geographical feature, and its highest elevation is only 2,380 feet. Established in 1635 by disgruntled English settlers who didn't like the way things were going at Plymouth Colony, it has long seemed spiritually divorced from the rest of New England—an appendage of New York, or a place to be traversed on the way to Boston.

All this might appear to constitute an identity crisis and hardly makes Connecticut seem an appealing vacation destination. But a closer look reveals an abundance of reasons to slow down and linger.

To a great extent, the state owes its existence to the presence of water. In addition to having Long Island Sound along its entire southern coast, several significant rivers and their tributaries slice through the hills and coastal plain: the Housatonic, Naugatuck, Quinnipiac, Connecticut, and Thames. They provided power for the mills along their courses and the towns and cities that grew around them. Industry still drives most of the economy, despite the bucolic image that mention of the state often conjures, and the pollution that industry has caused in the rivers and the sound is being scoured away.

Development, too, appears to have slowed, helping to preserve Connecticut's scores of classic Colonial villages, from the Litchfield Hills in the northwest to the Mystic coast in the opposite corner. They are as placid and timeless as they have been for more than 3 centuries, or as polished and sophisticated as transplanted urbanites can make them. And the state's salty maritime heritage is palpable in the old boat-building and fishing villages at the mouths of its rivers, especially those east of New Haven.

Connecticut is New England's front porch. Pull up a chair and stay awhile.

1 The Gold Coast: Fairfield County

Mansions, marinas, and luxury apartment blocks nudge up against each other along the deeply indented Long Island Sound shoreline in the southwestern corner of the state. This is one of the most heavily developed stretches of the coast, and, in terms of

Connecticut

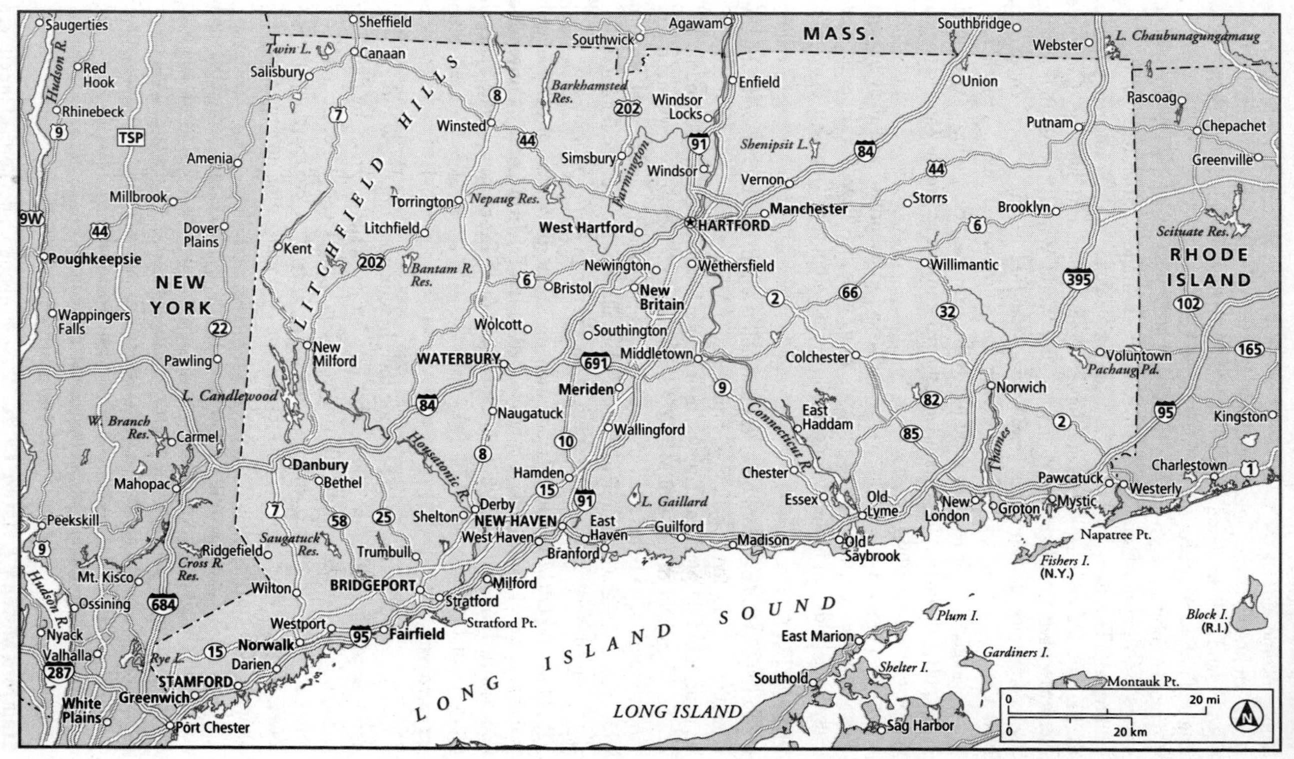

family income, one of the wealthiest. Not for nothing has coastal Fairfield County long been known as the Gold Coast, especially to real-estate agents. As the land rises slowly inland from the water's edge, woods thicken, roads narrow, and pockets of New England unfold. Yacht country becomes horse country.

The first suburbs began to form in the middle of the last century, when train rails started radiating north and east from New York's Grand Central Terminal into the countryside. This part of the state was made accessible for summertime refugees from the big city, and eventually weekend houses became permanent dwellings. Corporate executives liked the life of the gentry, so after World War II, they started moving their companies closer to their new homes. Stamford became a city; Greenwich, New Canaan, Darien, and Westport were the bedroom communities of choice—pricey, haughty, redolent of the good life. (Of course, Fairfield County also contains Bridgeport, a depressed city that once considered filing for bankruptcy and has a penchant for political scandal.)

But for visitors, the fashionable "exurbs" (beyond suburban) and their beaches, restaurants, and upscale shops are the draw, along with the villages farther north, especially Ridgefield, that hint of Vermont, all within 1½ hours of Times Square.

ESSENTIALS

GETTING THERE From New York and points south, take I-95 or, preferably, the Hutchinson and Merritt parkways. From eastern Massachusetts and northern Connecticut, take I-84 south to Danbury, then Route 7 south into Fairfield County.

The **Metro North** (✆ **800/METRO-INFO** or 212/532-4900; www.mta.nyc.ny.us/mnr) commuter line has many trains daily from New York's Grand Central Terminal, with stops at Greenwich, Stamford, Darien, Norwalk, Westport, and additional stations all the way to New Haven. Express trains make the trip in 45 to 65 minutes.

VISITOR INFORMATION Information on the northern part of the county is available at www.litchfieldhills.com, while the **Coastal Fairfield County Convention and Visitor Bureau** (✆ **800/866-7925;** www.coastalCT.com) can provide materials on the coastal towns.

STAMFORD

A trickle of corporations started moving their headquarters from New York 38 miles northeast to Stamford in the 1960s. That flow became a steady stream by the 1980s, and more than a dozen Fortune 500 companies, including General Electric and Xerox, continue to direct their operations from here. They have erected shiny mid-rise towers that give the city of 117,000 residents an appearance more like the new urban centers of the Sun Belt than those of the Snow Belt.

One result is a lively downtown that other, less prosperous Connecticut cities surely envy. Roughly contained by Greylock Place, Tresser Boulevard, and Atlantic and Main streets, it has two theaters, tree-lined streets with many shops and a large mall, pocket parks and plazas, and a number of stylish restaurants, sidewalk cafes, and clubs patronized by the city's large cohort of young single professionals.

For further information, check www.coastalCT.com.

WHAT TO SEE & DO

Stamford Museum & Nature Center ★ Kids About 5 miles north of the city center is this fine family-oriented resource. The center has a large lake, an open pen with a pair of river otters, and a real working farm with goats, sheep, cattle, and peacocks.

May and June mark the arrival of newborn chicks, kids, calves, and lambs. On the grounds are a country store, nature trails, a small planetarium, and an oddball Tudor-Gothic house with galleries of art, natural history, and Indian lore.

39 Scofield Town Rd.(at High Ridge Rd.) ✆ **203/322-1646.** Admission $6 adults, $5 seniors and children 4–14. Mon–Sat and holidays 9am–5pm; Sun 11–5pm. Feeding time is 9am. The center is 1 mile north of Exit 35 off the Merritt Pkwy. (Rte. 15).

SHOPPING

United House Wrecking, 535 Hope St. (✆ **203/348-5371;** www.unitedhousewrecking.com), is a find for dedicated antiques hounds who will want to make time for this sprawling emporium of oddments. The name may not sound promising, but the company got its start selling architectural remnants salvaged from building demolitions. For years, it featured such items as 1930s gas pumps, stone pigs, and pagodas. Now it showcases far less bizarre imported antiques and reproductions. It's open Monday through Saturday from 9:30am to 5:30pm, Sunday from noon to 5pm. It's also tough to find. From Exit 9 of I-95, pick up Route 1, then Route 106 north; make a left on Glenbrook Road, which becomes Church Street, and turn right on Hope Street. Be sure you have a map or detailed directions.

WHERE TO STAY

Stamford Marriott ★★ One of the posher breed of Marriotts, this relative newcomer piles on the extras. Most notable is the new Agora day spa, off the second floor, with six treatment rooms for facials, body wraps, and waxing, among other services. Steam rooms and 13-head full-body showers are additional attractions. What's more, it has an indoor golf training center with its own staff pro. All rooms have high-speed Internet access.

243 Tresser Blvd. (Exit 7, I-95), Stamford, CT 06901. ✆ **800/732-9689** or 203/357-9555. Fax 203/324-6897. www.marriottstamford.com. 506 units. $149–$295 double. AE, DC, DISC, MC, V. **Amenities:** 2 restaurants (American, Continental); lounge; heated indoor/outdoor pool; fitness center and spa; concierge; business center; limited room service; same-day dry cleaning/laundry. *In room:* A/C, TV w/pay movies, dataport, coffeemaker, hair dryer, iron.

Westin Stamford ★ This outpost of the always reliable international chain does nothing to diminish the expectations of business travelers. Everything is in place, from the executive floors with club lounge to the airport shuttle van. The more expensive rooms have high-speed Internet connections.

1 Stamford Place (Exit 7, I-95), Stamford, CT 06902. ✆ **800/937-8461** or 203/967-2222. Fax 203/967-3475. www.westin.com. 481 units. $255–$369 double. AE, DC, DISC, MC, V. **Amenities:** Restaurant (international); lounge; heated indoor pool; tennis court; health club; concierge; business center; 24-hr. room service; same-day dry cleaning/laundry. *In room:* A/C, TV, dataport, minibar, coffeemaker, hair dryer, iron, safe.

WHERE TO DINE

Oceans 211 ★ NEW AMERICAN/SEAFOOD First, know that the hands-on owner put in his apprenticeship at the venerable Oyster Bar in New York's Grand Central Terminal. It shows: The ground-floor bar has a Manhattan sheen, with a curving black marble bar and a long display case of featured wines. The menu (changed daily) is deceptively plain, the entrees listed only by their central ingredients—halibut, Dover sole, wild salmon, snapper—with unflowery descriptions of their preparation. The delights come with what shows up on the plate. One memorable dish was Pacific escolar crusted in Parmesan and served with marinated tomatoes and a purée of broccoli rabe. You might have trouble getting past the delectable appetizers, and the large selection (most nights) of oysters from the raw bar. Upstairs is a less cozy dining room that seats up to 70.

211 Summer St. ✆ **203/973-0494.** Reservations suggested on weekends. Main courses $28–$35. AE, DC, MC, V. Mon–Thurs noon–2:30pm and 5:30–10pm, Fri noon–2:30pm and 5:30–11pm; Sat 5:30–11pm.

Smokey Joe's BARBECUE Smack on the Stamford-Darien line, this wouldn't pass a Fort Worth authenticity test, but it's close enough. Upstairs is a down-and-dirty bar with pool table; downstairs is a classic barbecue joint. Stand in the cafeteria line and select from confusing lists of ribs, brisket, pulled pork, sausage, and birds; then retire to the oil-clothed picnic tables to gorge.

1308 E. Main St. (Rte. 1). ✆ **203/406-0605.** Main courses $9.95–$25. MC, V. Mon–Thurs 11:30am–9:30pm; Fri–Sat 11:30am–10:30pm; Sun 11:30am–9pm (bar daily until 1:30am).

Zinc FRENCH BISTRO Habitues of the Summer Street restaurant row were happy to note the arrival of this take on the Left Bank bistro model. All the doors in front open onto a raised streetside terrace, the floor inside is covered in tiny black-and-white tiles, and the bar has the requisite zinc top. The theme carries through with a menu that features onion soup, escargot, pâté, braised lamb shank, beef bourguinon . . . and more like that. There are even actual French people in attendance! It's all competently done, and the conviviality ushered in during the 5-to-7pm happy hour (Mon–Fri) continues to flow throughout the evening.

222 Summer St. ✆ **203/252-2352.** Reservations suggested on weekends. Main courses $17–$27. AE, DC, MC, V. Mon–Sat 11:30am–10pm (until 10:30pm Fri–Sat); Sun 5–9:30pm.

STAMFORD AFTER DARK

The **Stamford Center for the Arts,** Atlantic Street and Tresser Boulevard (✆ **203/325-4466;** www.onlyatsca.com) has three venues. The **Rich Forum** is the best known, presenting professional productions, with boldface name actors, of successful Broadway and off-Broadway plays as well as musical and dance presentations, while the **Palace Theatre,** 61 Atlantic St. (✆ **203/325-4466;** www.onlyatsca.com), offers musicals; rotating appearances by the Stamford Symphony Orchestra, the Connecticut Grand Opera and Orchestra, and the Connecticut Ballet; and one-night stands by solo acts and traveling troupes like B. B. King, Tom Jones, and the Alvin Ailey Dance Theater. Smaller, often experimental plays and related performances are given in **The Studio at Rich Forum.**

NORWALK

Given the despair that pervades many New England cities, the continuing betterment of this city's once notorious South Norwalk neighborhood gladdens the heart. The rehabilitation of several blocks of 19th-century row houses is transforming the waterfront into a trendy precinct that has come to be called, inevitably, "SoNo." The **Norwalk Seaport Oyster Festival** (✆ **203/838-9444;** www.seaport.org), held in early September, attracts over 90,000 visitors to its tall ships, oyster boats, crafts show, and food court. There are even skydivers. Bounded roughly by Washington, Water, and North and South Main streets, SoNo is readily accessible from the South Norwalk railroad station.

WHAT TO SEE & DO

Lockwood-Mathews Mansion Museum Erected in 1864, this granite mansion in the Second Empire style is covered with peaked and mansard slate roofs and has 62 rooms arranged around a stunning sky-lit octagonal rotunda. Marble, gilt, marquetry, and frescoes were commissioned and incorporated with abandon. Visits are by guide or audio tour. It has been designated a National Historic Landmark.

295 West Ave. © **203/838-9799.** www.lockwoodmathewsmansion.org. Admission $8 adults, $5 seniors and students, free for children under 12. Mid-Mar to New Year's Day Wed–Sun noon–5pm. From I-95 southbound, take Exit 15; from I-95 northbound, take Exit 14.

The Maritime Aquarium at Norwalk ★★ This facility remains the centerpiece of revitalized SoNo. The present name isn't inclusive, as part of the complex incorporates a section of boat-builders at work as well as exhibits of model ships and full-size vessels, including the *Tango,* which was *pedaled* across the Atlantic. While they don't call it a thrill ride, a submarine simulator takes 18 passengers at a time down to the ocean depths, shaking and shuddering all the way; the climax is a battle between a whale and a giant squid. The main attractions, though, are the marine creatures and mammals on view. Five harbor seals are fed at 11:45am, 1:45pm, and 3:45pm, when they wriggle up on the rocks and even rest their heads in their handler's lap. Additional exhibits include a pair of river otters, an open pool of cow-nosed rays, and tanks alive with creatures found in Sound waters, including sea turtles and sharks. A giant IMAX screen shows nature films that aren't necessarily confined to the seven seas.

10 N. Water St. © **203/852-0700.** www.maritimeaquarium.org. Admission $11 adults, $9.50 seniors, $8.50 children 2–12; IMAX $8.50 adults, $7.50 seniors, $6 children; combination packages (aquarium plus IMAX movie) $16 adults, $15 seniors, $12 children. July–Aug daily 10am–6pm; Sept–June daily 10am–5pm.

CRUISES

Excursions to **Sheffield Island** and its historic lighthouse are offered by the ***Seaport Islander*** (© **888/547-6863** or 203/854-4656), a 60-passenger vessel that departs from Hope Dock, near The Maritime Aquarium. Weather permitting, the boat sets out two to four times daily, on Saturdays and Sundays from Memorial Day weekend to late September as well as Monday through Friday from late June to Labor Day. The round-trip takes about 2½ hours, with a 15-minute layover on the island. Fares are $16 for adults, $14 for seniors (Mon–Tues), $12 for ages 4 to 12, and $5 for ages 3 and under. Thursday evenings from 6 to 9:30pm in season bring clambakes to the island ($60 per person). Other outings include sunset cruises and occasional Sunday picnics. Always call ahead for schedule.

Similarly, the research vessel ***Oceanic*** has "creature cruises" on many winter weekends to spot seals and bird life, as well as marine study cruises at other times, a service of The Maritime Aquarium. Fares are $18 per person. Reserve ahead by calling © **203/852-0700,** ext. 2206.

SHOPPING

Serious shoppers have several choices, primarily among the boutiques and galleries along Washington and Main streets. One shop that may produce a bargain or at least a surprise is **Saga,** 119 Washington St. (© **203/855-1900**). It specializes in folk arts and crafts as well as jewelry and furnishings from the southwestern United States, Mexico, and points south. **And Company, Inc.,** 108 Washington St. (© **203/831-8855**), offers bedding and bath products, but carries whimsical Oaxaca carvings and Mata Ortiz pottery, too.

WHERE TO DINE

For a break from shopping and strolling, drop into **SoNo Caffeine,** 133 Washington St. (© **203/857-4224**), an eccentric java joint that serves breakfast and lunch, offers live jazz and pop Sunday, Tuesday, Wednesday, and Thursday, and sticks a price tag on virtually every piece of furniture on the place.

Barcelona ★ MEDITERRANEAN Tapas are the featured attraction here, but the kitchen isn't doctrinaire about recipes, which range all over the Mediterranean and even down to South America for inspiration. Two or three tapas per person make a meal, and sharing is inevitable. Start, perhaps, with charcuteria, either an assortment of Spanish cheeses, which changes daily, or of cured meats and sausages, usually including nutty-tasting Serrano ham. The day's additional delectables might be chorizo with sweet and sour figs, garlic shrimp, or triangular piquillo peppers stuffed with potato-cod brandade. Other options include the half-chicken cooked in white wine with hot cherry peppers, and paella for two to six people. The patio is open year-round.

63–65 N. Main St. (north of Washington St.). © **203/899-0088.** Reservations suggested on weekends. Tapas $3.50–$14; main courses $20–$27. AE, DC, DISC, MC, V. Daily 5pm–1am.

Kazu JAPANESE The bountiful bento box displayed near the entrance mesmerizes diners awaiting seats. It contains a crispy shrimp and calamari salad, salmon skin roll, two vegetable dumplings, a crispy tofu salad, and a chicken katsu pizza. For $12 at lunch, it's easily enough for two. And given the indifferent decor of plastic room dividers and scant representations of irises and lotus blossoms, it's a good thing the focus is the food to come. Three or four chefs operate at the sushi bar in back, employing truly fresh fish to turn out dumplings and rolls both traditional and cross-cultural in character. In the latter category are jalapeño shrimp with ponzu sauce and the mango chicken roll with cilantro, hot peppers, lettuce, and mayo. (Mayo?) Odd or conventional, most items work to happy satisfaction.

64 North Main St. (near West Ave.). © **203/866-7492.** Main courses $15–$23. AE, DC, MC, V. Mon–Fri noon–2pm; daily 5–10pm.

Match ★★ NEW AMERICAN You know a restaurant is hot when the patrons are as young and good-looking as the staff, and they certainly are here (or at least they were when I last visited). It's been named to every "Best Newcomer" list in the state, and those tributes are justified. Don't expect elegance: most of the walls are bare brick, the ceiling is exposed wood joists, and industrial lamps provide most of the lighting. There is the expected martini menu, including pineapple and white chocolate versions for those who don't like the taste of alcohol. Pizzas emerge from the brick oven at the back, delivered to the counter that surrounds it. There is as much eating as drinking going on at the steel-topped main bar, happy diners making the most of such mmm-inducing edibles as the agnolotti pasta stuffed with goat cheese and served with chewy threads of veal confit and a wilted arugula garnish.

98 Washington St. (between Broad and Main sts.). © **203/852-1088.** Reservations strongly recommended on weekends. Main courses $21–$34. AE, DC, MC, V. Daily 5–10pm (and later).

SOUTH NORWALK AFTER DARK

Several of SoNo's restaurants offer musical entertainment on weekends. **SoNo Caffeine,** mentioned above, has presented folkies, Brazilian bands, and pop singer-songwriters. The new **Black Bear Saloon,** 80 Washington St. (© **203/299-0711**), delves into karaoke and brings on cover bands of various enthusiasms, and **Shacojazz Art Café,** 21 North Main St. (© **203/853-6124**), favors jazz. **Relish,** 86 Washington St. (© **203/854-5300**), hires folksingers and related performers.

WESTPORT

After World War II, the housing crunch had young couples scouring the metropolitan area for affordable housing along the three main routes of what is now known as the Metro North transit system. Some of them wound up in this pretty village beside the Saugatuck River, several miles inland from Long Island Sound (47 miles northeast of New York City, 29 miles southwest of New Haven). Most of the new commuter class found Westport to be too far away from Manhattan (1–1½ hr. each way on the train), and it was deemed the archetype of the far-out bedroom communities that were dubbed the exurbs.

Notable for its large contingent of people in the creative crafts, primarily commercial artists, advertising copywriters, art directors, and their fellows, the town was also appealing to CEOs and higher-level executives, many of whom solved their commuting problem by moving their offices to nearby Stamford. The result is a bustling community with surviving elements of its rural New England past wrapped in a sheen of Big Apple panache.

For more information, check out www.coastalCT.com.

GETTING OUTSIDE

Sherwood Island State Park, Green Farms (✆ **203/566-2305**), has two long swimming beaches separated by a grove of trees sheltering dozens of picnic tables with grills. Surf fishing is a possibility from designated areas, and the park has concession stands, restrooms, and an amateurish "nature center." The park is open from Memorial Day to Labor Day, daily from 8am to sunset. Pets are not allowed. By car, take Exit 18 off I-95 or U.S. 1, following the road called the Sherwood Island Connector. Admission for out-of-state cars from Memorial Day to September is $10 Monday through Friday, $14 Saturday and Sunday. Cars with CT plates are charged $7 weekdays, $9 weekends.

You can get to Sherwood Island by taking a train to Westport and a taxi from the station to the park. If you don't have a car, you might prefer to use that method to get to **Compo Beach,** the long municipal strand not far from downtown.

West of the town center is **Earthplace** (formerly called the Nature Center for Environmental Activities), 10 Woodside Lane (✆ **203/227-7253;** www.earthplace.org). Its 62 acres offer several trails, a wildlife rehab center, and a building with live animals and an aquarium. Open Monday through Saturday from 9am to 5pm, Sunday from 1 to 4pm. Admission $1 adults, 50¢ for children.

The **New Canaan Nature Center,** Old Route 7 (✆ **203/966-9577**), is in Weston, north of Westport (take Rte. 7 to Old Rte. 7). With the Nature Conservancy, it overlooks the **Devil's Den Preserve,** an undeveloped tract of more than 1,700 acres in the heart of densely populated Fairfield County. It is a refuge of rare value, with 15 miles of trails beside ponds and waterways rich with birds and other wildlife. Cross-country skiing is permitted, but there are no picnic or toilet facilities. Open daily from sunrise to sunset. Admission is free, but donations are welcome.

Rent a sailboat or kayak or arrange a lesson at the **Longshore Sailing School,** Longshore Club Park, 260 S. Compo Rd. (✆ **203/226-4646**), about 2 miles south of the Boston Post Road (U.S. 1). Small boat private lessons are $65 per hour.

SHOPPING

The long Main Street has plenty of shops, but they are increasingly being taken over by national chains, Talbot's, The Gap, Brooks Brothers, Pottery Barn, and Williams-Sonoma among them. Individuality is more likely to be found in antiques shops, such as the two below.

Kocian Depasqua Antiques New to the block is this purveyor of Centennial Chippendale (late-19th-c. reproductions of earlier furniture styles), as well as various bibelots, silverware, and Staffordshire and other porcelain. 19 Post Rd. ✆ **203/227-7308.**

The Stuart Collection On the west end of the bridge over the Saugatuck is a row of fetching shops. This one trumpets its taste for dazzlingly colorful ceramics and blown glassware, most of it Italian, often from Deruta and Vietri. 11 Winter St. ✆ **203/221-7102.**

WHERE TO STAY

For some years, the luxurious **Inn at National Hall** (2 Post Rd.; ✆ **800/629-4255** or 203/221-1351) was mentioned in the same breath with only a few other Connecticut hostelries. It is still operating (at this writing) but the owner has been seeking permission to turn it into condominiums. In the meantime, room rates have not declined, with doubles from $295 to $345 and suites from $495 to $650. Your call.

The Westport Inn The building housing this motor hotel has been on the scene since 1935, and while it can't claim the style and elegance of the Inn at National Hall (above), it will likely be around a lot longer. It provides more facilities and services than most motels, including an indoor pool, laundromat, and fitness room. Wi-Fi Internet access is available in all rooms. Guests with a romantic occasion to celebrate can request a room with red satin sheets scattered with rose petals at turndown. Guests have access to the town beach and a nearby golf course. Find it east of the town center. Pets are welcome.

1595 Post Rd. E., Wesport, CT 06880. ✆ **203/259-5236.** Fax 203/254-8439. www.westportinn.com. 116 units. $169–$199 double. Rates include breakfast. AE, DC, DISC, MC, V. **Amenities:** Restaurant (steakhouse); bar; heated indoor pool, small fitness room w/sauna; 24-hr. business center; same-day dry cleaning/laundry. *In room:* A/C, TV, dataport, coffeemaker, hair dryer, iron.

WHERE TO DINE

Acqua ★ MEDITERRANEAN/SEAFOOD A light touch does wonders with immaculately fresh ingredients such as striped bass, halibut, crab, skate, and clams. Presentations are inviting, yet without the appearance of excessive pushing and prodding in the kitchen. The decor consists of murals depicting cherubim, aged-looking tiles, and a bar facing the wood-burning oven, used to bake good designer pizzas and a customer favorite, roasted chicken. Among other possibilities is the open seafood ravioli with shrimp, lobster chunks, scallops, and roasted fennel. An express lunch in the street-level bar costs only $10, and the midday menu upstairs is far less expensive than dinner.

43 Main St. (near east end of Saugatuck Bridge). ✆ **203/222-8899.** Reservations recommended on weekends. Main courses, dinner $15–$36. AE, DC, MC, V. Mon–Thurs noon–2:30pm and 5:30–9:30pm; Fri–Sat noon–2:30pm and 5:30–10:30pm.

Tavern on Main ★ AMERICAN BISTRO Westporters don't come in too many different ages, sizes, or colors, but most of them mount the Tavern's front steps with regularity. Local merchants, widows who lunch, executives, and young moms crowd into the clubby bar to wait for a table. The main room has fragments of the building's earliest 19th-century years—hand-hewn beams and a brick fireplace. While menu items are neither over-the-top nor particularly daring, the kitchen does toy with convention. For example, the trademark lobster roll consists of warm (not cool) buttery chunks and shreds of the crustacean filling the cavity of a hollowed-out, seeded roll. Similar twists are taken with house-cured duck confit, five-vegetable couscous, and potato-wrapped sea bass.

146 Main St. ✆ **203/221-7222.** Reservations recommended. Main courses, dinner $20–$29. AE, DC, MC, V. Daily 11:30am–4pm and 5:30–10pm (Fri–Sat until 11pm).

WESTPORT AFTER DARK

One of the oldest theaters on the straw-hat circuit, the **Westport Country Playhouse,** 25 Powers Ct. (✆ **203/227-4177;** www.westportplayhouse.com), had its first performance in 1931. Revitalized under the leadership of Artistic Director Joanne Woodward and other new administrators, the theater produces a full schedule of comedies, dramas, and musicals from mid-June to mid-September, with performances Monday through Saturday evenings and Wednesday and Saturday matinees. There are single-night or short-term events through the winter season, as well. Famous or at least vaguely familiar actors appear in almost every production (Ms. Woodward even persuaded her husband to appear in a production of *Our Town* that went on to Broadway). A music series brings in such diverse acts as Arlo Guthrie, the Preservation Hall Jazz Band, and doo-wop groups. Tickets are priced from about $15 to $48.

RIDGEFIELD

No town in Connecticut has a grander, more imposing main street. Ridgefield's is 132 feet wide, lined with ancient elms, maples, and oaks, and bordered by massive 19th-century houses, most of them in Classical Revival and late Victorian styles. Impressive at any time of the year, it is in its glory during the brief blaze of the October foliage season. Only a little over an hour from New York City (58 miles northeast), the town (pop. 24,000) is nonetheless a true evocation of the New England character.

WHAT TO SEE & DO

Aldrich Contemporary Art Museum ★★★ Larry Aldrich was a fashion designer who used his superb collection of paintings and sculptures from the second half of the 20th century to establish this museum. The original 18th-century clapboard structure in which he housed his collection soon doubled in size. But when Aldrich died in 2001, the museum took a sharp turn in another direction. It was decided that it would now be devoted exclusively to "emerging and mid-career artists" and to work no more than 5 years old. To that end, the original collection was almost completely sold off, and in April 2003, the museum was closed for the construction of yet another building to carry out the new mission. The angular, blazingly white, copper-roofed new structure opened in summer 2004. Set back from the road, it contains 12 galleries on two floors, a screening room, and performance spaces. It is a singular contribution to the cultural life of western Connecticut.

258 Main St. (near the intersection of Routes 35 and 33 at the south end of Main St.). ✆ **203/438-4519.** www.aldrichart.org. Admission $7 adults, $4 seniors and students, free for youths under 18; Tues free to all. Tues–Sun noon–5pm.

Keeler Tavern This 1713 stagecoach inn was providing sustenance to travelers between Boston and New York long before the Revolutionary War, but that conflict provided it with its object of greatest note. A British cannonball is imbedded in one of its walls, presumably fired during the Battle of Ridgefield in 1777. It's now a museum of Colonial life, with period furnishings and costumed guides. And the tavern has another claim to fame: It was long the summer home of architect Cass Gilbert (1849–1934), who designed the Supreme Court Building in Washington, DC, and was a key figure in the construction of the George Washington Bridge in New York. Visits are by guided tour.

132 Main St. © **203/431-0815.** Admission $5 adults, $3 seniors, $2 children under 12. Feb–Dec Wed and Sat–Sun 1–4pm.

SHOPPING

Apart from the usual antiques shops and the strip malls north of town on Route 35, **Balducci's**, 21 Governor St. (© **203/431-4400**), formerly Hay Day Market, is a good stop for devoted food lovers. Hidden in a shopping center behind Main Street, it is about as fancy a food market as exists outside of Manhattan. Sections are devoted to produce, prepared foods, baked goods, charcuterie, cheeses, and fresh flowers. It's open Monday to Saturday 8am to 8pm, and until 7pm on Sundays. There are also branches in Westport, 1385 Post Rd. (© **293/254-5400**) and Greenwich, 1050 E. Putnam Ave. (© **203/637-7600**).

WHERE TO STAY & DINE

The Elms ★ Ridgefield's oldest (1799) operating inn has the ambience of a small contemporary hotel with the conveniences most travelers desire, as well as newly decorated guest rooms with canopied beds. Included among the 20 units are five suites. All have Wi-Fi Internet access. The **dining room and tavern** ★★ (© **203/438-9206**) are in the capable hands of star chef Brendan Walsh, who administers fresh twists on regional ingredients without masking their origins. In the main dining room, Connecticut seafood stew and lobster shepherd pie are staples, and the mixed grill of lamb, venison, and sausage is a Sunday dinner fixture. The tavern serves pub grub along the lines of bangers and mash and grilled fish and chicken. Reservations are essential on weekends.

500 Main St. (Rte. 35, at the north end of town), Ridgefield, CT 06877. ©/fax **203/438-2541.** www.elmsinn.com. 20 units. $155–$215 double. Rates include in-room breakfast. AE, DC, MC, V. **Amenities:** Restaurant (New American); tavern; same-day dry cleaning; laundry. *In room:* A/C, TV, dataport, hair dryer, iron

West Lane Inn ★★ An inn that fit most images of a romantic country getaway, this one also works for businesspeople, as it offers wireless Internet access, voice mail, and express checkout. For longer stays, there are two rooms with kitchenettes. A couple of rooms have fireplaces, and all have four-poster beds. The 1849 house stands on a property blessed with giant shade trees. Take breakfast on the porch in good weather; the continental version is included, but hot a la carte dishes are extra. Snacks are available until 9pm. Bernard's (below), just across the driveway, serves lunch and dinner. The management makes a point of declaring itself gay friendly.

22 West Lane (off Rte. 35), Ridgefield, CT 06877. © **203/438-7323.** Fax 203/438-7325. www.westlaneinn.com. 18 units. $145–$190 double. Rates include breakfast. AE, DC, DISC, MC, V. Driving north from Wilton on Rte. 33, turn west on Rte. 35 at the edge of town. **Amenities:** Concierge; limited room service; laundry service; dry cleaning. *In room:* A/C, TV/VCR, dataport, fridge, coffeemaker, hair dryer.

WHERE TO DINE

Bernard's ★ FRENCH A piano in the main dining parlor is played Friday and Saturday nights and for the festive Sunday brunch, but the primary interests of the owners clearly lie in the kitchen. Imagine galette of snails with wild mushrooms, salsify, fava beans, and a parsley coulis! Main courses are about 50-50 land- and ocean-based proteins. Among the most successful are roasted monkfish *osso buco* wrapped in rosemary pancetta and the venison chop and medallion with spaetzel and braised cabbage. Several dinner choices appear as half-priced versions at lunch, but the romance of music and flickering lights is reserved for evenings.

20 West Lane (near the junction with Rte. 7). ✆ **203/438-8282.** Reservations recommended on weekends. Main courses $26–$32. AE, DC, MC, V. Tues–Fri noon–2:30pm and 6–9pm; Sat 6–10pm; Sun noon–2:30pm and 5–8pm.

2 The Litchfield Hills ★★

When the Hamptons got too pricey, too visible, and too chichi back in the 1980s, a lot of stockbrokers, CEOs, and celebs started discovering the Litchfield Hills, arguably the most fetchingly rustic yet still sophisticated part of Connecticut.

The topography and, to an extent, the microculture of the region are defined by the river that runs through it, the Housatonic. Broad but not deep enough for vessels larger than canoes, it waters farms and villages and forests along its course, provides opportunities for recreational angling and float trips, and, over the millennia, has helped to shape these foothills, which merge with the Massachusetts Berkshires.

Men in overalls and CAT caps still stand on the porches of general stores, their breath steaming in the bracing autumn air. Churches hold pancake-breakfast fundraisers; neighbors squabble about development. That's one side of these bucolic hills, less than 2 hours from Times Square.

Increasingly, the other side is fashioned by refugees from New York. These chic seekers of tranquillity and real estate fled to pre-Revolutionary saltboxes and Georgian Colonials on Litchfield's warren of back roads and brought Manhattan-bred expectations with them. Boutiques fragrant with designer coffees and cachets opened in spaces once occupied by luncheonettes and feed stores. Restaurants discovered sushi and sun-dried tomatoes and just how much money they could get away with charging the newcomers.

Compromises and city-country conflicts aside, the Litchfield Hills remain a satisfying all-season destination for day trips and overnights from metropolitan New York and Connecticut.

ESSENTIALS

GETTING THERE From New York City, take the Hutchinson River Parkway to I-684 north to I-84 east, taking Exit 7 onto Route 7 north. Continue on Route 7 for New Milford, Kent, West Cornwall, and Canaan. For Washington Depot, New Preston, and Litchfield, branch off onto Route 202 at New Milford. An especially attractive entrance into the region is Route 44 from the Taconic Parkway, through Millerton and into Lakeville and Salisbury.

From Boston, take the Massachusetts Turnpike west to the Lee exit, picking up Route 7 south from nearby Stockbridge.

VISITOR INFORMATION The useful 40-page *Unwind* brochure is produced by the **Litchfield Hills Visitors Bureau** (✆ **860/567-4506;** fax 860/567-5214; www.litchfieldhills.com). Also see www.housatonic.org and www.litchfieldcty.com.

NEW MILFORD

A gateway to the Litchfield Hills, New Milford was founded in 1703 and functions as a commercial center for the smaller villages that surround it—Roxbury, Bridgewater,

Washington, and Brookfield. It is also at the high end of a long stretch of overdeveloped Route 7, which is clogged with strip malls.

New Milford is a welcome stop on the drive north, if only for lunch and a short stroll. Turn right on Route 202 where it splits from Route 7 and crosses the Housatonic River and a railroad track. Up on the left is one end of the long town green. A 1902 fire destroyed many of the buildings around the green, so this isn't one of those picture-book New England settings. Rather, it is a mix of late Victoriana, early Greek Revival, and Eisenhower-era architecture, not to ignore the requisite Congregational church.

Otherwise, there are no obligatory sights, so a walk down Bank Street, west of the green and along Railroad Street, with its crafts shops, a bookstore, and an Art Moderne movie house, won't take long.

GETTING OUTSIDE

Candlewood Lake (✆ **860/354-6928**) is the third-largest man-made lake in the eastern United States. It has a finger that pokes into New Milford, but the area with the most recreational facilities is a few miles to the west. From New Milford, drive north on Route 7 about 2½ miles, turn west on Route 37 toward and through Sherman, then south on Route 39 to **Squantz Pond State Park** (✆ **203/797-4165**). With over 170 acres along the lakeshore, it offers swimming, ice-skating, fishing, hiking and cycling trails, picnic grounds, rental canoes, and a boat launch.

WHERE TO DINE

There are many dining choices along Bank and Railroad streets and out on nearby Route 7.

The Cookhouse ★ BARBECUE Inexplicably, Connecticut is home to some thumping-good barbecue joints. This is the current champ. It's set, appropriately enough, in a converted barn on often-tacky Route 7. Ribs, chicken, pulled pork, and beef brisket are slow-smoked for 10 hours or more. Heaping portions come with sides such as baked beans, collard greens, and mashed potatoes. Separate menu categories list grills, fish, and "comfort foods," the last including burritos, fajitas, macaroni and cheese, and chicken-fried steak. But go for the 'cue.

31 Danbury Rd. (Rte. 7). ✆ **860/355-4111.** Main courses $17–$26. AE, DC, MC, V. Daily 11:30am–10pm (Fri–Sat until 11pm, Sun until 9pm).

WOODBURY ★

The chief distinction of this attractive town strung along Route 6, west of Waterbury, is its number of high-end antiques stores. On weekends in good weather, the main road is clogged with cars trolling for treasures, and progress can be slow.

ANTIQUING

Shoppers are drawn here for antiques and collectibles of every sort, from funky to obscure to elegant. To winnow down the list, pick up the directory produced by the **Woodbury Antiques Dealers Association** (www.antiqueswoodbury.com) at one of the member stores.

Start off in the building at 289 Main St., at the intersection of Routes 6 and 317, which contains **Jennings & Rohn Antiques** (✆ **203/263-3775**). European paintings and furnishings from the 16th century to 1960 are on view, as well as lighting fixtures and some Art Deco. At **Martell & Suffin Antiques** (✆ **203/263-1913**), the owners favor 18th- and early-19th-century European furniture as well as Asian works of art.

The Litchfield Hills

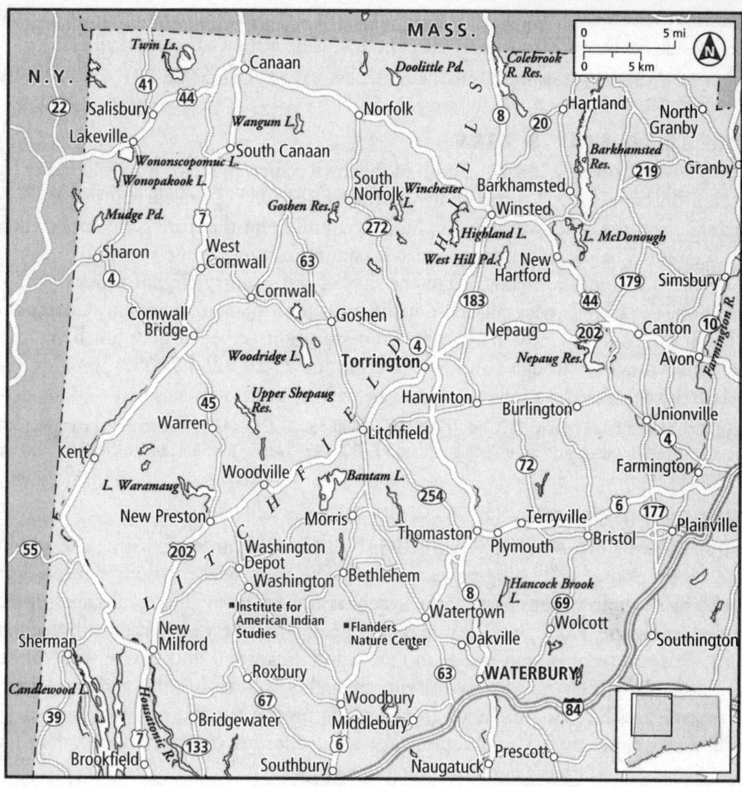

Drive south on Main Street (Rte. 6) to the notable **Wayne Pratt Antiques,** 346 Main St. (✆ **203/263-5676**), which specializes in 18th-century American furniture, much of it museum-level Chippendale and Queen Anne pieces. Some items are within reach for the rest of us, like the Chinese porcelain boxes for $12.

Of similar high order are the offerings at **Country Loft Antiques,** 557 Main St. (✆ **203/266-4500**), largely 19th-century French furnishings and *objets* displayed in a fine old barn. Wares run from biscuit tins to armoires, bolts of fabric to 18th-century dining tables. Be sure to look into the basement, outfitted as a wine cellar.

On most Saturdays in decent weather, the **Woodbury Antiques & Flea Market** (✆ **203/263-2841**) sets up in a parking lot at the south end of town.

WHAT TO SEE & DO

Flanders Nature Center North of Woodbury on Route 6, watch for Flanders Road forking to the left. Three miles along, on the right, is the office building for this 1,400-acre nature center. Yearly events include maple syrup and wreath making, along with a fall festival. Maps of hiking trails are available.

Church Hill and Flanders Rd. ✆ **203/263-3711**. Free admission. Office Mon–Fri 9am–5pm; trails daily dawn–dusk.

Glebe House About the only scrap of surviving history worth mentioning in town is this 1750 house of an Episcopal bishop, west of Route 6 on a street of fine 18th-century houses. A *glebe* was a property given to a preacher as partial compensation for his services. Inside are furnishings true to the period; outside is the Gertrude Jekyll Garden.

Hollow Rd. ✆ **203/263-2855.** www.glebehouse.org. Admission $5 adults, $2 children 6–12. Apr–Oct Wed–Sun 1–4pm; Nov Sat–Sun 1–4pm.

WHERE TO STAY & DINE

Longwood Country Inn ★ South of the town center, this 2-century-old house has been a B&B since 1951, once known as Merryvale. One of the current owners is an architect and the other worked in fashion, accounting for the spare good taste evident throughout. The considerably upgraded accommodations include room no. 3, with a four-poster bed and a fireplace, and the smaller but country-elegant room no. 2. In addition, the owners have pushed out the walls for a 48-seat restaurant, **Coriander.** The food is contemporary in aspiration and execution, served at both lunch and dinner from Tuesday through Saturday (reservations ✆ **203/263-7005**). Smoking and pets aren't permitted, and children must be over 10 years old.

1204 Main St. (Rte. 6), Woodbury, CT 06798. ✆ **203/266-0800.** Fax 203/263-4479. www.longwoodcountryinn.com. 5 units. $135–$250 double. Rates include breakfast. AE, DC, MC, V. **Amenities:** Restaurant (creative American). *In room:* A/C, TV.

WHERE TO DINE

Good News Café ★★ NEW AMERICAN This is a fun spot, with a cheery staff and rooms doused in blazing primary colors. The food? Make it Europe meets Asia, touching down in various parts of the Americas along the way. The results are spirited, but never bizarre. Examples: Venison filet mignon with celery root, caramelized chestnuts, Brussels sprouts, and pears, and an "adult" macaroni and cheese with lobster chunks and Swiss chard. Most of the entrees qualify as heart-healthy, and ingredients, whenever possible, are purchased from local farmers. Desserts, however, tend to be rich, gooey, and caloric—apple spice cake is splediforous. Saturday nights often feature live jazz, and there's outdoor dining in summer.

694 Main St. (Rte. 6). ✆ **203/266-4663.** Reservations recommended on weekends. Main courses $17–$30. AE, DC, MC, V. Wed–Mon 11:30am–10pm.

WASHINGTON ★★ & WASHINGTON DEPOT

Settled in 1734, its name changed in 1779 to honor the first American president, Washington occupies the crown of a hill beside Route 47. Its village green, with the impressive 1802 Congregational Meeting House surrounded by white buildings and sheltered by shade trees, is an example of a municipal arrangement found all over New England—but rarely to such near-perfection.

Adjacent Washington Depot, down the hill beside the Shepaug River, serves as the commercial center, with a bank and a small cluster of shops. Stop in at the beguiling **Hickory Stick Bookshop,** 2 Greenhill Rd. (✆ **860/868-0525**).

Nearby **Steep Rock Reservation** (✆ **860/868-9131**) is a lovely spot for hiking, fly-fishing, or cross-country skiing. (Unfortunately for pet owners, dogs must now be leashed.)

Institute for American Indian Studies A worthwhile detour takes drivers down Curtis Road to this small repository of Native American crafts and artifacts. They are presented with sensitivity and, for the most part, without polemics. Down a nearby path is a re-creation of an Algonquian village. There's a picnic area on the grounds.

38 Curtis Rd. (off Rte. 199). ✆ **860/868-0518.** www.birdstone.org. Admission $4 adults, $3.50 seniors, $2 children 6–16. Mon–Sat 10am–5pm; Sun noon–5pm (closed Mon–Tues Jan–Mar).

WHERE TO STAY & DINE

Mayflower Inn ★★ Galaxies of stars have already been scattered in abundance over this, one of the state's courtliest manor inns. While the main building is almost entirely new, some elements survive from the original 1894 structure, the most delightful of which is the richly paneled library. Porches look out across manicured lawns to deep woods. Most bedrooms have fireplaces, the bathrooms are done with tapestry rugs and mahogany wainscoting—all is as close to perfection as such an enterprise is likely to be, *almost* justifying the breathtaking prices. The clientele can't be described as youthful.

The accomplished restaurant features top-drawer ingredients drawn from New England producers and Atlantic fisheries. Execution can be uneven. Perhaps needless to say, the cellar is extensive, meticulously chosen, and pricey.

118 Woodbury Rd. (Rte. 47), Washington, CT 06793. ✆ **860/868-9466.** Fax 860/868-1497. www.mayflowerinn.com. 25 units. $400–$640 double; $700–$1,300 suite. AE, MC, V. Take Rte. 202 north 2 miles past New Preston, turn south on Rte. 47 through Washington Depot and up the hill past Washington Common. The entrance is on the left. Children over 12 welcome. **Amenities:** Restaurant (eclectic); pub; heated outdoor pool; nearby golf course; tennis court; extensive health club; sauna; bike rental; massage; same-day dry cleaning/laundry. *In room:* A/C, TV w/pay movies, fax, dataport, minibar, hair dryer.

WHERE TO DINE

One dining option is the restaurant at the **Mayflower Inn** (see above). For a more casual meal, put together a picnic from the delectable array of quiches, pizzas, and salads at **The Pantry,** 5 Titus Rd., Washington Depot (✆ **860/868-0258**).

G. W. Tavern ★ ECLECTIC AMERICAN The tavern's atmospheric bar has booths and a fireplace, while the simulated attached barn is airier, with a deck that looks down on the Shepaug River. The kitchen is dedicated to interpretations of such robust Americana as crab cakes, meatloaf, chicken potpie, and fish and chips. Daily specials nearly outnumber the items on the regular menu (plus a short card of lighter fare 2:30–5:30pm). It is all quite satisfying, if hardly revelatory. Weekend brunches are popular, as is live jazz Thursday evenings, blues on Mondays. and a variety of rock, pop, and folk performers on weekends. Find the tavern a block north of the Washington Depot shopping center.

20 Bee Brook Rd. (Rte. 47). ✆ **860/868-6633.** Main courses $9.75–$32. AE, MC, V. Daily 11:30am–10pm (Fri–Sat until 11pm).

NEW PRESTON & LAKE WARAMAUG ★★

Never more than a few houses and retailers at the junction of two country roads, the hamlet of New Preston long served primarily as a supplier for locals and, starting in the mid–19th century, the families who summered on nearby Lake Waramaug. More recently, New Preston's small grocery and hardware stores have been converted to antiques emporia of high order, and they find themselves surrounded on weekends by BMWs and Volvos.

EXPLORING THE LAKE WARAMAUG AREA

At the northwest tip of the L-shaped lake, 95-acre **Lake Waramaug State Park** ★, Lake Waramaug Road (✆ **860/868-0220**), gives the public access to a beautiful body of water that is otherwise monopolized by the private homes and inns that border it. Canoes and paddle boats are for rent, and there's a swimming beach as well as picnic tables, food concessions, and a total of almost 80 camping and RV sites.

Hopkins Vineyard A former dairy farm on a promontory above Lake Waramaug was converted into a vineyard and winery in 1979. Headquartered in a 19th-century barn across the street from the Hopkins Inn (see "Where to Stay & Dine," below), it produces about a dozen bottlings. They won't make anyone forget the Napa Valley, but prices are fair. Overlooking the lake is a wine bar, where selections of pâtés and cheese can accompany samples of the primary product.

25 Hopkins Rd. ✆ **860/868-7954.** www.hopkinsvineyard.com. Jan–Feb Sat–Sun 10am–5pm; Mar–Apr Wed–Sat 10am–5pm, Sun 11am–5pm; May–Dec Mon–Sat 10am–5pm, Sun 11am–5pm.

SHOPPING

In no time, the intersecting streets that form the center of the village have gone from sleepy to spiffy. Notable among the shops is **J. Seitz & Co.,** Main Street/East Shore Road (✆ **860/868-0119**), featuring bedding, bath products, and clothing of silk, velvet, cashmere, and suede. Two doors over is **New Preston Kitchen Goods,** 11 East Shore Rd. (✆ **860/868-1264**), selling a wide variety of what you think.

WHERE TO STAY & DINE

The Boulders ★★ This once rustic lakeside inn, with a private swimming beach, has scrambled steadily upward in both price and quality. With its sale for $4.3 million in 2002, it took a great leap. The outlying "guesthouses"—four buildings with two spacious units each plus a new carriage house—enjoy private decks, fireplaces, Jacuzzis, and refrigerators. These have contemporary furnishings, while the tone of the bedrooms in the 1895 main house is set by a massive stone fireplace, an elkhorn chandelier, and country antiques and reproductions. Drinks at the handsome bar or in the large sitting room precede dinner in the main dining room or on the porch, all with lake views. A serious wine cellar complements the acclaimed cuisine, based on seasonal and local ingredients. Smoking isn't permitted.

E. Shore Rd. (Rte. 45), New Preston, CT 06777. ✆ **800/552-6853** or 860/868-0541. Fax 860/868-1925. www.bouldersinn.com. 20 units. $350–$425 double. Rates include breakfast, Sunday brunch, and afternoon tea. AE, DISC, MC, V. Drive north from New Preston about 2 miles on Rte. 45. No pets. No children under 12. **Amenities:** Restaurant (New American); golf course nearby; tennis court; spa; small fitness room; lake swimming; free canoes and rowboats; game room; limited room service; in-room massage. *In room:* A/C, TV/DVD/CD, dataport, hair dryer.

Hopkins Inn A family named Hopkins started farming this land in 1787, and its descendants turned the farm into a vineyard and winery in 1979. The farmhouse sits atop a hill with the best views of Lake Waramaug. Food is the main event, since most of the guest rooms are on the spartan side, with phones and TV only in the two-bedroom suite in the annex. Dishes from the Swiss and Austrian Alps are served in hefty portions, with Wiener schnitzel and trout bleu among the options. The restaurant is closed from January to late March, but breakfast is still served to overnight guests. No smoking.

22 Hopkins Rd., New Preston, CT 06777. ✆ **860/868-7295.** Fax 860/868-7464. www.thehopkinsinn.com. 13 units, 11 with private bathroom. $95–$170 double. AE, DISC, MC, V. From New Preston, take Rte. 45 north about 2½ miles and look for the sign on the left. **Amenities:** Restaurant (contemporary Austrian). *In room:* A/C.

LITCHFIELD ★★

Possessed of a long common with stately trees reconfigured around the turn of the 20th century by the Frederick Law Olmsted landscaping firm (Olmstead designed New York's Central Park), Litchfield is testimony to the taste and affluence of the Yankee entrepreneurs who built it up in the late 18th and early 19th centuries from a Colonial farm community to an industrial center. The factories and mills were dismantled toward the end of the 19th century, and the men who built them settled back to enjoy their riches in their uncommonly large homes.

In recent decades, the town has been discovered by fashionable New Yorkers, who find it less frenetic than the Hamptons. Their influence is seen both in the quality of store merchandise and restaurant fare, as well as in the lofty prices houses command.

A WALK THROUGH HISTORY

Litchfield's houses and tree-lined streets reward leisurely strollers. From the stores and restaurants along West Street, walk east (to the right when facing the common), and then turn right on South Street. On the opposite corner is the recently expanded **Litchfield History Museum,** at South and East streets (✆ **860/567-4501**), containing an eclectic array of local historical artifacts, including the world's largest collection of works by the 18th-century portraitist Ralph Earl. It's open from April to mid-November, Tuesday through Saturday from 11am to 5pm and Sunday from 1 to 5pm. Admission is $5 for adults, $3 for seniors, and free for children under 14; includes admission to the Tapping Reeve House.

Walking down South Street, on the right, are the **Tapping Reeve House and Law School** (✆ **860/567-4501**). One of the few historic houses regularly open to the public, the Reeve house was built in 1773, while the adjacent 1784 building was the earliest American law school, established before independence. It counted among its students Aaron Burr and Noah Webster. Hours are the same as those of the Litchfield History Museum, which maintains it; one ticket buys admission to both museums.

When the street starts to peter out into more modern houses, walk back toward the common and cross over to the north side. Over here on the right is the magisterial **First Congregational Church,** built in 1828. Turn left, then right on North Street, where the domestic architecture matches the quiet splendor of South Street.

NEARBY ATTRACTIONS

Haight Vineyard Chardonnays and merlots don't spring to mind as likely Connecticut products, but this winery established in 1978 has grown and prospered, presently offering 11 drinkable bottlings. The tasting room is open year-round. It's east of town, off Route 118. There's a second winery in Mystic.

29 Chestnut Hill Rd. ✆ **860/567-4045.** Mon–Sat 10:30am–5pm; Sun noon–5pm.

GETTING OUTSIDE

The **White Memorial Foundation,** Route 202 (✆ **860/567-0857;** www.whitememorialcc.org), is a 4,000-acre wildlife sanctuary and nature conservancy about 3 miles southwest of Litchfield. It has campsites and 35 miles of trails for hiking, cross-country skiing, and horseback riding. On the grounds is a small museum of natural history. The Holbrook Bird Observatory looks out on a landscape specifically planted to attract birds. The museum is open year-round, Monday through Saturday from 9am to 5pm and Sunday from noon to 4pm. Admission is $4 for adults, $2 for children 6 to 12.

This is horse country, so consider a canter across the meadows and along the wooded trails of **Topsmead State Forest,** Buell Road (✆ **860/567-5694**). The park has a wildlife preserve and a Tudor-style mansion that can be toured the second and fourth weekends of each month from June to October. To get here, follow Route 118 for a mile east of town. The grounds are open from 8am to sunset. Horses can be hired nearby at **Lee's Riding Stable,** 57 East Litchfield Rd., off Route 118 (✆ **860/567-0785**).

SHOPPING

Most of the interesting shops are in the row of late-19th-century brick buildings on the south side of the town green. One such is **Kitchenworks,** 23 West St. (✆ **860/567-5011**) with a good selection of cookware and tableware, as well as some non-culinary gifts. Nearby is **Litchfield Gourmet,** 33 West St. (✆ **860/567-4882**), selling quality baked goods, ice cream, smoothies, espresso, and sandwiches at separate stations. Tables are available. Around the corner and down a few steep stairs is **Bella Cosa,** corner of West and South streets (✆ **860/567-4606**), purveyors of exemplary hand-painted Italian ceramics, pottery, and table linens.

WHERE TO STAY & DINE

Toll Gate Hill Inn ★ The centerpiece of this red-barn complex is a 1745 structure known as the Captain William Bull Tavern in the National Register of Historic Places. It houses the bar and restaurant, and it's as atmospheric as all get out, with random-width floors and walls, a marvelously worn old bar with a fireplace inglenook, and two dining rooms. New owners had to bring the kitchen up to code before turning their attention to the bedrooms in the newer outlying buildings. Do inspect your room before accepting it, for there are substantial variations in size and configuration. Wi-Fi Internet access is standard at no extra charge. Children and well-behaved pets are welcome.

With relatively few local options, the rejuvenated **restaurant** ★★ was instantly in demand, not least because of a chef who has put in years manning stoves from Asia to Europe. He conjures up such delights as barbecued pork crostini with crayfish aioli on polenta teacakes. His domain is open Wednesday through Saturday for lunch and dinner, for brunch and dinner on Sunday.

571 Torrington Rd. (Rte. 202), Litchfield, CT 06759. ✆ **866/567-1233** or 860/567-1233. Fax 860/567-1230. www.tollgatehill.com. 20 units. $95–$170 double. Rates include breakfast. AE, DC, MC, V. **Amenities:** Restaurant (international); bar. *In room:* A/C, TV.

WHERE TO DINE

West Street Grill ★ NEW AMERICAN When this contemporary bistro opened well over a decade ago, it was showered with stars by local and big-city reviewers. Known as an incubator for some of Connecticut's best chefs, several of whom went off to open their own places, it hasn't always merited the raves. But despite several important changes, the restaurant's fortunes have more often waxed than waned, and continue on an upswing following the hiring of a CIA-trained chef. Entrees tend toward fusion renditions of meats, poultry, and fish, and portions are substantial. It remains the trendiest spot for miles, some of its patrons bearing familiar faces from TV and newspapers.

43 West St. (on the Green). ✆ **860/567-3885.** Reservations recommended for dinner, essential on weekends. Main courses $19–$35. AE, MC, V. Mon–Thurs 11:30am–3pm and 5:30–9pm; Fri–Sat 11:30am–4pm and 5:30–10:30pm.

KENT

A prominent prep school of the same name, a history as an iron-smelting center, and a continuing reputation as a gathering place of artists and writers define this town of fewer than 2,000. Noted 19th-century landscape painter George Inness helped establish that assessment, and several galleries represent the works of his creative descendants. They are joined by a multiplicity of antiques shops and bookstores, most of them strung along Route 7. South of town on the same road is the hamlet of Bull's Bridge, named for one of the two remaining covered bridges in the state that can be crossed by cars.

Talk of the town is the recent federal recognition of the barely viable Schaghticoke (SKAT-a-cokes) Indian tribe. Ten members occupy a 400-acre reservation next to the prestigious Kent School. It is the fourth tribe in Connecticut to receive formal sovereignty, and controversy is rife locally over what it might do with that status. The prospect of yet another casino looms.

A super-sweet local landmark is **Belgique,** 1 Bridge St. (© **860/927-3681**), which gained rapturous reviews when it was a restaurant. Unhappily, the chef-owner tired of the workload, and turned the dining room into a catering operation. All was not lost, for he then focused on his calling as chocolatier and pastry chef. Stop in for a superb hot chocolate and examine glass cases full of the most delicate and creative tarts, cakes, mousses, chocolates, and other confections to have passed your teeth. There are freshly baked baguettes and croissants, too.

Four miles northeast of Kent is **Kent Falls State Park,** on Route 7 (© **860/927-3238**). Its centerpiece, a 250-foot cascade, is clearly visible from the road, and picnic tables are set about the grounds. A path mounts the hill beside the falls. Restrooms are available. A parking fee of $10 per out-of-state car ($7 per Connecticut car) is charged on weekends and holidays between June and October.

WEST CORNWALL

Not to be confused with Cornwall, 4 miles to the southeast, nor with Cornwall Bridge, 7 miles to the south, this tiny village is best known for its picturesque covered bridge, one of only two in the state that still permits the passage of cars. The bridge connects Routes 7 and 128, crossing the Housatonic. With a state forest to the north and a state park to its immediate south, West Cornwall enjoys a piney seclusion that remains welcoming to passersby.

Housatonic Meadows State Park, on Route 7 (© **860/672-6772** in summer, or 860/927-3238 the rest of the year), is comprised of 452 acres bordering both sides of the Housatonic River immediately south of West Cornwall. With 95 campsites, it offers access to fishing, canoeing, picnicking, and cross-country skiing. **Housatonic Anglers,** Route 7 (© **860/672-4457;** www.housatonicanglers.com), offers float trips, fly-fishing schools, and guided fishing trips.

Just outside Cornwall proper, off Route 4, is **Mohawk Mountain Ski Area,** 46 Great Hollow Rd. (© **800/895-5222** or 860/672-6100; www.mohawkmtn.com). "Mountain" is an overstatement, but this is the state's oldest ski resort, with five lifts, 23 trails, snowmakers, and night skiing. All-day lift tickets are $42 for adults, $22 for night skiing (6–10pm). Skis and snowboards are available for rent.

WHERE TO DINE

The Wandering Moose Café *Value* AMERICAN With more prior incarnations than most people can remember, this location has been serving food of one quality or another for decades. These days, the emphasis on comforting, familiar, and well-prepared meals leaves little room for innovation. Pizza can be topped with some less-usual—but hardly startling—toppings such as scallops, jalapeños, and artichoke hearts. Almond-crusted trout, beef stroganoff, and crab cakes are some of the best bets. Count on clam chowder, burgers, nachos, and baby back ribs, too. Most of it is quite affordable, ensuring that locals of all ages make it their HQ.

Rte. 128 (east end of the covered bridge). © **860/672-0178.** Main courses $15–$26. MC, V. Mon–Tues 6:30am–2pm; Wed–Fri 6:30am–3pm and 5:30–9pm; Sat 8am–3pm and 5:30–9pm; Sun 8am–4pm and 5–8pm.

SHARON

This hamlet near the New York border is primarily residential, a picturesque village with many houses made of brick or fieldstone in a region where wood-frame houses prevail.

Sharon Audubon Center The 2,000-acre nature preserve has gardens, a shop and interpretive center, and 11 miles of trails. Injured birds are brought to the center for rehabilitation, and there are usually some recuperating raptors and other animals in house.

Rte. 4. ✆ **860/364-0520.** Trails $3 adults, $1.50 seniors and children under 12. Main building Tues–Sat 9am–5pm, Sun 1–5pm; grounds dawn–dusk.

LAKEVILLE & SALISBURY

These two attractive villages share a main street lined with 19th-century houses stretching along Route 44. The "lake" in question is Wononscopomuc, slightly south of the town center.

The discovery in the area of a particularly pure iron ore led to the development of mines and forges as early as the mid-1700s. One of the ironworkers was the eccentric Ethan Allen, later to become the leader of the Green Mountain Boys and a hero for his capture of Fort Ticonderoga from the British in 1775.

Holley-Williams House One wealthy forge owner, John Milton Holley, bought a 1768 mansion and doubled its size in 1808. The result is a Federal and Greek Revival mix. It contains furnishings assembled by Holley and his descendants over the 173 years the family lived there. There were a lot of them—the outhouse has seven holes.

15 Millerton Rd. (Rte. 44). ✆ **860/435-2878.** Free admission; guided tours $3 adults, $2 seniors and students, free for children under 5. Late June to Labor Day Sat–Sun and holidays noon–5pm.

WHERE TO STAY

Interlaken Inn ★ Guest rooms here are divided among five buildings, including Sunnyside, with a B&B feel; Main, with its pleasant-enough double rooms; and the Townhouse Suites, fully equipped with washer/dryers, fireplaces, and kitchens. Room sizes and styles vary, so be clear about your needs before booking. For a splurge, consider the Woodside building's Executive Suite, complete with two TV/VCRs, a granite bathroom, and French doors opening out to a private patio with hot tub. Pets are allowed in some units ($10 per night).

74 Interlaken Rd. (Rte. 112), Lakeville, CT 06039. ✆ **800/222-2909** or 860/435-9878. Fax 860/435-2980. www.interlakeninn.com. 82 units. $139–$249 double; from $269 suite. Packages available. AE, MC, V. **Amenities:** Restaurant (New American); bar; outdoor pool; nearby golf course; 2 tennis courts; health club; 2 saunas; canoes, paddle boats, kayaks, and rowboats; game room; business center; limited room service; massage and facials by reservation; babysitting. *In room:* A/C, TV/VCR, dataport, coffeemaker, hair dryer, iron.

White Hart ★ This inn's fortunes have fluctuated in its 180-plus years, but the white-clapboard lodging at the end of Salisbury's main street is continuing its recent rise without a bump. The front porch is a prime summertime perch. Apart from the three suites and the large Ford Room, most of the guest rooms are on the small side. Both the dining rooms and the wine cellar have received excellent notices. Rates have remained stable for some time. VCRs and fridges are available for rent.

Village Green (P.O. Box 545), Salisbury, CT 06068. ✆ **800/832-0041** or 860/435-0030. Fax 860/435-0040. www.whitehartinn.com. 26 units. $120–$295 double. AE, DC, DISC, MC, V. Pets allowed ($10). **Amenities:** Restaurant (New American); cafe; bar. *In room:* A/C, TV, hair dryer.

WHERE TO DINE

You may also want to consider a meal at the **White Hart,** reviewed above.

West Main ★ FUSION The team that started out together in a more modest setting in Sharon picked up and moved here a few years ago. This is a far more attractive venue, with the big beams and old stones of a former barn fitted out with a striking fireplace and what they claim is the longest bar in the state. Such items as summer rolls with sesame-chile-mustard sauce, sensational frites with aioli, and spicy Shandong noodles have caused a lot of *ooh*ing and cross-table sampling. Live jazz is featured most Thursdays and some Friday evenings.

8 Holley Place, Lakeville. ✆ **860/435-1450.** Main courses $17–$24. AE, MC, V. Wed–Mon 5:30–9pm (Fri–Sat until 10pm). Closed 2 weeks in Mar and 2 weeks in Nov.

NORFOLK

Founded in 1758, Norfolk (pronounced NOR-fork) was long popular as a vacation destination for industrialists who owned mills and factories along Connecticut's rivers. At the very least, drive into the center for a look at the village green. It is highlighted by a monument that involved the participation of two of the late 19th century's most celebrated creative people—sculptor Augustus Saint-Gaudens and architect Stanford White.

At the opposite corner is the 90-year-old "Music Shed," the venue for an eagerly awaited series of summer events, the **Norfolk Chamber Music Festival** ★ (✆ **860/542-3000;** www.yale.edu/norfolk). Held from July to August, it hosts performances by such luminaries as the Tokyo String Quartet and the Vermeer Quartet.

Two prime recreational areas are near each other on Route 272, north of town. A mile from the village green is **Haystack Mountain State Park,** Route 272 (✆ **860/482-1817**). Its chief feature is a short trail leading to a 3-story stone tower at the 1,715-foot crest. On clear days, the views from the top take in a panorama stretching from the Catskill Mountains to Long Island Sound.

Another 5 miles farther north, on the Massachusetts border, you can enjoy the abundant streams, rapids, and cascades at **Campbell Falls,** Route 272 (✆ **860/482-1817**). Fishing, hiking, and picknicking are all possibilities.

WHERE TO STAY

Manor House ★ This gabled 1898 manse doesn't fit into a stylistic cubbyhole; just call it "Late Victorian Bavarian Tudor." Inside, it manages to be both stately and homey, with authentic Tiffany windows and fireplaces in the main salon, dining room, and four bedrooms. The most desirable rooms are on the second floor, notably the English Room, with a king-size bed, and the Lincoln Room, with a half-canopied antique queen-size bed. The least expensive room is on the third floor, tucked under the eaves—when even the owner says the room is very small, believe it.

69 Maple Ave., Norfolk, CT 06058. ✆ **860/542-5690.** Fax 860/542-5690. www.manorhouse-norfolk.com. 9 units. $130–$255 double. Rates include breakfast. AE, DISC, MC, V. *In room:* No phone.

3 New Haven

While New Haven suffers the generalized afflictions of many of Connecticut's cities—nearly a quarter of its citizens live at or below the poverty line—there has been a noticeable uptick in attitude in recent years, a palpable sense that things are getting better. All along, the city has had much to offer the leisure traveler: several performing-arts centers and theaters, outstanding museums, autumnal renewals of college football rivalries that date back over 120 years, and a growing number of notable restaurants.

Much of what is worthwhile about New Haven can be credited to the presence of one of the world's most prestigious universities. Yale both enriches its community and exacerbates the usual town-gown conflicts—a paradox with which the institution and civic authorities have struggled since the Colonial period.

Relatively little serious history has happened here, but there are a number of "firsts" that boosters love to trumpet. Yale awarded the first Doctor of Medicine degree in 1729 to a man who never practiced medicine. Noah Webster compiled his first dictionary here, Eli Whitney perfected his cotton gin, and a local man named Colt invented a revolver in 1836. The first telephone switchboard was made here, necessitated by a Reverend John E. Todd, who was the first person in the world to request telephone service. And, the first hamburger was allegedly made and sold here, as was—even less certainly—the first pizza.

ESSENTIALS

GETTING THERE Interstate 95 between New York and Providence skirts the shoreline of New Haven; I-91 from Springfield, MA, and Hartford ends here. Connections can also be made from the south along the Merritt and Wilbur Cross parkways. Downtown traffic isn't too congested, except at the usual rush hours, and there are ample parking lots and garages near the Green and Yale University, where most visitors spend their time.

Tweed–New Haven Airport (✆ **203/466-8888**) primarily handles commuter and charter traffic, as well as feeder flights of **US Air Express** (✆ **800/428-4322**). It's located southeast of the city, near Exits 50 and 51 off I-95.

Amtrak (✆ **800/USA-RAIL;** www.amtrak.com) has several trains daily that run between Boston and New York and stop in New Haven. To or from New York takes 1½ hours; to or from Boston, about 3 hours. **Metro North** (✆ **800/638-7646** or 212/532-4900; www.mta.nyc.ny.us/mnr) commuter trains make many daily trips between New Haven and New York. Metro North tickets are much cheaper than Amtrak's, but its trains take longer.

VISITOR INFORMATION The **Greater New Haven Convention & Visitors Bureau** (✆ **203/777-8550**) maintains an office at 169 Orange St. Downtown, **INFO New Haven,** at 1000 Chapel St. (✆ **203/773-9494;** www.infonewhaven.com), is open daily, all year. In addition to stocks of useful brochures, attendants can make theater and restaurant reservations and there is a computer terminal at which visitors can check their e-mail.

A bus designed to resemble an electric trolley makes a circuit of downtown, with frequent stops outside important attractions. In operation from 11am to 6pm Monday through Saturday, it passes along its fixed route every 15 or 20 minutes. At this writing it is free, but check before boarding or call the **New Haven Trolley Line** (✆ **203/288-6282**).

SPECIAL EVENTS Important events are the new **International Festival of Arts & Ideas** (www.artidea.org), held at many sites around the city in late June, and a free **jazz festival** on the Green from late July to early August. Call INFO New Haven for dates and details.

New Haven

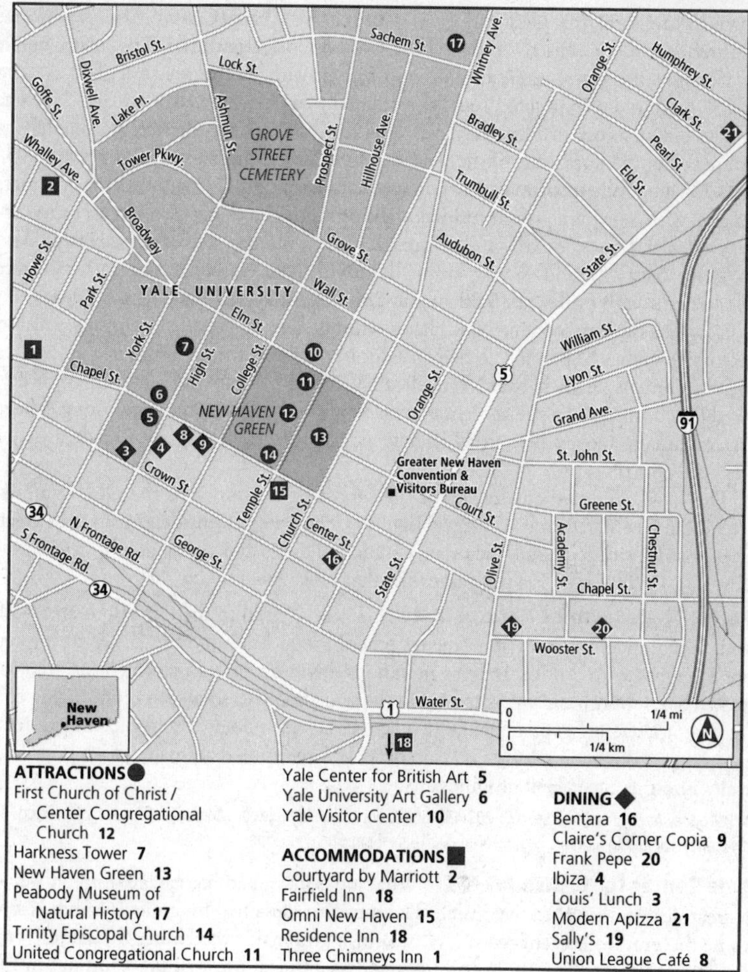

EXPLORING YALE & NEW HAVEN

Most of the major attractions are associated with Yale University, and, except for the Peabody Museum, are within walking distance of one another near the **New Haven Green,** which is bounded by Elm, Church, Chapel, and College streets.

The Green, about a third the size of Boston Common, is divided into two unequal parts by north-south Temple Street. Government and bank buildings, including the Gothic Revival City Hall, border it on the east, a retail district on the south, and some older sections of the vast Yale campus to the north and west.

Facing Temple Street are three historic churches, all dating from the early 19th century. Next to Chapel Street is **Trinity Episcopal Church,** a brownstone Gothic

Revival structure; the Georgian **First Church of Christ/Center Congregational Church;** and the essentially Federal-style **United Congregational.** The First Church of Christ is of greatest interest, built atop a crypt with tombstones inscribed as early as 1687. Tours are conducted Tuesday through Friday between 10:30am and 2:30pm.

The oldest house in New Haven is now the **Yale Visitor Center,** a Colonial-era house facing the north side of the Green at 149 Elm St., near College Street (© **203/432-2300**). While its primary mission is to familiarize prospective students and their parents with Yale on a 1-hour **guided walking tour,** the center also has an introductory video and maps for self-guided tours. It's open Monday through Friday from 9am to 4pm, Saturday and Sunday from 10am to 4pm. Guided tours are available Monday through Friday at 10:30am and 2pm, Saturday and Sunday at 1:30pm.

It is impossible to imagine New Haven without Yale, so pervasive is its physical and cultural presence. After all, it helped educate our last three presidents, as well as Gerald Ford, William Howard Taft, Noah Webster, Nathan Hale, and Eli Whitney. Established in 1702 in the shoreline town now known as Clinton, the young college was eventually moved here in 1718 and named for Elihu Yale, who made a major financial contribution.

The most evocative quadrangle of the sprawling institution is the **Old Campus,** which can be entered from College, High, or Chapel streets. Inside, the mottled green is enclosed by Federal and Victorian Gothic buildings and dominated by **Harkness Tower,** a 1920 Gothic Revival campanile that looks much older.

Peabody Museum of Natural History ★ Kids Head to the third floor and work your way down, especially if a raucous school group has just entered. Up at the top are dioramas with stuffed animals in various environments: bighorn sheep, Alaskan brown bears, bison, and musk oxen. On the same floor is a small but illuminating collection of ancient Egyptian artifacts. The second floor doesn't hold much of general interest, but down on the first is a "bestiary" of large stuffed animals, which leads logically into the Great Hall of Dinosaurs.

170 Whitney Ave. (at Sachem St.). © **203/432-5050.** www.peabody.yale.edu. Admission $7 adults, $6 seniors, $5 children 3–18; free to all Thurs 2–5pm. Mon–Sat 10am–5pm; Sun noon–5pm.

Yale Center for British Art ★★ What looks like a parking garage from outside is a great deal more impressive inside. The museum, designed by Louis I. Kahn, is said to be the most important repository of British art outside the United Kingdom, with holdings of more than 1,400 paintings and sculptures. Most of the paintings in the permanent collection are from the 16th through the early 19th centuries. It's a dazzling array, with canvases by such luminaries as Hogarth, Gainsborough, Joshua Reynolds, David Hockney, and the glorious Turner.

1080 Chapel St. (at High St.). © **203/432-2800.** www.yale.edu/ycba. Free admission. Tues–Sat 10am–5pm; Sun noon–5pm.

Yale University Art Gallery ★★ The artworks of many epochs and regions are on display, but the museum is most noted for its collections of French Impressionists and American realists of the late 19th and early 20th centuries. It's a satisfying collection for connoisseurs, and won't test the patience of reluctant museum-goers. Architect Louis I. Kahn, also responsible for the nearby Center for British Art, designed the larger of these two buildings. Take the elevator to the fourth floor and work your way down. Asian arts and crafts command the top floor. The tiny Netsuke ivories at the center bear close examination. On the third floor are 14th- to 18th-century Gothic ecclesiastical panels and 16th-century Italian and Dutch portraits, among them paintings by Rubens and Frans Hals. In sharp contrast are adjoining galleries of 20th-century works—Rothko and Rauschenberg as well as Braque, Picasso, and Mondrian.

1111 Chapel St. (at High St.). ✆ **203/432-0600.** www.artgallery.yale.edu. Free admission ($5 suggested donation). Tues–Sat 10am–5pm (Thurs until 8pm); Sun 1–6pm.

SHOPPING

Atticus Bookstore & Cafe It might as easily be listed under "Where to Dine," for half of this store consists of a lunch counter and takeout section, locally famous for its scones. The rest of the space is devoted to what many call the best bookstore in town. Open daily from 8am to midnight. 1082 Chapel St. ✆ **203/776-4040.**

WHERE TO STAY

New Haven lodgings are both limited and, with one notable exception, devoid of either charm or distinctiveness. Still, its motels and hotels fill up far in advance for football weekends, alumni reunions, and graduation.

Among the chains in town are the **Courtyard by Marriott,** 30 Whalley Rd. (✆ **203/777-6221**); **Fairfield Inn,** 400 Sargent Dr. (✆ **203/562-1111**); and **Residence Inn,** 3 Long Wharf Dr. (✆ **203/777-5337**). The visitor center has a **hotel reservations service** (✆ **800/332-7829**).

Omni New Haven ★★ This is a conventional member of the reliable Omni chain. Its location couldn't be improved, next to the Green and within easy walking distance of the theaters, much of the campus, and two of the Yale museums. Galileo's, the 19th-floor restaurant, offers fine views of the Green and surrounding cityscape.

155 Temple St. (south of Chapel St.), New Haven, CT 06510. ✆ **800/444-OMNI** or 203/772-6664. Fax 203/974-6780. www.omnihotels.com. 306 units. $139–$209 double. AE, DC, DISC, MC, V. **Amenities:** Restaurant; bar; exercise room; concierge; business center; limited room service; same-day dry cleaning/laundry. *In room:* A/C, TV/VCR, dataport, minibar, coffeemaker, hair dryer, iron

Three Chimneys Inn ★★ Once known as the Inn at Chapel West, this 1870 mansion is a favorite of Yalies and their parents. All rooms are outfitted with mahogany four-poster beds. On chilly days, gas fires burn in seven of the bedrooms and in the dining room and parlor, where a tray of cordials is set out. An honor bar and guest pantry are also at hand. Businesspeople are more in evidence than is usual at inns, many of them here to interview Yale students for jobs. The inn is nonsmoking.

1201 Chapel St. (between Park and Howe sts.), New Haven, CT 06511. ✆ **800/443-1554** out of state, or 203/789-1201. Fax 203/776-7363. www.threechimneysinn.com. 11 units. $210–$275 double. Rates include full breakfast and afternoon tea. AE, DISC, MC, V. No pets. No children under 6. **Amenities:** Exercise room; access to nearby health club; same-day dry cleaning. *In room:* A/C, TV/VCR, dataport, hair dryer.

WHERE TO DINE

Bentara ★ SOUTHEAST ASIAN In business for over 8 years, Bentara now finds itself benefiting from a surge in gentrification to its once shabby street. Bare teak tables occupy the spare, roomy front; the back room has tableclothed tables and a second bar. Shadow puppets hang behind opaque panels; carved fertility figures stand along one wall. Billed as Malaysian, the menu encompasses Thai, French, and Vietnamese ingredients and techniques, as well. Expect punchy, often fiery flavors, not for those with timid palates (nor, in all likelihood, those with nut or peanut allergies). *Ikan goring pedas,* for example, is a memorable golden-fried whole fish in a sweet-spicy sauce;

Tips The New Haven Pizza Wars

On the scene for most of the last century, **Frank Pepe** ★, 157 Wooster St. (between Olive and Brown sts.) (✆ **203/865-5762**) has long laid claim to the local pizza crown in the face of substantial competition. In exchange for super, almost unimaginably thin-crusted pies, pilgrims put up with long lines, nothing decor, and an often sullen staff the management prefers to think of as "seasoned." A big fave is the white clam pie.

You can do every bit as well at **Sally's** ★, 237 Wooster St. (✆ **203/624-5271**), just down the street (reservations accepted), and many knowledgeable pizza lovers (including this one) believe that **Modern Apizza** ★, 874 State St. (✆ **203/776-5306**), holds the edge over both of them.

precede it with the pan-simmered mussels in a coconut-curry sauce with slivered onions and red peppers.

76 Orange St. (at Center St.) ✆ **203/562-2511.** Main courses $8.95–$19 (but market price for several dishes). MC, V, AE, DISC, Diners. Daily noon–2:30pm and 5:30–10pm.

Claire's Corner Copia *Value* VEGETARIAN Few college towns are without at least one low-cost vegetarian restaurant. This one has ruled in New Haven since 1975. Options include curried couscous, eggplant rollatini, barbecue soy chicken, and a number of Mexican entrees, but the stars might well be the award-winning quiches. Fish-eaters will enjoy the tuna salad and open-faced albacore melt sandwiches on offer. Breakfast brings a bounty of plump scones and massive muffins. Place your order at the counter after perusing the very long blackboard menu, pay the cashier, and claim a table. Presently, someone emerges from the kitchen and shouts your name.

1000 Chapel St. (at College St.). ✆ **203/562-3888.** Most items under $10. No credit cards. Sun–Thurs 8am–9pm; Fri–Sat 8am–10pm.

Ibiza ★★ SPANISH This used to be Pika Tapas, a casual spot to indulge in versions of Spain's tastiest culinary invention. It didn't get all that much attention until the owners decided to go upmarket. Chef Bollo, who trained in San Sebastián in the Spanish Basque Country, introduced a now-primed clientele to the high-flying modern cuisine and wines of his native land. His menu includes a few traditional dishes, among them *caldo Gallego,* a Galician potato-and-cabbage soup, and *espinacas a la Catalana,* sautéed spinach with raisins and pine nuts. But he ups the ante with vigor, as when he pairs grilled sea scallops with squid-ink pasta or duck breast with diced polenta, bacon, apples, prunes, and tomatoes. To get a better idea of his range, spring for the $55 tasting menu (available Mon–Thurs).

39 High St. (south of Chapel St.). ✆ **203/865-1933.** Reservations essential. Main courses $22–$27. AE, MC, V. Tues 5–10pm; Wed–Sat 11:30–2:30pm and 5–10pm (until 11pm Fri–Sat).

Louis' Lunch BURGERS/SANDWICHES The claim, unprovable but gaining strength as the decades roll on, is that America's very first hamburger sandwich was sold in 1900 at this little luncheonette. Although Louis' was moved from its original location to escape demolition, not much else has changed. The wooden counter and tables are carved with the initials of a century of patrons. The beef is freshly ground each day, thrust into gas-fired ovens, and then served (medium rare, usually) on two slices of white toast. The only allowable garnishes are slices of tomato, onion, or cheese. There's no mustard and no ketchup, so don't even ask. And there's no fries, either, just potato chips. On the upside, soup is served, and, on Fridays only, tuna sandwiches.

261–263 Crown St. (between High and College sts.). ✆ **203/562-5507.** All items under $8. No credit cards. Tues–Wed 11am–4pm; Thurs–Sat noon–2am. Closed Aug.

Union League Café ★★ CREATIVE FRENCH These grand salons retain an air of their aristocratic origins, which date back to 1854. Even the name fairly shrieks of its former status as a bastion of WASP privilege, the Union League Club. It has loosened up considerably, and denim-clad Yalies, their doting parents, philosophizing profs, and deal-making execs are all equally comfortable here. With waiters in aprons and tables covered with butcher paper, the atmosphere is now closer to an updated brasserie than to that of a gentlemen's sanctuary. The chef routinely tinkers with Gallic culinary tradition. Entrees on the order of cod and sweet-potato brandade, saffron monkfish, and braised veal cheeks seem both familiar and fresh. A daily cheese card is proffered instead of, or in addition to, dessert. The wine list is almost exclusively French. Service is informed and proficient.

1032 Chapel St. (between High and College sts.). ✆ **203/562-4299.** Main courses $18–$32. AE, DC, MC, V. Mon–Fri 11:30am–2:30pm and 5–9:30pm; Sat 5–10pm.

NEW HAVEN AFTER DARK

The presence of Yale and a highly educated faction of the general population ensures a cultural life equal to that of many larger cities. A reliable source of information on cultural events and nightlife is the free weekly newspaper, the *New Haven Advocate* (www.newhavenadvocate.com).

THE PERFORMING ARTS Within a couple of blocks of the Green, the **Shubert Performing Arts Center,** 247 College St. (✆ **800/228-6622** or 203/562-5666; www.shubert.com), presents musicals, opera, plays, cabaret, concerts, and such touring troupes as the Alvin Ailey Dance Theater. The well-regarded **Yale Repertory Theatre** (✆ **203/432-1234;** www.yalerep.org) mounts an October-to-May season of modern productions as well as classics by Shakespeare, George Bernard Shaw, and Tennessee Williams. It uses three venues: University Theater, 222 York St., the New Theatre, 1156 Chapel St., and The Rep, 1120 Chapel St.

Away from downtown, but worth the cab fare, is the prestigious **Long Wharf Theatre,** 222 Sargent Dr. (✆ **203/787-4282;** www.longwharf.org), known for its success in producing new plays that often make the jump to off-Broadway and even Broadway itself. The season runs from October to June. The Long Wharf spawned the smaller **Stage II.**

Several venues on the Yale campus, including **Sprague Memorial Hall,** 470 College St., and **Woolsey Hall,** College and Grove streets, host the performances of many resident organizations, including the New Haven Symphony Orchestra, New Haven Civic Orchestra, Yale Concert Band, Yale Glee Club, Yale Philharmonia, and Yale Symphony Orchestra. For upcoming events, call the **Yale Concert Information Line** (✆ **203/432-4157**).

THE CLUB SCENE The biggest and best venue for live rock and pop is **Toad's Place,** 300 York St. (✆ **203/621-TOAD**), which has welcomed the likes of the Rolling Stones, U2, and Bob Dylan, although the usual fare is tribute bands and regional groups.

For something less frenetic, the popular **BAR,** 254 Crown St. (✆ **203/495-1111**), has a lounge in front—open to the street on warm nights—and a pool table, terrace, and dance floor in back. On Sundays, listen to live jazz or blues. **The Brü Rm,** a brewpub tacked onto the slightly older nightclub, produces rich beers and poses a naked challenge in the eternal New Haven pizza wars. Its thinnest-crust pies are leading contenders for the crown long held by Frank Pepe's.

4 Hartford

115 miles NE of New York; 103 miles SW of Boston

Dissidents fleeing the rigid religious dictates of the Massachusetts Bay Colony founded Hartford in 1636. Three years later, they drafted what were called the "Fundamental Orders," the basis of a subsequent claim that Connecticut was the first political entity on earth to have a written constitution, hence the nickname "Constitution State."

Unfortunately, Connecticut's capital and second-largest city endures a drooping uneasiness it hasn't been able to shake. Visitors can't help noticing the miles of distressed housing, weed-strewn lots, and hollow-eyed office structures that radiate out from the center.

After frequent disappointments, though, hopes are rising once again. Hartford has always pointed gamely to its grand edifices—the divinely overwrought gold-domed capitol, the High Victorian Mark Twain House, and the august Wadsworth Atheneum. Now, though, downtown is experiencing a construction boomlet, with hundreds of housing units, a couple of new hotels, and a new convention center at riverside among the results. The gracious Old State House enjoyed a 4-year renovation, and across the street, a shed has been provided for a farmers' market where noontime rock concerts are staged in summer. These efforts have encouraged new investments and the establishment of a dozen or so cosmopolitan restaurants, so most of a day trip or overnight visit can be contained within only a few square blocks.

ESSENTIALS

GETTING THERE Interstates 84 and 91 intersect in central Hartford, halfway between New York and Boston. Downtown Hartford has plenty of convenient parking.

Bradley International Airport, in Windsor Locks, about 12 miles north of the city, is served by several major airlines, including **American** (✆ 800/433-7300), **Continental** (✆ 800/525-0280), **Delta** (✆ 800/221-1212), **Northwest** (✆ 800/225-2525), **Southwest** (✆ 800/435-9792), **United** (✆ 800/241-6522), and **US Airways** (✆ 800/428-4322). Buses, cabs, and limousines shuttle passengers into the city and to other points in the state.

Amtrak (✆ **800/USA-RAIL;** www.amtrak.com) has several trains daily following the inland route between New York City and Boston, stopping at Hartford and Windsor Locks. The trip to either New York or Boston takes about 2½ hours.

VISITOR INFORMATION The Greater Hartford subdivision of the Connecticut Convention & Visitors Bureau provides useful details on www.enjoyhartford.com.

SPECIAL EVENTS Hartford makes the most of its association with one of America's most beloved authors, Mark Twain. His image is seen everywhere, and the city puts on **Mark Twain Days** in mid-August, with such events as frog jumping, riverboat rides, and performances of plays based on Twain's life or works. In late July, there's a **Festival of Jazz** with free performances at the pavilion in Bushnell Park.

Hartford

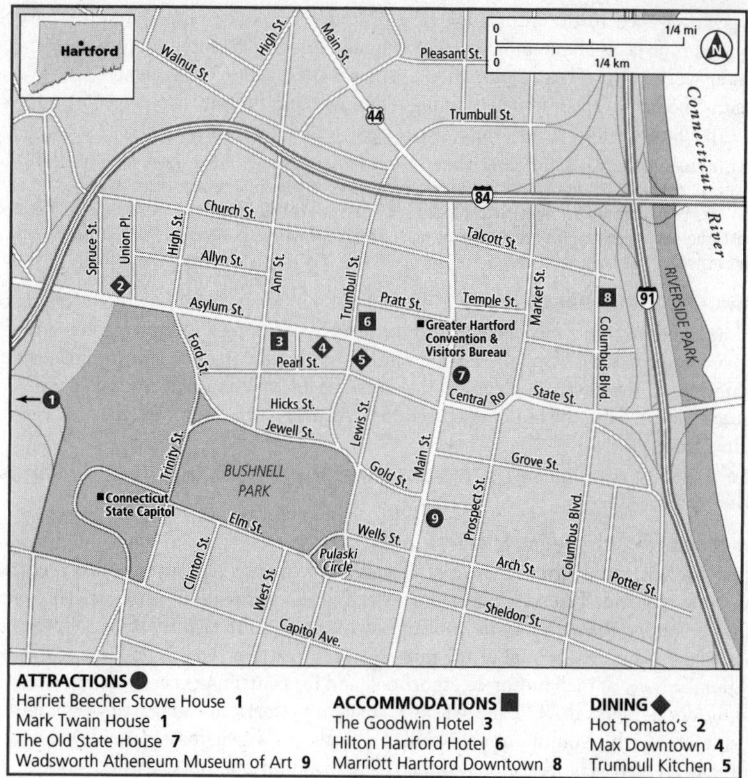

WHAT TO SEE & DO

Harriet Beecher Stowe House On the adjacent property, across the lawn from the Twain residence, this is a smaller version of its neighbor, built in 1871. Stowe, the author of *Uncle Tom's Cabin,* lived here for most of the time Twain resided in his house. The authors moved in within a year of each other, when she was in her 60s and Twain was nearing 40, approaching the zenith of his career.

77 Forest St. ✆ **860/522-9258.** www.harrietbeecherstowecenter.org. Admission $8 adults, $7 seniors, $4 children 6–16, free 5 and under. Tues–Sat 9:30am–4:30pm; Sun noon–4:30pm. Closed Mon Jan–May. Visits by guided tour only; last tour begins at 4pm.

Mark Twain House ★★ Kids This 19-room house is a fascinating example of the late-19th-century style sometimes known as "Picturesque Gothic," with several steeply peaked gables and brick walls whose varying patterns are highlighted by black or orange paint.

Samuel Clemens, whose pseudonym was a term used by Mississippi River pilots to indicate a water depth of 2 fathoms, lived here from 1874 to 1891. The High Victorian interior was the work of distinguished designers of the time, including Louis Comfort Tiffany, who provided both advice and stained glass. Twain's enthusiasm for newfangled gadgets—*Life On The Mississippi* is said to be the first novel written on a typewriter—led to the installation of a primitive telephone in the entrance hall. A guided tour takes about an hour and eventually leads to the top floor and the writer's main workroom, a large space that also has a pool table. Twain would often walk across the hall in the middle of the night and wake up his butler to play a few games.

An education and visitor center houses galleries, a small cinema, a cafe, and a shop.

351 Farmington Ave. ✆ **860/247-0998.** www.marktwainhouse.org. Admission $12 adults, $11 seniors, $10 students, $8 children 6–12, free for children 5 and under. Mon–Sat 9:30–5:30pm; Sun noon–5:30pm. Closed Mon Jan–May. Visits by guided tour only; last tour begins at 4:45pm. Take Exit 46 off I-84, turn right onto Sisson Ave., then right onto Farmington Ave. The house is on the right. From downtown, drive west on Asylum St., bearing left on Farmington Ave. The house is on the left.

The Old State House After a 4-year, $12-million restoration, the 1796 State House opened in time to celebrate its bicentennial. Costumed interpreters stand ready to answer questions. Upstairs on the right is the Senate chamber, with a full-length painting of the first president by the indefatigable Washington portraitist Gilbert Stuart. These days, the building is used for temporary art exhibitions, changed two or three times yearly.

800 Main St. (at Asylum Ave.). ✆ **860/522-6766.** www.ctosh.org. Free admission. Mon–Fri 10am–4pm; Sat 11am–4pm.

Wadsworth Atheneum Museum of Art ★★★ Opened in 1842, this was the first public art museum in the United States and remains a repository with few equals in New England. The strength of the collection lies primarily in its American paintings, spanning the period from landscape artists of the 19th century through luminaries of the New York School of the mid–20th century. On the top floor are works by Thomas Cole, of the Hudson River School, and his contemporaries Frederick Church and Albert Bierstadt. On the balcony are more Americans—Frederic Remington, Andrew Wyeth, Milton Avery, Norman Rockwell. Watch for the shadow box by Joseph Cornell. The first floor contains rule-bending multimedia works, as well as canvases by abstract expressionists and pop and op artists of the 1950s and 1960s like de Kooning and Rauschenberg. The **Museum Cafe** has surprisingly good light items and tables out on the terrace in fair weather.

600 Main St. (1 block west of The Old State House). ✆ **860/278-2670.** www.wadsworthatheneum.org. Admission $10 adults, $8 seniors, $5 students, free for children 12 and under (free to all until noon Sat); surcharges for some special exhibitions. Wed–Fri 11am–5pm; Sat–Sun 10am–5pm (until 8pm 1st Thurs of most months).

WHERE TO STAY

The Goodwin ★ This quiet hostelry opposite the Civic Center is housed in a Queen Anne–style Victorian built in 1881 as a residence for J. P. Morgan. Its understated public areas are attractive, while its cautiously decorated bedrooms are fully equipped. Valet parking is often slow, but still a blessing along this crowded block. The in-house restaurant has an erratic reputation, but some of the city's best dining options are short walks away.

1 Haynes St. (at Asylum St.), Hartford, CT 06103. ✆ **800/922-5006** or 860/246-7500. Fax 860/244-2669. www.goodwinhotel.com. 124 units. $145–$259 double. Weekend packages available. AE, DC, DISC, MC, V. Valet parking $15. **Amenities:** Restaurant (American); lounge; modest fitness center; concierge; limited room service; same-day dry cleaning. *In room:* A/C, TV, VCR on request, dataport, hair dryer, iron.

Hilton Hartford ★★ Kids This 22-story slab used to be a Sheraton. It closed for months to undertake a recent multimillion-dollar expenditure on both substantive and cosmetic renovations. Hotel chains have been competing with each other to install comfortable mattresses, and guest will love the ones here. Over a hundred adjoining rooms make it attractive to families. The hotel connects with the Civic Center and is readily visible to drivers entering the city from I-84. High-speed Internet access is available.

315 Trumbull St., Hartford, CT 06103. © **800/445-8667** or 860/728-5151. Fax 860/240-7246. www.hartford.hilton.com. 390 units. $161–$209 double. AE, DC, DISC, MC, V. **Amenities:** 2 restaurants (international); sports bar; indoor pool; fully equipped health club; Jacuzzi; sauna; limited room service; same-day dry cleaning/laundry. *In room:* A/C, TV, dataport, coffeemaker, hair dryer, iron.

Marriott Hartford Downtown ★★ New in town, this Marriott opened next to the Connecticut Convention Center in 2005. It challenges the existing big guys (above) on every front, with luxury s"s, a concierge level, and two splashy restaurants. Guest rooms compete with cushy mattresses as well as 27" flatscreen TVs that have high-speed Internet access and games. Morning newspapers are delivered to the door. Its main restaurant, **Vivo,** goes in for highly imaginative interpretations of the Tuscan oeuvre, employing wood-fired ovens. The designers were responsible for the commendable Octagon restaurant in the Marriott in Groton (p. 401).

200 Columbus Blvd., Hartford, CT. © **860/249-8000.** Fax 860/249-8181. www.hartfordmarriott.com. 409 units. $199–$249 double. AE, DC, DISC, MC, V. **Amenities:** Restaurant (contemporary Italian); bar/lounge; concierge; indoor pool and Jacuzzi; modest fitness room and spa; limited room service; same-day dry cleaning/laundry. *In room:* A/C, TV w/pay movies, dataport, coffeemaker, hair dryer, iron.

WHERE TO DINE

Hot Tomato's ITALIAN The renovation of Union Station spawned this popular trattoria in one wing. Dine in the glass-sided dining room or on the terrace. A casually dressed crowd tucks into big bowls of garlicky pasta, the primary offerings here. There is lobster *pinchiori,* for one, heaping chunks of the shellfish with portobellos and asparagus in lobster cream sauce over tagliatelle. Atkins followers have six equally hearty portions of beef and pork to choose among, notably the 18-ounce "Cowboy Cut" rib-eye. Especially spicy dishes are marked with a star. Sides are extra. The bar stays open late.

1 Union Place (corner of Asylum St.). © **860/249-5100.** Reservations advised for patio and on weekends. Main courses $16–$32. AE, DC, DISC, MC, V. Mon–Thurs 11:30am–11pm; Fri 11:30am–midnight; Sat 4pm–midnight; Sun 4–10pm.

Max Downtown ★★ NEW AMERICAN Hartford's prime-time power epicenter has a crowd that looks essentially interchangeable with the one that frequents the Trumbull Kitchen (see below), albeit with a few more suits at midday and a lot of air-kissing at night. Too bad patrons don't pay much attention to the bar menu, for its treats are along the lines of mulligatawny and mahimahi with mango-papaya sauce. The main room has banquettes arrayed behind expanses of glass, with a flashy mural on the back wall. Diners are indulged with hefty chophouse favorites—double pork chops and porterhouse steaks for two—and flightier efforts, such as zucchini-wrapped Atlantic halibut with white asparagus and morels. An exception to the prices listed below is the Kobe beef rib-eye, at $60.

185 Asylum St. (opposite City Center). © **860/522-2530.** Reservations advised on weekends. Main courses $22–$35. AE, DC, MC, V. Mon–Fri 11:30am–2:30pm and 5–10:30pm (Fri until 11:30pm); Sat 5–11:30pm; Sun 4:30–9:30pm.

Trumbull Kitchen ★ ECLECTIC Looking as though it belongs in a hipper city, this member of the highly successful Max chain (see Max Downtown, above) appears to be building upon its initial rush of popularity. Young execs and lawyers frequent it, enjoying a menu sprinkled with such global grazing categories as fondues and tapas-like noshes on the lines of marinated lamb skewers and miso chicken dumplings. Main plates include such possibilities as a perked-up meatloaf and blackened tuna with baby bok choy and soy mustard sauce. This is fun, diverting food—tasty enough without distracting from the primary mingling. The bar stays open after the kitchen closes.

150 Trumbull St. (near Asylum St.). © **860/493-7412.** Main courses $17–$25. AE, DC, DISC, MC, V. Mon–Wed 11:30am–11pm; Thurs–Fri 11:30am–midnight; Sat 5pm–midnight.

HARTFORD AFTER DARK

The free weekly *Hartford Advocate* (www.hartfordadvocate.com) provides useful information on cultural, sports, and musical events.

The **Bushnell Center for the Performing Arts,** 166 Capitol Ave. (© **860/987-5900;** www.bushnell.org), is expanding, the project to include a new 918-seat theater added to the 2,800-seat main stage. They serve as venues for the Hartford Symphony, Connecticut Opera, Hartford Pops, and smaller traveling groups, when not hosting visiting symphony orchestras or road companies of Broadway plays. The **Hartford Stage,** 50 Church St. (© **860/527-5151;** www.hartfordstage.org), mounts a variety of mainstream plays.

At the **Arch Street Tavern,** 85 Arch St. (© **860/246-7610**), nationally known bands of the second magnitude appear from time to time, but local groups dominate. Subject to frequent change, live bands—jazz, rock, whatever—perform Mondays, Wednesdays, and Saturdays. The **Brickyard Cafe,** 113 Allyn St. (© **860/249-2112**), contains a bar, dance floor with DJ mixes, sports bar, pool tables, patio, and a lot of people looking to hook up. Jello shots fuel the action.

Black-Eyed Sally's, 350 Asylum St. (© **860/278-7427**), known for its ribs and other Southern-style gustatorial treats, presents live blues bands Thursday through Saturday nights.

City Steam Brewery, 942 Main St. (© **860/525-1600**), serves food that goes well with the dozens of home-brews. On the premises are pool tables, frequent live music, and the Brew HA HA Comedy Club (Thurs–Sat). For beer by the pitcher along with Monday Night Football or the Final Four, where better than **Coach's,** 187 Allyn St. (© **860/522-6224**), a place founded by the UConn basketball coach himself? Open daily, it has 38 TVs, bar snacks, video games, and live music Thursday through Saturday (usually).

5 From Guilford to Old Saybrook

Usually ignored by vacationers anxious to get on to Essex and Mystic and the casinos, the stretch of coast between New Haven and the Connecticut River, known simply as the Shoreline, has its gentle pleasures, enough to justify a short detour for lunch, a walk on a beach, a spell of shopping, or even a proper British high tea (in Madison). When lodgings are difficult to find at the better-known destinations, the Shoreline's inns and resorts are logical alternatives within easy driving distance.

ESSENTIALS

GETTING THERE The Shoreline can be reached from Exit 57 off I-95. Pick up Route 1 (aka the Boston Post Rd.), which serves as the main street of several Shoreline towns.

Several daily **Amtrak** (✆ **800/USA-RAIL;** www.amtrak.com) trains stop at Old Saybrook. The **Shore Line East** (✆ **800/255-7433;** www.shorelineeast.com) commuter line uses the same tracks to service towns between New Haven and New London, but only Monday through Friday.

VISITOR INFORMATION A source of pamphlets, maps, and related materials for the towns described in this section is www.newhavencvb.org, the Greater New Haven website.

GUILFORD

One of the state's oldest Colonial settlements (1639), this village, 13 miles east of New Haven, is embraced by the West and East rivers and has an uncommonly large public green. There are dozens of historic houses to see in town, most of them privately owned and a few others open to the public on a limited basis, typically from Memorial Day to Columbus Day. **Hyland House,** 84 Boston St. (✆ **203/453-9477**), built around 1690, and the **Thomas Griswold House,** 171 Boston St. (✆ **203/453-3176**), from 1774, are two of these.

Henry Whitfield State Museum The Whitfield Museum bills itself as the oldest house in Connecticut and the oldest stone house in New England. Most of what you see now, though, including the leaded windows, dates from a 1930s reconstruction and not from the mid-1600s, so it is really more a museum than a historic home. It is still worth a brief visit, however, and the furnishings are authentic to the period.

248 Old Whitfield St. ✆ **203/453-2457.** Admission $4 adults, $3 seniors and students, $2.50 children 6–17. Feb 1–Dec 14 Wed–Sun 10am–4:30pm; Dec 15–Jan 30 by appointment only.

WHERE TO DINE

Martin's ★ NEW AMERICAN Occupying a space that formerly contained a restaurant called Esteve, this is a once-over-lightly refreshment of its predecessor. The contemporary artwork is still eye-catching, the staff still amiable, the menu similar, but now it is open daily for breakfast, lunch, and dinner. The food takes a long step toward memorable, finding delectable twists on familiar items. Fried calamari, for example, comes with sliced cherry peppers and a hoisin sauce. The lunch specials, changed daily, include a quiche, a soup, a panino, and an omelet. In the evening, the card lists conventional meats creatively addressed, on the lines of sea bass served over a sweet-potato cake with roasted corn and passion fruit beurre blanc or veal scallopini rolled with three cheeses over angel-hair pasta and tomato sauce.

25 Whitfield St. ✆ **203/458-1300.** Reservations advised. Main courses $20–$29. MC, V. Daily 8am–3:30pm and 5:30–9pm.

The Place ★ SEAFOOD There's no place like this place so this must be . . . What's different? It's outdoors, under a striped tent if the weather is threatening. The food is cooked over open wood fires. You sit on tree stumps and can buy a T-shirt that confirms that you "Put Your Rump On A Stump." You are invited to bring along beer, wine, salad, chips, or whatever to fill out your meal. It's open only 6 months a year. In essence, what's served is a clambake, so you are morally obligated to begin with a raft of that bivalve. They are roasted over those smoky coals, popped open, dabbed with hot sauce, and run back over the fire as a finish. Corn cooked in the husk and dipped in margarine is another must. You can get bluefish or chicken with that, but why would you? Go for the lobster. There are several desserts, including slices of pecan pies and hot fudge sundaes, but the carrot cake is a winner. You will leave grinning. 901 Boston Post Rd. (Rte. 1). ✆ **203/453-9276.** Main courses $9–$19. No credit cards. Late Apr to mid-Oct Mon–Thurs 5–10pm; Fri 5–11pm; Sat 1–11pm; Sun noon–10pm. From I-95, take Exit 58 onto Rte. 77 to Rte. 1, turn left (east). The Place is opposite a shopping mall.

MADISON

Madison, 19 miles east of New Haven, is home to a historic architectural district that stretches west of the business district along the Boston Post Road, from the main green to the town line, and contains many examples of 18th- and 19th-century domestic styles.

The well-to-do town has completed the transition from colony to seaside resort to year-round community, a process begun when the first house was built in 1651. Today, there are two dwellings from the early years that can be visited on limited summer schedules. **Deacon John Grave House,** 581 Boston Post Rd. (✆ **203/245-4798**), dates from 1685, and the **Allis-Bushnell House,** 853 Boston Post Rd. (✆ **203/245-4567**), from 1785.

Off the Boston Post Road east of the town center, also reached from Exit 62 off I-95, is **Hammonasset Beach State Park** (✆ **203/245-2785**), a 900-plus-acre peninsula jutting into Long Island Sound that has the only public swimming beach in the area, and it's over 2 miles long. It has a nature center, picnic areas, campgrounds, fishing, and boating. From Memorial Day to Labor Day, cars with Connecticut plates are charged $7 Monday through Friday, $9 on weekends and holidays; out-of-state plates are charged $10 Monday through Friday, $14 on weekends and holidays.

SHOPPING

Madison's commercial district may look ordinary at first glance, but several shops along Boston Post Road and intersecting Wall Street provide entertaining browsing. **R. J. Julia Booksellers,** 768 Boston Post Rd. (✆ **203/245-3959**), holds frequent author readings and poetry slams.

The British Shoppe, 45 Wall St. (✆ **203/245-4521**), stocks such favorites as kippers, pork pies, and sublime cheeses. Classic ploughman's lunches recall those in English pubs. (Tough licensing requirements don't allow for pints of English beer, but you can bring your own.)

Exit 63 off 1-95 west leads directly to **Clinton Crossing,** 20-A Killingsworth Tpk. (✆ **860/664-0700**), a "premium" outlet mall with more than 80 shops. Clothing stores by such designers as Calvin Klein, Donna Karan, and Ralph Lauren are augmented by Coach leather goods and Le Creuset cookware.

WHERE TO STAY & DINE

The Inn at Lafayette ★ Cafe Allegre ★★ The stately Greek Revival portico in the middle of the business district promises a touch of elegance, and the interior delivers. Since 1998, the ground floor has housed Cafe Allegre, a soothing setting for northern Italian and European food of considerable accomplishment. Fresh regional ingredients are paramount. Main courses, such as lemon chicken and veal saltimbocca, run from $16 to $22. The bar is a low-key gathering place, popular for lunch, with a piano player on Thursday and Friday nights; closed Monday. The owners haven't done much with the guest rooms upstairs, which are clearly secondary to their restaurant, but they're comfortable enough, with marble bathrooms and king- or queen-size beds.

725 Boston Post Rd., Madison, CT 06443. © **866/623-7498** or 203/245-7773. Fax 203/245-6256. www.allegre cafe.com. 5 units. Late May to early Oct $125–$185 double; Columbus Day to late May $95–$155 double. AE, DC, MC, V. No children under 12. **Amenities:** Restaurant (Italian/European); bar. *In room:* A/C, TV, dataport, hair dryer.

WHERE TO DINE

Lenny & Joe's Fish Tale SEAFOOD At this rough-and-ready fish shack, fish rules, most of it fried. And while it is sure to elevate triglyceride counts, the nutty coating on super-fresh clams, oysters, shrimp, and calamari is hard to resist. Chowders and seafood rolls are the way to go. In this branch, you give your order at the counter and carry it to a table. The one in Westbrook, at 86 Boston Post Rd. (© **860/669-0767**), has table service and a bar.

1301 Boston Post Rd., Madison © **860/245-7289.** Main courses $10–$19. MC, V, Disc. Daily 11am–9pm (Fri–Sat until 10pm).

OLD SAYBROOK

Its location at the mouth of the Connecticut River (35 miles east of New Haven, 26 miles west of Mystic) is this otherwise nondescript town's principal lure. Get off Route 1 to see it at its best. Pick up Route 153 south at the western edge, following the nearly circular route as it touches the shore and passes through the hamlets of Knollwood and Fenwick and across the causeway to Saybrook Point before ending up back in the main business district.

WHERE TO STAY & DINE

Saybrook Point Inn & Spa ★★ Resort hotels have existed at this location since the late 19th century, and they've gotten the formula down pat at the current facility. It has one of the largest marinas along the coast, an ingratiating restaurant with a clubby bar and a summer dining terrace, a fully equipped fitness room, and a spa offering a full range of body and skin-care services, including mud and seaweed wraps. Dishes like chipotle-orange marinated hanger steak and blackened escarole with lobster mashed potatoes and sautéed broccoli rabe elevate the cuisine at the Terra Mar Grille far above the bland country club fare often associated with shore resorts. Their definitive versions of clam chowder and lobster roll aren't to be missed. Sunday buffet brunch is especially popular. Bedrooms are spacious, all with wet bars and sitting areas, some of the more expensive with working fireplaces and whirlpool tubs. A shuttle carries guests to and from the Shore Line East railroad station.

2 Bridge St., Old Saybrook, CT 06475. © **800/243-0212** or 860/395-2000. www.saybrook.com. 80 units. Apr–Oct $179–$339 double; Nov–Mar $159–$269 double. AE, DC, DISC, MC, V. Take Rte. 154 south from the Old Saybrook business district. **Amenities:** Restaurant (New American); bar; limited room service; indoor and outdoor pool; health club and spa. *In room:* A/C, TV, dataport, unstocked fridge, hair dryer, iron.

6 The Connecticut River Valley

New England's longest river originates in the far north near the Canadian border, 407 miles from Long Island Sound. It separates Vermont from New Hampshire, splits Massachusetts in half, then takes a 45-degree turn at Middletown, south of Hartford, to make its final run to the sea.

Native Americans of the region called the river *Quinnetukut,* which, to the tin ears of the English settlers, sounded like "Connecticut." The colonists encroached upon Indian territory as far north as present-day Windsor, which ignited a brief war with the Pequot, who occupied the land.

Because the river was navigable by relatively large ships as far as Hartford, the sheltered lower Connecticut became important for boat-building and industries associated with the international clipper trade. The Connecticut River retains that nautical flavor, and the valley has miraculously avoided the industrialization, development, and decay that afflict most of the state's other rivers.

Cruising, boating, and kayaking are obvious attractions, supplemented by rides on a steam-powered train, a selection of worthy B&Bs, antiques shops, a venerable musical theater, even a bizarre castle on a hilltop.

ESSENTIALS

GETTING THERE Limited-access state highway 9 runs parallel to the river, along the west side of the valley, connecting I-91 south of Hartford with I-95 near Old Saybrook. The lower valley is therefore readily accessible from all points in New England and from the New York metropolitan area and points south.

Amtrak (✆ **800/USA-RAIL;** www.amtrak.com) trains stop at Old Saybrook, at the mouth of the river, several times daily on runs between New York and Boston. In addition, **Shoreline East** (✆ **800/255-7433**) commuter trains operate Monday through Friday between New Haven and New London.

VISITOR INFORMATION A source of pamphlets, maps, and related materials for the **Connecticut River Valley** is www.newhavencvb.org, the greater New Haven site.

OLD LYME

As quiet a town as the coast can claim, Old Lyme (40 miles east of New Haven, 21 miles west of Mystic) was the favored residence of generations of seafarers and ship captains. Many of their 18th- and 19th-century homes have survived, some as inns and museums. Preservationists and community activists proudly point out that their main street is the only one cut by I-95 that continues to thrive. With its many tree-lined streets largely free of traffic, stressless biking is an attractive option here.

Florence Griswold Museum ★ After the shipbuilding and merchant trade had all but flickered out at the end of the 19th century, artists who came to be known as the "American Impressionists" took a fancy to this area. They received encouragement, patronage, and even food and shelter from Ms. Griswold, the wealthy daughter of a sea captain. Falling upon hard times later in life, she decided to open her Georgian-Federal 1817 mansion to boarders. It became the temporary home for a number of painters, many of whom left samples of their work in gratitude, sometimes painting directly on the walls of the dining room. Among her grateful guests was Childe Hassam, considered the grand master of the American Impressionists. Woodrow Wilson was also a visitor, in 1910, when he was president of Princeton University. Now, The Flo Gris has a new building behind the mansion with three light-filled galleries. The first two spaces are usually devoted to changing exhibits, the third to paintings rotated from the Griswold permanent collection. Visitors can walk across the mansion's 6 acres to the Lieutenant River.

96 Lyme St. (Rte. 1). ✆ **860/434-5542.** www.flogris.org. Admission $7 adults, $6 seniors and students, $4 children 6–12. Tues–Sat 10am–5pm; Sun 1–5pm.

GETTING OUTSIDE

One of several state parks at the edge of Long Island Sound, **Rocky Neck State Park,** Route 156 (✆ **860/739-5471**), east of Old Lyme, has a crescent-shaped beach and over 560 acres for camping, picnicking, fishing, and hiking. Take I-95 to Exit 72 and follow Route 156 south. Open daily from 8am to sunset.

WHERE TO STAY & DINE

Bee and Thistle Inn On more than 5 acres beside the Lieutenant River, the Bee and Thistle has a core structure that dates from 1756, with the usual later wings and additions. Every corner of the public areas is an enjoyable jumble of antiques and collectibles. The bedrooms, on the other hand, are run-of-the-mill—think faded Laura Ashley. That aside, the focus of most guests is the **dining room** ★★. Year after year, it is voted "best overall" and "most romantic" in the state by reader polls. It's open Wednesday through Monday; reservations are essential. Musicians are on hand weekend evenings; appropriate attire is requested.

100 Lyme St. (Rte. 1), Old Lyme, CT 06371. ✆ **800/622-4946** or 860/434-1667. Fax 860/434-3402. www.beeandthistleinn.com. 11 units. $130–$239 double. AE, DC, DISC, MC, V. From the south, take Exit 70 off I-95; turn left, then right on Rte. 1 (Halls Rd.) north. No pets. No children under 12. **Amenities:** Restaurant (creative American). *In room:* A/C.

ESSEX ★★

It is difficult to imagine what improvements might be made to bring this dream of a New England waterside town any closer to perfection. In fact, a published survey, *The 100 Best Small Towns in America,* ranked the waterside village number one. Among the criteria were low crime rates, per-capita income, proportion of college-educated residents, and number of physicians.

Tree-bordered streets are lined with shops and homes that retain an early-18th-century flavor without the unreal frozen-in-amber quality that often afflicts other towns as postcard-pretty as this. People live and work and play here, and bustle busily along a Main Street that runs down to Steamboat Dock and its flotilla of working vessels and pleasure craft.

Clustered along the harbor end of Main Street are three historic houses that are open to the public on limited seasonal schedules. No. 40 is the **Richard Hayden House,** an 1814 brick Federal. Next door, at no. 42, is the **Noah Tooker House,** an 18th-century center-hall Colonial. And at no. 51 is the **Robert Lay House,** completed around 1730 and thought to be the oldest original structure in town.

In winter, bald eagles come to the lower reaches of the river, and Essex holds an **Eagle Festival** in mid-February in celebration, with music, Native American dancers, and guided boat and land-based viewing of the raptors. Call ✆ **800/714-7201** or log on to www.ctaudubon.org for information and to make tour reservations.

Connecticut River Museum ★ Anglers cast lines from the dock while gulls and ducks hang around hoping for a discarded tidbit. Steamboat service was fully operational here from 1823, and the existing dock dates from 1879. Designated a National Historic Site, the museum proper features model ships, marine paintings, and artifacts that relate the story of shipbuilding in the valley, which began in 1733 and helped make this a center of world trade far into the 19th century. A replica of America's first submarine (1775), the *Turtle,* is also on display. The museum usually has walking-tour maps of Essex, too, making this a good first stop on your visit.

A small cruise boat, the **River Quest** (✆ **860/662-0577;** www.ctriverexpeditions.com), makes 90-minute trips during the day and 2-hour sunset cruises in the warmer months, and eagle-sighting cruises on a less regular basis in February. Fares can include admission to the museum: $17 for adults, $10 for children 8 to 12.

Steamboat Dock (at foot of Main St.). ✆ **860/767-8269.** www.ctrivermuseum.org. Admission $6 adults, $5 seniors and students, $3 children 6–12. Tues–Sun 10am–5pm.

Essex Steam Train *Kids* Steam locomotives from the 1920s chug along to a boat landing in the hamlet of Deep River, a diverting excursion of about an hour. It can be combined with an optional cruise on the river. Dinner trains include five-course meals and a 2½-hour ride; call for fare and schedule.

1 Railroad Ave. (Rte. 154). ✆ **860/767-0103.** www.essexsteamtrain.com. Train and boat $24 adults, $12 children 3–11; train only $16 adults, $8 children 3–11. Daily trips mid-June to Labor Day, less frequently Sept–May.

WHERE TO STAY & DINE

Griswold Inn ★★ Nobody doesn't like "The Gris." Gloss over the assertion that it's the oldest inn in America (there are other claimants). What's more important is that some years ago local people rescued the inn from outside buyers. That was a relief, for it is difficult to imagine this corner of New England without the Gris. Rumpled, cluttered, folksy, and forever besieged by drop-in yachties, anglers, locals, and tourists, the main building dates to 1776. The atmospheric taproom started life as a schoolhouse and was moved here in 1800. There's live entertainment every night, be it a Dixieland band or just a man with a banjo. The colorful dining rooms are named for their displays of books, antique weapons, or marine paintings. Food, while still hearty, has taken a turn toward the less conventional, recently featuring maple-glazed scallops with smoked cod potato cake, pumpkin seed-crusted halibut, and cowboy steak with Gorgonzola. And now, they've inaugurated a new wine bar with leather furniture and a card of small plates. The often plain and unadorned bedrooms scattered throughout six buildings are slowly being upgraded; some have fireplaces. *Viva Gris!*

36 Main St. (center of town), Essex, CT 06426. ✆ **860/767-1776.** Fax 860/767-0481. www.originalinns.com. 30 units. $100–$220 double. Rates include breakfast. AE, MC, V. **Amenities:** Restaurant (American); bar. *In room:* A/C.

IVORYTON

Once a center for the ivory trade, where factories fabricated piano keys and hair combs, Ivoryton has since subsided into a residential quietude. A virtual suburb of the only slightly larger Essex, a few miles east, the town perks up a bit in summer, when the **Ivoryton Playhouse,** 103 Main St. (✆ **860/767-7318;** www.riverrep.com), conducts its theatrical season. The repertoire runs to revivals of Broadway musicals, dramas, and comedies.

WHERE TO STAY & DINE

Copper Beech Inn ★★ Despite comparisons with the Griswold Inn in nearby Essex, these are two very different animals. Where the Gris is decidedly populist and perennially busy, the stately Copper Beech has much less traffic, and not a single figurative hair out of place. The rooms in the converted barn are roomy, with TVs, Jacuzzis, and decks, while those in the 19th-century main building have most of the character, with plenty of antiques. The Copper Beech was already the home to one of the most honored restaurants in the region, but the new owners have raised the stakes even higher, and the chef they hired is garnering ecstatic reviews. He joins French techniques and recipes with high-quality seasonal ingredients. Service is seamless, the wine list impressive.

46 Main St., Ivoryton, CT 06442. ✆ **888/809-2056** or 860/767-0330. www.copperbeechinn.com. 13 units. $195–$325 double. Rates include breakfast. AE, DC, DISC, MC, V. Closed 1st week in Jan. Take Exit 3 from Rte. 9 and head west on Main St. No children under 10. **Amenities:** Restaurant (country French); bar. *In room:* A/C, TV (9 units), hair dryers.

CHESTER

Hardly more than a 3-block business center, Chester can be dismissed easily enough. But pause a moment, for this riverside hamlet deserves savoring. Along Main Street are antiques shops, galleries, and several eateries. **Ceramica,** 36–38 Main St. (✆ **860/526-9978**), an outlet of a small chain, carries a line of uniformly gorgeous hand-painted bowls, pitchers, vases, and teapots. Nearby is **Devil's Hopyard State Park,** 366 Hopyard Road, East Haddam (✆ **860/873-8566**), with 15 miles of hiking trails, picnic grounds, and the Chapman Falls.

WHERE TO DINE

The Wheatmarket (✆ **860/526-9347**), next door to Fiddlers (see below), will make up picnic baskets, or you can put together your own from the appetizing array of breads, cheeses, soups, salads, and sandwiches.

Fiddlers ★ SEAFOOD Have your fish any way you want—poached, sautéed, broiled, baked, or grilled over mesquite—or leave it up to the skillful kitchen staff, for they can come up with some eye-openers. If "lobster au pêché" (fat chunks of lobster meat married to peach nubbins, shallots, mushrooms, cream, and peach brandy) is still on the menu, go for it. Not for lobster purists, certainly, but a revelatory example of what an imaginative chef can do. A separate small plates menu lists things like smoked salmon and zucchini tartare, while the main dishes get as intriguing as five-spice ahi and porcini-crusted sea scallops. The dining rooms are cheerfully unremarkable.

4 Water St. (behind Main St.). ✆ **860/526-3210.** Main courses $21–$25. AE, MC, V. Tues–Sat 11:30am–2pm and 5:30–9pm; Sun 4–8pm.

EAST HADDAM

Hadlyme (a jurisdiction of the town of East Haddam), hardly more than a wide spot in a country road, wouldn't have attracted much attention at all if a wealthy thespian hadn't decided to build his hilltop redoubt here.

To get here, take the **Chester-Hadlyme Ferry,** at the end of Route 148, slightly less than 2 miles from Chester. A ferry has operated here since 1769, and the current version takes both cars and pedestrians ($2.25 for vehicles plus $1.50 for trailers, 75¢ for walk-on passengers). It operates (when the owners feel like it) from 7am to 6:45pm Monday through Friday, 10:30am to 5pm Saturday through Sunday from April through November 30th. If it's closed, there will be a sign posted at the intersection of Routes 148 and 154, in which case you'll have to drive north on Route 154 to Haddam and take the bridge.

Gillette Castle State Park ★ William Gillette was a successful actor and playwright known primarily for his portrayals of Sherlock Holmes. He took the money and ran to this hill rearing above the Connecticut River, where he had his castle built. It's difficult to believe that he really thought the result resembled the Norman fortresses that allegedly were his inspiration. Rock gardens by roadside eccentrics in South Dakota or Death Valley are closer relations. Gillette felt it necessary, for one example, to design a dining-room table that slid into the wall, an inexplicable space-saving effort by a bachelor rattling around in 24 oddly shaped rooms.

But whatever Gillette's deficiencies as an architect and designer, no one can argue with his choice of location. The castle sits atop a hill above the east bank, with superlative vistas upriver and down. Nowhere else is the blessed underdevelopment of the estuary more apparent. After 2 years of renovations, which involved replacing rotted ceiling beams and repairing extensive water damage, the castle was reopened in 2002.

The 184-acre grounds have picnic areas, nature trails, and fishing sites. Because the terrace of the "castle" can be entered for free, many visitors come just to take in those **views** ★★.

67 River Rd. ✆ **860/526-2336.** www.cttourism.org. Admission $5 adults, $2.50 children 6–11. Grounds daily 8am–sunset; castle Memorial Day to Labor Day Fri–Sun 10am–5pm.

RIVER CRUISES

A voyage on the river is an irresistible outing. Cruises of a variety of lengths, times, and themes are offered by **Camelot Cruises,** 1 Marine Park (✆ **860/345-8591;** www.camelotcruises.com). The pride of its fleet is the MV *Camelot,* a 160-foot vessel carrying as many as 400 passengers. In addition to dinner and mystery cruises, there are summer and fall excursions to Greenport, Long Island.

EAST HADDAM AFTER DARK

From Gillette Castle State Park, turn north on Route 82 and make the short drive to East Haddam proper. The dominant building is a restored 1877 Victorian of splendid proportions that is now the **Goodspeed Opera House** ★★, Goodspeed Landing (✆ **860/873-8668;** www.goodspeed.org). It mostly stages revivals of Broadway musicals on the order of *The Boy Friend* and *Seven Brides for Seven Brothers,* but always makes room for more experimental or original shows that have often made it all the way to the Big Apple. The smaller Norma Terris Theatre has an additional schedule of more experimental plays. The season for both runs usually from April into December.

7 Mystic & the Southeastern Coast

Mystic: 55 miles E of New Haven

This section of the shoreline is studded with towns that still bear the stamp of their maritime pasts, a string of fishing ports and inlets that segues into the mainland beach resorts of Rhode Island. Inland are a number of still semi-rural villages, but their futures are uncertain due to the presence of two enormously successful and steadily expanding Indian casino complexes, Foxwoods and Mohegan Sun. They produce gushers of money that are altering forever the character of this region.

The town of Mystic and its twin attractions, Mystic Aquarium and the living museum that is Mystic Seaport, are the prime reasons for a stay—the Seaport alone can easily occupy most of a day, and the two-part town itself sustains a nautical air, with fun shops and restaurants to suit most tastes.

But that's not a complete list of the region's charms. The tranquil neighboring village of Stonington is home to a small but active commercial fishing fleet, the last in the state; there are several enchanting inns in the area; and many companies offer their vessels for whale-watching, dinner cruises, and deep-sea fishing excursions. And yes, for those with a taste for the adrenaline rush of a winning streak, there are those casinos.

If at all possible, avoid July, August, and weekends from May to Columbus Day, when the crowds are oppressive, restaurants are packed, and rooms are booked months in advance at very high rates.

ESSENTIALS

GETTING THERE From New York City, take I-95 to Exit 84 (New London), Exit 86 (Groton), Exit 90 (Mystic), or Exit 91 (Stonington). Or, to avoid the heavy truck

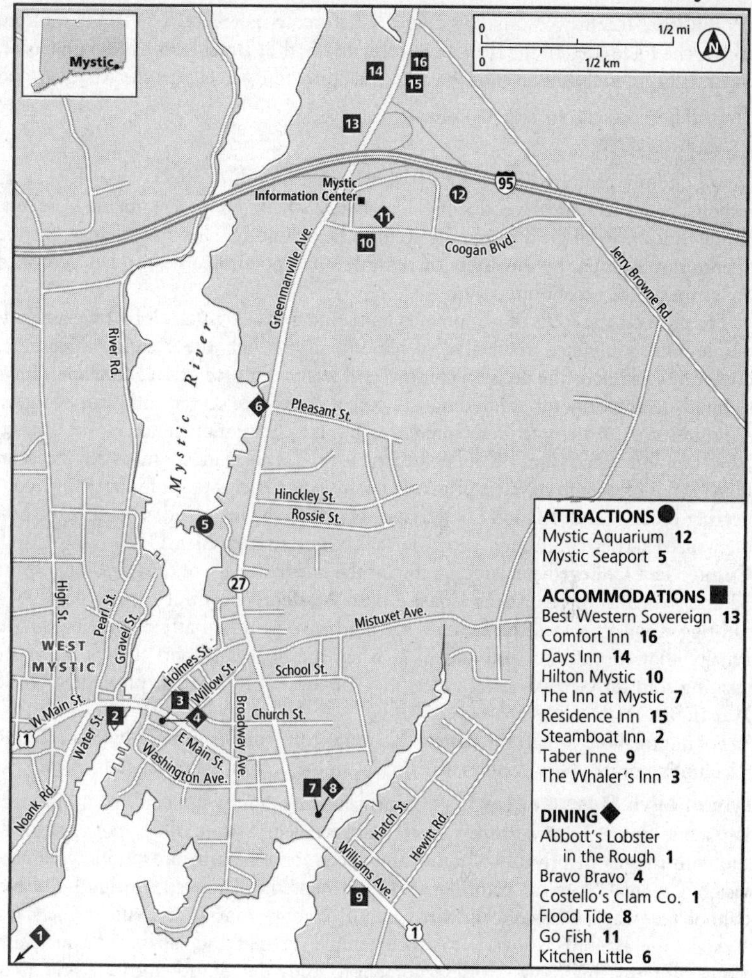

and commercial traffic of the western segment of I-95, use the Hutchinson River Parkway, which becomes the Merritt Parkway (Rte. 15) and merges with the Wilbur Cross Parkway. Continue to Exit 54, connecting with I-95 for the rest of the trip. From Boston, take the Massachusetts Turnpike to I-395 south to Exit 75, then south on Route 32 to New London and I-95.

Amtrak (© **800/USA-RAIL;** www.amtrak.com) runs several trains daily on its Northeast Direct route between New York, Providence, and Boston, with intermediate stops at New Haven, Old Saybrook, New London, and Mystic.

SEAT (© **860/886-2631**), the regional bus company, connects the more important towns and villages of the district, except for North Stonington.

VISITOR INFORMATION Two helpful sources of information are **Mystic & More** (© **800/873-6569;** www.mysticmore.com) and **Mystic Coast & Country**

(© **800/692-6278;** www.mycoast.com). If the many motels off I-95 aren't for you, ask for the folder describing the loosely affiliated **Bed & Breakfasts of Mystic Coast,** which lists 23 establishments in the area, including four just across the Rhode Island state line.

NEW LONDON

New London's protected deep-draft harbor at the mouth of the Thames River was responsible for its long and influential history as a whaling port. That heritage lingers, although its years of great prosperity seem to be behind it. That may change, for the opening of a global headquarters of the Pfizer Corporation in 2001 has provoked hopes for a rosier economic future.

The city was the focus of a Supreme Court ruling in 2005 that cleared the authorities to raze a blighted residential neighborhood through the exercise of eminent domain. What made the decision controversial was that it gave private developers leave to build a complex of office buildings, a hotel, a conference center, and luxury condos.

Possessed of an architecturally interesting but largely somnolent downtown district, New London, which lies 46 miles east of New Haven and 45 miles southeast of Hartford, is of note to travelers primarily because it's a transit point for ferry lines connecting Block Island, RI, and Long Island, NY, with the mainland, as well as the new high-speed ferries connecting with Martha's Vineyard and Glen Cove, Long Island. **Connecticut College** has a large campus at the northern edge of the city, along Route 32 and Williams Street. At the **Coast Guard Academy,** north of Exit 84 off I-95, a full-rigged sailing vessel, the *Eagle,* is the academy's principal attraction. Boarding is usually allowed only in April and May, when the boat is in port. It was built as a training ship for German naval cadets in 1936 and taken as a war prize after World War II.

For information, contact the **Eastern Regional Tourism District** (© **860/444-2206**), 32 Huntington St., New London, CT 06329, or log on to www.mysticcountry.com.

Lyman Allyn Museum of Art This neoclassical granite pile stands on a hill looking across Route 32 toward the Coast Guard Academy. Its holdings are the result of the enthusiasms of private collectors and therefore adhere to no specific curatorial vision. Colonial American paintings are supplemented by landscapes by Hudson River School landscapists Frederic Edwin Church, George Inness, and Albert Bierstadt. Upstairs are exhibits as diverse as Asian temple castings and Japanese lacquerware, along with traveling shows. Pause a moment to study the robustly intricate ship models of a local folk artist. A notable collection of 19th-century dolls and dollhouses, arranged in detailed room settings right down to tiny ladles on the kitchen counter, is now in the nearby Deshon-Allyn House.

625 Williams St. © **860/443-2545.** Admission $5 adults, $4 seniors and students, free for children under 8. Tues–Sat 10am–5pm; Sun 1–5pm. From Exit 83 off I-95, follow brown signs to museum.

GETTING OUTSIDE

Not far from downtown is **Ocean Beach Park,** at the south end of Ocean Avenue (© **800/510-7263** or 860/447-3031), a 40-acre recreational facility with a broad sand beach, boardwalk, 50m saltwater pool, miniature golf, water slide, bathhouse with lockers and showers, concession stands, and lounge. Open Memorial Day weekend through Labor Day, daily from 9am to 11pm.

The ferries that ply the Long Island Sound from New London have a recreational aspect, as well as simply serving as transport between Block Island and Long Island. **Cross Sound Ferry** (© **860/443-5281** for reservations and information; www.longislandferry.com) provides year-round service for both passengers and cars to Orient Point on Long Island. There are four to six departures a day, and the one-way voyage takes about an hour and 20 minutes. Round-trip fares are $25 for adults, $13 for children. Call ahead to make reservations, especially when taking a car. The **Fishers Island Ferry** (© **860/443-6851**) also has daily departures for Long Island. From late May to mid-October, **Block Island Express** (© **860/444-4624**) operates its high-speed catamaran daily between New London and the Old Harbor on Block Island, with five daily trips from mid-June to mid-September. The one-way trip takes a little over an hour. Round-trip rates are $25 for adults, $13 for children. Passengers and bicycles only. Reservations are essential.

WHERE TO STAY

Lighthouse Inn ★★ The former 1902 Sound-side mansion of a steel magnate is at the center of this multistructure property. It became an inn over 70 years ago and new owners have poured $1.2 million into its renovation. One of the outbuildings is a day spa providing salon services and massage therapy, another is a large cottage suitable for families, and a third contains 24 rooms—these, in addition to the 27 in the mansion. While the public rooms preserve a late Victorian flavor, all with working fireplaces, the bedrooms are more in country-home style, with a variety of antiques and reproductions, including some four-posters with crocheted tops. Eight suites have water views. Chef Timothy Grills (see review of Timothy's below) ensures that the several dining rooms are forever full. Meals are also served in the atmospheric tavern, where there is live music, mostly jazz, almost every night. Getting there is a challenge; the directions below lead from downtown's Bank Street.

6 Guthrie Place, New London, CT 06320. © **860/443-8411.** Fax 860/437-7027. www.lighthouseinn-ct.com. 52 units. $99–$379 double. Rates include breakfast. Packages available. AE, DC, MC, V. Drive west on Bank St. and turn left (south) on Howard St. This soon arrives at a rotary; take the 3rd exit, which goes under a railroad bridge. At the second traffic circle, take the 1st exit onto Pequot Ave. Follow Pequot about 1½ miles to Guthrie Place. Turn right. **Amenities:** Restaurant (New American); bar; heated outdoor pool; access to nearby health club and golf course. *In room:* A/C, TV, dataport, coffeemaker, hair dryer, iron.

WHERE TO DINE

Timothy's ★★ NEW AMERICAN Chef-owner Timothy Grills (talk about names as predestination) was doing just fine in his original contemporary bistro downtown. He's doing even better now, in his more expansive digs in the Lighthouse Inn. While there are always a couple of perky pastas on offer—a recent pasta primavera with scallops was particularly good—his menu now has fewer Italian touches. In fact, at first glance, it appears to be entirely conventional, with such stalwarts as Long Island duckling, salmon, and filet mignon. Obviously, he doesn't go in for mind-bending innovation, but shoots instead for a high level of execution. He brought along his signature creamy lobster and crabmeat bisque, hardly a rarity in these parts, but with supernal flavorings. Crab cakes on red pepper coulis and fried calamari with a chipotle dipping sauce are regulars, and very good. All of it is brightly seasoned, with daring combinations of fresh herbs. New London needs more operations like this.

In the Lighthouse Inn, 6 Guthrie Place. © **860/443-8411.** Reservations recommended. Main courses $18–$28. V, MC, Disc, AE. Daily 11:30am–2:30pm and 5:30–9:30pm (Fri until 10pm).

GROTON

The future is more promising for this naval-industrial town on the opposite side of the Thames from New London. It has long been dependent on the presence of the Electric Boat division of General Dynamics and the Navy's submarine base. There were threats to close the base, and, by extension, Electric Boat, but a federal commission issued a reprieve in 2004.

The principal tourist attraction remains the USS *Nautilus,* the world's first nuclear-powered vessel. After a visit to the submarine museum, history buffs may wish to stroll around **Fort Griswold Battlefield State Park,** Monument Street and Park Avenue (✆ **860/445-1729** or 860/449-6877). It was here, in 1781, that the traitor Benedict Arnold led a British force against American defenders, ruthlessly ordering the massacre of his 88 prisoners after they had surrendered. The free museum is open from Memorial Day to Labor Day, daily from 10am to 5pm; and from Labor Day to Columbus Day, Saturday and Sunday from 10am to 5pm.

Submarine Force Museum The entry hall and adjoining galleries display models of submarines, torpedoes, missiles, deck guns, periscopes, and a full-scale cross section of Bushnell's *Turtle,* the "first submersible ever used in a military conflict," in 1776. Out back, the 362-foot-long USS *Nautilus* itself stands at its mooring, ready for inspection. The claustrophobic walk through the control rooms, attack center, galley, and sleeping quarters is aided by listening devices handed out to each visitor. Passing through, it is difficult to imagine how it could possibly contain a crew of 116 men, especially on its fabled cruises between New London and San Juan and from Pearl Harbor to the North Pole.

Naval Submarine Base, 1 Crystal Lake Rd. ✆ **800/343-0079** or 860/694-3174. www.submarinemuseum. Free admission. May 15–Oct 31 Wed–Mon 9am–5pm, Tues 1–5pm; Nov 1–May 14 Wed–Mon 9am–4pm. Take Exit 86 from I-95, drive north on Rte. 12, and follow signs to the USS *Nautilus.*

FISHING TRIPS

A number of companies offer full- and half-day fishing trips. Typical of the party boats is the 114-foot ***Hel-Cat II,*** 181 Thames St. (✆ **860/535-2066** or 860/535-3200; www.visitconnecticut.com/helcat), operating from its own pier about 2 miles south of Exit 85 north or Exit 86 south off I-95. Trips are from 6 to 8½ hours at fares of $30 to $48. Tackle is available for rent.

Both charter and party boats are available from the **Sunbeam Fleet,** based at **Captain John's Sport Fishing Center,** 15 First St., Waterford (✆ **860/443-7259;** wwwsunbeamfleet.com). Fishing party boats sail twice daily Friday through Sunday from mid-May to mid-June, Thursday through Tuesday from late June to Labor Day. The same firm has whale-watching voyages three times a week in July and August. Nature cruises go eagle-watching in February and March, and search for harbor seals March through May. Adult fares are $40 to $68. Waterford is the town immediately south of New London; the dock is next to the Niantic River Bridge.

WHERE TO STAY

Mystic Marriott Hotel & Spa ★★ Filling a perceived gap in area lodgings, Marriott brings a measure of big-town pizzazz to an otherwise colorless intersection in a triangle occupied at the other corners by the casinos and Mystic. At a cost of $47 million, they obviously didn't stint, and there is little more that a business or leisure traveler might ask. Rooms adhere to corporate cookie-cutter standards, but are no less comfortable for that. Room safes are large enough for laptop computers; voice mail and high-speed Internet access are standard. On the sixth-floor concierge level, robes, fridges, and cordless phones are among the extras. The big deal is the Elizabeth Arden spa, which shares facilities with the excellent fitness center. In addition to the nail, skin-care, and hair salons are two hydrotubs, supplemented by seaweed wraps, herbal mud masks, massages, and stone therapy. Shuttles make frequent trips to both casinos.

625 North Rd. (Rte. 117), Groton, CT 06340. ✆ **866/449-7390** or 860/446-2600. Fax 860/446-2696. www.mysticmarriot.com. 291 units. $99–$279 double. Packages available. AE, DC DISC, MC, V. **Amenities:** 2 restaurants (steakhouse, bistro); bar; heated indoor 50m pool; exhaustively equipped health club and spa; business center; 24-hr. room service; same-day dry cleaning/laundry. *In room:* A/C, TV w/pay movies, PlayStation, dataport, coffeemaker, hair dryer, iron, safe.

WHERE TO DINE

Octagon ★ STEAKHOUSE After a stuttering start in its first months as the Mystic Marriott's formal restaurant, this ambitious steakhouse has hit its stride. While It's not as heavy-handedly masculine as others of its type, its dark, leathery tones still manage to look as if midtown Manhattan is just beyond the door. Beef is prime and grilled to the requested degree of doneness, but there are options beyond the expected T-bones, porterhouses, and New York strips. An interesting sidebar is the selection of "composed plates" for $17 to $27—various meats and fish paired with starches or vegetables, such as scallops with a leek and corn risotto and shellfish tossed with fettucini and artichokes. Starters include local oysters and clams from the raw bar, typically followed by beef with the usual preparations, in 8- to 24-ounce sizes. Salmon and tuna are also available. The short dessert list of cheesecake and cobblers is complemented by a longer selection of ports, cognacs, and single-malt scotches.

In the Mystic Marriott Hotel, 625 North Rd. ✆ **860/326-0300.** Reservations recommended. Main courses $16–$36. AE, DC, DISC, MC, V. Daily 7:30–11am, noon–2:30pm, and 6–10pm.

Olio CONTEMPORARY BISTRO Even the week after its opening, this spiffy little roadhouse needed nothing but word-of-mouth to pack in eager diners nightly. Ranging in age from barely legal to decidedly mature, patrons drop by on a whim for an hour or two of leisurely grazing (although it's wise to have a reservation). Pastas (14 of them) dominate the offerings, with an equal number of international standards like fried calamari, chicken satays, quesadillas, and bruschettas filling out the menu—tasty and quick for all their familiarity. With bare tables and hard surfaces everywhere, it's loud. And take the reading glasses, because the menu is written in a tiny hand and there are only guttering candles and a few dim pinlights for illumination. The waitstaff is young and appealing enough that it's easy to forgive their lack of efficiency in keeping glasses full.

33 Kings Hwy. (Rte. 395, exit 86N off I-95). ✆ **860/445-6546.** Reservations advised. Main courses $13–$29. AE, MC, V. Mon–Sat 11:30am–4:30pm and 5–9pm (until 10pm Fri–Sat); Sun 5–9pm.

MYSTIC ★★★

The spirit and texture of the maritime life and history of New England are captured in many ports along its indented coast, but nowhere more cogently than beside the Mystic River estuary and its harbor. This was a dynamic whaling and shipbuilding center during the Colonial period and into the 20th century, but the discontinuation of the first industry and the decline of the second haven't adversely affected the community. No derelict barges or rotting piers degrade the views and waterways (or at least not many).

Mystic and West Mystic are stitched together by a drawbridge, the raising of which, mostly for sailboats, causes traffic stoppages at a quarter past every hour but rarely shortens tempers, except for visitors who don't leave their urban impatience behind. There are complaints by some that the two-part town has been commercialized, but the incidence of T-shirt shops and related tackiness is limited, and the more garish motels and attractions have been restricted to the periphery, especially up near Exit 90 off I-95.

The town is home to one of New England's most singular attractions, the Mystic Seaport museum village. Far more than the single building the name might suggest, it is a re-created seaport of the mid-1800s, with dozens of buildings and watercraft of that romantic era of clipper ships and the China trade.

A **visitor center** is in Building 1D of the Olde Mistick Village shopping center, at Route 27 and Coogan Boulevard, near the Interstate (✆ **860/536-1641**).

WHAT TO SEE & DO

Mystic Aquarium ★★ Kids If you've never seen a marine show, the Marine Theater here is the place. It features alternating dolphins, sea lions, and orcas. Less gimmicky than similar commercial enterprises in Florida and California, the show illuminates as it entertains, and at 15 minutes in length, doesn't test the attention spans of the very young.

While the rest of the exhibits are in the shadow of the stars, they are enough to occupy at least another hour. In the outdoor "Alaskan Coast," see five beluga whales squeal and twirl and otherwise perform for their trainers at feeding time. Next door is a facsimile of the Bering Strait's Pribilof Islands, home to fur seals and endangered Steller sea lions, and out back are African black-footed penguins, with underwater viewing windows. A $52-million expansion was completed in 1999 under the direction of the legendary undersea explorer Robert Ballard, who discovered the sunken *Titanic,* represented here by a detailed 18-foot mode. Even newer is a re-creation of a Louisiana bayou stocked with "Swamp Things:" frogs, turtles, carp, largemouth bass, and small alligators. Elsewhere, visitors are eye to eye with such creatures as sea horses, jellyfish, and the pugnacious yellow-head jaw fish, which spends its hours digging fortifications in the sand. Dozens of rays flutter like butterflies and translucent jellyfish billow and flex in slow motion dance, a hypnotic display.

55 Coogan Blvd. (at Exit 90 off I-95). ✆ **860/572-5955.** www.mysticaquarium.org. Admission $18 adults, $17 seniors, $13 children 3–12. July to Labor Day Sun–Thurs 9am–7pm, Fri–Sat 9am–6pm; Sept–Dec daily 9am–6pm; Jan–Feb Mon–Fri 10am–5pm, Sat–Sun 9am–6pm; Feb–June daily 9am–6pm.

Mystic Seaport ★★★ Kids Few visitors fail to be enthralled by this evocative museum village. It encompasses an entire waterfront settlement, more than 60 buildings on and near a 17-acre peninsula poking into the Mystic River. Plan to set aside at least 2 or 3 hours—if not an entire day—for a visit. A useful map guide is available at the ticket counter in the **visitor center** in the building opposite the museum stores (which stay open later than the village most of the year, so make them your last stop).

Exit the visitor center and bear right along the path leading between the Galley Restaurant and the village green. It bends to the left, intersecting with a street of shops, public buildings, and houses. At that corner is an 1870s hardware and dry-goods store.

Turning right here, you'll pass a schoolhouse, a chapel, and an 1830s home. Stop at the **children's museum,** which invites youngsters to play games characteristic of the seafaring era. It faces a small square that is the starting point for **horse-drawn wagon tours.**

From here, the three-masted barque ***Charles W. Morgan,*** one of the proudest possessions of the Seaport fleet of over 400 craft, is only a few steps away. It was built in 1841.

If you're a fan of scrimshaw and ship models, continue along the waterfront to the right until you reach the **Stillman Building,** which contains fascinating exhibits of both. Otherwise, head left toward the lighthouse. Along the way, you'll encounter a tavern, an 1833 bank, a cooperage, and other shops and services that did business with the whalers and clipper ships that put in at ports such as this.

The friendly docents in the village are highly competent at the crafts they demonstrate and are always ready to impart as much information as visitors care to absorb. The fact that they aren't dressed in period costumes (except during special events like the Christmas lamplight tours) paradoxically enhances the village's feeling of authenticity by avoiding the contrived air of many such enterprises.

The next vessel encountered is the iron-hulled square-rigger ***Joseph Conrad,*** which dates from 1881. Up ahead is a small **lighthouse,** which looks out across the water toward the large riverside houses that line the opposite shore. Round the horn, go past the boat sheds, the fishing shacks, and the ketches and sloops that are moored along here in season until you come to the dock for the perky little 1908 **SS *Sabino.*** This working ship gives half-hour river rides from mid-May to early October, daily from 11am to 4pm, and 1½-hour evening excursions Monday through Thursday leaving at 5pm, Friday and Saturday at 7pm. A few steps away is the 1921 fishing schooner ***L. A. Dunton.***

And still the village isn't exhausted. A few steps south is the **Henry B. Du Pont Preservation Shipyard,** where the boats are painstakingly restored. One recent project was the re-creation of the schooner *Amistad,* which inspired an exhibit exploring the historical incident.

Also on the grounds are the **Galley Restaurant,** which serves pretty good fish and chips, fried clam strips, and lobster rolls; and **Sprouter's Tavern,** which offers snacks and sandwiches.

When you exit for the day, ask the gatekeeper to validate your ticket so you can come back the next day for free.

Across the brick courtyard with the giant anchor is a building containing several **museum stores** as well as an art gallery. These superior shops stock books, kitchenware, fresh-baked goods, nautical prints and paintings, and ship models.

75 Greenmanville Ave. (Rte. 27). ✆ **888/9-SEAPORT** or 860/572-5315. www.visitmysticseaport.org. Admission $17 adults, $9 children 6–12 (2nd day included with validation). AE, MC, V. Ships and exhibits Apr–Oct daily 9am–5pm, Nov–Mar daily 10am–4pm; grounds 9am–5pm. Closed Dec 25. Take Exit 90 off I-95, going about 1 mile south on Rte. 27 toward Mystic. Parking lots are on the left, the entrance on the right.

GETTING OUTSIDE

Several operators offer **sailing and fishing cruises.** One of the most convenient is the ***Argia*** (✆ **860/536-0416;** www.voyagermystic.com), a replica of a 19th-century schooner that docks 100 feet south of the drawbridge in Mystic. Offered are sunset cruises, harbor tours, and half-day sailing trips. Fares are $25 to $38 for adults, $22 to $35 for seniors, $15 to $28 for children under 18 years. For longer trips, outings on the ***Mystic Whaler*** (✆ **800/697-8420;** fax 860/536-4219; www.mysticwhaler.com) include dinner sails, day trips, and extended cruises that can last 2, 3, or 5 days. Corresponding rates go from $80 up to $835. Voyages set out from a pier at 15 Holmes St., off Route 27, 1 mile south of Mystic Seaport.

SHOPPING

Downtown Mystic has limited shopping, a situation made worse by a fire in 2000 that destroyed a 19th-century building with eight storefronts next to the famous drawbridge. Of the survivors, an engaging choice is **Bank Square Books,** 53 W. Main St. (© **860/536-3795**), which has remodeled and expanded since the fire.

WHERE TO STAY & DINE

The Inn at Mystic ★★ A variety of lodgings are on offer at this property occupying 13 acres overlooking Long Island Sound. At the crest of the hill a 1904 Classical Revival mansion has public rooms as grand as the exterior. Bedrooms are humbler; antique furniture mixed with merely old stuff, but many have four-poster beds and some have whirlpools. Porches and decks take in both sunrises and sunsets. Down the hill is the intimate Gatehouse, similarly accoutered. Some, but not all, of the units in the motel sections are equally well appointed.

The complex also incorporates one of the area's better restaurants, **Flood Tide** (© **860/536-8140**), newly renovated, with an exhibition kitchen containing a wood-burning grill and brick oven and a menu that claims to serve all natural and organic foods. The dining rooms look out over the sound, so ask for a table by the window.

Routes 1 and 27, Mystic, CT 06355. © **800/237-2415** or 860/536-9604. www.innatmystic.com. 67 units. $95–$295 double. Rates include afternoon tea. Packages available. AE, DC, DISC, MC, V. Pets accepted in 6 units ($10). **Amenities:** Restaurant (contemporary bistro); bar; outdoor pool; 2 putting greens; tennis court; access to nearby health club; free kayaks and boats; limited room service; same-day dry cleaning/laundry. *In room:* A/C, TV, dataport, fridge, coffeemaker, hair dryer.

WHERE TO STAY

There are plenty of ho-hum but adequate area motels that can soak up the traffic at all but peak periods, meaning weekends from late spring to early fall plus weekdays in July and August, when it is necessary to have reservations. Pick of the litter may be the **Best Western Sovereign,** north of Exit 90 (© **860/536-4281**), with a pool and restaurant. Nearby competitors are the **Comfort Inn** (© **860/572-8531**), **Days Inn** (© **860/572-0574**), and **Residence Inn** (© **860/536-5150**).

Hilton Mystic ★ Unlike the motels clustered around the I-95 interchange, this is a full-service hotel, providing the amenities expected of its big-city cousins, though without much personality. The front desk is often willing to negotiate prices. A pianist entertains many evenings in the lounge. The hotel is owned by the Pequot tribe, so it's no surprise to see posters announcing coming attractions at Foxwoods Casino and a shuttle van to take you there. High-speed Internet access is available.

20 Coogan Blvd., Mystic, CT 06355. © **800/445-8667** or 860/572-0731. Fax 860/572-0328. www.hiltonmystic.com. 183 units. $85–$250 double. AE, DC, DISC, MC, V. Free valet parking. Take Exit 90 off I-95 and drive south, following signs to the Mystic Aquarium; the hotel is opposite. **Amenities:** Restaurant (Continental); lounge; heated indoor pool; fitness room; bike rental; children's programs; video arcade; limited room service; same-day dry cleaning/laundry. *In room:* A/C, TV w/pay movies, dataport, coffeemaker, hair dryer, iron.

Steamboat Inn ★★ Mystic's most ingratiating lodging is easily overlooked from land, but readily apparent from the river. Perched on the riverbank, the yellow-clapboard structure has apartment-size downstairs bedrooms, with Jacuzzis and wet bars, while the upstairs units have wood-burning fireplaces. Every room is decorated differently—Laura Ashley must have been a muse—and all but one have water views. They are, it must be said, starting to look just a bit tired. A nonsmoking policy is enforced. The inn commissioned the 97-foot luxury yacht, *Valiant,* that is moored at its dock. The five staterooms can be rented when the yacht isn't chartered; log on to www.valiantcharters.com.

73 Steamboat Wharf, Mystic, CT 06355. ✆ **860/536-8300.** Fax 860/536-9528. www.visitmystic.com/steamboat. 10 units. Late May to Nov $165–$300 double; Dec to mid-May $140–$260 double. Rates include breakfast. AE, DISC, MC, V. Validated parking available in a gated lot. Look for the sign pointing down an alley on the west bank of the Mystic River, just before the drawbridge. No children under 9. *In room:* A/C, TV, dataport, fridge, coffeemaker, hair dryer, iron.

Taber Inne ★ Not quite an inn but more than a motel, this place has something to suit most tastes and budgets, with seven immaculate buildings containing both simple units and hedonistic suites with fireplaces and decks. A recently erected cottage with a cathedral ceiling has two bedrooms, a sitting room, and a kitchen, and a new building with an indoor pool and fitness center opened in 2004. Most rooms have fireplaces and twenty have whirlpools; high-speed Internet access is available.

66 Williams Ave. (Rte. 1; 2 blocks east of the intersection with Rte. 27), Mystic, CT 06355. ✆ **860/536-4904.** Fax 860/572-9140. www.taberinn.com. 34 units. Mid-Apr to Nov $155–$169 double; Nov to mid-Apr $95–$139 double. Rates include breakfast. AE, MC, V. **Amenities:** Heated indoor pool; exercise room, access to nearby health club w/tennis court. *In room:* A/C, TV, dataport, coffeemaker, hair dryer.

The Whaler's Inn ★ Acquired by people who also have interests in the estimable Steamboat Inn in Mystic (above) and The Inn at Stonington (below), the previously dispirited aspect of the venerable Whaler's has been banished. The five structures that constitute the property have all been addressed, with fresh fabrics and furnishings and new bathrooms. Best of all (and most expensive) are the eight bedrooms of Hoxie House, all with gas fireplaces, Jacuzzis, and Bose table radios. Sleigh beds and four-posters are common, and some rooms have VCRs. Breakfast is taken in the spacious Hospitality Room, which also has an Internet terminal for guest use.

20 E. Main St., Mystic, CT 06355. ✆ **800/243-2588** or 860/536-1506. Fax 860/572-1250. www.whalersinnmystic.com. Apr to late Nov $110–$249 double; Dec–Mar $99–$179 double. V, MC, Disc, AE. Rates include breakfast. Packages available. *In room:* A/C, TV, dataport, coffeemaker, hair dryer.

WHERE TO DINE

Abbott's Lobster in the Rough ★ SEAFOOD It's as if a wedge of the Maine coast had been punched into the Connecticut shore. This nitty-gritty lobster shack has plenty of picnic tables and not a frill to be found. While many options, including hot dogs and chicken, are available, the classic shore dinner rules. That means clam chowder, boiled shrimp, steamed mussels, and a tasty lobster, with coleslaw, chips, and drawn butter thrown in. Bring your own beer. Nearby is **Costello's Clam Co.,** owned by the same family, where scallops and the eponymous bivalves are featured. (Get it? Abbott's? Costello's?)

117 Pearl St., Noank. ✆ **860/536-7719.** Reservations not accepted. Main courses $16–$34 (prices subject to market availability). AE, MC, V. First Fri in May to Memorial Day and after Labor Day weekend to Columbus Day weekend Fri–Sun noon–7pm; Memorial Day to Labor Day weekend daily noon–9pm. From downtown Mystic, go south on Rte. 215 and cross a railroad bridge. At Main St. in Noank, turn left, and take an immediate right on Pearl St. Be prepared to ask for directions anyway.

Bravo Bravo ★ NEW ITALIAN/AMERICAN Ask locals about the best restaurant in town, and they'll probably send you here. It's a money machine for the owners, even on a frigid off-season night. Reserve or plan to wait, for even a recent expansion into a bakery next door only made room for more people to squeeze in. It can get as noisy as a disco, aided by bare wood tables and floors, and the waitstaff can get a little scattered.

Warm, coarse country bread arrives with drinks, supplemented with marinated olives and a white-bean red pepper spread. Order antipasti and get a plate crowded with salami, provolone, tuna chunks, artichoke hearts, and sliced tomatoes. At least half the entrees involve pasta—lobster ravioli, shrimp with fusilli, linguine and clams—but cool weather choices usually include braised lamb shanks and *osso buco.*

20 E. Main St. ✆ **860/536-3228.** Reservations recommended. Main courses $16–$25. AE, DC, MC, V. Sun and Tues–Thurs 5–9pm; Fri–Sat 5–10pm.

Go Fish ★ SEAFOOD Brash and boisterous, Go Fish is dominated by a sprawling granite bar at its center, often surrounded by younger drinkers and grazers. At the far end is an enclosed sushi bar, while near the door is a room usually populated by older folks and families. Local or regional fishery products are employed as much as possible, including Stonington sea scallops and Point Judith calamari. A long list of daily specials relies on fresh catches. The choice is yours: baked, roasted, grilled, deep-fried, or pan-blackened, and meals invariably arrive exactly as ordered. Portions are abundant, so you might want to skip appetizers, enticing though they are (the creamy bisque, for one). Each day has featured beers and wines.

Olde Mistick Village, at Exit 90 off I-95. ✆ **860/536-2662.** Reservations not accepted. Main courses $17–$26. AE, DC, DISC, MC, V. Sun–Thurs 11:30am–9:30pm; Fri–Sat 11:30am–10:30pm.

Kitchen Little ★ AMERICAN Not much more than a shack by the water, this is the sort of place dismissed and passed every day by hundreds of tourists hurrying on to the Seaport. They're missing not only 45 distinct breakfast choices, including at least a dozen three-egg omelets, but also some of the coast's tastiest clam and scallop dishes. At lunch, you must have the clear broth clam chowder, maybe the whole belly clam rolls, and absolutely the fried scallop sandwich. Or the lobster roll, with no fillers, only tail and claw flesh. Expect a wait in summer and tight quarters inside. They serve only breakfast on weekends. Try to snare a table out back, in view of the tall ships.

Rte. 27, 1 mile south of I-95. ✆ **860/536-2122.** Reservations not accepted. Main dishes $3.45–$13. MC, V. Mon–Fri 6:30am–2pm; Sat–Sun 6:30am–1pm.

STONINGTON & NORTH STONINGTON

Not much seemed to happen in these slumbering villages, only lightly brushed by the 21st century despite all the thrashing about in heavily touristed Mystic. That suited the residents just fine, explaining why most of them are not thrilled by the continual rumors of projected expansions of the nearby Foxwoods complex, not to mention the federal recognition of a third tribe, the Eastern Pequots, in 2002.

It is difficult to imagine what the flexing of the established gambling empire might do, eventually, to inland North Stonington, as peaceful a New England hamlet as can be found, with hardly any commercialization beyond a couple of inns. Sound-side Stonington has a pronounced maritime flavor, sustained by the presence of the state's only remaining (albeit dwindling) fishing fleet. Its two lengthwise streets are lined with well-preserved Federal-style and Greek Revival homes. The town marked its 350th anniversary in 1999.

EXPLORING THE AREA

For an introduction, drive south to **Cannon Square** along Stonington's **Water Street.** Standing in the grassy main square are two cannons that were used to fight off an attack by British warships during the War of 1812. Opposite is a lovely old granite house and, on the corner, a neoclassical bank.

Continue south to the end of Water Street, where there's a small **town beach** (admission $2–$3, or $5–$6 per family). The misty blue headland directly south across the sound is Montauk Point, the eastern extremity of New York's Long Island. Return along Main Street, which is almost exclusively residential except for a few government buildings.

You might check out the **Old Lighthouse Museum,** 7 Water St. (✆ **860/535-1440**). Built of stone in 1823, it was moved here from 100 yards away and deactivated. Most of its exhibits relate to the maritime past of the area, with scrimshaw tusks and the export porcelain that constituted much of the 19th-century China trade. Most interesting is the carved ivory pagoda. Admission is $5 for adults, $3 for children 6 to 12. Open May through October, Tuesday through Sunday from 10am to 5pm.

One of the Nutmeg State's handful of earnest wineries, **Stonington Vineyards,** 523 Taugwonk Rd., Stonington (✆ **860/535-1222**), has a tasting room in a barn beside its vineyard. There are usually five or six pressings to be sampled, with an aged-in-oak chardonnay leading the pack. Bring a picnic, buy a bottle, and take them to tables overlooking the vineyards or the brook than runs past. Open daily from 11am to 5pm, with a cellar tour at 2pm. To get here, take Exit 91 off I-95 and drive north 2½ miles.

WHERE TO STAY & DINE

Randall's Ordinary ★ The oldest structure on this 250-acre estate dates from 1685. The three bedrooms upstairs have fireplaces and four-poster or canopied beds, though no TVs or phones. Those conveniences are provided in the rooms in the nearby 1819 barn. All meals are cooked at an open hearth and served by a staff in period costumes. Considering the primitive circumstances under which the food is prepared, it is always hearty, if simple. The fixed-price dinner is $39 per person. Go for the romantic setting, not the food.

Rte. 2, North Stonington, CT 06359. ✆ **877/599-4540.** Fax 860/599-3308. www.randallsordinary.com. 18 units. $140–$250 double. Packages available. AE, MC, V. Take Exit 92 off I-95 and head north on Rte. 2. *In room:* A/C.

WHERE TO STAY

The Inn at Stonington ★★ Built on the site of a restaurant leveled by fire a few years ago, this inn harmonizes nicely with its neighbors on the town's main street. Combining the intimacy of a small inn with the comforts of a luxury hotel, it abounds in felicitous flourishes that exceed the expected. Every unit has a gas fireplace, six have balconies, and 10 have Jacuzzis. While rooms reflect a single design sensibility, with tailored contemporary interpretations of country decor, no two are alike. They recently annexed the building next door and added six more rooms, most of them even larger than the originals. It's so quiet guests might think they are alone, until they enter the bar and find that everyone else has shown up for the evening wine-and-cheese gathering.

60 Water St., Stonington, CT 06378. ✆ **860/535-2000.** Fax 860/535-8193. www.innatstonington.com. 18 units. Spring/summer $155–$440 double; fall/winter $140–$395 double. Rates include breakfast and evening wine and cheese. AE, DC, MC, V. Take Exit 91 off I-95; follow signs into Stonington village. **Amenities:** Small, well-equipped exercise room; bikes and kayaks available; computer for guests' use. *In room:* A/C, TV, dataport, hair dryer.

WHERE TO DINE

Boom ★ NEW AMERICAN With a spate of closings in recent years, it's a challenge picking new restaurants in Stonington that have the wherewithal to survive. This one,

A Casino in the Woods

What has been wrought in the woodlands north of the Mystic coast in the last decade is astonishing. There was little but trees here when the Mashantucket Pequot tribe received clearance to open a gambling casino on their ancestral lands in rural Ledyard. Virtually overnight, the tribal bingo parlor was expanded into a full-fledged casino, and a hotel was built.

That was in 1992. Within 3 years, it had become the single most profitable gambling operation in the world, with a reported 40,000 visitors a day. Money cascaded over the Pequot (pronounced *Pee*-kwat) in a seemingly endless torrent. Expansion was immediate—another hotel, then a third, more casinos, golf courses, and the $139-million **Mashantucket Pequot Museum and Research Center,** devoted to Native American arts and culture. The tribe bought up adjacent lands and at least four nearby inns and hotels, and then opened a shipworks to build high-speed ferries. All that hasn't sopped up the cascades of money, and the tribe has made major contributions to the Mystic Aquarium and Smithsonian Museum of the American Indian.

And that isn't the end of it. The Mashantucket Pequot Tribal Nation has announced a new $700-million project, scheduled for completion in mid-2008. Included will be a fourth high-rise hotel, another parking garage, two new golf courses, and more shops, restaurants, and gambling spaces.

All this prosperity came to a tribe of fewer than 520 acknowledged members, nearly all of them of mixed ethnicity. Residents of surrounding communities were ambivalent, to put the best face on it. When it was learned that one of the tribe's corporate entities was to be called Two Trees Limited Partnership, a predictable query was, "Is that all you're going to leave us? Two trees?"

But while there is a continuing danger of damage to the fragile character of this authentically picturesque corner of Connecticut, it is also a fact

though, has spawned a sibling by the same name at Brewer's Pilots Point Marina in Westbrook (© **860/399-2322**). The original is a companionable, under-decorated little room looking out over a marina. Often, there are irresistible fried oysters among the appetizers, and the roasted tomato bisque with a Stonington scallop and chèvre is a surprise. Seafood is the way to go, as with the seafood risotto and lobster ravioli. Salmon, tuna, and flounder are regulars, in various guises, but you can order hanger steak or sirloin, if you insist. They come in manageable portions. In good weather, tables are set up outside with a raw bar. Local purveyors are employed for seafood, and the restaurant moves a lot of lobster in summer.

Dodson Boatyard, 194 Water St. © **860/535-2588.** Reservations recommended on weekends. Main courses $16–$25. AE, MC, V. Tues–Sat 11:30am–3pm; Sun 10am–3pm; Tues–Sun 5:30–9:30pm. Closed Mar.

Water Street Café NEW AMERICAN It's easy to spot this place with its painted ocher-and-blue exterior on the main drag. Inside, exposed pipes and industrial-type lighting contrast with rustic walls and banquettes. A blackboard lists daily specials, and those are often the best choices. Otherwise, hunger pangs can certainly be that because of the recent development, thousands of non-Pequots have found employment in their various enterprises.

The complex is reached through forested countryside of quiet hamlets that give little hint of the behemoth rising above the trees in Ledyard township. There are no signs screaming FOXWOODS. Instead, watch for plaques with the symbols of tree, wolf, and fire above the word RESERVATION. As you enter the property, platoons of attendants point the way to parking and hotels. Ongoing construction surrounds the glassy, turquoise-and-violet towers of the hotels and casino. Though bustling, it doesn't look like Vegas from the outside—happily, it lacks sphinxes, fake volcanoes, and neon palm trees.

Inside, the glitz gap narrows, but it is still relatively restrained as such temples to chance go. The gambling rooms have windows, for example, even though the prevailing wisdom among casino designers is that they should not give customers any idea of what time of day or night it is.

And no one is allowed to forget that this whole eye-popping affair is owned and operated by Native Americans. Prominently placed around the main buildings are larger-than-life sculptures by artists of Chiricahua and Chippewa descent, depicting Amerindians in a variety of poses and artistic styles. One other Indian-oriented display is *The Rainmaker,* a glass statue of an archer shooting an arrow into the air. Every hour on the hour, he is the focus of artificial thunder, wind-whipped rain, and lasers pretending to be lightning bolts, the action described in murky prose by a booming voice-of-Manitou narrator. That's as close as the chest thumping gets to going over-the-top.

Two dozen bus companies provide daily service to Foxwoods from Boston, Hartford, Providence, New York, Philadelphia, and Albany, among many other cities—too many to list here. For information on transit from particular destinations, call ✆ **860/885-3000.**

assuaged by such reliables as Buffalo wings, barbecue pork sandwiches, burgers, and lobster spring rolls. Expect comforting edibles, shorn of artifice, not artistry.

143 Water St. ✆ **860/535-2122.** Reservations advised on weekends. Main courses $10–$19. MC, V. Daily 11:30–2:30pm and 5–10pm (until 11pm Fri–Sat).

FOXWOODS RESORT CASINO

This casino-hotel complex (✆ **800/369-9003;** www.foxwoods.com) is forever changing, adding, renovating, and expanding. There are six cavernous gambling rooms, one of the most popular being the hall containing 4,500 slot machines (out of a total of 6,400). The 3,200-seat Bingo Hall is huge, and the high-tech horse parlor is a dazzler. All the usual methods of depleting wallets are at hand—blackjack, bingo, keno, craps, baccarat, roulette, money wheels, and several variations of poker.

WHAT TO SEE & DO

Mashantucket Pequot Museum and Research Center ★★ A $139-million trickle of the floods of cash washing over southeastern Connecticut and its resurgent

Indian Nation was diverted to create this museum. Opened in 1998 to substantial fanfare, it has justified the hoopla with a carefully conceived mix of film, murals, models, dioramas, and re-creations of scenes of Native American life. The Pequot Village exhibit is complete with wigwams and life-size figures shown fishing, hunting, cooking, butchering game, and making baskets and ceramics. An observation tower supplies views of the reservation. Lunch and snacks are served in the restaurant, and there's a shop with books, jewelry, and crafts. A shuttle bus carries visitors between the museum and the casinos.

110 Pequot Trail. ✆ **800/411-9671.** www.mashantucket.com. Admission $15 adults (16–54), $13 seniors, $10 children 6–15. Daily 10am–4pm.

WHERE TO STAY

The resort has three hotels, with another on the way, the newest and most luxurious of which became operational in 1998, more than doubling Foxwoods' housing capacity. Unlike Las Vegas and other gambling centers, rates aren't kept artificially low as an inducement to gamblers.

To get to the resort from Boston, take I-95 south to Exit 92 onto Route 2 west. From New Haven and New York, take I-95 to I-395 north to Exit 79A onto Route 2A east, picking up Route 2 east. Don't bother trying to park your car in the huge garage. It takes forever, and the valet parking at the front door is swift and free.

Grand Pequot Tower ★★ The Grand Pequot Tower handily takes its place among New England's elite resort hotels. The newest of Foxwoods' hotels (so far) is the grandest in space and concept, yet it is also the most tasteful of the three. Polished granite and imported woods and marbles feature extensively in the handsome lobby. The tower's main restaurants, Fox Harbour and Al Dente, surpass all the resort competition. In back is a 50,000-square-foot casino, containing a plush Club Newport International open only to big-money players.

Rte. 2, Mashantucket, CT 06339. ✆ **800/369-9663** or 860/885-3000. Fax 860/312-7474. www.foxwoods.com. 824 units. July to Labor Day $220–$295 double, from $400 suite; Sept–June $145–$270 double, from $400 suite. AE, DC, DISC, MC, V. Free valet parking. **Amenities:** 2 restaurants (seafood, Italian); bars; indoor pool; golf course on property; health club and spa; video arcade; concierge; shopping arcade; 24-hr. room service; babysitting; same-day dry cleaning/laundry. *In room:* A/C, TV, dataport, hair dryer.

Great Cedar Hotel ★ Well maintained despite the heavy foot traffic, this hotel has eight floors adjoining the casinos. Guest rooms are colorful, but not too gaudy (except for the suites for high rollers on the top floor).

Rte. 2, Mashantucket, CT 06339. ✆ **800/369-9663** or 860/885-3000. Fax 860/885-4040. www.foxwoods.com. 312 units. July to Labor Day $160–$220 double, from $500 suite; Sept–June $175–$265 double, from $500 suite. AE, DC, DISC, MC, V. Free valet parking. **Amenities:** Restaurant; bars; indoor pool; golf course on the property; health club and spa; video arcade; shopping arcade; limited room service; babysitting; same-day dry cleaning/laundry. *In room:* A/C, TV, dataport.

Two Trees Inn This was the first Foxwoods lodging, built in less than 3 months, now a short shuttle-bus ride or 10-minute walk from the casino complex. A conventional motor hotel, it attracts large numbers of bus tours.

240 Lantern Hill Rd. (off Rte. 2), Mashantucket, CT 06339. ✆ **800/369-9663** or 860/312-3000. Fax 860/885-4050. www.foxwoods.com. 280 units. Nov–Mar $99–$225 double, suites from $210; Apr–June $125–$210 double, suites from $180; July–Aug $150–$225 double; suites from $280; Sept–Oct $125–$220 double, suites from $250. AE, DC, DISC, MC, V. **Amenities:** Restaurant; bar; heated indoor pool; fitness room; sauna; same-day dry cleaning/laundry. *In room:* A/C, TV.

Kids A Break from Gambling

If you want to temporarily escape the whirring of slots at Foxwoods, or simply need to occupy underage kids, check out **Cinetropolis,** an entertainment center that looks like a cleaned-up futuristic Gotham. **Turbo Ride** lets you pretend you're experiencing the rumbling takeoffs and powerful G-forces of jets taking off. **Fox Giant Screen Theatre** is an IMAX-like production that features front-row rock concerts and exploding volcanoes, and **Virtual Adventures** lets you take control of an undersea vessel.

WHERE TO DINE

Twenty-four restaurants and fast-food operations situated throughout the hotel-casino complex cover the most popular options. Only a couple aspire to even moderately serious culinary achievement, and unlike Atlantic City or Vegas there are no bargains to be found. Except at the Festival Buffet (below), expect to pay at least $50 for dinner for two, not including drinks, taxes, or tip.

Cedars Steak House grills Angus beef and native seafood, **Al Dente** does designer pizzas and pastas, and **Paragon** traffics in French-Asian–influenced cuisine. All three expect guests to be dressed at least a notch better than tank tops and shorts, and they accept reservations. Call ✆ **860/885-3000** and ask for the desired extension.

The most popular dining room is the **Festival Buffet** (ext. 3172), with an extensive all-you-can-eat spread. Other self-explanatory possibilities are **Han Garden** (ext. 4093), **Pequot Grill** (ext. 2690), and **The Deli** (ext. 5481).

FOXWOODS AFTER DARK

Just as in Vegas and Atlantic City, big showbiz names are whisked onto the premises, usually on weekends. Even Wayne Newton makes the scene, as do the likes of Chris Rock, Tony Bennett, Jon Stewart, the Dixie Chicks, and Jay Leno. For information, call ✆ **800/200-2882.** A recent addition to the complex is Connecticut's first Hard Rock Cafe.

UNCASVILLE & THE MOHEGAN SUN CASINO

About halfway between New London and Norwich, this blue collar town was once hardly worth downshifting your car for. That's changed, for good.

In 1996, the barely-extant Mohegan tribe opened its gambling casino, the **Mohegan Sun,** Mohegan Sun Boulevard (✆ **888/226-7711;** www.mohegansun.com). Sitting in the middle of a potential $1-billion annual market, it was drawing 20,000 gamblers a day away from Foxwoods within a few weeks of opening. Obviously, the initial outlay of over $300 million for land and construction paid off handsomely, for the tribe announced soon after its inauguration that it was committing another $400 million for a new 1,200-room hotel, a marina, and non-gambling entertainment facilities. Those undertakings were soon completed and the complex now also includes a 10,000-seat sports arena (with its own professional basketball team, the WNBA's Connecticut Sun), a planetarium, and a "Casino of the Sky" to complement the original "Casino of the Earth."

Both casinos bulge with eager gamblers. "Earth" is circular, with four entrances named for the seasons. The core of 150,000 square feet is devoted to the games, everything from blackjack to craps, supplemented by keno, a race book, and thousands of slot machines. In the center is a nightclub, the Wolf's Den, featuring free entertainment with weekend headliners on the order of Seal and Crystal Gayle. Overhead are simulated log constructions meant to suggest ancient lodge houses. It's an aesthetically pleasing space, as casinos go, although few of the avid players seem to notice. They can even park their kids in the child-care center. "Sky" directly adjoins the hotel, and is more splashily Vegas in style. It contains over thirty pricey shops and the 300-seat Cabaret, venue of choice for such headliners as Tony Bennett. The sports arena handles basketball, boxing matches, bull riders, and luminaries on the order of David Bowie, Keith Urban, and Bette Midler.

The casino is right off I-395, Exit 79A, which makes for easy on/off access for gamblers who don't want to deal with that onerous 20-minute drive to Foxwoods before emptying their bank accounts.

WHERE TO STAY

Mohegan Sun Hotel ★★ This asymmetrical grouping of soaring silver-skinned wedges provokes the *Wow!* response on first sight, exactly as intended. Every bit the equal of its rival, the Grand Pequot Tower at Foxwoods, it indulges in jaw-dropping design that begins with the slanting columns arrayed around a reflecting pool in abstract homage to woodland ponds. The front desk is over to the right, the escalators down to the restaurants and shops of the new Casino of the Sky on the far side. Rooms are conventionally attractive, albeit utilizing irregular shapes that echo design that was called "Modern" in the 1950s. Extras include Nintendo and high-speed Internet access through the TV with a wireless keyboard.

1 Mohegan Sun Blvd. (Off Rte. 2A), Uncasville, CT 06382. ✆ **888/226-7711** or 860/862-8000. www.mohegansun.com. 1,200 units. $150–$375 double. Packages available. AE, DC, DISC, MC, V. Free valet parking. **Amenities:** 9 restaurants (steakhouse, fusion, Italian, seafood, American); 4 bars; large indoor pool; extensive health club and spa; shopping arcade; concierge; 24-hr. room service; babysitting; same-day dry cleaning/laundry. *In room:* A/C, TV w/pay movies, dataport, hair dryer, fridge, coffeemaker, iron.

WHERE TO DINE

Of the thirty dining options now available at the expanded complex, those in the new Casino of the Sky are the more impressive. The ambitious **Rain** gets some of the best notices for its fusion cuisine and dazzling setting of cascades, glass, and gleaming metals. It is followed closely by an outpost of **Michael Jordan's Steakhouse** and those of celebrity chefs Jasper White and Todd English with the casual seafood of **Summer Shack** and contemporary Italian edibles of **Tuscany,** respectively. The quality of the food is unexpectedly good, too, within the limits of their missions, at **Big Bubba's BBQ, The Longhouse** (beef and fish), **Bamboo Forest** (Southeast Asian), **Uncas American Indian Grill,** and **Pompeii and Caesar.** For reservations for Rain, Tuscany, The Longhouse, Pompeii and Caesar, or Bamboo Forest, call ✆ **888/777-7920;** for Summer Shack, call ✆ **860/862-9500;** for Michael Jordan's, call ✆ **860/862-8600;** or for Big Bubba's BBQ, call ✆ **860/862-9800.**

NORWICH

This area, where the Yantic and Shetucket rivers converge to form the Thames, has potential. Blocks of Broadway and Union Street are lined with substantial mansions from the city's golden era. However, despite the nearby presence of the Mohegan Sun Casino, this old mill town remains in the doldrums, so far seeing little spillover effect.

Until efforts to reverse that decline take hold, the principal reason for a visit is the fine lodging described below.

WHERE TO STAY & DINE

The Spa at Norwich Inn ★★★ The complex is set on 40 acres, the main building augmented by outlying "villas" with 160 condo units. A typical suite has a kitchen, a sitting area with fireplace, a separate bedroom, and a deck overlooking the woods and a pond. Inn rooms aren't as large and don't have fireplaces, but they are hardly spartan. Terry robes and nightly turndowns are standard. Kensington's, the dining room, enjoys a versatile kitchen staff capable of producing meals either conventional or fitness-minded. The hotel and full-service spa have attracted the diverse likes of Barbra Streisand, Mary J. Blige, Michael Douglas, and Bob Dylan. The property is owned by the Mashantucket Pequot tribal organization, and its Foxwoods Casino, visible from the front door, is about 15 minutes away, making this inn a soothing and convenient respite from the glitz.

607 W. Thames St. (Rte. 32), Norwich, CT 06360. ✆ **800/275-4772** or 860/886-2401. Fax 860/886-9483. www.thespaatnorwichinn.com. 103 units. Inn $150–$325 double; villas $200–$350 suite. Packages available. AE, DC, MC, V. From New Haven, take Exit 76 off I-95 onto I-395 north, Exit 79A onto Rte. 2A east, then exit onto Rte. 32 north and drive 1½ miles to the inn. **Amenities:** Restaurant (spa/eclectic); bar; indoor and outdoor pools; adjacent golf course; fully equipped health club and spa (w/exercise classes, steam rooms, sauna, and massage); bicycle rental; limited room service; babysitting; same-day dry cleaning/laundry. *In room:* A/C, TV, dataport, fridge, coffeemaker, hair dryer, iron.

10

Rhode Island

by Herbert Bailey Livesey

Water defines "Little Rhody" as much as mountain peaks characterize Colorado. The Atlantic thrusts all the way to the Massachusetts border, cleaving the state into unequal halves and filling the geological basin that is Narragansett Bay. That leaves 400 miles of coastline and several large islands.

A string of coastal towns runs in a northeasterly arc from the Connecticut border up to Providence, the capital, which lies at the point of the bay, 30 miles from the open ocean. It was here that Roger Williams, banned from the Massachusetts Bay Colony in 1635 for his outspoken views on religious freedom, established his colony. Little survives from that first century, but a large section of the city's East Side is composed almost entirely of 18th- and 19th-century buildings.

Another group of Puritan exiles established their settlement a couple of years after Providence, on an island known to the Narragansett tribe as "Aquidneck." Settlers thought their new home resembled the Isle of Rhodes in the Aegean, so the official name became "Rhode Island and Providence Plantations," a moniker that was subsequently applied to the entire state and remains the official name.

The most important town on Aquidneck is Newport, and it's the best reason for an extended visit to the state. Its first era of prosperity was during the Colonial period, when its ships not only plied the new mercantile routes to China but also engaged in the reprehensible "Triangular Trade" of West Indies molasses for New England rum for African slaves. Their additional skill at smuggling and evading taxes brought them into conflict with their British rulers, whose occupying army all but destroyed Newport during the Revolution.

After the Civil War, the town began its transformation from commercial outpost to resort, with the arrival of the millionaires whose lives spawned what Mark Twain sneeringly described as the "Gilded Age." They built astonishingly extravagant mansions, their contribution to Newport's bountiful architectural heritage. Winning the America's Cup and subsequent defenses of yachting's most famous trophy made the town into a recreational sailing center with a packed summer cultural calendar. As a result, travelers who want nothing more than a deep tan by Monday can coexist with history buffs and music lovers, who come to attend concerts held against a seductive backdrop of waves moving across packed sand.

Finally, there is Block Island, a 1-hour ferry ride from Point Judith. A classic summer resort, it has avoided the imposition of Martha's Vineyard chic and Provincetown clutter. It has also sidestepped history (even though it was first settled in 1661), so there are few mandatory sights. That leaves visitors free simply to explore its lighthouses, hike its cliff-side trails, and hit the beach.

Note: Smoking is banned in all Rhode Island bars and restaurants.

1 Providence ★★

45 miles S of Boston; 55 miles NE of New London

Providence delights in its sobriquet, "Renaissance City." No question, the city is moving on up, counter to the trend of so many small and midsize New England cities. *Money* magazine even declared it the "Best Place to Live in the East." Revival is in the air and prosperity is returning, evident in the resurgent "downcity" business district. Rivers have been uncovered to form canals and waterside walkways; distressed buildings of the last century have been reclaimed; and continued construction has added a new hotel behind Union Station as well as Providence Place, a monster mall that brings national department stores to town for the first time. Adjacent to downcity is the Downtown Arts District, newly designated to the National Register of Historic Places, attracting restaurants, shops, a new boutique hotel, and several theater and repertory companies.

Much of the credit for Providence's boom, grudging or exuberant, went to the ebullient six-term mayor, Vincent A. "Buddy" Cianci, Jr. But he is now in prison, having been caught in an FBI probe into the bribery of local officials. A 97-page federal indictment charged Cianci and others with racketeering, extortion, witness tampering, and mail fraud. Buddy tried to laugh it off, right up until the verdict. Called Operation Plunder Dome, the investigation revived Providence's reputation for tolerance of corruption at high levels.

Still, continued local pride in the city's revitalization is palpable. A burgeoning dining scene includes ambitious new restaurants that are nearly always less expensive than their counterparts in Boston and New York. College Hill is one of only 26 National Historic Districts, the calendar is full of special events, and the presence of the young people attending the city's 12 colleges and universities guarantees a lively nightlife.

Roger Williams knew what he was doing. Admired for his fervent advocacy of religious and political freedom in the early Colonial period, he obviously had good instincts for town building as well. He planted the seeds of his settlement on a steep rise overlooking a swift-flowing river at the point where it widened into a large protected harbor. That part of the city, called the East Side and dominated by the ridge now known as College Hill, remains the most attractive district of a New England city second only to Boston in the breadth of its cultural life and rich architectural heritage.

College Hill is so named because it is the site of Rhode Island College, which started life in 1764 and was later renamed Brown University. The Hill is further enhanced by the presence of the highly regarded Rhode Island School of Design, whose buildings are wrapped around the perimeter of the Brown campus. In and around these institutions are several square miles of 18th- and 19th-century houses, Colonial to Victorian, lining often gaslit streets. At the back of the Brown campus is the funky shopping district along Thayer Street, while at the foot of the Hill is the largely commercial Main Street.

While most points of general interest are found on the East Side, the far larger collection of neighborhoods west of the river has its own attractions. The level downtown area is the center for business, government, and entertainment, with City Hall, a new convention center, the three best large hotels, some small parks and historic buildings, and several venues for music, dance, and theatrical productions. To its north, across the Woonasquatucket River, is the imposing State House, as well as the Amtrak station. And to its west, on the other side of Interstate 95, is Federal Hill, a residential area bearing a strong ethnic identity, primarily Italian, but increasingly leavened by numbers of more recent immigrant groups.

ESSENTIALS

GETTING THERE I-95, which connects Boston and New York, runs right through the city. From Cape Cod, pick up I-195 west.

T. F. Green/Providence Airport (© **888/268-7222** or 401/737-8222; www.pvdairport.com) in Warwick, south of Providence (Exit 13, I-95), is served by feeder and major airlines, including **American** (© 800/433-7300), **Continental** (© 800/525-0280), **Delta** (© 800/221-1212), **Northwest** (© 800/225-2525), **Southwest** (© 800/435-9792), **United** (© 800/241-6522), and **US Airways** (© 800/428-4322). The Rhode Island Public Transit Authority (RIPTA) provides transportation between the airport and the city center. Taxis are also available, costing about $20 for the 20-minute trip.

Amtrak (© **800/USA-RAIL;** www.amtrak.com) runs several trains daily between Boston and New York, stopping at the attractive new station at 100 Gaspee St., near the State House.

GETTING AROUND Traffic on local streets isn't bad, even at rush hour. Taxis are not easy to come by, with few to be found outside even the largest hotels. They can take 15 minutes to an hour to arrive when called from restaurants. Alternatives are the **RIPTA buses** of the Green and Gold Lines (© **401/781-9400;** www.ripta.com). Made to look like old-time trolleys, these buses have routes that reach most major hotels and tourist destinations. Each ride costs $1.50. RIPTA (the Rhode Island Public Transit Authority) also provides ferry service between Providence and Newport.

A singular attraction is **La Gondola** (© **401/421-8877;** www.gondolaRI.com). A faithful replica of the Venetian original, it carries up to 6 passengers along the Woonasquatucket and Providence rivers. Especially popular for rides during the Waterfire events, its rates run from $79 to $139 for two persons, about what it would cost in the Italian city itself, minus the airfare.

VISITOR INFORMATION For advance information, contact the **Providence Warwick Convention & Visitors Bureau,** 1 West Exchange St. (© **800/233-1636** or 401/274-1636; www.providencecvb.com). In town, consult the new visitor center in the Rhode Island Convention Center, 1 Sabin St. (© **800/233-1636** or 401/751-1177), or check with the helpful park rangers at the visitor center of the Roger Williams National Park, at the corner of Smith and North Main streets, open daily from 9am to 4:30pm.

EXPLORING PROVIDENCE

STROLLING THE HISTORIC NEIGHBORHOODS

This is a city of manageable size—the population is about 170,000—that can easily occupy 2 or 3 days of a Rhode Island vacation. Two leisurely walks, one short, another longer, pass most of the prominent attractions and provide a sense of the city's evolution from a colony of dissidents to a contemporary center of commerce and government.

Downtown, chart a route from the 1878 City Hall on Kennedy Plaza along Dorrance Street 1 block to Westminster. Turn left, then right in 1 block, past The Arcade (see "Quick Bites," later in this section), then left on Weybosset.

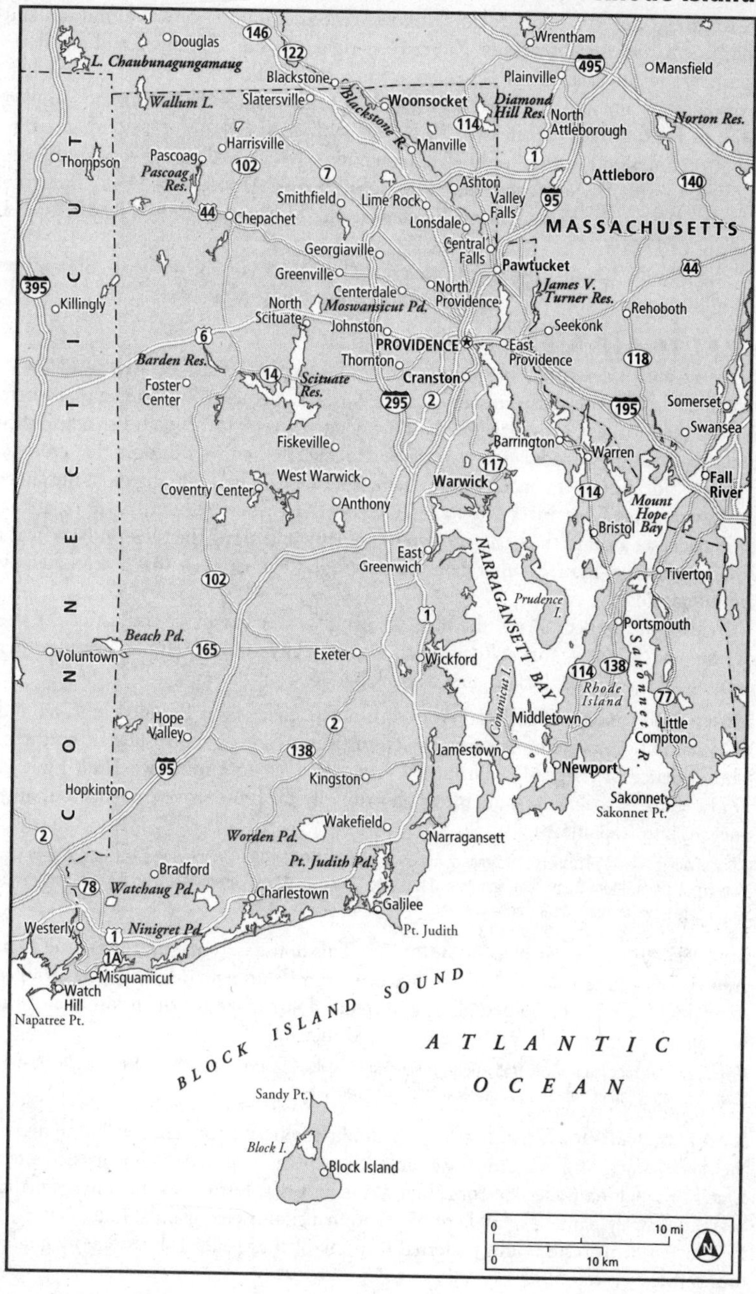
Douglas
L. Chaubunagungamaug
Blackstone
Slatersville
Wallum L.
Woonsocket
Blackstone R.
Manville
Wrentham
Plainville
Mansfield
Diamond Hill Res.
North Attleborough
Norton Res.
Attleboro
MASSACHUSETTS
Harrisville
Thompson
Pascoag
Pascoag Res.
Smithfield
Lime Rock
Ashton
Valley Falls
Lonsdale
Chepachet
Georgiaville
Central Falls
Pawtucket
Greenville
Centerdale
North Providence
James V. Turner Res.
Rehoboth
Seekonk
Killingly
North Scituate
Moswansicut Pd.
Johnston
PROVIDENCE
East Providence
Thornton
Barden Res.
Foster Center
Scituate Res.
Cranston
Somerset
Swansea
Barrington
Warren
Fiskeville
West Warwick
Coventry Center
Warwick
Anthony
Fall River
Mount Hope Bay
Bristol
East Greenwich
NARRAGANSETT BAY
Prudence I.
Tiverton
Portsmouth
Sakonnet R.
Beach Pd.
Voluntown
Exeter
Wickford
Conanicut I.
Rhode Island
Middletown
Little Compton
Hope Valley
Jamestown
Newport
Kingston
Hopkinton
Sakonnet
Sakonnet Pt.
Wakefield
Worden Pd.
Narragansett
Pt. Judith Pd.
Bradford
Watchaug Pd.
Charlestown
Galilee
Westerly
Ninigret Pd.
Pt. Judith
Misquamicut
Watch Hill
Napatree Pt.
CONNECTICUT
BLOCK ISLAND SOUND
ATLANTIC OCEAN
Sandy Pt.
Block I.
Block Island
146
122
495
114
1
102
7
140
95
44
395
6
118
14
295
2
195
117
165
138
77
78
1A
0
10 mi
10 km
N

To extend this into a longer walk, follow Weybosset until it joins Westminster and continue across the Providence River. Turn right on the other side, walking along South Water Street as far as James Street, just before the I-195 overpass. Turn left, cross South Main, and then turn left on Benefit Street. This is the start of the so-called **Mile of History** ★★. Lined with 18th- and 19th-century houses, it is enhanced by gas streetlamps and sections of brick herringbone sidewalks. Along the way are opportunities to visit, in sequence, the 1786 **John Brown House,** the **First Unitarian Church** (1816), the **Providence Athenaeum,** and the **Museum of Art, Rhode Island School of Design.**

The **Rhode Island Historical Society** (✆ **401/438-0463;** www.rihs.org) offers 90-minute guided tours of four different neighborhoods of interest.

WHAT TO SEE & DO

Boosters are understandably proud of their **Waterplace Park & Riverwalk** ★★, which encircles a tidal basin and borders the Woonasquatucket River down past where it joins the Moshassuck to become the Providence River. It incorporates an amphitheater, boat landings, landscaped walkways, and vaguely Venetian bridges that cross to the East Side. Summer concerts and other events are held here, among them the enormously popular **WaterFires** ★★ (✆ **401/272-3111**), when 97 bonfires are set ablaze in braziers set around the basin of Waterplace Park and along the river on New Year's Eve and on more than 20 other dates July through October, their roar accentuated by amplified music.

Nearby, in Kennedy Plaza, the **Fleet Skating Center** has an ice rink twice the size of the one in New York's Rockefeller Center, fully utilized almost every winter evening. Skate rentals, lockers, and a snack bar are available.

Brown University The nation's seventh-oldest college was founded in 1764 and has a reputation as the most experimental institution among its Ivy League brethren. The evidence of its pre-Revolutionary origins is seen in **University Hall,** built in 1771. Tours of the campus are intended primarily for prospective students, but anyone can join (call ahead).

Office of Admissions, 45 Prospect St. (corner of Angell St.). ✆ **401/863-1000.** Campus tours, late Nov to early Sept Mon–Fri at 10am, 11am, 1pm, 3pm, and 4pm (11am and 3pm only during Christmas and spring vacations); early Sept to late Nov, Sat 10am, 11am, and noon.

Gov. Henry Lippitt House Museum ★ This house is as magnificently true to its grandiose Victorian era as any residence on the Continent. Meticulously detailed stenciling, expanses of stained glass, and inlaid floors make this mansion one of the treasures of College Hill. Visits are by guided tour only.

199 Hope St. (at Angell St.). ✆ **401/453-0688.** Admission $4 adults, $2 seniors and students. Tours Apr–Dec Tues–Fri 11am–3pm on the hour; Sat–Sun and Jan–Mar by appointment only.

John Brown House Museum Quite unlike the fiery 19th-century abolitionist of the same name, *this* John Brown was an 18th-century slave trader who amassed a fortune in the China trade. He contributed much of that fortune to the university that bears the family name. The style of his 1786 mansion is Georgian, although after the Revolution, Brown no doubt preferred to think of it as Federal. Visits are by guided tour only.

52 Power St. (at Benefit St.). ✆ **401/331-8575.** Admission $7 adults, $5.50 seniors and students, $4 children 7–17. Tues–Sat 10am–5pm; Sun noon–4pm. Closed Jan–Feb.

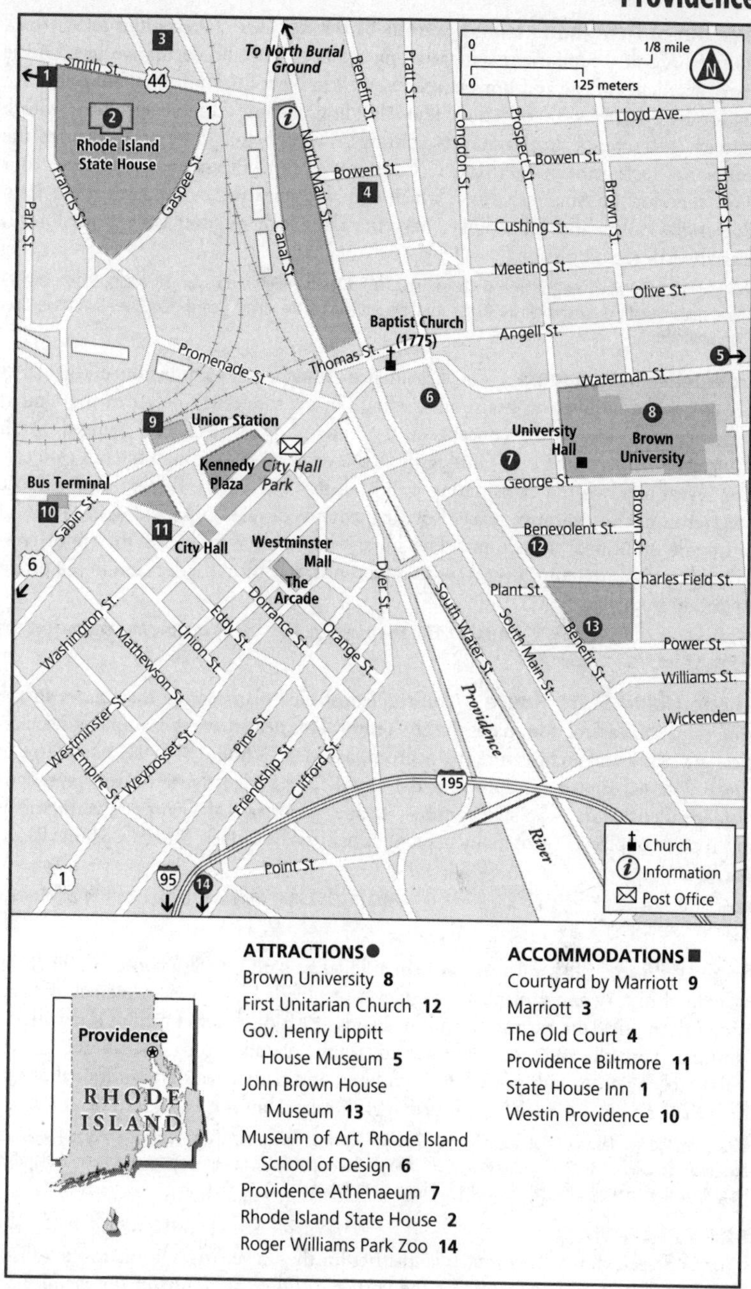

ATTRACTIONS ●

Brown University **8**
First Unitarian Church **12**
Gov. Henry Lippitt House Museum **5**
John Brown House Museum **13**
Museum of Art, Rhode Island School of Design **6**
Providence Athenaeum **7**
Rhode Island State House **2**
Roger Williams Park Zoo **14**

ACCOMMODATIONS ■

Courtyard by Marriott **9**
Marriott **3**
The Old Court **4**
Providence Biltmore **11**
State House Inn **1**
Westin Providence **10**

Museum of Art, Rhode Island School of Design ★★ Prestigious RISD (pronounced *Riz*-dee) supports this ingratiating center of fine and decorative arts. Of the many excellent college and university museums in New England, this ranks near the top for the breadth of its collection. Those holdings include Chinese terra cotta, Greek statuary, and French Impressionist paintings. Probably of greatest interest are the works by such masters as Monet, Cézanne, Rodin, Picasso, and Matisse. But allow time for the American wing, which contains paintings by Gilbert Stuart, John Singleton Copley, and John Singer Sargent. The Gorham silver collection alone is nearly worth the admission.

224 Benefit St. (between Waterman and College sts.). ✆ **401/454-6500.** Admission $8 adults, $5 seniors, $3 college students with ID, $2 children 5–18; free to all the 3rd Thurs of the month from 5–9pm. Tues–Sun 10am–5pm (Thurs until 9pm).

Providence Athenaeum The Providence Athenaeum commissioned this 1838 Greek Revival building to house its lending library, the fourth oldest in the United States and an innovative concept at the time. Edgar Allan Poe courted Sarah Whitman, his "Annabel Lee," among these shelves. Glances through the old card catalog reveal handwritten cards dating well back into the 1800s. Bibliophiles will lose themselves in this evocative place. Rotating exhibits of rare books and works by local artists are additional attractions. The library has money problems that have contributed to a contretemps over ways to raise funds, specifically a decision to sell off an Audubon folio valued at $7 million.

251 Benefit St. (at College St.). ✆ **401/421-6970.** Free admission. Mon–Thurs 9am–7pm; Fri–Sat 9am–5pm; Sun 1–5pm. Closed first 2 weeks in Aug.

Rhode Island State House Constructed of Georgian marble that blazes in the sun, the 1900 capitol dominates the city center. This near-flawless example of neoclassical governmental architecture (by McKim, Mead & White, 1891–92) boasts one of the largest self-supported domes in the world. The gilded figure on top represents "Independent Man," the state symbol. Inside, a portrait of George Washington is given pride of place, one of many depictions painted by Gilbert Stuart, a Rhode Island native.

82 Smith St. (between Francis and Hayes sts.). ✆ **401/277-2357.** Free admission. Guided tours by appointment Mon–Fri 8:30am–noon.

Roger Williams Park Zoo ★ *Kids* In a 430-acre park that also contains a museum of natural history and a planetarium, the zoo is divided into three principal habitats: Tropical America, the Farmyard, and the Plains of Africa. A newer exhibit is devoted to Australia, with the zoo's first saltwater aquarium. A walk-through aviary and underwater viewing areas with polar bears, sea lions, and harbor seals are additional attractions. The facility has looked a bit bedraggled of late, but not enough to deter visits.

1000 Elmwood Ave. (at Exit 17 off I-95). ✆ **401/785-3510.** www.rogerwilliamsparkzoo.org. Admission $10 adults, $8 seniors, $6 children 3–12. Mid-May to mid-Oct Mon–Fri 9am–5pm, Sat–Sun 9am–6pm; mid-Oct to mid-May daily 9am–4pm. Driving south on I-95, take Exit 17; driving north, take Exit 16.

SHOPPING

Thayer Street, the main commercial district for the university, is home to the official **Brown Bookstore,** at no. 244 (at the corner of Olive St.). Also in the vicinity are **Silverberry's,** at no. 220, with dressy and casual clothes for college-age women, and

Hillhouse, no. 135, long in the business of providing male Brownies with Ivy dress-up clothes for interview weeks and parents' days.

WHERE TO STAY

The clusters of motels around most of the exits from I-95 and I-195 offer decent value. Among these possibilities are the **Days Hotel,** 220 India St. (✆ **401/272-5577**), and the **Ramada Inn,** 940 Fall River Ave., Seekonk, MA (✆ **508/336-7300**). Rates at area inns and motels invariably go up on alumni and parents' weekends and during graduation weeks.

Courtyard by Marriott ★ This downcity hotel's style and exterior materials harmonize with the adjacent former Union Station complex. As a mid-priced entry designed primarily for businesspeople, its rooms are equipped with two-line phones, high-speed Internet access, and well-lit desks. It is just as comfortable for leisure travelers, with several of our recommended restaurants, the new Providence Place mall, and WaterFires only minutes away. While the on-site cafe doesn't serve dinner, meals can be delivered from nearby restaurants.

32 Exchange Terrace, Providence, RI 02903. ✆ **800/321-2211** or 401/272-1191. Fax 401/272-1416. www.courtyard.com. 216 units. $139–$259 double. AE, DC, DISC, MC, V. **Amenities:** Cafe/bar (breakfast and cocktails); indoor pool w/whirlpool; exercise room; business center; coin-op laundry; same-day dry cleaning. *In room:* A/C, TV w/pay movies, dataport, coffeemaker, hair dryer, iron.

Hotel Providence ★★ A dazzling contribution to the still-emerging Downtown Arts District, this new boutique hotel, combining two buildings, gained instant membership in the selective Small Luxury Hotels of the World marketing group. The owners filled the lobby and main halls with fine 18th- and 19th-century European antiques and artworks and commissioned custom reproductions for the bedrooms to carry through with the image thus created. They completed the picture by luring the much-honored **L'Epicureo** restaurant (see below) from its former Federal Hill address to a spacious new setting—with parklike terrace—just off the lobby. There are wireless hotspots in public areas. Guests are serenaded at 15-minute intervals by the pealing of the 16 bells of Grace Church, across the street.

311 Westminster St., Providence, RI 02903. ✆ **800/861-8990** or 401/861-8000. Fax 401/861-8002. www.thehotelprovidence.com. 80 units. $189–$279 double. Packages available. AE, DC, DISC, MC, V. Valet parking $18. **Amenities:** Restaurant (Italian); piano bar; small fitness room; concierge; business center; room service; same-day dry cleaning/laundry. *In room:* A/C, TV, dataport, hair dryer, iron.

Marriott This busy motor hotel is popular with both business and leisure travelers. It's north of downtown, but within a 10-minute drive of most of the city's attractions. Rooms have high-speed Internet access. Shuttle service to and from the airport and the bus and train stations can be arranged when booking and the hotel is within walking distance of the Providence Place Mall and the convention center. Parking is free. No pets.

1 Orms St., Providence, RI 02904. ✆ **800/228-9290** or 401/272-2400. Fax 401/273-2686. www.marriotthotels.com/pvdri. 351 units. $169–$209 double. AE, DC, DISC, MC, V. Free parking. **Amenities:** Restaurant (seafood/American); bar; indoor/outdoor pool; exercise room w/Jacuzzi and sauna; concierge; business center; limited room service; dry cleaning. *In room:* A/C, TV w/pay movies, dataport, coffeemaker, hair dryer, iron.

The Old Court This was once a rectory, built in 1863, and the furnishings reflect that use and period. You'll find secretaries embellished with marquetry, Oriental rugs, and wide-ranging Victoriana, with furnishings and oddments executed in sub-styles from bumptious Rococo Revival to massively elegant Eastlake. Traces of its tenure as a boardinghouse for students have been expunged. Families or longer-term visitors may be interested in the apartment across the street. Some rooms have wet bars. Unlike downtown hotels, rates are lower during the week but higher on weekends, especially those involving events at Brown and RISD.

144 Benefit St., Providence, RI 02903. © **401/751-2002.** Fax 401/272-4830. www.oldcourt.com. 10 units. $115–$195 double. Rates include breakfast. AE, DISC, MC, V. No children under 12. *In room:* A/C, TV.

Providence Biltmore ★★ A grand staircase beneath the stunning Deco bronze ceiling dates the centrally located building to the 1920s, and a plaque in the lobby shows the nearly 7-foot-high water level of the villainous 1938 hurricane. From the lobby, the dramatic glass elevator literally shoots skyward, exiting outdoors to scoot up the side of the building. Most guest rooms are large, half of them with more than 600 square feet of floor space; some of the 20 suites have kitchenettes. The entire property has received more than $10 million of overdue attention over the last 3 years, and another 50 rooms have been added. An Elizabeth Arden Red Door Spa should be open by the time you read this.

11 Dorrance St., Providence, RI 02903. © **800/294-7709** or 401/421-0700. Fax 401/455-3127. www.providence biltmore.com. 291 units. $249–$289 double; from $289 suite. AE, DC, MC, V. Valet parking $16. **Amenities:** Restaurant; bar; fitness center; concierge; business center; limited room service; babysitting; laundry; dry cleaning. *In room:* A/C, TV, VCR available, dataport, coffeemaker, hair dryer.

Westin Providence ★★★ This is easily the city's most important hotel, with a luxurious interior and a downtown location. Skyways connect the hotel with the new Providence Place mall and the convention center. Bedrooms are equipped with the patented "Heavenly Bed" sheets, pillows, and mattresses. The architectural grandeur of the lobby rotunda and other public spaces are only improved by the sunny dispositions of the staff. Off the lobby is a lounge with the buffed glow of an exclusive men's club. **Agora,** the main dining room, gets excellent reviews from critics, and serves all meals. A 31-story, 200-unit tower was recently added to the main building.

1 West Exchange St., Providence, RI 02903. © **800/937-8461** or 401/598-8000. Fax 401/598-8200. www.westin.com. 564 units. $199–$339 double. AE, DC, DISC, MC, V. Valet parking $18. **Amenities:** 2 restaurants (eclectic, American); 2 bars; indoor pool; fully equipped health club w/Jacuzzi and sauna; concierge; business center; limited room service; babysitting; same-day dry cleaning/laundry. *In room:* A/C, TV w/pay movies, VCR available, Nintendo, dataport, minibar, coffeemaker, hair dryer, iron, safe.

WHERE TO DINE

Providence has a sturdy Italian heritage, resulting in a profusion of tomato-sauce and pizza joints, especially on Federal Hill, the district west of downtown and I-95. Because these are so prevalent, the suggestions below focus instead on restaurants that break away from the red-gravy imperative.

One fruitful strip to explore for lower-cost dining options is that part of **Thayer Street** bordering the Brown University campus. It counts Thai, Tex-Mex, barbecue, and Indian restaurants among its possibilities.

Cafe Nuovo ★★★ MEDITERRANEAN FUSION This spacious room of glass, marble, and burnished wood occupies part of the ground floor of a downtown office tower that overlooks the confluence of the Moshassuck and Woonasquatucket rivers. Unlike its local competitor, Al Forno, which gets the greater share of praise and ink (largely undeserved), Cafe Nuovo takes reservations, is open for lunch *and* dinner, and impresses with every course, from dazzling appetizers to stunning pastries. The fare is grounded in the Italian repertoire, but skips lightly among other inspirations, too—Thai, Greek, and Portuguese among them. That culinary restlessness leads to such dishes as the appetizer of fried calamari and popcorn shrimp with hot cherry peppers and tartar sauce and the entree of lamb two ways involving rack of lamb crusted with goat cheese and almonds and Moroccan lamb tagine. There's music on weekends and outdoor dining in warm weather. Restaurants come and go, but Café Nuovo endures, steady and embracing.

1 Citizens Plaza (access is from the Steeple St. bridge). ✆ **401/421-2525.** Reservations advised. Main courses $22–$32. AE, DC, DISC, MC, V. Mon–Fri 11:30am–3pm; Mon–Thurs 5–10:30pm; Fri–Sat 5–11pm. Closed 1st week in Jan.

CAV ★★ ECLECTIC No corporate design drudge had a hand in *this* warehouse interior, a Jewelry District pioneer. CAV is an acronym for "Coffee/Antiques/Victuals," and patrons are surrounded by tribal rugs, African carvings, and assorted antiques (most for sale). Turkish kilims under glass cover the tables. The resulting bohemian air is not unlike Greenwich Village in the 1960s, complete with live jazz or blues on weekends ($5 cover). Attractive servers bring dishes prepared by folks quite accomplished at their craft. Select from such strenuous menu swings as pan-seared foie gras to the delectable overkill of roasted venison rack with grilled venison sausage, potato and fruit samosa, long beans, and anise-star demi-glace. Every day brings a choice of special soup, appetizer, pasta, and a pizza or two.

14 Imperial Place (near Basset St.). ✆ **401/751-9164.** Reservations recommended. Main courses $19–$31. DISC, MC, V. Mon–Thurs 11:30am–10pm; Fri–Sat 11:30am–1am; Sun 10:30am–10pm.

Gracie's ★ NEW AMERICAN Moved to the Downtown Arts District from its former Federal Hill address, this longtime favorite hasn't lost a smidgen of its old verve. Pinlights in the ceiling hint at the night sky, a theme carried out with rather too much enthusiasm in the proliferation of five-pointed stars scattered over the rest of the room. That aside, there are unlikely to be legit complaints about either the food or the people who bring it. It all starts with an *amuse bouche*—on one occasion, a tiny cup of broccoli soup with lemon oil, on another, a taste of lobster and crab salad. The first course can be the cheese tasting "with treats and surprises," consisting of five cheeses (one from Tasmania) accompanied by pistachios, pepper jelly, and blueberry compote.

Carnivores will be more than sated by the pork trio, which brings together maple-glazed tenderloin with warm peaches, smoked shoulder with white beans, and barbecue pork belly with potato salad. While the entrees mostly involve grilled or roasted meats, an elaborate tasting of fruits and vegetables is also available.

194 Washington St. ✆ **401/272-7811.** Reservations advised. Main courses $20–$32. AE, DC, MC, V. Tues–Fri 11:30am–3pm and 5–10pm; Sat 5–10pm; Sun 2–10pm.

L'Epicureo ★★ ITALIAN Long the odds-on top Italian restaurant on Federal Hill, this stalwart is still working its magic as the in-house dining room of the new downtown luxury Hotel Providence. Enter the spacious piano bar and continue into a main room that is just short of cavernous, with slate floors and crystal chandeliers. But it doesn't end there: Diners can also sit at tables out on the edge of a small park. The experience begins with a menu blessedly free of cutes and hyperbole. At lunch, there are superior panini and individualized pizzas, but the star is the antipasti salad. That platter comes with zucchini-corn fritters, pickled beets, artichoke hearts, roasted peppers, and a zesty chickpea spread on grilled bread. It's available at dinner, too, but with loads of competition, from lobster fritters to braised snails with porcini mushrooms to

Tips Big Tastes Hide In Little Rhody

You'd think, in an age of instant communication, that no ingratiatingly flavorful edible tidbit or preparation would stay unknown for long. Worthy regional specialties fast become national staples—think Buffalo wings, Carolina blooming onions, Texan burritos. But Rhode Islanders are tightfisted about their food secrets, and even residents of neighboring states are in the dark. So while you're visiting, try to check out some of the following:

- **Rhode Island clam chowder** is a clear broth, neither tomato- or cream-based, as are, respectively, the far better-known Manhattan and New England versions.
- **Stuffies** come in as many versions as there are cooks. At Flo's Clam Shack in Newport, quahog clams are chopped up with hot and sweet peppers and bread crumbs, packed inside the two shell halves and shut, the whole held together by a rubber band and baked. The mixture assumes the consistency of setting plaster, but is no less tasty for that.
- **Johnnycakes** (aka jonnycakes) are breakfast fodder, some as thin as crepes, others as thick as standard griddlecakes. The difference from the conventional pancakes is the primary ingredient, cornmeal. Honey is a common topping.
- **Clam cakes** are as inaccurately named as Brooklyn egg creams (which have neither eggs nor cream). These aren't cakes, but deep-fried fritters, and the clams therein are notable primarily for their virtual absence.
- **Coffee milk** and **cabinets** are the obligatory beverages to go with Rhody chow. The first is made with sweet coffee syrup, while the second is what the rest of America thinks of as a milkshake.
- **New York System Wieners** have only a passing acquaintance with Big Apple franks. In Rhode Island, the wieners are short—3 or 4 inches long—served on soft steamed buns and topped (usually) with a chili-type meat sauce, minced onion, and mustard. Nobody eats just one—the typical ration is four or more per person.

So step up to the counter and demand "Four all the way, extra sauce, and a coffee milk." You thus commence your initiation into the mysteries of the Rhode Island food culture. And did I mention doughboys and Gray's Ice Cream (p. 427)?

chilled capellini with clams and caviar. A meal of appetizers is a distinct option, but the entrees beckon—staples like *osso buco,* chicken Milanese, and very slowly braised pork belly, all done to near-perfect turn.

311 Westminster St. ✆ **401/521-3333.** Reservations advised. Main courses $23–$40. AE, DC, MC, V. Daily 11:30am–2:30pm and 5:30–10pm.

Mill's Tavern NEW AMERICAN Mill's Tavern isn't as hot and happening as it was a couple of years ago, and the restaurant is forced now to rely on other attributes: That isn't working as well as might be hoped. Wood roasting and grilling are fairly simple techniques, so it's difficult to understand why the kitchen so easily gets overwhelmed. Salmon with French lentils and a tomato-citrus jam is typical, as is the rabbit and peppardale stew with wild mushrooms, olives, and prunes. The wood-burning oven is employed for slow-braised ribs and roasted cod. The restaurant is almost always crowded with attractive young to middle-aged professionals, augmented with families and Providence's version of a bridge-and-tunnel crowd on weekends. A spread-out space with a ceiling crossed with dark beams, it has a black marble-topped bar and a large exhibition kitchen off to the right. Free valet parking is offered.

101 N. Main St. ✆ **401/272-3331.** Reservations essential. Main courses $17–$26. AE, DC, MC, V. Mon–Thurs 5–10pm; Fri–Sat 5–11pm; Sun 4–9pm.

Rue de l'Espoir AMERICAN BISTRO When every place else on College Hill is closed, full, or downright tacky, there's always The Rue. It serves breakfast or brunch, lunch, and dinner every day, a rebuke to those restaurateurs who can barely bring themselves to open 5 nights a week for a couple of hours. The interior is decked in warm, woody tones, with every type of seating configuration and not a square inch of wasted space. It is filled with people of all ages, from Brown frosh and grad students to profs to retirees. Easily the most popular brunch in town proffers "Rue Melt," an irresistible assemblage of English muffin, Thai crab cake, poached eggs, home fries, and lemon-grass aioli. The brunch prices don't hurt, either, only $9 to $12 for main courses. During the week, lunch can be any of a dozen small plates—peel-and-eat shrimp and lobster and mushroom crepes, among them—and dinners run to bouillabaisse, rack of lamb, and roasted salmon.

99 Hope St. ✆ **401/751-8890.** Reservations recommended, essential on weekends. Main courses $20–$30. AE, DC, MC, V. Daily 7:30–11am, 11:30am–2:30pm, and 5–9pm.

XO Café ★ ECLECTIC A younger, more casual crowd than that drawn to Mill's Tavern (above) keeps the staff moving at a fast evening-long pace. A modest redecoration effort laid new carpets on the floors and nonobjective sculptures on the walls. Behind the copper-topped bar are female mixologists in clothes not meant to conceal their gender. They serve almost as many meals as drinks, and their customers have some interesting choices. A note at the top of the menu insists "Life is short, order dessert first." That would mean crème brulée, tart tatin, and molten chocolate cake, and some diners happily take that advice. Slaves to tradition can order the "Pre Fixe"—their spelling—which on one occasion listed seared foie gras in brioche with candied shallots and citrus-honey glaze. The "Greatest Burger On Earth"—their hyperbole—is ground sirloin stuffed with barbecued duck confit and shaved truffle topped with pâté de foie gras. It is served on grilled brioche with a side of Parmesan truffled fries. There's free valet parking Thursday through Saturday.

125 N. Main St. ✆ **401/273-9090.** Reservations advised. Main courses $20–$31. AE, DC, MC, V. Daily 5–10pm (Fri–Sat until 11pm.)

QUICK BITES

Providence claims the invention of the diner, starting with a horse-drawn wagon transporting food down Westminster Street in 1872. The tradition is carried forward by the likes of the **Seaplane Diner,** 307 Allens Ave. (✆ **401/941-9547**), a silver-sided classic with tableside jukeboxes, and **Richard's Diner,** 377 Richmond St. (✆ **401/331-8541**), so small you can walk across it in six strides.

A bona fide National Historic Landmark is an unlikely venue for snarfing up cookies, souvlaki, and egg rolls, but **The Arcade,** 65 Weybosset St. (✆ **401/598-1199**), is a 19th-century progenitor of 20th-century shopping malls, an 1828 Greek Revival structure that runs between Weybosset and Westminster streets. Its main floor is given over largely to fast-food stands and snack counters of the usual kinds—yes, the Golden Arches, too—while the upper floor is primarily boutiques and souvenir shops.

Another local culinary institution arrives in Kennedy Plaza on wheels every afternoon around 4:30pm. The grungy aluminum-sided **Haven Bros.** (✆ **401/861-7777**) is a food tractor-trailer with a counter and six stools inside and good deals on decent burgers and even better fries sold from its parking space next to City Hall. No new frontiers here, except that it hangs around until way past midnight to dampen the hunger pangs of club-goers, lawyers, night people, and workaholic pols.

PROVIDENCE AFTER DARK

This being a college town, there is no end of music bars, small concert halls, and pool pubs. A good source of information is the free weekly *Providence Phoenix* (www.providencephoenix.com).

THE PERFORMING ARTS The **Opera Providence** (✆ **401/331-6060;** www.operaprovidence.org) stages three or four productions a season at various locations, including the Veterans Memorial Auditorium. The **Rhode Island Philharmonic** (✆ **401/831-3123;** www.ri-philharmonic.org) usually appears at the Providence Performing Arts Center or the Veterans Memorial Auditorium. Big-ticket touring musicals on the order of *Rent, Lion King,* and *Evita,* as well as traveling dance companies and other attractions, are showcased at the **Providence Performing Arts Center,** 220 Weybosset St. (✆ **401/421-ARTS;** www.ppacri.org), while new plays share space with Ibsen and Shakespeare at the **Trinity Repertory Company,** 201 Washington St. (✆ **401/351-4242;** www.trinityrep.com). The **Dunkin' Doughnuts Center,** 1 La Salle Sq. (✆ **401/331-2211**), between the Convention Center and the Holiday Inn Downtown, hosts stellar performers and acts, Bruce Springsteen, among them, along with up-and-comers.

THE CLUB & MUSIC SCENE **The Green Room,** 145 Clifford St. (✆ **401/351-7665**), usually has DJs Wednesdays and Thursdays, live rock Fridays and Saturdays, and a comedy showcase on Sundays.

Lupo's Heartbreak Hotel, 79 Washington St. (✆ **401/272-5876**), formerly at 239 Westminster St., still hosts a variety of live concerts. **The Call,** 15 Elbow St. (✆ **401/751-2255**), showcases mostly regional bands, supplemented by acts in the attached **Century Lounge,** 150 Chestnut St. (same phone). At the **Custom House Tavern,** 36 Weybosset St. (✆ **401/751-3630**), an open mic is on Monday and Wednesday, with live jazz or blues on Saturday and Sunday. Connected to the popular Café Paragon, **Club Viva,** 234 Thayer St. (✆ **401/272-7600**), has food from the same kitchen, but in a lounge environment that turns into dance club on weekends.

Many restaurants in the city engage musical groups 2 or more nights a week. These include CAV described under "Where to Dine," above. At the **Trinity Brewhouse,** 186 Fountain St. (✆ **401/453-2337**), live jazz and blues share attention with boutique beers, a pool table, and a deck.

MOVIES For art-house films and midnight cult movies, there is the **Avon Cinema,** 260 Thayer St., near Meeting St. (✆ **401/421-3315**). Curl up in the comfy sofas at the **Cable Car,** 204 South Main St. (✆ **401/272-3970**) for an art-house flick accompanied by free popcorn refills.

2 A Bucolic Detour to Sakonnet Point

As a break from the urbanity of Providence or the concentration of sights and activities that is Newport, a side trip down the length of the oddly isolated southeastern corner of Rhode Island is a soothing excursion.

No one has thought to throw a bridge or run a ferry across the water between Newport and Sakonnet Point, prospects the reclusive residents would no doubt resist to the last lawsuit. They have been known to steal road signs to discourage summer visitors, and almost no enterprises are specifically geared to attract tourists. Things are quiet in these parts, and they intend to keep it that way.

To get here from Providence or Boston, pick up I-195 east, then Route 24 south, toward Newport. Take Exit 4 for Route 77 south, just before the Sakonnet River Bridge. From Newport, take Route 138 toward Fall River, and exit on Route 77 south immediately after crossing the bridge.

After a welter of small businesses, most of them involved in some way with the ocean, Route 77 smooths out into a pastoral Brigadoon, not quite rural, but more rustic than suburban. Colonial farmhouses, real or replicated, bear sidings of weathered shakes the color of wood smoke. They are centered in tidy lawns, bordered by miles of low stone walls. No plastic deer, no tomato plants in front yards—it's as if a requirement of residence were attendance at a school of good taste.

There are a few antiques shops and roadside farm stands along the way, and a cluster of shops and eating places at Tiverton Four Corners, about halfway down the point. The building on the near right corner of that intersection is **Provender,** 3883 Main Rd. (✆ **401/624-8084**), a lunch counter famed for its veggie sandwich, the "Great Garbanzo." It's closed from Christmas until spring. On the far left corner, at the edge of the parking lot, is a destination dear to the hearts of Rhode Islanders. **Gray's Ice Cream,** 16 East Rd. (✆ **401/624-4500**) scoops out 32 flavors of the super-premium dessert, along with 11 more sherbets and frozen yogurts. A big cone or cupful costs $2.75; coffee is the best-selling flavor. It's open daily from 6:30am to 7pm in winter, until 9pm in summer.

Another good reason to pull off the road is **Sakonnet Vineyards** ★, 162 W. Main Rd. (✆ **401/635-8486;** www.sakonnetwine.com), with an entrance road on the left, about 3 miles south of Tiverton Four Corners. In operation for more than 20 years, it is one of New England's oldest wineries, and produces 50,000 cases of creditable wines annually. Types range from a popular pinot noir to an honored vidal blanc. Bring along a picnic lunch, then buy a bottle and retire to one of the tables beside the pond. The hospitality center is open daily from 10am to 6pm in summer, 11am to 5pm in winter, with tours on the hour.

Continuing south on Route 77, the road skirts Little Compton and heads on to **Sakonnet Point,** where the inland terrain gives way to stony beaches and coastal marshes. There's a wetlands wildlife refuge, a small harbor with working boats, and not much else.

Now head back north on Route 77, watching for the sign pointing toward Adamsville. Take the right turn at the triangular traffic island just beyond, onto a road that seems to have neither name nor number. Shortly, it arrives at a T intersection with a Congregational church and the C.R. Wilbur general store. This is downtown **Little Compton.** Long situated next to the store was a communal gathering spot, the **Common's** restaurant. It burned to the ground in 2005, but has been rebuilt and is the likeliest place for a snack or lunch in the area. Turn left (north) and you're back in the country. In less than 2 miles, the road ends at Peckham Road. Turn left to return to Route 77, and turn right (north) to return to your original destination.

WHERE TO STAY ALONG THE WAY

Stone House Club From the last stop in Sakonnet Point, return along Route 77, and you'll shortly note the entrance to this restaurant/tavern/inn. It's open to the public, but long observed the wink-wink subterfuge of proclaiming itself a private club because it serves spirits and there was a church next door. That means a $25 membership fee for individuals and $40 for couples, in addition to room rates. Furnishings are worn and un-stylish, but look oddly right for their location. Two private beaches are available to guests. The cellar Tap Room and the more formal restaurant upstairs traipse all over the gastronomic map, with an emphasis on seafood. They are open Tuesday through Sunday in summer, Friday through Sunday from October to December and March to April.

122 Sakonnet Point Rd., Little Compton, RI 02837. ✆ **401/635-2222.** Fax 401/635-2822. www.stonehouseclub.com. 14 units, 4 with shared bathroom. Summer $85–$175 double; Nov–Dec and Mar–Apr $60–$115 double. Rates include breakfast. **Note:** Additional membership fee as noted above. MC, V. Closed Jan–Feb. **Amenities:** Restaurant; bar. *In room:* No phone.

WHERE TO DINE ALONG THE WAY

Boat House ★ SEAFOOD Opened in 2005, largely as a service to the occupants of the condo development rising on the hill behind it, the restaurant emphasizes fish. Originally a tented, open-sided pavilion with a patio of umbrella tables, it was on a May-to-Columbus-Day schedule. It proved so popular, though, there was soon talk of enclosing at least part of the space and extending the season. That's understandable. There's that wide vista of Sakonnet Bay out there, and the food is fresh, clean, and varied. Raw clams and oysters are native, the seafood stew has local ingredients, and the salads, often seafood based, are large enough to serve as light lunches. One such is the salt cod with romaine, roasted peppers, red onion, olives, and chickpeas. Most of the entrees are simplicity itself, an exception being the Jamaican jerk tautog with tropical fruit salsa, red beans, and rice. This is good place to try out the wines of Sakonnet Vineyards, especially chardonnay and vidal blanc. Be sure to call ahead for details of changes.

227 Schooner Dr., Tiverton. ✆ **401/624-6300.** Reservations recommended. Main courses $14–$30. AE, DISC, MC, V. Mon–Sat 11:30am–9pm (until 10pm Fri–Sat); Sun 11am–9pm. Take Exit 5 coming from Newport; the restaurant is north of the bridge.

3 Newport ★★★

75 miles S of Boston; 115 miles NE of New Haven

"City by the Sea" is the unimaginative nickname an early resident unloaded on Newport. At least it was accurate, because for a time during the Colonial period it rivaled Boston and even New York as a center of New World trade and prosperity. Newport occupies the southern tip of Aquidneck Island in Narragansett Bay, and is connected to the mainland by three bridges and a ferry.

Wealthy industrialists, railroad tycoons, coal magnates, financiers, and robber barons were drawn to the area in the 19th century, especially between the Civil War and World War I. They bought up property at the ocean's rim to build what they called summer "cottages"—which were in fact mansions of immoderate design and proportions patterned after European palaces.

The principal toys of the Newport elite were equally extravagant yachts meant for pleasure, not commerce, and competition among them established Newport's reputation as a sailing center. In 1851, the schooner *America* defeated a British boat in a race around the Isle of Wight. The prize trophy became known as the America's Cup, which remained in the possession of the New York Yacht Club (with an outpost in Newport) until 1983. In that shocking summer, *Australia II* snatched the Cup away from *Liberty* in the last race of a four-out-of-seven series. An American team regained the cup in 1987, but in 1995 a New Zealand crew won it back. The strong U.S. yachting tradition has endured despite the loss of the Cup, and Newport continues as a bastion of world sailing and a destination for long-distance races.

The perimeter of the city resembles a heeled boot, its toe pointing west, not unlike Italy. About where the laces of the boot would be is the downtown business and residential district. Several wharves push into the bay, providing support and mooring for flotillas of pleasure craft. Much of the strolling, shopping, eating, quaffing, and gawking is done along this waterfront and its parallel streets: America's Cup Avenue and Thames Street. (The latter used to be pronounced "Tems," in the British manner, but was Americanized to "Thaymz" after the Revolution.)

The navy pulled out its battleships, causing a decline in the local economy, but it hasn't proven to be the disaster predicted by some, and Newport has been spared the coarser intrusions that afflict so many coastal resorts. Monster RVs rarely add to the heavy traffic of July and August, and T-shirt emporia have kept within reasonable limits—a remarkable feat, considering that Newport has nearly 4 million visitors a year.

Immediately east and north of the business district are blocks of Colonial, Federal, and Victorian houses of the 18th and 19th centuries, many of them designated National Historic Sites. Happily, they are not frozen in amber but are very much in use as residences, restaurants, offices, and shops. Taken together, they are as visually appealing in their own way as the 40-room cottages of the super-rich.

So, despite Newport's prevailing image as a collection of stupefyingly ornate mansions and regattas of sailing ships inaccessible to all but the rich and famous, the city is, for the most part, middle class and moderately priced. Scores of inns and B&Bs assure lodging even during festival weeks, at rates and fixtures from budget to luxury level. In almost every respect, this is the "First Resort" of the New England coast.

ESSENTIALS

GETTING THERE From New York City, take I-95 to the third Newport exit, picking up Route 138 east (which joins briefly with Route 4) and crossing the Newport toll bridge slightly north of the downtown district. From Boston, take Route 24 through Fall River, picking up Route 114 into town.

T. F. Green/Providence Airport (✆ **401/737-8222**) in Warwick, south of Providence (Exit 13, I-95), handles national flights into the state. Major airlines serving this airport include **American** (✆ 800/433-7300), **Continental** (✆ 800/525-0280), **Delta** (✆ 800/221-1212), **Northwest** (✆ 800/225-2525), **United** (✆ 800/241-6522), and **US Airways** (✆ 800/428-4322). A few of the larger Newport hotels provide shuttle service, as does **Cozy Cab** (✆ 401/846-2500).

The **Rhode Island Public Transit Authority,** or **RIPTA** (✆ **800/244-0444** or 401/781-9400; www.ripta.com), runs up to 28 buses a day on the 70-minute ride between Providence's Kennedy Plaza and the Newport Gateway Visitor Center. One-way fare is $1.50.

Newport

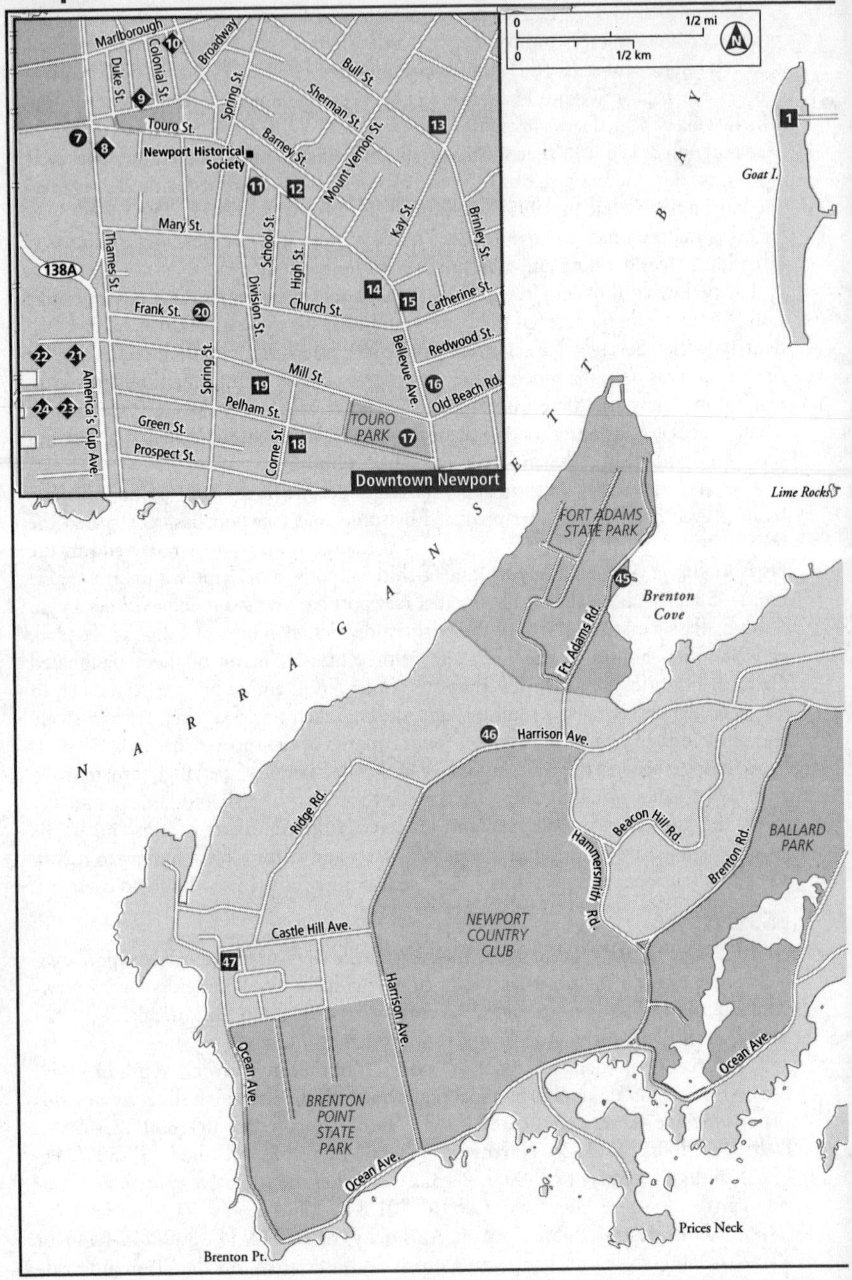

0
1/2 mi
0
1/2 km
N
Marlborough
Colonial St.
Duke St.
Broadway
Spring St.
Bull St.
Sherman St.
Touro St.
Barney St.
Mount Vernon St.
Newport Historical Society
Mary St.
School St.
Kay St.
Brinley St.
Thames St.
138A
High St.
Division St.
Frank St.
Church St.
Catherine St.
Bellevue Ave.
Redwood St.
Spring St.
Mill St.
America's Cup Ave.
Pelham St.
Old Beach Rd.
Green St.
TOURO PARK
Prospect St.
Corne St.
Downtown Newport
Goat I.
N A R R A G A N S E T T B A Y
Lime Rocks
FORT ADAMS STATE PARK
Brenton Cove
Ft. Adams Rd.
Harrison Ave.
Ridge Rd.
Beacon Hill Rd.
Hammersmith Rd.
Brenton Rd.
BALLARD PARK
NEWPORT COUNTRY CLUB
Castle Hill Ave.
Harrison Ave.
Ocean Ave.
Ocean Ave.
BRENTON POINT STATE PARK
Ocean Ave.
Prices Neck
Brenton Pt.

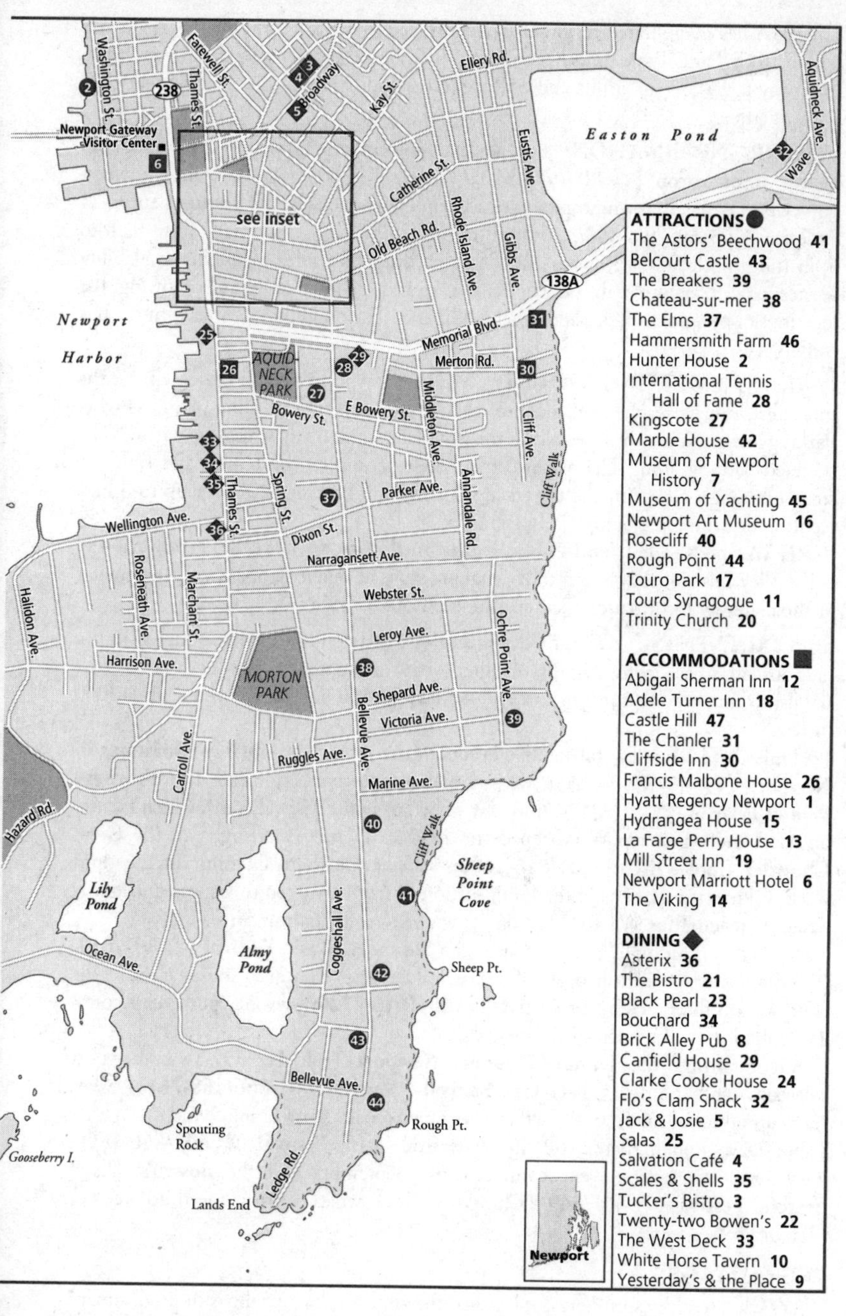

Washington St.
Farewell St.
Thames St.
238
Broadway
Kay St.
Ellery Rd.
Easton Pond
Aquidneck Ave.
Wave
Eustis Ave.
Newport Gateway Visitor Center
Catherine St.
Rhode Island Ave.
see inset
Old Beach Rd.
Gibbs Ave.
138A
Newport Harbor
Memorial Blvd.
Merton Rd.
AQUIDNECK PARK
Bowery St.
E Bowery St.
Middleton Ave.
Cliff Ave.
Cliff Walk
Spring St.
Parker Ave.
Annandale Rd.
Wellington Ave.
Dixon St.
Narragansett Ave.
Roseneath Ave.
Marchant St.
Halidon Ave.
Webster St.
Leroy Ave.
Ochre Point Ave.
Harrison Ave.
MORTON PARK
Shepard Ave.
Bellevue Ave.
Victoria Ave.
Ruggles Ave.
Carroll Ave.
Marine Ave.
Hazard Rd.
Lily Pond
Almy Pond
Sheep Point Cove
Coggeshall Ave.
Ocean Ave.
Sheep Pt.
Bellevue Ave.
Rough Pt.
Spouting Rock
Gooseberry I.
Ledge Rd.
Lands End
Newport
ATTRACTIONS
The Astors' Beechwood 41
Belcourt Castle 43
The Breakers 39
Chateau-sur-mer 38
The Elms 37
Hammersmith Farm 46
Hunter House 2
International Tennis Hall of Fame 28
Kingscote 27
Marble House 42
Museum of Newport History 7
Museum of Yachting 45
Newport Art Museum 16
Rosecliff 40
Rough Point 44
Touro Park 17
Touro Synagogue 11
Trinity Church 20
ACCOMMODATIONS
Abigail Sherman Inn 12
Adele Turner Inn 18
Castle Hill 47
The Chanler 31
Cliffside Inn 30
Francis Malbone House 26
Hyatt Regency Newport 1
Hydrangea House 15
La Farge Perry House 13
Mill Street Inn 19
Newport Marriott Hotel 6
The Viking 14
DINING
Asterix 36
The Bistro 21
Black Pearl 23
Bouchard 34
Brick Alley Pub 8
Canfield House 29
Clarke Cooke House 24
Flo's Clam Shack 32
Jack & Josie 5
Salas 25
Salvation Café 4
Scales & Shells 35
Tucker's Bistro 3
Twenty-two Bowen's 22
The West Deck 33
White Horse Tavern 10
Yesterday's & the Place 9

RIPTA has inaugurated **ferry service** between Point Street Landing in Providence and Perrotti Park. From mid-May to mid-October, there are five departures daily. One-way fare is $7 for adults and $5 for seniors and children 5 to 11; younger children ride free.

VISITOR INFORMATION For advance information available 24 hours, call **visitor information** (© **800/976-5122** outside RI, 800/556-2484 in RI; www.goNewport.com). In town, stop by the excellent **Newport Gateway Visitor Center,** 23 America's Cup Ave. (© **800/326-6030** or 401/849-8048). Open daily from 9am to 5pm (until 6pm Fri–Sat), it has attendants on duty, brochures, a lodging-availability service, a cafe, a souvenir stand, restrooms, and panoramic photos showing the locations of mansions, parks, and other landmarks. The building is shared with the bus station.

PARKING & GETTING AROUND Most of Newport's attractions, except for the mansions, can be reached on foot, so leaving your car at your hotel or inn is wise. Parking lots aren't cheap, especially at the waterfront, and many streets are narrow. The metered parking along Thames Street is closely monitored by police, and fines are steep (although Nov–Apr the meters are hooded and parking is free for up to 3 hr.). Renting or bringing a bicycle is an attractive option.

RIPTA, the **Rhode Island Public Transit Authority** (© **401/781-9400**), has several trolley/bus routes through town, making stops at major sights. Service originates at the Gateway Information Center. Fare is $1.50.

SPECIAL EVENTS Arrive any day in summer and you can expect to find at least a half-dozen festivals, competitions, or other events in progress. Following is only a partial list. (Call ahead to confirm dates: © **800/263-4636** outside RI, or 401/848-2000 in RI).

While there are a few substantive events in the off season, notably **Christmas in Newport** (© **401/849-6454;** www.christmasinnewport.org) and the **February Winter Festival** (© **401/847-7666;** www.newportwinterfestival.com), which focuses on food and winter sports, the pace ratchets up in June, starting with the **Great Chowder Cook-Off** (© **401/846-1600;** www.newportfestivals.com). In the third week of June, the gardens of the Point section of town are open to visitors during the **Secret Garden Tour** (© **401/847-0514;** www.secretgardentour.com).

During the middle 2 weeks in July, the **Newport Music Festival** (© **401/849-0700;** www.newportmusic.org), offers classical concerts daily at various venues. In the third week is the **Black Ships Festival** (© **401/846-2720;** www.newportevents.com), a celebration of all aspects of Japanese culture.

August brings the **Dunkin' Donuts Newport Folk Festival** (www.newportfolk.com) and the 4-day **JVC Jazz Festival—Newport** (© **866/468-7619;** www.festivalproductions.net), both held at Fort Adams State Park. Things wind down after Labor Day, though there's still the **Waterfront Irish Festival** (© **401/846-1600;** www.newportwaterfrontevents.com) in early September and the **Bowen's Wharf Seafood Festival** (© **401/849-2120;** www.bowenswharf.com) in the third week of October.

THE COTTAGES

That's what wealthy summer people called the almost unimaginably sumptuous mansions they built in Newport in the last decades before the 16th Amendment to the Constitution permitted an income tax.

Say this for the wealthy of the Gilded Age, many of whom obtained their fortunes by less than honorable means: They knew a good place to put down roots when they saw it. These are the same ones, after all, who developed Palm Beach in winter, the Hudson Valley in spring, the Berkshires in autumn, and Newport in summer, sweeping from house to luxurious house with the insouciance of a bejeweled matron dragging her sable down a grand staircase.

When driving or biking through the cottage district (walking its length is a serious trek for most people), consider the fact that most of these astonishing residences are still privately owned. That's almost as remarkable as the grounds and interiors of the nine that are open to the public.

Also, resolve to visit only one or two estates per day: The sheer opulence of the mansions can soon become numbing. Each residence requires 45 minutes to an hour for its guided tour. If at all possible, go during the week to avoid crowds and traffic.

Six of the mansions are maintained by the **Preservation Society of Newport County,** 424 Bellevue Ave. (✆ **401/847-1000;** www.newportmansions.org), which also operates the 1748 Hunter House, the 1860 Italianate Chepstow villa, the 1883 Isaac Bell House, and the Green Animals Topiary Gardens in Portsmouth. The Society sells a **combination ticket,** good for a year, to five of its properties; the cost is $31 for adults, $10 for children 6 to 17. Individual tickets for The Breakers are $15 for adults, $4 for children, and for Hunter House $25 for adults, $4 for children. Individual tickets for Kingscote, The Elms, Chateau-sur-mer, Marble House, and Rosecliff are $10 for adults, $4 for children. They can be purchased at any of the properties. Credit cards are accepted at most, but not all, of the cottages. Special events, such as the festive Thanksgiving and Christmas celebrations, cost extra. The Society conducts an hour-long walking tour past the mansions for $25 for adults and $10 for children. Parking is free at all the Society properties.

The mansions that aren't operated by the Preservation Society but are open to the public are Belcourt Castle, Beechwood, and Rough Point.

During the winter, the mansions of the Society take turns each year staying open through the period, with an additional one or two openings on weekends. Following are descriptions of the cottages in the order in which they're encountered when driving south from Memorial Boulevard along Bellevue Avenue, then west on Ocean Drive.

Kingscote ★ This mansion (on the right side of the avenue) is a reminder that well-to-do Southern families often had second homes north of the Mason-Dixon line to avoid the sultry summers of the deep South. Kingscote was built in 1841, nearly 40 years before the Gilded Age (usually regarded as the era between the end of the Civil War and the beginning of World War I). But it is considered one of the Newport Cottages because it was acquired in 1864 by the sea merchant William Henry King, who furnished it with porcelains and textiles accumulated in the China trade. Architect Richard Upjohn designed the mansion in the same Gothic Revival style he used for Trinity Church in New York. The firm of McKim, Mead & White was commissioned to design the 1881 dining room, notable for its Tiffany glass panels. As you drive down Bellevue, the Isaac Bell House is between Kingscote and The Elms.

Bowery St. (west of Bellevue Ave.). Late Mar to Apr Sat–Sun 10am–5pm; May to Columbus Day daily 10am–5pm. See above for admission details.

The Elms ★★ Architect Horace Trumbauer is said to have been inspired by the Château d'Asnieres outside Paris, and a first look at the ornate dining room of The Elms, suitable for at least a marquis, buttresses that claim. So do the sunken gardens, laid out and maintained in the formal French manner. The owner was a first-generation millionaire, a coal tycoon named Edward J. Berwind. His cottage was completed in 1901, and he filled it with Louis XIV and XV furniture as well as paintings and accessories true to the late 18th century. It was one of the first fully electrified mansions in Newport. Visitors can opt for a self-guided audio tour.

Bellevue Ave. Daily 10am–5pm. Closed Thanksgiving and Dec 24–25. See above for admission details.

Chateau-sur-mer ★ William S. Wetmore was yet another merchant who made his fortune in the China trade. The entrance to this "Castle by the Sea" is on the left side of Bellevue, driving south. High Victorian in style, which means it drew from many inspirations (including Italian Renaissance and French Second Empire), the Chateau features a central atrium with a skylight and balconies at every level. A park designed in a style true to the period of the cottage has copper beech and weeping willow trees standing around its garden pavilion.

Bellevue Ave. Jan to mid-Apr Sat–Sun and holidays 10am–4pm; mid-Apr to Oct daily 10am–5pm. See above for admission details.

The Breakers ★★★ If you have time to see only one of the cottages, make it this one. Architect Richard Morris Hunt was commissioned to create this replica of a generic Florentine Renaissance palazzo, replacing a wood structure that burned down in 1892. He was unrestrained by cost considerations. The high iron entrance gates alone weigh over 7 tons. The 50×50-foot great hall has 50-foot-high ceilings, forming a giant cube, and is sheathed in marble. Such mind-numbing extravagance shouldn't really be surprising—Hunt's patron was, after all, Cornelius Vanderbilt II, grandson of railroad tycoon Commodore Vanderbilt.

Had Vanderbilt been European royalty, The Breakers would have provided motive for a peasant revolt. Vanderbilt's small family and their staff of 40 servants had 70 rooms in which to roam. The mansion's foundation is approximately the size of a football field, and The Breakers took nearly 3 years to build (1892–95). Platoons of artisans were imported from Europe to apply gold leaf, carve wood and marble, and provide mural-size baroque paintings. The furnishings on view are original. The bathrooms, far from common at the time, were provided with both fresh and salt running water, hot and cold.

To get here, turn left on Ruggles Avenue after Chateau-sur-mer, then left again on Ochre Point Avenue. The Breakers is on the right; a parking lot is on the left.

Ochre Point Ave. (east of Bellevue Ave.). ✆ **401/847-1000.** Mid-Apr to Jan 1 daily 10am–5pm (until 6pm Fri–Sat in July–Aug); Nov 24 and Dec 1, 8, 15, and 29 also 6–8pm. See above for admission details.

Rosecliff ★ From The Breakers, return to Bellevue Avenue and turn left (south); Rosecliff is on the left. Stanford White thought the Grand Trianon of Louis XVI at Versailles a suitable model for this 1902 commission for the flamboyant Tessie Fair Oelrichs, heiress to the Comstock Lode. With a middling 40 rooms, it doesn't overwhelm, at least not on the scale of The Breakers. But it has the largest ballroom of all the cottages, not to mention a storied heart-shaped grand staircase. All this was made possible by one James Fair, an immigrant who made his fortune after he unearthed the thickest gold and silver vein of Nevada's Comstock Lode and bought this property for his daughters.

In 1941, the mansion and its contents were sold for $21,000. It was used as a setting for some scenes in the Robert Redford movie of Fitzgerald's *The Great Gatsby*

(1974) and for a ballroom scene in Arnold Schwarzenegger's *True Lies* (1994). On a humid summer day, keep in mind that the mansion is air-conditioned.

Bellevue Ave. Mid-Apr to late Oct daily 10am–5pm. See above for admission details.

The Astors' Beechwood ★★ Mrs. William Backhouse Astor—*the* Mrs. Astor, as every brochure and guide feels compelled to observe—was, during her active life, the arbiter of exactly who constituted New York and Newport society. "The 400" list of socially acceptable folk was influenced or perhaps even drawn up by her, and that roster bore meaning, in some quarters, well into the second half of the 20th century. Being invited to Beechwood was absolutely critical to a social pretender's sense of self-worth, and elaborate machinations were set in motion to achieve that goal.

Rebuilt in 1857 after a fire destroyed the original version, the mansion isn't as large or impressive as some of its neighbors. But unlike those managed by the Preservation Society, it provides a little theatrical pizzazz with a corps of actors who pretend to be friends, children, and servants of Mrs. Astor. In set pieces, they share details about life in the late Victorian era. Frequent special events are held, often replicating those that took place when she held court, including costume balls and specially decorated banquets with Victorian music and dancing.

There are several regularly scheduled tours and events—Living History, Murder Mystery, Speakeasy (no minors), and the Christmas tours. Many involve vignettes performed by the resident acting troupe, and admission prices vary.

580 Bellevue Ave. ✆ **401/846-3772.** www.astors-beechwood.com. Admission $18–$30 adults, $8–$15 children 6–12. Mid-May to early Nov daily 10am–5pm (tours every 20 min.); Christmas events Nov–Dec Wed–Sun; Feb to mid-May Fri–Sun 10am–4pm (tours every 30 min.). Closed Jan.

Marble House ★★★ Architect Richard Morris Hunt outdid himself for his clients William and Alva Vanderbilt. Several types of marble were used both outside and in, with a lavish hand that rivals the palaces of the Sun King, especially Le Petit Trianon at Versailles. It reaches its apogee in the ballroom, which is encrusted with three kinds of gold. It cost William $11 million to build and decorate Marble House, but Alva divorced him 4 years after the project was finished. She got the house, which she soon closed after marrying William's friend and neighbor. When her second husband died, Alva discovered the cause of female suffrage, and reopened Marble House in 1913 to hold a benefit for the campaign for women's right to vote. (Dishes in the scullery bear the legend "Votes for Women.")

Bellevue Ave. Mid-Apr to Jan 1 daily 10am–5pm (Fri–Sat until 6pm); Nov Sat–Sun 10am–4pm; Jan–Mar Sat–Sun and holidays 10am–4pm. See above for admission details.

Belcourt Castle ★★ This was the only slightly less grand mansion down the road from Marble House to which Alva Vanderbilt repaired after her second marriage. While the Vanderbilts were avid yachtsmen, her new husband, Oliver Hazard Perry Belmont, was a fanatical horseman. His 60-room house contained extensive stables on the ground floor where his beloved steeds slept under monogrammed blankets (the Belmonts were instrumental in building New York's famed Belmont Racetrack).

The castle, intended to resemble a European hunting lodge, has a ponderously masculine character, understandable in that it was designed for the bachelor Belmont before he won over vivacious Alva. It contains artifacts from the medieval era through the 19th century, including stained glass, Japanese and Chinese cabinetry, a full-size replica of a gaudy Portuguese coronation carriage, and French Renaissance furniture.

Thomas Edison designed the lighting. There are 14 secret doors and a tunnel to the kitchens, which were located 2 blocks away for fear of fire. The castle sold for a mere $25,000 in the early 1940s to the family of Harold B. Tinney, members of which still live here.

There are evening ghost and candlelight tours on some nights much of the year; tickets are $15 and reservations are wise. Leave the young ones at home. Call or check the website for dates.

657 Bellevue Ave. (at Lakeview Ave.). ✆ **401/846-0669.** www.belcourtcastle.com. Admission $10 adults, $8 seniors and college students, $7 children 13–18, $3.50 children 6–12. Feb–May Sat–Sun and holidays 10am–3pm; Memorial Day to mid-Oct daily 9:30am–4:30pm; mid-Oct to Nov daily 10am–4pm; Dec (special tours) 10am–3pm daily. Closed Jan.

Rough Point ★★ The fabled 1887 Gothic-Tudor home of the late tobacco heiress Doris Duke made its long-awaited opening in 2000. Only a portion of the 105 rooms are currently open for viewing, and by only 96 visitors per day. They may be greeted by Chairman Mao, the last of Duke's many pets. The heiress's collections include a wealth of Ming-dynasty vases, Flemish and French tapestries, and paintings by Van Dyck and Gainsborough. Watch for the ivory inset side tables bearing the marks of Catherine the Great in what is called the Yellow Room.

While those who knew her reject suggestions that Duke was reclusive or troubled, hers was, at the least, an often darkly eventful life. It was here at Rough Point in 1967 that the story of the tobacco heiress and her interior decorator/companion unfolded. Eduardo Tirella was killed after being crushed against the iron entrance gates by Duke's station wagon. Duke later claimed that she accidentally hit the accelerator when Tirella got out of the car to open the gates. The police chief declared it "an unfortunate accident," but local tongues wagged.

Duke died in 1993, bequeathing Rough Point to the Newport Restoration Foundation, along with all clothing, jewelry, and furniture in the house. To get here from Belcourt Castle, continue south on Bellevue. Rough Point is on the left, just before a sharp turn west along what becomes Ocean Drive. The mansion is fully air-conditioned.

Individual visits aren't allowed. The only source for tickets is the Newport Gateway Visitor Center, where parking is also available (no parking at the mansion). Minibuses shuttle visitors to Rough Point every 20 minutes between 10am and 3:20pm; tours are limited to 12 people each and take about 60 minutes.

Bellevue Ave. ✆ **401/849-7300.** www.newportrestoration.org. Admission $25, free under 12 years. Visits by guided tour only; mid-Apr to early Nov Tues–Sat.

ADDITIONAL ATTRACTIONS

Historic Hill is the large district of Colonial Newport that rises from America's Cup Avenue, along the waterfront, to Bellevue Avenue, the beginning of Victorian Newport. **Spring Street** ★ serves as the Hill's main drag, and it's a treasure-trove of Colonial, Georgian, and Federal structures. Chief among its visual delights is the 1725 **Trinity Church** ★, at the corner of Church Street. Said to have been influenced by the work of the legendary British architect Christopher Wren, it certainly reflects that inspiration in its belfry and distinctive spire, seen from all over downtown Newport and dominating Queen Anne Square, a greensward that runs down to the waterfront.

Hammersmith Farm Built for John W. Auchincloss in 1887, this shingled Victorian mansion was used for the wedding reception of John F. Kennedy and Jacqueline

Bouvier (whose mother was married to an Auchincloss), in 1953. It subsequently became the unofficial summer White House of the short Kennedy presidency. Hammersmith was sold in 1997 for over $6.6 million to a Chicago businessman who sold it again 2 years later, and it is no longer open to the public. The house can still be seen from the road, however.

Ocean Dr. (past Castle Hill Ave.).

Hunter House ★ Another property of the Preservation Society, this 1754 Georgian Colonial is one of the most impressive dwellings in the neighborhood known as the Point, north of downtown. Above the doorway is a carved wooden pineapple. This symbol of welcome derived from the practice of placing a real pineapple at the door to announce that the sea-captain owner had returned from his long voyage and was ready to receive guests. The interior displays furniture crafted by Newport's famed 18th-century cabinetmakers, Townsend and Goddard.

54 Washington St. (at Elm St.). ✆ **401/847-1000.** See "The Cottages," above, for admission details. Late May to early Oct daily 10am–5pm.

International Tennis Hall of Fame On Bellevue Avenue, there was (and is) an exclusive men's club called the Newport Reading Room. One member was James Gordon Bennett, Jr., the wealthy publisher of the *New York Herald.* He persuaded a friend to ride a horse into the club. The outraged members reprimanded Bennett, who had an instant snit that they hadn't enjoyed his little jest. He went right out and bought a property on the other side of Memorial Boulevard, and ordered a structure built for his own social and sports club.

McKim, Mead & White produced a shingle-style edifice of lavish proportions, with turrets and verandas and an interior piazza for lawn games, equestrian shows, and a new game called tennis. It is now given to a permanent grass court. As Bennett hoped, his Newport Casino swiftly became the premier gathering place of his privileged compatriots.

Now the pavilion hosts professional tournaments, and its courts are open to the public for play (call ahead to make reservations May–Oct). The building itself houses the Hall of Fame, of interest primarily to fans of the game. A restaurant (✆ **401/847-0418**) serves lunch, sunset dinners, and weekend brunch.

194 Bellevue Ave. (at Memorial Blvd.). ✆ **800/457-1144** or 401/849-3990. www.tennisfame.org. Admission $8 adults, $6 seniors and students, $4 children 16 and under. Daily 9:30am–5pm (except during tournaments and major holidays).

Museum of Newport History Maintained by the Newport Historical Society, this museum is in the refurbished 1772 Brick Market (not to be confused with the nearby shopping mall Brick Marketplace). The architect was Peter Harrison, also responsible for the Touro Synagogue (see below). The museum houses boat models, marine charts, antique silverware, and a ship figurehead, and also features videos on Newport history.

127 Thames St. (at Touro St.). ✆ **401/841-8770.** www.newporthistorical.org. Donation only. Thurs–Sat 10am–4pm; Sun 1–4pm.

Newport Art Museum Across the avenue from Touro Park, this was the first Newport commission of Richard Morris Hunt, who went on to design many of the cottages along Bellevue Avenue. Unlike most of his later Newport houses, the 1862 main structure is in the Victorian stick style, a wood construction that had origins in earlier Carpenter Gothic. It now mounts art exhibitions and serves as a venue for concerts.

76 Bellevue Ave. (at Old Beach Rd.). ✆ **401/848-8200**; www.newportartmuseum.com. Admission $6 adults, $5 seniors, and $4 students, but these are technically voluntary donations. Memorial Day to Columbus Day Mon–Sat 10am–5pm, Sun noon–5pm; Columbus Day to Memorial Day Tues–Sat 10am–4pm, Sun noon–4pm.

Touro Park Opposite the Newport Art Museum, this small park provides a shaded respite. At its center is the Old Stone Mill. Dreamers like to believe that its eight columns were erected by Vikings. Realists say it was built by Benedict Arnold, a governor of the colony long before his great-great-grandson committed his infamous act of treason during the War of American Independence.

Bellevue Ave. (between Pelham and Mill sts.).

Touro Synagogue The oldest existing synagogue in the United States dates from 1763. A Sephardic Jewish community, largely refugees from Portugal, lived in Newport from the mid–17th century, over 100 years before this building was erected. It was designed by Peter Harrison, who was also responsible for the Brick Market (see Museum of Newport History, above). The synagogue was designated a National Historic Site in 1946.

Next door is the **Newport Historical Society,** 82 Touro St. (✆ **401/846-0813**), which features displays of Colonial furnishings and sponsors walking tours (see "Organized Tours & Cruises," below).

85 Touro St. (Spring St.). ✆ **401/847-4794**. Free admission. July 1 to Labor Day Sun–Fri 10am–5pm; Labor Day to June 30 Sun 11am–3pm, Mon–Fri 1–3pm; Nov 1–Apr 30 Sun 11am–3pm, Mon–Fri at 1pm (groups of 10 or more by appointment only). Guided tours only, beginning every half-hour; call for the current schedule.

OUTDOOR PURSUITS: THE BEACH & BEYOND

Fort Adams State Park, Harrison Avenue (✆ **401/841-0707;** www.fortadams.org), is on the thumb of land that partially encloses Newport Harbor. It can be seen from the downtown docks and reached by driving or biking south on Thames Street and west on Wellington Avenue (a section of Ocean Dr., which becomes Harrison Ave.). The sprawling 1820s fort for which the park is named is under restoration, work that can be viewed by guided tour. Admission is $10 for adults, $5 for ages 6 to 18, and free for 5 and under. Boating, ocean swimming, fishing, and sailing are all possible in the park's 105 acres. Open from Memorial Day to Labor Day. Also on the grounds is the **Museum of Yachting** (✆ **401/847-1018**), housed in a stone barracks from the early 19th century. Open from mid-May to October daily from 10am to 5pm, by appointment the rest of the year. Admission is $5 for adults, $4 for seniors and children under 12.

Farther along Ocean Drive, past Hammersmith Farm, is **Brenton Point State Park** ★★, a scenic preserve that borders the Atlantic, with nothing to impede the waves rolling in and collapsing on the rock-strewn beach. Scuba divers are often seen surfacing offshore, anglers enjoy casting from the long breakwater, and on a windy day the sky is dotted with colorful kites.

There are other beaches more appropriate for swimming. The longest and most popular is **Easton's Beach** ★, which lies along Route 138A, the extension of Memorial Boulevard, east of town. There are plenty of facilities, including a bathhouse, eating places, picnic areas, lifeguards, a carousel, and the **Newport Aquarium** (✆ **401/849-8430**). Parking costs $8 weekdays, $10 on weekends.

On Ocean Drive, less than 2 miles from the south end of Bellevue Avenue, is **Gooseberry Beach** ★, which is privately owned but open to the public. Parking costs $8 Monday through Friday, $12 Saturday and Sunday.

Cliff Walk ★★ skirts the edge of the southern section of town where most of the cottages were built, and provides better views of many of them than can be seen from the street. Traversing its length, high above the crashing surf, is more than a stroll but less than an arduous hike. For the full 3.5-mile length, start at the access point near the intersection of Memorial Boulevard and Eustis Avenue. For a shorter walk, start at the Forty Steps, at the end of Narragansett Avenue, off Bellevue. Leave the walk at Ledge Road and return via Bellevue Avenue. Figure 2 to 3 hours for the round-trip, and be warned that there are some mildly rugged sections to negotiate, no facilities, and no phones. The walk is open from 9am to 9pm.

A recently inaugurated enterprise, the outdoor **Børn Family Skating Center** (✆ **401/846-1600**) is set up at the Newport Yachting Center, on America's Cup Avenue. An oval rink about 120 feet long, it's open from mid-November into March, depending upon weather. Skate rentals are available.

Biking is one of the best ways to get around town, especially out to the mansions and along **Ocean Drive** ★★. Among several rental shops are **Firehouse Bicycle,** 25 Mill St. (✆ **401/847-5700**); **Ten Speed Spokes,** 18 Elm St. (✆ **401/847-5609**); and **Scooters,** 411 Thames St. (✆ **401/619-0573**).

Adventure Sports Rentals, at the Inn on Long Wharf, 142 Long Wharf (✆ **401/849-4820**), rents not only bikes and mopeds, but also outboard boats, kayaks, and sailboats; parasailing outings can be arranged.

Guided fly-fishing trips and fly-casting instruction are offered by the **Saltwater Edge,** 561 Lower Thames St. (✆ **401/842-0062;** www.saltwateredge.com). Anglers are taken out on half- and full-day quests for yellowfin tuna, bluefish, striped bass, and white marlin.

ORGANIZED TOURS & CRUISES

Several organizations conduct tours of the mansions and the downtown historic district. Between May 15 and October 15, the **Newport Historical Society,** 82 Touro St. (✆ **401/846-0813**), offers a few different itineraries of considerable variety and length. Tickets cost as little as $4 and as much as $12. They can be purchased at the Society or at the Gateway Visitor Center (see "Visitor Information," earlier in this section).

Viking Tours, based at the Gateway Visitor Center, 23 America's Cup Ave. (✆ **401/847-6921**), has narrated bus tours of the mansions and harbor cruises on the excursion boat *Viking Queen.* Bus tours—daily in summer, Saturdays from November to March—are 1½ to 4 hours and cost $22 to $47 for adults, $13 to $21 for children 5 to 11. Boat tours, from late May to early October, are 1 hour in length and cost $12 for adults, $10 for seniors, and $6 for kids. In July and August, the cruise can be extended to include a stop and tour of Fort Adams; $17 for adults, $15 for seniors, and $9 for children.

Classic Cruises of Newport ★, Bannister's Wharf, schedules narrated cruises on its 72-foot schooner *Madeleine* (✆ **401/847-0298;** www.cruisenewport.com). There are daily departures from spring to late fall; fares are $25 or $30 (children under 12 $5 off). The company's classic powerboat *RumRunner II* (✆ **401/847-0299;** same website) offers cruises daily over the same period. Rates are $17 per person for most outings, $22 for the cocktail cruise.

The ***Spirit of Newport*** ★, 2 Bowen's Wharf (✆ **401/849-3575**), offers daily 1½-hour cruises of the bay and harbor from May 1 to Columbus Day; Fares are $13 for adults, $11 for seniors, $7 for children ages 4 to 12. Another possibility is the ***Adirondack*** ★, a 78-foot schooner that makes 2-hour cruises from the Newport Yachting Center (✆ **401/846-3018**). Its ticket booth is on America's Cup Avenue at Commercial Wharf; reservations must be made in advance. Daily departures cost $25 to $30, depending on the time of day.

The **Newport Touring Company,** 19 America's Cup Ave. (✆ **800/398-7427** or 401/841-8700; www.newportdinnertrain.com), features 90-minute round-trip excursions in vintage railroad trains along the edge of the bay. Fares are $15 for adults; kids 10 and under are free, but only one per paying adult; additional kids are charged $7.95. The company also has a **dinner train** that operates Thursdays through Saturdays, mid-April to mid-December. Variations include a rail-and-cruise luncheon, and cabaret and murder mystery dinners, with prices per person from $43 to $54.

SHOPPING

At the heart of the downtown waterfront, **Bannister's Wharf, Bowen's Wharf,** and **Brick Marketplace** have about 60 stores among them, few of them especially compelling.

More interesting, if only for their quirky individuality, are the shops along **Lower Thames Street.** For example, **J. T.'s Ship Chandlery** (no. 364) outfits recreational sailors with sea chests, ship lanterns, and foul-weather gear. **Aardvark Antiques** (no. 475) specializes in salvaged architectural components. Books, nautical charts, and sailing videos are offered at **Armchair Sailor** (no. 543); for vintage clothing, visit **Cabbage Rose** (no. 493).

Spring Street is noted for its antiques shops and purveyors of crafts, jewelry, and folk art. One of these is **MacDowell Pottery** (no. 140), a studio selling ceramics and gifts by Rhode Island artisans; the nearby **J.H. Breakell & Co.** (no. 132) is a good source for handcrafted jewelry. Antique boat models are displayed along with marine paintings and navigational instruments at **North Star Gallery** (no. 105). **The Drawing Room/The Zsolnay Store** (nos. 152–154) stocks estate furnishings and specializes in Hungarian Zsolnay ceramics. Folk art and furniture are the primary goods at **Liberty Tree** (no. 104).

Spring intersects with **Franklin Street,** which harbors even more antiques shops in its short length. **Newport China Trade Co.** (no. 8) deals in export porcelain and objects associated with 19th-century China. Take a fat wallet to the **John Gidley House** (no. 22) for European antiques of high order. **Patina** (no. 26) is another dealer in Americana and folk art.

WHERE TO STAY

The **Gateway Visitor Center** (✆ **800/976-5122** or 401/849-8040; www.gonewport.com) lists vacancies in motels, hotels, and inns. Most can be called from free direct-line phones located nearby. Less impulsive travelers should reserve in advance, especially on weekends (2 months ahead for weekends from Memorial Day to Labor Day).

Newport Reservations (✆ **800/842-0102** or 401/842-0102; www.newportreservations.com) is a free service representing a number of hotels, motels, inns, and B&Bs. **Bed & Breakfast Newport, Ltd.** (✆ **800/800-8765** or 401/846-5408; www.bbnewport.com) claims to offer 350 choices of accommodations.

Many of the better motels are located in Middletown, about 2 miles north of downtown Newport. Possibilities include the **Courtyard by Marriott,** 9 Commerce Dr. (✆ **401/849-8000**); **Newport Ramada Inn,** 936 W. Main Rd. (✆ **401/846-7600**); **Newport Gateway Hotel,** 31 W. Main Rd. (✆ **401/847-2735**); and **Howard Johnson,** 351 W. Main Rd. (✆ **401/849-2000**). Newport itself has a **Marriott,** 25 America's Cup Ave. (✆ **401/849-1000**).

The rates given below generally have very wide ranges depending upon seasonal demand, so a $200 room on weekends in July might be half that in spring. The summer season is usually defined as Memorial Day to Columbus Day, with lower prices in effect the rest of the year.

VERY EXPENSIVE

Abigail Sherman Inn ★★ The third property of the company that also operates the Cliffside Inn and Adele Turner Inn (below), this inn, the smallest of the group, displays trademark fixtures and services of its siblings. These include exquisite decor; marble bathrooms with double Jacuzzis in every room; pre-breakfast room delivery of juice, coffee, and newspaper of your choice; and extraordinary afternoon teas with scones, cakes, and finger sandwiches. But it also has distinctive touches: a bar set up like a little pub . . . for designer waters, and an intimate room where couples can have tea for just two. And the level of sensuality has been amped up. Separate menus list long rosters of soaps and bath products, dozens of teas, and over 20 different kinds of pillows to add to or substitute for those already on the bed. And at bedtime, not a tired pillow mint, but strawberries and cream with the turndown. Guests who can't relax here need medical help.

A surcharge of $50 applies on weekends and holiday Sundays from May 1 through October. No smoking.

102 Touro St., Newport, RI 02840. ✆ **800/845-1811**. www.legendaryinnsofnewport.com. 5 units. $295–$645 double. Rates include breakfast and afternoon tea. AE, DC, DISC, MC, V. No pets. No children under 12. **Amenities:** Concierge; limited room service; same-day dry cleaning/laundry. *In room:* A/C, TV/VCR/CD, dataport, hair dryer.

Castle Hill ★★★ The setting—40 oceanfront acres on a near-island—is the overwhelming attraction of this, the highest profile resort in Newport. But after roof-to-foundation renovations of the 1874 Victorian mansion and its outbuildings, even a visit in foul weather is a treat. There is no more enticing ritual in Newport than taking to one of the Adirondack chairs that dots the slope from the inn down toward the water, cocktail in hand, watching boats returning from the fishing grounds while the sun turns the water to gold. Best values are the Harbor Houses, which have been gutted and overhauled, with new furniture, Jacuzzis, and porches overlooking the bay. The handsome taproom offers a riveting view (shared by the dining areas, deck, and many of the bedrooms) of sailing ships on Narragansett Bay.

Breakfast buffets are expansive, and dinners in the dining rooms of the nameless restaurant and on the terrace are among the most accomplished in Newport. The kitchen applies Asian and European notions and techniques to largely regional ingredients, the menu delineating provenance, as with Hudson Valley duck, Farmstead artisan cheese, and Georges Bank scallops. They braise short ribs in Newport Storm Porter. Venturesome diners with few food prejudices might choose the "Chef's Inspiration" menu—three surprise courses created by the chefs. Service is wise and anticipatory. The Inn is completely nonsmoking, and pagers and cellphones are *verboten* in the restaurant.

590 Ocean Dr., Newport, RI 02840. © **888/466-1355** or 401/849-3800. Fax 401/849-3838. www.castlehillinn.com. 27 units. Summer $395–$1,450 double; fall–spring $145–$699 double (higher prices are for suites). Rates include breakfast and afternoon tea. AE, DISC, MC, V. Open weekends only Nov–Apr. Closed Jan. Children under 12 not accepted in main house. **Amenities:** Restaurant (eclectic); bar; laundry; dry cleaning. *In room:* A/C, TV, hair dryer.

The Chanler ★★★ Newport hoteliers keep topping themselves, but it will be a long while before they can best what has been wrought here. A boutique hotel with only 20 units, the main structure dates from 1873. It stands above the northern end of the Cliff Walk, overlooking the surf that rolls through the bay and onto Eaton's Beach. Extensive and very costly renovations have brought the French Empire mansion and three outlying villas to a level of opulence they never knew. All rooms have DVD and CD players, gas fireplaces, two TVs, separate sitting areas, and, except for one suite, double Jacuzzis, supplemented by multi-nozzled shower stalls. Each is jaw-droppingly decorated to a different theme—Mediterranean, Renaissance, Tudor—but chairs, sofas, and mattresses are uniformly plush, deep, and all-but-impossible to leave. In peak season, there are about three staff members for every guest. Be sure to get a tutorial on the controls of the shades, TV, door lock, and showers, none of which work the way they do in a Hilton.

After a rocky start, the restaurant, **Spiced Pear** (© **401/847-2244**), has surged back to elite status. The finest ingredients—foie gras, Kobe beef, Kurobuta pork, Iranian caviar, Dover sole—are deployed in refined (occasionally precious) arrangements that you might be reluctant to disturb. But do, and savor carefully. Portions look deceptively small, but by the time you finish that last bite of dessert, a bit of magic mastered by the most accomplished chefs, you'll be more than satisfied.

117 Memorial Blvd., Newport, RI 02840. © **401/847-1300.** wwwthechanler.com. 20 units. June–Oct $495–$1,195; Nov–May $350–$750 double. Rates include breakfast. AE, DC, MC, V. **Amenities:** Restaurant (fusion); bar; concierge; access to nearby health club; in-room massage; dry cleaning; laundry. *In room:* A/C, TV/DVD, dataport, hair dryer, safe.

EXPENSIVE

Adele Turner Inn ★★ The 1855 Admiral Benbow Inn was transformed into this sister property of the estimable Cliffside (see below). That meant that surroundings and services took an instant upward turn. While it is unlikely that the Adele Turner will ever match its sibling virtue for virtue—its rooms are smaller, for one thing—it comes close enough to merit this high recommendation. And in one area, it is preferable: Once you are here, most of the downtown attractions are within walking distance. Each room has a fireplace; some have been restored, others are newly installed. Some of the units have hot tubs. Full breakfasts and afternoon teas are nothing less than sumptuous. Room rates are $50 higher on weekends from May to October.

93 Pelham St., Newport, RI 02840. © **800/845-1811** or 401/857-1811. Fax 401/848-5850. www.adeleturnerinn.com. 13 units. $150–$500 double. Rates include breakfast and afternoon tea. AE, DC, MC, V. **Amenities:** Concierge; limited room service; same-day dry cleaning/laundry; free video library. *In room:* A/C, TV/VCR, hair dryer.

Cliffside Inn ★★★ This tops the list of grand Newport inns. All units now have at least one working fireplace, and most have whirlpool baths. A suite in the Seaview Cottage has a bathroom that has to be seen: The tub features both standard and hand-held showerheads, eight spray nozzles, and a built-in TV and CD player! Antiques are generously deployed, including Eastlake and Tiffany originals and Victorian fancies that include (in room no. 11) an amusing "bird cage" shower from 1890. A favorite unit is the Garden Suite, a duplex with private garden and big double bathroom with radiant heat beneath the Peruvian tile floors. Coffee, juice, and the newspaper of your choice are delivered to your room even before the full breakfast. From May to October, there is a room surcharge of $50 on weekends, as well as winter holiday weekends.

2 Seaview Ave. (near Cliff Ave.), Newport, RI 02840. ✆ **800/845-1811** or 401/847-1811. Fax 401/848-5850. www.cliffsideinn.com. 16 units. $245–$395 double. Rates include breakfast and afternoon tea. AE, DISC, MC, V. No children under 13. **Amenities:** Limited room service; laundry; same-day dry cleaning. *In room:* A/C, TV/VCR, dataport, hair dryer, iron.

Francis Malbone House ★★ A few years ago, nine modern rooms were added in a wing attached to the original 1760 Colonial house. They are very nice, with king-size beds and excellent reproductions of period furniture. Four of them share two sunken gardens, and three have Jacuzzi tubs built for two. Given a choice, take a room in the old section, where antiques outnumber repros, Oriental rugs adorn buffed wide-board floors, and silks and linens are deployed unsparingly. All but two units enjoy gas fireplaces. The most interesting parts of the waterfront are right outside the door.

392 Thames St. (east of Memorial Blvd.), Newport, RI 02840. ✆ **800/846-0392** or 401/846-0392. Fax 401/848-5956. www.malbone.com. 18 units. Apr–Oct $245–$345 double; Nov–Mar $99–$260 double. Midweek discounts available. Rates include breakfast and afternoon tea. AE, MC, V. No children under 12. *In room:* A/C, TV/VCR, CD player, dataport, hair dryer, iron.

Hyatt Regency Newport ★ More than 25 years old, the Hyatt is notable for its complete roster of hotel services, its location on an island at the northern end of Newport Harbor, and its full-service spa. You might expect such a place to be impersonal, but the staff endeavors to be pleasant. Delightful views of the harbor and town can be had from the restaurant and most of the guest rooms. Wireless Internet access is available. Morning newspaper delivery.

1 Goat Island, Newport, RI 02840. ✆ **800/233-1234** or 401/851-1234. Fax 401/846-7210. www.hyatt.com. 264 units. Summer $279–$479 double; winter $199–$329 double. AE, DC, DISC, MC, V. Parking $16. No pets. **Amenities:** 2 restaurants (American, regional); bar; indoor freshwater and outdoor saltwater pools; 2 tennis courts; well-equipped health club and spa; concierge; airport courtesy van; business center; limited room service; massage; babysitting; same-day laundry; dry cleaning. *In room:* A/C, TV w/pay movies, dataport, coffeemaker, hair dryer, iron.

Hydrangea House ★ Across the street from The Viking Hotel, this long-established inn can't quite match up with its more expensive competitors, but don't assume you'll feel deprived here. The deep violet exterior catches the eye, and the front door opens onto a dim common area furnished with antiques and a fireplace. That leads in turn into the breakfast room, with one long table beneath a glass chandelier. Fourteen upholstered chairs surround it, which leads easily into conversation. Morning coffee can be taken on the veranda in back. Upstairs bedrooms and suites are named rather than numbered, each distinctively decorated; all have steam showers and gas fireplaces, and some have Jacuzzis. The ample parking lot in back has enough space for all guests.

16 Bellevue Ave., Newport 02840. ✆ **800/945-4667** or 401/846-4435. www.hydrangeahouse.com. 9 units. $250–$425 double. Rates include breakfast. AE, DC, MC, V. *In room:* A/C, TV, hair dryer.

La Farge Perry House ★★ The first thing you're likely to notice upon entering this 1852 Federal-style home is the pristine housekeeping, and immediately after, the muted elegance of the superb furnishings. Crystal chandeliers, plush fabrics, and nautical artifacts fill both public and private rooms. That isn't to imply early-19th-century austerity: Unlike many of Newport's lesser B&Bs, no sacrifices in new-millennium conveniences are made. All units are suites with poster or sleigh beds; three have double Jacuzzis and one has a fireplace. The lavish breakfasts are memorable. Weekday discounts are often available, starting at $175.

24 Kay St. (at Bull St.), Newport, RI 02840. ✆ **877/736-1100** or 401/847-2223. www.lafargeperry.com. 5 units. May–Oct $195–$425 suite; Nov–Apr $125–$375 suite. Rates include full breakfast. AE, MC, V. No pets. No children under 12. *In room:* A/C, TV/VCR, dataport, fridge, hair dryer.

MODERATE

Mill Street Inn Something different from most Newport inns, this 19th-century sawmill was scooped out and rebuilt from the walls in. Apart from exposed expanses of brick and an occasional wood beam, all of it is new. An all-suite facility, even its smallest unit has a queen-size bed and a sofa bed. The duplexes have private balconies, but everyone can use the rooftop decks, where breakfast is served on warm days.

75 Mill St. (2 blocks east of Thames), Newport, RI 02840. ✆ **800/392-1316** or 401/849-9500. Fax 401/848-5131. www.millstreetinn.com. 23 units. June–Sept $169–$199 suite; Oct–May $119–$149 suite. Rates include breakfast and afternoon tea. Packages available. Children under 16 stay free in parent's room. Packages available. AE, DC, MC, V. Free adjacent parking. **Amenities:** Access to nearby health club; dry cleaning. *In room:* A/C, TV w/pay movies, dataport, minibar, hair dryer, safe.

The Viking On the Newport scene since 1926, this neo-Georgian sprawl of a hotel was built to accommodate the summer guests of Newport's wealthiest families. Today, its assets outnumber deficiencies, although it poses no challenge to Castle Hill or The Chanler, described above. On the plus side, it is cheaper than its rivals, has a modest new fitness room and spa, an indoor pool, a good location, and a pleasant, if sometimes distracted, staff. On the other, its bland Reagan-era furnishings and fixtures don't allow for many extras—no VCRs and only 11 channels on the TV. The rooftop bar with views of the harbor is an outstanding feature.

1 Bellevue Ave., Newport, RI 02840. ✆ **800/556-7126** or 401/847-3300. www.hotelviking.com. 237 units. $119–$389 double. Packages available. AE, DC, DISC, MC, V. **Amenities:** Restaurant (regional); bar; health club and spa; limited room service; laundry/dry cleaning. *In room:* A/C, TV, dataport, hair dryer.

WHERE TO DINE

There are far too many restaurants in Newport to give full treatment to even just the best among them. Equal in many ways to those recommended below are **Canfield House,** 5 Memorial Blvd. (✆ **401/847-0416**); **Yesterday's & the Place,** 28 Washington Sq. (✆ **401/847-0116**); **The Bistro,** 41 Bowen's Wharf (✆ **401/849-7778**); and **The West Deck,** 1 Waites Wharf (✆ **401/847-3610**). And for bargain dining in pricey Newport, the bountiful pastas of **Salas,** 343 Thames St. (✆ **401/845-8772**), are a perfect choice for hungry families.

The dining rooms at Castle Hill and The Chanler ("Where to Stay" above) are unsurpassed in this resort town of many good restaurants. They are open to any members of the public who are unintimidated by the expenditures required. Do make reservations. Figure about $200 to $300 for dinner for two.

In general, note that winter hours and days of operations vary considerably. Call ahead to avoid disappointment.

EXPENSIVE

Asterix ★ CONTEMPORARY FRENCH Named (for no obvious reason) for a famous French cartoon character, this cheerful place does render classic Gallic bistro dishes. Come and remember how delectable a near-perfect roast herbed chicken or sole meunière can be. To add a note of Lyonnaise authenticity, bluepoints, Wellfleets, and littlenecks are opened to order on weekend evenings. Daily specials are considerably more venturesome. Crispy duck with jasmine rice, Asian veggies, and Thai sweet-and-hot sauce was a recent one. A short bar menu lists sandwiches, pizzas, and pastas. What was once a car-repair shop has been given splashes of color, with an open kitchen in back. Sunday dinners are served to live jazz from 7pm. Excellent breads are provided by the chef/owner's **Boulangerie,** 382 Spring St. (✆ **401/846-3377**).

599 Lower Thames St. ✆ **401/841-8833.** Reservations recommended on summer weekends. Main courses $21–$32. MC, V. Daily 5–10pm (Sat–Sun until 11pm).

Black Pearl ★ SEAFOOD/AMERICAN This long building near the end of the wharf has you covered. The main building is divided into two sections. The Tavern contains an atmospheric bar and a room with marine charts on the walls. The pricier Commodore's Room is more formal, with linens and candles. In either setting, most of the preparations of fish, duck, and beef are familiar but of good quality, with an occasional lurch in exotic directions, such as ostrich steak. In the popular Tavern, don't miss the definitive Newport chowder, followed by a Pearlburger or one of the other overstuffed sandwiches. In summer, the menu is similar at the patio and open-air bar on the wharf, and there is a separate "Hot Dog Clam Chowder Annex."

30 Bannister's Wharf. ✆ **401/846-5264.** Reservations and jackets for men required for dinner in Commodore's Room. Main courses $16–$23 in Tavern, $19–$38 in Commodore's Room. AE, MC, V. Tavern daily 11:30am–1am; Commodore daily 11:30am–3pm and 6–10pm. Closed Jan and 1st 2 weeks in Feb.

Bouchard ★★ CREATIVE FRENCH Settle in for the evening on comfortable Empire chairs, while an efficient waiter takes your coat and your cocktail order. It's a polished performance, under the alert eye of the hostess, and what issues from the kitchen validates that promise. Presentations are thoughtfully conceived, attractive without voguish excesses—no heavily embellished towers of food as high as your chin. Here comes roasted wild boar redolent with a peppery currant sauce or sautéed scallops with a delicate red-wine and truffle butter sauce. You are asked when you place your order if you'll be having the Grand Marnier soufflé. If you do, you won't regret it. This is dining in a grand tradition. The only silly affectation is menu prices written out, as "Twenty Six dollars."

505 Lower Thames St. ✆ **401/846-0123.** Reservations recommended in high season. Main courses $18–$38. AE, DISC, MC, V. Wed–Mon 5:30–9pm (Sat–Sun until 10pm). Closed 1st 2 weeks in Jan.

Clarke Cooke House ★★★ ECLECTIC For many, this is the quintessential Newport restaurant. The picturesque 19th-century structure was moved to the wharf from America's Cup Avenue in the 1970s. Most of its several levels are open to the air in summer and glassed-in in winter. Several bars lubricate conversation. Up on the formal third floor, the staff sautés your lobster out of the shell while you put away such appetizers as stuffed zucchini blossoms, perhaps moving on to a rack of lamb *persillade* with minted tarragon glaze. If that seems too rich, spare the walk upstairs and stop in at the Grille, which wraps around a fireplace and center bar. The main floor, called the Candy Store, serves full meals, snacks, sandwiches, and drinks, and below that is the Boom Boom Room, with dancing on weekends from 9pm to whenever. All levels have access to the wide choices of a big wine cellar. No cellphones in the dining areas.

Bannister's Wharf. ✆ **401/849-2900.** Reservations recommended on summer weekends. Main courses $17–$33 in Candy Store and Grille, $27–$39 in the Porch. AE, DC, DISC, MC, V. Candy Store and Grille, summer daily 11:30am–10:30pm, winter Fri–Sun 11:30am–10:30pm; dining rooms, summer daily 6–10pm, winter Wed–Sun 6–10pm.

Tucker's Bistro ★★ CONTEMPORARY BISTRO You can't miss it at night—cascades of tiny lights swirl around the long facade. The eponymous owner is an avid yard-sale attendee who has filled his red walls with prints and mirrors in ornate gold frames and crowded his shelves with books, ceramics, and glassware. Little of it are you likely to covet, but the accumulation is oddly harmonious in its entirety. Anyway, Mr. Harris keeps the lights so low his staff provides flashlights to read the menu. The food is up to the visual extravagance, crying out for a meal of the provocative appetizers. Snapping taste buds to attention are the Thai shrimp nachos, actually crisp wontons topped with the grilled prawns, garnished with scallions and red pepper strips and leeks in a coconut red curry broth! Exclamation points are warranted as well for the mustard-crusted pork rillette with celeriac salad (!) and the entree of black pepper fettuccini with duck confit! By then, the rococo environment looks downright restrained.

150 Broadway. ✆ **401/846-3449.** Reservations strongly advised. Main courses $20–$33. AE, DC, MC, V. Daily 6–10pm (until 10:30pm Fri–Sat).

Twenty-Two Bowen's ★★ STEAKHOUSE On a wharf? Surrounded by water and fishing boats and unlimited tureens of clam chowder? Counter-intuitive though it might seem, that's where the owners of the Castle Hill inn decided to open their unabashed beef emporium. They guessed right: It's been full since the first day, and unlike many of its competitors, busy enough to stay open straight through the winter. The three rooms and bar have the burnished dark wood and polished brass of an old-time yacht club. Patrons are of an age and apparent prosperity to be comfortable with the steep prices, and possessed of sufficient knowledge to make assured choices from the extensive wine list. Light, briny oysters from the raw bar are the preferable preface to a pound or two of perfectly charred prime sirloin or porterhouse. Thick veal and lamb chops are possible alternatives, as are lobsters. All meats are served alone on the plate—sides are extra. In spring and summer, there's an outdoor patio. Service is as professional as any in Newport.

22 Bowen's Wharf. ✆ **401/841-8884.** Reservations advised for dinner and weekends. Main courses $24–$44. AE, DC, MC, V. Daily 11:30am–3:30pm and 5–10pm (Fri–Sat until 11pm).

White Horse Tavern ★ NEW AMERICAN Still going strong after almost 330 years, the White Horse makes a credible claim to be the oldest operating tavern in America. On the ground floor are a bar and two dining rooms, with a big fireplace once used for cooking, and they recently added another room with bar food upstairs. Given the picturesque Ye Olde setting, the kitchen could have coasted on New England boiled dinners and Indian pudding. But the food is quite good, from the daily lunch specials to the spice-rubbed venison with pears poached with rosemary and the cognac and cider-glazed duck breast. About a third of the dishes involve seafood, but rack of lamb is even more expensive than butter-poached lobster. Prices are significantly lower on the Pub menu ($10–$24 for entrees) available from 5pm Sunday through Thursday.

25 Marlborough St. (at Farewell). ✆ **401/849-3600.** Reservations recommended, essential for dinner. Jackets required for men at dinner. Main courses $28–$40. AE, DC, DISC, MC, V. Mon–Fri 6–9pm; Sat–Sun noon–2:30pm and 6–9pm.

MODERATE

Brick Alley Pub ★ *Kids* ECLECTIC The Brick is loud and good-natured, Newport's favorite hangout. Families, tourists, working stiffs, and yachtsmen squeeze through the doors into the thronged dining rooms, the bar, and the terrace. Just so you know what you're getting into, the cab of a 1938 Chevy pickup truck is next to the soup-and-salad bar. Decor, such as it is, also incorporates kid-size trucks, license plates, vintage photos, and a model train. The voluminous menu is pub grub squared: stuffed clams, Cajun catfish, nachos, burgers, pizzas, steaks, stuffies, meatloaf, and squid-ink spaghetti with cream, scallops, and crabmeat. Entrees include salad or the soup/salad/bread buffet *plus* potatoes and vegetables. Newport Storm Amber Ale is on draft.

140 Thames St. ✆ **401/849-6334.** Reservations recommended for dinner. Main courses $19–$28. AE, DISC, MC, V. Mon–Fri 11:30am–10pm (Fri until 11pm); Sat 11am–11pm; Sun 11am–10pm. Closed the week after Super Bowl.

Salvation Café ★ ECLECTIC As funky-hip as Newport gets, this is a gathering place so popular with locals that the tourists who discover it are barely visible. A monster Gulf sign and amateurish oil paintings occupy the walls. The steel-topped bar is given primarily to diners, at least in the early evening hours. The stereo gets your attention, playing 1940s big bands or Tom Jones or Gene Autry, and the menu, too, hops and skips around the map. It plucks pad Thai here, *malai kofta* there, and the no-doubt tasty spinach and tofu concoction from a place not known. But unfocused though it might be, a lot of satisfying food can be had here. Linguine with chipotle shrimp gets a nod, as do pork vindaloo over lemon coconut rice and the meltingly tender flesh from long-braised short ribs topped with mole sauce. Truth to tell, though, most people probably wind up with the 10-ounce Salvation burger with bacon and cheddar.

140 Broadway. ✆ **401/847-2620.** Main courses $9.50–$21. AE, DC, MC, V. Mon–Thurs 5–10pm; Fri–Sat 5–11pm; Sun 10am–2:30pm and 5–10pm.

Scales & Shells ★★ SEAFOOD That graceless name reflects the uncompromising character of this clangorous fish house. Diners who insist on a modicum of elegance should head for the upstairs room, called Upscales. Myriad fish and shellfish, listed on the blackboard, are offered in guileless preparations that allow the natural flavors to prevail. Substantial portions, too: The "large" appetizer of fried calamari is enough for four. Swordfish grilled over hardwood and topped with roasted sweet peppers is typical. Or, have linguini with your choice of clams, calamari, or shrimp. Expect no meat or fowl, but there are some vegetarian pastas. Note that credit cards aren't accepted.

527 Lower Thames St. ✆ **401/846-3474** for main floor, 401/847-2000 for Upscales. Reservations recommended May–Sept. Main courses downstairs $11–$21, Upscales $16–$29. No credit cards. Sun–Thurs 5–10pm; Fri–Sat 5–11pm; Sun 4–10pm (slightly shorter hours in winter). Closed Mon Jan–May and from last week in Dec to 1st 2 weeks in Jan.

INEXPENSIVE

Flo's Clam Shack SEAFOOD Just past Easton's Beach over the Newport/Middletown line, this old-timer is more than a lopsided strand-side shanty—but not *much* more. Step up to the order window, choose from the handwritten menu, and receive a stone with a number painted on it. What you'll get, if you're wise, are clams, on a plate or on a roll. Cooked swiftly to order, they're as tender as any to which you might have set your teeth. This is the place, also, to sample "chowda" and that Rhode Island specialty, stuffies. Clam cakes are inexplicably tasty, given the lack of clams therein. "Find a clam, get a prize," jokes the owner. The menu also suggests two hot dogs with a bottle of Moët for $50. Few patrons take that opportunity. Upstairs are a raw bar and deck even more happily ramshackle than below. Sundays feature live music from 2 to 6pm.

4 Wave Ave., Middletown, RI ✆ **401/847-8141.** Main courses $7.75–$17. No credit cards. Apr–Dec 11am–9pm. Closed Jan–Mar.

Jack & Josie NEW AMERICAN Fun is on the menu at this quirky corner spot, a sort of poolroom-luncheonette-sports-bar-Internet-cafe. Within the airy, well-lit space are five computer terminals ($10 per hour), a pool table, plasma TVs, and an eating area with brushed aluminum tables. Food? Mostly soups, salads, and sandwiches, along with contemporary twists, as in the warm pear and goat cheese salad and "The Jack," thin slices of sirloin with caramelized onions, fig compote, and arugula saga blue cheese. But the dishy owner—who is neither Jack nor Josie, which are actually the names of her dogs—has added several entrees, including a quiche of the day, roasted pork tenderloin, meatloaf, and a roasted salmon filet wrapped in prosciutto. Bring your own wine or beer: She doesn't have a liquor license and doesn't intend to get one. Herbal teas, smoothies, and specialty coffee drinks are options.

111 Broadway. ✆ **401/851-6900.** All items under $10. AE, MC, V. Sun–Mon 10am–5pm; Wed–Sat 10am–10pm. Closed 1 week in Mar.

NEWPORT AFTER DARK

The most likely places to spend an evening lie along **Thames Street.** One of the most obvious possibilities, **The Red Parrot,** 348 Thames St., near Memorial Boulevard (✆ **401/847-3140**), has the look of an Irish saloon and features jazz combos Thursday through Sunday. **One Pelham East** ★, at Thames and Pelham streets (✆ **401/847-9460**), has a cafe, a small dance floor, a pool table, and another bar upstairs, with mostly college-age patrons attending to rockers on the stage at front. Free pizza is served some evenings. **Aidan's,** 1 Broadway (✆ **401/845-9311**), is one of several local Irish taverns, enhanced by above-average pub grub to go with the Porter. Live music is heard most of the year, usually on Wednesday, Saturday, and Sunday.

A full schedule of live music is on the plate at the **Newport Blues Café** ★, 286 Thames St., at Green Street (✆ **401/841-5510**), plus a Sunday gospel brunch. With its fireplace, dark wood, and massive steel back door that used to guard the safe of this former bank, the cafe has a lot more class than most of the town's bars. Meals are available nightly in summer, Thursday through Sunday nights off season. It might close for 2 or 3 months in winter. **Area,** 3 River Lane (✆ **401/849-2315**), has music most nights, except in winter.

The Garden, 206 Thames St. (✆ **401/849-9300**), has pool, foosball, and live rock 3 to 4 nights a week, when there is a modest cover charge. **Mudville,** 8 W. Marlborough St. (✆ **401/849-1408**), is a bar for guys and the women who put up with them. A dozen TVs, including a couple of big-screen plasmas, are fed by both satellite and cable, insuring that no sporting event, anywhere, will be unavailable. A fireplace and fake Tiffany lamps constitute the decor.

Several restaurants offer music, as with the three-piece combo at Asterix, and disco at the Clarke Cooke House's Boom Boom Room. Also check out **Christie's,** 351 Thames St. (✆ **401/847-5400**); **The Landing,** 30 Bowen's Wharf (✆ **401/847-4514**); and **The West Dock,** 1 Waites Wharf (✆ **401/847-33610**).

4 South County: From Narragansett to Watch Hill

Narragansett: 32 miles SW of Providence; 14 miles W of Newport

Travelers rushing along the Boston–New York corridor inevitably choose I-95 to get from Providence to the Connecticut border. They either do not have the time for a detour or don't know that the nearby shore has some of the best beaches and most congenial fishing and resort villages of New England. This is called South County, a designation that has no official status, but refers to the coast that is the southerly edge of Bristol County. Bypassed by the inland I-95, it has escaped much of the commercial development that besets many parts of the New England coast.

Rhode Islanders certainly know about the beguilements of South County, though, so try to avoid weekends in July and August, when the crush of day-trippers can turn these two-lane roads into parking lots.

Definitions are fuzzy, but for our purposes, South County runs from Narragansett, a little over 30 miles south of Providence, west to Westerly, nudging Connecticut. See the map on p. 417 to locate towns discussed in this section.

ESSENTIALS

GETTING THERE To get to South County from Providence or Boston, take I-95 south, leaving it at Exit 9 to pick up Route 4, also a limited-access highway. This merges with Rte. 4, arriving in Narragansett in about 20 miles. From Newport, cross the Newport and Jamestown bridges on Route 138 to Route 1A south, and follow it to Narragansett, the center of South County's beach country. It is 14 miles west of Newport.

VISITOR INFORMATION The attendants at the **tourist information office** (© **401/783-7121**), in the landmark Towers on Route 1A in Narragansett, can help visitors find lodging. Contact the **South County Tourism Council,** 4808 Tower Hill Rd., Wakefield (© **800/548-4662** or 401/789-4422; www.southcountyri.com), to request the useful brochure *South County Style.*

NARRAGANSETT & THE BEACHES ★★

Continuing south on 1A from the Casey Farm, the pace quickens, at least from late spring to foliage season. After crossing the Narrow River Inlet, the road bends around toward **Narragansett Pier.** Along here and several miles on south to Port Judith and Jerusalem are some of the most desirable beaches in New England, with swaths of fine sand, relatively clean waters, and summer water temperatures that average about 70°F (21°C). When there are storms down south, the water kicks up enough to justify getting out the surfboard, and this is thought to be the best place in the state to catch the waves.

After a few blocks, Route 1A makes a sharp right turn (west), but stick to the shore, proceeding south on Ocean Road. Straight ahead is the **Towers,** a massive stone structure that spans the road between cylindrical towers with conical roofs. It is all that remains of the Gilded Age Narragansett Casino, designed by McKim, Mead & White, but lost in a 1900 fire. In the seaward tower is the Narragansett **tourist information office** (see "Essentials," above).

WHERE TO STAY

Village Inn ★ Several inns and hotels are in the vicinity, many of them looking out over the water across wide lawns. This is one of the largest and most obvious, a couple of blocks from the Towers. Despite the humble name, it is large and almost new, part of a complex that incorporates a cinema, a gas station, and a dozen shops. It has an oceanview deck, ready access to the beach, and modest resort facilities.

1 Beach St., Narragansett, RI 02882. © **800/843-7437** or 401/783-6767. www.v-inn.com. Fax 401/782-2220. 61 units. $131–$239 double. Packages available. V, MC, AE. Closed Nov–Mar. **Amenities:** Restaurant (Continental); bar; heated indoor pool w/Jacuzzi. *In room:* A/C, TV, dataport, fridge, coffeemaker, hair dryer, iron, microwave.

WHERE TO DINE

Amalfi MEDITERRANEAN BISTRO At least three restaurants preceded this one, in this same space, but Amalfi seems to have the stuff for survival. Its bank of windows look out over Route 1A to the beach and ocean. On yet another menu that encourages a meal of appetizers, the carpaccio of beef is sliced as thin as butterfly wings and the calamari frito are tossed with a savory mix of sun-dried tomatoes, Kalamata olives, and spicy peppers. Main dishes swing from paella to lobster ravioli to a hearty Thessaloniki salad with shrimp and feta. A less expensive bistro menu in the bar area has pastas and sandwiches. The staff is pleasant, if not terribly professional.

1 Beach St. ✆ **401/792-3999.** Main courses $16–$30. AE, DC, MC, V. Daily 5–9pm (until 10pm Fri–Sat).

Coast Guard House SEAFOOD/AMERICAN Adjacent to the Towers is this 1888 former Coast Guard headquarters, now a locally popular restaurant that enjoys unobstructed views of the beach and breakers crashing a few feet below its windows. Despite the venue, the menu features as many meat dishes as seafood, all executed with a measure of sophistication. Seafood stew packs in lobster, fish, mussels, Italian sausage, kale, fennel, and potatoes in a tomato-saffron broth. Lobster comes steamed, broiled, or baked. Another bar is on the deck upstairs.

40 Ocean Rd. ✆ **401/789-0700.** Main courses $20–$36. AE, DC, DISC, MC, V. Mon–Thurs 11:30am–3pm and 5–9pm; Fri–Sat 11:30am–3pm and 5–10pm; Sun 10am–2pm and 4–10pm (shorter hours in winter; call ahead). Closed Jan.

Spain ★ SPANISH South of Scarborough Beach, this restaurant is deservedly the most popular on this stretch of shore. Partly it's the congenial staff, partly the terraces overlooking the sea. But the greatest share of credit goes to the stellar interpretations of the Spanish tapas tradition and such favorites as *paella Valenciana.* Authenticity doesn't head the list of the kitchen's concerns: The irresistible fried calamari are tossed with very un-Spanish hot peppers. Do sample the *espinacas a la Catalana*—spinach sautéed with garlic, raisins, and pine nuts. Arrive early to avoid the nightly rush.

1144 Ocean Rd. ✆ **401/783-9770.** Reservations accepted only for parties of 6 or more. Main courses $13–$30. AE, DC, DISC, MC, V. Tues–Sat 4–10pm (Fri–Sat until 11pm); Sun 1–9pm.

FROM NARRAGANSETT TO POINT JUDITH

Follow scenic Ocean Road south from the Towers, soon arriving at **Scarborough State Beach** ★★. Noticeably well kept, with a row of pavilions for picnicking and changing, it has ample parking and surroundings unsullied by brash commercial enterprises. The beach is largely hard-packed sand. While the mild surf makes this a good option for families with young children, sections are often also jammed with teenagers and college students.

Continuing on Ocean Road to the end, you'll reach the **Point Judith Lighthouse,** 1460 Ocean Rd. (✆ **401/789-0444**). Built in 1816, the brick beacon is a photo op that can be approached but not entered.

GALILEE

Backtrack along Ocean Road, turning left on Route 108, then left again on Sand Hill Cove Road, past the dock of the only year-round ferries to Block Island, and into the Port of Galilee. At the end, past a cluster of restaurants beside the channel connecting Point Judith Pond with the ocean, is the redundantly named **Salty Brine State Beach.** Protected by a breakwater, it is a good choice for families with younger children, but popular with teenagers as well. Parking costs $6 weekdays and $7 on weekends. On the opposite side of the channel is popular **East Matunuck State Beach,** where waves break upon the sand at an angle, producing enough action to permit decent surfing on some summer days. Parking is $6 on weekdays, $7 on weekends.

To get a better sense of the area from the water, consider the 1¾-hour tour on the ***Southland*** (✆ **401/783-2954;** www.southlandcruises.com), which departs from State Pier in Galilee. Cruises are on Saturday and Sunday only from Memorial Day to mid-June and after Labor Day until mid-October; there are daily departures from mid-June to Labor Day. Prices are $14 to $16 for adults, $8 to $10 for children 4 to 12, free for ages 3 and under.

Numerous **party and charter boats** leave for fishing expeditions from Point Judith. Another possible excursion is a **whale-watching cruise** with the **Frances Fleet,** 2 State St., Point Judith (✆ **800/662-2824** or 401/783-4988; www.francesfleet.com). Cruises launch in July and August, Monday through Saturday from 1 to about 5:30pm. It isn't cheap, at $35 for adults and $25 for children under 12, but the sight of a monster humpback leaping from the water is unforgettable. Tuesdays and Thursdays are "family days," when two parents and two kids under 12 cost $95.

WHERE TO DINE

Very similar in atmosphere, food, and situation, **Champlin's Seafood,** 256 Great Island (✆ **401/783-3152**), is an entirely acceptable alternative to George's of Galilee (below) and only a short walk away. Main courses are $10 to $19, and all food is made to order.

George's of Galilee SEAFOOD/AMERICAN The impulse to drive as far as you can without winding up in the drink may account for part of the popularity of George's, in business for over 50 years. It can't be the food, which is good enough but unexceptional, despite the accolades of enthusiastic readers of regional magazines. Anyway, the decks serve as a good vantage point to watch the boat traffic in the channel. As for food, give the fried smelts, stuffies, fish and chips, and clam and cod cakes a thought, perhaps carrying them from the takeout window over to the picnic tables by the beach. After Labor Day, the twin lobsters go for $25.

250 Sand Hill Cove Rd. ✆ **401/783-2306.** Main courses $11–$19 (market prices for lobster). AE, DISC, MC, V. May–Oct daily noon–10pm; Nov–Apr Thurs–Sun noon–2:30pm and 6–9:30pm.

WATCH HILL ★

Although much of Westerly township remains peacefully semi-rural, it contains more than a dozen villages, notably the peninsular resort of Watch Hill, and several contiguous public beaches on slender barrier islands enclosing large saltwater ponds.

A pretty land's-end village that achieved its resort status during the post–Civil War period, Watch Hill has retained it ever since. It helped that it is the closest of South County's beach towns to New York. Many grand summer mansions and Queen Anne gingerbread houses remain from that time. The north side of the point occupied by the village is the harbor, packed with pleasure boats. Stretching from the eastern edge of Westerly township to the southwesternmost tip of the state at Watch Hill are **Dunes Park Beach** ★ and **Atlantic Beach,** followed by **Misquamicut State Beach** ★, a gathering place for large numbers of adolescents, and **Napatree Point Barrier Beach** ★, a wildlife preserve notable for its white crescent beach. While you can enter the Napatree preserve for free, there are no facilities, a reason for its generally sparser crowds. All the beaches are noted for their fine-grained sand and gentle surf with gradual drop-offs.

South of town on Watch Hill Road is the picturesque 1856 **Watch Hill Lighthouse,** open from 1 to 3pm Tuesday and Thursday. Back in town at the small **Watch Hill Beach,** younger children get a kick out of the nearby **Flying Horse Carousel,** which dates to 1867. Only kids are allowed to ride; tickets are 50¢. The carousel is open daily from mid-June to early September. Parents will have to settle for the more than 50 boutiques that fill the commercial blocks.

To get to Watch Hill from Providence and points north, take Exit 1 off I-95, south on Route 3, which passes through Westerly and continues to Watch Hill. From

Connecticut, take Exit 92 from I-95, going south briefly on Route 2, picking up Route 78 (the Westerly Bypass) down along Airport Road into Watch Hill. Free parking is extremely limited, so if you arrive after 8am, expect to pay up to $15 in the commercial lot behind the main street.

Amtrak trains from Boston and New York stop in Westerly several times daily. There is a pull-over **information office** on I-95 near the Connecticut border, and a **Chamber of Commerce** office at 74 Post Rd. in Westerly (✆ **800/732-7636**).

WHERE TO STAY

Pleasant View Inn ★ Two miles east of Watch Hill, this is a small resort with a private strand that adjoins 4 miles of Misquamicut Beach. The front desk can arrange guaranteed tee times at a nearby course. Five categories of rooms are assigned, most of the better ones facing the ocean, with balconies; some have fridges and microwaves. The cheapest rooms overlook a parking lot.

65 Atlantic Inn, Westerly, RI 02891. ✆ **800/782-3224** or 401/348-8200. www.pvinn.com. 112 units. May–June and Sept–Oct $85–$175 double; July–Aug $172–$272 double. Packages available. AE, MC, V. Closed Nov–Apr. No pets. **Amenities:** 2 restaurants (American); bar; heated outdoor pool and Jacuzzi; fitness room w/Jacuzzi and sauna; game room. *In room:* A/C, TV.

Shelter Harbor Inn ★ If it's time to stop for the night, for dinner, or for a spectacular Sunday brunch (reservations essential), watch for the entrance to this venerable inn off U.S. 1, about 6 miles east of Westerly. Parts of the main building date to 1810, and a genteel tone prevails. Several bedrooms have fireplaces, decks, or both. A shuttle takes guests to the private beach a mile away. A cautiously creative restaurant and honored wine cellar round out the picture, sullied only by uneven service; dinner entrees top out at a reasonable $25. Children are welcome. The inn and restaurant are open 365 days a year.

10 Wagner Rd., Westerly, RI 02891. ✆ **800/468-8883** or 401/322-8883. Fax 401/322-7907. www.shelterharborinn.com. 24 units. May–Oct $198–$228 double; Nov–Apr $96–$156 double. Rates include breakfast. AE, DC, DISC, MC, V. **Amenities:** Restaurant (regional); bar; rooftop hot tub. *In room:* A/C, TV, dataport.

The Villa ★ A Dutch Colonial manor with many Italianate overlays on Route 1A outside of town, The Villa is most often recommended for its extensive gardens and warm hospitality. All units are suites—they have fridges and microwaves, and DVD players. Three have Jacuzzi tubs built for two, and a couple have gas fireplaces. The breakfasts are continental during the week, but enhanced with hot dishes on weekends. Unlike most lodgings in the area, it is open all year. The inn is nonsmoking.

190 Shore Rd., Westerly, RI 02891. ✆ **800/722-9240** or 401/596-1054. Fax 401/596-6268. www.thevillaatwesterly.com. 6 units. Memorial Day to Columbus Day $150–$295 double; rest of year $105–$220 double. Rates include breakfast. Packages available. AE, DISC, MC, V. **Amenities:** Outdoor pool w/Jacuzzi. *In room:* A/C, TV/VCR/CD, fridge, coffeemaker, hair dryer.

Watch Hill Inn Savor sunsets from the veranda of this century-old clapboard lodge. Bedrooms are mostly of good size, with nothing special by way of decor, apart from the four-posters and occasional antiques. There's access to a beach. Meals are largely in the seafood-and-pasta tradition, but with superb views, taken in from the Grille Room and four decks.

38 Bay St., Watch Hill, RI 02891. ✆ **800/356-9314** or 401/348-6300. Fax 401/348-6301. www.watchhillinn.com. 16 units. Mid-June to early Sept $175–$275 double; Sept to mid-June $100–$185 double. Rates include breakfast. Packages available. MC, V. **Amenities:** Restaurant. *In room:* A/C, TV, dataport.

WHERE TO DINE

Olympia Tea Room ★ NEW AMERICAN The genteel tone of Watch Hill is undergirded by the Olympia, long a favorite meet-and-eat retreat. This version of an even older restaurant opened in 1939, and long retained its soda fountains and wooden booths. The fountain is now a full bar, but the kitchen continues to crank out pretty imaginative food. If available, jump for the appetizer of plump, lightly fried oysters on wilted spinach and corn salsa. The stuffies and lobster rolls are as good as you're likely to enjoy in coastal New England, and the "easy lobster casserole" contains more meat than a whole lobster

74 Bay St. ✆ **401/348-8211.** Reservations not accepted. Main courses $12–$31. AE, MC, V. June to Columbus Day daily 11am–10pm; mid-Oct to Nov and Apr–May Thurs–Sun 11am–9pm. (Hours vary frequently; call ahead.) Closed Dec–Easter.

The Up River Café ★ NEW AMERICAN An up-and-down history as a restaurant under other names and chefs has preceded in this converted old woolen mill cantilevered over the river that runs through town. The current occupant chooses to avoid experimentation, with a resulting menu that strides along a workmanlike path. The main dining room is a two-tiered affair allowing water views; the smaller adjacent room has a fireplace. It all has a North Woods look, with bare wide-board floors, carried through in the homey tavern beside the entry hall. The rich lobster bisque is a fine starter, while the fried calamari tossed with banana peppers, peanuts, and crisp rice noodles in a Thai chile sauce is a virtual meal in itself. Entrees are half sea-, half land-based on a card that changes seasonally. Sea scallops harvested by the local Stonington fleet are reliable, as is the New Zealand lamb that is usually on offer.

37 Main St. ✆ **401/348-9700.** Reservations suggested on weekends. Main courses $16–$30. AE, MC, V. Mon–Sat 11:30am–10pm (until 11pm Fri–Sat); Sun 5–9pm (closing an hour earlier after Labor Day).

5 Block Island ★★

Viewed from above or on a map, Block Island looks like a pork chop with a big bite taken out of the middle. Only 7 miles long and 3 miles wide, it is edged with long stretches of beach lifting at points into dramatic bluffs. The interior is dimpled with undulating hills, only rarely reaching above 150 feet in elevation. Its hollows and clefts cradle over 300 sweet-water ponds, some no larger than a backyard swimming pool. That "bite" out of the western edge of the "chop" is **Great Salt Pond,** which almost succeeds in cutting the island in two, but, as it is, serves as a fine protected harbor for fleets of pleasure boats.

The only significant concentration of houses, businesses, hotels, and people is at **Old Harbor,** on the lower eastern shore, where the ferries from the mainland arrive and most of the remaining fishing boats moor.

Named for Adrian Block, a Dutch explorer who briefly stepped ashore in 1641, the island's earliest European settlement was in 1661, and it has since attracted the kinds of people who nurture fierce convictions of independence, fueled in part by the streaks of paranoia that lead them to live on a speck of land with no physical connection to the mainland. In the past, that has meant farmers, pirates, fishermen, smugglers, scavengers, and entrepreneurs, all of them willing to deal with the realities of isolation, lonely winters, and occasional killer hurricanes. Today, there are about 875 permanent residents of similar pluck and enterprise who tough it out 9 months a year waiting for the sun to stay awhile.

The challenges of island living aren't readily apparent to the tens of thousands of visitors who arrive every summer. They aren't likely to worry that the water supply is fragile or that generator-provided electricity is hugely expensive. Vacationers are wont to describe this as paradise—and they are correct, at least if sun and sea and zephyrs are paramount considerations. Those elements transformed the island from an offshore afterthought into an accessible summer retreat for the urban middle class after the Civil War, in America's first taste of mass tourism.

Unlike other such regions throughout the country that have lost their sprawling Victorian hotels to fire or demolition, Block Island has preserved many of its buildings from that time. They crowd around Old Harbor, providing most of the lodging base. Smaller inns and B&Bs add more tourist rooms, most in converted houses built at the same time as the great hotels. There are only a few establishments that even resemble motels, and building stock is marked, with few exceptions, by tasteful Yankee understatement. Despite the ominous presence of a few houses that resemble those plunked down in potato fields in ultra-chic precincts of New York's Long Island, development so far remains under control, and there exist no franchised eateries or shops of any kind—this is not the place to have a Big Mac attack.

Away from the sand and surf, it is an island of peaceful pleasures and gentle observations. Police officers wear Bermuda shorts and ride bikes. Children tend lemonade stands in front of picket fences and low hedges. Clumps of hydrangeas tangle with beach roses and honeysuckle, hiding the foundations of saltboxes and Victorian farmhouses with shingles scoured gray by sea winds. No squirrels, chipmunks, possums, or raccoons live on the Block, but the island is in the middle of a prominent flyway for migratory birds, and egrets, ducks, goldfinches, and kingfishers are seen in abundance. Deer were introduced about 30 years ago, to the islanders' current regret, bringing Lyme disease and an enthusiasm for turning flowerbeds into salad bars.

ESSENTIALS

GETTING THERE The **Interstate Navigation Company,** New London, CT (✆ **860/442-7891** or 401/783-4613; www.blockislandferry.com), provides most of the surface service, including passenger-only ferries on daily runs between Newport and Block Island from July 1 to September 5. They leave Fort Adams in Newport at 9:15am and return from Old Harbor on Block Island at 4:45pm. Sailing time is 2 hours. Bicycles may be taken on board for a $2.50 fee. While reservations aren't required for passengers, get to the dock early, as the boats tend to fill up quickly. Round-trip fares at press time were $13 for adults and $5.80 for children under 12.

Getting a car to Block Island is something of a hassle and considerably more expensive—at press time, $78 per standard-size passenger vehicle round-trip (SUVs and pickups cost more) in addition to fares of $20 per adult and $10 for each child under 12, or a total of $138 for a family of four. It's safe to assume that these fares will continue to increase from year to year. Car ferries depart from the Port of Galilee at Point Judith, RI. Departures are daily year-round, as few as one or two a day in winter to as many as nine a day from early June to late August. Sailing time is about an hour. Drivers, be prepared: You are expected to *back* your car into the close quarters of the ferry's main deck.

High-speed passenger-only service is in operation from both Point Judith and New London, CT. **Island Hi-Speed Ferry,** Port of Galilee, RI (✆ **877/733-9425;** www.islandhighspeedferry.com), makes several daily round-trips from May 12 to October 10. Sailing time is about 30 minutes; round-trip passenger fare is $29 adults, $16 children.

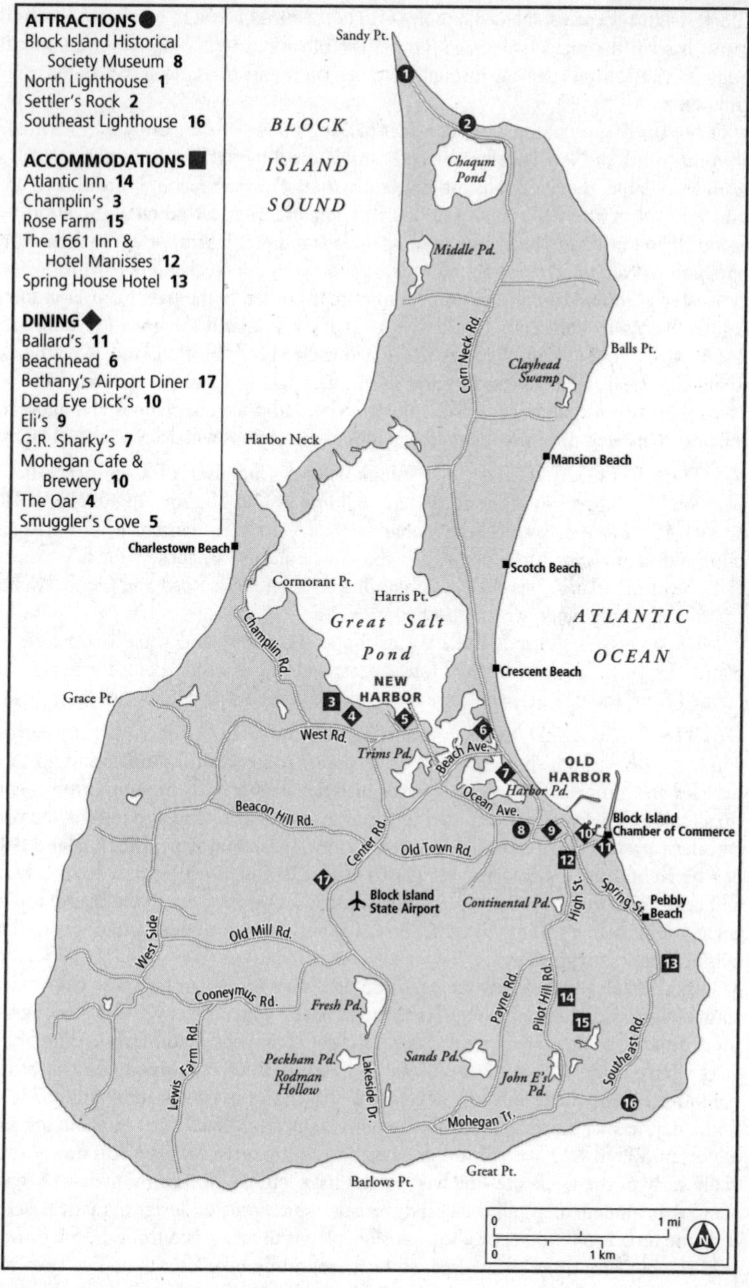
ATTRACTIONS
Block Island Historical Society Museum 8
North Lighthouse 1
Settler's Rock 2
Southeast Lighthouse 16
ACCOMMODATIONS
Atlantic Inn 14
Champlin's 3
Rose Farm 15
The 1661 Inn & Hotel Manisses 12
Spring House Hotel 13
DINING
Ballard's 11
Beachhead 6
Bethany's Airport Diner 17
Dead Eye Dick's 10
Eli's 9
G.R. Sharky's 7
Mohegan Cafe & Brewery 10
The Oar 4
Smuggler's Cove 5
Sandy Pt.
BLOCK ISLAND SOUND
Chaqum Pond
Middle Pd.
Corn Neck Rd.
Balls Pt.
Clayhead Swamp
Harbor Neck
Mansion Beach
Charlestown Beach
Scotch Beach
Cormorant Pt.
Harris Pt.
Great Salt Pond
ATLANTIC OCEAN
Champlin Rd.
Crescent Beach
NEW HARBOR
Grace Pt.
West Rd.
Trims Pd.
Beach Ave.
OLD HARBOR
Harbor Pd.
Ocean Ave.
Beacon Hill Rd.
Block Island Chamber of Commerce
Center Rd.
Old Town Rd.
Block Island State Airport
Continental Pd.
High St.
Spring St.
Pebbly Beach
Old Mill Rd.
West Side
Payne Rd.
Pilot Hill Rd.
Cooneymus Rd.
Fresh Pd.
Southeast Rd.
Peckham Pd.
Rodman Hollow
Lakeside Dr.
Sands Pd.
John E's Pd.
Lewis Farm Rd.
Mohegan Tr.
Great Pt.
Barlows Pt.
0
1 mi
0
1 km
N

Block Island Express, New London, CT (© **860/444-4624;** www.goblockisland.com), has cut the previous average time to the Block nearly in half, to a little over an hour. Service is from late May through October 10; round-trip fares are $34 adults, $15 children.

Given the cost of taking a car, consider parking in one of the nearby long-term lots at Point Judith or New London. Block Island is small, rental bicycles and mopeds are readily available, there are cabs for longer distances ($6 flat fee), and most hotels and inns are within a few blocks of the docks. There are even car-rental agencies on the island. If you intend to take a car anyway, understand that it's important to make ferry reservations well in advance—2 months isn't too early for weekend departures.

Westerly State Airport, near the Connecticut border, is the base for over a dozen regular flights to and from Block Island via **New England Airlines** (© **800/243-2460,** 401/596-2460 in Westerly, or 401/466-5881 on Block Island; www.block-island.com/nea). Flights depart hourly in summer, taking 12 to 15 minutes. Fares are $84 round-trip for adults, $69 for children. Make advance reservations and allow for the possibility that not-infrequent coastal fogs or high winds will delay or cancel flights.

VISITOR INFORMATION The **Block Island Chamber of Commerce** has a year-round information office at the ferry landing at Old Harbor (© **800/383-BIRI** or 401/466-2474; www.blockislandchamber.com). Its attendants can answer questions and help visitors find lodging. In the same building are lockers for day-trippers and one of the island's few ATMs. A building at Corn Neck Road and Ocean Avenue contains the only bank, which also has an ATM.

Most streets on Block Island have no house numbers, and some roads have no names. Leave your dog at home: Hotels, inns, and B&Bs won't accept them, they are banned from the beaches, and they are supposed to be leashed at all times.

GETTING AROUND Cars are allowed on the island, but roads are narrow, winding, and without shoulders, and drivers must contend with runners and flocks of bicycles and mopeds. Unless your party includes people with mobility problems or small children, we recommend leaving your car on the mainland and joining the two-wheelers. If you'd like to rent a car after you arrive by boat or plane, **Block Island Bike & Car Rental,** on Ocean Avenue (© **401/466-2297**), has offices near Payne's Dock and at the airport; reserve ahead. If you decide to bring your car to the island, top off the gas tank before rolling onto the ferry. There is only one rudimentary gas station, behind Sharky's restaurant.

Rental bikes and mopeds are available at several shops and stands. Convenient sources near Old Harbor include **The Moped Man,** Water Street (© **401/466-5444**), on the main business street, renting bikes as well as mopeds; **Old Harbor Bike Shop,** at the ferry dock (© **401/466-2029**); and **Island Bike & Moped,** Chapel Street, behind the Harborside Inn (© **401/466-2700**). Rates for bikes are typically $18 to $30 a day, less with widely available discount coupons. Moped rates vary, but are usually from $75 to $90 for half to full days. Bargaining often brings prices down, especially early in the week after the weekenders have left, or for 3 or more days. Keep in mind that mopeds aren't allowed on dirt roads, which provide access to many beaches.

Some inns also rent bicycles, so a possible plan is to take a taxi from the ferry or airport to your inn, drop off luggage, and get around by bike after that. Two such inns are the **Seacrest,** 207 High St. (© **401/466-2882**), and **Rose Farm,** on Roslyn Road (© **401/466-2034**), but inquire about rentals when making room reservations at other places as well.

Tips A Note on Accommodations

If you arrive on Block Island without reservations, one approach to getting a bed for the night is to show up at an inn an hour or so after the last ferry has departed, when management will often lower quoted rates if rooms are still available.

EXPLORING THE ISLAND

With no golf course and a lone museum that takes only about 15 minutes to see, little on the island distracts from the central missions of sunning, cycling, hiking, lolling, and ingesting copious quantities of lobster, clams, chowder, and alcohol. Add a couple of lighthouses, a wildlife refuge, and three topographical features of note, and that's about it, enough to provide destinations for a few leisurely bike trips. A driving tour of every site on that list takes no more than 2 hours.

A couple of miles south of Old Harbor on what starts out as Spring Street is the **Southeast Lighthouse** (**✆ 401/466-5009**). A tablet by the road claims that in 1590, the Manisseans, the Indians of Block Island, drove a war-party of 40 Mohegans over the bluffs. An undeniably appealing Victorian structure, built in 1874, the lighthouse's claim for attention lies primarily in the fact that it had to be moved 245 feet back from the eroding precipice a few years ago to save it. That was expensive, and now another $1 million is desperately needed to renovate this National Historic Landmark. While a small exhibit on the ground floor can be seen for free, the admission fee to the top is $5.

Continuing along the same road, which goes through other names and soon makes a sharp right turn inland, watch for the left turn onto West Side Road. In a few hundred yards, pull over near the sign for **Rodman's Hollow,** a geological dent dug by a passing glacier. It's deeper than it looks, the bottom a few feet below sea level and laced with walking trails beneath a thick mantle of low trees. Much of what you see here is designated forever wild, for the Nature Conservancy has purchased about a third of the island's surface to protect it from development. A map of the 12-mile trail network can be purchased at the Chamber of Commerce building at the ferry landing.

From Old Harbor, proceed north on Corn Neck Road, skirting Crescent Beach, on the right. The paved road eventually ends at **Settler's Rock** ★★★, with a plaque naming the English pioneers who landed here in 1661. This is one of the loveliest spots on the island, with mirrored **Chaqum Pond** behind the Rock and a scimitar beach curving out to **North Lighthouse,** erected in 1867. In between is a **national wildlife refuge** that is of particular interest to birders. The lighthouse, best reached by foot along the rocky beach, is now an interpretive center of local ecology and history, open from July 5 to Labor Day daily from 10am to 4pm.

Back in Old Harbor, the **Block Island Historical Society Museum,** Old Town Road and Ocean Avenue (**✆ 401/466-2481**), was an 1871 inn that now contains a miscellany of photos, ship models, and tools. Upstairs is a room set up to reflect the Victorian period.

The beaches on Block Island will suit every taste. Immediately south of the Old Harbor, past the breakwater, is the northern end of **Pebbly Beach,** a section informally known as **Ballard's Beach** for the popular restaurant located there (see "Where To Dine," below). Crowded with sunbathers and swimmers, it is one of only two on the island with lifeguards. The surf is often rough. Drinks are served at your towel.

North of Old Harbor, beyond the Surf Hotel, starts the 3-mile-long **Crescent Beach** (aka Frederick J. Benson Town Beach or simply Town Beach). The southern section, with a sandy bottom that stays shallow well out into the gentle surf, is known as **Kid Beach** because of its relative safety for children. Farther along is the main part, a broad strand served by a pavilion with a snack bar, bathrooms, and showers. Chairs, umbrellas, and boogie boards can be rented. The surf is higher along here and rolls straight in; lifeguards are on duty. Continuing north, and with a small parking lot reached by a dirt road off Corn Neck Road, is **Scotch Beach.** Consider this grown-up and R-rated, dominated by young summer workers and residents. Still farther north is **Mansion Beach,** with a dirt road of the same name leading in from Corn Neck Road. Somewhat more secluded, it is usually less crowded than the others. On the west side of the island, running south from the jetty that marks the entrance to New Harbor, is **Charlestown Beach.** Uncrowded and relatively tranquil during the day, it draws anglers from dusk and into the night surf-casting for striped bass.

Apart from sunbathing, the island's most popular pursuit is **bicycling.** The ferries allow visitors to bring their own bikes (for a small fee), but several local agencies rent bikes as well (see "Getting Around," above).

Parasailing has become popular here, and chutes can be seen lifting riders up to heights of 1,200 feet above the ocean. Call **Block Island Parasail** (✆ **401/864-2474;** www.blockislandparasail.com) with questions, but you must make reservations in person at the office near the Old Harbor ferry landing. Fares start at $70 and go up, gauged by altitude; observers are charged $20 each. The company also offers banana boat and jet boat rides, as well as dive trips.

A more old-fashioned form of transportation is provided by **Rustic Rides Farm,** on West Side Road (✆ **401/466-5060**). A walking attendant handles the reins and protects the littlest ones on the trail. A 1-hour slow ride costs $40; a 1-hour sunset ride costs $65, and a 2-hour beach ride is $100.

Fishing, kayaking, and canoeing are hugely popular, and the name to know is **Oceans & Ponds,** at Ocean and Connecticut avenues (✆ **401/466-5131**). The owners possess encyclopedic knowledge of the island; their quality stock features Orvis clothing and fishing gear. Rental kayaks and canoes put in at the head of the gentle inland ponds off the Great Salt Pond (New Harbor). Charters can be arranged on three sportfishing boats. Another source of boat rentals is **Champlin's Resort,** on Great Salt Pond (✆ **401/466-5811**), which has bumper boats and Zodiacs as well as kayaks.

WHERE TO STAY

Atlantic Inn ★★ Perched upon 6 rolling acres south of downtown, this 1879 Victorian hotel beguiles with its long veranda and broad views. Bedrooms are furnished mostly with antiques. Drawn by the promise of spectacular sunsets and the restaurant's changing menu of tapas, joined with the most diverse beer and wine selection on the island, people start assembling on the veranda and lawn at 4pm each summer day. President Clinton stopped by for dinner a few years ago, drawn by the reputation of the kitchen, one of the two most accomplished on Block Island. He had no trouble getting a table, it can be assumed, but the rest of us need reservations from June to September. Fish, fowl, and vegetables are smoked on the premises, and the chef comes up with such attractions as grilled striped bass with orzo salad. The inn is nonsmoking.

High St., Box 188, Block Island, RI 02807. ✆ **800/224-7422** or 401/466-5883. Fax 401/466-5678. www.atlanticinn.com. 21 units. Mid-Apr to mid-Oct $159–$279 double. Rates include breakfast. DISC, MC, V. Closed Nov–Apr. **Amenities:** Restaurant (eclectic); bar; 2 tennis courts; bike rental. *In room:* Dataport.

Champlin's ★★ Kids Families are welcome at this all-inclusive resort, with 225 slips in the marina for visiting yachters. Those who are put off by the idiosyncratic adornments of Victorian inns will be pleased by the simpler lines and muted fabrics of the bedrooms here. All rooms have fridges and microwaves (another plus for families). There's live music in the bars on weekends, picnic grounds with grills, a pizza bar and ice-cream parlor, even a theater showing first-run movies. Once you've unpacked, there isn't much to compel you to leave, but a shuttle van is provided for trips to other parts of the island. Cars, mopeds, kayaks, and pontoon boats are available for rent. Drawbacks include an under-staffed reception area that can be annoyingly empty for minutes at a time, and a slap-dash approach to maintenance.

Great Salt Pond, P.O. Box J, Block Island, RI 02807. ✆ **800/762-4541** or 401/466-7777. Fax 401/466-2638. www.champlinsresort.com. 30 units. $185–$475 double. AE, MC, V. Closed mid-Oct to early May. From Old Harbor, drive west on Ocean Ave. and turn left on West Side Rd. The entrance road to Champlin's is on the right. The ferry from Long Island docks here. **Amenities:** Restaurant; 2 bars; large outdoor pool; 2 tennis courts; kayak, bumper boat, and paddle-boat rentals; moped and bike rentals; game room; car rental; coin-op washers and dryers. *In room:* A/C, TV, fridge.

Rose Farm ★ The 1897 farmhouse that was the original inn is complemented by an additional house across the driveway. Four of the rooms in the new building feature Jacuzzis and decks. Some have canopied beds, most have ocean views, and their furnishings are often antique. Afternoon refreshments, usually iced tea and pastries, are served.

Roslyn Rd., Box E, Block Island, RI 02807. ✆ **401/466-2034.** Fax 401/466-2053. www.rosefarminn.com. 19 units, 2 with shared bathroom. $109–$289 double. Rates include breakfast. AE, DISC, MC, V. Closed Nov–Mar. From Old Harbor, drive west on High St. and turn left on paved driveway past the Atlantic Inn. Children over 12 welcome. **Amenities:** Bike rental; coin-op washers and dryers.

The 1661 Inn & Hotel Manisses ★★★ Emus, llamas, black swans, two camels, and a Scottish Highland ox graze in the meadow behind the Victorian Hotel Manisses, only the most visible part of a small hospitality empire. Other properties include The 1661 Inn & Guest House, up the hill, and the Dodge, Dewey, and Nicholas Ball cottages. (Children are welcome in five of the six buildings; smoking is allowed in one.) Guest rooms in the hotel utilize oak antiques and lots of wicker; some units have TVs and/or fireplaces. The median age in the hotel is noticeably grayer than in the other buildings, where families tend to gather. Common rooms in The 1661 Inn host an afternoon "wine and nibble" hour, while the Manisses parlor serves desserts and flaming coffees in the evening. Stylish dining is featured in the main dining room, with comparable fare in the more casual Gatsby Room. Picnic lunches are also prepared for guests. The inn is now open year-round, although the restaurants are closed in winter.

1 Spring St., P.O. Box 1, Block Island, RI 02807. ✆ **800/626-4773** or 401/466-2421/2063. Fax 401/466-3162. www.blockislandresorts.com. 17 units in hotel, plus 43 units (some with shared bathroom) in satellite buildings. $70–$410 double. Rates include breakfast. MC, V. **Amenities:** 2 restaurants; bar; concierge; babysitting. *In room:* Minibar, hair dryer, no phone.

Spring House Hotel ★ Marked by its mansard roof and wraparound porch, the island's oldest hotel (1852) has hosted the Kennedy clan, Ulysses S. Grant . . . and Billy Joel. The young staff is congenial, if occasionally a bit scattered. Bedrooms come in three styles, with queen-size beds and pullout sofas; most are large. A significant attraction is the all-you-can-eat barbecue lunch on the veranda. More formal meals are served in the all-white dining room. Swimming is allowed in the freshwater pond on the property. The hotel sponsors concerts of classical and pop music on its grounds in July and August.

902 Spring St., P.O. Box 902, Block Island, RI 02807. ✆ **800/234-9263** or 401/466-5844. www.springhousehotel.com. 50 units. $125–$450 double. Rates include breakfast. AE, MC, V. Closed mid-Oct to Mar. **Amenities:** Restaurant; bar.

WHERE TO DINE

Expect mostly lobsters, fried and grilled fish and chicken, and routine burgers and beef cuts. Chowders are usually surefire, especially the creamy New England version. Clam cakes appear less frequently on menus than before, but are still a staple. Actually deep-fried fritters containing more dough than clams, they are still fun eating, especially when dipped in tartar sauce.

Several inns and hotels have dining rooms worth noting (see "Where to Stay," above, for reviews of the **Atlantic Inn, The 1661 Inn & Hotel Manisses,** and **Spring House Hotel**), but even there, neither jackets nor ties are required. Due to the seasonal nature of the resort island, its restaurants can change policies, menus, and, most important, chefs in a twinkling. Keep that in mind if any of the observations below prove to undervalue or overstate a restaurant's virtues.

Ballard's ★ Kids AMERICAN/SEAFOOD Sooner rather than later, everyone winds up at Ballard's. Behind the long front porch is a warehouse-like hall where a monster whale skeleton hangs, and beyond that a terrace beside a crowded beach. Several bars and frequent live bands fuel drinkers and diners from lunch until midnight. The menu is all over the map, with something for everyone. Complementing the lobster rolls and fish and chips are yellowfin tuna *au poivre* and roasted monkfish medallions with shrimp and sweet pepper dressed in a tarragon hollandaise. Kids have their own menu, and they can make as much noise and mess as they want. It gets pricey for families, though, so you might want to go for lunch, not dinner, and have sandwiches, not entrees.

Old Harbor. ✆ **401/466-2231.** Main courses $9–$28. AE, MC, V. Daily 11:30am–11pm. Closed Oct to mid-May.

Beachhead ★ Kids ECLECTIC After changes in management, the menu has been expanded from the former tavern limitations to one of the more ambitious slates on the island. The casual atmosphere remains, making this a likely destination for families in afternoon and early evening (dinner prices are steep, though). In peak season, at least, the noise level is high enough to mask childish squeals. Plenty of seating is available inside and on the porch. There's a pizza of the day, seafood and meats are prepared in more imaginative ways than before, and the selection of beers and wines is attractive.

Corn Neck Rd. ✆ **401/466-2249.** Main courses $11–$26. MC, V. Daily 11:30am–9pm (later in summer).

Bethany's Airport Diner Kids AMERICAN "Ramshackle" is too grand a word for this relic of the 1940s. That's good, if your party includes little ones, for even the most destructive 2-year-old can't do much damage, especially out at the tables beside the runway. Decent chili and chowder come in Styrofoam cups, preceding tuna melts and quesadillas. Such specials as the Monte Cristo—a toasted ham and cheese sandwich—are about as fancy as it gets. Decor is confined to the model airplanes hanging from the ceiling, several of them fashioned from beer cans.

Center Rd. (at the airport). ✆ **401/466-3100.** All items under $10. No credit cards. Daily 5:30am–5pm (shorter hours in off season).

Tips DIY Shore Dinners

Should you have housekeeping facilities in your lodging, you might wish to put together a New England shore dinner. Lobster is the central component, of course, and you can buy yours straight off the fishing boats. Each afternoon from about 4 to 5:30pm, boats put in at both Old Harbor and the Great Salt Pond. Depending upon their catches of the day, they charge from $6 to $8 per pound. A more reliable source is **Finn's Fish Market,** at the Old Harbor ferry landing (✆ **401/466-2102**). Its lobster prices are similar, and it also carries oysters, clams, shrimp, and fish.

For the other fixings—corn, tomatoes, bread, sausage, chicken—stop at either the **Block Island Grocery** (known as the B.I.G.) near Ocean Avenue and Corn Neck Road (✆ **401/466-2949**), a conventional supermarket; or **Block Island Depot,** Ocean Avenue (✆ **401/466-2403**), which carries a line of cheeses and organic foods. The best-stocked wine and liquor store is the **Red Bird Package Store,** on Dodge Street (✆ **401/466-2441**), around the corner from the north end of Water Street. **Seaside Market,** toward the other end of Water Street (✆ **401/466-5876**), has a good wine selection and some grocery products.

Dead Eye Dick's *Kids* SEAFOOD/AMERICAN Despite the name and the logo of a shark with an eye patch, which might suggest beer blasts and wet T-shirt contests, this is a PG-rated restaurant with good eats and a welcome for all ages. Swordfish is high on the honors list, often grilled with a tomato-ginger relish. A twist on the Rhode Island stuffie is the minced Quahog crammed back into its shell with andouille sausage and sweet pepper. Lunch is mostly tasty wraps and meat salads. The kids' menu suggests pasta with butter or chicken tenders. Arrive early for a table on the deck.

Water St. (near Payne's Dock). ✆ **401/466-2473.** Main courses $16–$28. AE, MC, V. Memorial Day to Labor Day daily 5–10pm (Sun until 9pm); July–Aug also open noon–3pm daily. Closed rest of the year.

Eli's ITALIAN/AMERICAN This place used to be just a spaghetti-and-grinders drop-in, but it's evolved into one of the island's most popular eateries. Problem is, it can serve only 50 voracious diners at a time, and the no-reservations policy means waits of up to 2 hours. One duck dish brought together half of that bird with apples, pheasant sausage, and brandy. Such combinations are undeniably full-flavored, although the diverse ingredients are often mashed together as if in a thick stew, losing some of their individuality. Huge portions defy anyone to finish.

456 Chapel St. ✆ **401/466-5230.** Main courses $21–$28. AE, MC, V. May–Oct daily 6–9pm (Sat–Sun until 10pm); Nov–Dec Sat–Sun 5:30–10pm. Closed Jan–Apr.

G.R. Sharky's AMERICAN With its kicked-back atmosphere and pub-style menu, this entry opposite Crescent Beach has a clear kinship with at least a dozen casual eateries on the island. Mounted fish, deer heads, and sports memorabilia decorate the bar. Expect the usual burgers and cheesesteak pretenders, but know that the people handling the fried-fish dishes have a superbly light hand—go for the definitive fish and chips. Daily specials lean to the likes of blackened this or that—mako shark, for one—while dinner entrees run to fettuccine and prime rib. Children are welcome.

Corn Neck Rd. ✆ **401/466-9900.** Main courses $14–$27. MC, V. Summer daily 11:30am–10pm; hours vary substantially spring and fall. Closed late Oct to mid-May.

Mohegan Café & Brewery ECLECTIC Follow the crowds straight across from the Old Harbor ferry landing to this agreeable tavern. Featured microbrews are listed on the blackboard. They are made on the premises, usually four or five types from Pilsener to stout. Most of the daytime menu is standard pub fare, with chowder, burgers, burritos, and fried clams featured. That's the time to go, for the kitchen has a sure hand with its luncheon familiars, but looks a little too far afield for dinner ideas (pad Thai and red curried chicken). This is one of the few public places with air-conditioning, something to remember on a muggy July day.

Water St. ✆ **401/466-5911.** Main courses $16–$23. AE, DISC, MC, V. Summer Sun–Thurs 11:30am–9pm, Fri–Sat 11am–10pm; shorter hours during spring and fall shoulder seasons.

The Oar ★ AMERICAN This good-time bar is now open for a buffet breakfast and full-service lunch and dinner, and the menu has been plumped up with a few more choices. Grilled swordfish, sirloin, and fried chicken flesh out the old roster of nachos, lobster rolls, and calamari. A deck and a bar with a picture window take in dramatic views of storms over the mainland and of the fleet of pleasure boats in the Great Salt Pond. The ceiling and walls are hung with scores of oars—all of them painted with cartoons, graffiti, and assorted messages of obscure or ribald intent.

West Side Rd. (Block Island Marina). ✆ **401/466-8820.** Main courses $12–$24. AE, MC, V. Daily 8am–midnight (bar until 1am). Closed late Oct to May.

BLOCK ISLAND AFTER DARK

Nightlife isn't of the raunchy, rollicking, south Florida variety, but the bars don't close at sunset, either. Among the prime candidates for a potential rockin' good time is **Captain Nick's,** on Ocean Avenue (✆ **401/466-5670**), opposite the Block Island Grocery. It has pool, 3 more bars, and a large dance floor inside, as well as dollar beers, cheap burgers, and live music most nights in season out on the terrace. A block away, **McGovern's Yellow Kittens,** on Corn Neck Road (✆ **401/466-5855**), also presents live bands in summer, inside or out on the deck. Darts, pool tables, foosball, and video games help fill the winter nights. Pub food, pool tables, video games, and foosball are also attractions at **Club Soda,** on Connecticut Avenue (✆ **401/466-5397**), supplemented by live music once or twice a week.

Ballard's (see "Where to Dine," above) has live rock or pop most afternoons out on the terrace and nightly inside. An occasional live-music venue is the lounge of the **National Hotel,** on Water Street (✆ **401/466-2901**). Yachtsmen and other sailors docked or moored at Champlin's Marina settle in on the end of the main dock at **Trader Vic's,** at New Harbor (✆ **401/466-2641**). The bar is downstairs, with a DJ or band out on the deck most afternoons. In addition to the sunset drinks and tapas on the front lawn of the **Atlantic Inn** (see "Where to Stay," above), many visitors settle in on the porch of the equally well-situated (and less expensive) **Narragansett Inn,** on Water Street (✆ **401/466-2626**).

Island residents try to keep **Mahagony Shoals,** on Payne's Dock at the end of Water Street (✆ **401/466-5572**), to themselves. What they come for is the barbed humor of Wally McDonough. He sings Irish folk ballads and banters with the audience, invariably giving better than he gets. Wally occupies his corner Wednesday, Thursday, Saturday, and Sunday nights, as well as Fridays, when he feels like it. Get there around 10pm.

11

Vermont

by Paul Karr

Vermont's rolling, cow-spotted hills, shaggy peaks, sugar maples, and towns clustered along river valleys give it a distinct sense of place. Still primarily rural, the state is filled with dairy farms, dirt roads, and small-scale enterprises. The towns here are home to an intriguing mix of old-time Vermonters, back-to-the-landers who showed up in VW buses in the 1960s and stayed (many getting involved with municipal affairs; think Ben and Jerry), and newer, moneyed arrivals from New York or Boston who came to ski or stay at B&Bs and could never quite leave.

This place captures a sense of America as it once was—because, here, it still *is.* Vermonters continue to share a sense of community, and they respect the ideals of thrift and parsimony above those of commercialism (it took years for Wal-Mart to get approval to build in Vermont, for instance). Locals prize their villages, and they understand what makes them special. Vermont's governor once said that one of the state's strengths was knowing "where our towns begin and end." That seems a simple notion, but it speaks volumes when one considers the erosion of identity that has afflicted so many East Coast small towns swallowed up by a creeping megalopolis.

Though it is the closest part of northern New England to New York City, southern Vermont has mostly resisted the encroachment of progress (except at ski resorts on winter weekends). This area remains a great introduction to one of America's most wonderful states. Southern and central Vermont are defined by rolling hills, shady valleys, and historic villages. Throughout you'll find antiques shops and handsome inns, fast-flowing streams and inviting restaurants. The area is anchored at each corner by the towns of Bennington and Brattleboro; between them and running northward is the spine of the Green Mountains, much of which is part of the Green Mountain National Forest, all of which rewards explorers who consider dirt roads an irresistible temptation. The steep hills also host many of the state's popular ski resorts, such as Okemo, Killington, Sugarbush, and Mount Snow.

Northern Vermont is different, and well represented on both ends of the development spectrum. On the region's western edge, along the shores of Lake Champlain, Burlington, the state's largest, most lively city, is ringed by fast-growing suburban communities. But drive an hour or two east, and you're deep in the Northeast Kingdom, the state's least developed and most remote region.

1 Bennington, Manchester & Southwestern Vermont

Bennington: 143 miles NW of Boston; 126 miles S of Burlington. Manchester: 24 miles N of Bennington.

BENNINGTON ★

Bennington, Vermont's third-largest city, owes its fame (such as it is) to a handful of eponymous moments, places, and things: The Battle of Bennington, fought in 1777 during the American War of Independence; Bennington College, a small, prestigious liberal arts school; and Bennington pottery, which traces its ancestry back to the first factory in 1793, and is prized by collectors for its superb quality.

Today, visitors will find two Benningtons. Historic Bennington, with its white clapboard homes, sits atop a hill west of town off Route 9. (Look for the miniature Washington Monument.) Modern downtown Bennington is a pleasant, if no-frills, commercial center with restaurants and stores that still sell what people actually need—not so much a tourist destination as a handy supply depot.

ESSENTIALS

GETTING THERE Bennington is at the intersection of Routes 9 and 7. If you're coming from the south, the nearest interstate access is via the New York Thruway at Albany, about 35 miles away. From the east, I-91 is about 40 miles away at Brattleboro. **Vermont Transit** (✆ **800/552-8737** or 802/254-6066; www.vermonttransit.com) offers bus service to Bennington from Albany, Burlington, and other points. Buses arrive and depart from 126 Washington St.

VISITOR INFORMATION The **Bennington Area Chamber of Commerce,** 100 Veterans Memorial Dr. (✆ **800/229-0252** or 802/447-3311; www.bennington.com), has an information office on Route 7 North near the veterans' complex and a small park. This office is open weekdays from 9am to 5pm, Saturday and Sunday from 10am to 4pm. There's also a **downtown welcome center** (✆ **802/442-5758**) in town, at South and Elm streets; it's open Monday through Saturday from 9am to 5pm.

EXPLORING THE TOWN

One of Bennington's claims to history is the Battle of Bennington, which took place August 16, 1777. A relatively minor skirmish, it had major implications for the outcome of the American Revolution. That battle is commemorated by northern New England's most imposing monument. You can't miss the **Bennington Battle Monument** ★★ (✆ **802/447-0550**) if you're passing through the countryside. This 306-foot obelisk of blue limestone atop a low-rise was dedicated in 1891. It resembles a shorter, paunchier Washington Monument. Note also that it's about 6 miles from the site of the actual battle; the monument marks the spot where the munitions were stored. The monument's viewing platform, which is reached by elevator, is open from 9am to 5pm daily mid-April through October. A minimal fee is charged.

Near the monument, you'll find distinguished old homes lushly overarched with ancient trees. Be sure to spend a few moments exploring the old burying ground, where several Vermont governors and the poet Robert Frost are buried. The chamber of commerce (see above) provides a walking tour brochure that will help you make sense of the neighborhood's vibrant past.

Bennington College ★ was founded in the 1930s as an experimental women's college. It has since gone coed and garnered a national reputation as a leading liberal arts school. Bennington has a great reputation for the teaching of writing; W. H. Auden,

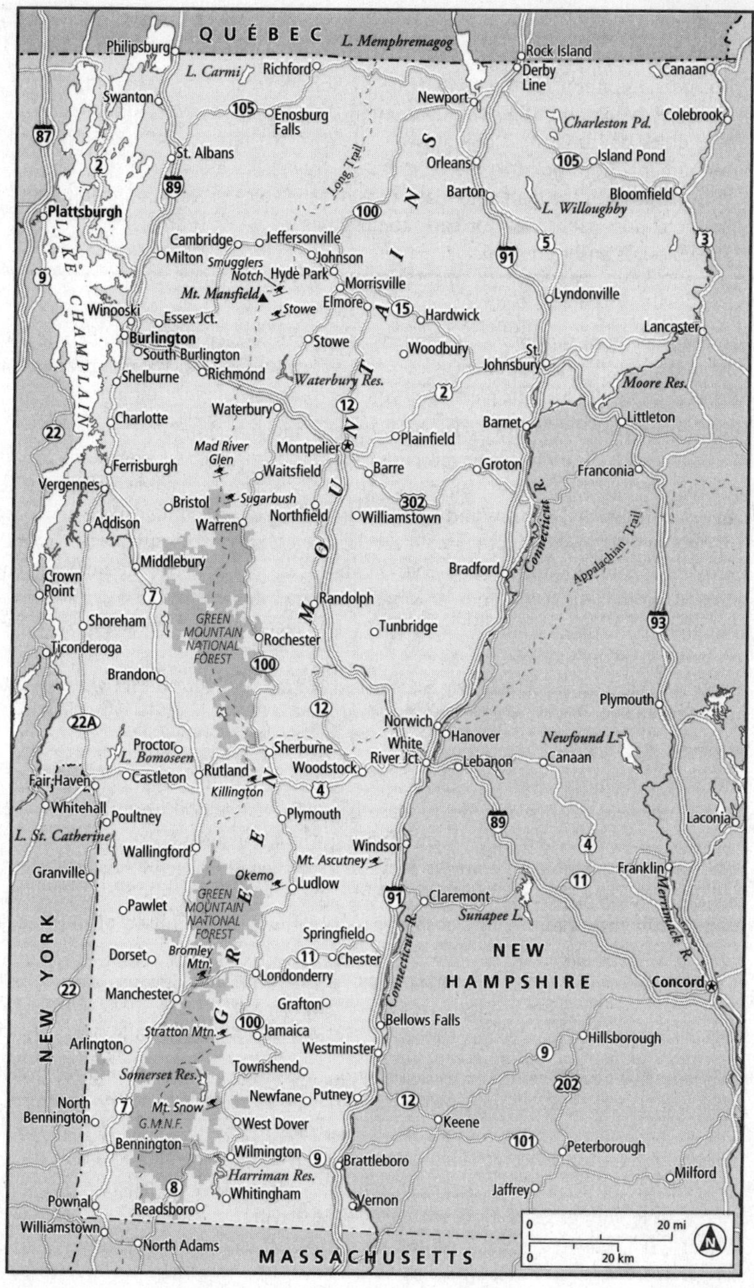
QUÉBEC
L. Memphremagog
Philipsburg
L. Carmi
Richford
Rock Island
Derby Line
Canaan
Swanton
105
Enosburg Falls
Newport
Charleston Pd.
Colebrook
87
St. Albans
Orleans
105
Island Pond
2
89
Long Trail
Barton
Bloomfield
L. Willoughby
Plattsburgh
100
LAKE CHAMPLAIN
Cambridge
Jeffersonville
5
3
Milton
Smugglers Notch
Johnson
91
9
Hyde Park
Morrisville
Lyndonville
Mt. Mansfield
Elmore
15
Stowe
Hardwick
Winooski
Essex Jct.
Lancaster
Burlington
Stowe
Woodbury
South Burlington
St. Johnsbury
Shelburne
Richmond
Waterbury Res.
Moore Res.
2
Waterbury
12
Charlotte
Barnet
Littleton
22
Mad River Glen
Montpelier
Plainfield
Ferrisburgh
Waitsfield
Barre
Groton
Franconia
Vergennes
Sugarbush
302
Bristol
Northfield
Williamstown
Addison
Warren
Connecticut R.
Appalachian Trail
Middlebury
Bradford
Crown Point
7
Randolph
GREEN MOUNTAIN NATIONAL FOREST
Tunbridge
93
Shoreham
Rochester
Ticonderoga
100
Brandon
Plymouth
12
22A
Norwich
Hanover
Proctor
L. Bomoseen
Sherburne
White River Jct.
Newfound L.
Lebanon
Canaan
Fair Haven
Castleton
Rutland
Woodstock
Killington
4
Whitehall
Poultney
Plymouth
89
Laconia
L. St. Catherine
Windsor
Wallingford
Mt. Ascutney
4
Franklin
Okemo
Ludlow
11
Granville
91
Claremont
GREEN MOUNTAIN NATIONAL FOREST
Pawlet
Sunapee L.
Springfield
Merrimack R.
NEW YORK
Dorset
Bromley Mtn.
11
Chester
NEW HAMPSHIRE
Connecticut R.
Londonderry
22
Manchester
Concord
Grafton
Stratton Mtn.
100
Jamaica
Bellows Falls
Arlington
Hillsborough
Westminster
9
Somerset Res.
Townshend
202
North Bennington
7
Mt. Snow
Newfane
Putney
12
G.M.N.F.
West Dover
Keene
Bennington
101
Peterborough
Wilmington
9
Brattleboro
Harriman Res.
Milford
8
Whitingham
Jaffrey
Pownal
Readsboro
Vernon
Williamstown
North Adams
MASSACHUSETTS
0
20 mi
0
20 km
N
GREEN MOUNTAINS

Moments **"I Had a Lover's Quarrel with the World."**

That's the epitaph on the tombstone of Robert Frost, who is buried in the cemetery behind the 1806 First Congregational Church. (It's where Rte. 9 makes two quick bends west of downtown and down the hill from the Bennington Monument. Signs point to the Frost family grave.) Travelers often stop to pay their respects to the man who many consider the voice of New England. Closer to the church itself, look for early tombstones (some with urns and skulls) of the voiceless and forgotten.

Bernard Malamud, and John Gardner have all taught here. In the 1980s, Bennington produced a number of prominent young authors, including Donna Tartt, Bret Easton Ellis, and Jill Eisenstadt. The pleasant campus north of town is worth wandering about.

The Bennington Museum ★★ This eclectic and intriguing collection traces its roots back to 1875, although the museum has occupied the current stone-and-column building overlooking the valley only since 1928. The expansive galleries feature a wide range of exhibits on local arts and industry, including early Vermont furniture, glass, paintings, and Bennington pottery. Of special interest are the colorful primitive landscapes by Grandma Moses (1860–1961), who lived much of her life nearby. (The museum has the largest collection of Moses's paintings in the world.) Look also for the glorious 1925 luxury car called the Wasp, 16 of which were handcrafted in Bennington between 1920 and 1925.

75 W. Main St. (Rte. 9 between Old Bennington and the current town center). ✆ **802/447-1571.** www.benningtonmuseum.org. Admission $8 adults, $7 seniors and students, free for children under 12, $19 family. Daily 10am–5pm.

WHERE TO STAY

The Four Chimneys Inn ★ This Colonial Revival building is among the first to catch your eye as you arrive in Bennington from the west. Set off from Route 7 on an 11-acre, nicely landscaped lot, it's an imposing white, three-story structure with—no surprise—four prominent chimneys. Built in 1912, the inn is at the edge of Historic Bennington; the towering Bennington Monument looms over its backyard. Guest rooms are inviting and homey, but the overall sensibility can be mildly off-putting, as if you were visiting somebody else's relatives.

21 West Rd., Bennington, VT 05201. ✆ **802/447-3500.** Fax 802/447-3692. www.fourchimneys.com. 11 units. $115–$230 double. Rates include breakfast. 2-night minimum stay foliage and holiday weekends. AE, DISC, MC, V. Children 12 and over accepted. **Amenities:** Restaurant. *In room:* A/C, TV, dataport, hair dryer, iron/ironing board.

Paradise Motor Inn ★ This is Bennington's best motel, with tidy and generously sized accommodations, though prices have shot up in recent years. Try to reserve a spot in the North Building, despite its dated 1980s styling—each room here has an outdoor terrace or balcony. The more up-to-date Office Building has a richer Colonial Revival style. The motel is uncommonly clean and well managed. It's across from the Hemmings gas station, within walking distance of town.

141 W. Main St., Bennington, VT 05201. ✆ **802/442-8351.** Fax 802/447-3889. www.theparadisemotorinn.com. 76 units. $85–$240 double. DC, DISC, MC, V. **Amenities:** Outdoor pool; 2 tennis courts. *In room:* A/C, TV, Jacuzzis (some).

South Shire Inn ★★ A locally prominent banking family hired architect William Bull in 1880 to design and build this impressive Victorian home. The spacious downstairs has leaded glass on its bookshelves and intricate plasterwork in the dining room. The guest rooms are richly hued, most with canopied beds and working fireplaces (with Duraflame-type logs only). The best of the bunch is the old master bedroom, with a king-size canopied bed, tile-hearth fireplace, and beautiful bathroom with hand-painted tile. Four more modern guest rooms are in the carriage house, where the downstairs rooms are slightly more formal and upstairs rooms more intimate, with low eaves and skylights over the tubs.

124 Elm St., Bennington, VT 05201. ✆ **802/447-3839.** Fax 802/442-3547. www.southshire.com. 9 units. $89–$200 double. Rates include breakfast. AE, MC, V. No children under 12. *In room:* A/C, hair dryer.

WHERE TO DINE

Alldays & Onions ECLECTIC ★ This casual spot was named after an early-20th-century British automobile manufacturer. Locals flock here to enjoy wholesome, tasty sandwiches, deli salads, and tasty soups; the atmosphere is that of a small-town restaurant gussied up for a big night out. Expect anything from pot roast and turkey with all the fixin's to Cajun seafood pasta, grilled steaks or shrimp, pastrami sandwiches, burgers, tortellini, and the like. (More ambitious entrees might include Southwest cowboy steak with skillet corn sauce and soba and stir-fried vegetables.)

519 Main St. ✆ **802/447-0043.** Reservations accepted for dinner, but not often needed. Breakfast $2–$8; sandwiches $2.50–$7.25; dinner $15–$19. AE, DISC, MC, V. Mon–Wed 7:30–10am and 11am–3pm; Thurs–Sun 9am–1pm and 5–9pm.

Blue Benn Diner ★ *Value* DINER Diner aficionados make pilgrimages to enjoy the ambience of this 1945 Silk City classic. Blue-plate dinner specials include vegetables, rice, soup or salad, rolls, and rice pudding for dessert. A bit incongruously, fancier and vegetarian fare is also available; especially good is the grilled portobello on sourdough. But you come here for diner staples such as turkey with gravy, big slabs of cornbread French toast, or butterscotch Indian pudding with vanilla ice cream.

314 North St. (Rte. 7). ✆ **802/442-5140.** Breakfast $1.50–$5.95; sandwiches and entrees $1.95–$5.75; dinner specials $7.95–$8.95. No credit cards. Mon–Tues 6am–5pm; Wed–Fri 6am–8pm; Sat 6am–4pm; Sun 7am–4pm.

ARLINGTON, MANCHESTER & DORSET ★★★

This trio of quintessential Vermont villages makes an ideal destination for romantic getaways, aggressive antiquing, and serious outlet shopping. Each of the towns is worth visiting, and each has its own unique charm. **Arlington** ★ has a town center that borders on microscopic. With its auto-body shops and redemption center (remnants of a time when the main highway artery passed through town), it gleams a bit less than its sibling towns to the north.

To the north, **Manchester** ★★ and **Manchester Center** share a blurred town line, but maintain distinct characters. The more southerly Manchester has an old-world, old-money elegance, with a campuslike town centered around the resplendently columned Equinox Hotel. Just to the north, Manchester Center is a major mercantile center with dozens of national outlets offering discounts on brand-name clothing, accessories, and housewares.

A worthy detour off the beaten track is **Dorset** ★★, an exquisitely preserved town of white clapboard architecture and marble sidewalks.

ESSENTIALS

GETTING THERE Arlington, Manchester, and Manchester Center are north of Bennington on Historic Route 7A, which runs parallel to and west of Route 7. Dorset is north of Manchester Center on Route 30, which diverges from Route 7A in Manchester Center. **Vermont Transit** (✆ **800/552-8737;** www.vermonttransit.com) provides bus service to Manchester.

VISITOR INFORMATION The **Manchester and the Mountains Chamber of Commerce** (✆ **800/362-4144** or 802/362-2100; www.manchestervermont.net) maintains a year-round information center at 5080 Main St. (Rte. 7A) beside the small village green in Manchester Center. Hours are Monday through Saturday from 10am to 5pm; from Memorial Day weekend through October, it's also open Sundays from 10am to 5pm, and to 7pm Fridays and Saturdays. If you're staying in Arlington, this hamlet maintains its own small self-serve visitor information center next to the Stewart's shop on Route 7A.

For information on outdoor recreation, the **Green Mountain National Forest** maintains a district ranger office (✆ **802/362-2307**) in Manchester on Routes 11 and 30 east of Route 7. It's open Monday through Friday from 8am to 4:30pm.

MUSEUMS & HISTORIC HOMES

American Museum of Fly Fishing ★ *Finds* If you loved *A River Runs Through It* and you're crazy about fly-fishing, you've come to the right place: Manchester is home to the world's largest collection of angling art and items. The complex, which includes a gallery space, library, reading room, store, and historical resources, was specially built for the purpose. Browse through antique rods (including those of Daniel Webster, Ernest Hemingway, and Winslow Homer), reels, and 200-year-old flies, as well as photos, sketchbooks, and historical items—a Greek historian wrote of a fly-fishing-like practice in A.D. 200. The museum is on Route 7A, just south of the Orvis flagship store.

4104 Main St. (Rte. 7A) Manchester. ✆ **802/362-3300.** www.amff.com. $5 adults, $3 children ages 5–14. Daily 10am–4pm (closed major holidays).

Hildene ★★ Robert Todd Lincoln was the only son of Abraham and Mary Todd Lincoln to survive to maturity. He's also noted for his own achievements, earning millions of dollars as a prominent corporate attorney, and serving as secretary of war and ambassador to Britain under three presidents. He was president of the Pullman Company (makers of deluxe train cars) from 1897 to 1911, stepping in after the death of company founder George Pullman.

What did one do with a million bucks in an era when it was more than chump change? Build lavish summer homes, for the most part. And Lincoln, the son of a man who grew up in famously modest circumstances, was no exception. He summered in this stately, 24-room Georgian Revival mansion between 1905 and 1926 and delighted in showing off its remarkable features, including a sweeping staircase and a 1908 Aeolian organ with 1,000 pipes (you'll hear it played on the tour). Still, it's more regal than ostentatious, and made with an eye to quality. Lincoln had formal gardens designed after the patterns in a stained-glass window and planted on a gentle promontory with outstanding views of the flanking mountains. The home is viewed on group tours that start at an informative visitor center; allow time following the tour to explore the grounds.

Historic Rte. 7A off Rte. 30, Manchester. ✆ **802/362-1788.** www.hildene.org. Tours $10 adults, $4 children 6–14, free for children under 6. Grounds only $5 adults, $2 children 6–14. Tours given mid-May to Oct daily on the half-hour 9:30am–4pm; grounds close at 5pm. Winter, tours Thurs–Mon only, from 11am–3pm. Special holiday tours Dec 27–29.

Southern Vermont Art Center ★★ This fine-art center is well worth the short detour from town. Located partly in a striking Georgian Revival home surrounded by more than 400 pastoral hillside acres (it overlooks land that once belonged to Charles Orvis of fly-fishing fame), the center features a series of galleries displaying works from its well-regarded collection, as well as frequently changing exhibits of contemporary Vermont artists. An inventive and appealing modern building across the drive, designed to display more of the 800-piece permanent collection, opened in 2000. (It was designed by noted contemporary architect Hugh Newell Jacobsen.) Check the schedule before you arrive; you may be able to sign up for an art class while you're in town. Also, leave time to enjoy a light lunch at the **Garden Cafe** and to wander the grounds, exploring both the sculpture garden and woods beyond.

West Rd. off Rte. 30 (P.O. Box 617), Manchester. ✆ **802/362-1405.** www.svac.org. Admission in summer $6 adults, $3 students, free for children under 13. Tues–Sat 10am–5pm; Sun noon–5pm.

AREA SKIING

Bromley Mountain Ski Resort ★ *Kids* Bromley is a great place to learn to ski. Gentle and forgiving, the mountain also has long, looping, intermediate runs that are tremendously popular with families. The slopes are mostly south-facing, which means they receive the warmth of the sun and some protection from the harshest winter winds. (It also means the snow may melt more quickly than at other ski resorts.) The base lodge scene is mellower than at many resorts, and your experience is almost guaranteed to be relaxing.

3984 Rte. 11, Peru (mailing address: P.O. Box 1130, Manchester Center, VT 05255). ✆ **800/865-4786** for lodging, or 802/824-5522. www.bromley.com. Vertical drop: 1,334 ft. Lifts: 6 chairlifts (including 1 high-speed detachable quad), 3 surface lifts. Skiable acreage: 175. Adult day lift tickets $25–$59.

Stratton ★★ Founded in the 1960s, Stratton labored in its early days under the belief that Vermont ski areas had to be Tyrolean to be successful—hence, the Swiss chalet architecture and overall feel of being Vail's younger, less affluent sibling. In recent years, Stratton has worked to leave the image of alpine quaintness behind in a bid to attract a younger, edgier set. New owners added $25 million in improvements, mostly in snowmaking, with coverage now up over 80%. The slopes are especially popular with snowboarders, a sport that was invented here when bartender Jake Burton slapped a big plank on his feet and aimed down the mountain. Expert skiers should seek out Upper Middlebrook, a fine, twisting run off the summit.

Stratton Mountain, VT 05155. ✆ **800/STRATTON** for lodging, or 802/297-4000. www.stratton.com. Vertical drop: 2,003 ft. Lifts: 1 tram, 9 chairlifts (including 2 6-person high-speed), 2 surface lifts. Skiable acreage: 583. Adult day lift tickets $59–$72.

OTHER OUTDOOR ACTIVITIES

HIKING & BIKING Scenic hiking trails ranging from challenging to relaxing can be found in the hills a short drive from town. At the Green Mountain District Ranger Station (see "Visitor Information," above), ask for the free brochure *Day Hikes on the Manchester Ranger District,* which lists 19 hiking trails easily reached from Manchester.

A scenic drive 30 to 40 minutes northwest of Manchester Center takes you to the **Delaware and Hudson Rail-Trail,** approximately 20 miles of which have been built in two sections in Vermont. The southern section of the trail runs about 10 miles from West Pawlet to the state line at West Rupert, over trestles and past vestiges of former industry, such as the old Vermont Milk and Cream Co. Like most rail-trails, this one is perfect for exploring by mountain bike. You'll bike sometimes on the original ballast, other times through grassy growth. To reach the trail head, drive north on Route 30 from Manchester Center to Route 315, then continue north on Route 153. In

West Pawlet, park across from Duchie's General Store (a good place for refreshments), then set off on the trail southward from the old D&H freight depot across the street.

The hills around Manchester are full of other great touring rides, too, and your headquarters should be **Battenkill Bicycle Shop** (✆ **800/340-2734** or 802/362-2734) at 1240 Depot St. in downtown Manchester. It's a wonderful little place, with free local route maps and a range of rentals from hybrids to touring cycles to mountain bikes.

CANOEING For a duck's-eye view of the rolling hills, stop by **BattenKill Canoe Ltd.** in Arlington (✆ **800/421-5268** or 802/362-2800; www.battenkill.com). This friendly outfit offers daily canoe rentals for exploring the Battenkill River and surrounding areas. Trips range from 2 hours to a day, but the firm specializes in multiple-night, inn-to-inn canoe packages. The shop is open daily in season (May–Oct) from 9am to 5:30pm, but for more limited hours during the rest of the year.

FLY-FISHING Aspiring anglers can sign up for fly-fishing classes taught by skilled instructors affiliated with **Orvis** (✆ **888/235-9763**), the noted fly-fishing supplier and manufacturer. The 2½-day classes include instruction in knot tying and casting, practicing catch-and-release fishing on the company pond and the Battenkill River. Classes are held from mid-April to Labor Day.

WHERE TO STAY

Expensive

The Equinox ★★★ Since 2000, The Equinox has been owned and managed by the upscale Rockresorts. It remains a blue-blood favorite, with acres of white clapboard behind a long row of stately columns that define lovely Manchester Village. Its roots extend back to 1769, but don't be misled by its lineage: The Equinox is a full-blown modern resort, complete with the full-service Avanyu spa. You'll find extensive sports facilities scattered about its 2,300 acres, four dining rooms, scheduled events (such as guided hikes up Mount Equinox), and a sense of settled graciousness. The rooms are tastefully appointed, though not terribly large.

Rte. 7A (P.O. Box 46), Manchester Village, VT 05245. ✆ **800/362-4747** or 802/362-4700. Fax 802/362-1595. www.equinoxresort.com. 183 units. Peak season $279–$449 double, $449–$639 suite; off season $179–$399 double, $399–$629 suite; Orvis Inn section wing $609–$899 suite. Ask about packages. AE, DISC, MC, V. **Amenities:** 4 restaurants; indoor pool; outdoor pool; golf course; 3 tennis courts; spa; sauna; croquet; concierge; shopping arcade; salon; limited room service; babysitting; laundry service; dry cleaning; falconry school. *In room:* A/C, TV, dataport, hair dryer, iron.

Barrows House ★★ Within easy strolling distance of Dorset stands this compound of eight Early American buildings set on 12 nicely landscaped acres studded with birches, firs, and maples. Built in 1784, the main house has been an inn since

---

Finds **Birds of a Feather**

The Equinox offers a variety of esoteric activities, ranging from archery to off-road driving, but one of the most thrilling experiences you can have is handling and flying a bird of prey at the British School of Falconry. Trained falconers give participants (singly or in groups) an up-close-and-personal look at these beautiful raptors, mostly Harris hawks, with programs ranging from an introductory lesson ($85 for 45 min.) to a half-day hunt ($319). For more information call ✆ **802/362-4780** or e-mail falconry@equinoxresort.com.

1900. Its primary distinctions are its historic lineage and its convenience to Dorset; the rooms are more comfortable than elegant, though some have gas or wood fireplaces. Not all few units have phones—check in advance if it's important to you. Some have wireless Internet access. This place will please history buffs; those looking for more pampering may prefer The Equinox or the Inn at Ormsby Hill.

Rte. 30, Dorset, VT 05251. ✆ **800/639-1620** or 802/867-4455. Fax 802/867-0132. www.barrowshouse.com. 28 units. Peak season $205–$300 double MAP. Off season lower. Rates include breakfast and dinner. B&B rates available. Midweek and off-season discounts also available. 2-night minimum stay weekends and some holidays. AE, DISC, MC, V. Pets allowed in 2 cottages. **Amenities:** Restaurant (contemporary New England); outdoor pool; 2 tennis courts; sauna; bike rental; game room. *In room:* A/C, no phone (some).

Inn at Ormsby Hill ★★ The oldest part of the striking Inn at Ormsby Hill dates to 1764 (the Revolutionary Ethan Allen is rumored to have hidden out here). Today, it's a harmonious medley of eras and styles, with inspiring views of the Green Mountains. Guests enjoy those views along with gourmet breakfasts in the dining room, built by prominent 19th-century attorney Edward Isham to resemble the interior of a steamship. Among the best units: the Taft Room, with its vaulted wood ceiling, and the first-floor Library, with many of Isham's books still lining the shelves. Nine rooms have two-person Jacuzzis and fireplaces.

1842 Main St. (Rte. 7A, near Hildene south of Manchester Village), Manchester Center, VT 05255. ✆ **800/670-2841** or 802/362-1163. Fax 802/362-5176. www.ormsbyhill.com. 10 units. Weekdays $205–$270 double; weekends $265–$330 double; foliage season and holidays $320–$385. Rates include breakfast. 2-night minimum stay on weekends. DISC, MC, V. Closed briefly in Apr. Children 14 and older welcome. *In room:* A/C, hair dryer.

Moderate

Arlington Inn ★★ This stout, multicolumned, Greek Revival house (1848) would be perfectly at home in the Virginia countryside, but it anchors this village well, set back from Historic Route 7A on a lawn bordered with sturdy maples. Inside, the inn boasts a similarly courtly feel, with unique wooden ceilings adorning the first-floor rooms and a tavern that borrows its atmosphere from an English hunt club. If you prefer modern comforts, ask for a room in the 1830 parsonage next door, where you'll find phones and TVs. The quietest units are in the detached carriage house, most removed from the sound of Route 7A.

Historic Rte. 7A and Rte. 313 W. (P.O. Box 369), Arlington, VT 05250. ✆ **800/443-9442** or 802/375-6532. Fax 802/375-6534. www.arlingtoninn.com. 18 units. $95–$315 double. Rates include breakfast. 2-night minimum stay most weekends. AE, DISC, MC, V. **Amenities:** Restaurant (regional); tennis court; babysitting. *In room:* A/C, TV, dataport.

Barnstead Inn ★ *Value* If you're looking for a bit of history with your lodging, but are feeling shell-shocked by area room rates, consider this congenial place within walking distance of Manchester. All but two of the guest rooms are in an 1830s hay barn; many are decorated in a rustic country style, some with exposed beams. Expect vinyl bathroom floors, industrial carpeting, and a mix of motel-modern and antique furniture. Among the more desirable units are room B, which is the largest and most requested, and the two rooms (nos. 12 and 13) above the office, each with two double beds and original round beams. A few rooms are priced around $100, and all are a good value.

Rte. 30 (P.O. Box 988), Manchester Center, VT 05255. ✆ **800/331-1619** or 802/362-1619. www.barnsteadinn.com. 14 units. $99–$229 double and suite; foliage season rates higher. AE, MC, V. Children over 12 welcome. **Amenities:** Outdoor pool. *In room:* A/C, TV, dataport, coffeemaker.

1811 House ★★★ This inn, one of the best in southern Vermont, is certain to appeal to those drawn to early regional history. A historic home built in the mid–1770s, it began taking guests in 1811 (hence the name), and it seems that little has changed in the intervening centuries. The cozy, warrenlike common rooms are steeped in the past—uneven pine floors, out-of-true doors, and everything painted in earthy, Colonial tones. The antique furniture re-creates the feel of the house during the Federal period. A delightful English-style pub lies off the entryway, complete with tankards hanging from the beams. One of the best units is the Robinson Room, with a private deck and great view.

Rte. 7A (P.O. Box 39), Manchester Village, VT 05254. ✆ **800/432-1811** or 802/362-1811. www.1811house.com. 13 units. $140–$280 double. Rates include breakfast. AE, DISC, MC, V. *In room:* A/C.

The Inn at Manchester ★★ *Finds* One of the best B&B's in New England sits on 4 acres of lawns and gardens, just a half-mile from the budget shopping that draws so many visitors to the village of Manchester. Rooms are in the main inn, built as a private home in 1889, and in an adjacent carriage house that dates from the mid-1800's. (Both are listed on the National Register of Historic Places, and all units are named for flowers or herbs.) Rooms are immaculately clean and fresh, with bright, cheerful patterns, antiques, and quality reproductions; they're also decorated with art and sculpture from around the world. All have private bathrooms; some have fireplaces and separate sitting rooms. Buoyant, hardworking innkeepers Frank and Julie Hanes are always available and can never do enough for their guests.

Rte. 7A (P.O. Box 41), Manchester Village, VT 05254. ✆ **800/273-1793** or 802/362-1793. www.innatmanchester.com. 18 units. $145–$265 double and suite; foliage season slightly higher. Rates include full breakfast. AE, MC, V. No children under 13. **Amenities:** Outdoor pool. *In room:* A/C, TV (2 suites), hair dryer.

The Reluctant Panther ★★ A short walk from The Equinox, this lodging is easy to spot, painted a pale eggplant color with faded yellow shutters, making it stand out in this staid village of white clapboard. This 1850s home is elegantly furnished throughout (as are guest rooms in an adjacent building, built in 1910) and has nice touches, including goose-down duvets in every room. The place is operated with couples in mind, so 12 of the rooms have fireplaces (some more than one), and some suites, such as the Mark Skinner, even have wood-burning fireplaces or double Jacuzzis in the bathrooms. Many visitors plan their stay around a romantic meal at the **restaurant** ★, which serves European fare.

39 West Rd. (P.O. Box 678), Manchester Village, VT 05254. ✆ **800/822-2331** or 802/362-2568. Fax 802/362-2586. www.reluctantpanther.com. 21 units, 1 with detached private bathroom. $149–$349 double; $459 suite. Off-season rates lower; holiday and foliage season rates higher. Rates include breakfast. AE, DISC, MC, V. Children 14 and older welcome. **Amenities:** Restaurant. *In room:* A/C, TV, hair dryer, iron.

West Mountain Inn ★ Sitting atop a grassy bluff at the end of a dirt road ½ mile from Arlington center, this rambling, white-clapboard building dates back a century and a half. It's a perfect place for travelers striving to get away from the irksome hum of modern life. The guest rooms, named after famous Vermonters, are nicely furnished with country antiques and Victorian reproductions. The rooms vary widely in size and shape, but even the smallest has plenty of charm and character. Several rooms in outlying cottages have kitchenettes and are popular among attendees of family reunions, who also use the 100-year-old post-and-beam barn for gatherings.

River Rd. and Rte. 313, Arlington, VT 05250. ✆ **802/375-6516.** Fax 802/375-6553. www.westmountaininn.com. 18 units. Summer, spring, and winter weekends $189–$269 double; foliage season $224–$304 double; winter midweek

$149–$269 double; town houses $185–$299. Rates include breakfast, MAP plans also available. 2-night minimum stay on weekends. AE, DISC, MC, V. **Amenities:** Restaurant; massage (by arrangement); babysitting. *In room:* A/C, no phone.

Wilburton Inn ★★ This impressive Tudor estate (built in 1902) is sumptuously appointed and the common spaces filled with European antiques, Persian carpets, and even a baby grand piano. Throughout the brick manor house you'll find works from the modern-art collection amassed by the inn's owners, Albert and Georgette Levis. The guest rooms are divided among the main house and several outbuildings of various vintages, sizes, and styles. In the outbuildings, my favorite unit is spacious room no. 24, which has a private deck with views of Mount Equinox and quirky outdoor sculptures. Three rooms have fireplaces; the units in the mansion lack TVs.

River Rd., Manchester Village, VT 05254. ✆ **800/648-4944** or 802/362-2500. Fax 802/362-1107. www.wilburton.com. 35 units, 1 with detached private bathroom. Midweek $115–$205 double; weekends $150–$250 double; holiday and foliage season, $180–$315 double. Rates include breakfast. 2- to 3-night minimum stay on weekends and holidays. AE, MC, V. **Amenities:** Restaurant; outdoor pool; 3 tennis courts. *In room:* A/C, TV (some), hair dryer, iron.

Inexpensive

Dorset Inn ★★ Set in the center of genteel Dorset, this former stagecoach stop was built in 1796 and claims to be the oldest continuously operating inn in Vermont. With 31 rooms, it's fairly large and impersonal (by Vermont standards, that is), and may not give the completely rustic experience you're after, but it's certainly professionally run. The carpeted guest rooms, some of which are in a well-crafted addition built in the 1940s, are furnished in an upscale country style, with a mix of reproductions and antiques, including canopied and sleigh beds. All rooms are air-conditioned, though only the two suites and a few other rooms have TVs and telephones.

8 Church St. at Rte. 30, Dorset, VT 05251. ✆ **877/367-7389** or 802/867-5500. Fax 802/867-5542. www.dorsetinn.com. 31 units. $120–$220 double B&B, $220–$330 double MAP. Rates include breakfast. AE, MC, V. No pets. No children under 5. **Amenities:** Restaurant; pub. *In room:* A/C, no phone (most).

Palmer House Resort ★ This is actually a motel, but several notches above the run-of-the-mill. Owned and operated by the same family for nearly 50 years, its rooms are furnished with antiques and other unexpected niceties. Ask for one of the somewhat larger rooms in the newer rear building. Added in 2000 were eight spacious suites, each with a gas fireplace, wet bar, and private deck overlooking a trout-stocked pond and the mountains beyond. The buildings are set on 22 nicely tended acres, and the motel even has its own small golf course. (No charge to play golf or borrow fishing rods.) Rooms tend to book up early in the season.

Rte. 7A, Manchester Center, VT 05255. ✆ **800/917-6245** or 802/362-3600. Fax 802/362-3600. www.palmerhouse.com. 58 units. Summer $85–$175 double; $190–$300 suite. 2-night minimum stay some weekends. AE, DISC, MC, V. **Amenities:** Outdoor pool; golf course; 2 tennis courts; Jacuzzi; sauna; fishing pond. *In room:* A/C, TV, fridge, coffeemaker, hair dryer.

WHERE TO DINE

Most inns listed above offer good to excellent dining, often in romantic settings.

Chantecleer ★★★ CONTINENTAL If you like superbly prepared Continental fare, but are put off by the stuffiness of highbrow Euro-wannabe restaurants, this is the place for you. Rustic elegance is the best description for this century-old dairy barn. The oddly tidy exterior, which looks as if it could house a chain restaurant, doesn't offer a clue to how pleasantly romantic the interior is. Swiss-born chef Michel Baumann, who has owned and operated the inn since 1981, changes his menu every 3 weeks. He specializes in game and may feature veal with a roasted garlic, sage, and balsamic demi-glaze, Swiss air-dried beef, veal chops, Wiener schnitzel, or slow-roasted duck with sesame seeds and hoisin sauce. Especially good is the whole Dover sole, which is filleted tableside.

Rte. 7A (3½ miles north of Manchester Center). ✆ **802/362-1616.** Reservations recommended. Main courses $26–$35. AE, MC, V. Wed–Mon 6–9:30pm. Closed Mon in winter and for 2–3 weeks in both Nov and Apr.

Little Rooster Cafe ★ CONTEMPORARY/REGIONAL You've got to love a place where the seats are painted like birds' nests. They really take the farm motif to the extreme at this appealing spot near the outlets, which is open only for breakfast and lunch—but it's the best choice in town for either of these meals. Breakfasts include flapjacks served with real maple syrup, a Cajun omelet, and a luscious corned-beef hash with béchamel sauce (go ahead—your doctor won't know). Lunches feature a creative sandwich selection, such as a commendable roast beef with pickled red cabbage and a horseradish dill sauce.

Rte. 7A S., Manchester Center. ✆ **802/362-3496.** Breakfast items $4.50–$6.75; lunch $6.50–$8.25. No credit cards. Daily 7am–2:30pm. Closed Wed in off season.

Mistral's at Toll Gate ★★ FRENCH The best tables at Mistral's are along the windows, which overlook a lovely creek that's spotlighted at night. In a tollhouse of a long-since-bypassed byway, the restaurant is a romantic mix of modern and old. The menu changes seasonally, with dishes such as salmon cannelloni stuffed with lobster or grilled filet mignon with Roquefort ravioli. The kitchen is run with great aplomb by chef/owner Dana Markey, who does an admirable job ensuring consistent quality. The restaurant has been recognized with the *Wine Spectator* excellence award since 1994.

Toll Gate Rd. (east of Manchester off Rte. 11/30). ✆ **802/362-1779.** Reservations recommended. Main courses $22–$32. AE, MC, V. July–Oct Thurs–Tues 6–10pm; Nov–June Thurs–Mon 6–10pm.

SHOPPING

Manchester Center has the best concentration of high-end outlets in New England. Among the noted retailers are Baccarat, Jones New York, Nine West, Giorgio Armani, Coach, and Cole-Haan. Other retailers include Hickey Freeman, Brooks Brothers, Crabtree & Evelyn, Levi's, Movado, Giorgio Armani, Timberland, and J. Crew. The shops are in tasteful minimall clusters in and around a T-intersection in the heart of Manchester Center. Hungry from all the shopping? There's an outdoor scoop shop purveying Ben & Jerry's ice cream in season.

The **Orvis Company Store** ★ (✆ **802/362-3750**) is between Manchester and Manchester Center and sells housewares, men's and women's clothing, both for daily wear and sturdy outdoor clothing, and—of course—fly-fishing equipment. Two small ponds just outside the shop allow prospective customers to try the gear before buying. A sale room, with even more deeply discounted items, is directly behind the main store.

2 Brattleboro & the Southern Green Mountains

Brattleboro is 105 miles NW of Boston and 148 miles SE of Burlington.

The hills and valleys around the bustling town of Brattleboro in Vermont's southeast corner have some of the state's best-hidden treasures. Driving along the main valley floors—on roads along the West or Connecticut rivers, or on Route 100—tends to be fast and only moderately interesting. To really soak up the region's flavor, turn off the main roads and wander up and over rolling ridges into the narrow folds in mountains hiding peaceful villages. If it looks as though the landscape hasn't changed all that

Tips Looking for More Information?

The best source of information for the region is the great **state visitor center** (✆ **802/254-4593**) right off I-91 in Guilford, south of Brattleboro; you can only reach it by traveling north on I-91, however, not south. This beautiful building, inspired by Vermont's barns, is filled with maps, brochures, and videos on activities in the region. Helpful staff dole out up-to-the-minute information, make reservations, and otherwise guide you. There are even bake sales outside in good weather, and the vending machines and spotless bathrooms are priceless to traveling families.

much in the past 2 centuries, well, you're right. It really hasn't.

THE WILMINGTON/MOUNT SNOW REGION ★

Wilmington has a nice selection of antiques shops, boutiques, and pizza joints. Except on busy holiday weekends when it's inundated by visitors driving oversize SUVs, Wilmington feels like a gracious mountain village untroubled by modern times. From Wilmington, the ski resort of Mount Snow/Haystack is easily accessible via Route 100 which is brisk, busy, and close to impassable on sunny weekends in early October. Heading north, you'll first pass through West Dover, an attractive, classic New England town with a prominent steeple and acres of white clapboard.

ESSENTIALS

GETTING THERE Wilmington is at the junction of Route 9 and Route 100. Route 9 offers the most direct access. The Mount Snow area is north of Wilmington on Route 100.

VISITOR INFORMATION The **Mount Snow Valley Chamber of Commerce** (✆ **877/887-6884** or 800/451-4211; www.visitvermont.com) maintains a visitor center at 21 W. Main St. in Wilmington. Open year-round daily from 10am to 5pm, the chamber offers a room-booking service, which is helpful for smaller inns and B&Bs. For on-mountain accommodations, check with the **Mount Snow Lodging Bureau and Vacation Service** (✆ **800/245-7669**).

THE MARLBORO MUSIC FESTIVAL

The renowned **Marlboro Music Festival** ★★★ has classical concerts, performed by accomplished masters as well as highly talented younger musicians, on weekends from mid-July to mid-August in the agreeable town of Marlboro, east of Wilmington on Route 9. The retreat was founded in 1951 and has hosted countless noted musicians, including Pablo Casals, who participated between 1960 and 1973. Concerts take place in the 700-seat auditorium at Marlboro College, and advance ticket purchases are strongly recommended. Call or write for a schedule and a ticket order form. Ticket prices usually range from about $15 to $30. Between September and June, contact the festival's winter office at Marlboro Music, 135 S. 18th St., Philadelphia, PA 19103 (✆ **215/569-4690**). In summer, write Marlboro Music, Box K, Marlboro, VT 05344, or call the box office (✆ **802/254-2394**). The website is **www.marlboromusic.org**.

MOUNTAIN BIKING

Mount Snow was among the first resorts to foresee the widespread appeal of mountain biking, and the region remains one of the leading destinations for those whose vehicle of choice has knobby tires. The first mountain-bike school in the country was established here in 1988 and still offers a roster of classes that are especially helpful to novices. Clinics and guided tours are also available.

Mount Snow Sports (✆ **802/464-4040**), at the Grand Summit Hotel, offers bike rentals, maps, and advice from late May to mid-October. The resort has some 45 miles of trails; bikers can explore an additional 140 miles of trails and abandoned roads that lace the region. For a fee, take your bike to the mountaintop by gondola and coast your way down along marked trails, or earn the ride by pumping out the vertical rise to the top. Fanning out from the mountain are numerous abandoned town roads that make for less challenging, but no less pleasant excursions.

DOWNHILL SKIING

Mount Snow ★ Mount Snow is noted for its widely cut runs on the front face (disparaged by some as "vertical golf courses"), yet also remains an excellent destination for intermediates and advanced intermediates. More advanced skiers migrate to the North Face, which is its own little world of bumps and glades. This is also an excellent spot for snowboarding. Because it's the closest Vermont ski area to Boston and New York (a 4-hr. drive from Manhattan), however, the mountain can be especially crowded on weekends—and lift ticket prices have surged in recent years.

Mount Snow's village is attractively arrayed along the base of the mountain. The most imposing structure is the balconied hotel overlooking a small pond, but the overall character is shaped more by the unobtrusive smaller lodges and homes. Once famed for its groovy singles scene, the hill's post-skiing activities have mellowed somewhat and embraced the family market, although 20-somethings will still find a good selection of après-ski activities.

Mount Snow, VT 05356. ✆ **800/245-7669** or 802/464-2151. www.mountsnow.com. Vertical drop: 1,700 ft. Lifts: 18 chairlifts (3 high-speed), 5 surface lifts. Skiable acreage: 749. Adult day lift tickets Mon–Fri $61; Sat–Sun and holidays $69–$71.

WHERE TO STAY

Deerhill Inn and Restaurant ★ The Deerhill Inn, on a hillside above Route 100 with views of the rolling mountains, was built as a ski lodge in 1954, but always helpful innkeepers Linda and Michael Anelli have given it a more gracious country gloss. In summer, it features attractive gardens and a stonework pool; in winter, the slopes are a short drive away. Guests have access to two comfortable sitting areas upstairs, stocked with a television and books. The guest rooms vary from very cozy to reasonably spacious, and most are decorated with a light country flair; four are in a motel-like addition with balconies. The best of the lot are rooms nos. L1 and L2, both of which have cathedral ceilings.

14 Valley View Rd. (P.O. Box 136), West Dover, VT 05356. ✆ **800/993-3379** or 802/464-3100. Fax 802/464-5474. www.deerhill.com. 14 units. $140–$335 double; $260–$370 suite. Rates include breakfast. 2-night minimum stay on weekends. AE, MC, V. Children 8 and older welcome. **Amenities:** Restaurant; outdoor pool; bike rental; massage (advance notice). *In room:* Jacuzzis (some), fireplaces (some), no phone.

The Hermitage Inn ★★ I love this place not so much for its unpretentious sense of style—the 19th century as interpreted by the 1940s—but for the way it combines the stately with the quirky. On 25 acres of meadow and woodland, the inn feels a bit like one of those British summer estates that P. G. Wodehouse wrote about. Out back are cages filled with game birds, some quite exotic, which are raised for eating, hunting, and show. The guest rooms are designed to satisfy basic comfort more than a thirst for elegance, and some are a bit past their prime. But they're still far from shabby—and the faded charm is part of the inn's appeal.

20 Handle Rd., Wilmington, VT 05363. ✆ **802/464-3511.** Fax 802/464-2688. www.hermitageinn.com. 15 units. Winter $185 double; rest of the year $125 double. Rates include breakfast and dinner. 2- or 3-night minimum stay on weekends and holidays in winter. AE, MC, V. $15 charge for dogs. **Amenities:** Restaurant; cross-country ski center; trout pond. *In room:* TV.

Inn at Quail Run ★ *Kids* Quail Run is a hybrid of the sort New England could use more of: an intimate B&B that welcomes families (and even pets). Set on 13 acres in the hills east of Route 100, the converted ski lodge features guest rooms in a contemporary country style. Family accommodations include king-size and bunk beds; the standard rooms are motel-size, and four have gas fireplaces. The inn also sports an attractive heated outdoor pool and eight-person Jacuzzi.

106 Smith Rd., Wilmington, VT 05363. ✆ **800/343-7227** or 802/464-3362. www.theinnatquailrun.com. 13 units. Summer $110–$180 double; foliage season $115–$210 double; ski season $115–$190 double. Rates include full breakfast. 3-night minimum stay holiday weekends; 2-night minimum stay foliage season. AE, DISC, MC, V. Pets allowed in some rooms ($15 per night). **Amenities:** Outdoor pool; Jacuzzi; sauna; game room. *In room:* TV.

Inn at Sawmill Farm ★★ The Inn at Sawmill Farm is a Relais & Châteaux property spread over 28 acres, and one of the first inns in New England to cater to affluent travelers. (The impressive wine cellar is a tip-off.) Guest rooms in this old farmhouse, parts of which date back to 1797, are distinctive, but all share a similar look, with contemporary country styling and Colonial reproduction furniture. Among the best are Cider House No. 2, with its rustic beams and oversize canopy bed, and the Woodshed, a quiet cottage with a beautiful brick fireplace and a cozy loft. In recent years the inn has lost a bit of its burnish, and service is not as good as it could be, especially given the high room rates.

Crosstown Rd. and Rte. 100 (P.O. Box 367), West Dover, VT 05356. ✆ **802/464-8131.** Fax 802/464-1130. www.theinnatsawmillfarm.com. 21 units. $375–$850 double MAP; foliage season $450–$900 MAP. Rates include breakfast and dinner. AE, DC, MC, V. Closed Apr–May. **Amenities:** Restaurant (see below); outdoor pool; tennis court. *In room:* A/C, hair dryer, iron/ironing board, no phone or TV.

Trail's End ★ Just a short drive off Route 100 on 10 nicely tended acres, this establishment is an updated 1960s ski lodge with attractive rooms and abundant common space. The guest rooms are spotlessly clean and styled in a modern country fashion. Six feature fireplaces, two have Jacuzzis, and the suites are perfect for midwinter cocooning, with microwaves, refrigerators, and VCRs. The best? Maybe it's room no. 6, with a lovely fireplace and nice oak accents. Other good spots to linger include the main common room, with a 22-foot stone fireplace, the stone-floored library and game room, and the informal second-floor loft.

5 Trail's End Lane (look for the turn between Haystack and Mount Snow), Wilmington, VT 05363. ✆ **800/859-2585** or 802/464-2727. www.trailsendvt.com. 15 units. Summer $110–$160 double; winter and holidays $130–$200 double. Rates include breakfast. 2- to 3-night minimum stay on weekends and holidays. AE, DISC, MC, V. Children 7 and older welcome. **Amenities:** Outdoor pool; tennis court; Jacuzzi; game room. *In room:* TV, no phone.

Vintage Motel *Value* A good budget choice for those planning to spend little time in their rooms, this has basic, motel-size rooms with industrial carpeting, durable furniture, and a few nice touches, such as quilts on the beds and a family room with microwave and VCR. Bathrooms have curious 4-foot-square tubs (with showers), which are weird and appealing at the same time, and this is one of the few budget motels you'll ever book with its own on-site driving range. The place is popular with snowmobilers and skiers in winter.

195 Rte. 9 (P.O. Box 222), Wilmington, VT 05363. ✆ **800/899-9660** or 802/464-8824. www.vintagemotel.net. 18 units. $45–$105 double; $130–$200 suite. 2-night minimum stay some weekends; 3 nights on holidays. AE, DISC, MC, V. Pets allowed in 4 units. **Amenities:** Outdoor pool, driving range. *In room:* TV.

White House of Wilmington ★ This grand Colonial Revival mansion sits atop the crest of an open hill just east of Wilmington. Built in 1915 by a lumber baron, the interior has hardwood floors, arched doorways, and nice detailing throughout. It's often lively and bustling, especially in winter, with cross-country skiers, snowshoers, and snow tubers (there's a great hill out front) all milling about. The guest rooms are simply furnished in Colonial Revival style; nine have wood fireplaces and four have whirlpools. The best choices include room no. 1, a corner unit with fireplace and vintage white-tile bathroom, and room no. 3, which has its own balcony and sitting room with fireplace.

178 Rte. 9, East Wilmington, VT 05363. ✆ **800/541-2135** or 802/464-2135. Fax 802/464-5222. www.whitehouseinn.com. 25 units. Mid-Sept to mid-Dec $145–$285 double; rest of the year $98–$262 double. Rates include breakfast. 2-night minimum stay on weekends. AE, MC, V. Children 8 and older welcome in main inn; all ages welcome in guesthouse. **Amenities:** Outdoor pool; indoor pool; sauna; steam room; snowshoe rental; cross-country ski trails. *In room:* No phone.

WHERE TO DINE

Dot's ★ *Value* DINER Wilmington is justly proud of Dot's, an institution that has stubbornly remained loyal to its longtime clientele, offering good, cheap food in the face of creeping boutique-ification elsewhere in town. (A second, more modern Dot's is in Dover.) This Dot's, right in the village, is a classic, with pine paneling, swivel stools at the counter, and checkerboard linoleum tile. It's famous for its chili and pancakes, but don't overlook other breakfast fare, such as the Cajun skillet—a medley of sausage, peppers, onions, and home fries sautéed and served with eggs and melted Monterey Jack cheese.

West Main St., Wilmington. ✆ **802/464-7284.** Breakfast $2.95–$7.25; lunch $2.75–$7.50; dinner $2.75–$13. DISC, MC, V. Daily 5:30am–8pm (until 9pm Fri–Sat).

Inn at Sawmill Farm ★★ CONTINENTAL More than 32,000 bottles of wine lurk in the custom-made wine cellar of this inn, which earned a coveted "Grand Award" from *Wine Spectator* magazine. The wine is only one of the reasons the inn consistently attracts well-heeled diners. The food is deftly prepared, with entrees ranging from roasted poussin breast stuffed with shallots and salmon filet with a sorrel cream sauce to potato-crusted sea bass with wild mushrooms, oven-roasted cod, and Indonesian curried chicken breast. A new bistro menu adds lighter items such as skate wing and grilled pork loin. The converted barn-and-farmhouse atmosphere is romantic, the service superb.

Crosstown Rd. and Rte. 100, West Dover. ✆ **802/464-8131.** www.theinnatsawmillfarm.com. Reservations recommended. Main courses $28–$39; prix fixe $44; bistro prix fixe $30. AE, DC, MC, V. Daily 6–9:30pm. Closed mid-Apr to Memorial Day weekend.

Maple Leaf Malt & Brewing Co. PUB FARE This is the place for those nights you don't feel like anything fancy, but Dot's is a bit too, well, authentic for your mood. This neighborly bar, just around the corner from Dot's, serves oversize sandwiches, burgers, wraps, and the occasional pasta special. All perfectly fine if unexciting, the food makes a nice accompaniment to the 16 brews crafted on the far side of the glass walls in the downstairs dining room.

3 N. Main St., Wilmington. ✆ **802/464-9900.** Main courses $6.95–$16. AE, DISC, MC, V. Daily 11:30am–10pm (sometimes later).

BRATTLEBORO ★

Set in a scenic river valley, the commercial town of Brattleboro is not just a good spot for provisioning; it has a funky, slightly dated charm that's part 19th century, part 1960s. The rough brick texture of this compact, hilly city has aged nicely, its flavor enhanced since its adoption by ex-flower children who moved here, grew up, cut their hair, and settled in, operating many of the best local enterprises.

ESSENTIALS

GETTING THERE From the north or south, Brattleboro is easily accessible by car via exits 1 and 2 on I-91. From the east or west, Brattleboro is best reached via Route 9. Brattleboro is also a stop on the **Amtrak** (✆ **800/872-7245**) line from Boston to northern Vermont.

VISITOR INFORMATION The **Brattleboro Chamber of Commerce,** 180 Main St. (✆ **877/254-4565** or 802/254-4565; www.brattleborochamber.org), provides travel information year-round, Monday through Friday between 8:30am and 5pm.

EXPLORING THE TOWN

The commercially vibrant downtown is blessedly compact, and strolling is the best way to appreciate its human scale and handsome commercial architecture. A town of cafes, bookstores, antiques stores, and outdoor recreation shops, it invites browsing. One shop of note is **Sam's Outdoor Outfitters,** 74 Main St. (✆ **802/254-2933**), filled to the eaves with camping and fishing gear.

Enjoyable for kids and curious adults is the **Brattleboro Museum & Art Center** (✆ **802/257-0124;** www.brattleboromuseum.org) at the Union Railroad Station, 10 Vernon St. (it's the stone building downtown near the bridge to New Hampshire). Wonderful exhibits highlight the history of the town and the Connecticut River Valley. The museum is open from mid-May to early February, Wednesday through Monday from 11am to 5pm. Admission is $4 for adults, $3 for seniors, $2 for students, and free for children under 18.

About 1½ miles outside of town on Route 30 is **Tom and Sally's Handmade Chocolates,** 485 W. River Rd. (✆ **802/254-4200**), a boutique chocolate shop with delicious handmade confections. Of note is the chocolate body-paint kit, which comes complete with two brushes. Tours are given daily (except Sun) between 10am and 2pm; they cost $5 per adult, $2 per child.

OUTDOOR PURSUITS

A soaring aerial view of Brattleboro can be found atop **Wantastiquet Mountain,** which is just across the Connecticut River in New Hampshire (figure on a round-trip of about 3 hr.). To reach the base of the "mountain" (a term that's just slightly grandiose), cross the river on the two green steel bridges, then turn left on the first dirt road; go ⅕ mile to a parking area on your right. The trail begins here via a carriage road (stick to the main trail and avoid the side trails) that winds about 2 miles through forest and past open ledges to the summit, which is marked by a monument dating from 1908. From here, you'll be rewarded with sweeping views of the river, the town, and the landscape beyond.

Vermont Canoe Touring Center (✆ **802/257-5008**) is at the intersection of Route 5 and the West River north of town. This is a fine spot to rent a canoe or kayak to poke around for a couple of hours, half a day, or a full day. Explore locally, or arrange for a shuttle upriver or down. The owners are helpful about providing information and maps to keep you on track. Among the best spots, especially for birders, are the marshy areas along the lower West River and a detour off the Connecticut River locally called "the Everglades." Get a lunch to go at the Brattleboro Food Co-op (see "Where to Dine," below) and make a day of it.

Bike rentals and advice on day-trip destinations are available at the **Brattleboro Bicycle Shop,** 165 Main St. (✆ **800/272-8245** or 802/254-8644; www.bratbike.com). Hybrid bikes ideal for exploring area back roads can be rented by the day ($25) or week ($125).

WHERE TO STAY

Several chain motels flank Route 5 north of Brattleboro. The top choice is **Quality Inn & Suites,** 1380 Putney Rd. (✆ **866/254-8701** or 802/254-8701; www.qualityinnbrattleboro.com), featuring a restaurant and indoor/outdoor pool. Double rooms run $49 to $129, depending on size and season.

Chesterfield Inn ★★ Just a 10-minute drive east of Brattleboro in New Hampshire, this attractive inn sits in a field just off a busy state highway, but inside it's more quiet and refined than you would imagine. The original farmhouse dates back to the 1780s, but has been expanded and modernized and today has a casual contemporary sensibility with antique accents. Nine guest rooms are located in the main inn, and six in cottages nearby. All are spacious and comfortably appointed with a mix of modern and antique furniture. Eight have wood-burning fireplaces, and two have gas fireplaces. The two priciest units have fireplaces, double Jacuzzis, and a private deck with mountain and meadow views.

Rte. 9, Chesterfield, NH 03443. ✆ **800/365-5515** or 603/256-3211. Fax 603/256-6131. www.chesterfieldinn.com. 15 units. $150–$295 double; foliage season and holidays $175–$320 double. 2-night minimum stay foliage season and holidays. AE, DC, DISC, MC, V. Pets allowed with prior permission. **Amenities:** Restaurant; babysitting. *In room:* A/C, TV, dataport, minibar, coffeemaker, hair dryer, iron.

Colonial Motel & Spa *Value* Operated by the same family since 1975, this sprawling compound is well maintained and offers the town's best value. Opt for the back building's larger and quieter rooms, which are furnished with armchairs and sofas. The motel's best feature is the 75-foot indoor lap pool in the spa building. ***Note:*** Skiers who present their lift tickets receive a $20 discount.

Putney Rd., Brattleboro, VT 05301. ✆ **800/239-0032** or 802/257-7733. www.colonialmotelspa.com. 73 units. $60–$140 double and suite. Rates include continental breakfast (served Mon–Fri only). AE, DISC, MC, V. Take Exit 3 off I-91; turn right and proceed ½ mile. **Amenities:** Restaurant (Italian); indoor pool; Jacuzzi; sauna. *In room:* A/C, TV.

Forty Putney Road ★★ Built in the early 1930s, this compact French château–style home has five guest rooms, including one two-room suite in an adjacent cottage. All are attractively appointed with a mix of modern country furnishings and reproductions. Two units have gas fireplaces; room no. 4 is a spacious minisuite. The cottage suite, with a foldaway sofa in the living room, is popular with small families

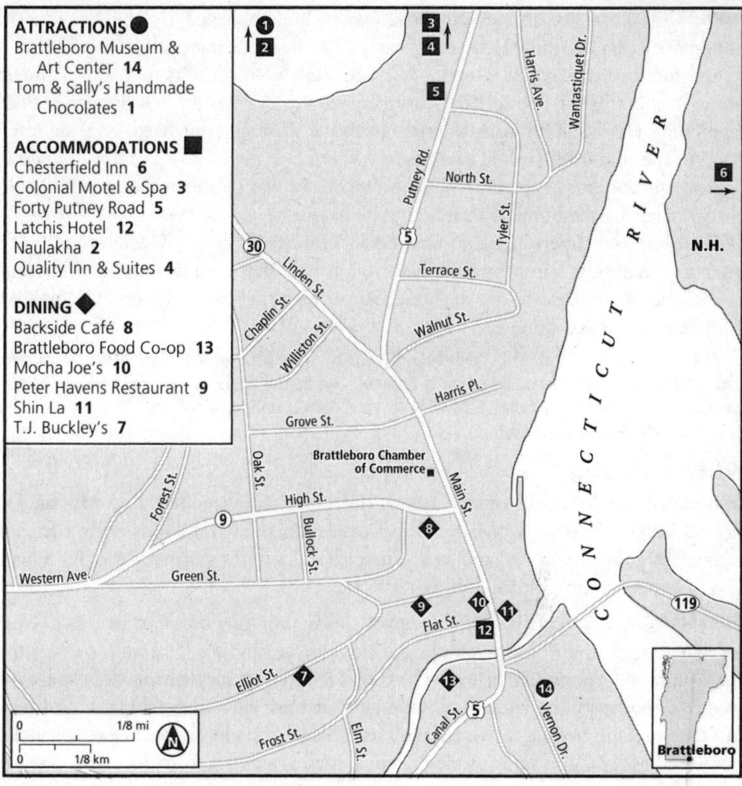

and pairs of couples traveling together. The inn is a short stroll to town, but is situated along a busy road.

40 Putney Rd., Brattleboro, VT 05301. ✆ **800/941-2413** or 802/254-6268. Fax 802/258-2673. www.putney.net/40putneyrd. 5 units. $120–$219 double; $215–$250 cottage. Rates include breakfast. AE, DISC, MC, V. Pets allowed with prior permission. **Amenities:** Pub. *In room:* A/C, TV/VCR, dataport, fridge, hair dryer, iron.

Latchis Hotel ★ *Value* This downtown hotel fairly leaps out in Victorian-brick Brattleboro. Built in 1938 in an understated Art Deco style, the Latchis was once the cornerstone for a small chain of hotels and theaters. It no longer has its own orchestra or commanding dining room (though the theater remains), but it still has an authentic if funky and somewhat outdated flair. That may be one reason construction scaffolding sometimes covers the side. For the most part, the guest rooms are compact and comfortable, if not luxurious. About two-thirds of the rooms have limited views of the river, although those come with the sounds of cars on Main Street. If you want quiet, sacrifice the view and ask for a room in back. From the hotel, it's easy to explore town on foot.

50 Main St., Brattleboro, VT 05301. ✆ **800/798-6301** or 802/254-6300. www.brattleboro.com/latchis. 30 units. $75–$125 double, $115–$165 suite; foliage season, $85–$155 double, $145–$180 suite. AE, MC, V. **Amenities:** Restaurant; movie theater. *In room:* A/C, TV, fridge, coffeemaker.

Naulakha ★ This unique property, owned and managed by the British-based Landmark Trust, is available for rent only by the week during peak season. (It can be rented for shorter stays in winter.) What makes this forthright, two-story shingled home in the hills outside of Brattleboro so extraordinary is its rich literary heritage. The home was built for British writer Rudyard Kipling, who lived here for several years in the mid-1890s while working on *The Jungle Book* and *Captains Courageous.* Kipling never quite fit in rural Vermont, where he was considered eccentric. He left abruptly, selling the home with much of its furniture.

Naulakha is a superb place to unwind in summer, with its 55-acre grounds. The price may cause the fainthearted to blanch, but note that even during the prime summer season, the rate works out to about $90 per night per room. Three bedrooms have twin beds; one has a double.

Landmark Trust, R.R. 1, Box 510, Brattleboro, VT 05301. ✆ **802/254-6868.** Fax 802/257-7783. www.landmarktrust.co.uk. 1 4-bedroom house (up to 8 people). Summer–fall $2,450–$2,780 per week; winter–spring available per night (minimum 3 nights) $233–$258 per night. Rates are estimated; billing is in British pounds. MC, V. Pets allowed. **Amenities:** Tennis court.

WHERE TO DINE

In addition to the choices listed below, the subterranean coffee shop **Mocha Joe's** (✆ **802/257-7794**) at 82 Main St. is a collection point for locals with a friendly, funky feel, good cup of joe, and fresh-squeezed -ades in the summertime. Try a maple latté if you're looking for something different.

Backside Café ★ AMERICAN A great choice for either breakfast or lunch. Nothing fancy here; everything is simple and homemade, and it's less, well, *crunchy* than the Common Ground (see below). The cafe is in an open, airy second-floor space with wooden booths in the back of a building that once housed a Chrysler dealership. Lunches include familiar favorites such as grilled ham and Swiss cheese, spicy chili, homemade soups, and some modest exotica, such as spinach, tomato, and roasted red pepper on focaccia.

Midtown Mall, 22 High St. (between High and Elliot sts., off the public parking lot). ✆ **802/257-5056.** Main courses $1.75–$4.75 at breakfast, $3.25–$5.25 at lunch. AE, DISC, MC, V. Mon–Fri 7:30am–3:30pm; Sat 8am–3:30pm; Sun 9am–3pm.

Brattleboro Food Co-op ★ DELI This co-op has been selling wholesome foods since 1975, and its location, in a small strip mall downtown near the New Hampshire bridge, has plenty of parking (it's a bit tricky to spot from the main road). The huge store has a deli counter great for takeout; snag a quick, filling lunch that won't necessarily be tofu and sprouts—you can get a smoked turkey and Swiss cheese sandwich, or opt for a crispy salad. Check out the eclectic wine selection and the cheeses in the store section, too, especially the award-winning Vermont Shepherd cheeses, made nearby in Putney. Other interesting finds here include natural bath products, house-made sausages, and hand-cut steaks.

Brookside Plaza, 2 Main St. ✆ **802/257-0236.** Sandwiches $3.50–$6; prepared foods around $4–$5 per pound. MC, V. Mon–Sat 8am–9pm; Sun 9am–9pm.

Peter Havens Restaurant ★★ REGIONAL/AMERICAN Chef-owned Peter Havens has been serving up reliable fare since 1989. Situated downtown in a pleasantly contemporary building, Peter Havens may not bowl you over with its menu, but you'll be impressed by what you're served. You're likely to feel instantly at home in this friendly spot, which has just 10 tables. Meals are prepared with choice ingredients and served with panache. Seafood is the specialty, with such offerings as salmon with a chipotle pepper rémoulade. The jazz playing in the background makes a nice accompaniment.

32 Elliot St. © **802/257-3333.** Reservations strongly recommended. Main courses $19–$24. MC, V. Tues–Sat 6–9pm.

Shin La *Value* KOREAN/JAPANESE With wooden booths and mismatched furniture, Shin La has the character of a pizza shop, but consistently good fare. Half the menu features a range of sushi rolls and plates, along with other traditional Japanese bar fare such as yakitori, katsus, and tempura; the other half, meanwhile offers something pretty hard to find in New England: simple Korean country fare such as *bool ko ki* (sliced sirloin) and *shu mai* (steamed dumplings). Meals are both tasty and inexpensive.

57 Main St. © **802/257-5226.** Entrees $5.50–$9.75. MC. V. Mon–Sat 11am–9pm.

T. J. Buckley's ★★★ NEW AMERICAN Brattleboro's best restaurant, and one of the better choices in all of Vermont, the Lilliputian T. J. Buckley's is housed in a classic old diner on a dim side street. Renovations such as slate floors and golden lighting have created an intimate restaurant that seats about 20. No secrets exist between the chef, the sous-chef, and the server, all of whom work within a couple dozen feet of one another (and you) throughout the meal—the entire place is smaller than the kitchen of many restaurants. The menu is limited, with just four entrees each night—beef, poultry, shellfish, and fish. Ingredients are fresh and select, the preparation concerned more with subtly melding flavors than dazzling with architectural flourishes.

132 Elliot St. © **802/257-4922.** Reservations strongly recommended. Main courses $25–$32. No credit cards. Winter Thurs–Sun 6–9pm; rest of year Wed–Sun 6–9pm (sometimes later on busy nights).

NEWFANE ★ & TOWNSHEND ★

These two villages, about 5 miles apart on Route 30, are the picture-perfect epitome of Vermont. Set within the serpentine West River Valley, both are built around town greens. Both towns contain impressive white-clapboard homes and public buildings that share the grace and scale of the surrounding homes. And both boast striking examples of Early American architecture, notably Greek Revival.

Don't bother looking for strip malls, McDonald's, or video outlets hereabouts. Newfane and Townshend feel as though they've idled on a sidetrack for decades while the rest of America steamed blithely ahead. For visitors, inactivity is often the activity of choice. Guests find an inn or lodge that suits their temperament, then spend days strolling the towns, undertaking aimless back-road driving tours, soaking in a mountain stream, hunting up antiques at the many shops, or striking off on foot for one of the rounded, wooded peaks that overlook villages and valleys.

ESSENTIALS

GETTING THERE Newfane and Townshend are located on Route 30 northwest of Brattleboro. The nearest interstate access is off Exit 3 from I-91.

VISITOR INFORMATION No formal information center serves these towns. Brochures are available at the **state visitor center** (© **802/254-4593**) on I-91 in Guilford, south of Brattleboro. The website **www.newfanevermontusa.com** provides good local information.

EXPLORING THE AREA

Newfane was originally founded on a hill a few miles from the current village in 1774; in 1825, it was moved to its present location on a valley floor. Some of the original

Fun Fact Maple Syrup & How It Gets That Way

Maple syrup is at once simple and extravagant: simple, as it's made from the purest ingredients available; extravagant, as it's an expensive luxury.

Two elemental ingredients combine to create maple syrup: sugar-maple sap and fire. Sugaring season slips in between northern New England's long winter and short spring; it usually lasts around 4 or 5 weeks, typically beginning in early to mid-March. When warm and sunny days alternate with freezing nights, the sap in the maple trees begins to run from roots to the branches overhead. Sugarers drill shallow holes into the trees and insert small taps. Buckets (or plastic tubing) are hung from the taps to collect the sap that drips out bit by bit.

The collected sap is then boiled off. The equipment for this ranges from a simple backyard fire pit cobbled together of concrete blocks to elaborate sugarhouses with oil or propane burners. It requires between 32 and 40 gallons of sap to make 1 gallon of syrup, and that means a fair amount of boiling. The real cost of syrup isn't the sap; it's in the fuel to boil it down.

Vermont is the nation's capital of maple syrup, producing some 550,000 gallons a year, with a value of about $12 million. The fancier inns and restaurants serve native maple syrup with breakfast. Other breakfast places charge $1 or so for real syrup, rather than the flavored corn syrup that's so prevalent elsewhere. (You may have to ask if the real stuff is available.)

You can pick up the real thing in almost any grocery store in the state, but I'm convinced it tastes better if you buy it right from the farm. Look for handmade signs touting syrup posted at the end of driveways around the region throughout the year. Drive on up and knock on the door.

A number of sugarers invite visitors to inspect the process and sample some of the fresh syrup in the early spring. Ask for the brochure "Maple Sugarhouses Open to Visitors," available at information centers, or by writing or calling the **Vermont Agency of Agriculture, Food, and Markets** (Drawer 20, 116 State St., Montpelier, VT 05620; ✆ **802/828-2416;** www.vermontagriculture.com). The list is also posted online at **www.vermontmaple.org** by the **Vermont Maple Sugar Makers' Association** in South Royalton (✆ **802/763-7435**).

buildings were dismantled and rebuilt, but most date from the early to mid–19th century. The **National Historic District** ★★ is comprised of some 60 buildings around the green and on nearby side streets. You'll find styles ranging from Federal through Colonial Revival, although Greek Revival dominates. A strikingly handsome courthouse—where cases have been heard for nearly 2 centuries—dominates the shady green. This structure was originally built in 1825; the imposing portico was added in 1853. For more details on area buildings, get a copy of the free walking-tour brochure at the Moore Free Library on West Street or at the Historical Society (see below).

Explore Newfane's history at the engaging **Historical Society of Windham County** ★ on Route 30 across from the village common. Housed in a handsome

1930s Colonial Revival brick building, it has an eclectic assemblage of local artifacts (dolls, melodeons, rail ephemera), along with changing exhibits that give intriguing snippets of local history. Open from late May to mid-October, Wednesday through Sunday from noon to 5pm; admission by donation.

More than two dozen **antiques shops** on or near Route 30 in the West River Valley allow for good grazing on lazy afternoons; they are also fine resources for serious collectors. At any of the shops, look for the free brochure *Antiquing in the West River Valley,* which provides a good overview of what's out there.

Treasure hunters should time their visit to coincide with the **Newfane Flea Market** ★ (✆ **802/365-7771**), which features 100-plus tables of assorted stuff, including some of the 12-tube-socks-for-8-bucks variety. The flea market is held on Sundays from May through October on Route 30 just north of Newfane Village.

On Route 30 between Townshend and Jamaica, you'll pass the **Scott Covered Bridge** ★ below the Townshend Dam. It dates from 1870 and is an example of a Town lattice-style bridge with an added arch. At 166 feet, it's the longest single-span bridge in the state.

OUTDOOR PURSUITS

Townshend State Park (✆ **802/365-7500**) and Townshend State Forest are at the foot of Bald Mountain, 3 miles outside Townshend. The park is a solidly built campground constructed by the Civilian Conservation Corps in the 1930s. Park here to hike **Bald Mountain,** one of the better short hikes in the region. A 3.1-mile loop trail begins behind the ranger station, following a bridle path along a brook. The ascent soon gets steeper, and at 1.7 miles, you arrive at the 1,680-foot summit, which is not bald at all. Open ledges offer views toward Mount Monadnock to the east and Bromley and Stratton mountains to the west. The descent is a steeper 1.4-mile trail that ends behind the campground. Open from early May to Columbus Day; the park charges a small day-use fee, and camping costs $14 to $21 per site. Ask for trail maps at the park office. To get to the park, cross the Townshend Dam (off Rte. 30), then turn left and continue to the park sign.

WHERE TO STAY & DINE

Four Columns Inn ★★ You can't help but notice the Four Columns Inn in Newfane: It's the regal, white-clapboard building with four Ionic columns just off the green. This perfect village setting hides an appealing inn within. Rooms in the Main House and Garden Wing are larger (and more expensive) than those above the restaurant. Four units have been made over as luxury suites, with double Jacuzzis. The best choice in the house may be room no. 12, with a Jacuzzi, skylight, gas fireplace, sitting area, and private deck with a view of a small pond. Out of doors, the inn owns 150 acres of property interlaced by hiking trails.

21 West St. (P.O. Box 278), Newfane, VT 05345. ✆ **800/787-6633** or 802/365-7713. Fax 802/365-0022. www.fourcolumnsinn.com. 15 units. Weekdays $160–$225 double; $265–$385 suite. Rates include continental breakfast. AE, DISC, MC, V. Pets allowed with prior permission ($10 per pet per night). **Amenities:** Restaurant; outdoor pool; hiking trails; babysitting. *In room:* A/C, hair dryer.

Three Mountain Inn ★★ The lovely Three Mountain Inn is in the middle of the appealing village of Jamaica, in a historic white clapboard home. It has benefited from a major upgrading under ambitious innkeepers, who are refurbishing the rooms one by one in a restrained country style. Accommodations range from cozy and basic to the outright sumptuous, with whirlpools and gas fireplaces. The inn is a good base for exploring southern Vermont; in winter, skiing at Stratton is a short drive away. Guests can walk from the inn to Jamaica State Park and from there follow an easy and serpentine hike along the river on an old rail bed. The **dining room** ★★ serves wonderful prix-fixe meals.

Rte. 30 (P.O. Box 180), Jamaica, VT 05343. ✆ **800/532-9399** or 802/874-4140. Fax 802/874-4745. www.threemountaininn.com. 15 units. $165–$235 double; $295 suite; $325 cottage. Rates include breakfast. AE, MC, V. Pets allowed with restrictions (call first). Children 12 and older welcome. **Amenities:** Restaurant. *In room:* A/C, TV/VCR, dataport, hair dryer.

Windham Hill Inn ★★★ This inn is about as good as it gets, especially if you're in search of a romantic getaway. Situated on 160 acres at the end of a dirt road in a high upland valley, the inn was built in 1823 as a farmhouse and remained in the same family until the 1950s, when it was converted to an inn. The inn today melds the best of the old and new. The guest rooms are wonderfully appointed in an elegant country style; 6 have Jacuzzis or soaking tubs, 9 have balconies or decks, 13 have gas fireplaces, and all have views. Especially nice: the Jesse Lawrence Room, with soaking tub and gas woodstove, and Forget-Me-Not, with soaking tub and four-poster bed. The excellent **dining room** ★★ features fresh, seasonal menus.

311 Lawrence Dr., West Townshend, VT 05359. ✆ **800/944-4080** or 802/874-4080. Fax 802/874-4702. www.windhamhill.com. 21 units. $195–$380 double; foliage season $245–$435 double. Midweek and off-season rates lower. Rates include breakfast. 2- to 3-night minimum stay on weekends and some holidays. AE, DISC, MC, V. Closed the week prior to Dec 27. Turn uphill across from the country store in West Townshend and climb 1¼ miles to a marked dirt road; turn right and continue to end. Children 12 and older welcome. **Amenities:** Restaurant; outdoor heated pool; clay tennis court; game alcove; 6 miles of groomed cross-country ski trails. *In room:* A/C, hair dryer, iron, Jacuzzi (some).

3 Woodstock & Environs ★

Woodstock is 16 miles W of White River Junction, 140 miles NW of Boston, and 98 miles SE of Burlington.

For more than a century, the resort community of Woodstock has been considered one of New England's most exquisite villages, and its attractiveness has benefited from the largess of some of the country's affluent citizens. Even the surrounding countryside is, by and large, unsullied—you simply can't drive to Woodstock on a route that *isn't* pastoral and scenic. Few New England villages can top Woodstock's sheer grace and elegance. The tidy downtown is compact and neat, populated largely by galleries and boutiques. The superb village green is surrounded by handsome homes, creating what amounts to a comprehensive review of architectural styles from the 19th and early 20th centuries.

In addition to Woodstock, the region also takes in White River Junction and Norwich, two towns of distinctly different lineage along the Connecticut River on the New Hampshire border.

WOODSTOCK ★★

A Vermont senator in the late 19th century noted that "the good people of Woodstock have less incentive than others to yearn for heaven," and that still applies today. Much of the town is on the National Register of Historic Places, and the Rockefeller family has deeded 500 acres surrounding Mount Tom (see below) to the National Park Service. In fact, locals sometimes joke that downtown Woodstock itself could be renamed Rockefeller National Park, given the attention and cash the Rockefeller family has

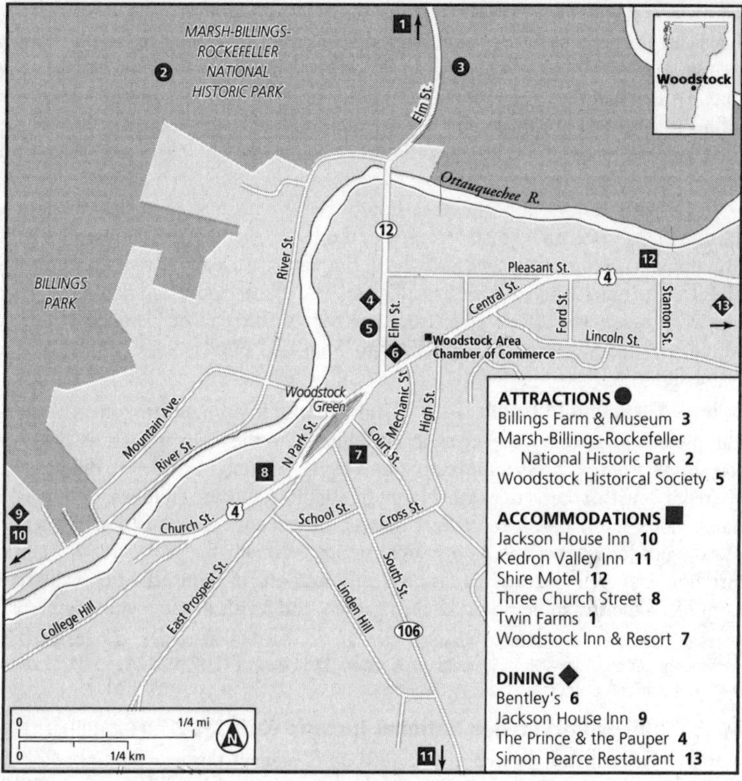

lavished on the town in the interest of preservation. (For starters, Rockefeller money built the faux-historic Woodstock Inn and paid to bury the unsightly utility lines around town.)

Woodstock is also notable as a historic center of winter outdoor recreation. The nation's first ski tow (a rope tow powered by an old Buick motor) was built in 1933 at the Woodstock Ski Hill near today's Suicide Six ski area. While no longer the skiing center of Vermont, Woodstock remains a worthy destination during the winter months for skating, cross-country skiing, and snowshoeing.

ESSENTIALS

GETTING THERE Woodstock is 13 miles west of White River Junction on Route 4 (take Exit 1 off I-89). From the west, Woodstock is 20 miles east of Killington on Route 4. **Vermont Transit** (**© 800/451-3292;** www.vermonttransit.com) provides daily bus service to Woodstock, with connections to Boston and Burlington.

VISITOR INFORMATION The **Woodstock Area Chamber of Commerce,** 18 Central St. (**© 888/496-6378** or 802/457-3555; www.woodstockvt.com), staffs an information booth on the green, open June through October daily from 9:30am to 5:30pm.

EXPLORING THE TOWN

The heart of the town is the shady, elliptical Woodstock Green. The famous Admiral George Dewey spent his later years in Woodstock, and local folks may explain very convincingly that the green was laid out in the shape of Dewey's flagship. This is such a fine and believable explanation for the odd, cigar-shaped green that it causes no small amount of distress to note that the green was in place by 1830, or 7 years before Dewey was born.

To put local history in perspective, stop by the **Woodstock Historical Society** ★, 26 Elm St. (✆ **802/457-1822**). Housed in the 1807 Charles Dana House, this beautiful home has rooms furnished in Federal, Empire, and Victorian styles, and displays of dolls, costumes, and early silver and glass. The Dana House and adjoining buildings with more exhibits are open from late May to the end of October. Hours are Monday through Saturday from 10am to 5pm and Sunday from noon to 4pm. Admission is $5.

Billings Farm and Museum ★★★ This remarkable working farm offers a striking glimpse of a grander era, as well as an introduction to the oddly interesting history of scientific farming. This extraordinary spot was the creation of Frederick Billings, who is credited with completing the Northern Pacific Railroad. (Billings, Montana, is named after him.) The 19th-century dairy farm was once renowned for its scientific breeding of Jersey cows and its fine architecture, especially the gabled 1890 Victorian farmhouse. A tour includes hands-on demonstrations of farm activities, exhibits of farm life, a look at an heirloom kitchen garden, and a visit to active milking barns.

River Rd. (about ½ mile north of town on Rte. 12), P.O. Box 489, Woodstock. ✆ **802/457-2355.** www.billingsfarm.org. Admission $9.50 adults, $8.60 seniors, $7.50 children 13–17, $5 children 5–12, $2 children 3–4, free for children under 3. Apr–Oct daily 10am–5pm.

Marsh-Billings-Rockefeller National Historic Park ★★★ The Billings Farm and the National Park Service have teamed up to manage this new park, the first and only national park focusing on the history of conservation. You'll learn about the life of George Perkins Marsh, the author of *Man and Nature* (1864), considered one of the first and most influential books in the history of the environmental movement. You'll also learn how Woodstock native and rail tycoon Frederick Billings, who read *Man and Nature,* eventually returned and purchased Marsh's boyhood farm, putting into practice many of the principles of good stewardship that Marsh espoused. The property was subsequently purchased by Mary and Laurance Rockefeller, who in 1982 established the nonprofit farm; a decade later, they donated more than 500 acres of forest land and their mansion, filled with exceptional 19th-century landscape art, to the National Park Service. Visitors can tour the elaborate Victorian mansion, walk the graceful carriage roads surrounding Mount Tom, and view one of the oldest professionally managed woodlands in the nation. Mansion tours accommodate a limited number of people; advance reservations are recommended.

54 Elm St. (P.O. Box 178), Woodstock. ✆ **802/457-3368.** www.nps.gov/mabi. Free admission to grounds; mansion tour $6 adults, $3 children 16 and under. Late May to Oct daily 10am–5pm.

WHERE TO STAY

Jackson House Inn ★★★ A comfortable and elegant choice just a 5-minute drive west of the village center, this home was built in 1890 by a lumber baron who hoarded the best wood for himself; the cherry and maple floors are so beautiful, you'll feel guilty for not taking off your shoes. The guest rooms are well appointed with antiques,

Tips Beer Here Now!

In Bridgewater Corners, a few miles west of downtown Woodstock on Route 4—it's just past the junction with Route 100A—sits the newish brewery that is headquarters to the **Long Trail Brewing Co.** (✆ **802/672-5011**; www.longtrail.com). The company's ales are renowned throughout the state of Vermont, and if you visit, you'll soon learn why.

Drop by for some free samples of the various seasonal brews (ask the bartender to set you up), nosh on a basket of free popcorn, buy a six-pack or T-shirt at the small gift shop, or hunker down for some burgers and beer on the patio, enjoying the woodsy views. The surrounding hillsides are especially beautiful in autumn and winter.

though some of the older rooms are rather small. A well-executed 1997 addition created four one-room suites with fireplaces and Jacuzzis. The inn welcomes guests with a series of pleasant surprises, including complimentary evening hors d'oeuvres and champagne and a 3-acre backyard with formal English gardens. This inn deserves three stars for elegance and attentive service; only its location, a stone's throw off a busy stretch of Route 4, detracts from the tranquil surroundings.

114-3 Senior Lane, Woodstock, VT 05091. ✆ **800/448-1890** or 802/457-2065. Fax 802/457-9290. www.jacksonhouse.com. 15 units. $195–$260 double; $290–$380 suite. Rates higher in foliage season. Rates include breakfast. 2-night minimum stay most weekends. AE, MC, V. No children under 14. **Amenities:** Restaurant (see below); fitness room; steam room; limited room service. *In room:* A/C, hair dryer, no phone (except in suites).

Kedron Valley Inn ★★ In a complex of Greek Revival buildings at a country crossroads, 5 miles south of Woodstock, the inn is run by Max and Merrily Comins, a cordial couple who offer guests a mix of history and country style. The attractive guest rooms in three buildings are furnished with both antiques and reproductions, and all have heirloom quilts from Merrily's collection; 15 have wood-burning fireplaces and 4 have Jacuzzis. The rooms in the newer, motel-like log building by the river are equally well furnished (and less expensive), with canopied beds, custom oak woodwork, and fireplaces. Room no. 37 even has a private streamside terrace. Room nos. 12 and 17 are among the most popular; both suites have fireplaces and double Jacuzzis. Some Frommer's readers have noted that the inn's rooms can be on the cool side in deep winter.

Rte. 106, South Woodstock, VT 05071. ✆ **800/836-1193** or 802/457-1473. Fax 802/457-4469. www.kedronvalleyinn.com. 24 units. $133–$299 double; foliage season and Christmas week $171–$337 double. Rates include breakfast. Discounts available spring and midweek. AE, DISC, MC, V. Closed Apr and briefly prior to Thanksgiving. Pets allowed with prior permission. **Amenities:** Restaurant; swimming pond. *In room:* TV, no phone.

Shire Motel ★ The convenient Shire Motel is within walking distance of the green and the rest of the village; with its attractive Colonial decor, it's better appointed than your average motel. The rooms are bright and have more windows than you might expect, most facing the river that runs behind the property. (The downside: thin sheets and some scuffed walls.) At the end of the second-floor porch is an outdoor kitchen where you can sit on rockers overlooking the river and enjoy a cup of coffee. The yellow clapboard house next door has three spacious and modern suites, all with gas fireplaces and Jacuzzis.

46 Pleasant St., Woodstock, VT 05091. ✆ **802/457-2211.** www.shiremotel.com. 36 units. $78–$218 double; $200–$318 suite. AE, MC, V. *In room:* A/C, TV, dataport, fridge.

Three Church Street *Value* A night here feels more like staying at a relative's house than staying at a fancy inn. This sturdy brick Greek Revival B&B with a white clapboard ell is just off the west end of the Woodstock green, and is well situated for launching an exploration of the village. It offers excellent value, especially if you don't mind sharing a bathroom and can overlook small imperfections like the occasional water stain on the ceiling. In the back is a lovely porch overlooking the inn's 3 acres, great for enjoying breakfast or sitting quietly. Guest rooms are furnished comfortably and eclectically with country antiques.

3 Church St., Woodstock, VT 05091. ✆ **802/457-1925.** Fax 802/457-9181. 11 units, 5 share 2 bathrooms. $75–$105 double. Higher rates during foliage season and Christmas week. Rates include breakfast. MC, V. Closed Apr. Pets allowed ($5 per pet per night). **Amenities:** Outdoor pool; tennis court. *In room:* No phone.

Twin Farms ★★★ Twin Farms offers uncommon luxury at an uncommon price. Housed on a 300-acre farm that was once home to Nobel prize–winning novelist Sinclair Lewis and his journalist wife, Dorothy Thompson, this is a very private, exceptionally tasteful small resort. The compound consists of the main inn, with 4 guest rooms, and 10 outlying cottages—which are quite expensive—each with a fireplace. (You can even rent the entire property for $24,000 a night if you're really feeling flush.) The owners are noted art collectors, and some of the work on display includes originals by David Hockney, Roy Lichtenstein, Milton Avery, and William Wegman. Rates here include gourmet meals, an open bar, and use of all the resort's recreational equipment.

Barnard, VT 05031. ✆ **800/894-6327.** www.twinfarms.com. 14 units. $1,050–$1,650 double; $1,650–$2,700 cottage. Rates include all meals and liquor. AE, MC, V. Closed Apr. No children under 18. **Amenities:** Restaurant; lake swimming; 2 tennis courts; fitness center; Jacuzzi; watersports equipment rental; bike rental; game room; concierge; car rental; courtesy car; limited room service; in-room massage. *In room:* A/C, TV/VCR, minibar, coffeemaker, hair dryer, iron.

Woodstock Inn & Resort ★★★ This is central Vermont's best full-scale resort. In an imposing brick structure off the town green, the inn at first glance appears to be a venerable and long-established institution, but it's not—it wasn't built until 1969. The inn adopted a Colonial Revival look well suited for Woodstock. Inside, guests are greeted by a broad stone fireplace and sitting areas tucked throughout the lobby. Guest rooms are tastefully decorated in either country pine or a Shaker-inspired style. The best units, in the wing built in 1991, have plush carpeting, refrigerators, and fireplaces.

14 The Green, Woodstock, VT 05091. ✆ **800/448-7900** or 802/457-1100. Fax 802/457-6699. www.woodstockinn.com. 141 units, 3 suites. $149–$434 double, $360–$664 suite; off season rates lower. Ask about packages. 2-night minimum stay on weekends. AE, MC, V. **Amenities:** 2 restaurants; indoor pool; outdoor pool; golf course; 12 tennis courts; fitness center (squash, racquetball, steam rooms); bike rental; concierge; limited room service; babysitting; laundry service; dry cleaning; cross-country ski trails. *In room:* A/C, TV w/pay movies, dataport, hair dryer, iron, safe.

WHERE TO DINE

Bentley's ★ AMERICAN Bentley's adopts an affluent English gentleman's club feel and is Woodstock's best choice for lunch. The dining room, set beyond an Anglophilic bar, affects a Victorian elegance, but not ostentatiously so. Lunch is the time for one of the juicy burgers or creative sandwiches (grilled chicken in mango sauce with almonds, anyone?). The dinner menu leans more toward resort standards, such as chicken and shrimp pescatore or steak flambéed with Yukon Jack bourbon, but also cracks its doors to slightly more ambitious fare, such as farm-raised duck with apricot and plum sauce. It's very often quite crowded at night, so reserve ahead if you can. At the fine brunch on Sunday, I gravitate toward the New England corned beef hash with poached eggs and hollandaise sauce.

3 Elm St. ✆ **877/457-3232** or 802/457-3232. www.bentleysrestaurant.com. Reservations recommended for parties of 4 or more. Main courses $9–$14 at lunch, $17–$22 at dinner. AE, DC, DISC, MC, V. Mon–Sat 11:30am–9:30pm; Sun 11am–9:30pm. Open later for drinks and dancing on weekends.

Jackson House Inn ★★★ CONTINENTAL The Jackson House dining room is a modern addition to the original inn (see above). Its centerpiece is a 16-foot-high stone fireplace, and it boasts soaring windows with views of the gardens. Once settled, you'll sample some of the most exquisite dishes in New England, ingeniously conceived, deftly prepared, and artfully arranged. The three-course meals begin with offerings such as Maine crabmeat and field greens with shaved fennel. The main courses do an equally good job combining the earthy with the celestial. Expect dishes such as crispy-skin salmon with a shiitake compote, an Angus filet with creamy white-corn polenta and a three-onion marmalade, deep-fried softshell crab, achiote-rubbed lamb loin, or roasted day boat scallops. For dessert, you might find a delicate banana-walnut soufflé or crème brûlée with a cranberry compote. The wine list is extensive.

114-3 Senior Lane. ✆ **800/448-1890** or 802/457-2065. Reservations highly recommended. 3-course prix-fixe dinner about $55; chef's tasting menu about $95. AE, MC, V. Wed–Sun 6–9pm.

The Prince and the Pauper ★★★ NEW AMERICAN It takes a bit of sleuthing to find this place, down Dana Alley (next to the Woodstock Historical Society's Dana House), but it's well worth the effort. This is one of Woodstock's best restaurants, with an intimate but informal setting and great food. It's also a bit more casual than the Jackson House. Ease into the evening with a libation in the taproom, then move over to the rustic but elegant dining room. The menu changes often; you may start with a lobster gazpacho, a piece of barbecued duck, or some seafood crepes, then move on to grilled ahi tuna with sweet-and-sour sauce and a jasmine rice cake, baked swordfish with a roasted pepper aioli, or the house specialty: a boneless rack of lamb baked in puff pastry with spinach and mushroom duxelles. The fixed-price dinner is a good value. Those on a tight budget can enjoy the lounge and the bistro menu.

24 Elm St. ✆ **802/457-1818.** www.princeandpauper.com. Reservations recommended. Prix-fixe dinners $43; bistro prix fixe $13–$20. AE, DISC, MC, V. Sun–Thurs 6–9pm; Fri–Sat 6–9:30pm. Lounge opens at 5pm.

Simon Pearce Restaurant ★★ NEW AMERICAN The setting can't be beat. Housed in a restored 19th-century woolen mill with wonderful views of a waterfall, Simon Pearce is a collage of exposed brick, pine floorboards, and handsome wooden tables and chairs. Meals are served on Simon Pearce pottery and glassware—if you like your place setting, you can buy it afterward at the sprawling retail shop in the mill. The atmosphere is a wonderful concoction of formal and informal. Lunch dishes include madras curry chicken salad, beef and Guinness stew, lamb burgers, and crispy calamari with field green. At dinner, look for entrees such as horseradish-rusted cod, roast duck with mango chutney, roasted chicken with a sage bread pudding, and pan-roasted wild salmon.

The Mill, Quechee. ✆ **802/295-1470.** www.simonpearce.com. Reservations recommended for dinner. Main courses $8.75–$13 at lunch, $22–$28 at dinner. AE, DC, DISC, MC, V. Daily 11:30am–2:45pm and 6–9pm.

4 Killington & Rutland

Killington is 12 miles E of Rutland, 160 miles NW of Boston, and 93 miles SE of Burlington.

In 1937, a travel writer described the town near Killington Peak as "a small village of a church and a few undistinguished houses built on a highway three corners." The rugged and remote area was isolated from Rutland to the west by imposing mountains and accessible only through the daunting Sherburne Pass.

That was before Vermont's second-highest mountain was developed as the Northeast's largest ski area. And before a wide, 5-mile-long access road was slashed through the forest to the mountain's base. And before Route 4 was widened and upgraded, improving access to Rutland. In fact, that early travel writer would be hard-pressed to recognize the region today.

Killington is plainly not the Vermont pictured on calendars and place mats. But the region around the mountain boasts Vermont's most active winter scene, with loads of distractions both on and off the mountain. The area has a frenetic, where-it's-happening feel in winter. (That's not the case in summer, when the vast, empty parking lots can trigger melancholia.) Those most content here are skiers who like their skiing BIG, singles in search of aggressive mingling, and travelers who want a wide selection of amenities and are willing to sacrifice quintessential New England charm for a broader range of diversions.

About a dozen miles to the west, the rough-hewn city of Rutland lacks the immediate charm of other Vermont towns, but has a rich history and an array of convenient services for travelers. If you like the action of Killington but want a lower-budget alternative, bivouacking in Rutland and traveling by day to the ski area is a popular option, with even a ski bus from Rutland to the slopes.

KILLINGTON

Killington lacks a town center, a single place that makes you feel you've arrived. Killington is wherever you park. Since the mountain was first developed for skiing in 1957, dozens of restaurants, hotels, and stores have sprouted along Killington Road to accommodate the legions of snow bunnies who descend upon the area during the skiing season, which typically runs October through May, sometimes into June.

Killington's current owner has heard the complaints about the lack of village ambience and is setting out to make some changes. Until they are made, though, Killington *is* the access road. Brightly lit and highly developed, there's not much to remind visitors of classic Vermont between Route 4 and the base lodge. Suburban-style theme restaurants dot the route (The Grist Mill has a water wheel; Casey's Caboose a red caboose), along with dozens of hotels and condos ranging from high-end fancy to low-end dowdy.

ESSENTIALS

GETTING THERE Killington Road extends southward from Routes 4 and 100 (marked on some maps as Sherburne). It's about 12 miles east of Rutland on Route 4. Many of the inns offer shuttles to the Rutland airport. **Amtrak** (© **800/USA-RAIL;** www.amtrak.com) provides service from New York to Rutland, with connecting shuttles to the mountain and various resorts.

The **Marble Valley Regional Transit District** (© **802/773-3244;** www.thebus.com) operates the **Skibus,** with $2 shuttle rides service between Rutland and Killington daily in winter.

VISITOR INFORMATION The **Killington Chamber of Commerce** (© **800/773-4181** or 802/773-4181; www.killington-chamber.org) has information on lodging and travel packages, and staffs an information booth on Route 4 at the base of the access road, open Monday through Friday from 9am to 5pm, and Saturday through Sunday from 10am to 2pm. For information on accommodations in the area and travel to Killington, contact the **Killington Lodging and Travel Service** (✆ **877/4KTIMES**).

DOWNHILL SKIING

Killington ★★ A love-it or hate-it kind of place, New England's largest and busiest ski area offers a greater vertical drop than any other New England mountain. For the big mountain experience, with lots of evening activities and plenty of challenging terrain, it's a good choice. For a less overwhelming experience and a more local sense of place, more intimate resorts such as Sugarbush, Stowe, and Suicide Six are better options. You'll find the broadest selection of slopes, with trails ranging from long, narrow, old-fashioned runs to killer bumps high on its flanks. Thanks to this diversity, it has long been the destination of choice for serious skiers. That said, it's also the skier's equivalent of the Mall of America: a huge operation run with efficiency and not much personal touch. It's easy to get lost and separated from friends and family, and seems to attract boisterous groups of young adults. To avoid getting lost, ask about free tours of the mountain, led by ski ambassadors based at Snowshed.

Killington, VT 05751. ✆ **877/4KTIMES** for lodging, or 800/734-9435. www.killington.com. Vertical drop: 3,050 ft. Lifts: 2 gondolas, 31 lifts. Skiable acreage: 1,182. Day lift tickets $69 adults, $54 ages 13–18, $45 children 6–12 and seniors; holidays 5% higher.

CROSS-COUNTRY SKIING

Nearest to the ski area (just east of Killington Rd. on Rte. 100/Rte. 4) is **Mountain Meadows Cross Country Ski Resort** ★ (✆ **800/221-0598** or 802/775-7077; www.xcskiing.net), with 36 miles of trails groomed for both skating and classic skiing. The trails are largely divided into three pods, with beginner trails closest to the lodge, an intermediate area a bit farther along, and an advanced 6-mile loop farthest away. Rentals and lessons are available at the lodge. For adults, a 1-day pass is $18, and a half-day (after 1pm) pass is $15. Kids ages 6 to 12 pay $8 per day, $6 per half-day.

The intricate network of trails at **Mountain Top Inn** ★★ (✆ **802/483-6089**) has long had a loyal local following. The 66-mile trail network offers pastoral views through mixed terrain groomed for traditional and skate skiing. Adults pay $19 for 1-day trail passes, $16 for half-day passes (after 1pm). With more challenging and picturesque terrain, Mountain Top is the better value of the two options.

OTHER OUTDOOR PURSUITS

MOUNTAIN BIKING Mountain biking comes in two forms at Killington—organized on the mountain and on-your-own on the back roads. On Killington's mountain, around 45 miles of trails are open for biking, and one eight-passenger gondola line is equipped to haul bikes and riders to the summit, delivering great views. Riders give their forearms a workout applying brakes while bumping down the slopes. A trail pass is $8; a trail pass with a two-time gondola ride is $22; unlimited gondola rides are $32 per day.

The **Mountain Bike Shop** (✆ **802/422-6232**) at the Killington Base Lodge is open from June to mid-October. Bike rentals (with suspension) start at around $30 for 2 hours, up to $45 for a full day. Helmets are required ($3 additional per day).

Bikes are also available for rent—along with sound advice on local trails—from **True Wheels Bike Shop** (✆ **802/422-3234**), in the Basin Ski Shop near the top of the Killington Access Road. Rentals range from around $45 a day for a low-end bike to about $65 for a bike with rock shocks and disc brakes (half-day rates also available;

helmets are included). Bikes are available from April to mid-October; reservations are helpful during holidays and busy times.

GOLF Vermont is loaded with fine golf courses, public and private, lovely in summer and outstandingly scenic in fall. The acknowledged top course is **Green Mountain National Golf Course** ★★ (✆ **888/483-4653** or 802/422-4653; www.greenmountainnational.com) on Route 100 in Killington. Greens fees, without cart, are $43 to $49 per adult midweek, $59 weekends and holidays, plus required cart fee. There are discounts after 3pm; rentals, instruction, and a driving range are also available.

A HISTORIC SITE

President Calvin Coolidge State Historic Site ★★ When told that Calvin Coolidge had died, literary wit Dorothy Parker is said to have responded, "How can they tell?" Even in his death, the nation's most taciturn president had to fight for respect. A trip to the Plymouth Notch Historic District should redeem Silent Cal's reputation among visitors, who'll get a strong sense of the president reared in this mountain village, a man shaped by harsh weather, unrelieved isolation, and a strong sense of community and family.

Situated in a high upland valley, the historic district consists of a group of about a dozen unspoiled buildings open to the public and a number of other private residences that may be observed from the outside only. At the Coolidge Homestead (now open for tours) in August 1923, Vice President Coolidge, on a vacation from Washington, was awakened and informed that President Warren Harding had died. His own father, a notary public, administered the presidential oath of office. Coolidge is buried in the cemetery across the road. He remains the only president to have been born on Independence Day, and every July 4th, a wreath is laid at his simple grave in a quiet ceremony.

Be sure to stop by the **Plymouth Cheese Factory** (✆ **802/672-3650**), just uphill from the Coolidge Homestead. Founded in the late 1800s as a farmer's cooperative by President Coolidge's father, the business was owned by the former president's son until the late 1990s. Excellent cheeses here include a spicy pepper cheddar. Hours are daily from 9:30am to 5pm.

Rte. 100A, Plymouth. ✆ **802/672-3773.** Admission $7.50 adults, $2 children 6–14, free for children 13 and under, $20 family. Daily 9:30am–5pm. Closed mid-Oct to late May.

WHERE TO STAY

Blueberry Hill Inn ★★★ The wonderfully homey Blueberry Hill Inn lies in the heart of the Moosalamoo recreation area, on 180 acres along a quiet road about 45 minutes northwest of Killington. With superb hiking, biking, canoeing, swimming, and cross-country skiing, it's an extraordinary destination for anyone who wants to spend time outdoors and away from the bother of everyday life. (From the inn's brochure: "We offer you no radios, no televisions, no bedside phones to disturb your vacation.") The inn dates to 1813; one graceful addition is the greenhouse walkway,

---

Value Budget Hints for Skiers

Skiers on a budget should consider basing in Rutland, at one of the chain motels, and commuting to the mountain via car or the $2 shuttle bus. See the "Rutland" section below for suggestions on motels.

---

leading to the cozy guest rooms. Family-style meals are served in a rustic dining room, with a great stone fireplace and homegrown herbs drying from the wooden beams.

Goshen-Ripton Rd., Goshen, VT 05733. ✆ **800/448-0707** or 802/247-6735. Fax 802/247-3983. www.blueberryhillinn.com. 12 units. $110–$190 double. Rates include breakfast and dinner. MC, V. **Amenities:** Sauna; bike rental; babysitting; cross-country ski trails. *In room:* No phone.

Butternut on the Mountain Motor Inn *Value* Butternut is a short remove from the access road, just enough to lend a little quiet, although winter guests tend to make up for that with a dose of boisterousness. I recommend it more as a budget option than an especially noteworthy spot. The rooms are motel-size with motel decor, but unexpected facilities such as a fireplace lounge area on the second floor and a restaurant with full bar and darts on the first floor add to the appeal.

Killington Rd. (P.O. Box 306), Killington, VT 05751. ✆ **802/422-2000.** www.butternutlodge.com. 18 units. $56–$120 double. Lower off-season rates. AE, DISC, MC, V. **Amenities:** Restaurant; lounge; indoor pool; Jacuzzi; game room. *In room:* A/C (some), TV.

Cortina Inn & Resort ★ The staff here does a fine job making this inn, with nearly 100 rooms, feel like a smaller and more intimate place. Especially appealing is the attention paid to service and detail—down to brushing off guests' car windows the morning after a snow. The lodge, set back slightly from busy Route 4 between Pico and Rutland, was built in 1966, with additions in 1975 and 1987. The interior has retro ski chalet charm dating from the original construction, including a sunken conversation pit with a two-sided fireplace and a spiral staircase twisting up to a second level. Guest rooms vary slightly in their modern country style, but all are nicely furnished.

103 U.S. Rte. 4 (1½ miles west of Pico), Killington, VT 05751. ✆ **800/451-6108** or 802/773-3333. Fax 802/775-6948. www.cortinainn.com. 96 units. $179–$369 double; $274–$384 suite (discounts for multiple days). Rates include breakfast. 5-night minimum stay Christmas week; 3-night minimum stay Columbus and Presidents' Day weekends. AE, DC, DISC, MC, V. Pets allowed ($5 per pet per night). **Amenities:** Restaurant; tavern; indoor pool; 8 tennis courts; fitness room; Jacuzzi; sauna; mountain-biking center; 2 game rooms; children's center; concierge; courtesy shuttle (ski season only); limited room service; babysitting; laundry service; dry cleaning; canoeing pond. *In room:* A/C, TV, dataport, hair dryer, iron.

Inn at Long Trail ★ The Inn at Long Trail is in an architecturally undistinguished building at the intersection of Route 4 and the Long and Appalachian trails (about a 10-min. drive from Killington's ski slopes). The interior of this rustic inn is far more charming than the exterior. Tree trunks support the beams in the lobby, which sports log furniture and banisters of yellow birch along the stairway. The older rooms in this three-floor hotel (built in 1938 as an annex to a long-gone lodge) are furnished simply, in ski-lodge style. Comfortable, more modern suites with fireplaces, telephones, and TVs are in a motel-like addition. The dining room is fun and appealing, maintaining the Keebler-elf theme with a stone ledge that juts through the wall from the mountain behind.

709 U.S. Rte. 4, Killington, VT 05751. ✆ **800/325-2540** or 802/775-7181. Fax 802/747-7034. www.innatlongtrail.com. 19 units. Summer $68–$98 double; fall $75–$224 double; winter $75–$300 double. Rates include breakfast. 2-night minimum stay most weekends and during foliage season. AE, MC, V. Closed late Apr to late June. Pets allowed with prior permission (with damage deposit). **Amenities:** Dining room; pub; Jacuzzi; laundry service. *In room:* No phone.

Inn of the Six Mountains ★ With its profusion of gables and dormers, the Inn of the Six Mountains stands among the more architecturally memorable of the numerous hotels along Killington Road. The lobby is welcoming in a modern, Scandinavian sort of way, with lots of blond wood and stone, and the location is convenient to

Killington's base lodge, just a mile up the road. The guest rooms are tastefully decorated, but for a luxury hotel that offers only "deluxe" rooms and suites, the attention to detail can come up short.

2617 Killington Rd., Killington, VT 05751. ✆ **800/228-4676** or 802/422-4302. www.sixmountains.com. 103 units, including 4 suites. Winter $149–$239 double, $199–$250 suite; winter holidays $259–$289 double, $309–$330 suite; foliage season $149–$239 double, $199–$250 suite; spring, summer, and other off season $138–$168 double, $188–$220 suite. Rates include continental breakfast. AE, DC, DISC, MC, V. **Amenities:** Restaurant; indoor pool; outdoor pool; tennis court; fitness center; Jacuzzi; sauna; game room; business center; limited room service. *In room:* TV, dataport, fridge, coffeemaker, hair dryer, safe.

Killington Grand Resort Hotel ★★ Kids This is a good (though pricey) choice for travelers seeking contemporary accommodations right on the mountain. More than half of the units have kitchen facilities, and most are quite spacious, though decorated in a generic country-condo style. Some units can sleep up to six people, and the resort has an emphasis on catering to families. You pay a premium for convenience compared with other spots near the mountain, but that convenience is hard to top during ski season. The helpful service is a notch above that typically experienced at large ski hotels.

228 E. Mountain Rd. (near Snowshed base area), Killington, VT 05751. ✆ **877/4KTIMES.** Fax 802/422-6881. www.thekillingtongrand.com. 200 units. Fall–winter $336–$395 double, suites from $508; off peak $129–$310 double, suites from $175. Ask about packages. 5-night minimum stay during Christmas and school holidays; 2-night minimum stay on weekends. AE, DISC, MC, V. **Amenities:** 2 restaurants; outdoor pool; 2 tennis courts; fitness center; Jacuzzi; sauna; children's programs; concierge; limited room service; massage; dry cleaning. *In room:* A/C, TV, coffeemaker, hair dryer, iron.

Mountain Top Inn & Resort ★★ An expansive front porch with Adirondack chairs, croquet games, and horseback rides contribute to this inn's relaxing summery feel. Carved out of a former turnip farm in the 1940s, this pond-side inn has wonderful views of the Green Mountains. Even the lowest-priced rooms have been wonderfully updated in woods, leathers, and tartans, while six expanded suites—including HighMeadow (with an entire wall of windows looking out on the gorgeous scenery) and comfy Mamey's Retreat (across the hall from where Ike stayed for a week back in 1955)—come outfitted with such modern amenities as flat-screen TVs, sofas, double-sided fireplaces, jetted tubs, and kitchenettes. Activities abound here, including clay bird shooting, and fly fishing lessons, free canoes and kayaks at a little dock (no lifeguard), 50 miles (80km) of cross-country ski trails, and performances of jazz and classical music. The cuisine at the Highlands dining room and its associated tavern, each serving regional American fare with a Continental twist, continues to improve under chef Shawn Casey. The Mountain Top Inn is about a 25-minute drive from the slopes of Killington.

195 Mountain Top Rd., Chittenden, VT 05737. ✆ **800/445-2100** or 802/483-2311. Fax 802/483-6373. www.mountaintopinn.com. 55 units, including 20 suites with 1–4 bedrooms. Spring and late fall $130–$265 double; summer and winter $170–$410 double; foliage season and holidays $210–$465 double. AE, MC, V. **Amenities:** Restaurant; spa; outdoor pool; private beach; golf course; driving range; horseback riding; cross-country skiing trails. *In room:* A/C, TV, dataport, Jacuzzi (some), kitchenette (some), fireplace (some).

The Summit Lodge ★ Think plaid carpeting and Saint Bernards. Those two motifs set the tone at this inviting spot on a knoll just off the access road. Though built only in the 1960s, the inn has a more historic character, with much of the common space constructed of salvaged barn timbers. The guest rooms are less distinguished, with clunky pine furniture and little ambience, though all have balconies or terraces. You may not spend much time in your room, however, as the numerous common spaces are so inviting. The Summit has more character than most self-styled resorts along the access road, and it offers decent value.

Killington Rd. (P.O. Box 119), Killington, VT 05751. ✆ **800/635-6343** or 802/422-3535. Fax 802/422-3536. www.summitlodgevermont.com. 45 units. Summer–fall, midweek $66–$98, weekends $80–$154; winter–spring, $74–$219 double. Winter rates include breakfast. Minimum-stay policy on holidays. AE, DC, MC, V. **Amenities:** Restaurant; 2 outdoor pools; 5 tennis courts; Jacuzzi; game room; limited room service; massage. *In room:* TV.

WHERE TO DINE

Charity's 1887 Saloon PUB FARE Rustic, crowded, bustling, and boisterous, Charity's is the place if you like your food big and your company young. The centerpiece of this barnlike restaurant adorned with stained-glass lamps and Victorian prints is a handsome old bar crafted in Italy and then shipped to West Virginia, where it stayed for nearly a century before being dismantled and shipped to Vermont in 1971. The menu offers a selection of burgers, plus a half-dozen vegetarian choices such as veggie stir-fry and red-pepper ravioli.

Killington Rd. ✆ **802/422-3800.** Reservations not accepted. Main courses $5.95–$8.95 at lunch, $13–$19 at dinner. AE, MC, V. Daily 11:30am–10pm.

Choices Restaurant and Rotisserie ★ BISTRO Locals enjoy the consistently good, unpretentious fare at Choices, located on the access road across from the Outback. Full dinners come complete with salad or soup and bread and will amply restore calories lost on the slopes or the trail. Fresh pastas are a specialty (I like the Cajun green-peppercorn fettuccine); other inviting entrees include meats from the rotisserie. The atmosphere is nothing to write home about and the prices are higher than at nearby burger joints, but the high quality of the food and care taken in preparation make up for that.

Killington Rd. (at Glazebook Center). ✆ **802/422-4030.** Main courses $13–$22. AE, MC, V. Sun 11am–2:30pm; Sun–Thurs 5–10pm; Fri–Sat 5–11pm.

Hemingway's ★★★ NEW AMERICAN Hemingway's is an elegant spot—and one that ranks among the best restaurants in New England. Located in the 1860 Asa Briggs House, a former stagecoach stop, Hemingway's seats guests in three formal areas. The two upstairs rooms are well appointed with damask linen, crystal goblets, and fresh flowers. Diners tend to dress causally but neatly (no shorts or T-shirts). The three- or four-course dinners are offered at a price that turns out to be rather reasonable given the quality of the kitchen and the unassailable service. The menu changes often to reflect available stock. A typical meal may start with seared diver scallops, roast quail, cream of garlic soup, seared tuna with a rice cake, or confit of duck strudel with blood oranges. Then it's on to the splendid main course: perhaps filet of red snapper with grilled shrimp and a risotto of bacon and chanterelles in fall; cod with lobster, corn, and vanilla in summer; or partridge, roasted arctic char, or pork tenderloin in winter. You can finish with tangerine fruit soup and chocolate sorbet, a poached pear in a port syrup with Vermont cheese, banana bread with maple walnut ice cream, or the chocolate mousse cake.

4988 Rte. 4 (between Rte. 100 N. and Rte. 100 S.). ✆ **802/422-3886.** www.hemingwaysrestaurant.com. Reservations strongly recommended. Prix-fixe menu $42–$60; wine-tasting prix-fixe menu more expensive. AE, MC, V. Sun and Wed–Thurs 6–9pm; Fri–Sat 6–10pm. (Also open selected Mon–Tues during ski and foliage seasons; call first.) Closed mid-Apr to mid-May and early Nov.

Ppeppers ★ PASTA/ECLECTIC This 1950s-retro restaurant is a festive and upbeat place—almost always crowded with visitors and locals who've just enjoyed a long day on the slopes or the trails. Situated in a strip-mallish complex near the top of Killington Road, Ppeppers sets the mood with black-and-white tile floors, red lampshades, and red chile-pepper accent lighting. Take a seat at a genuine Naugahyde booth, or grab a stool at the wooden counter. Despite the name, the food isn't all spicy—the menu is diner fare, expanded for a more sophisticated clientele, but the hamburgers are great, the pasta above average, and the service far friendlier than in many ski mountain establishments.

Killington Rd. ✆ **802/422-3177.** Reservations not accepted. Main courses $3.95–$7.95 at breakfast, $4–$7.95 at lunch, $9.95–$15 at dinner. AE, DC, MC, V. Sun–Thurs 7am–9pm; Fri–Sat 7am–midnight.

RUTLAND

Rutland is a no-nonsense, blue-collar town that never had a reputation for charm. Today, it's undergoing a low-grade renaissance, attracting new residents who like the small-city atmosphere and easy access to the mountains, especially nearby Killington in winter.

Set in the wide valley flanking Otter Creek, Rutland was built on the marble trade, which was mined out of bustling quarries in nearby Proctor and West Rutland. By 1880, Rutland boasted more residents than Burlington, and had the distinguished honorific of "Marble City." Many fine homes from this era still line the streets, and the intricate commercial architecture, which naturally incorporates a fair amount of marble, hints at a former prosperity.

Rutland remains the regional hub for central Vermont, with much of the economic energy along bustling Route 7 north and south of downtown. The downtown itself shares its turf with an oddly incongruous strip mall, which appeared during one of those ill-considered spasms of 1950s urban renewal. That said, Rutland has the feel of a real place with real people, a good antidote for those who feel they've spent too much time in tourist-oriented ski resorts.

ESSENTIALS

GETTING THERE Rutland is at the intersection of Route 7 and Route 4. Burlington is 67 miles to the north; Bennington is 56 miles south. **Amtrak** (✆ **800/USA-RAIL;** www.amtrak.com) offers daily train service from New York via the Hudson River Valley. Surprisingly, Rutland is also served by daily air service from Boston by **Continental Connection** (✆ **800/523-FARE;** www.continental.com).

VISITOR INFORMATION The **Rutland Regional Chamber of Commerce,** 256 N. Main St., Rutland, VT 05701 (✆ **802/773-2747;** www.rutlandvermont.com), staffs an information booth at the corner of Route 7 and Route 4 West from Memorial Day to Columbus Day, open daily from 10am to 6pm. The chamber's main office is open year-round Monday through Friday from 8am to 5pm.

FESTIVALS The **Vermont State Fair** ★ (✆ **802/775-5200;** www.vermontstatefair.net) has attracted fairgoers from throughout Vermont for over 150 years. It's held from late August through the first week of September at the fairgrounds on Route 7, south of the city. Gates open at 8am daily.

EXPLORING THE TOWN

A stroll through Rutland's historic downtown will delight architecture buffs. Look for the detailed marblework on many of the buildings, such as the Opera House, the Gryphan's Building, and along Merchant's Row. Note especially the fine marble exterior of the Chittenden Savings Bank at the corner of Merchant's Row and Center Street. Nearby South Main Street (Rte. 7) also has a good selection of handsome homes built in elaborate Queen Anne style.

A stop worth making, especially as a rainy-day diversion, is the **Chaffee Center for the Visual Arts** ★, 16 S. Main St. (✆ **802/775-0356**). Housed in a Richardsonian structure dating from 1896, with a characteristically prominent turret and a mosaic floor in the archway vestibule, it showcases abundant artistic talent from Rutland and beyond. While it owns no permanent collections, it does feature changing exhibits of local artists, and much of the work is for sale. The building is on the National Register of Historic Places, and the glorious parquet floors have been restored to their original luster. Open daily except Tuesdays from 10am to 5pm (Sun noon–4pm); admission is by donation.

OUTSIDE OF TOWN

A worthwhile detour from Rutland is the amiable town of **Proctor,** about 6 miles northwest of Rutland center. (Take Rte. 4 west, then follow Rte. 3 north to the town.) It's home to the expansive, popular **Vermont Marble Museum** ★ (✆ **800/427-1396** or 802/459-2300; www.vermont-marble.com). View an 11-minute video about marble, walk through the "Earth Alive" displays about geology, see a sculptor working in marble, and explore the Hall of Presidents, with life-size bas-relief sculptures of all past presidents. The vast size of this former factory is impressive in itself. The gift shop has a great selection of reasonably priced marble products.

It's open from Memorial Day to late October daily, 9am to 5:30pm (closed the rest of the year). Admission is $7 for adults, $5 for seniors, $4 for students 13 to 18, and free for children under 13. ***A tip:*** Prices are cheaper than this if you buy in advance. Look for signs to the exhibit from Route 3 in Proctor.

WHERE TO STAY

Rutland has a selection of basic roadside motels and chain hotels, mostly clustered on or along Route 7 south of town. Rates at the **Comfort Inn at Trolley Square,** 19 Allen St. (✆ **800/432-6788** or 802/775-2200; www.comfortinn.com), include continental breakfast. **The Holiday Inn,** 476 Rte. 7 S. (✆ **800/448-2296** or 802/775-1911; www.holiday-inn.com), has an indoor pool, hot tub, and sauna. Likewise, the **Red Roof Inn,** 401 Rte. 7 S. (✆ **802/775-4303;** www.hojo.com), features an indoor pool and sauna, with the familiar orange-roofed restaurant next door. The **Best Western Inn & Suites,** on Route 4 East (✆ **802/773-3200**), has a pool and tennis court.

Inn at Rutland ★ Built as a family home in the 1890s by the grain empire Burdett family, the Inn at Rutland is an imposing Victorian B&B overlooking Route 7 on the north side of town. It's elaborate on the outside, and even more so on the inside. Gracefully curving walls, stamped plaster wainscoting, oak trim, and leather wallpaper are among the noteworthy details. The downstairs parlors are formal in an Edwardian sort of way, and guest rooms are unusually spacious. Rooms facing Route 7 are a bit noisier, but the house was solidly wrought and seems to buffer most of the noise. The third-floor rooms are generally less detailed, but among my favorites are Washington and Rutland, which are large and quiet.

70 N. Main St. (Rte. 7), Rutland, VT 05701. ✆ **800/808-0575.** www.innatrutland.com. $120–$175 double; foliage season and holidays, $150–$220 double. Rates include breakfast. AE, MC, V, Disc. *In room:* TV.

WHERE TO DINE

The Coffee Exchange (✆ **802/775-3337**) is a casually hip cafe housed in a former downtown bank at 100 Merchant's Row. You've got your choice here: Grab a seat at a sidewalk table or move inside and pick a room. (The bank vault is tiny and painted enchantingly, and you can have a lively conversation with an echo.) A good selection of coffees is available, along with delectable baked goods such as banana-nut tarts, croissants, and cheese Danishes.

Little Harry's ★ GLOBAL The dishes here will appeal to anyone with an adventurous palate. This offshoot of the popular Harry's outside of Ludlow is in downtown Rutland on the first floor and basement of a strikingly unattractive building. The menu is wonderfully eclectic, with main selections ranging from grilled steak sandwich to duck in a "searing" red Thai curry (Thurs is Thai night). Appetizers are equally eclectic, with choices along the lines of marinated green olives, gazpacho, pad Thai, and hummus.

121 West St. ✆ **802/747-4848.** Reservations recommended. Main courses $11–$17. AE, MC, V. Daily 5–10pm.

Royal's 121 Hearthside AMERICAN Royal's Hearthside, a local institution since 1962, falls under the category of "old reliable." At the busy intersection of Route 4 and Route 7, Royal's is calming and quiet on the inside, done up in a sort of Ye Olde Colonial American style. Expect spindle-backed chairs, faux pewter sugar bowls, and Brandenburg concertos playing in the background. Meals don't tax the staff in the creativity department, but are solidly prepared. All the sauces are homemade, as are the popovers, breads, and pastries. They even butcher their own meat. Selections run along the lines of baked stuffed shrimp, grilled rack of lamb, broiled salmon, an assortment of grilled meats, and an array of specials. Lunches include sandwiches, burgers, and omelets. The restaurant is also noted for its traditional puddings, such as Grapenut, Indian, and bread.

37 N. Main St. ✆ **802/775-0856.** Reservations recommended on weekends. Main courses $6.95–$14 at lunch, $15–$23 at dinner. AE, MC, V. Mon–Sat 11am–3pm and 5–9:30pm; Sun noon–9pm.

5 Middlebury ★★

Middlebury is a gracious college town amid rolling hills and pastoral countryside, its town center idyllic in a New-England-as-envisioned-by-Hollywood sort of way. For many, it provides the perfect combination of small-town charm, access to the outdoors (the Adirondacks and Green Mountains are both close at hand), and a dash of sophistication. The influence of college students and out-of-staters has resulted in a natural foods store, ethnic restaurants, and more arts, crafts, and books than you would expect to find in a place several times the size of Middlebury.

ESSENTIALS

GETTING THERE Middlebury is on Route 7 about midway between Rutland and Burlington. **Vermont Transit** (✆ **800/552-8737** or 802/773-2774; www.vermonttransit.com) has bus service to town. From upstate New York by car, you can short-circuit Lake Champlain by driving to Fort Ticonderoga and taking the cable ferry (✆ **802/897-7999**) across the lake. The ferry operates from early May to late October; the cost is a steep $8 one-way, $12 round-trip per car.

VISITOR INFORMATION The **Addison County Chamber of Commerce,** 2 Court St. (✆ **800/733-8376** or 802/388-9300; www.midvermont.com), is in a handsome, historic white building just off the green, facing The Middlebury Inn. Brochures and assistance are available from Monday through Friday during business hours (9am–5pm), and often on weekends from early June to mid-October. Ask for

Middlebury

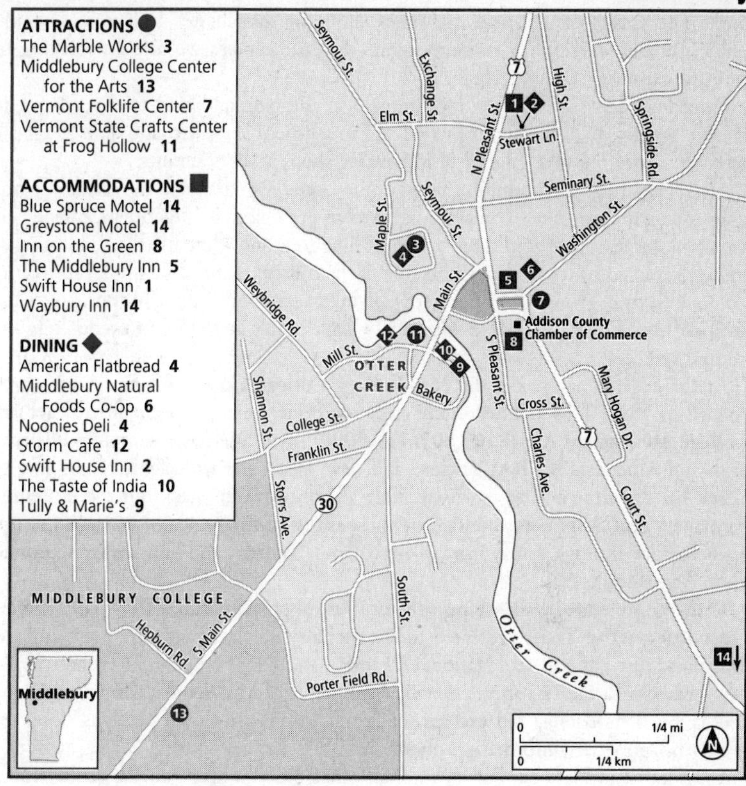

the map and guide to downtown Middlebury. It lists town shops and restaurants and is published by the Downtown Middlebury Business Bureau.

EXPLORING THE TOWN

The best place to begin a tour of Middlebury is the Addison County Chamber of Commerce; be sure to request the chamber's self-guided walking-tour brochure.

The **Vermont Folklife Center** ★, 3 Court St. (✆ **802/388-4964;** www.vermontfolklifecenter.org), in the 1823 Masonic Hall, is a short walk from Middlebury Inn. You'll find a gallery of changing displays of various folk arts from Vermont and beyond, including music and visual arts. The small gift shop has intriguing items, such as heritage foods and traditional crafts. Open summers Tuesday through Saturday from 10am to 4pm. Admission is by donation.

The historic **Otter Creek** ★★ district, set on a steep hillside by the rocky creek, is well worth exploring. Here you can peruse top-flight Vermont crafts at the **Vermont State Crafts Center at Frog Hollow** ★★, 1 Mill St. (✆ **888/388-3177;** www.froghollow.org). In a picturesque setting overlooking the tumbling stream, the center is open daily (closed Sun in winter) and shows the work of some 300 Vermont craftspeople. Their wares range from extraordinary carved wood desks to metalwork to glass and pottery. There's also a pottery studio and a resident potter who's often busy at work. The Crafts Center also maintains shops in Manchester Village and at the Church Street Marketplace in Burlington. Visit the center's website for a listing of monthly exhibits.

From Frog Hollow, take the footbridge over the river and find your way to **The Marble Works,** an assortment of wood and rough-marble industrial buildings on the far bank, converted to a handful of interesting shops and restaurants.

Atop a low ridge with beautiful views of the Green Mountains to the east and farmlands rolling toward Lake Champlain in the west, prestigious **Middlebury College** ★★ has a handsome, well-spaced campus of gray limestone and white marble buildings that are best explored by foot. The architecture of the college, founded in 1800, is primarily Colonial Revival, giving it a rather stern Calvinist demeanor. Especially appealing is the prospect from the marble Mead Memorial Chapel, built in 1917 and overlooking the campus green.

At the edge of campus is the **Middlebury College Center for the Arts,** which opened in 1992. This architecturally engaging center houses the small **Middlebury College Museum of Art** ★ (© **802/443-5000**), with a selective sampling of European and American art, both ancient and new. Classicists will savor the displays of Greek painted urns and vases; modern-art aficionados can check out the museum's permanent and changing exhibits. The museum is on Route 30 (S. Main St.) and is open Tuesday through Friday from 10am to 5pm, Saturday and Sunday from noon to 5pm. Admission is free.

One recommended walk—especially for those of poetic sensibilities—is the **Robert Frost Interpretive Trail,** dedicated to the memory of New England's poet laureate. Frost lived in a cabin (now a National Historic Landmark.) on a farm near here for 23 summers. On Route 125 approximately 6 miles east of Middlebury, this relaxing loop trail is just a mile long, and excerpts of Frost's poems are placed on signs along the trail. Also posted is information about the trail's natural history. Managed by the Green Mountain National Forest, the trail offers pleasant access to the gentle woods of these lovely intermountain lowlands.

WHERE TO STAY

The outskirts of Middlebury are home to a handful of motels and several inns. The 1960s-era **Blue Spruce Motel,** 2428 Rte. 7 S. (© **802/388-4091**), has 22 basic rooms; families lingering in the area for a few days should inquire about Room no. 122, a large suite with full kitchen, sleeping loft, and carport. Rates run from $75 to $95 for a double room ($135 for the suite). The **Greystone Motel,** 1395 Rte. 7 S. (© **802/388-4935**), has 10 clean rooms with small bathrooms; rates run from around $79 to $95 in summer, from around $65 to $90 in winter.

Inn on the Green ★★ This handsome village inn occupies a house that dates to 1803 (it was Victorianized with a mansard tower later in the century). It's both historic and comfortable. The rooms are furnished with a mix of antiques and reproductions; wood floors and boldly colored walls of harvest yellow, peach, and burgundy lighten the architectural heaviness of the house. The suites are naturally the most spacious, but all units offer plenty of elbow room. Those in the front of the house are wonderfully flooded with afternoon light.

71 S. Pleasant St., Middlebury, VT 05753. © **888/244-7512** or 802/388-7512. www.innonthegreen.com. 11 units. $98–$189 double; $149–$275 suite. Midweek discounts available. Rates include continental breakfast. 2-night minimum stay on weekends. AE, DC, DISC, MC, V. *In room:* A/C, TV, dataport, hair dryer, iron.

The Middlebury Inn ★ The historic Middlebury Inn traces its roots to 1827, when Nathan Wood built the Vermont Hotel, a brick public house. It now consists of four buildings containing 75 modern guest rooms. Rooms are on the large side, and most are outfitted with a sofa or upholstered chairs, Colonial-reproduction furniture, and some vintage bathroom fixtures. Room nos. 116 and 246 are spacious corner units entered via a dark foyer/sitting room. Room no. 129, while smaller, has a four-poster bed, a view of the village green, and a Jacuzzi. The 10 guest rooms in the Porterhouse Mansion next door also have a pleasant, historic feel. An adjacent motel with 20 units is decorated in an Early American motif, but underneath the veneer, it's just a standard-issue motel. Stick with the main inn if you're seeking a taste of history.

14 Courthouse Sq., Middlebury, VT 05753. ✆ **800/842-4666** or 802/388-4961. www.middleburyinn.com. 75 units. Midweek $88–$245 double, $235–$240 suite; weekends $98–$270 double, $270–$375 suite. Rates include continental breakfast. AE, DC, MC, V. Pets allowed in some rooms. **Amenities:** Restaurant; tavern; laundry service. *In room:* A/C, TV, dataport, hair dryer, iron.

Swift House Inn ★★ This historic complex of three whitewashed houses sits on a hillside 2 blocks from downtown Middlebury. New owners have improved it, with touches like chai tea in the rooms, a friendly barkeep just across from the reception desk, and improved pricing of the inn's fine restaurant. The five lower-priced rooms in the roadside gatehouse have a B&B feel and have been updated with upscale carpets, gorgeous wooden floors, and bathrooms. The 9 rooms in the main, Federal-style inn (built in 1814) are thoroughly imbued with the intriguing history of the place: a Vermont governor lived here at one time. Inside, it's decorated in a simple, historic style of antiques and reproduction furnishings, including the Clark Room—two former rooms combined into one, it has a love seat and looks out over lovely lawns and grounds. The carriage house's six suites are the inn's most luxurious, and most have Jacuzzis and fireplaces.

25 Stewart Lane, Middlebury, VT 05753. ✆ **866/388-9925** or 802/388-9925. Fax 802/388-9927. www.swifthouseinn.com. 20 units. Main inn $110–$185 double; gate house $110–$135 double; carriage house $235–$255 suite. Rates include full breakfast. 2-night minimum stay some weekends. AE, MC, V. **Amenities:** Restaurant; limited room service (breakfast only). *In room:* A/C, TV, dataport, hair dryer, iron, fireplace (some), Jacuzzi (some).

Waybury Inn ★ Photos of Bob Newhart and "Larry, his brother Darryl and his other brother, Darryl," grace the wall behind the desk at this 1810 inn. This inn was featured in the classic *Newhart* show—at least the exterior; the interior was created on a sound stage. The architecturally handsome Waybury has loads of integrity in that simple farmhouse kind of way. Rooms vary in size, as they do in most old inns. The more you pay, the more space you'll get. The inn is close to the road, and the front-facing rooms can be a bit noisy at night; the two attic rooms are cozy, but a bit dark and garretlike.

457 E. Main St. (Rte. 125), East Middlebury, VT 05753. ✆ **800/348-1810** or 802/388-4015. Fax 802/388-1248. www.wayburyinn.com. 15 units, 1 with detached private bathroom. $100–$180 double; $175–$250 suite. Rates include breakfast. Call for information about packages. AE, DISC, MC, V. Pets allowed with restrictions (call first). **Amenities:** Restaurant. *In room:* A/C, no phone.

WHERE TO DINE

In addition to the eateries listed below, Middlebury possesses an abundance of delis, sandwich shops, and the like—perfect for a quick lunch or a picnic.

Among the best are **Noonies Deli** (✆ **802/388-0014**), in The Marble Works complex, the locals' choice for sandwiches; **The Taste of India** (✆ **802/388-4856**), hidden away down 1 Bakery Lane, with inexpensive lunch specials; and **American Flatbread** ★ (✆ **802/388-3300**), also in The Marble Works, open Friday and Saturday evenings only from 5 to 9:30pm and cooking some of the best pizzas I've tasted. All do takeout. There's also a small, good natural foods store, **Middlebury Natural Foods Co-op** (✆ **802/388-7276**), at 1 Washington St. just uphill from The Middlebury Inn.

Storm Cafe ★ NEW AMERICAN A tiny, casual spot with great river views, Storm Cafe is one of the town's best fine-dining spots, popular with locals and travelers alike. The menu is simple, but tremendous care is taken in the selection of ingredients and the preparation; salads are especially good. Meal selections may include smoked salmon, jerk chicken, or pasta; there's also a changing fish entree nightly.

3 Mill St. ✆ **802/388-1063.** Reservations recommended, especially on weekends. Main courses $7–$13. MC, V. Tues–Sat 5–9pm.

Swift House Inn ★★ NEW AMERICAN This inn restaurant consists of two dining rooms on the ground floor of the main house. It's a wonderfully homey place to get a fancy meal. I like to start with a fresh strawberry-brie salad in poppyseed dressing, followed by a grilled lamb top round with delicately grilled zucchini, or maybe an oven-roasted duck breast over garlic polenta, grilled strip steak, cut of Scottish salmon with soba noodles, or some basil pasta with eggplant "meatballs." Two wonderful desserts are the boca negra chocolate cake with coconut whipped cream or a wonderful cappuccino-flavored crème brûlée with caramelized pecans. Some tables look out onto the grounds (and sunset over the mountains).

25 Stewart Lane, Middlebury, VT 05753. ✆ **802/388-9925.** Reservations recommended. Main courses $15–$21. AE, MC, V. Thurs–Mon 6–9pm.

Tully and Marie's ★ NEW AMERICAN/GLOBAL Tully and Marie's is not Ye Olde New Englande. It's a bright and colorful, Art Deco–inspired restaurant overlooking the creek, made all the more appealing by its surprising location down a small, dark alley. It's a fun, low-key place that puts you in a good mood the moment you walk in. Angle for a table perched over the creek. The menu specializes in New American cuisine, with clear influences from Asia and Mexico. At lunch, expect pad Thai, vegetable linguini, and a variety of hearty meals (for instance, burgers or grilled apple, bacon, and cheddar, served over baked beans). At dinner, you can find chicken saltimbocca, bourbon shrimp, and grilled strip steak with caramelized shallots and leeks.

7 Bakery Lane (on Otter Creek upstream from the bridge in the middle of town). ✆ **802/388-4182.** www.tullyandmaries.com. Reservations recommended for weekends and college events. Main courses $6.50–$10 at lunch, $10–$20 at dinner. AE, MC, V. Summer daily 11:30am–3pm and 5–9pm (to 10pm Fri–Sat); winter daily 11:30am–3pm, Sun–Mon and Thurs 5–9pm, Fri–Sat 5–10pm.

6 Mad River Valley ★★

Warren is 3 miles S of Waitsfield, 205 miles NW of Boston, and 43 miles SE of Burlington.

But for a couple of telltale signs, you could drive Route 100 past the sleepy villages of Warren and Waitsfield and not realize that you're close to some of the choicest skiing in the state. The region hasn't fallen prey to unbridled condo or strip-mall developers, and the valley seems to have learned some lessons from the haphazard development that afflicts Mount Snow and Killington to the south. Note the Mad River Green, a tidy strip mall disguised as an old barn on Route 100 just north of Route 17. It's scarcely noticeable from the main road. Longtime Vermont skiers say the valley today resembles the Stowe of 25 years ago.

The region's character becomes less pastoral along the Sugarbush Access Road, but even at the base of Sugarbush, the valley's preeminent ski area, signs of development aren't obvious. The better lodges and restaurants tend to be tucked back in the forest or set along streams; make sure you have good directions before setting out in search of accommodations or food. Hidden up a winding valley road, Mad River Glen, the area's older and grumpier ski area, has a pleasantly dated quality that eschews glamour for rustic charm.

The valley maintains a friendly and informal attitude, even during peak ski season; residents hope to keep it that way, even in the face of certain growth.

ESSENTIALS

GETTING THERE Warren and Waitsfield are on Route 100 between Killington and Waterbury. The nearest interstate access is from Exit 10 (Waterbury) on I-89; drive south on Route 100 for 14 miles to Waitsfield.

VISITOR INFORMATION The **Mad River Valley Chamber of Commerce** (✆ **800/828-4748** or 802/469-3409; www.madrivervalley.com) is at 4601 Main St. (Rte. 100) in the General Wait House, next to the elementary school. It's open daily from 9am to 5pm; during slow times, expect limited hours and days.

SKIING & OTHER WINTER SPORTS

Clearwater Sports (✆ **802/496-2708;** www.clearwatersports.com) on Main Street in Waitsfield offers telemark ski rentals and advice in the winter, as well as guided snowshoe hikes into the backcountry. Ask about the Mad River Rocket sled trip, involving snowshoeing up and sledding down a nearby hill.

Mad River Glen ★★★ Mad River Glen is the curmudgeon of the Vermont ski world—just what you'd expect from a place whose motto is "Ski it if you can." High-speed detachable quads? Forget it. The main lift is a 1948 *single*-chair lift that creaks its way 1 mile to the summit. Snowmaking? Don't count on it. Only 15% of the terrain benefits from the fake stuff; the rest is dependent on Mother Nature. Snowboarding? Nope. It's forbidden at Mad River. Mad River's slopes are twisting and narrow and hide some of the steepest drops in New England (nearly half the slopes are classified as expert). Mad River Glen long ago attained the status of a cult mountain among serious skiers, and its fans seem determined to keep it that way. Owned and operated by a cooperative of Mad River skiers since 1995, it's the only cooperative-owned ski area in the country. The owners are proud of the mountain's funky traditions (how *about* that single chair?) and say they're determined to maintain the spirit. Waitsfield, VT 05763. ✆ **802/496-3551.** www.madriverglen.com. Vertical drop: 2,000 ft. Lifts: 4 chairlifts. Skiable acreage: 115. Day lift tickets $50 adults.

Sugarbush ★★ This is a good choice if you find the sprawl of Killington overwhelming, but don't want to sacrifice great skiing for a quieter and more intimate resort. Sugarbush a fine intermediate-to-advanced ski resort, comprised of two ski mountains linked by a 2-mile, 10-minute high-speed chairlift that crosses three ridges. (A shuttle bus offers a warmer way to traverse the mountains.) The number of high-speed lifts (four) and excellent snowmaking make this a desirable destination for serious skiers. Despite large-scale improvements that began in the mid-1990s, Sugarbush

Finds **Stop by a Classic**

The **Warren General Store** (✆ **802/496-3864**) anchors the little town of Warren, once a timber warren but now HQ for legions of quiet-loving Mad River skiers. Set along a stream, the store has uneven floorboards, a potbellied stove, and merchandise updated for the 21st century, including a good selection of sandwiches (with names like the "Turkey Tumble" and the "Montpeculia"), gourmet foods, and wines. Get coffee or sandwich at the back deli counter, then enjoy it on the deck overlooking the water. The store is in Warren Village just off Route 100 south of the Sugarbush Access Road. It's open daily from 8am until 7pm, Sundays to 6pm.

remains a low-key area with great intermediate cruising runs on the north slopes and some challenging, old-fashioned expert slopes on Castlerock.

Warren, VT 05674. ✆ **800/537-8427** for lodging, or 802/583-6300. www.sugarbush.com. Vertical drop: 2,650 ft. Lifts: 14 chairlifts (4 high-speed), 4 surface lifts. Skiable acreage: 432. Lift tickets $50–$65 adults.

EXPLORING THE VALLEY

An unusual way to explore the region is atop an Icelandic pony. The **Vermont Icelandic Horse Farm** ★ (✆ **802/496-7141;** www.icelandichorses.com), on North Fayston Road in Waitsfield (turn west off Rte. 100 near the airport), specializes in tours on these small, sturdy horses. Full- and half-day rides are available daily, but to really appreciate both the countryside and the horses, sign up for a multiday trek, ranging from 1 to 5 nights and including lodging at area inns, all meals, your mount, and a guide to lead you through the lush hills around Waitsfield and Warren. In winter, try **skijoring,** best described as sort of like water-skiing behind a horse. Call for pricing information and reservations.

BIKING A rewarding 14-mile **bike trip** ★★ along paved roads begins at the village of Waitsfield. Park your car near the covered bridge, then follow East Warren Road past the Inn at Round Barn Farm and up into the hilly, farm-filled countryside. (Don't be discouraged by the unrelenting hill at the outset.) Near the village of Warren, turn right at Brook Road to connect back to Route 100. Return north on bustling, but generally safe and often scenic Route 100 to Waitsfield.

Clearwater Sports, at 4147 Main St. (Rte. 100) in Waitsfield north of the covered bridge (✆ **802/496-2708;** www.clearwatersports.com), offers mountain-bike rentals from a blue-and-white Victorian-era house. The staff is helpful, with suggestions for other routes and tours.

HIKING Hikers in search of good exercise and a spectacular view should strike out for **Mount Abraham** ★★, west of Warren. Drive west up Lincoln Gap Road (it leaves Rte. 100 just south of Warren Village) and continue until the crest, where you cross the intersection with the Long Trail. Park here and head north on the trail; about 2 miles along, you hit the Battell Shelter. Push on another .8 mile up a steep ascent to reach the panoramic views atop 4,006-foot Mount Abraham. Enjoy. Retrace your steps to your car. Allow 4 or 5 hours for the round-trip hike.

For a less demanding adventure that still yields great views, head *south* from Lincoln Gap Road on the Long Trail. In about .6 mile, look for a short spur trail to **Sunset Rock** ★, with sweeping westward vistas of the farms of the Champlain Valley, along with Lake Champlain and the knobby Adirondacks beyond. A round-trip hike requires a little more than an hour.

WHERE TO STAY

While Sugarbush isn't overrun with condos and lodges, it has its share. Some 200 of the condos nearest the mountain are managed by the **Sugarbush Resort** (✆ **800/537-8427;** www.sugarbush.com), with accommodations ranging from one to four bedrooms. Guests have access to amenities that include a health club and five pools. The resort also manages the 46-unit Sugarbush Inn. Shuttle buses deliver guests to and from the mountain and other facilities. Major winter holidays may require a minimum stay of up to 5 days. Rates vary widely, and most rooms are sold as packages that include lift tickets in winter.

Inn at the Mad River Barn ★ *Value* This classic 1960s-style ski lodge attracts a clientele that's nearly fanatical in its devotion to the place. It's best not to come here expecting anything fancy—carpets and furniture both tend toward the threadbare. Do come expecting to have some fun once settled. It's all knotty pine; spartan guest rooms and rustic common rooms help visitors feel at home putting their feet up. Accommodations are in the two-story barn behind the white clapboard main house and in an annex building, which is a bit fancier but with less character. In winter, dinners ($15) are served in boisterous family style. In summer, the mood is slightly more sedate, but enhanced by a beautiful pool a short walk away in a grove of birches.

2849 Mill Brook Rd. (Rte. 17), Waitsfield, VT 05673. ✆ **800/631-0466** or 802/496-3310. Fax 802/496-6696. www.madriverbarn.com. 15 units. $77–$115 double. Holiday and foliage season rates higher. Midweek discounts available. Rates include breakfast. 2-night minimum stay holiday and winter weekends. AE, DISC, MC, V. **Amenities:** Restaurant (winter only); lounge; outdoor pool; fitness room; sauna; game room. *In room:* TV (most), fridge (some), no phone.

Inn at Round Barn Farm ★★ You pass through a covered bridge just off Route 100 to arrive at one of my favorite romantic B&Bs in northern New England, a regal barn and farmhouse on 235 sloping acres with views of fields all around. The centerpiece of the inn is the Round Barn, a strikingly beautiful 1910 structure that's used for weddings, art exhibits, and Sunday church services. Each guest room is furnished with an understated country elegance. The less expensive rooms in the older part of the house are comfortable, if small; larger luxury units in the attached horse barn have soaring ceilings under old log beams and include extras such as steam showers, gas fireplaces, and phones.

1661 E. Warren Rd., Waitsfield, VT 05673. ✆ **802/496-2276.** Fax 802/496-8832. www.innattheroundbarn.com. 11 units. $160–$280 double; holidays and foliage season $190–$315 double. Rates include breakfast. 3-night minimum stay during holidays and foliage season. AE, DISC, MC, V. Closed Apr 15–30. No children under 15. **Amenities:** Indoor pool; game room; 18-mile cross-country ski center. *In room:* Hair dryer, no phone (except luxury rooms).

The Pitcher Inn ★★★ This Relais & Châteaux property is one of Vermont's finest. Set in the timeless village of Warren, the inn was built in the 1990s from the ground up following a fire that leveled a previous home; only the barn is original. Architect David Sellars created an inn that seamlessly blends modern conveniences, whimsy, and classic New England styling. The common areas fuse several styles: a little Colonial Revival, a little mission, and a little Adirondack sporting camp. You won't find a bad room in the house; each is designed with such wit that they're almost like elegant puzzles. (My favorite feature: The carved goose in flight on the ceiling of the Mallard Room is attached to a weathervane on the roof, and it rotates to indicate wind direction.) Nine units have fireplaces (seven wood-burning, two gas), and five have steam showers.

275 Main St. (P.O. Box 347), Warren, VT 05674. ✆ **802/496-6350.** Fax 802/496-6354. www.pitcherinn.com. 11 units. $350–$600 double; $700 suite. Rates include breakfast. 2-night minimum stay on weekends, 3 nights on holiday weekends, 5 nights at Christmas. AE, MC, V. Children under 16 accepted in suites only. **Amenities:** Restaurant; spa; Jacuzzi; game room; limited room service; in-room massage; babysitting. *In room:* A/C, TV/VCR, dataport, hair dryer, Jacuzzi (some).

West Hill House ★ This is among the more casual and relaxed inns in the valley, partly because of its quiet hillside location, partly because of the easy camaraderie among guests. Set on a lightly traveled country road, West Hill House offers a quintessential New England experience, just a few minutes from the slopes at Sugarbush. Built in the 1850s, this farmhouse boasts three common rooms, including a bright, modern addition with a handsome fireplace for warmth in winter and an outdoor patio for summer lounging. The guest rooms are decorated in an updated country style, and all have gas fireplaces or gas woodstoves; three are air-conditioned. The more modern units include steam showers and Jacuzzis.

1496 W. Hill Rd., Warren, VT 05674. ✆ **800/898-1427** or 802/496-7162. Fax 802/496-6443. www.westhillhouse.com. 7 units. $135–$190 double. Rates include breakfast. Check website for specials. 3-night minimum stay for foliage and holiday weekends; 2-night minimum stay on other weekends. AE, DISC MC, V. No children under 12. **Amenities:** Honor-system bar; in-room massage; snowshoes. *In room:* TV/VCR, dataport, hair dryer, iron, Jacuzzi (some).

WHERE TO DINE

Friday and Saturday nights in Waitsfield, the **American Flatbread** ★★ bakery (✆ **802/496-8856**) on Route 100 serves terrific organic-flour pizzas to the public from 5:30 to 9:30pm. Come early to place your name on the waiting list.

Bass Restaurant ★★ *Value* NEW AMERICAN The Bass Restaurant is in a multilevel former dinner theater with a circular stone fireplace and a blond-wood bar. Light jazz plays in the background, and sculpture enlivens the space. The main courses range from oven-roasted duck with black currant and orange jus to crabmeat-stuffed whole trout to a macadamia-crusted tuna loin on coconut rice. It's a quiet, romantic spot that offers excellent value, delivering more than you would expect for the price. (Most entrees are less than $16.)

527 Sugarbush Access Rd., Warren. ✆ **802/583-3100.** www.bassrestaurant.com. Main courses $13–$25. AE, MC, V. Sun–Thurs 5–10pm; Fri–Sat 5–11pm.

The Common Man ★ EUROPEAN The Common Man is in a century-old barn, and the interior is soaring and dramatic. Chandeliers, floral carpeting on the walls (weird, but it works), and candles on the tables meld successfully and coax all but coldhearted guests into a relaxed frame of mind. You'll be halfway through the meal before you notice there are no windows. The menu strives to be as ambitious and appealing as the decor. It doesn't hit the mark as consistently as it once did, and guests often find themselves poking at a bland offering or two. Yet it remains a local favorite, probably for the atmosphere. Entrees range from Vermont-raised rabbit braised with white wine and aromatic vegetables to duck with port sauce, trout amandine, and New Zealand lamb roasted and served with a tomato, garlic, and rosemary sauce.

3209 German Flats Rd., Warren. ✆ **802/583-2800.** www.commonmanrestaurant.com. Reservations recommended in season. Main courses $17–$27. AE, DISC, MC, V. Daily 6–9pm in ski season; closed Sun–Mon rest of the year.

The Den ★ AMERICAN In a nutshell: good food, decent service, no frills. A local favorite since 1970 for its well-worn, neighborly feel, it's the kind of spot where you can plop down in a pine booth, help yourself to the salad bar while awaiting your main course, then cheer on the Red Sox on the tube over the bar. The menu offers usual pub fare, including burgers, Reubens, roast-beef sandwiches, meal-size salads, and pork chops with applesauce and french fries.

Junction of Routes 100 and 17, Waitsfield. © **802/496-8880.** Main courses $4.95–$6.95 at lunch, $8.95–$14 at dinner. AE, MC, V. Sun–Thurs 11:30am–10pm; Fri–Sat 11:30am–11pm.

John Egan's Big World Pub & Grill ★ GRILL Gonzo extreme skier John Egan starred in 10 Warren Miller skiing films, but *really* took a risk when he opened this restaurant on Route 100 in the valley. In a 1970s-style motel dining room decorated with skiing mementos (including a bar made of ski sections signed by skiing luminaries), the Big World Pub compensates with a small but above-average pub menu that the chef often pulls off with unexpected flair: Menu options include snow crab cakes with chipotle sauce, duck-and-scallion wontons, and salads with Vermont chèvre, demonstrating a real effort to rise above pub fare. The wood-grilled items are always crowd pleasers, including chicken breast glazed with Vermont cider, ginger, and lime.

Rte. 100, Warren. © **802/496-3033.** Main courses $11–$17; burgers and sandwiches $6.50. AE, MC, V. Daily 5–9:30pm.

The Spotted Cow ★★ NEW AMERICAN/FRENCH Set on the ground floor of a small, rustic retail complex in Waitsfield, The Spotted Cow is a low-ceiling, modern, natural-wood spot with cherry banquettes and windows facing out onto a walkway. The place has the cozy feel of a bistro that only locals know about, with a more cultivated than funky air. The kitchen shines with creative approaches to old favorites. Venison is always on the menu, as is fresh fish. The duck and lamb cassoulet is a good choice, as is the Bermuda fish chowder, made with a splash of black rum. A vegetarian special is available.

Bridgestreet Marketplace (at corner of Rte. 100 and E. Warren Rd.), Waitsfield. © **802/496-5151.** Reservations recommended. Main courses $18–$24. MC, V. Tues–Sun 5:30–9pm.

The Warren House Restaurant ★ NEW AMERICAN With a cozy location in a 1958 sugarhouse, this is a popular and casual spot not far from the slopes. The menu is creative but doesn't stray too far from the familiar—call it eclectic comfort food. Starters include crab cakes made with herbed rémoulade, as well as several salads, including goat cheese wrapped in walnuts and served on baby greens. For main courses, look for roasted rack of lamb, chile-coffee beef ribs, merlot-braised duckling, filet mignon grilled and served with a fresh pesto aioli, and grilled swordfish with red curry over soba noodles.

2585 Sugarbush Access Rd., Warren. © **800/817-2055** or 802/583-2421. Reservations recommended. Main courses $14–$20. AE, MC, V. Wed–Sun 5:30–9:30pm (until 10pm Fri–Sat). Call first in summer and fall. Closed 1st 2 weeks of May and Nov.

7 Montpelier, Barre & Waterbury

Montpelier is 13 miles SE of Waterbury, 9 miles NW of Barre, 178 miles NW of Boston, and 39 miles SE of Burlington.

Montpelier ★★ may very well be the most down-home, low-key state capital in the U.S. Rising up behind the gold dome of the capitol isn't a bank of mirror-sided skyscrapers, but a thickly forested hill. Montpelier, it turns out, is no self-important center of politics, but a small town that just happens to be home to a state government. It's an agreeable place to pass an afternoon, or spend a night, if you want to see just how small-town Vermont really ticks.

Montpelier centers on two main boulevards: State Street, lined with state government buildings; and Main Street, with many of the town's shops. It's all very compact, manageable, and cordial. The downtown sports a pair of hardware stores next door to each another, good bookstores, and the **Savoy,** 26 Main St. (✆ **802/229-0509** or 802/229-0598), one of the best art movie houses in northern New England. A large cup of cider and popcorn slathered with real, unclarified butter costs less than a small popcorn at a mall cinema.

Nearby **Barre** (pronounced *Bar*-ry) is more commercial and less charming, but shares an equally vibrant past. Barre has more of a blue-collar demeanor than Montpelier. The historic connection to the thriving granite industry is glimpsed occasionally, from the granite curbstones lining the long Main Street to the signs for commercial establishments carved out of locally hewn rock. Barre attracted talented stone workers from Italy and Scotland (it has a statue of Robert Burns), who helped give the turn-of-the-20th-century town a lively, cosmopolitan flavor.

About 10 miles west of Montpelier, **Waterbury** ★ is at the juncture of Route 100 and I-89, making it a commercial center by default, if not by design. Set along the Winooski River, it tends to sprawl more than other Vermont towns, perhaps in part because of the flood of 1927, which came close to leveling the town. It's also because the town has attracted an inexplicable number of food companies (including Ben & Jerry's Ice Cream Store and Green Mountain Coffee) that have built factories and outlets in outlying former pastures. With its location between Montpelier and Burlington and easy access to Stowe and Sugarbush, Waterbury has started to attract more émigrés looking for the good life.

Downtown, with its brick commercial architecture and sampling of handsome early homes, is worth a brief tour, but most travelers are either passing through or looking for "that ice-cream place." Despite its drive-thru quality, Waterbury makes a decent home base for further explorations in the Green Mountains, in Burlington, 25 miles to the west, and in Montpelier to the east.

ESSENTIALS

GETTING THERE Montpelier is accessible via Exit 7 off I-89. For Barre, take Exit 8. Waterbury is at Exit 10 off I-89. For bus service to Montpelier, contact **Vermont Transit** (✆ **800/451-3292** or 802/229-9220; www.vermonttransit.com).

For bus service to Waterbury, call **Vermont Transit;** for train service to Waterbury, contact **Amtrak** (✆ **800/872-7245;** www.amtrak.com), whose *Vermonter* makes daily departures from New York.

VISITOR INFORMATION The **Central Vermont Chamber of Commerce** (www.central-vt.com) is on Stewart Road off Exit 7 of I-89. Turn left at the first light; it's a half-mile farther on the left. The chamber is open Monday through Friday from 9am to 5pm.

The **Waterbury Tourism Council** (www.waterbury.org) operates a small, unstaffed booth stocked with helpful brochures on Route 100 just north of I-89. It's open daily from 7am to 10pm.

EXPLORING MONTPELIER & BARRE

Start your exploration of Montpelier with a visit to the gold-domed **State House** ★ at 115 State St. (✆ **802/828-2228**), guarded out front by a statue of Ethan Allen. Three capitol buildings have risen on this site since 1809; the present building retained the portico designed during the height of Greek Revival style in 1836.

Fun Fact The Story of Ben & Jerry

Doleful cows standing amid a bright green meadow on Ben & Jerry's ice cream pints have almost become a symbol for Vermont, but Ben & Jerry's cows—actually, they're Vermont artist Woody Jackson's cows—also symbolize friendly capitalism ("hippie capitalism," as some prefer).

The founding of the company is legend in business circles. Two friends from Long Island, New York, Ben Cohen and Jerry Greenfield, started the company in Burlington in 1978 with $12,000 and a few mail-order lessons in ice-cream making. The pair experimented with flavor samples obtained free from salesmen and sold their product out of an old downtown gas station. Embracing the outlook that work should be fun, they gave away free ice cream at community events, staged free outdoor films in summer, and plowed profits back into the community. Their free-spirited approach, along with the exceptional quality of their product, built a successful corporation, with sales rising into the hundreds of millions of dollars.

The main factory in Waterbury is one of Vermont's most popular tourist attractions. The plant is located about a mile north of I-89 on Route 100, and the grounds have a festival marketplace feel to them. During summer season, crowds mill about waiting for the 30-minute **factory tours.** Tours are first-come, first-served, and run every 10 minutes from 9am to 8pm in July and August (open daily with shorter hours and tours on the half-hour in the off season, but always open at least from 9am–5pm); afternoon tours fill up quickly, so get there early to avoid a long wait.

Once you've got your ticket, browse the small **ice-cream museum** (learn the long, strange history of Cherry Garcia), buy a cone of your favorite flavor at the scoop shop, or lounge along the promenade. Tours are $3, $2 for seniors, and free for children under 12. A $20 package deal includes a tour, a T-shirt, and a pint of the good stuff.

Kids enjoy the "Stairway to Heaven," which leads to a playground, and a "Cow-Viewing Area," which is self-explanatory. The tours are informative and fun, and conclude with a sample of the day's featured product. For more information, call ✆ **866/BJTOURS** or 802/882-1240.

Modeled after the temple of Theseus in Athens, it's made of Vermont granite. Self-guided tours are offered whenever the capitol is open, Monday through Friday (except holidays) from 8am to 4pm. Guided tours are run between July and mid-October, Monday through Friday from 10am to 3:30pm and Saturday from 11am to 2:30pm, every half-hour. The tour is informative and fun (and free); it's worthwhile if you're in the area, but not worth a major detour.

A short stroll from the State House is the **Vermont Historical Society Museum** ★, 109 State St. (✆ **802/828-2291;** www.vermonthistory.org). The museum is housed in a replica of the elegant old Pavilion Building, a prominent Victorian hotel, and contains a number of artifacts, including a gun once owned by Ethan Allen. It's normally open Tuesday to Saturday, from 10am to 4pm, and from May to October, it's also open

Sundays from noon to 4pm. Admission is $5 for adults, $3 for students or seniors. There's also a store on the premises.

Rock of Ages Quarry ★★ When in or around Barre, listen for the deep, throaty hum of industry. That's the Rock of Ages Quarry, set on a hillside high above town near the aptly named hamlet of Graniteville. A free visitor center presents informative exhibits, a video about quarrying, a glimpse of an old granite quarry (no longer active), and a selection of granite gifts. Self-guided tours of the old quarry are free. For a look at the active quarry (the world's largest), sign up for a guided half-hour tour. An old bus groans up to a viewer's platform high above the 500-foot, man-made canyon, where workers cleave huge slabs of fine-grained granite and hoist them out using 150-foot derricks anchored with a spider's web of 15 miles of steel cable. It's an operation to behold.

773 Graniteville Rd. (P.O. Box 482, Barre, VT 05641), Graniteville. © **802/476-3119.** www.rockofages.com. Guided tours $4 adults, $3.50 seniors, $1.50 children 6–12. Visitor center (free) May–Oct Mon–Sat 8:30am–5pm; Sun noon–5pm (in foliage season Sun 8:30am–5:30pm). Guided tours offered late May to mid-Oct Mon–Fri 9:15am–3pm, also Sat during foliage season. Closed July 4. From Barre, drive south on Rte. 14, turn left at lights by McDonald's; watch for signs to quarry.

WHERE TO STAY

IN MONTPELIER

Capitol Plaza Hotel ★ The favored hotel of folks on business with the state government, it's also well located (across from the capitol) to serve visitors exploring the town. The small lobby has a Colonial cast to it; guest rooms on the three upper floors adopt a light, faux-Colonial tone, and more amenities than you may expect. Bottom line: nothing fancy, but clean, comfortable, and convenient.

100 State St., Montpelier, VT 05602. © **800/274-5252** or 802/223-5252. Fax 802/229-5427. www.capitolplaza.com. 58 units. $98 double; foliage season from $119 double, $118–$168 suite. AE, DISC, MC, V. **Amenities:** Restaurant. *In room:* A/C, TV, dataport, hair dryer, iron.

Inn at Montpelier ★ Two historic in-town homes comprise the Inn at Montpelier, and both are welcoming accommodations appealing to those who enjoy historic architecture. The main, cream-colored Federal-style inn, built in 1827, has a mix of historical and up-to-date furnishings, along with a sunny sitting room and deck off the rear of the second floor. (Room no. 27 is especially pleasant, with a large private deck.) The property is somewhat more sparely furnished than other historic inns in the area (you're better off heading to Waitsfield or Warren if you're in search of the quintessential Vermont inn), but it offers comfortable lodging and is an easy stroll from downtown.

147 Main St., Montpelier, VT 05602. © **802/223-2727.** Fax 802/223-0722. www.innatmontpelier.com. 19 units. $109–$194 double. Rates include continental breakfast. AE, DC, DISC, MC, V. **Amenities:** Bike rental; in-room massage; dry cleaning. *In room:* A/C, TV, dataport.

IN WATERBURY

The Old Stagecoach Inn ★ This handsome, gabled home, within walking distance of downtown, is full of wonderful details such as painted wood floors, a pair of upstairs porches, an old library with a stamped tin ceiling, and a chessboard. Originally built in 1826, the house was gutted and revamped in 1890 in ostentatious period style by an Ohio millionaire. After some years of quiet disuse, it was converted to an inn in the late 1980s by owners who preserved the historical detailing. Guest rooms are furnished in an understated Victorian style, mostly with oak and pine furniture and antiques. It's not a polished inn (expect some worn carpeting), but it's quite comfortable. The two third-floor rooms have the original exposed beams and skylights, and are pleasant and open. The three back rooms share a bathroom and offer guests the feel of a friendly farmhouse.

18 N. Main St., Waterbury, VT 05676. ✆ **800/262-2206** or 802/244-5056. Fax 802/244-6956. www.oldstagecoach.com. 11 units, 3 rooms share 1 bathroom. $65–$120 double; foliage season, Christmas week, and Presidents' Day weekend $75–$180 double. Rates include breakfast. 2-night minimum stay during peak periods. AE, DISC, MC, V. Pets allowed ($10 per pet per night). **Amenities:** Restaurant.

Thatcher Brook Inn ★ On busy Route 100 near the Ben & Jerry's factory, guests have the illusion they are considerably farther away from this major artery. The late-19th-century, white clapboard building has a pleasing historical character, though it has undergone significant renovations and expansions. The additions have kept its Queen Anne–style architectural integrity intact. The common areas downstairs are worn to a nice patina. The guest rooms are all carpeted and decorated with furniture varying from Ethan Allen new to flea-market oak, but the overall character takes its cue from a somewhat fussy country look. Room nos. 14 through 17 are larger and more spacious; room nos. 8 through 11 have back balconies that face a wooded hillside. Some rooms have air-conditioning.

Rte. 100, Waterbury, VT 05676. ✆ **800/292-5911** or 802/244-5911. www.thatcherbrook.com. 22 units. $80–$175 double; foliage season, holidays, Christmas week, and Presidents' Day weekend $135–$225 double; $305–$399 suite. Rates include breakfast. 2-night minimum stay during foliage season; 3-night minimum stay during Christmas. AE, DC, DISC, MC, V. **Amenities:** Restaurant; access to fitness center. *In room:* Jacuzzi (some), fireplace (some).

WHERE TO DINE

A creation of the New England Culinary Institute, **La Brioche Bakery & Cafe** (✆ **802/229-0443**) occupies the corner of Montpelier's State and Main streets. A deli counter offers baked goods such as croissants and baguettes. Get them to go, or settle into a table in the afternoon sun outdoors.

I've spent many a cold afternoon inside the cleverly named **Capitol Grounds** ★ at 45 State St. (✆ **802/223-7800**), a stone's throw from the gold dome of the state capitol. It's one of my favorite coffeehouses in New England: a great, youthful spot for an espresso, hot chocolate, soup, delicious sandwich, or baked goods while peering out windows at the goings-on of town, watching the snow fall, or leafing through one of the newspapers or free papers they leave out. You'll find everyone from mothers and their kids to State House interns to Greenpeace members hanging out here.

IN MONTPELIER

Main Street Grill & Bar ★★ AMERICAN/ECLECTIC This modern, comfortable restaurant serves as classroom and ongoing exam for students of the New England Culinary Institute, just down the block. It's not unusual to see knots of students, toques at a rakish angle, walking between the restaurant and class. You can eat in the first-level dining room, watching street life through the broad windows, or burrow in the homey bar downstairs. Dishes change every 3 months, but vegetarian dishes are always on the menu.

Also of note is the second-floor **Chef's Table** ★★ (✆ **802/229-4202**), which is also owned by the culinary institute, but operates on a different schedule. (It's open Tues–Sat for dinner.) This intimate and well-appointed dining room offers more refined fare, such as a smoked pork chop with apple-fennel salad, rosemary lamb chops, grilled swordfish with an olive tapenade, five-spiced quail, and interesting treatments of lobster.

118 Main St., Montpelier. ✆ **802/223-3188** or 802/229-9202 (Chef's Table). Limited reservations accepted. Lunch $6.50–$8.95; dinner $12–$17. AE, DISC, MC, V. Tues–Fri 11:30am–2pm and 5:30–9pm; Sat 9am–2pm and 5:30–9pm; Sun 10am–2pm and 5:30–9pm. Closed Mon.

IN WATERBURY

Marsala Salsa ★ INDIAN/MEXICAN The owner is from Trinidad, was raised on the cuisine of India, and worked at a Mexican restaurant in Nevada. The result? Marsala Salsa, an unexpected oasis that offers two international cuisines, both well prepared at reasonable prices. The restaurant, in a funky storefront in Waterbury's historic downtown, is decorated with a light and culturally ambiguous touch. Service is friendly and informal. Mexican entrees include carne asada and *bistec picado,* strips of sirloin charbroiled with homemade avocado-lime butter. If you're more tempted by the Asian subcontinent, try the curries or tandoori chicken, or a wonderful shrimp *shaag*—a light curry with sautéed shrimp, spinach, and carrots.

15 Stowe St. ✆ **802/244-1150.** Reservations recommended on weekends. Main courses $6.95–$13. MC, V. Tues–Sat 5–9:30pm.

8 Stowe

Stowe is a wonderful destination, summer, fall, and winter. One of Vermont's first winter destination areas, it has managed the decades-long juggernaut of growth with patience and aplomb. Condo developments and strip-mall-style restaurants are around, to be sure. Yet the village has preserved its essential character nicely, including trademark views of surrounding mountains and vistas across the fertile farmlands of the valley floor. Thanks to its history and charm, Stowe tends to attract a more affluent clientele than, say, Killington or Okemo.

Stowe is quaint, compact, and home to what may be Vermont's most gracefully tapered church spire, atop the Stowe Community Church. Because the mountain is a few miles from the village, the town doesn't suffer that woebegone emptiness that many ski villages do in summer. You can actually park your car and explore on foot by or bike, which isn't the case at ski resorts that have developed around large parking lots and condo clusters.

Most of the growth in recent decades has taken place along Mountain Road (Rte. 108), which runs northwest of the village to the base of Mount Mansfield and the Stowe ski area. Here you'll find an array of motels, restaurants, shops, bars, and even a three-screen cinema, with many establishments nicely designed or at least tastefully tucked out of view. The road has all the convenience of a strip-mall area, but with little of the aesthetic blight.

ESSENTIALS

GETTING THERE Stowe is on Route 100 north of Waterbury and south of Morrisville. In summer, Stowe can also be reached via Smugglers Notch on Route 108. This pass, which squeezes narrowly between rocks and is not recommended for RVs or trailers, is closed in winter.

Stowe has no direct train or bus service. Go to Waterbury, 10 miles south of Stowe, via **Amtrak** (✆ **800/USA-RAIL;** www.amtrak.com), then connect to Stowe via a rental car from **Thrifty** (✆ **802/244-8800;** www.thrifty.com), a ride from **Richard's Limousine Service** (✆ **800/888-3176** or 802/253-5606), or a taxi from **Peg's Pick Up** (✆ **802/253-9490**).

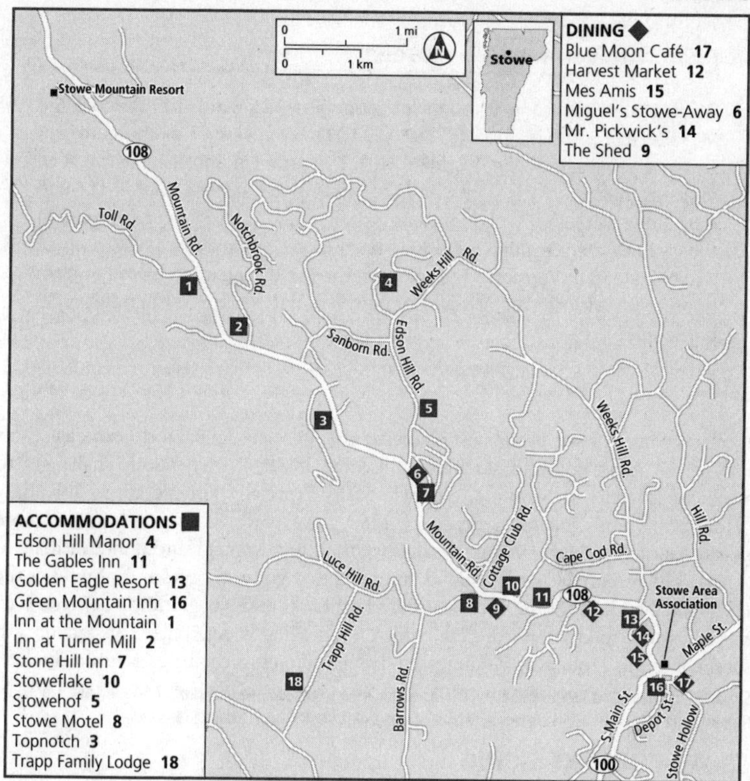

VISITOR INFORMATION The **Stowe Area Association** (© **877/603-8693** or 802/253-7321; www.gostowe.com) maintains a handy office on Main Street in the village center. It's open Monday through Friday from 9am to 8pm, Saturday and Sunday from 10am to 5pm (limited hours during slower seasons).

The **Green Mountain Club** (© **802/244-7037**), a venerable statewide association devoted to building and maintaining backcountry trails, has a visitor center on Route 100 between Waterbury and Stowe.

SPECIAL EVENTS The weeklong **Stowe Winter Carnival** (© **802/253-7321**) has taken place annually, from the middle to the end of January, since 1921. The fest features a number of wacky events involving skis, snowshoes, and skates, as well as nighttime entertainment. Don't miss the snow sculpture contest or "turkey bowling," which involves sliding frozen birds across the ice.

DOWNHILL SKIING

Stowe Mountain Resort ★★★ Stowe was one of the first, one of the classiest, and one of the most noted ski resorts in the world when it opened in the 1930s. Its regional dominance has eroded somewhat—Killington, Sunday River, and Sugarloaf, among others, have all captured large shares of the New England market. But this historic resort, first developed in the 1930s, still has loads of charm and plenty of

Tips The Vermont Ski Museum

When you're schussing through little downtown Stowe, the **Vermont Ski Museum** at 1 South Main St. (© **802/253-9911**; www.vermontskimuseum.org) makes a serviceable stop; it's filled with memorabilia and exhibits on such topics as the history of ski lifts, and the interesting Vermont Ski Hall of Fame is on the mezzanine level. Inductees include Mead Lawrence (two medals in the 1950 Winter Olympics) and Billy Koch (silver medalist in 1976), both of whom trained in Vermont. The museum is open daily except Tuesdays, from noon to 5pm (closed all of Nov). Suggested donations are $3 per adult or $5 per family.

excellent runs. It's one of the best places for the full New England ski experience, it's one of the most beautiful ski mountains, and it offers tremendous challenges to advanced skiers, with winding, old-style trails. Especially notable are its legendary "Front Four" trails (National, Starr, Lift Line, and Goat), which have humbled more than a handful of skiers attempting to grope their way from advanced intermediate to expert. The mountain has four good, long lifts that go from bottom to top—not the usual patchwork of shorter lifts you find at other ski areas. Beginning skiers can start out across the road at Spruce Peak, which has gentler, wider trails. This section will soon change its look, as townhomes are being built across the base of Spruce Peak.

Stowe, VT 05672. © **800/253-4754** or 802/253-3000. www.stowe.com. Vertical drop: 2,360 ft. Lifts: 1 gondola, 8 chairlifts (1 high-speed), 2 surface lifts. Skiable acreage: 480. Adult day lift tickets $76–$78.

CROSS-COUNTRY SKIING

Stowe is an outstanding destination for cross-country skiers, offering three groomed ski areas with a combined total of more than 100 miles of trails traversing everything from gentle valley floors to challenging mountain peaks.

The **Trapp Family Lodge Cross-Country Ski Center,** on Luce Hill Road, 2 miles from Mountain Road (© **800/826-7000** or 802/253-8511; www.trappfamily.com), was the nation's first cross-country ski center. It remains one of the most gloriously situated in the Northeast, set atop a ridge with views across the broad valley and into the folds of the mountains flanking Mount Mansfield. The center offers 30 miles of groomed trails (plus 60 miles of backcountry trails) on its 2,700 acres of rolling forestland. Rates are $16 for a trail pass, and $20 for equipment rental.

The **Edson Hill Manor Ski Touring Center** (© **800/621-0284** or 802/253-7371) has 33 miles of wooded trails just off Mountain Road (about $10 for a day pass). Good ski touring is also enjoyed at the **Stowe Mountain Resort Cross-Country Touring Center** (© **800/253-4754** or 802/253-3000), with 48 miles at the base of Mount Mansfield; passes cost $15 for adults, $8 for kids ages 6 to 12.

SUMMER OUTDOOR PURSUITS

Stowe's history is linked to winter recreation, but it's also a great fair-weather destination, surrounded by lush, rolling green hills and open farmlands, and dominated by craggy **Mount Mansfield,** Vermont's highest peak at 4,393 feet.

Deciding how to get atop Mount Mansfield is half the challenge. The **toll road** ★ (© **802/253-7311**) traces its lineage back to the 19th century, when it served horse-drawn vehicles bringing passengers to the old hotel sited near the mountain's crown. (The hotel was demolished in the 1960s.) Drivers now wend their way up this road and park below the summit; a 2-hour hike along well-marked trails will bring you to the top for unforgettable views. The toll road is open from mid-May to mid-October. The fare is $18 per car with up to six passengers, $4 per additional person. Ascending on foot or by bicycle is free.

Another option is the **Stowe gondola** ★ (© **802/253-7311**), which whisks visitors to the summit at the Cliff House Restaurant. Hikers can explore the rugged, open ridgeline, then descend before twilight. The gondola runs from mid-June to mid-October. The round-trip cost is $16 for adults, $9 for children ages 6 to 12. (In winter, you can take a scenic ride to the top—*if* you're dressed in street clothes—for $19 per person, regardless of age.)

One of the most understated local attractions is the **Stowe Recreation Path** ★★, winding 5.3 miles from behind Stowe Community Church up the valley toward the mountain, ending behind the Topnotch Tennis Center. This exceptionally appealing pathway, completed in 1989, is heavily used by locals in summer; in winter, it serves as a cross-country ski trail. Connect to the pathway at either end or at points where it crosses side roads that lead to Mountain Road. No motorized vehicles or skateboards are allowed.

All manner of recreational paraphernalia is available for rent at the **Mountain Sports & Bike Shop** (© **802/253-7919**) on the Rec Path, including full-suspension demo bikes, baby joggers, and bike trailers. Basic bike rentals are $16 for 4 hours, plenty long enough to explore the path. The shop is on Mountain Road (across from the Golden Eagle Resort), open from 9am to 6pm daily in summer. (It's also a good spot for cross-country ski and snowshoe rentals.)

WHERE TO STAY

EXPENSIVE

Stone Hill Inn ★★ With just nine rooms, the contemporary Stone Hill Inn (built in 1998) offers personal service and a handy location, along with room amenities such as Egyptian cotton towels, and double-sided gas fireplaces that front double Jacuzzis in the sizable bathrooms. Room layouts are roughly the same, each with a small sitting area. The high-ceilinged common rooms have fireplaces and billiard tables, and a well-stocked guest pantry has complimentary beverages. An outdoor hot tub provides a relaxing soak. Breakfast is in a bright morning room and hors d'oeuvres are set out each evening. Stonehill lacks a patina of age, but here you'll forego timeworn character in exchange for quiet, luxury, and romance.

89 Houston Farm Rd. (just off Mountain Rd. midway between village and ski area), Stowe, VT 05672. © **802/253-6282.** www.stonehillinn.com. 9 units. $265–$390 double; holidays and foliage season $350–$370 double. Rates include breakfast. 2-night minimum stay weekends and foliage season; 3-night minimum stay holiday weekends; 4-night minimum stay Christmas week. AE, DC, DISC, MC, V. Not suitable for children. **Amenities:** Jacuzzi; game room; self-service laundry; movie library; snowshoes and toboggan. *In room:* A/C, TV/VCR, hair dryer, safe, no phone.

Stoweflake ★★ Stoweflake is on Mountain Road 1¾ miles from the village. The newer guest rooms are nicer than those at Topnotch—they're regally decorated and have amenities such as two phones and wet bars. The resort has five categories of guest rooms in two wings; the "superior" rooms in the old wing are a bit cozy. They're okay for an overnight, but you're better off requesting "deluxe" or better if staying a few days. The spa and fitness facilities are adequate, but lack the over-the-top sybaritic elegance of Topnotch (what, no waterfalls?). Facilities include a decent-size fitness room with Cybex equipment, a squash/racquetball court, a coed Jacuzzi, and a small indoor pool.

1746 Mountain Rd. (P.O. Box 369), Stowe, VT 05672. ✆ **800/253-2232** or 802/253-7355. Fax 802/253-6858. www.stoweflake.com. 95 units, including 10 suites, plus 12 town houses. Peak winter season $170–$270 double, $390 suite; holiday season $180–$290 double, suite to $340; off season $150–$250 double, $360 suite. Call for town house or package info. 2-night minimum stay on most weekends; 4-night minimum stay during holidays. AE, DC, DISC, MC, V. **Amenities:** 2 restaurants; indoor pool, outdoor pool; 2 tennis courts; racquetball/squash court; health club; spa; bike rental; children's center; game room; business center; salon; limited room service; in-room massage; babysitting; laundry service; dry cleaning. *In room:* A/C, TV, dataport, fridge, coffeemaker, hair dryer, iron.

Topnotch ★★★ A boxy, uninteresting exterior hides a creatively designed interior at this upscale resort and spa. The main lobby is ski-lodge modern, with lots of stone and wood and a huge moose head hanging on the wall. The guest rooms are attractively appointed, most in country pine. Ten units have wood-burning fireplaces; 18 have Jacuzzis; and third-floor rooms have cathedral ceilings. The main attractions here are the resort's spa and activities, which range from horseback riding in summer to cross-country skiing and indoor tennis in winter. The spa has nice touches, such as fireplaces in the locker rooms.

4000 Mountain Rd., Stowe, VT 05672. ✆ **800/451-8686** or 802/253-8585. Fax 802/253-9263. www.topnotch-resort.com. 92 units. $180–$320 double, $315–$755 suite; holidays $380–$495 double, $500–$860 suite. 6-night minimum stay Christmas week. AE, DC, DISC, MC, V. Pets allowed. **Amenities:** 2 restaurants; indoor pool; outdoor pool; tennis courts (4 indoor, 10 outdoor); fitness room; spa; Jacuzzi; sauna; concierge; limited room service; horseback riding. *In room:* A/C, TV/VCR w/pay movies, dataport, fridge, coffeemaker, hair dryer, iron, safe.

Trapp Family Lodge The Trapp family of *Sound of Music* fame bought this sprawling farm high up in Stowe in 1942, just 4 years after fleeing the Nazi takeover of Austria. Descendants of Maria and Baron von Trapp continue to run this Tyrolean-flavored lodge on 2,700 mountainside acres. It's a comfortable resort hotel, though designed more for efficiency than elegance. Guest rooms are a shade or two better than run-of-the-mill hotel rooms, and most come complete with fine valley views and private balconies. Room prices are high; they offer access to nice facilities, but little else. Better value can be found elsewhere in the valley. Sunday concerts are held in the meadow in summer.

700 Trapp Hill Rd., Stowe, VT 05672. ✆ **800/826-7000** or 802/253-8511. Fax 802/253-5740. www.trappfamily.com. 120 units. $195–$585 double; $295–$880 suite. Rates include meals during holidays and foliage season. 3-night minimum stay Presidents' Day week and foliage season; 5-night minimum stay Christmas week. AE, DC, MC, V. Depart Stowe westward on Rte. 108; in 2 miles bear left at fork near white church; continue up hill following signs for lodge. **Amenities:** 2 restaurants; heated indoor pool; 2 outdoor pools (1 for adults only); 4 clay tennis courts; fitness center; sauna; children's programs; game room; limited room service; in-room massage; babysitting; coin-op washers/dryers; dry cleaning. *In room:* TV.

MODERATE

Edson Hill Manor ★★ The Edson Hill Manor sits atop a long, quiet drive 2 miles from Mountain Road and has an ineffably quirky charm. The main lodge dates to the 1940s; the four carriage houses just up the hill are newer. The compound is set amid a rolling landscape of lawns, hemlocks, and maples. The comfortable common room in the main house is like a movie set for a country retreat—tapestries, pastels, and oils adorn the walls. Most of the nine guest rooms in the main lodge have pine walls and floors, wood-burning fireplaces, Colonial maple furnishings, wingback chairs, and four-poster beds. The 16 carriage-house rooms are somewhat larger, but lack the cozy charm of the main inn and feel more like motel units (*really nice* motel units). Some units have TVs.

1500 Edson Hill Rd., Stowe, VT 05672. ✆ **800/621-0284** or 802/253-7371. www.edsonhillmanor.com. 25 units. $159–$219 double B&B. MAP plans also available. Off-season rates lower, foliage season and holiday rates higher. AE, DISC, MC, V. Pets and young children welcome in carriage-house units only. **Amenities:** Restaurant; access to nearby pool; riding stables (private lessons available). *In room:* A/C (some manor house rooms only).

Green Mountain Inn ★★★ This handsome, historic structure sits right in the village, and it's the best choice for those seeking a sense of New England history along with a bit of pampering. A sprawling hostelry with 100 guest rooms spread among several buildings old and new, it feels far more intimate, with accommodations tastefully decorated in an early-19th-century motif that befits the 1833 vintage of the main inn. More than a dozen units have Jacuzzis and/or gas fireplaces, and the Mill House has rooms with CD players, sofas, and Jacuzzis that open into the bedroom from behind folding wooden doors. The deluxe Mansfield House has double Jacuzzis, marble bathrooms, and 36-inch TVs with DVD players. The most expensive rooms are all superb.

Main St. (P.O. Box 60), Stowe, VT 05672. ✆ **800/253-7302** or 802/253-7301. Fax 802/253-5096. www.greenmountaininn.com. 100 units. $115–$305 double and suite; foliage season $165–$325 double and suite; holidays $225–$625 double and suite. 2-night minimum stay summer and winter weekends and in foliage season. AE, DISC, MC, V. Pets allowed in some rooms with restrictions (call first; $20 per night). **Amenities:** Restaurant; heated outdoor pool (year-round); fitness room; Jacuzzi; sauna; steam room; game room; limited room service; in-room massage; laundry service. *In room:* A/C, TV w/pay movies, hair dryer.

Inn at The Mountain ★ Kids This is the "official" hotel of Stowe Mountain Resort—near the base of the mountain (but not ski-in-ski-out) and owned and operated by the ski mountain. A low-key casual spot, more like an upscale motel than a fancy lodge, it has clean, attractive rooms that are more spacious than average motel rooms, with veneer furniture, small refrigerators, and tiny balconies that face the pool and woods. Ask about the 39 nearby condos, suitable for families. Some rooms have air-conditioning and fireplaces.

5781 Mountain Rd., Stowe, VT 05672. ✆ **800/253-4754** or 802/253-3000. www.stowe.com. 33 units (inn rooms, condos also available). $119–$359 double; apts and town houses higher. Holiday season rates higher. 5-night minimum stay Christmas week. AE, DC, DISC, MC, V. **Amenities:** Restaurant; outdoor pool; 9 tennis courts; fitness center; Jacuzzi; sauna; limited room service. *In room:* TV, fridge.

Stowehof ★ High on a hillside, this inn feels far removed from the hubbub of the valley floor. The exterior architecture has that aggressive, neo-Tyrolean ski-chalet styling, but inside, the place comes close to magical—it's pleasantly woodsy, folksy, and rustic, with heavy beams and pine floors, ticking clocks, and maple tree trunks carved into architectural elements. Guests may feel a bit like characters in *The Hobbit.* Furnished without a lot of fanfare, each guest room is decorated individually: some bold and festive with sunflower patterns, others subdued and quiet. Four have wood-burning fireplaces, 24 have air-conditioning, and all have good views. The lodge is next to Wiessner Woods, 80 acres laced with hiking and cross-country ski trails.

434 Edson Hill Rd. (P.O. Box 1139), Stowe, VT 05672. ✆ **800/932-7136.** www.stowehofinn.com. 40 units, 2 guesthouses. $83–$240 double; holidays and foliage season $150–$445 double. Rates include breakfast. 2-night minimum stay on some weekends; 4-night minimum stay during holidays. AE, DC, MC, V. **Amenities:** Restaurant; heated outdoor pool; 4 tennis courts; nearby health club; outdoor Jacuzzi; sauna; game room; business center; in-room massage; laundry service; dry cleaning; valet parking; safe; horseback riding (extra fee). *In room:* A/C (some), TV.

MODERATE/INEXPENSIVE

Golden Eagle Resort ★ Kids Of the numerous lodgings lined up along Mountain Road, few are more family-friendly than this one. The Golden Eagle gets it right with a children's play area, three pools, two ponds for fishing, regulation tennis court, 80 acres of private woods laced with hiking trails, and even a small spa offering kids' massages. Adults enjoy the place, too, particularly the romantic cottages and suites with fireplaces and whirlpools behind the main building. The spa also has a popular indoor Jacuzzi, and the mornings-only cafe serves breakfasts of fresh Stowe-raised eggs, dairy, and bacon. Don't come if you're expecting white-glove service, valet parking, and a fancy restaurant; the Golden Eagle is perfect at being a haven for family rustication. A few apartment units with full kitchens or kitchenettes and a house are also for rent.

511 Mountain Rd. (P.O. Box 1090), Stowe, VT 05672. ✆ **800/626-1010** or 802/253-4811. Fax 802-253-2561. www.goldeneagleresort.com. 94 rooms. $84–$180 double, $129–$359 suite; holidays and foliage season, $129–$285 double, $179–$479 suite. AE, DISC, MC, V. **Amenities:** Cafe; 2 outdoor pools; indoor pool; tennis court; Jacuzzi; spa. *In room:* Coffeemaker, fridge, fireplace (some), Jacuzzi (some).

INEXPENSIVE

Inn at Turner Mill ★ Set in a narrow wooded valley along a tumbling stream, this homey 1936 building was built as a residence and inn. In the winter, some of the rooms are combined into suites to accommodate groups, including one with a kitchen, two bathrooms, and a brick fireplace. The inn is eclectic in style, with everything from frightfully orange wall-to-wall carpeting to attractive and rustic log furniture. Most memorable is the monolithic stone walkway outside and the steep staircase to the upper floors. In summer, rooms rent separately (all have private bathrooms), and rates include breakfast. The inn is a short trip from the mountain and across the road from the Rec Path, making it a good destination for bike-trippers; snowshoes are also supplied upon request.

56 Turner Mill Lane, Stowe, VT 05672. ✆ **800/992-0016** or 802/253-2062. www.turnermill.com. 8 units. $60–$110 double, $100–$285 apartment; holidays and foliage season higher. Summer and fall rates include breakfast. AE, MC, V. *In room:* TV, fridge, coffeemaker.

Stowe Motel Value This is one of Stowe's best choices for those traveling on a budget. The motel has 60 units spread among three buildings; rooms are basic but slightly larger than average, and have some comfortable touches, such as couches and coffee tables. Efficiency units have two-burner stoves.

2043 Mountain Rd., Stowe, VT 05672. ✆ **800/829-7629** or 802/253-7629. Fax 802/253-9971. www.stowemotel.com. 30 units. Standard units $64–$89 double, foliage season $94–$120 double; efficiency units $74–$150 double. AE, DISC, MC, V. Pets allowed in some rooms ($10 per pet per night). **Amenities:** Outdoor heated pool; Jacuzzi; game room; snowshoes. *In room:* A/C, TV, dataport, fridge.

WHERE TO DINE

The **Harvest Market** ★, 1031 Mountain Rd. (✆ **802/253-3800**), is the place for gourmet-to-go. Browse Vermont products and imports, then pick up some fresh-baked goods, such as the pleasantly tart raspberry squares, to bring back to the ski lodge or take for a picnic along the bike path. High prices may cause your eyebrows to arch, but if you're not on a tight budget, it's a good place to splurge.

Blue Moon Cafe ★★★ NEW AMERICAN Delectable crusty bread on the table, Frank Sinatra crooning in the background, and vibrant local art on the walls are clues that this isn't your typical ski-area pub-fare restaurant. A short stroll off Stowe's main street in a contemporary setting in an older home, the Blue Moon offers the village's finest dining. The menu changes every Friday, but count on lamb, beef, and veggie dishes, plus seafood dishes. The kitchen staff has superb instincts for spicing and creates inventive dishes such as grilled yellowfin tuna with tomatillo salsa fresca and smoked yellow pepper coulis, a banana leaf-steamed halibut with Thai coconut curry, and sweet-and-sour braised rabbit. Desserts are pure delights, like a white chocolate mousse with caramelized banana.

35 School St. ✆ **802/253-7006.** Reservations recommended. Main courses $20–$26. AE, DISC, MC, V. Daily 6–9:30pm. In shoulder seasons, usually open weekends only; call first.

Mes Amis BISTRO The friendly Mes Amis is in a cozy structure above Mountain Road not far from the village. Once a British-style pub, it was pleasantly converted from half-timber Tudor decor to something more broadly European. A quiet, friendly spot, it lacks even an iota of pretension. The menu is rather limited (usually only five entrees), but the specials round out the offerings. The restaurant has three cozy dining rooms and a bar. Appetizers include smoked salmon on toast points and baked stuffed clams; entrees feature steaks and fish. The house specialty is a half-duck roasted with a hot-and-sweet sauce.

311 Mountain Rd. ✆ **802/253-8669.** Reservations accepted for 6 or more. Dinner $16–$20. DC, MC, V. Tues–Sun 5:30–10pm (open for appetizers at 4:30pm).

Miguel's Stowe-Away ★ MEXICAN/SOUTHWEST In an old farmhouse midway between the village and the mountain, Miguel's packs in folks looking for the spiciest Mexican and Tex-Mex food in the valley. Start off with a margarita or Vermont beer, then order up appetizers such as empanadas, nachos, or jalapeños. Follow up with sizzling fajitas, the good chicken Santa Fe or fish chimichangas, or a filling combo plate. Desserts range from the complicated (apple-mango compote with cinnamon tortilla and ice cream) to the simple (chocolate-chip cookies). Miguel's is popular enough to offer its own brand of chips, salsa, and other products. Expect a boisterous atmosphere on busy nights.

3148 Mountain Rd. ✆ **800/254-1240** or 802/253-7574. www.miguels.com. Reservations recommended on weekends and in ski season. Main courses $11–$18 (mostly under $14). AE, DISC, MC, V. Daily 5–10pm (from 5:30pm in summer); lunch in winter only noon–3pm.

Mr. Pickwick's ★★ PUB FARE/ECLECTIC Mr. Pickwick's is a pub and restaurant that's part of Ye Old English Inne. It could justly be accused of being a theme-park restaurant, with the theme being "ye olde Englande" all the way. But it's been run since 1983 with such creative gusto by British ex-pats Chris and Lyn Francis that it's hard not to enjoy yourself here. Start by admiring the Anglo gewgaws while relaxing at handsome wood tables at the booths (dubbed "pews"). You can try one of the 150 beers (many British) before ordering longtime house specialties such as bangers and mash (sausages and potatoes), fish and chips, and beef Wellington, or perhaps something from the newer, more upscale selection: Glenlivet-smoked shrimp, a Kobe beef burger, Szechuan stir-fried lobster.

433 Mountain Rd. ✆ **802/253-7558.** Reservations accepted for parties of 6 or more. Main courses $6.95–$13 at lunch, $14–$24 at dinner. AE, DC, MC, V. Daily 11am–1am.

The Shed ★ PUB FARE Stowe has plenty of options for pub fare, but The Shed is the most consistently reliable. Since it opened more than 3 decades ago, this friendly, informal place has won fans by the sleighload with filling fare and feisty camaraderie. It has a bar area with free popcorn and a good selection of beverages, ranging from craft beers brewed on the premises to frozen rum drinks to homemade root beer. The dining room has a chain-restaurant feel, but the bright solarium in the rear is a perfect spot to perch during sunny Sunday brunch. Meals are pub-fare eclectic: nachos (a bit soggy), burgers (including veggie burgers), chicken Alfredo, grilled tuna, prime rib, Asian stir-fry noodles, and taco salads.

1859 Mountain Rd. ✆ **802/253-4364.** Reservations recommended weekends and holidays. Main courses $5–$9.95 at lunch, $11–$19 at dinner. AE, DC, DISC, MC, V. Sun–Thurs 11:30am–10pm; Fri–Sat 11:30am–11pm.

9 Burlington

Burlington is 215 miles NW of Boston, 98 miles S of Montreal, and 154 miles NE of Albany, NY.

Burlington is a vibrant college town—home to the University of Vermont, known as UVM—that's continually, valiantly resisting the onset of middle age. It's the birthplace of hippies-turned-corporation Ben & Jerry's. (Look for the sidewalk plaque at the corner of St. Paul and College sts. commemorating the first store.) It elected a socialist mayor in 1981, Bernie Sanders, who's now Vermont's lone representative to the U.S. Congress. Burlington was also the birthplace of the jam rock band Phish.

It's no wonder that Burlington has become a magnet for those seeking an alternative to big-city life. Burlington has a superb location overlooking Lake Champlain and the Adirondacks of northern New York. To the east, the Green Mountains rise dramatically, with two of the highest points (Mount Mansfield and Camel's Hump) stretching above the undulating ridge.

The pedestrian mall (Church St.), a creation that has failed in so many other towns, works here. New construction has brought large-scale department stores right smack downtown, reversing the flight to the mall that has plagued other small cities. The city's scale is pleasantly geared toward pedestrians—park your car and walk when you can.

ESSENTIALS

GETTING THERE Burlington is at the junction of I-89, Route 7, and Route 2. **Burlington International Airport,** about 3 miles east of downtown, is served by **Continental Connection** (✆ **800/532-3273;** www.continental.com), **Delta Connection** (✆ **800/221-1212;** www.delta.com), **JetBlue** (✆ **800/538-2583;** www.jetblue.com), which flies in daily from New York City, **United** (✆ **800/864-8331;** www.united.com), and **US Airways Express** (✆ **800/428-4322;** www.usair.com).

The **Amtrak** (✆ **800/USA-RAIL;** www.amtrak.com) ***Vermonter*** offers daily departures for Burlington from Washington, Baltimore, Philadelphia, New York, New Haven, and Springfield, MA.

Vermont Transit Lines (✆ **802/864-6811;** www.vermonttransit.com), with a depot at 345 Pine St., has bus connections from Albany, Boston, Hartford, New York's JFK Airport, and other points in Vermont, Massachusetts, and New Hampshire.

VISITOR INFORMATION The **Lake Champlain Regional Chamber of Commerce,** 60 Main St. (✆ **877/686-5253** or 802/863-3489; www.vermont.org), maintains an information center in a stout 1929 brick building just up from the waterfront and a short walk from Church Street Marketplace. Hours are Monday through Friday from 8am to 5pm. On weekends, helpful maps and brochures are left in the entryway for visitors. A summer-only information booth is also staffed at the Church Street Marketplace at the corner of Church and Bank streets (no phone).

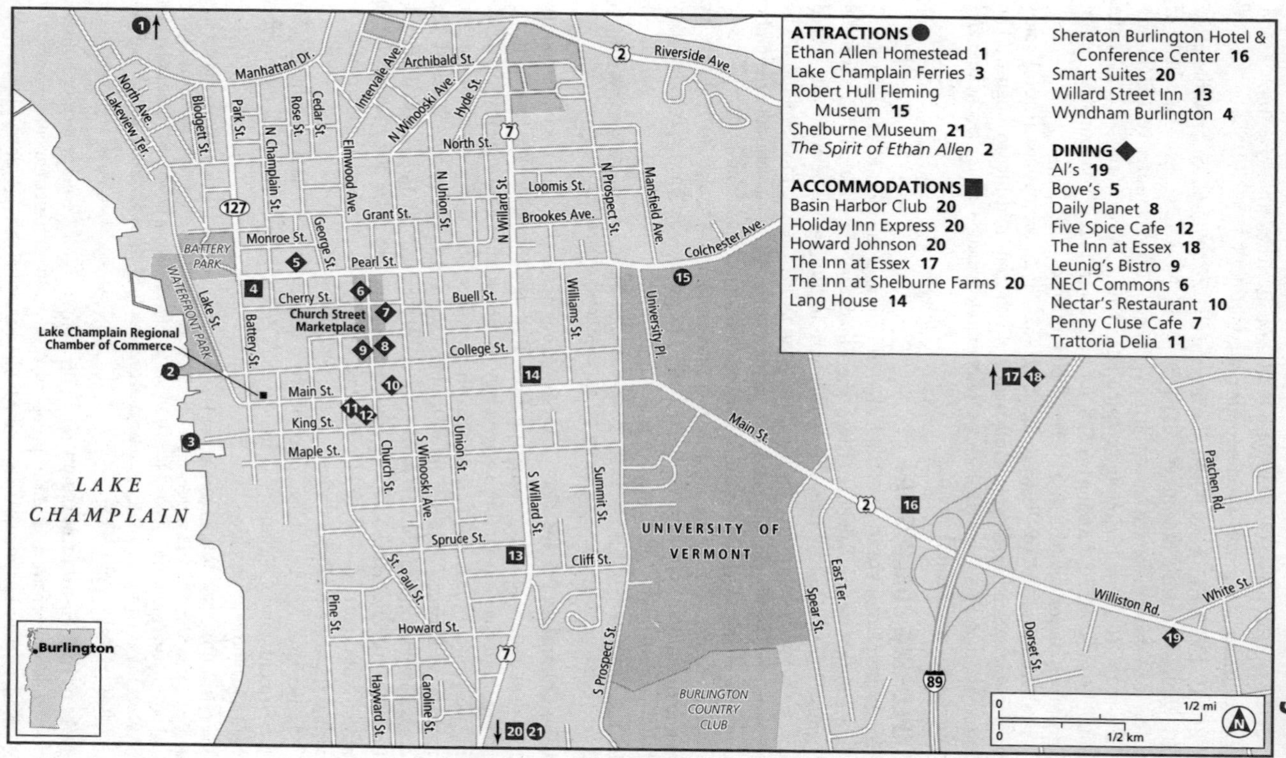

ATTRACTIONS
Ethan Allen Homestead 1
Lake Champlain Ferries 3
Robert Hull Fleming Museum 15
Shelburne Museum 21
The Spirit of Ethan Allen 2
ACCOMMODATIONS
Basin Harbor Club 20
Holiday Inn Express 20
Howard Johnson 20
The Inn at Essex 17
The Inn at Shelburne Farms 20
Lang House 14
Sheraton Burlington Hotel & Conference Center 16
Smart Suites 20
Willard Street Inn 13
Wyndham Burlington 4
DINING
Al's 19
Bove's 5
Daily Planet 8
Five Spice Cafe 12
The Inn at Essex 18
Leunig's Bistro 9
NECI Commons 6
Nectar's Restaurant 10
Penny Cluse Cafe 7
Trattoria Delia 11
LAKE CHAMPLAIN
UNIVERSITY OF VERMONT
BURLINGTON COUNTRY CLUB
BATTERY PARK
WATERFRONT PARK
Church Street Marketplace
Lake Champlain Regional Chamber of Commerce
Manhattan Dr.
Intervale Ave.
Archibald St.
N Winooski Ave.
Hyde St.
Riverside Ave.
North Ave.
Lakeview Ter.
Blodgett St.
Park St.
N Champlain St.
Rose St.
Cedar St.
Elmwood Ave.
North St.
N Union St.
N Willard St.
Loomis St.
Brookes Ave.
N Prospect St.
Mansfield Ave.
Grant St.
George St.
Monroe St.
Pearl St.
Colchester Ave.
Cherry St.
Buell St.
Williams St.
University Pl.
Lake St.
Battery St.
College St.
Main St.
King St.
Maple St.
Church St.
S Winooski Ave.
S Union St.
S Willard St.
Summit St.
Spruce St.
Cliff St.
St. Paul St.
Pine St.
Howard St.
Hayward St.
Caroline St.
S Prospect St.
East Ter.
Spear St.
Patchen Rd.
Dorset St.
Williston Rd.
White St.
0
1/2 mi
1/2 km
Burlington

The free local weekly *Seven Days* (www.sevendaysvt.com) carries topical and lifestyle articles, along with a very good list of events.

SPECIAL EVENTS **First Night Burlington** (✆ **802/863-6005;** www.firstnight burlington.com) turns downtown into a stage on New Year's Eve. Hundreds of performers—from rockers to vaudevillians—play at nearly three dozen venues (mostly indoors) for 10 hours beginning at 2pm. The evening finishes with a bang at the midnight fireworks. Admission is $20 for adults (or $12 if you purchase before Christmas), $6 for children, and covers all performances.

The **Vermont Mozart Festival** (✆ **802/862-7352;** www.vtmozart.com) takes place in and around Burlington (and farther afield) from mid-July to August. (The festival also has a winter series.) Ticket prices range widely. Call for a schedule and information, or check the website.

EXPLORING BURLINGTON

Ethan Allen Homestead ★ A quiet retreat on one of the most idyllic, least developed stretches of the Winooski River, the Ethan Allen Homestead is a shrine to Vermont's favorite son. While Allen wasn't born in Burlington, he eventually settled here on property confiscated from a British sympathizer during the Revolution. The reconstructed farmhouse is an enduring tribute to this Vermont hero; an orientation center gives an intriguing multimedia accounting of Allen's life and other points of regional history. The house is open for tours from mid-October to mid-May by appointment only (a day's notice is required). The grounds are open year-round daily from dawn to dusk. Park admission is free.

Rte. 127. ✆ **802/865-4556.** Admission $3 adults, $4 seniors, $2.50 children 5–17, $15 per family. May–Oct daily 9am–5pm; Nov–Apr Sat–Sun 9am–5pm. Take Rte. 127 northward from downtown; look for signs.

Lake Champlain Ferries ★★ Car ferries chug across the often placid, sometimes turbulent waters of Lake Champlain from Burlington to New York between late spring and foliage season; this is a good way to cut out miles of driving if you're heading west toward the Adirondacks, and a pleasant, inexpensive way to see the lake and mountains. Between June and mid-October, several daily 90-minute narrated lake cruises are also offered; the cost is $8.95 to $9.50 for adults, and up to $4.20 for children. No reservations are accepted; travelers are advised to arrive 20 to 30 minutes in advance of departure. Call ✆ **802/864-9669** for details of these narrated cruises, as well as brunch and dinner cruises.

Ferries also cross Lake Champlain between Grande Isle, VT, and Plattsburgh, NY (year-round), and Charlotte, VT, and Essex, NY (Apr to early Jan). Call the number below for more information.

King St. Dock. ✆ **802/864-9804.** www.ferries.com. $15 one-way fare for car and driver from Burlington to Port Kent. Round-trip fares $7.75 adults, $3.45 children 6–12, free for children under 6. Burlington ferry operates mid-May to mid-Oct. Frequent departures in summer 7:30am–7:30pm. Charlotte to Essex and Grande Isle to Cumberland Head, $8.50 one-way for car and driver, $5.25 round-trip adult passenger, $4.50 seniors, $2 children. Schedule varies seasonally; call or check website for times.

Robert Hull Fleming Museum ★ This University of Vermont facility houses a fine collection of art and anthropological displays, with a permanent collection of African, ancient Egyptian, Asian, and Middle Eastern art. A selection of paintings by 20th-century Vermont artists is on permanent display, and changing exhibitions reflect varied cultures. Nearby metered parking is available weekends only. Call or check the website for a schedule of lectures and other special events.

Ethan Allen, Patriot & Libertine

In 1749, the governor of New Hampshire began giving away land to settlers willing to brave the howling wilderness of what is now Vermont. Two decades later, New York State courts decreed those grants void, opening the door for New York speculators to flood into the region, vowing to push the original settlers out of the valleys and up into the Green Mountains.

Not surprisingly, this decision didn't sit well with those already there, who established a network of military units, the Green Mountain Boys, and swore to drive out the New Yorkers. A hale fellow named Ethan Allen headed up the new militia, which launched a series of effective harrying raids against the impudent New Yorkers. The Green Mountain Boys destroyed homes, drove away livestock, and chased the New York sheriffs back across the border.

The American Revolution soon intervened, and Ethan Allen and the Green Mountain Boys took up the Revolutionary cause with vigor. They helped sack Fort Ticonderoga in New York in 1775, rallied to the cause at the famed Battle of Bennington, and generally continued to make nuisances of themselves to the British effort throughout the war.

Allen's fame grew as word spread about him and his Green Mountain Boys. A hard-drinking, fierce-fighting, large-living sort of guy, Allen became a legend in his own time. He could bite the head off a nail, one story claimed; another said that he was once bitten by a rattlesnake, which promptly belched and died.

While Allen's apocryphal exploits lived on following his death in 1789, he also left a more significant legacy. Vermont's statehood in 1791 was due in large part to the independence and patriotism the region showed under Allen; today you can't drive very far in Vermont without a reminder of Allen's historic presence—parks are named after him, inns boast that he once slept there, and you'll still hear the occasional story about his bawdy doings.

61 Colchester Ave. (UVM campus). ✆ **802/656-0750.** www.flemingmuseum.org. Admission $5 adults, $3 seniors and students, $10 family. Year-round Sat–Sun 1–5pm; Labor Day to Apr Tues–Fri 9am–4pm; May to Labor Day Tues–Fri noon–4pm.

Shelburne Museum ★★★ Kids Established in 1947 by Americana collector Electra Havenmeyer Webb, this museum contains one of the nation's most singular collections of American decorative, folk, and fine art, occupying some 37 buildings spread over 45 rolling acres, just 7 miles south of Burlington. The more mundane exhibits include quilts, early tools, decoys, and weather vanes. But the museum also collects and displays *whole* buildings from around New England and New York, such as an 1890 railroad station, a lighthouse, a stagecoach inn, an Adirondack lodge, and a round barn from Vermont. Even a 220-foot steamship is eerily landlocked on the museum's grounds. Additions over the years include a wonderful 1950s ranch house, furnished in period style, and an architecturally engaging Collector's House, made creatively of prefab metal structures and other materials, and featuring folk art displays.

Rte. 7 (P.O. Box 10), Shelburne. © **802/985-3346.** www.shelburnemuseum.org. Summer admission $18 adults, $9 children 6–18. Half-day rates after 3pm. May–Oct daily 10am–5pm. Selected buildings open Apr to late May and mid-Oct to Dec 31; call for information.

The *Spirit of Ethan Allen III* ★ Accommodating 500 passengers on three decks, The *Spirit of Ethan Allen III* offers a more genteel touring alternative to the ferry. The vistas of Lake Champlain and the Adirondacks haven't changed much since Samuel de Champlain first explored the area in 1609. The enclosed decks are air-conditioned, and food is available from a full galley, including dinner served nightly and Sunday brunch. The scenic cruise departs daily every other hour from 10am through 4pm. Parking is available at additional cost. New in 2006 will be scenic Art Cruises for $65 per person.

Burlington Boathouse. © **802/862-8300.** www.soea.com. Narrated cruises (1½ hr.) $9.95 adults, $3.95 children 3–11. Specialty cruises (dinner, brunch, mystery theater) priced higher; call for details. Daily mid-May to mid-Oct.

WHERE TO STAY

A number of chain motels are along Route 7 (Shelburne Rd.) in South Burlington, about a 5- to 10-minute drive from downtown. While they lack any trace of New England charm, they're modern, clean, and reliable. Among the better choices are these three, which are clustered together: **Holiday Inn Express,** 1712 Shelburne Rd. (© **866/762-7870** or 802/860-1112; www.hojo.com); **Smart Suites,** 1700 Shelburne Rd. (© **802/860-9900**); and **Howard Johnson,** 1720 Shelburne Rd. (© **800/874-1554** or 802/860-6000).

Basin Harbor Club ★★★ On 700 rolling lakeside acres, 30 miles south of Burlington, the Basin Harbor Club offers a detour into a slower-paced era. Established in

Moments No Business Like Snow Business

If you're a lover of science or nature, one of the more interesting day trips from Burlington is to the little hamlet of **Jericho,** about a 15- to 20-minute drive northeast on Route 15. Once there, you'll find the **Old Red Mill craft shop and museum** ★ (© **802/899-3225;** www.snowflakebentley.com).

This museum showcases America's finest repository of snowflake photographs, courtesy of one Wilson Bentley, the local farmer and amateur naturalist who lived here from 1885 until 1931, devising the world's first camera designed to capture images of snowflakes. He photographed some 5,000 snowflakes in his lifetime, publishing articles in *National Geographic* and first advancing the idea that no two of them are identical. The story of Bentley's determined pursuit of his studies is as entrancing as the photographs lining the walls, which reveal the amazing variety of crystalline structures created in snowstorms—many of them breathtakingly beautiful.

The museum is open daily from April to December (from 10am–5pm most days, from 1pm Sun), open Wednesday through Saturday only during the rest of the year. There's no admission charge.

1887, this is the sort of resort where you can spend a week and not get bored—that is, if you're a self-starter and don't need a perky recreational director to plan your day. The property has historic gardens, including the largest collection of annuals in Vermont. The trademark Adirondack chairs are scattered all over the property, inviting indolence. The main lodge has 38 rooms, though I prefer the rustic cottages, tucked along the shore and in shady groves. Nothing's too fancy, yet nothing's shabby; it's all comfortable in a New England-y old-money kind of way. From art classes to a lecture series, you're never far away from the pleasant sensation that you've stepped into an upscale summer camp for grown-ups. The staff even caters three meals daily. Living really high on the hog? You're in luck: This place even has its own private airstrip.

Basin Harbor Rd., Vergennes, VT 05491. ✆ **800/622-4000** or 802/475-2311. Fax 802/475-6545. www.basinharbor.com. 105 units. Summer $225–$450 double, $300–$1,500 cottage; spring and fall $150–$250 double, $200–$350 cottage. Rates include breakfast, lunch, and dinner in summer. Ask about B&B and MAP plans and rates. 2-night minimum stay on weekends. MC, V. Closed mid-Oct to mid-May. Pets allowed in cottages ($6.50 per pet per night). **Amenities:** 2 restaurants; outdoor pool; golf course; 5 tennis courts; fitness center; bike rentals; children's programs (summer); concierge; limited room service; babysitting; laundry service; dry cleaning; boat rentals (windsurfers, kayaks, canoes, day sailors, outboards); cruises. *In room:* A/C, dataport, hair dryer, iron.

The Inn at Essex ★★ Touted as "Vermont's Culinary Resort," this inn makes a persuasive case for that praise: Its chefs come straight from the New England Culinary Institute in Montpelier. The 120 rooms are every bit as impressive, and 20 acres of grounds on a majestic hillside setting only enhance the experience of staying here. Rooms and suites are fitted with reproduction furniture and decked in flowery wallpaper and bed covers; many are further gussied up by fireplaces, CD players, Jacuzzis, four-poster beds, and rocking chairs or full kitchens with Hearthstone gas stoves, in some cases.

70 Essex Way, Essex, VT 05452. ✆ **800/727-4295** or 802/878-1100. Fax 802/878-0063. www.innatessex.com. 120 units. May–Oct $209–$309 double, $249–$529 suite; Nov–Apr $169–$239 double, $209–$479 suite. AE, DC, MC, V. **Amenities:** 2 restaurants; outdoor pool; golf course; fitness center; spa; bike rentals; massage. *In room:* TV, dataport, fridge (some), Jacuzzi (some), fireplace (some).

The Inn at Shelburne Farms ★★ The numbers behind this elaborate mansion on the shores of Lake Champlain tell the story: 60 rooms, 10 chimneys, 1,400 acres of land. Built in 1899, this sprawling Edwardian "farmhouse" is the place to fantasize about the lifestyles of the *truly* rich and famous. From your first glimpse of the mansion from the winding drive, you'll know you've left the rest of the world behind. That's by design—noted landscape architect Frederick Law Olmsted had a hand in shaping the grounds. The 24 guest rooms vary in terms of decor and upkeep; some are overdue for a makeover. If you're feeling flush, ask for Overlook, with the great views of the grounds. Of the budget units (with shared bathroom), I like the Oak Room with its lake view.

Harbor Rd., Shelburne, VT 05482. ✆ **802/985-8498.** www.shelburnefarms.org. 24 units, 7 units share 4 bathrooms. $225–$395 double with private bathroom; $135–$195 double with shared bathroom; $225–$335 cottage. 2-night minimum stay on weekends. AE, DC, DISC, MC, V. Closed mid-Oct to mid-May. **Amenities:** Restaurant; lake swimming; tennis court; children's farmyard; babysitting; farm tours.

Lang House ★ This stately, white Queen Anne mansion (1881) sits on the hillside between downtown and the University of Vermont. Not as extravagant as the Willard Street Inn (whose owners are co-owners here), it's still very comfortably appointed and lavish, with rich cherry and maple woodwork. Rooms vary, but most have small bathrooms and small TVs. I like two corner units: Room no. 101, on the first floor, has a wonderfully old-fashioned bathroom with wainscoting, and room no. 202 has a cozy sitting area tucked in the turret, which gets lots of afternoon light.

360 Main St., Burlington, VT 05401. ✆ **877/919-9799** or 802/652-2500. Fax 802/651-8717. www.langhouse.com. 11 units. $145–$225 double. Rates include breakfast. AE, DISC, MC, V. *In room:* A/C, TV.

Sheraton Burlington Hotel & Conference Center ★ The largest conference facility in Vermont, the Sheraton also does a decent job catering to individual travelers and families. This sprawling and modern complex (with 15 conference rooms) just off the interstate, a 5-minute drive east of downtown, features a sizable indoor garden area. All guest rooms have two phones and in-room Nintendos; rooms in the newer addition are a bit nicer, furnished in a simpler, lighter country style. Ask for a room facing east (no extra charge) to enjoy the views of Mount Mansfield and the Green Mountains.

870 Williston Rd., Burlington, VT 05403. ✆ **800/866-6117** or 802/865-6600. Fax 802/865-6670. 309 units. $89–$229 double. AE, DC, DISC, MC, V. **Amenities:** Restaurant; lounge; indoor pool; fitness room; 2 Jacuzzis; concierge; limited room service; laundry service; video rentals (extra charge). *In room:* A/C, TV w/pay movies, dataport, coffeemaker, hair dryer, iron.

Willard Street Inn ★★ This impressive, historic inn is in a splendid Queen Anne–style brick mansion a few minutes' walk from the university. The inn has soaring first-floor ceilings, cherry woodwork, and a beautiful window-lined breakfast room. The home was built in 1881 by a bank president and once served as a retirement home before its conversion to an inn. Among the best units are room no. 12, which boasts a small sitting area and views of the lake, and spacious room no. 4, which has a sizable bathroom and lake views.

349 S. Willard St. (2 blocks south of Main St.), Burlington, VT 05401. ✆ **800/577-8712** or 802/651-8710. Fax 802/651-8714. www.willardstreetinn.com. 15 units, 1 with detached private bathroom. $125–$225 double. Rates include breakfast. 2-night minimum stay on weekends. AE, DC, DISC, MC, V. *In room:* A/C, TV, dataport.

Wyndham Burlington ★★ *Kids* This nine-story hotel has great views (if you spend $20 extra on a lakeside room), as well as a terrific downtown location between the waterfront and Church Street Marketplace. Five cabana rooms open up to the pool area and are ideal for families.

60 Battery St., Burlington, VT 05401. ✆ **802/658-6500.** Fax 802/658-4659. www.wyndhamburlington.com. 256 units. Summer $159–$269 double; winter $139–$179 double. Ask about packages. AE, DISC, MC, V. Parking in attached garage $5 per day. **Amenities:** 2 restaurants; indoor pool; fitness room; Jacuzzi; concierge; free airport shuttle; limited room service; babysitting; laundry service; dry cleaning. *In room:* A/C, TV w/pay movies, dataport, coffeemaker, hair dryer, iron, safe.

WHERE TO DINE

Al's ★ *Kids* BURGERS & FRIES Al's is where Ben and Jerry (yes, *the* Ben and Jerry) go to satisfy french-fries cravings. This classic roadside joint is both fun and efficient. The vats of fries draw people back time and again; the other offerings (hamburgers, hot dogs, sloppy-joe-like barbecue) are okay, but nothing special.

1251 Williston Rd. (Rte. 2, just east of I-89), South Burlington. ✆ **802/862-9203.** Sandwiches $1–$3.95. No credit cards. Mon 10:30am–10pm; Tues–Thurs 10:30am–11pm; Fri–Sat 10:30am–midnight; Sun 11am–10pm.

Bove's ★ *Value* ITALIAN A Burlington landmark since 1941, Bove's is a classic spaghetti joint a couple of blocks from the Church Street Marketplace—and nothing costs more than 9 bucks. The facade is black and white, its octagonal windows closed to prying eyes by Venetian blinds. Step through the doors and into a lost era, grab a seat at a vinyl-upholstered booth and browse the menu: spaghetti with meat sauce, spaghetti with meatballs, and . . . well, you get the idea. The red sauce is rich and tangy, while the garlic sauce packs a punch strong enough to knock you out of your booth. Cocktails are inexpensive.

68 Pearl St. ✆ **802/864-6651.** www.boves.com. Sandwiches $1.75–$6.95; dinner items $6.50–$8.85. No credit cards. Tues–Fri 2–9pm; Sat 11am–9pm. Closed Sun–Mon.

Daily Planet ★ ECLECTIC This popular spot often brims with college students and downtown workers on evenings and weekends. The mild mayhem adds to the charm, enhancing the eclectic, interesting menu. The meals are better prepared than you might expect from a place that takes its cues from a pub. Look for lamb stew, seafood Newburg, strip steak with a Gorgonzola and green-peppercorn sauce, or rainbow trout with peach and red-onion relish.

15 Center St. ✆ **802/862-9647.** Reservations recommended for parties of 5 or more. Main courses $5.75–$7.95 at lunch, $11–$20 at dinner. AE, DISC, MC, V. Sun–Thurs 5–9:30pm; Fri–Sat 5–10pm.

Five Spice Cafe ★★ *Finds* PAN-ASIAN With an intimate setting of wood floors and aquamarine wainscoting, Five Spice is a popular spot among college students and professors. They come not for the lively scene, but for the inventive chef's Asian-fusion cuisine, which draws on Thai, Vietnamese, and Chinese dishes. I usually start with the superb, spicy hot-and-sour soup, then move on to Thai tilapia or the robust kung-pao chicken. The dish with the best name on the menu—Evil Jungle Prince with Chicken—is also one of the best, featuring a light sauce of coconut milk, chiles, and lime leaves. Or simply do dim sum: The owners claim this is the only place you can find it between Boston and Montreal. Finish with a piece of ginger-tangerine cheesecake or one of the many liqueur-accented desserts.

175 Church St. ✆ **802/864-4045.** www.fivespicecafe.com. Reservations recommended on weekends and in summer. Main courses $4.50–$9.95 at lunch, $12–$18 at dinner. AE, DISC, MC, V. Mon–Thurs 11:30am–3pm and 5–9:30pm; Fri–Sat 11:30am–10pm; Sun 11am–9pm.

Inn at Essex ★★ REGIONAL/CONTINENTAL The Inn at Essex, about a 15-minute drive from Burlington, is the auxiliary campus of the Montpelier-based New England Culinary Institute. It offers both formal and informal dining rooms with meals prepared and served by New England's rising culinary stars. Both restaurants are housed in a large faux-farmhouse complex along the fringe of Burlington's suburban sprawl. Inside, the setting is quiet and comfortable. In the light and airy tavern, you may be tempted by the Caribbean grilled chicken with black-bean salsa, chicken puff pie, Tuscan salad, or honey-glazed pork chop. Amid the more intimate, country inn elegance of Butler's, the dinner fare is a bit more ambitious, with entrees that might run to Dijon-peppered rack of lamb, pan-seared salmon with a sorrel beurre blanc, oven-roasted veggies with goat cheese burritos, and a number of seafood specials. Ask about the kitchen tours.

70 Essex Way, Essex Junction. ✆ **800/727-4295** or 802/878-1100. www.innatessex.com. Reservations recommended at Butler's; not needed at The Tavern. Tavern main courses $4.50–$6.95 at lunch, $4.50–$9.95 at dinner. Butler's lunch $6.95–$13, dinner $15–$25. AE, DC, DISC, MC, V. Tavern daily 2–11pm. Butler's daily 11:30am–10pm.

Leunig's Bistro ★★ REGIONAL/CONTINENTAL This boisterous, fun place on the pedestrian mall has a retro old-world flair, with washed walls, a marble bar, crystal chandeliers, and oversize posters. The inventive, large menu features regional foods prepared with a Continental touch. Brunch is available on weekends; lunch includes sandwiches such as turkey cranberry melt. Dinner offerings change seasonally; in summer, you may find poached asparagus with smoked salmon or soft-shell crabs with a lemon-grass and coconut broth; in fall, look for hearty fare such as pork chops with green-peppercorn apple-cider sauce.

115 Church St. ✆ **802/863-3759.** Reservations recommended on weekends and holidays. Main courses $5.95–$7.95 at lunch, $8.95–$28 at dinner. AE, DISC, MC, V. Mon–Thurs 11am–10pm; Fri 11am–11pm; Sat 9am–11pm; Sun 9am–10pm.

NECI Commons ★★ *Value* BISTRO NECI Commons is a popular stop both for foodies sniffing out new trends and for those who like good value. Also a part of the New England Culinary Institute empire (The Inn at Essex and Montpelier's Main Street Grill & Bar are others), this lively, spacious, and busy spot is a training ground for aspiring chefs and restaurateurs. You can eat upstairs in the main dining room, which has soaring windows overlooking the Church Street Marketplace, or downstairs, where you can watch the chef-trainees prepare meals in the open kitchen. At Sunday brunch, look for wood-fired breakfast pizza, with eggs, bacon, tomato, and cheddar. Lunchtime offers delectable pizzas, soups, sandwiches (such as crab cake with chipotle sauce on a toasted roll), and more filling dishes such as salmon cake salad. For dinner, look for sirloin or filet of salmon served with the restaurant's famous Vermont cheddar potatoes or perhaps a pan-seared halibut with a shrimp–lemon grass broth. Prices are reasonable, the service excellent.

25 Church St. ✆ **802/862-6324.** Call before arrival for priority seating. Brunch $5.95–$7.95; lunch $6.95–$8.95; bistro $6.50–$8.95; dinner $8.50–$19. AE, DC, DISC, MC, V. Tues–Thurs 11:30am–3pm and 5:30–10pm; Fri–Sat 11:30am–3pm and 5:30–10:30pm; Sun 11am–3pm and 5:30–9:30pm. Closed Mon.

Nectar's Restaurant and Lounge CAFETERIA Burlington in microcosm parades through Nectar's over the course of a long day. In the morning, you'll find blue-collar workers and elderly gentlemen in ties enjoying heaping plates of eggs and hash browns. In midday, downtown office workers come in for lunch; and late in the evening, Nectar's adopts a sort of retro chic as clubbers from nearby clubs and Nectar's own lounge next door file through the cafeteria line for hamburgers, a plate of meatloaf, or a local microbrew and gravy fries, and to hang with friends.

188 Main St. ✆ **802/658-4771.** Breakfast $1.75–$6; lunch and dinner $2.50–$7.50. No credit cards. Mon–Fri 6am–2am; Sat–Sun 7am–2pm.

Penny Cluse Cafe ★★ CAFE/LATINO This gets my vote as the city's best choice for lunch or breakfast. A block off the Church Street Marketplace, Penny Cluse is a casual, bright, and popular spot decorated in a vaguely Southwestern motif. Among the better breakfasts is the Zydeco, with eggs, black beans, andouille sausage, and corn muffins. Lunch ranges from salads and sandwiches (the veggie Reuben with mushrooms, spinach, and red onions is excellent) to more elaborate fare such as adobo pork chops with plantain cake.

169 Cherry St. ✆ **802/651-8834.** Reservations recommended (dinner only). Breakfast $3.50–$6.50; sandwiches and lunch $6.25–$8. MC, V. Breakfast and lunch Mon–Fri 6:45am–3pm; Sat–Sun 8am–3pm.

Trattoria Delia ★★ ITALIAN If the idea of locally foraged mushrooms served over polenta with fontina causes you to sit up and take notice, this is your place. Serving the best Italian food in Burlington, Trattoria Delia is in a low-traffic location, almost hidden through a speak-easy-like door beneath a large building. But locals never fail to find it; be sure to reserve ahead if you're coming. Inside is pure culinary magic, with wild boar, filet mignon with white truffle butter, and classic pasta dishes, such as tagliatelle alla Bolognese. After your meal, you can choose from Italian dessert wines and traditional desserts such as tiramisu and *panna cotta.*

152 Saint Paul St. ✆ **802/864-5253.** Reservations recommended. Main courses $14–$20. DC, MC, V. Daily 5–10pm.

10 The Northeast Kingdom

Vermont's Northeast Kingdom has a more wild and remote character than much of the rest of the state. Consisting of Orleans, Essex, and Caledonia counties, the region was given its memorable nickname in 1949 by Sen. George Aiken, who understood the area's allure at a time when few others paid it much heed. What gives this region its character is stubborn, old-fashioned insularity.

In contrast to the dusky narrow valleys of southern Vermont, the Kingdom's landscape is open and spacious, with rolling meadows ending abruptly at the hard edge of dense boreal forests. The leafy woodlands of the south give way to spiky forests of spruce and fir. Accommodations and services for visitors aren't as plentiful or easy to find here as in the southern reaches of the state, but a handful of inns are tucked among the hills and in the forests.

Visitor information is available from the **Northeast Kingdom Chamber of Commerce,** 51 Depot Square, Suite 3 in St. Johnsbury (✆ **800/639-6379** or 802/748-3678; www.nekchamber.com).

DRIVING TOUR THE NORTHEAST KINGDOM

Start: **Hardwick**
Finish: **St. Johnsbury**
Time: **1 full day**

Start your tour at Hardwick, which is at the intersection of Routes 14 and 15, about 23 miles northwest of St. Johnsbury and 26 miles northeast of Montpelier:

❶ Hardwick

A small town with rough edges set on the Lamoille River, Hardwick has a compact commercial main street, some intriguing shops, a couple of casual, family-style restaurants, and one of Vermont's best natural food co-ops. (***Note:*** A Nov 2005 fire claimed part of this downtown block.)

From here, head north on Route 14 about 7 miles to the turnoff to Craftsbury and:

❷ Craftsbury Common

An uncommonly graceful village, Craftsbury Common is home to a small academy and a large number of historic homes and buildings spread along a green and the village's main street. The town occupies a wide upland ridge and offers sweeping views to the east and west. Be sure to stop by the old cemetery on the south end of town, where you can wander among historic tombstones of the pioneers, which date back to the 1700s. Craftsbury is an excellent destination for mountain biking and cross-country skiing.

From Craftsbury, continue north to reconnect to Route 14. You'll wind through the towns of Albany and Irasburg as you head north. At the village of Coventry, veer north on Route 5 to the lakeside town of:

❸ Newport

This commercial outpost (pop. 4,400) is set on the southern shores of Lake Memphremagog, a stunning 27-mile-long lake that's just 2 miles wide at its broadest point and the bulk of which lies across the border in Canada. From Newport, continue north on Route 5, crossing under I-91, for about 7 miles to the border town of Derby Line (pop. 2,000). This outpost has a handful of restaurants and antiques shops; you can usually park and walk across the bridge to poke around the Canadian town of Rock Island with simple ID such as a driver's license, though additional documents couldn't hurt. (That's for U.S. residents; travelers from other countries must ask at the U.S. Customs and Border Protection booth about returning before crossing the line.)

Back in Derby Line, look for the:

❹ Haskell Free Library & Opera House

At the corner of Caswell Avenue and Church Street (✆ **802/873-3022**), this handsome neoclassical building contains a public library on the first floor and an elegant opera house on the second, which is modeled after the old Boston Opera House. The theater opened in 1904 with advertisements promoting a minstrel show featuring "new songs, new jokes, and beautiful electric effects." It's a beautiful theater, with a scene of Venice painted on the drop curtain and carved cherubim adorning the balcony.

What's most curious about the structure, however, is that it lies half in Canada and half in the U.S. (The Haskell family donated the building jointly to the towns of Derby Line and Rock Island.) A thick black line runs beneath the seats of the opera house, indicating who's in the U.S. and who's in Canada. Because the stage is set entirely in Canada, apocryphal stories abound from its early days of frustrated U.S. officers watching fugitives perform on stage. More recently, the theater has been used for the occasional extradition hearing.

From Derby Line, retrace your path south on Route 5 to Derby Center and the juncture of Route 5A. Continue south on Route 5A to the town of Westmore on the shores of:

❺ Lake Willoughby

This glacier-carved lake is best viewed from the north, with the shimmering sheet of water pinched between the base of two low mountains at the southern end. With a distinctive alpine feel to the whole scene, this underappreciated lake is one of the most beautiful in the Northeast. Route 5A along the eastern shore is lightly traveled and ideal for biking or walking. To ascend the mountains by foot, see the "Getting Outdoors" section, below.

Head southwest on Route 16, which departs from Route 5A just north of the lake. Follow Route 16 through the peaceful villages of Barton and Glover. A little over a mile south of Glover, turn left on Route 122. Very soon on your left, look for the farmstead that serves as home to the:

❻ Bread & Puppet Theater

For nearly 3 decades, until 1998, Polish artist and performer Peter Schumann's Bread and Puppet Theater staged an elaborate annual summer pageant at this farm, attracting thousands. Attendees participated, watched, and lounged about the hillsides as huge, brightly painted puppets crafted of fabric and papier-mâché marched around the farm, acting out a drama that typically featured rebellion against tyranny of one form or another. It was like Woodstock without the music.

Alas, the summer event became so popular—and attracted so many people who weren't in the spirit of the event (drugs and surly dogs were a problem)—it overwhelmed the farm; in 1998, a killing at the adjacent campground during the annual pageant prodded Shumann to shut down the circus for good. The troupe periodically travels and stages shows on the road; for details about upcoming events, check the website www.theater-of-memory.com. Between June and October, you can still visit the venerable, slightly tottering barn, home to the **Bread and Puppet Museum** ★, with many of the puppets used in past

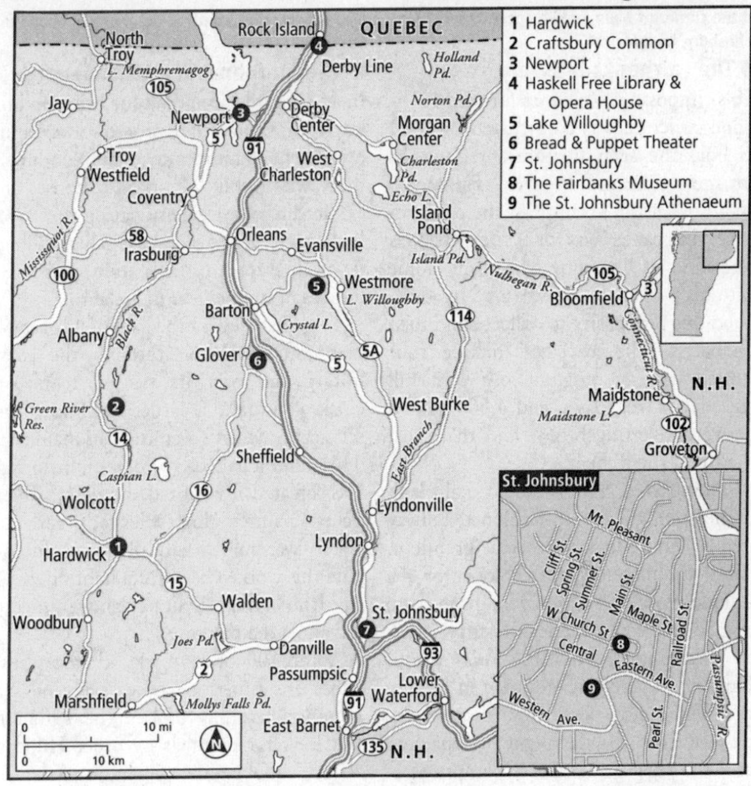

events. This remarkable display shouldn't be missed if you're near the area. Downstairs, in former cow-milking stalls, smaller displays include mournful washerwomen doing laundry and King Lear addressing his daughters. Upstairs, the vast hayloft is filled with soaring, haunting puppets, some up to 20 feet tall. Witty and eclectic, it seems a joint endeavor of David Lynch, Red Grooms, and Hieronymus Bosch. Admission is free, though donations are encouraged.

From Glover, continue south through serene farmlands to Lyndonville, where you pick up Route 5 south to:

❼ St. Johnsbury

This town of 7,600 inhabitants is the largest in the Northeast Kingdom and the major center of commerce. First settled in 1786, the town enjoyed a buoyant prosperity in the 19th century, largely stemming from the success of platform scales (invented—and still manufactured—here in 1830 by Thaddeus Fairbanks). The town, which has not suffered from the depredations of tourist boutiques and brewpubs, has an abundance of fine commercial architecture in two distinct areas, joined by steep Eastern Avenue. The more commercial part of town lies along Railroad Street (Rte. 5) at the base of the hill. The more ethereal part of town, with the library, St. Johnsbury Academy, and grand museum, is along Main Street at the top of the hill. The north end of Main Street is notable for its grand residential architecture.

At the corner of Main and Prospect streets in St. Johnsbury, look for:

❽ The Fairbanks Museum

This imposing Romanesque red-sandstone structure was constructed in 1889 to hold the accumulations of obsessive amateur collector Franklin Fairbanks, grandson of the inventor of the platform scale. Fairbanks was once described as "the kind of little boy who came home with his pockets full of worms." In adulthood, his propensity to collect continued unabated. His artifacts include four stuffed bears, a huge moose with full antlers, art from Asia, and 4,500 stuffed native and exotic birds—and that's just the tip of the iceberg.

The soaring, barrel-vaulted main hall, reminiscent of an old-fashioned railway depot, embodies Victorian grandeur. Amid the assorted clutter, look for the unique mosaics by John Hampson, who crafted scenes of American history—such as Washington bidding his troops farewell—entirely of mounted insects. In the Washington scene, for instance, iridescent green beetles form the epaulets, and the regal great coat is comprised of hundreds of purple moth wings. Words fail me; these works alone are worth the price of admission.

Open Tuesday through Saturday from 9am to 5pm, and Sunday from 1 to 5pm (© **802/748-2372;** www.fairbanksmuseum.org), admission is $5 for adults, $4 for seniors and children ages 5 to 17; $15 per family (maximum of three adults).

Also in town, just south of the museum on Main Street, is:

❾ The St. Johnsbury Athenaeum

In an Edward Hopper-esque brick building with truncated mansard tower and prominent keystones over the windows, the town's public library also houses an extraordinary art gallery dating to 1873. It claims to be the oldest art gallery still in its original form in the nation, and I see no reason to question that claim.

Your first view of the gallery is spectacular: After winding through the cozy library and past its ticking regulator clock, you round a corner and find yourself gazing across Yosemite National Park. This luminous 10×15-foot oil painting was created by noted Hudson River School painter Albert Bierstadt, and the gallery was built specifically to accommodate this work. The natural light flooding in from the skylight above nicely enhances the painting.

Some 100 other works fill the walls. Most are copies of other paintings (a common teaching tool in the 19th c.), but look for originals by other Hudson River School painters, including Asher B. Durand, Thomas Moran, and Jasper Cropsey.

The Athenaeum, 1171 Main St. (© **802/748-8291;** www.stjathenaeum.org), is open Monday and Wednesday from 10am to 8pm; Tuesday, Thursday, and Friday from 10am to 5:30pm; and Saturday from 9:30am to 4pm. Admission is free, but donations are encouraged.

GETTING OUTDOORS

MOUNTAIN BIKING The Craftsbury ridge has several excellent variations for bikers in search of easy terrain. Most of the biking is on hard-packed dirt roads through sparsely populated countryside. Views are sensational, and the sense of being well out in the country is very strong. The **Craftsbury Outdoor Center at Craftsbury Common** (© **802/586-7767;** www.craftsbury.com) rents mountain bikes and is an excellent source for maps and local information about area roads. A small fee is charged for using bikes on the cross-country ski trail network.

CROSS-COUNTRY SKIING The same folks who offer mountain biking at the Craftsbury Outdoor Center also maintain 61 miles of groomed cross-country trails through the gentle hills surrounding Craftsbury. The forgiving, old-fashioned trails, maintained by **Craftsbury Nordic Center** ★★ (✆ **802/586-7767**), emphasize pleasing landscapes rather than fast action. Another option is **Highland Lodge** ★ (✆ **802/533-2647;** www/highlandlodge.com) on Caspian Lake, with more than 30 miles of trails (about 10 miles of which are groomed) through rolling woodlands and fields. Should you care to stay, double rooms at the lodge run $222 to $310 in winter.

DOWNHILL SKIING

Jay Peak ★★ Just south of the Canadian border, Jay is Vermont's best choice for those who prefer to avoid all the modern-day glitz and clutter that seem to plague ski resorts elsewhere. While some new condo development has been taking place at the base of the mountain, Jay still has the feel of a remote, isolated destination, accessible by a winding road through unbroken woodlands. Thanks to its staggering snowfall (an average of 340 in., more than any other New England ski area), Jay has developed extensive glade skiing; the ski school also specializes in running the glades, making it a fitting place for advanced intermediates to learn how to navigate these exciting, challenging trails.

Rte. 242, Jay, VT 05859. ✆ **800/451-4449** or 802/988-2611. www.jaypeakresort.com. Vertical drop: 2,153 ft. Lifts: 1 60-person tram, 4 chairlifts, 2 surface lifts. Skiable acreage: 385 acres. Day lift tickets $58 adults, cheaper for Vermont residents.

WHERE TO STAY

Comfort Inn & Suites ★ This modern property consists of more than 100 units and has a number of nice touches, such as granite vanity counters and high-backed desk chairs. The rooms are pleasantly appointed (more like an inn than a motel), and the basement houses an appealing, if small, pool and fitness room, along with a game room outfitted with air hockey and a pool table. The hotel is just off I-91 about a mile south of downtown St. Johnsbury.

703 Rte. 5 S. (off Exit 20 of I-91), St. Johnsbury, VT 05819. ✆ **877/424-6423** or 802/748-1500. Fax 802/748-1243. 107 units. June to mid-Oct $139–$399 double and suite; mid-Oct to May $89–$139 double and suite. Rates include continental breakfast. AE, DISC, MC, V. **Amenities:** Indoor pool; fitness room; game room; coin-op washers/dryers. *In room:* A/C, TV, dataport, coffeemaker, hair dryer, iron.

Highland Lodge ★ Kids Built in the mid–19th century, this lodge has been accommodating guests since 1926. Just across the road from lovely Caspian Lake, it has 11 rooms furnished in a comfortable country style. Nearby are 11 cottages, 9 of which are equipped with kitchenettes. A stay here is supremely relaxing—the main activities include swimming and boating in the lake in summer, along with tennis on a clay court; in winter, the lodge maintains its own cross-country ski area with 30 miles of groomed trails. Behind the lodge is an attractive nature preserve that invites quiet exploration.

Caspian Lake, Greensboro, VT 05841. ✆ **802/533-2647.** Fax 802/533-7494. www.thehighlandlodge.com. 22 units, including 11 cottages. $240–$280 double. Call for summer rates. Rates include breakfast and dinner. DISC, MC, V. Closed mid-Mar to May and mid-Oct to Christmas. From Hardwick, take Rte. 15 east 2 miles to Rte. 16; drive north 2 more miles to East Hardwick. Head west and follow signs to the inn. **Amenities:** Restaurant; tennis court; watersports equipment rental; bike rental; children's program; game room; babysitting; laundry service; cross-county ski trails. *In room:* No phone.

Inn on the Common ★★★ This exceedingly handsome complex of three Federal-era buildings anchors the charming ridge-top village of Craftsbury Common, one of the most quintessential of New England villages. This is a stunning inn, and offers just the right measure of history and pampering. It tends to be a rather social place, attracting both families and couples seeking a romantic getaway. Dinner starts with cocktails at 6pm, guests seated family-style amid elegant surroundings at 7:30pm. The menu changes nightly, but includes well-prepared contemporary American fare. Some deluxe guest rooms have fireplaces.

Craftsbury Common, VT 05827. ✆ **800/521-2233** or 802/586-9619. Fax 802/586-2249. www.innonthecommon.com. 16 units. $135–$225 double; $235–$255 suite. Holiday and foliage season rates higher. 2-night minimum stay during foliage season, weekends, and Christmas week. AE, MC, V. Pets allowed with prior permission ($25 per visit). **Amenities:** Outdoor pool; tennis court; massage; babysitting; croquet. *In room:* Hair dryer, no phone.

Willoughvale Inn ★★ An elegant inn on a low-rise at the north end of Lake Willoughby, it has stunning views across the water to the twin mountains at the south end of the lake. This is an ideal location for a quiet retreat, especially in one of four cottages with kitchens right on the lake. (Available by the week only in July–Aug.) The 11 rooms in the lodge are tastefully appointed, with much of the furniture crafted in Vermont. The cottages tend to have more of a rustic Adirondack-lodge feel. (This sister property of the well-managed Green Mountain Inn in Stowe has a similar attention to detail.) It's hard to imagine a better place to spend a few days with books and a bicycle. The restaurant is also unpretentious, serving well-prepared meals along with a superb view of the lake.

793 Rte. 5A, Orleans, VT 05860. ✆ **800/594-9102** or 802/525-4123. Fax 802/525-4514. www.willoughvale.com. 15 units, including 4 lakeside cottages. $85–$245 double; $149–$265 cottage. Rates include continental breakfast. Ask about ski packages. 2-night minimum stay July–Aug, as well as foliage weekends. AE, MC, V. 1 pet with restrictions (call ahead) permitted per room or cottage ($20 per night). **Amenities:** Restaurant; lake swimming; bike rentals; watersports equipment (canoes and kayaks) rental. *In room:* A/C, TV.

12

New Hampshire

by Paul Karr

Okay, I admit it. I love New Hampshire. Oh, I know it's not as postcard-pretty as Vermont, nor as tourist-friendly as Maine. The state charges everyone, even residents, an annoying 2 bucks to traverse a measly 15 miles of coastal interstate highway (with no views). The fields here are mostly full of rocks, and the winter is much too long.

And that "Live Free or Die" license plate? It's for real. New Hampshire stands behind its words. It regards zoning as a conspiracy to undermine property rights. Last I knew, the state did not have a bottle-deposit law, a law banning billboards, a bill requiring motorcyclists to wear helmets, or a sales or income tax on its books.

But that's what makes it so wonderful to visit: its authenticity. New Hampshire savors its reputation as an outpost of plucky, heroic, independent citizens fighting the good fight against intrusive laws and irksome bureaucrats—the same sort of folks who took up arms and thumbed their noses at King George way back when.

This rebellious attitude has had some consequences. State legislators have had to become very creative in financing public services. Many services are funded either by lottery sales or through a "tourist tax" (8% on meals and lodging), along with a hefty local property tax that hits residents a bit too hard. Candidates for virtually every local, state, or national office must also take The Pledge, vowing to fight any effort to impose sales or income tax. To shirk The Pledge is tantamount to political suicide.

Get beyond New Hampshire's affable crankiness, though, and you find pure New England. At its core is a mistrust of outsiders, a premium placed on independence, a belief that government should be frugal, and a laconic acceptance that, no matter what, you can't change the weather. Travelers exploring the state with open eyes will find these attitudes in spades—along with pickup trucks, pancake houses, hunting caps, and country and rock music. (Granite Staters know how to have fun: The band Aerosmith and actor-comedian Adam Sandler had their starts here.)

It's not all about flannel shirts and rifle racks. You will also find wonderfully diverse terrain—from beaches to broad lakes to impressive hills and mountains. Without leaving the state's borders, you can toss a Frisbee on a sandy beach, ride bikes along quiet country lanes, hike rugged granite hills blasted by some of the most severe weather in the world, or canoe on a placid lake in the company of moose and loons. You'll also find good food and country inns.

But most of all, you'll find a strong taste of the independence that has defined New England since the first settlers ran up their flags 3½ centuries ago.

1 Portsmouth

11 miles N of Hampton, 10 miles NE of Exeter, 55 miles N of Boston, and 54 miles S of Portland.

New Hampshire's tiny sliver of coast manages to pack a lot of variety into a little space. The coast has honky-tonk beach towns, impressive mansions, vest-pocket state parks with swaths of warm sand, and a historic seaport city with a vibrant maritime history and culture. Ecologically, it has low dunes, lush hardwood forests, and a complex system of salt marshes that has prevented development from overtaking the region entirely.

A short drive inland, more historic towns and a slower way of life have, so far, resisted the inexorable creep of Boston suburbs. While strip malls are belatedly appearing throughout the region (particularly on Rte. 1), the quiet downtowns are holding their own, several establishing themselves as fertile breeding grounds for small-scale entrepreneurs who've shunned the hectic life of bigger cities.

PORTSMOUTH ★★

Portsmouth is a civilized little seaside city of bridges, brick, and seagulls, and quite a little gem. Filled with elegant architecture that's more intimate than intimidating, this bonsai-size city projects a strong, proud sense of its heritage without being overly precious. Part of the city's appeal is its variety: Upscale coffee shops and art galleries stand alongside old-fashioned barbershops and tattoo parlors. Despite a steady influx of money in recent years, the town still retains an earthiness that serves as a tangy vinegar for more saccharine coastal spots. Portsmouth's humble waterfront must actually be sought out; when found, it's rather understated.

The city's history runs deep, a fact that is evident on a walk through town. For the past 3 centuries, the city has been the hub for the region's maritime trade. In the 1600s, Strawbery Banke (it wasn't renamed Portsmouth until 1653) was a major center for the export of wood and dried fish to Europe. Today, Portsmouth's maritime tradition continues with a lively trade in bulk goods (look for scrap metal and minerals stockpiled along the shores of the Piscataqua River on Market St.). The city's de facto symbol is the tugboat, one or two of which are almost always tied up near the waterfront's picturesque "tugboat alley."

In October 2003, city sewer builders discovered wooden coffins containing the remains of 13 18th-century Africans, probably slaves. The city plans to create a memorial and park area to preserve the site, the only known African-American cemetery of its age in New England.

Visitors to Portsmouth will find a lot to see in such a small space, including good shopping in the boutiques that now occupy much of the historic district, good eating at many small restaurants and bakeries, and plenty of history to explore among the historic homes and museums set on almost every block.

ESSENTIALS

GETTING THERE Portsmouth is served by exits 3 through 7 on I-95. The most direct access to downtown is via Market Street (Exit 7), which is the last New Hampshire exit before crossing the river to Maine.

Amtrak (© **800/872-7245;** www.amtrak.com) operates several trains daily from Boston's North Station to downtown Dover, NH; a one-way ticket is about $16 per person, and the trip takes about 1½ hours. You then take the no. 2 **COAST** bus (© **603/743-5777;** www.coastbus.org) to the center of downtown Portsmouth, a 30-minute trip that costs just $1.

New Hampshire

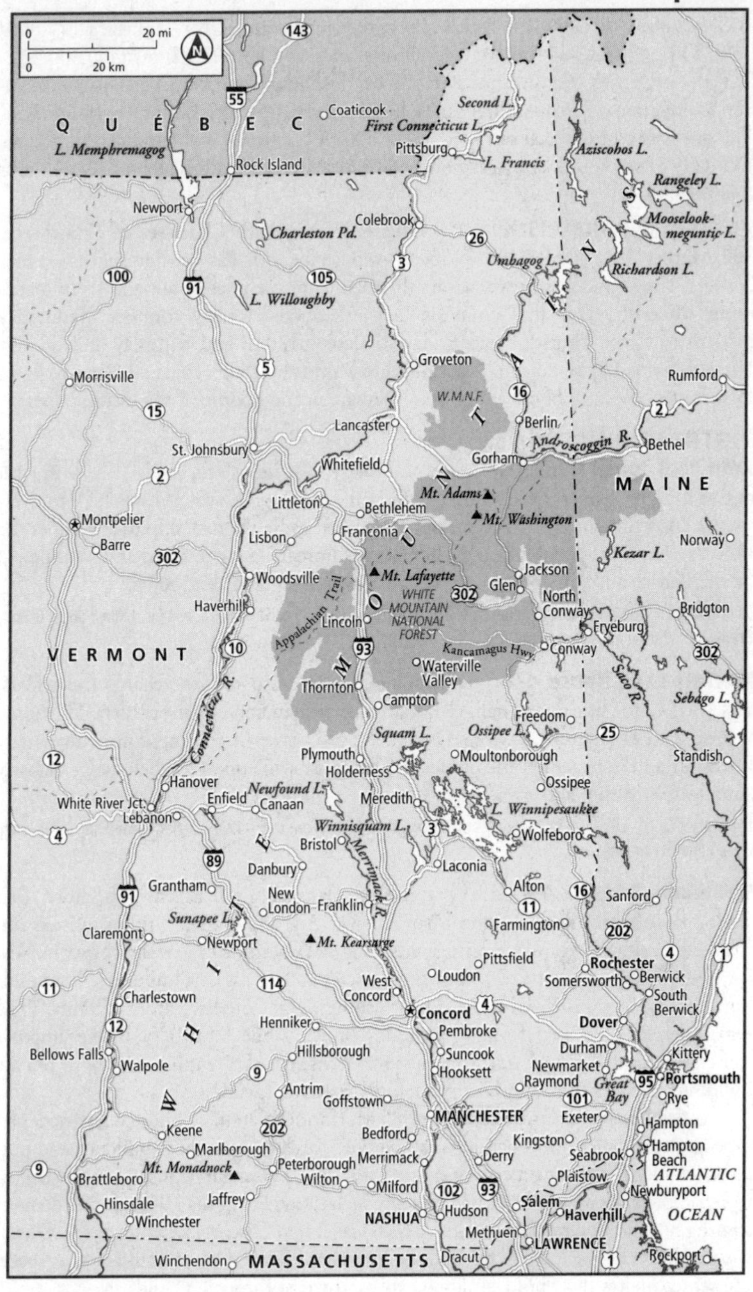

Greyhound (✆ **800/231-2222;** www.greyhound.com), **C&J Trailways** (✆ **800/258-7111** or 603/430-1100; www.cjtrailways.com), and **Vermont Transit** (✆ **800/552-8737;** www.vermonttransit.com) all run about five buses daily from Boston's South Station to downtown Portsmouth, plus one to three daily trips from Boston's Logan Airport. The one-way cost for each service is about $16. A one-way Greyhound trip from New York City's Port Authority bus station to downtown Portsmouth is about $48 and takes about 6½ hours.

VISITOR INFORMATION The **Greater Portsmouth Chamber of Commerce,** 500 Market St. (✆ **603/436-3988;** www.portcity.org), has an information center between Exit 7 and downtown across the road from the piles of salt and scrap metal. From Memorial Day to Columbus Day, it's open Monday through Wednesday 8:30am to 5pm; Thursday and Friday 8:30am to 7pm; and Saturday and Sunday 10am to 5pm. The rest of the year, hours are Monday through Friday 8:30am to 5pm. In summer, a second booth is at Market Square in the middle of the historic district.

HISTORIC BUILDINGS

John Paul Jones House ★★ Revolutionary War hero John Paul ("I have not yet begun to fight") Jones lived in this 1758 home during the war. He was here to oversee the construction of his sloop, *Ranger,* believed to be the first ship to sail under the U.S. flag (a model is on display). The house is immaculately restored and maintained by the Portsmouth Historical Society, and costumed guides lead tours.

43 Middle St. ✆ **603/436-8420.** Admission $10 adults, $8 seniors, $5 children 6–14, free for children under 6. Daily 11am–5pm. Closed mid-Oct to mid-May.

Moffatt-Ladd House ★★ Built for a family of prosperous merchants and traders, this 1763 home has a great hall, elaborate carvings, and an elegant garden. The home belonged to one family between 1763 and 1913, when it became a museum; many furnishings have never left the premises. The house will appeal to aficionados of Early American furniture and painting.

154 Market St. ✆ **603/436-8221.** Admission $5 adults, $2.50 children under 12. Mon–Sat 11am–5pm; Sun 1–5pm. Closed mid-Oct to mid-June.

Strawbery Banke ★★★ In 1958, the city planned to raze this neighborhood, first settled in 1653, to make way for urban renewal. A group of local citizens resisted and won, establishing an outdoor history museum that's become one of the largest in New England. Today it consists of 10 downtown acres and 46 historic buildings. Ten buildings have been restored with period furnishings; eight others feature exhibits. (The remainder may be seen from the exterior only.) While Strawbery Banke employs staffers to assume the character of historic residents, the emphasis is more on the buildings, architecture, and history than the costumed reenactors.

The neighborhood surrounds an open lawn (formerly an inlet) and has a settled, picturesque quality. At three working crafts shops, watch coopers, boat builders, and potters at work. The most intriguing home is the split-personality Drisco House, half of which depicts life in the 1790s and half of which shows life in the 1950s, nicely demonstrating how houses grow and adapt to each era. A new Discovery Center at the Wheelwright House is scheduled to open in the summer of 2006. A playful, interactive, space, the center invites the whole family to explore the past through a child's eyes.

Hancock St. ✆ **603/433-1100.** www.strawberybanke.org. Summer admission $15 adults, $10 seniors, $5 children 7–17, free for children under 6, $35 per family; winter $10 adults, $9 seniors, $5 ages 5–17, $25 family. May–Oct

Portsmouth

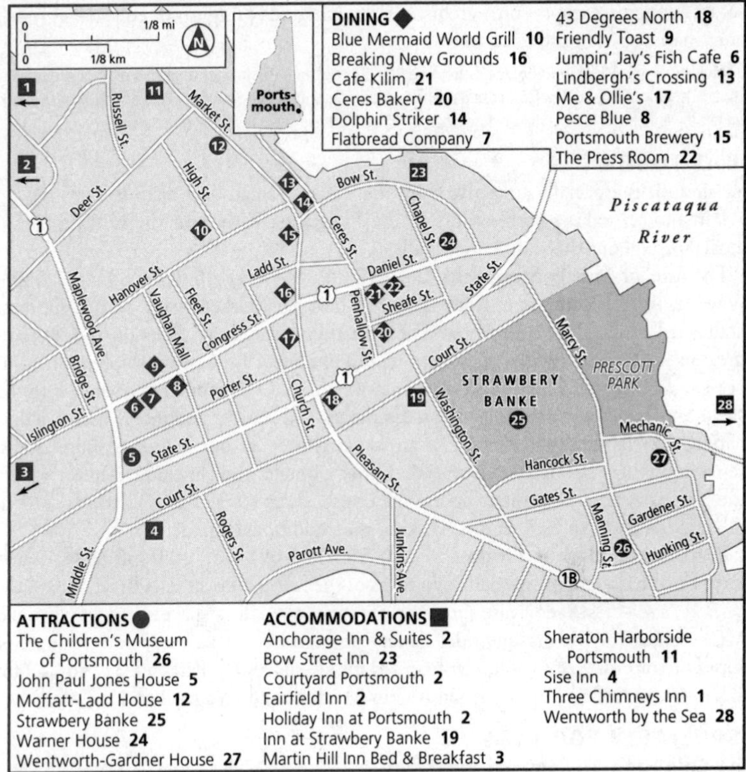

Mon–Sat 10am–5pm, Sun noon–5pm; winter Sat 10am–2pm, Sun noon–2pm. Look for directional signs posted around town.

Warner House ★ This house, built in 1716, was the governor's mansion in the mid–18th century when Portsmouth was the state capital. After a time as a private home, it has been open to the public since the 1930s. This stately brick structure with graceful Georgian architectural elements is a favorite among architectural historians for its wall murals (said to be the oldest murals still in place in the U.S.), early wall marbleizing, and original white pine paneling.

150 Daniel St. ✆ **603/436-8420.** www.warnerhouse.org. Admission $5 adults, $2.50 children 7–12, free for children 6 and under. Mid-June–Oct Mon–Sat 11am–4pm; Sun noon–4pm. Closed Nov to early June.

Wentworth-Gardner House ★★★ Arguably the most handsome mansion in the Seacoast region, this is considered one of the nation's best examples of Georgian architecture. The 1760 home features many period elements, including pronounced *quoins* (blocks on the building's corners), pedimented window caps, plank sheathing (to make the home appear as if made of masonry), an elaborate doorway with Corinthian pilasters, a broken scroll, and a paneled door topped with a pineapple, symbol of hospitality. Perhaps most memorable is its scale—though a grand home of the Colonial era, it's modest in scope; some architectural circles today might not consider it much more than a pool house.

50 Mechanic St. ✆ **603/436-4406.** Admission $4 adults, $2 children 6–14, free for children 5 and under. Tues–Sun 1–4pm. Closed mid-Oct to May. From rose gardens on Marcy St. across from Strawbery Banke, walk south 1 block, turn left toward bridge, make a right before crossing bridge; house is down the block on your right.

BOAT TOURS

Portsmouth is especially attractive from the water. A small fleet of tour boats ties up at Portsmouth, taking scenic tours of the Piscataqua River and the historic Isle of Shoals throughout the summer and fall.

The **Isle of Shoals Steamship Co.** ★★ (✆ **800/441-4620** or 603/431-5500; www.islesofshoals.com) sails from Barker Wharf on Market Street and is the best established of the tour companies. The firm runs a variety of tours on the 90-foot, three-deck *Thomas Laighton* (a modern replica of a late-19th-c. steamship) and the 70-foot *Oceanic,* especially designed for whale-watching. One popular excursion is to the Isle of Shoals, at which passengers can disembark and wander about Star Island, a dramatic, rocky landmass that's part of an island cluster far out in the offshore swells. Reservations are strongly encouraged. Other popular trips include 6-hour whale-watching voyages and a sunset lighthouse cruise. Fares are $24 to $32 adults, $14 to $22 children, $21 to $27 seniors. Parking is an additional charge.

Portsmouth Harbor Cruises ★ (✆ **800/776-0915** or 603/436-8084; www.portsmouthharbor.com) specializes in tours of the historic Piscataqua River aboard the *Heritage,* a 49-passenger cruise ship with plenty of open deck space. Cruise by five old forts or enjoy the picturesque tidal estuary of inland Great Bay, a scenic trip upriver from Portsmouth. Trips run daily; reservations are suggested. Fares are $11 to $19 for adults, $9.50 to $17 for seniors, and $7 to $11 for children ages 2 to 12.

ESPECIALLY FOR KIDS

The Children's Museum of Portsmouth ★★ Kids The Children's Museum is a bright, lively, arts and science museum that offers a morning's worth of hands-on exhibits of interest to younger artisans and scientists (it's designed to appeal to children between ages 1–11). Popular displays include exhibits on earthquakes, dinosaur digs, and lobstering, along with the miniature yellow submarine and space shuttle cockpit, both of which invite clambering.

280 Marcy St., 2 blocks south of Strawbery Banke. ✆ **603/436-3853.** www.childrens-museum.org. Admission $6 adults and children, $5 seniors, free for ages 1 and under. Tues–Sat 10am–5pm; Sun 1–5pm. Also open Mon during summer and school vacations.

WHERE TO STAY

Downtown accommodations are preferable, as everything is within walking distance, but prices tend to be higher. For budget accommodations, less-stylish chain hotels are at the edge of town along I-95. Among these are the **Anchorage Inn & Suites,** 417 Woodbury Ave. (✆ **603/431-8111**); the **Fairfield Inn,** 650 Borthwick Ave. (✆ **800/228-2800** or 603/436-6363); and the **Holiday Inn of Portsmouth,** 300 Woodbury Ave. (✆ **603/431-8000**). The **Courtyard Portsmouth,** 1000 Market St. (✆ **603/436-2121**), just outside town, is of a higher class than those, with simple clean rooms and is right off I-95, but I've noted service is sometimes unfriendly at best; hopefully it will improve soon. It also books up fast, so specify and confirm your room type in advance.

In addition to the options below, see the Portsmouth Harbor Inn and Spa on p. 588.

Bow Street Inn This is a decent option for travelers willing to sacrifice charm for convenience. The former brewery was made over in the 1980s in a bit of inspired recycling: Condos occupy the top floor, while the **Seacoast Repertory Theatre** (✆ **603/433-4472**) occupies the first. The second floor is the Bow Street Inn, a 10-room hotel that offers good access to historic Portsmouth. Guest rooms, set off a rather sterile hallway, are clean, comfortable, small, and, for the most part, unexceptional. Only room nos. 6 and 7 provide good views of the harbor, and a premium is charged for these. Parking is on the street or at a nearby paid garage; a parking pass is included with harbor-view rooms.

121 Bow St., Portsmouth, NH 03801. ✆ **603/431-7760.** Fax 603/433-1680. www.bowstreetinn.com. 10 units. Peak May–Oct $140–$180 double; off season $99–$160 double. Rates include continental breakfast. 2-night minimum stay on some holidays. AE, DISC, MC, V. *In room:* A/C, TV, dataport, hair dryer.

Inn at Strawbery Banke ★ This historic inn is tucked away in an 1814 home on Court Street, an ideal base for exploring Portsmouth: Strawbery Banke is a block away, and Market Square (the center of the action) is 2 blocks away. The friendly innkeepers have done a nice job of taking a cozy antique home and making it comfortable for guests. Rooms are tiny but bright and feature stenciling, wooden shutters, and beautiful pine floors; one has a bathroom down the hall. Common areas include two sitting rooms with TVs, lots of books, and a dining room where a full breakfast is served each morning.

314 Court St., Portsmouth, NH 03801. ✆ **800/428-3933** or 603/436-7242. www.innatstrawberybanke.com. 7 units. Mar–Sept $145–$150 double; Nov–Feb $100–$115 double. Rates include breakfast. 2-night minimum stay Aug and Oct weekends. AE, DISC, MC, V. No children under 10. *In room:* A/C, no phone.

Martin Hill Inn Bed & Breakfast ★★ This friendly B&B (said to be the original in Portsmouth) sits in a residential neighborhood a short walk from downtown. The inn consists of two period buildings: a main house (built around 1815) and a second guesthouse built 35 years later. All rooms have queen-size beds, writing tables, and sofas or sitting areas, and are variously appointed with distinguished wallpapers, porcelains, antiques, love seats, four-poster or brass beds, and the like. Each has its own character—from the Master Bedroom with pine floors to the mahogany-lined Library Room (the only room with two beds). The relaxing Greenhouse Room (really a suite) has a sitting room, solarium, and access to the outdoors. A stone path leads to a small, beautiful garden, and the gourmet breakfast is a highlight.

404 Islington St., Portsmouth, NH 03801. ✆ **603/436-2287.** www.martinhillinn.com. 7 units. May 15–Nov 1 $130–$200 double; Jan 1–May 14 $105–$145 double. Holiday rates higher. Rates include full breakfast. MC, V. No children under 16. *In room:* A/C, hair dryer.

Sheraton Harborside Portsmouth ★★ This five-story, in-town brick hotel is nicely located—the attractions of downtown Portsmouth are virtually at your doorstep (Strawbery Banke is about a 10-min. walk), and with parking underground and across the street, a stay here can make for a relatively stress-free visit. It's a modern building inspired by the low brick buildings of the city, and it wraps around a circular courtyard. This is a well-maintained, well-managed property popular with business travelers, as well as leisure travelers looking for the amenities of a larger hotel. Some rooms have views of the working harbor.

250 Market St., Portsmouth, NH 03801. ✆ **888/627-7138** or 603/431-2300. Fax 603/431-7805. www.sheratonportsmouth.com. 200 units. Summer $200–$255 double; suites higher. Ask about off-season discounts. AE, DISC, MC, V. **Amenities:** Restaurant; fitness center; business center; limited room service; executive rooms. *In room:* A/C, TV w/pay movies, dataport, minibar, coffeemaker, hair dryer, iron.

Sise Inn ★★ A modern, elegant hotel in the guise of a country inn, this solid Queen Anne–style home was built for a prominent merchant in 1881; the hotel addition was constructed in the 1980s, amid other renovations. The effect is happily harmonious, with antique stained glass and copious oak trim meshing well with the more contemporary elements. An elevator serves the three floors; modern carpeting is throughout, but many rooms have antique armoires, updated Victorian styling, and whirlpool or soaking tubs. I like room no. 302, a bi-level, two-bedroom suite with a claw-foot tub; no. 406, a suite with soaking tub and private sitting room; no. 120, with a private patio; and no. 216 (in the carriage house), with an actual working sauna, a two-person whirlpool, and lovely natural light. This is a popular hotel for business travelers. New owners recently added free Wi-Fi access.

40 Court St. (at Middle St.), Portsmouth, NH 03801. ✆ **877/747-3466** or 603/433-0200. Fax 603/433-1200. www.siseinn.com. 34 units. Summer–fall $189 double, $229–$269 suite; off season $129 double, $159–$199 suite. Rates include continental breakfast. AE, DISC, MC, V. **Amenities:** Laundry service. *In room:* A/C, TV, iron, Jacuzzis (some).

Three Chimneys Inn ★★ About 20 minutes northwest of Portsmouth at the edge of the pleasant university town of Durham, this is a wonderful retreat. The main part of the inn dates back to 1649, but later additions and a full-scale renovation in 1997 have given it more of a regal Georgian feel. All units are above average in size and lushly decorated with four-poster or canopied beds, mahogany armoires, and Belgian carpets. In 17 rooms are either gas or Duraflame log fireplaces. One favorite is the William Randolph Hearst Room, with photos of starlets on the walls and a massive bed that's a replica of one at San Simeon. Five rooms are on the ground-floor level beneath the restored barn and have outside entrances, Jacuzzis, and gas fireplaces; these are a bit cavelike, but luxurious. ***Note:*** The inn is a popular spot for weddings on summer weekends, and is booked full for University of New Hampshire events such as graduation and homecoming.

17 Newmarket Rd., Durham, NH 03824. ✆ **888/399-9777** or 603/868-7800. Fax 603/868-2964. www.threechimneysinn.com. 23 units. $169–$239 double ($30 less midweek). Rates include breakfast. 2-night minimum stay on weekends Sept–Oct. AE, DISC, MC, V. No children under 6. **Amenities:** 2 restaurants. *In room:* A/C, TV, coffeemaker.

Wentworth by the Sea ★★★ Kids I consider this to be one of the top resorts in New England. The photogenic grand hotel is operated jointly with Marriott in professional, luxurious fashion. Rooms vary in size, but most are spacious, with good views of the ocean or harbor. My favorites are the suites in the three turrets. Eighteen rooms have gas-powered fireplaces, while 15 have private balconies; all have luxury bath amenities, new bathroom fixtures, and beautiful detailing and furnishings. Free high-speed Internet access is a welcome addition. Families should note that many units here contain two queen-size beds. Just downhill, beside the marina, is a set of truly outstanding bi-level luxury suites with a private pool, water views, modern kitchens with pots and utensils, and marble bathrooms with Jacuzzis. The full-service spa offers a full range of treatments, while the adjacent privately operated country club is reserved for hotel guests. The **dining room** ★ is first-rate.

Wentworth Rd. (P.O. Box 860), New Castle, NH 03854. ✆ **866/240-6313** or 603/422-7322. Fax 603/422-7329. www.wentworth.com. 161 units. Peak season midweek double from $259, suite from $419; weekend double $349–$369, suite $489–$659. Off season midweek double from $169, suite from $219; weekend double from $179, suite from $229. Ask about packages. AE, DISC, MC, V. **Amenities:** 2 restaurants; indoor pool; outdoor pool; spa. *In room:* A/C, TV, coffeemaker, hair dryer.

WHERE TO DINE

Portsmouth has perhaps the best cafe scene in New England; in at least 10 places downtown, you can get a good cup of coffee and decent baked goods. There's a Starbucks, of course, but my favorites are **Breaking New Grounds** (✆ **603/436-9555**), 14 Market Sq., with outstanding espresso shakes, good tables for chatting, and late hours; **Caffe Kilim** (✆ **603/436-7330**) at 79 Daniel St., across from the post office, a bohemian choice; and **Me and Ollie's** (✆ **603/436-7777**) at 10 Pleasant St., well known locally for its bread, sandwiches, and homemade granola.

If you want a bit more of a bite with your coffee, two other outstanding places leap to mind. The tie-dyed **Friendly Toast** (✆ **603/430-2154**), at 121 Congress St., serves a variety of eggs and other breakfast dishes all day long, plus heartier items such as burgers. Funky **Ceres Bakery,** 51 Penhallow St. (✆ **603/436-6518**), on a side street, has a handful of tiny tables; you may want to get a cookie or slice of cake to go and walk to the waterfront rose gardens.

Downtown Portsmouth now also has an outlet of the terrific **Flatbread Company** at 138 Congress St. (✆ **603/436-7888**); it's the perfect place for an organic-wheat crust pizza.

Blue Mermaid World Grill ★★ *Value* GLOBAL/ECLECTIC The Blue Mermaid is a Portsmouth favorite for its good food, good value, and refusal to take itself too seriously. A short stroll from Market Square, in a historic area called the Hill, it's not pretentious—locals congregate here, Tom Waits drones on in the background, and the service is casual but professional. The menu is adventurous in a low-key global way—you might try entrees such as beef filet with an ancho-cilantro compound butter; skewers of Moroccan lamb; chicken breast with mole sauce; a guava-soy flavored braised pork shank; and a short menu of barbecued items such as ribs, chicken, and even swordfish. There are seafood, burgers, pasta, and pizza from the wood grill, plus a fun cocktail menu and homemade fire-roasted salsa.

The Hill (at Hanover and High sts., facing the municipal parking garage). ✆ **603/427-2583.** www.bluemermaid.com. Reservations recommended for parties of 6 or more. Main courses $5.95–$14 at lunch, $13–$21 at dinner (most around $15–$17). AE, DISC, MC, V. Sun–Thurs 11:30am–9pm; Fri–Sat 11:30am–10pm.

Dolphin Striker ★ NEW ENGLAND In a historic brick warehouse in Portsmouth's most charming area, the place serves traditional New England seafood dishes such as haddock filet piccata and lobster potpie. Grilled meat dishes like strip steak, beef tenderloin, rack of lamb, and duck breast are also available. The main dining room has a rustic, public house atmosphere with wide pine-board floors and wooden furniture; or order meals downstairs in a comfortable pub.

15 Bow St. ✆ **603/431-5222.** www.dolphinstriker.com. Reservations recommended. Main courses $10–$18 at lunch, $20–$34 at dinner. AE, DC, DISC, MC, V. Tues–Sun 11:30am–2pm and 5–10pm.

43 Degrees North ★★★ ECLECTIC Right off the city's main square, this eatery pulls off the neat trick of being both a classy restaurant and a capable wine bar. Chef Evan Hennessey works magic with local seafood, Continental sauces, and game meats. You can fill up on a selection of his small plates, such as cumin-fried oysters, seared Maine crabs, or blackberry-juniper braised short ribs; or go straight to a main course, such as chile-spiced tuna steak, grilled tenderloin of pork, rabbit, boar, or even ostrich, or a grilled five-spice duck in a blood orange reduction with a duck confit crepe. Beguiling side dishes could be anything from apple-wood bread pudding to andouille-scallion potato cake. You can get plenty of wines by the glass or half-bottle. In December, lunch is served 3 days a week.

75 Pleasant St. ✆ **603/430-0225.** www.fortythreenorth.com. Reservations recommended. Small plates $8.50–$12; entrees $17–$27. AE, MC, V. Daily 5–9pm.

Jumpin' Jay's Fish Café ★★ SEAFOOD One of Portsmouth's more urbane eateries, Jay's is a welcome destination for those who prefer sophistication to the deep-fryer when it comes to seafood. A sleek and spare spot dotted with splashes of color, it also has an open kitchen and a polished-steel bar. Jay's attracts a younger, culinary-attuned clientele. The day's fresh catch is posted on blackboards; you pick the fish, and pair it up with sauces, such as salsa verde, ginger-orange, or roasted red pepper. Pasta dishes are also an option—add scallops, mussels, or chicken as you like. The food is great, and the attention to detail by the kitchen and waitstaff is admirable.

150 Congress St. ✆ **603/766-3474.** www.jumpinjays.com. Reservations recommended (call by Wed for weekends). Dinner $18–$24. AE, DISC, MC, V. Mon–Thurs 5:30–9:30pm (closes at 9pm in winter); Fri–Sat 5–10pm; Sun 5–9pm.

Lindbergh's Crossing ★ BISTRO For exotic comfort food, head to this restaurant, which serves what it calls hearty French country fare. In an old waterfront warehouse, this intimate, two-story restaurant has a bistro menu that's subtly creative without calling too much attention to itself. Starters include seared rare tuna with rice cake and scallop crepes in poblano-corn mushroom cream sauce. For main courses you may want to try the Portuguese seafood stew, mahimahi over yellow bean salad, or a seared elk steak. If you don't have reservations, ask about sitting in the bar.

29 Ceres St. ✆ **603/431-0887.** www.lindberghscrossing.com. Reservations recommended. Main courses $18–$29. AE, DC, MC, V. Sun–Thurs 5:30–9:30pm; Fri–Sat 5:30–10pm. Bar opens 4pm daily, with a limited menu.

Pesce Blue ★★ SEAFOOD/ITALIAN Yet another upscale seafood eatery in Portsmouth, yet another smashing success. Lunch might be a piece of grilled flatbread topped with maple smoked salmon and white bean purée, a smoked trout salad, or a crispy Icelandic char with roasted fingerling potatoes and lemon caper sauce. Dinner options include grilled tuna, lobster with basil gnocchi, crispy salmon with roasted shallots and root vegetables, or a small plate of seafood-inflected pasta such as linguine with Maine peekytoe crab. The house desserts range from goat cheese-mascarpone crepes with berries to *panna cotta,* molten chocolate cake, and gelati.

106 Congress St. ✆ **603/430-7766.** www.pesceblue.com. Small plates and entrees $9.50–$27. Lobsters market price. AE, DISC, MC, V. Mon–Tues 5–9pm; Wed–Sun 11:45am–2pm and 5–9pm.

Portsmouth Brewery PUB FARE In the heart of the historic district (look for the tankard suspended over the sidewalk), New Hampshire's first brewpub opened in 1991 and draws a clientele loyal to the superb beers. The tin-ceiling, brick-wall dining room is open, airy, echoey, and redolent of hops. Brews are made in 200-gallon batches and include specialties such as Old Brown Ale and a delightfully creamy Black Cat Stout. While not up to the standard set by the beer, the eclectic food offerings include burgers, veggie jambalaya, hickory-smoked steak, and London broil with white-bean cassoulet.

56 Market St. ✆ **603/431-1115.** www.portsmouthbrewery.com. Reservations accepted for parties of 10 or more. Main courses $6.50–$8.95 at lunch, $13–$22 at dinner. AE, DC, DISC, MC, V. Daily 11:30am–12:30am.

The Press Room PUB FARE Locals flock here more for the convivial atmosphere and easy-on-the-budget prices than for creative cuisine. An in-town favorite since 1976, The Press Room boasts that it was the first in the area to serve Guinness stout, so it's appropriate that the atmosphere has rustic Gaelic charm. On cool days, a fire burns in the woodstove, and quaffers flex their elbows at darts amid brick walls, pine floors, and heavy wooden beams overhead. Choose from a bar menu of inexpensive selections, such as burgers, fish and chips, and stir-fries.

77 Daniel St. ✆ **603/431-5186.** Reservations not accepted. Sandwiches $3.50–$6.50; main courses $7.50–$13. AE, DISC, MC, V. Sun–Thurs 5–11pm; Fri–Sat 11:30am–11pm.

PORTSMOUTH AFTER DARK

Performing Arts

The Music Hall This historic theater dates back to 1878 and was thankfully restored to its former glory by a local nonprofit arts group. A variety of shows are staged here, from magic festivals and comedy revues to concerts by visiting symphonies and pop artists. Call for the current lineup. 28 Chestnut St. ✆ **603/436-2400.** www.themusichall.org. Tickets $12–$50 (average price about $25).

Bars & Clubs

Dolphin Striker Live jazz, classical guitar, and low-key rock is offered most evenings Tuesday through Sunday. 15 Bow St. ✆ **603/431-5222.**

Muddy River Smokehouse Blues are the thing at Muddy River's downstairs lounge, which is open evenings, Wednesday through Saturday. Weekends offer reggae and blues with well-known performers from Boston, Maine, and beyond. Cover charges vary, but admission is free for some shows if you arrive before 7:30pm. 21 Congress St. ✆ **603/430-9582.** www.muddyriver.com.

The Press Room A popular local bar and restaurant (see "Where to Dine," above), The Press Room offers casual entertainment almost every night, either upstairs or down. Tuesday nights are the popular Hoot nights, with an open mic hosted by local musicians. Friday nights are for contemporary folk, starring name performers from around the region; but The Press Room may be best known for its live jazz on Sunday, when the club brings in quality performers from Boston and beyond. 77 Daniel St. ✆ **603/431-5186.** No cover charge Mon–Thurs; around $5 Fri–Sun (2nd floor only).

2 The Monadnock Region & the Connecticut River Valley ★

Peterborough is 71 miles NW of Boston and 38 miles SW of Manchester, NH.

New Hampshire's southwestern corner is a pastoral region of rolling hills, small villages, rustic farmsteads, and winding back roads. What the area lacks in major attractions it makes up for in peacefulness and bucolic charm. The inns tend to be more basic and less elegant than those across the river in southern Vermont, but prices appeal to budget travelers looking for a taste of history with their room and board. This is a popular area for Bostonians seeking a respite from city life.

For most visitors, chief activities include woodland walks, porch sitting, and idle drives to nowhere in particular. In fact, the best strategy for exploring the area may be to put away the map and turn randomly on a side road to see where you'll end up. Odds are good you'll find a gentle Currier and Ives quality wherever you go.

PETERBOROUGH & ENVIRONS ★★

Peterborough (pop. 5,000), settled in 1749, is no quaint Colonial town gathered primly around a village green. Rather, it has the feel of a once-prosperous commercial center, where the hum of industry provided harmony for a thriving economy. While the hum is a bit quieter these days, Peterborough is still a beautiful town with diverse architecture, set in a valley at the confluence of the Contoocook and Nubanusit rivers. Improbably enough, Peterborough has carved out a niche in the high-tech world as a publishing center for computer magazines.

ESSENTIALS

GETTING THERE Peterborough is between Keene and Nashua on Route 101. A decent map is essential for exploring the outlying villages and towns on winding state and county roads . . . unless, of course, you choose to get lost.

VISITOR INFORMATION The **Greater Peterborough Chamber of Commerce,** P.O. Box 401, Peterborough, NH 03458 (✆ **603/924-7234;** www.peterboroughchamber.com), provides advice either over the phone or at a year-round information center at the intersection of Route 101 and Route 202.

OUTDOOR PURSUITS

Mount Monadnock stands impressively amid the gentler hills of southern New Hampshire. Though only 3,165 feet high (about half the height of Mount Washington to the north), it has a solitary grandeur that has attracted hikers for more than 2 centuries. The knobby peak has been ascended by New England luminaries such as Ralph Waldo Emerson and Henry David Thoreau. Today, more than 100,000 hikers head for the summit each year.

Some 40 miles of trails lace the patchwork of public and private lands on the slopes of the mountain. The most popular (and best-marked) trails leave from near the entrance to **Monadnock State Park** ★★ (✆ **603/532-8862**), about 4 miles northwest of Jaffrey Center. (Head west on Rte. 124; after 2 miles, follow the park signs to the north.) A round-trip on the most direct routes will take someone in decent shape about 3 to 4 hours. Admission to the park is $3 for adults and children 12 and older, $1 for children age 6 to 11, free for children age 5 and under and New Hampshire seniors. No pets are allowed in the park.

WHERE TO STAY

Benjamin Prescott Inn ★ Col. Benjamin Prescott fought at the Battle of Bunker Hill before retiring to Jaffrey in 1775. This three-story home built by his sons dates to 1853 and is a handsome yellow Greek Revival farmhouse along an (often busy) road in a pastoral area 2 miles east of the village. Throughout this pleasant inn, you'll find a strong sense of history and a connection to the past. All guest rooms have ceiling fans and phone jacks (phones provided on request), and two suites have air-conditioning. The best room in the house? The Col. Prescott, bright and airy and furnished with two comfortable armchairs and a writing desk. Guests can wander the farmlands beyond the inn or set off to hike Mount Monadnock, a short drive down the road.

433 Turnpike Rd. (Rte. 124), Jaffrey, NH 03452. ✆ **888/950-6637** or 603/532-6637. www.benjaminprescottinn.com. 10 units, including 3 suites. $90–$165 double. Rates include breakfast. 2-night minimum some holidays and peak-season weekends. AE, MC, V. *In room:* No phone.

Birchwood Inn ★ *Value* This quiet retreat offers good rooms at good prices. Thoreau visited the inn on his travels; neither the town nor the inn feels as if they've changed that much since. This handsome brick farmhouse with white-clapboard ell is in the middle of the country crossroads town of Temple, near the Grange and a park with three war memorials (including one to the heroes of 1776). It's also an easy stroll to a historic cemetery with headstones dating back to the 18th century. The inn is decorated in a pleasantly informal country style. Each of the seven rooms has a different theme (musical instruments, train memorabilia, and country store), bordering on kitschy without overdoing it. Of note is the spacious, bright, and summery Seashore Room.

Rte. 45 (1½ miles south of Rte. 101), Temple, NH 03084. ✆ **603/878-3285.** 7 units, 1 with detached private bathroom. $79–$89 double. Rates include breakfast. 2-night minimum stay during foliage season. No credit cards. No children under 10. **Amenities:** Restaurant. *In room:* TV, no phone.

Hancock Inn ★ The austere and simple Hancock Inn sits on Main Street in a small town that doesn't appear to have changed much since the inn was built in 1789. You'll find classic Americana inside, from creaky floors and braided oval rugs to guest rooms appointed with understated Colonial decor. The Rufus Porter Room has an evocative wall mural from the inn's early days. Three rooms have gas fireplaces; three have soaking tubs. The inn has four suites, including the new Ballroom and the Bell Tower Room, the former with a domed ceiling, the latter with a cannonball king-size bed and gas fireplace; both have soaking tubs. While other nearby inns are equally historic and charming, this one is more upscale.

33 Main St., Hancock, NH 03443. ✆ **800/525-1789** or 603/525-3318. Fax 603/525-9301. www.hancockinn.com. 15 units. $105–$250 double. Rates include breakfast. AE, DC, DISC, MC, V. Pets allowed with prior permission. Children 12 and older welcome. **Amenities:** Restaurant. *In room:* A/C, TV.

The Inn at Jaffrey Center ★ In the middle of one of New Hampshire's most gracious villages, this historic, architecturally eclectic inn was built in 1830. Rooms are in traditional New England style, some with four-poster or canopy beds and old claw-foot tubs.

379 Main St., Jaffrey Center, NH 03452. ✆ **877/510-7019** or 603/532-7800. Fax 603/532-7000. www.theinnatjaffreycenter.com. 11 units, 1 with private bathroom across hall. May–Oct $100–$150 double; Nov–Apr $65–$100 double. Rates include continental breakfast. Minimum stay policy during foliage and holiday weekends. MC, V. **Amenities:** Restaurant. *In room:* No phone, TV (some).

WHERE TO DINE

Acqua Bistro ★★ MEDITERRANEAN/BISTRO Founded by a Boston restaurant consultant who had wearied of telling other people what to do, Acqua is Peterborough's best choice for a well-crafted meal. Hidden off Peterborough's main thoroughfares (near Twelve Pine and the Sharon Arts Center), this place is modern and agreeable, overlooking a river (more of a stream, really), and offering a contemporary Mediterranean twist on regional fare. Entrees may include cavatelli with braised artichokes and arugula or a veal meatloaf. Creative pizzas (think: lamb sausage) are also offered nightly. Sunday mornings feature a rustic, country brunch.

9 School St., Peterborough. ✆ **603/924-9905.** Reservations accepted for parties of 5 or more. Main courses $12–$25. MC, V. Tues–Sat 5–11pm; Sun 11am–2:30pm and 5–8pm.

Peterborough Diner ★ DINER This classic 1940s throwback is hidden on a side street. Behind the faded yellow-and-green exterior is a beautiful interior of wood, aluminum, tile, and ceiling fans, along with one of the best easy-listening jukeboxes in New England. The meals are just what you'd expect: filling, cheap, and basic. Look for the great hot-oven grinders (served with cheese and chips), Reubens, burgers, and grilled-cheese-and-bacon at lunchtime. (Though blasphemous to diner aficionados, croissant sandwiches are on the menu.) Dinner selections include Yankee pot roast, meatloaf, chicken Kiev, pasta, and fried fish.

10 Depot St., Peterborough. ✆ **603/924-6202.** Breakfast $2.95–$12; lunch and dinner $1.95–$13. AE, DISC, MC, V. Daily 6am–9pm.

Twelve Pine ★ Value UPSCALE DELI This inviting deli and market is in an airy former railroad building behind Peterborough's main street. It's a great place to nosh and linger. Simply select a pre-made meal (say, chicken burritos or one of four homemade soups) from a deli counter and bring it to a table. Sandwiches are on homemade bread with heaping fillings; excellent cheeses are available by the pound, and fresh juices round out a meal. It's a relaxed place with good value.

11 School St. (Depot Sq.), Peterborough. ✆ **603/924-6140.** www.twelvepine.com. Sandwiches around $5; other items priced by the pound, generally $6–$8 for a meal. MC, V. Mon–Fri 8am–7pm; Sat–Sun 9am–4pm.

CORNISH & ENVIRONS

Artists flocked to this bucolic region in the late 19th century and the subtle beauty of the area makes it abundantly clear why. The first artistic immigrants to arrive were painters and sculptors, who showed up in the late 1880s and early 1890s, building modest homes in the hills. They were followed by politicians and the affluent, who eventually established a summer colony. Among those who populated the hills that look across the river toward Mount Ascutney were sculptor Daniel Chester French, painter Maxfield Parrish, and *New Republic* editor Herbert Crowley. Visitors included Ethel Barrymore and presidents Woodrow Wilson and Theodore Roosevelt.

ESSENTIALS

GETTING THERE Don't bother looking for Cornish proper or a main street; you won't find either. Cornish is just a few scattered villages with names such as Cornish Flats and, somewhat grandiloquently, Cornish City. The best route for exploring the area is Route 12A along the Connecticut River north of Claremont.

VISITOR INFORMATION The **Greater Claremont Chamber of Commerce,** Tremont Square, Claremont, NH 03743 (✆ **603/543-1296;** www.claremontnhchamber.org), dispenses travel information from the Moody Building in town.

EXPLORING THE CORNISH AREA

The region's premier monument to the former arts colony is the **Saint-Gaudens National Historic Site** ★★ (✆ **603/675-2175;** www.sgnhs.org), off Route 12A. Sculptor Augustus Saint-Gaudens first arrived in this valley in 1885, shortly after receiving an important commission to create a statue of Abraham Lincoln. His friend Charles Beaman, a lawyer who owned several houses and much land in the Cornish area, assured him he would find a surfeit of "Lincoln-shaped men" in the area. Saint-Gaudens came and pretty much stayed the rest of his life.

His home and studio, which he called Aspet, after the village in Ireland where he was raised, is a superb place to learn more about this extraordinary artist. A brief tour of the house, which is kept mostly as it was when Saint-Gaudens lived here, provides a brief introduction to the man. Visitors learn about Saint-Gaudens the artist at several outbuildings and on the grounds, where many replicas of his most famous statues are on display.

The 150-acre grounds also have short nature trails, where visitors can explore the hilly woodlands, passing by streams and a millpond. The historic site is open daily from 9am to 4:30pm from late May to October. Admission is $5 for adults, free for children under 17.

Covered-bridge aficionados should seek out the **Cornish-Windsor Covered Bridge,** the nation's longest covered bridge. Spanning the Connecticut River between Vermont and New Hampshire, this bridge has an ancient, interesting lineage. A toll bridge was first built in 1796 to replace a ferry; the current bridge was built in 1866 and restored in 1989. When late afternoon light hits it just right, it also vies for the title of most handsome covered bridge in New England.

WHERE TO STAY

Home Hill Inn ★★ This superbly renovated 1811 Federal-style brick house is set on 25 acres near the Connecticut River. Owners Victoria and Stéphane du Roure have turned this property into one of the region's most inviting retreats. Rooms are elegantly appointed with a Continental country flair that's not too delicate, not too rustic. The main house has four guest rooms and a two-room suite; six guest rooms are in the carriage house, and one (seasonal) is in the pool house located steps from the inviting pool. Most rooms have fireplaces. An added-on **dining room** ★ blends nicely with the lines and interior of the original home and serves mostly provincial French cooking: fish, game, and the like.

River Rd., Plainfield, NH 03781. ✆ **603/675-6165**. Fax 603/675-5220. www.homehillinn.com. 11 units. $235–$425 double. Rates include continental breakfast. AE, DISC, MC, V. **Amenities:** Restaurant; outdoor pool; putting green; tennis court; free bikes. *In room:* A/C.

HANOVER ★★

If your idea of New England involves a sweeping green edged with stately brick buildings, be sure to visit Hanover, a thriving university town in the Connecticut River Valley. First settled in 1765, the town was home to early colonists who were granted a charter by King George III to establish a college. The school was named after the second Earl of Dartmouth, its first trustee. Since its founding, Dartmouth College has had a large hand in shaping the community.

This Ivy League school has produced more than its share of celebrated alumni, including Robert Frost, Vice President Nelson Rockefeller, former surgeon general C. Everett Koop, and Dr. Seuss. Another noted son of Dartmouth was the 19th-century politician and orator Daniel Webster. In arguing for the survival of Dartmouth College in a landmark case before the U.S. Supreme Court in 1816 (when two factions vied for control of the school), Webster offered his famous closing line: "It is a small college, gentlemen, but there are those who love it."

That has served as an informal motto for school alumni ever since. Today, a handsome, oversize village green marks the permeable border between college and town. In summer, the green is an ideal destination for strolling and lounging. The best way to explore Hanover is on foot, so your first endeavor is to park your car, which can be trying during peak seasons (fall foliage and whenever school is in session). Try the municipal lots west of Main Street.

ESSENTIALS

GETTING THERE Hanover is north of Lebanon, NH, and I-89 via Route 10 or Route 120. Amtrak serves White River Junction, Vermont, across the river.

VISITOR INFORMATION Dartmouth College alumni and chamber volunteers maintain an **information center** on the green in summer. It's open daily from 10am to 5pm in June and September, daily from 9:30am to 5pm in July and August. In the off season, head to the **Hanover Chamber of Commerce** (✆ **603/643-3115**) on Main Street across from the post office. It's open Monday through Friday from 9am to 4:30pm.

SPECIAL EVENTS In mid-February, look for the fantastic and intricate ice sculptures of the annual **Dartmouth Winter Carnival;** call Dartmouth College (✆ **603/646-1110**) for more information on this traditionally beer-soaked event.

Tips Exploring Newport & Lake Sunapee

While visiting Hanover, Concord, or Cornish, don't neglect the Newport–Lake Sunapee region. The commercial center of the area is **Newport** ★, a former mill town with grit, character, and substantial history in a valley setting. This is the town that produced Sarah Josepha Hale, authoress of the children's poem "Mary Had a Little Lamb" and creator of the Thanksgiving holiday; President Lincoln was sufficiently impressed by her persistence to make it so. Hale was also one of the first women in the United States to serve as editor of a national publication.

Today the town's historical attractions include a quilt project documenting Newport's industrial past and the immigrants (including healthy numbers of Finns, Polish, Greeks, and Italians) who pitched in to turn the engines of commerce; an antique 1815 Hunnemen "handtub," a wheeled apparatus built by an apprentice of Paul Revere and originally used by town firemen to pump water while fighting blazes (on display at the Lake Sunapee Bank); and a wooden covered bridge painstakingly built by a craftsman to replace the priceless original, torched by an unknown arsonist.

Drop by the town's **Richards Free Library** ★ (**✆ 603/863-3430**) on North Main Street to get oriented; for my money, it's one of the best small-town libraries in America. (Tantalizing historical tidbit: President Kennedy was invited to accept a writing award at this library on the night of Nov 22, 1963.) Equally tantalizing is the pizza down the street at **Newport Village Pizza** (**✆ 603/862-3400**), 7 S. Main St. Contact the Newport Chamber of Commerce (**✆ 603/863-1510**) for more details on the area; there's a good volunteer-run kiosk beside the town green in summer months.

EXPLORING HANOVER

Hanover is a superb town to explore on foot, by bike, and even by canoe. Start by picking up a map of the campus, available at the Dartmouth information center on the green or at The Hanover Inn. (Free guided tours are also offered in summer.) The expansive, leafy campus is a delight to walk through.

South of the green next to The Hanover Inn is the modern **Hopkins Center for the Arts** ★ (**✆ 603/646-2422;** http://hop.dartmouth.edu). The center attracts national acts to its 900-seat concert hall and stages top-notch performances at the Moore Theater. Wallace Harrison, the architect who later went on to fame for his Lincoln Center in New York, designed the building.

Hanover's compact downtown not only has excellent gift and clothing shops, but two outstanding bookstores stand nearly shoulder to shoulder. The huge **Dartmouth Bookstore** at 33 S. Main St. (**✆ 603/643-3616**) was sold to Barnes & Noble's college bookstore division in 2005, but it remains mostly the same as before: a maze of rooms filled with children's books, travel books, calendars, and a bargain-basement section heavy on poetry, literature, and foreign language titles. The newspaper and magazine selection is exemplary, and the staff is unfailingly helpful.

Good as it is, though, I'm partial to **Left Bank Books** just up the street at 9 S. Main St. (**✆ 603/643-4479;** go up the stairs). Owner Corlan Johnson runs this one-woman

Six miles away, big **Lake Sunapee** ★ is said to be one of the purest in the nation (it's much deeper than it looks, which helps), and has excellent swimming, boating, and fishing. It's a longtime favorite summer resort of Bostonians. The short, steep mountain across the way—also part of **Sunapee State Park** (✆ **603/763-5561**)—is a fine place to hike, ski, snowboard, or catch a gondola ride for expansive foliage and lake views. There's a $3-per-adult charge to enter either the beach or mountain portion of the park in summer; rent skis at **Bob Skinner's Ski & Sports** (✆ **603/763-2303**). August brings an outstanding arts event, the weeklong **Craftsman's Fair** ★ (✆ **603/224-3375**), to the park: Expect quality handcrafted art pieces. Two-day admission tickets cost $8 per adult, $6 per senior or student, free for children under 12.

The main commercial harbor for the lake, a few miles away at the junction of Routes 103B and 11, is the place to put in your boat, grab an ice-cream cone at sunset, and watch the lakeside cottage light up. You might even see a famous face; several members of the band Aerosmith and their families own lakefront or island homes. On the back side of the lake, pretty **New London** is an attractive college town with more than its share of fine homes and upscale restaurants. Without ever straying off Main Street, you can settle down for a full meal at the tony **Millstone** (✆ **603/526-4201**); relax over java or light bistro meals at **Jack's Coffee** (✆ **603/526-8003**); or go mid-level with an English-style board of bread, cheese, and beer at **Peter Christian's Tavern** (✆ **603/526-4042**).

show, stocking a small space (with nice Hanover views) with a changing selection of mostly used poetry, fiction, philosophy, art books, cookbooks, and more. The leftward tilt of the place is unmistakable, and so is Johnson's eye for a good read; I never leave empty-handed.

Enfield Shaker Museum ★★ This cluster of historic buildings on Lake Mascoma is about a 20-minute drive southeast of Hanover. "The Chosen Vale," as its first inhabitants called it, was founded in 1793; by the mid-1800s, it had 350 members and 3,000 acres. From that peak, the community dwindled, and by 1927, the Shakers abandoned the Chosen Vale and sold the village lock, stock, and barrel. Today, much of the property is owned by either the state of New Hampshire or the museum.

Dominating the village is the **Great Stone Dwelling,** an austere but gracious granite structure erected between 1837 and 1841. When constructed, it was the tallest building north of Boston, and it remains the largest dwelling house in any of the Shaker communes. The Enfield Shakers lived and dined here, with as many as 150 Shakers at once eating at trestle tables. In 1997, the museum acquired the stone building, and in 2005 moved the museum into it, presumably for good. The self-guided walking tour of the village is free with admission. The historic feel is compromised by

Tips Orozco Art at Dartmouth

Dartmouth's **Baker Memorial Library** houses a wonderful treasure: a set of murals by Latin American painter José Orozco, who painted *The Epic of American Civilization* while teaching here between 1932 and 1934. The huge paintings wrap around a basement study room and are as colorful as they are metaphorical. Ask for a printed interpretation at the front desk.

a recent condominium development along the lakeshores, although the scale and design of these structures are sympathetic to the original village.

447 Rte. 4A, Enfield. ✆ **603/632-4346.** www.shakermuseum.org. Admission $7 adults, $6 seniors, $3 students or children 10–18, free for children under 10. Memorial Day to Halloween Mon–Sat 10am–5pm, Sun noon–5pm; winter–spring Sat 10am–4pm, Sun noon–4pm.

Hood Museum of Art ★ This modern, open building next to the Hopkins Center houses one of the oldest college museums in the nation. Its current incarnation—an austere and modern three-story structure—was built in 1986 and features special exhibits as well as examples from the permanent collection, which includes a superb selection of 19th-century American landscapes.

Wheelock St. ✆ **603/646-2808.** http://hoodmuseum.dartmouth.edu. Free admission. Tues and Thurs–Sat 10am–5pm; Wed 10am–9pm; Sun noon–5pm.

Ledyard Canoe Club ★★ An idyllic way to spend a lazy afternoon is to drift along the Connecticut River in a canoe. Dartmouth's historic boating club is just down the hill from the campus. While much of the club's focus is on competitive racing, it's a good place for travelers to rent a boat for a few hours and explore the tree-lined river. Instruction is also available.

Off W. Wheelock St. (turn upstream at the bottom of the hill west of bridge; follow signs to the clubhouse). ✆ **603/643-6709.** www.dartmouth.edu/~lcc. Canoe and kayak rentals $5 per hour, $15 per day ($25 on weekends). Summer Mon–Fri 10am–8pm, Sat–Sun 9am–8pm; spring and fall Mon–Fri noon–6pm, Sat–Sun 10am–6pm. Open when river temperature is higher than 50°F (10°C).

WHERE TO STAY

Several hotels and motels are just off the interstate in Lebanon and West Lebanon, about 5 miles south of Hanover. Try the **Airport Economy Inn,** at 45 Airport Rd. (Exit 20 off I-89; ✆ **800/433-3466** or 603/298-8888; www.airporteconomyinn.com); **Days Inn,** at 135 Rte. 120 (Exit 18 off I-89; ✆ **603/448-5070;** www.daysinn.com); **Fireside Inn and Suites,** at 25 Airport Rd. (Exit 20 off I-89; ✆ **800/962-3198** or 603/298-5906; www.afiresideinn.com); or **Sunset Motor Inn,** at 305 N. Main St. (Rte. 10, 4 miles off Exit 19 off I-89; ✆ **603/298-8721**).

Alden Country Inn ★ Ten miles north of Hanover is the pretty, quiet crossroads village of Lyme, with its tidy commons and handsome church. Overlooking the commons is this 1809 inn, a regal four-story building with a high triangular gable. Over the years, it has served as a stagecoach stop and housed a milliner and a tinsmith. Guest rooms are varied, and decorated with light historic styling; some are simply furnished with white walls and stenciling, others are more floral in character. Most have painted floors that show off the wide boards. Room no. 9 has mustard-yellow floors and a somewhat larger bathroom. (Common to many old inns, bathrooms here are on the small side, often tucked into closets.) Be aware that stairs get narrower and steeper the higher your room is in the building.

On the Common, Lyme, NH 03768. © **800/794-2296** or 603/795-2222. Fax 603/795-9436. www.aldencountryinn.com. 15 units. Summer–fall $130–$195 double; off season $95–$155 double. Rates include breakfast or Sun brunch. 2-night minimum on weekends Apr to mid-Oct. AE, DC, DISC, MC, V. **Amenities:** Restaurant. *In room:* A/C, TV, hair dryer, iron.

The Hanover Inn ★★★ The Hanover Inn is the Upper Connecticut Valley's best managed and most up-to-date hotel, perfectly situated for exploring both the campus and the town. Established in 1780, most of the current five-story inn was added later—1924, 1939, or 1968—and this large, modern hotel now offers professional service, attractive rooms, excellent dining, and subterranean walkways to the art museum and theater. Yet the inn somehow manages to maintain an old-world graciousness, informed by that mildly starchy, neo-Georgian demeanor trendy in the 1940s. Most rooms have canopy or four-poster beds and down comforters; some overlook the green.

Wheelock St. (P.O. Box 151), Hanover, NH 03755. © **800/443-7024** or 603/643-4300. Fax 603/643-4433. www.hanoverinn.com. 92 units. $259 double; $309 suite. AE, DISC, MC, V. Valet parking $12 per day. Pets allowed ($15 per night). **Amenities:** 2 dining rooms (see below); access to fitness equipment; limited room service; massage; babysitting; dry cleaning. *In room:* A/C, TV, dataport, coffeemaker, hair dryer, iron.

WHERE TO DINE

If you're in a hurry, the **Dirt Cowboy Cafe** at 9 S. Main St. (© **603/643-1323**) is a good choice for coffee and a snack. The beans are roasted downstairs and served upstairs, along with smoothies and good baked items; sit at a table and eavesdrop on professors and students.

Daniel Webster Room ★★ CONTEMPORARY AMERICAN The Daniel Webster Room of The Hanover Inn appeals to those looking for fine dining in a formal New England atmosphere. The inn's Colonial Revival dining room is reminiscent of a 19th-century resort hotel, with fluted columns, floral carpeting, and regal upholstered chairs. The dinner menu isn't extensive, but that doesn't make it any less appealing. Produce from the college's organic farm is used seasonally. The changing entrees are eclectic and creative and may include braised rabbit leg with truffled pappardelle. Off the lobby is **Zins,** a more informal wine bistro offering 30 wines by the glass (open daily 11:30am–10pm).

Hanover Inn, Wheelock St. © **603/643-4300.** Reservations recommended. Main courses $3.95–$11 at breakfast, $4.50–$13 at lunch, $20–$30 at dinner. AE, DISC, MC, V. Mon 7–10:30am and 11:30am–1:30pm; Tues–Fri 7–10:30am, 11:30am–1:30pm, and 6–9pm; Sat 7–10:30am and 6–9pm; Sun 11am–1:30pm.

Lou's ★ *Value* BAKERY/COMFORT FOOD Lou's has been a Hanover institution since 1947, attracting hungry crowds for breakfast on weekends and a steady local clientele for lunch throughout the week. The mood is no-frills New Hampshire, with a black-and-white linoleum checkerboard floor, maple-and-vinyl booths, and a harried but efficient crew of waiters. Breakfast is served all day (real maple syrup on your pancakes is extra), and the sandwiches, served on fresh-baked bread, are huge and delicious.

30 S. Main St. © **603/643-3321.** Breakfast $3–$7; lunch $5–$8. AE, MC, V. Mon–Fri 6am–3pm; Sat–Sun 7am–3pm (opens 8am Sun in winter). Bakery open for snacks until 5pm.

3 The Lake Winnipesaukee Region ★

Lake Winnipesaukee is the state's largest lake, convoluted with coves and dotted with islands. Yet when you're out on the lake, it rarely seems all that huge. The 180-mile shoreline is edged with dozens of inlets, coves, and bays, and further fragmented by 274 islands. As a result, intermittent lake views from shore give the illusion of a chain of smaller lakes and ponds rather than one massive body of water that measures 12×20 miles at its broadest points.

How to best enjoy the lake? If you're traveling with kids, try basing yourself at Weirs Beach. If you're looking for solitude, consider renting a lakeside cabin on the eastern shore for a week, tracking down a canoe or sailboat, and then exploring in much the same way travelers did a century ago. If time is limited, a driving tour around the lake with a few well-chosen stops will give you a nice taste of the region's woodsy flavor.

Lake Winnipesaukee's western shore has a more frenetic, working-class atmosphere than its refined sibling shore across the lake. That's partly for historic reasons—the main stage and rail routes passed along the western shore—and partly for modern reasons: I-93 runs west of the lake, serving as a sluice for harried visitors streaming in from the Boston megalopolis to the south.

MEREDITH

The village of Meredith sits at the northwest corner of Winnipesaukee, with views across a nice bay throughout the town. It lacks the quaintness and selection of activities that many travelers seek—a busy road cuts off the tidy downtown from the lakeshore, and strip malls have intruded—but it has good services and is home to several desirable inns. Foremost among its qualities is its superb location. I'd choose Meredith as a home base to explore the lakes area and the White Mountains in just 2 or 3 days, as both are within striking distance for day trips (Franconia Notch is about 50 miles north).

ESSENTIALS

GETTING THERE Interstate access to Meredith is via Exit 23 off I-93. Drive 9 miles east on Route 104 to Route 3, then turn left down the hill into town.

VISITOR INFORMATION The **Meredith Area Chamber of Commerce** (© **877/279-6121** or 603/279-6121; www.meredithcc.org) maintains an office in the white house on Route 3 (on the left when driving down the hill from Rte. 104). It's open daily in summer from 9am to 5pm; closed weekends in winter.

EXPLORING THE AREA

Meredith's attractive, if now largely bypassed, Main Street ascends a hill from Route 3 at an elbow in the middle of town. A handful of shops, galleries, and boutiques offer low-key browsing. The creative re-adaptation of an early mill at the **Mill Falls Marketplace** ★ (© **800/622-6455** or 603/279-7006) has 18 shops, including a well-stocked bookstore. It's connected to The Inns at Mill Falls, at the intersection of Route 3 and Route 25.

An excellent fair-weather trip is an excursion to 112-acre **Stonedam Island** ★★, one of the largest protected islands in the lake. Owned by the Lakes Region Conservation Trust (© **603/279-7278**), the island has a trail that winds through wetlands and forest. Approximately 2½ miles southeast of downtown Meredith, it's an ideal destination for a picnic, though it takes some doing to get there. Rent a canoe or kayak at **Sports & Marine Parafunalia,** Route 11B, Gilford (© **603/293-8998**), and make a day of it.

WHERE TO STAY

The Inns at Mill Falls ★★ This ever-expanding complex is gradually dominating Meredith, but thus far has managed its growth with considerable flair. The accommodations are spread among four buildings, each subtly different, but all uncommonly well tended and comfortable. The main inn is in a former mill complex (a small, tasteful shopping mall is adjacent) and has attractive but simple rooms. All rooms in the more upscale Chase House have gas fireplaces; most have balconies and porch rockers with views of the lake. The Inn at Bay Point is on 2,000 feet of lakefront, and most rooms have balconies with sensational views of Winnipesaukee. Ten rooms have Jacuzzis. In May 2004, the inn unveiled its latest expansion, Church Landing. The converted church, right on the lakefront and in front of two beaches, offers 58 rooms and suites with gas fireplaces (some also sport double Jacuzzis and balconies). Hallelujah! A pool and health club with massage services, Jacuzzi, and sauna are included in this new section, as well as marina space for 25 boats and a restaurant. The church wing will be connected to the other inns by a lakeside walking path.

Rte. 3, Meredith, NH 03253. ✆ **800/622-6455** or 603/279-7006. www.millfalls.com. 159 units. Main inn spring–fall $109–$289 double, winter $99–$209 double; Inn at Bay Point spring–fall $179–$319 double, winter weekends and holidays $129–$289 double; Chase House spring–fall $169–$329 double, winter weekends and holidays $129–$279 double. Call for Church Landing rates. Bay Point and Chase House closed weekdays, Nov–Apr. Minimum stay required some weekends. AE, DC, DISC, MC, V. **Amenities:** 5 restaurants; indoor pool; fitness center; shopping arcade; limited room service; massage; babysitting; laundry service; dry cleaning. *In room:* A/C, TV, dataport, hair dryer, iron.

Manor on Golden Pond ★★★ This regal stucco-and-shingle mansion, 9 miles north of Meredith in Holderness, was built between 1903 and 1907 and sits on a low hill overlooking Squam Lake. The Manor is wonderfully situated on 14 landscaped acres studded with white pines. Inside, it has the feel of an English manor house, with oak paneling and leaded windows; the options to play croquet and horseshoes add to the summery feel. Most rooms have wood-burning fireplaces, and all first-floor rooms have been enlarged and upgraded. Among the best rooms: Savoy Court, Buckingham, and Stratford, all lavishly appointed. Four annex suites have French doors that open onto views of the lake. The top-notch dining room is "dressy casual" (no shorts or jeans).

Rte. 3, Holderness, NH 03245. ✆ **800/545-2141** or 603/968-3348. Fax 603/968-2116. www.manorongoldenpond.com. 25 units (fewer in winter). Summer $235–$450 double; winter $190–$450 double. Rates include breakfast and afternoon tea. 2-night minimum stay on holidays and in foliage season. AE, DISC, MC, V. No children under 12. **Amenities:** Restaurant; outdoor pool; lake swimming; tennis court; watersports equipment rental; limited room service; massage. *In room:* A/C, TV, dataport, fridge (some), coffeemaker (some), hair dryer, iron/ironing board.

WHERE TO DINE

Abondante ★ ITALIAN/DELI This casual storefront market and deli has a delightful atmosphere—maple floors, copper-topped tables, herbs drying from the joists overhead, classical music. Both table service and to-go orders are available, with an inviting selection of fresh pastas (the lobster ravioli is popular) and rustic breads, not to mention imported chocolates. This is a good spot for a casual dinner, or to pick up a lunch for a boating picnic.

30 Main St., Meredith. ✆ **603/279-7177.** Main courses $7.95–$19. AE, DISC, MC, V. Summer daily 5–9pm (until 10pm Fri–Sat); off season Wed–Sat 5–9pm, Sun 4–8pm.

Hart's Turkey Farm Restaurant TURKEY/AMERICAN Hart's Turkey Farm Restaurant is bad news if you're a turkey. On a typically busy day, this place dishes up more than a ton of America's favorite bird. Judging by name alone, Hart's Farm sounds more rural than it is. In fact, it's in a nondescript building on busy Route 3. Inside, it's comfortable in a faux Olde New Englande sort of way—a classic family restaurant (founded 1954) that borders on kitsch, but with turkey too good to write off as a mere retro experience. The service is afflicted with the same rushed efficiency found in other places that attract bus tours, but it's still New Hampshire–friendly. Diners don't return time and again for the charm, anyway—they come for the turkey. There's a good gift shop, too.

Junction of Routes 3 and 104, Meredith. ✆ **603/279-6212.** www.hartsturkeyfarm.com. Main courses $9.50–$22 (mostly $13–$15). AE, DISC, MC, V. Summer daily 11:15am–9pm; fall–spring daily 11:15am–8pm.

WOLFEBORO ★★

The lovely town of Wolfeboro on Lake Winnipesaukee's eastern shore claims to be the first summer resort in the U.S., and the supporting documentation is pretty persuasive. In 1763, John Wentworth, nephew of a former governor, built a summer estate on what's now called Lake Wentworth (east of Winnipesaukee). The house burned in 1820, and its site now attracts mainly archaeologists.

Where western Winnipesaukee tends to be more raucous, with the populist attractions of Weirs Beach, Wolfeboro has more of a blue-blood sensibility. You'll find impeccably maintained 19th-century architecture, attractive downtown shops, and a more refined sense of place.

ESSENTIALS

GETTING THERE Lake Winnipesaukee's east shore is best explored on Route 28 (from Alton Bay to Wolfeboro) and Route 109 (from Wolfeboro to Moultonborough).

VISITOR INFORMATION The **Wolfeboro Chamber of Commerce** (✆ **800/516-5324** or 603/569-2200; www.wolfeborochamber.com) provides regional information and advice from its offices in a converted railroad station at 32 Central Ave., a block off Main Street in Wolfeboro. It's open in summer daily from 10am to 5pm, in the off season Monday through Friday from 10am to 3pm.

EXPLORING WOLFEBORO

Wolfeboro (pop. 2,800) has a vibrant, homey downtown, easily explored on foot. Park near Depot Square and the Victorian train station, and stock up on brochures and maps at the chamber of commerce office. Behind the train station, running along the former tracks of the rail line, is the **Russell C. Chase Bridge-Falls Path** ★, a rail trail that runs along Back Bay to a set of small cascades.

Several boat tours depart from docks behind the shops of Main Street. The best: a wind-in-the-face, half-hour tour on the ***Millie B.*** ★★ (✆ **603/569-1080**), a 28-foot mahogany speedboat constructed by Hacker-Craft ($7 for adults, $4 for children under 5). Also available are chartered excursions on the ***Winnipesaukee Belle*** ★ (✆ **603/569-3796**), a faux 65-foot steamship with a canopied upper deck, owned and operated by the Wolfeboro Inn—however, they start at $800 a pop.

The impressive **MS *Mount Washington*** ★★ (✆ **888/THE-MOUNT** or 630-366-5531; www.cruisenh.com) is a handsome, 230-foot-long vessel that sails out of Wolfeboro several times weekly in summer ($16 for adults, $8 for children ages 4–12).

For a self-propelled afternoon, kayak rentals and guided tours are available from **Winnipesaukee Kayak** ★, 17 Bay St., at Back Bay Marina (✆ **603/569-9926**). On a relatively windless day, few activities beat exploring by paddle from Wolfeboro Bay to the cluster of islands just to the south.

Quieter lake swimming is available at **Wentworth State Beach** ★ (✆ **603/569-3699**), which also has a shady picnic area. The park is 5 miles east of Wolfeboro on Rte. 109. It's open daily mid-June to Labor Day, weekends only from mid-May through mid-June. The entrance fee is $3 per adult, $1 per child ages 6 to 11.

Castle in the Clouds ★★ About 15 miles north of Wolfeboro is a rather unusual sight. Cranky millionaire Thomas Gustav Plant built an eccentric stone edifice atop a mountain overlooking Lake Winnipesaukee in 1913, at a cost of $7 million. The home is a sort of rustic, smaller San Simeon East, with cliff-hugging rooms, stained-glass windows, and unrivaled views of surrounding hills and lakes. Park at the carriage house; from there you are taken through the house by knowledgeable guides. If the castle holds no interest, the 5,200-acre grounds are worth the admission. The long access road is harrowingly narrow and winding, with wonderful vistas and turnouts for stopping along the way. Take time to explore on the way; a separate exit road is fast, straight, and uninteresting.

Rte. 171 (4 miles south of Rte. 25), Moultonborough. ✆ **800/729-2468** or 603/476-2352. www.castleintheclouds.org. Admission $10 adults, $8 seniors, $5 students 7–17, free for children under 6. Grounds only $6 adults, free for children. Mid-May to mid-June Sat–Sun 10am–4:30pm; June to mid-Oct daily 10am–4:30pm. Closed mid-Oct to mid-May.

New Hampshire Boat Museum Winnipesaukee is synonymous with classic wooden powerboats—sleek wooden Chris-Crafts and other icons of a more genteel era—and the New Hampshire Boat Museum brings that era to life with a collection of early boats and artifacts. The museum is in a barn about 2 miles from downtown Wolfeboro. (Drive north on Rte. 109/28 from downtown.). Try to plan your trip to coincide with one of the summer regattas that bring boat restorers and aficionados out of the woodwork to show off their obsessions. Check the website for upcoming events.

397 Centre St., Wolfeboro. ✆ **603/569-4554**. www.nhbm.org. Admission $5 adults, $4 seniors, $3 students, free for children under 13. Memorial Day to Columbus Day Mon–Sat 10am–4pm; Sun noon–4pm.

WHERE TO STAY & DINE

Wolfeboro Inn ★★ This small, elegant hotel mixes modern and traditional remarkably well. Within an easy stroll of downtown Wolfeboro, the inn dates back to 1812 but was expanded and updated in the mid-1980s. The modern lobby has a small atrium with wood beams, a slate floor, and a brick fireplace, but retains an old-world elegance. Most of the comfortable guest rooms are furnished with Early American reproductions and quilts. Deluxe rooms have better views, and a dozen have balconies as well. The downside: For an inn of this price and quality, it has only a disappointing sliver of lakeshore and just a tiny beach for guests.

On-site, casual **Wolf's Tavern** serves pubby meals at breakfast, lunch, and dinner daily.

90 N. Main St. (P.O. Box 1270), Wolfeboro, NH 03894. ✆ **800/451-2389** or 603/569-3016. Fax 603/569-5375. www.wolfeboroinn.com. 44 units. Summer–fall $145–$315 double; spring $135–$260 double; winter $95–$195 double. Rates include continental breakfast. 2-night minimum stay in peak season. AE, DISC, MC, V. **Amenities:** 2 restaurants; watersports equipment rental; concierge; limited room service; babysitting; laundry service; dry cleaning. *In room:* A/C, TV, coffeemaker, hair dryer, iron.

4 The White Mountains ★★★

The White Mountains range is northern New England's outdoor recreation capital. This cluster of ancient mountains is a sprawling, rugged playground that attracts kayakers, mountaineers, rock climbers, skiers, mountain bikers, bird-watchers, and especially hikers.

The **White Mountain National Forest** encompasses 773,000 acres of rocky, forested terrain, more than 100 waterfalls, dozens of backcountry lakes, and miles of clear brooks and cascading streams. An elaborate network of 1,200 miles of hiking trails dates to the 19th century, when city folk took to the mountains to build character (and trails) and experience nature. Trails ranging from easy to demanding lace the hillside forests, run along valley rivers, and traverse barren ridgelines where weather can change quickly and dramatically.

The center of the White Mountains, in spirit if not in geography, is its highest point: 6,288-foot **Mount Washington,** an ominous, brooding peak that's often cloud-capped and mantled with snow both early and late in the season. This blustery peak is accessible by cog railway, car, and foot, making it one of the more popular destinations in the region. You won't find utter wilderness here, but you will find abundant natural drama.

Flanking this peak is the brawny **Presidential Range** of the White Mountains, a series of wind-blasted granite peaks named after U.S. presidents and offering spectacular views. Surrounding these are many other rocky ridges that lure hikers looking for challenges and a place to experience nature at its most elemental.

If your idea of fun doesn't involve steep cliffs or icy dips in mountain streams, you can still enjoy the mountain scenery via spectacular drives. Route 302 carries travelers through Crawford Notch to the pleasant towns of Bethlehem and Littleton. Route 16 travels from southern New Hampshire through congested North Conway before twisting up dramatic Pinkham Notch at the base of Mount Washington. Wide and fast Route 2 skirts the northern edge of the mountains, with wonderful views en route to the town of Jefferson. I-93 may be the most scenic interstate in northern New England, passing through spectacular Franconia Notch as it narrows to two lanes in deference to its natural surroundings (and local political will). The most scenic drive, though, is the **Kancamagus Highway,** which links Conway with Lincoln and provides frequent roadside pull-offs to admire cascades, picnic along rivers, and enjoy sweeping mountain views.

North Conway is the region's motel capital, with hundreds of rooms—many lacking charm, but usually reasonably priced. The Loon Mountain and Waterville Valley areas possess a sort of planned condo-village graciousness that delights some and gives others the creeps. Jackson, Franconia Notch, Crawford Notch, and the Bethlehem-Littleton area are the best places to find old-fashioned hotels and inns.

BACKCOUNTRY FEES

The White Mountain National Forest requires anyone using the backcountry—whether for hiking, mountain biking, picnicking, skiing, or any other activity—to pay a recreation fee. Anyone parking at a trail head must display a backcountry permit on the car dashboard. Those lacking a permit face a fine. Permits are available at ranger stations and many stores in the region. An annual permit costs $20, and a 7-day pass is $5. You can also buy a day pass for $3, but it covers only one site. If you drive somewhere else later in the afternoon and park, you'll have to pay $3 again. You're much better off with a 7-day pass. For information, contact the **Forest Service's White Mountains office** (✆ **603/528-8721;** www.fs.fed.us/r9/white).

RANGER STATIONS & INFORMATION

The Forest Service's **central White Mountains office** is at 719 N. Main St. in Laconia (✆ 603/528-8721), near Lake Winnipesaukee. Your best general source of information is the **Saco Ranger Station,** 33 Kancamagus Hwy., 100 yards west of Route 16,

The White Mountains

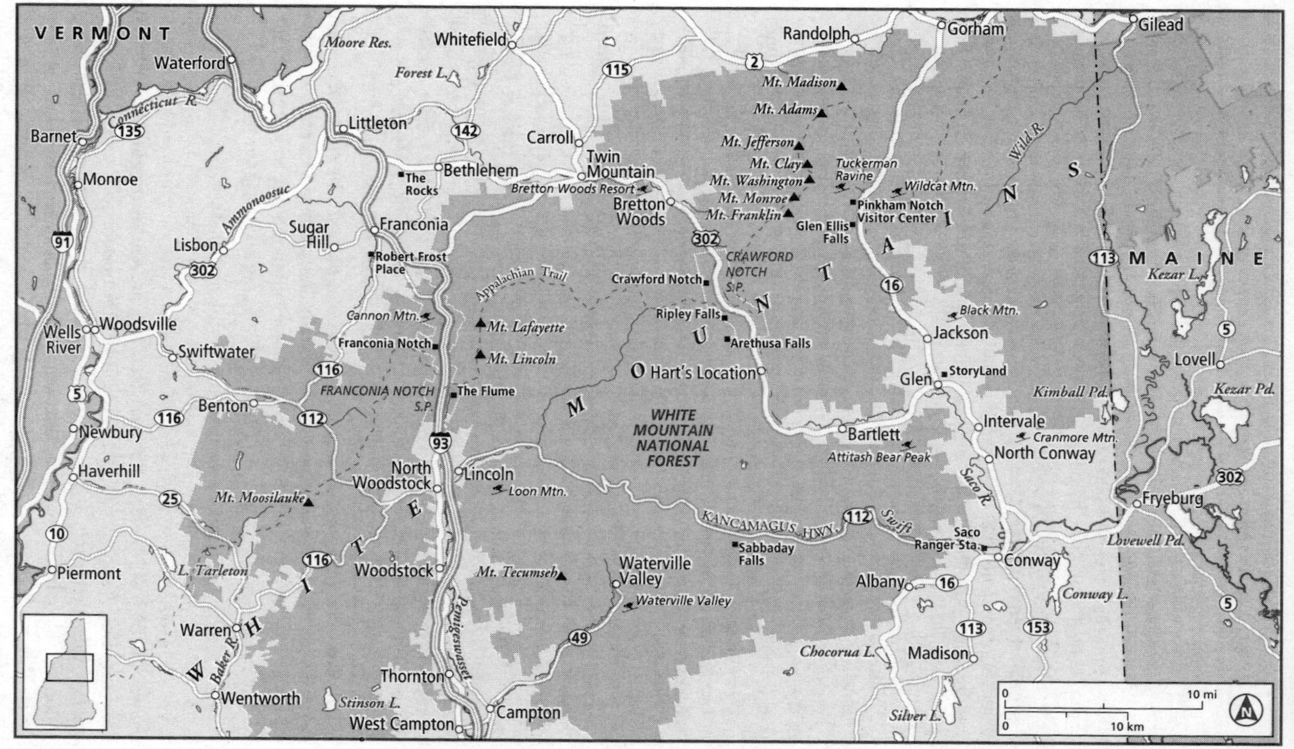

Activities in the White Mountains

BACKPACKING The White Mountains of northern New Hampshire allow for some of the most challenging and scenic backpacking in the Northeast. The best trails are within the 773,000-acre **White Mountain National Forest,** encompassing several 5,000-plus-foot peaks and more than 100,000 acres of designated wilderness. Trails range from easy lowland walks along bubbling streams to demanding ridgeline paths buffeted by fierce winds. The **Appalachian Mountain Club** (✆ **603/466-2727;** www.amc-nh.org) is an excellent source of general information about the New Hampshire outdoors; its huts offer basic shelter and a certain spartan comfort in eight dramatically situated cabins. Reservations are essential.

In addition, a number of three-sided Adirondack-style shelters throughout the backcountry are on a first-come, first-served basis. Some are free; others have a small fee. Pitching a tent in the backcountry is free, subject to certain restrictions, and no permits are required. Check with the **White Mountain National Forest** headquarters (✆ **603/528-8721;** www.fs.fed.us/r9/white) or a district ranger station for rules and regulations. The Appalachian Trail passes through New Hampshire, entering the state at Hanover, running along the highest peaks of the White Mountains, and exiting into Maine along the Mahoosuc Range northeast of Gorham. The trail is well maintained, though it tends to attract teeming crowds along the highest elevations in summer.

Everything, including sleeping bags and pads, tents, and backpacks, is available for rent at **Eastern Mountain Sports** (✆ **603/356-5433**) in North Conway, at reasonable rates.

FISHING Fishing licenses are required for freshwater fishing, but not for saltwater fishing. For detailed information on regulations, request the free *Freshwater Fishing Digest* from the **New Hampshire Fish and Game Department,** 11 Hazen Dr., Concord, NH 03301 (✆ **603/271-3421**). Fishing licenses for nonresidents range from $15 for 3 days to $35 for 15 days. Another helpful booklet, available free from the fish and game department, is *Fishing Waters of New Hampshire.* For online information, go to www.wildlife.state.nh.us.

HIKING The White Mountains have 1,200 miles of trails. The essential guide to hiking trails is the Appalachian Mountain Club's *White Mountain Guide,* which contains up-to-date and detailed descriptions of every trail in the area. The guide is available at most bookstores and outdoor shops in the state.

Conway (✆ 603/447-5448). Other district offices are **Androscoggin Ranger Station,** 300 Glen Rd., Gorham (✆ 603/466-2713); **Ammonoosuc Ranger Station,** 660 Trudeau Rd., Bethlehem (✆ 603/869-2626); and **Pemigewasset Ranger Station,** Route 175, Holderness, near the Plymouth town line (✆ 603/536-1310). The **Evans Notch Ranger Station** (✆ 207/824-2134), which covers the Maine portion of the White Mountains (about 50,000 acres), is in Bethel at 18 Mayville Rd., off Route 2 north of town.

ROCK CLIMBING The White Mountains are renowned for their impressive, towering granite cliffs, especially Cathedral and White Horse ledges, attracting legions of rock climbers from throughout the U.S. and Europe. Ascents range from rather easy to extraordinarily difficult. The North Conway area hosts three climbing schools, and experienced and aspiring climbers alike have plenty of options for improving their skills. Classes range from 1 day to a week.

Contact the Eastern Mountain Sports Climbing School (✆ **603/356-5433;** www.emsclimb.com), the International Mountain Climbing School (✆ **603/356-7064;** www.ime-usa.com/imcs), or the Mountain Guides Alliance (✆ **603/356-5310**) for more information.

SKIING The best ski areas in the White Mountains are Cannon Mountain, Loon Mountain, Waterville Valley, Wildcat, and Attitash Bear Peak, with vertical drops of 2,000 feet and services one would expect of a professional ski resort.

The most impressive ski run in New Hampshire isn't served by a lift. **Tuckerman Ravine** drops 3,400 feet from a lip on the shoulder of Mount Washington down to the valley floor. Skiers arrive from all over to venture here in the early spring (it's dangerously avalanche-prone during the depths of winter), first hiking to the top and then racing to the bottom of this dramatic glacial cirque. The slope is sheer and unforgiving; only very advanced skiers should attempt it. Careless or cocky skiers are hauled out every year on stretchers, and few years go by without at least one death. The AMC's **Pinkham Notch Visitor Center** (✆ **603/466-2721**) has information on current conditions.

The state boasts some 26 cross-country ski centers, which groom a combined total of more than 500 miles of trails. The state's premier cross-country destination is **Jackson** (✆ **800/XC-SNOWS**), with 55 miles of groomed trails in and around an exceptionally scenic village in a valley near the base of Mount Washington. Other favorites include **Bretton Woods Resort** (✆ **800/314-1752** or 603/278-3322) at the western entrance to Crawford Notch, also with more than 55 miles of groomed trails, and the spectacularly remote **Balsams/Wilderness** cross-country ski center (✆ **800/255-0600** or 603/255-3400) in the northerly reaches of the state.

Additional info and advice on recreation in the White Mountains are available at the **AMC's Pinkham Notch Visitor Center** (✆ **603/466-2721**), on Route 16 between Jackson and Gorham. The center is open daily from 6am to 10pm.

CAMPING

CAMPING Car campers shouldn't have any problem finding a place to pitch a tent or park an RV, especially in the northern half of the state. The White Mountain National Forest maintains 23 campgrounds with more than 850 total sites (no hookups), some very small and personal, others quite large and noisy. Sites tend to be fairly easy to come by midweek, but on summer or foliage weekends, you're taking a chance if you arrive without reservations.

For National Forest Campground reservations, call the **National Recreation Reservation Service** (✆ **877/444-6777**). Reservations may also be made at **www.reserveusa.com**, a useful and sophisticated site that enables you to read up on individual campsites (including distance to the nearest water faucet and suitability for RVs or those with disabilities) and reserve your campsite online.

For advance **reservations** at one of the state parks in or around the White Mountains, call ✆ **603/271-3628** between January and May; during the summer season, call the campground directly or, better yet, reserve online at www.nhstateparks.org. Some campgrounds are first-come, first-served. A list of parks and phone numbers is listed in the *New Hampshire Visitor's Guide,* available at information centers, or from the **Division of Travel and Tourism Development,** P.O. Box 1856, Concord, NH 03302 (✆ **800/386-4664;** www.visitnh.gov).

For the latest updates on campsite openings and closures, consult the Forest Service website www.fs.fed.us/r9/forests/white_mountain/recreation/camping/camp_status.php.

NORTH CONWAY ★

North Conway is 150 miles N of Boston and 62 miles NW of Portland.

North Conway is the commercial heart of the White Mountains. Shoppers are drawn by the outlets along Routes 302 and 16. (The two state highways overlap through town.) Outdoor purists abhor the town, considering it a garish interloper to be avoided at all costs, except when seeking pizza and beer.

North Conway itself won't strike anyone as nature's wonderland. The shopping strip south of the village is basically one long turn lane flanked with outlet malls, motels, and chain restaurants of every architectural stripe. On rainy weekends and during foliage season, the road can resemble a linear parking lot.

Sprawl notwithstanding, North Conway is beautifully situated along the eastern edge of the broad and fertile Saco River valley (also called the Mount Washington Valley). Gentle, forest-covered mountains, some with sheer cliffs that suggest the distant, stunted cousins of Yosemite's rocky faces, border the bottomlands. Northward up the valley, the hills rise in a triumphant crescendo to the blustery, tempestuous heights of Mount Washington.

The village is trim and attractive (if often congested), with an open green, some colorful shops, Victorian frontier-town commercial architecture, and a distinctive train station. It's a good place to park, stretch your legs, and find a cup of coffee or a snack. (A Ben & Jerry's Ice Cream Store is off the green near the train station.)

ESSENTIALS

GETTING THERE North Conway and the Mount Washington Valley are on Route 16 and Route 302. Route 16 connects to the Spaulding Turnpike, which intersects with I-95 outside of Portsmouth, NH. Route 302 begins in Portland, ME. **Concord Trailways** (✆ **800/639-3317;** www.concordtrailways.com) provides service from points south, including Boston.

Traffic can be vexing in the Mount Washington Valley on holiday weekends in summer and foliage weekends in fall, when backups of several miles are common. Try valiantly to plan around these busy times to preserve your own sanity.

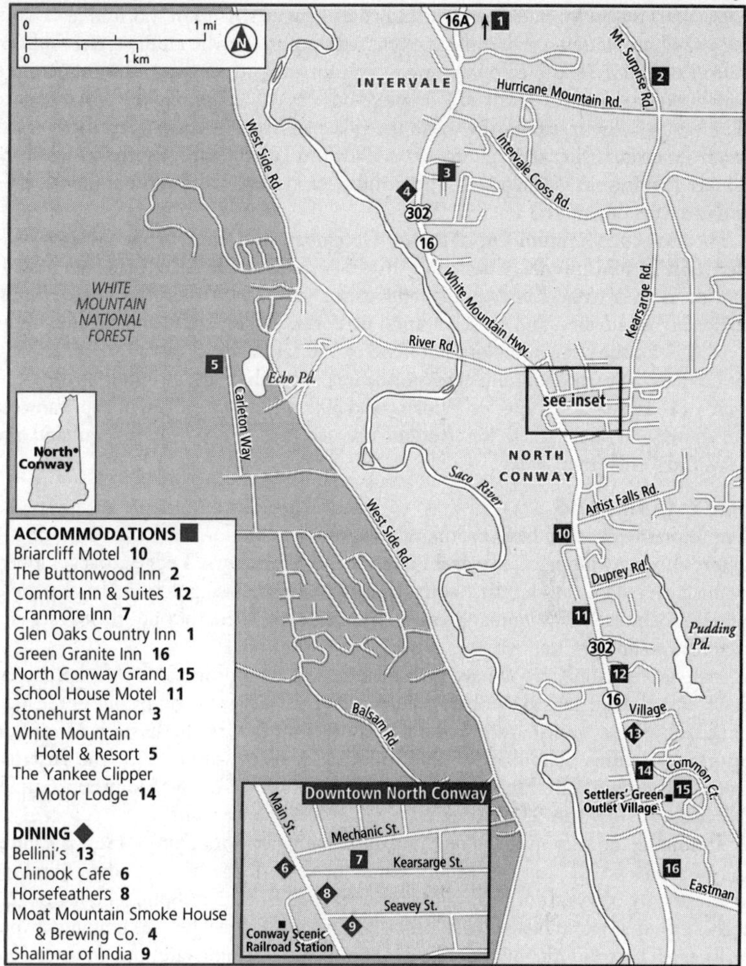

VISITOR INFORMATION Contact the **Mount Washington Valley Chamber of Commerce** (© **800/367-3364** or 603/356-5701; www.mtwashingtonvalley.org), which operates a seasonal information booth opposite the village green. Staff can help arrange for local accommodations. It's open in summer daily from 9am to 6pm, in winter on Saturday and Sunday only.

The state of New Hampshire also operates an **information booth** with restrooms and phones at a spot with fine views of Mount Washington on Routes 16 and 302 north of North Conway.

RIDING THE RAILS

The **Conway Scenic Railroad** ★★ (© **800/232-5251** or 603/356-5251; www.conwayscenic.com) provides mountain excursions in comfortable rail cars (including a dome car) pulled by either steam or early diesel engines. Trips depart from a distinctive 1874 train station, off the village green, recalling an era when tourists arrived from Boston and New York to enjoy the country air for a month or two each summer. The 1-hour excursion heads south to Conway; you're better off signing up for the more picturesque 1¾-hour trip northward to the village of Bartlett. For the best show, select the 5½-hour excursion through dramatic Crawford Notch, with stupendous views of the mountains from high along this beautiful glacial valley. Ask also about the railway's dining excursions.

The train runs from mid-April to mid-December, with more frequent trips scheduled daily in midsummer. Coach and first-class fares are available; first-class passengers sit in "Gertrude Emma," an 1898 parlor car with wicker and rattan chairs, mahogany woodwork, and an observation platform. Tickets are $10 to $22 for adults ($38–$58 for the Crawford Notch trip), $8 to $16 for children ages 4 to 12 ($22–$36 for Crawford Notch). Kids under age 4 ride free in coach on the two shorter trips, but there's a charge of $6 to $26 for toddlers who take the Crawford Notch trip. Fares for the dining car are higher. Reservations are accepted for the dining car and the Crawford Notch train only.

ROCK CLIMBING

The impressive granite faces on the valley's west side are for more than admiring—they're also for climbing. **Cathedral Ledge** ★ and **Whitehorse Ledge** attract climbers from all over who consider these cliffs (along with the Shawangunks in New York and Seneca Rocks in West Virginia) a sort of eastern troika where they put their grace and technical acumen to the test.

Experienced climbers will have their own sources of information on the best access and routes. Inexperienced climbers should sign up for a class taught by one of the local outfitters, whose workshops run from 1 day to 1 week. Try the **Eastern Mountain Sports Climbing School** (✆ **603/356-5433;** www.emsclimb.com), the **International Mountain Climbing School** (✆ **603/356-7064**), or the **Mountain Guides Alliance** (✆ **603/356-5310;** www.mountainguidesalliance.com).

To tone up or keep in shape on rainy days, the **Cranmore Family Fitness Center** (✆ **603/356-6301**) near the Mount Cranmore base lodge has an indoor climbing wall open weekdays from 5 to 8pm and weekends from 2 to 8pm. The fee is $20, including equipment. Newcomers must pass a belay test (free) before climbing; if your skills aren't up to snuff, you can take a lesson. Private, semiprivate, and group lessons are available. You can also play tennis on the courts here for a fee, or buy a day pass that allows free-run access of the center.

DOWNHILL SKIING

Cranmore Mountain Resort ★ *Kids* *Value* Mount Cranmore is the oldest operating ski area in New England. The slopes are unrepentantly old-fashioned, but the mountain has restyled itself as a snow-sports mecca—look for snow tubing, snow-scooters, and ski-bikes. The slopes aren't likely to challenge advanced skiers, but the resort will delight beginners and intermediates, as well as those who like a little diversion with the ski toys. It's highly recommended for families, thanks to the relaxed attitude, range of activities, and budget ticket prices ($15 for kids ages 6–12).

North Conway Village, NH 03860. ✆ **800/SUNNSKI** or 603/356-5543. www.cranmore.com. Vertical drop: 1,200 ft. Lifts: 10. Skiable acreage: 192. Day lift tickets $45.

WHERE TO STAY

Route 16 through North Conway is packed with basic motels, reasonably priced in the off season (around $40–$50), but more expensive in peak travel times such as summer and ski-season weekends and fall foliage season. Fronting the commercial strip, these motels don't offer much in the way of a pastoral environment, but most are comfortable and conveniently located. Try the budget **School House Motel** (✆ **800/638-6050** outside New Hampshire, or 603/356-6829), with a heated outdoor pool; **The Yankee Clipper Motor Lodge** (✆ **800/343-5900** or 603/356-5736; www.blueberrymuffin.com), with a pool and miniature golf (the cheaper rooms lack phones); or the slightly pricier **Green Granite Inn** (✆ **800/468-3666** or 603/356-6901; www.greengranite.com), with 88 rooms, suites with whirlpool, and a free continental breakfast.

Briarcliff Motel *Value* Among North Conway's dozens of roadside motels, the Briarcliff is one of the better options. A basic U-shaped motel with standard-size rooms, all its units have been redecorated in rich colors, more like B&B rooms. A $10 premium is necessary for a room with a "porch" and mountain view, but these are a little peculiar—the porches are really part of a long enclosed sitting area with each unit separated from its neighbor by cubicle-height partitions. (Save your money.) Get over the traffic noise and the nagging signs, and the Briarcliff is decent value.

Rte. 16 (½ mile south of village center, P.O. Box 504), North Conway, NH 03860. ✆ **800/338-4291** or 603/356-5584. www.briarcliffmotel.com. 30 units. Summer–fall $59–$156 double; off season $59–$112 double. 2-night minimum stay holidays and foliage season. AE, DISC, MC, V. **Amenities:** Outdoor pool. *In room:* A/C, TV, fridge.

The Buttonwood Inn ★★ Just a couple minutes' drive from the outlets and restaurants, the Buttonwood has more of a classic country-inn feel than any other North Conway inn. It's set on 17 quiet acres on the side of Mount Surprise in an 1820s-era home, and has a tastefully appointed interior inspired by the Shaker style. Most guest rooms tend toward the small and cozy, but two common rooms (one with a TV) allow guests plenty of space to unwind. Two units have gas fireplaces, and one has a large Jacuzzi as well. The hosts are uncommonly helpful with planning day trips, no matter what your interests. Breakfasts tend toward country elegant: Think cornmeal waffles with strawberry rhubarb sauce.

Mt. Surprise Rd., North Conway, NH 03860. ✆ **800/258-2625** or 603/356-2625. Fax 603/356-3140. www.buttonwoodinn.com. 10 units, 2 with detached private bathroom. Peak season $120–$255 double; off season $95–$170 double. Rates include breakfast. 2- to 3-night minimum stay on weekends and holidays. AE, DISC, MC, V. Closed Apr. Children 6 and older are welcome. **Amenities:** Outdoor pool; cross-country ski trails. *In room:* A/C, dataport.

Comfort Inn & Suites ★ *Kids* This tidy chain hotel has all "suites" (mostly large single rooms, actually) spread among three stories, giving travelers a bit more elbowroom than at most area motels. It's a good choice for families: close to outlet shopping and with its own elaborate, pirate-themed miniature golf course (slight discount for hotel guests). Four executive suites have separate sitting areas; two rooms have gas fireplaces.

2001 White Mountain Hwy. (Rte. 16), North Conway, NH 03860. ✆ **800/647-8483** or 603/356-8811. Fax 603/356-7770. 58 units. $99–$199 double; executive suites to $249. Rates include continental breakfast. AE, DISC, MC, V. **Amenities:** Indoor pool; fitness room. *In room:* A/C, TV, dataport, fridge, coffeemaker, hair dryer, iron.

Cranmore Inn ★ *Value* The Cranmore Inn feels just like what it is—a 19th-century boardinghouse. Open since 1863, this three-story Victorian home is a short walk from North Conway's village center. Its heritage as the oldest continuously operating hotel in North Conway adds charm and quirks, but also the occasional drawback, such as uneven water pressure in the showers. That said, the Cranmore Inn is a good value thanks to its handy location and the hospitality of the innkeepers.

80 Kearsarge St. (P.O. Box 1349), North Conway, NH 03860. ✆ **800/526-5502.** www.cranmoreinn.com. 21 units, including 3 kitchen units with private bathroom. Peak season $74–$124 double, $134–$164 kitchen unit; off season $59–$89 double, $114–$134 kitchen unit. Rates include breakfast except in kitchen units. 2-night minimum stay weekends, holidays, foliage season. AE, DISC, MC, V. **Amenities:** Outdoor pool.

Glen Oaks Country Inn ★ Just 10 minutes north of North Conway is a spur road that leads through the village of Intervale, which has several lodges and feels slightly removed from the clutter of nearby outlet shops. Glen Oaks was built in 1850, with a mansard-roofed third floor added when it opened as an inn in 1890. Typical for the era, the rooms are more cozy than spacious. They are decorated mostly with reproductions and some country Victorian antiques. The best units are the two in the nearby stone cottage, the Arrow Room and the Cottle Room. I prefer the latter, with its wood-burning fireplace, wing chairs, and small porch with Adirondack chairs.

Rte. 16A (P.O. Box 37), Intervale, NH 03845. ✆ **877/854-6535** or 603/356-9772. Fax 603/356-5652. www.glenoaksinn.com. 11 units. $85–$165 double; $110–$185 cottage. Rates include breakfast. 2-night minimum stay most weekends and holidays. AE, DISC, MC, V. Closed Apr. No children under 6. **Amenities:** Outdoor pool. *In room:* A/C, CD players (some), fireplace (some).

North Conway Grand ★ If you're looking for convenience, amenities, and easy access to outlet shopping, this former Sheraton is your best bet. Built on the site of North Conway's former airfield, the Grand is a four-story, gabled hotel adjacent (and architecturally similar) to Outlet Village Plus, one of the outlet centers based in North Conway. The Grand offers clean, comfortable, basic hotel rooms with the usual chain-hotel amenities, and a brick-terraced indoor pool.

Rte. 16 at Settler's Green (P.O. Box 3189), North Conway, NH 03860. ✆ **800/648-4397.** Fax 603/356-6028. www.northconwaygrand.com. 200 units. Summer $99–$229 double; off season $69–$199 double. AE, DC, DISC, MC, V. **Amenities:** Restaurant; indoor pool; outdoor pool; tennis court; fitness room; Jacuzzi; executive rooms. *In room:* A/C, TV w/pay movies, dataport (some), fridge, coffeemaker, hair dryer, iron/ironing board.

Stonehurst Manor ★ This imposing, architecturally eclectic Victorian stone-and-shingle mansion is set amid white pines on a rocky knoll above Route 16, 1 mile north of North Conway. It wouldn't seem at all out of place in either the south of France or the moors of Scotland. One's immediate assumption is that it caters to the stuffy and affluent, but the main focus here is on outdoor adventures, and it attracts a youngish crowd. Request one of the 14 rooms in the regal 1876 mansion (another 10 are in a comfortable, but less elegant, wing built in 1952).

Rte. 16 (1¼ miles north of North Conway Village; P.O. Box 1937), North Conway, NH 03860. ✆ **800/525-9100** or 603/356-3113. www.stonehurstmanor.com. 24 units, 2 with shared bathroom. Midweek $136–$216 double; weekend $146–$236 double. Holidays and foliage season rates higher. 2-night minimum stay on weekends, 3-night minimum on holiday weekends. MC, V. Pets allowed in some rooms ($25 per pet per night). **Amenities:** Restaurant; outdoor pool; tennis court; Jacuzzi. *In room:* A/C, TV, Jacuzzi (some), no phone.

White Mountain Hotel and Resort ★★ This contemporary resort has the best location of any North Conway–area hotel: It's at the base of dramatic White Horse Ledge near Echo Lake State Park, in a modern golf-course community. The White Mountain Hotel was built in 1990, but its style borrows from classic area resorts. Its designers have managed to take some of the more successful elements of a friendly country inn—a nice deck with a view, comfortable seating in the lobby, a clubby tavern area—and incorporate them into a thoroughly modern resort. The comfortably appointed guest rooms are a solid notch or two above what you'd find in a standard hotel.

West Side Rd. (5½ miles west of North Conway; P.O. Box 1828), North Conway, NH 03860. © **800/533-6301.** Fax 603/356-7100. www.whitemountainhotel.com. 80 units. $99–$229 double; $99–$269 suite. 2-night minimum stay on weekends. AE, DISC, MC, V. **Amenities:** Dining room; tavern; outdoor pool; golf course; 2 tennis courts; fitness center; Jacuzzi; sauna; limited room service; babysitting; laundry service; dry cleaning. *In room:* A/C, TV, dataport, coffeemaker, hair dryer, iron.

WHERE TO DINE

North Conway is the turf of family-style restaurants, fast-food chains, and bars that serve food. If you want more refined dining, you're best off heading for The Inn at Thorn Hill in Jackson, about 10 minutes north (see below).

Bellini's ★ SOUTHERN ITALIAN Now in a new location, Bellini's is run by the third generation of the Marcello family, who opened their first place in Rhode Island in 1927. The food runs from fettuccine chicken pesto and braciola to beef carpaccio and stuffed quahogs, and almost everything is homemade—soups, breads, pastas, and desserts. Particularly good are the toasted ravioli appetizers. Drinks include espresso martinis.

Rte. 16, North Conway. © **603/356-7000.** www.bellinis.com. Reservations not accepted. Main courses $12–$22. AE, DISC, MC, V. Mon–Sat 4:30–11pm; Sun 4:30–10pm.

Chinook Café ★ ECLECTIC The Chinook Café opened in 1998 in Conway (a 10-min. drive south of North Conway) as a small, mostly takeout place, but its popularity led it to move down the street and expand. You'll find healthy fare for breakfast and lunch, with a good selection of vegetarian items. The chicken wraps are delicious (especially Thai style with peanut sauce) and the homemade baked goods are a fitting conclusion to a hike.

80 Main St. (across from fire station), Conway. © **603/447-6300.** Main courses, breakfast $1.75–$3.75, lunch $4.85–$6.25. MC, V. Mon–Sat 7am–4pm; Sun 7am–3:30pm.

Horsefeathers ★ PUB FARE In a town where pub food is the rule, Horsefeathers has been leading the pack since 1976. Set in the village, across from the train station, this local hangout is often loud and boisterous, filled with everyone from families to off-duty bartenders. The fare is hard to pin down, ranging from tortilla soup to eggplant ravioli with a red-pepper cream sauce, but tends to gather strength in the middle, with chicken wings, grilled steaks, and the like. The apple-smoked bacon cheddar burger is a good choice, as is the smoked chicken ravioli, lobster-crab cakes, the Harvey (a pastrami sandwich with onion, tomato, and poppyseed dressing), or the scallop pie.

Main St., North Conway. © **603/356-2687.** www.horsefeathers.com. Reservations not accepted. Main courses $6.95–$18. AE, MC, V. Daily 11:30am–11:45pm.

Moat Mountain Smoke House and Brewing Co. ★ Kids BARBECUE/PUB FARE Moat Mountain is the place for fresh, on-site brewed beer, smoked meat, and wood-fired pizza. It's casual and relaxed, and has a more intriguing variety of eats than other North Conway beer joints. You can choose from a selection of barbecued meats or smoked trout and salmon. Other options include burgers, quesadillas, and wraps. A dozen beers are on tap, including six house-brewed. There's also a children's menu.

3378 White Mountain Hwy. (Rte. 16), North Conway (about 1 mile north of the village). © **603/356-6381.** www.moatmountain.com. Reservations not accepted. Main courses $12–$24. AE, MC, V. Daily 11:30am–9pm (until 10pm Fri–Sat).

Shalimar of India ★ Kids NORTHERN INDIAN Shalimar is a pleasant surprise in a town where adventurous ethnic cuisine once meant "nachos fully loaded." Shalimar offers a wide variety of tasty, tangy dishes of northern India. The meals are well prepared, and the chef is very accommodating in ensuring just the right spice level for your palate. The restaurant, a short walk from the village green, offers several tandoori dishes and a wonderfully spicy lamb vindaloo. A kids' menu is available.

27 Seavey St., North Conway. ✆ **603/356-0123.** www.shalimarofindia.com. Reservations recommended in peak summer and winter seasons. Main courses $6–$7 at lunch, $10–$17 at dinner. DISC, MC, V. Sat–Sun noon–3pm and 5–9:30pm; Mon 5–9:30pm; Tues–Fri 11am–2:30pm and 5–9:30pm.

JACKSON & ENVIRONS ★★

Jackson is 8 miles N of North Conway.

Jackson is a quiet village in a picturesque valley off Route 16 about 15 minutes north of North Conway. The village center, approached on a single-lane covered bridge, is tiny, but touches of old-world elegance remain—vestiges of a time when Jackson was a favored destination for the East Coast upper middle class, who fled the summer heat to relax at rambling wooden hotels or country homes.

Thanks to a revamped golf course and one of the most elaborate and well-maintained cross-country ski networks in the country, Jackson is again a thriving resort in summer and winter. While no longer undiscovered, it still feels a shade out of the mainstream and is a peaceful spot, especially when compared to commercial North Conway.

ESSENTIALS

GETTING THERE Jackson is just off Route 16, about 11 miles north of North Conway. Heading north, look for the covered bridge on the right.

VISITOR INFORMATION The **Jackson Chamber of Commerce** (✆ **800/866-3334** or 603/383-9356; www.jacksonnh.com), based in offices at the Jackson Falls Marketplace, can answer questions about area attractions and make lodging reservations.

EXPLORING MOUNT WASHINGTON ★★★

Mount Washington, just north of Jackson amid the national forest, is described with numerous superlatives. At 6,288 feet, it's the highest mountain in the Northeast. It's said to have the worst weather in the world outside of the polar regions. It holds the world's record for the highest surface wind speed ever recorded—231 mph in 1934. Winds over 150 mph are routinely recorded every month except June, July, and August, in part the result of the mountain's location at the confluence of three major storm tracks.

Mount Washington may also be the mountain with the most options for getting to the summit. Visitors can ascend by cog railway (see the "Crawford Notch" section, below), by car, by guide-driven van, or on foot.

Despite the raw power of the weather, Mount Washington's summit is not the best destination for those seeking untamed wilderness. The summit is home to a train platform, parking lot, snack bar, gift shop, museum, and handful of outbuildings, some of which house the weather observatory that's staffed year-round. There also are the crowds, which can be thick on a clear day. Then again, on a clear day, the views can't be beat, with vistas extending into four states and to the Atlantic Ocean.

The best place to learn about Mount Washington and its approaches is rustic **Pinkham Notch Visitor Center** (✆ **603/466-2721**), operated by the Appalachian Mountain Club. At the crest of Route 16 between Jackson and Gorham, the center offers overnight accommodations and meals (see below), maps, a limited selection of outdoor supplies, and plenty of advice from the helpful staff. A number of hiking trails also depart from here, with several loops and side trips. About a dozen trails in all lead to the mountain's summit, ranging in length from about 4 to 15 miles. (Detailed information is available at the visitor center.) The most direct and dramatic is the **Tuckerman Ravine Trail** ★★★, which departs from Pinkham Notch. It's a full day's endeavor: Healthy hikers should allow 4 to 5 hours for the ascent, an hour or two less for the return trip. Be sure to allow enough time to enjoy the dramatic glacial cirque of Tuckerman Ravine, which attracts extreme skiers to its snowy chutes and sheer drops as late as June, and often holds patches of snow well into summer.

The **Mount Washington Auto Road** ★★ (✆ **603/466-3988;** www.mountwashingtonautoroad.com) opened in 1861 as a carriage road and has since remained one of the most popular White Mountain attractions. The steep, winding 8-mile road (with an average grade of 12%) is partially paved and incredibly dramatic; your breath will be taken away at one curve after another. The ascent will test your will; the descent will test your car's brakes. The trip is not worth doing if the summit is in the clouds; wait for a clear day.

If you'd prefer to leave the driving to someone else, van tours ascend throughout the day, allowing you to relax, enjoy the views, and learn about the mountain from informed guides. The cost is $24 for adults, $22 for seniors, and $10 for children ages 5 to 12, and includes a half-hour stay on the summit.

The Auto Road, on Route 16 north of Pinkham Notch, is open from early May to late October from 7:30am to 6pm (limited hours early and late in the season). The cost for cars is $18 for vehicle and driver, $7 for each additional adult ($4 for children ages 5–12), or $10 for a motorcycle and its operator. The fee includes audiocassette narration pointing out sights along the way (available in English, French, and German). Management has imposed some restrictions on cars; for example, Acuras, Hondas, Saturns, and Jaguars with automatic transmissions must show a "1" or "L" on the shifter to be allowed on the road, and no Lincoln Continentals made before 1969 are permitted.

One additional note: The average temperature atop the mountain is 30°F (1°C). (The record low was –43°F/–6°C, and the warmest temperature ever recorded atop the mountain, in Aug, was 72°F/22°C.) Even in summer, visitors should come prepared for blustery, cold conditions.

EXPLORING PINKHAM NOTCH ★★★

The Pinkham Notch Visitor Center is at the height of land on Route 16. Just south, look for signs for **Glen Ellis Falls** ★★, a worthwhile 10- to 15-minute stop. From the parking area, you'll pass through a pedestrian tunnel and walk along the Glen Ellis River for a few minutes until it seemingly falls off the face of the earth. The stream plummets 64 feet down a cliff; observation platforms are at the top and near the bottom of the falls, one of the region's most impressive after a torrential rain. From the parking lot to the base of the falls is less than a half-mile.

From the visitor center, it's about 2.5 miles up to **Hermit Lake and Tuckerman Ravine** ★★★ via the Tuckerman Ravine Trail (see above). Even if you're not planning to continue on to the summit, the ravine, with its sheer sides and lacey cataracts, may be the most dramatic destination in the White Mountains. It's well worth the 2-hour ascent in all but the most miserable weather. The trail is wide and only moderately demanding. Bring a picnic and lunch on the massive boulders that litter the ravine's floor.

In summer, an **enclosed gondola** ★ at Wildcat ski area (see below) hauls passengers up the mountain for a view of Tuckerman Ravine and Mount Washington's summit. The lift operates Saturday and Sunday from Memorial Day to mid-June, then daily through October. The base lodge is just north of Pinkham Notch on Route 16.

CROSS-COUNTRY SKIING

Jackson regularly ranks among the top five cross-country ski resorts in the nation. That's due to nonprofit **Jackson Ski Touring Foundation** ★★★ (✆ **800/XC-SNOWS** or 603/383-9355; www.jacksonxc.com), which created and now maintains the extensive trail network of 93 miles (55 miles of which are regularly groomed). The terrain is wonderfully varied; many of the trails are rated "most difficult," which will keep advanced skiers from getting bored. Novice and intermediate skiers have good options spread out along the valley floor.

Start at the base lodge near the Wentworth Resort in the center of Jackson. There's parking, and you can ski through the village and into the hills. Gentle trails traverse the valley floor, with more advanced trails winding up the mountains. One-way ski trips with shuttles back to Jackson are available; ask if you're interested. Given how extensive and well maintained the trails are, passes are a good value at $15 for adults, $8 for children ages 10 to 15. Rentals are available in the ski center. Ticket/rental packages are available, as are snowshoe rentals and trails specifically for snowshoers.

DOWNHILL SKIING

Black Mountain ★ Kids Dating back to the 1930s, Black Mountain is one of the White Mountains' pioneer ski areas. It remains the quintessential family mountain—modest in size, thoroughly nonthreatening, ideal for beginners—although there's also glade skiing for more advanced skiers. A day here feels a bit like you've trespassed onto a farmer's unused hayfield, which adds to the charm. The ski area also offers two compact terrain parks for snowboarders, as well as lessons, rentals, a nursery, and a base lodge with cafeteria and pub.

Jackson, NH 03846. ✆ **800/475-4669** or 603/383-4490. www.blackmt.com. Vertical drop: 1,100 ft. Lifts: 2 chairlifts, 2 surface lifts. Skiable acreage: 143. Adult day lift tickets Mon–Fri $20; Sat–Sun $32.

Wildcat ★★ Set high within Pinkham Notch, Wildcat Mountain has a rich heritage as a venerable New England ski mountain, with the best views of any ski area in the White Mountains. Wildcat has a bountiful supply of intermediate trails, as well as some challenging expert terrain. This is skiing as it used to be—no base area clutter, just a lodge. While that also means no on-slope accommodations, there are many options within a 15-minute drive. Skiers can save a few dollars by purchasing advance tickets online.

Rte. 16, Pinkham Notch, NH 03846. ✆ **888/SKI-WILD** or 603/466-3326. www.skiwildcat.com. Vertical drop: 2,100 ft. Lifts: 4 chairlifts (1 high-speed lift). Skiable acreage: 225. Adult day lift tickets $55; ages 13–18 $49; ages 6–12 and seniors $29.

ESPECIALLY FOR KIDS

Children ages 10 and under will enjoy **StoryLand** ★★, at the northern junction of Routes 16 and 302 (✆ **603/383-4186;** www.storylandnh.com). This old-fashioned (around 1954) fantasy village is filled with 30 acres of improbably leaning buildings, magical rides, fairy-tale creatures, and other enchanted beings. A "sprayground" features a 40-foot water-spurting octopus. StoryLand is open from Memorial Day to mid-June, Saturday and Sunday only from 10am to 5pm; from mid-June to Labor Day, daily from 9am to 6pm; and from Labor Day to Columbus Day, Saturday and Sunday only from 10am to 5pm. Admission is a flat $22 ages 4 and older; free for 3 and under.

WHERE TO STAY

Covered Bridge Motor Lodge ★ *Value* This pleasant, family-run motel, on 5 acres between Route 16 and the burbling river, is next to Jackson's covered bridge. Rooms are priced well for this area. The best units have balconies that overlook the river; the noisier rooms facing the road are a bit cheaper. Ask about the two-bedroom apartment units with kitchen and fireplace. While basic, the lodge has gardens and other appealing touches that make it a good value.

Rte. 16, Jackson, NH 03846. ✆ **800/634-2911** or 602/383-9151. Fax 603/383-4146. www.jacksoncoveredbridge.com. 32 units, including 6 apt suites. $79–$139 double; $109–$229 suite. Rates include continental breakfast. AE, DISC, MC, V. **Amenities:** Outdoor pool; tennis court; Jacuzzi. *In room:* A/C, TV.

Eagle Mountain House ★★ The Eagle Mountain House is a handsome relic that has survived the ravages of time, fire, and the capricious tastes of tourists. Built in 1916, this five-story, gleaming white wooden classic is set in an idyllic valley above Jackson. The guest rooms are furnished in a country pine look with stenciled blanket chests, armoires, and feather comforters. You'll pay a premium for rooms with mountain views, but it's not really worth the extra cash. Just plan to spend your free time lounging on the wide porch with the views across the golf course toward the mountains beyond.

Carter Notch Rd. (P.O. Box E), Jackson, NH 03846. ✆ **800/966-5779** or 603/383-9111. Fax 603/383-0854. www.eaglemt.com. 96 units. Mid-June to mid-Oct $99–$179 double, $119–$209 suite; off season $79–$109 double, $99–$139 suite. Ask about packages. AE, DISC, MC, V. **Amenities:** Dining room; tavern; outdoor pool; golf course; 2 tennis courts; health club; Jacuzzi; sauna; massage; dry cleaning. *In room:* TV.

The Inn at Thorn Hill ★★★ This elegant inn is a great choice for a romantic getaway. The classic shingle-style home (now swathed in yellow siding) was designed by architect Stanford White in 1895, and sits just outside the village center surrounded by wooded hills. Inside, the place has a comfortable Victorian feel. Rooms are luxuriously appointed; my favorites are Catherine's Suite, with a fireplace and two-person Jacuzzi, and Notch View Cottage, with a screened porch and Jacuzzi with a forest view. The hospitality is top-notch, and the meals (see review below) are among the best in the Mount Washington Valley.

Thorn Hill Rd. (P.O. Box A), Jackson, NH 03846. ✆ **800/289-8990** or 603/383-4242. www.innatthornhill.com. 19 units. Main inn $60–$410 double; carriage house $195–$310 double; cottage $320–$410 double. Rates include breakfast and dinner. 2- to 3-night minimum stay on weekends and some holidays. AE, DISC, MC, V. No children under 8. **Amenities:** Restaurant; outdoor pool; Jacuzzi; spa; limited room service; babysitting; laundry service. *In room:* A/C, TV.

Joe Dodge Lodge at Pinkham Notch Guests come to the Pinkham Notch Visitor Center more for the camaraderie than the accommodations. Situated spectacularly at the base of Mount Washington, far from commercial clutter and with easy access to many hiking and skiing trails, the center is operated by the Appalachian Mountain Club like a tightly run youth hostel, with guests sharing spartan bunk rooms, dorm-style bathrooms, and meals at family-style tables in the main lodge. (Some private rooms provide double beds or family accommodations.) The pluses: a festive atmosphere and an unbeatable location.

Rte. 16, Pinkham Notch, NH. (Mailing address: AMC, P.O. Box 298, Gorham, NH 03581.) ✆ **603/466-2721.** www.outdoors.org. 108 beds in bunkrooms of 2, 3, and 4 beds, all with shared bathroom. $74 double. Bunkrooms peak season $49 per adult, $26 per child 15 and under (discount for AMC members); off season $43 per adult, $25 per child. MAP plans also available. MC, V. No children under 3. **Amenities:** Cafeteria; weekend activities. *In room:* No phone.

Wentworth Resort Hotel ★★ The venerable Wentworth sits in the middle of Jackson Village, all turrets, eaves, and awnings. Built in 1869, this Victorian shingled

Value Gorham: Budget Beds, Bargain Meals

White Mountain travelers on a lean budget would do well to look at **Gorham** as a base for mountain explorations. This tidy commercial town 10 minutes north of Pinkham Notch lacks charm, but has a great selection of clean mom-and-pop motels and family-style restaurants. After all, if you're planning to spend your days hiking or canoeing, where you rest your head at night won't matter much. **Moriah Sports,** 101 Main St. (✆ **603/466-5050**), sells a wide range of sporting equipment (bikes, cross-country skis, rain gear) and is a good stop for suggestions on area activities.

The top motel choice is the **Royalty Inn,** 130 Main St. (✆ **800/437-3529** or 603/466-3312; www.royaltyinn.com), which has a restaurant, larger-than-average, if plain, rooms, two pools, and a large fitness club; rates for a double are $45 to $78. **Top Notch Inn,** 265 Main St. (✆ **800/228-5496** or 603/466-5496; www.topnotchinn.com), has an outdoor pool and hot tub and in-room fridges. Rates start at $79 for a double; small pets are accepted.

For basic family dining, **Wilfred's,** 117 Main St. (✆ **603/466-2380**), serves steaks, chops, and a variety of seafood. The **Moonbeam Café,** 19 Exchange St. (✆ **603/466-5549**), has hearty meals such as potato pancakes and cups of coffee; a visit to the antique bathroom (complete with pull-chain) is mandatory. **Libby's Bistro,** at 115 Main St. (✆ **603/466-5330**), is in a handsomely renovated bank and serves dinners better than any place in North Conway.

inn once had 39 buildings (including a dairy and electric plant), but edged to the brink of deterioration in the mid-1980s. The seven remaining buildings were refurbished, with a number of condominium clusters added around the expanded and upgraded golf course. The inn has upgraded again, and the owner and chef were both formerly with the Four Seasons hotel chain. The large standard and superior double rooms are decorated with Victorian-inspired furnishings. Suites (all with king-size beds) have such amenities as propane fireplaces, whirlpools, outdoor hot tubs, and claw-foot tubs. Visitors of stout constitution can stroll up the road and plunge into the waters of Jackson Falls.

Carter Notch Rd. (P.O. Box M), Jackson, NH 03846. ✆ **800/637-0013** or 603/383-9700. Fax 603/383-4265. www.thewentworth.com. 76 units. Peak season $185–$245 double, $305–$355 suite; off season $155–$185 double, $225–$265 suite. Rates include full breakfast and 5-course dinner. B&B and no-meal rates also available. AE, DC, DISC, MC, V. **Amenities:** Restaurant; outdoor pool; golf course; tennis court; cross-country ski center. *In room:* A/C, TV, Jacuzzi (some).

Wildcat Inn & Tavern ★ The Wildcat Inn occupies a three-story farmhouse-style building in the middle of Jackson. It's a comfortable, informal place better known for its cozy restaurant and tavern than for its accommodations. Guest rooms are mostly small, two-room suites, carpeted and furnished with a mishmash of furniture. Sitting rooms typically have contemporary sofas, chairs, and pine furniture, and offer cozy sanctuary after a day of hiking or skiing. The downstairs dining room resembles a traditional country farmhouse, with old wood floors and pine furniture. In the winter, stake out a toasty spot in front of the tavern fireplace—one of the most popular gathering spots in the valley—to sip soothing libations and order from the bar menu.

Rte. 16A, Jackson, NH 03846. ✆ **800/228-4245** or 603/383-4245. www.wildcattavern.com. 14 units, 2 with shared bathroom. $129–$199 double. Rates include full breakfast. $10 surcharge during foliage season. AE, DC, MC, V. *In room:* A/C, TV.

WHERE TO DINE

Inn at Thorn Hill ★★★ NEW AMERICAN The romantic Inn at Thorn Hill is a great choice for a memorable meal. The candlelit dining room faces the forested hill behind the inn. Start with a glass of wine (the restaurant has won the *Wine Spectator* award of excellence), then browse the menu selections that change weekly, but often have Asian accents. Appetizers may include Nigerian prawn pad Thai, a lobster vichyssoise, bacon-wrapped scallops over truffled polenta, or coconut-steamed mussels. Entrees can be a lobster-and-scallop risotto in lobster cream with wasabi caviar, sake-marinated halibut over crispy noodles, lamb loin poached in olive oil, or Peking duck. Quail or pheasant are also great choices.

Thorn Hill Rd., Jackson. ✆ **603/383-4242.** www.innatthornhill.com. Reservations recommended. Main courses $25–$30. AE, DISC, MC, V. Daily 6–9pm.

Thompson House Eatery ★★ ECLECTIC This friendly, old-fashioned spot in a 19th-century farmhouse at the edge of Jackson's golf course attracts crowds, not only for its well-prepared fare, but also for its reasonable prices. Dining is both indoors and out. For lunch, there are salads and good sandwiches. (Pork-and-pears and beef-and-boursin are two.) Dinner features fresh fish, ginger-cured pork tenderloin, crab cakes, lamb chops, steak, and several vegetarian entrees. An adjacent ice-cream parlor is worth a stop.

Rte. 16A, Jackson (near north intersection with Rte. 16). ✆ **603/383-9341.** Reservations recommended for dinner. Main courses $4–$9 at lunch, $19–$25 at dinner. AE, DISC, MC, V. Sun–Mon 5:30–9pm; Wed–Thurs 11:30am–3:30pm and 5:30–9pm; Fri–Sat 11:30am–3:30pm and 5:30–10pm.

CRAWFORD NOTCH ★★

Crawford Notch is a wild, rugged mountain valley that angles through the heart of the White Mountains. Within the notch itself is a surplus of legend and history. For years after its discovery by European settlers in 1771, it was an impenetrable wilderness, creating a barrier to commerce by blocking trade between the upper Connecticut River Valley and harbors in Portland and Portsmouth. This was eventually surmounted by a plucky crew who hauled the first freight through.

Nathaniel Hawthorne immortalized the notch with a short story about a real-life tragedy that struck in 1826. One night (dark and stormy, naturally), the Willey family fled its home when they feared an avalanche would roar toward the valley floor. As fate would have it, the avalanche divided above their home and spared the structure; the seven who fled were killed in tumbling debris. You can still visit the site today—watch for signs when driving through the notch.

The notch is accessible via Route 302, which is wide and speedy on the lower sections, becoming steeper as it approaches the narrow defile of the notch itself. Modern engineering has taken most of the kinks out of the road, so you need to remind yourself to stop from time to time and enjoy the panoramas. The views up the cliffs from the road can be spectacular on a clear day; on an overcast or drizzly day, the effect is nicely foreboding.

ESSENTIALS

GETTING THERE Route 302 runs through Crawford Notch for approximately 25 miles between the towns of Bartlett and Twin Mountain.

VISITOR INFORMATION The **Twin Mountain Chamber of Commerce** (✆ **800/245-8946;** www.twinmountain.org) provides general information and lodging referrals at its booth near the intersection of Routes 302 and 3. Open year-round; hours vary.

HIKING

The **Highland Center at Crawford Notch** ★★ (✆ **603/278-HIKE**) on Route 302 in Bretton Woods is a new, multipurpose facility on 26 acres of AMC-owned land. It's a great headquarters for hikes into the surrounding mountains: under one roof, you can book a tour, hike a path that passes nearby, bunk down for the night, eat communal dinners, and use L.L.Bean gear for free. It's open year-round.

From June through mid-October, two useful, though pricey, **hiker shuttles** (✆ **603/466-2727**) operated by the Appalachian Mountain Club cruise the mountains, depositing and picking up hikers. Rides cost $12 one-way, regardless of length; AMC members get a $2 discount.

SKIING

Attitash Bear Peak ★★ Attitash Bear Peak is a good mountain for families and skiers at the intermediate-edging-to-advanced level; look for great cruising runs and a handful of more challenging drops. The ski area includes two peaks, 1,750-foot Attitash and the adjacent 1,450-foot Bear Peak, and is among New England's most scenic ski areas—dotted with rugged rock outcroppings, with sweeping views of Mount Washington and the Presidential Range (an observation tower is on the main summit). The base area tends to be sleepy in the evenings; those looking for nightlife can head 15 minutes away to North Conway.

Rte. 302, Bartlett, NH 03812. ✆ **877/677-SNOW** or 603/374-2368. www.attitash.com. Vertical drop: 1,750 ft. Lifts: 12 chairlifts (including 2 high-speed quads), 3 surface lifts. Skiable acreage: 280. Adult day lift tickets $59; ages 13–18 $49; ages 6–12 and seniors $39.

Bretton Woods Resort ★ Bretton Woods continues its expansion of lifts and expert glade skiing; the resort has also added Olympic medalist Bode Miller to its staff, tapping him as director of skiing. These newer trails and lifts and young blood bring a welcome vitality and edge to the mountain, which has long been popular with beginners and families. The trails include glades and wide cruising runs, along with more challenging options for advanced skiers. (The challenge level still doesn't rival the more demanding slopes of Vermont or Maine, but that is being fixed: One new section features "Bode's Run," an expert trail partly designed by Miller.) The resort continues to do a fine job with kids and has a low-key attitude that families adore. Accommodations are available on the mountain and nearby, notably at the Mount Washington Hotel, but evening entertainment tends to revolve around hot tubs, TVs, and going to bed early. An excellent cross-country ski center is nearby.

Rte. 302, Bretton Woods, NH 03575. ✆ **800/314-1752** or 603/278-3333. www.brettonwoods.com. Vertical drop: 1,500 ft. Lifts: 8 chairlifts (including 2 high-speed quads), 2 surface lifts. Skiable acreage: 375. Adult day lift tickets Mon–Fri $57; Sat–Sun and holidays $64.

WATERFALLS & SWIMMING HOLES

Much of the mountainous land flanking Route 302 falls under the jurisdiction of **Crawford Notch State Park** ★★, which was established in 1911 to preserve land that elsewhere had been decimated by overly aggressive logging. The headwaters of the Saco River form in the notch, and what's generally regarded as the first permanent trail up Mount Washington also departs from here. Several turnouts and trail heads invite a more leisurely exploration of the area. The trail network on both sides of Crawford Notch is extensive; consult the *AMC White Mountain Guide* or *White Mountains Map Book* for detailed information.

Up the mountain slopes that form the valley, hikers will spot a number of lovely waterfalls, some more easily accessible than others.

Arethusa Falls ★★ has the highest single drop of any waterfall in the state, and the trail to the falls passes several attractive smaller cascades, especially beautiful in the spring or after a heavy rain, when the falls are at their fullest. You can enjoy a 2.6-mile round-trip to the falls and back on Arethusa Falls Trail, or a 4.5-mile loop that includes views from Frankenstein Cliffs (named not after the creator of the monster, but after a noted landscape painter).

If arriving from the south, look for signs to the trail parking area after passing the Crawford Notch State Park entrance sign. From the north, the trail head is a half-mile south of the Dry River Campground. At the parking lot, look for the sign and map to get your bearings, then cross the railroad tracks to start up the falls trail.

Continue north on Route 302 to the trail head for tumultuous **Ripley Falls** ★. This easy hike is a little more than 1 mile round-trip. Look for the sign to the falls on Route 302 just north of the trail head for Webster Cliff Trail. (If you pass the Willey House site, you've gone too far.) Park at the site of the Willey Station. Follow trail signs for the Ripley Falls Trail, and allow about a half-hour to reach the cascades. The most appealing swimming holes are at the top of the falls.

A HISTORIC RAILWAY

Mount Washington Cog Railway ★★ The cog railway was a marvel of engineering when it opened in 1869, and it remains so today. Part moving museum, part slow-motion roller-coaster ride, the cog railway steams to the summit at a determined "I think I can" pace of about 4 mph. But you'll feel a bit of excitement on the way up and back, especially when the train crosses Jacob's Ladder, a rickety-seeming trestle 25 feet high that angles upward at a grade of more than 37%. Passengers enjoy the expanding view on this 3-hour round-trip (including stops to add water to the steam engine, to check the track switches, and to allow other trains to ascend or descend). A 20-minute stop at the summit allows you to browse around. Be aware that the ride is noisy and sulfurous; dress warmly and expect to acquire a patina of cinder and soot.

Rte. 302, Bretton Woods. ✆ **800/922-8825** or 603/278-5404. www.thecog.com. Fare $57 adults, $52 seniors, $37 children 4–12, free for children 3 and under. MC, V. Runs daily Memorial Day to late Oct, plus weekends in May. Frequent departures; call for schedule. Reservations recommended.

WHERE TO STAY & DINE

The Bernerhof Inn ★ Overlooking busy Route 302 en route to Crawford Notch, The Bernerhof occupies a century-old home that's all gables and squared-off turrets on the outside. Inside, the guest rooms are eclectic and fun, crafted with odd angles and corners. All are tastefully furnished in a simple country style that's sparing with the froufrou. Spacious room no. 7 (a suite) is tucked under the eaves on the third floor and has a two-person Jacuzzi and in-room sauna. Room no. 8 (not a suite) is also romantic and appealing, with a Jacuzzi under a skylight, wood floors, a brass bed, and a handsome cherry armoire.

Rte. 302, Glen, NH 03838. ✆ **800/548-8007** or 603/383-9132. Fax 603/383-0809. www.bernerhofinn.com. 9 units. Midweek $79–$145 double; weekends $99–$179 double. Rates include breakfast. 2-night minimum stay peak season and weekends. AE, DISC, MC, V. **Amenities:** Restaurant; pub. *In room:* A/C, TV, hair dryer.

The Mount Washington Resort at Bretton Woods ★★ This five-story resort at the foot of New Hampshire's highest peak, with its gleaming white clapboards and cherry-red roof, was built in 1902. In its heyday, the resort attracted luminaries such as Babe Ruth, Thomas Edison, and Woodrow Wilson. Guest rooms vary in size and decor; many have grand views of the surrounding mountains and countryside. A 900-foot-long veranda makes for relaxing afternoons. Meals are enjoyed in an impressive octagonal dining room. A house orchestra provides entertainment during the meal, and guests often dance between courses. The decor isn't lavish, and while the innkeepers are making overdue improvements, the hotel can feel a bit unfinished in parts. However, it remains a favorite spot in the mountains, partly for the sheer improbability of it all, and partly for its direct link to a lost era. Recent visits noted encouraging signs, including renovations to the smallish indoor pool and fly-casting lessons outside on the tennis court.

Rte. 302, Bretton Woods, NH 03575. ✆ **800/314-1752** or 603/278-1000. www.mtwashington.com. 200 units. $145–$525 double; $910–$1,750 suite. Rates include breakfast and dinner. Minimum stay during holidays. AE, DISC, MC, V. **Amenities:** 2 restaurants; indoor pool; outdoor pool; 2 golf courses; 12 tennis courts; Jacuzzi; sauna; bike rental; children's programs (summer); concierge; shopping arcade; room service; babysitting. *In room:* TV.

Notchland Inn ★★ Off Route 302 in a wild section of Crawford Notch, this inn looks every bit like a redoubt in a Sir Walter Scott novel. Built of hand-cut granite in the mid-1800s, Notchland is classy yet informal, perfectly situated for exploring the wilds of the White Mountains. Guest rooms are outfitted with antiques, wood-burning fireplaces, high ceilings, and individual thermostats. Three suites have Jacuzzis; two units are in the adjacent schoolhouse, where the upstairs room has a wonderful soaking tub. (All but three rooms have air-conditioning.) The inn is also home to affable Bernese mountain dogs and llamas. You may want to add the five-course dinner to your plan ($30 per person)—a good value, since the closest restaurant is a long, dark drive away.

Rte. 302, Hart's Location, NH 03812. ✆ **800/866-6131** or 603/374-6131. www.notchland.com. 13 units. $195 double, $230–$260 suite; foliage season and holidays $245 double, $280–$310 suite. Rates include breakfast. 2- to 3-night minimum stay weekends, foliage season, and some holidays. AE, DISC, MC, V. No children under 12. **Amenities:** Restaurant; Jacuzzi; babysitting. *In room:* Hair dryer, iron, no phone.

Finds **All Aboard! For Dinner, That Is**

Surprisingly, the best dining hereabouts is aboard **Cafe Lafayette** ★★, in three restored Pullman rail cars that chug along a scenic tour through the western White Mountains while diners enjoy a five-course meal with white tablecloths and fresh flowers. The evening tour lasts a little more than 2 hours, and includes homemade dinner rolls, salad, sorbet, entree, and dessert. (Wine and cocktails are available at extra cost.) Meals are prepared aboard, and main courses include New American fare such as grilled salmon with cranberry walnut salsa or pork tenderloin with pinot noir demi-glaze. The train runs from mid-May through October. Boarding is at 5:15pm Tuesdays, Thursdays, and Saturdays, an hour earlier Sundays, at the Eagle's Nest on Route 112 in North Woodstock; reservations are advised, but not essential. Cost is $60 to $70 per adult, $40 to $50 for children ages 6 to 11 (✆ **800/699-3501** or 603/745-3500; www.cafelafayette.com).

FRANCONIA NOTCH ★★

Franconia Notch is rugged New Hampshire writ large. As travelers head north on I-93, the Kinsman Range to the west and Franconia Range to the east begin to converge, and the road swells upward. Soon, the flanking mountain ranges press in on either side, forming dramatic Franconia Notch, which offers little in the way of civilization and services, but a whole lot in the way of natural drama. Most of the notch is in a well-managed state park that to most travelers will be indistinguishable from the national forest. Travelers seeking the sublime should plan on a leisurely trip through the notch, allowing enough time to get out of the car and explore forests and craggy peaks. Franconia Notch is more developed for recreation (and thus more crowded with day-trippers) than equally rugged Crawford Notch to the northeast (see above).

ESSENTIALS

GETTING THERE I-93 runs through Franconia Notch, narrowing from four lanes to two (becoming the Franconia Notch Pkwy.) in the most scenic and sensitive areas of the park. Several scenic roadside pull-offs dot the route.

VISITOR INFORMATION Information on the park and surrounding area is available at the **Flume Information Center** (✆ **603/745-8391**), at Exit 1 off the parkway, open daily in summer from 9am to 4:30pm. North of the notch, the **Franconia Notch Chamber of Commerce** (✆ **603/823-5661;** www.franconianotch.org) on Main Street next to town hall is open spring through fall, Tuesday through Sunday from 10am to 5pm (days and hours often vary).

EXPLORING FRANCONIA NOTCH STATE PARK ★

Franconia Notch State Park's 8,000 acres, nestled within the surrounding White Mountain National Forest, host an array of scenic attractions easily accessible from I-93 and the Franconia Notch Parkway. At the Flume Information Center (see above), a free 15-minute video summarizes the park's attractions. For information on the following, contact the park offices (✆ **603/745-8391**).

The Flume ★★ is a rugged 800-foot gorge through which the Flume Brook tumbles. A popular attraction in the mid–19th century, it's 800 feet long, 90 feet deep, and as narrow as 20 feet at the bottom; visitors explore by means of a network of boardwalks and bridges on a 2-mile walk. Early photos of the chasm show a boulder wedged in overhead; this was swept away in an 1883 avalanche. If you're looking for easy, quick access to natural grandeur, it's worth the money. Otherwise, set off into the mountains and seek your own drama with fewer crowds. Open May through October; admission is $8 for adults, $5 for children ages 6 to 12. Walk or snowshoe the grounds for free in the off season.

Echo Lake ★ is a picturesquely situated recreation area, with a 28-acre lake, a handsome swimming beach, and picnic tables scattered about, all within view of Cannon Mountain on one side and Mount Lafayette on the other. A bike path runs alongside the lake and meanders up and down the notch for a total of 8 miles. (Mountain bikes, canoes, and paddle boats may be rented at the park for $10 per hour.) Admission to the park is $3 for all visitors over age 12, $1 for visitors under 12. It's open from mid-June through Labor Day only.

For a high-altitude view of the region, set off for the alpine ridges on the **Cannon Mountain Tramway** ★★ (✆ **603/823-8800**). The old-fashioned cable car serves skiers in winter; in summer, it whisks up to 80 travelers at a time to the summit of the 4,180-foot mountain. Once at the top, you can strike out on foot along the Rim Trail for superb views. Be prepared for cool, gusty winds. The tramway costs $10 round-trip for adults, $6 for children ages 6 to 12. It's at Exit 2 of the parkway.

HIKING

The Franconia Notch region is one of the most varied and more challenging destinations for White Mountain hikers. It's easy to plan hikes ranging from gentle valley walks to arduous ascents of blustery granite peaks. Consult the *AMC White Mountain Guide* for a comprehensive directory of area hiking trails, or ask for suggestions at the information center.

Among my recommendations: A pleasant woodland detour of 2 hours or so can be found at the **Basin-Cascades Trail** ★★ (look for well-marked signs off I-93 about 1½ miles north of The Flume). A popular roadside waterfall and natural pothole, the Basin attracts crowds who come to see pillows of granite scoured smooth by glaciers and water. Relatively few visitors continue to the series of cascades beyond. Look for signs for the trail, then head off into the woods. After about .5 miles of easy hiking, you'll reach **Kinsman Falls,** a beautiful 20-foot cascade. Continue another .5 mile beyond that to **Rocky Glen,** where the stream plummets through a craggy gorge.

For a more demanding hike, set off for **Mount Lafayette,** with its spectacular views of the western White Mountains. Hikers should be well experienced, well equipped, and in good condition. Allow 6 to 7 hours to complete the hike. A popular and fairly straightforward ascent begins up the **Old Bridle Trail,** which departs from the Lafayette Place parking area off the parkway. This trail climbs steadily to the AMC's **Greenleaf Hut** (about 3 miles), with expanding views along the way. From here, continue to the summit of Lafayette on the **Greenleaf Trail.** It's a little over 1 mile farther, but it covers rocky terrain and can be demanding and difficult, especially if the weather turns on you. If in doubt about conditions, ask other hikers or the AMC staff at Greenleaf Hut.

DOWNHILL SKIING

Cannon Mountain ★ One of New England's first ski mountains, Cannon remains famed for its challenging runs and exposed faces, and the mountain still attracts skiers serious about getting down the hill in style. (During skiing's formative years, this state-run ski area was *the* place to ski in the East.) Many of the old-fashioned New England–style trails are narrow and fun (if often icy, scoured by the notch's winds), and the enclosed tramway is an elegant way to get to the summit. With no base scene to speak of, skiers retire to inns around Franconia or retreat southward to the condo villages of Lincoln.

Franconia Notch Pkwy., Franconia. ✆ **603/823-8800.** www.cannonmt.com. Vertical drop: 2,146 ft. Lifts: 70-person tram, 6 chairlifts, 2 surface lifts. Skiable acreage: 165. Adult day lift $42–$54.

WHERE TO STAY & DINE

Breakfast aficionados must not miss a chance to experience **Polly's Pancake Parlor** ★ (✆ **603/823-5575**), in a wooden-sided building (dating from around 1830) on Route 117 a few miles outside Sugar Hill. This is one of my favorite breakfast stops in America. Besides possessing possibly the best views of any pancake house in the western world, the restaurant also serves wonderful assortments of pancakes (order a combo of three kinds; I like chocolate chip and cornmeal) with—of course—real New Hampshire maple syrup from the Hildex Sugar Farm of which it's part.

Kids love this place, and there's also a good gift shop for adults, which doubles as a display for antique farm implements. However, it's only open from early May through late October, daily from 7am to 2pm.

Moments **Frost, You Say?**

Robert Frost lived in New Hampshire from the time he was 10 until he was 45. The Frost Place is a humble farmhouse, where Frost once lived with his family; today, appropriately, it's an arts center and a gathering place for writers. Wandering the grounds, it's not hard to see how his granite-edged poetry evolved at the fringes of the White Mountains. First editions of Frost's works are on display; a nature trail in the woods nearby is posted with excerpts from his poems.

The farm is on Ridge Road in Franconia (© **603/823-5510**; www.frostplace.org), and it's open from late May through June Saturday through Sunday 10am to 5pm, then from July to mid-October Wednesday through Monday 10am to 5pm. To find it, head south on Route 116 from Franconia 1 mile to Ridge Road (which is gravel); follow signs a short way to the house and park in a lot below the house. Admission costs $4 for adults, $3 for seniors, $2 for children 6 to 12 (free for children under 6).

Franconia Inn ★ This welcoming inn is set on a quiet road in a bucolic valley 2 miles from the village of Franconia. Built in 1934 after a fire destroyed the original 1886 structure, the inn has an informal feel, with wingback chairs around the fireplace in one common room, and jigsaw puzzles half completed in the paneled library. Guest rooms are appointed in a relaxed country fashion; three have gas fireplaces and four have Jacuzzis. The inn is a haven for cross-country skiers—38 miles of groomed trails start right outside the front door.

1300 Easton Rd., Franconia, NH 03580. © **800/473-5299** or 603/823-5542. www.franconiainn.com. 32 units. $91–$185 double; $146–$310 suite. Rates include breakfast in fall. MAP rates available. 3-night minimum stay on holiday weekends. AE, MC, V. Closed Apr to mid-May. **Amenities:** Restaurant; outdoor pool; 4 tennis courts; Jacuzzi; sauna; free bikes; bridle trails; horse rentals; cross-country ski trails. *In room:* No phone.

Sugar Hill Inn ★★ A classic inn, with wraparound porch and sweeping mountain panoramas occupying 16 acres on lovely Sugar Hill, this welcoming, comfortable spot is a great base for exploring the western White Mountains. Rooms are graciously appointed in antique country style, some influenced by Shaker sensibility. Most have gas Vermont Castings stoves for heat and atmosphere. The restaurant, one of the area's best, serves upscale regional fare.

Rte. 117, Franconia, NH 03580. © **800/548-4748** or 603/823-5621. Fax 603/823-5639. www.sugarhillinn.com. 15 units. $140–$290 double; $155–$380 suite and cottage. Rates include breakfast. AE, MC, V. Closed Apr. No children under 12. **Amenities:** Restaurant. *In room:* No phone.

5 The North Country

New Hampshire's North Country is an ideal destination for those who find the White Mountains too commercialized. Tiny communities—such as **Errol,** at a crossroads of two routes to nowhere—regard change with high suspicion. The land surrounding the town is an outpost of rugged, raw grandeur that has been little compromised. The piney shoreline around spectacular Lake Umbagog is protected as a National Wildlife Refuge.

Of course, a problem with lost-in-time areas can be a nothing-to-see/nothing-to-do syndrome. You can drive for miles and not see much more than spruce and pine, an infrequent bog, a glimpse of a shimmering lake, and—if you're lucky—a roadside moose chomping on sedges.

But you *can* find plenty to do if you're self-motivated and oriented toward the outdoors, including white-water kayaking on the Androscoggin River, canoeing on Lake Umbagog, and bicycling along the wide valley floors. Or visit one of the Northeast's grandest, most improbable historic resorts, thriving against considerable odds.

ESSENTIALS

GETTING THERE Errol is at the junction of Route 26 (accessible from Bethel, ME) and Route 16 (accessible from Gorham, NH). **Concord Trailways** (✆ **800/639-3317**) provides service to Berlin from points south, including Boston.

VISITOR INFORMATION The **Northern White Mountains Chamber of Commerce,** 164 Main St., Berlin (✆ **800/992-7480** or 603/752-6060), provides information from Monday through Friday between 8:30am and 4:30pm.

OUTDOOR PURSUITS

Dixville Notch State Park ★ (✆ **603/538-6707**) has several hiking trails, including a 2-mile round-trip to Table Rock. Look for the parking area east of the Balsams Resort on the edge of Lake Gloriette. The loop hike (it connects with a .5-mile return along Rte. 26) ascends a scraggy trail to an open rock with fine views of the resort and the flanking wild hills. It's open year-round.

Learn the fundamentals of white water at **Saco Bound's Northern Waters** ★★ (✆ **603/447-2177;** www.sacobound.com), a white-water school located where the Errol bridge crosses the Androscoggin. With 2- to 5-day workshops in the art of getting downstream safely, if not dryly, classes involve videos, dry-land training, and frequent forays onto the river—both Class I to III rapids at the bridge and more forgiving rips downstream. Two-day classes cost about $180, including equipment and a riverside campsite.

Excellent lake canoeing may be found at Lake Umbagog, which sits between Maine and New Hampshire. The lake, home to the newly created **Umbagog Lake State Park** ★★ (✆ **603/482-7795**), has some 40 miles of shoreline, most of which is wild and remote. The day-use fee is $3, $1 for kids ages 6 to 11. You'll need a boat of some sort to properly see the lake. Canoes and flatwater kayaks are available for rent at Saco Bound's Errol outpost for $25 to $30 per day (see above). Saco Bound also offers pontoon boat tours to get a glimpse of the complex river system that feeds both into and out of the lake.

More than 20 primitive **campsites** are scattered around the shoreline and on the lake's islands. Most of these backcountry sites are managed by New Hampshire parks; call the park for more information.

The area around Errol has excellent roads for **bicycling**—nearly all routes out of town make for good exploring (though it's mighty hilly heading east). One nice trip is south on Route 16. The occasional logging truck can be unnerving, but mostly it's an easy and peaceful riverside trip. Consider pedaling as far as the Brown Co. Bridge—a simple, wooden, logging road bridge that crosses the Androscoggin River, a good spot to leap in and float through a series of gentle rips. Some ledges on the far side of the bridge are good for sunning and relaxing.

Biking information and rentals are available in Gorham at **Moriah Sports,** 101 Main St. (✆ **603/466-5050**).

WHERE TO STAY & DINE

Balsams Grand Resort Hotel ★★★ Kids The Balsams is a grand gem deep in the northern forest. On 15,000 acres in a valley surrounded by 800-foot cliffs, it's one of a handful of great 19th-century New England resorts still in operation; its survival is all the more extraordinary given its remote location. The Donald Ross golf course and surrounding scenery are so lovely that you won't even notice the prim, whitewashed rooms—more like what you'd find in a country B&B or summer cabin than a luxury resort or boutique hotel. Expect solid wood furniture and smallish work desks, rather than luxury duvets and first-class toiletries.

Also notable is this Victorian grande dame's refusal to compromise or bend to the trend of the moment. Bathing suits and jeans are prohibited in public areas, you'll be ejected from the tennis courts or golf course if not neatly attired, and men are *required* (not requested) to wear jackets at dinner. The resort maintains strict adherence to the spirit of the "American plan"—everything but booze is included in room rates, including greens fees, boats on Lake Gloriette, and evening entertainment in the lounges. (Even ski tickets at the inn's downhill area are included.) Meals are an event—especially the summer luncheon buffet.

1000 Cold Spring Rd., Dixville Notch, NH 03576. ✆ **800/255-0600,** 800/255-0800 in NH, or 603/255-3400. www.thebalsams.com. 204 units. Summer $219–$259 double; fall–winter $189–$215 double; off season $149–$199 double. Ask about MAP plan rates and packages. 4-night minimum July–Aug weekends. AE, DISC, MC, V. Closed Apr–May and mid-Oct to mid-Dec. **Amenities:** Restaurant; 3 lounges; outdoor pool; 2 golf courses; 6 tennis courts; health club; Jacuzzi; sauna; free watersports equipment; bike rental; children's programs (summer); concierge; shopping arcade; salon; limited room service; massage; babysitting; laundry service; dry cleaning; cross-country ski trails; downhill ski area. *In room:* TV (some), dataport, iron.

Philbrook Farm Inn ★★ Finds This New England period piece traces its lineage to the 19th century, when farmers opened their doors to summer travelers to earn extra cash. Set on 1,000 acres between the Mahoosuc Range and Androscoggin River, it has been owned and operated by the Philbrook family since 1853, with additions in 1861, 1904, and 1934. The cozy rooms are eclectic; some have a farmhouse feel, others a more Victorian flavor. Guests can swim, play croquet or badminton, explore trails in the hills, or simply read on the porch. This is a relaxing retreat, well out of the mainstream and worthy of protection as a local cultural landmark. ***Note:*** Credit cards are not accepted.

881 North Rd. (off Rte. 2 between Gorham, NH, and Bethel, ME), Shelburne, NH 03581. ✆ **603/466-3831.** www.philbrookfarminn.com. 24 units, 6 with shared bathroom. $120–$150 double (including breakfast and dinner). No credit cards. Closed Apr and Nov–Dec 25. Pets allowed in cottages. **Amenities:** Restaurant; outdoor pool; badminton; shuffleboard. *In room:* No phone.

13

Maine

by Paul Karr

Professional funny guy Dave Barry once suggested that Maine's state motto should be "Cold, but damp."

Cute, but true. Spring tends to last a few blustery, rain-soaked days; November has arctic winds that alternate with gray sheets of rain; and winter brings a character-building mix of blizzards and ice storms to the fabled coast and rolling mountains.

Ah, but summer. Summer in Maine sees osprey diving for fish off wooded points, gleaming cumulus clouds building over steely-blue rounded peaks of western mountains, the haunting whoop of loons echoing off the dense forest walls bordering the lakes. Summer brings languorous days when the sun rises well before most visitors; by 8am, it seems like noon. Maine summers offer a measure of tranquillity; a stay in the right spot can rejuvenate the most jangled nerves.

The trick is finding that right spot. Those who arrive here without a clear plan may find themselves regretting their decision. Maine's Route 1 along the coast has its moments, but it's mostly an amalgam of convenience stores, tourist boutiques, and restaurants catering to bus tours. Acadia National Park can be congested, Mt. Katahdin's summit overcrowded, and some of the more popular lakes have become *de facto* racetracks for jet skis; but Maine's size works to your advantage.

Maine is roughly as large as the other five New England states combined. It has 5,500 miles of coastline, some 3,000 coastal islands, and millions of acres of undeveloped woodland. In fact, more than half of the state exists as "unorganized territories," where no town government exists, and the few inhabitants look to the state for basic services. With all this space and a little planning, you'll be able to find your piece of Maine.

1 The Southern Maine Coast

Maine's southern coast runs roughly from the state line at Kittery to Portland, and is the destination of most travelers to the state (including many day-trippers from the Boston area). While it takes some doing to find privacy and remoteness here, two excellent reasons for a detour are the long, sandy beaches, and the sense of history in some of the coastal villages.

Thanks to quirks of geography, nearly all of Maine's sandy beaches are in this 60-mile stretch of coastline. It's not hard to find a relaxing sandy spot, whether you prefer dunes and the lulling sound of the surf or the carnival-like atmosphere of a festive beach town. Waves depend on the weather—during a good Northeast blow (especially prevalent in spring and fall), they pound the shores and threaten beach houses built decades ago. During balmy midsummer days, the ocean can be as gentle as a farm pond, barely audible waves lapping timidly at the shore.

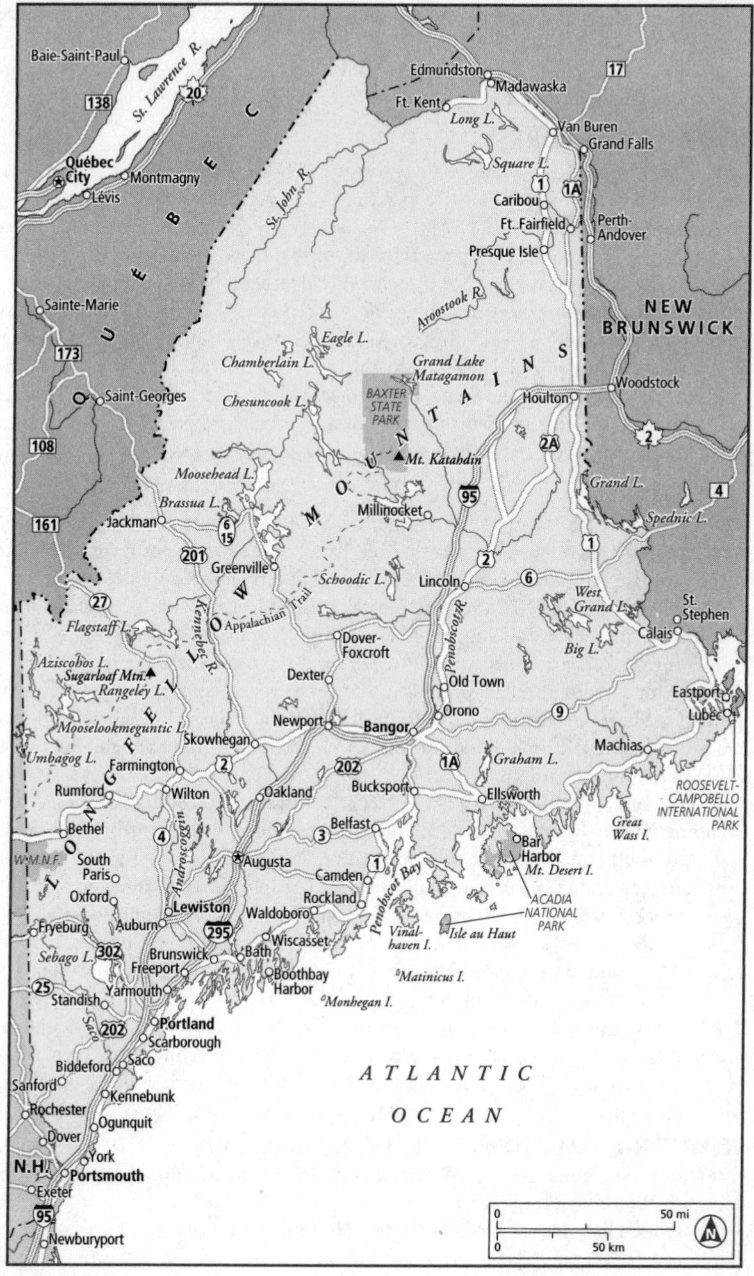
Baie-Saint-Paul
138
St. Lawrence R.
20
Québec City
Montmagny
Lévis
QUÉBEC
Sainte-Marie
173
Saint-Georges
108
161
Jackman
St. John R.
Edmundston
Madawaska
17
Ft. Kent
Long L.
Van Buren
Grand Falls
Square L.
1
1A
Caribou
Ft. Fairfield
Perth-Andover
Presque Isle
Aroostook R.
NEW BRUNSWICK
Eagle L.
Chamberlain L.
Grand Lake Matagamon
BAXTER STATE PARK
Chesuncook L.
Houlton
Woodstock
2
2A
Mt. Katahdin
LONGFELLOW MOUNTAINS
Moosehead L.
Brassua L.
95
Grand L.
4
Millinocket
Spednic L.
6
15
201
Greenville
Schoodic L.
Lincoln
6
27
Appalachian Trail
West Grand L.
St. Stephen
Flagstaff L.
Kennebec R.
Dover-Foxcroft
Calais
Penobscot R.
Big L.
Aziscohos L.
Sugarloaf Mtn.
Rangeley L.
Dexter
Old Town
Eastport
Orono
9
Lubec
Newport
Bangor
Mooselookmeguntic L.
Skowhegan
Machias
Umbagog L.
Farmington
202
1A
Graham L.
Rumford
Wilton
Oakland
Bucksport
Ellsworth
ROOSEVELT-CAMPOBELLO INTERNATIONAL PARK
Bethel
Belfast
Great Wass I.
4
Androscoggin
3
W.M.N.F.
South Paris
Augusta
Bar Harbor
Mt. Desert I.
Camden
Oxford
Rockland
Penobscot Bay
ACADIA NATIONAL PARK
Lewiston
Waldoboro
Fryeburg
Auburn
295
Vinalhaven I.
Isle au Haut
Wiscasset
Sebago L.
302
Brunswick
Bath
Freeport
Boothbay Harbor
Matinicus I.
25
Yarmouth
Standish
Monhegan I.
Saco
202
Portland
Scarborough
Biddeford
Saco
ATLANTIC OCEAN
Sanford
Kennebunk
Rochester
Ogunquit
Dover
York
N.H.
Portsmouth
Exeter
95
Newburyport
0
50 mi
50 km
N

One thing all beaches share in common: a season that is generally brief and intense, running from July 4th to Labor Day. While an increasing number of beach towns see visitors well into the fall, shorefront communities tend to adopt a slower, more somnolent pace after Labor Day.

KITTERY & THE YORKS

Driving into Maine from the south, as most travelers do, **Kittery** ★ is the first town to appear. Once famous for its (still operating) naval yard, it's now better known for dozens of factory outlets.

"The Yorks," just to the north, are three towns that share a name, but little else. In fact, it's rare to find three such well-defined and diverse New England archetypes within such a compact area. **York Village** ★ is full of early (17th-c.) American history and architecture, and has a good library. **York Harbor** ★★ reached its zenith during America's late Victorian era, when wealthy urbanites constructed cottages at the ocean's edge; it's the most relaxing and scenic of the three. However, I like **York Beach** ★★ the best: a beach town with amusements, taffy shops, a small zoo, gabled summer homes set in crowded enclaves, a great lighthouse, and two good beaches.

ESSENTIALS

GETTING THERE Kittery is accessible from **I-95** or **Route 1,** with well-marked exits. The Yorks are reached most easily from Exit 1 of the Maine Turnpike. Just south of the turnpike exit, look for Route 1A, which connects all three York towns.

Amtrak (✆ **800/872-7245;** www.amtrak.com) operates four trains daily from Boston's North Station to southern Maine, stopping outside Wells, about 10 miles away from the Yorks; a one-way ticket is $17, and the trip takes 2 hours. You'll need to phone for a taxi or arrange for a pickup to get to your destination if you arrive by train. The **Shoreline Explorer** (✆ **207/324-5762;** shorelineexplorer.com), will pick you up at the Wells station and drop you at your lodgings in the Kennebunks, Wells, Oqunquit, York, or Sanford.

Greyhound (✆ **800/229-9424**), **C&J Trailways** (✆ **800/258-7111**), and **Vermont Transit** (✆ **800/552-8737**) all run a few buses daily from Boston's South Station to southern Maine, but they only stop in Wells, and not even in the beach or commercial area. Bus fare is comparable to train fare, but the trip can be up to a half-hour shorter. Buses also run a bit more frequently from South Station to downtown Portsmouth, NH, which is close to Kittery and a more convenient place to get off. Taking a Greyhound from New York City's Port Authority to Portsmouth is about $44 one-way and takes about 6½ hours.

A trackless trolley (a bus retrofitted to look like an old-fashioned trolley) links all three York towns and is a convenient way to explore without the hassle of parking. Hop on the trolley (✆ **207/748-3030**) at one of the well-marked stops; an all-day pass costs $7 per adult, $4 for kids (children age 3 and under ride free).

VISITOR INFORMATION The **Kittery Information Center** (✆ **207/439-1319**) is at a well-marked rest area on I-95. It's open daily from 8am to 6pm in summer, from 9am to 5:30pm the rest of the year.

The **York Chamber of Commerce** (✆ **207/363-4422**) operates an information center at 571 Rte. 1, a short way from the turnpike exit. It's open in summer daily from 9am to 5pm (until 6pm Fri), limited days and hours the rest of the year.

Southern Maine

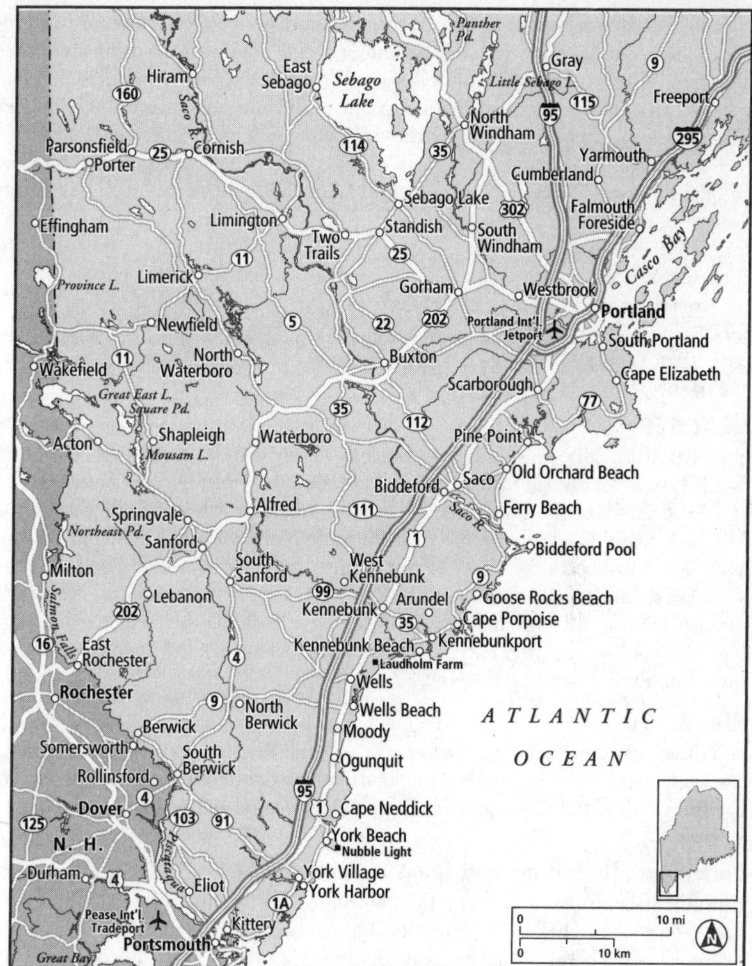

SHOPPING

Kittery's consumer mecca is 4 miles south of York on Route 1. Some 120 factory outlets flank the highway, scattered among more than a dozen strip malls.

Name-brand retailers include Dansk, Eddie Bauer, Calvin Klein, and Polo/Ralph Lauren, among others. Information on current outlets is available from the **Kittery Outlet Association.** Call © **888/KITTERY,** or visit the website at www.thekittery outlets.com.

DISCOVERING LOCAL HISTORY IN YORK

Old York Historical Society This historical society oversees the bulk of York's collection of historic buildings, some of which date to the early 18th century and most of which are astonishingly well preserved or restored.

John Hancock is famous for his oversize signature on the Declaration of Independence, his tenure as governor of Massachusetts, and the insurance company named after him. What's not so well known is his earlier checkered past as proprietor of Hancock Wharf, a failed enterprise that is but one of the intriguing historic sites in **York Village** ★★★, a fine destination for those curious about early American history.

The two don't-miss buildings in the society's collection are the intriguing **Old Gaol** and the **Emerson-Wilcox House.** The **Old Gaol** ★★, a former jail with now-musty dungeons, was built in 1719 as a jail for criminals and debtors. It is the oldest surviving public building in the United States. Just down the knoll from the jail is the **Emerson-Wilcox House** ★, built in the mid-1700s and added to periodically over the years. It's a virtual catalog of architectural styles and early decorative arts.

207 York St., York. ✆ **207/363-4974.** Admission per building $5 adult, $4 senior, $3 children 3–15; pass to all buildings $10 adult, $7 senior, $5 children 4–15. Free for children under 4. Mon–Sat 10am–5pm; Sun 1–5pm. (Last tour leaves at 4pm.) Closed mid-Oct to mid-June.

BEACHES

York Beach actually consists of two beaches—**Long Sands Beach** ★★ and **Short Sands Beach**—separated by a rocky headland. Both have plenty of room for sunning and Frisbees when the tide is out. When the tide is in, they're both narrow and cramped. Short Sands fronts the town of York Beach with its candlepin bowling and video arcades. It's the better bet for families traveling with kids who have short attention spans. Long Sands runs along Route 1A, across from a profusion of motels, summer homes, and convenience stores. Parking at both beaches is metered in summer (50¢ per hour, quarters only); pay heed, as enforcement is strict and you must pay from 9am until 9pm, 7 days a week.

WHERE TO STAY

York Beach has a number of motels facing Long Sands Beach. Reserve ahead during high season. Among those with simple accommodations on or near the beach are the **Anchorage Inn** (✆ **207/363-5112**) and **Sea Latch** (✆ **800/441-2993** or 207/363-4400).

In Kittery

Portsmouth Harbor Inn and Spa ★★ This handsome 1899 home is a pleasant, half-mile walk across a drawbridge from downtown Portsmouth, NH (p. 538). Guests here get a taste of small coastal town life, but can access the restaurants and shopping of a small city. Though some rooms are on the small side, all are boldly furnished and fun—the Valora room has ruby red walls, harbor views, attractive antiques, and a bigger-than-average bathroom with historic accents. The King George comes with a king-size bed (of course) and kingly skyline and bridge views. The Dido's two single beds can be adapted into an extra-long king-size. The whimsically decorated sitting room has two couches, where you can sprawl and browse through intriguing books. Innkeepers Nat and Lynn Bowditch are incredibly friendly, extending homey touches such as fresh chocolate chip cookies and complimentary port and sherry.

6 Water St., Kittery, ME 03904. ✆ **207/439-4040.** Fax 207/438-9286. www.innatportsmouth.com. 5 units. Midweek $110–$185 double; weekend $120–$220 double. Rates include full breakfast. 2-night minimum in summer, holidays. MC, V. No children under 16. **Amenities:** Jacuzzi; spa. *In room:* A/C, dataport, hair dryer.

In the Yorks

Dockside Guest Quarters ★ David and Harriet Lusty established this quiet retreat in 1954, and recent additions (mostly new cottages) haven't changed the friendly, maritime flavor of the place. Situated on an island connected to the mainland by a small bridge, the inn occupies nicely landscaped grounds shady with maples and white pines. Five of the rooms are in the main house, built in 1885, but the bulk of the accommodations are in small, modern town house–style cottages constructed between 1968 and 1998. These are simply furnished, bright, and airy, and most have private decks that overlook the entrance to York Harbor. (Several rooms also have woodstoves and/or kitchenettes.)

Harris Island (P.O. Box 205), York, ME 03909. © **888/860-7428** or 207/363-2868. Fax 207/363-1977. www.docksidegq.com. 25 units. Mid-June to mid-Oct $120–$190 double, $230–$256 suite; May to mid-June and mid-Oct to Dec $95–$120 double, $190 suite. Closed Jan–Apr. Weekends only May and Nov–Dec. 2-night minimum July–Sept. DISC, MC, V. Drive south on Rte. 103 from Rte. 1A in York Harbor; after bridge over York River, turn left and follow signs. **Amenities:** Restaurant; ocean swimming; rowboats; bike rentals; badminton; croquet; laundry service; sun deck. *In room:* A/C, kitchenette (some).

Edwards' Harborside Inn ★ *Finds* Work your way downhill off Route 1A toward the sprawling Stage Neck Inn, and before you get there, you'll stumble across a beautifully kept home right on the water, with a private dock and a lawn with wonderfully quaint views. This is Jay Edwards's place, and he runs it as his father and grandfather did. Ten units vary from simple to elegant (the York Suite is otherwise known as the "Spoil Me Suite," with a tiled Jacuzzi and water views on all sides), but all are lovely and homey with touches such as welcoming chocolates.

Stage Neck Rd., York Harbor, ME 03911. © **800/273-2686** or 207/363-3037. www.edwardsharborside.com. 13 units, 3 with shared bathroom. July–Aug and holidays, $200 double, $270 suite; May–June and Sept–Oct $140–$170 double, $210–$240 suite; Nov–Apr $100–$130 double, $180–$210 suite. Rates include breakfast. Extra 8% service charge in addition to tax. Holidays and weekends higher. Minimum stay some times of year. MC, V. *In room:* A/C, Jacuzzi (1 room).

Stage Neck Inn ★★ Since about 1870, a hotel in one form or another has been housing guests on this windswept bluff between the harbor and the open ocean. The most recent incarnation was constructed in 1972, and furnished with an understated, country club–like elegance. The hotel, while indisputably up-to-date, successfully creates a sense of old-fashioned intimacy and avoids the overbearing grandeur to which many modern resorts aspire. Almost every room has a view of the water, and guests enjoy low-key recreational pursuits. York Harbor Beach is only steps away. The inn has two dining rooms: the Sandpiper Bar and Grille and Harbor Porches. Both serve three meals daily.

Stage Neck (P.O. Box 70), York Harbor, ME 03911. © **800/340-1130** or 207/363-3850. www.stageneck.com. 58 units. Mid-May to Labor Day $235–$275 double; spring $165–$200 double; fall $185–$255 double; winter $135–$185 double. Ask about off-season packages. AE, DISC, MC, V. Head north on 1A from Rte. 1; make 2nd right after York Harbor post office. **Amenities:** 2 restaurants; indoor and outdoor pools; ocean swimming; tennis courts; fitness room; Jacuzzi; sauna. *In room:* A/C, TV/VCR, CD player.

Union Bluff Hotel ★ With its stumpy turrets, dormers, and prominent porches, the Union Bluff has the look of an old-fashioned beach hotel, so it's a bit of a surprise to learn that it was built in 1989. Inside is a generic-modern building; rooms have oak furniture, wall-to-wall carpeting, and small refrigerators. There's a comfortable and quiet deck on the top floor for getting away from it all (alas, no ocean view). Step outside and you're virtually at the beach and the Fun-O-Rama arcade. Twenty-one rooms are in a motel annex next door, and the rooms here are also simply furnished. Stick to the main inn for better views; the best rooms are the suites on the top floor, which have beach vistas. There's also a lounge and a restaurant, both of which are open daily during the warmer months (weekends only in the off season).

Beach St. (at the north end of Short Sands Beach), York Beach, ME 03910. ✆ **800/833-0721** or 207/363-1333. www.unionbluff.com. 61 units. Summer $139–$209 double and suite; rest of the year, $59–$169 double, $129–$219 suite. AE, DISC, MC, V. **Amenities:** Restaurant; lounge. *In room:* A/C, some fridges.

York Harbor Inn ★★ This compound sits on a hill overlooking a lovely bay and beach, it's a great pick in the Yorks if you're trying to avoid the honky-tonk of both Short and Long Sands. Rooms are scattered throughout several buildings. The main inn's 22 rooms are simplest, but it has the advantage of containing both a very good dining room and a convivial basement pub. Adjacent Harbor Hill Inn contains the inn's seven best units: all have Jacuzzis, gas fireplaces, heated bathrooms, CD players, and sea views, plus a hot tub out back. Harbor Cliffs is also a great choice, with an included breakfast and a variety of choices among its seven rooms—and some mighty distinctive quirks, such as a pull-out shoe closet in one room.

Rte. 1A (P.O. Box 573), York Harbor, ME 03911. ✆ **800/343-3869** or 207/363-5119. Fax 207/363-7151. www.yorkharborinn.com. 54 units. $119–$289 double, $179–$349 suite; ask about off-season rates and packages. Some rates include breakfast. AE, DISC, MC, V. **Amenities:** Restaurant; bar. *In room:* A/C, TV, dataport, iron/ironing board.

WHERE TO DINE

In Kittery

Bob's Clam Hut *Value* FRIED FISH Operating since 1956, Bob's manages to retain an old-fashioned flavor—despite now being surrounded by slick new factory outlet malls—while serving up heaps of fried clams and other diet-busting enticements with great efficiency. Order at the front window, get a soda from a vending machine, then stake out a table inside or on the deck (with a Rte. 1 view) while waiting for your number to be called. The food is surprisingly light, cooked in cholesterol-free vegetable oil; the onion rings are especially good. To ensure the irrevocable undermining of your diet, Bob's also serves Ben & Jerry's ice cream.

Kittery. ✆ **207/439-4233.** Reservations not accepted. Sandwiches $1.50–$3.95; dinners $3.95–$18. AE, MC, V. Memorial Day to Labor Day daily 11am–9pm; closing times vary in off season, call ahead. Located just north of the Kittery Trading Post.

Chauncey Creek Lobster Pier ★★ *Finds* LOBSTER It's not on the wild, open ocean, but Chauncey's remains one of the most scenic lobster pounds in the state. You reach the pound by walking down a wooden ramp to a broad deck on a tidal inlet, where some 42 festively painted picnic tables await. Lobster, served hot and fresh, is the specialty, but they also serve steamed mussels (in wine and garlic) and clams. This place is a la carte—buy a crock of baked beans and sodas and a bag of ice while waiting for your lobsters to cook. Want a drink? BYOB.

Kittery Point. ✆ **207/439-1030.** No reservations. Lobsters priced to market; other items $1.50–$8.95. MC, V. Daily 11am–8pm (until 7pm during shoulder seasons). Closed Mon after Labor Day and Columbus Day to Mother's Day. Located between Kittery Point and York on Rte. 103; watch for signs.

In the Yorks

Goldenrod Restaurant *Kids* TRADITIONAL AMERICAN This beach-town classic is *the* place for local color—it has been a summer institution in York Beach since it first opened in 1896. It's easy to find: Look for visitors gawking through plate-glass windows at the ancient taffy machines hypnotically churning out taffy in volumes enough (9 million candies a year) to make busloads of dentists very wealthy. The restaurant is behind the taffy and fudge operation and is low on frills and long on atmosphere. Diners sit on stout oak furniture around a stone fireplace, or at the antique soda fountain. Breakfast offerings are standard egg and waffle dishes; at lunch you'll find soups, burgers, and somewhat overpriced sandwiches. But the real reason to come that outstanding candy counter.

Railroad Rd. and Ocean Ave., York Beach. ✆ **207/363-2621.** www.thegoldenrod.com. Breakfast $2.65–$5.25; lunch and dinner entrees $2.75–$7.50. MC, V. late May to early Sept 8am–10pm (until 9pm in June); mid Sept to mid-Oct Wed–Sun 8am–3pm. Closed late Oct to mid May.

Lobster Cove SEAFOOD/FAMILY-STYLE Right across the street from the pounding Atlantic, dependable Lobster Cove is a good choice when you don't want to stray from the beach for lunch or dinner. Breakfast consists of standard, though surprisingly inexpensive, choices like omelets, pancakes, and eggs Benedict. Lunch runs to burgers and sandwiches, but I prefer dinner, when a standard shore dinner of lobster, corn on the cob, clam chowder, and steamed clams is hefty and good. The lobster pie is an old-fashioned New England favorite, and the Captain's Platter is a selection of fried seafood. They also do lobster rolls, clam rolls, and traditional Maine desserts like wild blueberry pie, and warm bread pudding with whiskey sauce.

756 York St., York (south end of Long Sands Beach). ✆ **207/351-1100.** Breakfast items $2–$6; main courses $6–$30 (for lobster dinner). AE, MC, V. Daily 7:30am–9pm.

Stonewall Kitchen Café CAFE Stonewall Kitchen's York-based gourmet foods operation has taken a step to the front with this cafe, smartly located in its York headquarters/store and just beside the local tourist information office. The cafe serves simple, hearty meals of fish chowder, crispy duck confit with Damson plum and a balsamic glaze, chicken potpie, steak fries, and sandwiches. For dessert I like the house-made chai ice cream topped with bittersweet chocolate sauce. The kitchen also prepares gourmet meals to go.

Stonewall Lane, York. ✆ **207/351-2719.** www.stonewallkitchen.com. Entrees $8–$14. AE, DC, DISC, MC, V. Mon–Sat takeout 8am–6pm, lunch 11am–3pm; Sun takeout 9am–6pm, brunch 10am–3pm.

OGUNQUIT

Ogunquit is a bustling beachside town that's attracted vacationers and artists for more than a century. While notable for its abundant and elegant summer-resort architecture, Ogunquit is most famous for its 3½-mile white-sand beach, backed by grassy dunes. The beach serves as the town's front porch, and most everyone drifts by at least once a day when the sun is shining.

Ogunquit's fame as an art colony dates to around 1890, when Charles H. Woodbury arrived and declared the place an "artist's paradise." He was followed by artists Walt Kuhn, Elihu Vedder, Yasuo Kuniyoshi, and Rudolph Dirks, the last of whom is best known for creating the "Katzenjammer Kids" comic strip.

In the latter decades of the 19th century, the town found quiet fame as a destination for gay travelers, at a time when one's sexual orientation was not publicly acknowledged. Ogunquit has retained its appeal for gays through the years; many local enterprises are run by gay entrepreneurs. The scene is very low-key and understated. Despite its architectural gentility and overall civility, the town feels overrun with tourists during the peak summer season, especially on weekends. If you don't like crowds, you would do well to visit here in the off season.

ESSENTIALS

GETTING THERE Ogunquit is on Route 1 between York and Wells. It's accessible from either Exit 1 or Exit 2 of the Maine Turnpike.

VISITOR INFORMATION The **Ogunquit Welcome Center,** P.O. Box 2289, Ogunquit, ME 03907 (© **207/646-2939;** www.ogunquit.org), is on Route 1 south of the village center. It's open daily 9am to 5pm Memorial Day to Columbus Day (until 8pm weekends during the peak summer season), and Monday to Saturday during the off season—and it has restrooms.

GETTING AROUND Ogunquit centers on a 3-way intersection (with no traffic lights) that seems fiendishly designed to cause massive traffic foul-ups in summer. Parking in and around the village is tight and relatively expensive for small-town Maine ($6 per day or more). As a result, Ogunquit is best navigated on foot or by bike.

EXPLORING OGUNQUIT

The village center is good for an hour or two of browsing among the boutiques, or sipping a cappuccino at one of the several coffee emporia.

From the village, you can walk to scenic Perkins Cove along **Marginal Way** ★, a mile-long oceanside pathway that departs across from the Seacastles Resort on Shore Road. It passes tidepools, pocket beaches, and rocky, fissured bluffs, all worth exploring. The seascape can be spectacular, but Marginal Way can also be extremely crowded during fair-weather weekends, so head out in the early morning.

Perkins Cove ★, accessible either from Marginal Way or by driving south on Shore Road and veering left at the Y intersection, is a small, well-protected harbor that attracts many visitors and is often heavily congested. A handful of galleries, restaurants, and T-shirt shops cater to the tourist trade from a cluster of quaint buildings between harbor and sea. An intriguing pedestrian drawbridge is operated by whoever happens to be handy.

Not far from the cove is **The Ogunquit Museum of American Art** ★★★, 543 Shore Rd. (© **207/646-4909;** www.ogunquitmuseum.org), one of the best small art museums in the nation. Set back from the road in a grassy glen overlooking the rocky shore, the museum's spectacular view initially overwhelms the artwork as visitors walk through the door. But stick around a few minutes—the changing exhibits in this architecturally engaging modern building of cement block, slate, and glass will get your attention soon enough, since the curators have a track record of staging superb shows and attracting national attention. The museum is open July 1 to October 15 from 10:30am to 5pm Monday to Saturday, and 2 to 5pm on Sunday. Admission is $5 for adults, $4 for seniors, $3 for students, and free for children under 12.

Tips Trolley Ho!

A number of trackless "trolleys" (© **207/646-1411**)—actually buses—with names like Dolly and Ollie (you get the idea) run all day from mid-May to Columbus Day between Perkins Cove and the Wells town line to the north, with detours to the sea down Beach and Ocean streets. A day pass costs $5 per adult, $3 per child under 10, though it might be worth the expense to avoid driving and parking hassles.

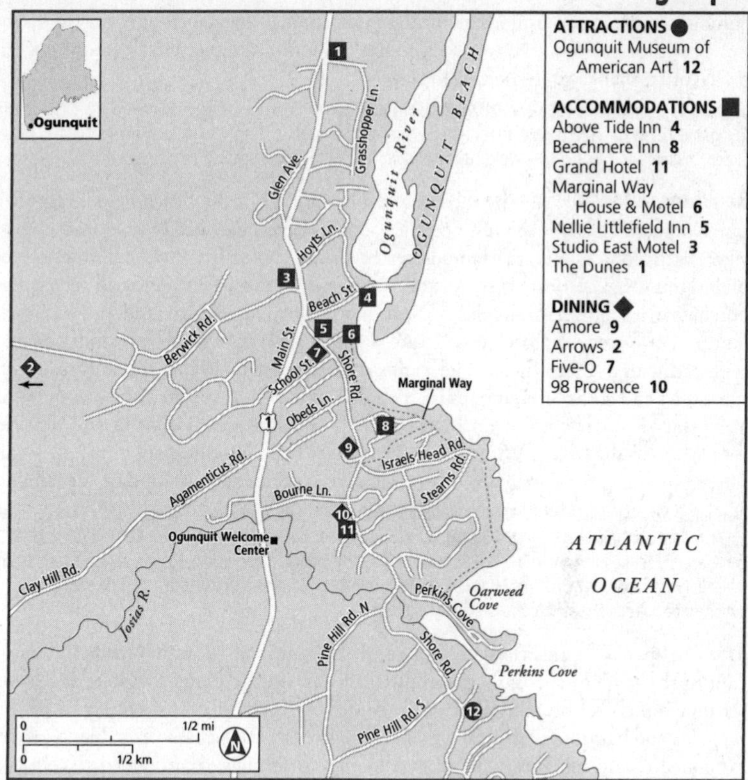

For evening entertainment, head to the **Ogunquit Playhouse** ★, Route 1 (© **207/646-5511**), a 750-seat summer stock theater that has garnered a solid reputation for its careful, serious attention to stagecraft. The theater has entertained Ogunquit since 1933, attracting noted actors such as Bette Davis and Tallulah Bankhead. Tickets generally cost $29 to $45 per person.

WHERE TO STAY

Just a few steps from Ogunquit's main downtown intersection is the meticulously maintained **Studio East Motel,** 267 Main St. (© **207/646-7297**). It's open April to mid-November, with peak-season rates running $129 to $159 double. The rooms are basic, but all have refrigerators, telephones, and televisions, and there are a few two-bedroom suites for $20 to $30 more per night. Microwaves are free to those staying 3 nights or more.

Above Tide Inn ★ This nicely sited inn rises from where a lobster shack once stood . . . until a 1978 blizzard took it to sea. That fact (and the inn's name) should suggest its great setting—on a lazy tidal river between town and the main beach, which is an easy stroll away. It's right by the start of Marginal Way, the town's popular walking path. The terrific location offsets rooms that are a bit smaller and darker than one might wish. If the weather's good, you're in luck—each room has its own outdoor sitting area, most located off the room (though two tables are reserved on the front deck for guests in the two back rooms that don't face the water). Room no. 1 is my favorite, thanks to its view of the river.

66 Beach St. Ogunquit, ME 03907. ✆ **207/646-7454.** www.abovetideinn.com. 9 units. Summer $170–$250 double; spring and fall $110–$180 double. Rates include continental breakfast. 3-night minimum stay in summer. MC, V. Closed Columbus Day to mid-May. No children. *In room:* A/C, TV, fridge, no phone.

Beachmere Inn ★ Run by the same family since 1937, the Beachmere Inn sprawls across a grassy hillside (the inn occupies about 4 acres) and nearly every room has a view north along Ogunquit's famous beach. Guests choose from two buildings on the main grounds. The Beachmere Victorian dates from the 1890s and is all turrets and porches; two rooms have fireplaces. Next door is the mid-century modern Beachmere South, a two-story motel-like structure designed in 1960s style, featuring concrete slathered with a stucco finish. The rooms at Beachmere South are spacious (some are minisuites and cost more), interestingly angled, and all have private balconies or patios and great views. The inn is on Marginal Way, which is great for walks and provides foot access to the beach. When rooms in the two main buildings are filled, guests are offered rooms in the cottages nearby, which are spacious and appropriate for families.

Beachmere Rd., Ogunquit, ME 03907. ✆ **800/336-3983** or 207/646-2021. Fax 207/646-2231. www.beachmereinn.com. 53 units. Summer $105–$230 double, cottage $140–$360; late spring and fall $75–$180 double, $75–$255 cottage; early spring and winter, $65–$130 double, $60–$180 cottage. Rates include continental breakfast. 3-night minimum in summer. AE, DC, DISC, MC, V. Closed mid-Dec to late Mar. **Amenities:** Beach access. *In room:* A/C, some patios, some balconies, some fireplaces, some kitchenettes.

The Dunes ★★ This classic motor court (built around 1936) has made the transition to the modern age more gracefully than any vintage motel I've seen. It has one six-unit motel-like building, but most of the rooms are in gabled cottages with full kitchens and bathrooms, and all have been updated in the past 12 years. Plenty of old-fashioned charm remains, with vintage maple furnishings, oval braided rugs, maple floors, knotty pine paneling, and louvered doors. All but one of the cottages has a wood-burning fireplace. The Dunes is set on 12 peaceful acres (away from Rte. 1).

518 U.S. Rte. 1, Ogunquit, ME 03907. ✆ **207/646-2612.** www.dunesmotel.com. 36 units. Summer $100–$285 double, $180–$335 cottage; spring $75–$190 double, $130–$255 cottage. MC, V. July–Aug 1-week minimum stay in cottages; 3-night minimum stay in motel. All other weekends, 2-night minimum stay in motel. Closed Nov to late Apr. **Amenities:** Outdoor pool; watersports equipment rental. *In room:* A/C, TV, dataport, fridge, coffeemaker.

Grand Hotel ★ The modern Grand Hotel, built in 1990, seems a bit ill at ease in Victorian Ogunquit; frankly, it's a bit jarring at first glance. But the hotel centers on a three-story atrium and consists of 28 two-room suites. All rooms have refrigerators and VCRs (tapes available for rent). The modern, tidy guest rooms have a generic, chain-hotel character, and each has a private deck from which to enjoy the Maine air (no ocean views). The five top-floor penthouses are airy and bright, with cathedral ceilings and Duraflame-log fireplaces. The hotel is about a 10-minute walk to the beach.

276 Shore Rd. (P.O. Box 1526), Ogunquit, ME 03907. ✆ **800/806-1231** or 207/646-1231. www.thegrandhotel.com. 28 suites. Late June to early Sept $149–$269 double; Apr–June and Sept–Nov $69–$219. Rates include continental breakfast. 2- or 3-night minimum on weekends and peak season. AE, DISC, MC, V. Underground parking. Closed early Nov to early Apr. **Amenities:** Indoor pool; video rental. *In room:* A/C, TV/VCR, fridge, some fireplaces.

Marginal Way House and Motel ★ This old-fashioned, nothing-fancy compound centers on a four-story, mid-19th-century guesthouse with summery, basic rooms and white-painted furniture. Room no. 7 is one of the best, with a private porch and canopy and an ocean view. The guesthouse is surrounded by four contemporary buildings that lack charm and have motel-style rooms, yet are generally comfortable and bright. The whole affair is situated on a large, grassy lot on a quiet cul-de-sac. It's hard to believe that you're smack in the middle of Ogunquit, with both the beach and the village just a few minutes' walk away.

Wharf Lane (P.O. Box 697), Ogunquit, ME 03907. ✆ **207/646-8801.** www.marginalwayhouse.com. 30 units, 1 with private bathroom down hall. Mid-June to early Sept $99–$192 double; shoulder seasons $49–$144 double. Minimum stay requirements on some weekends. MC, V. Closed mid-Oct to mid-Apr. Pets allowed off season; advance notice required. *In room:* A/C, fridge, some balconies.

Nellie Littlefield House ★★ A prime location at the edge of Ogunquit's compact commercial district and the handsome Queen Anne architecture are the main draws of this 1889 home. All rooms are carpeted and have a mix of modern and antique reproduction furnishings; several have refrigerators. Four rooms to the rear have private decks, but views are limited—mostly to the unlovely motel next door. The most spacious room is the third-floor J. H. Littlefield suite, with two TVs and a Jacuzzi. The most unique? The circular Grace Littlefield room, in the upper turret and overlooking the street.

27 Shore Rd., Ogunquit, ME 03907. ✆ **207/646-1692.** www.visit-maine.com/nellielittlefieldhouse. 8 units. July to Labor Day $165–$220 double; Memorial Day to June and Labor Day to Columbus Day $95–$170 double; late Apr, May, and late Oct $85–$140 double. Rates include full breakfast. 2-night minimum weekends, 3 nights on holidays. DISC, MC, V. Closed late Oct to late Apr. No children under 12. **Amenities:** Fitness center. *In room:* A/C, TV.

WHERE TO DINE

For breakfasts in Ogunquit, it's hard to beat **Amore** (178 Shore Rd.; ✆ **207/646-6661**). This isn't the place for dainty pickers and waist-watchers, but hey . . . you're on vacation. Look for numerous variations on the eggs Benedict theme, along with Belgian waffles and omelets. Breakfast is served daily until 1pm.

Arrows ★★★ NEW AMERICAN When owner/chefs Mark Gaier and Clark Frasier opened Arrows in 1988, they quickly put Ogunquit on the national culinary map. They've done so not only by creating an elegant and intimate atmosphere, but by serving up some of the freshest, most innovative cooking in New England. The emphasis is on local products—the salad greens are grown in gardens on the grounds. The menu changes nightly, and entrees may include wild salmon in four preparations; a pair of roasted quail with preserved lemon; a plate of six pastas, six cheeses and six herbs; and grilled Maine lobster tail with crispy shallots, lime leaf-cilantro vinaigrette and coconut "jello." The wine list is top-rate. Jackets are required for men and no shorts are allowed.

Berwick Rd. ✆ **207/361-1100.** www.arrowsrestaurant.com. Reservations strongly recommended. Main courses $40–$44; tasting menu $95. MC, V. Generally open Apr to mid-Dec 6–9:30pm daily. Days of the week that Arrows is open vary widely. We strongly recommend you call ahead for specifics. Closed mid-Dec to Mar. Turn uphill at the Key Bank in the village; the restaurant is 2 miles on your right.

Five-O ★★ FRENCH/NEW AMERICAN A fine choice if you're looking for a more casual alternative to the two more formal restaurants listed, Five-O is one of those spots where just reading the menu is a decent evening's entertainment. New chef Zachary Crosby has transformed a formerly Caribbean-inspired menu into one that is classically French: witness escargot with shallots, chargrilled filet mignon, a rack of lamb in garlic and chiles with pink lentil sauce, and freshly caught local haddock stuffed with seafood. Of course, you can get a Maine lobster, too, steamed and served over a bed of mussels steamed with blue cheese, sweet cream, and cracked pepper.

50 Shore Rd. ✆ **207/646-5001.** Reservations recommended in summer. Main courses $23–$34. AE, DISC, MC, V. Daily 5–9pm.

98 Provence ★★ BISTRO Candlelight reflects off the warm wood interior and infuses the surroundings with a romantic glow; tables are covered with two layers of Provençal-style linens, lace curtains drape the windows, and diners eat off colorful china. 98 Provence is charming, if a bit on the precious side. The decor almost, but not quite, distracts one from the delicious food. The menu changes thrice yearly to reflect the seasons. You might start with the seared duck foie gras with cheese buccatini, green peas, and morel mushrooms, scallops seared in Basque pepper—or just simple, fresh Nova Scotia mussels. Entrees wander the barnyard, from rabbit to cassoulet to lamb in puff pastry; potential offerings could include veal mignon wrapped in smoked bacon or stewed rabbit daube with porcini, country olives, and papardelle. The roasted venison is quite popular; in fall, it's prepared with stuffed pumpkin and dried fruits.

262 Shore Rd. ✆ **207/646-9898.** www.98provence.com. Reservations recommended. Main courses $24–$31; table d'hôte (appetizer, main course, and dessert) $32. AE, MC, V. Summer Wed–Mon 5:30–9:30pm; off season Thurs–Mon 5:30–9pm.

THE KENNEBUNKS

"The Kennebunks" consist of the side-by-side villages of **Kennebunk** and **Kennebunkport,** both situated along the shores of small rivers, and both claiming a portion of rocky coast. The region was first settled in the mid-1600s and flourished after the American Revolution, when ship captains, boat builders, and prosperous merchants constructed imposing, solid homes. The Kennebunks are famed for their striking historical architecture and expansive beaches.

ESSENTIALS

GETTING THERE Kennebunk is off Exit 3 of the Maine Turnpike. Kennebunkport is 3½ miles southeast of Kennebunk on Port Road (Rte. 35).

VISITOR INFORMATION **The Kennebunk-Kennebunkport Chamber of Commerce,** 17 Western Ave. (P.O. Box 740), Kennebunk, ME 04043 (✆ **800/982-4421** or 207/967-0857), can answer your questions year-round by phone or at its offices on Route 9 next to Meserve's Market. The **Kennebunkport Information Center** (✆ **207/967-8600**), operated by an association of local businesses, is off Dock Square (next to Ben & Jerry's) and is open daily throughout the summer and fall.

GETTING AROUND The local trolley (actually a bus) makes several stops in and around Kennebunkport and also serves the beaches. The fare, a day pass costing $10 per adult or $5 per child ages 3 to 14, includes unlimited trips. Call (✆ **207/967-3686**) or check www.intowntrolley.com for details.

EXPLORING KENNEBUNK

Kennebunk's downtown is inland, just off the turnpike, and is a dignified, small commercial center of white clapboard and brick. The **Brick Store Museum** ★, 117 Main St. (✆ **207/985-4802**), hosts shows of historical art and artifacts throughout the summer, switching to contemporary art in the off season. The museum is housed in a historic former brick store—yes, a store that once sold bricks!—and three adjacent buildings. The buildings have been renovated and all have the polished gloss of a

The Kennebunks

well-cared-for gallery. Admission is free, but tours cost $5 per person. The museum is open Tuesdays to Fridays 10am to 4:30pm and Saturdays from 10am to 1pm from March to December. Call for winter hours.

Tom's of Maine (© **800/FOR-TOMS** or 207/985-2944), a toothpaste company, is headquartered here. Tom and Kate Chappell sell their all-natural toothpaste and other personal-care products worldwide, but they are almost as well known for their green, socially conscious business philosophy. Tom's factory outlet sells firsts and seconds of its own products, as well as a other natural goods. The shop is at Lafayette Center (corner of Main and Water sts.), a historic industrial building converted to shops and offices. It's open Monday to Saturday 10am to 5pm. Another store is nearby at 1 Storer St.

When en route to or from the coast, be sure to note the extraordinary homes that line Port Road (Rte. 35). These include the famously elaborate **Wedding Cake House** ★, which you should be able to identify all on your own. Local lore claims that the house was built by a guilt-ridden ship captain who left for sea before his bride could enjoy a proper wedding cake.

EXPLORING KENNEBUNKPORT

Kennebunkport is the summer home of President George Bush, Sr., whose family has summered here for decades, and it has the tweedy, upper-crust feel that one would expect. The tiny historic downtown, whose streets were laid out during days of travel by boat and horse, is subject to monumental traffic jams. If the municipal lot off the square is full, go north on North Street a few minutes to the free long-term lot and catch the trolley back into town, or go about on foot—it's a pleasant walk of 10 or 15 minutes back to Dock Square.

Dock Square ★ has an architecturally eclectic, wharflike feel, with low buildings of mixed vintages and styles, but the flavor is mostly clapboard and shingles. Today, it's *haute tourist,* with boutiques of arts and crafts and a lot of trinkets. Kennebunkport's deeper appeal is found in the surrounding blocks, where the side streets are lined with some of the nation's best-preserved Early American homes.

Ocean Drive from Dock Square to **Walkers Point** ★ and beyond is lined with opulent summer homes overlooking surf and rocky shore. You'll likely recognize the Bush family compound right out on Walkers Point when you arrive (look for the shingle-style Secret Service booth at the head of a drive). There's nothing to do here but park for a minute, snap a picture, and then push on.

The Seashore Trolley Museum ★ A short drive north of Kennebunkport is a local marvel: a scrap yard masquerading as a museum ("world's oldest and largest museum of its type"). Quirky and engaging, this museum was founded in 1939 to preserve a disappearing way of life, and today the collection boasts more than 200 trolleys, including specimens from Glasgow, Moscow, San Francisco, and Rome. (Naturally, there's also a streetcar named Desire from New Orleans.)

About 40 of the cars still operate, and the admission charge includes rides on a 2-mile track. Other cars, some of which still contain early-20th-century advertising, are on display outdoors and in vast storage sheds.

195 Log Cabin Rd., Kennebunkport. ✆ **207/967-2800.** www.trolleymuseum.org. Admission $7.50 adults, $5.50 seniors, $5 children 6–16. June to mid-Oct daily 10am–5pm; May and late Oct weekends only. Closed Nov–Apr. Head north from Kennebunkport on North St. for 1¾ miles; look for signs.

BEACHES

The coastal area around Kennebunkport is home to several of the state's best beaches. Southward across the river (technically, this is Kennebunk, though it's much closer to Kennebunkport) are **Gooch's Beach** ★★ and **Kennebunk Beach** ★★. Head eastward on Beach Street (from the intersection of Routes 9 and 35) and you'll soon wind into a handsome colony of eclectic shingled summer homes. The narrow road twists past sandy beaches and rocky headlands. It may be congested in summer; avoid gridlock by exploring on foot or by bike.

Goose Rocks Beach ★★★ is north of Kennebunkport off Route 9 (watch for signs), a good destination if you like your crowds light and prefer actual beaches to beach scenes. An enclave of beach homes is set amid rustling oaks off a fine-sand beach. Offshore, a narrow barrier reef often attracts flocks of geese.

WHERE TO STAY

Beach House Inn ★★ This is a good choice if you'd like to be amid the action of Kennebunk Beach. The inn was built in 1891 but has been extensively modernized and expanded—in 1999, it was purchased by the same folks who own the legendary White Barn Inn and was upgraded with down comforters and pillows. The rooms aren't necessarily historic, but they are carpeted and most have Victorian furnishings and accenting. The main draw is the lovely porch, where you can stare out at the pebble beach across the road and idly watch the bikers and in-line skaters. The inn has bikes and canoes for guests to use and provides beach chairs and towels.

211 Beach Ave., Kennebunk Beach, ME 04043. ✆ **207/967-3850.** Fax 207/967-4719. www.beachhseinn.com. 35 units. Late June to mid-Sept $255–$390 double; June and mid-Sept to Oct $185–$390 double; Nov–Dec $155–$300 double. Closed Jan–May. Rates include continental breakfast. 2-night minimum on weekends. AE, MC, V. **Amenities:** Bikes; canoes; beach chairs. *In room:* TV/VCR, CD player.

Captain Jefferds Inn ★★ This 1804 Federal home was fully redone in 1997, and the innkeepers have done a superb job of coaxing out the historic feel of the place while giving each room its own personality. Fine antiques abound throughout, and guests will need some persuading to come out of their wonderful rooms once they've settled in. Among the best are the Manhattan, with a four-poster bed, fireplace, and beautiful afternoon light; and the Assisi, with a restful indoor fountain and rock garden (sounds weird, but it works). The Winterthur is the only room with a television (though there is a TV in the common room), and the Winterthur and the Santa Fe both have whirlpools. The price range reflects the varying room sizes, but even the smallest rooms—like the Katahdin—are comfortable and far exceed the merely adequate.

5 Pearl St. (P.O. Box 691), Kennebunkport, ME 04046. ✆ **800/839-6844** or 207/967-2311. Fax 207/967-0721. www.captainjefferdsinn.com. 15 units. Memorial Day to Oct $170–$345 double; rest of the year $120–$295 double. Rates include full breakfast. 2-night minimum weekends. AE, MC, V. Dogs $20 additional by advance reservation. *In room:* A/C, hair dryer, some Jacuzzis, some fireplaces, CD player.

The Captain Lord Mansion ★★★ Housed in a pale-yellow Federal-style home that peers down a shady lawn toward the river, this is one of the most architecturally distinguished inns in New England. You know this is the genuine article once you spot the grandfather clocks and Chippendale highboys in the front hall. Guest rooms are furnished with antiques and gas fireplaces, and not a single one is an unappealing room (although the Union room is a little dark). Among my favorites: the Excelsior, a large corner unit with a massive four-poster bed, a gas fire, and two-person Jacuzzi; Hesper, the best of the lower-priced rooms; and Merchant, a spacious first-floor with a large Jacuzzi.

Pleasant St. and Green St. (P.O. Box 800), Kennebunkport, ME 04046. ✆ **800/522-3141** or 207/967-3141. Fax 207/967-3172. www.captainlord.com. 16 units. $248–$419 double; $439–$499 suite. Rates include full breakfast. 2-night minimum weekends and holidays year-round (some holidays 3-night minimum). DISC, MC, V. No children under 12. **Amenities:** Lounge; conference room. *In room:* A/C, some Jacuzzis, some fireplaces.

The Colony Hotel ★★ One of a handful of oceanside resorts that has preserved the classic New England vacation experience, this mammoth white Georgian Revival (from 1914) lords over the ocean and the mouth of the Kennebunk River. All rooms in the three-story main inn have been renovated over the last 3 years. The rooms are bright and cheery, simply furnished with summer cottage antiques. Rooms in two of the three outbuildings carry over the rustic elegance of the main hotel; the exception is the East House, a 1950s-era motor hotel at the back edge of the property with 20 uninteresting motel-style rooms that do at least have televisions. Staff encourages guests to socialize in the evening downstairs in the lobby, on the porch, or at the shuffleboard court, which is lighted for nighttime play.

140 Ocean Ave. (P.O. Box 511), Kennebunkport, ME 04046. ✆ **800/552-2363** or 207/967-3331. Fax 207/967-8738. www.thecolonyhotel.com/maine. 123 units. $145–$545 double. Rates include breakfast. 3-night minimum on summer weekends and holidays in main hotel. Closed late Oct to mid-May. AE, MC, V. Pets allowed. **Amenities:** Restaurant; cocktail lounge; afternoon tea in lobby; heated saltwater pool; small beach; putting green; health club nearby; bike rental; social director; library; room service; free newspaper. *In room:* A/C (some rooms), TV (some rooms), safe.

Franciscan Guest House ★ *Finds* This former dormitory on the 200-acre grounds of St. Anthony's Monastery is a unique lodging choice. The 60 or so rooms are institutional, basic, and clean, with private bathrooms; guests can stroll the very attractive riverside grounds or walk to Dock Square, about 10 minutes away. Only drawback? It's not nearly as inexpensive as it used to be—the brothers have wised up to modern times, and rates have slowly escalated as a result. They even have suites here now. Nevertheless, the place is still an outstanding bargain, especially given the fine walking trails.

28 Beach Ave. (P.O. Box 980), Kennebunk, ME 04046. ✆ **207/967-4865.** www.franciscanguesthouse.com. 60 units. $50–$144 double; $79–$279 suite. No credit cards. Closed mid-Oct to mid-May. *In room:* A/C, TV.

Old Fort Inn ★★ The sophisticated Old Fort Inn is on 15 acres in a quiet and picturesque neighborhood of magnificent late-19th-century summer homes about 2 blocks from the ocean and not far from The Colony Hotel. Guests check in at a tidy antiques shop, and most park around back at the large carriage house, an interesting amalgam of stone, brick, shingle, and stucco. Rooms are delightfully decorated with antiques and reproductions. About half have in-floor heated tiles in the bathrooms. Two large suites are in the main house; light-filled no. 216 faces east and looks out over the pool. A full buffet breakfast is served in the main house.

Old Fort Rd. (P.O. Box M), Kennebunkport, ME 04046. ✆ **800/828-3678** or 207/967-5353. Fax 207/967-4547. 16 units. High season $160–$375 double; low season $99–$295 double. Rates include full breakfast. AE, DC, DISC, MC, V. 2-night minimum weekends and July to Labor Day. **Amenities:** Heated outdoor pool; beach within walking distance; tennis court (1 hr. free daily); laundry service and self-serve laundry; dry cleaning. *In room:* A/C, minibar, fridge, coffeemaker, hair dryer, iron, robe.

White Barn Inn ★★★ Part of the exclusive Relais & Châteaux group, the White Barn Inn pampers its guests like no other in Maine. Upon checking in, guests are shown to one of the parlors and served port or brandy while valets gather luggage and park cars. The rooms are individually decorated in an upscale country style, and I know of no other inn of this size that offers as many unexpected niceties such as fresh flowers in the rooms and turndown service at night. Nearly half the rooms have wood-burning fireplaces, while the suites (in a separate facility across from the main inn) are truly spectacular; each has a separate color theme, and most have LCD televisions, whirlpools, or similar perks. A handful of cottages on the tidal Kennebunk River are cozy, and nicely equipped with modern kitchens and bathrooms. Future plans include the addition of a spa.

Ocean Ave. (¼ mile east of junction of Routes 9 and 35; P.O. Box 560-C), Kennebunk, ME 04043. ✆ **207/967-2321.** Fax 207/967-1100. www.whitebarninn.com. 25 units, 4 cottages. $280–$540 double; $565–$785 suite; $630–$1,260 cottage. Rates include continental breakfast and afternoon tea. 2-night minimum weekends; 3 nights holiday weekends. AE, MC, V. Valet parking. **Amenities:** Outdoor heated pool; nearby ocean beach; bikes; concierge; conference rooms; room service (breakfast only); in-room massage; free newspaper; twice-daily maid service. *In room:* A/C, safe, robes, some fireplaces.

The Yachtsman Lodge & Marina ★★ This riverfront motel within walking distance of Dock Square is an appealing base from which to explore the southern Maine coast. Nice touches abound, such as down comforters, granite-topped vanities, high ceilings, CD players, and French doors that open onto patios just above the river. Every room is on the first floor and is a standard motel size, but their simple, classical styling is far superior to anything you'd find at a chain motel.

Ocean Ave. (P.O. Box 2609), Kennebunkport, ME 04046. ✆ **207/967-2511.** Fax 207/967-5056. www.yachtsmanlodge.com. 30 units. $149–$299 double. Rates include continental breakfast. AE, MC, V. 2-night minimum stay on weekends and holidays. *In room:* A/C, TV/VCR, dataport, fridge, coffeemaker, hair dryer, iron.

WHERE TO DINE

Federal Jack's Restaurant and Brew Pub ★ PUB FARE This light, airy, and modern restaurant, named after a schooner built at Cape Porpoise a century ago, is in a retail complex of recent vintage, which sits a bit uneasily amid the boatyards lining the south bank of the Kennebunk River. From the second-floor perch (look for a seat on the spacious three-season deck in warmer weather), you can gaze across the river toward the shops of Dock Square. The upscale pub menu features regional fare with a creative twist and also standards like hamburgers. This is a good bet for a basic meal without any pretensions. The restaurant is best known for its Shipyard ales, lagers, and porters, which are among the best in New England.

8 Western Ave., Lower Village (south bank of Kennebunk River), Kennebunk, ME 04043. ✆ **207/967-4322.** www.federaljacks.com. Main courses (lunch or dinner) $2.95–$16; lobster dinners priced to market. AE, DISC, MC, V. Daily 11:30am–9pm (bar to 1am); also Sun brunch served 10:30am–2pm.

Grissini ★★ TUSCAN Opened by the same folks who run the White Barn Inn, Grissini is a handsome trattoria that offers great value for the money. Oversize Italian advertising posters line the walls of the soaring, barnlike space, and burning logs in the handsome stone fireplace take the chill out of a cool evening. The menu changes weekly; meals are likewise luxuriously sized and nicely presented, and include a wide range of pastas and pizzas served with considerable flair: Think fresh fettuccine with chicken breast and garlic tomato sauce, or linguini tossed with mahogany clams, leeks, and fennel in a pinot grigio sauce.

27 Western Ave., Kennebunk, ME 04043. ✆ **207/967-2211.** www.restaurantgrissini.com. Reservations encouraged. Entrees $2.95–$14. AE, MC, V. Sun–Fri 5:30–9:30pm; Sat 5–9:30pm. Closed Wed Jan–Mar.

Hurricane ★★★ AMERICAN/ECLECTIC Originally an offshoot of Brooks MacDonald's award-winning Hurricane in Ogunquit, this became the flagship when the other branch closed its doors for good. A meal may start with a cup of lobster chowder, the "Ice Cube" (a block of iceberg lettuce with blue-cheese dressing, toasted pecans, roasted pears, and croutons), or a bento box of shrimp, scallop, and salmon lumpia. The main course could be a gourmet sandwich, some pan-roasted halibut over coconut purple rice, or seared diver-caught scallops. Dinner entrees run to items like lobster cioppino, grilled veal chops, or baked or boiled lobster. Vanilla-bean crème brûlée and Key lime tart with coconut rum sauce are two of my favorite desserts.

29 Dock Sq., Kennebunkport. ✆ **207/967-1111.** www.hurricanerestaurant.com. Reservations recommended. Main courses $19–$39; small plates $6–$22. AE, DC, DISC, MC, V. Daily 11:30am–10:30pm (winter to 9:30pm).

Pier 77 Restaurant ★★ CONTEMPORARY NEW ENGLAND Long a tony restaurant with a wonderful ocean view, Pier 77 is run by husband-and-wife team Peter and Kate Morency. The food, drawing on Peter's training at the Culinary Institute of America and 20 years in top kitchens in Boston and San Francisco, is more contemporary and skillful than almost anything else in Maine. The menu has traditional favorites along with more adventurous dishes, such as cashew-crusted Chilean sea bass served with citrus-tamari sauce and pan-roasted haddock with spinach gnocchi. The restaurant has earned *Wine Spectator*'s award of excellence annually since 1993.

77 Pier Rd., Cape Porpoise, Kennebunkport. ✆ **207/967-8500.** www.pier77restaurant.com. Reservations recommended. Main courses $14–$23. AE, MC, V. Tues–Sat 11:30am–2:30pm and 5–10pm; Sun 10am–2pm.

White Barn Inn ★★★ REGIONAL/NEW AMERICAN The restaurant is housed in a rustic barn attached to the inn (p. 600), with a soaring interior and eclectic collection of country antiques displayed in a hayloft. One window throws in coastal light, and staff gussies it up with changing window dressings (bright pumpkins, corn stalks, and other reminders of the harvest in fall, for example). Chef Jonathan Cartwright's menu also changes frequently, nearly always incorporating local ingredients: You may start with a lobster spring roll of daikon, carrots, snow peas, or local scallops seared with a beet-chorizo crust; glide through an *intermezzo* course of fruit soup or sorbet; then graduate to a roasted New England duck with a juniper sauce, grilled beef tenderloin glazed in chestnuts over a pumpkin pancake, or a simply steamed Maine lobster over fettuccine. Service is astonishingly attentive and knowledgeable. This was recently selected one of America's finest inn restaurants by the readers of *Travel + Leisure* magazine.

Beach Ave., Kennebunkport. © **207/967-2321.** Reservations recommended. Fixed-price dinner $89; tasting menu $105 per person. AE, MC, V. Mon–Thurs 6:30–9:30pm; Fri 5:30–9:30pm. Closed 2 weeks in Jan.

2 Portland ★

106 miles N of Boston.

Maine's largest city, Portland sits on a peninsula extending into scenic Casco Bay. It's easy to drive right past on I-295, admire the skyline at 60 mph and be on your way to the villages and headlands farther up the coast. After all, one doesn't usually think of urban life when envisioning Maine.

However, Portland is well worth an afternoon detour or overnight stay. This historic city has plenty of charm—especially the renovated Old Port, with its brick sidewalks and cobblestone streets. In addition, travelers who stop here are rewarded with ferries to islands, boutique shops, some top-notch historic homes, graceful neighborhoods—and the food. Portland is a culinary mecca of Maine, blessed with an uncommonly high number of excellent restaurants for a city its size (65,000).

ESSENTIALS

GETTING THERE Coming from the south by car, downtown Portland is most easily reached by taking Exit 6A off the Maine Turnpike (I-95), then following I-295. Exit at Franklin Street and continue straight uphill and downhill until you arrive at the ferry terminal. Turn right onto Commercial Street, and continue several blocks to the visitor center on the right (see below).

Amtrak (© **800/872-7245;** www.amtrak.com) runs its Downeaster service from Boston's North Station to Portland. The train makes four round-trips daily, for about $22 one-way. Take a short Metro bus ride to reach downtown from the station.

Concord Trailways (© **800/639-3317** or 207/828-1151) and **Vermont Transit** (© **800/552-8737** or 207/772-6587) provide bus service to Portland from Boston and Bangor. The Vermont Transit bus terminal is at 950 Congress St., about a mile downhill from, and south of, the downtown core. Concord Trailways, which is a few dollars more expensive, has movies and headsets on its trips; its terminal is inconveniently set on Thompson Point Rd. (a 35-min. walk from downtown), but it is served by local buses from nearby Congress Street.

Portland International Jetport (© 207/774-7301; www.portlandjetport.org) is served by **Delta** (© 800/212-1212; www.delta-air.com), **Continental** (© 800/525-0280; www.continental.com), **Independence Air** (© 800/FLY-FLYI; www.flyi.com), **Northwest** (© 800/225-2525; www.nwa.com), **US Airways** (© 800/428-4322; www.usairways.com), and **United** (© 800/241-6522; www.ual.com). The

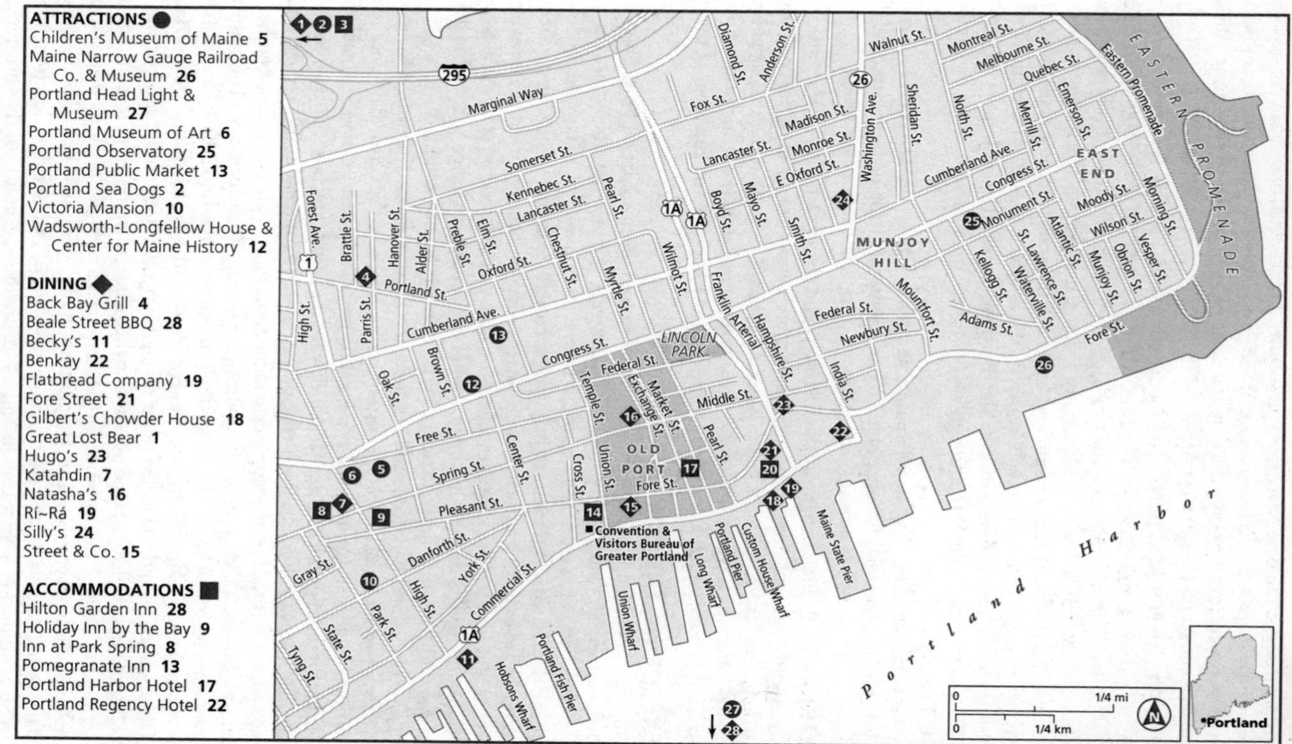
ATTRACTIONS
Children's Museum of Maine 5
Maine Narrow Gauge Railroad Co. & Museum 26
Portland Head Light & Museum 27
Portland Museum of Art 6
Portland Observatory 25
Portland Public Market 13
Portland Sea Dogs 2
Victoria Mansion 10
Wadsworth-Longfellow House & Center for Maine History 12
DINING
Back Bay Grill 4
Beale Street BBQ 28
Becky's 11
Benkay 22
Flatbread Company 19
Fore Street 21
Gilbert's Chowder House 18
Great Lost Bear 1
Hugo's 23
Katahdin 7
Natasha's 16
Rí~Rá 19
Silly's 24
Street & Co. 15
ACCOMMODATIONS
Hilton Garden Inn 28
Holiday Inn by the Bay 9
Inn at Park Spring 8
Pomegranate Inn 13
Portland Harbor Hotel 17
Portland Regency Hotel 22
EASTERN PROMENADE
Eastern Promenade
EAST END
MUNJOY HILL
OLD PORT
LINCOLN PARK
Portland Harbor
Maine State Pier
Custom House Wharf
Portland Pier
Long Wharf
Union Wharf
Portland Fish Pier
Hobsons Wharf
Convention & Visitors Bureau of Greater Portland
Marginal Way
Diamond St.
Anderson St.
Fox St.
Walnut St.
Montreal St.
Melbourne St.
Quebec St.
Emerson St.
Merrill St.
North St.
Sheridan St.
Washington Ave.
Madison St.
Monroe St.
E Oxford St.
Lancaster St.
Somerset St.
Kennebec St.
Pearl St.
Boyd St.
Mayo St.
Smith St.
Cumberland Ave.
Congress St.
Monument St.
Moody St.
Wilson St.
Morning St.
Vesper St.
Obrion St.
Munjoy St.
Atlantic St.
St. Lawrence St.
Waterville St.
Kellogg St.
Adams St.
Mountfort St.
Fore St.
Federal St.
Newbury St.
India St.
Hampshire St.
Franklin Arterial
Wilmot St.
Myrtle St.
Chestnut St.
Oxford St.
Elm St.
Preble St.
Alder St.
Hanover St.
Brattle St.
Forest Ave.
Portland St.
Parris St.
High St.
Brown St.
Oak St.
Temple St.
Exchange St.
Market St.
Middle St.
Free St.
Center St.
Cross St.
Union St.
Spring St.
Pleasant St.
Danforth St.
York St.
Commercial St.
Gray St.
Park St.
State St.
Tyng St.
1/4 mi
1/4 km
Portland

airport is across the Fore River from downtown. Local Metro buses ($1) connect the airport to downtown; cab fare runs about $15. The airport has grown in fits and starts in recent years (ongoing construction and tight parking can be frustrating at times), but it is small and easily navigated.

VISITOR INFORMATION The **Convention and Visitor's Bureau of Greater Portland,** 245 Commercial St., Portland, ME 04101 (© **207/772-5800** or 207/772-4994; www.visitportland.com), stocks a large supply of brochures and is happy to dispense information about local attractions, lodging, and dining. The center is open in summer on weekdays 8am to 6pm and Saturdays 10am to 5pm; hours are shorter in the off season. Ask for the free "Greater Portland Visitor Guide" with map. There's also a tourist information kiosk at the **Portland International Jetport** (© **207/775-5809**), open mid-May through mid-October from around 10am to around 10:30pm daily.

Portland has a free weekly alternative newspaper, the *Portland Phoenix,* offering close-to-comprehensive listings of local events, films, nightclub performances, and the like. Copies are widely available at restaurants, bars, and convenience stores.

PARKING Parking is tight in the Old Port, and the city's parking enforcement is notoriously efficient. Several parking garages are convenient to the Old Port, with parking fees less than $1 per hour; you can also park in some residential neighborhoods, often for a maximum of 2 hours. Read signs carefully for nighttime street-sweeping hours; you *will* be towed (don't ask how I know) if you run afoul of them.

EXPLORING THE CITY

Any visit to Portland should start with a stroll around the historic **Old Port.** Bounded by Commercial, Congress, Union, and Pearl streets, this area near the waterfront has the city's best commercial architecture, a mess of boutiques, fine restaurants, and one of the thickest concentrations of bars on the Eastern Seaboard. (The Old Port tends to transform as night lengthens, the crowds growing younger and rowdier.) Its narrow streets and intricate brick facades reflect the mid-Victorian era; most of the area was rebuilt following a devastating fire in 1866. Leafy, quaint Exchange Street is the heart of the Old Port, with other attractive streets running off and around it.

The city's finest harborside stroll is along the **Eastern Prom Pathway** ★★, which wraps for about a mile along the waterfront beginning at the Casco Bay Lines ferry terminal (corner of Commercial and Franklin sts.). The paved pathway is suitable for walking or biking, and offers expansive views of the islands and boat traffic on the harbor. The pathway skirts the lower edge of the **Eastern Promenade** ★★, a 68-acre hillside park with broad, grassy slopes extending down to the water. Tiny East End Beach is here, but the water is often off-limits for swimming (look for signs). The pathway continues on to Back Cove Pathway, a 3.5-mile loop around tidal Back Cove.

Atop Munjoy Hill, above the Eastern Promenade, is the distinctive **Portland Observatory,** a quirky shingled tower dating from 1807, used to signal the arrival of ships into port. After 4 years of extensive structural repairs, the tower reopened in the summer of 2000. Exhibits inside provide a quick glimpse of Portland's past, but the real draw is the **expansive view** ★ from the top of the city and the harbor. It is open daily (when flags are flying from the cupola), Memorial Day to Labor Day, from 10am to 5pm; admission is $5 for adults and $4 for children ages 6 to 16. (For more information, call © **207/774-5561.**)

Children's Museum of Maine ★ *Kids* The centerpiece exhibit here is the camera obscura, a room-size "camera" on the top floor of this stout, columned downtown building next to the art museum. There's plenty more to do here, though, from running a supermarket checkout counter to sliding down the firehouse pole, to piloting a mock space shuttle from a high cockpit. The Explore Floor has a series of interactive science exhibits focusing on Maine's natural resources. Make a deal with your kids: If they behave during a trip to the art museum (just next door), they'll be rewarded with a couple of hours in their own museum.

142 Free St. (next to the Portland Museum of Art). © **207/828-1234.** www.childrensmuseumofme.org. Admission $6. Free 5–8pm first Fri of each month. AE, MC, V. Tues–Sat 10am–5pm; Sun noon–5pm. Closed Mon fall–spring. Discounted parking at Spring St. parking garage.

Maine Narrow Gauge Railroad Co. & Museum ★ *Kids* In the late 19th century, Maine was home to several narrow-gauge railways, operating on rails 2 feet apart. Most of these versatile trains have disappeared, but this nonprofit organization is dedicated to preserving the examples that remain. Admission is free, with a charge for a short ride on a train that chugs on a rail line along Casco Bay at the foot of the Eastern Promenade. Views of the islands are outstanding; the ride itself is slow-paced and somewhat dull, unless you're very young.

58 Fore St. © **207/828-0814.** www.mngrr.org. Museum free admission; train fare $8 adults, $7 seniors, $5 children, free for children 3 and under. Daily 10am–4pm; trains run on the hour from 11am. Closed Jan to mid-Feb. From I-295, take Franklin St. exit and follow to Fore St.; turn left, continue to museum, on the right.

Portland Head Light & Museum ★★ A short drive (15–20 min. depending on traffic) from downtown Portland, this 1794 lighthouse is one of the most picturesque in the nation. (You'll probably recognize it from its cameo role in numerous advertisements and posters.) The light marks the entrance to Portland Harbor and was occupied continuously from its construction until 1989, when it was automated and the graceful keeper's house (1891) was converted to a small town-owned museum focusing on the history of navigation. The lighthouse itself is still active and thus closed to the public, but visitors can stop by the museum, or browse for lighthouse-themed gifts at the gift shop.

Fort Williams Park, 1000 Shore Rd., Cape Elizabeth. © **207/799-2661.** www.portlandheadlight.com. Free admission for grounds; museum admission $2 adults, $1 children 6–18. Park grounds year-round daily sunrise–sunset (until 8:30pm in summer); museum June–Oct daily 10am–4pm; open weekends only in spring and late fall. From Portland, follow State St. across bridge to South Portland; bear left on Broadway. At 3rd light, turn right on Cottage Rd. (Rte. 77), which becomes Shore Rd.; follow until you arrive at the park, on your left.

Portland Museum of Art ★★ This bold, modern museum was designed by I.M. Pei & Partners in 1983, and it features selections from its own fine collections along with a parade of touring exhibits. (Summer exhibits are usually targeted at a broad audience.) The museum is particularly strong in American artists with Maine connections, including Winslow Homer, Andrew Wyeth, and Edward Hopper, and it has fine displays of Early American furniture and crafts. The museum shares the Joan Whitney Payson Collection with Colby College (the college gets it one semester every other year), which includes wonderful European works by Renoir, Degas, and Picasso. Guided tours are daily at 2pm.

7 Congress Sq. (corner of Congress and High sts.). © **207/775-6148.** www.portlandmuseum.org. Admission $8 adults, $6 students and seniors, $2 children 6–17. (Free admission Fri 5–9pm.) Tues–Sun 10am–5pm (Fri to 9pm); Memorial Day to mid-Oct also open Mon 10am–5pm.

Portland Public Market *Kids* The Portland Public Market has some of the best food that Maine is producing, and it's the perfect place to lay in supplies for a picnic or snacks. There are more than two dozen vendors selling fresh foods and flowers, much of which is Maine-grown. The architecturally distinctive building is at once classic and modern, and it houses fishmongers, butchers, fresh fruit dealers, a seafood cafe, and a wine shop. There's free parking (with validated ticket) at the connected garage on the west side of Cumberland Avenue; ask any merchant to stamp your ticket.

25 Preble St. (½ block west of Monument Sq.). ✆ **207/228-2000.** www.portlandmarket.com. Open year-round. Mon–Sat 9am–7pm; Sun 10am–5pm.

Victoria Mansion ★★ *Finds* This home is a must for architecture buffs and is often mentioned in books on the history of American architecture. Widely regarded as one of the most elaborate Victorian brownstone homes in the United States, this mansion (also known as the Morse-Libby House) is a remarkable display of high Victorian style. Built between 1858 and 1863 for a Maine businessman who made a fortune in the New Orleans hotel trade, the towering, slightly foreboding home is a prime example of the Italianate style. Inside, it appears that not a square inch of wall space was left untouched by craftsmen or artisans (11 painters were hired to create the murals).

109 Danforth St. ✆ **207/772-4841.** www.victoriamansion.org. Admission $10 adults, $9 seniors, $3 children 6–17, free for children under 6. Christmas slightly higher. May–Oct Tues–Sat 10am–4pm, Sun 1–5pm; July–Oct also Mon 10am–4pm. Tours offered at quarter past and quarter of each hour. Closed Nov–Apr, except for holiday tours from end of Nov to mid-Dec. From the Old Port, head west on Fore St., and veer right on Danforth St. at light near Giobbi's restaurant; proceed 3 blocks to the mansion, at the corner of Park St.

Wadsworth-Longfellow House & Center for Maine History Maine Historical Society's "history campus" includes three widely varied buildings on busy Congress Street in downtown Portland. The austere brick Wadsworth-Longfellow House dates from 1785 and was built by Gen. Peleg Wadsworth, father of noted poet Henry Wadsworth Longfellow. It's furnished in an early-19th-century style, with many samples of Longfellow family furniture on display. Adjacent to the home is the Maine History Gallery, in a garish postmodern building, formerly a bank. Changing exhibits here explore the rich texture of Maine history. Just behind the Longfellow house is the library of the Maine Historical Society, a popular destination among genealogists.

489 Congress St. ✆ **207/774-1822** or 207/879-0427. www.mainehistory.org. $7 adults, $6 seniors and students, $3 children (6–18). Longfellow House May–Oct Mon–Sat 10am–5pm; Sun noon–5pm. Also open Dec daily (except Christmas) noon–4pm.

ON THE WATER

Casco Bay Lines Six of the Casco Bay islands have year-round populations and are served by scheduled ferries from downtown Portland. Except for Long Island, the islands are part of the city of Portland. The ferries provide an inexpensive way to view the bustling harbor and get a taste of island life. Trips range from a 20-minute (one-way) excursion to Peaks Island (the closest thing to an island suburb, with 1,200 year-round residents), to the 5½-hour cruise to Bailey Island (connected by bridge to the mainland south of Brunswick) and back. All of the islands are well suited for walking; Peaks Island has a rocky back shore that's easily accessible via the island's paved perimeter road (bring a picnic lunch). Cliff Island is the most remote of the bunch and has a sedate turn-of-the-20th-century island retreat character. Peaks is easily biked, and there's a rental outfit right on the island, a few blocks from the ferry: Brad's Bike Shop, at 115 Island Ave. (✆ **207/766-5631**).

Commercial and Franklin sts. ✆ **207/774-7871.** www.cascobaylines.com. Fares vary depending on the run and the season; summer rates typically $6–$9 round-trip. Frequent departures 6am–10pm daily.

Eagle Island Tours ★ Eagle Island was the summer home of famed arctic explorer and Portland native Robert E. Peary, who claimed in 1909 to be the first person to reach the North Pole. (His accomplishments have been the subject of exhaustive debates among arctic scholars, some of whom insist he inflated his claims.) In 1904, Peary built a simple home on a remote, 17-acre island at the edge of Casco Bay; in 1912, he added flourishes in the form of two low stone towers. After his death in 1920, his family kept up the home; they later donated it to the state, which has since managed it as a state park. The home is open to the public, maintained much as it was when Peary lived here. Eagle Tours takes one trip daily from Portland. The 4-hour excursion includes a 1½-hour stopover on the island.

Long Wharf (Commercial St.) ✆ **207/774-6498.** www.eagleislandtours.com. $24 adults, $22 seniors, $13 children under 12 (includes state park fee of $2.50). 1 departure daily at 10am, daily late June to Labor Day, weekends June and Sept.

Olde Port Mariner Fleet This fleet of three boats tied up off Commercial Street provides a number of ways to enjoy the bay. The *Indian II* runs deep-sea fishing trips far beyond Portland Harbor in search of cod, cusk, hake, pollack, and more. Most are daylong trips (8am–5pm), but several times each summer they offer marathons (5am–5pm) for real die-hards. On the *Odyssey* you search for whales by day, and on Friday evenings you can enjoy music and food, including a 4-hour Downeast lobster bake. Book these cruises in advance if you're set on going.

Commercial St. (Long Wharf and Custom House Wharf). ✆ **800/437-3270** or 207/774-2022. www.marinerfleet.com. Excursions $30–$60, short cruises $10. Several departures daily.

WHERE TO STAY

If you're looking for something central, though not particularly special, the **Hilton Garden Inn,** 65 Commercial St. (✆ **207/780-0780**) is convenient to the Old Port's restaurants, bakeries, and pubs—not to mention the islands of Casco Bay. Double rooms run from about $89 to $289 per night.

The **Holiday Inn by the Bay,** 88 Spring St. (✆ **207/775-2311**), has great views of the harbor from about half the rooms, along with the usual chain-hotel creature comforts. Peak-season rates are approximately $140 for a double.

Kids Seeing the Sea Dogs

The Portland Sea Dogs are a minor league Double-A team affiliated with the Boston Red Sox (a perfect marriage in baseball-crazy northern New England). They play through summer at Hadlock Field (217 Park Ave.; ✆ **800/936-3647** or 207/879-9500; www.seadogs.com) a small stadium near downtown that still retains an old-time feel despite aluminum benches and other updating. Activities are geared toward families, with lots of entertainment between innings and a selection of food that's a couple of notches above basic hot dogs and hamburgers. (Try the tasty french fries and grilled sausages.) You might even catch future pro stars—Josh Beckett, Brad Penny, Alex Gonzalez, Charles Johnson, and Kevin Millar all did time here as farmhands before they made "the show." Tickets cost $3 to $10 and the season runs April to Labor Day.

Budget travelers seeking chain hotels typically head toward the area around the Maine Mall in South Portland, about 8 miles south of the attractions of downtown. Try **Days Inn** (© **207/772-3450**) or **Coastline Inn** (© **207/772-3838**). The new **Extended Stay America,** 2 Ashley Dr., Scarborough (© **207/883-0554;** fax 207/883-1705; www.exstay.com) is a few minute's drive south of the Maine Mall and 6 miles from downtown Portland. Doubles start at about $50.

Inn at Park Spring ★★ This small, tasteful B&B is on a busy downtown street in an 1835 brick home. The Portland Museum of Art is just 2 blocks away, the Old Port is about 10 minutes away, and great restaurants are also within easy walking distance. The rooms are all corner rooms; most are bright and sunny. I especially like "Spring," with its great morning light and wonderful views of the historic row houses on Park Street, and "Gables," on the third floor, which gets abundant afternoon light and has a nice bathroom.

135 Spring St., Portland, ME 04101. © **800/437-8511** or 207/774-1059. www.innatparkspring.com. 6 units. Mid-June to Oct and holidays $149–$175 double; mid-Apr to mid-June $129–$165 double; Nov to mid-Apr $109–$135 double. Rates include full breakfast and off-street parking. 2-night minimum weekends. AE, MC, V. No children under 10. *In room:* A/C, hair dryer.

Pomegranate Inn ★★ This is one of the best choices in all of northern New England. Housed in an imposing, dove-gray 1884 Italianate home in the architecturally distinctive Western Prom neighborhood, the interiors are wondrously decorated with whimsy and elegance—a fatally cloying combination when attempted by someone without impeccably good taste. Look for the bold and exuberant wall paintings by a local artist, and the eclectic antique furniture. If you have the chance, peek in some of the unoccupied rooms—they're all different with painted floors and boisterous faux-marble woodwork. Most rooms have gas fireplaces; the best of the lot is in the carriage house, which has its own private terrace, kitchenette, and fireplace.

49 Neal St., Portland, ME 04102. © **800/356-0408** or 207/772-1006. Fax 207/773-4426. www.pomegranateinn.com. 8 units. Memorial Day to Oct $175–$265 double; off season $95–$165 double. Rates include full breakfast. 2-night minimum summer weekends and holidays. AE, DISC, MC, V. On-street parking. From the Old Port, take Middle St. (which turns into Spring St.) to Neal St. in the West End (about 1 mile); turn right and proceed to inn. No children under 16. **Amenities:** Tea; wine. *In room:* A/C, 1 kitchenette, some fireplaces.

Portland Harbor Hotel ★★ On the corner of Fore and Union streets and just steps from a long row of bars and restaurants, this semicircular town-house-like structure—designed to fit in with the brick facades you'll see prevailing throughout the Old Port—goes for the boutique crowd with lots of amenities. The interior courtyard and garden project European ambience; large, exquisite rooms are furnished with comfy queen-size and king-size beds (each with 250-count thread sheets) and spacious work desks. Even the standard rooms are outfitted with big, deep bathtubs in granite-faced bathrooms; armoires; comfy duvets and down coverlets. Deluxe rooms and suites have Jacuzzis and sitting areas, and many units look out onto an attractive central garden area where guests dine or sip drinks in good weather.

468 Fore St., Portland, ME 04101. © **888/798-9090** or 207/775-9090. Fax 207/775-9990. www.portlandharborhotel.com. 100 units. Mid-May to mid-Oct $229–$249 double, $329 suite; off season $159–$179 double, $259 suite. AE, DC, DISC, MC, V. Parking $10 per day. **Amenities:** Dining room; bar; fitness center; concierge; limited room service; dry cleaning. *In room:* A/C, digital TV, Internet access, hair dryer, safe, Jacuzzi (some).

Portland Regency Hotel ★★★ On a cobblestone courtyard in the middle of the trendy Old Port, the Regency boasts one of the city's premier hotel settings, but it's also one of the most architecturally striking and better-managed hotels in the state. Housed in an 1895 brick armory, the interior is thoroughly modern with attractive guest rooms nicely appointed and furnished with all the expected amenities. The architects have had to work within the quirky layout of the building; as a result, the top-floor rooms lack windows but have skylights, and the windows are knee-high in some other rooms. The hotel has several different types of rooms and suites; for a splurge, ask for one of the luxurious corner rooms with handsome (nonworking) gas log fireplaces. Staff is extremely professional, the health club is a good one, and the hotel houses not only a good fine-dining restaurant, **The Armory,** but a **bar** ★ that's the best (quiet) place in Portland to sip a drink.

20 Milk St., Portland, ME 04101. ✆ **800/727-3436** or 207/774-4200. Fax 207/775-2150. www.theregency.com. 95 units. Early July to late Oct $249–$269 double, $289–$389 suite; off season $159–$219 double, $209–$329 suite. AE, DISC, MC, V. Valet parking $8 per day. **Amenities:** Restaurant; bar; fitness club; aerobics classes; Jacuzzi; sauna; courtesy car to airport; business center; conference rooms; limited room service; babysitting (with prior notice); dry cleaning (Mon–Fri). *In room:* A/C, CD player, minibar, safe, Jacuzzis (some).

WHERE TO DINE

EXPENSIVE

Back Bay Grill ★★ NEW AMERICAN Back Bay Grill is one of Portland's consistently best restaurants, with an upscale, contemporary ambience in a rather downscale neighborhood near the main post office. Light jazz is on the stereo; bold artwork is on the walls. The menu is revamped seasonally, although dishes change more frequently to emphasize available local produce and meats. I like to start with Maine crab cakes with lemon-pepper crème fraîche, or potato soup with a salmon mousse, then move on to such heavenly dishes as rack of lamb with foie gras and lingonberry sauce, or a plate of soft-shell crab and seared jumbo scallops served with basmati rice and a truffle sauce. The fresh pastas are also memorable, including hand-rolled fettuccini with smoked tomatoes and oyster mushrooms, or that same fettuccini with Maine chèvre, spring peas, and pine nuts.

65 Portland St. ✆ **207/772-8833.** www.backbaygrill.com. Reservations recommended. Main courses $17–$33. AE, DC, DISC, MC, V. Mon–Thurs 5–9pm; Fri–Sat 5–9:30pm.

Fore Street ★★ CONTEMPORARY GRILL The secret is simplicity at one of New England's most celebrated restaurants. Local ingredients are used when possible (note the rustic vegetable cooler overflowing with what's fresh), and the kitchen shuns fussy presentations. The menu changes nightly; some of the most memorable meals are prepared over an applewood grill, such as Maine pheasant, or two-texture duckling with grilled pears. During the long summer evenings, light floods in through this loftlike space's huge windows; later at night, soft lighting against the brick walls, buttery narrow-plank maple floors, and copper-topped tables lends a more intimate glow. But the place is always bustling; it centers on a sprawling, busy open kitchen. Though it can be mighty hard to snag a reservation here, particularly on a summer weekend, Fore Street sets aside a few tables each night for walk-ins.

288 Fore St. ✆ **207/775-2717.** www.forestreet.biz. Reservations recommended. Main courses $13–$29. AE, MC, V. Sun–Thurs 5:30–9:30pm; Fri–Sat 5:30–10:30pm.

Hugo's ★★★ ECLECTIC/NEW AMERICAN New England-native chef Rob Evans and partner Nancy Pugh use locally produced ingredients wherever possible. The result is a set of experimental, exciting menus that begin in familiar New American territory and then take off into the stratosphere. Even a more basic prix-fixe menu might include such twists as "four-textured mini-lobster," "a love affair with cod," and four treatments of duck. The full Chef's Menu includes a whopping 13 courses—four of which could be considered desserts. Representative stops along this epic journey may include parsnips soup, lobster cannelloni, Maine matsutake mushrooms, bay scallops with angel-hair pasta, and duck breast sided by a balsamic poached pear, walnut-fenugreek milk, and popped wild rice. Dessert could be a roasted apple French toast, pistachio buttermilk ice cream, or a unique house-created dark chocolate bar with peanuts, taffy, nougat, and crème anglaise. A tapas menu is also available at the bar.

88 Middle St. © **207/774-8538.** www.hugos.net. Reservations strongly recommended (required for Chef's Menu). Prix-fixe menus $58–$120 per person; bar tapas menu $9–$12 per item. AE, MC, V. Tues–Thurs 5:30–9:30pm; Fri–Sat 5:30–9:30pm.

Street & Co. ★★★ MEDITERRANEAN/SEAFOOD A pioneering establishment on now-bustling Wharf Street, Dana Street's intimate, brick-walled bistro specializes in seafood cooked just right. You'll pass the open kitchen as you're seated, where you'll see the talented chefs performing magic in their tiny space. The kitchen specializes in seafood that's fresh as can be (the docks are close by) and cooked just right. Diners sit at copper-topped tables, designed so that the waiters can deliver steaming skillets directly from the stove. Looking for lobster? Try it grilled and served over linguini in a butter-garlic sauce. If you're partial to calamari, they know how to cook it here so that it's perfectly tender. Otherwise, go for seared tuna, fresh mussels, or a grilled piece of whatever has come in (swordfish, perhaps). This place often fills up early, so reservations are strongly recommended.

33 Wharf St. © **207/775-0887.** Reservations recommended. Main courses $14–$24. AE, MC, V. Sun–Thurs 5:30–9:30pm; Fri–Sat 5:30–10pm.

MODERATE

Beale Street BBQ ★ *Finds* BARBECUE Of all the barbecue joints in Maine, this is my favorite, with its appealing roadhouse atmosphere, friendly staff, and great smoked meats. Owner Mark Quigg once operated a takeout grill on Route 1 outside Freeport, but he chucked that life when notables like author Stephen King got wind of his cooking. Soon he joined forces with his two brothers and began to cater movie shoots. Though I like everything here—check the board for intriguing daily specials, which usually include a fish preparation as well as Creole or Cajun offerings—I usually order the barbecue sampler (subtitled "All You Really Need to Know About BBQ"). Two people can comfortably split it. This location, in South Portland's commercial Mill Creek and Knightville neighborhoods, is a bit hard to find (it's almost beneath the Casco Bay Bridge). There's another fancier location (© **207/442-9514**) at 215 Water St. in Bath, a half-hour north up Route 1.

90 Waterman Dr., South Portland. © **207/767-0130.** Reservations not accepted. Main courses $9–$18. MC, V. Mon–Sat 11:30am–10pm; Sun 11:30am–9pm.

Benkay ★ *Value* JAPANESE/SUSHI Of Portland's sushi restaurants, Benkay is the hippest, usually teeming with a lively crowd lured by good value. Ask about special sushi nights where pieces go for as little as $1 (usually weeknights). Chef Seiji Ando's regular sushi platter is inexpensive and delivers a lot for the money, though nothing very exotic. Teriyaki and tempura round out the menu. Expect harried service on busy nights. It stays open until 1am Thursdays through Saturdays—a boon in early-closing Portland.

2 India St. (at Commercial). © **207/773-5555.** www.sushiman.com. Reservations not accepted. Main courses $7.95–$17. AE, MC, V. Mon–Fri 11:30am–2pm; Mon–Sat 5–10pm; Sun noon–9pm.

Flatbread Company ★ PIZZA This upscale, hippie-chic pizzeria—an offshoot of the original Flatbread Company in Waitsfield, VT—may have the best waterfront location in town. It sits on a slip overlooking the Casco Bay Lines terminal, so you can watch fishermen at work while you eat. (Picnic tables are on the deck in fair weather.) The inside brings to mind a Phish concert, with Tibetan prayer flags and longhaired staffers stoking wood-fired ovens and slicing nitrate-free pepperoni and organic vegetables. The laid-back atmosphere makes the place; the pizza is quite good, though toppings tend to be skimpy.

72 Commercial St. ✆ **207/772-8777.** Reservations accepted for parties of 10 or more. Pizzas $12–$15. AE, MC, V. Mon–Tues 5–9pm; Wed–Sun 11:30am–9pm.

Katahdin ★ *Value* CREATIVE NEW ENGLAND Katahdin is a lively, often noisy spot that prides itself on its eclectic cuisine. Artists on slim budgets dine on the nightly blue-plate special, which typically features something basic like meatloaf or pan-fried catfish. Wealthy business folks may opt for more delicate fare, like the restaurant's crab cakes. Nightly specialties could include a plate of grilled sea scallops with an apricot-lobster reduction, or a London broil marinated in a ginger, scallion, and garlic mix. Sometimes the kitchen nods, but for the most part, food is good, made more palatable by the reasonable prices.

106 High St. ✆ **207/774-1740.** www.katahdinrestaurant.com. Reservations not accepted. Main courses $12–$18. DISC, MC, V. Tues–Thurs 5–9:30pm; Fri–Sat 5–10:30pm.

Natasha's ★ NEW AMERICAN Lobster stew with leek and potatoes or a Maine crab and goat cheese Rangoon are typical starters at Natasha's. Dinner entrees (served Tues–Sat) include lobster and crab ravioli served with leeks and lemon, pork loin grilled and served with a spicy pepper jam, and a crispy peanut tofu with pad Thai seasoning. Lunch is inviting, with creative sandwiches (my pick: the vegetarian napoleon with artichoke hearts, mozzarella cheese, portobello mushrooms, and roasted red peppers) and salads, along with wraps and noodles.

82 Exchange St. ✆ **207/774-4004.** Reservations recommended. Main courses lunch $4.50–$9.95 (mostly $5–$6), dinner $13–$20. AE, DISC, MC, V. Mon–Fri 11am–2:30pm and 5–9:30pm; Sat 5–9:30pm.

Rí~Rá ★ IRISH This fun restaurant and bar (next to Flatbread Company) is styled after a friendly Irish pub. The doors were imported from a shop pub in Kilkenny, and the back bar and counter are from County Louth. Old and new blend seamlessly; it sometimes seems more Irish than the real thing—save for a lack of smoke and a large-screen TV with football and baseball, not soccer. Upstairs beyond the pub is a nice dining room with a great view of the ferry slip; look for basic pub fare, along with some more upscale dishes acceptably done.

72 Commercial St. ✆ **207/761-4446.** www.rira.com. Main courses pub fare $6.95–$9.95, entrees $18–$22. AE, MC, V. Mon–Sat 11:30am–10pm; Sun 11am–10pm.

INEXPENSIVE

Becky's *Value* BREAKFAST/LUNCH This waterfront institution is in a squat maroon building of concrete block on the not-so-quaint end of the waterfront; it has drop ceilings, fluorescent lights, and scruffy counters, booths, and tables. Local fishermen often show up early to grab a cup of joe and a plate of eggs before setting off. The menu is extensive, but is most noted for its breakfasts.

390 Commercial St. ✆ **207/773-7070.** www.beckysdiner.com. Main courses breakfast $2.25–$7.50; sandwiches $1.95–$5.25; dinners $2.25–$7.95. AE, DISC, MC, V. Daily 4am–9pm.

Gilbert's Chowder House CHOWDER/SEAFOOD Gilbert's is an unprepossessing waterfront spot that's nautical without being too cute. Angle for the outdoor tables overlooking a parking lot and the working waterfront; sometimes it smells pleasantly marine, sometimes unpleasantly so. The chowders are flavorful, if pasty. If you're looking to bulk up, you can get your chowder in a bread bowl. Other meals include fried clams and haddock sandwiches, and a lot of other seafood broiled or fried. A basic lobster dinner includes corn on the cob and a cup of clam chowder.

92 Commercial St. ✆ **207/871-5636.** Reservations not accepted. Chowders $2.50–$9.75; sandwiches $2.25–$9.95; main courses $6.95–$23. DISC, MC, V. Mon–Thurs 11am–10pm; Fri–Sat 11am–11pm; Sun 11am–9pm (closed earlier in winter).

Silly's ★ *Finds* *Kids* ECLECTIC/TAKEOUT Silly's is the favored cheap-eats joint for Portlanders. Situated on a ragged commercial street, the interior is informal, bright, and funky, with mismatched 1950s dinettes and an equally hodgepodge back patio beneath improbable trees. There's also a weird fascination with Einstein here. Like Einstein, the menu is creative, everything made fresh and from scratch. The place is noted for its roll-ups ("fast Abdullahs"), a series of tasty fillings piled into fresh tortillas. Among the best: the shish kabob with feta and the sloppy "Diesel," made with pulled pork barbecue and coleslaw. Don't overlook the playful, changing dessert menu of pies, ice creams, and cakes—and absolutely do not leave without sampling one of the huge milkshakes.

40 Washington Ave. ✆ **207/772-0360.** www.sillys.com. Lunch and dinner $3.25–$7.50; pizza $8.50–$11. MC, V. Tues–Thurs 11:30am–9pm; Fri–Sat 11:30am–10pm; Sun 11:30am–8pm.

PORTLAND AFTER DARK

FILM

Downtown Portland is still blessed with two downtown movie houses, enabling travelers in the mood for a flick to avoid the disheartening slog out to the boxy, could-be-anywhere mall octoplexes. **Nickelodeon Cinemas,** 1 Temple St. (✆ **207/772-9751**), has six screens showing first- and second-run films at reasonable prices. **The Movies** ★, 10 Exchange St. (✆ **207/772-9600** or 207/772-8041), is a compact art-film showcase in the heart of the Old Port featuring a lineup of foreign and independent films of recent and historical vintage.

MUSIC

Portland is usually lively in the evenings, especially on summer weekends when the hormone level in the Old Port seems to rocket into the stratosphere, with young men and women prowling the dozens of bars and spilling out onto Fore Street and the surrounding alleys and streets.

Among the Old Port bars favored by locals are **Three-Dollar Dewey's,** at the corner of Commercial and Union streets (the popcorn is free); atmospheric **Gritty McDuff's Brew Pub** ★ on Fore Street at the foot of Exchange Street, where you'll find live music and a cast of regulars quaffing great beers brewed on-site; and the slightly rowdy Irish pub **Brian Ború,** on Center Street, with a rooftop patio.

A gay club, **Styxx,** 3 Spring St. (✆ **207/828-0822;** www.styxxportland.com) is just uphill from the Old Port. Half of the place is a tidy, friendly bar and hangout with pool table; the other half is a dance club with pulsing lights and music. It has movie nights, karaoke, and other special promotions and is open daily until 1am.

Finds On Tap at the Great Lost Bear

The **Great Lost Bear,** 540 Forest Ave. (✆ **207/772-0300;** www.greatlostbear.com) has the best brew selection in all of northern New England, around 50 on offer at any given time, including most of the local brews crafted in Maine. Some of the choicest ales are dispensed from one of three cask-conditioned hand pumps. Every Thursday the bartender showcases a particular brewer or style—a good way to get educated about the nuances of good beer. As if that weren't enough, an eclectic menu ranges from juicy burgers to vegetarian dishes. To find the Bear, head about 2 miles out Forest Avenue (*away* from the Old Port).

PERFORMING ARTS

Portland has a growing creative corps of performing artists. Theater companies typically take the summer off, but it doesn't hurt to call or check the local papers for special performances.

Center for Cultural Exchange ★ The center is devoted to bringing acts from around the globe to Portland. Venues range from area theaters and churches to the center's small, but handsome performance space in a former dry-cleaning establishment facing a statue of the pensive poet Henry Wadsworth Longfellow. Acts range from pan-Caribbean dance music to klezmer bands, to Quebecois step-dancing. It's worth stopping by the center (it hosts a tiny cafe) to see what's coming up. You just never know. Longfellow Sq. (corner of Congress and State sts.) ✆ **207/761-1545.** www.centerforculturalexchange.org. Tickets $8–$32.

Portland Stage Company The most polished and consistent of the Portland theater companies, Portland Stage offers crisply produced shows starring local and imported equity actors in a handsome, second-story theater just off Congress Street. About a half-dozen shows are staged throughout the season, which runs from October to May. Recent productions have included *Proof, Arcadia,* and *Fences.* Performing Arts Center, 25A Forest Ave. ✆ **207/774-0465.** www.portlandstage.com. Tickets $20–$32.

Portland Symphony Orchestra ★★ The well-regarded Portland Symphony, headed by Toshiyuki Shimada, offers a variety of performances throughout the season (typically Sept–May), ranging from pops to Mozart. Summer travelers should consider a Portland detour in the week of July Fourth, when the "Independence Pops" is held (weather permitting) at various sites around southern Maine, including the grounds of the Portland Head Lighthouse in Cape Elizabeth. The latter is a memorable outdoor picnic concert that features the "1812 Overture" and concludes with fireworks. 477 Congress St. ✆ **207/842-0800** for tickets, or 207/773-6128 for more information. www.portlandsymphony.com. Tickets $15–$50.

A SIDE TRIP TO OLD ORCHARD BEACH

About 12 miles south of Portland is the unrepentantly honky-tonkish beach town of Old Orchard Beach, a venerable Victorian-era resort famed for its amusement park, pier, and long, sandy beach. Be sure to spend time and money on the stomach-churning rides at the beachside amusement park of **Palace Playland** (✆ **207/934-2001**), and then walk on the 7-mile-long beach past the mid-rise condos that sprouted in the 1980s.

The beach is broad and open at low tide; at high tide, space to place your towel is at a premium. In the evenings, teens and young adults dominate the town, spilling out of video arcades and cruising the main strip. Do as the locals do for dinner: Buy hot dogs, pizza, and cotton candy, saving your change for the arcades.

Old Orchard is just off Route 1 south of Portland; leave the turnpike at Exit 5 and follow I-195 and the signs to the beach. Don't expect to be alone here: Parking is tight, and traffic can be horrendous during peak summer months.

3 Mid-Coast Maine

Bath 33 miles NE of Portland; Boothbay Harbor 23 miles E of Bath, 41 miles W of Rockland.

Veteran Maine travelers contend that this part of the coast is fast losing its native charm—it's too commercial, too developed, too much like the rest of the United States. The grousers do have a point, especially regarding Route 1's roadside, but get off the main roads and you'll find pockets where you can catch glimpses of another Maine.

The best source of information for the region in general is at the **Maine State Information Center** (**© 207/846-0833**), off Exit 17 of I-95 in Yarmouth. This state-run center is stocked with hundreds of brochures and a selection of free newspapers, and is staffed by a helpful crew who can provide information on the entire state, but are particularly well informed about the mid-coast region. It's open daily from 8am to 6pm (8:30am–5pm in winter).

FREEPORT

If Freeport were a mall (not a far-fetched analogy), L.L.Bean would be the anchor store. It's the business that launched Freeport, elevating its status from just another town off the interstate to one of Maine's two outlet capitals (the other is Kittery). Freeport still has the form of a classic Maine village, but it's a village that's been largely taken over by the national fashion industry. Most of the old homes and stores have been converted to upscale shops, and now sell name-brand clothing and housewares. Banana Republic occupies an exceedingly handsome brick Federal-style home; even the McDonald's is in a tasteful, understated Victorian farmhouse—you really have to look for the golden arches.

While a number of more modern structures have been built to accommodate the outlet boom, strict planning guidelines have managed to preserve much of the local charm, at least in the village section.

ESSENTIALS

GETTING THERE Freeport is on Route 1, but is most commonly reached via I-95 from either Exit 19 or 20.

VISITOR INFORMATION The **Freeport Merchants Marketing Association,** P.O. Box 452, Freeport, ME 04032 (**© 800/865-1994** or 207/865-1212; www.freeportusa.com), publishes a map and directory of businesses, restaurants, and overnight accommodations. The free map is widely available around town, or you can contact the association to have one sent to you.

SHOPPING

Freeport has more than 100 retail shops between Exit 19 of I-95 at the far lower end of Main Street and Mallett Road, which connects to Exit 20. Shops have recently

Mid-Coast Maine

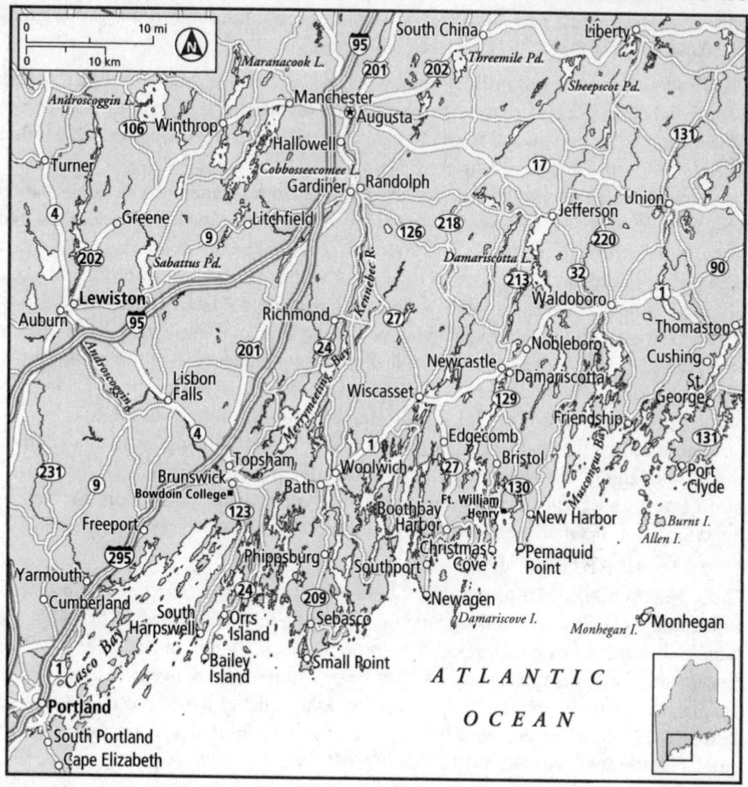

begun to spread south of Exit 19 toward Yarmouth. If you don't want to miss a single shopping opportunity, get off at Exit 17 and head north on Route 1. The bargains can vary from extraordinary to expensive, so plan on racking up some mileage if you're intent on finding outrageous deals. The national chains in Freeport include Abercrombie & Fitch, Banana Republic, Gap, Levi's, and J. Crew, among many others.

Stores in Freeport are typically open daily 9am to 9pm during the busy summer and close much earlier (at 5 or 6pm) in other seasons; between Thanksgiving and Christmas, they remain open late once more. To avoid hauling your booty around for the rest of your vacation, stop by the **Freeport Trading & Shipping Co.,** 18 Independence Dr. (© **207/865-0421**), which can pack and ship everything home.

Cuddledown of Maine Cuddledown started producing down comforters in 1973 and now makes a whole line of products much appreciated in northern climes and beyond. Down pillows are made right in the outlet shop, which carries a variety of European goose-down comforters in all sizes and weights. Look also for linens and home furnishings. Another outlet is in Kittery. 475 U.S. Rte. 1 (between exits 17 and 19). © **888/235-3696** or 207/865-1713. www.cuddledown.com.

Freeport Knife Co. This store sports a wide selection of knives for kitchen and camp alike. Look for the custom knives, and bring your dull camp blade for sharpening. It also sells replacement parts and do repairs on any knives, not just its own brand. 148 Main St. ✆ **800/645-8430** or 207/865-0779. www.freeportknife.com.

L.L.Bean ★★ Monster outdoor retailer L.L.Bean traces its roots from the day Leon Leonwood Bean decided that what the world really needed was a good weatherproof hunting shoe. He joined a watertight gum shoe with a laced leather upper. Hunters liked it. The store grew. An empire was born.

Today L.L.Bean sells millions of dollars' worth of clothing and outdoor goods nationwide through its well-respected catalogs, and it continues to draw hundreds of thousands of customers through its doors. This modern, multilevel store is the size of a regional mall, but it's tastefully done with its own indoor trout pond and lots of natural wood. L.L.Bean is open 365 days a year, 24 hours a day (note the lack of locks or latches on the front doors), and it's a popular spot even in the dead of night, especially in summer and around holidays. Selections include Bean's own trademark clothing, along with home furnishings, books, shoes, and plenty of outdoor gear for camping, fishing, and hunting. Just next door is the L.L.Kids store, with goods for the younger set.

In addition to the main store, L.L.Bean stocks an **outlet shop** ★ with a relatively small, but rapidly changing inventory at discount prices. It's in a back lot between Main Street and Depot Street—ask at the front desk of the main store for walking directions. L.L.Bean also has outlets in Portland and Ellsworth. 95 Main St. (at Bow St.). ✆ **877/552-3268.** www.llbean.com.

Thos. Moser Cabinetmakers ★ Classic furniture reinterpreted in lustrous wood and leather is the focus at this shop, which, thanks to a steady parade of ads in *The New Yorker* and elsewhere, has become almost as much an icon of Maine as L.L.Bean. Shaker, mission, and modern styles have been wonderfully reinvented by the shop's designers and woodworkers, who produce heirloom-quality signed pieces. Nationwide delivery is easily arranged. As a bonus, there's great **Maine art** ★ on display at the shop. 149 Main St. ✆ **207/865-4519** or 800/708-9041. www.thomasmoser.com.

WHERE TO STAY

Harraseeket Inn ★★ The Harraseeket Inn is a large, thoroughly modern hotel 2 blocks north of L.L.Bean. It's to the inn's credit that, despite its size, a traveler could drive down Main Street and not immediately notice it. A late-19th-century home is the soul of the hotel, but most of the rooms are in later additions built in 1989 and 1997. Guests can relax in the well-regarded dining room, read the paper in the common room with the baby grand player piano, or sip a cocktail in the homey Broad Arrow Tavern, with its wood-fired oven and grill. The guest rooms are on the large side and tastefully done, with quarter-canopy beds and a nice mix of contemporary and antique furniture.

162 Main St., Freeport, ME 04032. ✆ **800/342-6423** or 207/865-9377. www.harraseeketinn.com. 84 units. July–Oct $189–$285 double, $285–$295 suite; mid-May to June $140–$245 double, $235–$260 suite; winter $115–$249 double, $225–$295 suite. All rates include breakfast buffet and afternoon tea. MAP plans also available. AE, DC, DISC, MC, V. Take Exit 20 off I-95 to Main St. **Amenities:** Dining room; indoor pool; concierge; business center; conference rooms; room service; laundry service; dry cleaning. *In room:* A/C, coffeemaker, some hair dryers, safe, some fireplaces, some whirlpools.

Kendall Tavern Bed & Breakfast If you want to be out of the bustle of town but not too far from the shopping, this is a good choice. This handsome B&B is in a cheerful yellow farmhouse on 3½ acres at a bend in the road a half-mile north of the center of Freeport. The rooms are all plushly carpeted and comfortable. Everything is decorated in a bright and airy style, with framed prints of New England scenes and Victorian ladies on the walls and a mix of antique and new furniture. The rooms facing Route 1 (Main St.) are be a bit noisier than the others, but the traffic shouldn't be too disruptive.

213 Main St., Freeport, ME 04032. ✆ **800/341-9572** or 207/865-1338. Fax 207/865-3544. www.kendalltavern.com. 7 units. Peak season $120–$180 double; off-season and midweek discounts. Rates include full breakfast. AE, DISC, MC, V. **Amenities:** Hot tub.

Maine Idyll Motor Court *Value* The 1932 Maine Idyll Motor Court is a Maine classic—a cluster of 20 cottages scattered about a grove of beech and oak trees. Each has a tiny porch, a wood-burning fireplace (birch logs provided), a TV, modest kitchen facilities (no ovens), and timeworn furniture. The cabins are not lavishly sized, but are comfortable and spotlessly clean. The only interruption to an idyll here is the omnipresent sound of traffic: I-95 is just through the trees on one side, and Route 1 is on the other side. Get past the drone, and you'll find good value for your money.

1411 U.S. Rte. 1, Freeport, ME 04032. ✆ **207/865-4201.** www.maineidyll.com. 20 cottages. $55–$95 double; spring rates lower. Rates include continental breakfast. No credit cards (checks okay). Closed early Nov to late Apr. Pets on leash allowed. *In room:* Kitchenette, fireplace (some), no phone.

WHERE TO DINE

For a quick and simple meal, head down Mechanic Street (near the Mangy Moose, at 112 Main St.) to the **Corsican Restaurant** ★, 9 Mechanic St. (✆ **207/865-9421**), for a surprisingly healthful, 10-inch pizza, calzone, or king-size sandwich. The **Lobster Cooker,** 39 Main St. (✆ **207/865-4349**), serves daily seafood, sandwich, and chowder specials on an outdoor patio with views of the shopping hordes; go for salmon, lobster, or crab. Also nearby is **Morrison's Maine Chowder House,** 2 Mechanic St. (✆ **207/865-3404**), with counter seating for about a dozen. It serves somewhat pricey fish, lobster, and clam chowder in paper bowls with plastic spoons.

Harraseeket Lunch & Lobster ★ *Finds* LOBSTER At a boatyard on the Harraseeket River about a 10-minute drive from Freeport's main shopping district, this lobster pound is an especially popular destination on sunny days—although, with its heated dining room, it's a worthy destination anytime. Order a crustacean according to how hungry you are (1 lb. on up), and then take in the river view from the dock while waiting for your number to be called. Be prepared for big crowds.

Main St., South Freeport. ✆ **207/865-4888.** Lobsters market price (typically $8–$12). No credit cards. Daily 11:30am–8:30pm. Closed mid-Oct to May 1. From I-95, take Exit 17 and head north on Rte. 1; turn right on S. Freeport Rd. at the huge Indian statue; continue to stop sign in South Freeport; turn right to waterfront. From Freeport, take South St. (off Bow St.) to Main St. in South Freeport; turn left to waterfront.

Jameson Tavern ★ AMERICAN In a handsome historic farmhouse just north of L.L.Bean, the Jameson Tavern touts itself as the birthplace of Maine. In 1820, the papers were signed here legally separating Maine from Massachusetts. Today, it has dual restaurants under the same ownership. As you enter the door, you can head left to the historic Tap Room, a compact, often crowded spot filled with the smell of fresh popcorn. The other part of the house is the Dining Room, which is more formal in a country-Colonial sort of way. Meals here are sedate and gussied up, with an emphasis on steak and hearty fare. Entrees include filet mignon Oscar (with asparagus, crabmeat, and hollandaise), seafood fettuccini, and pan-blackened haddock.

115 Main St. ✆ **207/865-4196.** Reservations encouraged. Main courses tap room and lunch $6.95–$18, dining room dinner $13–$25. AE, DC, DISC, MC, V. Tap room daily 11am–11pm; dining room daily in summer 11am–10pm, winter 11:30am–9pm.

WISCASSET ★★ & THE BOOTHBAYS ★

Wiscasset is a lovely riverside town on Route 1, and it's not shy about letting you know: THE PRETTIEST VILLAGE IN MAINE boasts the sign at the edge of town and on many brochures. Whether or not you agree, the town *is* attractive (though the sluggish line of traffic snaking through diminishes the charm) and makes a good brief lunch stop en route to coastal destinations farther along.

The Boothbays, 11 miles south of Route 1 on Route 27, consist of several small and scenic villages—**East Boothbay, Boothbay Harbor,** and **Boothbay,** among them—that are closer than Wiscasset to the open ocean.

ESSENTIALS

GETTING THERE Wiscasset is on Route 1 midway between Bath and Damariscotta. Boothbay Harbor is south of Route 1 on Route 27. Coming from the west, look for signs shortly after crossing the Sheepscot River at Wiscasset.

VISITOR INFORMATION As befits a place where tourism is a major industry, the Boothbay region has three visitor information centers in and around town. At the intersection of Routes 1 and 27 is a center that's open May to October; it's a good place to stock up on brochures. A mile before you reach the village is the seasonal **Boothbay Information Center** on your right (open June–Oct). If you zoom past or it's closed, don't fret. The year-round **Boothbay Harbor Region Chamber of Commerce,** P.O. Box 356, Boothbay Harbor, ME 04538 (© **800/266-8422** or 207/633-2353; www.boothbayharbor.com), is at the intersection of Routes 27 and 96.

EXPLORING WISCASSET

Castle Tucker ★ This fascinating mansion at the edge of town overlooking the river was first built in 1807 and then radically added to and altered in a more ostentatious style in 1860. The home remains more or less in the same state as when reconfigured by cotton trader Capt. Richard Tucker; one of his descendants, Jane Tucker, still lives on the top floor. Tours of the lower floor are offered by the Society of New England Antiquities, which was given the house by Ms. Tucker in 1997. The detailing is exceptional and offers insight into the life of an affluent sea captain in the late 19th century. Be sure to note the extraordinary elliptical staircase and the painted plaster trim (it's not oak).

Lee and High sts. © **207/882-7169.** Admission $5. Tours leave on the hour 11am–4pm Fri–Sun. Open June to mid-Oct only.

EXPLORING THE BOOTHBAY REGION

The best way to see the timeless Maine coast around Boothbay is on a boat tour. Nearly two dozen tour boats berth at the harbor or nearby. **Balmy Days Cruises** (© **800/298-2284** or 207/633-2284; www.balmydayscruises.com) runs several trips from the harbor, as many as five daily in summer. If you'd rather be sailing, ask about the 90-minute cruises on the *Bay Lady,* a 15-passenger Friendship sloop ($18). It's a good idea to call ahead for reservations.

Coastal Maine Botanical Garden This 128-acre waterside garden is relatively new and a work in progress, but it's already worth exploring. It's not a fancy, formal garden like you'll find elsewhere in Maine, but rather a natural habitat that's being gently coaxed into a more mannered state. Those overseeing this nonprofit organization have blazed several short trails through the mossy forest, good for a half-hour's worth of exploring, cutting through terrain that's delightfully quiet and lush. One trail follows along much of the 3,600 feet of tidal shoreline that's part of the property.

Barters Island Rd., Boothbay (near Hogdon Island). ✆ **207/633-4333.** www.mainegardens.org. Free admission. Mon–Fri 8:30am–4:30pm; Sat–Sun 9am–6pm. From Rte. 27 in Boothbay Center, bear right at the monument at the stop sign, and then make the first right on Barters Island Rd.; drive 1 mile and look for the stone gate on your left.

Marine Resources Aquarium Operated by the state's Department of Marine Resources, this compact aquarium provides a context for life in the sea around Boothbay and beyond. You can view rare albino and blue lobsters and get your hands wet at a 20-foot touch tank—a sort of petting zoo of the slippery and slimy. Parking is tight at the aquarium, which is on a point across the water from Boothbay Harbor, so visitors are urged to use the free shuttle bus (look for the Rocktide trolley) that connects to downtown and runs frequently in summer.

McKown Point Rd., West Boothbay Harbor. ✆ **207/633-9542.** Admission $5 adults, $3 children 5–18 and seniors. Daily 10am–5pm. Closed Oct to Memorial Day.

WHERE TO STAY

Five Gables Inn ★ The handsome Five Gables Inn was painstakingly restored in the late 1980s and now sits proudly amid a small colony of summer homes on a quiet road above a peaceful cove. It's nicely isolated from the confusion and hubbub of Boothbay Harbor. The rooms are pleasantly appointed, and five have fireplaces that burn manufactured logs; some also sport four-poster beds. Room no. 8 is a corner room with brilliant morning light; room no. 14 is the most requested, with a great view and a fireplace with a marble mantle. (Some of the first-floor rooms open onto a common deck and lack privacy.) The breakfast buffet is sumptuous.

Murray Hill Rd. (P.O. Box 335), East Boothbay, ME 04544. ✆ **800/451-5048** or 207/633-4551. www.fivegablesinn.com. 15 units. $140–$210 double. Rates include breakfast buffet. MC, V. Closed Nov to mid-May. Drive through East Boothbay on Rte. 96; turn right after crest of hill on Murray Hill Rd. Children 12 and older are welcome. *In room:* Fireplace (some).

The Inn at Lobsterman's Wharf *Value* This is my budget pick for the region. A clean, comfortable, no-frills place adjacent to a working boatyard, this nine-room inn was originally a coal depot and later a boardinghouse. It still has a little boardinghouse informality to it (although all rooms now have small private bathrooms), but you get a lot for your money. The innkeeper invited locals to decorate each of the rooms to reflect local history, giving them a unique, homespun flair. Seven face the water. Hodgon Suites is the largest, located under the eaves with a view of the Hodgon Yacht boatyard.

Rte. 96, East Boothbay. ✆ **207/633-5481.** 9 units. $75–$95 double. Rates include continental breakfast. MC, V. Closed in winter. Pets allowed in 2 rooms. *In room:* TV.

Lawnmeer Inn & Restaurant The Lawnmeer, a short hop from Boothbay on the northern shore of Southport Island (accessed via a bridge) has a restful environment. This was originally built as a guesthouse in the late 19th century, and the main inn has been updated with some loss of charm. More than half of the guest rooms are in a motel-like annex, with private balconies and views of the placid waterway that separates Southport Island from the mainland. Regional and global cuisine is served in a comfortable, homey dining room with windows overlooking the waterway. The inn serves some of the most consistently reliable food in a town that has come to expect high restaurant turnover. Look for contemporary fare, with entrees like grilled venison with a cranberry chutney and poached salmon with dill hollandaise sauce. Reservations are recommended.

Rte. 27 (P.O. Box 29), Southport, ME 04576. ✆ **800/633-7645** or 207/633-2544. www.lawnmeerinn.com. 32 units. Summer $100–$230 double; spring and fall $90–$210 double. 2-night minimum on holiday weekends. MC, V. Closed mid-Oct to mid-May. Pets accepted on limited basis; $10 extra per pet. **Amenities:** Dining room. *In room:* A/C (some).

Newagen Seaside Inn ★ This 1940s-era resort has seen more glamorous days, but it's still a superb small, low-key resort with stunning ocean views and a fragrant spruce forest for walks. The inn is housed in a low, wide, white-shingled building and has simple country pine furniture, a classically austere dining room, narrow cruise ship–like hallways with pine wainscoting, and a lobby with a fireplace. Rooms have polished wood floors and simple Amish-style quilts; country-themed decorations adorn the walls. The 85-acre grounds are filled with decks, gazebos, and walkways that border on the magical. The magnificent ocean views are some of the best of any Maine inn.

Rte. 27 (P.O. Box 29), Newagen, ME 04576. ✆ **800/654-5242** or 207/633-5242. www.newagenseasideinn.com. 30 units, 3 cottages. $110–$250 double, including full breakfast; cottages $1,500 weekly. Ask about off-season discounts. AE, MC, V. Closed mid-Oct to mid-May. Located on south tip of Southport Island. Take Rte. 27 from Boothbay Harbor and continue on until the inn sign. **Amenities:** Dining room; freshwater and saltwater pools; tennis courts; badminton; horseshoes; free rowboats; bikes.

Spruce Point Inn ★ The Spruce Point Inn was originally built as a hunting and fishing lodge in the 1890s, and it evolved into a summer resort in 1912. Those looking for historic authenticity could be disappointed. Those seeking modern resort facilities (Jacuzzis, carpeting, updated furniture) along with accenting to provide a bit of historical flavor will be delighted. Anyway, it's hard to imagine being let down by the scenic 15-acre grounds, situated on a rocky point facing west across the harbor. Although more of a couples' place, children's programs accommodate a growing number of families who vacation here. Also laudable is the recent addition of a spa facility.

Atlantic Ave. (P.O. Box 237), Boothbay Harbor, ME 04538. ✆ **800/553-0289** or 207/633-4152. www.sprucepointinn.com. 93 units. July–Aug $165–$355 double, spring and fall $135–$250 double; cottages and condos $250–$550. 3–6 night minimum stay summer, weekends, and holidays. AE, DC, DISC, MC, V. Closed mid-Oct to Memorial Day. Turn seaward on Union St. in Boothbay Harbor; proceed 2 miles to the inn. Pets not allowed. **Amenities:** Dining room; 2 outdoor pools; 2 tennis courts; fitness center; spa; Jacuzzi; lawn games (shuffleboard, tetherball, and so on); game room; concierge; conference rooms; massage; babysitting; laundry service; dry cleaning. *In room:* Kitchenette (some), fridge, coffeemaker, iron/ironing board, safe, Jacuzzi (some).

Topside The old gray house on the hilltop looming over the dated motel buildings may bring to mind the Bates Motel, especially when a full moon is overhead. But forget about that. Topside has spectacular ocean views at a reasonable price from a quiet hilltop compound right in downtown Boothbay. The inn itself—a former boardinghouse for shipyard workers—has several comfortable rooms, furnished with a somewhat discomfiting mix of antiques and contemporary furniture. At the edge of the inn's lawn are two outbuildings with basic motel units. These are on the small side, furnished simply with dated paneling and furniture. Room nos. 9 and 14 have the best views, but most rooms allow a glimpse of the water and many have decks or patios.

60 McKown Hill, Boothbay Harbor, ME 04538. ✆ **877/486-7466** or 207/633-5404. Fax 207/633-2206. http://home.gwi.net/topside. 21 units. $100–$165 double. Rates include continental breakfast. DISC, MC, V. Closed late Nov to Apr. *In room:* Patio (some).

WHERE TO DINE

In Wiscasset

Red's Eats TAKEOUT Red's is an innocuous roadside stand smack in downtown Wiscasset that's probably received more than its fair share of media ink about its famous lobster rolls. (They often crop up in "Best of Maine" surveys.) They *are* good, consisting of moist and plentiful chunks of chilled lobster placed in a roll served with a little mayo on the side. Be aware that they're on the pricey end of the scale—you can find less expensive (although less meaty) versions elsewhere.

Water St. (Rte. 1 just before the bridge). © **207/882-6128.** Sandwiches $2–$5.25; lobster rolls typically $13–$14. No credit cards. Mon–Thurs 11am–11pm; Fri–Sat 11am–2am; Sun noon–6pm. Closed Oct–Apr.

Sarah's Café SANDWICHES/TRADITIONAL Sarah's is a hometown favorite. Expect personable service and filling, well-prepared (if unremarkable) food. It's usually crowded for lunch, with items such as pita pockets, croissant sandwiches, and a local favorite called a whaleboat. The lobsters are fresh, hauled daily by Sarah's brother and father. This is my choice for an informal lunch break when motoring up Route 1—at least when I don't feel like splurging on a lobster roll at Red's.

Water St. and Rte. 1 (across from Red's). © **207/882-7504.** Sandwiches $5–$6.25; pizzas $4.95–$17. AE, DISC, MC, V. Daily 11am–8pm (until 9pm Fri–Sat).

In the Boothbays

When wandering through Boothbay Harbor, watch for "King" Brud and his famous hot-dog cart. Brud started selling hot dogs in town in 1943, and he's still at it. He's usually at the corner of McKown and Commercial streets from 10am until 4pm from June to October.

More innovative dining can be found in the dining rooms at Spruce Point Inn and Lawnmeer Inn, listed in "Where to Stay," above.

Boothbay Region Lobstermen's Co-op SEAFOOD WE ARE NOT RESPONSIBLE IF THE SEAGULLS STEAL YOUR FOOD reads the sign at the ordering window of this casual, harborside lobster joint, and that sets the tone pretty well. Across the harbor from downtown Boothbay, the lobstermen's co-op offers no-frills lobster and seafood. This is the best pick from among the cluster of usually dependable lobster-in-the-rough places that line the waterfront nearby. Lobsters are priced to market (figure $8–$12), with extras like onion rings ($2.10) or coleslaw ($1). This is a fine place for a lobster on a sunny day, but it's uninteresting in rain or fog.

Atlantic Ave., Boothbay Harbor. © **207/633-4900.** Reservations not accepted. Fried and grilled foods $2–$10; dinners $7–$15. DISC, MC, V. May to mid-Oct daily 11:30am–8:30pm. By foot: Cross footbridge and turn right; follow road for ⅓ mile to co-op.

Lobsterman's Wharf SEAFOOD On the water in East Boothbay, the Lobsterman's Wharf has the comfortable, pubby feel of a popular neighborhood bar, complete with a pool table. But it's that rarest of pubs—a place that's popular with the locals, but also serves up a decent meal and knows how to make travelers feel at home. Entrees include a mixed-seafood grill, a barbecue shrimp and ribs platter, grilled swordfish with béarnaise, and succulent fresh lobster served four different ways. At lunch, there's hamburger, baked haddock, lobster rolls, and steamed lobster.

Rte. 96, East Boothbay. © **207/633-3443.** Reservations accepted for parties of 6 or more only. Lunch $5–$14; dinner $14–$25 (mostly $14–$16). AE, MC, V. Apr–Oct daily 11:30am–10pm. Closed Nov–Mar.

PEMAQUID PENINSULA ★★★

Pemaquid Peninsula is an irregular, rocky wedge driven deep into the Gulf of Maine. Far less commercial than Boothbay Peninsula across the Damariscotta River, it's more inviting for casual exploration. Rugged and rocky Pemaquid Point, at the extreme southern tip of the peninsula, is one of the most dramatic destinations in Maine when the ocean surf pounds the shore.

ESSENTIALS

GETTING THERE The Pemaquid Peninsula is accessible from the west by turning southward on Route 129/130 in Damariscotta, just off Route 1. From the east, head south on Route 32 just west of Waldoboro.

VISITOR INFORMATION The **Damariscotta Region Chamber of Commerce,** P.O. Box 13, Main Street, Damariscotta, ME 04543 (© **207/563-8340**), is a good source of local information and maintains a seasonal information booth on Route 1 during the summer months. To get there, follow Route 27 south, leaving Route 1 just east (across the bridge) after Wiscasset.

EXPLORING THE PEMAQUID PENINSULA

The Pemaquid Peninsula invites slow driving and frequent stops. South on Route 129 toward Walpole is Damariscotta, a sleepy head-of-the-harbor village. On the left is the austerely handsome Walpole Meeting House, dating from 1772. Services are held here during the summer to which the public is welcome.

Just north of the unassuming fishing town of South Bristol on Route 129, watch for the **Thompson Ice Harvesting Museum** ★ (© **207/644-8551**). The grounds are open during daylight hours year-round; the museum exhibits are open 1 to 4pm Wednesday, Friday, and Saturday only, and only in July and August. A $1 donation (50¢ for children) is requested.

Continue on Route 129 and arrive at picturesque **Christmas Cove,** so named because Capt. John Smith (of Pocahontas fame) anchored here on Christmas Day in 1614. While wandering about, look for the rustic **Coveside Bar and Restaurant** (© **207/644-8282**), a popular marina with a pennant-bedecked lounge and basic dining room open from mid-June to mid-September.

About 5 miles north of South Bristol, turn right on Pemaquid Road, which will take you to Route 130. Along the way, look for the **Harrington Meeting House** (the other 1772 structure), open to the public on occasional afternoons in July and August. It's an architectural gem inside, almost painfully austere, with a small museum of local artifacts on the second floor. Head south on Route 130 to the village of New Harbor and look for signs to **Colonial Pemaquid** (© **207/677-2423**). Open daily from Memorial Day to Labor Day, 9am to 5pm, this state historic site has exhibits on the original 1625 settlement here; archaeological digs take place in the summer.

Pemaquid Point ★★★, which is owned by the town of Bristol, is the place to while away an afternoon (© **207/677-2494**). Bring a picnic and a book, and find a spot on the dark, fractured rocks to settle in. The ocean views are superb, and the only distractions are the tenacious seagulls that might take a profound interest in your lunch. While here, be sure to visit the **Fishermen's Museum** ★ (© **207/677-2494**) in the handsome lighthouse (open daily 9am–5pm). There's a small fee to enter the park; admission to the museum is by donation.

WHERE TO STAY

Bradley Inn ★ The Bradley Inn is within easy hiking or biking distance to the point, but there are plenty of reasons to lag behind at the inn. Start by wandering the nicely landscaped grounds or settle in for a game of Scrabble at the pub. The rooms are tastefully appointed; only the carriage house has a television. The third-floor rooms are the best, despite the climb, thanks to distant glimpses of John's Bay.

The inn is popular for summer weekend weddings, so ask in advance if you're seeking solitude.

Rte. 130, 3063 Bristol Rd., New Harbor, ME 04554. © **800/942-5560** or 207/677-2105. Fax 207/677-3367. www.bradleyinn.com. 15 units, 1 cottage. Late May to Oct $155–$235 double, $250–$275 suite; Apr to late May $145–$195 double, $225 suite. Rates include full breakfast. AE, MC, V. Closed Nov–Mar. **Amenities:** Restaurant; pub; access to nearby beach; free use of bikes; room service (7am–10pm).

WHERE TO DINE

Shaw's Fish and Lobster Wharf ★ LOBSTER Shaw's attracts hordes of tourists, and it's no trick to figure out why: It's one of Maine's best-situated lobster pounds, with postcard-perfect views of the working harbor. You can stake out a seat on either the open deck or the indoor dining room (go for the deck), or order up some appetizers from the raw bar. This is one of the few lobster joints in Maine with a full liquor license.

On the water, New Harbor. © **207/677-2200.** Lobster priced to market (typically $7 per pound). MC, V. Mid-May to mid-Oct daily 11am–8pm (until 9pm July–Aug). Closed mid-Oct to mid-May.

MONHEGAN ISLAND ★★★

Monhegan Island is Maine's premier island destination. Visited by Europeans as early as 1497, the wild, remote island was settled by fishermen attracted to the sea's bounty in offshore waters. In the 1870s, artists discovered the island and stayed for a spell, including Rockwell Kent (the artist most closely associated with the island), George Bellows, Edward Hopper, and Robert Henri. Jamie Wyeth, scion of the Wyeth clan, claims the island as his part-time home.

It's not hard to figure out why artists have been attracted to the place, with its mystical quality and remarkable sense of tranquillity. In addition, it's a superb destination for hikers, as most of the island is undeveloped and laced with trails.

Be aware—there are no ATMs, few pay phones, and even electricity is scarce. An overnight at one of the several hostelries is strongly recommended. Day trips are easily arranged, but the island's true character doesn't emerge until the last day boat sails away and the rustic appeal of the place percolates to the surface.

ESSENTIALS

GETTING THERE Access to Monhegan Island is via boat from New Harbor, Boothbay Harbor, or Port Clyde. The picturesque trip from Port Clyde is the favored route of longtime island visitors; the boat passes the Marshall Point Lighthouse and goes by a series of spruce-clad islands before reaching open sea.

Two boats make the run to Monhegan from Port Clyde. The *Laura B* is a doughty workboat (building supplies and boxes of food are loaded on first; passengers fill in the available niches on the deck and in the small cabin). A newer boat—the faster (50-min.), passenger-oriented *Elizabeth Ann*—also makes the run, offering a large heated cabin and more seating. You'll need to leave your car behind. The fare is $27 round-trip for adults, $14 for children ages 2 to 12, and $2 for pets. Reservations are advised: **Monhegan Boat Line,** P.O. Box 238, Port Clyde, ME 04855 (© **207/372-8848;** www.monheganboat.com). Parking is available near the dock for an additional $4 per day. After mid-October, there's only one trip per day to Monhegan.

VISITOR INFORMATION Monhegan Island has no formal visitor center, but it's small and friendly enough that you can make inquiries of just about anyone you meet on the island pathways. The clerks at the ferry dock in Port Clyde are also quite helpful. Be sure to pick up the inexpensive map of the island's hiking trail at the boat ticket office or at the various shops around the island. An informal website maintained by island resident Clare Durst gives helpful information to first-time visitors: **www.briegull.com/monhegan**.

EXPLORING MONHEGAN

Walking is the chief activity on the island; it's genuinely surprising how much distance you can cover on these 700 acres (about 1½ miles long and ½ mile wide). The village clusters tightly around the harbor; the rest of the island is mostly wildland, laced with 17 miles of **trails** ★★★. Much of the island is ringed with high, open bluffs atop fissured cliffs.

The inland trails are appealing in a far different way. Deep, dark **Cathedral Woods** ★★ is mossy and fragrant; sunlight only dimly filters through the evergreens to the forest floor.

Birding is a popular spring and fall activity. The island is on the Atlantic flyway, and a wide variety of birds stop at the island along their migration routes.

The sole formal attraction on the island is the **Monhegan Museum** ★ (www.monheganmuseum.org), next to the 1824 lighthouse on a point above the village. The museum, open for a few hours in the middle of each day, from July through September, has a quirky collection of historical artifacts and provides some context for this rugged island's history. Also near the lighthouse is a small and select art museum displaying the works of Rockwell Kent and other island artists.

WHERE TO STAY & DINE

Things have changed, a little, since the days when you had zero options for sleeping or dining. In a pinch, you can also hit the **North End Market** (✆ **207/594-5546**).

Monhegan House The handsome Monhegan House has been accommodating guests since 1870, and it has the comfortable, worn patina of a venerable lodging house. The accommodations at this four-floor walk-up are austere, but comfortable, more so after renovations; there are no closets, and everyone uses clean dormitory-style bathrooms. The downstairs lobby with fireplace is a welcome spot to sit and take the fog-induced chill out of your bones (even in Aug, it can be cool here). The restaurant serves three meals a day.

Across from church, Monhegan Island, ME 04852. ✆ **207/594-7983.** www.monheganhouse.com. 33 units, all with shared bathroom. Peak season $119–$225 double; off season $99 double. MC, V. Closed Columbus Day to Memorial Day. **Amenities:** Dining room. *In room:* No phone.

Trailing Yew At the end of long summer afternoons, guests congregate near the flagpole in front of the main building of this rustic hillside compound. They're waiting for the ringing of the bell that signals the start of the included-with-the-price dinner, just like at summer camp. Inside, guests sit around long tables, introduce themselves to their neighbors, and then pour an iced tea and wait for the delicious family-style repast. This is a friendly, informal place that's popular with hikers and birders. Guest rooms are eclectic and simply furnished in a pleasantly dated, summer-home style. Only one of the four guest buildings has electricity; guests in rooms without electricity are provided a kerosene lamp and instruction in its use. Most, but not all, bathrooms have electricity. Rooms are unheated.

Lobster Cove Rd., Monhegan Island, ME 04852. ✆ **800/592-2520** or 207/596-0440. 37 units in 4 buildings, all but 1 share bathrooms. May–June and Sept–Oct $99 double; July–Aug $123–$134 double. Rates include breakfast, dinner, taxes, and tips. No credit cards. Closed mid-Oct to mid-May. Pets allowed. **Amenities:** Dining room. *In room:* No phone.

4 Penobscot Bay

Camden 230 miles NE of Boston; 8 miles N of Rockland; 18 miles S of Belfast.

When traveling east along the Maine coast, those who pay attention to such things will notice they're suddenly heading almost due north around Rockland. The culprit behind this geographic quirk is Penobscot Bay, a sizable bite out of the Maine coast that forces a lengthy northerly detour to cross the head of the bay where the Penobscot River flows in at Bucksport. You'll find some of Maine's most distinctive coastal scenery in this region, which is dotted with broad offshore islands and high hills rising above the mainland shores. Though the mouth of Penobscot Bay is occupied by two large islands, its waters can still churn with vigor when the tides and winds conspire.

ROCKLAND & ENVIRONS

On the southwest edge of Penobscot Bay, Rockland has long been proud of its brick-and-blue-collar waterfront reputation. Built around the fishing industry, Rockland historically dabbled in tourism on the side, but with the decline of fisheries and the rise of Maine's tourist economy, the balance has shifted. In the last decade, Rockland has been colonized by creative restaurateurs, innkeepers, and other small-business folks who paint it with an unaccustomed gloss.

ESSENTIALS

GETTING THERE Route 1 passes directly through Rockland. Rockland's tiny airport is served by **Colgan Air** (© **800/428-4322**) with daily flights from Boston and Bar Harbor. **Concord Trailways** (© **800/639-3317**) has bus service from Rockland to Bangor and Portland.

VISITOR INFORMATION The **Rockland/Thomaston Area Chamber of Commerce,** P.O. Box 508, Rockland, ME 04841 (© **800/562-2529** or 207/596-0376; www.therealmaine.com), staffs an information desk at Harbor Park. It's open daily 9am to 5pm Memorial Day to Labor Day, and on weekdays the rest of the year.

SPECIAL EVENTS The **Maine Lobster Festival** (© **800/LOB-CLAW** or 207/596-0376) takes place at Harbor Park the first weekend in August (plus the preceding Thurs–Fri). Entertainers and vendors of all sorts of Maine products—especially the local crustacean—fill the waterfront parking lot and attract thousands of festivalgoers who enjoy this pleasant event with a sort of buttery bonhomie. The event includes the Maine Sea Goddess Coronation Pageant. Admission is $7 to $10 per day; food, of course, costs extra.

MUSEUMS

Farnsworth Museum ★★★ Rockland, for all its rough edges, has long and historic ties to the arts. Noted sculptor Louise Nevelson grew up in Rockland, and in 1935, philanthropist Lucy Farnsworth bequeathed a fortune large enough to establish the Farnsworth Museum, which has since become one of the most respected art museums in New England. In the middle of downtown, the Farnsworth has a superb collection of paintings and sculptures by renowned American artists with a connection to Maine. This includes not only Nevelson and three generations of Wyeths (N. C., Andrew, and Jamie), but also Rockwell Kent, Childe Hassam, and Maurice Prendergast. The exhibit halls are modern, spacious, and well designed, and the shows are professionally prepared. In 1998, the museum expanded with the opening of the **Farnsworth Center for the Wyeth Family,** housed in the former Pratt Memorial Methodist Church.

The Farnsworth also owns two other buildings open to the public. The **Farnsworth Homestead,** behind the museum, offers a glimpse into the life of prosperous coastal Victorians. Just a 25-minute drive away, in the village of Cushing, is the **Olson House,** perhaps Maine's most famous home, immortalized in Andrew Wyeth's noted painting *Christina's World.*

356 Main St., Rockland. ✆ **207/596-6457.** www.farnsworthmuseum.org. $10 adults, $8 seniors and students 18 and older, free for 17 and under. MC, V. Memorial Day to Columbus Day daily 10am–5pm; off season, closed Mon.

Owls Head Transportation Museum ★ *Finds* You don't have to be a car or plane buff to enjoy a day at this museum, 3 miles south of Rockland on Route 73. Founded in 1974, the museum has an extraordinary collection of cars, motorcycles, bicycles, and planes, nicely displayed in a tidy, hangarlike building at the edge of the Knox County Airport. Look for the beautiful early Harley Davidson and the sleek Rolls-Royce Phantom dating from 1929.

Rte. 73, Owls Head. ✆ **207/594-4418.** www.ohtm.org. $7 adults and children 12–17, $6 seniors, $5 children 5–12, $18 families. Apr–Oct daily 10am–5pm; Nov–Mar daily 10am–4pm.

WHERE TO STAY

Capt. Lindsey House Inn ★ The three-story, brick Capt. Lindsey House is just a couple minutes' walk from the Farnsworth Museum. It was originally erected as a hotel in 1835, but it's gone through several incarnations, including one as headquarters of the Rockland Water Co. (The inn's front desk is where folks once paid their water bills.) Guests enter through a doorway a few steps off Rockland's Main Street into an opulent first-floor common area done up in rich tones, handsome dark-wood paneling, and a well-selected mix of antique and contemporary furniture. The upstairs rooms are also tastefully decorated in a contemporary country style. Even the smaller rooms like no. 4 are well done (this in a sort of steamship nouveau style); the rooms on the third floor all have yellow pine floors and antique Oriental carpets. All but two rooms have showers only, and a few rooms have twin beds.

5 Lindsey St., Rockland, ME 04841. ✆ **800/523-2145** or 207/596-7950. Fax 207/596-2758. www.lindseyhouse.com. 9 units. Peak season $99–$190 double. Rates include continental breakfast. AE, DISC, MC, V. *In room:* A/C, hair dryer, robe.

East Wind Inn ★ The inn itself, formerly a sail loft, is perfectly situated next to the harbor with water views from all rooms and the long porch. It's a classic seaside hostelry with busy wallpaper, simple Colonial reproduction furniture, and tidy rooms. (The 10 guest rooms across the way at a former sea captain's house have most of the private bathrooms.) The atmosphere is relaxed almost to the point of ennui, and the service is good.

P.O. Box 149, Tenants Harbor, ME 04860. ✆ **800/241-8439** or 207/372-6366. Fax 207/372-6320. www.eastwindinn.com. 26 units, 7 with shared bathroom. $89–$109 double (shared bathroom), $119–$159 double (private bathroom); $149–$189 suite; $169–$299 apartment and cottage. Dec–May, open only by prior arrangement. Rates include full breakfast. 2-night minimum on suites and apts. AE, DISC, MC, V. Drive south on Rte. 131 from Thomaston to Tenants Harbor; turn left at post office. $15 extra for pets (by reservation). **Amenities:** Dining room.

LimeRock Inn ★★ This beautiful Queen Anne–style inn is on a quiet side street just 2 blocks from Rockland's Main Street. The innkeepers have done a commendable job converting what could be a gloomy manse into one of the region's better choices for overnight accommodations. Attention has been paid to detail throughout, from the choice of country Victorian furniture to the Egyptian cotton bed sheets. All the guest rooms are welcoming, but among the best choices is the Island Cottage Room, a bright and airy chamber wonderfully converted from an old shed, with a private

Penobscot Bay

deck and Jacuzzi; the Turret Room, with French doors into the bathroom, which has a claw-foot tub and a separate shower; and the elegant Grand Manan Room, with a large four-poster bed, fireplace, and double Jacuzzi.

96 Limerock St., Rockland, ME 04841. ✆ **800/546-3762** or 207/594-2257. www.limerockinn.com. 8 units. $110–$215 double. Rates include breakfast. DISC, MC, V. *In room:* Jacuzzi (some).

WHERE TO DINE

Cafe Miranda ★★ *Finds* WORLD CUISINE Hidden away on a side street, this tiny contemporary restaurant has a huge menu with big flavors and a welcoming, hip attitude. The fare draws liberally from cuisines around the globe and given its wide-ranging culinary aspirations, it's surprising just how well prepared everything is. The chargrilled pork and shrimp cakes served with a ginger-lime-coconut sauce are superb. Other creative entrees are pork ribs with smoked jalapeño sauce, Indian almond chicken, and Ducks of Spanish Pleasure (a sort of duck curry). Or just go for some of the many small plates, dishes like gazpacho, roasted corn with pickled banana peppers, grilled rare beef with wasabi, or fried oysters with buttermilk sherry vinegar. All things considered, I'd say that Cafe Miranda provides the best value—and opportunity for gustatory exploration—per your buck of any restaurant in Maine. Wash it down with beer or wine.

15 Oak St., Rockland. ✆ **207/594-2034**. www.cafemiranda.com. Reservations strongly encouraged. Small plates $5–$11; main courses $12–$22. DISC, MC, V. Daily 5:30–9:30pm (until 8:30pm in winter).

Cod End Cookhouse *Finds* LOBSTER POUND Part of the allure of Cod End is its hidden, scenic location—it seems as though you've stumbled upon a secret. Situated between the Town Landing and the East Wind Inn, Cod End is a classic lobster joint with fine views of tranquil Tenants Harbor. You walk through the fish market (where you can buy fish or lobster to go, along with various lobster-related souvenirs) and then place your order at the outdoor shack. Lobsters are the draw here, naturally, but there's plenty else to choose from, including chowders, stews, linguini with seafood, rolls (like the clam or haddock rolls), and simple sandwiches for younger tastes (even peanut butter and jelly).

Next to the Town Dock, Tenants Harbor. ✆ **207/372-6782.** www.codend.com. Lunch entrees $2.50–$8; dinner $7.95–$14. DISC, MC, V. July–Aug daily 11am–8:30pm; limited hours June and Sept–Oct. Closed Nov–May.

Market on Main ★ *Kids* CONTEMPORARY DELI Run by the folks at Cafe Miranda (see above), this lively and hip spot is a great choice for a midday break or easy dinner if you're driving up the coast or spending the day at the Farnsworth Art Museum down the block. Half-deli, half-restaurant, it's casual, with brick walls, exposed heating ducts, and galvanized steel tabletops. Selections range from sandwiches (including choices such as baked eggplant) to burgers to seafood, as well as salads and a children's menu.

315 Main St. ✆ **207/594-0015.** Main courses $5.50–$14. DISC, MC, V. Mon–Thurs 11am–7pm; Fri–Sat 11am–8pm; Sun 10am–3pm.

Primo ★★★ MEDITERRANEAN/NEW AMERICAN Primo, owned by executive chef Melissa Kelly and pastry chef Price Kushner, occupies two deftly decorated floors of a century-old home a short drive south of downtown Rockland (no views to speak of). Kelly graduated first in her class at the Culinary Institute of America and won the 1999 James Beard Foundation award for "best chef in the Northeast." The menu reflects the seasons and draws from local products wherever available. I like to start with an appetizer such as foie gras or wood oven-roasted Raspberry Point oysters with creamy leeks, tomato, bacon, and tarragon. For the main course, you can choose from one of the inventive daily pastas—ricotta Cavatelli with Italian sausage, kale, and eggplant in a tomato sauce, or spaghetti tossed with baby calamari, chiles, and roasted tomatoes in an almond pesto. Alternatively, try pepper-crusted venison with a rosemary spaetzle, grilled muscovy duck, or one of the great wood-fired pizzas with matzoh-thin crusts. Finish with one of Kushner's fabulous desserts. The wine list is also outstanding.

2 S. Main St. (Rte. 173), Rockland. ✆ **207/596-0770.** www.primorestaurant.com. Reservations strongly suggested. Main courses $16–$30. AE, DC, DISC, MC, V. Summer daily 5:30–9pm; off season Thurs–Sun 5:30–9pm.

CAMDEN ★★

A quintessential coastal Maine village at the foot of wooded Camden Hills on a picturesque harbor, the affluent village of Camden has attracted the gentry of the Eastern Seaboard for more than a century. The mansions of the moneyed set still dominate the shady side streets (many are now bed-and-breakfasts), and Camden is possessed of a grace and sophistication that eludes many other coastal towns. Don't miss the hidden town park (look behind the library), designed by the landscape firm of Frederick Law Olmsted, the nation's most lauded landscape architect.

ESSENTIALS

GETTING THERE Camden is on Route 1, and from the south, you can shave a few minutes off your trip by turning left onto Route 90, 6 miles past Waldoboro,

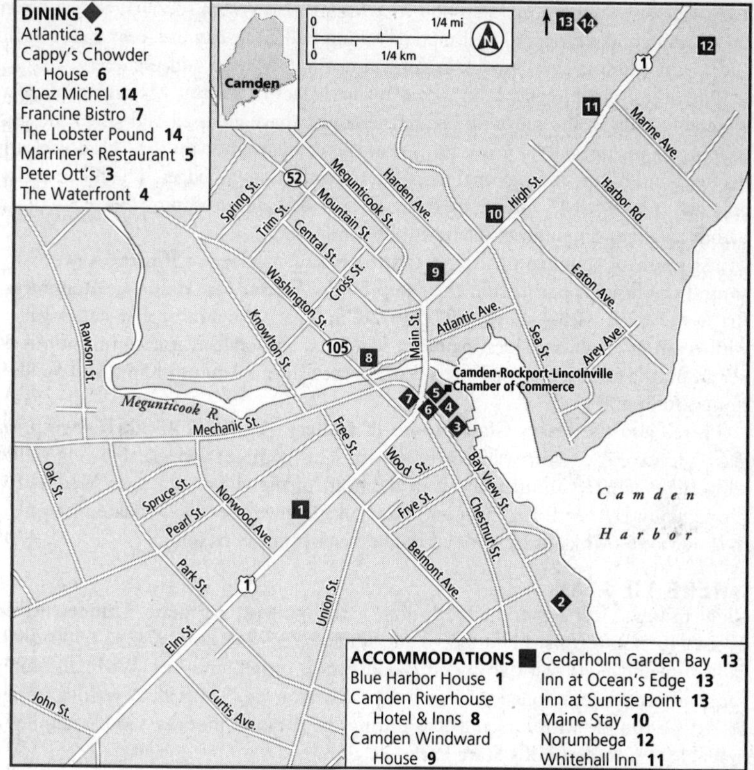

bypassing Rockland. The best traffic-free route from southern Maine is to Augusta via the Maine Turnpike, then via Route 17 to Route 90 to Route 1.

Concord Trailways (© **800/639-3317**) has bus service from Camden to Bangor and Portland.

During the fall, use the new **Maine Eastern Railroad** (© **866-MERAILS;** www.maineeasternrailroad.com) excursion train to see foliage between the towns of Brunswick and Rockland from mid-September through mid-November. Round-trip fares run about $55 per adult, half price for children ages 5 to 12. The line also operates a limited Santa train service in December at a lower cost.

VISITOR INFORMATION The **Camden-Rockport-Lincolnville Chamber of Commerce,** P.O. Box 919, Camden, ME 04843 (© **800/223-5459** or 207/236-4404; www.camdenme.org), dispenses helpful information from its center at the Public Landing in Camden, which also has free parking (although spaces are scarce in summer). The chamber is open year-round weekdays from 9am to 5pm, and Saturdays 10am to 5pm. In summer, it's also open Sundays 10am to 4pm.

EXPLORING CAMDEN

Camden Hills State Park ★★ (© **207/236-3109**) is about a mile north of the village center on Route 1. This 6,500-acre park has an oceanside picnic area, camping at

107 sites, a winding toll road up 800-foot Mount Battie with spectacular views from the summit, and a variety of well-marked hiking trails. The day-use fee is $3 for adults and $1 for children ages 5 to 11. It's open from mid-May to mid-October.

One hike I recommend is an ascent to the ledges of **Mount Megunticook** ★★, preferably early in the morning before the crowds have amassed and when the mist still lingers in the valleys. Leave from near the campground (the trail head is clearly marked) and follow the well-maintained trail to these open ledges. The hike requires only about a 30- to 45-minute exertion. Spectacular, almost improbable views of the harbor await, as do glimpses inland to the gentle vales.

Just south of Camden on Route 1 is the pleasant village of **Rockport** ★. Snoop around the historic harbor and then stop by the **Center for Maine Contemporary Art** ★★, 162 Russell Ave. (✆ **207/236-2875;** www.artsmaine.org), a stately gallery with rotating exhibits of local painters, sculptors, and craftspeople. Admission is $5 per adult; the gallery is open Tuesday to Saturday from 10am until 5pm and Sundays from 1 to 5pm.

There's also the **Prism Glass Studio & Gallery** (✆ **207/230-0061;** www.prism glassgallery.com) to visit while in Rockport. This combination glassblowing gallery and cafe is at 297 Commercial St. in the heart of the village; it's open Wednesdays through Sundays. Patti Kissinger and Lisa Sojka opened the 6,500-square-foot gallery to showcase blown glass by some of the best artists in the country.

WHERE TO STAY

Right in town, just across the footbridge, is the modern, if generic, **Camden Riverhouse Hotel and Inns,** 11 Tannery Lane (✆ **800/755-7483** or 207/236-0500; www.camdenmaine.com), with an indoor pool, fitness center, and new Wi-Fi and high-speed Internet access (open year-round; peak season $179–$219). A warning: High Street is a-rumble with cars and RVs during the summer months. Good camping is available at **Camden Hills State Park** (see above).

Blue Harbor House ★ On busy Route 1 just south of town, this pale-blue 1810 farmhouse has been an inn since 1978, decorated throughout with a sprightly country look. Guest rooms vary in size; some are rather small and noisy (earplugs and white-noise machines are in some rooms). Room no. 3 is especially nice, with wood floors, a handsome quilt, a bright alcove with plants, and a small TV. (Seven rooms have TVs, and two have Jacuzzis). The quietest and most spacious quarters are the two suites in the rear of the house; these offer the best value.

67 Elm St., Camden, ME 04843. ✆ **800/248-3196** or 207/236-3196. Fax 207/236-6523. www.blueharborhouse.com. 10 units. $95–$205 double. Rates include breakfast. AE, DISC, MC, V. Closed mid-Oct to mid-May. Pets allowed in suite with prior permission. **Amenities:** Dining room (by reservation only). *In room:* A/C, TV, hair dryer.

Camden Windward House ★ One of the frequent complaints about travelers staying in B&Bs on Camden's High Street is the noise from passing traffic. The Windward solved that problem by installing double windows in the front of this historic 1854 house to dampen the drone (all rooms are air-conditioned). As a result, when you walk in and close the door behind you, it feels as if you're miles away. The welcoming common rooms are decorated with a light Victorian touch and display a great collection of cranberry glass; in the library, you'll find a guest refrigerator, icemaker, and afternoon refreshments. The guest rooms are varied in size, but all have televisions and phones with dataports. Four rooms have gas fireplaces.

6 High St., Camden, ME 04843. © **877/492-9656** or 207/236-9656. Fax 207/230-0433. bnb@windwardhouse.com. 8 units. Peak season $190–$280 double; off season $120–$240 double. Rates include full breakfast. AE, MC, V. No children under 12. **Amenities:** Library. *In room:* A/C, TV/VCR (1 room), some fireplaces, Jacuzzi (1 room).

Cedarholm Garden Bay ★★ Owners Joyce and Barry Jobson—the daughter of the former owner and her husband—took over the inn in 1995, built a road down to the 460 feet of dramatic cobblestone shoreline, and constructed two modern, steeply gabled cedar cottages (named Loon and Puffin), each with two bedrooms. These are wonderful places, with great detailing like pocket doors, cobblestone fireplaces, wet bars, phones, handsome kitchenettes, and Jacuzzis. They're easily among the region's most quiet and peaceful retreats. There are also now two smaller, simpler waterfront cottages (Osprey and Tern) that are quite suitable for couples; these lack the aforementioned kitchens, fireplaces, and Jacuzzis, but have microwaves and great views.

Rte. 1, Lincolnville Beach, ME 04849. © **207/236-3886.** www.cedarholm.com. 6 units. Peak season $165–$350 double and cottage; off season $165–$250 double and cottage. Rates include breakfast. 2-night minimum in some cottages. Closed late Nov to late Apr. MC, V. *In room:* Kitchenette (some), Jacuzzi (some), fireplaces (some), no phone.

Inn at Ocean's Edge ★★★ This is as friendly, personable, and well-kept a place as you'll find along the coast. On 24 gorgeous acres, this inn has committed to remaking itself into one of Maine's premier oceanfront properties, taking full advantage of windjammer views and a position close to the Isleboro ferry. The inn is in the process of adding new buildings, rooms, gardens, an in-ground vanishing-edge pool, and an inlaid hot tub overlooking the sea. Units in the main inn and the newer hilltop annex are nearly identical: all have Jacuzzis, four-poster beds, ocean views, and tasteful wallpaper prints and art. The hilltop units add fridges, coffeemakers, and balconies, but are farther from the pleasant common room overlooking the bay and gardens. The on-site restaurant, **Edge** ★, is excellent.

Rte. 1, Lincolnville Beach (P.O. Box 74, Camden, ME 04843). © **207/236-0945.** Fax 207/236-0609. www.innatoceansedge.com. 33 units. $159–$295 double. AE, DISC, M, V. Rates include full breakfast. **Amenities:** Pub; fitness room. *In room:* A/C, TV/VCR, coffeemaker (some), fridge (some), Jacuzzi, fireplace.

Inn at Sunrise Point ★★ This peaceful, private sanctuary 4 miles north of Camden Harbor seems a world apart from the bustling town. The service is crisp and helpful, and the setting can't be beat. Situated on the edge of Penobscot Bay down a long, tree-lined gravel road, the Inn at Sunrise Point consists of a cluster of contemporary yet classic shingled buildings set amid a nicely landscaped yard. Guest rooms are spacious and comfortable and full of amenities, including fireplaces and individual heat controls. The cottages are at the deluxe end of the scale, and all have double Jacuzzis, fireplaces, wet bars, and private decks.

Route 1 (P.O. Box 1344), Camden, ME 04843. © **207/236-7716.** Fax 207/236-0820. www.sunrisepoint.com. 8 units, 4 in cottages. $225–$250 double; $250–$405 suite; $265–$495 cottage. Rates include full breakfast. AE, MC, V. Closed Nov to late May. No children. *In room:* TV/VCR, minibar, fridge (some), fireplace, Jacuzzi (some).

Maine Stay ★★ The Maine Stay is one of Camden's premier bed-and-breakfasts. Set in a home dating from 1802, but expanded in Greek Revival style in 1840, the Maine Stay is a classic slate-roofed New England homestead set in a shady yard within walking distance of both downtown and Camden Hills State Park. The eight guest rooms on three floors all have ceiling fans and are distinctively furnished with antiques and special decorative touches. Our favorite: the downstairs Carriage House Room, which is away from the buzz of traffic on Route 1 and boasts its own stone patio. Of note to families is the Amelia Huse Suite, which occupies the whole third floor.

22 High St., Camden, ME 04843. © **207/236-9636.** www.mainestay.com. 8 units. Late May to Oct $135–$250 double, $230–$250 suite; rest of the year, $110–$180 double, $165–$180 suite. Rates include breakfast. AE, MC, V. No children under 10. **Amenities:** Kitchen.

Norumbega ★★ You'll have no problem finding Norumbega. Just head north of the village and look for travelers taking photos of this Victorian-era stone castle overlooking the bay. The 1886 structure is both wonderfully eccentric and finely built, full of wondrous curves and angles. The lobby has extravagant carved-oak woodwork and a stunning oak-and-mahogany-inlaid floor. The downstairs billiards room is the place to pretend you're a 19th-century railroad baron. Guest rooms have been meticulously restored and furnished with antiques. Five of the rooms have fireplaces, and the three "garden-level rooms" (they're off the downstairs billiards room) have private decks. Two rooms rank among the finest in New England—the Library Suite, housed in the original two-story library with an interior balcony, and the sprawling penthouse, with its superlative views, king-size bed, and oversize soaking tub.

63 High St., Camden, ME 04843. © **207/236-4646.** Fax 207/236-0824. www.norumbegainn.com. 12 units. July to mid-Oct $160–$365 double; mid-May to June $125–$275 double; mid-Oct to mid-May $95–$250 double. Suite $250–$475. All rates include full breakfast and evening refreshments. 2-night minimum in summer, weekends, and holidays. AE, DISC, MC, V. Children age 7 and older welcome. **Amenities:** Billiards room. *In room:* Fireplace (some).

Samoset Resort ★★ *Kids* The Samoset is a something of a Maine coast rarity—a modern, self-contained resort with contemporary styling, ocean views, and lots of golf. Both the hotel and town houses are surrounded by the handsome golf course, with expansive views of it from almost every window on the property. The lobby is constructed of massive timbers (recovered from an old grain silo in Portland), and the guest rooms all have balconies or terraces. Bathrooms are extra-big, many with soaker tubs. Golfers like the place for its scenic 18-hole course with several waterside holes, and there's a new golf school. Families will always find plenty of activities for kids (there's a summer camp during high season, and babysitting the rest of the year). The Flume Cottage is a recent luxury addition.

Rockport, ME 04856. © **800/341-1650** outside Maine, or 207/594-2511. www.samoset.com. 178 hotel units, plus 72 town-house units. Early July to late Aug from $259–$289 double, from $369 suite; mid-Apr to early July and late Aug to early Oct from $179–$289 double, from $259–$289 suite; winter starting at $129 double, from $209 suite. Cottage $539–$769. Meals not included; ask about MAP packages. AE, DC, DISC, MC, V. Valet parking. **Amenities:** 4 restaurants; indoor and outdoor pools; 18-hole golf course ($95 for 18 holes); 4 tennis courts (night play); modern health club; Jacuzzi; sauna; jogging and walking trails; children's program; indoor video golf driving range; concierge; courtesy car; business center; gift shops; massage; babysitting; laundry service; dry cleaning; free newspaper. *In room:* A/C, safe.

Whitehall Inn ★ The Whitehall is a venerable Camden establishment. Set at the edge of town on Route 1 in a structure that dates from 1834, this three-story inn has a striking architectural integrity with its columns, gables, and long roofline. The only downside is its location on Route 1—the traffic noise tends to persist through the evening and then start up early in the morning. (Ask for a room away from the road.) Inside, the antique furnishings—including the handsome Seth Thomas clock, Oriental carpets, and cane-seated rockers on the front porch—are cared for impeccably. Guest rooms are simple but appealing.

52 High St., Camden, ME 04843. © **800/789-6565** or 207/236-3391. Fax 207/236-4427. www.whitehall-inn.com. 50 units, 8 units share 4 bathrooms. July to mid-Oct $149–$199 double ($110–$120 shared bathroom); mid-May and

June $99–$159 double. Rates include full breakfast. AE, MC, V. Closed mid-Oct to mid-May. **Amenities:** Dining room; tennis court; nature trails; tour desk; conference rooms; babysitting. *In room:* Afternoon tea, safe, no phone (some).

WHERE TO DINE

Atlantica ★★ SEAFOOD/ECLECTIC Atlantica gets high marks for its innovative seafood menu and consistently well-prepared fare under the management of executive chef Ken Paquin, a graduate of the Culinary Institute of America. On the waterfront with a small indoor seating area and an equally small deck, Atlantica serves subtly creative fare like porcini-dusted black bass, morel mushroom- and scallion-encrusted tuna, or scallops glazed with ginger and brown sugar. Lunch is served on Sunday.

1 Bayview Landing. ✆ **888/507-8514** or 207/236-6011. www.atlanticarestaurant.com. Reservations suggested. Lunch $5–$13; dinner main courses $19–$26. AE, MC, V. Thurs–Mon 5:30–9pm (Sun also 12:30–2:30pm). Closed Nov–Mar.

Cappy's Chowder House *Finds* *Kids* SEAFOOD/AMERICAN "People always remember their meal here," say fans of Cappy's, a local institution smack in the middle of Camden. Travelers—especially families—tend to drift in here more to drink up the atmosphere than to sample rarified cuisine. Prime rib is served every day, there's a hearty seafood stew flavored with kielbasa, and there's also the famous chowder (it's been recognized by *Gourmet* magazine). Cappy's is well worth a stop if you're looking for a reasonably priced and filling meal, and if you don't expect to be treated like a member of the House of Windsor.

1 Main St. ✆ **207/236-2254.** www.cappyschowder.com. Main courses, lunch and dinner $5.95–$14. MC, V. Daily 7:30am–11pm.

Chez Michel ★ *Value* FRENCH/SEAFOOD This restaurant, right across the road from the Isleboro ferry in Lincolnville Beach, offers good value amid a sea of higher-priced area options. The menu successfully blends in elements of Maine and American cooking for those a bit too shy to go for, say, bouillabaisse. I like to begin with some mussels steamed in wine or a pâté of rabbit or locally smoked salmon, then move on to lamb kabobs, duck au poivre, or haddock in a meunière sauce. If those sound too adventurous, choose a lobster dinner or some fried oysters instead.

Rte. 1, Lincolnville Beach. ✆ **207/789-6500.** Entrees $13–$18; lobster dishes market price. AE, DC, DISC, MC, V. Tues–Sat 4–9:30pm (sometimes later); Sun 11:30am–9pm.

Francine Bistro ★ FRENCH BISTRO At this hot new local bistro, chef-owner Brian Hill's meals could start with fish, onion, or lentil soup, or skewers of grilled lamb served with white pesto, orange, and endive. The evening's entrees may run to roast chicken with a chèvre gratin or a cauliflower-cheese hash, a roasted sea bass in caramelized garlic sauce, or steak frites (the only constant on the menu).

55 Chestnut St., Camden. ✆ **207/230-0083.** www.francinebistro.com. Reservations recommended. Entrees $17–$25. MC, V. Tues–Sat 5:30–10pm.

The Lobster Pound ★ LOBSTER POUND Among the many lobster shacks up and down the mid-coast, this one holds its own by offering a variety of surf-and-turf combos, shore dinners, and variations on, well, lobster. But it also serves noncrustacean meals, such as grilled steaks, roast turkey with all the trimmings, and your usual set of straightforward fish and shellfish dishes. A takeout shack is adjacent.

U.S. Rte. 1, Lincolnville Beach. ✆ **207/789-5550.** Sandwiches $5.95–$7.20; lunch portions $9.95–$15; dinner entrees $12–$37. AE, DISC, MC, V. Daily 11:30am–8:30pm.

Marriner's Restaurant LUNCHEONETTE "The last local luncheonette" is how Marriner's sums itself up, along with the legend DOWN HOME, DOWN EAST, NO FERNS, NO QUICHE. As you might guess, this is a fairly small and simple affair, done up in a not-very-subtle nautical theme with pine booths and vinyl seats, some of which are held together with duct tape. Marriner's has been dishing up filling breakfasts and lunches since 1942, and it's the place for early risers to get a quick start on the day. Lunches are basic and good. The lobster and crab rolls are superb, as are the homemade pies.

35 Main St., Camden. ✆ **207/236-4949.** Breakfast $3.75–$5.95; lunch $4.25–$12 (mostly under $7). MC, V. Daily 6am–2pm.

Peter Ott's ★ AMERICAN Peter Ott's has attracted a steady stream of satisfied local customers and repeat-visitor yachtsmen since it opened smack in the middle of Camden in 1974. While it poses as a steakhouse with its simple wooden tables and chairs and its manly meat dishes (like charbroiled Black Angus with mushrooms and onions, and sirloin steak Dijonaise), it has grown beyond that to satisfy more diverse tastes. In fact, the restaurant serves some of the best prepared seafood in town, including a pan-blackened seafood sampler and grilled salmon with a lemon caper sauce.

16 Bayview St., Camden. ✆ **207/236-4032.** Main courses $17–$26. MC, V. Daily 5:30–9pm.

The Waterfront SEAFOOD/AMERICAN The Waterfront disproves the restaurant rule of thumb that "the better the view, the worse the food." Here you can watch multimillion-dollar yachts and handsome windjammers come and go (angle for a harborside seat on the deck), yet still be pleasantly surprised by the food. The house specialty is fresh seafood of all kinds. Lunch and dinner menus are an enterprising mix of old favorites and creative originals. On the old-favorites side are fried clams, crab cakes, and a fisherman's platter piled with fried seafood. On the more adventurous side: a warm duck breast salad sautéed with spinach, kalamata olives, roasted red peppers, balsamic vinaigrette, pine nuts, and feta cheese. More earthbound fare for non-seafood eaters includes burgers, pitas, and strip steaks.

Bayview St. on Camden Harbor. ✆ **207/236-3747.** Main courses lunch $6.95–$15, dinner $16–$18; lobsters market price. AE, MC, V. Daily 11:30am–2:30pm and 5–10pm. Closes earlier in off season.

5 The Blue Hill Peninsula

136 miles NE of Portland; 23 miles N of Stonington; and 14 miles SW of Ellsworth.

The Blue Hill Peninsula is a back-roads paradise. If you like to get lost on country lanes that dead-end at the sea or inexplicably start to loop back on themselves, this is the place. In contrast to the western shores of Penobscot Bay, the Blue Hill Peninsula has more of a lost-in-time character. The roads are hilly, winding, and narrow, passing through forests, along saltwater farms, and touching on the edge of an inlet here or there. The peninsula is overlooked by most of Maine's visitors, especially those who like itineraries well structured and destinations simple.

CASTINE & ENVIRONS ★★

Castine has my vote for Maine's most gracious village. It's not so much the stunningly handsome and meticulously maintained mid-19th-century homes, or its setting on a quiet peninsula, 16 miles south of RV-clotted Route 1. No, what lends Castine its charm are splendid, towering elm trees that still overarch many of the village streets. And, for American history buffs, Castine offers much more. This outpost served as a strategic town in various battles between British, Dutch, French, and feisty Colonials in the centuries following its settlement in 1613.

ESSENTIALS

GETTING THERE Castine is 16 miles south of Route 1. Turn south on Route 175 in Orland (east of Bucksport) and follow it to Route 166, which winds its way to Castine. Route 166A offers an alternate route along Penobscot Bay.

VISITOR INFORMATION Castine lacks a formal information center, but the clerk at the **Town Office** (✆ **207/326-4502**) is often helpful. The office is open Monday to Friday, 11am to 3pm only. The **Blue Hill Peninsula Chamber of Commerce** (see below) handles tourist inquiries.

EXPLORING CASTINE

One of the town's more intriguing attractions is the **Wilson Museum** ★ (✆ **207/326-1247;** www.wilsonmuseum.org) on Perkins Street, an appealing and quirky, small anthropological museum constructed in 1921. It contains the collections of John Howard Wilson, an archaeologist and collector of prehistoric artifacts from around the globe. His gleanings are neatly arranged in a staid, classical arrangement of the sort that proliferated in the late 19th and early 20th centuries. The museum is open from the end of May to the end of September every day except Monday 2 to 5pm; admission is free.

Next door is the **John Perkins House** (✆ **207/326-9247**), Castine's oldest home. It was occupied by the British during the Revolution and the War of 1812, and a tour includes demonstrations of old-fashioned cooking techniques. The Perkins House is open in July and August, Wednesday and Sunday only, from 2 to 5pm. Admission is free. Castine is also home to the **Maine Maritime Academy** (✆ **207/326-4311**), which trains sailors for the rigors of life at sea with the merchant marine. The campus is on the western edge of the village, and the 498-foot vessel TV *State of Maine,* the hulking gray training ship, is often docked in Castine, all but overwhelming the village. Free half-hour tours of the ship are led in summer whenever the ship is in port, on the hour from 10am to noon and from 1 to 4pm.

WHERE TO STAY

Castine Harbor Lodge ★ *Kids* This is a great seasonal spot for families. Housed in a grand 1893 mansion (the only inn on the water in Castine), it's run with an informal good cheer that allows kids to feel at home amid the regal architecture. The main parlor is dominated by a pool table. The spacious rooms are eclectically furnished, with some antiques and some modern furniture. Two of the guest rooms share an adjoining bathroom—of note to traveling families. And speaking of bathrooms, these just may have the best views of any in the state.

Perkins St. (P.O. Box 215), Castine, ME 04421. ✆ **207/326-4335.** www.castinemaine.com. 16 units (2 with shared bathrooms), 1 cottage. $85–$245 double; cottage $1,250 weekly. Rates include continental breakfast. MC, V. Pets allowed ($10 per night). **Amenities:** Dining room; bar; pool table.

Castine Inn ★ The Castine Inn is a Maine Coast rarity: a hotel that was originally built as a hotel (not as a residence)—in this case, in 1898. This handsome, cream-colored village inn, designed in an eclectic Georgian Federal Revival style, has a fine front porch and attractive gardens. Inside, the lobby takes its cue from the 1940s, with wingback chairs and loveseats and a fireplace in the parlor. The guest rooms on the two upper floors are attractively, if unevenly, furnished in Early American style—the innkeepers are revamping the rooms one by one to an even gloss, adding deluxe touches. The elegant dining room (see below) serves Castine's best fare and some of the best in the state.

Main St. (P.O. Box 41), Castine, ME 04421. ✆ **207/326-4365.** Fax 207/326-4570. www.castineinn.com. 19 units. Peak season $90–$245 double; off season lower. Rates include full breakfast. Closed early Oct to Apr. 2-night minimum July–Aug. MC, V. Children 8 and older are welcome. **Amenities:** Dining room; sauna.

Pentagöet Inn ★ Here's the big activity at the Pentagöet: Sit on the wraparound front porch on cane-seated rockers and watch the slow-paced activity on Main Street. This quirky, yellow-and-green 1894 structure with its prominent turret is tastefully furnished downstairs with hardwood floors, oval braided rugs, and a woodstove. It's comfortable without being overly fussy, professional without being chilly, personal without being overly intimate. The rooms on the upper two floors of the main house are furnished eclectically, with a mix of antiques and collectibles. The five guest rooms in the adjacent Perkins Street building—a more austere Federal-era house—are furnished simply and have painted floors.

Main St. (P.O. Box 4), Castine, ME 04421. ✆ **800/845-1701** or 207/326-8616. Fax 207/326-9382. www.pentagoet.com. 16 units, 2 with private hallway bathrooms. Peak season $95–$225 double; off season lower. Rates include full breakfast. MC, V. Closed Nov–Apr. Pets by reservation. Suitable for older children only. **Amenities:** Dining room; pub; bikes. *In room:* Fireplace (some).

WHERE TO DINE

Castine Inn ★★ NEW AMERICAN This handsome hotel dining room has Castine's best fare and some of the better food in the state. Chef/owner Tom Gutow worked at both Bouley and Verbena in New York, and isn't timid about experimenting with local meats and produce. Expect dishes such as lobster with vanilla butter, mango mayonnaise, and tropical-fruit salsa; or lamb loin with eggplant, green lentils, tomatoes, and rosemary jus. One night each week, the restaurant has a buffet; that night, you're better off heading to Dennett's Wharf.

Main St. ✆ **207/326-4365.** Reservations recommended. Main courses $26–$33. MC, V. Daily 6–9pm. Closed mid-Dec to May.

Dennett's Wharf PUB FARE In a soaring waterfront sail loft with dollar bills tacked all over the high ceiling, Dennett's Wharf serves upscale bar food amid a lively setting leavened with a good selection of microbrews. If the weather is decent, there's outside dining under a bright yellow awning with superb harbor views. Look for grilled sandwiches, roll-ups, and salads at lunch; dinner includes lobsters, stir-fries, and steak teriyaki. And how did all those bills get on the ceiling? Ask your server. It will cost you exactly $1 to find out.

15 Sea St. (next to the Town Dock). ✆ **207/326-9045.** Reservations recommended in summer and for parties of 6 or more. Lunch $4.75–$13; dinner $8.95–$27. AE, DISC, MC, V. Daily 11am–midnight. Closed mid-Oct to Apr 30.

BLUE HILL ★

Blue Hill (pop. 1,900) is fairly easy to find—look for the gently domed Blue Hill Mountain, which lords over the northern end of Blue Hill Bay. Set between the mountain and the bay is the quiet and historic town of Blue Hill. The town never seems to have much going on, which may be exactly what attracts summer visitors time and again. Blue Hill offers several excellent options for lodging. A good destination for an escape, it especially appeals to those deft at crafting their own entertainment.

Tips Community Radio

When in the area, tune to the local community radio station, WERU at 89.9 FM. Started by Noel Paul Stookey (the Paul in Peter, Paul, and Mary) in a chicken coop, its idea was to spread good music and provocative ideas. It's slicker and more professional in recent years, but still maintains a pleasantly homespun flavor, with an eclectic range of music and commentary.

ESSENTIALS

GETTING THERE Blue Hill is southeast of Ellsworth on Route 172. Coming from the west, take Route 15 south 5 miles east of Bucksport (it's well marked with road signs).

VISITOR INFORMATION Blue Hill does not maintain a visitor information booth. Look for the "Blue Hill, Maine" brochure and map at state information centers, or write the **Blue Hill Peninsula Chamber of Commerce** (© **207/374-3242**), P.O. Box 520, Blue Hill, ME 04614. The staffs at area inns and restaurants are usually able to answer any questions you may have.

EXPLORING BLUE HILL

From the open summit of **Blue Hill Mountain** ★★ are superb views of the bay and the rocky balds on Mount Desert Island just across the way. To reach the trail head from the village, drive north on Route 172, then turn west (left) on Mountain Road at the Blue Hill Fairgrounds. Drive .8 mile and look for the marked trail. An ascent of the "mountain" (elevation 940 ft.) is about a mile and requires about 45 minutes. Bring a picnic and enjoy the vistas.

Even if you're not given to swooning over historic homes, you owe yourself a visit to the intriguing **Parson Fisher House** ★ (© **207/374-2459;** www.jonathanfisher house.org), on Routes 176 and 15, a half-mile west of the village. Fisher, Blue Hill's first permanent minister, was a countrified version of a Renaissance man when he settled here in 1796. Educated at Harvard, Fisher not only delivered sermons in six different languages, including Aramaic, but was also a writer, painter, and minor inventor whose energy was evidently boundless. The Parson Fisher House is open from July to mid-September on a rather odd schedule: Tuesdays and Fridays from 1 to 4pm, and Saturdays from 11am to 2pm. Admission is by donation; $5 per person is suggested.

If you're an ardent antiques hunter or bibliophile, it's worthwhile to detour to the **Big Chicken Barn** (© **207/667-7308**), on Route 1 between Ellsworth and Bucksport (it's 9 miles west of Ellsworth and 11 miles east of Bucksport). This sprawling antiques mall and bookstore is of nearly shopping-mall proportions—more than 21,000 square feet of stuff in an old poultry barn. It's open daily from 9am to 6pm during summer, shorter hours in the off season.

WHERE TO STAY

Blue Hill Farm Country Inn Comfortably situated on 48 acres and 2 miles north of the village of Blue Hill, the Blue Hill Country Farm Inn has some of the most relaxing and comfortable common areas you'll find anywhere. The first floor of a vast barn has been converted to a spacious living room for guests, with a handful of sitting areas arrayed so that you can opt for privacy or the company of others. The guest rooms tend to be small and lightly furnished. The more modern rooms are upstairs in the barn loft and are nicely decorated in a country farmhouse style, but these are a bit motel-like, with rooms set off a central hallway. The seven older rooms in the farmhouse have more character and share a single bathroom with a small tub and hand-held shower.

Rte. 15 (P.O. Box 437), Blue Hill, ME 04614. ✆ **207/374-5126.** www.bluehillfarminn.com. 14 units, 7 with shared bathroom. $85–$95 double (no shared bathroom in off season). Rates include continental breakfast. AE, MC, V.

Blue Hill Inn ★★ The Blue Hill Inn has been hosting travelers since 1840. On one of Blue Hill's main thoroughfares and within walking distance of almost everything, this Federal-style inn displays a convincing Colonial American motif, with the authenticity enhanced by creaky floors. The friendly innkeepers have furnished all the rooms pleasantly with antiques and down comforters; the four rooms in the main house have wood-burning fireplaces, although these rooms are open only from mid-May through the end of October. A large contemporary suite in an adjacent, free-standing building has a cathedral ceiling, fireplace, full kitchen, living room, and deck; this Cape House Suite is available to guests year-round. Ask about packages that include kayaking, hiking, or sailing.

Union St. (P.O. Box 403), Blue Hill, ME 04614. ✆ **207/374-2844.** Fax 207/374-2829. www.bluehillinn.com. 11 units, 1 cottage. $138–$195 double; $165–$285 suite. Rates include breakfast. 2-night minimum in summer. DISC, MC, V. Main inn closed Dec to mid-May. Children 13 and older are welcome. **Amenities:** Free hors d'oeuvres; wine dinners. *In room:* A/C, kitchen (1), fireplace.

WHERE TO DINE

Arborvine Restaurant ★★ FINE DINING In recent years, Blue Hill saw the closing of two of its longtime favorite dining spots (Firepond and the Left Bank Cafe). Fortunately, the Arborvine has stepped in to fill the gap, once again giving this sleepy town a top-flight eatery. Ensconced in a beautifully renovated Cape Cod–style house, the restaurant's interior is warm and inviting—think rough-hewn timbers, polished wooden floors, and a cozy bar area. The husband-and-wife team that owns the place is careful to use locally grown and procured ingredients for appetizers, such as Damariscotta River oysters on the half-shell. Among the entrees are crispy roast duckling with an amaretto glaze, rack of lamb with a basil pine-nut crust, and five-spiced grilled sirloin. Reservations are highly recommended.

Main St., Blue Hill, ME 04614. ✆ **207/374-2119.** www.arborvine.com. Dinner $22–$28. MC, V. Summer daily 5:30–8:30pm; off season Fri–Sun 5:30–8:30pm.

6 Mount Desert Island & Acadia National Park ★★★

Mount Desert Island is home to spectacular Acadia National Park, and for many visitors, the two places are one and the same. Yet the park holdings are only part of the appeal of this popular island, connected to the mainland via a short, two-lane causeway. Beyond the parklands are scenic harborside villages and remote backcountry roads, lovely B&Bs and fine restaurants, oversize 19th-century summer "cottages," and the historic tourist town of Bar Harbor.

Mount Desert (pronounced Des-*sert,* like what you have after dinner) is divided into two lobes separated by Somes Sound, the only true fjord—that is, a valley carved out by a glacier and then subsequently filled in with rising ocean water—in the continental U.S. Most of the parkland is on the east side of the island, though large swaths of park exist on the west, too. The east side is much more heavily developed, with Bar Harbor the center of commerce and entertainment. The west side has a quieter, more

Mount Desert Island & Acadia National Park

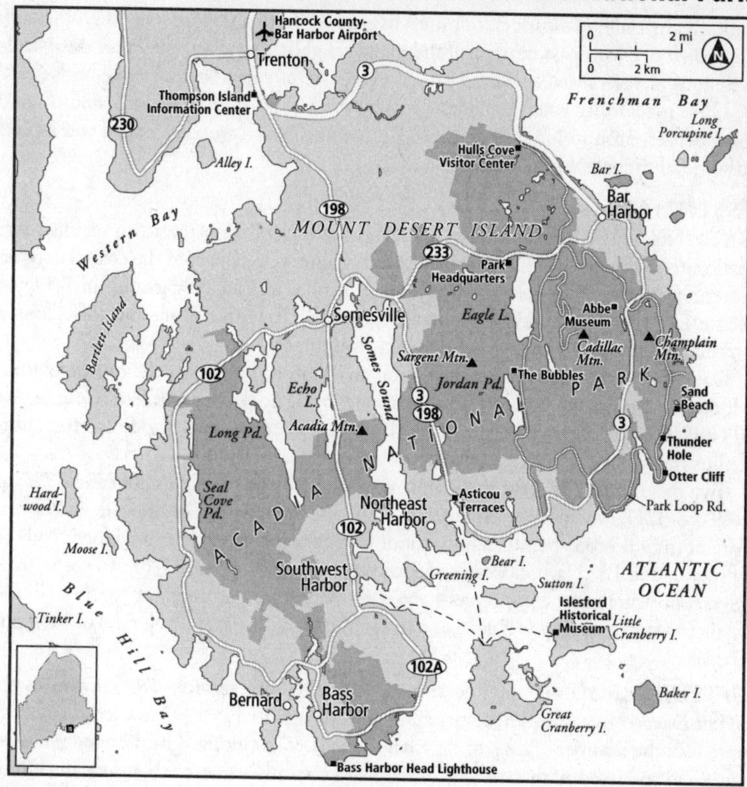

settled air, and teems more with wildlife than tourists. This island isn't huge—about 15 miles from the causeway to the southernmost tip at Bass Harbor Head—yet you can do an awful lot of adventuring in such a compact space. The best plan is to take it slowly, exploring whenever possible by foot, bicycle, canoe, or kayak, and taking up to a week to do it. You'll be glad you did.

ACADIA NATIONAL PARK ★★★

It's not hard to fathom why Acadia is one of the biggest draws in the national park system. Its landscape is a rich tapestry of rugged cliffs, restless ocean, and quiet woods. Acadia's terrain, like so much of the rest of northern New England, was carved by glaciers 18,000 years ago. A mile-high ice sheet shaped the land, scouring valleys into U shapes, rounding many of the once-jagged peaks, and depositing boulders around the landscape, including the famous 10-foot-high Bubble Rock, which appears to be perched precariously on the side of South Bubble Mountain.

By the early 1900s, the island's popularity and growing development began to concern its most ardent supporters. Boston textile heir and conservationist George Dorr and Harvard president Charles Eliot, aided by the largesse of John D. Rockefeller, Jr., started acquiring large tracts for the public's enjoyment. These parcels were eventually donated to the government, and in 1919, the land was designated Lafayette National

Park, the first national park east of the Mississippi. Renamed Acadia in 1929, the park has grown to encompass nearly half the island. Highlights include an elaborate 57-mile system of private carriage roads, with a dozen gracefully handcrafted stone bridges.

These roads, open today to pedestrians, bicyclists, and equestrians, are concentrated most densely around Jordan Pond, but also wind through wooded valleys and ascend to some of the most scenic open peaks.

ESSENTIALS

GETTING THERE Acadia National Park is reached from the town of Ellsworth via Route 3. If you're coming from southern Maine, you can avoid the coastal congestion along Route 1 by taking the Maine Turnpike to Bangor, picking up I-395 to Route 1A, then continuing south on Route 1A to Ellsworth. While this looks longer on the map, it's by far the quickest route in summer.

Daily flights from Boston to the airport in Trenton, just across the causeway from Mount Desert Island, are offered year-round by U.S. Airways affiliate **Colgan Air** (**© 207/667-7171;** www.colganair.com). From here, call a taxi or ride the free shuttle bus (late June to mid-Oct only) to downtown Bar Harbor.

Two major bus lines serve the island. **Vermont Transit Lines** (**© 800/552-8737** or 207/288-3211; www.vermonttransit.com) is affiliated with **Greyhound** and serves Bangor from Boston's South Station, continuing onward (in summer only) once daily to Ellsworth and Bar Harbor. **Concord Trailways** (**© 800/639-3317** or 207/945-5000; www.concordtrailways.com) serves Bangor from Boston, but does not continue to the smaller towns onward; you'll need to transfer at Bangor via taxi (a long ride) or Vermont Transit.

GETTING AROUND A free **summer shuttle bus service** ★★ known as the *Island Explorer* (www.exploreacadia.com) was inaugurated in 1999 as part of an effort to reduce the number of cars on the island's roads. It's working. The propane-powered buses are equipped with racks for bikes, serve six routes that cover nearly the entire island, and will stop anywhere you request outside the village centers, including trail heads, ferries, small villages, and campgrounds. Just be prepared to share the ride with garrulous fellow passengers—and/or bring a book; there are lots of stops. All routes begin or end at the Village Green in Bar Harbor, but you're encouraged to pick up the bus wherever you're staying, whether motel or campground, to avoid parking hassles in town. Route no. 3 goes from Bar Harbor along much of the Park Loop, offering easy access to some of the park's best hiking trails. The buses operate from late June to mid-October (there are fewer, but still enough, buses from Sept to mid-Oct); ask for a schedule at any of the island information centers.

GUIDED TOURS **Acadia National Park Tours** (**© 207/288-0300;** www.acadiatours.com) offers 2½-hour park tours departing twice daily (10am and 2pm) from downtown Bar Harbor. The bus tour includes three stops (Sieur De Monts Springs, Thunder Hole, and Cadillac Mountain) and plenty of park trivia, courtesy of the driver. This is an easy way for first-time visitors to get a quick introduction to the park before setting out on their own. Tickets are available at Testa's Restaurant, 53 Main St., Bar Harbor; $20 adults, $10 children under 14.

ENTRY POINTS & FEES A 1-week park pass, which includes unlimited trips on Park Loop Road (closed in winter), costs $20 per car, $10 in the off season; there's no additional charge per passenger. Pedestrians, cyclists, and others traveling without a vehicle must pay a $5-per-person fee.

Tips Cost-Effective Acadia

No daily pass to Acadia is available, so if you'll be here more than 2 weeks, purchase a $40 annual Acadia pass for your car instead of buying repeat $20 access passes. Or, better yet, buy a $50 National Parks Pass, allowing you entry to *all* the nation's national parks during the current calendar year.

The main point of entry to Park Loop Road, the park's most scenic byway, is at the visitor center at **Hulls Cove.** Mount Desert Island consists of an interwoven network of park and town roads, allowing visitors to enter the park at numerous points. A glance at a park map (available free at the visitor center) will make these access points self-evident. The entry fee is collected at a tollbooth on Park Loop Road, a half-mile north of Sand Beach.

VISITOR CENTERS & INFORMATION Acadia staffs two visitor centers. The **Thompson Island Information Center** (✆ **207/288-3411**) on Route 3 is the first you'll pass as you enter Mount Desert Island. This center is maintained by the local chambers of commerce, but park personnel are often on hand to answer inquiries. It's open daily May to mid-October from 6am until 10pm, and is a good stop for general lodging and restaurant information.

If you're interested primarily in information about the park itself, continue on Route 3 to the National Park Service's **Hulls Cove Visitor Center,** about 7½ miles beyond Thompson Island. This attractive, stone-walled center has professionally prepared park service displays, such as a large relief map of the island, natural history exhibits, and a short introductory film. You can also request free brochures about hiking trails and the carriage roads, or purchase postcards and more detailed guidebooks. The center is open daily mid-April through October, 8am to 4:30pm (to 6pm July–Aug, to 5pm Sept–Oct). Information is available year-round, by phone or in person, from the park's **headquarters** (✆ **207/288-3338**) on Route 233 between Bar Harbor and Somesville, open 8am to 4:30 daily. Your questions may also be answered in advance on the park's Web page at **www.nps.gov/acad**.

DRIVING TOUR DRIVING THE PARK LOOP ROAD

The 20-mile **Park Loop Road** ★★★ is Acadia's premier attraction, and magnet for the largest crowds. This remarkable roadway starts near the Hulls Cove Visitor Center and follows the high ridges above Bar Harbor before dropping down along the rocky coast. Here, earthy tones and spires of spruce and fir cap dark granite, making a sharp contrast with the white surf and steely-blue sea. After following the picturesque coast and touching on several coves, the road loops back inland along Jordan Pond and Eagle Lake, with a detour to the summit of the island's highest peak.

Ideally, visitors make two circuits on the loop road. The first is for the sheer exhilaration of it and to check out the lay of the land. On the second trip, plan to stop frequently and poke around on foot by setting off on trails or scrambling along the coastline. Scenic pull-offs are staggered at frequent intervals. The two-lane road is one-way along coastal sections; the right-hand lane is set aside for parking, so you can stop wherever you'd like to admire the vistas.

From about 10am to 4pm in July and August, anticipate large crowds along the loop road, at least on those days when the sun is shining. Parking lots may fill at some of the more popular destinations.

From the Hulls Cove Visitor Center, the Park Loop initially runs atop:

❶ Paradise Hill

The tour starts with sweeping views eastward over Frenchman Bay. You'll see the town of Bar Harbor far below, and just beyond it the Porcupines, a cluster of islands that look like, well, porcupines.

Following the Park Loop Road clockwise, you'll dip into a wooded valley and come to:

❷ Sieur de Monts Spring

Here you'll find a rather uninteresting natural spring, unnaturally encased, along with a botanical garden with some 300 species showcased in 12 habitats. The original **Abbe Museum** (✆ **207/288-3519**) is here, featuring a small but select collection of Native American artifacts. It's open daily from mid-May to mid-October, 9am to 4pm; admission is $2 for adults, $1 for children ages 6 to 15. ***Note:*** A larger, more modern branch is open in Bar Harbor year-round, with more and better-curated displays, and a ticket here gets you $2 off admission there.

The Tarn is the chief reason to stop here; a few hundred yards south of the springs via a footpath, it's a slightly medieval-looking and forsaken pond sandwiched between steep hills. Departing from the south end of the Tarn is the fine **Dorr Mountain Ladder Trail** (see "Hiking," below).

Continue the clockwise trip on the loop road; views eastward over the bay soon resume, almost uninterruptedly, until you get to:

❸ The Precipice Trail ★

The park's most dramatic trail ascends sheer rock faces on the east side of Champlain Mountain. Only about .8 of a mile to the summit, it's rigorous, and involves scrambling up iron rungs and ladders in exposed places (those with a fear of heights or under 5 ft. tall should avoid this trail). The trail is often closed midsummer to protect nesting peregrine falcons. Rangers are often on hand in the trail head parking lot to point out the birds and suggest alternative hikes.

Between the Precipice Trail and Sand Beach is a tollbooth where visitors pay the park fee of $10 per car, good for 1 week.

Picturesquely set between the arms of a rocky cove is:

❹ Sand Beach ★

Sand Beach is the only sand beach on the island, although swimming these cold waters (about 50°F/10°C) is best enjoyed on extremely hot days or by those with a freakishly robust metabolism. Midday when it's sunny out, the sandy strand is crowded. (***Tip:*** The water at the far end of the beach—where a gentle stream enters the cove—is often a few degrees warmer than the end closer to the access stairs.)

Two worthwhile hikes start near the beach. **The Beehive Trail** overlooks Sand Beach (see "Hiking," below); its trail head is across the loop road. From the east end of Sand Beach, look for the **Great Head Trail,** a loop of about 2 miles that follows on the bluff overlooking the beach, then circles back along the shimmering bay before cutting through the woods back to Sand Beach.

About a mile south of Sand Beach is:

❺ Thunder Hole ★

Thunder Hole is a shallow oceanside cavern into which surf surges, compresses, and bursts out (a walking trail on the road allows you to leave your car parked at the beach). When the bay is as quiet as a millpond (it often is during the lulling days of summer), it's a drive-by. Spend your time elsewhere.

However, on days when the seas are rough and large swells roll in off the Bay of Fundy, it's a must-see, three-star attraction; you can feel the ocean's power and force resonating under your sternum. (***Tip:*** The best viewing time is 3 hr. before high tide.)

Just before the road curves around Otter Point, you'll be driving atop:

❻ Otter Cliffs

This set of 100-foot-high precipices is capped with dense spruce that plummet down into roiling seas. Look for whales spouting in summer; in early fall, thousands of eider ducks can sometimes be seen floating in flocks just offshore. A footpath follows the brink of the crags.

At Seal Harbor, the loop road veers north and inland back toward Bar Harbor. On the route is:

❼ Jordan Pond ★★

This small but uncommonly beautiful body of water is encased by gentle, forested hills. A 3-mile hiking loop follows the pond's shoreline (see "Hiking," below), and a network of splendid carriage roads converge at the pond. After a hike or mountain-bike excursion, spend some time at a table on the lawn of the Jordan Pond House restaurant (see "Where to Dine," below).

Shortly before the loop road ends, you'll pass the entrance to:

❽ Cadillac Mountain ★

Reach this mountain by car, ascending an early carriage road. At 1,528 feet, it's the highest peak on the Eastern Seaboard between Canada and Brazil. But because Cadillac Mountain is the only mountaintop in the park accessible by car, and because it's also the island's highest point, the parking lot at the summit can be jammed, and drivers testy. Views are undeniably great, but the shopping-mall-at-Christmas atmosphere can put a serious crimp in your enjoyment of the place. Some lower peaks accessible only by foot—such as Acadia or Champlain mountains—have equally good views and fewer crowds.

GETTING OUTSIDE

CARRIAGE RIDES ★★ Carriage rides are offered by **Wildwood Stables (© 207/276-3622;** www.acadia.net/wildwood), about a half-mile south of Jordan Pond House. The 1-hour trip departs three times daily and takes in sweeping ocean views; it costs $14 for adults, $7 for children ages 6 to 12, and $4 for children ages 2 to 5. Longer tours are available, as is a special carriage designed for passengers with disabilities. Reservations are recommended.

HIKING Acadia National Park has 120 miles of hiking trails, plus 57 miles of carriage roads suitable for walking. The park is studded with low "mountains" (called hills elsewhere), and almost all have trails with superb views of the ocean. Many pathways were crafted by stonemasons and others with high aesthetic intent, and thus the routes aren't the most direct—but they're often the most scenic, taking advantage of fractures in the rocks, picturesque ledges, and sudden vistas.

The Hulls Cove Visitor Center has a brief chart of area hikes; combined with the park map, this is all you'll need to explore the well-maintained, well-marked trails. It's not hard to cobble together loop hikes to make your trips more varied. Coordinate your hiking with the weather; if it's damp or foggy, you'll stay drier and warmer strolling the carriage roads. If it's clear and dry, head for the highest peaks with the best views.

MOUNTAIN BIKING The 57 miles of **carriage roads** ★★★ built by John D. Rockefeller, Jr., are among the park's most extraordinary hidden treasures. These were maintained by Rockefeller until his death in 1960, after which they became shaggy and overgrown. A major restoration effort was launched in 1990, and today the roads are superbly restored and maintained. With their wide hard-packed surfaces, gentle grades, and extensive directional signs, they make for very smooth biking. Note that bikes are also allowed on the island's free shuttle buses (see "Getting Around," earlier).

A useful map of the roads is available free at visitor centers; more detailed guides may be purchased at area bookshops, but aren't necessary. Where carriage roads cross private land (generally between Seal Harbor and Northeast Harbor), they're closed to mountain bikes, which are also banned from hiking trails.

Mountain bikes can be rented along Cottage Street in Bar Harbor, with rates around $17 to $18 for a full day, $12 to $13 for a half-day (which is actually only 4 hr. in the bike-rental universe). Most bike shops include locks and helmets as basic equipment, but ask what's included before you rent. Also ask about closing times, since you'll be able to get in a couple of extra hours with a late-closing shop. **Bar Harbor Bicycle Shop** (✆ **207/288-3886**), at 141 Cottage St., gets my vote for the most convenient and friendliest; you could also try **Acadia Outfitters** (✆ **207/288-8118**), at 106 Cottage St., or **Acadia Bike & Canoe** (✆ **800/526-8615** or 207/288-9605), at 48 Cottage St.

CAMPING

The National Park Service maintains two campgrounds within Acadia National Park. Both are extremely popular; during July and August, expect both to fill by early to midmorning.

The more popular of the two is **Blackwoods** (✆ **207/288-3274**), on the island's eastern side. Access is from Route 3, 5 miles south of Bar Harbor. Bikers and pedestrians have easy access to the loop road from the campground via a short trail. The campground has no public showers, but an enterprising business just outside the campground entrance provides clean showers for a modest fee. Camping fees are $20 per night and reservations are accepted; **reservations** can be made up to 5 months in advance by calling ✆ **800/365-CAMP.** (This is to a national reservation service whose contract is revisited from time to time by the park service; if it's nonworking, call the campground directly to ask for the current toll-free reservation number.) Reservations can also be made online between 10am and 10pm only at http://reservations.nps.gov. Sites cost $20 each, and a park pass is also required for park entry; see above for details.

Seawall (✆ **207/244-3600**) is on the quieter western half of the island near the fishing village of Bass Harbor. This is a good base for road biking, and several short coastal hikes are within easy striking distance. Many of the sites are walk-ins, which require carrying your gear 300 feet or so to the site. The campground is open mid-May through the end of September on a first-come, first-served basis—and lines form early. In general, if you get here by 9 or 10am, you'll be pretty much assured of a campsite, especially if you're a tent camper. Camping fees are $14 to $20 per night, depending on whether you want to drive directly to your site or pack a tent in for a distance of up to 450 feet. As with Blackwoods, possession of a park pass is also required to stay at the campground.

WHERE TO DINE

Jordan Pond House ★★ *Finds* AMERICAN The secret to the Jordan Pond House? Location, location, location. The restaurant traces its roots from 1847, when a farm was established on this picturesque property at the southern tip of Jordan Pond looking north toward The Bubbles, a picturesque pair of glacially sculpted mounds. In 1979, the original structure and its birch-bark dining room were destroyed by fire. A more modern, two-level dining room was built in its place—it has less charm, but it still has the island's best dining location, on a nice lawn. Afternoon tea with popovers is a hallowed Jordan Pond House tradition. The lobster and crab rolls are abundant and filling; the lobster stew is expensive but very good. Dinners include classic entrees like prime rib, steamed lobster, and baked scallops with a crumb topping.

Park Loop Rd. (near Seal Harbor), Acadia National Park. ✆ **207/276-3316.** www.jordanpond.com. Advance reservations not accepted; call before arriving to hold a table. Main courses: lunch items $8.50–$18; dinner entrees $13–$19. AE, DISC, MC, V. Mid-May to late Oct daily 11:30am–8pm (until 9pm July–Aug).

BAR HARBOR ★

After a period of quiet decay, Bar Harbor has been revived and rediscovered by both visitors and entrepreneurs. The less charitable regard Bar Harbor as another tacky tourist mecca, with T-shirt vendors, ice-cream shops, and souvenir palaces; crowds spill off the sidewalk and into the street in midsummer, and the traffic can be appalling. Yet Bar Harbor's history, distinguished architecture, and beautiful location on Frenchman Bay make it a desirable base for exploring the island, and it has the best selection of lodging, meals, supplies, and services in the area.

ESSENTIALS

GETTING THERE Bar Harbor is on Route 3 about 10 miles southeast of the causeway onto Mount Desert Island. Daily flights from Boston to the airport in Trenton, just across the island causeway, are offered year-round by U.S. Airways affiliate **Colgan Air** (✆ **800/428-4322**). From here, call a taxi or ride the free shuttle bus (late June to mid-Oct only) to downtown Bar Harbor.

Two major bus lines serve the island. **Vermont Transit Lines** (✆ **800/552-8737** or 207/288-3211; www.vermonttransit.com) is affiliated with **Greyhound** and serves Bangor from Boston's South Station, continuing onward (in summer only) once daily to Ellsworth and Bar Harbor.

Concord Trailways (✆ **800/639-3317** or 207/945-5000; www.concordtrailways.com) serves Bangor from Boston, but does not continue to the smaller towns onward; you'll need to transfer at Bangor via taxi (a long ride) or Vermont Transit.

VISITOR INFORMATION The **Bar Harbor Chamber of Commerce,** P.O. Box 158, Bar Harbor, ME 04609 (✆ **207/288-5103;** www.barharborinfo.com), stockpiles a huge arsenal of information about local attractions at its offices at 93 Cottage St. Write, call, or e-mail in advance for a directory of area lodging and attractions. The chamber's website is chock-full of information and helpful links.

EXPLORING BAR HARBOR

The best water views in town are from the foot of Main Street at grassy **Agamont Park,** which overlooks the town pier and Frenchman Bay. From here, set off past The Bar Harbor Inn on the **Shore Path** ★★, a wide, winding trail that follows the shoreline for half a mile along a public right-of-way. The pathway passes in front of many elegant summer homes (some converted to inns), offering a superb vantage point to view the area's architecture.

The **Abbe Museum** ★, 26 Mount Desert St. (✆ **207/288-3519;** www.abbemuseum.org), opened an extensive 17,000-square-foot gallery in late 2001, showcasing a top-rate collection of Native American artifacts. It has an orientation center and a glass-walled lab where visitors can see archaeologists at work preserving recently recovered artifacts, along with changing exhibits and videos that focus largely on Maine and other New England tribes.

The museum is open almost year-round; in summer, it opens daily from 9am to 4pm, while from April to mid-May, it's open Thursdays to Sundays only. In 2006, the museum closed from January until April, but this may change in subsequent years—check ahead if you plan a winter visit. Admission is $6 for adults, $2 for children ages 6 to 15.

A short stroll around the corner from the new Abbe Museum is the **Bar Harbor Historical Society,** 33 Ledgelawn Ave. (© **207/288-0000** or 207/288-3807). The society moved into this handsome 1918 former convent in 1997, where it has showcased artifacts of life in the old days—dishware and photos from the grand old hotels, and exhibits on noted landscape architect Beatrix Farrand. Leave enough time to spend a few minutes thumbing through the scrapbooks about the devastating 1947 fire. The museum is open June to October, Monday to Saturday from 1 to 4pm; admission is free.

WHALE-WATCHING

Bar Harbor is a base for several ocean endeavors, including whale-watching tours. Operators lead excursions in search of humpbacks, finbacks, minkes, and the infrequently seen endangered right whale. The sleekest is the ***Friendship V,*** operated by the **Bar Harbor Whale Watching Co.** (© **800/942-5374** or 207/288-2386; www.whalesrus.com), which operates from the municipal pier in downtown Bar Harbor. Tours are on a fast, twin-hulled, three-level excursion boat that can hold 200 passengers in two heated cabins. The tours run 3 hours plus; the cost is $46 per adult, $25 per child ages 6 to 14, and $8 per child age 5 and under.

A puffin- and whale-watching tour is also offered for the same prices, and shorter seal-watching tours for about half the price. There's free on-site parking and a money-back guarantee that you'll see whales. Tours begin in May and run throughout the summer; call ahead for the exact dates.

WHERE TO STAY

Bar Harbor is the bedroom community for Mount Desert Island, with hundreds of hotel, motel, and inn rooms. They're invariably filled during the busy days of summer, and even the most basic of rooms can be quite expensive in July and August. It's essential to reserve as early as possible.

Reputable motels in or near town that have some rooms under $100 in peak season include the conveniently located **Villager Motel,** 207 Main St. (© **207/288-3211**) ; the in-town, pet-friendly **Rockhurst Motel,** 68 Mount Desert St. (© **207/288-3140**); and the smoke-free **Highbrook Motel,** 94 Eden St. (© **800/338-9688** or 207/288-3591). About 4 miles west of Bar Harbor on Route 3 is **Hanscom's Motel and Cottages** (© **207/288-3744;** www.hanscomsmotel.com), an old-fashioned motor court with 12 units (some two-bedroom) that have been well maintained. Its rates range from $86 to $120 in summer; from $68 off season.

Expensive

Bar Harbor Grand Hotel ★ The Grand nicely fills a lodging gap between quaint, expensive inns and B&Bs and the family-owned motels, hotels, and cottages scattered about the island. It's owned by the Witham family, the same folks behind the Bar Harbor and Bluenose hotels (see below). It has spacious bathrooms and rooms, the latter decked out in the same floral bedspreads and curtains you'd expect in any upscale business hotel, but the access to downtown Bar Harbor and the nearby ocean are big pluses. Concessions to business and tourist travelers include a guest laundry facility, gift shop, and high-speed Internet access. Not surprisingly, they're getting a lot of tour groups. Expect comfort, not island character.

Bar Harbor

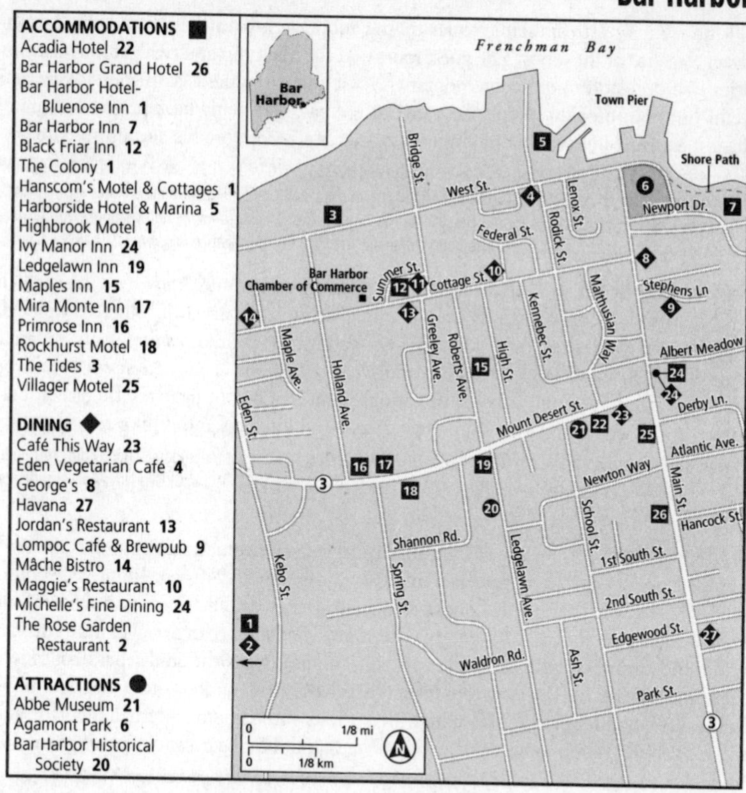

269 Main St. ✆ **888/766-2529** or 207/288-5226. www.barharborgrand.com. 70 units. Late June to early Oct $145–$195 double; mid-Apr to late June and early Oct to mid-Nov $99–$139 double. Suites $20–$70 extra. Rates include continental breakfast. AE, DISC, MC, V. Closed mid-Nov to mid-Apr. **Amenities:** Outdoor pool. *In room:* A/C, fridge, coffeemaker, DVD player.

Bar Harbor Hotel–Bluenose Inn ★★ Owned by the same folks who operate the waterside Bar Harbor Inn (see below), this resort-style complex—situated in two buildings topping a small rise—has even better views of the surrounding terrain than its companion property. Facilities here are more modern, too: Expect spacious carpeted rooms with huge bathrooms, balconies, and one of the island's best dining rooms (see "Where to Dine," below). Upper-floor rooms with sea views are definitely worth the extra cost, particularly if the weather is good, and the staff here is professional and friendly.

90 Eden St., Bar Harbor, ME 04609. ✆ **800/445-4077** or 207/288-3348. www.bluenoseinn.com. 97 units. Mid-June to early Oct $159–$405 double; late Apr to mid-June and mid Oct $75–$299 double. AE, DC, DISC, MC, V. Closed Nov–mid Apr. **Amenities:** Restaurant; 2 pools; fitness center; Jacuzzi. *In room:* A/C, fridge, coffeemaker, hair dryer, iron/ironing board, robe, balcony.

The Bar Harbor Inn ★★ The Bar Harbor Inn, just off Agamont Park, nicely mixes traditional and contemporary style, along with convenience and gracious charm. The main shingled inn, which dates from the turn of the 19th century, has a settled, old-money feel, with its semicircular dining room with ocean views and the button-down elegance of the lobby. The guest rooms, in the main inn and two additional structures, are decidedly more contemporary. Guest rooms in the Oceanfront Lodge and Main Inn both provide spectacular views of the bay, and many have private balconies; the less expensive Newport Building lacks views but is comfortable and up-to-date.

Newport Dr. (P.O. Box 7), Bar Harbor, ME 04609. ✆ **800/248-3351** or 207/288-3351. www.barharborinn.com. 153 units. Early June to late Oct $155–$369 double; late Mar, mid June, and Nov $79–$245 double. Rates include continental breakfast. AE, DISC, MC, V. Closed Dec to late Mar. **Amenities:** Dining room; heated outdoor pool; Jacuzzi; conference space; limited room service; afternoon coffee and cookies; free newspaper. *In room:* A/C, balcony (some).

Harborside Hotel & Marina ★ Once a family-style motel known as the Golden Anchor, the Harborside is slowly transforming itself into luxury digs. When completed, it promises a wide variety of studios and two- and three-bedroom suites sporting fancy bathrooms, business-hotel amenities, and large televisions. The priciest suites will be more like condominium units, with various combinations of Jacuzzis, fireplaces, balconies, water views, and even—in a few cases—full kitchens and dining rooms.

55 West St., Bar Harbor, ME 04609. ✆ **800/328-5033** or 207/288-5033. www.theharborsidehotel.com. 160 units. $139–$259 double; $225–$850 suite. Off-season rates sometimes lower. DISC, MC, V. Closed Nov–Apr. **Amenities:** Outdoor pool. *In room:* A/C, TV, dataport.

Ivy Manor Inn ★ The Ivy Manor quickly proved a welcome addition to Bar Harbor's upscale lodging pool when it opened in 1997. Located in a 1940s-era Tudor-style house, the Ivy Manor was thoroughly done over in an understated French Victorian style, mostly in lush, rich colors such as burgundy. The rooms are larger than average; most are carpeted and furnished with attractive, tasteful antiques from the innkeeper's collection. Some rooms have antique claw-foot tubs; others have small outdoor sitting decks. Among my favorite rooms: no. 6, a small suite with a private sitting room and small fireplace; and no. 1, the honeymoon room, with an imposing walnut headboard and matching armoire.

194 Main St., Bar Harbor, ME 04609. ✆ **888/670-1997** or 207/288-2138. www.ivymanor.com. 7 units. Mid-June to Oct $200–$325 double; Apr to mid-June $185–$275 double. Rates include full breakfast. Closed Nov–Mar. 2-night minimum on holiday weekends. AE, DISC, MC, V. No children under 12. **Amenities:** Restaurant; lounge. *In room:* A/C.

Mira Monte Inn A stay at this grayish-green Italianate mansion, built in 1864, feels a bit like a trip to grandmother's house—a grandmother who inherited most of her furniture from *her* grandmother. The antiques are more intriguing than elegant, and the common rooms are furnished in a pleasant country Victorian style. The 2-acre grounds, within a few minutes' walk of Bar Harbor's restaurants and attractions, are nicely landscaped. The brick terrace set away from the street is a fine place to enjoy breakfast on warm summer mornings. Most guest rooms have a balcony or a fireplace, or both. The room styles vary widely; some are heavy on the Victorian, others have the feel of a country farmhouse. If you're a light sleeper, avoid the rooms facing Mount Desert Street; those facing the gardens in the rear are far more peaceful. Families should inquire about the suites in the adjacent outbuilding.

69 Mount Desert St., Bar Harbor, ME 04609. ✆ **800/553-5109** or 207/288-4263. Fax 207/288-3115. www.miramonte.com. 12 units. Late June to mid-Oct $160–$230 double, $220–$290 suite; spring and fall $95–$166 double, $130–$204 suite. Rates include breakfast. 2-night minimum stay in midsummer. AE, DC, DISC, MC, V. Closed Nov to early May. **Amenities:** Garden; Internet access. *In room:* A/C, fireplace (some), balcony (some).

The Tides ★ The Tides has just four guest rooms (three of which are suites) in a sprawling yellow mansion dating from 1887. It's at the head of a long, lush lawn that descends to the water's edge in a neighborhood of imposing homes within easy strolling distance of the village center. Guests can unwind in one of the two spacious living rooms (one upstairs and one down) or, even better, on the veranda, which has a unique outdoor fireplace. Breakfast is served on the porch in good weather; otherwise, it's in the regal dining room, with polished wood floors and views out to Bar Island.

119 West St., Bar Harbor, ME 04609. ✆ **207/288-4968.** www.barharbortides.com. 4 units. $225 double; $375–$395 suite. Rates include full breakfast. DISC, MC, V. Closed Nov to mid-June. *In room:* TV/VCR, dataport, fireplace (some).

Moderate

Acadia Hotel ★ *Value* The Acadia Hotel is nicely situated overlooking the Village Green, easily accessible to in-town activities and free shuttles to elsewhere on the island. This handsome, simple home dating from the late 19th century has a wraparound porch and guest rooms decorated with busy floral motifs. Rooms vary widely in size and amenities; two have whirlpools, two have phones, one has a kitchenette. Ask for the specifics when you book. The smaller rooms are a good value for those who don't plan to spend much time inside.

20 Mt. Desert St., Bar Harbor, ME 04609. ✆ **207/288-5721.** www.acadiahotel.com. 10 units. Summer $100–$160 double; fall $80–$130 double; winter and spring $55–$100 double. MC, V. *In room:* A/C, TV, no phone.

Black Friar Inn *Value* The Black Friar Inn, tucked on a side street near the municipal building parking lot, is easily overlooked. This yellow-shingled structure with quirky pediments and a somewhat eccentric air is a good deal in Bar Harbor. A former owner "collected" interiors and installed them throughout the house. Among them is a replica of the namesake Black Friar Pub in London, complete with elaborate carved-wood paneling (it's now a common room), stamped-tin walls in the breakfast room, and a doctor's office (now a guest room). The Black Friar's rooms are carpeted and furnished with a mix of antiques, and most are rather small. The least expensive are the two garret rooms on the third floor, each of which has a detached private bathroom down the hall. Staff can also arrange for kayak and fly-fishing tours.

10 Summer St., Bar Harbor, ME 04609. ✆ **207/288-5091.** Fax 207/288-4197. www.blackfriar.com. 7 units. Peak season $110–$160 double; off season lower. Rates include full breakfast. 2-night minimum mid-June to mid-Oct. DISC, MC, V. Closed Dec–Apr. Children 12 and older welcome. *In room:* A/C.

Ledgelawn Inn ★ If you want great location with considerably more flair than a motel, this is a good bet. This hulking cream-and-maroon 1904 "cottage" sits on a village lot amid towering oaks and maples and has an early-20th-century elegance, updated with modern amenities. The Ledgelawn first gets your attention with a handsome sun porch lounge with full bar. Guest rooms vary somewhat in size and mood, but all are comfortably, if not stylishly furnished with antiques and reproductions. Room no. 221 has a working fireplace, a shared balcony, and a pair of oak double beds; room no. 122 has an appealing sitting area with fireplace.

66 Mt. Desert St., Bar Harbor, ME 04609. ✆ **800/274-5334** or 207/288-4596. Fax 207/288-9968. www.ledgelawninn.com.. 33 units. July–Aug $125–$275 double; off season lower. Rates include breakfast. AE, DISC, MC, V. Closed late Oct to early May. Pets allowed ($15 per day).

Maples Inn ★ The Maples is a popular destination among those attracted to outdoor activities. You'll often find guests swapping stories of the day's adventures on the handsome front porch or lingering over breakfast to compare notes about the best hiking trails. The rather modest (by Bar Harbor standards) yellow farmhouse-style home is tucked away on a leafy side street among other B&Bs; it's an easy walk downtown to a movie or dinner. The innkeepers have a nice way of making guests comfortable, with board games and paperbacks scattered about, and down comforters in all rooms. Rooms are small to medium-size and all have private bathrooms. The two-room White Birch has a fireplace and is the largest; Red Oak has a private deck with plastic patio furniture. Breakfasts are appropriately filling for a full day outdoors.

16 Roberts Ave., Bar Harbor, ME 04609. ✆ **207/288-3443.** www.maplesinn.com. 6 units. Mid-June to mid-Oct $110–$165 double; May to mid-June and mid- to late Oct $75–$115 double. Memorial Day weekend $20 higher. Rates include full breakfast. 2-night minimum on holiday weekends. DISC, MC, V. Closed Nov–Apr. No children under 12.

Primrose Inn ★ *Kids* This handsome, pale-green-and-maroon Victorian stick–style inn, originally built in 1878, is one of the more notable properties on mansion row along Mount Desert Street. Its distinctive architecture has been not only preserved, but even improved upon, with an addition in 1987 that added 10 rooms with private bathrooms and a number of balconies. The inn is comfortable and furnished with "functional antiques" and more modern reproductions, and many rooms have a floral theme and thick carpets. Two guest rooms have whirlpools or fireplaces. The suites in the rear are spacious and comfortable, and the efficiencies make sense for families that could benefit from a kitchen (for rent by the week only).

73 Mount Desert St., Bar Harbor, ME 04609. ✆ **877/846-3424** or 207/288-4031. www.primroseinn.com. 10 units plus 5 efficiencies. Peak season $135–$215 double; spring and fall $95–$160 double; apartments $650–$1,200 per week. Daily rates include breakfast. 2-night minimum summer weekends. DISC, MC, V. Closed late Oct to Apr. Pets allowed ($75 fee; call first). **Amenities:** Piano. *In room:* A/C, kitchenette (some), hair dryer, iron/ironing board, Jacuzzi (some), fireplace (some).

Inexpensive

The Colony *Value* The Colony is a vintage motor court consisting of a handful of motel rooms and a battery of cottages arrayed around a long green. It will be most appreciated by those with a taste for the authentically retro; others might decide to look for accommodations more lavishly appointed. The rooms are furnished in a simple '70s style that won't win any awards for decor, but all are comfortable; many have kitchenettes. It's just across Route 3 from a cobblestone beach, and a 10-minute drive from Bar Harbor. The Colony offers one of the better values on the island.

Rte. 3 (P.O. Box 56), Hulls Cove, ME 04644. ✆ **800/524-1159** or 207/288-3383. www.acadiainfo.com/colony.htm. 55 units. $65–$125 double (discounts in Oct). AE, DC, DISC, MC, V. Closed mid-Oct to early June. *In room:* A/C, kitchenette (some), fridge (some).

WHERE TO DINE

Expensive

George's ★★ CONTEMPORARY MEDITERRANEAN This is a Bar Harbor classic, offering fine dining in classy but informal surroundings for more than 2 decades. George's takes some sleuthing to find, but it's worth the effort. (It's in the small clapboard cottage behind Main St.'s First National Bank.) The place captures the joyous feel of summer with four smallish dining rooms and plenty of open windows, plus additional seating on the terrace outside—the best place to watch the gentle dusk settle over town. The service is upbeat and the meals are wonderfully prepared. All entrees sell for one price and include salad, vegetable, and potato or rice. Offerings change with the season and availability. You won't go wrong with basic choices like steamed lobster, roast chicken, or grilled beef with ancho chile sauce and masa cakes, but you're better off opting for the more adventurous fare, like lobster strudel or "To Die For" mustard shrimp. The house specialty is lamb. Delicious desserts include coconut *panna cotta,* speckled chocolate cake with orange Bavarian cream, maple sugar crème brûlée, and black currant sorbet.

7 Stephens Lane. ✆ **207/288-4505.** www.georgesbarharbor.com. Reservations recommended. Entrees $25; appetizer, entree, and dessert packages $37–$40. AE, DISC, MC, V. Daily 5:30–10pm; shorter hours after Labor Day. Closed Nov to early May.

Michelle's Fine Dining ★★ FRENCH Michelle's is in the graceful Ivy Manor Inn (p. 648). The three dining rooms are elegant and the extensive menu of chef William Sellner, Jr., elaborates on traditional French cuisine with subtle New England twists. The appetizers include smoked salmon layered with a chervil mousse, and foie gras with black truffle. Main courses are elaborate affairs, like chateaubriand for two carved at the table, roasted lobster in basil cream sauce, rack of lamb, and Michelle's bouillabaisse for two. Finish with the unique "bag of chocolate," which comes served in an edible chocolate bag, or one of several outstanding soufflés.

194 Main St. ✆ **207/288-0038.** www.michellesfinedining.com. Reservations required during peak season. Main courses $26–$40. AE, DISC, MC, V. Daily 6–9pm. Closed late Oct to early May.

The Rose Garden Restaurant ★★★ NEW AMERICAN One of only a handful of fine-dining establishments in Bar Harbor that actually delivers a big-league dining experience, this unassuming room—within the Bluenose Inn (p. 647)—turns out wonderful meals. The prix-fixe isn't cheap, but the chef's seared tenderloin is perfectly done and paired with tender pot-roast vegetables; a tasty hunk of grilled salmon comes with mustard sauce, caramelized onions, and a potato cake. Another choice is peppercorn-seared venison with wild rice, squash purée, and cranberry sauce. Inventive appetizers include a strudel filled with asparagus, toasted walnuts, and Gruyère, and a chilled mango soup with jumbo shrimp and fresh mint. Dessert doesn't let up, either—the chocolate mousse cake and the unusual sweet-potato crème brûlée with shortbread are out of sight.

90 Eden St. ✆ **800/445-4077** or 207/288-3348. Reservations recommended. Breakfast $10–$17; prix-fixe dinner $63. MC, V. Breakfast 7–10:30am; dinner 5:30–9:30pm. Closed Nov–Apr.

Moderate

Café This Way ★ NEW AMERICAN This is the kind of place that does wonderful things with relatively simple ingredients. Café This Way feels like a casually hip coffeehouse and is tucked on a side street down from the Village Green. Bookshelves line one wall, and a small bar is tucked in a nook. It serves breakfast and dinner, but no lunch. The breakfasts are excellent and mildly sinful. Dinners are equally appetizing, with tasty starters that may run to a spicy Portuguese stew of mussels and sausages or a small flatbread pizza of pears and blue cheese, followed by main courses such as lemon-vodka lobster cooked in Absolut citron, a Thai seafood pot, or grilled and peppered lamb chops.

14½ Mount Desert St. ✆ **207/288-4483.** www.cafethisway.com. Reservations recommended for dinner. Main courses breakfast $4.95–$7.50, dinner $13–$23. MC, V. Mid-Apr to Oct Mon–Sat 7–11am; Sun 8am–1pm; dinner daily 5:30–9pm.

Mâche Bistro ★ BISTRO Relative newcomer Mâche has developed a devoted following among those who know quality food and preparation. The small restaurant (nine tables) with soothing but plain decor hides a sophisticated kitchen. The menu changes monthly; appetizers could include a salad with bleu cheese, apples, and truffle oil; or a smoked-lobster bisque. Main courses recently featured a seared steak with black trumpet infused jus, pan-fried tempeh, and a fisherman's stew made with local seafood. Duck is often on the menu, and it's usually a good choice.

135 Cottage St. ✆ **207/288-0447.** www.machebistro.com. Reservations recommended. Main courses $16–$22. AE, MC, V. Tues–Sun 5–9pm.

Maggie's Restaurant ★ SEAFOOD The slogan for Maggie's is "Notably fresh seafood," and the place invariably delivers on that understated promise. (Only locally caught fish is used.) It's a casually elegant spot tucked off Cottage Street, good for a romantic evening with soothing music and attentive service. Appetizers include smoked salmon and steamed oysters with a saffron hollandaise. Main courses range from basic boiled lobster and simple grilled salmon to Maine seafood Provençal. Desserts are homemade and it's worth leaving room for them.

6 Summer St. ✆ **207/288-9007.** www.maggiesbarharbor.com. Reservations recommended July–Aug. Main courses $16–$24. MC, V. Mon–Sat 5–9:30pm.

Havana ★★ LATINO/FUSION Havana established a new creative standard for restaurants when it opened in 1999 in this town of fried fish and baked stuffed haddock. The spare but sparkling decor is sophisticated, and the menu could compete in any urban area. While the offerings change weekly, expect appetizers like monkfish seviche or Thai tofu with a plantain crust. Recent entrees included Chilean black-bean stew, grilled pork chops rubbed with maple sugar and chiles, and filet mignon rubbed with Cuban coffee and black pepper. Finish with an equally dazzling dessert such as pistachio-mousse popovers with chocolate Cointreau sauce.

318 Main St. ✆ **207/288-2822.** www.havanamaine.com. Reservations recommended. Main courses $16–$33. AE, DC, DISC, MC, V. Daily 5–10pm.

Inexpensive

Eden Vegetarian Café ★ *Finds* VEGETARIAN Right across the street from the bay, chef Mark Rampacek operates Bar Harbor's only vegetarian eatery, bringing high culinary flair and atmosphere to the cause; most dishes here use organic and/or locally grown ingredients, and you may want to dress up a bit if you dine here. Dinners are surprisingly elaborate; starters include roasted fig bruschetta and a beet tartare with capers and a delicate arrangement of "stained-glass" potato. The main course could be a bento box of tofu, edamame, and seaweed salad; grilled vegetables, tempeh, or seitan; or bright red lentil dal paired with eggplant. For dessert, try chocolate fondue for two.

78 West St. ✆ **207/288-4422.** www.barharborvegetarian.com. Reservations strongly recommended. Main courses $9–$17. MC, V. Daily 5–9:30pm. Closed Dec–Mar.

Jordan's Restaurant *Value* DINER This unpretentious breakfast and lunch joint has been dishing up filling fare since 1976, and it offers a glimpse of old Bar Harbor before the local economy was dominated by T-shirt shops. It's a popular haunt of working folks in town on one errand or another, but the staff is also genuinely friendly to tourists. Diners can settle into one of the pine booths or at a laminated table and order off the place-mat menu, choosing from basic fare. Breakfast is the specialty here, with a broad selection of three-egg omelets, along with muffins and pancakes made with wild Maine blueberries.

80 Cottage St. ✆ **207/288-3586.** Breakfast $2.95–$6.75; lunch $2.25–$8.25. MC, V. Daily 4:30am–2pm. Closed Feb–Mar.

Lompoc Cafe and Brewpub AMERICAN/ECLECTIC The Lompoc Cafe has a well-worn, neighborhood bar feel to it—little wonder, since waiters and other workers from around Bar Harbor congregate here after-hours. The cafe consists of three sections—there's the original bar, a tidy beer garden just outside (try your hand at bocce), and a small and open barnlike structure at the garden's edge to handle the overflow. The brewery next door produces several unique beers, including a blueberry ale (intriguing concept, but ask for a sample before ordering a full glass) and the smooth Coal Porter, available in sizes up to the 20-ounce "fatty." Bar menus are usually yawn-inducing, but this one has some pleasant surprises, like the Persian plate (hummus and grape leaves), Szechuan eggplant wrap, and crab and shrimp cakes. Alas, the kitchen's executions don't always live up to its aspirations. Live music is offered some evenings, when there's a small cover charge.

36 Rodick St. © **207/288-9392.** www.lompoccafe.com. Reservations not accepted. Sandwiches $4.25–$14; dinner items $8.50–$19. MC, V. May–Nov daily 11:30am–1am. Closed Dec–Apr.

ELSEWHERE ON THE ISLAND ★★

You'll find plenty to explore outside of Acadia National Park and Bar Harbor. Quiet fishing villages, deep woodlands, and unexpected ocean views are among the jewels that turn up when one peers beyond the usual places.

ESSENTIALS

GETTING AROUND The east half of the island is best navigated on Route 3, which forms the better part of a loop from Bar Harbor through Seal Harbor and past Northeast Harbor before returning up the eastern shore of Somes Sound. Route 102 and Route 102A provide access to the island's western half. See information on the free *Island Explorer* shuttle service under "Getting Around" in the section on Acadia National Park, earlier.

VISITOR INFORMATION The best source of information on the island is at the **Thompson Island Information Center** (© **207/288-3411**), on Route 3 just south of the causeway connecting Mount Desert Island with the mainland (see above). Another source of local information is the **Mount Desert Chamber of Commerce,** P.O. Box 675, Northeast Harbor, ME 04662 (© **207/276-5040**).

EXPLORING THE REST OF THE ISLAND

On the tip of the eastern lobe of Mount Desert Island is the staid, prosperous community of **Northeast Harbor,** long a favored retreat among the Eastern Seaboard's upper crust. Those without personal invitations to come as house guests will need to be satisfied with glimpses of the shingled palaces set in the fragrant spruce forests and along the rocky shore, but the village itself is worth investigating. Situated on a scenic, narrow harbor, with the once-grand Asticou Inn at its head, Northeast Harbor possesses a refined elegance that's best appreciated by finding a vantage point, and then sitting and admiring.

One of the best, least publicized places for enjoying views of the harbor is from the understatedly spectacular **Asticou Terraces** ★. Finding the parking lot can be tricky: Head ½ mile east (toward Seal Harbor) on Route 3 from the junction with Route 198, and look for the small gravel lot on the water side of the road with a sign reading ASTICOU TERRACES. Park here, cross the road on foot, and set off up a magnificent path made of local rock that ascends the sheer hillside, with expanding views of the harbor and the town. This pathway, with its precise stonework and the occasional bench and gazebo, is one of the nation's hidden marvels of landscape architecture. Created by Boston landscape architect Joseph Curtis, who summered here for many years prior to his death in 1928, the pathway seems to blend in almost preternaturally with its spruce-and-fir surroundings, as if it were created by an act of God rather than of man. Curtis donated the property to the public for quiet enjoyment.

Continue on the trail at the top of the hillside and you'll soon arrive at Curtis's cabin (open to the public daily in summer), behind which lies the formal **Thuya**

Gardens, which are as manicured as the terraces are natural. These wonderfully maintained gardens, designed by noted landscape architect Charles K. Savage, attract flower enthusiasts, students of landscape architecture, and local folks looking for a quiet place to rest. It's well worth the trip. A donation of $2 is requested of visitors to the garden; the terraces are free.

WHERE TO STAY

Asticou Inn ★ The once-grand Asticou Inn, which dates from 1883, occupies a prime location at the head of Northeast Harbor. Its weathered gray shingles and profusion of overhanging eaves give it a stern demeanor, but it also has elements of eccentricity. The Asticou is more elegant in its location and on the exterior rather than interior. The rooms are furnished in a simple summer-home style, as if a more opulent decor were somehow too ostentatious. The dinner dance and elaborate "grand buffet" on Thursday nights in summer remain hallowed island traditions and worth checking out. (Expect smoked seafood, lobster Newburg, salads and relishes, a dessert tray, and more.)

Rte. 3, Northeast Harbor, ME 04662. ✆ **800/258-3373** or 207/276-3344. www.asticou.com. 41 units, 2 cottages. July–Aug $215–$330 double; May and Sept–Oct $130–$235 double. Rates include breakfast; MAP plans available July–Aug only. MC, V. Valet parking. Closed Nov to late Apr. No children under 6. **Amenities:** Outdoor pool; tennis court; concierge; business center; limited room service; babysitting; laundry; Thurs dances.

Claremont ★ Early prints of the 1884 Claremont show an austere four-story wooden building with a single gable overlooking Somes Sound from a grassy rise, and the place hasn't changed all that much since. The Claremont offers nothing fancy or elaborate—just simple, classic New England grace. Most of the guest rooms are bright and airy, furnished with antiques and some old furniture that doesn't quite qualify as "antique." The bathrooms are modern. Guests opting for the full meal plan at the inn are given preference in reserving rooms overlooking the water; it's almost worth it, although dinners are lackluster. There's also a series of cottages, available for a 3-day minimum—some are set rustically in the piney woods, while others have pleasing views of the sound.

P.O. Box 137, Southwest Harbor, ME 04679. ✆ **800/244-5036** or 207/244-5036. www.theclaremonthotel.com. 30 inn rooms, 14 cottages. Inn rooms: summer $180 double, spring and fall $120–$170 double. Cottages: mid-June to mid-Sept $195–$265 double; late May to mid-June and mid-Sept to mid-Oct $155–$195 double. Rates include breakfast. MAP rates also available (inn rooms only). MC, V. Closed mid-Oct to late May. **Amenities:** Dining room; tennis court; bicycles (free to guests); babysitting; croquet; rowboats; library.

Inn at Southwest There's a decidedly late-19th-century air to this mansard-roofed Victorian home, but it's restrained on the frills. The guest rooms are named after Maine lighthouses and furnished with both contemporary and antique furniture. All rooms have ceiling fans and down comforters. Among the most pleasant rooms is Blue Hill Bay on the third floor, with its large bathroom, sturdy oak bed and bureau, and glimpses of the scenic harbor. Breakfasts are ample reason to rise and shine, with specialties like vanilla Belgian waffles with raspberry sauce, and crab potato bake.

371 Main St. (P.O. Box 593), Southwest Harbor, ME 04679. ✆ **207/244-3835.** www.innatsouthwest.com. 7 units. Mid-June to early Oct $125–$175 double; late Apr to mid-June and mid- to late Oct $95–$135 double. All rates include full breakfast. DISC, MC, V. Closed Nov–Apr. *In room:* No phone.

Lindenwood Inn ★★ The Lindenwood offers a refreshing change from the fusty, overly draperied inns that proliferate along Maine's coast; affable innkeeper Jim King gave up cabinetmaking to open a string of successful B&Bs in Southwest Harbor, and his latest is his best, one of my favorites in Maine. Staying here feels as though you've rented an island home for the summer with a bunch of your friends. Housed in a handsome 1902 Queen Anne–style home at the harbor's edge, the inn has modern and uncluttered rooms, with colors that are simple and bold. Most rooms have balconies, some have fireplaces, and all possess wonderfully comfy mattresses. The adornments are few and mostly from King's wonderful collection of African and Pacific art and artifacts, but clean lines and bright natural light more than create a relaxing mood—you'll even begin to view the cobblestone doorstops as works of art. The spacious suite with its great harbor views is especially appealing, with a deck, cathedral ceiling, and Jacuzzi.

118 Clark Point Rd. (P.O. Box 1328), Southwest Harbor, ME 04679. ✆ **800/307-5335** or 207/244-5335. www.lindenwoodinn.com. 8 units, 1 bungalow. Mid-June to mid-Oct $105–$195 double; $245–$275 suite. Closed mid-Oct to mid-June. Rates include full breakfast. AE, MC, V. **Amenities:** Bar; outdoor pool; Jacuzzi. *In room:* Kitchenette (some), fireplace (some), Jacuzzi (1).

WHERE TO DINE

Beal's Lobster Pound *Finds* LOBSTER POUND Purists claim this is among the best lobster shacks in Maine. It's certainly got the atmosphere: creaky picnic tables on a plain deck, overlooking a working-class harbor and right next to the Coast Guard base. Don't wear a tie. You go inside to pick out and order your lobster from tanks (pay by the pound), then choose sides (corn on the cob, slaw, steamed clams—the usuals—are good), then wait for your number to be called. There are absolutely no pretensions here; your meal will arrive on Styrofoam or paper plates, but you won't care a bit.

182 Clark Point Rd., Southwest Harbor. ✆ **207/244-7178** or 207/244-3202. www.bealslobster.com. Lobsters market price. AE, DISC, MC, V. Summer daily 9am–8pm; after Labor Day 9am–5pm daily. Closed Columbus Day to Memorial Day.

The Burning Tree ★★ *Finds* REGIONAL/ORGANIC On busy Route 3 between Bar Harbor and Northeast Harbor, The Burning Tree is an easy restaurant to speed right by—but that's a mistake. This low-key restaurant, with its bright, open, and sometimes noisy dining room, serves up the freshest food in the area. Much of the produce and herbs comes from its own gardens, with the rest of the ingredients supplied locally whenever possible. Seafood is the specialty, and it's consistently prepared with imagination and skill. The menu changes often to reflect local availability.

Rte. 3, Otter Creek. ✆ **207/288-9331.** Reservations recommended. Main courses $18–$23. DISC, MC, V. Mid-June to Columbus Day Wed–Mon 5–9pm. Closed day after Columbus Day to mid-June.

Fiddlers' Green ★ CREATIVE AMERICAN/SEAFOOD Derek Wilbur's bistro is something different in these parts, and very welcome indeed. Begin with a selection from the cold seafood bar: smoked salmon wrapped in gravlax and horseradish chèvre, or Wilbur's unique "sashimi martini," a cup of smoked mussels, scallop seviche, and raw tuna in a pear-tahini marinade. There are always a few good pasta dishes on the menu. Meatier main dishes nightly could include steak frites, a bacon-wrapped saddle of rabbit, or venison chops.

411 Main St., Southwest Harbor. ✆ **207/244-9416.** www.fiddlersgreenrestaurant.com. Reservations recommended. Main courses $18–$26. AE, DISC, MC, V. Tues–Sun 5:30–9pm. Closed Columbus Day to Memorial Day.

Red Sky ★★ CREATIVE AMERICAN Terry Preble closed his former Preble Grill but, after a spell, reopened right off Southwest Harbor's main drag; like the other two gourmet restaurants in the area, it brings a big-city sensibility to the island. Meals begin with intriguing starters such as carrot-red curry soup, "lollipop" lamb chops dusted with bitter chocolate and minty vinaigrette, or house-fashioned duck-and-pork sausages served with dipping sauces. Main courses run to lobster risotto with asparagus and porcini mushrooms, panko-crusted sea scallops in tamari sauce, or a simple pan-roasted breast of duck served with a plum wine demiglace.

14 Clark Point Rd., Southwest Harbor. © **207/244-0476.** www.redskyrestaurant.com. Entrees $16–$25. AE, DISC, MC, V. Wed–Sat 5:30–9pm; open additional days in summer (call to check). Closed Jan.

7 The Western Lakes & Mountains ★

Maine's western mountains comprise a rugged, brawny region that stretches northeast from the White Mountains to the Carrabassett Valley. Maine's coast is more commercialized, and villages here aren't as quaint as in Vermont's Green Mountains, but you'll find azure lakes, forests of spruce, fir, and lichens, and hills and mountains that take on a sapphire hue in summer hiking season. Moosehead Lake and Baxter State Park in the North Woods allow for numerous outdoor pursuits. About half of Maine is made up of northern forest lands with no formal government—"unorganized townships." While timber companies own and maintain much of the land, visitors will find much to explore on foot or by canoe.

BETHEL ★★

Until recently, Bethel was a sleepy resort town with one of those family-oriented ski areas that seemed destined for extinction. But then the Sunday River ski area was bought and dusted off by a brash young entrepreneur, who turned it into one of New England's most vibrant and challenging ski destinations.

With the rise of Sunday River, the white-clapboard town of Bethel (about 7 miles from the ski area) has been dragged into the modern era, though it hasn't (yet) taken on the artificial, packaged flavor of many other New England ski towns. The village (pop. 2,500) is still defined by the stoic buildings of the respected prep school Gould Academy, the broad village common, and The Bethel Inn, a sprawling, old-fashioned resort that's managed to stay ahead of the tide by adding condos without losing its pleasant, timeworn character.

ESSENTIALS

GETTING THERE Bethel is at the intersection of Routes 26 and 2. It's accessible from the Maine Turnpike by heading west on Route 26 from Exit 11. From New Hampshire, drive east on Route 2 from Gorham.

VISITOR INFORMATION The **Bethel Area Chamber of Commerce,** 30 Cross St., Bethel, ME 04217 (© **800/442-5826** for reservations or 207/824-2282; www.bethelmaine.com), has offices behind the Casablanca movie theater. It's open year-round Monday through Friday from 8am to 8pm, Saturday from 10am to 6pm, and Sunday from noon to 5pm.

GRAFTON NOTCH STATE PARK

Grafton Notch ★★ straddles Route 26 as it angles northwest from Newry toward Errol, NH. The 33-mile drive is one of my favorites, both picturesque and dramatic. You pass through farmland in a fertile river valley before ascending through bristly forest to a glacial notch hemmed in by rough, gray cliffs on the hillsides above. Foreboding Old Speck Mountain towers to the south; views of Lake Umbagog open to the north as you continue into New Hampshire. This route attracts few crowds, though it's popular with Canadians headed to the Maine coast.

Public access to the park consists of a handful of roadside parking lots near scenic areas. The best of the bunch is **Screw Auger Falls,** where the Bear River drops through several small cascades before tumbling dramatically into a narrow, corkscrewing gorge carved long ago by glacial runoff through granite bedrock. Picnic tables dot the forested banks upriver of the falls, and kids are inexorably drawn to splash and swim in the smaller pools on warm days. Admission to the park is $1; look for self-pay stations at the parking lot.

DOWNHILL SKIING

Sunday River Ski Resort ★★★ Sunday River has grown at lightening speed, swiftly becoming one of the best ski mountains in New England for its terrain and conditions. (The resort scene, however, sorely lags, and staff can be brusque.) Unlike ski areas that have developed around a single tall peak, Sunday River expanded along an undulating ridge some 3 miles wide that encompasses seven peaks. Just traversing the resort, stitching runs together with chairlift rides, can take an hour or more. As a result, you're rarely bored making the same run time and again. The descents offer something for virtually everyone, from deviously steep bump runs to wide, wonderful intermediate trails. Sunday River is also blessed with plenty of water for snowmaking, making tons of the stuff using a proprietary snowmaking system. The superb skiing conditions are, alas, offset by an uninspiring base area. The lodges and condos (total capacity 6,000) tend toward the architecturally dull, and the less-than-delicate landscaping is of the sort created by bulldozers. Sunday River's trails are often crowded on weekends; weekdays, you'll pretty much have the place to yourself.

P.O. Box 450, Bethel, ME 04217. © **800/543-2754** for lodging, or 207/824-3000. www.sundayriver.com. Vertical drop: 2,340 ft. Lifts: 15 chairlifts (4 high-speed), 3 surface lifts. Skiable acreage: 654. Lift tickets Mon–Fri $52; Sat–Sun $56.

Ski Mt. Abram Mount Abram is a welcoming and friendly intermediate mountain, perfect for families still ascending skiing's learning curve. It has an informal atmosphere that sharply contrasts with bustling and impersonal Sunday River nearby. It's suffered from the usual financial ups and downs of small ski areas in recent years, but its current owners seem to have put it on a good course, adding a 500-foot snow tube park for kids, and capitalizing on its popularity among telemark skiers by offering telemark rentals and weekend lessons. The day care and other family programs are worth noting.

P.O. Box 240, Greenwood, ME 04255. © **207/875-5002.** www.skimtabram.com. Vertical drop: 1,030 ft. Lifts: 2 chairlifts, 3 T-bars. Skiable acreage: 135. Lift tickets Mon–Fri $21; Sat–Sun $37.

OTHER OUTDOOR PURSUITS

GOLF Head for **The Bethel Inn and Country Club** (© **207/824-2175**), an unusually scenic, 18-hole golf course next to the inn, if you feel the urge to play 9. Equipment and golf carts are for rent, and the club also has a driving range.

HIKING The **Appalachian Trail** ★★ crosses the Mahoosuc mountains northwest of Bethel. Many who have hiked the entire 2,000-mile trail say this stretch is the most demanding on knees and psyches. The trail doesn't forgive; it generally foregoes switchbacks in favor of sheer ascents and descents. It's also hard to find water along the trail during dry weather. Still, it's worth the knee-pounding effort for the views and the unrivaled sense of remoteness.

One stretch crosses Old Speck Mountain, Maine's third-highest peak. Views from the summit are all but nonexistent since the old fire tower closed, but an easy-to-moderate spur trail on the lower end of the trail ascends an 800-foot cliff called "The Eyebrow," and provides a good vantage point for Bear River Valley and the rugged terrain of Grafton Notch. Look for the well-signed parking lot where Route 26 intersects the trail in Grafton Notch State Park. Park your car and then head south on the A.T. toward Old Speck; in .1 mile, you'll intersect the Eyebrow Trail, which you can follow to the overlook.

The Appalachian Mountain Club's *Maine Mountain Guide* is highly recommended for detailed information about other area hikes.

WHERE TO STAY

The Bethel Inn ★ A classic, old-fashioned resort set on 200 acres in the village, this inn has a quiet, settled air, which is appropriate because it was built to house patients of Dr. John Gehring, who put Bethel on the map by treating nervous disorders through a regimen of healthy country living. (Bethel was once known as "the resting place of Harvard" for the legions of faculty treated here.) The quaint, homey rooms aren't terribly spacious, but they are pleasingly furnished with country antiques. More luxurious are the 16 modern rooms and suites added to the inn in the late 1990s. You give up some of the charm of the old inn, but gain elbowroom.

On the Common, Bethel, ME 04217. ✆ **800/654-0125** or 207/824-2175. www.bethelinn.com. 62 units. Summer $198–$418 double; winter $158–$454 double. Rates include breakfast and dinner. Ski packages available. 2-night minimum stay summer weekends and ski season; 3-night minimum stay during winter school vacations. AE, DISC, MC, V. Pets allowed ($10 per night). **Amenities:** Dining room; outdoor pool; golf course; tennis court; fitness center; Jacuzzi; sauna; shuttle to ski areas; watersports equipment rental; babysitting; laundry service; cross-country skiing. *In room:* TV, hair dryer, iron.

Jordan Grand Resort Hotel ★ Kids The anchor for expanded development in the far-flung Jordan Bowl area, this hotel feels miles away from the rest of the resort, largely because it is—even the staff makes *The Shining* jokes about its remoteness. A modern if sprawling hotel, it offers little personal touch or flair, but boasts a great location for skiers who want to be first on untracked slopes each morning. Owing to the quirky terrain, parking is inconvenient; you often have to walk some distance to your room (opt for valet parking). Rooms are simply furnished in a durable condo style. Many are quite spacious and most have balconies. It's a popular destination with families, so not the best choice for couples seeking a quiet getaway. Sunday River improved its food service; its two restaurants, though not outstanding, are a notch above typical ski-area hotel fare.

Sunday River Rd. (P.O. Box 450), Bethel, ME 04217. ✆ **800/543-2754** or 207/824-5000. Fax 207/824-2111. www.sundayriver.com. 195 units. $117–$332 double. AE, DC, DISC, MC, V. **Amenities:** 2 restaurants; outdoor pool; fitness room; Jacuzzi; sauna; steam room; children's center; concierge; business center; limited room service; in-room massage; babysitting; dry cleaning; valet parking. *In room:* A/C, TV, dataport, coffeemaker.

The Victoria ★★ Built in 1895, the inn has been restored with antique lighting fixtures, period furniture, and the original formidable oak doors. The guest rooms have a luxurious William Morris feel, with richly patterned wallpaper and handmade duvet covers. Room no. 1 is the luxurious master suite, with a turret window and a sizable bathroom; room no. 3 is the only unit with wood floors (the others are carpeted), but it has a tiny bathroom. Most intriguing are the four loft rooms in the attached carriage house, each with a gas fireplace, Jacuzzi, and soaring ceilings revealing old beams. The suites also have lofts; they can sleep up to eight guests.

32 Main St., Bethel, ME 04217. ✆ **888/774-1235** or 207/824-8060. www.thevictoria-inn.com. 15 units. Winter weekend $109–$179 double, $179–$279 suite; midweek $79–$129 double, $149–$199 suite; summer and foliage season $89–$159 double, $159–$259 suite; spring and late fall $75–$139 double, $139–$239 suite. Rates include breakfast. 2-night minimum stay on weekends and holidays. AE, MC, V. Pets sometimes allowed ($30 per night). **Amenities:** Restaurant (see below). *In room:* A/C, TV, dataport, hair dryer, Jacuzzi (some).

WHERE TO DINE

Great Grizzly American Steakhouse ★ STEAKHOUSE These two restaurants share a handsome timber-frame structure a couple of minutes from the ski area. It's casual, with pinball, a pool table, and a bar. The atmosphere is more relaxed, the food is significantly better than at the Sunday River Brewing Company, and the beer-on-tap selection is pretty good.

Sunday River Rd. ✆ **207/824-6271** or 207/824-6836. Pizzas $7.95 and up; other entrees $6.95–$17. MC, V. Daily pizza menu 3–10pm; steakhouse menu from 5pm. Open only during ski season.

Sunday River Brewing Company PUB FARE This modern and boisterous brewpub, on prime real estate at the corner of Route 2 and the Sunday River access road, is a good choice if your primary objective is to quaff robust ales and porters. The brews are awfully good; the food (burgers, nachos, and chicken wings) doesn't strive for any culinary heights, and certainly doesn't achieve any. If you want good pub fare, you're better off headed up Sunday River Road to try Great Grizzly American Steakhouse (see above). Come early if you're looking for a quiet meal; it gets loud later in the evening when bands take the stage.

Rte. 2 (at Sunday River Rd.), Bethel. ✆ **207/824-4253.** Reservations not accepted. Main courses $5.95–$17. AE, MC, V. Daily 11:30am–12:30am.

The Victoria ★★ NEW AMERICAN The dining room on the first floor of Bethel's finest inn serves the town's best (and most romantic) dinners. Guests are seated in one of two intimate rooms, where they choose from a menu that's simple but generally delivers on its high aspirations. Starters may be lobster cakes, smoked salmon, or a salad; entrees could include lobster ravioli in a pink vodka sauce, or filet mignon served with a blueberry-and-port demiglace. Desserts are a treat, both visually and to the taste.

32 Main St. ✆ **888/774-1235** or 207/824-8060. www.thevictoria-inn.com. Reservations recommended on weekends. Main courses $9.95–$18. AE, MC, V. Wed–Mon 5:30–9pm.

8 The North Woods

Much of Maine's outdoor recreation takes place on private lands—especially in the North Woods, 9 million acres of which are owned by fewer than two dozen timber companies. This sprawling, uninhabited land is increasingly at the heart of a simmering debate over land-use policies.

Hunters, fishermen, canoeists, rafters, bird-watchers, and hikers have been accustomed to having the run of much of the forest, with the tacit permission of local timber companies, many of which have had long and historic ties to woodland communities. However, a lot has changed in recent years.

Among the biggest changes is the value of lakefront property, which has become far more valuable as second-home properties than as standing timber. A number of parcels have been sold off, and some formerly open land was closed to visitors.

A number of proposals to restore and conserve the forest have circulated in recent years. At press time, the governor of Maine had just authorized a land deal which will attach Baxter State Park to Katahdin Lake to the east, adding about 4,000 acres. Another 2,000 acres will allow hunting and snowmobiling and will be managed by the Maine Department of Conservation.

MOOSEHEAD LAKE REGION ★★

Thirty-two miles long and 5 miles across at its widest, Moosehead Lake is Maine's largest lake, a great destination for hikers, boaters, and canoeists. The lake was historically the center of the region's logging activity, a history that preserved the lake and kept it largely unspoiled by development.

The first thing to know about the lake is that it's not meant to be seen by car. Some great views can be had from a handful of roads—especially from Route 6/15 as you near Rockwood, and from the high elevations on the way to Lily Bay—but for the most part, the roads are a distance from the shores and driving is rather dull. To see the lake at its best, you should plan to get out on the water by steamship or canoe. If you prefer sightseeing by car, you'll find more rewarding drives in the western Maine mountains or along the coast.

ESSENTIALS

GETTING THERE Greenville is 158 miles from Portland. Take the Maine Turnpike to the Newport exit (Exit 39) and head north on Route 7/11 to Route 23 in Dexter, following it northward to Route 6/15 near Sangerville. Follow this to Greenville.

VISITOR INFORMATION The **Moosehead Lake Chamber of Commerce** (✆ **207/695-2702;** www.mooseheadlake.org) maintains a helpful information center. In addition to a good selection of the usual brochures, the center maintains files and bookshelves full of maps, trail information, wildlife guidebooks, and videos. From Memorial Day to mid-October, it's open Wednesday through Monday, 10am to 4pm; it's on your right as you come into Greenville, next to the Indian Hill Trading Post. Call for hours during the rest of the year.

OUTDOOR PURSUITS

CANOEING Follow Thoreau's footsteps into the Maine woods on a canoe excursion down the **West Branch of the Penobscot River** ★. This 44-mile trip is typically done in 3 days. Put in at Roll Dam, north of Moosehead Lake and east of Pittston Farm, and paddle northward on the generally smooth waters of the Penobscot. Pick one of several campsites along the river and spend the night, watching for moose as evening descends. On the second day, paddle to huge, wild Chesuncook Lake. Near where the river enters the lake is the Chesuncook Lake House, a farmhouse dating from 1864 and open to guests. Spend the night here (✆ **207/745-5330**). The final day brings a paddle down Chesuncook Lake with its views of Mount Katahdin to the east and take-out near Ripogenus Dam.

Allagash Canoe Trips (summers: P.O. Box 932, Greenville, ME 04441, ✆ **207/695-3668;** winters: 2314 G St., Carrabassett Valley, ME 04947, ✆ **207/237-3077;** www.allagashcanoetrips.com) has been leading guided canoe trips in the North Woods—including on the Allagash, Moose, Penobscot, and St. John's rivers—since 1953, with the next generation now taking over this family-run business. A 5-day guided camping trip down the West Branch—including all equipment, meals, and transportation—costs $500 for adults, $395 for children under 18.

HIKING One of my favorite hikes in the region is **Mount Kineo** ★★, marked by a massive, broad cliff that rises from the shores of Moosehead. This hike is accessible via water; near the town of Rockwood, look for signs advertising shuttles across the lake to Kineo from the town landing (folks offering this service seem to change from year to year, so ask around; it usually costs about $5 round-trip). Once on the other side, you can explore the grounds of the famed old Kineo Mountain House (alas, the grand,

500-guest-room hotel was demolished in 1938), then cut across the golf course and follow the shoreline to the trail that leads to the 1,800-foot summit. The views from the cliffs are dazzling; I know one hiker who says he has no problems on any mountain except Kineo, which afflicts him each time with vertigo. Be sure to continue on the trail to the old fire tower, which you can ascend for a hawk's-eye view of the region.

WHITE-WATER RAFTING Commercial white-water outfitters have trips in summer at a cost of about $85 to $115 per person (usually at the higher end on weekends). **Northern Outdoors** (© **800/765-7238;** www.northernoutdoors.com) is the oldest of the bunch and has rock-climbing, mountain biking, and fishing expeditions as well, plus snowmobiling in winter. Other reputable rafting companies include **Wilderness Expeditions** (© **800/825-9453**), which is affiliated with the rustic Birches Resort, and the **New England Outdoor Center** (© **800/766-7238**).

MOOSEHEAD BY STEAMSHIP & FLOAT PLANE

During the lake's golden days of tourism in the late 19th century, visitors could come to the lake by train from New York or Washington, then connect with steamship to the resorts and boardinghouses around the lake. A vestige of that era is found at the **Moosehead Marine Museum** (© **207/695-2716**) in Greenville. A handful of displays in the small museum suggest the grandeur of life at Kineo Mountain House, a sprawling Victorian lake resort that once defined elegance; but the museum's showpiece is the SS *Katahdin,* a 115-foot steamship that's been cruising Moosehead's waters since 1914. The two-deck ship (now run by diesel, rather than steam) takes a variety of sightseeing tours, including a twice-a-week excursion up the lake to the site of the former Kineo Mountain House. Fares vary depending on the length of the trip, ranging from $20 to $26 for adults and $12 to $15 for children age 6 and over (free for children under 6).

Moosehead from the air is a memorable sight. Stop by **Folsom's Air Service** (© **207/695-2821**) on the shores of the lake in Greenville just north of the village center on Lily Bay Road. Folsom's has been serving the North Woods since 1946 and has a fleet of five float planes, including a vintage canary-yellow DeHavilland Beaver. A 15-minute tour of the southern reaches of the lake costs $20 per person; longer flights over the region run up to about $60.

WHERE TO STAY & DINE

Blair Hill Inn ★★★ This unexpectedly classy inn amid the wilds occupies an 1891 hilltop Queen Anne mansion with dazzling views of Moosehead Lake and the surrounding hills. It's been sparely and elegantly decorated with a mix of rustic and classic appointments, such as Oriental carpets and deer-antler lamps. The bright first-floor common rooms, the drop-dead-gorgeous porch, and the handsome guest rooms invite loafing. All units provide terry robes, spring water, and locally made soaps. Room no. 1 is the best—the former master bedroom, featuring a panoramic sunset view and fireplace (Duraflame logs only). All guests can enjoy the outdoor Jacuzzi, Adirondack chairs on the lawn, and a small catch-and-release trout pond (ask about fly-fishing workshops).

Lily Bay Rd. (P.O. Box 1288), Greenville, ME 04441. © **207/695-0224.** www.blairhill.com. 8 units. June–Oct $195–$395 double. Rates include breakfast. 2-night minimum stay on weekends. DISC, MC, V. Closed Nov and Apr. No children under 10. **Amenities:** Restaurant; Jacuzzi. *In room:* Hair dryer, no phone.

Greenville Inn ★★ This handsome 1895 Queen Anne lumber baron's home sits regally on a hilly side street above Greenville's commercial district. The interiors are sumptuous, with wonderful cherry and mahogany woodworking and a lovely stained-glass window over the stairwell. At the handsome small bar, you can order a cocktail or Maine beer, then sit in front of the fire or retreat to the front porch to watch the evening sun slip over Squaw Mountain and the lake.

Norris St., Greenville, ME 04441. ✆ **888/695-6000** or 207/695-2206. www.greenvilleinn.com. 12 units. $250–$425 double. Rates include continental breakfast. 2-night minimum stay on holiday weekends. DISC, MC, V. No children under 8. **Amenities:** Restaurant. *In room:* No phone.

Little Lyford Pond Camps ★ This venerable backwoods logging camp is one of the more welcoming spots in the North Woods—at least for those looking to rough it a bit. Built in the 1870s to house loggers, each of its rustic cabins contains a small woodstove, a propane lantern, cold running water, and its own outhouse. At mealtimes, guests gather in the main lodge, which has books to browse and board games for evenings. During the day, activities aren't hard to find, from fishing for native brook trout (fly-fishing lessons available) and hiking with the lodge's llamas to canoeing at two nearby ponds or wandering on the Appalachian Trail to Gulf Hagas, a scenic gorge 2 miles away. In winter, cross-country skiing on the lodging's private network is superb, and time spent in the sauna will make you forget the cold weather. Access is via a rough logging road in summer (ski or snowmobile in winter), so factor in extra time for getting there.

P.O. Box 340, Greenville, ME 04441. ✆ **603/466-2727.** 8 units. $90–$120 double. Rates include all meals. 2-night minimum stay on weekends and holidays. No credit cards. **Amenities:** Sauna; canoes. *In room:* No phone.

The Lodge at Moosehead Lake ★★★ The Lodge at Moosehead Lake is a regal 1917 home on a hillside outside of town built for a wealthy summer rusticator. The inn is a mix of woodsy and modern resulting in upscale rustic elegance. Though guest rooms are carpeted, for instance, Adirondack-style stick furnishings are mixed in with wingback chairs and antique English end tables. The dining room, where a full breakfast is served year-round (dinner is only served once or twice weekly), has a brisk, modern feel in contrast to the rest of the inn. Beds in the main lodge are handcarved by local artist Joe Bolf, and the five rooms here are themed to North Woods creatures, such as bears, trout, and moose; the three luxurious suites in the carriage house have unique swinging beds—suspended from the ceiling by old logging chains—as well as chandeliers, sunken living rooms, and whirlpools fashioned from river stones. One suite, the Katahdin, even has a fireplace in the bathroom.

Lily Bay Rd. (P.O. Box 1167), Greenville, ME 04441. ✆ **207/695-4400.** Fax 207/695-2281. www.lodgeatmooseheadlake.com. 8 units. $205–$475 double. Rates include breakfast. 2-night minimum stay. AE, MC, V. Located 2½ miles north of Greenville on Lily Bay Rd. (head north through blinker). Children 14 and older are welcome. **Amenities:** Concierge. *In room:* A/C, TV/VCR, coffeemaker, hair dryer, iron, Jacuzzi.

Maynard's-in-Maine ★ Maynard's has long been one of my favorite places in the North Woods. This is the real thing—nothing the least faux, cute, or neo-rustic about it, sitting at the edge of Rockwood on the Moose River. While the sound of logging trucks can be a bit jarring, the more memorable sounds are wooden screen doors slamming and the clank of horseshoes. Chickens wander the grounds, and guests idle in birch and hickory chairs on cedar-post porches. Photos suggest that nothing has moved, much less been replaced, in the main lodge over the past 50 years. The compound has a handful of rustic cabins edging a lawn, most furnished eclectically with some classic camp furniture, as well as cheesy flea-market finds. Wildwood Cottage has three bedrooms, all sharing a bathroom, woodstove, and large screened porch; Birch Cottage is smaller and appropriate for a couple, and is less modernized than others. Note that not only are there no in-room phones, there's not even a pay phone on the premises. The dining room is equally classic and unchanged. Coffee is served before dinner, which is the old-school way. Two or more entrees are offered daily, usually New England favorites such as pot roast, along with fruit juice, soup, salad, relish tray, beverages, and dessert. (No alcohol is served, but feel free to BYOB.)

Rockwood, ME 04478. ✆ **207/534-7703.** www.maynardsinmaine.com. 14 units. $110 double. Rates include all meals (bag lunch). AE, DISC, MC, V. Drive across the bridge over Moose River in Rockwood, make 1st left, and continue to lodge. Pets allowed. **Amenities:** Watersports equipment rental. *In room:* No phone.

BAXTER STATE PARK & ENVIRONS ★★★

Baxter State Park is one of Maine's crown jewels, even more spectacular in some ways than Acadia National Park. This 204,000-acre state park in the remote north-central part of the state is unlike more elaborate state parks you may be accustomed to elsewhere—don't look for fancy bathhouses or groomed picnic areas. When you enter Baxter State Park, you enter near-wilderness. Former Maine governor and philanthropist Percival Baxter single-handedly created the park, using his inheritance and investment profits to buy the property and donate it to the state in 1930. Baxter stipulated that it remain "forever wild." Caretakers have done a good job fulfilling his wishes.

You won't find paved roads, RVs, or hook-ups at the eight drive-in campgrounds. (Size restrictions keep RVs out.) Even cellphones are banned. You will find rugged backcountry and remote lakes. You'll also find Mount Katahdin, a lone and melancholy granite monolith that rises above the sparkling lakes and severe boreal forest of northern Maine.

ESSENTIALS

GETTING THERE Baxter State Park is 86 miles north of Bangor. Take I-95 to Medway (Exit 56) and head west 11 miles on Route 11/157 to the mill town of Millinocket, the last major stop for supplies. Head northwest through town and follow signs to Baxter State Park. The less-used entrance is near the park's northeast corner. Take I-95 to the exit for Route 11, drive north through Patten, and then head west on Route 159 to the park. The speed limit in the park is 20 mph; motorcycles and ATVs are not allowed.

VISITOR INFORMATION Baxter State Park provides maps and information from its **headquarters,** 64 Balsam Dr., Millinocket, ME 04462 (✆ **207/723-5140;** www.baxterstateparkauthority.com). Note that no pets are allowed in Baxter State Park, and all trash you generate must be brought out.

For information on canoeing and camping outside of Baxter State Park, contact **North Maine Woods, Inc.,** P.O. Box 421, Ashland, ME 04732 (✆ **207/435-6213;** www.northmainewoods.org). Help finding cottages and outfitters is available through the **Katahdin Area Chamber of Commerce,** 1029 Central St., Millinocket, ME 04462 (✆ **207/723-4443**).

FEES Baxter State Park visitors with out-of-state license plates are charged a per-day fee of $12 per car. (It's free to Maine residents.) The day-use fee is charged only once per stay for those camping overnight. Camping reservations are by mail or in person only (see below). Private timberlands managed by North Maine Woods levy a per-day fee of $4 per person for Maine residents, $7 per person for nonresidents. Camping fees are additional (see below).

GETTING OUTDOORS

BACKPACKING Baxter State Park maintains about 180 miles of backcountry hiking trails and more than 25 backcountry sites, some accessible only by canoe. Most hikers coming to the park are intent on ascending 5,267-foot Mount Katahdin; but dozens of other peaks are well worth scaling, and just traveling through the deep woods is a sublime experience. Reservations are required for backcountry camping; many of the best spots fill up shortly after the first of the year. Reservations can be made by mail or in person, but not by phone.

En route to Mount Katahdin, the Appalachian Trail winds through the "100-mile Wilderness," a remote and bosky stretch where the trail crosses few roads and passes no settlements. It's the quiet habitat of loons and moose. Trail descriptions are available from the **Appalachian Trail Conference,** P.O. Box 807, Harpers Ferry, WV 25425 (✆ **304/535-6331;** www.appalachiantrail.org).

CAMPING Baxter State Park has eight campgrounds accessible by car and two backcountry camping areas, but don't count on finding anything available if you show up without reservations. The park starts taking reservations in January, and dozens of die-hard campers traditionally spend a cold night outside headquarters the night before the first business day in January to secure the best spots. Many of the most desirable sites sell out well before the snow melts from Mount Katahdin. The park is stubbornly old-fashioned about its reservations, which must be made either in person or by mail, with full payment in advance. No phone reservations are accepted. Don't even mention e-mail. The park starts processing summer camping mail requests on a first-come, first-served basis the first week in January; call well in advance for reservations forms. Camping at Baxter State Park costs $6 per person ($12 minimum per tent site), with cabins and bunkhouses available for $7 to $17 per person per night.

CANOEING The state's premier canoe trip is the Allagash River, starting west of Baxter State Park and running northward for nearly 100 miles, finishing at the village of Allagash. The **Allagash Wilderness Waterway** (✆ **207/941-4014**) was the first state-designated wild and scenic river in the country, protected from development in 1970. The river runs through heavily harvested timberlands, but a buffer strip of at least 500 feet of trees preserves forest views along the entire route. Eighty campsites are maintained along the route; most have outhouses, fire rings, and picnic tables. The camping fee is $4 per night per person for Maine residents, $5 for nonresidents.

Several outfitters have Allagash River packages, including canoes, camping equipment, and transportation. **Allagash Wilderness Outfitters,** Box 620, Star Route 76, Greenville, ME 04441 (it doesn't have a direct phone line in summer; call Folsom's Air Service at ✆ **207/695-2821** and an operator will relay messages/requests via shortwave radio), rents a complete outfit (including canoe, life vests, sleeping bags, tent, saw, axe, shovel, cooking gear, first-aid kit, and so on) for $23 per person per day. **Allagash Canoe Trips** (✆ **207/695-3668;** www.allagashcanoetrips.com) in Greenville leads 7-day guided descents of the river, including all equipment and meals, for $650 adults, $500 children under 18.

HIKING With 180 miles of maintained backcountry trails and 46 peaks (including 18 over 3,000 ft.), Baxter State Park is the destination of choice in Maine for serious hikers.

The most imposing peak is 5,267-foot **Mount Katahdin** ★★★—the northern terminus of the Appalachian Trail. An ascent up this rugged, glacially scoured mountain is a trip you'll not soon forget. Never mind that it's not even a mile high (though a tall cairn on the summit claims to make it so). The raw drama and grandeur of the rocky, windswept summit is equal to anything you'll find in the White Mountains of New Hampshire. Allow at least 8 hours for the round-trip, and be prepared to abandon your plans for another day if the weather takes a turn for the worse while you're en route.

Appendix: New England in Depth

by Paul Karr

Reduced to the simplest terms, New England consists of two regions: Boston and Not-Boston.

Boston, of course, is in the same league as other major metropolitan areas, and boasts first-class hotels, restaurants, and historic and modern architecture. Of all U.S. cities, Boston has perhaps the richest history, ranging from the days of America's settlement in the 17th century through the War of Independence in 1776 and on into the nation's cultural renaissance in the mid- and late 19th century. The Boston area is also a national seat of education, with dozens of prestigious colleges and universities. The presence of so many august institutions lends the city a youthful air in contrast to its staid heritage.

The extensive territory of Not-Boston arcs widely, from the Connecticut and Rhode Island shoreline through the rolling Berkshire Mountains of western Massachusetts on through the Green and White mountains and into the vast state of Maine. This region, while widely spread, traces it roots back to a Puritan ethic, and its longtime residents still tend to display shared traits and values such as a stubborn independence, a respect for thrift and straight-shooting, and an almost genetic mistrust of outsiders.

Some writers maintain that New England's character is still informed by a Calvinist doctrine, which decrees nothing will change one's fate and that hard work is a virtue. The New Englander's perverse celebration of the often-brutish climate is often trotted out as evidence of the region's enduring Calvinism.

But that's not to say travelers should expect rock-hard mattresses and nutritional but tasteless meals. Luxurious country inns and restaurants serving food rivaling what you'll find in Manhattan have become part of the landscape in the past 2 decades. Be sure to visit these places. But also set aside enough time to spend an afternoon rocking and reading on a broad inn porch, or to wander out of town on an abandoned county road with no particular destination in mind.

"There's nothing to do here," an inn manager in Vermont once explained. "Our product is indolence." That's an increasingly rare commodity these days. Take the time to savor it.

1 New England Today

It's a common question, so don't be embarrassed about asking it. You might be on Martha's Vineyard, or traveling through a pastoral Vermont valley, or exploring an island off the Maine coast. You'll see houses and people. And you'll wonder: "What do these people do to earn a living?"

As recently as a few decades ago, the answer was probably living off the land. They might have fished, harvested timber, or managed a gravel pit. Of course, many still do operate such businesses, but this work is no longer the economic mainstay it once was. Today, scratch a rural New Englander and you're just as likely to find an editor for a magazine that's published in Boston or New York, a farmer who grows specialized produce for gourmet restaurants, or a banking consultant who handles business by fax and e-mail. And you'll find lots of folks whose livelihood is dependent on tourism.

This change in the economy is but one of the tectonic shifts facing the region. The most visible and wracking change involves development and growth. For a region long familiar with economic poverty, a spell of recent prosperity and escalating property values has threatened to bring to New England that curious homogenization already marking much of the rest of the nation. Once a region of distinctive villages, green commons, and courthouse squares, New England's landscape in certain places is beginning to resemble suburbs everywhere else—a pastiche of strip malls dotted with fast-food chains, big-box discount and home-improvement stores, and the like.

This change pains longtime residents. New England towns have long maintained their identities in the face of considerable pressure. The region has always taken pride in its low-key, practical approach to life. In smaller communities, town meetings are still the preferred form of government. Residents gather in a public space to speak out about—sometimes rather forcefully—and vote on the issues of the day, such as funding for their schools, road improvements, fire trucks, or even symbolic gestures such as declaring their towns nuclear-free. "Use it up, wear it out, make do, or do without" is a well-worn phrase that aptly sums up the attitude of many longstanding New Englanders—and it's the polar opposite of the designer-outlet ethos filtering in.

It's still unclear how town meetings and that sense of knowing where your town starts and the next one begins will survive the slow but inexorable encroachment of Wal-Marts and Banana Republics. Of course, suburban Connecticut communities in the orbit of New York City and Boston have long since capitulated to sprawl, as have pockets elsewhere in the region—including mall-heavy areas outside Hartford, CT; Portland, ME; and Burlington, VT, not to mention Maine's Route 1 or the outlets along interstate highways in Massachusetts and Connecticut.

But the rest of New England is still figuring out how best to balance the principles of growth and conservation—how to allow the economy to edge into the modern age, without sacrificing those qualities that make New England such a distinctive place.

Development is a hot but not necessarily inflammatory issue—this isn't like the property rights movement in the West, where residents are manning the barricades and taking hostages for the cause. (At least not yet.) Few seem to think that development should be allowed at all costs. And few seem to think that the land should be preserved at all costs.

Pinching off all development means the offspring of longtime New England families will have no jobs, and New England will be fated to spend its days as a sort of quaint theme park. But if development continues unabated, many of the characteristics that make New England unique—and attract tourist dollars—will vanish. Will the Berkshires or the Maine coast be able to sustain their tourism industries if they're blanketed with strip malls and fast-food joints, making them look like every other place in the nation? Not likely. The question is how to respect the conservation ethic while leaving room for growth. And that question won't be resolved in the near future.

Except for a several-year slump in the early 1990s, New England has been enjoying a generally rosy period of economic growth since the mid-1980s; even when the economy has nosed back downward, as it has done of late, property values continue to rise as city folks increasingly seek a piece of whatever makes rural New England special. Commentators point out that this change, while welcome after decades of slow growth, will bring new conflicts. The rise of the information culture will make it increasingly likely that telecommuters and info-entrepreneurs will settle in New England's most remote and pristine villages, running their businesses via modem or satellite. How will these affluent newcomers adapt to clear-cutting in the countryside or increasing numbers of tour buses cruising their village greens?

Change doesn't come rapidly to New England. But there's a lot to sort out, and friction will certainly continue to build, one strip mall at a time.

2 History 101

Viewed from a distance, New England's history mirrors that of its namesake, England. The region rose from nowhere to gain tremendous historical prominence, captured a good deal of overseas trade, and became an industrial powerhouse and center for creative thought. And then the party ended relatively abruptly, as commerce and culture sought more fertile grounds to the west and south.

To this day, New England remains entwined with its past. Walking through Boston, layers of history are evident at every turn, from the church steeples of Colonial times (dwarfed by glass-sided skyscrapers) to verdant parklands that bespeak the refined sensibility of the late Victorian era.

History is even more inescapable in off-the-beaten-track New England. Travelers in Downeast Maine, northern New Hampshire, Connecticut's Litchfield Hills, the Berkshires, and much of Vermont will find clues to what Henry Wadsworth Longfellow called "the irrevocable past" every way they turn, from stone walls running through woods to Federal-style homes.

Here's a brief overview of some historical episodes and trends that shaped New England:

INDIGENOUS CULTURE Native Americans have inhabited New England

Dateline

- **1000–15** Viking explorers land in Canada, and may or may not have sailed southward to New England. Evidence is spotty.
- **1497** John Cabot, seeking to establish trade for England, reaches the island of Newfoundland in Canada and sails south as far as Maine.
- **1602** Capt. Bartholomew Gosnold lands on the Massachusetts coast. Names Cape Cod, Martha's Vineyard, and other locations.
- **1604** French colonists settle on an island on the St. Croix River between present-day Maine and New Brunswick. They leave after a single miserable winter.
- **1614** Capt. John Smith maps the New England coast, names the Charles River after King Charles I of England, and calls the area a paradise.
- **1616** Smallpox kills large numbers of Indians between Maine and Rhode Island.
- **1620** The *Mayflower,* carrying some 100 colonists (including many Pilgrims, fleeing religious persecution in England), arrives at Cape Cod.
- **1630** Colonists led by John Winthrop establish the town of Boston, named after an English village.

continues

since about 7000 B.C. While New York's Iroquois Indians had a presence in Vermont, New England was inhabited chiefly by Algonquins who lived a nomadic life. Connecticut was home to some 16 Algonquin tribes, who dubbed the region Quinnetukut.

After the arrival of the Europeans, French Catholic missionaries succeeded in converting many Native Americans, and most tribes sided with the French in the French and Indian Wars in the 18th century. Afterward, the Indians fared poorly at the hands of the British, and were quickly pushed to the margins. Today, they are found in greatest concentration at several reservations in Maine. The Pequots have established a thriving gaming industry in Connecticut. Other than that, the few clues left behind by Indian cultures have been more or less obliterated by later settlers.

THE COLONIES In 1604, some 80 French colonists spent a winter on a small island on what today is the Maine–New Brunswick border. They did not care for the harsh weather of their new home and left in spring to resettle in present-day Nova Scotia. In 1607, 3 months after the celebrated Jamestown, VA, colony was founded, a group of 100 English settlers established a community at Popham Beach, ME. The Maine winter demoralized these would-be colonists as well, and they returned to England the following year.

The colonization of the region began in earnest with the arrival of the Pilgrims at Plymouth Rock in 1620. The Pilgrims—a religious group that had split from the Church of England—established the first permanent colony, although it came at a hefty price: Half the group perished during the first winter. But the colony began to thrive over the years, in part thanks to helpful Native Americans.

The success of the Pilgrims lured other settlers from England, who established a constellation of small towns outside of Boston that became the Massachusetts Bay Colony. Roger Williams was expelled from the colony for his religious beliefs; he founded the city of Providence, RI. Other restless colonists expanded their horizons in search of lands for settlement. Throughout the 17th century, colonists from Massachusetts pushed northward into what are now New Hampshire and Maine, and southward into Connecticut. The first areas to be settled were lands near protected harbors along the coast and on navigable waterways.

The more remote settlements came under attack in the 17th and early 18th centuries in a series of raids by Indians conducted both independently and in

- **1635–36** Roger Williams is exiled from Massachusetts for espousing liberal religious ideas; he founds the city of Providence, RI.
- **1636** Harvard College is founded to educate young men for the ministry.
- **1638** America's first printing press is established in Cambridge.
- **1648** First labor unions are established by coopers and shoemakers in Boston.
- **1675–76** Native Americans attack colonists in New England in what is known as "King Philip's War."
- **1692** The Salem witch trials take place. Twenty people (including 14 women) are executed before the hysteria subsides.
- **1704** America's first regularly published newspaper, the *Boston News Letter,* is founded.
- **1713** The first schooner, a distinctively American sailing ship, is designed and built in Gloucester, MA.
- **1764** "Taxation without representation" is denounced in reaction to the Sugar Act.
- **1770** Five colonists are killed outside what is now the Old State House in an incident known as the Boston Massacre.

concert with the French. These proved temporary setbacks; colonization continued throughout New England into the 18th century.

THE AMERICAN REVOLUTION Starting around 1765, Great Britain launched a series of ham-handed economic policies to reign in the increasingly feisty colonies. These included a direct tax—the Stamp Act—to pay for a standing army. The crackdown provoked strong resistance. Under the banner of "No taxation without representation," disgruntled colonists engaged in a series of riots, resulting in the Boston Massacre of 1770, when five protesting colonists were fired upon and killed by British soldiers.

In 1773, the most infamous protest took place in Boston. The British had imposed the Tea Act (the right to collect duties on tea imports), which prompted a group of colonists dressed as Indians to board three British ships and dump 342 chests of tea into the harbor. This incident was dubbed the Boston Tea Party.

Hostilities reached a peak in 1775, when the British sought to quell unrest in Massachusetts. A contingent of British soldiers was sent to Lexington to seize military supplies and arrest two high-profile rebels—John Hancock and Samuel Adams. The militia formed by the colonists exchanged gunfire with the British, thereby igniting the Revolution ("the shot heard round the world").

Notable battles in New England included the Battle of Bunker Hill outside Boston, which the British won but at tremendous cost; and the Battle of Bennington in Vermont, in which the colonists prevailed. Hostilities formally ended in February 1783, and in September, Britain recognized the United States as a sovereign nation.

FARMING & TRADE As the new republic matured, economic growth in New England followed two tracks. Residents of inland communities survived by farming and trading in furs. Vermont in particular has always been an agrarian state, and remains a prominent dairy producer to this day.

On the coast, boatyards sprang up from Connecticut to Maine, and ship captains made tidy fortunes trading lumber for sugar and rum in the Caribbean. Trade was dealt a severe blow following the Embargo Act of 1807, but commerce eventually recovered, and New England ships could be encountered everywhere around the globe.

The growth of the railroad in the mid–19th century was another boon. The train opened up much of the interior, and led to towns springing up

---

- **1773** British ships are raided by colonists disguised as Indians during the Boston Tea Party. More than 300 chests of tea are dumped into the harbor from three British ships.
- **1775** On April 18, Paul Revere and William Dawes spread the word that the British are marching toward Lexington and Concord. The next day the "shot heard round the world" is fired. On June 17, the British win the Battle of Bunker Hill but suffer heavy casualties.
- **1783** Treaty of Paris is signed, formally concluding the American Revolution.
- **1788** Connecticut becomes the fifth, Massachusetts the sixth, and New Hampshire the ninth state to formally join the union.
- **1790** Rhode Island becomes the 13th state and the final colony to ratify the constitution.
- **1791** The short-lived Republic of Vermont (1777–91) ends and the state of Vermont joins the union.
- **1812** War of 1812 with England batters New England economy.
- **1814** The nation's first textile mill is built, in Waltham, MA.
- **1820** Maine, formerly a district of Massachusetts, becomes a state.

continues

A Literary Legacy

New Englanders have generated whole libraries, from the earliest days of hellfire-and-brimstone Puritan sermons to Stephen King's horror novels set in fictional Maine villages.

Among the more enduring writings from New England's earliest days are the poems of Massachusetts Bay Colony resident **Anne Bradstreet** (ca. 1612–72) and the sermons and essays of **Increase Mather** (1639–1723) and his son, **Cotton Mather** (1663–1728).

After the American Revolution, Hartford dictionary writer **Noah Webster** (1758–1843) issued a call to American writers: "America must be as independent in literature as she is in politics, as famous for arts as for arms." He struck an early blow for pragmatism by taking the "u" out of British words like "labour" and "honour."

The tales of **Nathaniel Hawthorne** (1804–64) captivated a public eager for a native literature. His most famous story, *The Scarlet Letter,* is a narrative about morality set in 17th-century Boston, but he wrote numerous other books that wrestled with themes of sin and guilt, often set in the emerging republic.

Henry Wadsworth Longfellow (1807–82), the Portland poet who settled in Cambridge, caught the attention of the public with evocative narrative poems focusing on distinctly American subjects. His popular works included "The Courtship of Miles Standish," "Paul Revere's Ride," and "Hiawatha." Poetry in the mid–19th century was the equivalent of Hollywood movies today—Longfellow could be considered his generation's Steven Spielberg (apologies to literary scholars).

The zenith of New England literature occurred in the mid- and late 19th century with the Transcendentalist movement. These writers and thinkers included **Ralph Waldo Emerson** (1803–82), **Bronson Alcott** (1799–1888), and **Henry David Thoreau** (1817–62). They fashioned a way of viewing nature

- **1835** Samuel Colt of Connecticut develops the six-shooter pistol.
- **1861** Massachusetts Institute of Technology is founded.
- **1892** America's first gasoline-powered automobile is built in Chicopee, MA.
- **1897** First Boston Marathon is run; Boston completes first American subway.
- **1903** The first World Series is played; Boston Red Sox win.
- **1918** The Red Sox celebrate another World Series victory.
- **1930** America's Cup sailing race is first held in Newport, RI.
- **1930s** The Great Depression devastates New England's already reeling industrial base.
- **1938** A major hurricane sweeps into New England, killing hundreds and destroying countless buildings and trees.
- **1942** A fire at Boston's Cocoanut Grove nightclub kills 491 people.
- **1946** John F. Kennedy is elected to Congress to represent Boston's first congressional district.
- **1957** Boston Celtics win their first NBA championship, laying the groundwork for a reign that will eventually include 16 championships.

and society that was uniquely American. They rejected the rigid doctrines of the Puritans, and found sustenance in self-examination, the glories of nature, and a celebration of individualism. Perhaps the best-known work to emerge from this period was Thoreau's *Walden.*

Among other regional writers who left a lasting mark on American literature was **Emily Dickinson** (1830–86), a native of Amherst, MA, whose precise and enigmatic poems placed her in the front rank of American poets. **James Russell Lowell** (1819–91), of Cambridge, was an influential poet, critic, and editor. Later poets were imagist **Amy Lowell** (1874–1925), from Brookline, MA, and **Edna St. Vincent Millay** (1892–1950), from Camden, ME.

The bestselling *Uncle Tom's Cabin,* the book Abraham Lincoln half-jokingly accused of starting the Civil War, was written by **Harriet Beecher Stowe** (1811–86) in Brunswick, ME. She lived much of her life as a neighbor of **Mark Twain** (himself an adopted New Englander) in Hartford, CT. Another bestseller was the children's book *Little Women,* written by **Louisa May Alcott** (1832–88), whose father, Bronson, was part of the Transcendentalist movement.

New England's later role in the literary tradition may best be symbolized by the poet **Robert Frost** (1874–1963). Though born in California, he lived his life in Massachusetts, New Hampshire, and Vermont. In the New England landscape and community, he found a lasting grace and rich metaphors for life. (Among his most famous lines: "Two roads diverged in a wood, and I— I took the one less traveled by, / And that has made all the difference.")

New England continues to attract writers drawn to the noted educational institutions and the privacy of rural life. Prominent contemporary writers and poets who live in the region at least part of the year include **John Updike, Nicholson Baker, Christopher Buckley, P. J. O'Rourke, Bill Bryson, John Irving,** and **Donald Hall.** Maine is also the home of **Stephen King,** who is considered not so much a novelist as Maine's leading industry.

- **1963** New Hampshire becomes first state to establish a lottery to support education.
- **1966** Edward Brooke of Massachusetts becomes the first African American elected to the U.S. Senate since Reconstruction.
- **1972** Maine's Indians head to court, claiming the state illegally seized their land in violation of a 1790 act. They settle 8 years later for $81.5 million.
- **1974** In Connecticut, Ella Grasso becomes the first elected woman governor.
- **1991** The Big Dig begins in Boston.
- **2001** The New England Patriots win the Super Bowl, stunning New Englanders.
- **2004** The Red Sox break the curse, winning the World Series for the first time in 86 years. The Patriots win the Super Bowl for the third time in 4 years.
- **2005** The Big Dig nears completion and Boston's downtown area has unobstructed access to the waterfront for the first time in 50 years.

Berkshires, the White and Green mountains, and Block Island were lifted by the tide of summer visitors. The tourism wave crested in the 1890s in Newport, RI, and Bar Harbor, ME, both of which were flooded by the affluent. Several grand resort hotels from tourism's golden era still host summer travelers in the region.

ECONOMIC DOWNTURN While the railways allowed New England to thrive in the mid–19th century, the train also played a role in undermining the region's prosperity. The driving of the Golden Spike in 1869 in Utah, linking America's Atlantic and Pacific coasts by rail, was heard loud and clear in New England, and it had a discordant ring. Transcontinental rail meant farmers and manufacturers could ship goods from the fertile Great Plains and California to faraway markets, making it harder for New England's hardscrabble farmers to survive. Likewise, the coastal shipping trade was dealt a fatal blow by this new transportation network. And the tourists set their sights on the Rockies and other stirring sites in the West.

Beginning in the late 19th century, New England lapsed into an extended economic slumber. Families commonly walked away from their farmhouses (there was no market for resale) and set off for regions with more promising opportunities. The abandoned, decaying farmhouse became almost an icon for New England, and vast tracts of open farmland were reclaimed by forest. With the rise of the automobile, the grand resorts further succumbed, and many closed their doors as inexpensive motels siphoned off their business.

BOOM TIMES In the last 2 decades of the 20th century, much of New England rode an unexpected wave of prosperity. A massive real-estate boom shook the region in the 1980s, driving land prices sky-high as prosperous buyers from New York and Boston acquired vacation homes or retired to the most alluring areas. In the 1990s, the rise of high-tech also sent ripples from Boston into the hinterlands. Tourism rebounded as harried urbanites of the Eastern Seaboard opted for shorter, more frequent vacations closer to home.

Travelers to the more remote regions will discover that many communities never benefited from the boom at all; they're still waiting to rebound from the economic malaise earlier in the century. Especially hard-hit have been places like northeastern Vermont and far Downeast Maine, where many residents still depend on local resources—timber, fisheries, and farmland—to eke out a living.

3 New England Style

You can often trace the evolution of a town by its architecture, as styles evolve from basic structures to elaborate Victorian mansions. The primer below should aid with basic identification.

- **Colonial** (1600–1700): The New England house of the 17th century was a simple, boxy affair, often covered in shingles or rough clapboards. Don't look for ornamentation; these homes were designed for basic shelter from the elements, and are often marked by prominent stone chimneys. You can see examples at Plimoth Plantation and in Salem, near Boston.
- **Georgian** (1700–1800): Ornamentation comes into play in the Georgian style, which draws heavily on classical symmetry. Georgian buildings were in vogue in England at the time, and were embraced by affluent colonists. Look for Palladian windows, formal pilasters, and elaborate projecting pediments. Deerfield (in the Pioneer Valley) is a good destination for seeing early Georgian homes; and

Providence, RI, and Portsmouth, NH, have abundant examples of later Georgian styles.

- **Federal** (1780–1820): Federal homes (sometimes called Adams homes) may best represent the New England ideal. Spacious yet austere, they are often rectangular or square, with low-pitched roofs and little ornament on the front, although carved swags or other embellishments are frequently seen near the roofline. Look for fan windows and chimneys bracketing the building. Excellent Federal-style homes are found throughout the region in towns such as Kennebunkport, ME.
- **Greek Revival** (1820–60): The most easy-to-identify Greek Revival homes feature a projecting portico with massive columns, like a part of the Parthenon grafted onto an existing home. The less dramatic homes may simply be oriented such that the gable faces the street, accenting the triangular pediment. Greek Revival didn't catch on in New England the way it did in the South, but some fine examples exist, notably in Newfane, VT.
- **Carpenter Gothic** and **Gothic Revival** (1840–80): The second half of the 19th century brought a wave of Gothic Revival homes, which borrowed their aesthetic from the English country home. Aficionados of this style and its later progeny featuring gingerbread trim owe themselves a trip to Oak Bluffs at Martha's Vineyard, where cottages are festooned with scrollwork and exuberant architectural flourishes.
- **Victorian** (1860–1900): This is a catchall term for the jumble of mid- to late-19th-century styles that emphasized complexity and opulence. Perhaps the best-known Victorian style—almost a caricature—is the tall and narrow Addams Family–style house, with mansard roof and prickly roof cresting. You'll find these scattered throughout the region.

  The Victorian style also includes squarish **Italianate** homes with wide eaves and unusual flourishes, such as the outstanding Victoria Mansion in Portland, ME.

  Stretching the definition a bit, Victorian can also include the **Richardsonian Romanesque** style, which was popular for railroad stations and public buildings. The classic Richardsonian building, designed by H. H. Richardson himself in 1872, is Trinity Church, in Boston.
- **Shingle** (1880–1900): This uniquely New England style quickly became preferred for vacation homes on Cape Cod and the Maine coast. They're marked by a profusion of gables, roofs, and porches, and are typically covered with shingles from roofline to foundation.
- **Modern** (1900–present): Outside of Boston, New England has produced little in the way of notable modern architecture. In the 1930s, Boston became a center for the stark **International Style** with the appointment of Bauhaus veteran Walter Gropius to the faculty at Harvard. Some intriguing experiments in this style are found on the MIT and Harvard campuses, including Gropius's Campus Center and Eero Saarinen's Kresge Auditorium.

4 A Taste of New England

All along the coast you'll be tempted by seafood in its various forms. You can get fried clams by the bucket at divey shacks along remote coves and busy highways. The more upscale restaurants offer fresh fish, grilled or gently sautéed.

Live lobster can be bought literally off the boat at lobster pounds, especially along the Maine coast. The setting is usually rustic—maybe a couple of picnic tables and a shed where huge vats of water are kept at a low boil.

Inland, take time to sample the local products. This includes delectable maple syrup, sold throughout the northern reaches. Cheese is a Vermont specialty, especially cheddar. Look also for Vermont's famed apple cider, and Maine's wild blueberries.

In summer, small farmers across New England set up stands at the end of their driveways offering fresh produce straight from the garden. You can usually find berries, fruits, and sometimes home-baked breads. These stands are rarely tended; just leave your money in the coffee can.

Restaurateurs haven't overlooked New England's bounty. Many chefs serve up delicious meals consisting of local ingredients—some places even tend their own gardens. Some of the fine dishes we've enjoyed while researching this guide include curried pumpkin soup, venison medallions with shiitake mushrooms, and wild boar with juniper berries.

But you don't have to have a hefty budget to enjoy the local foods. A number of regional classics fall under the "road food" category. Here's an abbreviated field guide:

- **Beans:** Boston is forever linked with baked beans (hence the nickname "Beantown"), which are popular throughout the region. A Saturday-night supper traditionally consists of baked beans and brown bread.
- **Lobster rolls:** Lobster rolls consist of lobster meat plucked from the shell, mixed with just enough mayonnaise to hold it all together, then served on a hot-dog roll.
- **Moxie:** Early in this century, Moxie outsold Coca-Cola. Part of its allure was the fanciful story behind its 1885 creation: A traveler named Moxie was said to have observed South American Indians consuming the sap of a native plant, which gave them extraordinary strength. The drink was "re-created" by Maine native and Massachusetts resident Dr. Augustin Thompson. It's still popular in New England, although some folks liken the taste to a combination of medicine and topsoil.
- **Necco wafers:** Still made in Cambridge by the New England Confectionery Company, these powdery wafers haven't changed a bit since 1847. The candies are available widely throughout New England.

Finally, no survey of comestibles would be complete without mention of something to wash it all down: beer. New England has more microbreweries than any other region outside of the Pacific Northwest. Popular brewpubs that rank high on the list include the Great Providence Brewing Co., the Commonwealth Brewing Co. (Boston's first brewpub), the Portsmouth Brewery, Federal Jack's Brewpub (Kennebunkport), Vermont Pub & Brewery (Burlington), the Windham Brewery at the Latchis Hotel (Brattleboro), and Portland, Maine's clutch of mini-breweries—at least a half-dozen, at last count, all making mighty good beer.

Index

See also Accommodations index, below.

General Index

ACCOMMODATIONS

IF YOU BOOK IT, IT SHOULD BE THERE.
Only Travelocity guarantees it will be, or we'll work with our travel partners to make it right, right away. So if you're missing a balcony or anything else you booked, just call us 24/7. 1-888-TRAVELOCITY.
travelocity
You'll never roam alone.